THE OXFORD HAND.

THE EUROPEAN
UNION

This is an authoritative, one-volume, and independent treatment of the history, functioning and nature of the European integration. Written by a selection of leading scholars, it covers the major institutions, policies, and events in the history of integration,
whilst also providing a guide to the major theoretical approaches that have been used to
study it over time. By bringing together such a distinguished cast covering such a wide
array of themes, the Handbook is intended as a one stop shop for all those interested in
the European Union and its predecessors. Written in an accessible style, the volume is
intended to shape the discipline of EU studies, and to establish itself as the essential
point of reference for all those interested in European integration, both in universities
and more broadly. It represents a timely guide to an institution that is much discussed
but often only imperfectly understood.

THE OXFORD HANDBOOK OF

THE EUROPEAN

UNION

Edited by
ERIK JONES, ANAND MENON,
and
STEPHEN WEATHERILL

OXFORD
UNIVERSITY PRESS

OXFORD
UNIVERSITY PRESS

Great Clarendon Street, Oxford, OX2 6DP,
United Kingdom

Oxford University Press is a department of the University of Oxford.
It furthers the University's objective of excellence in research, scholarship,
and education by publishing worldwide. Oxford is a registered trade mark of
Oxford University Press in the UK and in certain other countries

Published in the United States of America by Oxford University Press
198 Madison Avenue, New York, NY 10016, United States of America

British Library Cataloguing in Publication Data
Data available

ISBN 978-0-19-954628-2 (Hbk.)
ISBN 978-0-19-871479-8 (Pbk.)

Printed in Great Britain by
CPI Group (UK) Ltd, Croydon, CR0 4YY

CONTENTS

List of Figures   xi
List of Tables   xii
List of Abbreviations   xiii
List of Contributors   xxi

Preface   xxvii
ERIK JONES, ANAND MENON, AND STEPHEN WEATHERILL

PART I: PERSPECTIVES

1. Realist, Intergovernmentalist, and Institutionalist Approaches   3
   MARK A. POLLACK

2. Neo-Functionalism and Supranational Governance   18
   WAYNE SANDHOLTZ AND ALEC STONE SWEET

3. Constructivist Perspectives   34
   FRANK SCHIMMELFENNIG

4. Sociological Perspectives on European Integration   48
   CRAIG PARSONS

5. Multilevel Governance   62
   GEORGE PAGOULATOS AND LOUKAS TSOUKALIS

PART II: TREATIES

6. The Treaties of Paris   79
   BERTHOLD RITTBERGER

7. The Treaties of Rome   95
   MARK GILBERT

8. The Single European Act   107
   MARIA GREEN COWLES

9. The Treaty of Maastricht   121
   FINN LAURSEN

10. The Treaty of Amsterdam   135
    SOPHIE VANHOONACKER

11. The Treaty of Nice   149
    ALBERTA M. SBRAGIA

12. The Constitutional and Lisbon Treaties   163
    YOURI DEVUYST

PART III: MAJOR PERSONALITIES

13. The Founding Fathers   181
    RICHARD T. GRIFFITHS

14. Dynamic Franco–German Duos: Giscard–Schmidt
    and Mitterrand–Kohl   193
    CARINE GERMOND

15. Problematic Partners: de Gaulle, Thatcher, and their Impact   206
    N. PIERS LUDLOW

16. The Presidents and the Presidency of the European Commission   219
    HUSSEIN KASSIM

17. Famous Non-Performers: Franco Malfatti, Gaston Thorn,
    and Jacques Santer   233
    DESMOND DINAN

PART IV: MEMBER STATES (CLEAVAGES)

18. Large Versus Small States: Anti-Hegemony and the Politics
    of Shared Leadership   249
    SIMONE BUNSE AND KALYPSO AUDE NICOLAÏDIS

19. Old Versus New   267
    CHRISTIAN LEQUESNE

20. Rich Versus Poor   278
    WALTRAUD SCHELKLE

21. Coordinated Versus Liberal Market Economies   292
    ORFEO FIORETOS

22. Leaders and Followers: Leadership amongst Member States
    in a Differentiated Europe   306
    VINCENT DELLA SALA

PART V: INSTITUTIONS

23. Council of Ministers and European Council   321
    JEFFREY LEWIS

24. European Commission   336
    SUSANNE K. SCHMIDT AND ARNDT WONKA

25. The European Court of Justice and the Legal Dynamics
    of Integration   350
    LOÏC AZOULAI AND RENAUD DEHOUSSE

26. The European Parliament   365
    TAPIO RAUNIO

27. External Scrutiny Institutions   380
    IAN HARDEN

28. European Union Agencies   392
    R. DANIEL KELEMEN

PART VI: ECONOMIC COMPETENCES

29. Single Market   407
    MICHELLE EGAN

30. Trade Policy   422
    ALASDAIR R. YOUNG

31. Competition Policy   441
    IMELDA MAHER

32. Economic and Monetary Union   453
    KENNETH DYSON

33. Lisbon Strategy   469
    ANNETTE BONGARDT AND FRANCISCO TORRES

34. CAP   484
    FRANCIS SNYDER

35. Regional and Structural Funds   496
    DERMOT HODSON

PART VII: SUBSTANTIVE POLICY DEVELOPMENT

36. Environmental Policy   511
    CHARLOTTE BURNS AND NEIL CARTER

37. European Consumer Law   526
    HANS-W. MICKLITZ

38. Social Policy and Labor Market Regulation   542
    CATHERINE BARNARD AND SIMON DEAKIN

39. European Energy Policy   556
    DIETER R. HELM

40. The Constitutional Context of (Ever-Wider) Policy-Making   570
    STEPHEN WEATHERILL

PART VIII: COMPETENCES IN FOREIGN POLICY AND HOME AFFAIRS

41. Defense Policy   585
    ANAND MENON

42. The Shadow of Schengen   600
    JONATHON W. MOSES

43. Justice and Home Affairs   613
    JÖRG MONAR

44. Intelligence and the European Union   627
    RICHARD J. ALDRICH

45. The Common Foreign and Security Policy   643
    DAVID ALLEN

PART IX: POLITICAL CONCERNS

46. Democracy and Legitimacy in the European Union   661
    VIVIEN A. SCHMIDT

47. Policy Effectiveness and Transparency in European
    Policy-Making   676
    ADRIENNE HÉRITIER

48. Identity and Solidarity   690
    ERIK JONES

49. Political Time in the EU   703
    KLAUS H. GOETZ

50. Public Opinion and Integration   716
    SARA B. HOBOLT

51. Rights (and Obligations) in EU Law   734
    JOXERRAMON BENGOETXEA

52. Bringing the Territory Back In: Toward a New Understanding
    of the Regional Dimension of the EU   749
    CHARLIE JEFFEREY AND CAROLYN ROWE

53. Neither an International Organization nor a Nation State:
    The EU as a Supranational Federation   761
    ARMIN VON BOGDANDY

54. Comparative Regional Integration: Theoretical Developments   777
    WALTER MATTLI

PART X: EU AND THE MEMBER STATES

55. Coordination in the EU   795
    B. Guy Peters

56. Burden-Sharing   810
    Eiko Thielemann

57. Europeanization   825
    Ulrich Sedelmeier

58. Politicization   840
    Liesbet Hooghe and Gary Marks

Index   855

List of Figures

20.1   GDP per head (PPS) in 2007, EU-27 = 100 (Luxembourg excluded)   280

20.2   GDP per head (PPS) in member states and candidate countries
with regional extremes, 2007 (EU-27 = 100)   281

20.3   Productivity growth in member states, 1995–2005   282

20.4   Growth of GDP per head 2000–2004 and level of GDP per head 2004   282

20.5   Correlation between current account balance and income level   287

20.6   Correlation between current account balances and real income
growth 2000–2007   289

42.1   Net migration, EU-27   602

42.2   Net migration, percentage of population, 2007   603

50.1   Public support for EU membership   719

56.1   Absolute distribution of "asylum burdens" in 2009
(top twelve OECD countries)   815

56.2   Relative distribution of "asylum burdens" (per 1000 of population)
in 2009 (top twelve OECD countries)   816

58.1   The structure of political conflict (2006)   848

List of Tables

6.1 Fault lines in the literature on the ECSC and EDC   80

8.1 Timeline leading to the SEA   113

11.1 Distribution of seats in the European Parliament
under the Treaty of Nice   159

18.1 Evolution of the qualified majority (QM) in the Council of Ministers   254

18.2 The evolution of the composition of the European Parliament   258

18.3 Synopsis of small versus big divide and Convention/IGC outcomes   262

28.1 EU agencies   394

50.1 Explaining support for European integration   720

50. 2 Referendums on European Integration   725

54.1 Integration outcomes   783

54.2 Overview of theories of comparative regional integration   790

56.1 Types of international burden-sharing mechanisms   814

57.1 Mediating factors of the EU's adjustment pressures inside
and outside its membership   832

List of Abbreviations

ACER	EU Agency for the Cooperation of Energy Regulators
ACP	Asian, Caribbean, and Pacific Group of States
ADR	Alternative Dispute Resolution
AEC	Atomic Energy Commission
AFSJ	Area of Freedom, Security, and Justice
AGFISH	Agriculture and Fisheries Council
AIVD	Dutch Intelligence and Security Service
ALDE	Alliance of Liberals and Democrats for Europe
APEC	Asia-Pacific Economic Cooperation
ASEAN	Association of Southeast Asian Nations
BBQ	British Budgetary Question
BENELUX	Belgium, the Netherlands, and Luxembourg Economic Union
BEPGs	Broad Economic Policy Guidelines
BERs	Block Exemption Regulations
BIA	Security Information Agency of the Republic of Serbia
BIS	Bank for International Settlements
BM	Blocking Minority
BSE	Bovine Spongiform Encephalopathy
CACM	Central American Common Market
CAP	Common Agricultural Policy
CCM	Civilian Crisis Management
CCP	Common Commercial Policy
CCS	Carbon Capture and Storage
CdT	Translation Centre for the Bodies of the European Union
CDU	Christian Democratic Union (Germany)
CEAS	Common European Asylum System
Cedefop	European Centre for the Development of Vocational Training
CEE	Central and East European States

CEEC	Central and Eastern European Country
CEGB	Central Electricity Generating Board
CEN	European Committee for Standardization
CENELEC	European Committee for Electrotechnical Standardization
CEO	Chief Executive Officer
CEPOL	European Police College
CFCA	Community Fisheries Control Agency
CFI	Court of First Instance
CFSP	Common Foreign and Security Policy
CGS	Council Secretariat
CIA	Central Intelligence Agency
CJEU	Court of Justice of the European Union
COGs	National Chiefs of Government
COP	Copenhagen Conference of the Parties
CoR	Committee of the Regions
COREPER	Committee of Permanent Representatives
CPCC	Civilian Planning and Conduct Capability
CPVO	Community Plant Variety Office
CSP	Confederation of Socialist Parties of the European Community
CSU	Christian Social Union (Germany)
CTG	Counter Terrorist Group
DAS	*Déclaration d'assurance*
DCFR	Academic Draft Common Frame of Reference
DRC	Democratic Republic of Congo
EAFRD	European Agricultural Fund for Rural Development
EAGGF	European Agricultural Guarantee and Guidance Fund
EAP	Environmental Action Programme
EASA	European Aviation Safety Agency
ECA	European Court of Auditors
ECB	European Central Bank
ECDC	European Centre for Disease Prevention and Control
ECEP	European Climate and Energy Package
ECHA	European Chemicals Agency
ECHR	European Convention on Human Rights
ECJ	European Court of Justice

ECN	European Competition Network
ECOFIN	Council of Economics and Finance Ministers
ECSC	European Coal and Steel Community
ECtHR	European Court of Human Rights
ECU	European Currency Unit
EDA	European Defence Agency
EDC	European Defence Community
EDF	Electricité de France
EDPS	European Data Protection Supervisor
EEA	European Economic Area
EEA	European Environment Agency
EEAS	European External Action Service
EEC	European Economic Community
EES	European Election Studies
EES	European Employment Strategy
EFC	European Financial Coalition
EFGP	European Federation of Green Parties
EFSA	European Food Safety Authority
EFSF	European Financial Stability Facility
EFTA	European Free Trade Association
EGP	European Green Party
EIB	European Investment Bank
EIGE	European Institute for Gender Equality
ELDR	Federation of European Liberal, Democrat, and Reform Parties
EMA	European Medicines Agency
EMCDDA	European Monitoring Centre for Drugs and Drug Addiction
EMI	European Monetary Institute
EMS	European Monetary System
EMSA	European Maritime Safety Agency
EMU	European Monetary Union
ENGOs	Environmental Non-Governmental Organizations
ENISA	European Network and Information Security Agency
EPC	European Political Cooperation
EPP	Euro Plus Pact
EPP	European People's Party

EPRG	European Parliament Research Group
EPU	European Payments Union
ERA	European Railway Agency
ERDF	European Regional Development Fund
ERF	European Refugee Fund
ERG	European Regulators Group
ERM	Exchange Rate Mechanism
ERRIN	European Regions and Innovation Network in Brussels
ERT	European Roundtable of Industrialists
ESCB	European System of Central Banks
ESDP	European Security and Defence Policy
ESF	European Social Fund
ESM	European Stability Mechanism
ESPRIT	European Strategic Program on Research in Information Technology
ESRB	European Systemic Risk Board
ESS	European Security Strategy
ETF	European Training Foundation
ETS	Emissions Trading System
ETUC	European Trade Union Confederation
EU	European Union
EU OSHA	European Agency for Safety and Health at Work
EUCOM	United States European Command
EUETS	European Union Emissions Trading Scheme
EUFOR	European Force
Euratom	European Atomic Energy Community
EUREGHA	European Network of Regional and Local Health Authorities
EUREMA	EU Relocation Malta
Eurodac	European Dactyloscopy
Eurofound	European Foundation for the Improvement of Living and Working Conditions
EUROJUST	European Judicial Cooperation Unit
Europol	European Police Office
EUSC	European Union Satellite Centre
EUT	Draft Treaty on the European Union

EVCA	European Venture Capital Association
FBI	Federal Bureau of Intelligence
FDI	Foreign Direct Investment
FGD	Flue Gas Desulphurization
FRA	European Union Agency for Fundamental Rights
FRONTEX	European Agency for the Management of Operational Cooperation at the External Borders
FSU	Finnish Seaman's Union
FTA	Free Trade Area
FYROM	Former Yugoslav Republic of Macedonia
GAERC	General Affairs and External Relations Council
GAL	Green-Alternative-Libertarian
GATT	General Agreement on Trade and Tariffs
GDP	Gross Domestic Product
GMOs	Genetically Modified Organisms
GNI	Gross National Income
GNP	Gross National Product
GSA	European GNSS Agency
G7/8	Group of Seven or Eight
GTAZ	Germany's Joint Counterterrorism Centre
G20	Group of Twenty
HA	High Authority
HG	Headline Goal
HHG	Helsinki Headline Goal
HR	High Representative
IDOC	Investigation and Disciplinary Office
IEA	International Energy Agency
IGC	Intergovernmental Conference
IMF	International Monetary Fund
IMSC	Internal Market Support Committee
Intdiv	Intelligence Division of the European Military Staff
IPE	International Political Economy
IR	International Relations
ISS	European Union Institute for Security Studies

ITF	International Transport Workers' Federation
JHA	Justice and Home Affairs
JTAC	Joint Terrorism Analysis Centre
LAFTA	Latin American Integration Association
LCPD	Large Combustion Plant Directive
LI	Liberal Intergovernmentalism
MEPs	Members of the European Parliament
MERCOSUR	Mercado Común del Sur
MLG	Multilevel Governance
MP	Member of Parliament
MRP	Mouvement Républicain Populaire
MS	Member State
MTR	Mid-Term Review
NAFTA	North American Free Trade Agreement
NAP	National Allocation Plan
NATO	North Atlantic Treaty Organization
NCAs	National Competition Agencies
NGO	Non-Governmental Organization
NMS	New Member States
NRAs	National Regulatory Authorities
NRP	National Reform Programs
NSRF	National Strategic Reference Framework
NUTS	Nomenclature of Territorial Units for Statistics
OCA	Optimum Currency Area
ODS	Civic Democratic Party
OECD	Organization for Economic Cooperation and Development
OEEC	Organization for European Economic Cooperation
OHIM	Office for Harmonization in the Internal Market
OLAF	European Anti-Fraud Office
OLS	Ordinary Least Squares
OMC	Open Method of Coordination
OMS	Old Member State
OP	Operational Programmes
OPEC	Organization of the Petroleum Exporting Countries
OSCE	Organisation for Security and Cooperation in Europe

PCA	Partnership and Cooperation Agreement
PD	Prisoner's Dilemma
PECL	Principles of European Contract Law
PES	Party European Socialists
PiS	Party Law and Justice
PPEWU	Policy Planning and Early Warning Unit
PPS	Power Parity Standard
PSL	Polish Peasant's Party
QM	Qualified Majority
QMV	Qualified Majority Voting
R&D	Research and Development
RCI	Rational-Choice Institutionalism
rTPA	Regulated Third Party Access
RWE	Rhenish-Westphalian Electric Power Company
S&D	Group of the Progressive Alliance of Socialists and Democrats
SAPS	Single Area Payment Scheme
SBC	Schengen Borders Code
SBU	Security Service of Ukraine
SCA	Special Committee on Agriculture
SEA	Single European Act
SEM	Single European Market
SEPA	Single Euro Payment Area
SFP	Single Farm Payment
SFS	Small Farmers Scheme
SGP	Stability and Growth Pact
SHAPE	Supreme Headquarters Allied Powers Europe
SIRENE	Supplementary Information Request at the National Entry
SIS	Schengen Information System
SitCen	EU Joint Situation Centre
SME	Small- and Medium-Sized Enterprises
SVR	Foreign Intelligence Service (Russia)
TAN	Traditionalist-Authority-Nationalism
TARGET	Euro Payment and Settlement System
TCNs	Third-Country Nationals
TEC	Treaty Establishing the European Union

TEU	Treaty on European Union
TFEU	Treaty on the Functioning of the Union
TPA	Third-Party Access
TREVI	Terrorisme, radicalisme, extrémisme et violence internationale
TRIPS	Trade-Related Measures of Intellectual Property
UCLAF	Anti-Fraud Task Force
UK	United Kingdom
UNECE	United Nations Economic Commission for Europe
UNHCR	United Nations High Commissioner for Refugees
US	United States
VP	Vice President
WEU	Western European Union
WMD	Weapons of Mass Destruction
WTO	World Trade Organization

LIST OF CONTRIBUTORS

Richard J. Aldrich Professor of International Security, Department of Politics and International Studies, University of Warwick, Warwick, United Kingdom.

David Allen Professor of European and International Politics, School of Social, Political, and Geographical Sciences, Department of Politics, History, and International Relations, Loughborough University, Loughborough, United Kingdom.

Loïc Azoulai Professor of EU Law, European University Institute, Florence, Italy; Professor of EU Law, Panthéon-Assas University (Paris II), Paris, France.

Catherine Barnard Professor of European Union Law; Co-Director of CELS; Jean Monnet Chair of EU Law; Director of the LL.M. Course, Faculty of Law, University of Cambridge, Cambridge, United Kingdom.

Joxerramon Bengoetxea Professor of Jurisprudence and Sociology of Law, Department of Administrative and Constitutional Law and Professor of Philosophy of Law, University of the Basque Country (UPV/EHU), Donostia-San Sebastian, Spain.

Armin von Bogdandy Director, Max Planck Institute for Comparative Public Law and International Law, Heidelberg, Germany, and Professor, Goethe University, Frankfurt, Germany.

Annette Bongardt Professor of European Studies, Universidade Fernando Pessoa and INA, Portugal, and ESC, St Antony's Oxford University.

Simone Bunse Adjunct Visiting Assistant Professor, Georgetown Public Policy Institute, Georgetown University, Washington DC, United States.

Charlotte Burns Lecturer in Politics, School of Politics and International Studies, University of Leeds, Leeds, United Kingdom.

Neil Carter Professor of Politics, Department of Politics, University of York, York, United Kingdom.

Maria Green Cowles Associate Dean for Academic Affairs and Professor, School of International Service, American University, Washington DC, United States.

Simon Deakin Professor of Law, Faculty of Law, University of Cambridge, Cambridge, United Kingdom.

Renaud Dehousse Jean Monnet Professor of EU Law and Politics and Director, Centre d'études européennes, Sciences Po, Paris.

Vincent Della Sala Professor of Political Science, Department of Sociology, University of Trento, Trento, Italy; Adjunct Professor, The John Hopkins University SAIS Bologna Center, Bologna, Italy.

Youri Devuyst Professor of EU Politics and Law, Institute for European Studies, Vrije Universiteit Brussel, Brussels, Belgium.

Desmond Dinan Professor of Public Policy and ad personam Jean Monnet Professor; Director, International Commerce and Policy Program, School of Public Policy, George Mason University, Arlington, Virginia, United States.

Kenneth Dyson FBA, Research Professor in the School of European Studies, Cardiff University, Cardiff, Wales, United Kingdom.

Michelle Egan Associate Professor, School of International Service; Affiliate Faculty Member, Department of History; Coordinator, European and Russian Studies Program; Faculty Advisor, European Studies Certificate, American University, Washington, DC, United States.

Orfeo Fioretos Associate Professor, Department of Political Science, Temple University, Philadelphia, United States.

Carine Germond Lecturer in History of European Integration, Department of History, Maastricht University, The Netherlands, and Jean Monnet Fellow, Robert Schuman Center for Advanced Studies, European University Institute, Florence, Italy.

Mark Gilbert Visiting Associate Professor of Contemporary European History, the Johns Hopkins University SAIS Bologna Center, Bologna, Italy; Associate Professor in Contemporary European History, University of Trento, Trento, Italy.

Klaus H. Goetz Professor of German and European Politics and Government, Faculty of Economics and Social Sciences, University of Potsdam, Germany.

Richard T. Griffiths Professor of Social and Economic History, Institute for History, Faculty of Humanities, Leiden University, Leiden, Netherlands.

Ian Harden Secretary-General, Office of the European Ombudsman, Strasbourg, France; Honorary Professor, School of Law, University of Sheffield, Sheffield, United Kingdom.

Dieter R. Helm Professor of Energy Policy at the University of Oxford and Official Fellow in Economics, New College, University of Oxford, Oxford, United Kingdom.

Adrienne Héritier Joint Chair RSCAS/Political and Social Sciences Department, Professor of Comparative and European Public Policy, European University Institute, Fiesole, Italy.

Sara B. Hobolt Sutherland Chair in European Institutions, European Institute, London School of Economics and Political Science (LSE), London, United Kingdom.

Dermot Hodson Senior Lecturer in Political Economy, Department of Politics, School of Social Sciences, History and Philosophy, Birkbeck, University of London, London, United Kingdom.

Liesbet Hooghe W. R. Kenan Jr. Professor, University of North Carolina, Chapel Hill, United States; Chair in Multilevel Governance, Vrije Universiteit Amsterdam, Amsterdam, Netherlands.

Charlie Jefferey Professor of Politics and Director, Academy of Government, School of Social and Political Studies, University of Edinburgh, United Kingdom.

Erik Jones Director of European and Eurasian Studies, School of Advanced International Studies of The Johns Hopkins University, and Senior Research Fellow at Nuffield College, Oxford, United Kingdom.

Hussein Kassim Professor of Politics and Head of School, School of Political, Social, and International Studies, Faculty of Arts and Humanities, University of East Anglia, Norwich, United Kingdom.

R. Daniel Kelemen Associate Professor of Political Science, Jean Monnet Chair and Director of the Center for European Studies, Rutgers University, New Brunswick, New Jersey, United States.

Finn Laursen Canada Research Chair in European Union Studies and Professor, Department of Political Science, Dalhousie University, Halifax, Canada.

Christian Lequesne Director of the Centre d'études et de recherches internationales (CERI), Sciences Po, Paris, France.

Jeffrey Lewis Associate Professor of Political Science, Department of Political Science, Cleveland State University, Cleveland, Ohio, United States.

N. Piers Ludlow Reader, Department of International History, London School of Economics and Political Science (LSE), London, United Kingdom.

Imelda Maher Sutherland Professor of European Law, UCD School of Law, University College Dublin, Ireland.

Gary Marks Burton Craige Professor, University of North Carolina, Chapel Hill, United States; Chair in Multilevel Governance, Vrije Universiteit Amsterdam, Amsterdam, Netherlands.

Walter Mattli Professor of International Political Economy, Department of Politics and International Relations, University of Oxford, Oxford, United Kingdom.

Anand Menon Professor of European Politics and Foreign Affairs, Kings College, London, United Kingdom.

Hans-W. Micklitz Director of Graduate Studies and Professor of Economic Law, European University Institute, Fiesole, Florence, Italy.

Jörg Monar Professor of Contemporary European Studies, University of Sussex, Brighton, United Kingdom; Director of Political and Administrative Studies, College of Europe, Bruges, Belgium.

Jonathon W. Moses Professor of Comparative Politics, Department of Sociology and Political Science, Norwegian University of Science and Technology, Trondheim, Norway.

Kalypso Nicolaïdis Professor of International Relations, European Studies Centre, St Antony's College, University of Oxford; Chair, South East European Studies at Oxford (SEESOX); Chair, Global Trade Ethics Project, University of Oxford, Oxford, United Kingdom.

George Pagoulatos Professor of European Politics and Economy, Department of International and European Economic Studies, Athens University of Economics and Business, Athens, Greece; Visiting Professor, College of Europe, Bruges, Belgium.

Craig Parsons Professor of Political Science, Department of Political Science, University of Oregon, Oregon, United States.

B. G. Peters Maurice Falk Professor of American Government and Research Professor at the University Center for International Studies, University of Pittsburgh, Pittsburgh, Pennsylvania, United States.

Mark A. Pollack Professor and Jean Monnet Chair, Department of Political Science, Temple University, Philadelphia, Pennsylvania, United States.

Tapio Raunio Professor of Political Science, School of Management, University of Tampere, Tampere, Finland.

Berthold Rittberger Professor of International Relations, Geschwister-Scholl-Institute of Political Science, University of Munich, Munich, Germany.

Carolyn Rowe Lecturer in Politics, Aston Centre for Europe, Aston University, Birmingham, United Kingdom.

Wayne Sandholtz John A. McCone Chair in International Relations, School of International Relations, University of Southern California, United States.

Alberta M. Sbragia Professor of Political Science, Department of Political Science, and Vice-Provost for Graduate Studies, University of Pittsburgh, United States.

Waltraud Schelkle Senior Lecturer in Political Economy, European Institute, London School of Economics and Political Science (LSE), London, United Kingdom.

Frank Schimmelfennig Professor of European Politics, Center for Comparative and International Studies, Eidgenössische Technische Hochschule (ETH) Zurich, Zurich, Switzerland.

Susanne K. Schmidt Professor of Political Science, Institute of Political Science, University of Bremen, and Dean of the Bremen International Graduate School of Social Sciences (BIGSSS), Bremen, Germany.

Vivien A. Schmidt Jean Monnet Professor of European Integration, Departments of International Relations and Political Science, Boston University, Boston, Massachusetts, United States.

Ulrich Sedelmeier Reader in the International Relations of Europe, Department of International Relations, London School of Economics and Political Science (LSE), London, United Kingdom.

Francis Snyder C.V. Starr Professor of Law and Co-Director, Center for Research on Transnational Law and Jean Monnet Chair ad personam, Peking University School of Transnational Law, Shenzhen Graduate School, China; Visiting Professor, London School of Economics and Political Science (LSE), London, United Kingdom; Visiting Professor, College of Europe, Bruges, Belgium.

Alec Stone Sweet Leitner Professor of International Law, Politics, and International Studies, Yale Law School, New Haven, Connecticut, United States.

Eiko Thielemann Senior Lecturer in European Politics and Policy, Department of Government and European Institute, London School of Economics and Political Science (LSE), London, United Kingdom.

Francisco Torres Professor of European Studies, Universidade Católica Portuguesa, Lisbon, Portugal, and INA, Portugal, ESC, St Antony's, Oxford University.

Loukas Tsoukalis Professor of European Integration, University of Athens, and President of the Hellenic Foundation for European and Foreign Policy (ELIAMEP), Athens, Greece; Visiting Professor, College of Europe, Bruges, Belgium.

Sophie Vanhoonacker Jean Monnet Professor and Chair in Administrative Governance, Department of Politics, Faculty of Arts and Social Sciences; Head of the Department of Political Science, Maastricht University, Maastricht, Netherlands.

Stephen Weatherill Jacques Delors Professor of European Law, Faculty of Law and Somerville College, Oxford University, Oxford, United Kingdom.

Arndt Wonka Lecturer at the Bremen International Graduate School of Social Sciences (BIGSSS), Bremen, Germany.

Alasdair R. Young Associate Professor, The Sam Nunn School of International Affairs, Georgia Institute of Technology, Atlanta, United States.

PREFACE

ERIK JONES, ANAND MENON, AND
STEPHEN WEATHERILL

For more than half a century, the process of European integration has redrawn the map of Europe, both literally and figuratively. Credited by its supporters with helping entrench peace and prosperity, attacked by its enemies for undermining nation states that represent the cornerstone of political legitimacy, the EU continues to spark controversy and to defy easy understanding or explanation.

The institutions spawned by this process are both familiar and unusual at the same time. They combine elements recognizable from the politics that takes place within states with others that reflect more the politics between states. What is true in form is also true in function. European institutions share competence with their national counterparts in some areas and claim exclusive competence in others. Moreover, virtually every aspect of public policy falls somewhere within their remit.

The combination of unfamiliarity and ubiquity has provoked successive waves of scholarly interest. The 1960s and 1990s stand out as particularly intense moments of dynamism and scrutiny; the 1970s and early 2000s show some tapering off. Across these ebbs and flows of popularity, the literature has continued to deepen and expand. The number of academic journals devoted to the study of European integration is one indicator; the inclusion of articles on European integration in the most prominent disciplinary journals is another.

The objective of *The Oxford Handbook on the European Union* is to provide a survey of this rich field of scholarly endeavor. As a collection, *The Oxford Handbook* provides a comprehensive resource, bringing together acknowledged authorities in the area of EU Studies to provide original and up-to-date analyses of the study of the Union. Our intention as editors has been not only to address key perennial debates in the field, but also to cast light on issues that are often overlooked. We also aim to bring together a wide range of perspectives. Hence the individual chapters offer insights from economics, history, international relations, law, political science, and sociology.

The volume begins with the theoretical perspectives that have dominated academic debates about European integration. Examining, in turn, Realist, neo-functionalist, constructivist, sociological, and multilevel governance perspectives, the authors in Part I consider not only where controversy lay in the past, but also the potential of the various approaches to contribute to our understanding of the EU in years to come.

Part II considers the succession of treaties that have provided the building blocks for the European integration process. Many of these treaties are notable for their success; others are more significant for their failure. Therefore, this part covers not only the progression from Rome to Lisbon, but also early attempts to create an EDC and later attempts to ratify a Constitutional Treaty.

The workings of any political system are, of course, only partially determined by the formal rules put in place to govern its operation. Part III moves away from formal structures to look at the role of particular individuals in shaping the process of European integration. Again, we focus not only on those personalities who played a major role in the construction of the communities, but also consider the record, and determinants of the performance, of others who have long being considered as "non-performers."

Part IV shifts the focus from individuals to states. Rather than adopting a typical approach of examining individual countries and their attitudes toward European integration, we asked contributors to examine various groupings of states and to consider their role in either shaping or retarding the integration process. The intention here is to get a sense of how and why domestic politics and international relations have interacted to shape so many of the debates about the development of the EU.

The following section (Part V) goes on to look at the institutions of the Union, considering both their development over time and their contemporary workings. Here we have included both the "core" EU institutions whose study has been central to the intellectual interests of the sub-field, and those other institutions that are the subject of far less scholarly debate, including the Court of Auditors, the European Ombudsman, and the EU agencies.

Part VI moves us from what the EU is and how it works to what it does. Its focus is on economic policies—perhaps the core activities of the Union. Successive chapters examine the single market, external commercial policies, competition policy, EMU, the Lisbon Agenda, the CAP, and Structural and Regional Funds. Part VII, meanwhile, considers other areas of activity such as environmental policy, consumer and energy policy. Finally, in terms of policy areas, Part VIII deals with foreign policy and home affairs, looking at the EU's role in dealing with borders, migration, and security.

The penultimate section (Part IX) broadens our perspective again, looking at some of the key debates that have surrounded the development of the Union. Issues relating to the so-called democratic deficit, the presence, or absence, of a European identity, the nature and impact of public opinion, and the nature of the EU—whether a traditional international organization or a state in the making or something different again—have shaped both political and academic debates for many years.

Finally, no volume such as this would be complete without consideration of the relationship between the Union and its constituent member states (Part X). The ability of member states to coordinate their policies when dealing with the Union, debates between them as to what constitutes legitimate burden-sharing, and the impact of the Union on policies and politics within the member states are fundamental issues not only in the academic study of the EU but also loom increasingly large in public and political debates concerning its future. The conventional slogan "European integration" itself deserves deconstruction: what is being "integrated," what is left unaligned? The EU has no agreed end station.

This *Oxford Handbook* was several years in gestation. It goes without saying, therefore, that we would like to thank our editor at Oxford University Press, Dominic Byatt, and his colleagues for their hard work and dedication. Thanks go to our home institutions—the SAIS Bologna Center, the University of Birmingham, and Somerville College and the Law Faculty at Oxford—for the support and confidence that goes alongside a regular paycheck. Thanks go to Valeria Calderoni, who played a vital role in bringing the project to a close. Most important, this volume would not have been possible without the commitment and professionalism of our contributors. Although we believe that the collection is greater than the sum of its parts, we also recognize that it was built on a foundation of individual effort.

Erik Jones	Anand Menon	Stephen Weatherill
Bologna, Italy	Oxford, UK	Oxford, UK
		August, 2011

PART I

PERSPECTIVES

CHAPTER 1

··

REALIST, INTERGOVERNMENTALIST, AND INSTITUTIONALIST APPROACHES

··

MARK A. POLLACK

FOR many years, theoretical approaches to the study of the EU were dominated by theories of international relations (IR). For many IR theorists, the European Communities, and later the EU, were international organizations, albeit unusually well institutionalized ones,[1] and off-the-shelf theories such as realism sufficed to understand and explain the EU. Other IR theorists, such as Ernst Haas, argued that the distinguishing feature of the EU was an ongoing process of integration that was transforming the EU into a new polity, and neo-functionalist theorists subsequently developed new approaches that focused on interest groups, on transnational flows, and on supranational actors as important drivers of the integration process (see Chapter 2, this volume). When the European Community seemed to run into trouble in the 1960s, however, intergovernmentalist theorists reasserted the primacy of the nation state within EU institutions, and the intergovernmentalist approach was given further impulse in the 1990s by the liberal intergovernmentalism of Andrew Moravcsik, which remains influential even as other scholars have attempted to build more complex institutional models on the core assumptions of earlier theories.

This chapter examines a body of theories—realism, intergovernmentalism, liberal intergovernmentalism, and rational-choice institutionalism—that together represent a distinctive family of approaches to the study of the EU. While these various theories are often depicted, correctly, as rivals in explaining particular developments in EU politics, they share an intellectual starting point in international relations, as well as two common core assumptions, namely (1) the initial primacy and ongoing centrality of states (as opposed to transnational or supranational actors) in European integration and EU politics, and (2) the assumption that those states (and other actors) behave as utility-maximizing rational actors.[2] For this reason, I shall argue, the theories grouped in this chapter constitute a broad research program in EU studies, distinct from both constructivist and sociological analyses (which question the core rationality assumption—see Chapters 3 and 4, this volume) and multilevel governance approaches (which challenge the primacy of states as key actors in EU politics—see Chapter 5, this volume).

Despite these common assumptions, the various theories reviewed in this chapter also differ on three other assumptions, namely (1) the nature and derivation of state preferences, (2) the severity of the international security environment, and (3) the significance of international institutions in shaping the interactions of states and creating potentially powerful supranational agents. These different assumptions, in turn, explain the primary differences in the predictions of each theory about the workings of EU politics and the process of European integration.

Finally, this chapter can also be read, not only as a typological argument about the relationship of realist, intergovernmentalist, and institutionalist theories to each other, but also as an intellectual history argument, tracing an intellectual progression in the literature from realism to intergovernmentalism to liberal intergovernmentalism to rational-choice institutionalism. While useful as a heuristic device, however, this intellectual history argument should not be confused with an evolutionary argument: the "later" theories have not replaced or subsumed "earlier" theories like realism, which have continued to develop in recent years and remain more or less viable as theories of European integration and EU politics.

Reflecting this framework, the chapter is divided into three primary sections, discussing realism, intergovernmentalism and liberal intergovernmentalism, and rational-choice institutionalism in turn, with a particular focus on the less-studied realist EU literature. A brief final section concludes.

1.1. REALISM

Realism is, according to a widespread conventional wisdom, the oldest and arguably dominant theory of international relations. In fact, realism is not a single theory but a family of theories, commonly traced back to "classical" realist works by Thucydides, Machiavelli, and Hobbes, as well as twentieth-century realists like E. H. Carr, Hans Morgenthau, and Reinhold Niebuhr.[3] In the late twentieth century, Kenneth Waltz sought to systematize realist thought, articulating a parsimonious and influential "neorealist" theory of international politics, premised on the primacy of states and on a structural analysis of an anarchic international system that required states to focus on security, power, and relative gains.[4] From these basic assumptions Waltz derived a series of broad generalizations, including the ubiquity of power balancing, the greater stability of bipolar structures over multipolar structures, and the epiphenomenal nature of international institutions and international law, which were taken to be reflections of the underlying distribution of power and the preferences of the great powers.

Waltz's neo-realism or structural realism proved enormously influential, both among realists and among critics who often couched their own neo-liberal[5] or constructivist[6] theories as elaborations of or rejoinders to Waltz. However, followers of Waltz faced a dilemma in applying his theory to new questions and to real-world events. Waltz's theory was famously spare, focusing on just a few key variables and explicitly eschewing any formal theory of international institutions, domestic politics, or foreign policy. Furthermore, and even more problematic, Waltz's basic assumption about states' preferences—that states "at a minimum, seek their own preservation, and at a maximum, drive for universal domination"[7]—was frustratingly vague, requiring greater precision to serve as the basis of a theory that could generate specific, testable predictions about outcomes in international politics.[8]

Within the neo-realist camp, two competing approaches emerged, differentiated by their assumptions about the severity of the security dilemma and its impact on the prospects for war and the possibility of international cooperation. On the one hand, offensive realists like John Mearsheimer adopted relatively pessimistic assumptions about the implications of anarchy, arguing that the security dilemma requires each state to attempt to maximize its own power, seeking not only security but also hegemony, and distrusting the intentions of other states.[9] In this view, states must indeed be concerned about military power and relative gains, the prospects for international cooperation are bleak, and international institutions hold out only the "false promise" of mitigating the effects of anarchy.[10] By contrast, defensive realists "reasoned that under very common conditions the war-causing potential of anarchy is attenuated."[11] In this view, a number of factors such as military technology, geography, strategic beliefs, and modern nationalism may increase the costs of offensive war, making anarchy less threatening, security more plentiful, and defensive strategies more attractive than in Waltz's model.[12] In this view, the security dilemma, or anarchy itself, could be seen as a variable, and international cooperation might be particularly promising and robust insofar as technology, geography, and other factors favored defense over offense.[13]

Departing more decisively from Waltz, still another group of scholars, frequently grouped under the rubric of "neoclassical realists," have retreated from the purely structural approach of neo-realism, supplementing systemic factors with consideration of domestic factors that might act as intervening variables between systemic pressures, on the one hand, and state behavior, on the other hand, and thus offer a realist theory of foreign policy.[14] In Gideon Rose's influential formulation, the structural distribution of material capabilities sets the parameters of a state's foreign policy, and is given analytic primacy. However, "the impact of such power capabilities on foreign policy is indirect and complex, because systemic pressures must be translated through intervening variables at the unit level."[15] More specifically, domestic factors including socioeconomic interest-group coalitions, military doctrines, and elite perceptions, among others, can refract systemic pressures in different ways.

These elaborations of realist thought have occasioned a sharp inter-paradigm debate between realists and their critics, who accuse neo-classical realists in particular of theoretical "degeneration" and inconsistency. Drawing on Lakatosian analysis of the social sciences, for example, John Vasquez has argued that realist scholars after Waltz have amended the core assumptions of the theory in ways that violate the "hard core" of realism as a research program, engaging in a "degenerative" rather than a "progressive" research program in which assumptions are changed to "fit" the data, without generating additional novel insights about international politics.[16] Along similar lines, Jeffrey Legro and Andrew Moravcsik have argued that neoclassical realists regularly violate the three core assumptions that the authors argue distinguish realism as a school of thought: (1) states as unitary actors (units); (2) states as rational utility maximizers (preferences); and (3) the anarchic nature of the international system forcing states to place primacy on self-help, power, and relative gains (international structure). In practice, they argue, neoclassical realists frequently violate the second and third of these assumptions, for example by replacing the assumption of fixed preferences with liberal conceptions of domestic politics, or smuggling in systemic insights from neo-liberal regime theory. The result is a "minimal realism," difficult or impossible to distinguish from other rational-choice theories of politics and in no way distinctively realist.[17]

Not surprisingly, defenders of realist theory reject what Wohlforth calls the "monolithic myth" that all realist theory comprises a single research program, and that variation from strict neo-realist assumptions constitutes inconsistency and degeneration.[18] Recent work in both structural and neoclassical realism, they argue, constitutes a progressive research agenda, and one that benefits from mutual learning among theorists rather than a strict inter-paradigm debate among realism, liberalism, and other "grand theories" of international politics.[19]

We need not take sides in this dispute to assess the ways in which, and the extent to which, realist theory has examined and explicated developments in European integration and the workings of the EU both internally and as a foreign-policy actor. Beginning with neo-realism, it is striking that Waltz devoted only a few pages in his landmark text to the then-European Communities, which he explained as a side effect of the structural condition of US–Soviet bipolarity. Put simply, Waltz attributed the uneven progress of (West) European integration to the fact that the United States had emerged as the guarantor of West European security in the face of the Soviet threat, leaving the member states of the European Community free to pursue integration without concerns about security threats from their European partners.[20]

Following closely from Waltz's analysis is John Mearsheimer's offensive realist analysis of the prospects for the EU *after* the Cold War. Taking Waltz's account as his starting point, Mearsheimer predicted that the collapse of the Soviet Union and the departure of the United States from the defense of continental Europe would lead to an increase in concerns about relative gains among EU member states, most notably with respect to German power and intentions, and place a significant check upon the future course of European integration.[21]

Similarly, offensive realists predicted increasing tensions in the transatlantic US–EU relationship as "deep structural forces" produce divergent geopolitical interests in Europe and the United States.[22] Indeed, given American "hyper-power" after the Cold War, some scholars predicted European balancing, or "soft balancing," against the United States in a unipolar world.[23] Still other realists, noting the EU's relatively low levels of defense spending, slow economic growth rates, and demographic decline, argued that the relative decline of Europe's material power resources would condemn the EU to an ever-shrinking place in a world order likely to be dominated by the United States and by rising powers like China and India.[24]

In fact, despite occasional crises over the non-ratification of the Constitutional Treaty and the financial crisis of 2008–2010, the European Union has managed in the two decades since the end of the Cold War to engage in both widening (enlarging from 12 to 27 members) and deepening (four major treaties, institutional change, establishment of the euro, etc.), and critics of realism have pointed to the relative success of the EU during this period as a strong refutation of the theory.[25] The evidence of tension in the transatlantic relationship is more equivocal, with some realist scholars seeing the Franco–German campaign against the 2003 US invasion of Iraq as evidence of diverging geopolitical preferences between the US and the EU as well as among EU countries,[26] while critics argue that the US–EU and NATO relationships remain vital despite the rupture over Iraq. Indeed, in Moravcsik's analysis, the EU has confounded realist predictions on every front: the EU itself has not fractured under the strain of renewed geopolitical conflict, but deepened and widened substantially since the end of the Cold War; Europe has not declined but remains, alongside the US, one of the two most influential powers in the contemporary world; and the transatlantic relationship, rather than fragmenting, remains close, with disagreements and diplomatic crises having arguably *lessened* since the end of the Cold War.[27]

Notwithstanding this refutation of offensive realism, it is worth reiterating that realist work on the EU has been quite diverse, and should not be taken as synonymous with Mearsheimer's bleak offensive realist predictions. Defensive realists, for example, predicted that post-Cold War Europe might in fact be "primed for peace," given that the offense–defense balance in today's EU strongly favors defensive strategies.[28] Other defensive realists, like Joseph Grieco, went further, seeking to account for success of the integration process in post-Cold War Europe. In a widely cited article, Grieco posits a "neorealist voice opportunities hypothesis" which he argues is consistent with the core hypotheses of neo-realist theory and generates new insights into the "institutional rule trajectory" of the EU. When negotiating new international institutions, Grieco argues, "states—and especially relatively weak but still necessary partners—will seek to ensure that any cooperative arrangement they construct will include effective voice opportunities."[29] In empirical terms, Grieco argues that the French and Italian entrepreneurship in favor of Economic and Monetary Union can be explained largely by their eagerness to secure a voice in monetary policy through their representatives in the ECB. Grieco's thesis is arguably consistent with a broad defensive realism, but its core insight—that states seek to increase their influence through institutions—is not distinctive to realist theory, as Legro and Moravcsik point out.[30]

In recent years, a group of mostly neoclassical realist theorists have turned their attention to the study of the EU's Common Foreign and Security Policy. Typically these scholars have sought to rebut constructivist arguments about the EU as a so-called "normative power." As formulated by Ian Manners, the normative power argument constitutes two key claims: that the EU is *normatively distinctive*, embodying certain core norms (peace, liberty, democracy, the rule of law, and human rights) and championing those norms in its foreign policy; and that the EU is a *normative power*, diffusing its norms primarily through example and persuasion rather than through reliance on economic or military power.[31]

In response to such claims, various scholars have put forward a realist critique, suggesting that the EU is motivated, at least in part, by material interests as well as normative values (the problem of "mixed motives" or "hypocrisy"[32]), with material economic interests often trumping core values, as when the EU defends its Common Agricultural Policy despite that policy's pernicious trade-distorting effects on farmers in less developed countries. Indeed, Adrian Hyde-Price, citing E. H. Carr, argues that the EU's universalist claims often disguise particularistic material interests.[33] American neoconservative Robert Kagan goes further, suggesting that the EU's normative preference for international institutions and the rule of law actually reflects the EU's underlying military weakness and hence its preference to utilize the institutional frameworks most likely to secure its substantive preferences at the global level.[34] Still others question the extent of the EU's commitment to international law, suggesting that the EU—like the US and other states—is prepared to violate international law when doing so is in its interest.[35]

Looking beyond the EU's normative difference, realist and other rationalist scholars also dispute Manners' "normative power" argument, claiming that the most important mechanisms of the EU's normative diffusion actually rely on the use of material power resources, and most notably on economic conditionality. Other realist scholars adopt a similar approach to the EU's emerging ESDP. In this view, the EU's humanitarian and peacekeeping missions in Bosnia and Kosovo can be seen, not (only) as expressions of EU values, but (also, or primarily) as a reflection of the "milieu goal" of maintaining a stable geopolitical balance in Europe,[36] while the EU's halting and selective deployment of peacekeeping troops to the Congo and other African nations represents an effort to increase the credibility of ESDP, but only where that aim can be achieved at relatively low cost and high probability of success.[37]

Finally, turning from a positive to a normative analysis, Hyde-Price makes a realist argument that the EU should behave as a "calculator not a crusader." More specifically, he argues that the EU should focus primarily on its core material interests, avoiding crusades and taking heed of realist cautions about the frequently tragic and unintended impacts of moral crusades in an anarchic international realm. In keeping with defensive realism, Hyde-Price concedes that the structure of the international system is not fully determining of economic policies, allowing some space for EU countries to promote "second-order normative concerns." Even here, however, he counsels EU governments to learn from realist analysis about the potential ineffectiveness of international law and institutions, noting that reliance on such instruments is unlikely to yield "ethical" outcomes in practice.[38]

In sum, realist scholarship offers a cautionary analysis of both European integration and of the EU's role in the world, pointing to the importance of material interests and the significance of structural factors that may impede intra-EU relations as well as the transatlantic alliance. Nevertheless, we can identify two primary weaknesses in the realist literature reviewed above. First, it seems clear that the most pessimistic offensive realist predictions about the EU and its relations with the US have not (or not yet) been vindicated by events in the post-Cold War era. This has led many realists to embrace less parsimonious defensive realist and neoclassical realist theories better suited to explaining European developments. Second, however, while such realists have attempted to show that the progress of European integration is *not incompatible* with realist theory, it remains the case that realist theories of integration and internal EU politics remain relatively sparse, and many of these theories engage in "minimal realism" and generate few novel insights that draw directly on realist theory's emphasis on international structure, security, and material power as the primary determinants of international outcomes.[39] The solution to these weaknesses, according to Moravcsik and other critics, is to jettison realist theories in favor of an intergovernmentalist or liberal intergovernmentalist approach.

1.2. INTERGOVERNMENTALISM AND LIBERAL INTERGOVERNMENTALISM

As a matter of intellectual and disciplinary history, the first major theory of European integration to systematically question realist assumptions was the neo-functionalism of Ernst Haas and his followers. Haas's neo-functionalism rejected not only realism's pessimistic assumptions about the effects of anarchy, but also its core assumption of state-centrism, embracing instead a pluralist model that gave increasing prominence to societal as well as supranational actors, and positing a gradual process of integration in which individuals would gradually transfer their demands, expectations, and loyalties to a new center in Brussels.[40] Empirical developments of the 1960s, however, re-emphasized the importance of the EU's member governments as gatekeepers limiting the transfer of powers from member states to a new center.

Reflecting these developments, an "intergovernmentalist" school of integration theory emerged, beginning with Stanley Hoffmann's claim that the nation state, far from being obsolete, had proven "obstinate."[41] Most obviously with de Gaulle, but later with the accession of new member states such as the UK, Ireland, and Denmark in 1973, member governments made it clear that they would resist the gradual transfer of sovereignty to the Community, and that European Community decision-making would reflect the continuing primacy of the nation state. As William Wallace bluntly argued,

"The success of the neo-functional approach depended upon national governments not noticing—in effect—the gradual draining away of their lifeblood to Brussels."[42] Indeed, in the view of intergovernmentalists like Paul Taylor, the few decisive political agreements of the 1970s, such as the creation of the European Council in 1974, and the establishment of the European Monetary System in 1979, had actually taken the Community back to a traditional intergovernmentalist style of decision-making which retained the national veto and minimized the role of supranational actors like the Commission.[43]

Contemporary historical scholarship also pointed in large part to the central role and even the strengthening of EU member governments as a result of the integration process.[44] Studies of EU policy-making also appeared to support these claims, demonstrating for example that the EU's Structural Funds, often seen as the prototypical example of multilevel governance, in fact featured a strong and even growing gatekeeper role for national governments.[45] Under these circumstances, Haas himself pronounced the "obsolescence of regional integration theory," counseling students of European integration to focus instead on the emerging study of international regimes.[46]

Despite this empirical support, intergovernmentalist theories of the 1960s and 1970s were hobbled by vague assumptions about the preferences of EU member governments. Intergovernmentalists broadly shared a view of member governments as being jealous of their sovereignty and determined to retain control within the EU—making intergovernmentalism, in effect, a theory of brakes on the integration process. By and large, however, early intergovernmentalists failed to provide clear assumptions about the substantive policy preferences of EU member governments, including any possible preferences for further integration. Hence, when the European integration process was "relaunched" with the 1992 internal market program and the SEA, the theoretical debate about European integration was revived, with a number of scholars viewing the relaunching of the integration process as a vindication of earlier neo-functionalist models.[47] By contrast, Andrew Moravcsik argued in a series of articles and in a landmark book that even these steps forward could be accounted for by a revised intergovernmentalist model emphasizing the power and preferences of EU member states.[48]

In its most elaborate formulation, Moravcsik's "liberal intergovernmentalism" is a three-step model, which combines (1) a liberal theory of national preference formation with (2) an intergovernmental model of EU-level bargaining and (3) a "credible commitments" model of institutional choice. In the first or liberal stage of the model, national chiefs of government (COGs) aggregate the interests of their domestic constituencies, as well as their own interests, and articulate their respective national preferences toward the EU. Thus, national preferences are complex, reflecting the distinctive economics, parties, and institutions of each member state, and they are determined *domestically*, not shaped by participation in the EU as some neo-functionalists had proposed. In substantive terms, Moravcsik argues, national preferences are driven by issue-specific and generally economic interests, with at best a secondary role for geopolitical interests (*pace* realism) or ideology.[49]

In the second or intergovernmental stage, national governments bring their preferences to the bargaining table in Brussels, where agreements reflect the relative power of each member state, and where supranational organizations such as the Commission exert little or no influence. By contrast with neo-functionalists, who emphasized the entrepreneurial and brokering roles of the Commission and the upgrading of the common interest among member states, Moravcsik and other intergovernmentalists emphasize the hardball bargaining among member states and the importance of bargaining power, package deals, and side payments as determinants of intergovernmental bargains on the most important EU decisions.

Third and finally, Moravcsik puts forward a rational choice theory of institutional choice, arguing that EU member states adopt particular institutions—pooling sovereignty through QMV, or delegating sovereignty to supranational actors like the Commission and the Court—in order to increase the credibility of their mutual commitments. Pooling and delegating sovereignty through international organizations, he argues, allows states to commit themselves credibly to their mutual promises on which they might otherwise be tempted to renege, by monitoring state compliance and filling in the blanks of broad international treaties, such as those that have constituted the European Community/EU.

In empirical terms, Moravcsik argues that the EU's historic intergovernmental agreements, such as the 1957 Treaties of Rome and the 1992 TEU, were not driven primarily by supranational entrepreneurs, unintended spillovers from earlier integration, or transnational coalitions of interest groups, but rather by a gradual process of preference convergence among the most powerful member states, which then struck central bargains among themselves, offered side payments to smaller member states, and delegated strictly limited powers to supranational organizations that remained more or less obedient servants.

Overarching the three steps of this model is a "rationalist framework" of international cooperation.[50] Although sometimes mischaracterized as "realist" by critics, liberal intergovernmentalism (LI), like intergovernmentalism, shares only the core assumptions of state-centrism and rationality with realist theory. By contrast with realism, however, LI does not assume that states are characterized by identical preferences for national security and power, nor does it assume that the anarchical structure of the international system is sufficiently unforgiving to preclude deep cooperation or integration among states. Rather, "LI simply acknowledges a blunt empirical fact about contemporary institutions like the EU: member states are 'masters of the treaty' and continue to enjoy pre-eminent decision-making power and political legitimacy."[51]

1.3. Rational-Choice Institutionalism

By the early 2000s, Moravcsik and Schimmelfennig argue, LI had acquired the status of a "baseline theory" in EU studies, "an essential first cut explanation against which other theories are often compared."[52] Nevertheless, both the basic theoretical assumptions and the empirical claims of LI were questioned by international relations scholars coming from three different approaches. The core assumption of state-centrism was questioned by proponents of both neo-functionalism and multilevel governance (see, respectively, Chapters 2 and 5, this volume); the core assumption of states as rational actors with domestically determined preferences was questioned by constructivist and sociological scholars (see, respectively, Chapters 3 and 4, this volume); and the assumption that EU institutions exerted little influence over EU outcomes was questioned by rational-choice institutionalist (RCI) scholars.

This third school of thought was presented by its pioneers as a repudiation of inter-governmentalism and offered a distinctive set of theoretical and empirical claims.[53] Yet in fact RCI is largely consistent with and builds upon the core assumptions of LI, starting with a similar statist and rationalist set of assumptions, theorizing institutional choice, and then going one step further to analyze the *operation* of those institutions, including how they constrain states and produce unintended and path-dependent consequences in the long term.

Space precludes an extended review of RCI and its application to the EU, which has in any event been the subject of multiple review essays.[54] Suffice it to say here that RCI analyses have focused scholarly attention on two key questions that had been understudied in previous EU scholarship. First, RCI students of the EU have theorized and empirically studied the creation of EU institutions, including the decision to "pool" sovereignty through QMV and the decision to delegate powers and discretion to supranational "agents" such as the Commission, the ECJ, and the ECB. Simplifying slightly, such "principal–agent" accounts of delegation argue that member-state principals, as rational actors, delegate powers to supranational organizations primarily to allow member governments to commit themselves credibly to international agreements and to benefit from the speed and/or expertise provided by supranational actors. Despite differences in emphasis, the empirical work of these scholars has collectively demonstrated that EU member governments do indeed delegate powers to supranational agents largely to reduce the transaction costs of policy-making, in particular through the monitoring of member-state compliance, the filling-in of incomplete contracts, and the speedy and efficient adoption of implementing regulations.[55] By and large, these theories are compatible with, and arguably extend, the basic model of institutional choice in Moravcsik's liberal intergovernmentalism.

Second, however, nearly all rational-choice institutionalists go beyond the institutional choice stage and theorize about and empirically study the subsequent workings of the EU's legislative, executive, and judicial bodies. The scholarly literature on the EU's legislative process, for example, is overwhelmingly dominated by rational-choice institutionalists, who model the intergovernmental bargaining and voting processes of the Council, the legislative behavior of the European Parliament, and the interactions of the two branches of the EU legislature under various decision rules.[56]

With respect to executive politics, rational-choice scholars have theorized the principal–agent relationship between the EU's member states as principals and EU supranational actors like the Commission as agents. The determinants of supranational autonomy, in this view, can be found primarily in the administrative procedures that the principals may establish to define *ex ante* the scope of agency activities, as well as the oversight procedures that allow for *ex post* oversight and sanctioning of errant agents. Applied to the EU, principal–agent analysis leads to the hypothesis that agency autonomy is likely to vary across issue areas and over time, as a function of the preferences of the member states, the distribution of information between principals and agents, and the decision rules governing the application of sanctions or the adoption of new legislation. By and large, empirical studies of executive politics in the EU have supported these hypotheses, pointing in particular to the significance of decision rules as a crucial determinant of executive autonomy.[57]

Students of EU judicial politics, finally, have also drawn on principal–agent analysis, theorizing the ECJ as a politically insulated agent with an extraordinary degree of discretion vis-à-vis member governments, and the ability to shape not only legal but constitutional developments such as the direct effect and supremacy of European law. Such models have become progressively more sophisticated over time, progressing from simple principal–agent models of member state–court interaction to richer models that incorporate the Court's "other interlocutors," including national courts and individual litigants.[58]

What all three bodies of RCI literature share in common is that, proceeding from starting assumptions of rational state actors, they all theorize explicitly about the creation and the operation of supranational institutions and agents whose behavior may be controlled only imperfectly by the member states that created them. In this sense, RCI scholars could argue, rational-choice institutionalism has subsumed liberal intergovernmentalism, incorporating LI's core assumptions and insights and adding on a set of mid-range theories about the workings of EU institutions, principal–agent relations, and the EU policy-making process.[59] Moravcsik and Schimmelfennig dispute this claim, however, arguing that, "LI theory applies far more broadly than is supposed," insofar as "many decisions within the EU are taken by *de facto* consensus or unanimity, even when the formal rules seem to dictate otherwise."[60] Nevertheless, as the authors also point out, the distinction between LI and RCI should not be overdrawn, since they draw upon nearly identical core assumptions and fit within a broad rationalist framework, and since the primary differences between them are largely matters of empirical emphasis, with the former emphasizing intergovernmental bargaining about the core history-making decisions that established EU institutions, and the latter seeking to model the day-to-day workings of those institutions in practice.

1.4. Conclusions

Summing up this review, we may say that the relationship among realist, intergovernmentalist, and rational-choice institutionalist theories is one of theme and variation, with the core themes being the interactions of rational, self-interested states under anarchy, and the variation consisting in assumptions about the nature of state preferences, the severity of the security dilemma, and the role of international institutions in EU and world politics.

To some extent, I have suggested, we can also discern in this account an intellectual history progression, in which each successive theory—realism, followed by intergovernmentalism, liberal intergovernmentalism, and finally rational-choice institutionalism—adopts and adapts core assumptions from the previous one. Nevertheless, as tempted as an RCI scholar (such as myself) might be to claim the pinnacle of an evolutionary ladder, the evidence reviewed in this chapter is more equivocal, finding theoretical evolution and significant variation *within* each tradition, all of which remain legitimate approaches to the study of the EU.

The differences among these three groups of theories are significant, and disciplinary rivalries certainly encourage a focus on the variations rather than the common themes in these theories. Nevertheless, I remain convinced, as I wrote a decade ago, that realism, liberal intergovernmentalism, and rational-choice institutionalism

> are all part of an emerging rationalist research programme which is rapidly establishing itself as the dominant paradigm in European integration theory... Whether we label this research programme "liberal intergovernmentalism," "rational-choice institutionalism," "regime theory," or simply "rationalism" is less important for our purposes than the fact that there exists... a community of scholars operating with similar basic assumptions and with few or no systematic differences in empirical findings across the "isms." ... In any event, the differences in basic assumptions among these three approaches are minor in contrast to constructivist and sociological approaches, which question the basic assumptions underlying the rationalist approach, and indeed the very "ontology" of such rationalist studies.[61]

It is these, very different, theories of politics that are the focus of the chapters that follow.

NOTES

1. Hence Moravcsik's claim that the EU "is best seen as an international regime for policy coordination." Andrew Moravcsik, "Preferences and Power in the European Community: A Liberal Intergovernmentalist Approach," *Journal of Common Market Studies* 31, no. 4 (December 1993), 473–524, at 480.
2. State-centrism and rationality are not universal assumptions of realist theory, which remains diverse, but both assumptions are commonplace in modern realist theories and in neo-realist theory in particular. See Jeffrey Legro and Andrew Moravcsik, "Is Anybody Still a Realist?" *International Security* 24, no. 2 (Autumn 1999), 5–55. Similarly, state-centrism was the core assumption of early intergovernmentalists, whose assumptions about state preferences were broadly rationalist if not always clearly specified. See Ben Rosamond, *Theories of European Integration* (Basingstoke: Palgrave, 2000), 75–81. Finally, state-centrism and rationality are explicitly laid out as the core assumptions of both liberal intergovernmentalism and rational-choice institutionalism. See respectively Andrew Moravcsik

and Frank Schimmelfennig, "Liberal Intergovernmentalism," in Antje Wiener and Thomas Diez, eds, *European Integration Theory*, 2nd edition (Oxford: Oxford University Press, 2009), 67–87, at 68; and Mark A. Pollack, "International Relations Theory and European Integration," *Journal of Common Market Studies* 39, no. 2 (June 2001), 221–44, at 231.

3. See Michael Joseph Smith, *Realist Thought from Weber to Kissinger* (Baton Rouge: Louisiana State University Press, 1986).
4. Kenneth N. Waltz, *Theory of International Politics* (Reading, MA: Addison-Wesley Publishing Company, 1979).
5. See e.g. Robert O. Keohane, *After Hegemony: Cooperation and Discord in the World Political Economy* (Princeton: Princeton University Press, 1984).
6. See e.g. Alexander Wendt, *A Social Theory of International Politics* (New York: Cambridge University Press, 1999).
7. Waltz, *Theory of International Politics*, 118.
8. William C. Wohlforth, "Realism," in Christian Reus-Smit and Duncan Snidal, eds, *The Oxford Handbook of International Relations* (New York: Oxford University Press, 2008), 131–49, at 137.
9. John J. Mearsheimer, *The Tragedy of Great Power Politics* (New York: Norton, 2001).
10. John J. Mearsheimer, "The False Promise of International Institutions," *International Security* 19, no. 3 (Winter 1994/1995), 5–49.
11. Wohlforth, "Realism," 139.
12. See e.g. Robert Jervis, "Cooperation under the Security Dilemma," *World Politics* 30, no. 2 (January 1978), 167–214; Jeffrey W. Taliaferro, "Security Seeking Under Anarchy: Defensive Realism Revisited," *International Security* 25, no. 2 (Autumn 2000), 128–61; and Steven Van Evera, *Causes of War* (Ithaca: Cornell University Press, 2001).
13. Charles L. Glazer, "The Security Dilemma Revisited," *World Politics* 50, no. 1 (October 1997), 171–201.
14. See e.g. Stephen Brooks, "Dueling Realisms," *International Organization* 51, no. 3 (Summer 1997), 445–79; and Gideon Rose, "Neoclassical Realism and Theories of Foreign Policy," *World Politics* 51, no. 1 (October 1998), 144–72.
15. Rose, "Neoclassical Realism," 146
16. John Vasquez, "The Realist Paradigm and Degenerative versus Progressive Research Programs: An Appraisal of Neotraditional Research on Waltz's Balancing Proposition," *American Political Science Review* 91, no. 4 (December 1997), 899–913.
17. Legro and Moravcsik, "Is Anybody Still a Realist?"
18. Wolhlforth, "Realism," 138.
19. See e.g. Kenneth N. Waltz, Colin and Miriam Elman, Randall Schweller, and Stephen Walt, "Responses to Vasquez," *American Political Science Review* 91, no. 4 (December 1997), 899–913; Peter D. Feaver, Gunther Hellman, Randall L. Schweller, Jeffrey W. Taliaferro, William C. Wohlforth, Jeffrey W. Legro, and Andrew Moravcsik, "Correspondence: Brother, Can You Spare a Paradigm?" *International Security* 25, no. 1 (Summer 2000), 165–93; Randall L. Schweller, "The Progressiveness of Neoclassical Realism," in Colin Elman and Miriam Elman, eds, *Progress in International Relations Theory* (Cambridge, MA: MIT Press, 2003), 311–47; and Wohlforth, "Realism."
20. Waltz, *Theory of International Politics*, 70–1.
21. John J. Mearsheimer, "Back to the Future: Instability in Europe After the Cold War," *International Security* 15, no. 4 (Spring 1990), 5–56.

22. Stephen M. Walt, "The Ties that Fray: Why Europe and America are Drifting Apart," *The National Interest* 54 (Winter 1998–1999), 3–11.

23. Andrew Moravcsik "Europe: The Quiet Superpower," *French Politics* 7, nos. 3–4 (September–December 2009), 403–22.

24. Robert Kagan, "The End of the End of History: Why the 21st Century Will Look Like the 19th," *The New Republic* 238, no. 7 (April 23, 2008), 40–7.

25. Simon Collard-Wexler, "Integration Under Anarchy: Neorealism and the European Union," *European Journal of International Relations* 12, no. 3 (September 2006), 397–432; Andrew Moravcsik "Europe: The Quiet Superpower," *French Politics* 7, nos. 3–4 (September–December 2009), 403–22.

26. T. V. Paul, "Soft Balancing in the Age of U.S. Primacy," *International Security* 30, no. 1 (Summer 2005), 46–71.

27. Moravcsik, "Europe, the Quiet Superpower."

28. Jack Snyder, "Averting Anarchy in the New Europe," *International Security* 14, no. 4 (Winter 1990), 5–41; and Steven Van Evera, "Primed for Peace: Europe after the Cold War," *International Security* 15, no. 3 (Winter 1990–1991), 7–57.

29. Joseph M. Grieco, "State Interests and Institutional Rule Trajectories: A Neorealist Reinterpretation of the Maastricht Treaty and European Economic and Monetary Union," in Benjamin Frankel, ed., *Realism: Restatements and Renewal* (London: Frank Cass, 1995), 262–305, at 288–9.

30. Legro and Moravcsik, "Is Anybody Still a Realist?"

31. Ian Manners, "Normative Power Europe: A Contradiction in Terms?" *Journal of Common Market Studies* (2002), Vol. 40(, No. 2), (June 2002), 235–58.

32. Liesbeth Aggestam, "Introduction: Ethical Power Europe?" *International Affairs* 84, no. 1 (January 2008), 1–11.

33. Adrian Hyde-Price, "A 'Tragic Actor'? A Realist Perspective on 'Ethical Power Europe,'" *International Affairs* 84, no. 1 (January 2008), 29–44.

34. Robert Kagan, "Power and Weakness," *Policy Review* 113 (June/July 2002), 3–28.

35. Jack Goldsmith and Eric A. Posner, "Does Europe Believe in International Law?" *Wall Street Journal*, November 25, 2008, A15.

36. Aggestam, "Introduction: Ethical Power Europe?" 9.

37. Catherine Gegout, "Causes and Consequences of the EU's Military Intervention in the Democratic Republic of Congo: A Realist Explanation," *European Foreign Affairs Review* 10, no. 3 (2005), 427–43.

38. Hyde-Price, "A 'Tragic Actor'?" 36–41.

39. Legro and Moravcsik, "Is Anybody Still a Realist?"; Collard-Wexler, "Integration Under Anarchy."

40. Ernst B. Haas, *The Uniting of Europe* (Stanford: Stanford University Press, 1958; reprinted in 2004 by Notre Dame University Press).

41. Stanley Hoffmann, "Obstinate or Obsolete? The Fate of the Nation-State and the Case of Western Europe," *Daedalus* 95, no. 3 (Summer 1966), 862–915.

42. Quoted in Fritz W. Scharpf, "The Joint-Decision Trap: Lessons from German Federalism and European Integration," *Public Administration* 66, no. 3 (September 1988), 239–78.

43. Paul Taylor, *The Limits of European Integration* (New York: Columbia University Press, 1983).

44. See e.g. Alan S. Milward, *The European Rescue of the Nation-State*, 2nd edition (London: Routledge, 2000); and Alan S. Milward and Frances M. B. Lynch, eds, *The*

Frontiers of National Sovereignty: History and Theory 1945-1992 (London: Routledge, 1993).

45. Mark A. Pollack, "Regional Actors in an Intergovernmental Play: The Making and Implementation of EC Structural Policy," in S. Mazey and C. Rhodes, eds, *The State of the European Union, Vol. III* (Boston: Lynne Rienner, 1995), 361–90.

46. Ernst B Haas, "Turbulent Fields and the Theory of Regional Integration," *International Organization* 30, no. 2 (March 1976), 173–212.

47. See e.g. John Zysman and Wayne Sandholtz, "1992: Recasting the European Bargain," *World Politics* 41, no. 4 (July 1989), 95–128.

48. Moravcsik, "Preferences and Power"; and Andrew Moravcsik, *The Choice for Europe: Social Purpose and State Power from Messina to Maastricht* (Ithaca: Cornell University Press, 1998).

49. Moravcsik, *The Choice for Europe.*

50. Moravcsik, *The Choice for Europe*, 19–20; Moravcsik and Schimmelfennig, "Liberal Intergovernmentalism."

51. Moravcsik and Schimmelfennig, "Liberal Intergovernmentalism," 68.

52. Moravcsik and Schimmelfennig, "Liberal Intergovernmentalism," 67.

53. Geoffrey Garrett and George Tsebelis, "An Institutional Critique of Intergovernmentalism," *International Organization* 50, no. 2 (March 1996), 269–99.

54. See e.g. Joseph Jupille and James A. Caporaso, "Institutionalism and the European Union: Beyond International Relations and Comparative Politics," *Annual Review of Political Science* 2 (1999), 429–44; Keith Dowding, "Institutionalist Research on the European Union: A Critical Review," *European Union Politics* 1, no. 1 (February 2000), 125–44; Mark Aspinwall and Gerald Schneider, eds, *The Rules of Integration: Institutionalist Approaches to the Study of Europe* (New York: Manchester University Press, 2001); Mark A. Pollack, "The New Institutionalism and European Integration," in Antje Wiener and Thomas Diez, eds, *European Integration Theory*, 2nd edition (Oxford: Oxford University Press, 2009), 125–43.

55. Moravcsik, *The Choice for Europe*; Mark A. Pollack, *The Engines of Integration: Delegation, Agency and Agenda Setting in the European Union* (New York: Oxford University Press, 2003); and Fabio Franchino, *The Powers of the Union: Delegation in the EU* (New York: Cambridge University Press, 2007).

56. Gail McElroy, "Legislative Politics," in Knud Erik Jørgensen, Mark A. Pollack, and Ben Rosamond, eds, *The Handbook of European Union Politics* (New York: Sage, 2007), 175–94; Chapter 26, this volume.

57. Pollack, *The Engines of European Integration*; Franchino, *The Powers of the Union*; see also Chapters 46 and 28, this volume.

58. Lisa Conant, "Judicial Politics," in Knud Erik Jørgensen, Mark A. Pollack, and Ben Rosamond, eds, *Handbook of European Union Politics* (London: Sage, 2000), 213–29; Chapter 25, this volume.

59. Jonathan Slapin takes the empirical critique of intergovernmentalism a step further, venturing onto LI's home turf of major intergovernmental treaty negotiations and arguing that the EU's institutional rules provide small states with far greater power over outcomes than a purely intergovernmental model would suggest; see Jonathan B. Slapin, "Bargaining Power at Europe's Intergovernmental Conferences: Testing Institutional and Intergovernmental Theories," *International Organization* 62, no. 1 (January 2008), 131–62.

60. Moravcsik and Schimmelfennig, "Liberal Intergovernmentalism," 74.

61. Pollack, "International Relations Theory," 233.

CHAPTER 2

....

NEO-FUNCTIONALISM AND SUPRANATIONAL GOVERNANCE

....

WAYNE SANDHOLTZ AND ALEC STONE SWEET

THE transformation of the EEC stands as one of the remarkable political metamorphoses of modern times. Though the 1957 Treaty of Rome created an international organization with restricted authority, limited purposes, and a small membership, today's EU is an altogether different, quasi-constitutional, federal entity. It oversees a vast single market, but also a monetary union and a single currency, and it is pan-European in its scope. It produces common policies across a broad spectrum of domains touching on virtually every dimension of modern life.[1] Neo-functionalist theory offers a coherent, parsimonious explanation of this evolution.[2]

The chapter proceeds as follows. In section 2.1, we discuss the rebirth of neo-functionalist theory following its presumed death in the 1970s. In section 2.2, we clarify the aims and essential logic of the theory—what it proposes to explain and what it does not. Section 2.3 discusses how the present authors modified neo-functionalism, in particular, in light of theories of delegation and institutionalization. Section 2.4 briefly reviews some of the empirical research that, over the years, has confirmed neo-functionalism's primary causal claims. The final section (2.5) compares neo-functionalism with other theories of integration.

2.1 THE EARLY ABANDONMENT OF NEO-FUNCTIONALIST THEORY

....

By the 1980s, scholars of European integration almost without exception had discarded neo-functionalism as outmoded and disproven by events. By the early 1990s, neo-functionalism was virtually extinct. In the common narrative, de Gaulle's empty chair, the

Luxembourg compromise, and the failure of ambitious integration plans in the early 1970s refuted the neo-functionalist expectation that integration would be a relatively steady process. Further, member states, such as France, had shown that the EU could also be a site for the playing out of traditional international politics in Europe, centered on sovereignty and national interests.[3] We know now that the integration project did not stall in any real sense, and that the growth of supranational governance continued throughout the period of "Euro-sclerosis."[4]

Still, the abandonment of neo-functionalist theory by the 1980s seemed all the more complete in light of Haas's own declaration on *The Obsolescence of Regional Integration Theory*. But Haas offered evidence that the scope of the European Community's competences to govern had increased since its founding, and that the overall level of political integration was unchanged, having increased in some respects while declining in others.[5] Haas did note "the absence of much visible institutional movement toward further integration," and he recommended that future efforts be directed not toward repairing the deficiencies of regional integration theory, but rather toward devising new theories for new problems. Two interconnected forces were changing the world: intensifying international interdependence (what would later be called "globalization") and the rise of post-industrial problems in the wealthier countries.

Haas was right about the importance of globalization, but not about its implications for European integration. European institutions and organizations proved resilient and adaptive, and the EU today has well-developed authority in many of the domains that seemed so problematic in 1975 (like environmental protection and research and development). Haas also anticipated that globalization would reduce the drive for European integration, as problem-solving would have to take place at broader levels. Another possibility, however, was that globalization, in particular some of its implications for economic competitiveness, would provide a stimulus for further European integration.[6]

In short, the abandonment of neo-functionalism as a theory of European integration was premature.

2.2 THE AIMS AND LOGIC OF NEO-FUNCTIONALISM

Neo-functionalism is a theory of market and political integration within a specific region constituted by those states that have taken a formal decision to integrate. The theory accounts for the migration of rule-making authority from national governments to the EU. We refer to the EU's capacities to create, interpret, and enforce rules[7] as "supranational governance." As has been well documented,[8] these competences have deepened (the EU's rule systems have become denser, and more articulated within particular policy areas) and broadened (they cover an expanding range of substantive domains) over time. Further, the capacity of the EU's organs to monitor and enforce EU law has been steadily upgraded since the 1960s. Neo-functionalism claims to explain why, and how, that transformation occurred.

In seeking to explain the evolution of the EU over time, neo-functionalists locate the essential sources of the dynamism of integration in the EU's organs and institutional configuration. Haas proposed this key insight, as well as the core elements of a neo-functionalist theory of integration. On many of the major questions, we believe, Haas was right.

Haas conceived of integration as a product of transactions across borders, European institutions, and pluralist politics. First, the "the interests and values" of an emerging transnational society would be "defended by major groups involved in the process": political parties, industry associations, and labor federations, plus member-state governments.[9] Supranational organs of governance would possess "the formal attributes necessary to make [them] an agent of integration."[10] Integration would occur *to the extent that* (a) transnational activity and economic interdependence proceeded, revealing the potential both to reap joint gains and to deal with the negative externalities created by transnational activity; (b) European elites (private actors, firms, and public officials) were led to seek regional—rather than national—solutions to shared problems; and (c) supranational organs of governance supplied rules (law, procedures for the ongoing production of rules and dispute resolution) that satisfied these needs.[11] As will be readily apparent to contemporary social scientists, Haas was a pioneer of theorizing logics of institutionalization that are central both to sociological and historical brands of the new institutionalism.[12]

In neo-functionalism, the creation of supranational authority leads to changes in the expectations and behavior of social actors, who in turn shift some of their resources and policy efforts to the supranational level. Supranational bodies become the locus for a new kind of politics, spurring the formation of transnational associations and interest groups. As the supranational organs begin to deliver the coordinative solutions that societal groups want, those groups increasingly seek to influence supranational rules and policies. Haas also noticed that some forms of feedback produced new cycles of feedback, which he called "spillover." In its most basic form, spillover occurs when actors realize that the objectives of initial supranational policies cannot be achieved without extending supranational policy-making to additional, functionally related domains.

2.3   NEO-FUNCTIONALISM UPDATED

We developed our approach to integration with reference to generic materials that we found in institutional approaches to politics.[13] The three constituent elements of our theory are (1) actors and groups with transnational goals and interests (which we label "transnational society"), (2) supranational organizations with autonomous capacity to resolve disputes and to make rules, and (3) the rule system (or normative structure) that defines the polity. Haas focused on the same variables, and understood that, under specified conditions, they would become causally connected to one another to drive integration forward. The outcome to be explained by our modified neo-functionalism was the expansion of supranational governance. In this respect, we differed somewhat from Haas, who predicted that the integration process would lead political actors "to shift their national loyalties, expectations, and political activities to a new and larger center."[14] We left open the question of whether, and to what extent, the loyalties and identities of actors would shift from the national to the European level, and we insisted that there was substantial room for the expansion of supranational governance without that ultimate shift in identification.

2.3.1 Cross-Border Transactors

To explain movement toward supranational governance, our starting point is transnational society, in particular, non-state actors who engage in transactions and communications across national borders within the context of the institutional arrangements established in the Rome Treaty. These transactors—anyone seeking to exchange goods, services, ideas, information, or funds across national frontiers—are those who need European rules, standards, and dispute resolution mechanisms, in other words, those who need supranational governance. Separate national legal regimes hinder such interactions. Those who seek cross-border transactions experience the absence of European-level rules as a cost or an obstacle to the realization of greater gains. Increasing levels of cross-border transactions and communications by private actors increase the perceived need (or "functional demand") for European-level rules and policies and for supranational capacity to supply them. Transactors therefore exert pro-integration pressure on their own governments, but they also activate the Commission and the ECJ, frequently bypassing national officials.

What has repeatedly been found in empirical studies is that European integration is largely the product of a basic kind of Haasian feedback loop: (a) increasing cross-border transactions activate (b) supranational governance (dispute resolution and rule-making), which facilitate (c) a subsequent expansion of cross-border transactions, which translates into greater social demand for new forms of supranational governance (spillover). Feedback loops and spillover have been basic mechanisms of integration across the history of the EU. Our theory led to comprehensive collection of data (measures of processes associated with integration), across the life of the European Community. We now know that intra-European Community trade, litigation and dispute resolution, the production of European Community legislation (directives and regulations), and the formation of Europe-level lobbying groups all increased steadily throughout the 1960s and 1970s.[15]

The theory provides testable propositions about how integration proceeds, and why integration proceeds faster in some policy domains than in others. In sectors where the intensity and value of cross-national transactions were relatively low, the supply of EU-level rules and dispute resolution was correspondingly low. Conversely, in policy areas where the number and value of cross-border transactions rose, so did the supply of EU-level rules, and so did the investment of interest groups in Brussels. Supranational governance expanded earlier and advanced further in areas related to the internal market, because the number and intensity of cross-border trade ties grew early and rapidly, and because transnational business organized to defend their claims in Brussels.

We specified the spillover mechanism in light of the transaction-driven theory of integration. As the EU removed the most obvious hindrances to cross-national exchange and interaction, new obstacles to such transactions were revealed and became salient to transactors. For instance, after the most direct restrictions on trade—intra-European Community tariffs and quotas—were removed, then differences in national regulatory standards—for the environment, health and safety, technical compatibility, and so forth—become more apparent barriers to exchange. Transactors then targeted these obstacles, through litigation and through pressure on EU institutions to expand the reach of EU rules into new domains. This reformulated version of spillover emphasizes not functional linkages among different policy domains but the way in which the removal of barriers reveals additional layers of obstacles hindering cross-national transactions. This logic neatly explains the chain of developments leading from the *Dassonville* case, to *Cassis de Dijon*, to European Community mutual recognition legislation.[16]

2.3.2 Supranational Organizations

Even if transactors are a primary motor of the expansion of supranational governance in the EU, an alternative theory might (as intergovernmentalists do) posit that the demand for integration generated by transnational activity is funneled exclusively through national governments, who then establish European rules through intergovernmental bargaining. In what we would call "strong intergovernmentalism," EU bodies (like the Commission and the ECJ) are "perfectly reactive agents," carrying out the wishes of their masters, the member-state governments.[17] By now, however, the empirical record is decisive: the Court and the Commission have routinely produced rules and policies that the member governments would not have adopted through intergovernmental bargaining. We summarize some of the research on that point in the next section.

As every student of EU politics knows, businesses and other groups with an interest in pushing European integration are not limited to the domestic politics "game."[18] They can bypass national policy-making processes, directly activating organs like the Court and the Commission. One strong assumption of neo-functionalism is that both the ECJ and the Commission will consistently work to produce pro-integrative policies, even when these are resisted by the most powerful member states. The reason is straightforward: in many situations, the Court and the Commission are not simple agents of the member states, but trustees exercising fiduciary responsibilities under the treaties.[19] Trustees are a special kind of agent: they possess the authority to govern the principals themselves, and its decisions are effectively insulated from reversal by the principals.[20]

The Court operates in an exceptionally broad "zone of discretion." That is, the sum of the powers formally conferred upon the Court plus those that the Court has acquired through its own rulings far outweigh the "sum of control instruments available" to other centers of authority, including member states.[21] Governments cannot block litigation against them, and they cannot escape the Court's control; moreover, it is virtually impossible for the member states to reverse unwanted decisions. The decision rule that underpins intergovernmental modes of governance in the European Community—unanimity—also underpins supranational authority, when it comes to the Court. As is well known, the ECJ expanded its own zone of discretion through a series of now-famous decisions that gradually "constitutionalized" the Treaty of Rome, federalizing the system in all but name.[22] It bears emphasis that the Court's rulings on direct effect and supremacy took place "in the absence of express authorization of the Treaty, and despite the declared opposition of Member State governments."[23] Note also that this quantum increase in supranational authority was initiated and consolidated during the 1960s and 1970s, when the construction of supranational governance had supposedly stalled.

The Commission likewise has important trusteeship powers. The Treaties establish some of these directly, including the (exclusive) authority to propose legislation, the power to initiate infringement proceedings in the ECJ, and to fine the member states in certain contexts. The Commission can also issue binding directives in support of the EU's market competition rules. Of course, the Commission must work collaboratively with other EU bodies, especially the European Parliament and the Council of Ministers, and it interacts constantly with organized interest groups as well as member-state governments. Even so, the oversight tools that governments can use to rein in the Commission are sometimes costly and of limited effectiveness. In addition, the Commission can exploit divergent preferences among its multiple principals (the member states).[24]

Finally, the Commission acts as a political entrepreneur, mobilizing and organizing private-sector groups to support its policy objectives. The Commission regularly creates—and sometimes funds—roundtables, working groups, and committees composed of firms and other non-state actors. The working groups help the Commission design programs and draft legislation; these same groups then become advocates of the Commission's proposals vis-à-vis national governments and other actors.[25] The Commission, for example, put together a "roundtable" of the leading information technology companies to help design, and lobby for, European Community-level research and development programs in the 1980s.[26] Mid-level Commission officials were behind the early-1980s creation of the European Venture Capital Association (EVCA), the first pan-European group representing the interests of venture capital firms.[27] The EVCA played a vital role two decades later in bringing about the emergence of new smaller-company stock exchanges in Europe.

For Haas, as for us, supranational organizations with independent authority are at the heart of the expansive dynamism of European integration. We have argued, and the evidence shows, that market and political integration has proceeded, in significant part, through the activities of the Commission and the Court. These organs have routinely generated policy outcomes that would not have been adopted by the member states if left to their own devices, given existing decision-rules.

2.3.3 Institutionalization

Indispensable to neo-functionalism is the proposition that shifts toward supranational governance tend to propel the system forward, sometimes into uncharted areas. We call this dynamic "institutionalization." Institutions are systems of rules;[28] institutionalization is the process by which rules are created, applied, and interpreted by those who live under them. As actors collectively argue about rules and find modes of resolving disputes, they inevitably modify the rules, which then feed back into subsequent activity.[29]

The logic of institutionalization has long been at work in the EU, and it is crucial to understanding integration as a dynamic process. As European actors discovered the limits or ambiguities in EU rules, they pressed for new or modified rules. The new rules created legal rights and opened new arenas for politics, and thereby established the context for subsequent interactions, disputes, and rule changes. Actors–including governments, private entities, and EU bodies—adapted to the new rules, but subsequently encountered their limits and ambiguities, which led them to generate new dispute resolution and rule-making processes. Institutionalization thus has a cyclic character. The body of supranational rules expands in scope and becomes more formal and specific over time, in ways—and this point is crucial—that are not predictable or expected from the *ex ante* perspective of those who establish them.[30]

This logic of institutionalization helps to explain why we observe a high degree of stickiness, or ratcheting, in the development of supranational governance. As EU rules multiply and extend their coverage, actors adjust their behaviors. Because the purpose of EU rules is to facilitate cross-border transactions, they tend to generate new kinds and higher levels of transactions, which then become entrenched interests. The number of actors with a material stake in the supranational system therefore expands. The concept of path-dependence captures the logic of this stickiness quite well. As Pierson argues, institutional change is a path-dependent process.[31] Once institutional changes are in place, actors adapt to them and frequently make significant investments in them. Institutional reversal—an unwinding of supranational rules—is possible but difficult because it entails writing off those investments (sunk costs). Institutional and policy outcomes become "locked in," channeling behavior and politics down specific paths and rendering less feasible previously plausible alternatives.

2.4 EMPIRICAL RESEARCH

Neo-functionalism generates empirical hypotheses about the course and shape of the EU's development over time. Further, the hypotheses are directly at odds with the empirical implications of contending theories, like intergovernmentalism. Some of the key propositions are the following. If neo-functionalism is right, then we would expect that:

- Increasing cross-border transactions will lead to greater activity on the part of supranational organizations, and to the expansion of supranational rules.
- Expanding supranational rules should, in a recursive process, lead to higher levels of cross-border transactions.
- The growth of supranational rules should lead to increases in the number and activity of interest groups at the EU level.
- The expansion of EU rules should increase supranational dispute resolution (the activity of the ECJ).
- Those sectors in which cross-border transactions are more numerous and important should move faster and farther toward supranational governance (EU-level rules and regulations).
- EU organizations like the Commission and Court of Justice will routinely produce supranational outcomes that the member states would not have produced on their own.
- Supranational governance will routinely produce outcomes that conflict with the revealed preferences of the most powerful states.

We now briefly summarize empirical results that address one or more of these hypotheses. The survey below is representative, not comprehensive. We organize the discussion under two headings: macro-level processes and sectoral outcomes.

2.4.1 Macro-Level Processes

Stone Sweet and his collaborators have confirmed the predictions of neo-functionalist theory with respect to the ECJ and the broader process of integration. Stone Sweet and Brunell, in the first scholarly work in EU studies to test any theory of integration against comprehensive data collected across the life of the European Community, showed that the legal system, once constitutionalized, spurred transnational economic activity, which, as it grew, further activated the legal system.[32] Fligstein and Stone Sweet pushed this project further, modeling European integration as a series of feedback loops, and made use of comprehensive data providing relatively direct measures of processes associated with integration.[33] The econometric analysis demonstrated that the activities of market actors, lobbyists, legislators, litigators, and judges had become connected to one another in specific ways. These linkages constituted a self-reinforcing system that has given the EU its fundamentally expansionary character. *The Judicial Construction of Europe* presents a qualitative analysis of the Court's impact on EU governance, as a means of cross-checking quantitative results, to further refine and test hypotheses, and to explore processes and outcomes that can only be understood through detailed case studies, or "process tracing."[34]

Additional studies continue this line of inquiry. Pitarkis and Tridimas confirm that "the establishment of an EU-wide legal order and a system of dispute resolution with the ECJ at the top, leads to deeper economic integration expressed as a larger share of intra-European Community trade in economic activity."[35] Carrubba and Murrah also found that "transnational actors are using the preliminary ruling process to expand transnational economic activity."[36]

Neo-functionalist approaches have dominated analyses of the ECJ and its effects on integration since Burley and Mattli's seminal article.[37] The intergovernmentalism of Garrett and Moravcsik, as a body of theorizing about integration and EU governance,[38] has failed to produce a theory of law and courts in the EU capable of surviving empirical tests.[39]

2.4.2 Sectoral Outcomes

A growing body of research on specific policy sectors directly tests core neo-functionalist propositions. These studies focus on variables (cross-border transactions, supranational organizations) and outcomes (supranational rules that major states opposed or that would not have won approval in intergovernmental forums) that are at the heart of the theory. Increasing cross-border exchange generates political processes that lead to EU-level rule-making. This pattern appears in the EU-led liberalization of telecommunications and air transport; the development of EU-level higher education policies; the production of EU rules for financial services; and the emergence of EU transport policy.[40]

A rich array of studies confirms the neo-functionalist claim that the EU's *supranational organizations*, namely, the Court and the Commission, often play a decisive—and independent—role in advancing integration. This has occurred in criminal justice, the EU-level liberalization of telecommunications and air transport, rule-making for financial services, electricity market integration, and EU-wide rights for immigrants.[41] Schmidt has argued convincingly that the Commission's powers are not limited to agenda setting, but that it can sometimes alter the domestic preferences of some member states, divide the opposition to its proposals, and increase the unattractiveness of a failure to agree.[42]

The more the Commission's authority and leverage expanded, the more private actors and transnational interest groups dealt directly with the Commission; EU regulation of state aids for industry offers an example.[43] Numerous sectoral studies demonstrate the decisive role played by direct alliances between the Commission and European interest groups in producing EU rules and policies.[44] The Commission is not only the frequent ally of trans-European interest groups (transactors); it frequently takes active steps to *organize and mobilize those groups*. It has done so on behalf of high-technology research and development, telecommunications liberalization, air transport liberalization, EU-level financial services regulation, and the creation of smaller-company stock markets.[45]

The ECJ often reinforces or expands the Commission's authority. For example, key rulings from the ECJ strengthened the Commission's hand and helped it to overcome member state opposition to its pro-integrative efforts in telecommunications, air transport, the regulation of state aids, and EU transport policy (see previous citations). The Court has also been the key actor extending EU rules in specific policy domains, including the health sector, despite member state opposition.[46]

Finally, it is worth stressing that research on the impact of the ECJ on policy processes and outcomes has invalidated theories that predict that the EU's supranational organs never produce "unintended consequences" from the perspective of the governments of the member states. Both Tsebelis and Garrett and Moravcsik have advanced theories that treat as a theoretical impossibility the capacity of EU organs to change the "rules of the game" governing EU policy-making.[47] Yet the ECJ does so, in two obvious ways, each of which routinely provokes spillover. First, when the Court chooses to apply treaty law to policy areas that were formerly assumed to be in the domain of national and inter-governmental, not supranational, governance, it empowers the Commission and the Court. Important examples have already been noted. Second, the Court can "constitu-tionalize" policy when it holds that specific legislative dispositions are required by Treaty law.[48] One well-documented example is the sex equality domain.[49]

As neo-functionalist theory predicts, transnational exchange, the authority of EU organizations, and supranational rule-making move together often enough to matter a great deal to the overall course of integration. It is important to stress that the empirical domain of neo-functionalism includes treaty revision episodes, the extension of new competences to EU organs, and policy-making within established legislative processes. It is decidedly *not* limited to narrowly "technical" sectors, or "low politics" areas outside of intergovernmental control. The best neo-functionalist research never ignored inter-governmental modes of governance. Instead, it demonstrated how, and the extent to which, intergovernmental bargaining and decision-making are embedded in the larger flow of integration, as integration has been institutionalized over time as supranational authority.

2.5 CONCLUSION

Neo-functionalism seeks to account for market and political integration, and for the migration of rule-making authority from national governments to the EU. The EU's capacities to resolve disputes, and to make, monitor, and enforce rules (supranational governance), has become both deeper and broader over time. Neo-functionalism claims to explain why, and how, that expansion occurred. The theory also allows us to answer a second, related question: why the development of supranational authority has pro-ceeded more rapidly in some policy domains than in others.

These questions are not the only ones worth asking about the EU. Scholars have sought to account for virtually every aspect of the EU: policy outcomes in specific sec-tors; the expansion of membership; the legislative mechanism; inter-organizational rela-tions within the EU; the evolution of public opinion and national or European identities; the development of the EU as a global actor; and so on. These are all legitimate topics for systematic research. But the scope of neo-functionalism is different: to provide a dynamic account of European integration. Very few extant theories of integration share neo-functionalism's goal of explaining the broad course of institutional development in the EU.

Tsebelis and Garrett, for instance, propose a model of how EU organizations interact in legislative processes to produce specific treaty revisions and pieces of secondary legislation.[50] But there is nothing dynamic about their model; it does not explain the evolution of the EU's organizations and institutions. Their theory treats as a theoretical impossibility what we have shown to be endemic: the Commission and the Court have succeeded in changing both the "rules of the game" and the organizational capacities of supranational institutions.[51]

The "multilevel governance" approach assesses how policy-making authority is distributed and shared across sub-national regions, national governments, and the European Union (see Chapter 5, this volume). But the approach does not offer a theory of integration or change; multilevel governance is itself an outcome of integration processes that it cannot explain.

The main rival to neo-functionalism as a dynamic theory of the broad course of European integration remains liberal intergovernmentalism (see Chapter 1, this volume). What is at stake between the two is not some (imagined) debate about whether EU policy-making is more supranational or more intergovernmental. The EU will always possess both intergovernmental and supranational (or federal) elements and mechanisms for rule-making. It is thus important to distinguish between "intergovernmentalism" as a mode of governance (which one finds in all federal polities), and "intergovernmentalism" as a theory of, or framework for explaining, integration.

Moravcsik does claim that his "liberal intergovernmentalism" (LI) is a general theory of the evolution of the EU, though his claims have become less ambitious over time (compare the sweeping claims in the 1991 article with those in *The Choice for Europe*). There are two major problems with the current, scaled-back version of intergovernmentalism. First, it is non-falsifiable. When EU organizations carry out the preferences of the powerful member states, they supposedly confirm the theory that governments control EU development. But when EU organizations do not adhere to the preferences of member governments, they also supposedly confirm the theory (by carrying out member state desires for EU-level enforcement of incomplete contracts). Any possible outcome would "fit" the theory, rendering it immune to falsification.[52] Second, the current version of LI has lost much of its distinctiveness relative to neo-functionalism.[53] Moravcsik now appears to agree with us (and with Pollack, Tallberg, and a host of others) that the more states seek to enhance the credibility of commitments through extensive delegation to EU organs, the more EU organs can be expected to generate outcomes that governments would not have produced on their own, given existing decision-rules.[54]

Neo-functionalism offers a causal explanation of the development of EU institutions and the expansion of their authority. Until a new theory can better explain what neo-functionalism does, it will remain the most theoretically viable and empirically productive general theory of European integration.

NOTES

1. Jonas Tallberg, "The Anatomy of Autonomy: An Institutional Account of Variation in Supranational Influence," *Journal of Common Market Studies* 38 (2000), 843; and Jonas Tallberg, "Delegation to Supranational Institutions: Why, How, and with What Consequences?" *West European Politics* 25 (2002), 23.

2. Some have referred to the version of neo-functionalism developed in our work as "trans-actionalist" theory, presumably because cross-border transactions are a crucial motor of the dynamic process of integration we theorize.

3. Stanley Hoffman, "Obstinate or Obsolete: The Fate of the Nation State and the Case of Western Europe," *Daedalus* 95, no. 3 (1966), 862–915.

4. Neil Fligstein and Alec Stone Sweet, "Constructing Markets and Polities: An Institutionalist Account of European Integration," *American Journal of Sociology* 107 (2002), 1206–43.

5. Ernst B. Haas, *The Obsolescence of Regional Integration Theory* (Berkeley: Institute of International Studies, 1975), 1, 96–101.

6. Wayne Sandholtz and John Zysman, "1992: Recasting the European Bargain," *World Politics* 42, no. 1. (October 1989), 95–128; Wayne Sandholtz, *High-Tech Europe: The Politics of International Cooperation* (Berkeley: University of California Press, 1992); Wayne Sandholtz, "The Emergence of a Supranational Telecommunications Regime," in Wayne Sandholtz and Alec Stone Sweet, eds, *European Integration and Supranational Governance* (Oxford: Oxford University Press, 1998), 134–63.

7. For the sake of simplicity, we use the catch-all word, "rules," for legal norms that lawyers might divide into subcategories (rules, standards, principles, procedures, and so on).

8. Neil Fligstein and Jason McNichol, "The Institutional Terrain of the European Union," in Wayne Sandholtz and Alec Stone Sweet, eds, *European Integration and Supranational Governance* (Oxford: Oxford University Press, 2001), 58–91; Fligstein and Stone Sweet, "Constructing Markets and Polities"; Wayne Sandholtz and Alec Stone Sweet, eds., *European Integration and Supranational* Governance (Oxford: Oxford University Press, 1998); Alec Stone Sweet, Wayne Sandholtz, and Neil Fligstein, eds, *The Institutionalization of Europe* (Oxford: Oxford University Press, 2001).

9. Ernst B. Haas, *The Uniting of Europe: Political, Social, and Economic Forces, 1950–1957* (Notre Dame, IN: University of Notre Dame Press, 2004 [1968]), 13.

10. Haas, *The Uniting of Europe*, 29.

11. Ernst B. Haas, "International Integration: The European and the Universal Process," *International Organization* 15 (1961), 366–92.

12. Fligstein and Stone Sweet, "Constructing Markets and Polities."

13. James G. March and Johan P. Olsen, *Rediscovering Institutions* (New York: Free Press, 1989); Douglass R. North, *Institutions, Institutional Change, and Economic Performance* (Cambridge: Cambridge University Press, 1990); and Alec Stone Sweet, "Judicialization and the Construction of Governance," *Comparative Political Studies* 32, no. 2 (1999), 147–84.

14. Haas, "International Integration: The European and the Universal Process," 367.

15. Alec Stone Sweet and Thomas Brunell, "Constructing a Supranational Constitution: Dispute Resolution and Governance in the European Community," *American Political Science Review* 92 (1998), 63–81; Fligstein and Stone Sweet, "Constructing Markets and Polities."

16. For a full explication, see Alec Stone Sweet, *The Judicial Construction of Europe* (Oxford: Oxford University Press, 2004), ch. 3.

17. Andrew Moravcsik, "Liberal Intergovernmentalism and Integration: A Rejoinder," *Journal of Common Market Studies* 33 (1995), 616, 621; see also Geoffrey Garrett, "International Cooperation and Institutional Choice: The European Community's Internal Market," *International Organization* 46 (1992), 533–60.

18. Neil Fligstein and Iona Mara-Drita, "How to Make a Market: Reflections on the Attempt to Create a Single Market in the European Union," *American Journal of Sociology* 102 (1996), 1–33; Sonia Mazey and Jeremy Richardson, "Institutionalizing Promiscuity: Commission-Interest Group Relations in the EU," in Stone Sweet, Sandholtz, and Fligstein, eds, *The Institutionalization of Europe*, 71–93.

19. Giandomenico Majone, *Dilemmans of European Integration* (Oxford: Oxford University Press, 2005); Mark Thatcher and Alec Stone Sweet, "Theory and Practice of Delegation to Non-Majoritarian Institutions," *West European Politics* 25 (2002), 1; Stone Sweet, *The Judicial Construction of Europe*, ch. 1.

20. Mark A. Pollack, "The Engines of Integration? Supranational Autonomy and Influence in the European Union," in Wayne Sandholtz and Alec Stone Sweet, eds, *European Integration and Supranational Governance*, 217–49; Mark Pollack, *The Engines of Integration: Delegation, Agency, and Agenda Setting in the European Union* (Oxford: Oxford University Press, 2003); Tallberg, "Delegation to Supranational Institutions."

21. Stone Sweet, *The Judicial Construction of Europe*, 23–32.

22. Koen Lenaerts, "Constitutionalism and the Many Faces of Federalism," *American Journal of Comparative Law* 38 (1990), 205; Eric Stein, "Lawyers, Judges, and the Making of a Transnational Constitution," *American Journal of International Law* 75 (1981), 1–27; Joseph H. H. Weiler, "The Transformation of Europe," *Yale Law Journal* 100 (1991), 2403–83. For a summary of the most important doctrines and decisions, see Stone Sweet, *The Judicial Construction of Europe*, 64–81.

23. Stone Sweet, *The Judicial Construction of Europe*, 66.

24. Pollack, "The Engines of Integration?"

25. Mazey and Richardson, "Institutionalizing Promiscuity."

26. Sandholtz, *High-Tech Europe*.

27. Elliot Posner, *The Origins of Europe's New Stock Markets* (Cambridge, MA: Harvard University Press, 2009), 50.

28. Ronald Jepperson, "Institutions, Institutional Effects, and Institutionalism," in Paul J. DiMaggio and Walter W. Powell, eds, *The New Institutionalism in Organization Analysis* (Chicago: University of Chicago Press, 1991), 149, 157; North, *Institutions, Institutional Change, and Economic Performance*, 3, 6.

29. Wayne Sandholtz, *Prohibiting Plunder: How Norms Change* (New York: Oxford University Press, 2007); Stone Sweet, "Judicialization and the Construction of Governance."

30. See generally, Stone Sweet, Sandholtz, and Fligstein, eds, *The Institutionalization of Europe*.

31. Paul Pierson, "The Path to European Integration: A Historical-Institutional Analysis," in Sandholtz and Stone Sweet, eds, *European Integration and Supranational Governance*, 27–58.

32. Stone Sweet and Brunell, "Constructing a Supranational Constitution."

33. Fligstein and Stone Sweet, "Constructing Markets and Polities."

34. Stone Sweet, *The Judicial Construction of Europe*.

35. Jean-Yves Pitarkis and George Tridimas, "Joint Dynamics of Legal and Economic Integration in the European Union," *European Journal of Law and Economics* 16 (2003), 365. Curiously, Pitarkis and Tridimas state that their analysis does not provide support for neo-functionalist integration theory, even as their findings affirm some of neo-functionalism's core claims.

36. Clifford J. Carrubba and Lacey Murrah, "Legal Integration and Use of the Preliminary Ruling Process in the European Union," *International Organization* 59 (2005), 399–418.

37. Anne-Marie Burley and Walter Mattli, "Europe Before the Court: A Political Theory of Legal Integration," *International Organization* 47, no. 1 (Winter 1993), 41–76.

38. Garrett, "International Cooperation and Institutional Choice."

39. See Rachel Cichowski, "Integrating the Environment: The European Court and the Construction of Supranational Policy," *Journal of European Public Policy*, 5 (1998), 387; Rachel Cichowski, "Women's Rights, the European Court, and Supranational Constitutionalism," *Law and Society Review* 38 (2004), 489; Rachel Cichowski, *The European Court and Civil Society: Litigation, Mobilization and Governance* (Cambridge: Cambridge University Press, 2007); Joseph Jupille, *Procedural Politics: Influence and Institutional Choice in the European Union* (New York: Cambridge University Press, 2004); Margaret McCown, "The European Parliament before the Bench: ECJ Precedent and EP Litigation Strategies," *Journal of European Public Policy*, 10 (2003), 974; Stone Sweet, *The Judicial Construction of Europe*. The literature is surveyed in Alec Stone Sweet, "The European Court of Justice and the Judicialization of EU Governance," *Living Reviews in EU Governance*, 2010, <http://europeangovernance.livingreviews.org/Articles/lreg-2010-2>.

40. Sandholtz, "The Emergence of a Supranational Telecommunications Regime"; Dolores O'Reilly and Alec Stone Sweet, "The Liberalization and European Reregulation of Air Transport," in Wayne Sandholtz and Alec Stone Sweet, eds, *European Integration and Supranational Governance* (Oxford: Oxford University Press, 1998), 164–87; Eric Beerkens, "The Emergence and Institutionalization of the European Higher Education and Research Area," *European Journal of Education* 43, no. 4 (2008), 407–25; Lucia Quaglia, "The Politics of Financial Services Regulation and Supervision Reform in the European Union," *European Journal of Political Research* 46, no. 2 (2007), 269–90; Marco te Brömmelstroet and Tobias Nowak, "How a Court, a Commissioner, and a Lobby Group Brought European Transport Policy to Life in 1985," *GeoJournal* 72 (2008), 33–44.

41. Christian Kaunert, " 'Without the Power of Purse or Sword': The European Arrest Warrant and the Role of the Commission," *Journal of European Integration* 29, no. 4 (2007), 387–404; Sandholtz, "The Emergence of a Supranational Telecommunications Regime"; O'Reilly and Stone Sweet, "The Liberalization and European Reregulation of Air Transport"; Quaglia, "The Politics of Financial Services Regulation"; Rainer Eising, "Policy Learning in Embedded Negotiations: Explaining EU Electricity Liberalization," *International Organization* 56, no. 1 (2002), 85–120; Kerstin Rostenow, "The Europeanisation of Integration Policies," *International Migration* 47, no. 1 (2009), 133–59.

42. Susanne K. Schmidt, "Only an Agenda Setter?," *European Union Politics* 1, no. 1 (2000), 37–61.

43. Mitchell P. Smith, "Autonomy by the Rules: The European Commission and the Development of State Aid Policy," *Journal of Common Market Studies* 36, no. 1 (1998), 55–78.

44. Sandholtz, "The Emergence of a Supranational Telecommunications Regime"; O'Reilly and Stone Sweet, "The Liberalization and European Reregulation of Air Transport"; Smith, "Autonomy by the Rules"; Eising, "Policy Learning in Embedded Negotiations"; Quaglia,

"The Politics of Financial Services Regulation"; Brömmelstroet and Nowak, "How a Court, a Commissioner, and a Lobby Group."

45. Sandholtz, *High-Tech Europe*; Sandholtz, "The Emergence of a Supranational Telecommunications Regime"; O'Reilly and Stone Sweet, "The Liberalization and European Reregulation of Air Transport"; Quaglia, "The Politics of Financial Services Regulation"; Posner, *The Origins of Europe's New Stock Markets*.

46. Dorte Sindbjerg Martinsen, "Towards an Internal Health Market with the European Court," *West European Politics* 28, no. 5 (2005), 1035–56; Scott L. Greer, "Uninvited Europeanization: Neo-functionalism and the EU in Health Policy," *Journal of European Public Policy* 13, no. 1 (2006), 134–52; Cichowski, "Integrating the Environment."

47. George Tsebelis and Geoffrey Garrett, "The Institutional Foundations of Inter-governmentalism and Supranationalism in the European Union," *International Organization* 55, no. 2 (2001), 357–90; and Andrew Moravcsik, *The Choice for Europe: Social Purpose and State Power from Messina to Maastricht* (Ithaca, NY: Cornell University Press, 1998), 482–90. No important strain of empirical research on the Court and the EU's legal system has found any support for hypotheses derived from Tsebelis and Garrett or from Moravcsik.

48. Stone Sweet, *The Judicial Construction of Europe*, ch.4; see also Adrienne Héritier, *Explaining Institutional Change in Europe* (Oxford: Oxford University Press, 2007); Beate Kohler-Koch and Berthold Rittberger, "Review Article: The 'Governance Turn' in EU Studies," *Journal of Common Market Studies* 44 (2006), 27.

49. Cichowski, "Women's Rights"; Stone Sweet, *The Judicial Construction of Europe*, ch.4.

50. Tsebelis and Garrett, "The Institutional Foundations."

51. Henry Farrell and Adrienne Héritier, "Formal and Informal Institutions under Codecision: Continuous Constitution-Building in Europe," *Governance* 16, no. 4 (2003), 577–600; Jupille, *Procedural Politics*; McCown, "The European Parliament before the Bench"; Alec Stone Sweet and Wayne Sandholtz, "No Foundations, No Edifice: A Comment on Tsebelis and Garrett," September 2009, <www.socsci.uci.edu/~wsandhol/Sweet%20 and%20Sandholtz%20Reply%20to%20Tsebelis%20and%20Garrett.pdf>.

52. Careful empirical investigations of Moravcsik's interpretations of historical materials have cast serious doubts on the reliability of his empirical claims. Parsons writes that "the empirical evidence [Moravcsik] offers is substantially incomplete at practically every step (and sometimes simply wrong)"; Craig Parsons, *A Certain Idea of Europe* (Ithaca, NY: Cornell University Press, 2003), 29. Lieshout, Segers, and van der Vleuten carefully examine the sources Moravcsik cites in his account of de Gaulle's European policy, a section which Moravcsik himself sees as crucial to his overall argument (see Moravcsik, *The Choice for Europe*, 83–4). Lieshout et al. discover that Moravcsik regularly offers erroneous or misleading interpretations of the sources he cites. Out of 221 references cited in the crucial section on de Gaulle, more than half (116) do not say what Moravcsik claims they say. A further 11 references are only partly correct (Robert H. Lieshout, Mathieu L. L. Segers, and Anna M. van der Vleuten, "De Gaulle, Moravcsik, and *The Choice for Europe*: Soft Sources, Weak Evidence," *Journal of Cold War Studies* 6, no. 4 (2004), 94–5, 121–39). In an appendix, Lieshout et al. list every reference in the section and specify how Moravcsik's use of it diverges from what the source contains. Another review of *The Choice for Europe* finds that, in 386 pages covering the five case studies, only 2 percent of 917 footnotes contain references to hard primary sources. The remaining 98 percent of the references cite secondary and soft primary sources (like political memoirs) (Jeffrey

J. Anderson, "Review of *The Choice for Europe: Social Purpose and State Power from Messina to Maastricht*, by Andrew Moravcsik," *American Political Science Review* 94, no. 2 (2000), 516). The bottom line is that Moravcsik's central argument—that de Gaulle's European strategy was driven by narrow commercial interests—is not supported by the sources he cites and is, in fact, frequently contradicted by them.

53. Ernst Haas only addressed this issue on one occasion: "Andrew Moravcsik is the most visible defender of the continuing centrality of the nation-state and its government as the engine of integration...I find it at least very curious that despite great similarities in both ontological and epistemological assumptions my treatment and Moravcsik's turn out to be so different. His ontology is described in detail as 'liberalism' [yet] its core assumptions are identical with those of Neo-functionalism...It is difficult to understand why he makes such extraordinary efforts to distinguish his work from these sources" (Ernst B. Haas, "Does Constructivism Subsume Neo-functionalism?," in T. Christiansen, K. E. Jørgensen, and A. Wiener, eds, *The Social Construction of Europe* (Thousand Oaks, CA: SAGE Publications, 2001), note 4).

54. Moravcsik admits that his version of intergovernmentalism cannot explain constitutionalization of the Treaty, or the effects of direct effect, supremacy, and related doctrines downstream. He then treats the Court, constitutionalization, and the legal system as anomalies that somehow do not weaken his theory (Andrew Moravcsik, "Liberal Intergovernmentalism and Integration: A Rejoinder," *Journal of Common Market Studies* 33 (2005), 611–28).

CHAPTER 3

....

CONSTRUCTIVIST PERSPECTIVES

....

FRANK SCHIMMELFENNIG

CONSTRUCTIVIST perspectives are a comparatively recent addition to the portfolio of theoretical approaches to European integration. A 1999 special issue of the *Journal of European Public Policy* signaled that something like a "constructivist school" was form-ing in EU studies.[1] Since then, constructivism has firmly established itself with a secure place in the text- and handbook canon.[2] To this day, however, it has not consolidated as a theory of European integration on the same level as liberal intergovernmentalism or neo-functionalism—and some would deny the likelihood and, indeed, the desirability of such a development.[3]

The late arrival of constructivism is not to say that social constructions had not fea-tured in theorizing on the EU before. But they were prominent mainly in early theoreti-cal approaches. Federalism relied heavily on "ideas of Europe" and value-based commitments as a motivation and orientation for European integration movements.[4] Karl Deutsch's "transactionalism" defined an emerging "sense of community," a trans-formation of identities, as the essence of integration.[5] Neo-functionalism envisaged that European integration would lead to the socialization of actors involved in the integrated policy-making process and ultimately result in a shift of citizens' loyalties and identities from the nation state to the supranational community.[6] Even intergovernmentalism had a place for ideas such as the diversity of national traditions and the dominance of national identities—albeit as a limiting factor in European integration.[7]

By contrast, more recent theories of European integration were based on an explicitly "rationalist" foundation (see Chapter 1, this volume). Liberal intergovernmentalism accords ideas only a minor role in the formation of preferences for integration and con-ceives them predominantly as a residual explanatory factor in situations of uncertain or negligible material consequences.[8] Even the "supranationalist" successor theories to neo-functionalism started from rationalist micro-foundations.[9]

The arrival of constructivism in EU studies thus redirected the attention of scholars to the ideational and intersubjective underpinnings, driving forces, constraints, and outcomes of European integration. For the first time, it brought theoretical perspectives to EU studies that were not only sensitive to the role of ideas in integration but built on an intersubjectivist ontology and epistemology. As usual, these perspectives were imported from other disciplines—in this case international relations (IR) where constructivism had established itself a few years earlier as the counterpart of the rationalist mainstream. Indeed, most of the early proponents of constructivism in EU studies had their academic roots in IR.

Thanks in part to extensive prior debates in IR, constructivism arrived in EU studies without heavy meta-theoretical baggage. Constructivists mostly attacked the substantive explanatory limits of rationalism rather than its positivist epistemological foundations. Methodological debates were rare and focused on how to show empirically that, and in which way, ideas and discourses matter in European integration.[10] Constructivism in EU studies is not tied to critical or post-positivist meta-theory or to interpretative methods. This chapter can thus focus on substantive theory and empirical results.[11]

3.1 THEORY

Simply put, constructivism claims that social ideas and discourses matter for European integration. On the one hand, ideas and discourses regarding "Europe" are considered relevant objects of study in their own right. In other words, they constitute important *explananda* or "dependent variables" neglected in rationalist accounts. For instance, is there a European identity or public sphere? How strong are they? How can we explain their emergence or weakness? On the other hand, ideas and discourses are "independent variables," without which we cannot (sufficiently) explain important outcomes of European integration and EU politics. How and to what extent do ideas and discourses shape preferences and negotiations on European integration, the deepening and widening of the EU, or substantive EU policies?

Constructivism has two main theoretical foundations—one relating to structure, the other to agency. First, it assumes the primacy of intersubjective ideational structures such as collective identities, knowledge, culture, values, and norms in politics. Ideas and discourses shape social preferences, interactions, and outcomes, and they do so in ways that cannot be reduced to material structures and interests. Second, rather than behaving instrumentally or strategically, actors follow the "logic of appropriateness"[12] or the "logic of arguing."[13] They do not judge alternative courses of action by the consequences for their own utility but by their conformity to norms, rules, and identities, or by the validity of the arguments made in their favor. By contrast, constructivism does not take any particular stance regarding the relevant actors in European integration. Ideas can operate at the level of governments, society, and supranational organizations.

In the constructivist perspective, European integration is at its core a process of community building. Communities are groups or associations based on shared ideas. They share a collective identity, causal and normative beliefs, and structures of meaning. Over time, community building and institutional integration mutually influence and potentially reinforce each other. The constructivist research program in European integration studies has three distinct foci. The first is on the effects of ideas and discourses on integration preferences. The second asks how the intersubjective context of negotiations and decision-making in the EU affects integration outcomes. Finally, constructivists are interested in the effects of European integration and institutions on community building. Constructivist studies on the EU tend to cluster around one or another of these foci.

The main assumption of the first research focus is that institutional integration depends on the strength of transnational community: the stronger the collective, "European" identity and the larger the pool of common or compatible beliefs and meanings, the more institutional integration we will see. By contrast, weak European and strong national identities generate resistance to institutional integration, and without shared normative and causal beliefs common institutions and integrated policies are hard to agree on. This research focus follows the tradition of Karl Deutsch who stipulated compatible social values (together with mutual responsiveness) as essential conditions of functioning international communities.[14]

By contrast, the other two perspectives start from the assumption that institutional integration promotes community building and take up neo-functionalist expectations of upgrading the common interest, actor socialization, and shifting identities and loyalties.[15] Integrated policy-making generates intense and frequent contacts and cooperation and takes place in a distinct environment structured by community norms. This environment facilitates integration-friendly decisions and promotes social learning processes (such as imitation, persuasion, and social influence) that have the potential to transform identities, restructure discourses, and lead to common meanings and beliefs. Constructivists have established a widely accepted catalogue of conditions under which these processes are likely to be effective,[16] i.e. if

- actors face *novel* situations characterized by high *uncertainty*,
- a socializing agent possesses the *authority* to act on behalf of a community with which a particular actor *identifies* (or to which an actor aspires to belong),
- socialization concerns norms and rules which enjoy high *legitimacy* in the community,
- it takes place in an environment corresponding to an "ideal speech situation" which encourages *deliberation* and is characterized by the absence of external and political constraints, and
- the domestic or societal *resonance* of EU ideas is high.

In the longer run, this socialization process may generate momentum in favor of further integration but constructivist theories are by no means generally optimistic about "ever closer union." As a research program, constructivism is open to potential transformative effects of integration on identities, norms, and preferences, and rejects the rationalist assumption of exogenously given preferences. But the theorized conditions of such transformative effects may simply not obtain in the EU. Because identities and structures of meaning may be less compatible and more durable than the interests of

EU governments, constructivists may even come to more pessimistic conclusions about the prospects of European integration than intergovernmentalists.

While all constructivist approaches agree that ideas and discourses matter for European integration, they regard different kinds of ideas as relevant for community formation. What is the meaning of "Europe"? What does it mean to be a European or have a European identity? What is a European discourse, value, or norm? There are two main notions in the literature. The first one defines "European identity" in terms of *sense of belonging and allegiance.* The classical opposition here is between European and national identities and allegiances, although it is now generally recognized that identities are best conceived as multiple, layered or nested. This shifts the issue to how exclusive these multiple identities are and in which way they relate to each other.

The second conception of "Europe" is based on *political values and norms as well as constitutional principles.* In this view, "Europeanness" is defined by such principles as liberal democracy, national diversity, or multilateralism, which stand in contrast to illiberal, xenophobic, or national-protectionist values.[17] Or the focus is on constitutional principles such as the balance of supranational (federal) and intergovernmental (confederal) elements, appropriate democratic institutions, or the legal constitution of the EU. In this view, European integration does not require that individuals and political actors feel European as long as they adhere to shared principles. We can also distinguish these two conceptions of "Europe" as "thick" and "thin" European identities. Whereas a thick European identity resembles national identities in being based on group identification, a thin European identity requires identification with abstract transnational values and norms.

What do we know empirically about ideational effects in European integration, and which ideas matter most? The remainder of the chapter will first present empirical findings on integration preferences, then move on to ideational effects on collective integration decisions, and finally report results regarding the effects of institutional integration on identities and ideas.

3.2 Ideas and Integration Preferences

There is widespread evidence for the ideational nature of integration preferences in Europe. However, the relevant research differs vastly with regard to the kind, substance, and level of ideational effects. The following examples are by no means exhaustive but demonstrate the diversity of constructivist research.

Craig Parsons' study of French integration policy[18] is a prime example of a voluntarist (or anti-structuralist) analysis of ideas. Parsons shows that the supranationalist ideas of entrepreneurial French leaders brought about the supranational institutional model of European integration in the face of more intergovernmental alternatives and that these ideas cannot be reduced to structural economic or political factors. Because French preferences were decisive at the early stage of European integration, and because these early institutional choices shaped its subsequent institutional development, Parsons can indeed claim that the "origins of the European Union" were ideational. He also argues, however, that the presence of a community-minded leadership of the 1950s cannot be explained by deeper beliefs, cleavages, or membership in parties or other organizations. Moreover, these leaders were able to stand up against alternative visions of Europe not because they persuaded their proponents or obtained an electoral mandate for the community model but because they gained power for completely unrelated reasons. This ideational explanation thus builds strongly on historical contingency.

By contrast, most constructivist explanations build on the notion of culturally and discursively embedded ideas and account for preferences on European integration in terms of relatively stable group-based or organizational identities, ideologies, and discourses. Studies at the individual level seek to account for individual support for European integration. Rationalism does so in terms of the costs individuals incur, and the benefits they reap, from European integration.[19] Constructivists, however, attribute support to identity. More precisely, empirical research shows that *exclusive* national identities weaken support for the EU.[20] By contrast, having a national identity is not detrimental to support for European integration if people feel at least somewhat "European," too. Finally, European identity is correlated with age, education, and class. Young, educated, and well-to-do people are most likely to see themselves as Europeans.[21]

At the level of political parties, research shows that integration preferences vary with "polity-ideas," i.e. normative ideas about a legitimate political order, which are linked to the identity and normative orientations of the actors.[22] Quantitative studies of party contestation on the EU concur insofar as they do not only detect the classical left–right cleavage, representing distributional conflict about economic welfare, but an even more powerful cultural, "new politics" or GAL-TAN (green-alternative-libertarian vs traditionalist-authoritarian-nationalist) dimension regarding the desirability of integration.[23]

At the national level, Ole Waever describes different visions of Europe embedded in national identity discourses.[24] In his view, these national discourses and visions are not, and do not need to be, replaced by a harmonized European vision. For stable integration, it is sufficient if these visions are compatible and include the European project as a part of national identity.[25] This view corresponds to the relevance of inclusive identities stressed in public opinion research.

In addition, preferences on the constitution of the EU mirror national constitutional traditions and ideas. Across policy areas, federally organized member states are more likely to advocate supranational institutional solutions than unitary member states.[26] This is also true for individuals coming from a federal country.[27] Sieglinde Gstöhl argues that the reluctance of Scandinavian countries and Switzerland to join the EU cannot be adequately explained by economic costs and benefits alone but must additionally be attributed to ideational and institutional constraints—such as traditions of neutrality and direct democracy or ethno-linguistic cleavages in the Swiss case.[28] Finally, the fact that Denmark, Sweden, and the UK did not introduce the euro has less to do with a lack of economic convergence, or even incompatible monetary policy paradigms, than with identity- and resonance-based skepticism toward sovereignty transfers in the populations of these countries.[29]

In sum, there is abundant evidence that the integration preferences of individuals and political actors are informed by ideational factors. We can, however, draw two further conclusions from the state of research. First, the evidence in favor of ideational factors does not imply a refutation of rationalist accounts of preferences on integration. For one, most authors concede that these factors complement rather than replace economic interests and cost–benefit calculations in a complete account of preference formation. Moreover, ideational explanations mostly fill the gap left explicitly by liberal intergovernmentalism: they relate primarily to constitutional issues, that is, issues with weak or uncertain material or distributional implications for powerful domestic groups. On these issues, liberal intergovernmentalism does not claim to have to say much.[30]

Second, the research findings emphasize ideational diversity across actors. They thus help to explain why some countries are not members of the EU and why some members do not participate in individual EU policies. But diverse identities, institutional traditions, and discourses pose a problem for the constructivist explanation of progress in institutional integration. After all, it starts with the assumption that integration depends on transnational community. Therefore, constructivism proposes mechanisms of argumentation and persuasion for generating consensus in the face of diverse preferences.

3.3 IDEAS, ARGUMENTS, AND INTEGRATION OUTCOMES

In the rationalist perspective, integration outcomes result from constellations of interests and power. If national interests diverge, states with superior bargaining power are able to shape integration according to their interests. By contrast, constructivists claim that actors with conflicting preferences engage in a process of arguing, during which the actors with the "better" arguments prevail. According to the strong version of constructivism, the process of arguing results in the harmonization of actor preferences. By contrast, the weak version holds that actors do not necessarily change their conflicting preferences. Rather, those actors whose preferences are not (or less) in line with the community identity, norms, and values become subject to social influence and normative pressures and adapt their behavior as a result of the negotiations because their legitimacy is at stake.[31] This mechanism can be illustrated with examples from the study of Council decision-making, enlargement, and constitutionalization.

In contrast to the intergovernmentalist focus on hard intergovernmental bargaining and a rational-choice institutionalist focus on formal decision-making rules, constructivist analyses of the Council and its committee substructures show informal norms of deliberation and a commitment to compromise and consensus to guide the negotiations.[32]

More specifically, Jeffrey Lewis argues that the high density and intensity of interactions in COREPER as well as its insulation from domestic politics facilitate the internalization of group standards of behavior by member governments' permanent representatives.[33]

Studies of enlargement provide ample evidence for ideational effects on negotiations and their outcomes. Already in the early 1960s when the big member states favored giving Franco's Spain a membership perspective, the Parliamentary Assembly of the EEC invoked the liberal-democratic (and anti-fascist) identity of the Community to mobilize successfully against association.[34] In the early 1990s, the same liberal democratic identity worked in favor of Eastern enlargement. When a powerful majority of self-interested member states were reticent to give the CEECs a firm membership perspective, the CEECs' governments and their supporters in the European Community framed enlargement as an identity issue, referred to the pan-European and liberal-democratic enlargement norms of the European Community, and reminded the opponents of past promises made to the East.[35] This "rhetorical entrapment" compelled the reluctant member states to agree to enlargement (without harmonizing their enlargement preferences). The same mechanism has been at work in EU–Turkey relations.[36] Other constructivist explanations of Eastern enlargement refer to more specific identity constructions with regard to Central and Eastern Europe. This is true for the "special responsibility"[37] and the "sense of 'kinship-based duty' "[38] of the EU to Central and Eastern Europe, or the West's "collective guilt" for having failed the CEECs before and after World War II.[39]

Studies on the parliamentarization and the institutionalization of human rights provide evidence for similar processes of entrapment.[40] Berthold Rittberger argues that governments have undermined traditional channels of parliamentary representation and accountability by pooling sovereignty and delegating it to supranational institutions for reasons of efficiency. For the same efficiency reasons, governments have generally not been interested in empowering the European Parliament or other supranational institutions. In addition, their ideas about what constitutes a legitimate constitution for Europe diverge.[41] In this situation, actors with a preference for democratizing the EU have scandalized the democracy deficit, invoked shared standards of parliamentarism, and successfully put normative pressure on reticent member-state governments. Similarly, it can be shown that the institutionalization of human rights in the European Community has resulted from the competition between the ECJ and national constitutional courts, during which the ECJ introduced human rights to the supranational level in order to legitimize its claim for legal supremacy.[42]

These cases indicate the conditions under which normative effects are most likely to shape the outcome of integration negotiations: if the issues at stake are constitutive for the community, uncontested shared norms and values can be invoked, and a legitimate precedent has been established by past practice or rhetoric.[43] In addition, they support the weaker version of constructivism, which does not assume harmonized ideational preferences either at the beginning or the end of the negotiation process. But does a transformation of identities, norms, or discourses result from integration in the longer run?

3.4 INTEGRATION AND SOCIALIZATION

First of all, there is no evidence for a shift of mass loyalties and change of identities. Surveys show that national identities and allegiances clearly predominate in the European Union—either as purely national identities or as national identities with a modicum of European identity. Moreover, purely and moderately national identities have also remained extraordinarily stable since the early 1990s—a period of dynamic institutional integration.[44] As expected by neo-functionalism, mass attitudes toward European integration have indeed become more politicized during this period. But rather than strengthening European identity and loyalty, politicization has ended up undermining the "permissive consensus" on European integration, reasserting territorial and national identities and divisions, and has led to the proliferation of Euro-skeptic parties.[45] Even in the case of the young, educated, and well-to-do Europeans, it is unclear whether their more strongly European identity results from their primary, national socialization in the privileged social strata and institutions of higher education or from positive transnational interaction and the experience of transnational solidarity. While it is true that these people are more likely to know and use a second language, and to interact with people from other EU countries, the strongest factor is class.[46]

Weak socialization effects of European integration are confirmed by studies on the preferences and identities of various types of political and administrative actors. The "ideas of Europe" of the major parties in the major member states have remained remarkably stable over the decades.[47] National bureaucrats involved in Commission and Council committees do develop expanded role conceptions but their primary allegiance remains with their state of origin.[48] Roger Scully shows that the views on integration of members of the European Parliament are little different from those of the members of national parliaments. Moreover, the length of service in the European Parliament has no significant effect.[49] Jan Beyers finds that the extensive exposure of participants in Council Working Groups to the EU does not systematically lead to supranational role-playing. Rather than the intensity, duration, and density of contact, domestic factors affect the adoption of supranational role conceptions.[50] Furthermore, Liesbet Hooghe demonstrates that EU socialization is weak even in the (arguably most likely) case of the Commission. Although Commission officials identify themselves comparatively strongly with the EU, this is not a result of preference shifts or internalization generated by involvement in EU policymaking but a result of previous socialization in national contexts. Again, length of service is not significant (except for those who joined at a young age).[51]

Finally, the effects of European integration on the public sphere have been limited as well. It is clear that, because of the extreme linguistic diversity and the absence of EU-wide media, the development of a single European public sphere is not a realistic scenario. But the Europeanization of national public spheres, i.e. parallel debates on EU issues and mutual responsiveness to national debates, is limited to elite newspapers and "to relatively confined issues and time spans"[52] as well.

In sum, empirical studies generally show that the socialization effects of European integration and European institutions are weak. Whereas identities, ideas, and discourses do indeed shape the integration preferences of individuals and political actors, these intersubjective structures are primarily located below the supranational level and have proven to be resistant to the growth of institutional integration.

3.5 CONCLUSIONS

Constructivist approaches and explanations are indispensable for a thorough understanding and explanation of European integration. There is broad empirical evidence that European integration cannot be sufficiently accounted for by material, mainly economic, conditions, interests, or bargaining power. That ideas do indeed matter for European integration is, however, an admittedly trivial result. For a mature constructivist research program, it is essential to stipulate which ideas matter, and how and under which conditions they do. In this regard, the review of empirical studies also allows some general conclusions.

Regarding the three foci of constructivist research, we find ample evidence that ideas and discourses shape integration preferences and the negotiated outcomes of European integration. By contrast, the effects of European integration on identities and public spheres appear to be weak. To be sure, the limited evidence for transformative effects of institutional integration does not as such contradict constructivist assumptions. It merely shows that national identities, discourses, and public spheres are entrenched and persistent, and that the conditions stipulated by constructivist approaches for their transformation might be lacking. In particular, the fact that primary political socialization and systems of media and education have remained firmly national accounts for the weakness of identity transformation.[53]

Existing research further demonstrates that both thin (value-based) and thick (group-based) identities matter in European integration, but they do so in different and potentially conflicting ways.[54] Thick identity is predominantly national and strongest at the mass level. It is a latent constraint on European integration, which becomes a manifest obstacle under conditions of mass politicization and mobilization, e.g. during election campaigns or referenda on EU treaties. By contrast, a thin, post-national identity based on liberal values and norms is compatible with and conducive to European integration. It is enshrined in the EU's constitutional norms and constitutes a part of the identity of European elites. Its positive effects on European integration are most likely to materialize when EU negotiations and policy-making take place at the elite and supranational level and remain insulated from mass politics.

These two kinds of identity and identity effects also indicate two different limits of rational, liberal intergovernmentalism in the explanation of European integration. At the domestic level, and because it assumes that European integration is mainly driven by economic interest groups, liberal intergovernmentalism downplays the impact of national identities and constitutional ideas. Adding identity to the picture shows that the prospects of European integration are more limited domestically than liberal intergovernmentalism assumes. At the European level, however, their exclusive focus on interest constellations and bargaining power leads rationalist approaches to neglect the effects of common values and norms on the negotiation outcomes. Here, ideas and discourses enable more integration than liberal intergovernmentalism would expect.

On the whole, however, existing research points to a division of labor rather than the mutual exclusiveness of rationalist and constructivist theorizing on the EU.[55] Instead of making unconditional claims about identity effects, many constructivist analyses tell us when and how ideas should matter. For instance, Liesbet Hooghe and Gary Marks argue that "identity is more influential a) for the general public than for cognitively sophisticated individuals or functional interest groups, b) for populist *tan* parties than for radical left parties, and c) when regional integration is political as well as economic."[56] At the European level, the effect of community values and norms on negotiations is strongest when the issue at stake is constitutive for the community and when the relevant values and norms enjoy high international legitimacy and domestic salience.[57]

Constructivist approaches and analyses of European integration have thus arrived at increasingly detailed, differentiated, and empirically testable and corroborated conditional propositions about intersubjective ideational effects at all stages of the integration process from preferences to outcomes. There is less reason than ever for claiming that a constructivist theory of European integration is out of reach.

Notes

1. Published later by Thomas Christiansen, Knud Erik Jørgensen, and Antje Wiener, eds, *The Social Construction of Europe* (London: Sage, 2001).
2. Jeffrey T. Checkel, "Constructivism and EU Politics," in Knud Erik Jorgensen, Mark A. Pollack, and Ben Rosamond, eds, *Handbook of European Union Politics* (London: Sage, 2006), 57–76; Thomas Risse, "Social Constructivism and European Integration," in Antje Wiener and Thomas Diez, eds, *European Integration Theory*, 2nd edition (Oxford: Oxford University Press, 2009), 144–60; Antje Wiener, "Constructivism and Sociological Institutionalism," in Michelle Cini and Angela K. Bourne, eds, *European Union Studies* (Basingstoke: Palgrave Macmillan, 2006), 35–55.
3. Checkel, "Constructivism and EU Politics," 57; Risse, "Social Constructivism and European Integration," 158–9.
4. See, e.g. Michael Burgess, *Federalism and European Union. Political Ideas, Influences, and Strategies in the European Community 1972–1987* (London: Routledge, 1989); Walter Lipgens, *A History of European Integration* (Oxford: Clarendon Press, 1982).
5. Karl W. Deutsch, *Political Community and the North Atlantic Area: International Organization in the Light of Historical Experience* (Princeton: Princeton University Press, 1957), 5.

6. Haas, Ernst B., *The Uniting of Europe. Political, Social, and Economic Forces 1950-1957*, 2nd edition (Stanford: Stanford University Press, 1968), 16.

7. Stanley Hoffmann, "Obstinate or Obsolete? The Fate of the Nation-State and the Case of Western Europe," *Daedalus* 95, no. 3 (1966), 862-915.

8. Andrew Moravcsik, *The Choice for Europe. Social Purpose and State Power from Messina to Maastricht* (Ithaca: Cornell University Press, 1998), 486-9; Andrew Moravcsik and Kalypso Nicolaïdis, "Explaining the Treaty of Amsterdam: Interests, Influence, Institutions," *Journal of Common Market Studies* 37, no. 1 (1999), 59-85, 61.

9. See, e.g. Paul Pierson, "The Path to European Integration. A Historical Institutionalist Analysis," *Comparative Political Studies* 29, no. 2 (1996), 123-63. See also Chapter 2, this volume.

10. Andrew Moravcsik, "'Is Something Rotten in the State of Denmark?' Constructivism and European Integration," *Journal of European Public Policy* 6, no. 4 (1999), 669-81; Thomas Risse and Antje Wiener, "'Something Rotten' and the Social Construction of Social Constructivism," *Journal of European Public Policy* 6, no. 5 (1999), 775-82; Jeffrey T. Checkel and Andrew Moravcsik, "A Constructivist Research Program in EU Studies?," *European Union Politics* 2, no. 2 (2001), 219-49.

11. For more meta-theoretically oriented survey articles, see Checkel, "Constructivism and EU Politics" and Wiener, "Constructivism and Sociological Institutionalism." For an overview focusing more strongly on post-positivist, interpretivist work, see Ole Waever, "Discursive Approaches," in Antje Wiener and Thomas Diez, eds, *European Integration Theory*, 2nd edition (Oxford: Oxford University Press, 2009), 163-80.

12. James G. March and Johan P. Olsen, *Rediscovering Institutions. The Organizational Basis of Politics* (New York: Free Press, 1999), 160.

13. Thomas Risse, "'Let's Argue!' Communicative Action in World Politics," *International Organization* 54, no. 1 (2000), 1-39.

14. Deutsch, *Political Community and the North Atlantic Area*, 66.

15. See, e.g. Leon N. Lindberg and Stuart A. Scheingold, *Europe's Would-Be Polity. Patterns of Change in the European Community* (Englewood Cliffs: Prentice Hall, 1970), 117-20.

16. Jeffrey T. Checkel, "Why Comply? Social Learning and European Identity Change," *International Organization* 55, no. 3 (2001), 562-3; Alistair Iain Johnston, "Treating International Institutions as Social Environments," *International Studies Quarterly* 45, no. 4 (2001), 498-9; Risse, "Let's Argue!," 19; Frank Schimmelfennig, "Transnational Socialization: Community-Building in an Integrated Europe," in Wolfram Kaiser and Peter Starie, eds, *Transnational European Union. Towards a Common Political Space* (London: Routledge, 2005), 63-9.

17. See, e.g. Hartmut Kaelble, "Identification with Europe and Politicization of the EU since the 1980s," in Jeffrey T. Checkel and Peter J. Katzenstein, eds, *European Identity* (Cambridge: Cambridge University Press, 2009), 193-212.

18. Craig Parsons, "Showing Ideas as Causes. The Origins of the European Union," *International Organization* 56, no. 1 (2002), 47-84; Craig Parsons, *A Certain Idea of Europe* (Ithaca: Cornell University Press, 2003).

19. Matthew Gabel, *Interests and Integration: Market Liberalization, Public Opinion, and European Union* (Ann Arbor: University of Michigan Press, 1998).

20. Liesbet Hooghe and Gary Marks, "Calculation, Community and Cues: Public Opinion on European Integration," *European Union Politics*, 6, no. 4 (2005), 419-43.

21. Neil Fligstein, *Euroclash. The EU, European Identity, and the Future of Europe* (Oxford: Oxford University Press, 2008), 145; Matthew Gabel, *Interests and Integration*.

22. Markus Jachtenfuchs, Thomas Diez, and Sabine Jung, "Which Europe? Conflicting Models of a Legitimate European Political Order," *European Journal of International Relations* 4, no. 4 (1998), 409–45; Markus Jachtenfuchs, *Die Konstruktion Europas. Verfassungsideen und institutionelle Entwicklung* (Baden-Baden: Nomos, 2002).

23. Liesbet Hooghe, Gary Marks, and Carole J. Wilson, "Does Left/Right Structure Party Positions on European Integration?," *Comparative Political Studies* 35, no. 8 (2002), 965–89.

24. See, e.g. Ole Waever, "European Integration and Security: Analysing French and German Discourses on State, Nation, and Europe," in David R. Howarth and Jacob Torfing, eds, *Discourse Theory in European Politics: Identity, Policy and Governance* (Basingstoke: Palgrave Macmillan, 2005), 33–67.

25. Waever, "Discursive Approaches."

26. See, e.g. Mathias Koenig-Archibugi, "Explaining Government Preferences for Institutional Change in EU Foreign and Security Policy," *International Organization* 58, no. 1 (2004), 137–74; Thomas Risse, "Neofunctionalism, European Identity, and the Puzzles of European Integration," *Journal of European Public Policy* 12, no. 2 (2005), 291–309; Wolfgang Wagner, "The Subnational Foundations of the European Parliament," *Journal of International Relations and Development* 5, no. 1 (2002), 24–36.

27. Liesbet Hooghe, "Several Roads Lead to International Norms, but Few Via International Socialization: A Case Study of the European Commission," *International Organization* 59, no. 4 (2005), 879.

28. Sieglinde Gstöhl, "Scandinavia and Switzerland: Small, Successful, and Stubborn Towards the EU," *Journal of European Public Policy* 9, no. 4 (2002), 529–49; Sieglinde Gstöhl, *Reluctant Europeans. Norway, Sweden, and Switzerland in the Process of European Integration* (Boulder: Lynne Rienner, 2002).

29. Thomas Risse, Daniela Engelmann-Martin, Hans-Joachim Knopf, and Klaus Roscher, "To Euro or Not to Euro? The EMU and Identity Politics in the European Union," *European Journal of International Relations* 5, no. 2 (1999), 147–87.

30. See above, endnote 8.

31. Frank Schimmelfennig, "The Community Trap: Liberal Norms, Rhetorical Action, and the Eastern Enlargement of the European Union," *International Organization* 55, no. 1 (2001), 47–80; Daniel Thomas, "Explaining the Negotiation of EU Foreign Policy: Normative Institutionalism and Alternative Approaches," *International Politics* 46, no. 4 (2009), 339–57.

32. See, e.g. Christian Joerges and Jürgen Neyer, "From Intergovernmental Bargaining to Deliberative Political Processes," *European Law Journal* 3, no. 3 (1997), 273–99; Jeffrey Lewis, "Institutional Environments and Everyday EU Decision Making," *Comparative Political Studies* 36, no. 1–2 (2003), 97–124; Jeffrey Lewis, "Informal Integration and the Supranational Construction of the Council," *Journal of European Public Policy* 10, no. 6 (2003), 996–1019.

33. Jeffrey Lewis, "The Janus Face of Brussels: Socialization and Everyday Decision Making in the European Union," *International Organization* 59, no. 4 (2005), 937–71.

34. Daniel C. Thomas, "Constitutionalization through Enlargement: the Contested Origins of the EU's Democratic Identity," *Journal of European Public Policy* 13, no. 8 (2006), 1190–210.

35. Frank Schimmelfennig, "The Community Trap." See also Karin Fierke and Antje Wiener, "Constructing Institutional Interests: EU and NATO Enlargement," *Journal of European Public Policy* 6, no. 5 (1999), 721–42.

36. Frank Schimmelfennig, "Entrapped Again: the Way to EU Membership Negotiations with Turkey," *International Politics* 46, no. 4 (2009), 413–31.

37. Ulrich Sedelmeier, "Eastern Enlargement: Risk, Rationality, and Role-Compliance," in Maria Green Cowles and Michael Smith, eds, *Risks, Reforms, Resistance and Revival* (Oxford: Oxford University Press, 2000), 12041; Ulrich Sedelmeier, *Constructing the Path to Eastern Enlargement. The Uneven Policy Impact of EU Identity* (Manchester: Manchester University Press, 2005).

38. Helene Sjursen, "Why Expand? The Question of Legitimacy and Justification in the EU's Enlargement Policy," *Journal of Common Market Studies* 40, no. 3 (2001), 508.

39. Ainius Lasas, "Restituting Victims: EU and NATO Enlargements through the Lenses of Collective Guilt," *Journal of European Public Policy* 15, no. 1 (2008), 98–116.

40. Berthold Rittberger and Frank Schimmelfennig, "Explaining the Constitutionalization of the European Union," *Journal of European Public Policy* 13, no. 8 (2006), 1148–67; Frank Schimmelfennig, "The Normative Origins of Democracy in the European Union: Toward a Transformationalist Theory of Democratization," *European Political Science Review* 2, no. 2 (2010), 211–33.

41. Berthold Rittberger, *Building Europe's Parliament. Democratic Representation Beyond the Nation-State* (Oxford: Oxford University Press, 2005).

42. Frank Schimmelfennig, "Competition and Community: Constitutional Courts, Rhetorical Action, and the Institutionalization of Human Rights in the European Union," *Journal of European Public Policy* 13, no. 8 (2006), 1247–64.

43. Rittberger and Schimmelfennig, "Explaining the Constitutionalization," 1159–1160; Frank Schimmelfennig, "Strategic Action in a Community Environment: The Decision to Enlarge the European Union to the East," *Comparative Political Studies* 36, nos. 1–2 (2003), 162; Frank Schimmelfennig and Daniel Thomas, "Normative Institutionalism and EU Foreign Policy in Comparative Perspective," *International Politics* 46, no. 4 (2009), 491–504.

44. See, e.g. Neil Fligstein, *Euroclash*, 141; Daniel R. Kelemen, "Built to Last? The Durability of EU Federalism," in Sophie Meunier and Kathleen R. McNamara, eds, *Making History. European Integration and Institutional Change at Fifty* (Oxford: Oxford University Press, 2007), 5166.

45. Liesbet Hooghe and Gary Marks, "A Postfunctionalist Theory of European Integration: From Permissive Consensus to Constraining Dissensus," *British Journal of Political Science* 39, no. 1 (2009), 1–23.

46. Neil Fligstein, *Euroclash*, 147–54.

47. Markus Jachtenfuchs et al., "Which Europe?"

48. See, e.g. Morten Egeberg, "Transcending Intergovernmentalism? Identity and Role Perceptions of National Officials," *Journal of European Public Policy* 6, no. 3 (1999), 456–74; Jarle Trondal, "Re-Socializing Civil Servants: The Transformative Powers of EU Institutions," *Acta Politica* 39, no. 1 (2004), 4–30.

49. Roger Scully, *Becoming Europeans? Attitudes, Behaviour, and Socialization in the European Parliament* (Oxford: Oxford University Press, 2005).

50. Jan Beyers, "Multiple Embeddedness and Socialization in Europe: The Case of Council Officials," *International Organization* 59, no. 4 (2005), 899–936.

51. Liesbet Hooghe, "Several Roads Lead to International Norms, but Few Via International Socialization," 861–98.
52. Claes H. De Vreese, "The EU as a Public Sphere," *Living Reviews in European Governance* 2, no. 3 (2007), 11; see also Juan Díez Medrano, "The Public Sphere and the European Union's Political Identity," in Jeffrey T. Checkel and Peter J. Katzenstein, eds, *European Identity* (Cambridge: Cambridge University Press, 2009), 89; Thomas Risse, *A Community of Europeans? Transnational Identities and Public Spheres* (Ithaca: Cornell University Press, 2010).
53. Lars-Erik Cederman, "Nationalism and Bounded Integration: What It Would Take to Create a European Demos," *European Journal of International Relations* 7, no. 2 (2001), 139–74.
54. See, e.g. Jeffrey T. Checkel and Peter J. Katzenstein, "The Politicization of European Identities," in Jeffrey T. Checkel and Peter J. Katzenstein, eds, *European Identity* (Cambridge: Cambridge University Press, 2009), 11–12.
55. See Joseph Jupille, James A. Caporaso, and Jeffrey T. Checkel, eds, "Integrating Institutions: Rationalism, Constructivism, and the Study of the European Union," *Comparative Political Studies* 36, nos. 1–2 (2003), 7–40.
56. Liesbet Hooghe and Gary Marks, "Postfunctionalist Theory," 21.
57. See above, endnote 43.

....

CHAPTER 4

SOCIOLOGICAL PERSPECTIVES ON EUROPEAN INTEGRATION

....

CRAIG PARSONS

ANY close observer of EU studies will have noticed a rising volume of explicitly "sociological" work on European integration in recent decades. It reflects a growing engagement of sociologists with terrain long claimed by political scientists.

As unmistakable as the sociological wave may be, however, this chapter's task of identifying its perspective and contributions is not easy. At least by some definitions, "sociological" views have always been prominent in EU studies, and have become more prominent over time—quite separately from decisions of actual sociologists to enter the sub-field. I must begin, then, by considering what we might call a "sociological approach," and how the recent surge of work under that label (which *is* mostly from sociologists) carries its own understanding of European integration. The chapter makes no attempt to catalogue all writing about Europe by sociologists, or all invocations of the term "sociological."[1] Its goal, as part of our section on theoretical perspectives, is to identify a distinctive school of thought that carries this mantle.

4.1 WHAT'S "SOCIOLOGICAL" IN EU STUDIES?

....

To begin to identify "sociological" approaches to EU studies, we can take some hints—but only hints—from broader uses of the term. They only help a bit (as hints are wont to do), but discussing their limitations maps some of the scholarly space around the sociological wave.

4.1.1 A Focus on Society?

Our first hint comes from the most classic meaning of "sociological" approaches to action: those that are rooted in society. "Sociological" arguments have long been seen as "bottom-up," especially as opposed to a political science focus on the state and governance and its ostensibly more "top-down" logic. Several of the scholars discussed below contrast their society-focused "bottom-up" thinking to a "top-down" political science orthodoxy on the EU.[2]

Yet this remains only a hint, for the simple reason that most political science theorizing on the EU is actually quite "sociological" by this definition—at least in its theoretical logic. Much of the earliest scholarship on integration grew out of Karl Deutsch's transactionalism, which (despite Deutsch's two PhDs in political science) focused its most direct attention on quotidian transactions in society.[3] Ernst Haas's neo-functionalist theory drew strongly on Deutsch (despite Haas' PhD in public law and government), but shifted more to a liberal logic that made societal groups "the building blocks of a theory of politics."[4] Though Haas became known mainly for predicting a shift of power and loyalties to European institutions, his core argument about *why* this would happen flowed upward from a certain configuration of interests in pluralistic societies.[5] Admittedly, Haas also laid foundations for later institutionalist thinking in which delegations of power to European institutions feed back into society to encourage integration—more of a top-down logic—but his emphasis remained on the bottom-up side. As Wayne Sandholtz and Alec Stone Sweet summarized Haas's core thought, "social exchange across borders drives integration processes, generating social demands for supranational rules."[6] Their chapter in this volume nicely highlights both these neofunctionalist foundations and the more top-down institutional feedback mechanisms that they have added to them.

The approach that eventually became neo-functionalism's great rival, Andrew Moravcsik's "liberal intergovernmentalism" (LI), is even *more* bottom-up. In Moravcsik's early writings this was obscured by his origins in realist theory. Following earlier work by one of his advisors, Stanley Hoffmann, he initially criticized neo-functionalism mainly for understating top-down state control of the integration process.[7] But as Moravcsik fleshed out his theory, he—like Haas thirty years before—connected it to liberal, bottom-up foundations. While maintaining his emphasis on state control, he explained state choices as a function of social demands: "Groups articulate preferences; governments aggregate them."[8] Politicians—"agents" of societal "principals"—seek interest-group and electoral support, selecting policies that appeal to the best represented and most intensely expressed societal interests on each issue. Much as the EU obeys state control, states obey societal control. The whole resultant theory flows upward from society.

There is nonetheless one way in which the classic integration literature left space for new kinds of bottom-up, society-focused scholarship. Though the theoretical *logic* of both classic approaches is bottom-up, their empirical work has been less so. This is especially true for Moravcsik. Though he argues that the EU reflects the aggregation (through several levels) of social-group interests, he has paid little attention to social groups. Instead he has researched and written about top state leaders and their interactions. For a clear example, consider the two-part, 106-page article on the European policies of Charles de Gaulle that Moravcsik expanded from one of the chapters in his landmark book.[9] Only six pages even mention *any* evidence about demands or concerns from *anyone* in France besides de Gaulle himself. The 1998 book gives somewhat more attention to social groups, but it too spills much more ink on leaders' strategizing than on anything happening in society. In my view, scholars in the neo-functionalist line do better at matching theory and evidence, though sometimes they too display the same disjuncture. While many works in this approach study business, interest groups, and other non-state actors fairly closely,[10] it is fair to say that its main empirical focus has been on political actors in the EU institutions (especially the European Commission).

In recent decades, then, "sociological" students of the EU could not claim bottom-up theorizing for their own. At most they could stake a claim to direct investigations of integration in society outside of the EU institutions and national governments. This is indeed partly what they have done. They have looked at areas like Europe in the media and public opinion,[11] social mobility in and between European cities,[12] collective mobilization and contentious politics that relate to the EU,[13] school textbooks and curricula on European issues,[14] and football.[15] That said, this attention to processes outside of Brussels looks more like a disciplinary division of labor than a different theoretical perspective on integration. And another development—the broadest change in political science theorizing on the EU in the 1990s—obscures whether there is even a division of labor. By the mid-1990s, most new work was turning to a focus on "Europeanization." After decades of taking EU institutions and policies as outcomes to be explained, a new generation of political scientists shifted to ask about the effects of the EU outside of Brussels.[16] If much of this literature has looked for Europeanization in rather classic political science spaces—sectoral policies, sub-national government, political parties, interest groups—it has broadly redirected political science's attention to processes "out there" in European societies. Most of the more society-focused work by sociologists fits comfortably alongside, or within, the "Europeanization" research agenda.

4.1.2 Attention to Interpretation and Social Construction?

A second hint about the distinctiveness of "sociological approaches" lies in another common meaning of "sociological." Especially in recent years, the term often refers to constructivist or interpretive scholarship, wherein actors' subjective interpretations make a difference in how they act. In this usage (like in the modifier of "sociological institutionalism"[17]), "sociological" becomes a synonym of "ideational," and is contrasted to "materialist" or "objective-interest" approaches. This seems a promising lead: some of the sociologists in EU studies present social constructivism as definitional to their approach.[18]

Objections immediately arise, however, if we portray this as more than a hint about where sociological approaches stand. There is clearly a widespread perception that they are not simply a strand of constructivist or interpretivist approaches—as reflected by our editors' commission for this chapter alongside Frank Schimmelfennig's survey of constructivism (Chapter 3). As much as these scholars agree that "social representations," "social structures," and socially-defined practices form part of their shared tool kit, they are also frequently critical of political science constructivism.[19] As Kauppi puts it, in terms similar to some from Mérand,[20]

> despite its stated aims to study the social fabric of Europe and world politics, [constructivism] is only weakly sociological. Its protagonists are eager to example the discursive processes informing European integration, identity, norms of behavior, and so on, leaving largely untouched the social characteristics of the individuals and groups who, through their activities, construct this symbolic and material entity.[21]

In stronger terms, Favell presents constructivism as an outdated resurrection of thin cultural thinking from Parsonian sociology.[22] Guiraudon evokes the thinness of constructivism in another way, noting that sociologists "do not usually mobilize concepts that emphasize *either* material interests *or* ideals and norms. There is no 'either/or' way of thinking as in the debate between liberal intergovernmentalism, neofunctionalists and IR social constructivist"; sociologists bypass these dichotomies to "study the locus of action, the nature of the game and [actors'] position[s] within it."[23]

Where, then, do these two hints leave us? A closer look at this literature will show that a societal focus and attention to interpretation both have strong echoes within it, but that its real distinctiveness lies in a rejection of the dichotomies implied above. Rather than advancing bottom-up thinking against top-down statists or interpretivism against objective interests, these scholars problematize the spatial and interpretive context of action within the EU. As Saurugger puts it, "sociological approaches can be differentiated from other approaches by the fact that they question social categories such as integration, the state, identity or interests which are often taken for granted in most European integration theories."[24] Their novelty lies in posing open-ended questions about networks and "fields" of action within the EU project: how do various categories of Europeans perceive the political arenas through which they act, and what does this tell us about integration?

4.2 Charting the Spatial and Interpretive Context of Integration

An early leading edge of the sociological wave, and some of its most prominent publications, came from Neil Fligstein and his collaborators. Tracing his exemplary contributions helps illuminate the emergence of sociological approaches more broadly. As one of the first sociologists to take a direct interest in European integration since the 1960s, Fligstein's initial work was inserted strongly in political science debates, and connected with the transactionalist/neo-functionalist category that is presented in this volume by Sandholtz and Stone Sweet (Chapter 2). Yet he also posed somewhat distinctive questions early on, and his thinking is best understood as part of the school of sociologists that has emerged alongside him.

An economic sociologist who had worked mainly in American political economy, Fligstein was drawn to Europe by the "relaunch" of European integration around the single market project. He soon became a key figure in the rebirth of the transactionalist/ neo-functionalist approach.[25] Within that effort, though, his work was notable for traveling across bottom-up/top-down and ideational/objective-interest lines. On the one hand, his theoretical statement with Stone Sweet in the *American Journal of Sociology* (*AJS*) was dominated by objective-interest, bottom-up language:

> The underlying logic of our model can be stated simply: as problems and new circumstances arise, firms and other market actors will press governmental organizations, including legislators and courts, for rules to govern markets. To the extent that these organizations respond to the demands, new opportunities to expand markets will emerge. If market actors adapt their activities to exploit these new opportunities, then the feedback loop will be completed, and the cycle will begin anew.[26]

On the other hand, an earlier *AJS* piece cast the single market project in a more top-down and interpretive light, and effectively suggested that Fligstein is not quite simply a member of the neo-functionalist school. Fligstein and Iona Mara-Drita argued that the Delors Commission strategically repackaged pre-existing proposals to create an "elite social movement," and used "existing rules and meanings to reorganize concepts of interest" in governments and business.[27] That sounds like a creative process that originates substantially in the Berlaymont building, rather than bubbling up out of society— more like the avowedly constructivist work of Nicolas Jabko.[28]

The way in which Fligstein's research combines these different emphases is nicely displayed in his recent summary statement, *Euroclash*.[29] Taking the sociological notion of "field" as his organizing concept—of which more below—he is interested in the emergence of "Europe-wide fields of action." Descriptively, this means charting which sectors have been touched by EU rules and how; how trade and merger patterns have reoriented to intra-European ties; or how we can see the Europeanization of diverse areas like defense, telecommunications, and football. Analytically, he proposes a "more sociological view of the process" of integration—by which he means an approach that looks at the intersection of bottom-up and top-down dynamics, and recognizes that integration is shaped both by some rather objective constraints of prevailing economic and state interests and subjective elements of identity and framing.[30] He is not interested in a grand teleology or a precise historical explanation, but rather in mapping the constellation of "fields of action" that have or have not been Europeanized, and the political problems (the "Euroclash") that may result from disjunctures across them.

In my view, it is this focus on tracking the emergence of "Europe-wide fields of action" that forms the distinctive core of recent "sociological approaches." As we can see with Fligstein, this goal carries scholars across some of the analytic dichotomies that have organized other approaches to the EU. In theoretical terms, one figure looms particularly large behind the approach: Pierre Bourdieu. Bourdieu first developed the notion of "field," and also argued aggressively for transcending the many dichotomies with which other scholars structure their work. He is a rather distant inspiration for Fligstein, though the French theorist's thinking contributed substantially to the emergence of the US-based "sociological institutionalism" for which Fligstein has been a leading light.[31] For most of today's sociological approaches to European integration—a substantial current of which comes from Francophone sociologists—Bourdieu's influence is quite direct.

A quick introduction to Bourdieu, then, helps to clarify this school's foundations. Bourdieu was born in 1930, and defined his thinking in the polarized world of Parisian sociology in the 1950s and 1960s. Students were pressured to choose between Levi-Strauss's structuralism and Sartre's existentialism, which were overlaid with a bewildering number of theoretical and political dichotomies which need not detain us here.[32] Bourdieu's response was to seek "to transcend inherited oppositions and dichotomies and the limitations of vision they always entail."[33] He attempted to fashion tools for a sociology that would be "resolutely antidualistic" and "genuinely synthetic."[34] Over several decades he elaborated a vast opus around three innovative concepts: "capital," "field," and "habitus." In rough terms (with the caveat that a fair presentation of these ideas requires longer treatment), Bourdieusian capital includes all the material and symbolic resources for which people compete in society. People are motivated above all by a search for social recognition (or dignity, or "distinction"); capital is the various kinds of wealth and status that one can accumulate to obtain it. Societies are organized in many overlapping but analytically distinct fields, which are defined around the many kinds of capital for which people compete and the different resources and spaces of interaction that are relevant to these competitions. Habitus is the package of practical knowledge and interpretive filters that allow individuals to negotiate fields of action.

Bourdieu proposed to use these concepts to organize concrete studies of practical action. He opposed any attempt to establish the relative weight of objective or subjective factors in any context, or indeed in parsing capital, fields, or habitus into any of the dichotomies that so fascinated his colleagues. As his student Louis Pinto writes,

> [Bourdieu's] refusal to choose between opposites...is the refusal of someone who experiences an almost existential malaise when forced to engage totally in one of the innumeral social and intellectual games which have two inverse and symmetrical positions, or when asked to rejoin his socially granted place and share the illusions of all those complicitous adversaries who perpetuate the game by their disagreement, and their identity by their difference.[35]

He suggested that we use ethnographic methods to identify the kinds of capital people sought in a given context; the interlocutors, competitors, and resources that defined their fields of action; and the practical knowledge and meanings which allowed them to act effectively therein. Unlike many grand social theorists, he implemented his approach in wide-ranging empirical work, from consumer tastes to education, religion, language, science, and the study of academia itself.[36]

Sociological approaches to EU studies vary in how directly they invoke Bourdieu, but his project captures nicely what is distinctive about their work. Social constructivism is clearly central to such an agenda, as Kauppi and Rumford suggest, but Favell rightly stresses that it does not share constructivists' goal of separating out the impact of social construction on action. Some of these scholars indeed direct their attention squarely at society outside Brussels, but their collective theoretical project can be applied just as fruitfully to fields of action that stretch in and across the EU institutions themselves. Overall, today's sociological approaches are most distinctive relative to other currents in EU studies for an explicit avoidance of spatial or directional assumptions, and for setting aside objective/subjective, ideational/materialist dichotomies.

The result is a body of scholarship in EU studies with two notable strengths. First, it generates arguments that follow real dynamics of action across the national–supranational divide so entrenched in older EU theorizing. Taking the actors' points of view, these scholars reconstruct the logic of a field's norms, boundaries, and configurations of its internal networks, internal dynamics of opposition, competition, cooperation, or emulation, and intersections with other fields. If some such fields operate mainly out in society, many of the fields that relate to the elite-dominated, multilevel arena of the EU are situated almost entirely among policy elites—and when these scholars reconstruct them, they always seem to find political dynamics that stretch across Brussels and state capitals. Charting these fields reveals aspects of EU politics which older approaches tend to miss.

A good example is Virginie Guiraudon's work on immigration and asylum policies. She is best known for a forceful but nuanced argument about the emergence of EU immigration policies in the 1990s.[37] Guiraudon portrays the gradual appearance of partial EU authority in immigration and asylum as driven by state actors, but not as a product of Moravcsik-style coherent state strategies. Interior ministry bureaucrats found their attempts to manage migration problems blocked or complicated by anti-immigration electoral politics, national courts, and inter-ministerial arbitrage within governments, and seized EU opportunities to "go transnational" in order to escape the constraints of their national policy fields. In so doing they effectively constructed a new European field of action in this sector.

Another example comes from Frédéric Mérand, who invokes Bourdieusian approaches to "analyze the development of [ESDP] as the creation of a pan-European military field, a structured network of security and defense actors who look to each other, share social representations, and vie for influence over policy outcomes."[38] He tells the tale of the post-war emergence of a field of international defense interactions around NATO, the somewhat later emergence of a field of foreign policy interactions around the EU, and their progressive merger since the 1990s. Unlike in an LI story, no powerful actors consciously laid out these developments over time and pursued this result. Prominent in the story are horizontal interactions between militaries and governments, and cross-field bricolage at a relatively low-profile, quotidian level. Yet his account is driven by "the intentional actions of state actors, and precisely those who are seen as the carriers of state sovereignty: statesmen, diplomats and military officers"[39] Their increasingly quotidian interaction at the European level reorganized the possibilities for European military action.

A third set of examples comes from the extensive scholarship of Andy Smith. Smith developed his thinking out of the French political sociology tradition of scholars like Pierre Muller, Yves Mény, and Jean-Louis Quermonne.[40] Though their lineage connects to Michel Crozier, a political and theoretical rival of Bourdieu, their overall theorizing and methods are very similar.[41] In a subtly different vocabulary, they trace legitimation, power, and competition through networks and fields of action. Besides offering one of the stronger theoretical statements for a distinctive political sociology of the EU,[42] Smith has written a whole series of fine-grained studies that trace the concrete experience of EU-related action as it flows in and out of the Brussels institutions. They include close studies of networks in and around the Commission, densely-researched work on EU regional policy and sub-national government, analyses of wine and other agricultural sectors, and a book on football, rugby, and Europe as well.[43]

The second notable strength of this work is that it tends to produce careful, nuanced empirical narratives that render action concretely comprehensible without overly reducing its real complexity, open-endedness, and reliance on perception and meaning. As a European Union Studies Association committee wrote in presenting Guiraudon with a "best conference paper" award, her work "captures the complexity of contemporary EU policy formation in the immigration area … [and] is remarkable for its recognition and mastery of different streams of policy-making over time. It foregrounds real EU politics in an unstable, constantly changing set of institutional arenas without imposing artificial social science parsimony."[44] On my reading, the empirical work of Mérand, Andy Smith, or Niilo Kauppi merits the same description. Kauppi (one of the most incisive interpreters of Bourdieu and founder of the new political sociology section of the European Consortium for Political Research) has written a sophisticated study of how the growing power of the European Parliament drew new actors into politics, and fed back into national political life.[45] In a study of the European Parliament and Finnish and French politics, he stresses that European Parliament elections opened up a new channel for relatively marginal actors to enter electoral politics, allowing them "to challenge traditional careers and the dominant political culture."[46] Similar studies in a more fully ethnographic vein—seeking less to explain the emergence of new integrative dynamics than to document the practical lives of EU-related actors—include Marc Abélès's study of the European Parliament, George Ross's insider account of the Delors Commission, the contributions to Guiraudon's edited volume on *The Sociology of Europe*, Didier Georgakakis's edited collection on careers and professionalization within the EU, and Favell's work on transnational elites.[47]

4.3 BUT HOW DISTINCTIVE IS IT?

There can be no doubt that a distinct sociological approach now exists in EU studies. It draws on its own theoretical sources, follows its own concepts and methods, and produces studies with their own sociological "feel," whether they address action in society or on the traditional terrain of EU institution building and policy-making.

To consider this scholarship more critically, however, it can be difficult to specify where it makes a clear-cut theoretical contribution. What do these scholars tell us about the EU, or Europe more broadly, that other schools would contest or miss? The synthetic, dichotomy-surpassing ambitions of Bourdieu-style theorizing often leave it unable to spell out just how much it contributes in contrast to sparser alternatives. This is one of the most common criticisms of Bourdieu himself. As Rogers Brubaker put it, Bourdieu's approach "is particularly ill-suited to a conceptualist, logocentric reading, one that treats it as the bearer of a set of logically interconnected propositions framed in terms of precise, unambiguous concepts."[48] This is not just to say that Bourdieu's essays can be opaque. The real problem is that it is almost always difficult to ascertain how much he disagrees with other arguments.[49] Indeed, Pinto summarizes a short intellectual biography of Bourdieu under the heading, "The Refusal of Theoretical Alternatives."[50] As much as Bourdieu's abstract criticisms of other theories are often insightful, his refusal to recognize legitimate alternatives in empirical context—spelling out how his claims depart from other empirical claims—deprives him of contrasts that are necessary to communicate a position in scholarly debates. Given Bourdieu's central interest in the social embeddedness of academia, surely he should have better appreciated that we advance our arguments in debate with other scholars, not as direct illuminations of the world. That is not to say that we must dignify every alternative or reproduce every dichotomy, but our claims can only be as clear as the alternatives that accompany them.

Just how crippling such problems are to Bourdieu is not a question for this chapter, but an echo of similar issues is visible across all the sociological approaches discussed above. These scholars are critical of the separation of EU elites and institutions from deeper societal processes, or of national from supranational organizational actors, or more abstractly of trying to distinguish ideational from material elements of action, or power-seeking and resource competition from norms and ideas and appropriateness and legitimation. But without some reference to these dichotomies—false analytic cartoons though they may be—it can be hard for readers to see the alternatives to these scholars' claims. Mérand's work is worth considering as an example, since it stands out for theoretical explicitness and engagement with a wide range of American and European scholarship. Despite this engagement at an abstract or summary level, his Bourdieusian theoretical apparatus discourages him from seeking sharp analytic distinctions with other claims in empirical material. He tells a concrete, nuanced story about the separation of militaries from the notion and practice of state sovereignty, thereby permitting progress in European defense. But he is not interested in parsing out the intertwining threads of that story. Asking why state actors have accepted to begin defense integration, he summarizes:

the deep and broad interpenetration of European states has created strong incentives for state actors to coordinate their foreign and defence policies at the EU level. "Internationalization" and more specifically "Europeanization" have constituted a single strategy on the part of state actors to salvage their positions by giving them access to more resources and enhancing their legitimacy. By downplaying patriotism and stressing the 'politics of scale,' this strategy gave meaning to professional practices that would have otherwise been seen as antiquated in late 20th Century Europe. This is what the international defense field (through NATO) and the European foreign policy field (through the EU) provided diplomats and soldiers with since the early 1950s.[51]

An emphasis on meaning and legitimacy is evident here, as is one on apparently rational response to fairly clear incentives in the surrounding environment. Mérand's book does not try to tease out how much he sees of each, instead rejecting the interests/ideas dichotomy and advocating a concrete focus on whatever combination of material and ideational contexts action appears to reflect. The problem with this stance, let me reiterate, is not that its synthetic goal is unpromising overall. The problem is that we do not know how different it is from other positions, especially the old rationalist-materialist ones. Mérand criticizes the materialist baseline but does not swing entirely to the opposite pole; some material conditions matter in his account. Since he does not elaborate a "pure" materialist version of his story against which he can display the distinctiveness of his argument, though, we cannot see how much he parts company with older theorizing.

To perceive a choice between abstract analytic distinctions and complex, nuanced understandings of action, then—as Bourdieu did, and these scholars often do—may be to construct a new kind of false dichotomy. To achieve more genuine syntheses, showing and demystifying the interrelationships that undercut many dichotomies, we may actually need to give *sharper* attention to such analytic distinctions. In simple logical terms, the more we posit a world of multiple, complex dynamics, the more we must try to separate them out and recombine them to say anything organized about what is going on. It is certainly imaginable that this is a fool's errand—the world may resist such analytic disentanglement—but I am not sure that we have the real option of a direct path to understanding that bypasses such stylized disaggregation. At times, I will admit, the empirical mastery and elegant narratives of many recent sociological approaches to EU studies make me think otherwise. But I still suspect that they will become still more clearly distinctive, making an ever-growing contribution to EU studies, if they try to subvert dichotomies by unpacking rather than by ignoring them.

4.4 CONCLUSION

As many parts of this volume attest, the rarefied political science world of US-dominated, grand-theory-oriented, narrowly-elite-focused integration theory is no longer. That is not to say that grand old theories have left the scene, but the sub-field has broadened in disciplinary, geographical, and conceptual terms. The turn of sociologists toward the EU project, many of them Europeans, has brought in a newly concrete, open-ended, and theoretically synthetic approach. Their project of charting the spatial and interpretative "fields" of EU-related action has tremendous empirical promise, and their theoretical eclecticism should place them at the center of scholarly debates. Our collective understanding of the EU will be stronger for it.

Notes

1. For a more exhaustive review, see Sabine Saurugger, "Sociological Approaches in EU Studies," *Journal of European Public Policy* 16, no. 6 (2009), 935–49.
2. Niilo Kauppi, "Bourdieu's Political Sociology and the Politics of European Integration," *Theory and Society* 32 (2003), 775–89; Adrian Favell, "The Sociology of EU Politics," in K. E. Jørgensen, Mark Pollack, and Ben Rosamond, eds, *Handbook of EU Politics* (London: Sage: 2006), 122–8; Adrian Favell and Virginie Guiraudon, eds, *Sociology of the European Union* (London: Palgrave, 2009); Gerard Delanty and Chris Rumford, *Rethinking Europe: Social Theory and the Implications of Europeanization* (New York: Routledge, 2005).
3. Karl Deutsch, *Nationalism and Social Communication* (Cambridge, MA: MIT Press, 1953).
4. Ernst Haas, *The Uniting of Europe: Political, Social and Economic Forces, 1950–1957* (Stanford, CA: Stanford University Press, 1958); Ernst Haas, *Beyond the Nation-State: Functionalism and International Organization* (Stanford, CA: Stanford University Press, 1964), 30–50.
5. Craig Parsons, "Domestic Interests, Ideas, and Integration: Lessons from the French Case," *Journal of Common Market Studies* 38, no. 1 (2000), 45–70.
6. Wayne Sandholtz and Alec Stone Sweet, "Integration, Supranational Governance, and the Institutionalization of the European Polity," in Sandholtz and Stone Sweet, eds, *European Integration and Supranational Governance* (New York: Oxford University Press, 1998), 1–26, at 5.
7. Stanley Hoffmann, "Obstinate or Obsolete? The Fate of the Nation State and the Case of Western Europe," *Daedalus* 95 (1966), 862–915; Andrew Moravcsik, "Negotiating the Single European Act: National Interests and Conventional Statecraft in the European Community," *International Organization* 45, no. 1 (1991), 19–56.
8. Andrew Moravcsik, "Preferences and Power in the European Community: A Liberal Intergovernmentalist Approach," *Journal of Common Market Studies* 31, no. 4 (1993), 473–524; 483.
9. Andrew Moravcsik, *The Choice for Europe: Social Purpose and State Power from Messina to Maastricht* (Ithaca, NY: Cornell University Press, 1998); Andrew Moravcsik, "De Gaulle Between Grain and *Grandeur*: The Political Economy of French EC Policy, 1958–1970 (Part I)," *Journal of Cold War Studies* 2, no. 2 (2000), 3–43, and Part II, *Journal of Cold War Studies* 2, no. 3 (2000), 4–68.
10. For example, Wayne Sandholtz, *High-Tech Europe* (Berkeley: University of California Press, 1992); Anne-Marie Burley and Walter Mattli, "Europe Before the Court: A Political Theory of Legal Integration," *International Organization* 47 (1993), 41–76.

11. Olivier Baisnée and Dominique Marchetti, "Euronews: Un laboratoire de la production de l'information 'européenne'," in Virginie Guiraudon, ed., *Sociologie de l'Europe: Mobilisations, élites et configurations institutionnelles* (Paris: L'Harmattan, 2000), 121–52; Juan Diez Medrano, *Framing Europe: Attitudes to European Integration in Germany, Spain and the United Kingdom* (Princeton, NJ: Princeton University Press, 2003).

12. Patrick Le Galès, *European Cities, Social Conflicts and Governance* (Oxford: Oxford University Press, 2002); Adrian Favell, *Eurostars and Eurocities* (Oxford: Blackwell, 2008).

13. Doug Imig and Sidney Tarrow, eds, *Contentious Europeans* (Lanham, MD: Rowman & Littlefield, 2001).

14. Yasmin Soysal and Hanna Schissler, eds, *The Nation, Europe, and the World: Textbooks and Curricula in Transition* (Oxford: Berghahn, 2004).

15. Anthony King, *The European Ritual: Football in the New Europe* (Hampshire: Ashgate, 2003); Neil Fligstein, *Euroclash: The EU, European Identity, and the Future of Europe* (New York: Oxford University Press, 2008).

16. Among many, Claudio Radaelli, "Whither Europeanization? Concept Stretching and Substantive Change," *European Integration Online Papers* 4, no. 8 (2000), <http://eiop.or.at/eiop/texte/2000-008a.html>; Maria Green Cowles, James Caporaso, and Thomas Risse, eds, *Transforming Europe: Europeanization and Domestic Change* (Ithaca, NJ: Cornell University Press, 2001); Paolo Graziano and Maarten Vink, eds, *Europeanization: New Research Agendas* (Basingstoke: Palgrave Macmillan, 2006); see also Craig Parsons, "Puzzling out the EU Role in National Politics," *Journal of European Public Policy* 14, no. 7 (2007), 1135–49.

17. Walter Powell and Paul DiMaggio, eds, *The New Institutionalism in Organizational Analysis* (Chicago: University of Chicago Press, 1991).

18. Niilo Kauppi, *Democracy, Social Resources and Political Power in the European Union* (Manchester: Manchester University Press, 2005); Delanty and Rumford, *Rethinking Europe*.

19. Frédéric Mérand and Sabine Saurugger, "Does European Integration Theory Need Sociology?" *Comparative European Studies* 8, no. 1 (2010), 1–18.

20. Frédéric Mérand, *European Defence Policy: Beyond the Nation State* (Oxford: Oxford University Press, 2008).

21. Kauppi, "Bourdieu's Political Sociology," 777.

22. Favell, "Sociology of EU Politics."

23. Virginie Guiraudon, "The EU Through Europeans' Eyes: Political Sociology and EU Studies," *EUSA Review* 19, no. 1 (2006), 1–5, at 3.

24. Saurugger, "Sociological Approaches," 936.

25. Sandholtz and Stone Sweet, *European Integration and Supranational Governance*.

26. Neil Fligstein and Alec Stone Sweet, "Constructing Polities and Markets: An Institutionalist Account of European Integration," *American Journal of Sociology* 107, no. 5 (2002), 1206–43, at 1213.

27. Neil Fligstein and Iona Mara-Drita, "How to Make a Market: Reflections on the Attempt to Create a Single Market in the European Union," *American Journal of Sociology* 102, no. 1 (1996), 1–33.

28. Nicolas Jabko, "In the Name of the Market: How the European Commission Paved the Way for Monetary Union," *Journal of European Public Policy* 6, no. 3 (1999), 475–95; and *Playing the Market* (Ithaca, NY: Cornell University Press, 2006).

29. Neil Fligstein, *Euroclash: The EU, European Identity, and the Future of Europe* (New York: Oxford University Press, 2008).

30. Fligstein, *Euroclash*, 26.

31. Paul DiMaggio, "On Pierre Bourdieu," *American Journal of Sociology* 84, no. 6 (1979), 1460–74.

32. Rogers Brubaker, "Rethinking Classical Theory: The Sociological Vision of Pierre Bourdieu," *Theory and Society* 14, no. 6 (1985), 745–75; Loic Wacquant, "Pierre Bourdieu," in Robert Stones, ed., *Key Sociological Thinkers* (Houndmills: Macmillan, 1998), 215–29.

33. Craig Calhoun, Edward LiPuma, and Moishe Postone, eds, *Bourdieu: Critical Perspectives* (Chicago: University of Chicago Press, 1993), 2.

34. Wacquant, "Pierre Bourdieu," 217.

35. Louis Pinto, "Theory in Practice," in Richard Shusterman, *Bourdieu: A Critical Reader* (Oxford: Blackwell, 1999), 94–112, at 102.

36. Among many, Pierre Bourdieu, *Distinction* (Cambridge, MA: Harvard University Press, 1984); *Homo Academicus* (Stanford, CA: Stanford University Press, 1988); *La noblesse d'Etat: Grands corps et grandes écoles* (Paris: Editions de Minuit, 1989); *The Field of Cultural Production* (New York: Columbia University Press, 1993).

37. Virginie Guiraudon, "The Constitution of a European Immigration Policy Domain: A Political Sociology Approach," *Journal of European Public Policy* 10, no. 2 (2003), 263–82.

38. Mérand, *European Defence Policy*, 2.

39. Mérand, *European Defence Policy*, 4.

40. Yves Mény, Pierre Muller, and Jean Louis Quermonne, eds, *Politiques publiques en Europe* (Paris: L'Harmattan, 1995).

41. Michel Crozier, *Le phénomène bureaucratique* (Paris: Seuil, 1964).

42. Andy Smith, *Le gouvernement de l'Union européenne: une sociologie politique* (Paris: Librairie générale de droit et de jurisprudence, 2004).

43. Andy Smith, *L'Europe politique au miroir du local* (Paris, l'Harmattan, 1995); Jean Joana and Andy Smith, *Les commissaries européens: technocrats, diplomats ou politiques?* (Paris: Presses de Sciences Po, 2002); *La passion du sport. Le football, le rugby et les appartenances en Europe* (Rennes: Presses universitaires de Rennes, 2002); Andy Smith, ed., *Politics and the European Commission* (London, Routledge, 2004); Andy Smith, Jacques de Maillard, and Olivier Costa, *Vin et politique: Bordeaux, la France, la mondialisation* (Paris: Presses de Sciences Po, 2007).

44. Cited in editors' "Note to Guiraudon," "Constitution of a European Immigration Policy Domain," 263.

45. Niilo Kauppi, *The Politics of Embodiment: Habits, Power, and Pierre Bourdieu's Theory* (New York: Peter Lang, 2000).

46. Niilo Kauppi, *Democracy, Social Resources and Political Power in the European Union* (Manchester: Manchester University Press, 2005), 5.

47. Marc Abélès, *La vie quotidienne au Parlement européen* (Paris: Hachette, 1992); George Ross, *Jacques Delors and European Integration* (London: Polity, 1995); Virginie Guiraudon, ed., *Sociologie de l'Europe: Mobilisations, élites et configurations institutionnelles* (Paris: L'Harmattan, 2000); Didier Georgakakis, ed., *Les métiers de l'Europe politique* (Strasbourg: Presses universitaires de Strasbourg, 2002); Adrian Favell, *Eurostars and Eurocities* (Oxford: Blackwell, 2008).

48. Brubaker, "Rethinking Classical Theory," 217.

49. See the contributions to Calhoun, LiPuma, and Postone, *Bourdieu: Critical Perspectives*, especially Edward LiPuma, "Culture and the Concept of Culture in a Theory of Practice, 14–34, and also Richard Shusterman, ed., *Bourdieu: A Critical Reader* (Oxford: Blackwell, 1999).

50. Pinto, "Theory in Practice," 95.

51. Mérand, *European Defence Policy*, 149.

CHAPTER 5

MULTILEVEL GOVERNANCE

GEORGE PAGOULATOS AND LOUKAS TSOUKALIS

In the broader universe of EU theoretical approaches, multilevel governance (MLG) should be located along the intergovernmentalism/supranationalism dimension, rather than on either the sociological or the constructivist approaches, which draw on a different methodological vocabulary. In the continuum between state-centric theories (see Chapter 1, this volume) and supranationalist theories (see Chapter 2, this volume), MLG is clearly placed on the side of neo-functionalism/supranationalism, with which it shares common hypotheses. Contrary to either intergovernmentalism or neo-functionalism, however, MLG should not be regarded as a macro-theory of European integration, though some of the leading MLG exponents would claim it as such. MLG does not explain why European integration happens. It is rather a middle-range, meso-level theoretical approach that accounts for the day-to-day workings of European integration and the EU.

The term multilevel governance (MLG) was initially launched by Gary Marks[1] in order to conceptualize the evolving EU structural policy after its 1988 reform, which had aimed to render the internal market compatible with the wider regional disparities resulting from Southern enlargement. In his early work, Marks[2] found out that while liberal intergovernmentalism could account for the 1988 decision to double the size of funds, the implementation of the funds gradually ended up escaping state control in many different ways. Wishing to ensure the effective use of these funds, governments (willingly or reluctantly) agreed with the Commission to have funds administered through partnerships established domestically, comprising representatives of national actors, regional/local actors, and supranational actors (the Commission).

Based on the partnership principle, sub-national actors like local authorities formed alliances with supranational bodies like the Commission, in circumventing or operating outside the purview of their respective national governments. They established their own channels of communication, such as an autonomous Brussels representation or collaboration with pan-European lobbying groups. Moreover, once created, these policy networks linking sub-national with supranational or transnational actors could not be easily controlled by national governments, assuming a life of their own in order to promote interests and preferences often diverging from those of national governments. Thus, with reference to the EU, Marks argued, structural funds are "part of a new political (dis)order that is multilateral, constitutionally open-ended, and programmatically diverse."[3] In one of the early definitions of MLG, Marks[4] spoke of "supranational, national, regional, and local governments...enmeshed in territorially overarching policy networks."

5.1 THE MLG THEORETICAL PROJECT AND THE "NEO-FUNCTIONALISM VS INTERGOVERNMENTALISM" DEBATE

MLG was well founded on empirical grounds. Both structural funds and the SEA were changing the reality of integration and the nature of the European Community. The SEA gradually transformed what was until then a closed, top-driven, elite-handled integration process insulated from public pressures into one that drew domestic groups directly into the European policy arena. National and sub-national collective interests mobilized at European Community-level, seeking to influence the copious production of single market legislation. The introduction of QMV, the increase of European Parliament legislative powers following the SEA, and later the introduction of co-decision by the TEU, were all transforming the European Community/EU into a kind of EU polity in the making. Its evolutionary dynamics now defied the traditional toolbox of government-centered international relations scholars, calling for approaches that would address it in terms of what was evolving into a *sui generis* political system. Indeed, the MLG approach has advanced the broader theoretical project of viewing the EU through the lenses of comparative politics as a political system, rather than as an international organization undergoing a process of integration.

Though MLG develops a different focus, asking different questions, it does share a similar world view with neo-functionalism, from which it can be claimed to have evolved. Some have taken the point even further, arguing that MLG is identical to neo-functionalism in the hypotheses it generates, "because it is nothing more than a partial restatement of neofunctionalism without the functionalism."[5] Echoing neo-functionalists, the world of MLG is one in which the EU is polycentric, states are not unitary, national governments are fragmented, having lost control to actors at different levels (EU supranational, national- and sub-national). The plurality of collective interests and actors assumed by MLG is compatible with the pluralist conceptualization espoused by neo-functionalism. So is the understanding that state and non-state actors may form alliances with their counterparts in other member states, transnational networks potentially promoting the agenda and preferences of other supranational actors like the Commission. Contrary to neo-functionalism, however, MLG does not seek to explain the occurrence and progress of integration, but to understand "the nature of the beast" itself, the EU and EU policy-making.

Starting from the modest background of an approach that was meant to make sense of EU structural policy, MLG theorizing has built up an impressive dynamic. Recent formulations of MLG theory have fully appropriated the neo-functionalist conceptual tradition, except perhaps for the notion of functional spillover, which is considered as dated.[6] Speaking for MLG, Hooghe and Marks[7] confront state-centric theories by pointing out that governments no longer monopolize European-level policy-making or the aggregation of domestic interests, as decision-making competences are shared by actors at different levels. MLG scholars point out that supranational institutions, especially the European Parliament, the Commission, and the Court, have independent influence in policy-making that cannot be derived from their role as agents of national executives, as rational-choice institutionalism (RCI) would have it. Though national governments and national arenas are important, and remain the most important pieces of the European puzzle, "one must analyze the independent role of European-level actors to explain European policy making."[8] State-centric approaches claim that EU decisions reflect the lowest common denominator among national government positions, as unanimity provisions on important issues allow them to maintain individual and collective control over outcomes. MLG contradicts the state-centric view, by pointing out that lowest common denominator outcomes are available only on a subset of EU decisions mainly concerning the scope of integration; on the contrary, much of EU regulation such as single market rules is zero-sum, inevitably involving gains and losses for individual states. Finally, MLG disputes the state-centric conceptualization of policy-making in the EU as "determined primarily by national governments constrained by political interests nested within autonomous national arenas."[9] Hooghe and Marks[10] argue that political arenas are interconnected rather than nested: sub-national actors operate in both national and supranational arenas, creating transnational associations in the process. The separation between domestic and international politics, pivotal in state-centric theories, is rejected by MLG. Instead, the MLG approach views national governments as an integral and powerful part of the EU, but no longer providing the sole interface between supranational and sub-national arenas; governments "share, rather than monopolize, control over many activities that take place in their respective territories."[11]

Though the EU must be viewed as a political system, defying the traditional separation between international and domestic, it challenges standard state-centric, comparative politics conceptualizations. Any state-centric approach, positing a hierarchically organized and functionally divided state polity around which political parties compete seeking to respond to pressures and interests of domestic society, would fail to fully capture a *sui generis* EU. While the EU is much more than an international organization, it also falls short of being a federal state, lacking a proper government—though some have optimistically described it as an "emerging federation."[12] Condominio[13] or confederal consociation[14] have been some of the concepts employed to delineate the institutional complexity of the EU polity. It represents a negotiated order[15] rather than one defined by a formal legal framework. For such reasons, an MLG approach is suitable at capturing the institutional and functional complexity and indeterminacy of the EU. MLG focuses on systems of governance involving transnational, national, and sub-national institutions and actors; it draws attention to negotiations and networks, instead of legal and constitutional frameworks, as the defining feature of institutional relationships; it emphasizes the role of "satellite organizations" such as NGOs and agencies, which are not formally part of the governmental framework.[16]

Part of the MLG theoretical project is to emphasize the importance and strength supranational EU institutions have gradually acquired since the SEA. MLG theory posits that the sovereignty of individual states is diluted both by collective decision-making among governments and by the autonomous role of the European Parliament, the Commission, the ECJ, and the ECB. The Commission provided over the years ample evidence of its tendency to operate autonomously in many different ways, transforming e.g. structural policy from a simple side payment transferring money from richer to poorer member states into an interventionist instrument of regional policy. On its part, the ECJ developed into a formidable supranational actor, engaging in systematic activism that brought about the constitutionalization of EU treaties in a way that has repeatedly challenged national governments.[17] As Sandholtz and Stone Sweet point out in this volume (Chapter 2), there is ample evidence that supranational EU institutions such as the Commission and the ECJ have routinely produced rules and policies that the member states would not have adopted through intergovernmental bargaining.

In the MLG world view, national governments are far from omnipotent. Neither the treaties nor the Council give governments full control over policy-making. In addition to the autonomous function of EU supranational actors, EU intergovernmental decision-making has often been confronted and derailed by the participation and opposition of a wide range of domestic actors. This happened in a number of cases, from the opposition of British national members of parliament (MPs) to the Maastricht Treaty ratification, to the German regional governments' attempts to thwart it in the Constitutional Court, to the 1992 TEU rejection by Danish citizens, to the 2005 negative referenda in France and the Netherlands that led to the rejection of the EU Constitutional Treaty, to the public opinion of Ireland that obstructed ratification of the Nice Treaty in 2001 and the Lisbon Treaty in 2008. With growing frequency since the 1990s, the "permissive consensus" that had nurtured European integration until the single market has given way to "constraining dissensus." An increasingly politicized, internally fragmented EU has emerged, where a rising number of issues are addressed not just in cross-national terms, nor only in pro- or anti-integration terms, but along the left–right ideological continuum.[18] All such instances are taken by the MLG scholarship as limitations on collective national government control over the EU decision-making process, limitations arising from parliaments, regional governments, and public pressures, in tandem with the increased public scrutiny of EU decision-making especially since the 1990s. Hooghe and Marks[19] have proposed a "post-functionalist" research program that seeks to account for the varying degrees of politicization of the EU across EU countries, by refocusing attention to domestic political conflict as one driven by questions of identity rather than economic preferences of interest groups.

5.2 From Macro- to Meso-Level, From Government to Governance

In drawing attention to the EU and EU policy-making, MLG also represents a certain fatigue with grand-theorizing as the EU reality has grown increasingly fluid and complex. Along with its associated conceptual approaches of *governance* and *policy networks*, MLG is a leading example of the ascendance of meso-level theorizing in EU studies, concerned with hitherto overlooked issues of content, process, context, and bargaining. MLG serves to direct attention from the most visible, "history-making" moments in the evolution of the EU (intergovernmental agreements and Treaties, major Council decisions), where states are indeed the dominant actors, to what follows after history-making decisions have been made, that is the day-to-day reality of integration, the "practice of policy." In stark contrast to liberal intergovernmentalism, the emphasis on the "post-decisional" processes, Treaty interpretation, and policy implementation echoes the neo-functionalist focus on the supranational functional councils, advisory groups, and technical committees operating as mechanisms of a closer and denser integration.

MLG is thus part of a wider turn from government to *governance*. Governance implies a shift of emphasis from the institution to the process, from state authority and government resources to the coordinated collective action and "governing activities of social, political and administrative actors"[20] and the sharing of tasks and responsibilities between public and private actors, guiding and steering in a more or less continuous process of interaction.[21] EU governance is organized through multiple, overlapping jurisdictions. Authority is dispersed both vertically (across different territorial levels) and horizontally (shared between government- and non-state actors). Through the dispersion of decision-making competences, the political systems of member states are not separate but interconnected in various ways.

Multilevel governance reflects the context of globalization in which the EU develops. Global interdependence, the erosion of national sovereignty and traditional state hierarchical structures, the emergence of transnationalized policy regimes and networks, sectoral and functional differentiation, have been distinct features of globalization that also shape the content of multilevel governance. The challenge to traditional state authority has been summarized by Rhodes as a process of "hollowing out" the state.[22] The declining capacity of governments to control the flows of goods, capital, services, and people within and across their borders correlates with the proliferation of various forms of governance. On the supply side, a multiplying array of organizations, associations, regulatory agencies, and all sorts of public and private entities at sub-national, national and transnational level, emerge to participate in sharing authority. On the demand side, the swelling demands for governance derive from the "simultaneous, diverse, and contradictory forces that can be summarized in the clash between globalization, centralization, and integration on the one hand and localization, decentralization, and fragmentation on the other."[23]

Following the standard typology, the MLG approach distinguishes EU policy-making into four sequential stages: initiation, decision-making, implementation, and adjudication. The policy *initiation* stage is a multi-actor activity, where the Commission operates as a conditional agenda setter, holding the pen but subject to pressures from many actors (European Council and Council of Ministers, European Parliament, interest groups, and individual member states). The *decision-making* stage is that in which the legislative powers of national governments are relatively at their highest. However, MLG scholars find national government control eroded by the European Parliament legislative power, the Commission, and interest groups.[24] Even in policy areas prescribed by the treaties as intergovernmental (formerly second and third pillar policies) the Commission has occasionally managed to turn the incomplete contract of treaty stipulations to its benefit. MLG scholars have provided evidence of that even in "high" policy areas: the Commission, for example, has asserted a key presence in decision-making on the EU defense industry by linking Community policies (industry and internal market) to CFSP measures.[25] The incorporation of immigration policy into the Community pillar of the EU also testifies to the Commission's ability to promote integration in policy areas where intergovernmental decision-making fails to function in the most efficient manner.

MLG is stereotypically regarded as being prominent at the *implementation* stage of the EU policy process. Day-to-day implementation in a number of areas brings the Commission into close regularized contact with regional governments and all kinds of interest groups. Comitology, initially designed for national governments to monitor the Commission's executive work, ended up increasing the participation of sub-national actors, interest groups, and technical experts, in the policy-making and implementation process. Finally, *adjudication* brings to the fore an activist Court in a supranational legal order, ECJ decisions often taken up and acted upon by other actors such as the Commission and national courts.[26] All four stages of the EU policy-making process demonstrate how national states in the EU, rather than being explicitly challenged, "are being melded into a multi-level polity by their leaders and the actions of numerous sub-national and supranational actors."[27]

5.3 Applications of MLG

MLG has been boosted by the spreading process of regional devolution and decentralization of authority in Europe, especially since the 1980s, in the EU and beyond. This has been the case particularly with Southern European countries (Spain, Greece), Scandinavian countries, as well as the UK after 1998.[28] Hooghe and Marks[29] have shown that no EU-15 country became more centralized since 1980, and half decentralized authority to a regional tier of government. A large number of transnational regimes were created over the 1980s and 1990s, some exercising real supranational authority, while diverse public/private networks multiplied from local to international level.[30]

The MLG theoretical approach has inspired an extensive research program, especially but not exclusively in the field of structural and regional policy.[31] Bache[32] finds that EU cohesion policy has made a crucial contribution to emerging MLG in Britain, increasing both vertical and horizontal interdependence, the latter particularly at the sub-national level. Though structural and regional policy remained the par excellence domain of MLG, the concept was developed further to apply to EU policy-making in general.[33] MLG has opened up new avenues of research in areas such as the governance of the single market,[34] industrial relations,[35] environmental policy,[36] financial and monetary governance,[37] or the broad Europeanization literature.[38] In the case of Europeanization, the empowerment of technocratic actors, sub-national actors and institutions, and the strengthening of civil society, are all outcomes associated with the dynamics of MLG. In the field of economic policy, Perraton and Wells[39] locate three general trends over the last sixty years, each of which informs debates on MLG: the ceding of economic policy-making power to supranational institutions, the decentralization of economic policy functions to the regional level, and a pressure to reduce the size of government and promote new governance and partnership agreements involving market and civil society agents. They propose fiscal federalism, dealing with the optimal allocation of economic policy-making functions, as the closest economics corollary of MLG. MLG has even been extended to areas of high politics like common foreign policy, normally constituting the *locus classicus* of state-centrism. Smith[40] finds significant progress during the 1990s toward a multilevel governance of EU foreign policy, governance mechanisms influencing domestic foreign policy cultures of EU member states, and interacting with domestic politics to produce specific policy outcomes. That said, policy areas traditionally branded as "high politics" (foreign policy, economic policy) remain the least susceptible to MLG, subject to a prevailing logic of government interest and a dominant role of state and institutional actors (like the ECB), characterized by a formal layering of authority and far more limited involvement of non-state actors.

In its standard form, the emergence of MLG has been identified with the single market process, relying on European regulation and "hard" policy, as well as self-regulation and delegation of decision-making authority to non-state actors, and public–private networks of actors at various levels of governance for policy implementation.[41] MLG can be claimed to have been given a new boost by the ascendance of "soft law" in the 2000s under the Lisbon agenda and the Open Method of Coordination (OMC), based on intergovernmental voluntary compliance with goals, benchmarking-driven mutual adjustment without application of formal power. The OMC is compatible with MLG in that several different layers of government and sub-national actors coordinate—and compete—with each other, jointly define objectives and instruments, with the Commission empowered to assess the member states' relative performance in attaining the consensually determined agreed objectives.[42] On the other hand, other EU supranational institutions (European Parliament and the Court) are absent, member states rule, and the real OMC impact on national policy has remained lamentably limited.

The tension between state-centric and multilevel governance increases at moments of history-making decisions or crises; there, traditional state leadership takes the lead. The

2008–2009 economic crisis, for example, demonstrated the limits of diffused authority and shared control. This was even more so since the effects of the crisis were asymmetrically felt across the EU. Workers, businesses, and disaffected socio-economic groups turned to their national governments for response. At hard times, politics is primarily national (even the Commission's EU stimulus was actually the sum of national spending plans); national popular demand and democratic government control carry the day. In such cases, efficient policy responses require not only vertical government power but also that most Westfalian of policy instruments and political resources, the national budget. Government is called into the game again, to stabilize, cushion the vulnerable, and redistribute. As long as these functions in the EU polity remain primarily or exclusively national, the moment when they are most in demand will represent a retreat of blurred policy boundaries and MLG. On the other hand, it could be noted that European regulatory initiatives on post-crisis banking re-regulation have evolved along the lines of MLG, featuring hybrid regulatory authority and public–private forms of transnational governance, non-state actors drawing up rules adopted by states as legally binding—basic rules having been agreed by national governments.

5.4 CRITIQUES OF MLG

The real impact of MLG is perhaps that it has become an inextricable part of our conceptual vocabulary and understanding of how the EU functions. Even EU leaders, like former Commission President Prodi,[43] have defined the EU as a MLG structure. Regardless of whether one subscribes to MLG theory or not, the majority of European scholars today, including MLG critics, accept that the EU (if not generally, at least in particular sectors) operates at several different administrative levels and exhibits some features of "governance."[44] This alludes to a necessary (and fairly obvious) distinction between MLG as a theoretical approach and MLG and as a real-world phenomenon. We may add here a third distinct version of MLG as prescriptive approach adopted by European policy-makers for its enhanced capacity to address the complex governance requirements of the modern era, in the EU and beyond. One may accept the second (MLG as phenomenon) without subscribing to the first (MLG theory). And one may conceivably employ MLG as theoretical approach and recognize MLG as a phenomenon, while remaining skeptical about its normative superiority and capacity to deliver in the real policy world.

For one thing, the theoretical potency and scope of MLG have been seriously questioned. MLG scholars have been criticized for offering more of a concept than a theory. Jordan[45] argued that MLG "lacks a causal motor of integration or a set of testable hypotheses," thus providing an EU description but not a theory. Jessop[46] has claimed that work on governance often remains at a pre-theoretical stage, as it is much clearer what the notion of governance excludes than what it contains. Pointing out its indeterminate nature, Peters and Pierre[47] maintain that MLG lacks a clear conceptual analysis,[48] and "appears incapable of providing clear predictions or even explanations (other than the most general) of outcomes in the governance process."[49] Sandholtz and Stone Sweet in this volume (Chapter 2) argue that MLG is an approach which does not offer a theory of integration or change, since MLG "is itself an outcome of integration processes that it cannot explain."

MLG scholars have countered such critiques, arguing that MLG theory does provide testable hypotheses. According to MLG scholars, MLG is validated when state sovereignty is compromised in collective national decision-making, and individual state executives cannot deliver the policy outcomes they wish through European policy-making; when the European Council and Council of Ministers share power with supranational actors; when sub-national interests mobilize beyond the reach of national governments directly in the European arena, seeking to use the EU to pressure state executives into particular actions.[50]

Moreover, Hooghe and Marks[51] offer three alternative causal explanations of why national central governments relinquish authority to sub-national or supranational actors. First, domestic diffusion of power by government enhances its intergovernmental bargaining power by allowing it to claim that its hands are tied, and it can only make limited concessions. Second, government leaders may wish to tie the hands of their successors by making the reversal of their policies more difficult. This applies particularly for amending EU legislation on the adoption of which a national government has agreed. Third, transferring authority to the supranational level may be a self-binding strategy for governments seeking to eschew the political cost of necessary but unpopular decisions (for example, the adoption of Maastricht-prescribed policies of macroeconomic discipline by South European governments in the 1990s). In all such ways the transfer of authority from central government to the sub-national or supranational level is not just a result of external necessities but a conscious political choice.

Another line of criticism has argued that MLG focuses excessively on sub-national authorities at the expense of other actors like pressure groups, and that MLG scholars tend to overstate the impact of sub-national actors anyway. Their bypassing state authorities and operating independently in Europe is not necessarily tantamount to their having the power to shape outcomes, as mobilization and influence are not necessarily synonymous.[52]

Others have pointed out that, except for the decentralization already mentioned, MLG has not been paralleled by corresponding constitutional reforms. Sub-national authorities undertaking initiatives such as signing agreements with cross-border authorities do so against the proper constitutional definition of their competences.[53] This latter is an argument well-taken by MLG scholars, who concede that MLG represents a substantive transformation of governance towards a network mode, but less so of formal legal–institutional structures.[54]

A serious weakness of the MLG theoretical approach is that it tends to underplay the renationalization of policy. The emergence of MLG coincided with a period of optimism of supranationalists about the depth of integration, its transformative impact on national polities, and the leading role of the Commission in that process. On the road to Eastern enlargement such optimism dissipated. National governments asserted their control in a process where EU resources were becoming increasingly scarce and contested. The Commission itself, at the turn of the twenty-first century, adopted a more pragmatic stance and lowered its requirements vis-à-vis new member states during the accession negotiations. Instead of devolution and the creation of local and regional authorities as interlocutors and partners in the administration of structural and cohesion funds, the Commission now prioritized the sound and efficient management of structural and regional policy, preferring national governments over untested and inefficient sub-national actors.[55] Thus, structural funds were increasingly featuring a stronger gate-keeper role for national governments, as also argued by Pollack in this volume (Chapter 1). Such signs of reversal, retrenchment, and renationalization were evinced even in the "old" cohesion countries, where EU structural and regional policy had carried a notable earlier impact toward decentralization.[56]

MLG raises important normative issues. On the positive side, it is the brainchild of dissatisfaction with hierarchical policy-making authority and the monopoly of power by central governments. On the negative side, with its spatial diffusion of power and control, MLG makes political legitimacy and accountability (traditional democratic control devices of government) harder to pursue. In a way, MLG represents a more functionalist and less political mode of governance than that encountered in traditional democratic government.

Consequently, MLG is susceptible to the critique that it tends to overstate outcome-oriented coordination and bargaining, which downplays the often politicized and conflictive nature of relations.[57] Behind a façade of horizontal and voluntary interaction, MLG may often conceal power relations, usually in the form of government ability to dominate by setting the governance agenda and (in the EU context) by predetermining the institutional milieu. Given the inherent power asymmetry in MLG relations, side-lining formal constraints for the sake of flexible informal interaction may end up depriving the less powerful of the institutional guarantees aimed to control and offset the power of the dominant parties. Hence the concern that MLG may be compromising democratic guarantees.[58]

The risks on democratic accountability have been raised by Peters and Pierre,[59] who have argued that MLG "could be a 'Faustian bargain' in which core values of democratic government are traded for accommodation, consensus and the purported increased efficiency in governance." Formal institutions have the advantage of being institutionally visible and subject to some form of democratic control. The prevalence of informality and opacity, the central role of non-state actors, public–private networks, and informal political coordination patterns may serve as a strategy for political interests to escape or bypass regulations. Excessive reliance on governance patterns of self-regulation could lead to democratically problematic outcomes of regulatory capture. Indeed, in a pluralistic EU arena of interest representation, MLG theory may be exhibiting the benign neglect of early pluralists over questions of power, overlooking the fact that some of the interests competing for influence are structurally endowed to prevail over their competitors. Governance arenas are not necessarily neutral, and participation of actors in MLG does not imply equal influence—not even necessarily a level playing field.

How have MLG scholars responded to these concerns? Eising and Kohler-Koch[60] posit that the very fragility of democratic legitimacy in the EU warrants the emergence of a network mode of governance, predicated on *consociation* as the central ordering principle of the relations between member states and EU institutions, and *interests* as the constitutive basis of the EU system. Marks and Hooghe[61] have argued that the dispersion of authority across multiple jurisdictions is both more efficient and normatively superior to the monopoly of authority by central government. By operating at multiple levels, governance is more capable of internalizing the externalities that arise from the provision of public goods. In addition, multiple jurisdictions better reflect the heterogeneity of preferences among citizens, facilitate credible policy commitments, foster jurisdictional competition, and encourage innovation and experimentation.[62]

5.5 Concluding Remarks

MLG is the brainchild of a period of optimism over the power of integration and the leading role of the Commission in transforming the EU political order. It remains highly questionable whether the buoyant mood prevailing in Brussels during the heroic era of launching the structural and cohesion funds has been vindicated by the developments that ensued in the 1990s and 2000s. Early expectations of a strengthening of sub-national authorities at the expense of national governments proved exaggerated. The process was reversed even in EU structural policy, where renationalization has been a powerful trend especially since the Eastern enlargement. Enlargement has also contributed to weakening the Commission and a resurgence of intergovernmentalism.

Nonetheless, as theoretical approach MLG offers a potent conceptual framework for understanding the wide-range EU transformation since the launch of the single market project. As a real-world phenomenon, MLG has been an offspring of functional integration revolving around mostly—but not exclusively—"low politics." It is a product of great integrationist ambition and its chain effects, unleashed by the mobilization of actors at sub-national, national, and transnational level.

With its emphasis on process, networks, informality of cooperation and negotiation, MLG informs comparative policy analysis. With its focus on horizontal and vertical diffusion of power, MLG contributes to comparative politics, blurring the distinction between state and society, and between domestic and international level.

At an EU constitutional level, MLG is far too informal and fluid to provide an adequate substitute for the lack of a strong EU-level party system that would integrate socio-economic interests along political, rather than functional or territorial lines. It does not adequately compensate for the underdevelopment of a European political space and the elusiveness of a European democracy. This democratic void is only partly covered by the participatory inclusiveness of MLG structures, which falls short of fulfilling the requirements of democratic legitimacy and accountability. MLG remains a positive factor in the "democratization" process of the European Union, bounded however by its inherent imperfections.

NOTES

1. Gary Marks, "Structural Policy in the European Community," in A. Sbragia, ed., *Europolitics: Institutions and Policymaking in the "New" European Community* (Washington: Brookings Institute, 1992), 191–224; Gary Marks, "Structural Policy and Multilevel Governance in the EC," in A. Cafruny and G. Rosenthal, eds, *The State of the European Community Vol. 2: The Maastricht Debates and Beyond* (Boulder: Lynne Rienner, 1993) 391–410.

2. Marks, "Structural Policy in the European Community."

3. Marks, "Structural Policy in the European Community," 221.

4. Marks, "Structural Policy and Multilevel Governance in the EC," 402–3.

5. S. George, "Multi-Level Governance and the European Union," in I. Bache and M. Flinders, eds, *Multi-Level Governance* (Oxford: Oxford University Press, 2004), 116.

6. George, "Multi-Level Governance and the European Union."

7. Liesbet Hooghe and Gary Marks, *Multi-Level Governance and European Integration* (Oxford: Rowman and Littlefield, 2001).

8. Hooghe and Marks, *Multi-Level Governance and European Integration*, 3.

9. Hooghe and Marks, *Multi-Level Governance and European Integration*, 3.

10. Hooghe and Marks, *Multi-Level Governance and European Integration*, 4.

11. Hooghe and Marks, *Multi-Level Governance and European Integration*, 4.

12. T. A. Börzel, and T. Risse, "Who is Afraid of a European Federation? How to Constitutionalise a Multi-Level Governance System," *Jean Monnet Working Paper* 7 (New York: NYU Jean Monnet Center for International and Regional Economic Law Justice, 2000) <http://centers.law.nyu.edu/jeanmonnet/papers/00/00f0101.html>.

13. P. C. Schmitter, "Examining the Present Euro-Polity with the Help of Past Theories," in G. Marks, F. W. Scharpf, P. Schmitter, and W. Streeck, eds, *Governance in the European Union* (London: Sage, 1996), 1–14.

14. D. Chryssochoou, *Democracy in the European Union* (London: I.B. Tauris, 1998).

15. M. Smith, "The European Union and the Changing Europe: Establishing the Boundaries of Order," *Journal of Common Market Studies* 34, no. 1 (1996), 5–28.

16. B. G. Peters and J. Pierre, "Multi-Level Governance and Democracy: A Faustian Bargain?" in Bache and Flinders, *Multi-Level Governance*, 77.

17. R. Dehousse, *The European Court of Justice. The Politics of Judicial Integration* (Basingstoke: Palgrave Macmillan, 1998).

18. L. Tsoukalis, *What Kind of Europe?* (Oxford: Oxford University Press, 2005).

19. Liesbet Hooghe and Gary Marks, "A Postfunctionalist Theory of European Integration: From Permissive Consensus to Constraining Dissensus," *British Journal of Political Science* 39 (2008), 1–23.

20. J. Kooiman, "Social-Political Governance: Introduction," in J. Kooiman, ed., *Modern Governance: New Government-Society Interactions* (London: Sage, 1993), 2.

21. R. Eising and B. Kohler-Koch, "Introduction: Network Governance in the European Union," in Kohler-Koch and Eising, eds, *The Transformation of Governance in the European Union* (London: Routledge, 1999), 312.

22. R. A. W. Rhodes, "The Hollowing Out of the State," *Political Quarterly* 65 (1994), 138–51; R. A. W. Rhodes, "Understanding Governance: Ten Years On," *Organization Studies* 28, no. 8 (2007), 1243–64.

23. J. N. Rosenau, "Strong Demand, Huge Supply: Governance in an Emerging Epoch," in Bache and Flinders, *Multi-Level Governance*, 34.

24. Hooghe and Marks, *Multi-Level Governance and European Integration*, 17ff.
25. Hooghe and Marks, *Multi-Level Governance and European Integration*, 22.
26. Dehousse, *The European Court of Justice*.
27. Hooghe and Marks, *Multi-Level Governance and European Integration*, 27.
28. I. Bache, *Europeanization and Multilevel Governance: Cohesion Policy in the European Union and Britain* (Plymouth: Rowman & Littlefield, 2008).
29. Hooghe and Marks, *Multi-Level Governance and European Integration*.
30. Gary Marks and Liesbet Hooghe, "Contrasting Visions of Multi-Level Governance," in Bache and Flinders, *Multi-Level Governance*, 15, 23.
31. e.g. Liesbet Hooghe, ed., *Cohesion Policy and European Integration: Building Multi-Level Governance* (Oxford: Oxford University Press, 1996); S. Bulmer, M. Burch, C. Carter, P. Hogwood, *British Devolution and European Policy-Making: Transforming Britain into Multi-Level Governance* (Basingstoke: Palgrave Macmillan, 2003); Bache, *Europeanization and Multilevel Governance*.
32. Bache, *Europeanization and Multilevel Governance*.
33. Gary Marks, Liesbet Hooghe, and Kermit Blank, "European Integration from the 1980s: State-Centric v. Multi-Level Governance," *Journal of Common Market Studies* 34 , no. 3 (1996), 341–78.
34. K. Armstrong and S. Bulmer, *The Governance of the Single European Market* (Manchester: Manchester University Press, 1998).
35. P. Marginson and K. Sisson, *European Integration and Industrial Relations: Multi-Level Governance in the Making* (Basingstoke: Palgrave Macmillan, 2004).
36. C. Paraskevopoulos, P. Getimis, and N. Rees, eds, *Adapting to EU Multi-Level Governance: Regional and Environmental Policies in Cohesion and CEE Countries* (Aldershot:Ashgate, 2006); C. Knill and D. Liefferink, *Environmental Politics in the European Union: Policy-Making, Implementation and Patterns of Multi-Level Governance* (Manchester: Manchester University Press, 2007).
37. A. Baker, ed., *Governing Financial Globalization: International Political Economy and Multi-Level Governance* (London: Routledge, 2008).
38. M. Cowles, J. Caporaso, and T. Risse, eds, *Transforming Europe: Europeanization and Domestic Change* (Ithaca: Cornell University Press, 2001).
39. Jonathon Perraton and Peter Wells, "Multi-Level Governance and Economic Policy," in Bache and Flinders, *Multi-Level Governance*, 17994.
40. M. Smith, "Toward a Theory of EU Foreign Policy-Making: Multi-Level Governance, Domestic Politics, and National Adaptation to Europe's Common Foreign and Security Policy," *Journal of European Public Policy* 11, no. 4 (2004), 740–58.
41. M. Egan, "Governing the Single Market: From Private Coordination to Public Regulation," in I. Tömmel and A. Verdun, eds, *Innovative Governance in the European Union* (Boulder: Lynne Rienner, 2009), 15978.
42. B. Jessop, "Multi-Level Governance and Multi-Level Metagovernance," in Bache and Flinders, *Multi-Level Governance*, 60.
43. "The Union, as we already hinted, is different from a traditional national state. It is a system of multi-level governance where the supranational, national and regional co-exist" (European Commission President Romano Prodi, speech on "The EU draft Constitutional Treaty" at the World Affairs Council in Philadelphia , USA, June 25, 2003).
44. Andrew Jordan, "The European Union: An Evolving System of Multi-Level Governance . . . or Government?" *Policy and Politics* 29, no. 2 (2001), 193–208.

45. Jordan, "The European Union," 201.
46. Jessop, "Multi-Level Governance and Multi-Level Metagovernance," 61.
47. Peters and Pierre, "Multi-Level Governance and Democracy: A Faustian Bargain?."
48. Peters and Pierre, "Multi-Level Governance and Democracy: A Faustian Bargain?," 76.
49. Peters and Pierre, "Multi-Level Governance and Democracy: A Faustian Bargain?," 88.
50. Marks, Hooghe, and Blank, "European Integration from the 1980s: State-Centric v. Multi-Level Governance," 356; Hooghe and Marks, *Multi-Level Governance and European Integration*, 12ff.
51. Hooghe and Marks, *Multi-Level Governance and European Integration*, 71–3.
52. Jordan, "The European Union," 201.
53. Peters and Pierre, "Multi-Level Governance and Democracy: A Faustian Bargain?," 80.
54. Eising and Kohler-Koch, "Introduction: Network Governance in the European Union."
55. Bache, *Europeanization and Multilevel Governance*.
56. e.g. G. Andreou, "EU Cohesion Policy in Greece: Patterns of Governance and Europeanization," *South European Society and Politics* 11, no. 2 (2006), 241–59.
57. Peters and Pierre, "Multi-Level Governance and Democracy: A Faustian Bargain?," 86.
58. Y. Papadopoulos, "Problems of Democratic Accountability in Network and Multilevel Governance," *European Law Journal* 13, no. 4 (2007), 469–86; J. DeBardeleben and A. Hurrelmann, eds, *Democratic Dilemmas of Multilevel Governance* (Houndmills: Palgrave Macmillan, 2007).
59. Peters and Pierre, "Multi-Level Governance and Democracy: A Faustian Bargain?," 85.
60. Eising and Kohler-Koch, "Introduction: Network Governance in the European Union," 269.
61. Marks and Hooghe, "Contrasting Visions of Multi-Level Governance."
62. Marks and Hooghe, "Contrasting Visions of Multi-Level Governance," 16.

PART II

TREATIES

CHAPTER 6

··

THE TREATIES OF PARIS

··

BERTHOLD RITTBERGER

WITHIN a period of thirteen months, the heads of state of Italy, France, Germany, and the Benelux countries signed two treaties, the Treaty establishing the ECSC in April 1951 and the Treaty establishing the EDC in May 1952 (known as the Treaties of Paris). Both were to leave their lasting imprint on the development and trajectory of European integration, albeit in very different ways. While the ECSC Treaty was ratified by all six founding member states and thus entered into force in 1952, establishing the first "supranational" community in the history of international cooperation, the EDC Treaty and the plan to create a common European army did not see the light of day—the majority of the French Assemblée Nationale denied passage on August 30, 1954. In the case of the ECSC, national governments decided to delegate domestic decision-making authority in the coal and steel sectors to a new supranational organization, thereby renouncing portions of their national sovereignty.[1] The plan to pool coal and steel resources and submit decisions in these sectors to a supranational High Authority was presented to the public by the French Foreign Minister Robert Schuman on May 9, 1950. Robert Schuman and Jean Monnet, the "mastermind" behind the Schuman Plan, referred to the plan as a "bold, constructive act" and François Duchêne, author of a much celebrated Monnet biography, referred to its contents as a "break with the past" in the light of its novel supranational quality.[2] The ultimate objective of the plan was to alleviate concerns that postwar Germany would employ its regained industrial strengths as a threat to French autonomy, both in economic and security terms.

Before the six prospective member states signed the ECSC treaty, the outbreak of the Korean War in June 1950 and the swelling fear of a Soviet attack on Western Europe prompted a change in perspective on the part of the Western Allies, especially with regard to the question of how the "German problem" should be addressed. The British and especially the US government were in favor of a substantial German contribution to the defense of Western Europe, which ultimately implied the rearmament of Germany. Unsurprisingly this proposal sent "shockwaves" through France.[3] However, ongoing US pressure made French political leaders rethink different solutions to the security problem posed by prospective German rearmament. The Pleven Plan—presented by

Prime Minister René Pleven in October 1950—proposed the setting up of a European army under an ECSC-style supranational institutional setting. The Pleven Plan was widely criticized for being too discriminatory against Germany and for its failure to provide sufficient supranational authority for a European army to act effectively.[4] During the negotiations leading to the adoption of the EDC treaty, most discriminatory measures were dropped and the supranational character of the European defense project was bolstered with the proposal to create a Board of Commissioners exercising responsibility for military command and procurement.[5] But even though the EDC treaty was signed by the six ECSC member states, it did not enter into force and kept attempts for a common European security and defense policy stalled for several decades.

The aim of this chapter is to shed light on four debates or "fault lines" in the literature on the ECSC and EDC treaties. First, scholarly accounts of the two treaties differ in their respective assessments of who the most relevant actors in driving European integration in its early phase were. Most historical or political science accounts are characteristic for their state-centric perspective, emphasizing either the role of diplomats and leading figures in government or, somewhat less prominently, domestically organized interest groups. More recently, scholars have started to depart from the state-centrism in the literature and turn to transnationally organized networks of policy-makers to analyze their impact on European integration. The debate about the origins of actors' preferences for European integration represents a second fault line in the literature. This chapter contrasts "materialist" accounts of preference formation—emphasizing economic and geopolitical conditions—with constructivist accounts of preference formation stressing the subjective interpretations of material conditions. The third issue addressed here discusses the dynamics of interstate bargaining and the sources of ratification successes and failures. These accounts employ—implicitly or explicitly—a rationalist bargaining approach, but disagree on whether actors' bargaining power is more centrally affected by domestic or systemic sources. Fourthly and finally, this chapter turns to a body of literature exploring the question of institutional design. What prompted policymakers to opt for a supranational organization in the cases of the ECSC and the EDC? The fault line in this section pits proponents of functionalist and rationalist explanations for institutional design against constructivism-inspired institutionalist accounts emphasizing the legitimacy-enhancing effects of institutional choices (see Table 6.1).

Table 6.1 Fault lines in the literature on the ECSC and EDC

Fault line	Contrasting perspectives and explanations
Actors	State-centric vs transnational perspectives
Preferences	Materialist vs ideational explanations
Bargaining and ratification	Systemic vs domestic pressures
Institutional design	Rational design vs constructivist explanations

6.1 Identifying the Key Actors: State-Centric and Transnational Perspectives

To introduce the first fault line, key assumptions of the dominant theories of European integration need to be recalled. Intergovernmentalist explanations are state-centric because states are considered to be the dominant actors. They shape European integration according to nationally defined goals and interests. In contrast, supranationalist theories of integration claim that transnational societal actors, in conjunction with supranational actors, are the most relevant players in initiating and steering the integration process.[6] With the exception of Ernst Haas' seminal work *The Uniting of Europe*, we find rather few studies on the early years of European integration, which are explicitly informed by either supranationalism (for which Haas' neo-functionalism was a precursor) or intergovernmentalist arguments.[7] This state of affairs is partially caused by the fact that the majority of important works on the ECSC and the EDC have been written by historians. These works are, nevertheless, quite explicit about the relative importance accorded to different actors in the integration process. As a matter of fact, the vast majority of accounts on the origins of the ECSC and the EDC adopt a state-centric perspective, emphasizing the role of "national" interests and conceptualizing governments as purposeful and (more or less) cohesive actors.[8] For instance, research in the "diplomatic history" tradition is characteristic of their "France and x" or "Germany's position towards y" treatises of integration.[9] The works of Alan Milward and William Hitchcock, as well as those of Michael Creswell and Marc Trachtenberg are representative of this approach, stressing the centrality of French political leaders and high-ranking officials, specifically in the Ministry of Foreign Affairs, in defining France's European policy.[10]

Most political scientists who have written on the early phase of European integration history can also be located inside the state-centric camp. In sync with the assumptions of a "liberal" interpretation of intergovernmentalism, these studies focus not merely on political elites as well as top-level officials and bureaucrats, but also on intermediary actors, such as interest groups and political parties.[11] Helen Milner, for example, emphasizes the relevance of domestic interest groups whose endorsement was required by governments in Germany and France for negotiating and adopting the ECSC treaty.[12] Craig Parsons places particular emphasis on the role of domestic party politicians and political parties represented in the French Assemblée National.[13]

More recently, historians have begun to depart from the state-centrism characteristic of most research on the ECSC and EDC. As one prominent critic of state-centric approaches has argued, "[m]ost integration history has ignored the importance of supranational institutions and transactional actors…in EU politics."[14] A new branch of the literature on European integration history thus places its work in the tradition of Ernst Haas and neo-functionalism/supranationalism by emphasizing the centrality of transnationally organized groups of political actors. According to Wolfram Kaiser, state-centric approaches overlook that "national actors and collective interests stand no realistic chance of influencing the policy-making process significantly unless they are well connected across borders in transnational political networks."[15] The conceptual turn proposed by these works, i.e. to conceive of the transnational arena as relevant in the politics of European integration, is not entirely new. Walter Lipgens, a pioneer in the study of European integration history, focused his research efforts on transnationally organized federalist movements in the post-war era and claimed that a politically relevant federalist agenda to advance European integration developed in the early 1950s. This agenda was spurred by post-war federalist movements, whose predecessors could often be found in war-time resistance movements, before these movements turned into a single movement, the Union of European federalists, in 1946.[16] According to Lipgens, the vast number of politicians who were part of the "private associations" of federalists successfully convinced majorities in both Socialist as well as Christian democratic parties to promote the federalist ideal, which found its clearest and most coherent expression in the plans to institute the European Political Community (EPC) in the first half of the 1950s.[17] Criticism against Lipgens has centered mostly on the decidedly normative orientation of much of his work and the importance he attributed to the "Federalist social movement" in influencing the course of European integration, which is not convincingly corroborated empirically.[18]

6.2 Forming Preferences: Material vs Ideational Worlds

What is the basis of political actors' preferences for European integration? Within the intergovernmentalist camp, a "realist" and a "liberal" variant can be distinguished to explain preference formation.[19] While realist intergovernmentalists assume that states' overall interest is to maximize autonomy, security, and influence,[20] the liberal variant of intergovernmentalism sets out with the assumption that states' preferences reflect the interests of dominant (economic) interest groups, which can mostly be found among producers.[21] While intergovernmentalism emphasizes the "material" underpinnings of state preferences, i.e. economic and geopolitical conditions, constructivist accounts emphasize the role societal norms and ideas play in affecting the ways political actors interpret the "material world."

These different approaches to account for the formation of actors' preferences are reflected in the literature on the origins of the ECSC and EDC. Realist interpretations highlight the mounting security threat posed to France by Germany. William Hitchcock has prominently argued that Germany's economic advances in the post-war era carried profound negative security externalities for France.[22] Moreover, the Anglo-American shift of focus from promoting economic recovery in Western Europe to planning European (including German) rearmament, following the Prague coup in 1948 and the Berlin blockade in 1948–1949, "gripped the Quai d'Orsay."[23] Hitchcock's analysis of France's European policy suggests that French foreign policy was at the time both autonomy- and influence-seeking. When, due to external events (such as the Berlin blockade, the Prague coup, or the Korean War), the goal to maximize France's autonomy by keeping Germany's economic and political development under allied control was no longer a viable option, Robert Schuman and the Foreign Ministry turned to influence-seeking policies and hence the proposal to create self- and other-binding supranational institutions, as expressed in the Schuman Plan.

The initial response to the Schuman Plan by the German government strongly mirrors the primacy of security- and autonomy-related preferences. Given its position in the international community after World War II, Germany possessed only limited external and internal sovereignty, since the majority of political decisions had to be approved by the allied High Commission. Therefore, the prospect of international cooperation signaled an opportunity for Germany to regain domestic and foreign policy-making capacity. The Schuman Plan offered an immediate opportunity to become an equal member in the European concert of states. Germany's governing political elite was relatively autonomous from domestic economic pressures in forging ahead with Schuman's proposal (though the major opposition force in the Bundestag, the Social Democrats, actually opposed the Schuman Plan). Hence, the supranational principle, enshrined in the institution of the High Authority, was readily accepted, as were economic concessions to obtain a successful negotiation outcome.[24] Even though some commentators argue that the German government's stance on the ECSC hardened as a result of domestic economic pressure and the prospect that allied controls of Germany would ease in the near future, Milward claims that "Adenauer insisted throughout on the prime political priority for the Federal Republic on the removal of the Ruhr Authority and the weakening of the Occupation Statute" to bolster German sovereignty.[25]

Akin to his analysis of the ECSC, Hitchcock also provides a realist intergovernmentalist-inspired account of preference formation in the EDC context.[26] Turning to France, he argues that the Pleven Plan applied the same logic as the Schuman Plan, which was announced half a year earlier. To influence and contain German rearmament, the French government proposed to create a European army under the command of a supranational European defense authority. Creswell and Trachtenberg add a feature to this picture by pointing out that most accounts of France's European policy mistake political rhetoric for underlying security interests.[27] Their assessment of the security threat faced by France differs from those presented hitherto in the literature. They argue that the primary security threat for France did not emanate from Germany but from the fear that the Soviet Union would take over a unified Germany. The "European turn" of French policy, which led to the creation of the ECSC and the proposal to create a European army, did not mean that French diplomats and political leaders altered their fundamental foreign policy goals, but merely their strategy. Contrary to the public rhetoric of "keeping Germany down," French political leaders pursued a more accommodating strategy towards Germany, which was, by and large, in sync with US and British policy.[28] The authors even argue that the security threat posed by Germany can be considered a "convenient myth," which "provided political cover for a course of action that was in fact directed against the Soviet threat."[29]

Turning to liberal intergovernmentalist accounts of preference formation, Frances Lynch argues that the economic externalities of a common coal and steel pool were driving French policy since they would directly contribute to France's economic modernization as spelled out in the Monnet Plan.[30] Other accounts see economic and security-related objectives to be inextricably connected. Monnet's proposed coal and steel pool has rather to be seen as a means to protect French security and promote economic reconstruction through the international control of Germany's heartland of heavy industry, the Ruhr.[31] With France being—at the time—the world's largest importer of coal and coke,[32] a common market for coal and steel promised to ensure sufficient and cheap supply of German combustible for French industry and for the realization of the French economic modernization plan.[33] Liberal intergovernmntalist theory not only stresses the relevance of economic interests in general but offers a "liberal" explanation for why economic interests play a crucial role in the formulation of state preferences: state preferences are considered to be sector-specific and reflect the interests of dominant societal interest groups in a particular sector.[34] For example, in energy policy, governmental preferences should reflect the interests of dominant energy producers and consumers. Yet, the historical literature on the ECSC attributes a rather limited role to the French coal and steel industry. It was only after the announcement of the Schuman Plan that the steel industry launched fierce campaigns against the way the negotiations were conducted. Nevertheless, they were mostly excluded from the talks which was mainly the result of the industry's lack of a concerted stance.[35] The literature thus points to a reading of French policy largely unconstrained by domestic interest group pressures. The motivation of the French governing elite to tie Germany's coal and steel industry to a supranational coal and steel pool was not driven by the sector- or issue-specific demands articulated by organized interests but rather by domestic economic policy objectives which were spelled out in the Monnet Plan. However, as argued in the previous section, these economic concerns existed alongside geopolitical and security ones.[36] As for preference formation in Germany, economic objectives were of secondary importance. Contrary to what liberal intergovernmentalism would have us expect, domestic interest groups had little influence on the formation of the government's preferences. For example, the German Iron and Steel Manufacturers' Association was informed by the government early in the negotiations that "the political aim was in the foreground, and economic aims were more or less subordinate to it."[37] Despite massive opposition from industrialists and labor unions, Chancellor Konrad Adenauer succeeded in imposing the crucial elements of the Schuman Plan even against considerable domestic opposition.

Macroeconomic objectives and domestic interest groups played a much more important role in the formation of state preferences in the Benelux countries. Rather than accepting an a priori commitment to supranational integration, the respective governments sought cooperation in policy areas in which the expected joint gains of integration would be highest and existing domestic social and economic policies would not be prohibitively affected. For example, Dutch import dependence on the one hand, Belgium's and Luxembourg's export dependence with regard to coal and steel on the other hand, led the respective governments and domestic interest groups to press for low common tariffs.

Especially Belgium and Luxembourg were more dependent on the steel market for their exports than the other negotiating partners because steel amounted to a fifth of their total exports. In another policy area, wage policy, macroeconomic policy objectives were seen to be under attack by the prospective ECSC. The prospect that the High Authority would be empowered to equalize living conditions and prevent countries that wished to catch up economically from pursuing a low-wage strategy, was rejected by the Dutch government whose low-wage policy was a cornerstone of its post-war recovery policy.[38] Similar examples could be provided for the highly contested questions about investment control, price levels, cartels/restrictive practices, or transitional agreements. In the Benelux cases, then, the liberal intergovernmentalist account for preference formation provides a good fit, while the preferences of the French and German governments are better explained with reference to the realist variant of intergovernmentalism.

More recently, attempts to explain governmental preferences on a "materialist" basis have come under attack. Some scholars argue that the historical literature in particular has ignored "the significance of ideas in early European integration as an independent variable."[39] Kaiser argues that the glue for transnational cooperation among Christian Democrats was a shared ideological predisposition, which eventually helped to spur supranational integration in Europe.[40] Through the informal Christian Democratic transnational party network, political leaders were in a position not only to debate and define common objectives, but also to effectively set the policy agenda on matters of European integration.[41] Parsons echoes Kaiser's argument that ideational variables are important to explain European integration.[42] He analyzes the impact of "cross-cutting ideas" on the formulation of European integration policy in France and juxtaposes his ideational account with "objective-interest theories."[43] How can it be explained that seemingly similar economic or geopolitical conditions led to radically different foreign and security policy trajectories? Since ideational approaches rest on the assumption that "actors interpret their interests through ideas that can vary independently from their objective positions,"[44] Parsons demonstrates that different sets of ideas about European institution building—traditionalist, confederalist, and community notions of cooperation—were all viable in the domestic political debate in France.[45] For instance, the EDC can by no means be explained solely by taking recourse to shifts in the geopolitical environment. Parsons argues that none of the three ideas was initially bound to fail: "All else equal, the French were selecting between outcomes as divergent as a European Army and simple German entry into NATO."[46]

6.3 NEGOTIATING AND RATIFYING TREATIES: SYSTEMIC AND DOMESTIC PRESSURES

The third fault line in the literature on the ECSC and EDC reflects different positions on the question about how negotiation and ratification success or failure—as in the case of the EDC—can be accounted for.[47] Most scholars argue that systemic or exogenous events altered the attractiveness of outside options for the different governments and hence affected their bargaining power during the treaty negotiations. Some scholars also point at domestic sources of bargaining strength or weakness, highlighting that political leaders engaged in playing "two-level games."[48]

In the case of France, several authors claim that the political leaders realized from the late 1940s onwards that isolationist or autonomy-seeking solutions to the "German question" could not be considered viable to achieve French economic recovery and security. To address the threat of an increasingly economically more powerful Germany, and given the prospect of an end to the system of domination of Germany, a solution to the "German problem" had to be found sooner rather than later. This was ever more pressing given the disappointing performances of the OEEC and the Council of Europe. In this regard, time was ticking against France. According to Milward, "[i]t was better for France to negotiate now while the West German state was in tutelage, before the extent of the Ruhr Authority's powers were fully discovered, and before the Federal German Republic was admitted more fully into the system of military alliances."[49] Consequently, the French government saw its outside options disappear rapidly. The French government's negotiating position was also hampered by different perceptions of the German security threat among the three Western Allies. An economically and militarily more powerful Germany was more threatening to the French government than to the British and American: "[G]iven that the bulk of western Germany was controlled by Britain and the Unites States, the outcome of that conflict was never in doubt. The French, to avoid total marginalization—that is, to have any impact at all on what was going on within Germany—were forced from concession to concession."[50] While the German government enthusiastically embraced the Schuman Plan, its negotiation stance hardened in the course of the negotiations. With the outbreak of the Korean War and the signals sent from across the Atlantic that German rearmament was a realistic option, the German delegation to the Schuman Plan negotiations changed its strategy and demanded more concessions. Had it not been for American pressure, some even argue that the ECSC might have ultimately failed. Besides these external changes and their effect on states' outside options (viz. bargaining power), other authors argue that domestic politics also played a role in the hardening of the German government's bargaining stance. John Gillingham states quite bluntly that Adenauer was playing a "two-level game": "The chancellor was hardly a starry-eyed idealist. A shrewd calculation underlay his apparent acquiescence to (sic) the French. Adenauer questioned neither the vigor of his producers nor their ability to stand up for their interests and was certain that time was on his side."[51]

Analyses of ratification success and failure in the cases of the ECSC and EDC take the "two-level game" concept even more seriously. Milner argues that ratification failure (of the EDC in France) and success (in the case of the ECSC) depended heavily on two factors. First, on the presence or absence of divided government in the key states (France and Germany) and, secondly, on the "presence or absence of endorsement from important domestic actors,"[52] such as well-organized interest groups. While in the case of the ECSC domestic politics was conducive to ratification, this was not the case for the EDC.

In the latter case, domestic actors failed to endorse the EDC; the French military, in particular, was ferociously opposed to the EDC treaty. This lack of endorsement by domestic actors is also considered to be the result of successive French governments' lack of willingness to make side payments in an attempt to win the military over to support the EDC. Furthermore, mounting divisions inside the French government in the period preceding Premier Mendès-France's lackluster attempt to ratify the EDC treaty constituted a growing obstacle for successful ratification. In the period 1953–1954, the centre of gravity of the governing coalitions shifted to the right, thereby undermining the parliamentary majority in the Assemblée Nationale supporting ratification.[53] Fleischer argues that the French government used the volatility in the assembly as bargaining leverage to obtain military aid from the US government, which made the flow of aid dependent on ratification of the EDC. Successive French governments delayed ratification while pretending the ratification was still possible, thereby reinforcing "US convictions that there was no alternative to the EDC" (Fleischer 2012:8). The end of the war in Indochina eased French independence on US military aid and hence the incentive by French politicians "to keep the treaty 'stuck'…was removed" (Fleischer 2012:8).[54] With regard to the ECSC, both factors that Milner considers to be crucial to explain ratification outcomes were more conducive to successful ratification in France and Germany. In order to win the endorsement of the key domestic groups—the unions as well as the respective coal and steel industries—the French and German chiefs of government successfully employed side payments. Furthermore, the French and German governments displayed low levels of internal division over the ECSC. In France, the Third Force government (Socialists, Christian Democrats, and smaller centrist parties) controlled the majority of votes in the French Assemblée Nationale and could thus ensure ratification. In Germany, the coalition government of Christian Democrats and Free Democrats supported the ECSC and also held a majority of votes in the Bundestag.

While Milner stresses the crucial position of domestic "endorsers" to ensure ratification, this argument is not undisputed in the literature. Note that most historical and political science accounts of preference formation have heavily discounted the relevance of domestic interest groups in affecting preferences or even the bargaining stance of governments in negotiating the ECSC and EDC treaties. Parsons, for example, argues that ratification of ECSC was ensured because "pro-community" leaders controlled the policy agenda with Monnet playing a key role.[55] Pro-community leaders were able to assemble majorities for their position by employing the standard arsenal of rational bargaining theory: issue linkages and side payments.[56] The failure of the EDC did not come about as a result of shifts in position on Europe but rather as the result of the collapse of the "Third Force" governing coalition, which removed coalitional pressures from a critical mass of "confederalists" and "traditionalists" inside the former governing coalition to play the "community" tune. While both Milner and Parsons present sophisticated analytical accounts of the ratification phase of the ECSC and EDC, their analyses differ on the role attributed to domestic endorsers. For Parsons, domestic interest groups did not affect the ratification success of the ECSC treaty even though they were strongly opposed to it. The government had to make side payments—e.g. offer policy compromises on colonial policy issues—to different groups of members of parliament who were threatening to jump ship in order to ensure their support. He furthermore argues that the government did not have to please interest groups.[57] Parsons claims that Robert Schuman had ample room for maneuver to realize his preferred European policy. In the absence of coherent party positions on the ECSC and given the observation that support for the ECSC cut across the different coalition partners, he "had the autonomy—not the mandate—to take a 'leap in the dark' toward his interpretation of the French interest."[58] Milner, in contrast, argues that in the ratification process of the ECSC treaty, the French and German governments had to make side payments to industry and labor, which opposed the Schuman Plan, in order to push the treaty through. The problem with both accounts is that they rely heavily on secondary and soft primary sources. The respective arguments need to be empirically bolstered to allow the jury to make an informed verdict on the sources of ratification success and failure.

6.4 Choosing Institutions: Institutions as Credible Commitment Devices vs Legitimate Design Solutions

This section addresses the choice of the particular set of institutions adopted by the member states. Two issues will be highlighted. First, how can we account for the supranational design of the ECSC and EDC, embodied by the High Authority (ECSC) and the Board of Commissioners (EDC)? Second, the institutional order includes additional organizations, such as a parliamentary assembly, a member state council, and a court. The scholarly literature has started to take issue with the broader institutional structure of these two communities. In the search for explanations, there is a dialogue between scholars who adopt a functionalist "rational design" approach and those who base their explanations on constructivist social theory.

Mark Pollack is the major proponent of a functionalist rational design approach to explain institutional delegation in the EU. According to Pollack, member-state governments delegate certain powers to supranational institutions with the expectation that these institutions efficiently address a set of collective action problems arising from international cooperation: monitoring compliance, filling in "incomplete contracts," or ensuring the credibility of policy commitments. Furthermore, Pollack argues that the member-state "principals" will—depending on the precise nature of the delegation problem—create a set of institutional checks and control mechanisms to limit the discretion of their supranational "agents."[59] According to Pollack, the creation of the High Authority follows the functionalist logic for delegation. The key concerns faced by policy-makers were precisely those alluded to by the functional rational design approach. Problems of delegation and discretion "were foremost in the minds of negotiators of the ECSC Treaty."[60] Besides monitoring compliance with ECSC policies, only an independent High Authority could "credibly and impartially regulate the coal and steel sector."[61] In the historical and political science literature on the ECSC and EDC, the partial delegation of sovereignty (in the areas of coal and steel as well as defense) is most commonly interpreted as a solution to the problem of ensuring the credibility of policy commitments. Individual security and economic concerns could be best addressed by a supranational organization to which the concerned states would delegate portions of their sovereignty. For the French government, delegated sovereignty implied that Germany could not use its economic power "unchecked." For the German government, delegated sovereignty implied that it would be able to act on a par with the other Western states.[62]

But the supranational High Authority could not be left to its own devices. With a view to limit its discretion, Pollack argues that the creation of the council, court, and parliamentary assembly primarily served a control or "checking" function. Karen Alter underlines this argument with regard to the court of the ECSC: "The ECJ was created as part of the European Coal and Steel Community in order to protect member states and firms by ensuring that the supranational high authority did not exceed its authority."[63] The concern that the High Authority could overstep its mandate was pointedly made by the leader of the Dutch delegation to the Schuman Plan negotiations, Dirk Spierenburg, who asked whether the High Authority actually embodied a dictatorship of experts. To circumscribe its powers and limit the High Authority's discretion, the Benelux countries insisted on the creation of a council in which the member-state governments would be represented.[64] In line with Pollack's rational design approach, the Schuman Plan negotiations demonstrated that "the concern for 'executive control' was unanimously shared among all participating [national] delegations, yet the delegations' *interpretation* of the norm of executive control as to *who* should control and *how* control should be exercised varied."[65] More recent empirical research based on the analysis of primary documents reveals the limitations of functional rational design explanations for institutional design of the ECSC as well as the EDC. While it can be argued that the creation of an inter-ministerial council provided a check on the High Authority by the "principals," not all actors perceived of the "control problem" in the same way. In sync with a constructivist argument, which points to the relevance of ideas in informing institutional design preference, the German delegation to the Schuman Plan negotiations interpreted the control problem in a radically different manner. Internal documents reveal that the proposal for creating a council was not primarily discussed in terms of an effective check on the High Authority's powers but was discussed in normative terms, i.e. whether it provided a "fit" with prevailing (domestic) notions of appropriate constitutional design. This implied the following reasoning on behalf of German delegates: if the High Authority constitutes a nascent executive of a European federal state (*Bundesstaat*), then a chamber representing the territorial interests of the constituent states is an appropriate constitutional design feature.[66] The federal state analogy was time and again expressed by members of the German delegation as a guide to institutional design. This became particularly apparent in the case of the creation of the parliamentary assembly of the ECSC and proposals to "federalize" the institutional structure of the EDC.[67] Berthold Rittberger and Frank Schimmelfennig have shown that the delegation of sovereignty from the domestic to the European level has repeatedly triggered a "normative spillover" process which arises when steps of functional supranational integration undermine the fundamental liberal democratic norms of the Western international community and when the resulting legitimacy deficit triggers demands to redress the situation.[68] These demands, in turn, generate a process of arguing, in which committed or interested actors draw on liberal democratic community norms to make the case for enhancing the powers of the European Parliament and put normative pressure on their reticent opponents. As a consequence of normative spillover, parliamentary competences at the European level have been regularly enhanced, which also holds in the cases of the ECSC and EDC.[69]

6.5 CONCLUSION

This chapter has approached the exploration of Europe's first two communities from an analytical perspective. Four debates or "fault lines" have been identified in the literature on the "Treaties of Paris," which are indicative of a wide range of scholarly differences in the ways actors and their preferences, the dynamics of negotiations and ratification, and institutional design processes are conceptualized. While the vast majority of work on the ECSC and EDC continues to be conducted by historians, political scientists have finally "rediscovered" the early treaties. From a theoretical–analytical perspective, the ECSC and EDC offer ample "material" to test and refine European integration and international relations theories. While political scientists working on European integration in the early 1950s are still predominantly locked in state-centric explorations, contemporary historians have broken out of state-centric and "diplomatic history"-driven conceptualizations of integration dynamics. The focus on transnational networks of political actors, such as particular political parties and their informal links across domestic borders corresponds to a broader trend among historians to study history from a boundary-transcending transnational perspective. While studying transnational relations and processes is obviously not unknown to political scientists and European integration scholars—neo-functionalism and supranationalist approaches offer precisely such a transnational perspective, after all—this is not (yet) reflected in the work carried out by political scientists studying the early era of European integration. Despite this "conceptual deficit," political scientists have made progress in consulting primary sources and the historical literature more extensively in order to scrutinize their theoretical claims more thoroughly. This review of the literature on the ECSC and EDC also demonstrates that our knowledge of the ECSC and EDC treaties in general, and of European integration theory in particular, has progressed remarkably in recent years as a result of the work accomplished by more "theory-sensitive historians and history-sensitive political scientists."[70]

NOTES

1. Guido Thiemeyer, "Supranationalität als Novum in der Geschichte der Internationalen Politik der Fünfziger Jahre," *Journal of European Integration History* 4, no. 2 (1998), 5–21.
2. See Francois Duchêne, *Jean Monnet. The First Statesman of Interdependence* (New York and London: Norton, 1994), 205.
3. See Richard T. Griffiths, *Europe's First Constitution. The European Political Community, 1952–1954* (London: Federal Trust, 2000), 56.
4. Walter Lipgens, "EVG and Politische Föderation," *Vierteljahreshefte für Zeitgeschichte* 32 (1984), 637–88.
5. Lipgens, "EVG and Politische Föderation," 654; Griffiths, *Europe's First Constitution. The European Political Community, 1952–1954*, 54–8; Hans-Erich Volkmann and Walter Schwengler, eds, *Die Europäische Verteidigungsgemeinschaft. Stand und Probleme der Forschung* (Boppard am Rhein: Harald Boldt Verlag, 1985).
6. See Frank Schimmelfennig and Berthold Rittberger, "Theories of European Integration. Assumptions and Hypotheses," in Jeremy Richardson, *European Union. Power and Policy-Making* (London: Routledge, 2006), 73–169.
7. Ernst B. Haas, *The Uniting of Europe* (Notre Dame: University of Notre Dame Press, 1958).
8. See Wolfram Kaiser and Brigitte Leucht, "Informal Politics of Integration. Christian Democratic and Transatlantic Networks in the Creation of ECSC Core Europe," *Journal of European Integration History* 14, no. 1 (2008), 35.
9. See Piers Ludlow, "Widening, Deepening and Opening Out. Towards a Fourth Decade of European Integration History," in Wilfried Loth, ed., *Experiencing Europe. 50 Years of European Construction 1957–2007* (Baden-Baden: Nomos, 2009), 37.
10. William I. Hitchcock, "France, the Western Alliance, and the Origins of the Schuman Plan, 1948–1950," *Diplomatic History* 21, no. 4 (1997), 604–5; William I. Hitchcock, *France Restored. Cold War Diplomacy and the Quest for Leadership in Europe, 1944–1954* (Chapel Hill: University of North Carolina Press, 1998); Michael Creswell and Marc Trachtenberg, "France and the German Question, 1945–1955," *Journal of Cold War Studies* 5, no. 3 (2003), 5–28; Alan S. Milward, *The Reconstruction of Western Europe* (London: Routledge, 1984); Alan S. Milward, *The European Rescue of the Nation-State* (Berkeley: University of California Press, 1992), 318.
11. Andrew Moravcsik, *The Choice for Europe. Social Purpose and State Power from Messina to Maastricht* (Ithaca: Cornell University Press, 1998).
12. Helen Milner, *Interests, Institutions, and Information* (Princeton: Princeton University Press, 1997).
13. Craig Parsons, "Showing Ideas as Causes. The Origins of the European Union," *International Organization* 56, no. 1 (2002), 47–84; Craig Parsons, *A Certain Idea of Europe* (Ithaca: Cornell University Press, 2003).
14. See Wolfram Kaiser, "From State to Society? The Historiography of European Integration," in Michelle Cini and Angela K. Bourne, eds, *Palgrave Advances in European Union Studies* (Basingstoke: Palgrave Macmillan, 2006), 196.
15. See Wolfram Kaiser, *Christian Democracy and the Origins of European Union* (Cambridge: Cambridge University Press, 2007), 1.
16. Walter Lipgens, *A History of European Integration 1945–47. The Formation of the European Unity Movement* (Oxford: Clarendon Press, 1982).

17. See Walter Lipgens, "Die Bedeutung des EVG-Projekts für die politische europäische Einigungsbewegung," in Hans-Erich Volkmann and Walter Schwengler, eds, *Die Europäische Verteidigungsgemeinschaft. Stand und Probleme der Forschung* (Boppard am Rhein: Harald Boldt Verlag, 1985), 13.

18. See Kaiser, *Christian Democracy and the Origins of European Union*, 8–9.

19. Schimmelfennig and Rittberger, "Theories of European Integration. Assumptions and Hypotheses," 78–84.

20. See, for example, Stanley Hoffmann, "Obstinate or Obsolete? The Fate of the Nation-State and the Case of Western Europe," *Daedalus* 95, no. 3 (1966), 862–915; Joseph Grieco, "State Interests and Institutional Rule Trajectories. A Neorealist Interpretation of the Maastricht Treaty and European Economic and Monetary Union," *Security Studies* 5 (1996), 261–306.

21. See Moravcsik, *The Choice for Europe*.

22. Hitchcock, "France, the Western Alliance, and the Origins of the Schuman Plan, 1948–1950."

23. See Hitchcock, "France, the Western Alliance, and the Origins of the Schuman Plan, 1948–1950," 610.

24. See Hans-Jürgen Küsters, "Die Verhandlungen über das institutionelle System zur Gründung der Europäischen Gemeinschaft für Kohle und Stahl," in Klaus Schwabe, ed., *Die Anfänge des Schuman-Plans 1950/51—The Beginnings of the Schuman Plan* (Baden-Baden: Nomos, 1988), 78; see Ulrich Lappenküper, "Der Schuman-Plan. Mühsamer Durchbruch zur deutsch-französischen Verständigung," *Vierteljahreshefte für Zeitgeschichte* 42, no. 3 (1994), 411–13.

25. See Milward, *The Reconstruction of Western Europe*, 413.

26. Hitchcock, *France Restored. Cold War Diplomacy and the Quest for Leadership in Europe, 1944–1054*.

27. Creswell and Trachtenberg, "France and the German Question, 1945–1955."

28. Creswell and Trachtenberg, "France and the German Question, 1945–1955," 6.

29. Creswell and Trachtenberg, "France and the German Question, 1945–1955," 13.

30. See Frances Lynch, "The Role of Jean Monnet in Setting Up the European Coal and Steel Community," in Schwabe, *Die Anfänge des Schuman Plans 1950/51—the Beginnings of the Schuman Plan*, 124–6.

31. See JohnGillingham, *Coal, Steel and the Rebirth of Europe, 1945–1955* (Cambridge: Cambridge University Press, 1991), 229.

32. See Lynch, "The Role of Jean Monnet in Setting Up the European Coal and Steel Community," 119.

33. See Lynch, "The Role of Jean Monnet in Setting Up the European Coal and Steel Community," 125.

34. See Moravcsik, *The Choice for Europe*.

35. See Milward, *The Reconstruction of Western Europe*, 419; see Philippe Mioche, "La Patronat de la Sidérurgie Française et le Plan Schuman en 1950–1952. Les Apparences d'un Combat et la Réalité d'une Mutation," in Schwabe, *Die Anfänge des Schuman Plans 1950/51—the Beginnings of the Schuman Plan*; see also William Diebold, *The Schuman Plan. A Study in Economic Cooperation 1950–59* (New York: Frederick A. Praeger, 1959), 16–17.

36. See Werner Abelshauser, "'Integration à la carte'. The Primacy of Politics and the Economic Integration of Western Europe in the 1950s," in Stephen Martin, ed., *The*

Construction of Europe—Essays in Honour of Emile Noël (Dordrecht: Kluwer Academic Publishers, 1994), 7.

37. Milward, *The Reconstruction of Western Europe*, 415–16.

38. See Richard T. Griffiths, "Die Benelux-Staaten und die Schumanplan-Verhandlungen," in Ludolf Herbst, Werner Bührer, and Hanno Sowade, eds, *Vom Marshallplan zur EWG. Die Eingliederung der Bundesrepublik Deutschland in die westliche Welt* (München: Oldenbourg, 1990), 271; Gillingham, *Coal, Steel and the Rebirth of Europe, 1945–1955*, 244.

39. See Kaiser and Leucht, "Informal Politics of Integration. Christian Democratic and Transatlantic Networks in the Creation of ECSC Core Europe," 36.

40. Wolfram Kaiser, "Institutionelle Ordnung und strategische Interessen. Die Christdemokraten und 'Europa' nach 1945," in Wilfried Loth, ed., *Das Europäische Projekt zu Beginn des 21. Jahrhunderts* (Opladen: Leske + Budrich, 2001), 81–98.

41. See Kaiser and Leucht, "Informal Politics of Integration. Christian Democratic and Transatlantic Networks in the Creation of ECSC Core Europe," 39–42.

42. Parsons, "Showing Ideas as Causes. The Origins of the European Union"; Parsons, *A Certain Idea of Europe*.

43. See Parsons, "Showing Ideas as Causes. The Origins of the European Union," 50.

44. See Parsons, "Showing Ideas as Causes. The Origins of the European Union," 50.

45. See Parsons, "Showing Ideas as Causes. The Origins of the European Union," 57–8.

46. See Parsons, "Showing Ideas as Causes. The Origins of the European Union," 63.

47. This section draws on Berthold Rittberger, "Which Institutions for Post-War Europe? Explaining the Institutional Design of Europe's First Community," *Journal of European Public Policy* 8, no. 5 (2001), 673–708.

48. Milner, *Interests, Institutions, and Information*.

49. See Milward, *The Reconstruction of Western Europe*, 378.

50. Creswell and Trachtenberg, "France and the German Question, 1945–1955," 6.

51. See Gillingham, *Coal, Steel and the Rebirth of Europe, 1945–1955*, 233.

52. Milner, *Interests, Institutions, and Information*, 200.

53. See Milner, *Interests, Institutions, and Information*, 197–200.

54. Bjorn Fleischer, "Negotiating the European Defence Community," European Political Science, advance online publication, doi: 10.1057/eps.2012.10 (2012).

55. See Parsons, "Showing Ideas as Causes. The Origins of the European Union," 63.

56. See Parsons, "Showing Ideas as Causes. The Origins of the European Union," 62.

57. See Parsons, *A Certain Idea of Europe*, 62–3.

58. See Parsons, *A Certain Idea of Europe*, 66.

59. Mark A. Pollack, "Delegation, Agency, and Agenda Setting in the European Community," *International Organization* 51, no. 1 (1997), 99–134; Mark A. Pollack, *The Engines of European Integration. Delegation, Agency, and Agenda Setting in the EU* (Oxford: Oxford University Press, 2003).

60. See Pollack, *The Engines of European Integration. Delegation, Agency, and Agenda Setting in the EU*, 77.

61. See Pollack, *The Engines of European Integration. Delegation, Agency, and Agenda Setting in the EU*, 78.

62. Mette Eilstrup-Sangiovanni and Daniel Verdier, "European Integration as a Solution to War," *European Journal of International Relations* 11, no.1 (2005), 99–135.

63. See Karen Alter, "Who Are the 'Masters of the Treaty'? European Governments and the European Court of Justice," *International Organization* 52, no.1 (1998), 124.

64. See Rittberger, "Which Institutions for Post-War Europe? Explaining the Institutional Design of Europe's First Community," 695–6.

65. See Rittberger, "Which Institutions for Post-War Europe? Explaining the Institutional Design of Europe's First Community," 696, emphasis in the original.

66. See Berthold Rittberger, *Building Europe's Parliament. Democratic Representation Beyond the Nation-State* (Oxford: Oxford University Press, 2005), 98.

67. See Rittberger, *Building Europe's Parliament. Democratic Representation Beyond the Nation-State*, 98–104; Berthold Rittberger, "'No Integration Without Representation!' European Integration, Parliamentary Democracy, and Two Forgotten Communities," *Journal of European Public Policy* 13, no. 8 (2006), 1211–29.

68. Berthold Rittberger and Frank Schimmelfennig, "Explaining the Constitutionalization of the European Union," *Journal of European Public Policy* 13, no. 8 (2006), 1148–67; Berthold Rittberger and Frank Schimmelfennig, "The Constitutionalization of the European Union. Explaining the Parliamentarization and Institutionalization of Human Rights," in Sophie Meunier and Kathleen R. McNamara, eds, *Making History. European Integration and Institutional Change at Fifty* (Oxford: Oxford University Press, 2008), 213–30.

69. Rittberger, *Building Europe's Parliament. Democratic Representation Beyond the Nation-State*; Rittberger, "'No Integration Without Representation!' European Integration, Parliamentary Democracy, and Two Forgotten Communities"; Berthold Rittberger, "The Historical Origins of the EU's system of Representation," *Journal of European Public Policy* 16, no. 1 (2009), 43–61; Frank Schimmelfennig et al., "Conditions for EU Constitutionalization. A Qualitative Comparative Analysis," *Journal of European Public Policy* 13, no. 8 (2006), 1168–89.

70. See Wolfram Kaiser, "History meets Politics. Overcoming Interdisciplinary Volapük in Research on the EU," *Journal of European Public Policy* 15, no. 2 (2008), 310.

CHAPTER 7

THE TREATIES OF ROME

MARK GILBERT

On 25 March 1957, in the course of an imposing ceremony in Rome, the representatives of Belgium, France, Italy, Luxembourg, the Netherlands, and West Germany signed a treaty instituting a European Economic Community (EEC Treaty) and a second accord establishing a European Community in Atomic Energy (Euratom). The two communities began operations in January 1958.

Since August 1952, the six countries had been collaborating together in the ECSC, but the two Treaties of Rome, especially the EEC Treaty, were not just a simple extension of their cooperation. The Treaties of Rome confirmed the desire of the "Six" to accelerate their post-war progress toward freer trade and greater economic integration and underscored their willingness to develop the peaceful use of atomic energy, which was seen at that time as the probable long-term substitute for fossil fuels. But the immediate goals of greater trade and cheaper energy were placed in a broader, political, context. As the now famous preamble of the EEC Treaty made clear, the treaties were intended to "lay the foundations" for "an ever closer union among the peoples of Europe."

Yet the treaties also made a virtue out of necessity. Lurking in European statesmen's minds was the fear that the post-war economic expansion might prove hard to sustain in the long-term. The size of the American market gave US companies a head start over their European rivals, while the United States was years ahead in nuclear technology. The Soviet bloc was growing even faster than Western Europe and also possessed advanced nuclear technology. The Treaties of Rome, in short, were undoubtedly in part a response to a position of perceived inferiority. As Guy Mollet, a Socialist who became prime minister of France in the spring of 1956, contended in a contemporary article in *Le Monde*, "[i]n the presence of the Russian and American colossi...a mosaic of European states leaves Europe's place empty."[1] Constructing Europe was explicitly seen as a way of remaining competitive, enhancing relative power, and hence of counting in the world.[2]

7.1 FROM MESSINA TO THE SPAAK REPORT

The process that led to the signature of the Rome Treaties began with the 30 August 1954 refusal of the French National Assembly to ratify the treaty establishing the EDC. The EDC Treaty, in brief, shifted sovereignty over defense questions from the six national governments and transferred it both to NATO and to an intergovernmental Council of Ministers. Article 38 of the EDC Treaty, moreover, asserted that the treaty would be the prelude to a subsequent "federal or confederal structure" for Europe. The Assembly of the ECSC, to which was entrusted the task of drawing up the institutional design of such a structure, produced in March 1953 a blueprint for a federal European polity, with a bicameral parliament as its centerpiece. Naturally, the six governments had no intention of transforming the Assembly's musings into reality, but the scale of the EDC's overall threat to national sovereignty, especially since the United Kingdom (UK) had made clear that it would not take part, piqued French national pride. The fact, too, that ratification was a prelude to West Germany's emergence as a fully independent nation state with its own armed forces caused alarm. After a rhetorically charged debate, Gaullists, communists, but also many socialists and radicals, united to vote the treaty down. Since any project of European unity was meaningless without France, the EDC debacle meant that other routes to greater cooperation between the Six had to be found (for the ECSC and the EDC treaties, see Chapter 6, this volume).

Instigated by Jean Monnet, the first President of the High Authority of the ECSC, the baton was picked up by the Low Countries, and in particular by the Belgian foreign minister, Paul-Henri Spaak. The Belgian government pressed Monnet's pet scheme for an atomic energy community on the other five member states in April 1955. In the same month, the Dutch foreign minister, Jan Willem Beyen, reprising a plan he had advocated two years earlier, maintained that the Six should construct a customs union as a prelude to full economic integration. On 18 May 1955, the Belgians and the Dutch wrote to their partners specifically proposing these two policies. The idea of a customs union was especially controversial. For protectionist nations like France, whose welfare costs were high, free trade within the Six represented a threat; for enthusiasts of *laissez faire* like the German economics minister, Ludwig Erhard, a customs union implied a deviation from the Six's commitment to work, through the OEEC, for freer trade throughout democratic Europe.

The Messina conference of the Six's foreign ministers (1–2 June, 1955) made the Belgian–Dutch proposals the centerpiece of their discussions. Spaak used his considerable talents for persuasion to convince the French that "Europe" had to set itself ambitious goals.[3] The final communiqué of the Messina conference stated that the six ministers believed it was necessary to establish a united Europe through the "development of common institutions," the "gradual fusion" of their economies, the "creation of a common market," and the "gradual harmonization of their social policies," though it conspicuously did not resurrect the notion of a federal West European polity. Such general objectives, the Six suggested, were "indispensable" if Europe were to "maintain the place that it holds in the world," to "regain its influence and prestige," and to ensure "continually rising living standards for its people."

In concrete terms, the Messina conference proposed, among other things, that the Six should "study" the creation of a "common organization" with "the responsibility and the means" to ensure the "peaceful development of atomic energy" and affirmed that the step-by-step establishment of a "common European market" free of tariffs and quantitative restrictions on trade was their common goal in the sphere of economic policy. Well aware that such objectives would require lengthy negotiation, that adjustments in member states' monetary, fiscal, and social policies would in all probability be necessary, and that the construction of any new customs union was subject to precise conditions by the GATT, to which Western Europe's nations were signatories, the foreign ministers opted to set up a committee of experts from the member states, chaired by a "political figure," to write a non-binding report setting out the main issues that the Six would face. Spaak was nominated as chair.

The Six also invited London to participate in the committee's labors; itself another sign that federalist ideas had been abandoned, for all knew that the British government would never stoop to join any form of arrangement that was not purely intergovernmental in scope. In general, the Messina conference clarified that though the will to cooperate on economic affairs existed between the Six, and though the Six's underlying economic philosophy was broadly coherent (all agreed, in the abstract, on the benefits of freer markets), there was no consensus on behalf of supranational institutions with strong powers.

Spaak's intergovernmental committee was a distinguished body. West Germany's delegation was headed by one of its most senior civil servants, Ambassador Carl Friedrich Ophuels, Belgium's by Baron Jean-Charles Snoy et d'Oppuers, Secretary General of the country's Ministry for Economic Affairs, France's by a strong proponent of European unity, Félix Gaillard, a former minister and parliamentary deputy, Italy's by Ludovico Benvenuti, who boasted similar credentials to Gaillard. Ambassador Lambert Schaus represented Luxembourg, while the Netherlands' delegation was led by Professor Gerard Marius Verrijn Stuart.

By contrast, the UK's chief representative was Russell Bretherton, a former Oxford University economics lecturer who held a second-tier position within the British trade ministry. Such a relatively low-profile choice was indicative of the suspicion with which the government of Anthony Eden viewed the Messina process. The Chancellor of the Exchequer, R. A. Butler, was dismissive of the Messina initiative. Then Foreign Secretary Harold Macmillan was more positive, but had no more than a pair of allies in Cabinet.[4] To the UK, which was still exercising significant global responsibilities in Africa, the Middle East, and Malaysia, the politics of West European trade appeared frankly boring and inimical to its traditional economic ties with Australia, Canada, and New Zealand. In any future atomic energy community, the UK was bound to be a net contributor of technology and know-how, not certainly a beneficiary.

For these reasons, British participation in the Spaak committee was of short duration. Bretherton, whose initial cynicism about the committee's work gave way over the summer of 1955 to a *personal* conviction that the proposed Economic Community was a sensible idea and would lead to an organization which the UK, if it was only prepared to make compromises, could aspire to lead, left the talks when Spaak made clear to the British government that a customs union would have to be part of the final package. He did so with a pithy summary of London's official position on November 7, 1955, asserting that "the treaty has no chance of being concluded; if it is concluded, it has no chance of being ratified; and if it is ratified, it has no chance of being applied."[5]

Once the UK was out of the frame, negotiations accelerated. Spaak was an able chairman who was decisive in keeping the project for a customs union in the foreground. In this regard, Spaak diverged from Jean Monnet, who left the presidency of the ECSC in January 1955 and set up in October 1955 an "Action Committee" composed of prominent politicians from the Six's Liberal, Socialist and Christian Democratic parties, as well as trade unionists. The Action Committee's second plenary meeting was in january 1956: its final communiqué laid great stress on the centrality of atomic energy for Europe's future and relegated the common market to secondary status, an emphasis that was repeated after its September meeting.[6] Spaak never fell into this error. He prodded the committee and its advisers to reach agreement on the most technical trade matters. As Laurent has written, for Spaak, "the free flow of goods, services, persons and capital was the keystone to progress, more important than transfers of sovereignty or political union."[7]

The final report of Spaak's committee was largely written by one of Jean Monnet's closest collaborators, Pierre Uri, and was presented to the foreign ministers on 21 April 1956. The document's "avant-propos" made no bones about the political imperatives pushing the Six toward greater economic and political integration. "Europe," its post-war economic growth notwithstanding, was falling behind and only a rapid increase in its economic potential, by exploiting the economies of scale brought by a common market and by developing atomic energy, would enable it to catch up with the United States, whose huge firms, single market, and nuclear prowess were plainly seen as a model to emulate.

The Spaak report was dominated by the committee's detailed recommendations on the common market, which took up over eighty pages of text (plans for Euratom, by contrast, were outlined in just twenty-five pages). So far as the common market was concerned, the report advocated the step-by-step full liberalization of internal commerce and an equally liberal approach to the common external tariff: high external protection should be rejected "a priori," the report insisted. Agriculture, always the thorniest of trade issues, was to be included: "The establishment of a common market in Europe is inconceivable if agriculture is not included therein."[8] The market thus created would be administered by four institutions: a decision-making Council of Ministers in which unanimity in voting would be "the rule"; a "Commission" of government nominees charged with administrating the common market and with "watching over" its development; a Court, shared with the ECSC, whose task would be to rule on breaches of the treaty by governments or firms and on appeals against the Commission's decisions. The fourth institution would be the "Common Assembly" of the new Economic Community and the ECSC which would possess the power to censure the Commission's performance.

The Spaak Committee's recommendations on atomic energy underlined that the colossal costs associated with its development made it a logical subject for supranational cooperation. Spaak proposed the creation of a body whose tasks would be to assist and coordinate the member states' private and public enterprises in the nuclear field by standardizing safety norms, developing research, creating a common market in technologies, materials, and specialist workers, and ensuring equal access to nuclear fuels by permitting the Euratom Commission to have priority of purchase of uranium ores and materials. The new organization should not, however, have "any power" to pronounce on the "economic rationality" or "location" of nuclear power stations, the report asserted.[9] The committee also made no attempt to discuss the military use of nuclear technology, declaring it to be a political question beyond its remit.

The Spaak report was approved as a basis for negotiation during a summit meeting of the Six's foreign ministers in Venice in May 1956. A tense intergovernmental negotiation lay ahead, but there is no doubt that Spaak, by producing a coherent and detailed blueprint for intergovernmental action, in effect dared the governments of the Six to turn their rhetoric in favor of European unity into reality. Unlike the EDC, the Spaak report did not require the member states to make sweeping renunciations of sovereignty to achieve European gains.

7.2 THE ROAD TO ROME

The chief stumbling block to acceptance of the Spaak report's conclusions was France. France was ready to accept Euratom, so long as it could carry on its military research, but feared that a customs union would expose the lack of competitiveness of its manufacturers. France had a generous welfare state which weighed upon its production costs; it therefore wanted its partners to raise their levels of social protection to French levels. France also raised the issue of its overseas colonies, whose economies provided abundant raw materials as well as markets for French products. Would such benefits now have to be shared? If so, France intended to ensure that the expense of developing living standards in its "dependencies" were shared by its European partners. Above all, France wanted a concerted agricultural policy that would raise farm incomes and ensure free trade in food products throughout the Six.

As a result, French leaders tried give priority to Euratom while presenting a lengthy list of reservations to the common market. West Germany refused to play. The Bonn government advocated a collective renunciation of the development of nuclear arms by the Six (Germany was forbidden to make nuclear weapons by the October 1954 Treaty of Paris that, after the debacle of the EDC, had permitted it to regain statehood and become a member of WEU). Bonn also insisted that the two treaties should be signed simultaneously: in the jargon of the time, there was a *Junktim* (link) between the two treaties. It was both or nothing. The intergovernmental negotiations, with Spaak once more in the chair, began in Brussels at the end of June, but bogged down by September 1956.[10]

The UK exploited this situation on October 3, 1956 by floating a proposal to create a free trade area (FTA) in manufactured goods throughout the seventeen member states of the OEEC. "Plan G," as the scheme was known inside the British government, would have positioned the British economy at the center of two free trade areas (the OEEC and the Commonwealth), enjoying the benefits of both. The UK would have been able to import Australian wool and export expensive sweaters, tariff-free, to its European partners. "Plan G" was also deftly designed to appeal to committed free traders like Erhard who disliked the "little Europe" separatism inherent in the idea of a customs union and to the many politicians within the Six who did not want free trade in agricultural products.[11]

For these reasons, "Plan G" has been portrayed as an attempt to undermine the EEC. Scholarship suggests, however, that British leaders simply had a different perspective on how Europe should organize itself. For them, a loose trading area administered by the OEEC was politically in keeping with the choices already made in the defense sphere (NATO, WEU) and also in Britain's immediate economic interests—it gave Britain the "best of both worlds." Moreover, British spokesmen were at pains both in October 1956 and subsequently to underline that the FTA was intended as a complement to the common market, not as a substitute.

The deadlock in the negotiations was broken by the other five nations, and especially West Germany, making the calculation that the benefits of "little Europe" were such that it made sense to give way to France on almost all key points. On agriculture, on the military use of nuclear energy, and on the question of development aid for the French empire, an issue that dominated the negotiations in January–February 1957, French leaders got much the treaty language they wanted. They had to cede on the issue of harmonization of social legislation, but this concession was softened by the realization that France's lack of competitiveness was as much due to the over-valued franc as to its generous welfare state and short working week. Devaluation, together with a restrictive fiscal policy to dampen the desire for imported goods, could solve the problem. This was, indeed, the solution adopted by Charles de Gaulle when he became president of France in the summer of 1958.

Why did the breakthrough occur? Some scholars have emphasized the role of the United States, which was important in two ways. First, the United States, by disowning, in the first week of November 1956, Franco–British military action against Egypt in the Suez canal zone, humiliated their allies and brought home the fact that American support could not be taken for granted. Suez certainly did reinforce the geopolitical rationale for building Europe, which, as this chapter has been at pains to suggest, was an ever-present factor in European leaders' minds. German Chancellor Konrad Adenauer was actually in Paris, for talks on the EEC impasse with French premier Guy Mollet, as the Suez crisis came to its embarrassing close. Specifically, it was in Paris on November 6, 1956 that Adenauer accepted that the French would build the bomb and that Mollet gave the green light for speeding up talks on the Economic Community.[12]

Second, the Eisenhower administration gave constructive encouragement to the Europeans' efforts to build both Euratom and the EEC. In a way, the chief US contribution lay in what it did *not* do. It did not interfere in the negotiating process to demand easier access for US products, or criticize the common market for the distortions to world trade that it would bring. This was partly due to the healthy state of the US economy, which still enjoyed a surplus in its balance of payments with the Six ($1,463 million in 1956; $1,636 million in 1957). As Federico Romero has pointed out "[a]s long as the American economy remained buoyant, and foreign trade growing, the U.S. positive attitude towards European integration was not vulnerable to domestic pressures for an assertion of the USA's immediate commercial interest."[13]

The United States also skillfully adjusted its own position on nuclear proliferation to accommodate the construction of Euratom. The United States and Great Britain had cornered the non-communist world's supplies of uranium in the post-war period by purchasing the entire production of uranium ore from the Belgian Congo, which was then the world's major producer. In 1955, the accord with Belgium was renewed to guarantee that the lion's share of Congolese ore would be sold to the Anglo-American consortium until 1960. Contemporaneously, the 1954 Atomic Energy Act relaxed the US stance on the transmission of nuclear technology by permitting bilateral treaties with nations that met US security standards. US firms stood to make export dollars from selling its know-how to approved buyers. West Germany and other European nations were the natural market.

Cutting a very complicated story to its bare bones, the United States, pushed by Secretary of State J. F. Dulles and President Eisenhower, in 1956–1957 opted to make Euratom its nuclear interlocutor in Europe, rather than establish a network of bilateral links with its European allies. Particularly in the case of West Germany, where powerful factions within the ruling coalition would have preferred a bilateral deal, this political pressure was of vital importance. After a visit to Washington by the persuasive Paul-Henri Spaak in February 1957, the United States also permitted Belgium to make Euratom the priority buyer of Congolese uranium ore from 1960, and to "Europeanize" its share before that date.[14]

Ideas mattered. Dulles and Eisenhower, strongly influenced by Monnet, were true believers in the historical significance of the European project. Both feared, moreover, that absent European integration, West Germany would become a loose cannon, trying to balance Washington and Moscow for its own advantage. Eisenhower consistently expressed his hope that a united Europe would become a 'third force' in world affairs, even if this meant some reduction in the United States' own relative power, and saw the construction of the two Communities as essential stepping stones toward this goal.

7.3 THE TREATIES AND THEIR SIGNIFICANCE

In the Euratom Treaty the Six created a Community that had eight specific objectives. Promoting research and disseminating technical information; establishing uniform safety standards in the nuclear industry; facilitating investment in nuclear plant; ensuring that all users in the Community received a 'regular and equitable' supply of ore;

supervising nuclear materials to make sure they were used for appropriate purposes; exercising the right of ownership of fissile materials; creating a common market in specialized materials and equipment, as well as free movement of capital for investment in the nuclear industry and freedom of movement for nuclear specialists; fostering relations with other countries and organizations. Euratom was given a nine-member Commission and a Council of Ministers; it shared its Assembly and Court of Justice with the ECSC. The possession of fissile materials for military use was authorized by juridical sleight of hand. Article 84 of the Euratom Treaty stated that the Community's rules safeguarding fissile materials "may not extend to materials intended to meet defense requirements"; Article 86, which stated that "all fissile materials shall be the property of the Community," exempted those not "subject to the safeguards" outlined in the previous chapter of the treaty (which included Article 84).

Euratom was greeted with great fanfare by Monnet's Action Committee and by the press. But it was not destined to impinge heavily upon European history. The proponents of nuclear energy had underestimated the costs involved in making nuclear power the mainstay of European electricity generation. Coal and oil remained far cheaper sources of energy than processed uranium and took the lion's share of national investment. When the oil shock hit in the mid-1970s, democratic Europe's economies were more, not less, dependent upon fossil fuels than they had been in the 1950s: a fact that had significant foreign and domestic policy repercussions.

The Treaty establishing the EEC, by contrast, unquestionably has impinged upon European history in a decisive manner. A hugely complex document, its objectives were clearly stated in its preamble and its opening articles. It would "lay the foundations of an ever closer union among the peoples of Europe." More specifically, by "establishing a common market" and "progressively approximating" its member states' economic policies, the Community would "promote" the "harmonious development of economic activities, a continuous and balanced expansion, an increase in stability, an accelerated raising of the standard of living and closer relations between the states belonging to it."

To this end, the six member states promised to construct a customs union and abolish "obstacles to freedom of movement for persons, services and capital" between them. The Community set itself a twelve-year timetable (or "transitional period") for the realization of the customs union, divided into three four-year stages (though some slippage was permitted for the first stage), with a "set of actions" being assigned to each stage. Tariff revenues on intra-Community trade, for instance, would be reduced by specified amounts at specified times and by 30 percent in all by the end of the first four-year period. Individual products were to have duties reduced by at least 50 percent by the end of the second four-year period. Quantitative restrictions on imported goods were to be entirely phased out within four years. The EEC Treaty moreover committed the member states not to introduce new customs duties and to promising that they would cut tariffs more rapidly if overall economic conditions were conducive (a promise they would eventually keep: the customs union was completed in July 1968, eighteen months ahead of the most optimistic schedule). Restrictions upon the movement of capital were also to be abolished by the end of the transitional stage. The EEC Treaty affirmed that the common external tariff would be the "arithmetical average" of the duties exacted on 1 January 1957 by the four customs regimes comprised in the Community (Belgium, Luxembourg, and the Netherlands were already a single territory for trade purposes) and it too was to be implemented over a twelve-year period. The member states themselves, via a unanimous vote of the Council of Ministers, would decide whether each stage's "set of actions" had been substantially fulfilled, although a state could not prevent unanimity by backsliding on its own obligations.

The EEC Treaty's liberalizing dispositions on trade were balanced with articles that reflected French concerns. On social policy, while the Community was not to have legal competence over welfare policy, broadly defined, the member states did explicitly commit themselves to ensuring the principle of "equal pay for equal work" between men and women. Member states' colonies would become associate members of the Community and have access to the common market on the same terms as member states. The member states promised to "contribute to the investments required for the progressive development of these countries or territories." In concrete terms, as an annex to the Treaty clarified, the member states committed themselves to investing some 580 million European Payments Union (EPU) "units of account" (i.e. dollars) over five years, with France and Germany being the largest contributors with 200 million apiece. French overseas territories, however, were to benefit from 511.25 million of this investment. In effect, the five other members of the EEC pledged themselves to subsidize the former French empire to the tune of $60 million per year until 1963. Guy Mollet made no bones about the advantages for France: "By opening our overseas populations to the broad opportunities offered by a union with Europe, by enabling them, through our good offices, to enter in this vast collectivity, we adroitly maintain our influence."[15] The French historian René Girault, however, has placed this development in a different light. By "obliging" its partners to "occupy themselves" with Europe's overseas territories, Girault has contended, France "made Europe address the question of aid for underdeveloped countries."[16]

Above all, the CAP was to be established alongside the common market in agricultural products. Its goals were to increase agricultural productivity, "ensure a fair standard of living for the agricultural community," "stabilize markets," and ensure that foodstuffs reached consumers at "reasonable" prices, a formulation that would in future cover a multitude of sins. As one of France's chief negotiators subsequently wrote, "France would never have accepted a Customs Union that did not include agriculture and did not guarantee French producers protection comparable to that which they were receiving under French law. Without a common agricultural policy, there would never have been a common market."[17]

The EEC's institutional structure mixed supranationalism and intergovernmentalism. The Community's executive was the Commission, whose nine members (two Germans, two French, two Italians, one each from the other countries) were however to be completely independent of the governments that had nominated them. The Commission's job was to propose new legislation, monitor compliance with the treaty, act as market regulator, and conduct, under the strict supervision of the Council, international trade negotiations. The ECJ was given a potentially significant role. Whereas under the ECSC Treaty, the Court of Justice provided judicial review only of the High Authority, under the EEC Treaty, the Court could rule upon breaches of the treaty by the member states. The Commission, the governments of member states, and lower courts within the member states could all refer cases to the Court for adjudication, though the ECJ had no powers to impose sanctions on a state that did not abide by its rulings. The EEC Treaty thus created two potentially powerful supranational institutions.

The Council of Ministers was the key legislative institution of the EEC Treaty: in the highly sensitive area of agriculture, its decisions were to be by unanimity for the first eight years. Many other areas of legislation, at least during the first stage, were to be decided by unanimous vote. Other votes were to be by "qualified majority." France, Italy, Germany were each given four votes in the Council; Belgium and the Netherlands disposed of two; Luxembourg of one. The qualified majority necessary was to be twelve votes out of seventeen, though, in practice, member states preferred from the first to find consensus where they could. The EEC Treaty, in short, while it gave the power of proposal to a supranational institution, and sketched the prospect of supranational judicial review, nevertheless placed political authority squarely in the hands of the member states acting by agreement.

It certainly made no concessions to the federalist vision of a sovereign European Parliament. The EEC's institutions were completed by an Assembly, designated by the various national parliaments, whose nominal task was to represent Europe's peoples. Its only substantive power in the original treaty was the power, by a two-thirds majority vote, to censure the Commission and oblige its collective resignation. This power was too sweeping to be used. This failure to give real power to the Assembly actually caused many European federalists to repudiate the EEC Treaty. In the words of Altiero Spinelli, an Italian socialist intellectual who regarded the superseding of national sovereignty as a necessary historical step for Europeans, keen federalists considered that "Europeans continue to be deprived of any institutional instrument that would permit them to be the European people and to act as the European people."[18]

What was the significance of the EEC Treaty? In the first place, it was a hard-nosed bargain, as many scholars have pointed out.[19] France got the promise of aid for its farmers and a free market in agricultural products and in exchange opened its markets to German (and Italian) manufactured goods. Insofar as this bargain gave an undeniable stimulus to economic activity, the EEC was an important development. It was significant, too, in that it established the Six as an economic and perhaps political bloc in a way that the ECSC had not. The creation of the EEC in 1958 coincided with the introduction of full convertibility of European currencies into US dollars in 1958. Once money could move more freely, the EEC swiftly became a magnet for US investment—on a scale, in fact, which both worsened the US balance of payments and aroused European, especially French, angst about American industrial hegemony. The worsening of the US balance of payments was to be a major concern of President Kennedy's when he entered the White House in 1961. The EEC Treaty also had significant effects on the UK, which suddenly found its pose of lofty disdain for continental commitments harder to sustain. When de Gaulle was elected President of France, he quickly scuppered the FTA talks and made clear his preference for "little Europe." Whitehall had to scrabble to establish the rival EFTA with Austria, Portugal, Ireland, and the Scandinavians—a worthy venture, but nevertheless something of a comedown. Prime Minister Harold Macmillan would soon conclude that Britain could not stay out of the EEC even if it wanted to.

The creation of the EEC is often depicted as the first step or milestone on the road to European unity in the EU of today. This kind of teleological approach should be treated with some caution. Making the EEC was a fraught process that might have had many different outcomes. The new Community also endured a somewhat querulous infancy. The first Commission, which was headed by the former German Foreign Minister Walter Hallstein, contained a number of first-rank political figures, notably the Frenchman Robert Marjolin and the Dutch Commissioner Sicco Mansholt, and its work, especially over the thorny issue of agriculture, established the EEC's credibility. Nevertheless, there was nothing inevitable about the progression of the Community from a first to a second stage: the EEC had to "stop the clock" for fifteen days in January 1962 while it conducted frantic efforts to make the birth pangs of the CAP less painful.

The legal status of the Community was still anything but clear. The member states assumed that the EEC Treaty was an international agreement between states that did not restrict their sovereign right to make law binding upon their citizens. The ECJ's famous *Van Gend end Loos* judgment in February 1963 dismissed this interpretation, in the face of strenuous objections from the Dutch, Belgian, and German governments and the Court's own advocate general, stating plainly that the "Community constitutes a new legal order…for the benefit of which the states have limited their sovereign rights…and the subjects of which comprise not only Member States *but also their nationals*" (italics mine).[20] In the terminology of international law, the Court ruled, in short, that the EEC Treaty's provisions had "direct effect" on the public authorities and in some circumstances the citizens of the signatory states. Thus, in this specific case, the Dutch government had had no right in 1959 to raise tariffs on imported German chemicals when the then Art. 12 of the EEC Treaty ruled out such an action. By doing so, the Netherlands was not only infringing the treaty, it was infringing the civil rights of the Dutch importer. Had the Court ruled otherwise, and had the member states not abided by this and other subsequent rulings, it is easy to conjecture that the EEC, like many customs unions before it, would have found protectionist impulses rearing their ugly head sooner or later.

Ultimately, the striking feature of the Treaties of Rome, and the negotiation process that preceded them, is precisely this novel willingness of the Six to subordinate their traditional sovereign rights. This perception of mutual interest ultimately derived from their leaders' judgment that they would not count in the world unless they colluded. At bottom, the Treaties of Rome derived from a shrewd assessment by the Six's leaders of their nations' diminished standing in the world and a shared determination that they would make "Europe" matter again.

NOTES

1. Guy Mollet, "Le Front Républicain et l'Europe," *Le Monde*, December 28, 1955, 3.
2. For a recent book that strongly emphasises the importance of prestige and the Six's perception of relative power, see Sebastian Rosato, *Europe United: Power Politics and the making of the European Community* (Ithaca NY : Cornell University Press, 2011) especially ch.5.

3. See Paul-Henri Spaak, *The Continuing Battle: Memoirs of a European* (London: Weidenfeld & Nicholson, 1971), 227–58 for Spaak's (somewhat skimpy) account of his role in the process launched at Messina.

4. Roger Bullen, "Britain and Europe, 1950–1957," in Enrico Serra, ed., *Il rilancio europeo e i trattati di Roma*, (Milan: Giuffré, 1989), 381.

5. Quoted in Craig Parsons, *A Certain Idea of Europe* (Ithaca NY: Cornell University Press, 2003), 105. For British policy during the negotiation, see John W. Young, "The 'Parting of Ways?' Britain, the Messina Conference and the Spaak Committee, June–December 1955," in Michael Dockrill and John W. Young, eds, *British Foreign Policy, 1945–1956* (Basingstoke: Macmillan, 1989), 197–220.

6. Political and Economic Planning, *Statements of the Action Committee for a United States of Europe* (London: Political and Economic Planning, 1969), 12–18.

7. Pierre-Henri Laurent, "Paul-Henri Spaak and the Diplomatic Origins of the Common Market," *Political Science Quarterly* 85, no. 3 (September 1970), 387.

8. *Rapport des Chefs de Délégation aux Ministres des Affaires Etrangères* (The Spaak Report), Brussels April 21, 1956, 44.

9. *Spaak Report*, 111.

10. An excellent account of these negotiations is Robert Lieshout, *Struggle for the Organization of Europe* (Cheltenham: Edward Elgar, 1999).

11. For "Plan G" see Martin Schaad, "Plan G: A 'Counterblast?' British Policy Towards the Messina Countries, 1956," *Contemporary European History* 7, no. 1 (1998), 39–60.

12. A point made by H. J. Küsters, "The Treaties of Rome, 1955–1957," in Roy Pryce, ed., *The Dynamics of European Union* (London: Routledge, 1989), 90–1. Pierre Mélandri, *Les Etats-Unis et le 'défi' européen, 1955–1958* (Paris: Presses Universitaires de France, 1975), 119, ironically comments that John Foster Dulles did more for European unity by opposing Suez than by supporting the EDC.

13. Federico Romero, "Interdependence and Integration in American Eyes: From the Marshall Plan to Currency Convertibility," in Alan S. Milward et al., *The Frontier of National Sovereignty* (London: Routledge, 1993), 168–9.

14. These paragraphs on the US and Euratom are indebted to Jonathan E. Helmreich, "The United States and the Formation of Euratom," *Diplomatic History* 15, no. 3 (1991), 387–410.

15. Mollet quoted in Frédéric Turpin, "Alle origini della politica europea di cooperazione allo sviluppo: la Francia e la politica di associazione Europa-Africa (1957–1975)," *Ventunesimo Secolo* 6, October 2007, 137.

16. René Girault, "La France entre l'Europe et l'Afrique," in Serra, *Il rilancio*, 377.

17. Robert Marjolin, *Architect of European Unity* (London: Weidenfeld & Nicholson, 1989), 303.

18. Daniele Pasquinucci, *Europeismo e democrazia. Altiero Spinelli e la sinistra europea, 1950–1986* (Bologna: Il Mulino, 2000), 142.

19. For a brief summary of the interpretative debate on the treaties of Rome, see Mark Gilbert, "The Treaties of Rome in Narratives of European Integration," in Michael Gehler, ed., *Von gemeinsamen Markt zur europäischen Unionsbildung. 50 Jahre Römische Verträge* (Vienna, Cologne, Weimar: Böhlau, 2008), 721–9. This book, which contains essays in English, French, and German, is a comprehensive evaluation of the treaties and their consequences.

20. Quoted in Anthony Arnull, *The European Union and its Court of Justice* (Oxford: Oxford University Press, 1999), 83.

....

CHAPTER 8

THE SINGLE EUROPEAN ACT

....

MARIA GREEN COWLES

THE Single European Act (SEA)—signed in February 1986—marked the first significant formal transformation of the Treaty of Rome. The SEA was instrumental in implementing the EU's single market program. The central feature of the SEA was the modification of the Community's decision-making procedures that allowed for majority voting on key internal market matters. This change signaled the end of the infamous 1965 "Luxembourg Compromise" that allowed member states to move away from the majority voting system called for in the Treaty of Rome and to effectively veto legislation in the name of national interest. Indeed, it is difficult to imagine that the European Community could have successfully pursued its "1992 program"—the initiative to implement almost 300 legislative acts to create a single market by December 31, 1992—without the SEA. No one understood this linkage better than the politically astute European Commission President Jacques Delors, who promoted the internal market while championing the institutional reforms needed to ensure its implementation.

The SEA modified the Treaties of Rome in other important ways. It expanded the competence of the then-European Community to the fields of research, environment, regional policy, and certain aspects of social policy. The treaty also formalized European political cooperation, establishing a secretariat for political cooperation and strengthening cooperation among embassies in third countries. In addition, the SEA gave expanded powers to the European Commission through the delegation of implementation powers by the Council. The European Parliament gained the right of assent on further European Community enlargement as well as the "cooperation procedure"—requiring the Council to consult with the European Parliament a second time in certain instances. A second court—the Court of First Instance (CFI)—was created through the SEA to allow the ECJ to focus on more critical matters.

Importantly, the SEA symbolized the relaunch of the European Community after a decade of "Eurosclerosis." The oil crisis of the 1970s coupled with stagflation in European economies prompted many European Community member states to focus on domestic economic issues, promote "national champions," and be wary of competition from outside firms. The single market program and SEA marked an explicit turn back to a European response to global economic challenges.

Finally, the SEA reintroduced the vigorous theoretical debate between scholars who espouse intergovernmentalism or neo-functionalism in explaining European integration. While intergovernmentalists[1] argued that national governments were largely responsible for the events leading to the SEA, others argued that transnational actors were critical in this phase of European integration.[2]

The emergence of the SEA, the key treaty reforms, and its impact are explored below.

8.1 Origins of the SEA

The nascent European Community showed much promise in the 1950s and early 1960s with the creation of the customs union and common external tariff; the early development of common policies in agriculture, commerce, transport, and competition; the establishment of the EIB; the functioning of supranational bodies such as Commission and Assembly; and the emergence of the ECJ that helped recognize the supremacy of European Community law over national laws.

When in 1965, European Commission President Walter Hallstein proposed an extension of the Commission's powers to include more QMV in the Council on commercial matters, French President Charles de Gaulle strongly opposed the measure. The French president opted to withdraw France's representative in Brussels and boycott any discussions of institutional change. The result was the "empty chair crisis"—with a missing French representative at the table—that dramatically slowed any progress on European matters. The crisis was resolved in January 1966 with the infamous "Luxembourg Compromise"—a tacit agreement that member states could require unanimity in voting when matters arose that were of national interest. This effectively slowed down the supranational decision-making in the European Community.

A few years later, the oil crisis and related stagflation of the member states' economies in the 1970s ushered in a new period of what was termed "Eurosclerosis." As the European economy weakened, member states began to look for national strategies to address economic growth. National business associations and governments alike focused less on the approximation of laws to create a functioning common market as called for in the Treaty of Rome, and instead sought more protectionist policies to counter the rise of Japanese companies and *"le défi américain"* (the American challenge)[3] in the European and global marketplace, and to promote national champions.

Yet two decades after the Luxembourg Compromise, member states of the European Community signed the SEA, the first major modification of the Treaty of Rome, on February 18, 1986, that brought about more supranational voting processes for single market regulation. What prompted the symbolic relaunch of Europe with the SEA? Observers of European integration have identified at least four critical developments that led to the SEA: (1) the directly elected European Parliament in 1980 and the resulting Draft Treaty on European Union in 1984;[4] (2) the recognition that member countries needed to develop stronger political cooperation in light of changing relations with the United States;[5] (3) a series of intergovernmental bargains that culminated in key member states supporting the creation of the SEA;[6] and (4) the mobilization of European business actors and support of the European Commission in promoting the creation of a single market.[7]

8.1.1 The European Parliament

One argument is that the first directly elected European Parliament in 1979 triggered the SEA initiative. The election brought together members (MEPs) who eagerly sought to carry out the European Parliament's powers of "own initiative" under the Treaty of Rome. The MEPs were also responding to concerns for Europe's future in light of the economic and political malaise of the 1970s and the recognition that critical reforms were needed to ensure that the European Community could constructively address these issues.[8] With the leadership of Altiero Spinelli and fellow members of the Crocodile Club (so named after the *Au Crocodile* restaurant in Strasbourg where the MEPs met), the new European Parliament created its own Draft Treaty on European Union (EUT) in July 1983. The European Parliament approved the EUT on February 14, 1984, by a vote of 237 MEPs for the treaty, and 31 against.

The Draft Treaty proposed a number of new institutional powers. Indeed, the Draft Treaty laid out an institutional arrangement in which the Parliament and Council would function much like the US Congress (with the Parliament approximating the House of Representatives and the Council, the Senate).[9] It also called for majority voting procedures and included European Political Cooperation as part of this supranational framework.

Spinelli had hoped that the Draft Treaty would capture the imagination of the general electorate in Europe who would, in turn, pressure governments to rally around the treaty. Several national parliaments expressed support for the Draft Treaty, as did French President François Mitterrand in an address to the European Parliament. When the European Council created a special ad hoc committee, the Dooge Committee, in June 1984 to examine institutional reform, the committee looked to the Draft Treaty for many of its agenda ideas.

The Dooge Committee, however, proved much less supportive of the core institutional reforms proposed by the European Parliament. Indeed, at the Brussels meeting in 1985, the Dooge Committee did not support the European Parliament's call for a new treaty (such as the Draft Treaty), and instead proposed that Article 125 allowing for the amendment of the existing treaty be used. The committee suggested that the governments create an IGC to be governed by the "spirit" of the Draft Treaty.[10] In the end, most of Draft Treaty's institutional proposals were never incorporated into the IGCs leading to the SEA. Despite laying some groundwork for discussions on expanding the European

Community, the SEA "fell far short" of the major transformation of the European Community as envisioned by the European Parliament.[11]

8.1.2 European Political Cooperation

Scholars have argued that the changing relationship between the United States and Europe in the 1980s also gave impetus to greater European collaboration. European governments expressed concern over the growing US budget and trade deficits and the possibility that the US might grow closer economically to Japan. At the same time, they were wary of the American security guarantee in NATO. The Soviet invasion of Afghanistan in 1979, coupled with the more militant-sounding American President Ronald Reagan who entered office in 1980, made a number of countries—notably West Germany—concerned that the carefully cultivated relations with its Eastern neighbors through *Ostpolitik* in the 1970s might be thwarted. European leaders also were not pleased when the October 1986 US–Soviet summit in Reykjavik, Iceland, nearly led to a breakthrough on eliminating all nuclear arms between the superpowers. While not opposed to arms control per se, the Western Europeans were upset that the Americans would support such a significant change without consulting its transatlantic allies. The Europeans, after all, had long relied on the nuclear threat to prevent conventional warfare on European soil again. These developments prompted the European Community countries to consider expanding the Community's scope to develop a stronger political/military profile, along with the WEU.[12]

With growing dissatisfaction with the United States and concern over the Soviet invasion of Afghanistan, the British presidency sponsored the "London Report" in 1981 which formalized many of the informal EPC practices that had developed in the previous five years. That same year, the German and Italian foreign ministers issued the "Genscher–Colombo Plan" calling for a European act that would commit governments to a common foreign policy and the development of a security policy.[13] At the 1983 European Council meeting in Stuttgart, the member states issued the Solemn Declaration on the European Union calling for greater attention to European integration and the strengthening of EPC procedures. This included coordination among embassies in third countries and common positions at international conferences and organizations. As noted above, the European Parliament sought to formalize EPC in its Draft Treaty as a regular function of the European Community.

While the 1984 Dooge Committee and subsequent IGC negotiations brought EPC into the SEA, they created it as a separate structure with no formal linkages to the voting mechanisms of the European Community. In many respects, while the changing relationship between the United States and Europe was important, the SEA simply appropriated much of what had already been agreed to in the earlier London Report. Whether the political climate alone was a key incentive for treaty reform is therefore open to debate.

8.1.3 Intergovernmental Bargaining

Some observers maintain that the origins of the SEA can be directly traced to a series of key agreements by member-state governments based on their own national inter-ests.[14] The fact that the 1983 European Council in Stuttgart issued the Solemn Declaration on European Union, calling for greater economic integration and politi-cal cooperation, did not suggest that a single market was a foregone conclusion. Rather, it is argued that the real démarche toward the single market occurred in February 1984 at the Brussels European Council meeting, the first of the French presi-dency, when the French and German presidents sought to reach agreement on the European budget. For a number of years, the British had complained that owing to the CAP, the British contribution to the European Community budget was not commen-surate to what it received in overall benefits from the Community. Consequently, the British remained tepid about moving forward with any major European initiatives. While Germany and France were open to negotiations, both German Chancellor Kohl and French President Mitterrand expressed strong frustration when British Prime Minister Thatcher refused to compromise on budgetary discussions at the Brussels European Council meeting in March 1984. Indeed, Chancellor Kohl threatened the British to "take it or leave it" and suggested that France and Germany would be willing to move ahead on initiatives in the future without the British. At the following Council meeting in June 1984 at Fontainebleau, a budget accord finally was reached. With the British now on-board, the Council agreed to create two committees that might explore further advances in European integration—the above-mentioned Dooge Committee to examine institutional reform, and the Adonnino Committee to examine ways in which to strengthen the notion of "a citizen's Europe." This budgetary compromise, therefore, allowed European integration to proceed.

The ensuing political bargaining and agreements of the government leaders led to further advances. At the Luxembourg summit in 1985, both France and Germany sup-ported an initiative to relaunch the European Community that would involve majority voting for internal market initiatives, thus limiting the Luxembourg compromise. In Brussels a few weeks later, the Council agreed that the European Community should commit itself to creating a single market by December 30, 1992, and called on the Commission to create a detailed action plan. Finally, at the Milan summit in 1985, the governments approved the White Paper, the document created by Lord Cockfield, the Internal Market Commissioner, who outlined over 300 specific proposals that were needed to create the single market. The Italian foreign minister called for the creation of an intergovernmental conference to identify the necessary revisions to the Treaty of Rome to support the single market initiative. Three member states—UK, Greece, and Denmark—opposed convening the IGC, but the Italians deemed that the majority had agreed to move forward on the initiative. Despite the protests of the three dissenting countries, when the first IGC took place in Luxembourg on September 9, 1985, all mem-ber states were present. The IGC met five times under European Council, with agreement in principle reached at the IGC conference on December 16–17, 1985.[15] The SEA was signed on February 1986.

In the end, this perspective of the origins of the SEA focuses on the negotiating positions of the three largest member states—France, Germany, and the United Kingdom. Accordingly, the French president's more pro-European stance in the mid-1980s allowed for the French and German governments to pressure the British government once the budget agreements were reached at Fontainebleau. While the role of these governments is clearly important, why the governments promoted these changes and what domestic pressures influenced their decision-making was less clearly defined.

8.1.4 Transnational Business and Commission Leadership

Other scholars argue that the mobilization of major business actors and the leadership of the European Commission largely account for the origin of the single market program and the resulting SEA. Sandholtz and Zysman argued that a "shift in the distribution of [global] economic power"—the rise of Japan and perceived decline of the United States, prompted European elites to reevaluate their economic roles in the world.[16] Cowles maintained that the mobilization of a key transnational business organization, the European Roundtable of Industrialists (ERT), encouraged the European Commission and later the member states to support a single market initiative.[17]

In 1982, Pehr Gyllenhammar, the Chief Executive Officer (CEO) of Swedish automaker Volvo, promoted a "Marshall Plan for Europe" and called on European industrial leaders to work together to promote a major European industrial initiative. Gyllenhammar was soon supported by Etienne Davignon, the European Community Industry Commissioner who later successfully launched the European Strategic Program on Research in Information Technology (ESPRIT) that brought together key high-tech firms to Brussels. The two men identified a number of key CEOs or board chairs to form the ERT. The ERT's creation marked the first time that major European companies openly mobilized to influence European Community developments. In 1983, the ERT held a series of meetings and issued a memorandum, "Foundations for the Future of European Industry" calling on political action to create a unified European market.[18] That same year, French ERT members played an important role in convincing French President Mitterrand to support a European initiative. Indeed, when the French government announced an industrial initiative in September 1983, it largely reflected the key goals articulated earlier in the ERT memorandum. In 1984, the ERT issued a report, *Missing Links*, that addressed the trans-European infrastructure—key goals articulated in the ERT and French initiatives—needed to support a single market.[19]

In 1984, Internal Market Commissioner Karl-Heinz Narjes produced a package containing hundreds of proposals needed to complete a common market. The document, however, received no strong support from government leaders. The ERT found the proposal to be "unwieldy," with no timetable, no overarching rationale for industrial growth, and no strategy to ensure its implementation.[20] Key ERT members agreed that a larger strategic approach was necessary. In January 1985, Philips CEO and ERT member Wisse Dekker unveiled such a plan, "Europe 1990," before 500 commission and industry officials in Brussels. The "Dekker Plan" laid out steps in four key areas—trade facilitation (elimination of border formalities), opening up of public procurement markets, harmonization of technical stands, and fiscal harmonization (eliminating the fiscal Value Added Tax frontiers) to create a European market in five years. Three days later, the new Commission President, Jacques Delors, announced the Commission's intention to create a single market by 1992. Delors soon invited ERT members to an "on the record" meeting to discuss mutual goals.

The Dekker Plan and *Missing Links* document generated considerable interest in ERT ideas. Soon the ERT developed it own Political Contact Program to target its messages and meetings with senior European officials as well as the heads of state and government. Wisse Dekker and other ERT members appeared on the front page of the *Financial Times* warning that European multinational corporations would take their businesses elsewhere if there was not strong support for an industrial initiative.

The European Council gave its general endorsement of the Commission's 1992 single market project in March 1985. Internal Market Commissioner Lord Cockfield set to work on the internal market White Paper, creating a strategic approach to the many proposals his predecessor had earlier identified, and proposing Delors's 1992 deadline.

In June 1985, the ERT issued another document, *Changing Scales*, featuring the Dekker paper and infrastructure projects, that was delivered to heads of state and government.[21] That same month, the Milan European Council gave its support to the Cockfield White

Table 8.1 Timeline leading to the SEA

Dates	Events
1980	First direct European Parliament elections
1981	London Report, Genscher–Colombo Plan
April 1983	European Roundtable of Industrialists created
June 1983	Solemn Declaration on EU
July 1983	Draft Treaty on EU: European Parliament approved February 14, 1984
June 1984	Fontainebleau European Council: budgetary compromise reached, creation of the Dooge and Adonnino Committees
December 1984	ERT publishes *Missing Links*
January 1985	Dekker calls for single market by 1990
January 1985	Delors calls for single market by December 30, 1992, the "1992 initiative"
March 1985	Brussels European Council: agreement to create a single market by December 30, 1992
June 1985	ERT document, *Changing Scales*
June 1985	Milan European Council: Cockfield White Paper accepted, creation of Intergovernmental Conference
February 1986	SEA signed

Paper and the Italian presidency launched the IGC process. While ERT members did not seek to influence the specific negotiations within the Dooge committee or the IGC, they continued to inform governments of the need to respond positively and forcefully to the single market initiative. Even after the SEA was passed, ERT members sought to meet with the Council presidencies to ensure that the efforts to address the single market initiatives were on track. As Delors himself noted, the market program came about "thanks to many people and actors in what became a process…the 1992 process. And I must admit the business actors mattered; they made a lot of it happen."[22]

Of course, there is scholarly debate as to whether or not transnationally organized business actors and Commission officials were the critical actors behind the SEA. Table 8.1 below highlights a number of key events in the timeline leading to the SEA. Indeed, one can argue—as Delors indicated—that many actors mattered, from the European Parliament that created a "rough draft" for the SEA, to the business leaders, Commissioners, and member states who responded to the economic and political challenges of the times.

8.1.5 A "Fait Accompli"?

While there are various explanations for the origins of the SEA, they are not necessarily mutually exclusive. After all, the European Parliament's actions along with developments in EPC set the stage for the Dooge Committee on institutional reform. The budgetary compromise among heads of state and government at the Fontainebleau Council meeting in June 1984 allowed the work of these committees to move forward. The Franco–German effort to relaunch the European project at the Luxembourg summit in 1985 was possible only after French ERT members convinced President Mitterrand of the need to move forward with a European industrial initiative.

Even after heads of state and government signed the treaty, however, it was not clear at the time if the SEA would be successfully implemented. Nor was the SEA's immediate impact understood. After all, the common market had yet to be created after thirty years of the Treaty of Rome. Why would government leaders, the Commission, and business believe a single market could be created in just eight years?[23]

ERT members, for example, were not convinced that the single market provisions would be carried out in an expeditious manner. The ERT members created the Internal Market Support Committee (IMSC) to monitor governments' response to the single market initiative and apply pressure to government leaders and domestic groups when progress was slow. In December 1987, the IMSC delivered a stern message to government leaders at the Luxembourg summit: [S]how political will, or European industry will invest elsewhere.[24]

Recognizing the slow movement on the SEA, the European Commission called together a group of experts, chaired by Paolo Cecchini, to examine the benefits and costs of a single market. The 1998 Cecchini report outlined the "costs of non-Europe"—the difficulties associated with having separate nationally fragmented markets. The report also made a forceful case for continued support of the single market initiative, for example, arguing that the European Community could expect between 2 ½ to 6 ½ per cent increase in output.[25] While not all observers concurred—then and now—with the underlying assumptions and economic analysis in the Cecchini report, the European Commission touted the report's findings as compelling evidence for completing the single market.

Commission President Jacques Delors also pushed the SEA's implementation along. In February 1988, the European Council accepted a financial package proposed by Delors that substantially increased the European Council structural funds which could compensate those countries less likely to immediately benefit from the single market program. This initiative helped solidify support for the SEA's provisions from all European Community countries. The turning point for the SEA became evident that same year during the German presidency when a number of single market initiatives were approved. Thus, three years after the SEA was signed, the single market program was finally moving in a purposive direction. By the end of 1992, over nine-tenths of the Cockfield White Paper measures had been adopted, with only a few key issues (company law, double taxation of companies, etc.) remaining to be addressed. While the SEA had an inauspicious start, the treaty's overall success is now evident in the European marketplace.

8.2 KEY PROVISIONS OF THE SEA

The SEA was the first major formal revision of the Treaty of Rome which resulted in significant changes to the then-European Community. Of course, the creation of a single European market—which is defined in Article 7A of the Treaty Establishing the European Community as "an area without internal frontiers in which the free movement of goods, persons, services and capital"—is arguably the important legacy. To ensure that the approximately 300 legislative actions in the Cockfield White Paper were implemented, it was necessary to end the Luxembourg compromise and to promote a different voting procedure for internal market matters—the QMV in Council. Under the SEA, numerous articles of the Treaty of Rome—Articles 8A, 8B, 8C, 28 57(2), 59, 70(1) and 83—were amended to replace unanimity with QMV. Moreover, a new Article 100a called for QMV in all harmonization measures except for fiscal policy, free movement of peoples, and the rights of employees.[26] This new article in particular is recognized for accelerating the adoption of the single market.

Institutional Change. While European Community institutional change was not as expansive as envisioned in the Draft Treaty on European Union, the SEA allowed for significant institutional change. For the Commission, the SEA provided a formal framework within which the Council can formally delegate powers to the Commission. For the Parliament, the SEA allowed for greater assent and "cooperation" powers. The end of unanimity voting and further pooling of sovereignty signaled to some that other steps were needed to address the growing "legitimacy deficit." National governments recognized that they would "need to compensate for the expected loss of national parliaments' capacity of holding national executives to account under qualified majority voting, by strengthening the legislative powers of the EP."[27] The European Parliament thus gained the "cooperation procedure" for those sections of the treaty amended to provide for majority voting. This complex procedure essentially gave the European Parliament a second reading to legislation where the Council is required to consult with the Parliament. The latter also gained two other important powers that it continues to wield today— assent over admission of new members of the European Community, and assent in final agreements between the European Community and other states or organizations. As Allen has noted, this assent ability "gave the European Parliament powers over international agreements similar to those exercised by the US Senate and enabled the Parliament to exercise a degree of political conditionality over concessions offered by the EC."[28]

The SEA also created a new CFI designed to reduce the backlog of the overburdened ECJ. Direct actions brought by natural and legal persons to challenge the validity of European Community measures were brought before the new CFI. The European Council is another institution that was "new" in the SEA. Indeed, the SEA mentions the European Council for the first time alongside the Council of Ministers, although its role was not defined.

New Competences. The SEA also introduced five new competences to the Treaties: monetary capacity, social policy, economic and social cohesion, research and technological developments, and the environment. All are recognized as important components in creating the larger European market. The SEA is also notable for the competences not included in the treaty, including culture and education, development, and energy policy.[29]

For the first time, the SEA—in its preamble and the monetary chapter—cites economic and monetary union as an objective of the Treaty of Rome. The SEA also refers to the EMS and the European Currency Unit (ECU) for the first time, basically enshrining developments that existed in practice. While these advances were important, the SEA was also restrictive by stipulating that any further developments in monetary policy-making must be done through an IGC and treaty amendment. These restrictions proved less difficult three years later with the signing of the Maastricht Treaty which called for the establishment of an EMU.

The new social policy provisions allows for directives that could articulate "minimum criteria on the working environment and to protect the safety and health of workers."[30] Importantly, the new Article 118A calls for the Council to act on these directives on a qualified majority basis in Council. The SEA also allows national governments to enact legislation that would be stricter than European Community policy in this domain.

The economic and social policy competence promotes the idea of improving citizens' living and working conditions by reducing the gap between rich and poor.[31] The Regional Fund is formally identified and defined in the Treaty, and agreement was reached to rationalize the existing funds (regional, structural, social) under the economic and social cohesion policy.

The research and technology development competence was inserted to improve the European Community's own competitiveness in light of the growing economic and technological prowess of Japan, coupled with the Commission's own success in creating the ESPRIT program. The SEA empowers the Commission to create multi-annual framework programs and participation in R&D programs by European Community members.

Finally, the European Community environmental policy was designed to "preserve, protect and improve" the quality of the environment, use resources rationally, and, importantly, support the principle of "polluter pays."[32] The treaty also notes that whereas the European Community is charged with setting minimum standards, member states may maintain or propose more stringent national standards, provided they do not impede the single market. Thus, the SEA ensured that environmental standards would not be a "race for the bottom" but would promote higher environmental norms.

European Political Cooperation. The inclusion of EPC under Title III of the SEA was also an important development. Some member states had suggested that EPC be a treaty separate from the SEA but the negotiating parties ultimately agreed to incorporate it in the SEA. Nonetheless, Title III distinguishes EPC from the regular Treaty of Rome and refers to the "high contracting parties" as opposed to the "member states" in its provisions.[33] Article 30 refers to European foreign policy for the first time and largely codifies EPC practices that had been agreed to in earlier reports and agreements such as the London Report (1981) and the Solemn Declaration on European Union (1983). As such, the treaty language continues to call on the high contracting parties to "inform" and "consult." At the same time, it was agreed that the Commission would have a role in EPC and that the Council of Ministers could discuss EPC matters. (In the early 1970s, the Council took considerable pains to separate economic from political matters, including a meeting where all the ministers met under the European Council to discuss economic issues and moved to a different location on the same day to discuss political issues. While the SEA would eliminate such meeting arrangements, the treaty did not provide further clarity on what international issues could be defined as purely political (EPC) or economic (European Council) in nature.)

The SEA created a Brussels-based EPC secretariat to assist the presidency. It also formally calls for the parties to develop common positions in international organizations, thus promoting the creation of a European voting bloc. Furthermore, while the SEA mentions the term "security" for the first time, it does so with the agreement that the parties "coordinate positions more closely on the political and economic aspects of security, with no mention of defense or military aspects of security."[34]

8.3 THE SEA'S IMPACT

While the SEA's import was not recognized in the early years after its signing, its significance and impact have grown over the years. By the end of 1992, the twelve member states could boast a market of 350 million people, with more than 15 percent of the world's exports. By 2010, the European Union's twenty-seven members report a single market of nearly half a billion people, with a Gross Domestic Product larger than that of the United States. In short, the SEA created the single largest market in the world.

The SEA is significant in other ways. The single market, coupled with the European Community's new competences in social policy, R&D, and the environment, prompted new stakeholders in European Community policy-making. Indeed, Brussels saw a significant growth in interest group mobilization and advocacy in the years following the treaty's adoption and the expansion of supranational decision-making. These developments, in turn, prompted changes in the organization of interest groups and business–government relations in the member states, as well as the implementation of national policies.[35]

Countries outside the European Community also started paying greater attention to European integration. In the United States, many companies and legislators initially feared that the SEA and single market program would create a "Fortress Europe," where American goods could no longer enter with ease. While the fear of "Fortress Europe" subsided, American companies and law firms recognized that they, too, needed to pay closer attention to European Community developments.

Scholarly debates also changed. A resurgence in European integration studies occurred both in Europe and the United States as the salience of the single market program became apparent. As noted above, scholars sought to account for the single market program through competing—but not necessarily mutually exclusive—explanations. The 1960s debates resurfaced between neo-functionalists who noted the role of supranational actors behind the 1992 program and the SEA[36] and intergovernmentalists who singled out the role of government actors.[37] This debate was short-lived, when other scholars argued that the implementation of the single market program could best be explained by the literatures on comparative politics and public policy.[38] For these scholars, the European Community was not to be understood merely as an exercise in integration. Rather, the European Community had become a polity whose decision-making and governance could be compared to and understood in terms similar to that of national polities.

In the end, the SEA signaled a significant shift in the supranational decision-making of the European Community. Indeed, it was anticipated that it would take many years for European governments and their citizens to become accustomed to the single market. The events of 1989, however, changed the European landscape once again. While the SEA did not automatically lead to the Maastricht Treaty, it clearly laid a foundation for the creation of the EU six years later.

NOTES

1. A. Moravcsik, "Negotiating the Single European Act: National Interests and Conventional Statecraft in the European Community," *International Organization* 45, no. 1 (1991), 19–56.
2. W. Sandholtz and J. Zysman, "1992: Recasting the European Bargain," *World Politics* 42, no. 1 (1989), 95–128; and M. G. Cowles, "Setting the Agenda for a New Europe: The ERT and EC 1992," *Journal of Common Market Studies* 33, no. 4 (1995), 501–26.

3. J. J. Schreiber, *Le Défi Américain* (Paris: De Noel, 1967).

4. R. Corbett, "The 1985 Intergovernmental Conference and the Single European Act," in R. Pryce, ed., *The Dynamics of the European Union* (New York: Croom Helm, 1987), 238–72; and J. Lodge, "The Single European Act: Towards a New Euro-Dynamism?" *Journal of Common Market Studies* 24, no. 3 (1986), 203–23.

5. D. Allen, "European Union, the Single European Act and the 1992 Programme," in Dennis Swann, ed., *The Single European Market and Beyond: A Study of the Wider Implications of the Single European Act* (New York: Routledge, 1992), 33–4.

6. Moravcsik, "Negotiating the Single European Act: National Interests and Conventional Statecraft in the European Community," 19–56.

7. Sandholtz and Zysman, "1992: Recasting the European Bargain," 95–128; and Cowles, "Setting the Agenda for a New Europe: The ERT and EC 1992," 501–26.

8. Lodge, "The Single European Act: Towards a New Euro-Dynamism?" 204.

9. Allen, "European Union, the Single European Act and the 1992 Programme," 35.

10. Allen, "European Union, the Single European Act and the 1992 Programme," 40.

11. Corbett, "The 1985 Intergovernmental Conference and the Single European Act," 259.

12. Allen, "European Union, the Single European Act and the 1992 Programme," 33–4.

13. A. Forster and W. Wallace, "Common Foreign and Security Policy," in H. Wallace and W. Wallace, *Policy-Making in the European Union*, 3rd edition (Oxford: Oxford University Press, 1996), 415.

14. Moravcsik, "Negotiating the Single European Act: National Interests and Conventional Statecraft in the European Community," 19–56.

15. For an overview of these negotiations, see J. De Ruyt, *L'Acte Unique Européen* (Éditions de l'Université de Bruxelles, 1987).

16. Sandholtz and Zysman, "1992: Recasting the European Bargain," 95.

17. M. G. Cowles, "Setting the Agenda for a New Europe: The ERT and EC 1992," 501–26. Contrary to the arguments of a number of scholars, individual European companies had not mobilized in Brussels in any coordinated manner in the early years of the European Community. Indeed, a number of large firms were opposed to the creation of the common market. See J. Meynaud and D. Sidjanski, *Les Groupes de Pression dans la Communauté Européen, 1958–68* (Bruxelles: Éditions de l'Institut de Sociologie, 1971).

18. Cowles, "Setting the Agenda for a New Europe: The ERT and EC 1992," 506.

19. European Roundtable of Industrialists, *Missing Links* (Brussels: ERT, 1984).

20. Cowles, "Setting the Agenda for a New Europe: The ERT and EC 1992," 514.

21. European Roundtable of Industrialists, *Changing Scales* (Brussels: ERT, 1985).

22. A. Krause, *Inside the New Europe* (New York: HarperCollins, 1991), 86.

23. Cowles, "Setting the Agenda for a New Europe: The ERT and EC 1992," 518.

24. Cited in Cowles, "Setting the Agenda for a New Europe: The ERT and EC 1992," 519.

25. P. Cecchini, *The European Challenge* (London: Wildwood House, 1988).

26. Corbett, "The 1985 Intergovernmental Conference and the Single European Act," 246.

27. B. Rittberger, "The Creation and Empowerment of the European Parliament," *Journal of Common Market Studies* 41, no. 2 (2003), 218.

28. Allen, "European Union, the Single European Act and the 1992 Programme," 45.

29. Corbett, "The 1985 Intergovernmental Conference and the Single European Act," 262.

30. Corbett, "The 1985 Intergovernmental Conference and the Single European Act," 251.

31. Lodge, "The Single European Act: Towards a New Euro-Dynamism?" 213.

32. Lodge, "The Single European Act: Towards a New Euro-Dynamism?" 217.

33. Allen, "European Union, the Single European Act and the 1992 Programme," 47.

34. Allen, "European Union, the Single European Act and the 1992 Programme," 48–9.

35. M. G. Cowles, "The Transatlantic Business Dialogue and Domestic Business-Government Relations," in M. G. Cowles, J. Caporaso, and T. Risse, eds, *Transforming Europe: Europeanization and Domestic Change* (Ithaca, NY: Cornell University Press, 2001), 159–79.

36. Sandholtz and Zysman, "1992: Recasting the European Bargain," 95–128; and Cowles, "Setting the Agenda for a New Europe: The ERT and EC 1992," 501–26.

37. Moravcsik, "Negotiating the Single European Act: National Interests and Conventional Statecraft in the European Community," 19–56.

38. S. Hix, "The Study of the European Community: The Challenge to Comparative Politics," *West European Politics* 17, no. 1 (1994), 1–30.

CHAPTER 9

....

THE TREATY OF MAASTRICHT

....

FINN LAURSEN

THE Treaty of Maastricht, which created the EU, was signed in Maastricht on February 7, 1992, and it entered into force on November 1, 1993 after being ratified by the then twelve member states of the European Communities. It amended the Treaty Establishing the European Economic Community (EEC) and established the European Community as the first pillar in the union (Title II of the treaty). It also amended the Treaty Establishing the European Coal and Steel Community (Title III) and the Treaty Establishing the European Atomic Energy Community (Title IV). It then added two pillars of intergovernmental cooperation, namely Common Foreign and Security Policy (CFSP) in a second pillar (Title V) and Justice and Home Affairs (JHA) cooperation in a third pillar (Title VI). Title I included common provisions and Title VII included final provisions.[1]

The pillar structure was adopted to make it possible to differentiate decision-making procedures. The Community pillar applies what has become known as the Community method, initiated by the Treaties of Rome (see Chapter 7, this volume). Under this method the European Commission plays an important role as agenda setter. It has an exclusive right of initiative when legislation is adopted. Further, a number of decisions in the Council of Ministers can be made by a QMV. And the ECJ interprets Community law. It is a real court making binding decisions. The intergovernmental cooperation in the second and third pillar involves the Commission less, normally consensus is required, and the ECJ is largely excluded. The three-pillar structure survived until entry into force of the Lisbon Treaty in 2009.

The first pillar contained the plans for EMU, including the introduction of a single currency. It added various new policies and enhanced the role of the European Parliament by introducing the new co-decision procedure (Article 189b). It also extended the use of QMV.

CFSP was an improved version of the pre-existing EPC, which had existed since 1970, and which had been given a treaty basis in the SEA in 1987. CFSP remained intergovernmental cooperation as EPC had been. It added defense policy to the scope, but delegated its elaboration and implementation to the WEU.

JHA bundled a number of issues together, including asylum policy, external border control, immigration policy, combating drug addiction, combating fraud on an international scale, judicial cooperation in civil matters, judicial cooperation in criminal matters, customs cooperation, and police cooperation. Previously the member states had cooperated informally in most of these areas.

Overall, the Maastricht Treaty constituted one of the most important treaty changes in the history of European integration.

9.1 How the Treaty was Adopted

The treaty was negotiated by two IGCs, one dealing with EMU and the other with political union. The IGC on EMU was relatively well prepared thanks to the work of the Delors Committee, which had produced a report outlining how an EMU could be established through three stages. The decision to have a committee, chaired by Commission President Jacques Delors and including also the central bankers, prepare a report was made at the June 1988 Hannover meeting of the European Council. The report was finished in April 1989.[2] The decision to call the IGC on EMU was made in principle at the meeting of the European Council in Madrid in June 1989, and confirmed by the European Council meeting in Strasbourg in December of that same year. The IGC dealing with political union was decided the following year by the European Council in June 1990 in Dublin. The European Parliament had suggested a wider treaty reform on November 23, 1989, in the aftermath of the Cold War. It was on November 8, 1989 that the Berlin Wall fell. On November 28, 1989 German Chancellor Helmut Kohl announced a ten-point plan for German unification. This announcement surprised the other European Community member states which had not been consulted. French President François Mitterrand and UK Prime Minister Margaret Thatcher were against German unification. Eventually Mitterrand realized that he was fighting a losing battle. In April 1999 Kohl and Mitterrand took a joint initiative in a letter to the Irish Presidency supporting the idea of a second IGC on political union. The French had now concluded that further integration in Europe was the best way to bind a united Germany, and Kohl favored more political integration, including the strengthening of the European Parliament.[3] In their letter dated April 19 to the Irish Presidency, Kohl and Mitterrand said:

> The European Council should initiate preparations for an intergovernmental conference on political union. In particular, the objective is to: - strengthen the democratic legitimation of the union, - render its institutions more efficient, - ensure

unity and coherence of the union's economic, monetary and political action, - define and implement a common foreign and security policy.[4]

Prior to the Kohl–Mitterrand letter the European Parliament had adopted the Martin Report, on March 14, 1990 arguing that it was "increasingly necessary, rapidly to transform the European Community into a European Union of a federal type."[5] The Belgian government issued a memorandum on March 19 suggesting that political union be put on the agenda, either of the EMU IGC or of a separate, second IGC. The memorandum gave three reasons, "the transformation of the political scene in Europe," "the internal development of the Community, in particular the completion of the internal market and economic and monetary union," and "the special responsibility which the Community is generally thought to have for seeking solutions to the problems of Central and Eastern Europe."[6] Eventually most member states produced memorandums or proposals.

The two IGC started on December 15, 1990 in Rome during the Italian Presidency. The IGC on political union was less well prepared than the one on EMU, partly because it was decided later. It also ended up with an agenda that included some controversial points, based on diverse proposals from the European Parliament, the Commission, and member states.[7] The five big themes on the agenda were:

(1) Democratic legitimacy,
(2) Common foreign and security policy,
(3) European citizenship,
(4) New common policies, such as health, education, culture, and improvement of some of the existing policies, such as environment and social policy,
(5) Improving the effectiveness and efficiency of the EC.[8]

The IGCs then continued during 1991, first through the Luxembourg Presidency in the first half of 1991. The Luxembourg Presidency presented the first draft negotiating text for the IGC on political union, a so-called Non-Paper, in April 1991, and it presented the first Draft Treaty text on June 18, 1991.[9] The Draft Treaty text was based on the pillar approach. Article A said inter alia: "This Treaty marks a new stage in the process leading gradually to a Union with a federal goal."[10] The European Council meeting in Luxembourg at the end of June decided to take this draft as the basis for further negotiations.

The IGCs then continued through the Dutch Presidency during the second part of 1991. The Dutch presented a new Draft Treaty on September 30, 1991, which abandoned the pillar approach for a more unified treaty structure.[11] This, however, was rejected by a majority of the member states. The Dutch then duly presented a second draft Treaty based on the pillar approach in November 1991. The IGCs finished in December in Maastricht with a meeting of the heads of state or government. Some of the most controversial issues were only sorted out in Maastricht.

The major difficulties during the negotiations turned out to be the defense dimension of CFSP, social policy, economic and social cohesion, co-decision of the European Parliament, and extended application of QMV in the Council.

9.2 Economic and Monetary Union

Arguably the most important novelty of the first pillar was EMU. EMU was supposed to be introduced through three stages. The first stage started already in 1990. The second stage followed in 1994, including the creation of a European Monetary Institute (EMI), which should help coordinate national monetary policy and prepare for stage three. The final stage three, the introduction of the single currency and creation of the ECB, was based on controversial convergence criteria. If a majority of the member states fulfilled the necessary conditions by December 31, 1996 a qualified majority could decide to introduce the single currency—referred to as the ECU in the Treaty, but later changed to the euro. If not, then stage three would start on January 1, 1999 involving the member states fulfilling the convergence criteria then. The heads of state or government would decide by a QMV which member states fulfilled the necessary conditions in 1998. The solution was a compromise between the states that insisted on a fixed timetable, including France and Italy, and those who insisted on convergence as a precondition, including Germany and the Netherlands.

For domestic politics reasons the UK had problems with the proposed EMU and asked for an opt-out. This was one of the difficult issues in the negotiations. Should opt-outs be allowed, should there be a general opt-out clause or should opt-outs be country specific? Late in the IGC it was agreed to give the UK an opt-out through a protocol to the treaty.[12] Denmark then joined and asked for and got one too.[13] The other member states committed themselves to introduce the single currency.

The convergence criteria were:

- Inflation rate may not be higher than 1.5 percent of the average inflation rate of the three best performing countries
- Nominal long-term interest rate may not be higher that 2 percent of the average of the three best performing countries in terms of price stability
- The government deficit may not exceed 3 percent of GDP
- The government debt may not exceed 60 percent of GDP
- Observance of the normal fluctuations margins in the European Exchange Rate Mechanism (ERM), without devaluation for at least two years.[14]

In 1996 there was no majority of member states meeting the convergence criteria. In 1999 the third stage started with eight of the then twelve member states. It had been decided that Greece was too far from meeting the criteria. The UK and Denmark had their opt-outs, and Sweden chose to stay out for the moment.

The Maastricht Treaty also created a governance system for EMU, including the ESCB and the ECB. "The ESCB shall be composed of the ECB and the national central banks" (Art. 106 TEC).

"The Governing Council of the ECB shall comprise the members of the Executive Board of the ECB and the Governors of the national central banks.... The executive

Board shall comprise the President, the Vice-President and four other members" (Art. 109a, TEC).

The primary objective of the ESCB is price stability. The ECB has legal personality. The ESCB and ECB are independent.[15] The emphasis on price stability, which was also the objective of the German *Bundesbank*, was not uncontroversial. Some countries like to use monetary policy for other objectives, like job creation. The role for Community institutions was also controversial. The treaty assigns the main role in monetary policy to the ECB, but it also gives the Council of Ministers powers to deal with exchange rate policy (Article 109). France wanted the ECOFIN to become a *gouvernement économique*.

Fiscal policy remains a national responsibility. But there are rules against excessive deficits including the possibility of the Council imposing fines against a member state with an excessive deficit. Treaty provisions on deficits were further developed in June 1997 by the European Council prior to the adoption of the Amsterdam Treaty in the form of a controversial SGP.[16]

9.3 Main Policy Changes

The treaty made the subsidiarity principle more visible. The SEA had included it for environmental policy. Now it became a general principle for the new union, mentioned in the preamble as well as in Article 3b under the first pillar: "In areas which do not fall within its exclusive competence, the Community shall take action, in accordance with the principle of subsidiarity, only if and in so far as the objectives of the proposed action cannot be sufficiently achieved by the Member States and can therefore, by reason of the scale or effects of the proposed action, be better achieved by the Community" (Art. 3b, TEC).

The principle was sufficiently vague to find support from both those who wanted to restrain European integration, like the UK, and those who wanted the European Community/EU to become more federal, like Germany.[17]

On the insistence of the British in particular the proposal to mention "a federal goal" in Article A was taken out in Maastricht. Instead, the treaty talks about "creating an ever closer Union among the peoples of Europe, where decisions are taken as closely as possible to the citizens."[18]

A new concept in the treaty was that of citizenship of the union, championed especially by Spain. It includes the following:

- Right to move and reside freely within the territory of the Member States (Art. 8a, TEC);
- Right to vote and to stand as a candidate at municipal elections in the Member State in which one resides (Art. 8b(1), TEC);
- Right to vote and to stand as a candidate in elections to the European Parliament in the Member State in which one resides (Art.8b(2), TEC); and

- Right to protection by diplomatic or consular authorities of any Member State on the same condition as nationals of that state (Art. 8c, TEC).

The treaty introduced changes in some of the existing policy chapters and added new ones. The new policy chapters added to the treaty were the following: education, culture, public health, consumer protection, trans-European networks, industrial policy, and development cooperation. Social policy was controversial because of British opposition. The new Prime Minister John Major, who had taken over from Margaret Thatcher, was not able to accept a social policy chapter in the treaty. In the end, eleven member states decided to develop social policy, but the UK was given an opt-out.[19] The eleven would use QMV for some decisions among themselves. But some decisions would require unanimity.

The objective of social policy was defined as "promotion of employment, improved living and working conditions, proper social protection, dialogue between management and labor, the development of human resources with a view to lasting high employment and the combating of exclusion."[20] In order to do that the European Community would "support and complement the activities of the Member States in the following fields":

> Improvement in particular of the working environment to protect workers' health; working conditions; the information and consultation of workers; equality between men and women with regard to labor market opportunities and treatment at work; and the integration of persons excluded from the labor market.[21]

The cooperation procedure would be applied to adopt directives. However, for some sensitive areas unanimity would be required and the European Parliament would only be consulted, namely the following:

> Social security and social protection of workers; protection of workers where their employment contract is terminated; representation and collective defense of the interests of workers and employers, including co-determination; conditions of employment for third-country nationals legally residing in Community territory; and financial contributions for promotion and job-creation, without prejudice to the provisions relating to the Social Fund.[22]

Energy, civil protection, and tourism are mentioned in Article 3, but no special chapter on these policy areas were included in the treaty, despite proposals to do so.

There were changes in some existing policy chapters, including common commercial policy, economic and social cohesion, research and technological development, and environment.

Economic and social cohesion was controversial, especially because Spain requested a treaty commitment to doubling the structural funds to be able to prepare for EMU. This was not granted but a new Cohesion Fund was created. It would contribute "to provide a financial contribution to projects in the fields of environment and trans-European networks in the area of transport infrastructure" (Art. 130d, TEC).

Concerning environmental policy, which first got a treaty chapter in the SEA, the use of QMV was now introduced, with the exception of the following which would still require unanimity:

Provisions primarily of a fiscal nature; Measures concerning town and country planning, land use with the exception of waste management and measures of a general nature, and management of water resources and measures significantly affecting a Member State's choice between different energy sources and the general structure of its energy supply. (Art. 130s(2), TEC)

As in the case of social policy we see that the member states insist on unanimity for policy areas considered sensitive in domestic politics.

Among the new policy areas included in the treaty, culture and industrial policy would be based on unanimity. France insisted on unanimity for culture, including the audiovisual area. Some countries, including France, wanted an European Community industrial policy. Others, including the UK, did not see the need for such a policy. It was included on condition that it would be based on unanimity.

All in all the policy scope of European integration was expanded substantially by the Maastricht Treaty.

9.4 THE NEW PILLARS

CFSP was also new, without being a radical departure from the existing trajectory of foreign policy cooperation. In the run-up to the IGC on political union it was clear that CFSP would be an important but controversial point on the agenda, especially because of British hesitation about a defense dimension. During the IGC in June 1991 the war broke out in Yugoslavia, reminding the European Community member states of the importance of the issue, but the views about what to do diverged considerably between them. On October 5 "An Anglo-Italian Declaration on European Security and Defense" was issued. It emphasized the Atlantic dimension of security, but the British accepted the idea of a European defense policy:

> Political union implies the gradual elaboration and implementation of a common foreign and security policy and a stronger European defense identity with the longer term perspective of a common defense policy compatible with the common defense policy we already have with all our allies in NATO.[23]

More concretely it was proposed that the

> WEU should be entrusted with the task of developing the European dimension in the field of defense, it will develop its role in two complementary directions: as the defense component of the Union and as the means to strengthen the European pillar of the Alliance.[24]

The Anglo–Italian Declaration also suggested the development by the WEU of a European reaction force.

A Franco–German Initiative on Foreign Security and Defense Policy followed on October 11, 1991. The objectives included a "common defense," not just defense policy:

To affirm its identity on the international scene, particularly with regard to the implementation of a common foreign and security policy which, in the long term, would include a common defense.[25]

The Initiative saw the WEU as an "integral part of the process of European Union" and called for the "development of a clear organic relationship between the WEU and the Union, and the operational organization of the WEU, which shall act in conformity with the Directives of the Union."[26] It further suggested that other countries could join the Franco–German Brigade. Eventually the IGC produced a text on CFSP, including defense.

Under CFSP the EU is supposed to establish systematic cooperation, define common positions, and adopt joint actions. The most novel aspect was that the treaty added defense policy, as a delicate compromise: "The common foreign and security policy shall include all questions related to the security of the Union, including the eventual framing of a common defense policy, which might in time lead to a common defense" (Art. J.4(1), TEU). The vagueness of the text suggests the lack of a common conception. A balance had to be found between pro-Atlantic/NATO countries and pro-European countries. The language also had to be acceptable to neutral Ireland. The compromise language found included the following: "The policy of the Union in accordance with this Article shall not prejudice the specific character of the security and defense policy of certain Member States and shall respect the obligations of certain Member States under the North Atlantic Treaty and be compatible with the common security and defense policy established within that framework" (Art. J.4(4), TEU).

JHA basically foresaw three instruments: joint positions and joint action (borrowed from CFSP) as well as the drawing up of conventions. The member states and the Commission would share the right of initiative. The possibility of negotiating separate conventions also included the possibility of involving ECJ through such conventions.

A special Coordinating Committee was created for JHA, known as the Article K.4 Committee. The Commission would be "fully associated with the work."

9.5 THE MAIN INSTITUTIONAL CHANGES

The Maastricht Treaty gave the European Parliament new powers:

1. It may request the Commission to submit a proposal (Art. 138b, TEC),
2. it may set up a temporary Committee of Inquiry to investigate alleged contraventions or maladministration (Art 138c, TEC),
3. citizens may address a petition to the Parliament (Art. 138d, TEC),
4. it shall appoint an Ombudsman (Art. 138e, TEC),
5. it shall approve the President and other members of the Commission (Art. 158(2), TEC), and
6. it gets a right of co-decision in some areas (Art. 189b, TEC).

The introduction of the new co-decision procedure, arguably the most important institutional novelty, took the EU towards a bicameral system. And the power to approve the
Commission President was also important, even if it did not amount to the kind of
power parliaments have to appoint prime ministers in parliamentary systems. Maastricht
did not create a full-fledged federal system, but it empowered the European Parliament
further and opened up new possibilities of accountability.

The question of efficiency was first of all dealt with through the extended use of QMV.
The treaty expanded the use of QMV to about thirty existing or new policy areas. These
included several aspects of EMU and many new policies, such as education, public
health, consumer protection, and development cooperation. It also included certain
environmental policy measures.[27] We should also mention QMV for certain aspects of
social policy among the eleven member states, minus the UK.

The new co-decision procedure, which enhanced the legislative role of the European
Parliament, included the fifteen following areas:

> Free movement of workers, right of establishment, coordination of provisions for
> special treatment of foreign nationals, mutual recognition of diplomas, coordina-
> tion of provisions for the self-employed, most provisions concerning services, har-
> monization of laws for the internal market, mutual recognition of non-harmonized
> provisions, education (incentive measures, excluding legislative harmonization),
> culture (incentive measures, excluding legislative harmonization), public health
> (incentive measures, excluding legislative harmonization), consumer protection
> (specific supplementary measures), trans-European networks (guidelines), multi-
> annual framework program for research and technology and general action pro-
> grams for some areas of the environment.[28]

Maastricht also created a new Committee of the Regions "consisting of representatives
of regional and local bodies." It has to be consulted by the Council and Commission on
certain questions.

With respect to the ECJ, the most important change was a provision including the
possibility of imposing "a lump sum or penalty payment" on a member state which
"failed to fulfill an obligation" under the treaty.

9.6 RATIFICATION OF MAASTRICHT

The ratification of the Maastricht Treaty did not go smoothly. On June 2, 1992 the Danes
voted "No" in a referendum. In France it was barely accepted in a referendum in
September 1992 and UK Prime Minister John Major had big problems getting it through
Parliament.[29]

The first shock for the political establishment came when 50.7 percent of the Danes
voted "No" to Maastricht on June 2, 1992. The Foreign Ministers of the member states
that happened to be in Oslo for a NATO meeting agreed on June 4 that the ratification

process should continue. So the Danish problem was a problem for Denmark to solve. The other country that needed a referendum to ratify the treaty, Ireland, was much more successful, with 69 percent of the Irish voting "Yes" on June 18.

When the Danes voted "No," President Mitterrand decided the following day that there should be a referendum in France too, expecting probably a relatively easy win. As the referendum day, September 20, approached, the opinion polls showed an increasingly narrow battle. In the end, the French accepted the treaty with only 51.05 percent of "Yes" votes. In the Benelux countries—Italy, Spain, and Portugal—parliamentary ratifications went smoothly.

To solve the Danish problem the leading opposition parties drafted a so-called national compromise which was accepted by the government parties with only minor changes. It was sent to the other member states on October 30, 1992. In it the Danish government sought four special arrangements, namely for defense policy, the single currency, citizenship of the Union, and supranational JHA cooperation.[30] The Edinburgh meeting of the European Council basically satisfied the Danish request. An agreement was reached that gave Denmark the four special arrangements—referred to in Denmark as *forbehold* (reservations).

A second referendum then took place in Denmark on May 18, 1993. This time the treaty supplemented with the special arrangements granted by the Edinburgh agreement was accepted by 56.7 percent of the Danish electorate. In the meantime the Conservative–Liberal government led by Prime Minister Poul Schlüter had been replaced by a four-party government led by Social Democrat Poul Nyrup Rasmussen. (The change of government was unrelated to the Maastricht issue.) The main difference between 1992 and 1993 was that a much larger proportion of the Social Democratic voters voted "Yes" in 1993. Important for the difference was also that the Socialist People's Party, which had been against the Maastricht Treaty in 1992, was actively involved in reaching the National Compromise and supported the treaty with the reservations in 1993.

Two days after the "Yes" victory in the second Danish referendum the UK House of Commons approved the treaty, and the House of Lords followed on July 20. On October 12 the German Constitutional Court ruled on the constitutionality of the treaty, so Germany could complete its ratification, as the last member state to ratify. The treaty entered into force on November 1, 1993.

9.7 EXPLAINING THE MAASTRICHT TREATY

Scholars give various reasons why the Maastricht Treaty was adopted and emphasize different factors influencing the negotiation process. They disagree on the relative importance of economic, geopolitical, and ideational factors. Andrew Moravcsik emphasized economic factors in his liberal intergovernmentalist interpretation. Starting from national preference formation, demands from economic actors were seen as very important. He admitted that geopolitical factors, including pro-European ideology, had played a role, but a secondary one. Concerning influence during the negotiations he focused on asymmetrical interdependence. Those who depend most on an agreement are willing to compromise most. Institutional choice, the pooling and delegation of sovereignty that had taken place in the European Community, was explained as a way to get "credible commitments." Pooling refers to the use of majority voting. Delegation refers to the powers given to supranational bodies, primarily to the Commission and the ECJ. His empirical research focused on France, Germany, and the UK.[31]

Other scholars have emphasized high-politics factors, the end of the Cold War and German unification.[32] Then there are scholars who go back to early integration theory, neo-functionalism, and see elements of spillover from preceding integration, including the internal market and the existing monetary cooperation, EMS, often combined with other factors.[33]

Derek Beach discussed the role of Community institutions in treaty reforms, including Maastricht. He admits that the Commission played less of a role in the Maastricht negotiations that in the previous reform, the SEA.[34]

One could also approach the question eclectically and say that a number of factors interacted to produce the Maastricht Treaty and that these factors do not fit neatly into any particular theory. Some were international systemic factors, like the end of the Cold War. Others were endogenous to the European Community system, like spillover and learning processes. Domestic politics is also an important factor. Nor should the question of agency, the role of particular leaders like Kohl, Mitterrand, and Delors, be ignored. Such leaders provided ideas and leadership for the process.[35]

The emphasis on explanatory factors also depends on the part of the Maastricht Treaty you try to explain. It can be argued that the explanation of EMU is not theoretically the same as the explanation of CFSP. Here it has to be mentioned that Moravcsik focused on the EMU part of Maastricht. The IGC on political union only "generated modest results," he said.[36] Explaining EMU consistently with liberal intergovernmentalism, he argued that "national preferences... were driven primarily by the enduring structural economic interests of strong- and weak-currency countries under conditions of increased capital mobility and macroeconomic convergence. They were essentially unchanged by German reunification." The national positions, he argued, were "consistently supported by a decisive majority in peak business groups in both France and Germany."[37]

Looking at influence during the interstate bargaining, Moravcsik argued that "the outcomes of distributive conflict... consistently reflected the preferences of Germany—the country with the tightest domestic win-set and the most to give up in the monetary negotiations." And, "finally, the choice of institutions reflected above all the need for credible commitments, in particular Germany's desire to 'lock in' a guarantee of low inflation by creating an autonomous ECB, by far the most contentious issue in the negotiations."[38]

Looking at the timing of events can be useful. The Delors Committee finished its report in the spring of 1989 before the end of the Cold War, but the decision to have a second parallel IGC on political union, which came in the first half of 1990, was influenced by the fall of the Berlin Wall on November 11, 1989 and the subsequent German unification. The end of the Cold War created a fundamentally new situation in Europe with new demands to and responsibilities of the European Community. The EMU plans followed the relatively successful monetary cooperation within the EMS, which however had produced an asymmetry in favor of the German currency, the *Deutschmark*, and the German central bank, the *Bundesbank*. Some European Community member states, France and Italy in particular, became increasingly dissatisfied with the system and called for a real monetary union. Alternatively, one could also see EMU as a kind of spillover from the internal market. The Commission produced a study entitled *One Market, One Money*, a title that suggested spillover. But in reality there was a strong element of power politics inside the Community. France and some other member states could not accept the fact that Germany was in the driving seat when it came to monetary policy.[39]

9.8 SIGNIFICANCE OF MAASTRICHT

Maastricht created the current EU. Many see EMU as the most important achievement of the treaty. But it also expanded the scope of European integration to several new policy areas and it improved the institutions in various ways. The introduction of co-decision empowered the European Parliament and it should in principle contribute to the democratic legitimacy of the EU. The extended use of QMV should in principle make it easier to arrive at decisions among an increasing number of member states and thus improve efficiency.

Maastricht further formalized intergovernmental cooperation in two new pillars, CFSP and JHA cooperation. Since decisions normally require unanimity these pillars have not been very efficient. But the member states were not ready to accept the use of the Community method for these areas in 1991.

The ratification problems gave impetus to the debate about a democratic deficit, accountability, and openness in the EU. They were to remain on the agenda of the subsequent treaty reforms, from the Amsterdam Treaty to the Lisbon Treaty, and they were central agenda points during the European Convention, 2003–2004.

Since the negotiators in Maastricht realized some of the shortcomings of their agreement, they decided that a new IGC should take place already in 1996. IGC 1996–1997 produced the next treaty reform, The Amsterdam Treaty, which started moving JHA to the first pillar, but only included minor reforms of CFSP (see Chapter 10, this volume). Eventually the Lisbon Treaty abolished the pillar structure, only to leave special procedures for CFSP, which de facto remained a kind of separate pillar (see Chapter 12, this volume).

NOTES

1. Council of the European Communities (1992), *Treaty on European Union*. Luxembourg: Office for Official Publications of the European Communities; also in *Official Journal of the European Communities*, No. C 224/1, August 31, 1992.

2. For chronology, see Richard Corbett, *The Treaty of Maastricht: From Conception to Ratification: A Comprehensive Reference Guide* (Harlow, Essex: Longman Current Affairs, 1993), pp. xvi–xxii.

3. See for instance Michael J. Baun, "The Maastricht Treaty as High Politics: Germany, France, and European Integration," *Political Science Quarterly* 110, no. 4 (1995–96), 605–24.

4. Text reproduced in Finn Laursen and Sophie Vanhoonacker, eds, *The Intergovernmental Conference on Political Union: Institutional Reforms, New Policies and International Identity of the European Community* (Maastricht: European Institute of Public Administration, 1992), 276.

5. Quoted from Finn Laursen, Sophie Vanhoonacker, and Robert Wester, "Overview of the Negotiations," in Laursen and Vanhoonacker, eds, *The Intergovernmental Conference on Political Union*, 5.

6. Text reproduced in Laursen and Vanhoonacker, *The Intergovernmental Conference on Political Union*, 269.

7. Corbett, *The Treaty of Maastricht*, 14–29.

8. Laursen et al., "Overview," 11–12; Yves Doutriaux, *Le Traité sur l'Union européenne* (Paris: Armand Colin, 1992), 50.

9. Reproduced in Laursen and Vanhoonacker, *The Intergovernmental Conference on Political Union*, 358–406.

10. Text in Laursen and Vanhoonacker, *The Intergovernmental Conference on Political Union*, 358.

11. External Relations part of text reproduced in Laursen and Vanhoonacker, *The Intergovernmental Conference on Political Union*, 407–12.

12. "Protocol on Certain Provisions Relating to the United Kingdom of Great Britain and Northern Ireland" in Council of the European Communities, *Treaty on European Union*, 191–3.

13. "Protocol on Certain Provisions Relating to Demark" in Council of the European Communities, *Treaty on European Union*, 194.

14. Article 109j and "Protocol on the Convergence Criteria," in Council of the European Communities, *Treaty on European Union*, 185–6.

15. For details, see "Protocol on the Statute of the European System of Central Banks and of the European Central Bank" in Council of the European Communities, *Treaty on European Union*, 148–71.

16. Loukas Tsoukalis, "Economic and Monetary Union: Political Conviction and Economic Uncertainty," in Helen Wallace and William Wallace, eds, *Policy-Making in the European Union*, 4th edition (Oxford: Oxford University Press, 2000), 168.

17. Brendan P. G. Smith, *Constitution Building in the European Union: The Process of Treaty Reforms* (The Hague: Kluwer Law International, 2002), 129.

18. Text in Laursen and Vanhoonacker, *The Intergovernmental Conference on Political Union*, 429

19. "Protocol on Social Policy" in Council of the European Communities, *Treaty on European Union*, 196.

20. "Agreement on Social Policy concluded the Member States of the European Community with the exception of the United Kingdom of Great Britain and Northern Ireland" in Council of the European Communities, *Treaty on European Union*, 197–201, Article 1.

21. "Agreement on Social Policy…," Article 2(1).

22. "Agreement on Social Policy…," Article 2(3).

23. Text in Laursen and Vanhoonacker, *The Intergovernmental Conference on Political Union*, 413–14.

24. Laursen and Vanhoonacker, *The Intergovernmental Conference on Political Union*, 413–14.
25. Text in Laursen and Vanhoonacker, *The Intergovernmental Conference on Political Union*, 416.
26. Laursen and Vanhoonacker, *The Intergovernmental Conference on Political Union*, 417.
27. Vaughne Miller, "The Extension of Qualified Majority Voting from the treaty of Rome to the European Constitution," *House of Commons Research Paper 2004/54* (7 July), 13–14.
28. Edward Best, "The Treaty on European Union: What Does it actually Say and Do?" in Finn Laursen and Sophie Vanhoonacker, eds, *The Ratification of the Maastricht Treaty: Issues, Debates and Future Implications* (Dordrecht: Martinus Nijhoff Publishers, 1994), 17–44.
29. Finn Laursen, and Sophie Vanhoonacker, eds, *The Ratification of the Maastricht Treaty: Issues, Debates and Future Implications* (Dordrecht: Martinus Nijhoff Publishers, 1994).
30. Finn Laursen, "Denmark and the Ratification of the Maastricht Treaty," in Laursen and Vanhoonacker, *The Ratification of the Maastricht Treaty*, 61–86.
31. Andrew Moravcsik, *The Choice for Europe: Social Purpose and State Power from Messina to Maastrich* (Ithaca, NY: Cornell University Press, 1998).
32. e.g. Baun, "The Maastricht Treaty"; see also Geoffrey Garrett, "The Politics of Maastricht," *Economics and Politics*, 5, no. 2 (July 1993), 105–23.
33. See for instance Wayne Sandholtz, "Choosing Union: Monetary Politics and Maastricht," *International Organization 47*, no. 1 (Winter 1993), 1–39.
34. Derek Beach, *The Dynamics of European Integration: Why and When EU Institutions Matter* (Basingstoke: Palgrave Macmillan, 2005).
35. Finn Laursen, "Explaining the Intergovernmental Conference on Political Union," in Laursen and Vanhoonacker, *The Intergovernmental Conference on Political Union*, 229–48.
36. Moravcsik, *The Choice for Europe*, 379.
37. Moravcsik, *The Choice for Europe*, 381.
38. Moravcsik, *The Choice for Europe*, 386.
39. See also Joseph M. Grieco, "The Maastricht Treaty, Economic and Monetary Union and the Neo-Realist Research Programme," *Review of International Studies 21*(1995), 21–40.

CHAPTER 10

THE TREATY OF AMSTERDAM

SOPHIE VANHOONACKER

10.1 FROM MAASTRICHT TO AMSTERDAM

As like any political system, the EU was not built in one day but its institutional structure, common policies, and rules have gradually been shaped on a day-to day basis with regular moments of consolidation and reform at IGCs. Between the signature of the Rome Treaties (1957) and the fall of the Berlin wall (1989), there was only one IGC, leading to the SEA (1987). In contrast, in the period 1991–2000 there have been three IGCs, respectively leading to the Treaties of Maastricht, Amsterdam, and Nice.

This increase in high number of revisions in just one decade is not accidental. The original Treaties had been signed in the context of a divided Europe (and Germany) and mainly concentrated on the creation of an internal market. Following the fall of the Berlin wall, the dramatically changed circumstances in Europe required a new response. Three main challenges stood out: the development of Europe's political muscle, the strengthening of its institutional foundations, and the relation with the European citizens. As there was no agreement on how to address these complex questions, it proved impossible to tackle all the issues at once in Maastricht. As a matter of fact the Maastricht Treaty explicitly foresaw that a number of issues would again be discussed at a new IGC in 1996.

The 1996–1997 IGC leading to the Amsterdam Treaty was therefore in the first place an attempt to deal with some of the leftovers of the 1991 IGC. At the same time, however, it is more than merely an extension of Maastricht as the deliberations took place against a changed background. In 1994 the Union had been enlarged to include Austria, Finland, and Sweden, three neutral and non-aligned countries with their own particular views on Europe's future development. Furthermore, the European Council of Copenhagen (June 1993) had given further urgency to the question of institutional reform by opening the prospect of enlargement to the Central and Eastern European countries.[1] In addition, a number of member states had entered the second stage of the EMU, bringing the single currency one step closer and increasing the pressure to conclude the IGC before moving to the third and final phase of EMU.[2]

Following a brief introduction on the preparatory stage of the 1996–1997 IGC, this chapter starts by giving an overview of its main players. Secondly, it examines the main themes that were discussed and presents the results. The conclusion takes stock of the outcome and presents some final remarks on how to make sense of the Amsterdam IGC.

10.2 GETTING READY

Negotiations in the EU are always a delicate balance of keeping both the more ambitious as well as the minimalist member states on board. One of the devices used to keep the maximalist countries at the Maastricht negotiation table was to create the prospect of revising some of the provisions at a later stage. The TEU did not only name the date of the next IGC (1996),[3] it also already identified a number of questions for further discussion. These included the extension of co-decision to new policy areas, questions related to the security of the Union and the CFSP more broadly, and issues such as energy, tourism, civil protection, and the hierarchy of norms. This was however not meant to be an exclusive agenda and in the run-up to the IGC, several other issues were added.

As had also been the case with Maastricht, especially EMU, the IGC was preceded by substantial preparations. Between June and December 1995, a Reflection Group chaired by the Spanish State Secretary for European Affairs Carlos Westendorp and composed by high-level national representatives of the member states, the European Commission and the European Parliament[4] brainstormed about the IGC's agenda. Its final report (December 1995) identified three main priorities: bringing Europe closer to its citizens; enabling the Union to function better and preparing it for enlargement; and endowing the EU with a greater capacity for external action.

The IGC officially started with a European Council meeting in Turin under the Italian Presidency (March 29, 1996) and was concluded almost one and a half years later in Amsterdam (June 16–17, 1997). Formally the ministers of foreign affairs were responsible for conducting the negotiations but in practice the greater part of the work was done by the Group of Representatives meeting on an almost weekly basis.[5] The most sensitive questions and key bargains were reserved for the highest level of the European Council.

The Treaty entered into force on May 1, 1999. For most member states, this implied approval by their national parliaments and in the case of Denmark and Ireland a referendum. In France the ratification also required constitutional revision.[6] Compared to both Maastricht—where the Danes initially rejected the Treaty (see Chapter 9, this volume)—and Lisbon with almost nine years between the Laeken declaration (December 2001) and its entering into force (December 2009), the ratification process was relatively smooth.

10.3 ACTORS AND PROCESSES

An IGC is in the first place a bargaining process. Using the metaphor of diplomatic Darwinism, Bobby McDonagh, the deputy to the Irish IGC representative, compares it to a slow evolutionary process in which only the fittest ideas survive.[7] At the core of any IGC negotiation are the national governments and their representatives. Member states, mainly in interaction with domestic public opinion, determine their preferences and identify their core priorities. These are translated into position papers, presented either on an individual basis or in cooperation with like-minded delegations. Although in principle all players are equal, history shows that size matters and that it is difficult to make progress if the bigger member states are not on board.[8] Also, during the Amsterdam IGC, the Franco–German axis led by the French President Jacques Chirac and the German Chancellor Helmut Kohl was again a force to count on, although it was not as forceful as it was in Maastricht. While they put forward joint proposals on flexibility and the reform of CFSP, they disagreed on institutional reform. Also domestic factors such as the unexpected victory of the French socialists in the parliamentary elections (May 1997) and opposition from the German *Länder* against further pooling of sovereignty negatively affected the Franco–German motor.

The role and position of the United Kingdom was a very good illustration of how domestic politics is never far away from the negotiation table.[9] The predilection of the conservative government of John Major for the status quo and the expectation of a change in leadership after the elections of May 1997 put London in a relatively isolated position. The victory of Tony Blair enabled agreement to be reached on the Employment Title and ended the opt-out on social policy but on most other issues there was continuity.[10]

In the 1996–1997 IGC, there were for the first time sixteen delegations sitting around the table (member states plus Commission). This large number made it imperative for delegations to look for allies; especially for the smaller member states, this was the most effective way to make their voice heard. Denmark, for example, forged a coalition with two of the new member states, Finland and Sweden. Together they managed to foster progress in "Nordic" priority areas such as the environment, employment, and fundamental rights and non-discrimination.[11] On the other hand, Belgium, Luxembourg, and The Netherlands tried to work together in a Benelux framework or joined forces with other players on the maximalist side of the spectrum, such as the European Commission, Italy, France, and Germany. Very often coalitions varied according to the issue. Portugal, for instance, teamed up with Ireland, Luxembourg, and the Nordic countries on institutional reform while on the flexibility dossier it collaborated with the UK, Greece, and Sweden.[12]

In any IGC, the country holding the Presidency occupies a key position. As chair of all the meetings, it does not only fulfill an important organizational and mediating role, but it is also in a privileged position to steer the negotiations and have an impact on the final outcome. Its papers and proposals are a key instrument to streamline the discussions and to identify common ground. The chair is helped by the experienced staff of the Council General Secretariat.[13] The three countries that chaired the 1996–1997 IGC were Italy (first half of 1996), Ireland (second half of 1996), and The Netherlands (first half of 1997). The Italian Presidency started with an initial exploration of the many issues on the table and summarized the findings in a Progress Report presented to the Florence European Council (June 21–22, 1996).[14] The contribution of Ireland consisted in bringing the different positions closer together and coming up with concrete suggestions for Treaty amendments. The result of these multiple discussions—including an extra European Council in early October (Dublin I)—was an outline draft treaty covering all the aspects of the Conference and on several issues already providing concrete draft treaty texts.[15]

It was clear, however, that the most sensitive issues would be left for the concluding Dutch Presidency. Important outstanding questions were the integration of Schengen into the Treaty, the transitional decision-making arrangements for asylum and migration, as well as institutional reform. On the former two it managed to hammer out a deal but on institutional reform the water between the small and big member states proved too deep and the issue was postponed to a later IGC (see above).

Last but not least, any account of the actors in an IGC should include the European Commission. Contrary to the European Parliament, which is only an associated member, the Commission is present at all meetings. Its task is to look at the reform process through European lenses. Having been criticized for overplaying its hand during the Maastricht negotiations, it decided to adopt a more pragmatic approach. Apart from a number of proposals on very specific dossiers, it mainly operated behind the scenes by closely cooperating with the Presidency and the Council General Secretariat.[16]

The next sections of this chapter examine in more detail the main issues on the IGC agenda. What did the treaty reform bring for the EU citizens? To what extent did it strengthen the EU's international role? What were the main achievements in terms of institutional reform? And finally, what were the provisions on flexible cooperation?

10.4 Bringing Europe Closer to its Citizens

All member states agreed that a key priority for the Amsterdam IGC was to address the increasingly loud criticism that the EU was doing too little for "the ordinary European citizen" and that it was important to deal with questions dominating the public debate such as migration, asylum, and the fight against crime. Despite the sensitivity of some of the issues, it was these areas where the IGC made the most important progress. Firstly, the national delegations agreed on a number of substantial steps in terms of fundamental rights, employment, and social policy. Secondly, there was an extensive revision of the heavily criticized third pillar.

The new Treaty explicitly referred to the fundamental rights of the EU citizens, now firmly enshrined into TEU, Title I, Article 6, and confirmed that the Union is based on the principles of liberty, democracy, respect for human rights and fundamental freedoms, and the rule of law. In the light of the upcoming enlargement with countries with a limited democratic tradition, the Fifteen introduced a mechanism whereby the rights (including the voting rights) of member states breaching fundamental rights could be suspended by QMV by the Council, meeting in the composition of the heads of state or government.[17] Furthermore a new general non-discrimination clause allowing the Council to adopt legislation combating discrimination based on sex, racial or ethnic origin, religion and belief, disability, age, or sexual orientation was introduced.[18]

In response to high levels of unemployment and the criticism that it was primarily the big firms that benefited from European integration, the IGC members agreed on the introduction of a new title on *employment* and further steps in the development of a *social policy*. Under the impulse of various proposals from Sweden, they decided to improve the coordination of the multiple national initiatives.[19] While the primary responsibility still remained with the national capitals, a high level of employment became an official EU objective, also to be taken into account in the development of other Community policies. As mentioned earlier, in the area of social policy the UK, under the new government of Tony Blair, gave up its opt-out leading to the integration of the Maastricht Social Protocol into the Treaty. This opened the prospect for new initiatives in areas such as social protection of workers, their representation, and employment conditions for third-country nationals. In addition, it was also agreed to introduce measures on combating social exclusion. To the regret of many, however, the UK was not ready to give up unanimity in these sensitive areas and partly in consequence of this there has been relatively little legislative activity in this area. On the more positive side, the Treaty introduced a legal basis for action in the area of equal opportunities and equal treatment of men and women at work.

The second block of measures addressing the direct concerns of the citizens related to the reform of the heavily criticized third pillar introduced at Maastricht (TEU, Title VI) (see Chapter 9, this volume). The complexity and sensitivity of the topic made the negotiation process very difficult but overall the results were rather impressive. Notwithstanding the strong opposition of the UK and Denmark, all provisions on the free movement of persons, asylum and immigration, and judicial cooperation in civil matters were moved to a new Treaty title in the first pillar (Title IV). The price to be paid for this communitarization, entailing the exclusive right of initiative for the European Commission[20] and judicial review by the ECJ, was an opt-out for Denmark, Ireland, and the UK. The third pillar itself was left with police cooperation and judicial cooperation in criminal matters. Its objectives were made more explicit and the legal instrument of the convention was replaced by the framework decision.[21]

A further important step was the integration of the Schengen *acquis*[22] into the EU legal framework by means of a protocol. This was mainly the result of the hard work of the Dutch Presidency and its Secretary of State for European Affairs Michiel Patijn for whom this was a top priority.[23] The 1985 Schengen agreement, whereby a small group consisting of the Benelux, France, and Germany had started the creation of a borderless zone, had been developed outside the EU Treaties and gradually been extended to all member states except for Ireland and the United Kingdom.[24] The protocol was a general agreement on integrating all the decisions and declarations adopted by the Schengen bodies into the Community legislation. Depending on whether it concerns freedom of movement or police cooperation, the acts are legally based on the first or third pillar. This "lock, stock, and barrel" or "big bang" approach has the advantage that all legislation has to be accepted by all future member states. Denmark had recently joined Schengen but it wanted to remain exempted from the part of the Schengen *acquis* that would become part of the legislation in the first pillar.[25] The UK and Ireland, who had their own Common Travel Area, maintained their right to exert border controls.

10.5 EUROPE ON THE INTERNATIONAL SCENE

Against the backdrop of the fall of the Berlin wall, uncertainties about transatlantic relations, and the Yugoslav conflict, the development of a more full-fledged European foreign policy had already been discussed extensively in Maastricht leading to the establishment of the CFSP.[26] Although a step forward compared to the earlier EPC, the intergovernmental character and the lack of military instruments to back up the EU's foreign policy efforts remained a source of weakness. This was well illustrated by the EU's incapacity to be a player in the bloody conflict in Bosnia and the instability in the Balkans more broadly. The gap between the EU's economic and political weight remained huge.

The deliberations leading to the Amsterdam Treaty revolved around two main questions. The first objective was to make the foreign policy-making process more effective. Secondly, the member states discussed how they could give shape to the security dimension of CFSP. In institutional terms the most important achievement was undoubtedly the creation of the post of a High Representative for the CFSP.[27] This "monsieur PESC,"[28] as the French called him, was not based in the European Commission but in the Council General Secretariat. He was to be assisted by a Policy Planning and Early Warning Unit (PPEWU), bringing together officials of the European Commission, the Council Secretariat, and the member states. Its task was to analyze and assess foreign policy events, and provide the High Representative with policy advice. This was a revolution for the Council General Secretariat, which traditionally had only fulfilled a purely supporting role.[29] On the ever-returning question of the communitarization of foreign policy cooperation, it was once again impossible to reach agreement. As a concession to the supranationalists, QMV could now be used for implementing decisions that before had been taken by unanimity. This also applied to the decisions implementing common strategies, a new instrument setting out general guidelines for a certain country or region and adopted by the European Council. Furthermore, it was also made possible for member states to abstain from a decision without blocking it (the so-called constructive abstention).

The most heated debates, however, revolved around the future EU role in the field of security and defense. The wording pertaining to common defense was slightly strengthened[30] and the so-called Petersberg tasks, earlier defined in the 1992 Petersberg declaration of the WEU as "humanitarian and rescue tasks, peace-keeping tasks and tasks of combat forces in crisis management, including peace-making," were included in the Treaty. A lot of time was spent on the future relationship with the WEU, with proposals ranging from maintaining the status quo to full integration into the EU. Inspired by the EMU model, Belgium, France, Germany, Italy, Luxembourg, and Spain proposed a timetable that would culminate in full integration. This, however, was unacceptable to the UK, which was concerned about the position of NATO and to the neutral and non-aligned member states such as Ireland, Austria, Finland, and Sweden. The compromise was that the WEU remained an autonomous body but strengthened its institutional relations with the EU. The door for full integration was kept open by leaving the decision to the European Council, taking into account the constitutional requirements of the different member states.[31] It would take the poor performance in the 1998–1999 Kosovo crisis for the member states to finally make a more serious attempt to back up their declaratory policy with operational means.

10.6 REFORM OF THE INSTITUTIONS

The prospect of a future Union of twenty-five or more member states and the realization that since the 1950s the EU institutions had only undergone marginal adaptations, had catapulted the question of institutional reform and enhanced decision-making capacities to the top of the IGC agenda. The debate related to a wide variety of issues, ranging from the extension of QMV and enhanced use of co-decision to the re-weighting of votes in the Council and the composition of the European Commission. Central concerns were to ensure a further increase of the legitimacy of the institutions and the efficiency of the decision-making process.

On a wide number of institutional issues, agreement was already reached during the Irish Presidency. Efficiency was to be further enhanced by measures such as the reduction of the number of decision-making procedures,[32] the reduction of the number of seats in the European Parliament to 700, a simplification of the co-decision procedure by abolishing the third reading, and a strengthening of the role of the President of the European Commission. The legitimacy question was mainly addressed by further extension of the scope of co-decision and—under the impulse of France—by the adoption of a protocol on the role of national parliaments.[33]

The three most delicate issues regarding the extension of QMV, the size of the Commission, and the future Council voting system were passed on to the Dutch

Presidency and kept the negotiators busy until the early hours in Amsterdam. The proposal put forward in the Reflection Group to make QMV the general rule did not prove feasible and therefore its extension was discussed on a case-by-case basis. Fourteen new areas were added to the QMV list but most of the more sensitive questions such as social security, professional services, culture, and indirect taxation were kept under unanimity.[34] The poor result can also partly be explained by the cautious attitude of Chancellor Kohl, who under pressure from the German *Länder* adopted a more conservative and inflexible stance.[35] The two other issues, viz. the size of the Commission and the re-weighting of votes, proved even more sensitive. Both were linked to the future influence of the member states and they radically pitted large and small countries against each other. The large players wanted a compensation for the loss of their second Commissioner[36] and for the fact that with every enlargement the population represented in QMV declined.[37] France, Italy, Spain, and the UK wanted to address the problem of their under-representation by increasing the number of votes allocated to the big member states. Germany, on the other hand, pleaded for a system of double majority, combining the existing system with the requirement that a majority would also represent the majority of the EU citizens.[38] The small states were especially opposed to the idea of applying a cap to the number of Commissioners. They feared that the principle of rotation would only apply to them and that they would no longer have a national in the College able to take into account specific domestic concerns.

All three questions were discussed by the heads of states or government in Amsterdam. On QMV the results were disappointing and on the re-weighting of votes and the size of the Commission no agreement was reached. As the enlargement with the Central and Eastern European countries was still several years away, the pressure to reach an agreement was probably not sufficiently strong.[39] The way out was once again a protocol attached to the Treaty. It stipulated that another IGC should be organized at least one year before the EU had exceeded the number of twenty members, carrying out "a comprehensive review of the provisions of the Treaties on the composition and functioning of the institutions."[40] It would only be in Nice in December 2000 that an agreement on these Amsterdam leftovers was reached (see Chapter 11, this volume).

10.7 FLEXIBILITY

As has been emphasized throughout this chapter, the negotiations for the Amsterdam Treaty were very much influenced by the upcoming enlargement. The prospect of more economic, political, and cultural diversity had raised concerns about the feasibility to move forward simultaneously with all the members of the EU club. The variable speed in EMU and the Maastricht opt-outs for the UK (social policy) and Denmark (security) were already a first illustration of flexible integration. The

Amsterdam Treaty tried to institutionalize the possibility whereby a number of member states could cooperate more closely in a particular area within the EU institutional framework.

The debate on flexible integration was first launched by the so-called Schäuble–Lamers paper on a hard core Europe of five member states (September 1994) and by Balladur's proposal for a Europe of concentric circles (August 1994).[41] Both proposals were very controversial but they had the merit of putting the long-lingering issue of flexible cooperation finally on the EU agenda. The negotiations on "enhanced cooperation" as the Treaty has labeled flexible cooperation, proved to be very difficult. There were not only different views on the form, the purpose, and effect of the flexibility principle, but also on its purpose.[42] While the Euro-enthusiast countries saw it as a way to deepen European integration, the Euro-skeptics hoped that it would institutionalize the opt-out mechanism.[43]

During the IGC itself, it was primarily France and Germany who were the most vocal defenders of a flexibility clause in the Treaty. Already at an early stage they presented several joint proposals both at the level of the heads of states and government (December 1995) and the ministerial level (February 1996). Progress was slow, however, because the formulation of the general flexibility provisions depended on what would be agreed on individual policy areas. It was therefore only under the Dutch Presidency that real progress was made.[44] Balancing on a narrow rope of multiple sensitivities, the final agreement consisted of the combination of a general TEU flexibility clause and specific provisions in the first and the third pillar. With its provision on "constructive abstention" (see above), the second pillar was deemed to have sufficient scope for its own variation of flexibility.

Trying to appease the fears of lack of coherence or marginalization, a general enabling clause specified a whole range of precise conditions for its application (TEU, Title VII). These included amongst others respect for the *acquis communautaire*, the involvement of the majority of member states, the use of flexibility as an instrument of last resort, and openness to all member states. In addition, specific provisions were introduced with regard to the conditions and decision-making mechanisms in the first and the third pillar. In the first pillar, the decision prompting flexibility was taken by QMV but it was up to the European Commission to ensure compliance with the flexibility criteria and to formulate the proposal. A so-called emergency break gave countries the possibility to refer the matter to the European Council for a decision by unanimity. The procedure for the third pillar was the same, but instead of a binding opinion, the European Commission was to give only non-binding opinions on the initiatives of the member states.

As has been pointed out by Alexander Stubb, the tone of the debate on flexibility was very defensive and, rather than focusing on the areas where enhanced cooperation could possibly be applied, the deliberations concentrated in the first instance on what should not be done.[45] The result was that the conditions were defined in such a restrictive way that they proved unworkable and have never been applied. It is therefore no surprise that the question reappeared for revision on the Nice agenda.

10.8 EVALUATING AND UNDERSTANDING AMSTERDAM

The negotiations leading to the Amsterdam Treaty were a lengthy and at times distressing process. Given the many issues on the table and the diverse national preferences, it was not easy to hammer out a package deal acceptable to all delegations. Looking back at the 1996–1997 IGC, two questions called for further consideration. First, what did the Treaty bring for the broader process of European integration? And second, how can we understand the process described in this chapter?

The final outcome of an IGC is always the result of compromise and since "one delegation's areas of dissatisfaction are . . . areas of satisfaction for another," any assessment will always be colored by one's own preferences.[46] It is therefore no surprise that the immediate reactions ranged from heralding the Treaty as a success to condemning it as an outright failure.

Going back to the three original IGC objectives of bringing Europe closer to its citizens, enabling the Union to function better and preparing it for enlargement, and endowing it with a greater capacity for external action, most would agree that the greatest progress was made with regard to the first goal. Besides provisions on fundamental rights and non-discrimination, the Treaty had made a number of important steps in areas such as employment, social policy, asylum and migration, and the fight against organized crime—all issues that were high on the public agenda. In the field of foreign policy, the results were more limited. The mechanism of "constructive abstention" could be seen as a first departure from unanimity, but overall decision-making in the second pillar remained intergovernmental. The failure to reach agreement on the integration of the WEU into the EU made the prospect of the development of a European crisis management role look rather gloomy. The biggest disappointment however was the IGC's incapacity to reach an agreement on institutional reform. The extension of QMV was limited and there was no consensus on the re-weighting of votes and the future size of the European Commission. Concerns about possible isolation had made "enhanced cooperation" conditional upon so many criteria that it proved unworkable in practice.

However, while at first sight these results may seem rather poor, this may be misleading; if one takes a more long-term perspective, the picture is more positive. Treaty texts are by definition concise and their future impact depends on how they are ultimately interpreted and implemented. In other words, constitutional change in Europe is not just a question of formal treaty reform but a continuous development, and if we want to understand the full impact of Amsterdam, we should look beyond the deal reached in the early hours of June 18, 1997.[47] A good example of how treaty texts do not tell the full story is the institutional innovation of the High Representative (HR). Although he was meant to be merely an assistant of the Presidency, Javier Solana, the first occupant of the new post, proved to be very good at exploiting his *marge de manoeuvre* and preparing the way for a much more powerful HR under the Lisbon Treaty (see Chapter 12, this volume). Furthermore, the fact that the Council General Secretariat was now headed by a political figure had an important impact on its functioning and role: it developed into an important force in the European foreign policy landscape.

The second question, of broader interest, is how to make sense of the IGC process leading to Amsterdam. Also here the answer may be more complex than suggested by the actor-centered debate between neo-functionalists and liberal intergovernmentalists.[48] Certainly the member states as representatives of national interests play a key role, and it makes a difference whether one represents the UK or Luxembourg. Undoubtedly it is important, as argued by neo-functionalists, to pay attention to the role of supranational actors such as the European Commission and even the Council Secretariat.[49] However it is also clear from this account on Amsterdam that these actors do not operate in a vacuum. They are part of a broader institutional and political context which structures their debate and influences the outcome in a wide variety of ways.[50] In other words, there are a whole series of factors that are beyond the control of the protagonists of the IGC and which all contribute to structuring and streamlining the process. These include questions such as the time horizon, formal and informal practices at IGCs, domestic developments, and last but not least the broader international, European, and domestic context.[51]

The Amsterdam agenda indeed did not start from scratch but was to some extent already pre-defined by the choices made in Maastricht. From the beginning of the negotiations it was foreseen that the conference would be concluded under the aegis of the Dutch Presidency in the second half of 1997 and this time horizon was important in the strategic calculations that were made. It took place against the broader backdrop of an upcoming enlargement, continuing instability in the Balkans, and increasing public disenchantment with European integration. It was partly held hostage by the British election and the expected victory of the Labour party. The Presidencies, while different in style and approach, were led by practices established in earlier IGCs. All the above factors are examples of elements structuring the environment in which the IGC members operate and constraining the possible choices. Any account of the Amsterdam Treaty should therefore also take these factors into account.

NOTES

1. Karen Smith, "Enlargement and European Order," in Christopher Hill and Michael Smith, eds, *International Relations and the European Union* (Oxford: Oxford University Press, 2006), 270–91.
2. Ulf Sverdrup, "An Institutional Perspective on Treaty Reform: Contextualizing the Amsterdam and Nice Treaties," *Journal of European Public Policy* 9, no. 1 (February 2002) 120–40.
3. TEU, Title VII, Article N states that "a conference of representatives of the governments of the Member States shall be convened in 1996 to examine those provisions of this Treaty for which revision is provided, in accordance with the objectives set out in articles A and B."

4. The European Parliament was represented by both Elisabeth Guigou (Party of European Socialists) and Elmar Brock (European People's Party).

5. For a list of the national representatives, see Finn Laursen, "Institutions and procedures: The Limited Reforms," in Finn Laursen, ed., *The Amsterdam Treaty. National Preference Formation, Interstate Bargaining and Outcome* (Odense: Odense Univeristy Press, 2002), 9. The group consisted of a mixture of Permanent Representatives (6), Ministers of State (5), and others. See also Bobby McDonagh, *Original Sin in a Brave New World: An Account of the Negotiation of the Treaty of Amsterdam* (Dublin: Institute of European Affairs, 1998).

6. Finn Laursen, "Introduction: Overview of the 1996–97 Intergovernmental Conference (IGC) and the Treaty of Amsterdam," in Laursen, *The Amsterdam Treaty*, 1–19.

7. McDonagh, Original Sin in a Brave New World.

8. Andrew Moravcsik *The Choice for Europe* (London: UCL Press, 1998)

9. Thomas Christiansen and Christine Reh, *Constitutionalizing the European Union* (Houndmills: Palgrave Macmillan, 2009).

10. Edward Best, "The United Kingdom: From Isolation towards Influence," in Laursen, *The Amsterdam Treaty*, 359–78.

11. Youri Devuyst, "Treaty Reform in the European Union: The Amsterdam Process," *Journal of European Public Policy* 5, no. 4, (December 1998) 615–31. See also Jonas Talberg, "First Pillar: The Domestic Politics of Treaty Reform in Environment and Employment," in Laursen, *The Amsterdam Treaty*, 453–72.

12. Clotilde Marinho, "Portugal: Preserving Equality and Solidarity among Member States," in Laursen, *The Amsterdam Treaty*, 291–310.

13. McDonagh, *Original Sin in a Brave New World*.

14. Laura Corrado, "Italy: From the Hard Core to Flexible Integration," in Laursen, *The Amsterdam Treaty*, 225–53.

15. McDonagh, *Original Sin in a Brave New World*.

16. Mark Gray, "The European Commission: Seeking the Highest Possible Realistic Line," in Laursen, *The Amsterdam Treaty*, 381–403.

17. The first step was a reasoned opinion by one third of the member states, the European Parliament, or the Commission, acting by a majority of four fifths of its members after obtaining the assent of the European Parliament.

18. Michelle Petite, "The Treaty of Amsterdam." *The Jean Monnet Working Papers*, no. 2 (New York: The Jean Monnet Centre for International and Regional Economic Law and Justice, 1998).

19. Karl Magnus Johansson and Anna-Carin Svensson, "Sweden: Constrained but Constructive," in Laursen, *The Amsterdam Treaty*, 341–57.

20. There was a five-year transitional period during which the Commission and the Council still shared the right of initiative.

21. McDonagh, *Original Sin in a Brave New World*. See also Michelle Petite, "The Treaty of Amsterdam."

22. The Schengen *acquis* refers to the 1985 Schengen agreement itself; the implementing Convention of 1990; the various Accession Protocols and Agreements; and the decisions and declarations adopted by the Executive Committee and acts adopted by the organs on which the Committee has conferred decision-making powers.

23. Colette Mazzucelli, "Understanding the Dutch Presidency's Influence at Amsterdam: A Constructivist Analysis," *European Union Studies Association 8th Biennial International Conference* (Nashville, March 2003).

24. Monica den Boer, "A New Area of Freedom, Security and Justice: The Shaping of a Hybrid Compromise," in Laursen, *The Amsterdam Treaty*, 509–35.
25. Michelle Petite, "The Treaty of Amsterdam."
26. Sophie Vanhoonacker, "A Critical Issue: From European Political Cooperation to a Common Foreign and Security Policy," in Finn Laursen and Sophie Vanhoonacker, eds, *The Intergovernmental Conference on Political Union. Institutional Reforms, New Policies and International Identity of the European Community* (Dordrecht: Martinus Nijhoff Publishers, 1992), 25–33.
27. The daily management of the Council Secretariat was handed over to the Deputy Secretary General.
28. PESC (Politque extérieure et de sécirité commune) is the French acronym for CFSP.
29. Hylke Dijkstra, "The Council Secretariat's Role in the Common Foreign and Security Policy," *European Foreign Affairs Review* 13, no. 2 (2008), 149–66.
30. While Maastricht talked about "the eventual framing of a common defense policy, which might in time lead to a common defense," the Amsterdam Treaty speaks about "the progressive framing of a common defense policy, which might lead to a common defense, should the European Council so decide" (TEU, Title V, Article 17).
31. Simon Duke and Sophie Vanhoonacker, "Administrative Governance of the CFSP: Theory and Practice," *European Foreign Affairs Review* 11, no. 2 (2006), 163–82.
32. The cooperation procedure was abolished except for EMU.
33. Laursen, *The Amsterdam Treaty*.
34. Andrew Moravcsik and Kalypso Nicolaïdis, "Explaining the Treaty of Amsterdam: Interests, Influence, Institutions," *Journal of Common Market Studies* 37, no. 1 (1999), 59–85.
35. Andrew Duff, *The Treaty of Amsterdam. Text and Commentary* (London: Federal Trust, 1997).
36. France, Germany, Italy, Spain, and the UK each had two Commissioners, while all the others had only one.
37. While in a Union of fifteen, QMV still represented 58.3 percent of the total population; it only stood for 50.29 percent in an EU of twenty-six. See Laursen, "Institutions and Procedures: The Limited Reforms."
38. Laursen "Institutions and Procedures."
39. Moravcsik and Nicolaïdis, "Explaining the Treaty of Amsterdam."
40. Protocol (no. 7) on the institutions with the prospect of enlargement of the European Union (Amsterdam, October 1997).
41. Wolfgang Schäuble and Karl Lamers, "Reflections on European Policy." Document by the CDU/CSU Group in the German *Bundestag* (September 1, 1994). Edouard Balladur presented his proposal for a Europe of concentric circles in an interview with the French newspaper *Le Figaro* on August 30, 1994.
42. McDonagh, *Original Sin in a Brave New World*.
43. Alexander Stubb, *Flexible Integration and the Amsterdam Treaty: Negotiating Differentiation in the 1996–7 IGC* (London: London School of Economics and Political Science, 1998).
44. McDonagh, *Original Sin in a Brave New World*.
45. Stubb, *Flexible Integration and the Amsterdam Treaty*.
46. McDonagh, *Original Sin in a Brave New World*.
47. Christiansen and Reh, *Constitutionalizing the European Union*.

48. Ernst B. Haas, *The Uniting of Europe. Political, Social and Economic Forces, 1950–1957* (Stanford: Stanford University Press, 1958). See also Moravcsik, *The Choice for Europe*.
49. Derek Beach, "The Unseen Hand in Treaty Reform Negotiations: The Role and Influence of the Council Secretariat," *Journal of European Public Policy* 11, no. 3 (2004), 408–39.
50. Christiansen and Reh, *Constitutionalizing the European Union*.
51. Christiansen and Reh, *Constitutionalizing the European Union*.

CHAPTER 11

....

THE TREATY OF NICE

....

ALBERTA M. SBRAGIA

THE Treaty of Nice will be viewed in the history of European integration as a "hinge" between the "old" EU of 15 West European states and the "new" EU of 27 + states symbolized by the Lisbon Treaty. Since it responded to a historic enlargement, it was perhaps not surprising that the Nice Summit was the longest in history, beginning at 9:45 a.m. on Thursday December 7, 2000 and ending at 4:25 a.m. local time on Monday December 11.

Nice was designed to cope with the institutional repercussions of an enlargement which would nearly double the EU's membership. Not surprisingly, it raised questions which had lain dormant during earlier, and in retrospect much less historic, enlargements. Enlargement in fact became the façade behind which the issues of "efficiency and power" were contested.[1]

Those questions—revolving around the issues of national representation as well as the expansion of QMV—formed the heart of the negotiations. The travails of the Nice negotiations emphasized that the EU was in the process of becoming a different organism, one no longer to be anchored in the understandings and patterns which had almost imperceptibly developed since 1958.

Those patterns were such that the four large states—Germany, France, Italy, and the United Kingdom—had been treated equally when it came to representation and the smaller states were given disproportionate voting weights. Enlargement was divisive both because it raised the question of the governance of a much larger entity as well as the apportionment of institutional power to states of very different sizes. Finally, it also raised the issue of how to accommodate a much larger Germany. Although Germany had traditionally been viewed as roughly equivalent in terms of population to France, Italy, and the UK, the "new," more populous post-unification Germany had to be accommodated.

How much weight should that Germany gain within an enlarged Union? In which institution should that greater weight be situated? That question was particularly sensitive for France (i.e. President Chirac), for whom parity was absolutely crucial. German unification had thus produced the "German Question"—in institutional garb. It was to be conclusively answered at Lisbon, but the contours of the debate surrounding the new role of Germany in Europe were foreshadowed at Nice.

Whereas previous treaty negotiations had focused on issues related to public policy, the Treaty of Nice was primarily concerned with institutional issues and the representation that each member state would enjoy within the Commission and the Council as well as the Parliament. It thus focused attention on the question of formal institutional power in a way which was new to the process of treaty negotiation. Nice did not settle basic conflicts—it bought time. That became clear once the conflicts began over the constitutional treaty and the subsequent Lisbon treaty (see Chapter 12, this volume). Nice had been a precursor rather than an oddity or an exception.

Given that basic questions of representation were on the negotiating table, it should not come as a surprise that the negotiations were both very tough and very messy. The messiness had something to do with the (widely criticized) performance of the French Presidency which was in place during the second half of 2000 and during the December summit. While the Portuguese Presidency was praised for its organization of the pre-summit negotiations in the first half of 2000, the French Presidency which followed it was severely criticized.[2] But it undoubtedly was also due to the neuralgic nature of the question of representation, a question which not surprisingly pitted the large states against the small states although neither group was consistently internally coherent.

As a whole, the large states wanted more representation than they had heretofore enjoyed, but that did not mean that all necessarily wanted equality with each other. In a similar vein, the less populous states wanted to protect as much of their over-representation as possible but did not necessarily want equality amongst each other. That is, big states competed with each other—the French and the Germans—as did small states (the Netherlands and Belgium).

The tension between the representation of territory versus population is a nearly universal one during the founding of systems of representation based on territorial units of widely varying population sizes. How should population be factored into a system of governance based on states? How "majoritarian" in terms of population should the system be? Federal systems have differed in their response to that question.[3] The US Senate, for example, dramatically over-represents the least populous states—all states have equal representation (two votes) regardless of population. The negotiations at Nice introduced the issue of population versus territory in a more explicit fashion than had been the case since the signing of the Treaty of Rome.

The drawn-out negotiations, however, did not lead to an easy ratification process. Ireland, required to hold a referendum, saw its voters refuse to ratify the Treaty. A second referendum—with a positive outcome—finally allowed the Treaty of Nice to come into force on February 1, 2003.

This chapter discusses the background to the Treaty of Nice and the context within which the Treaty of Nice was negotiated. It then discusses the actors, lays out the most contentious issues which had to be addressed, and concludes with the dynamics of bargaining.

11.1 BACKGROUND

The Treaty of Nice can best be understood as the third of a quartet of treaties which moved beyond the completion of market integration. The SEA, which came into force in 1987, set out the institutional and legal framework which culminated in the single market. The post-SEA period saw the ratification of the Treaty of Maastricht, the Treaty of Amsterdam, the Treaty of Nice, and the Treaty of Lisbon (see Chapters 9, 10, and 12, this volume). While Maastricht moved the process of European integration into the area of monetary integration (with the decision to create an ECB) as well as into foreign policy, Amsterdam moved it into the area of justice and home affairs. Those two treaties expanded the reach of European integration. The EU became a significant actor in policy areas which had been controlled by national governments acting individually rather than collectively.

Nice, however, moved the focus of European integration eastward, as well as highlighting the issue of representation. Enlargement drove the process which led to Nice, and Nice in turn began to lay out the institutional rules which were to shape the governance of an enlarged Union with new member states very different from its pre-Nice members. Nice had to deal with the issue of size—a larger EU was necessarily going to function differently from its smaller predecessor. It also had to deal with a Germany significantly larger than the Germany of 1958. While Germany and France in 1958 had roughly equal populations, in 2000 Germany's population of roughly 83 million contrasted with a French population of roughly 53.5 million.

11.2 THE CONTEXT

The negotiations for the Nice Treaty were taking place as Denmark voted against joining the Euro. The "No" vote of September 2000 reminded political elites of the fact that the process of integration could be rocky. The Danes had earlier voted against the Treaty of Maastricht and had only approved it after Denmark was allowed to "opt out" of defense and asylum policy. This second "No" vote confirmed that the process of integration would now not involve uniformity. Some countries would join the eurozone while others would not; some states would pursue a more integrationist path than others. The defeat highlighted the need for the possibility of "enhanced cooperation" which would permit some countries to move more quickly in an integrationist policy framework than others. As it turned out, enhanced cooperation never became a major point of contention in the negotiations, but the Danish "No" vote reminded all parties that an enlarged Union was unlikely to be able to integrate in a uniform fashion across policy areas.

Secondly, the Commission had undergone a major crisis in 1999. In March the entire Santer Commission had resigned, and a new Commission, led by President Prodi, was not in place until July. The Commission, therefore, was institutionally far weaker than it had been during previous treaty negotiations. Scholars argue that the Commission can try to promote its own positions or act as a mediator;[4] in the case of the Nice Treaty, it was ineffectual in both arenas.

Thirdly, the French Presidency was imbedded in a complex domestic political situation. The French government was experiencing "cohabitation" as French President Chirac and the French Prime Minister Jospin belonged to different political parties. George Ross has described such a political context as one in which the "President and Prime Minister [are] political rivals…With the Prime Minister a potential president, the sitting president has to fight for his political life."[5] During the French Presidency, each could use any misstep by the other to his political advantage. Furthermore, Chirac was facing a barrage of accusations having to do with political corruption and various scandals (he was ordered to stand trial on embezzlement charges in October 2009). During the negotiations at the Nice summit, Chirac represented the Presidency while Jospin negotiated as the representative of France.

Finally, by the time the IGC was convened in February 2000, negotiations had been ongoing since the spring of 1998 for the accession of Cyprus, Hungary, Poland, Estonia, the Czech Republic, and Slovenia. Enlargement was now becoming real to political leaders. In turn, they emphasized the necessity of institutional change in order to accommodate the accession of new states from the East.

The pressure of enlargement was increased as the IGC was launched. Accession negotiations were begun with six more states, and Turkey was accepted as a candidate state. In the words of the Council's Legal Advisor of the Intergovernmental Conference, "Member States definitely had their backs to the wall."[6] The IGC took place earlier than expected and was widely viewed as having been underprepared.[7] The rushed quality of the IGC, in fact, contrasts sharply with the extensive preparations which had preceded previous treaty reforms.

11.3 THE ACTORS

Small and Large Member States. In general, the Nice Treaty was negotiated in an atmosphere in which the small (i.e. less populous) states viewed themselves as being on the defensive. The five most populous states—France, the United Kingdom, Germany, Italy, and Spain—wished to increase their representation within the Council of Ministers as well as limit the Commission's size. The less populous states wished to protect the level of representation which they had historically enjoyed to the greatest extent possible, which included maintaining a Commissioner for each member state. The "small versus large" divide did not affect every issue (it did not shape the conflict over the extension to QMV for example) but it did shape the conflict over most contentious issues.[8]

Commission and Council Secretariat. Both the Commission and the Council Secretariat played a more limited role in the Nice negotiations than had been the case in previous IGCs.[9] The Commission's top representatives—Prodi and Barnier—had participated in previous summits as national political leaders and were unfamiliar with the kinds of relatively technical issues which the Commission tackles at IGCs.[10] Finally, the Commission's proposals were widely viewed as unrealistically ambitious, and the Commission was generally therefore viewed as unable to act as an "honest broker."[11] Its institutional weakness was compounded by the French Presidency's disregard for its role during the Nice Summit. In fact, Chirac "went out of his way in the Nice Summit to remove the Commission from all influence."[12]

Further, the Commission was not necessarily viewed as an ally by the smaller states. Given the distrust of France felt by the smaller states (exacerbated by the arrogance with which Chirac treated some of their leaders), French Commission officials were sometimes viewed as carrying forward a French agenda. Portugal, which held the presidency when the negotiations began in February 2000, was very suspicious of the Commission's representative to the IGC—Commissioner Michel Barnier—because he was French (and had been the French European Affairs Minister). In fact, Barnier, in the view of Portuguese State Secretary for European Affairs, was thought to be "'singing Chirac's tune'."[13] In a similar vein, the Portuguese Prime Minister, Antonio Guterres, viewed France as the leader of the "big" states which in his view were determined to change the balance of power within the Council to their advantage. He accused the big states of attempting an "'institutional coup d'Etat'."[14]

The Secretariat for its part was also viewed by the smaller states as favoring the large states. Further, it was noticed that key Secretariat officials were predominantly French.[15] The role of France, in fact, is one of the dominant themes in the scholarly literature on the Treaty of Nice. French officials working for the Secretariat were especially viewed with suspicion by those worried about the attempt to recalibrate the balance of power in favor of the large states.

The Secretariat itself, however, suffered as an institution from the fact that the French presidency was institutionally based in Paris rather than in the Brussels-based French Permanent Representation.[16] Coordination was therefore more difficult. Thus, the Nice negotiations were marked by the unusual dominance of the French Presidency.

11.4 Two Presidencies

Portugal and France held the presidencies during the negotiations which began in February 2000. Whereas the French Presidency is uniformly criticized, its Portuguese counterpart generally receives high marks. Gray and Stubb conclude that "a good Presidency needs three things—organization, objectivity, and leadership—and the Portuguese Presidency had all three."[17] Francisco Seixas da Costa, the Portuguese

Minister for European Affairs, was widely viewed as having done an excellent job. Once Portugal stepped out of the Presidency, it was free to act in defense of the small states. In fact, Costa and the Portuguese Prime Minister were important in organizing the small states to protect their status within the Council.[18]

By contrast, the academic literature is almost uniformly critical of the French Presidency, especially since all the crucial issues were decided at the Nice Summit where Chirac himself was in command. Whereas Pierre Vimont, the French Permanent Representative, receives high marks for his handling of the flexibility dossier (which however was not viewed as one of the most contentious issues),[19] Chirac's contribution has been judged far less favorably.

Cohabitation weakened the Presidency's institutional efficiency. The stand-off between Jospin and Chirac involved a good deal of infighting. The need for coordination between Chirac's camp and Jospin's camp was time-consuming. Meetings were badly organized and management skills were often invisible.[20] Ross concludes that "everything had to be done by two different, mutually suspicious teams whose main goal was not to make the French Presidency a success but to trip each other up where possible."[21]

Chirac, commemorating ten years of German unification in Dresden, had signaled his desire to move toward a German- and French-led "two-tier" EU.[22] The Commission should play a subordinate role in this view with the large states providing leadership. The small states' membership would be subject to rotation. Not surprisingly, such a vision was unacceptable to the smaller states.

The tension between the large and smaller states became very visible in mid-October 2000 at the informal European Council in Biarritz.[23] It became clear then that the Presidency's goal was to change "the balance between the Member States."[24] While the Biarritz meeting agreed that groups of countries could move ahead under the rubric of enhanced cooperation under certain conditions, the smaller states fought against the idea of a smaller Commission. They also opposed a re-weighting of votes in the Council. Both proposals were viewed as diluting their influence and unduly benefiting the larger states. The Presidency eventually suggested that all (including the large) states should rotate their Commissioners, with the number of Commissioners being restricted to twelve. While Portugal supported the idea of all members being forced to engage in rotations, the other members were not ready to agree to a smaller Commission.[25]

11.5 KEY ISSUES

Negotiations at the Nice Summit centered on four interrelated core issues which had to be resolved in order for enlargement to proceed: the composition of the Commission, the re-weighting of votes in the Council of Ministers, the number of MEPs allocated to each member, and the definition of QMV. The question of the size of the Commission was crucial. Should the Union move to a relatively small Commission which would be heavily tilted toward the larger member states? Should a smaller Commission be composed of

Commissioners appointed on a rotating basis with all members treated equally? Or should the Commission be a larger one with each member being represented?

Each state's voting strength was a particularly complex issue in part because it most clearly highlighted the unified Germany's new position. Should Germany be allocated more votes in the Council than any other member given that its population was now the largest? Should Spain be treated as one of the "large" countries (à la Germany, France, Italy, and the UK)? Upon accession, it had been treated as a large member when it came to Commission representation but not in terms of voting strength. Should the candidate states be allocated fewer votes than their counterparts from Western Europe?

The number of parliamentary seats raised many of the same questions. Germany had been allotted the largest number of seats in the European Parliament by the Treaty of Amsterdam. While that number was not questioned, the number of seats to be allocated to the accession states was contested. Furthermore, should the limit of 700 seats agreed to in the Treaty of Amsterdam be increased? How important should population be when deciding on the number of seats for the accession states?

Finally, the composition of QMV was very divisive. Although it was decided that the use of QMV would be expanded to only some extent, the question of how a qualified majority vote was to be constructed led to a complicated formula. Should population be taken into account over and above the role it played in the weighting of votes? Given that the large states were increasing their weight, how could the smaller states protect themselves?

These four questions formed the core of the conflicts and negotiations which had to be resolved before the Treaty of Nice could be concluded.

11.6 NEGOTIATIONS AT THE SUMMIT

Italian premier Amato came to the Nice Summit with unusual backing from Italy's political groups. All of the major parties voted to support Amato's negotiating position in Nice even though it was widely expected that his centre-left coalition would lose the next general election.[26] An expert on the EU as well as a skilled negotiator, Amato was able on the summit's first day to gain agreement that at least some of the candidate states would be able to join before the Parliamentary elections of 2004.[27] The decision reassured the candidate countries which were worried above all that the Nice summit would delay their accession.

However, the negotiations over the four issues which addressed the power each state would be able to wield under the new regime were far more contentious. In the pre-Nice period, the "big four"—France, UK, Germany, and Italy—had enjoyed parity when it came to voting. Small states, for their part, enjoyed a disproportionate say in the decision-making process. In a traditional international organization, large states are extremely dominant. Within the Council of Ministers, by contrast, small states had enjoyed an increasingly favorable situation. Their status had become more privileged as enlargement in the pre-1995 period proceeded because "in each accession, the larger Member States lost more than the smaller states."[28] The large states viewed the Nice negotiations as leading to the re-balancing of the large member states plus Spain on the one hand and the rest on the other. However, given that voting weights were to be allocated to new member states, Poland wanted to be treated the same as Spain. Finally, the smaller member states wanted to protect their privileged position.

11.7 COMPOSITION OF THE COMMISSION

Having refused to agree to a smaller Commission at Biarritz, the small states renewed their fight against the downsizing desired by the large states. The accession states, for their part, were very committed to having "their" Commissioner and argued that such representation was critical for maintaining popular support for accession. The Commission was particularly visible for the accession states because of its prominent role in managing the accession process.

The large states (France, Germany, Italy, Spain, and the United Kingdom) agreed that they would relinquish a Commissioner so that each member would have only one Commissioner on the condition that the five of them would have more voting weight within the Council. The small states finally agreed in principle to a smaller Commission—without however making any hard choices. That is, they very reluctantly agreed that once the accession treaty for the twenty-seventh member state was signed, the European Council would unanimously agree to the exact number of Commissioners and to a fair system of rotation. (The small states, however, have won as the ratification process for the Treaty of Lisbon concluded with a decision that each member would select a Commissioner.)

The Commission President would be chosen by QMV and his or her appointment would need to be approved by the Parliament. With the sad fate of the Santer Commission in mind, the power of the Commission President would be increased—being able, for example with the approval of the entire Commission, to ask for the resignation of an individual Commissioner.

11.8 RE-WEIGHTING VOTES AND PARLIAMENTARY REPRESENTATION

The most controversial issue faced by the summit concerned the distribution of votes in the Council and in the Parliament. Both issues had been discussed at Biarritz, and it was clear that agreement would be very difficult in Nice. Conflicts arose among current members as well with the accession states.

One of the most difficult negotiating dynamics developed between France and Germany over the issue of voting weights. Those two states had always been equals in terms of votes (along with Italy and the UK). However, post-unification Germany now wanted to be recognized as the "biggest of the big"[29] while Chirac was absolutely committed to maintaining parity with Germany in the Council. Amato and Blair were both willing to support the German position, but Chirac was unyielding in his demand that all four "big" states wield the same number of votes in the Council of Ministers.

The French had earlier pointed out that France had not asked for more votes than Germany in the early 1950s when France could have claimed a larger population by counting its colonies.[30] Furthermore, Chancellor Kohl and President Mitterrand had struck a "gentleman's agreement" in 1989 that if France accepted German unification, Germany would accept voting parity with France in the European Council.[31] Overall, the discussion about German–French parity was a difficult one. In the words of a German official, "the arrogance of the French was at times unbearable."[32]

Italy and the UK, for their part, wanted to maintain parity with France, and Spain wanted to join the "top four" by achieving parity with the four biggest states.[33] The original German position involved the weighting of population so that Germany would have thirty-three votes, France and Britain thirty, and Italy twenty-seven.[34] The end result was that the "big four" retained their equality in voting, but Germany received ninety-nine MEPs whereas France, Italy, and the UK each received eight-seven. Thus, German representation was not cut in spite of enlargement whereas that of the other three states was.

Spain, for its part, at the very least wanted to maintain the "semi-big" position it had negotiated upon its accession. It had been granted two Commissioners (like "the big") and had eight votes (rather than ten) in the Council. If enlargement were to cost it a Commissioner, it wanted to be compensated by strengthening its position in the Council. It finally accepted twenty-seven votes in the Council (compared to the twenty-nine granted to the "big four"), thereby improving its relative position. Cohesion and structural funds, of particular importance to Spain, were also kept under unanimity until 2013.

Allocating votes entailed a series of other battles. One of the most noteworthy involved Belgium and the Netherlands. Belgian Prime Minister Verhofstadt threatened to veto the entire agreement when the Presidency proposed that the Netherlands be allocated one vote more than Belgium. The exhausting negotiations over that issue stretched into the early hours of Monday morning. Verhofstadt finally accepted the disparity on the condition that, post-enlargement, formal European Council meetings would all be held in Brussels. Furthermore, the Benelux countries collectively had the same number of votes as the big countries. He was given credit for increasing Lithuania's weight from five to seven votes so that it would be equal to Ireland but was relatively unsuccessful in winning only one extra vote for Romania (the Presidency had given Romania the same thirteen votes as the Netherlands in spite of Romania's significantly larger population).[35]

The candidate countries above all viewed the IGC through the prism of enlargement. They did not want any issues to be added to the agenda which would extend the IGC and thereby delay their accession. However, once the Nice Summit began, the bargaining over the number of votes became far more intense. The initial Presidency position gave the accession states fewer votes than their population would justify. For example, Poland was allocated one fewer vote than Spain in spite of having roughly the same population. Polish officials were, however, intent on negotiating a status equivalent to that of their EU counterparts. They put up a furious fight, lobbying the German Chancellor as well as the Spanish, Danish, and Swedish prime ministers and issued a "press statement...demanding equal treatment."[36] In the end, Poland and Spain each received eight votes in the Council.[37] However, the Czech Republic and Bulgaria were both viewed as having been allocated fewer votes than their relevant counterparts (Belgium and Portugal) while Estonia and Cyprus did not fare as well as Luxembourg in spite of having significantly larger populations.[38]

The bargaining over parliamentary votes was also intense. Belgium received two more MEPs (for a total of twenty-two) than had been envisaged by the French Presidency. Portugal for its part received two more MEPs (for a total of twenty-two) than originally proposed so as to help balance its relationship with Spain. Greece (with a larger population than Portugal) then demanded—and received—the same.[39] However, Hungary and the Czech Republic only received twenty (but each received two more during the accession negotiations). The end result of the horse trading was an increase in the number of seats to 732 (rather than the 700 which had been agreed to at Amsterdam). That was a decision which was likely to lead to major logistical problems as new parliamentary buildings had been prepared to accommodate a maximum of 700 MEPs.[40]After the Hungarian and Czech accession, the total number of seats in the European Parliament in fact was set at 736 (see Table 11.1).

11.9 QMV

The final key question resolved by the Nice Summit had to do with the decision-rule to be used for those areas which were not to be decided by unanimity. How to define the super-majority—or what in EU-speak is known as QMV—necessary to pass legislation not subject to unanimity? The definition of QMV would shape decision-making in the post-Nice enlarged Union. Germany was determined to come away with a form of voting system which took demographics into account. Once it was clear that gaining more votes than the other three big countries was out of the question, the final decision about the composition of QMV was "not based on any clear and understandable principle but a pure matter of 'power poker' (*Machtpoker*)."[41]

The "triple majority" that emerged as the definition of QMV required a majority of the member states, between 71 and 74 percent of weighted votes (depending on the pace of accession), and most interestingly a provision that if a member state so requests, 62 percent of the total population. For the first time, a demographic factor was introduced, one which increased the power of the large states to block agreement. Three of the four largest states would be able to form a blocking minority. However, Germany was in a privileged position in that it would need the support of just one of the largest states plus any of the smaller states (other than Luxembourg).[42]

Table 11.1   Distribution of seats in the European Parliament under the Treaty of Nice

Member States	European Parliament Seats (*)
Germany	99
United Kingdom	72
France	72
Italy	72
Spain	50
Poland	50
Romania	33
Netherlands	25
Greece	22
Czech Republic	20 (+2)
Belgium	22
Hungary	20 (+2)
Portugal	22
Sweden	18
Bulgaria	17
Austria	17
Slovakia	13
Denmark	13
Finland	13
Ireland	12
Lithuania	12
Latvia	8
Slovenia	7
Estonia	6
Cyprus	6
Luxembourg	6
Malta	5
Total	732 (736)

* Parentheses denote the addition of European Parliament seats from Hungarian and Czech accession.

Source: European Communities

11.10 THE IRISH

Although EU leaders left Nice with an agreement, under the provisions of the Irish con-stitution, the Irish electorate had to approve it before Ireland could ratify the treaty. The first referendum led to a defeat—one which shocked political elites throughout the EU. At the Seville summit in June 2002, the Irish government obtained the Seville mandate which responded to Nice's new provisions in the area of defense. Due to Irish neutrality, the Irish would not be required to participate in any kind of EU-led military action unless approved by the UN, the Irish cabinet, and the Irish Parliament.

11.11 CONCLUSION

The Treaty of Nice finally went into effect on February 1, 2003, and its provisions guided the process of enlargement. The conflicts associated with it reflected the stresses of a particular period in post-war European integration. The role of France and Germany, of the applicant states, and the small member states were indicative of a European order which was still very much divided between "Western" and "Eastern" Europe. The Treaty of Lisbon came into force roughly ten years after the initiation of the negotiations which led to the Treaty of Nice. In those ten years, the EU changed in fundamental ways. While the Treaty of Nice will be viewed as a stopgap on the way to Lisbon, some of the conflicts associated with its negotiation pointed to important structural features of the EU governance system.

The crucial role of the Commission for the smaller states is one of those features, as was emphasized by the Irish vis-à-vis the Lisbon Treaty. Whatever the merits of a smaller Commission might be in the abstract, they do not outweigh the role of national presence in that institution. Secondly, the tension between the representation of population and territory is and will continue to be a recurring tension within the Union. And, finally, the importance of individual leaders should not be underestimated. The "small group" dynamics of the European Council colors the decision-making dynamics within the Union in complex ways.

NOTES

1. Mark Gray and Alexander Stubb, "The Treaty of Nice—Negotiating a Poisoned Chalice?" *Journal of Common Market Studies* 39, Annual Review (2001) pp. 5–23.
2. Andreas Dur and Gemma Mateo, "Bargaining Efficiency in Intergovernmental Negotiations in the EU Treaty of Nice vs. Constitutional Treaty," *Journal of European Integration* 28, no. 4 (2006), 381–98.
3. Alberta M. Sbragia, "Thinking about the European Future: The Uses of Comparison," in A. M. Sbragia, ed., *Euro-Politics: Institutions and Policy-Making in the New "European" Community* (Washington, DC: Brookings Institution Press, 1992), 257–91; and Sergio Fabbrini, "*Compound Democracies: Why the United States and Europe are Becoming Similar* (Oxford: Oxford University Press, 2007).
4. Thomas Christiansen, "The Role of Supranational Actors in EU Treaty Reform," *Journal of European Public Policy* 9, no. 1 (2002), 33–53.
5. George Ross, "France's European Tour of Duty, or Caution—One Presidency may Hide Another," *ECSA Review* 14, no. 2 (2001), 4–6, at 5.

6. Jean-Claude Piris, "The Treaty of Nice; An Imperfect Treaty but a Decisive Step Towards Enlargement," The *Cambridge Yearbook of European Legal Studies* (Cambridge: Centre for European Legal Studies, 2000), 15–36, at 17.

7. Dur and Mateo, "Bargaining Efficiency in Intergovernmental Negotiations in the EU Tereaty of Nice vs. Constitutional Treaty," 387.

8. David Galloway, "The Treaty of Nice and 'Small' Member States," *Current Politics and Economics of Europe* 11, no. 1 (2002), 11–29.

9. Derek Beach, "The European Commission and the Council Secretariat: How they Gained Some Influence," in F. Laursen, ed., *The Treaty of Nice: Actor Preferences, Bargaining and Institutional Choice* (Leiden/Boston: Martinus Nijhoff, 2006), 369–409.

10. Beach, "The European Commission and the Council Secretariat," 380.

11. Beach, "The European Commission and the Council Secretariat," 381; Christiansen, "The Role of Supranational Actors in EU Treaty Reform."

12 Beach, "The European Commission and the Council Secretariat," 381.

13 Beach, "The European Commission and the Council Secretariat," 377.

14 Ana Maria Guerra Martins, "Portugal: The Fight Against the 'Big' Ones," in Laursen, *The Treaty of Nice*, 247–62, at 254.

15. Beach, "The European Commission and the Council Secretariat," 377.

16. Beach, "The European Commission and the Council Secretariat," 385–6.

17. Gray and Stubb, "The Treaty of Nice—Negotiating a Poisoned Chalice?" 10.

18. Federiga Bindi, "Italy: When Individual Actors Make the Difference," Laursen, *The Treaty of Nice*, 97–218; Martins, "Portugal: The Fight Against the 'Big' Ones."

19. Adriaan Schout and Sophie Vanhoonacker, "France: Presidency Roles and National Interests," in Laursen, *The Treaty of Nice*, 133–62, at 148–9.

20. Ulf Sverdrup, "An Institutional Perspective on Treaty Reform: Contextualizing the Amsterdam and Nice Treaties," *Journal of European Public Policy* 9, no. 1 (2002), 120–45. For a more sanguine assessment, also see Schout and Vanhoonarcker, "France: Presidency Roles and National Interests," and Ross, "France's European Tour of Duty."

21. Ross, "France's European Tour of Duty," 5.

22. Haig Simonian and Michael Smith, "Chirac Repeats His Call for France and Germany to Lead Two-Tier EU," *Financial Times*, October 4, 2000, 1.

23. Martins, "Portugal: The Fight Against the 'Big' Ones."

24. Gray and Stubb, "The Treaty of Nice—Negotiating a Poisoned Chalice?" 11.

25. Vaughne Miller, "IGC 2000: From Feira to Biarritz," Research paper 00/83. House of Commons Library, October 27, 2000, 19.

26. Bindi, "Italy: When Individual Actors Make the Difference," 211; Martins "Portugal: The Fight Against the 'Big' Ones"; James Blitz, "Italian Parties Rally Behind Amato," *Financial Times*, November 30, 2000.

27. Peter Ludlow "The Treaty of Nice: Neither Triumph nor Disaster," *ECSA Review* 14, no. 2 (2001), 1–4.

28. George Tsebelis and Xenophon Yataganas, "Veto Players and Decision-Making in the EU After Nice," *Journal of Common Market Studies* 40, no. 2 (2002), 283–307, at 288.

29. Bindi, "Italy: When Individual Actors Make the Difference," 211.

30. Peter Norman, "France Damps Hopes of Pact on Services," *Financial Times*, December 6, 2000, 10.

31. Bart Kerremans, "Belgium: More Catholic than the Pope?" in Laursen, *The Treaty of Nice*, 41–56, at 50.

32. Lionel Barber, "Hearts and Minds," *Financial Times*, December 22, 2000, 18.

33. Leslie Crawford, "Spain Sees Last Chance to Assert its Status," *Financial Times*, December 4, 2000, 2.

34. Haig Simonian, "Chirac and Schroder at Odds over German Voting," *Financial Times*, December 4, 2000, 2.

35. Peter Norman, "Belgian PM's Altruism 'Heroic'," *Financial Times*, December 12, 2000, 10.

36. Michael J. Baun and Dan Marek, "The Candidate States and the IGC," *Journal of International Relations and Development* 4, no. 1 (2001), 13–37, at 27.

37. Baun and Marek, "The Candidate States and the IGC."

38. Jorg Monar, "Continuing and Building on Amsterdam: The Reforms of the Treaty of Nice," in J. Monar and W. Wessels, eds, *The European Union after the Treaty of Amsterdam* (New York: Continuum, 2001), 321–34, at 326.

39. Panos Tsakaloyannis and Spyros Blavoukos, "Greece: Continuity and Change," in Laursen, *The Treaty of Nice*, 163–78, at 171.

40. Alberta M. Sbragia, "The Treaty of Nice, Institutional Balance, and Uncertainty," *Governance* 15, no. 3 (2002), 393–411.

41. Christian Engel, "Germany: A Story of Saving Face," in Laursen, ed., *The Treaty of Nice*, 83–116, at 108.

42. Monar, "Continuing and Building on Amsterdam."

CHAPTER 12

THE CONSTITUTIONAL AND LISBON TREATIES

YOURI DEVUYST

THIS chapter examines the EU's failed attempt to approve the Treaty establishing a Constitution for Europe (hereafter Constitutional Treaty) and its successful replacement by the Treaty of Lisbon.

12.1 THE NEGOTIATION AND RATIFICATION PROCESS OF THE CONSTITUTIONAL AND LISBON TREATIES

12.1.1 Negotiating the Treaty Establishing a Constitution for Europe

The route toward the Constitutional Treaty was launched at the Laeken European Council on December 14–15, 2001.[1] In view of the EU's planned expansion from fifteen to twenty-seven member states, the heads of state or government considered further institutional reform essential. Earlier attempts to adjust the EU's functioning had produced only meager results. The Treaty of Nice, signed on February 26, 2001, formed the most notorious example of a complex agreement including only minimal achievements (see Chapter 11, this volume). The Treaty of Nice and its predecessors had been negotiated at diplomatic IGCs that operated largely behind closed doors. In an attempt to pave the way for the following IGC as broadly and openly as possible, the heads of state or government decided to convene a Convention. Its task was to consider the key issues arising for the EU's future development and to try to identify the various possible responses.[2] Former French President Valéry Giscard d'Estaing was appointed as chairman. In addition to the chairman and two vice-chairmen, the

Convention was composed of representatives of the heads of state or government and of the national parliaments of member states and candidate countries as well as delegates of the European Parliament and the European Commission. The Economic and Social Committee, the Committee of the Regions, the social partners, and the European Ombudsman were invited to attend as observers. Hoping to stimulate a public embrace of the European project, the Convention made a special effort of stimulating the dialogue with civil society. One of its vice-chairmen was made responsible for maintaining a regular exchange of view with citizens, associations, and organizations wishing to contribute to the debate on the future of Europe. A special *Futurum* website was created for this purpose. To also mobilize young people, a "Convention for the Young People of Europe" was set up to provide its view on the European construction.

Between February 2002 and July 2003, the Convention met once a month in plenary session open to the public, at the premises of the European Parliament in Brussels. The Convention's work was steered by the Praesidium which consisted of the chairman and the two vice-chairmen, two representatives each of the European Parliament, the Commission, and the national parliaments, and representatives of the Spanish, Danish, and Greek governments (the countries holding the EU Council Presidency during the Convention). A delegate of the candidate countries was also invited to the Praesidium meetings. While the Convention was allowed to work as a parliamentary discussion forum with input from civil society, Giscard kept strict control over its agenda. In addition, he summarized the debates and determined on which points a consensus existed. Due to the drive of the chair, the Convention succeeded in adopting—by consensus—a complete draft Treaty establishing a Constitution for Europe. It was submitted to the president of the European Council on July 18, 2003. This result had not initially been foreseen by the heads of state or government when launching the reform process at Laeken. In their declaration authorizing the start of the Convention, they had simply asked the question whether the simplification and reorganization of the EU treaties "might not lead in the long run to the adoption of a constitutional text in the Union."[3]

To turn the Convention's draft into an effective new Treaty, a follow-up IGC between the governments of the member states was needed. After a year of bargaining, the "IGC 2004" arrived at a political agreement at the Brussels European Council of June 18, 2004. It largely confirmed the outcome of the Convention. The resulting Treaty establishing a Constitution for Europe was formally signed by all member states in Rome on October 29, 2004.[4] While much of the Constitutional Treaty was taken directly from the earlier treaties, there were a number of novelties, such as the creation of a permanent post of President of the European Council, the establishment of the office of EU Foreign Minister, supported by a new External Action Service, and the incorporation of the EU's Charter of Fundamental Rights in the binding treaty language.

The Constitutional Treaty was supposed to replace all existing treaties that first established the European Communities and then reformed them over the years. This replacement never took place. While eighteen member states successfully ratified the Constitutional Treaty, it was voted down by referendums in France and the Netherlands.

In France, the referendum was held on May 29, 2005. With a turnout rate of 69 percent, 55 percent voted "No." The actual text of the Constitutional Treaty motivated only a fifth of the "No" voters. The domestic unemployment situation in France was given as the main reason for the "No" vote.[5] The Dutch referendum was held on June 1, 2005. With a turnout rate of 63 percent, 62 percent voted "No." Among the "No" voters, 28 percent indicated that their key motivation was the internal economic and social situation in the Netherlands, 23 percent voted "No" because of their negative overall opinion of the EU, and a further 21 percent stated that they specifically opposed the text of the Constitutional Treaty.[6] While the heads of state or government initially declared that the negative referendums in France and the Netherlands would not call into question the validity of continuing with the ratification processes, the British government decided on June 6, 2005 to suspend the ratification procedure indefinitely. Since it could legally enter into force only after the ratification by all EU member states, this effectively killed the Constitutional Treaty.[7]

12.1.2 Negotiating the Treaty of Lisbon

In reaction to the referendum results in France and the Netherlands, the European Council of June 16–17, 2005 called for a period of reflection. Serious work started again in 2007 when German Chancellor Angela Merkel assumed the Presidency of the European Council. In line with the plans of the newly elected French President Nicolas Sarkozy, Merkel's main idea was to recuperate as much as possible of the substance from the Constitutional Treaty, while throwing all constitutional symbolism overboard. By putting the changes in the format of a traditional amending treaty like the Treaties of Amsterdam and Nice, the heads of state or government explicitly wanted to avoid new referendums. The "IGC 2007" started its work on July 23, 2007. Thanks to the unprecedented level of detail in the political mandate, the negotiations could focus mainly on technical and legal aspects.[8] The new Treaty was formally signed by the governments of all member states in Lisbon on December 13, 2007.[9] But once again, its entry into force required the ratification by all member states.

As a simple amending treaty, referendums were avoided in all but one member state: Ireland. On June 12, 2008, the Irish voters rejected the Lisbon Treaty. With a turnout rate of 53 percent, 52 percent voted "No." A Eurobarometer poll found that a lack of information about the Lisbon Treaty was the main reason for voting against the treaty (22 percent of all answers), followed by the desire to protect Irish identity (12 percent of all answers).[10] This time, the negative referendum did not stop the ratification process in the other member states. From the start, the idea was to repeat the Treaty of Nice experience and ask the Irish people to vote a second time. In June 2009, the European Council agreed on a number of guarantees that were intended to put the main Irish concerns to rest.[11] First, the heads of state or government adopted a formal Decision clarifying that the Treaty would not affect (a) Ireland's constitutional protection of the right to life, family, and education, (b) the powers of the member states regarding taxation, and

(c) Ireland's traditional policy of military neutrality. Second, through a Solemn Declaration, the European Council reaffirmed its commitment to workers' rights, social policy, public services, and other related issues. Thirdly, a national Declaration by Ireland reaffirmed its specificity in security and defense policy. Finally, it was agreed that the European Commission would continue to include one national of each member state. On October 2, 2009, with a turnout of 58 percent, the Irish voters supported the Lisbon Treaty by a margin of 67 to 33 percent. It was generally assumed that the severe financial and economic crisis of 2008–2009 had made the Irish voters more aware of the importance of the protective European umbrella. The Irish referendum was followed by the signature of the Polish ratification documents by Euro-skeptic President Lech Kaczynski on October 10, 2009. This left Czech President Václav Klaus as the sole European leader to hold out against the Treaty in spite of its approval by the Czech Parliament. In a confusing last-minute request, Klaus demanded—and the other member states agreed to—an opt-out of the Charter of Fundamental Rights on the same terms that had already been agreed for Poland and the United Kingdom.[12] Klaus finally signed the ratification documents on November 3, 2009. Ten days later, the Czech prime minister deposited the instrument of ratification with the Ministry of Foreign Affairs of the Italian Republic, which is the depositary of the Treaty of Lisbon. This allowed the Treaty to enter into force on December 1, 2009.

12.2   THE IMPACT OF THE TREATY OF LISBON ON THE EU'S FUNCTIONING[13]

The main substantive changes introduced by the Treaty of Lisbon were taken from the Constitutional Treaty and therefore reflected the work of the Convention.[14]

12.2.1 The EU's Structure

Upon the entry into force of the Lisbon Treaty, the EU received explicit legal personality and replaced and succeeded the European Community. As a result, the word "Community" is replaced throughout the existing treaties by the word "Union." Furthermore, the Treaty establishing the European Community is renamed as the Treaty on the Functioning of the Union (TFEU). Together with the Treaty on the EU (TEU), the TFEU constitutes the primary law on which the Union is founded, and both have the same legal value.[15] The full integration of the old European Community in the Union is accompanied by the formal abolition of the EU's three-pillar structure created by the Treaty of Maastricht (see Chapter 9, this volume). Nevertheless, in spite of the abolition of the pillars, the CFSP—i.e. the former second pillar—continues to work under specific and more intergovernmental decision-making procedures. Judicial cooperation in criminal matters and police cooperation—i.e. the former third pillar—is brought under the "Community method" through the extension of the ordinary legislative procedure (co-decision), QMV in the Council, and jurisdiction of the ECJ. Still, a number of specific institutional arrangements, safeguards, and opt-outs continue to apply.[16]

12.2.2 The EU's Competences

In the wake of the Constitutional Treaty debacle, the Lisbon Treaty makes a special point of reconfirming that the EU enjoys only those competences which have been conferred on it by the member states in the Treaties. In other words, the basic principle of the EU's legal order is that competences rest with the member states, except in those cases where they transfer them to the Union. This point was underscored by the German Federal Constitutional Court (*Bundesverfassungsgericht*) in its Lisbon Treaty judgment of June 30, 2009. The Court emphasizes that the EU's constitutional system "remains a derived fundamental order" in which the member states "permanently remain the masters of the Treaties." As its empowerment to exercise supranational competences comes from the member states, the Court maintains that the EU cannot be seen as a sovereign entity under international and public law, but constitutes an association of sovereign national states (*Staatenverbund*). As a consequence, the EU does not have the possibility of taking possession of *Kompetenz-Kompetenz* (i.e. the power to decide autonomously over its own competences).[17] The exercise of the EU's competences is governed by the reinforced principles of subsidiarity and proportionality, whereby national parliaments get the possibility to voice their concern whenever they believe that a legislative proposal is not in compliance with those principles. Regarding the substance of the EU policies, the negotiators decided to explicitly incorporate the fight against climate change and energy solidarity in the new Treaty.

12.2.3 The Rights of the Citizens

In contrast with the Constitutional Treaty, the Treaty of Lisbon does not incorporate the full text of the EU's Charter of Fundamental Rights. It simply specifies that the Union recognizes the rights, freedoms, and principles set out in the Charter and that it shall have the same legal value as the Treaties. As such, the Charter has become legally binding for the EU institutions. Via a special Protocol, Poland, the United Kingdom, and the Czech Republic obtained the assurance that their laws, regulations, and practices cannot be declared inconsistent with the Charter. The new Treaty also foresees that the EU shall accede to the Council of Europe's European Convention for the Protection of Human Rights and Fundamental Freedoms. This will make the EU subject to the same external review as regards the obligation to respect human rights as its member states, via the mechanisms of the European Court of Human Rights in Strasbourg.

Apart from the question of fundamental rights, the Lisbon Treaty also promotes participative democracy. Firstly, the Council is to meet in public when deliberating or voting on draft legislative acts, thus allowing citizens to see how their governments act. Secondly, the Treaty encourages an open, transparent, and regular dialogue with representative associations and civil society, with social partners, and with churches, religious communities, and non-confessional organizations. Thirdly, an entirely new citizens' initiative right is created: one million citizens who are nationals of a significant number of member states may take the initiative of inviting the European Commission to submit a legislative proposal.

12.2.4 The Role of the European and the National Parliaments

The Treaty of Lisbon substantially enhances the role of the European Parliament. The existing co-decision procedure is extended to practically all areas of secondary law-making and elevated to the rank of "ordinary legislative procedure." In parallel, the European Parliament's consent is required on a broadened range of international agreements. On February 11, 2010, as an immediate indication that this new power should be taken seriously, the European Parliament rejected an agreement between the EU and the United States on the transfer of financial data for the purposes of the Terrorist Finance Tracking Program, thus forcing the reopening of the negotiations. In the new budget procedure, Parliament obtains powers on an equal footing with the Council of Ministers on all EU expenditures. It is also granted the right of consent for the approval of the EU's Multiannual Financial Framework. The President of the Commission will henceforth be formally elected by the European Parliament, on a proposal of the European Council taking into account the elections to the European Parliament. Via the formalization of the Convention procedure, the European Parliament will also be directly involved in the preparation of the future revisions of the EU treaties. The Lisbon Treaty also results in a growing role for the national parliaments in EU decision-making. They each obtain the right to issue a reasoned opinion indicating that a draft legislative proposal fails to comply with the subsidiarity principle. If supported by at least one third of the national parliaments, such an opinion leads to a fresh review of the draft. After the review, the Commission may decide to maintain, amend, or withdraw the draft.

12.2.5 EU Decision-Making and the Workings of the Institutions

Together with the European Parliament, the main institutional "winner" of the Treaty of Lisbon is the European Council. Composed of the heads of state or government, its

new full-time President, and the Commission President, the European Council is recognized for the first time as an official institution that is able to take formal decisions
on the EU's political future.[18] As a general rule, such decisions require consensus, thus
providing each member with a possibility to block the adoption of conclusions. The
elevation of the European Council to the rank of formal institution is accompanied by
the creation of the office of full-time President of the European Council. Former
Belgian prime minister Herman Van Rompuy was chosen as the first holder of this
new post. The President of the European Council—whom the media have already
inaccurately labeled as the "President of Europe"—has as his task to improve the continuity and consistency of the European Council's preparation and representation.
Operating as a facilitator and mediator rather than as a high profile President, Van
Rompuy immediately increased the frequency of European Council meetings and
successfully placed his institution at the center of the debate on the conception and
implementation of the EU's new economic governance. In August 2011, in response to
the crisis of the eurozone, French President Sarkozy and German Chancellor Merkel
proposed a further reinforcement of the role of the heads of state or government in the
form of regular meetings (twice a year) of the leaders of the member states that have
introduced the euro as their currency. Their function would be "to act as the cornerstone of the enhanced economic governance of the Euro area." Sarkozy and Merkel
also expressed the wish that Van Rompuy would be elected as chairman of these eurozone summits.[19] On October 26, 2011, the other heads of state or government of the
eurozone accepted these Franco–German proposals.[20] The systematic strengthening
of the role of the heads of state or government in EU governance has clearly reinforced
the EU's intergovernmental dimension.

At the level of the Council of Ministers, the Lisbon Treaty moves decision-taking in
forty-four instances from unanimity to QMV. It also defines a new method of achieving
QMV. Obtaining agreement on the new method turned out to be the most divisive issue
throughout the reform process. The new system abandons the Community's traditional
weighted voting method. Instead, qualified majority is defined as at least 55 percent of
the members of the Council and representing member states comprising at least 65 percent of the EU's population. In comparison with the QMV thresholds imposed by the
Treaty of Nice, the new system should make decision-making easier.[21] However, its practical functioning might be complicated by the addition of several safeguards. To protect
the smaller member states, the blocking minority must include at least four Council
members, failing which the qualified majority shall be deemed attained. This was added
to counterbalance the fact that the Lisbon Treaty replaces the old weighting of the votes
(that traditionally favored the smaller countries) by a system that takes into account the
real demographic situation of each member state. The most important difficulty during
the IGC 2004 and 2007 was the necessity to overcome Poland's opposition to the introduction of the new QVM system. During the Nice negotiations, Spain and Poland had
been treated exceptionally well in the attribution of weighted votes. The use of the real
population figures in Lisbon's QMV system significantly reduced the national blocking
power of both countries. For Poland, this proved a major problem till the very end.[22] To

accommodate its objections, the entry into force of the new system is delayed until November 2014. Furthermore, until March 2017, the request of any member state is sufficient to ensure that a vote is still governed by the weighted voting procedures of the Treaty of Nice. As an additional safeguard, the Lisbon Treaty incorporates a reinforced Ioannina compromise that allows a significant minority of member states (but below the blocking minority necessary to prevent the qualified majority) to delay the actual application of QMV.

12.2.6 The EU's External Relations and Defense Policy

The Lisbon Treaty's main innovation in the area of the EU's external relations is the creation of the office of High Representative for Foreign Affairs and Security Policy. The first holder of the new post is Baroness Catherine Ashton, the former EU Commissioner for Trade. She presides over the Council of Foreign Affairs Ministers and is, at the same time, one of the Vice-Presidents of the Commission responsible for handling external relations. The negotiators hoped that this function would help to increase the coherence and visibility of the EU's external action. However, several months after the Lisbon Treaty's entry into force, it remained unclear whether the new High Representative would be able to effectively enhance the EU's international role. The difficult process of setting up the unified European External Action Service (EEAS), characterized by a power struggle between Commission, Council, Parliament, and the national diplomatic services, underlined the thorny nature of the High Representative's tasks. The first major test for the EU's new foreign policy under the Lisbon Treaty—the formulation of a response to the revolutions in the Southern Mediterranean, and especially to the situation in Libya—failed to convince the observers that the Union had moved to a higher level of efficiency in international affairs. With the open rift between those in favor of a military intervention in Libya (notably France and the United Kingdom) and those against (notably Germany), the EU as collective actor "played no identifiable part in the war" to overthrow Colonel Gaddafi.[23]

The Lisbon Treaty also reinforces the EU's common structures in the field of security and defense policy. It creates a European Defence Agency to foster Europe's defense R&D and weapons acquisition capabilities. It provides for the establishment of "permanent structured cooperation" among member states which have the military capability and political will to be involved. For the first time, it brings a guarantee in the EU treaty framework stating that the member states have an obligation of aid and assistance by all the means in their power toward a member state which is the victim of armed aggression on its territory. This provision must be implemented in compliance with the defense commitments of those member states who also belong to NATO and it does not prejudice the specific character of the defense policy of the neutral member states. In addition, the Lisbon Treaty obliges solidarity and assistance for any member state that is the victim of terrorist attack or natural disaster.

12.2.7 The EU's Adaptability: The Process of Future Treaty Change

During the Convention, several proposals were advanced to make EU treaty revision, especially of provisions dealing with internal policies, more flexible and not necessarily subject to unanimous ratification. The Constitutional and Lisbon Treaties do not go that far. In the ordinary revision procedure, a positive outcome remains subject to a common accord at an IGC, followed by the ratification in all member states. An IGC must be prepared by a Convention, except if this is not justified in view of the limited scope of the reform. A first example of such an ordinary treaty revision without Convention was the mini-IGC of June 2010 that resulted in the addition of eighteen new members to the European Parliament.[24]

Smaller treaty modifications can be adopted through new simplified procedures that do not require the meeting of member-state representatives in an IGC. Thus, moving a subject from unanimity to QMV in the Council or from special legislative procedures to the ordinary co-decision procedure can be decided by the European Council, acting unanimously, with the consent of the European Parliament. This, however, is on condition that no national parliament objects. For the adaptation of the EU's internal policies in the TFEU, the European Council can also take the necessary decisions by unanimity, without IGC. The prime example is the European Council decision of March 2011 amending article 136 TFEU. It allows the member states whose currency is the euro to establish a stability mechanism that may be activated if indispensable to safeguard the stability of the eurozone.[25] While not necessitating an IGC, the amendment must still be ratified by all member states.

In other words, even the simplified reform procedures remain hostage to veto rights at multiple levels. As an alternative, the Lisbon Treaty facilitates the conditions for enhanced cooperation among a minimum of nine member states as a technique to move forward in policy areas blocked by unwilling partners. Immediately following the Lisbon Treaty's entry into force, the European Commission for the first time in the EU's history formally proposed enhanced cooperation in divorce and legal separation law. The initiative followed a request by nine member states to move forward together after a 2006 Commission proposal became deadlocked in the Council. The nine have meanwhile been joined by three further member states.

The Lisbon Treaty also provides its member states with the explicit right to withdraw from the Union in accordance with their own constitutional requirements. From a legal perspective, the explicit acknowledgment of the voluntary right of withdrawal from the EU confirms that it is still only a treaty between a group of countries, and not a federal European state. In the words of the German Federal Constitutional Court, withdrawal from the EU "is not a secession from a state union (*Staatsverband*), which is problematic under international law, but merely the withdrawal from a *Staatenverbund* which is founded on the principle of the reversible self-commitment."[26]

12.3 POLITICAL SCIENCE PERSPECTIVES ON THE CONSTITUTIONAL AND LISBON TREATIES

12.3.1 Procedures and Personalities

The negotiating history of the Constitutional and Lisbon Treaties resulted in a some-what surprising return of procedures and personalities as a main subject for research.[27] The outcome of the negotiations at Maastricht, Amsterdam, and Nice was credibly explained through a liberal intergovernmental perspective, with the final texts largely reflecting the relative bargaining power of the member states. In contrast, the substance of the Constitutional draft—and the resulting Lisbon Treaty—can, according to political scientists such as Thomas König and George Tsebelis only be understood in light of the particular rhetoric and procedures adopted by the Convention.[28] Dominated by the strong personality of Giscard and his Praesidium, the Convention "used every trick in the book" to expand the Convention's authority.[29] Once the importance of the Convention process became clear to the member states, several governments upgraded their representation to the level of the Minister of Foreign Affairs. Still, it was Giscard who ultimately shaped a consensus on a draft Constitutional Treaty even though the heads of state or government had not requested this. Daniel Finke correctly concludes that this outcome is not what member states would have been ready to accept in an ordinary IGC setting. Furthermore, this result cannot be adequately explained from a liberal intergovernmental perspective.[30] The particular context of the Convention—its public standing as a grand exercise in constitutional democracy and the rhetorical emphasis on transparency and democratic accountability—made it very awkward for skeptical member states to openly block Giscard's consensus.[31]

While a number of additional safeguards were subsequently added via the IGCs in 2004 and 2007, the Convention's draft was never totally reopened. As such, the Convention not only served as agenda setter, but it also proved to be the key source of the final compromise on the Treaty of Lisbon. Still, it is useful to add a nuance to this conclusion. As Wolfgang Wessels and Anne Faber point out, in the end it was only through a "renaissance" of the Monnet method, based on a business-like approach and confidential negotiations behind closed doors, that Chancellor Merkel was able to achieve a consensus on the detailed negotiating mandate of the IGC 2007 that resulted in the final version of the Lisbon Treaty.[32]

During the difficult ratification process of the Lisbon Treaty, the obstruction politics of the Polish and Czech presidents again drew attention to the role of individual personalities in the history of European integration. Especially the refusal by the Czech President Klaus to sign the Lisbon ratification documents, while his own parliament and all other member states had approved it, seemed to reinforce the view that actions by isolated individuals can make a difference. However, at the end of the day, Klaus himself admitted that he was unable to prevent the Treaty's entry into force. In his own words: "the train has already travelled so fast and so far that I guess it will not be possible to stop it or turn it around, however much we would wish to."[33] Ultimately, the Klaus episode also seems to indicate the limits of individual blocking power.

12.3.2 The Nature of the EU Polity

The negotiation and ratification of the Treaty of Lisbon has been another occasion to debate the democratic nature of the European constitutional settlement. According to the German Federal Constitutional Court, the EU "does, even upon the entry into force of the Treaty of Lisbon, not yet attain a shape that corresponds to the level of legitimation of a democracy constituted as a state."[34] Since the number of members in the European Parliament is fixed according to assigned national contingents (with some over-representation for the smaller countries), the Constitutional Court considers that the Parliament "is not laid out as a body of representation of the citizens of the Union as an undistinguished unity according to the principle of electoral equality." This, together with the observation that there is no "uniform European people," leads the Court to the conclusion that "the European Parliament is not a body of representation of a sovereign European people."[35] It adds, however, that this is not necessarily a problem: as a derived order, the EU is not required to democratically develop in analogy to a state. Long before the Court delivered its Lisbon judgment, Moravcsik had warned that the EU should not be held to the impossible standard of an idealized conception of Westminsterian democracy. In his view, the EU's so-called democratic deficit is a myth.[36] Taking into consideration the EU's limited competences, the great restrictions on the EU's fiscal, coercive, and administrative capacity, the EU's exceptional system of checks and balances, and the existing democratic accountability under which the EU's decision-makers work, Moravcsik concludes that the thesis of the democratic deficit lacks empirical support. Most practitioners have a similar view. As stated by the European Parliament in its resolution on the Lisbon Treaty, the adoption of EU legislation "will be subject to a level of parliamentary scrutiny that exists in no other supranational or international structure."[37] The debate on the nature of the EU's polity is intimately linked with the discussion on its politicization that was launched by Liesbet Hooghe and Gary Marks and which forms the subject of a specific chapter in this volume.[38]

With respect to the fundamental nature of the EU polity, Andrew Moravcsik, writing in 2008, came to the conclusion that the European integration process had reached an "institutional plateau" which he called the "European constitutional settlement."[39] He found that the Lisbon reform stayed largely within the institutional order fixed by the Treaty of Maastricht in 1992 and predicted that we were starting to see an endpoint of European integration based on the existing constitutional contours. The financial crisis that started in 2008 and, especially, the eurozone governance crisis of 2011 have demonstrated, however, that the Lisbon Treaty's institutional plateau is far from stable. As underlined by Joschka Fischer, Germany's former Foreign Minister and Vice-

Chancellor, the Euro area "now rests on the shaky basis of a confederation of states that are committed both to a monetary union and to retaining their fiscal sovereignty. At a time of crisis, that cannot work."[40] For Fischer and most other observers, the EU has the choice of trying to muddle through, which could lead to the end of monetary union, or to move forward to real economic and political union. This would require a decisive step in the federal direction that leaders such as Merkel and Sarkozy seem unwilling to take.[41]

12.4 RECOMMENDATIONS FOR THE EU'S TREATY REFORM PROCESS

The painful ratification process of the Lisbon Treaty has given rise to several recommendations on how to improve the efficiency of the treaty change mechanism. Moravcsik has noted that the effort to increase trust and support among the European public through greater politicization and democratization—via the Convention and its extensive dialogue with civil society—"was doomed to failure because it runs counter to our consensual social scientific understanding of how advanced democracies actually work."[42] In his view, forcing participation—as is the case when referendums are called—is likely to be counterproductive "because the popular response is condemned to be ignorant, irrelevant and ideological," thus playing into the hands of small bands of activists.[43] Gary Marks has drawn largely similar conclusions and believes that "referendums encourage polarization rather than compromise, and do little to encourage reasoned debate."[44] Marks describes the EU as a patient suffering from a "democratic surplus" characterized by "an unplanned, incoherent, and inappropriate application of direct democracy to European decision making." He proposes to redirect demand for democracy to representative institutions.[45] Moravcsik advocates to return to the traditional and successful strategy of developing the EU "through an incremental, piecemeal strategy of implementing effective policies and modest institutional reforms," thus avoiding referendums.[46] This could be coupled with the reform proposed by Italian President Giorgio Napolitano, who has suggested that—in an EU of twenty-seven member states—the entry into force of EU treaties should be possible when they are ratified by member states representing a large majority of the EU's population, not necessarily including all member states.[47]

After the decade-long Constitutional and Lisbon Treaty reform process, it was argued that Europe's politicians were suffering from a treaty change fatigue and preferred not to return to the negotiation and ratification ordeal any time soon. However, as indicated above, the first post-Lisbon amendment—on the addition of eighteen new members of the European Parliament—was signed less than a year after the new Treaty's entry into force. It was followed, in March 2011, by the amendment allowing the creation of a stability mechanism to safeguard the euro. In light of the ongoing eurozone governance crisis, more fundamental decisions on Europe's future are on the horizon. This is not surprising. As the Lisbon Treaty was shaped by a Convention that took place in 2002–2003, it is a pre-economic crisis treaty for a crisis and post-crisis world.[48] In other words, as in the past, European integration remains a continuing process, with permanent functional pressures for further institutional adaptations.

NOTES

1. Laeken European Council, "Presidency Conclusions," December 14–15, 2001, Annex I.
2. On the Convention and its functioning, see its website <http://european-convention.eu.int/bienvenue.asp?lang=EN>. See also Guy Milton and Jacques Keller-Noëllet with Agnieszka Bartol-Saurel, *The European Constitution. Its Origins, Negotiation and Meaning* (London: John Harper Publishing, 2005); Peter Norman, *The Accidental Constitution. The Making of Europe's Constitutional Treaty* (Brussels: EuroComment, 2005).
3. Laeken European Council, "Presidency Conclusions," December 14–15, 2001, Annex I.
4. Treaty Establishing a Constitution for Europe, October 29, 2004, O.J. C 310, December 16, 2004. See also Giuliano Amato, Hervé Bribosia, and Bruno De Witte, eds, *Genesis and Destiny of the European Constitution* (Brussels: Bruylant, 2007).
5. European Commission, "Flash Eurobaromètre 171: La Constitution européenne: sondage post-réferendum en France," June 2005.
6. European Commission, "Flash Eurobarometer 172: The European Constitution: Post-Referendum Survey in the Netherlands," June 2005.
7. Finn Laursen, ed., *The Rise and Fall of the EU's Constitutional Treaty* (Leiden: Martinus Nijhoff Publishers, 2008).
8. Desmond Dinan, "Governance and Institutional Developments: Ending the Constitutional Impasse," *Journal of Common Market Studies* 46, Annual Review (2008), 71–90.
9. Treaty of Lisbon amending the Treaty on European Union and the Treaty establishing the European Community, signed at Lisbon, December 13, 2007, O.J. C306, December 17, 2007.
10. European Commission, "Flash Eurobarometer 245: Post-Referendum Survey in Ireland," June 18, 2008.
11. Brussels European Council, "Presidency Conclusions," June 18–19, 2009, para. 1–5 and Annexes 1, 2, and 3. It can be noted that a similar technique had been used to convince Denmark in its second referendum on the Treaty of Maastricht. See Chapter 9, this volume.
12. Brussels European Council, "Presidency Conclusions," October 29–30, 2009, para. 2 and Annex I.
13. This summary of the Lisbon Treaty builds in large measure on the excellent overview by Richard Corbett and Inigo Mendez de Vigo, *Report on the Treaty of Lisbon*, European Parliament, Committee on Constitutional Affairs, A6-0013/2008, January 29, 2008. See also Paul Craig, *The Lisbon Treaty. Law, Politics, and Treaty Reform* (Oxford: Oxford University Press, 2010); Stefan Griller and Jacques Ziller, eds, *The Lisbon Treaty. EU Constitutionalism without a Constitutional Treaty?* (Vienna: Springer, 2008); Jean-Claude Piris, *The Lisbon Treaty. A Legal and Political Analysis* (Cambridge: Cambridge University Press, 2010).

14. Tim Corthaut, "Plus ça change, plus c'est la même chose? A comparison with the Constitutional Treaty," *Maastricht Journal of European and Comparative Law* 15, no. 1 (2008), 21–34.
15. For the currently applicable version of the TEU and TFEU, see Consolidated versions of the Treaty on European Union and the Treaty on the Functioning of the European Union, O.J. C115, May 9, 2008.
16. Andrea Ott, "Depillarisation: The Entrance of Intergovernmentalism through the Backdoor?" *Maastricht Journal of European and Comparative Law* 15, no. 1 (2008), 35–42.
17. German Federal Constitutional Court (Bundesverfassungsgericht), Judgment of the Second Senate, June 30, 2009–2 BvE 2/08, 2 BvE 5/08, 2 BvR 1010/08, 2 BvR 1022/08, 2 BvR 1259/08, 2 BvR 182/09, para. 239 and 231.
18. For a more detailed treatment, see Youri Devuyst, "The European Union's Institutional Balance After the Treaty of Lisbon: 'Community Method' and 'Democratic Deficit' Reassessed," *Georgetown Journal of International Law* 39, no. 2 (2008), 247–325.
19. Joint Letter by Nicolas Sarkozy and Angela Merkel to President Van Rompuy, Paris, August 17, 2011, available at <http://www.elysee.fr/president/root/bank/print/11871.htm>.
20. Euro Summit Statement, October 26, 2011, para. 31 and Annex 1.
21. Stefaan Van den Bogaert, "Qualified Majority Voting in the Council: First Reflections on the New Rules," *Maastricht Journal of European and Comparative Law* 15, no. 1 (2008), 97–108. For a comparison with the Treaty of Nice, see Chapter 11, this volume.
22. Maciej Wilga, "Poland and the Constitutional Treaty: A Short Story about a 'Square Root,'" in Finn Laursen, ed., *The Rise and Fall of the EU's Constitutional Treaty* (Leiden: Martinus Nijhoff Publishers, 2008), 225–48.
23. François Heisbourg, "Libya: A Small War with Big Consequences," *International Herald Tribune*, August 30, 2011, 6.
24. Protocol amending the Protocol on transitional provisions annexed to the Treaty on European Union, to the Treaty on the Functioning of the European Union and to the Treaty establishing the European Atomic Energy Community, signed at Brussels on June 23, 2010, O.J. C 263, September 29, 2010, 1.
25. European Council Decision of March 25, 2011 amending Article 136 of the Treaty on the Functioning of the European Union with regard to a stability mechanism for Member States whose currency is the euro, OJ L 91, April 6, 2011, 1 For an analysis, see Bruno de Witte, "The European Treaty Amendment for the Creation of a Financial Stability Mechanism," *Sieps European Policy Analysis*, no. 6 (2011), 1–8.
26. German Federal Constitutional Court, Judgment of the Second Senate, June 30, 2009, para. 233.
27. For an overview of the literature, see Christine Reh, "The Convention on the Future of Europe and the Development of Integration Theory: A Lasting Imprint," *Journal of European Public Policy* 15, no. 5 (2008), 781–94.
28. For the opposite point of view, namely that the European Convention did not systematically differ from previous IGC negotiations, see Paul Magnette and Kalypso Nicolaïdis, "The European Convention: Bargaining in the Shadow of Rhetoric," *West European Politics* 27, no. 3 (2004), 381–404.
29. George Tsebelis, "Thinking about the Recent Past and the Future of the EU," *Journal of Common Market Studies* 46, no. 2 (2008), 285. See also George Tsebelis and Sven-Oliver Proksch, "The Art of Political Manipulation in the European Convention," *Journal of*

Common Market Studies 45, no. 1 (2007), 157–86; Thomas König and Jonathan Slapin, "From Unanimity to Consensus: An Analysis of the Negotiations at the EU's Constitutional Convention," *World Politics* 58, no. 3 (2006), 413–46; Thomas König, A. Warntjen, and S. Burkhart, "The European Convention: Consensus without Unity?" in Thomas König and Simon Hug, eds, *Policy-Making Processes and the European Constitution: A Comparative Study in Member States and Accession Countries* (London: Routledge, 2006), 23–34.

30. Daniel Finke, "Challenges to Intergovernmentalism: An Empirical Analysis of EU Treaty Negotiations since Maastricht," *West European Politics* 32, no. 3 (2009), 482.

31. Dionyssis Dimitrakopoulos, "Norms, Strategies and Political Change: Explaining the Establishment of the Convention on the Future of Europe, *European Journal of International Relations* 14, no. 2 (2008), 319–41.

32. Wolfgang Wessels and Anne Faber, "Vom Verfassungskonvent zurück zur 'Methode Monnet'? Die Entstehung der 'Road map' zum EU-Reformvertrag unter deutscher Ratspräsidentschaft," *Integration* 30, no. 4 (2007), 370–81.

33. Rob Cameron, "Czech leader resigned to treaty," *BBC News*, October 17, 2009, <http://news.bbc.co.uk/2/hi/europe/8312778.stm>.

34. German Federal Constitutional Court, Judgment of the Second Senate, June 30, 2009, para. 276.

35. German Federal Constitutional Court, Judgment of the Second Senate, June 30, 2009, para. 280.

36. Andrew Moravcsik, "The Myth of Europe's 'Democratic Deficit'," *Intereconomics* 43, no. 6 (2008), 332.

37. European Parliament, "Resolution on the Treaty of Lisbon," February 20, 2008, para. 2.

38. Gary Marks and Liesbet Hooghe, Chapter 58, this volume. See also Liesbet Hooghe and Gary Marks, "A Postfunctionalist Theory of European Integration: From Permissive Consensus to Constraining Dissensus," *British Journal of Political Science* 39, no. 1 (2009), 1–23; Liebet Hooghe and Gary Marks, "Europe's Blues: Theoretical Soul-Searching after the Rejection of the European Constitution," *PS: Politics and Political Science* 39, no. 2 (2006), 247–50.

39. Andrew Moravcsik, "The European Constitutional Settlement," *The World Economy* 31, no. 1 (2008), 157–82.

40. Joschka Fischer, "Europe's Shaky Foundations," August 30, 2011 available at <http://www.project-syndicate.org/commentary/fischer65/English>.

41. Fischer, "Europe's Shaky Foundations."

42. Andrew Moravcsik, "What Can We Learn from the Collapse of the European Constitutional Project?" *Politische Vierteljahresschrift* 47, no. 2 (2006), 221. For an opposite viewpoint, see John E. Fossum and Agustín José Menéndez "The Constitution's Gift? A Deliberative Democratic Analysis of Constitution Making in the European Union," *European Law Journal* 11, no. 4 (2005), 380–410, who claim that the inclusiveness, openness, and deliberative nature of the Convention actively further democracy building and make the Convention's output more democratic.

43. Moravcsik, "What Can We Learn from the Collapse of the European Constitutional Project?", 227.

44. Gary Marks, "The EU's Direct Democratic Surplus," *EUSA Review* 21, no. 4 (2008), 12. For a similar view, see Renaud Dehousse, "One No Too Many," *EUSA Review* 21, no. 4 (2008), 8.

45. Marks, "The EU's Direct Democratic Surplus," 12. The suggestion is inspired by Simon Hix, *What's Wrong With the European Union and How to Fix It* (London: Polity, 2008).
46. Moravcsik, "What Can We Learn from the Collapse of the European Constitutional Project?", 227.
47. Giorgio Napolitano cited in *Bulletin Quotidien Europe* no. 9889 (April 25, 2009), item 1.
48. Wolfgang Münchau, "A Pre-Crisis Treaty for a Post-Crisis World," *Financial Times*, September 14, 2009, 11.

PART III

MAJOR PERSONALITIES

CHAPTER 13

....

THE FOUNDING FATHERS

....

RICHARD T. GRIFFITHS

To approach history through the lens of personalities, as Part III of this volume does, carries with it serious implications of historical interpretation. This is particularly true when we look at the so-called "founding fathers" of what became the EU. We cannot resolve these issues here, but we will explore the implications so that the reader is aware of the choices that this particular perspective may involve.

One of the most persistent debates in political science concerns the dichotomy between structure and agency, the difference between the circumstances shaping history and the agencies or actors enacting change, or not, as the case may be. To talk of the "founding fathers" places the discussion squarely in the agency camp. This does not necessarily mean, however, that one has to accept an "heroic" interpretation of the past when great men bent the future to their will. Historians who choose this direction concentrate on the influences that molded these personalities. Moreover, if we do decide to retain this focus, there are plenty of routes from which to choose. For example, much has been made of the fact that many of the actors had grown up in border areas and were presumably less attached to the concepts of nation states—Robert Schuman in Luxembourg, when it was part of the German Zollverein; Alcide de Gasperi in the Southern Tyrol, when it was part of the Austro-Hungarian Empire; and Konrad Adenaeur in the Rhineland. Schuman became foreign minister of France, de Gasperi became prime minster of Italy and, of course, Adenauer became chancellor of West Germany. Another line of thought links their shared Roman Catholicism as a factor binding them together, though quite how this translates into their subsequent adoption of the European cause it less clear. Another link lies less through their religious faith as through the religious-based mass political parties that emerged after the war and the network of contacts that these allowed, which enabled the growth of a shared rhetoric and experience.

There is a more direct route to their shared political goals toward Europe and that is through political ideology. Since the espoused goal of the EU is ever closer union, the most obvious place to start (though not necessarily the correct one) is the European federalist movement which found its roots in the United States between the wars but which gathered momentum and influence in the immediate post-war years. Alternatively, since the European federalist model was based on the earlier American one, one could skip the European movement altogether and seek the common factor in the inspiration, or alternatively the pressure, of American policy-makers and officials in Europe—a treasured gift from the new world for the old. However, if Americans "made Europe" (which they didn't) we would need a whole new list of founding fathers.

Placing the "founding fathers" at the crossroads of history is an easier task. They were all highly placed policy-makers, or their influential advisors, in a Europe emerging from five years of war, death, and destruction. All were concerned with the tasks of economic and political reconstruction and with avoiding the mistakes that had precipitated the war in the first place—the economic depression, and the accompanying trade wars, and the nationalistic, authoritarian, and aggressive militaristic regimes that they had spawned and nurtured. In addition, looming from the East was the emergence of new Communist states, backed by the armed might of the Soviet Union. Thus, in the late 1940s and early 1950s, the "founding fathers" were in positions of political power and able to take decisions that would help resolve current problems of Europe and shape the future course of history. And, by this route, we arrive at the structural side of the agency/structure debate.

One of the immediate problems facing post-war planners was the position of Germany. The initial policy of the occupying forces was to keep down Germany's industrial and military potential, by destroying plants and imposing restrictions on industrial production. This, however, entailed large costs for the occupiers and prolonged the economic dislocation in Europe that was dependent on German markets and supplies. At some point, Germany would have to be reintegrated into the normal economic and political life of the Continent, but under what terms? What was to prevent Germany in the future from adopting nationalistic trading policies and an aggressive, militaristic foreign policy?

In answering this question some historians have adopted a meta-stance, focusing on the German problem as some exogenous issue of equal concern to all and resolved by some creating institutional formulae, such as the institutions that eventually became the European Union. These historians have usually been able to align their analysis with the various agency approaches. Other historians, however, have stressed the different degrees to which states were affected by Germany's rehabilitation and they have concentrated on the domestic positions which each attempted to protect. Aggressively adopting a "national interest" label, they shattered the consensus that had hitherto prevailed in mainstream writings on the origins of European integration.

It would be nice to report that there had been a debate between the two approaches, and possibly a reinterpretation, but nothing could be further from the truth. Generally, both sides have studiously ignored each other's findings and, as the "national interest school" retired from the field, the old consensus had emerged virtually unchallenged. However, the dichotomy was a false one from the start. The national interest school have approached negotiations toward international agreements as attempts to secure (domestic) national interests. The fact that such interests were secured is then transmuted into the main driving force behind the agreement. On the other hand, if an international agreement is to be achieved (and ratified!) every party must be able to endorse it—an impossible feat, if vital national interests have not been secured. Thus, assuming that satisfaction of substantive issues is a precondition for agreement, one can then concentrate on the form and the thinking behind the institutional architecture adopted—whether it be a faith in the rule of law, or a belief in federalism or in supranationality—which brings the question back to the agents of change and, in our case, the founding fathers.

The following sections will be designed around the three main supranational treaties that were signed in the years 1951–1957—the ECSC, the EDC, and the EEC. Through these contexts, the main protagonists, the "founding fathers," will be introduced, each accompanied by a necessarily short description of his career to date. This might lead to a more complicated history, but hopefully one that is closer to reality.

13.1 THE EUROPEAN COAL AND STEEL COMMUNITY

Jean Monnet (1888–1979) was the architect of the ECSC which came into existence in 1952 and which is often viewed as the first European supranational institution. Monnet was the son of a Cognac merchant, who made his career as an international banker. After a brief spell with the League of Nations after the World War I, he spent most of the interwar period in the United States. It goes without saying that he was well aware of the American federal political system. He also built up an impressive network of political contacts that served him well later on. During the war itself, he helped the British negotiate aircraft contracts with the Americans, before joining the Free French forces in Algiers. In 1946 General de Gaulle created the *Commissariat du Plan* to oversee the economic reconstruction of the country and named Jean Monnet as its Director. In this position, Monnet was responsible for planning the priorities for the French economy and allocating the necessary resources. One of his targets was to realize a substantial increase in French heavy industry, making full use of the opportunity afforded by the elimination by the occupation authorities of German competition. In 1949, the assumptions underpinning this strategy were beginning to unravel.

In 1949, the control of the German heavy industry was placed in the hands of the International Ruhr Authority in which the Western Occupation Authorities were joined by the Benelux countries and in which Germany would also, eventually, take its place. The limits of its power and authority were still untested. In September 1949 Germany partially regained its sovereignty with its own democratically elected parliament and its own Chancellor, Konrad Adenauer. The Allies still maintained some control over the country through an agreement to maintain Occupation Statutes until the German government had replaced them with its own legislation. Again, it was uncertain how effective these measures would be on an ostensibly sovereign country. These were not idle concerns.[1] Already in early 1950 German steel production surpassed its supposed ceiling, not by much but there were still seven million tons of idle capacity ready to enter an already glutted market. Because of international shortages, German coal was being sold abroad at prices above those charged to domestic industry. Moreover, the practice of differential transport prices also served to distort the market in favor of domestic output. In addition, the break-up of vertical ownership of coal mines by steel mills, a long-held goal of Allied policy, had still not materialized. As long as this situation prevailed, producers could withhold supplies altogether, supplies upon which French steel production depended. A final problem lay in the future of the disputed Saar region, at that point linked to France by a customs union and its coal mines under French state control. The Saar helped alleviate the French coal shortage and should it revert to Germany, French dependence on German supplies would increase uncomfortably. It is little wonder that early in 1950, Jean Monnet should become concerned with the future of Germany.

Jean Monnet was not a prolific writer and not a great reader for that matter. He also had a poor memory, so his memoires were largely reconstructed by close associates and should be read as a political statement rather than an accurate work of historical record.[2] References to his political ideas in the period before 1950 are scarce. In his writings in the desert during the war, there are a couple of mentions of federalist solutions for the future of Europe and of the need for a joint organization for the Continent's heavy industry. Apart from that there is nothing, not at least until 1950. Monnet's original idea to control German heavy industry was to place French heavy industry alongside it and under the same regime. That regime would be depoliticized in so far as the supervision of the industry would be entrusted to a panel, to be known as the High Authority (HA), of technical experts, operating independently from their nationalities. The plan was modified early in the negotiations so that the institutional architecture acquired many of the organs associated with a neo-federalist structure—an assembly, a court, and a council of ministers in addition to the High Authority originally envisaged—but that did not necessarily mean that it was inspired by federalist thinking. The original structure had far more in common with the Tennessee Valley Authority, inaugurated in 1933 as part of the New Deal, allowing for the development of the river system in a desperately poor part of the United States, which was only possible if states surrendered part of their sovereignty over this one shared resource. The original plan was not quite so high-minded as later federalists would suggest for within the working document Monnet prepared for the launch of the negotiations was a clause suggesting that all other controls over Germany would be respected for as long as they were kept intact. Moreover there exists a memorandum to foreign minister Schuman setting out quite clearly how the arrangements would help control Germany and Monnet did have a considerable interest in controlling Germany. So too did the French Foreign Ministry. At the same time as Monnet's staff were preparing draft after draft of his proposals, the Foreign Ministry wanted to increase the powers of the International Ruhr Authority when the ministers met in London on May 12, 1950, but these efforts were unlikely to succeed. Time, therefore, was of the essence. On April 28, 1950 Monnet finally had his alternative plan ready, but he was not a government minister. He took a copy of the plan to Georges Bidault, the prime minster, who promptly ignored it. He also arranged for a copy to be received by Robert Schuman, the foreign minister. It was Schuman who introduced the scheme to the cabinet.

Robert Schuman (1886–1963) was born in Luxembourg. After the war, he was elected parliament deputy for Moselle. He was placed under house arrest by the Germans before escaping to non-occupied France and working for the resistance. After the war, he returned to mainstream politics on behalf of the Christian democrat MRP (Mouvement Républicain Populaire) and became foreign minister in July 1948. Schuman was an ardent federalist, but thought that, in the light of public opinion, it was premature to strive for a political federation in Europe, and certainly not one that included Germany. At the time, Monnet's more limited sectoral approach was more appealing. It was Schuman, therefore, who steered the plan through cabinet, who secured the backing of both the United States and West Germany for the scheme, and thus secured a majority even before the 12 May London conference had opened. On May 9, 1950, five years after the end of the war and almost ten years to the day after the German invasion of his country, Schuman made the dramatic radio announcement calling for the pooling of German and French heavy industry under a common High Authority and inviting all nations willing to accept the scheme to join. The plan would end the means and will to wage war, and would lay the foundations for a future federal Europe. The Benelux countries and Italy all responded positively.

For the plan to succeed, it required Germany's approval. That, in turn, depended upon Konrad Adenauer (1876–1967). Had the Social Democrats been in power, the response would probably have been very different since they were to hold aloof from entanglements that might jeopardize German reunification. Educated as a lawyer, Adenauer became mayor of Cologne in 1919 until the Nazis came to power in 1933. He was periodically imprisoned by them, but after the war he returned to his position as mayor of the first German city liberated by the Allies, that is until the British sacked him. He then became leader of a reconstituted Christian Democratic party and, at the age of 73, became the first Chancellor of West Germany. Adenauer was genuinely pleased with the Schuman Plan and positively endorsed it before the German public. In public, he ignored the unequal treatment that lay in the detail but from the start he was determined that if Germany submitted to control, it would only do it once—other forms of control, such as the International Ruhr Authority, would have to lose their powers. It was almost the last issue to be resolved in the subsequent negotiations.

The negotiations on the Schuman Plan were dominated by Monnet and his team. They chaired the most important committees and staffed the secretariat. Although Monnet had wanted a quick negotiation establishing the HA and its areas of competences, he accepted the need for some political control over it. He was also forced to respect the demands, especially by the Benelux countries, not only to define the areas of HA competences, but also to define the competences themselves—what price systems, what tariffs, when intervention, and so on. What emerged was a HA with considerable freedom of action, within the rules prescribed, over the coal and steel sectors. The Council of Ministers would be involved only when industrial policy conflicted with other policy areas, such as wages or defense strategies. The Court would arbitrate in cases of interpretation over the treaty and there would be an Assembly, with extremely limited powers. The Treaty of Paris was signed in April 1951 and the ECSC itself came into force in August 1952. Jean Monnet was nominated as its first president.

13.2 THE EUROPEAN DEFENCE COMMUNITY

As the negotiations for the ECSC were starting, another problem was emerging. The successful atomic test by the Soviet Union in August 1949 had scuppered the American hope that the United States could for much longer base its defense strategy on its nuclear monopoly. The president ordered the National Security Council to review the options and its report, NSC–68, completed in April 1950, painted a scenario of a defenseless Europe falling within months to a Soviet attack and, thereafter, posing a serious threat to Atlantic communications. Having surveyed various alternatives, the report concluded that the only solution was, with American help, to increase European defense capabilities, and to rearm Germany. Soon after the report was delivered to the president, the Korean War started and the decision was taken to press ahead with the demand for German rearmament.

If the idea of the re-emergence of German heavy industry had worried French policy-makers, it was nothing like the impact the prospect of a rearmed Germany had upon the French population. Schuman frankly told US policy-makers that the suggestion was completely unacceptable to French public opinion and the French Assembly. However, if supranationality could control German heavy industry, could not the same mechanism be used to control a German army? In haste, Monnet instructed his staff to prepare a scheme for a European army into which German forces would be integrated. Launched in October 1950, the Pléven Plan, as it became known after the prime minister, became the French alternative to the US scheme.[3] It set out the principle of a European army, with a single budget and a single minister of defense. However Article 38 left the details of its exact institutional framework to be elaborated later, after ratification, by a parliamentary assembly. Although the Pléven plan endorsed supranationality, it was not a particularly even treaty that emerged. It contained clauses that disadvantaged Germany and privileged France—there was to be no German army or German high command (unlike other nations, German troops would enlist directly into the European army); Germany unilaterally renounced the possession of nuclear weapons; there was to be no advanced military industry in strategically vulnerable areas (with a defense line initially envisaged along the Rhine, that meant most of Germany). The German Social Democrats were vehemently opposed to the plan, and opposed to rearmament generally. As with the ECSC, for the plan to work it required Adenauer's endorsement. It is interesting that throughout the long, tortuous, and ultimately futile negotiations for an EDC, the Germans never tried to claw back on these provisions.

Eventually the Americans withdrew their scheme and threw their backing behind the Pléven plan. Negotiations involving all six ECSC members produced a treaty, which was signed in Paris in May 1952. All that remained was to secure its ratification. Meanwhile, the Italian prime minister, Alcide de Gasperi (1881–1954), convinced Schuman that the period before ratification could usefully be employed if the Assembly envisaged in Article 38 were to start its work beforehand. De Gasperi was a local catholic politician in his native Austrian South Tyrol. When, in 1919, the area devolved to Italy, he went to Rome as one of its parliamentary deputies. He was imprisoned for eighteen months by the fascists, and upon his release he retired from public life to work in the Vatican library. After the overthrow of Mussolini he returned to politics. In 1944 he founded Italy's Christian Democratic Party and became Italy's foreign minister. Three years later he became the country's prime minster, a post which he held until his death. He was an ardent federalist, though it is doubtful whether he anticipated the effect of his actions in establishing a provisional assembly to give effect to Article 38. He certainly supported the outcome.

At the time, the ECSC had just come into effect and its Assembly, drawn from members of the Consultative Assembly of the Council of Europe, had yet to meet. Aside from reviewing association agreements, respectfully following the work of the HA and keeping an organic link with the Council of Europe, its powers were strictly limited. Under Article 38, this body, with its composition slightly amended to reflect the different composition of the ECSC and EDC Assemblies, would design an institutional framework to contain both existing treaties.[4] In September 1952 the "ad-hoc assembly" was given six months to prepare a draft text. The chairman of the Assembly was former Belgian foreign minister, Paul-Henri Spaak (1899–1972). A socialist politician, he became his country's foreign minister in 1936 and briefly prime minister. He spent the World War II in exile in London. After the war, he had two short stints as prime minister, but in 1949 he and his party were in opposition. As a member of parliament, he joined the newly formed Consultative Assembly of the Council of Europe and was elected as its first chairman. However, he quickly chaffed under the restrictions imposed on the Assembly's mandate and in December 1951 he resigned as its chairman. Although he initially opposed the more radical elements of the federalist movement, whilst fighting for more powers for the Consultative Assembly, he fell increasingly under their sway and turned his attention to the Six as a means for pioneering the constitutional reform of the Continent. In March 1952, even before the agreement to activate Article 38, he convened a group of lawyers to prepare the groundwork for the European Communities. When the Ad Hoc Assembly was convened, Spaak was elected as its chairman.

By this stage, Spaak was heavily under the influence of the radical Italian federalist, Altiero Spinelli (1907–1986). A communist political journalist, Spinelli fell foul of the Italian fascist authorities and spent most of the period after 1927 in prison. Whilst in prison, he broke with Stalin and was profoundly influenced by UK federalist writings. He became convinced that a federal Europe would not come about if it were entrusted to national politicians. What was needed was the immediate creation of a democratically elected constituent assembly that would design the constitution for a new Europe. With political legitimacy would come power and authority, and not the other way round— piecemeal surrenders of sovereignty leading to democratic responsibility. In 1943, immediately after the fall of Mussolini, he founded the European Federalist Movement, espousing this radical band of federalism. Forced to compromise in the Congress in The Hague in 1948, which created the Council of Europe, and as a member of its Consultative Assembly, he witnessed at first hand as his misgivings were confirmed. Now, together with Spaak, he formed part of the secretariat empowered to lead the Ad Hoc Assembly in designing a new constitution. The design went straight back to basic federalist principles, with a strict functional split between federal (i.e. European) and states (i.e. national) levels, and with a full panoply of institutions at the federal level—a court, a two-chamber legislature, an executive Council, and a Council of (national) Ministers (with the latter consigned to a subsidiary role). It was little less than an attempted coup d'état.

Meanwhile, the situation was further complicated by the Dutch demand for the inclusion in the new community of a customs union. The Netherlands was a highly trade-dependent economy, always strongly reliant on Germany for both markets and supplies. Since the war, and still smarting from the experience during the Great Depression, successive governments had struggled to reduce trade barriers, to control their re-erection in case of economic difficulties, and to obtain Germany's re-entry into the European trading network. They had used any and every available forum to push their cause.[5] It was only a matter of time before they devised a scheme for the six ECSC countries. The task fell to the new foreign minister, Jan-Willem Beyen (1987–1976). Beyen was an international financier who had worked with the Bank of International Settlements before the war and with the IMF after the war. He had no party allegiance and was brought into the government by prime minister Drees to counteract the pro-integration drift within his cabinet. It was a big mistake. Drees had not wanted a European army and he was not enamored by yet another layer of European institutions. It was not difficult to get him to tie Dutch demands for a customs union to Dutch acceptance of the latter. But what might have started as opportunism on Beyen's part soon transmuted to warm support for European integration.

While all these developments were taking place, the French political landscape was shifting radically. New elections increased the representation of Gaullist parliamentarians in the French Assembly and although the MRP remained in government, Robert Schuman's support for supranationality was no longer sustainable. In January 1953 he lost his post as minister of foreign affairs to his party colleague Georges Bedault. He remained in parliament and continued to support the EDC. In 1955 he returned to government for a short time as minister for justice, before becoming once more a parliamentarian, president of the European Movement, and president of the Assembly of the EEC. Meanwhile, events in Strasbourg were now moving far ahead of the original French design—a simple construction to contain German rearmament. They now embraced a nascent federal structure and a move toward economic integration. When the Ad Hoc Assembly presented a draft treaty to the ECSC ministers for an intergovernmental conference, in March 1953, the French government started to empty the draft treaty of its content while, at the same time, demanding additional safeguards to the EDC treaty itself. Only de Gasperi stayed true to the original design. In August 1954 the French government made a final set of demands on the EDC treaty signatories, including abandoning everything that had happened since the acceleration of Article 38, and starting the institutional design anew. When these demands were refused, the French Assembly rejected the EDC Treaty. De Gasperi died on the eve of that vote. Spinelli continued to fight actively for a federal Europe and in 1979 he became a member of the European Parliament. In this capacity, he single-mindedly set in motion a campaign for greater powers for the Parliament that led to the adoption in 1984 of a Draft Treaty of European Union. The draft was taken up by European governments but by the time it re-emerged as the SEA, most of the increased parliamentary powers had disappeared.

13.3 EUROPEAN ECONOMIC COMMUNITY

The rejection of the EDC treaty by the French Assembly made clear that, without a change in government, there was little point in pursuing any new integrationist schemes. The HA, still led by Jean Monnet, remained Europe's sole supranational institution. It had indeed overseen the creation of a single market in coal and steel, but was being criticized for weakness in the face of the steel barons and supine before the foot-dragging of the German government when it came to taking measures to dismantle the national coal cartel.[6] Monnet was a "doer;" he was not suited to administering what was basically a supranational regulator. He was impatient for action. When, in February 1955, the Mendes–France government, responsible for the EDC failure, collapsed, he accelerated his plans for a European "relaunch."

Monnet originally had two aims. The first was to remain as president of the HA but on condition that negotiations would start, hopefully under his leadership, that would mark the next steps toward European integration. The second was to determine the direction that those steps would take. To start with the second, Monnet considered that one should build on the experience of the HA and expand into areas that flanked its existing competences—all coal consumption, "traditional energy," or rail traffic. Viable and worthy though these initiatives seemed, they were not the stuff to set the world alight. What Monnet thought would clinch the deal was atomic energy—it was new, so there were few entrenched interests; it was expensive, so it paid to work together; it was exciting, so it would capture the public's imagination; and the French wanted it. By this time, Monnet was beginning to get signals that the French, in particular, were far from keen to have him run any new negotiations and that any "relaunch" emanating from the HA might be a liability. If there were to be a new initiative, it would have to come from elsewhere and therefore Monnet turned to Spaak, once more his country's foreign minister, to see whether the Benelux countries would be prepared to front the initiative. At this point, Beyen made it clear that if there were to be a Benelux memorandum, it would have to include a customs union. Beyen's argument was that in the negotiations around the draft treaty, five countries had been willing to countenance a move to further economic integration, even if not exactly in the form the Dutch were proposing. The only exception had been France, but therein lay the problem. Monnet was not opposed to a customs union, but he was wary of tying the new initiative to something that the French had already rejected and therefore inviting a further rebuff. Beyen's insistence ensured that economic integration remained on the table. Monnet also allowed his own candidature for HA president, and his offer to run the subsequent negotiations, to go forward, despite clear signals that this would be unacceptable to the French. Monnet's logic was that the French might start the new negotiations with one veto; they were unlikely to use two.

In May 1955 the ECSC ministers met in Messina in Italy.[7] Monnet's candidature was the first item on the agenda and it was, as expected, refused. His chosen successor was the Frenchman René Mayer. Monnet resigned his post shortly afterwards and created the Action Committee for the United States of Europe, which he ran until forced by ill health to retire in 1975. Through this means he tried to mobilize especially trade union support for European integration and he employed his considerable network of contacts in the higher echelons of the American administration to bolster support for the new communities. The Messina meeting did go on to accept virtually the whole raft of proposals as a basis for further negotiation, but significantly, it downplayed any mention of federalism or of supranationality. Spaak was chosen to lead the negotiations.

From the start, Spaak treated the common market and atomic energy as the twin prongs of his efforts, aided by the Germans who insisted throughout that the two treaties be negotiated and signed together. His efforts were greatly assisted by a change in government in France in January 1956, which produced a more positive approach toward economic integration, though still a cautious one (France was becoming increasingly embroiled in Algeria and its balance of payments position was precarious). The "Spaak Report" became the basis for the negotiations that led to the signing of the Treaty of Rome in March 1957. Beyen was not one of the signatories. He had lost his cabinet post in October 1956 and ended his career as Dutch ambassador to Paris. Spaak went on to become Secretary General of NATO in May 1957, and never returned to advocate the federalist cause.

13.4 REFLECTIONS

There are several observations that one can make following this review of the "founding fathers." The first is that we can debunk the common assertion that from the start they intended to achieve a political goal (European integration) by economic means (the ECSC and EEC). On the contrary, they intended to obtain political goals by political means. There are surely few things more political than linking armed forces and, by implication, foreign policy. These ambitions went further than anything attempted since, and it was the crushing failure to realize them that left the economic route as one of the few alternatives available.

The second fallacy that we can disprove is that there is a Darwinian link between the ECSC and the EEC. It is true that the institutional architecture is similar, but the constellation of power is radically different. The Messina meeting did not endorse the pattern of earlier integration, but decisively rejected it, and its embodiment, Jean Monnet. In place of a powerful, independent, and technocratic HA, the Treaty of Rome placed most of the decision-making in the hands of the states, represented by the Council of Ministers. The powers of initiative granted to the Commission were, in reality, severely circumscribed by the degree of support among the states.

The third observation lies in the working methods. Each of the three treaties was negotiated in a different way. For Monnet, the secret to success in the ECSC negotiations was to sideline the politicians, while technocrats worked together to solve practical problems. Spaak, by contrast, while directing the EEC negotiations, believed that it required a strong direction from a political personality to push innately conservative officials forward. In contrast, negotiations for the new institutional framework for the ECSC and EDC treaties were initiated and directed by a parliamentary assembly or, rather, by its secretariat. Whether working methods are instrumental to success is difficult to prove either way; successful outcomes almost by definition have successful methods. However, the parliamentary method does seem a questionable one. The Ad Hoc Assembly advanced so far outside what the member states were willing to accept that it was almost fifty years before the idea was tried again in a modified form in the European Convention leading to the Treaty establishing a Constitution for Europe that was rejected by referendums in France and the Netherlands in May–June 2005. The European Assembly's unsolicited draft constitution in 1984 was similarly stripped of most of its content by member states. If history can teach us little about the methods for success in intergovernmental conferences, it does suggest that the more democratic approach has not triumphed.

Looking back at the period covered in this chapter, there would be few at that time who would have believed the progress toward European integration made over the next fifty years. This is often heralded as a vindication of the "Monnet method," a gradual step-by-step functional approach involving concrete projects. Spinelli's one-step institutional approach to the creation of a federation was relegated to the history of ideas. Interestingly, the Monnet and Spinelli approaches clashed directly at the Conference of the European Union of Federalists early in 1956, at which Spinelli rejected a compromise resolution to support both approaches simultaneously. He established his own organization, European Federalist Action, whose 650,000 adherents, however, proved insufficient to attract government backing. Although the mantle of history belongs to the Monnet method, it is difficult, with hindsight, to refute Spinelli's analysis that member states, left to themselves, would be slow to surrender their powers to democratic bodies, let alone to federalist institutions. The "democratic deficit" is part of the price paid by the success of Monnet's approach.

At the start of this chapter, we introduced the structure/agent debate and suggested that history is best served by conflating the two approaches. This serves to pay attention to the constraints under which historical actors operated, the problems that had to be overcome, while holding on to some vision of a future. The founding fathers were not "European saints" or visionaries[8] but practical politicians dealing with real problems, and trying to solve them in institutional forms that would prove more attractive and more durable than those that had ended in economic depression, autarchy, militarism, and war. This makes their personal achievements more real than if we were to portray them as heroes of myth and legend.

NOTES

1. For details of the origins of the ECSC see J. Gillingham, *Coal, Steel and the Rebirth of Europe, 1945–1955* (Cambridge: Cambridge University Press, 1991); A. S. Milward, *The Reconstruction of Western Europe, 1945–1951* (London: Methuen, 1984); K. Schwabe, *Die Anfänge des Schuman-Plans 1950/51. The Beginnings of the Schuman Plan* (Baden-Baden: Nomos, 1988).
2. D. Brinkley and C. Hackett, *Jean Monnet: The Path to European Unity* (New York: St. Martin's Press, 1991).
3. For details of the European Defence Community see A. Clesse, *Le projet de C.E.D. du Plan Pléven au "crime" du 30 aout: Histoire d'un malentendu européen* (Baden-Baden, Nomos, 1989); M. Dumoulin, ed., *La communauté européenne de défence, leçons pours demains?* (Berne: Peter Lang, 2000); E. Fursdon, *The European Defence Community: A History* (London: Macmillan 1980); H. E. Volkmann and W. Schwengler, eds, *Die Europäische Verteidigungsgemeinschaft: Stand und Probleme der Forschung* (Boppard am Rhein, Boldt, 1985).
4. R. T. Griffiths, *The European Political Community, 1952–1954. Europe's First Federal Constitution* (London, Federal Trust, 2000); D. Preda, *Sulla soglia dell'unione: la vicenda della Comunità Politica Europea (1952–1954)* (Milan: Jacca Books, 1993).
5. W. Asbeek Brusse, *Tariffs, Trade and European Integration, 1947–1957. From Study Group to Common Market* (New York: St. Martin's Press, 1997).
6. D. Spierenburg and R. Poidevin, *Histoire de la Haute Autorité de la Communauté du charbon et de lácier, une expérience supranationale* (Brussels: Bruylant 1993).
7. For details of the relaunch and the subsequent negotiations see E. Serra, *Il Rilancio dell'Europa e i Trattati di Roma. La Relance Européenne et les traités de Rome. The Relaunching of Europe and the Treaties of Rome* (Brussels: Brulyant, 1989).
8. For an iconoclastic view see A. S. Milward, "The Lives and Teachings of the European Saints" in A. S. Milward, *The European Rescue of the Nation State* (London: Routledge, 1992) 318–44.

CHAPTER 14

......

DYNAMIC FRANCO–GERMAN DUOS: GISCARD–SCHMIDT AND MITTERRAND–KOHL

......

CARINE GERMOND

THERE is widespread agreement among scholars on the decisive role that France and Germany play in the European Community, based on a close, cooperative, and interdependent relationship.[1] The oft-used labels of the motor or engine of Europe suggest that the two countries together act as a driving force, while the imagery of the tandem, couple, or duo stresses the role of the leaders who embody it. These images are generally associated with dynamic pairs of statesmen who have promoted Franco–German cooperation and implemented an integrationist European agenda thanks to their personal entente and use of the institutional structures created by the Elysée Treaty signed in January 1963.

The successful duos formed by Valéry Giscard d'Estaing–Helmut Schmidt and François Mitterrand–Helmut Kohl shared a number of characteristics, such as excellent personal relations, a consensus on the necessity of a close cooperation to steer Europe in their desired direction, and the ability to take advantage of opportunities arising from the European and international context, which single them out from the many Franco–German couples, which have followed one another since the legendary couple of Charles de Gaulle and Konrad Adenauer.[2] By analyzing the personal, institutional and contextual factors that allowed the Giscard–Schmidt and Mitterrand–Kohl tandems to exert influence in the Community, this chapter intends to assess how their joint leadership shaped bilateral and European affairs and to clarify the role played by them in European integration.

14.1 THE PERSONAL VARIABLE: A SPECIAL RELATIONSHIP?

Both Giscard and Schmidt came to occupy the highest positions in France and Germany, respectively, in the spring of 1974. An essential characteristic of the Giscard–Schmidt era was the friendly, trustful, and constructive relationship between the two leaders, which they had developed initially while serving as the finance ministers of their respective countries. The two men also shared similar ideas on monetary issues, a crucial subject in a time of monetary instability after the collapse of the Bretton Woods system, as well as a certain "superiority complex" since they viewed themselves as finance experts. Giscard and Schmidt came from different political parties—Giscard belonged to the center, European-oriented right; Schmidt was a moderate social democrat—but this did not hinder their cooperation. They represented a new generation of politicians, who adopted a less formal style in the conduct of bilateral relations with organized meetings in their private houses and English as a common language. Their memoirs bear witness to truly good personal relations.[3]

Personal affinities were reinforced by a strong will to cooperate on both sides of the Rhine. Giscard wanted to move beyond reconciliation, which he believed had been achieved by de Gaulle and Adenauer, and toward a Franco–German entente that would reassert Europe's influence in the world. Schmidt, too, was interested in closer cooperation with France. Yet, conscious of the historical and political constraints limiting the Federal Republic's leeway, he formally left the leading role to Giscard in joint initiatives. Both men purposefully emphasized the privileged character of the Franco–German relationship. It is no accident that references to the Franco–German couple, axis, or tandem, which stressed both the dynamism and the centrality of the Franco–German relationship, began to flourish during the mid-1970s. Their excellent personal relations and particular division of responsibilities, as well as a shared outlook on the Franco–German role in Europe, enabled Giscard and Schmidt to form a close and dynamic alliance during Giscard's seven-year term.

The nomination of Helmut Kohl at the Federal Chancellery in October 1982, about a year and half after François Mitterrand's election to the French presidency in May 1981, marked the beginning of a new era in Franco–German relations. Relations between Mitterrand and Kohl's predecessor, Helmut Schmidt, were characterized by a lack of personal affinities and disagreements on the economic and social policies of the new French government. Moreover, Mitterrand showed at the beginning of his presidency a certain distance from the concept of a privileged partnership with Germany and attempted to establish closer relations with other neighboring countries. Yet, the French president was quickly forced to acknowledge the importance of preferential ties to Germany and the two countries' interdependence.

At first glance, Mitterrand and Kohl formed an odd couple.[4] The short, elegant, intellectual, sphinx-like Mitterrand, whose ambiguous political career had led him from working for the Vichy regime to joining the Socialist Party later on, stood in stark contrast to the tall, massive, and unsophisticated Kohl, whose career, from early engagement in the Christian Democratic Union to political leader to his election as chancellor, was comparatively straightforward. Despite different political allegiances and personal histories, both leaders came to share what looked like a genuine friendship. Although they belonged to different generations, Mitterrand and Kohl shared the same European will and a desire to cooperate. Mitterrand was a convinced European, not least because he saw the link between European integration and the answer to the German question.[5] Kohl, the self-styled grandson of Adenauer, like him a Rhinelander, wanted to preserve and build up the privileged partnership with France. Moreover, they both felt the—oft-tragic—community of destiny that united their countries. This sense of a community of shared fate is found in several of Mitterrand's writings[6] and is best captured in the image of the two statesmen, hand in hand, solemnly commemorating the soldiers who fell in the battle of Verdun during the World War I. This kinship explains much of the Mitterrand–Kohl relationship. It gave Franco–German ties a stability that outlasted day-to-day disagreements or divergences of interests. It gave their joint initiatives the momentum needed to achieve progress in Europe. Nevertheless, Mitterrand, just as his predecessors at the Elysée Palace, was unwilling to go beyond an asymmetrical relationship, in which France remained the senior partner.

The fruitful personal cooperation that existed between Giscard and Schmidt or Mitterrand and Kohl helped them transform a shared consensus on the necessity of bilateral cooperation into practical realizations and overcome diverging positions. Conversely, communication problems or lack of personal affinities, which existed between other couples, such as Charles de Gaulle and Ludwig Erhard,[7] or, currently exist between Nicolas Sarkozy and Angela Merkel, impeded common bilateral actions. The systematic emphasis of the Franco–German entente under Giscard–Schmidt and Mitterrand–Kohl also had a normative and performative function: the good personal relations were to epitomize and assert the far-reaching agreement between the two countries. If a close personal understanding is an important variable for a successful joint Franco–German leadership, the cooperation Treaty of 1963, which legally underpins and institutionally structures contemporary Franco–German relations, is a key parameter of the privileged partnership.

14.2 The Institutional Variable: The Elysée Treaty

Signed on January 22, 1963 by Charles de Gaulle and Konrad Adenauer, the Elysée Treaty established highly institutionalized structures and procedures of cooperation. It is the most important document governing the modern relationship between France and Germany.[8] The treaty's multilayered consultations provide a forum, in which Paris and

Bonn (and later Berlin) learned to negotiate and reach compromises and established the Franco–German dialogue as a pivotal element of post-war European politics.

During their term as finance ministers, Giscard and Schmidt had met regularly within the consultation framework of the Elysée Treaty. These institutionalized meetings encouraged a "coordination reflex"[9] that lived on after these two men became president and chancellor of their respective states. Yet, as heads of state, they developed a habit of meeting informally on the sidelines of European summits to agree on common policy positions and of bypassing the official—bilateral or European—channels when necessary. The EMS, which was devised during a tête-à-tête in Schmidt's private apartment before it was proposed to the European Community member states in July 1978, is the most significant example of this trend.[10]

A key characteristic of bilateral relations under Kohl and Mitterrand was the will to use the consultation mechanisms of the Elysée Treaty to find bilateral compromises that led to new political initiatives on a European level. Accordingly, the two statesmen took several initiatives to deepen and extend Franco–German cooperation in new areas such as culture, scientific research, education, and youth, which were frequently translated into European policies. The Franco–German couple thus emerged "as a sort of European laboratory."[11] Mitterrand and Kohl also further developed the institutional dialogue. The semi-annual summit consultations, which involved an ever-increasing number of ministers, evolved into a sort of Franco–German Council of Ministers. Following each Council, they held joint press conferences that established a "joint Franco–German discourse"[12] on Europe and served to underpin the engine role of the Franco–German tandem. In 1988, on the twenty-fifth anniversary of the Elysée Treaty, the two governments added a protocol to it that created new consultation instruments in the fields of culture, finance, and the military. This innovation, the first since the signature of the Elysée Treaty, not only broadened the scope of Franco–German bilateralism, but also highlighted the capacity to modernize and adapt consultation mechanisms and instruments in order to tackle new challenges posed to the Franco–German relationship in Europe and the world.

14.3 The Dependent Variable: The European and International Context

The dynamics of the political relationship in the Giscard–Schmidt and Mitterrand–Kohl eras depended on the European and international context, which more than often emphasized the need for greater bilateral solidarity and favored close cooperation in a European framework but sometimes hindered common actions.

Soon after Giscard's election, the French president and Helmut Schmidt agreed on the need to restart the process of European integration and to deepen it in the monetary and institutional arenas, which, against the backdrop of the economic crisis after the first oil shock of 1973 and a difficult international context, seemed crucial.[13] While ideological quarrels had hindered their predecessors' ability to act as Europe's engine, the pragmatism of both of these statesmen permitted certain breakthroughs. The difficult economic and monetary situation encouraged the need for bilateral initiatives and European solutions in these areas.

Institutional progress in the European Community was enabled by the pragmatic approach chosen by Giscard and Schmidt, as well as by a convergence in their visions. Although Giscard officially maintained the confederal line adopted by his predecessors, his understanding of the term was flexible enough to leave room for substantial advances. At the same time, Schmidt, whose country had been traditionally pushing for a federal Europe, did not pursue supranational objectives. This convergence in policy made a middle ground between the pro-federal German position and the pro-intergovernmental French position much easier to find.

During their terms, Giscard and Schmidt took on two major European institutional initiatives, which led to the creation of the European Council and the election of the European Parliament by direct suffrage. The European Council was the brain child of Jean Monnet[14] and institutionalized meetings between the heads of state and government of the European Community member states. After his election, Giscard wanted to make a strong sign of change in French European policy and supported the project. Schmidt was personally in favor of some sort of a European executive, but he was aware that the creation of a new European intergovernmental body would be problematic in his country. Hence, he suggested doubling this initiative with the election of the European Parliament by direct elections, an old German aspiration. The double Franco–German initiative was adopted in December 1974 at the Paris summit. Although the European Council was initially more of an impulse than a real institution, it proved decisive for the later evolution of European integration.

To a large extent, the new European Community institution mirrored the working method and practice of the Giscard–Schmidt duo that preferred discussing important issues in small groups at the highest levels of state unhindered by institutional mechanisms.[15] The European Council furthermore became the privileged institution for Franco–German cooperation and a forum in which Giscard and Schmidt could rally their partners to their joint projects, such as the EMS, or views, for instance on the Conference on the Security and Cooperation in Europe established after the Helsinki summit of 1975. Giscard and Schmidt also used the European Council to develop the EPC in two ways. Firstly, they initiated joint bilateral actions that resulted in actions of the Nine. This illustrated their preference for intergovernmental initiatives, whose implementation could be left to the Community institutions, however, as the example of the Euro–Arab dialogue showed. Secondly, the Franco–German tandem was to embody Europe's voice in the international arena. This was made possible by the convergence in the policies of both leaders that contributed to the emergence of a sort of Franco–German "third way" in the world arena characterized by non-alignment with US policy and the preservation of the dialogue and détente with the East. While this confirmed the existence of a genuine Franco–German entente on international issues, it also revealed a very Gaullist conception, in which the Franco–German duo was equated with Europe. For instance, the joint declaration issued by Paris and Bonn after the invasion of Afghanistan by Soviet troops was presented as the Community's position although the European Community partners had been neither consulted nor informed.

Two main elements characterized the working of the Giscard–Schmidt in the European Council and help explain their relative success: first, a flawless solidarity and mutual support that enabled them to either impose their views on their partners or limit the leeway of difficult partners such as Margaret Thatcher (see Chapter 15, this volume); second, a division of responsibility whereby Giscard acted as the representative of the Franco-German duo—this prevented eventual fears of a German domination in the European Community and corresponded to Giscard's own view of his role within the Franco–German tandem.[16]

Giscard and Schmidt did not limit their common actions to the European political realm but took several initiatives to promote economic and monetary governance in the European Community. The development of Franco–German economic and monetary cooperation was in large part a reaction against the consequences of the oil shock of 1973 and the end of the fixed exchange rate anchored to gold, with the resulting dollar volatility. Economic stagnation, rampant inflation, rising unemployment, and monetary instability affected both countries in a similar fashion and threatened to undermine the cohesion of the Community. For both statesmen, it was important that Europe present a united front. An important milestone in this regard was the creation of the G7, an idea of Giscard and Schmidt, who had recognized the growing economic interdependence of the West and hoped that this would provide a forum in which the leading Western economies could coordinate their economic and financial policies at the international level. Although the G7 did not fulfill all the hopes of its initiators, it embodied Giscard's and Schmidt's common approach to international problems: the preference for multilateral rather than national solutions and the affirmation of a Franco–German "community of destiny"[17] within Europe and beyond.

Monetary cooperation was by no means a new idea. As finance ministers, Giscard and Schmidt were both involved in the first attempts at monetary rapprochement through the creation of the "snake in the tunnel," which set fluctuation margins for the European currencies. Yet, the snake soon proved unsustainable, with currencies such as the French franc constantly leaving and rejoining. The snake eventually collapsed in 1973 when the dollar began to float freely. Yet, the two leaders were convinced that a monetary union would be the best instrument to shelter the Community from the fluctuations of American monetary policy and endow the Community with a common currency capable of measuring up to international currencies.

The EMS was pushed by Giscard in particular, whose aim was twofold: he hoped the EMS would stabilize the European currencies and establish monetary solidarity. Schmidt was at first reluctant about the project. He feared that the system would weaken Europe's stronger currencies, like the mark, without providing any substantial help to the weaker currencies such as the franc. Two main factors pushed him to rally for the idea. First, the economic policy of austerity adopted by Prime Minister Raymond Barre in 1976 aligned French economic and monetary policy with Germany's and steered France away from inflation and toward monetary stability, a chief objective of the Germans. Second, increasingly strained German–American relations after the election of President Jimmy Carter in 1976 and Schmidt's irritation with American monetary policy, which he felt was responsible for Europe's monetary problems and their economic consequences, tilted the German chancellor in favor of the monetary project.[18] In 1978, Giscard and Schmidt seized the political, economic, national, and international moment, successfully instrumentalizing their entente to advance European integration with the creation of the EMS.

Interestingly, the realization of this project embodied the working methods of the Giscard–Schmidt duo: the details of the project were elaborated in secret, "at the summit, in exclusive company, and outside institutional circuits."[19] The two statesmen worked closely together not only on general principles but, drawing on their own expertise, also on all important details. Hence, the blueprint for the European monetary system that was presented to the other European Community member states at the European Council of Bremen in July 1978 was a truly Franco–German project. The EMS came into force in March 1979. Although it initiated a form of European monetary solidarity, its effectiveness was undermined significantly by the severe deterioration of the economic and international contexts after the outbreak of the revolution in Iran and the resulting second oil shock.

Despite the progress achieved under Giscard and Schmidt, European integration had reached a plateau by the beginning of the 1980s. Disputes between the member states over the agricultural budget and the question of the British contribution were paralyzing the European Community. The Mitterrand–Kohl duo played a key role in the European revival of the 1980s. The Franco–German rapprochement on European issues was facilitated in the spring of 1983 by the readjustment of Mitterrand's domestic policy toward German monetary and economic orthodoxy. A bilateral agreement on the necessity to relaunch Europe in the key areas of military and security policy and economic and monetary integration took shape gradually in the second half of 1983.

In the course of the 1980s, France and Germany took a series of pragmatic and piecemeal bilateral initiatives that moved closer to European integration in the areas of defense and security.[20] The intensification of the Franco–German dialogue from the early 1980s onward was triggered primarily by the euromissiles crisis, which had underscored the vulnerability of Europe and the common strategic Franco–German interests. This strategic rapprochement constituted an innovation. While cooperation in the areas of defense and security was stipulated by the Elysée Treaty, it had remained limited. A milestone was set in January 1983 when Mitterrand supported the deployment of the US Pershing in a speech to the German Bundestag, and thereby signaled his support of Chancellor Kohl, who faced strong domestic opposition from the pacifist and neutralist movements. Mitterrand's speech is described by his close advisor Hubert Védrine as a "founding act,"[21] for it paved the way to closer Franco–German—and later European—collaboration in the area of defense and security. All projects did not come to fruition, and important strategic differences remained. Still, one can point to concrete examples of Franco–German collaboration.[22] In 1988, on the initiative of Helmut Kohl, the two governments jointly created the Franco–German brigade, which was intended to be a symbol of Franco–German military cooperation and form the core of a future European force. The Franco–German brigade was eventually subsumed under the Eurocorps. Particularly important was the creation of the Security and Defense Council in 1988, the aim of which was to develop common military conceptions and armaments, and increase military cooperation generally. Institutional improvements of the Elysée Treaty served to underpin their European initiatives. These various initiatives are indeed characteristic of the way Mitterrand and Kohl used their privileged partnership to advance European integration: Franco–German realizations were systematically designed to trigger a "spillover effect" from the bilateral to the European level and so deepen integration in the chosen area.

The renewal of Franco–German cooperation furthermore gave decisive impetus to the European *relance* of the mid-1980s.[23] Both statesmen played a key role in the settlement of the budgetary disputes at the European Community summit of Fontainebleau in June 1984. Thanks to the Franco–German entente, the Ten agreed on the European Community budget, on the limitation of agricultural expenditures, and on compensation for the British deficit to the Community budget. This agreement lifted the obstacle to the accession of Spain and Portugal and to the convocation of two committees charged with studying the possibility of a political union. The two statesmen agreed at Fontainebleau to appoint Jacques Delors as President of the European Commission.[24] They were also influential in convincing their partners to hold an IGC and adopt Delors' single market project. Convened at Rome in June 1985, the IGC resulted in the adoption of the SEA in February 1986. By establishing a genuine common market, in which goods, workers, capital, and services could move freely, the SEA took European integration to a new level. Mitterrand and Kohl led the way when they decided in the summer of 1984 to open the borders between France and Germany. This decision served as a forerunner to the Europe-wide freedom of movement introduced a year later with the Schengen agreement and provided another example of the avant-garde function of the Franco–German relationship under Mitterrand and Kohl.

As of 1986, the Franco–German couple seemed to be losing its momentum due to resurging disagreements over agriculture and the EMU. While Paris and Bonn agreed on the necessity to reform the CAP, they disagreed on how to achieve this. In February 1988, an agreement was finally reached after an exceptional summit meeting, thanks not least to the Franco–German entente. EMU remained a bone of contention, however. France, whose currency was tied to the German mark through the EMS, was in favor of EMU, which would give Paris more influence over monetary decisions. German authorities were divided over the issue. Under pressure from France, Kohl eventually agreed at a Council meeting in Hannover to launch the EMU project and Delors was charged with drafting a report. Presented in April 1989, the Delors report prescribed a three-stage economic and monetary union, and recommended the creation of an independent European central bank, a major concession to German wishes. EMU was adopted at the European summit in Madrid in June 1989. Kohl agreed to set a date for the implementation of its first stage, but he refused to set one to convene the IGC, which would decide on the next stages. While Mitterrand hoped to use his good relations with Kohl to overcome German hesitations toward the EMU, Kohl's desire for a slow monetary unification was reinforced by the prospect of German reunification.

Although a primary objective of German foreign policy, reunification remained an unlikely event until 1989. The division of Germany had been a defining parameter of the post-war Franco–German relationship: it provided the basis for an asymmetrical balance of power within the Franco–German couple, arguably a key element of the successful reconciliation between the two former enemies and stability of the bilateral partnership since 1945.

German reunification had been often discussed during the regular Franco–German meetings as of 1987, but for neither Bonn nor Paris was it a prospect that would be achieved in the near future. Mitterrand considered the German aspiration to reunification legitimate provided the process would be peaceful, democratic, European, and respectful of existing borders—in particular the German–Polish border.[25] While German reunification was certainly not on his European agenda, the sudden fall of the Berlin Wall on the night of November 9–10, 1989 forced him to deal with the new geopolitical reality. His first reaction was to anchor a Germany on its way to reunification into a deepening European Community. Kohl, too, was aware of the necessity to achieve a certain balance between progress toward European integration—also as a means to reassure his European and American partners—and German unity. Yet, Mitterrand and Kohl did not agree on how to pursue either of these aims. While neither the persistence of contradictions nor the *cohabitation* in France had derailed the bilateral relationship, German reunification caused enormous frictions between the two leaders and put the Franco–German couple to the test.[26] It thus proved a deeply destabilizing event for the Paris–Bonn duo.

Mitterrand's position vis-à-vis reunification was subtle and complicated, and the French president did not do much to clarify it. His cryptic and ambiguous attitude gave rise to many controversial interpretations.[27] Although he was often portrayed by contemporaries and scholars as opposing German reunification, above all he wished to frame the process while and through strengthening Europe. Mitterrand's concerns over the prospect of German unity were enhanced by several acts of Kohl, which undermined a crucial element of the relations between the two partners: trust. First, the German chancellor did not seem as eager to push for the realization of the EMU, while Mitterrand insisted on setting a date for the ICG on it. Second, a major turning point was Kohl's speech to the Bundestag on November 28, 1989, in which he outlined a ten-point plan for a German confederation. The speech, which opened the way for a gradual reunification of the two Germanys, made clear that German unity, rather than European integration, had become the top priority of the federal government. Moreover, although the chancellor's proposals were prudent, they called for a new organization of Europe. Still worse, Paris had been neither consulted nor informed of the speech's content beforehand. This was a clear rupture with the institutional constraints structuring the partnership. Third, Paris was worried by the Federal government's unwillingness to commit itself to the recognition of the Oder–Neisse Line as the ultimate German–Polish border, which was a prerequisite for reunification for Paris. For these reasons, Mitterrand's main objective was to keep the unification process under control and to Europeanize it.

Since December 1989, the French president had pressured Chancellor Kohl to agree to convene an IGC on the EMU. After protracted bilateral discussions, Kohl eventually consented to set a date for the start of these talks, thereby signaling his intention to achieve both German and European unification. Moreover, the German chancellor suggested that monetary union be linked to a deepening of political cooperation between the European Community member states.

From the spring of 1990 onward, the Franco–German motor was working again. Yet, it had undergone significant transformation. German reunification accelerated the rebalancing of the power relations within the relationship, which had started in the 1970s, when the economic recession tipped the power scales in Germany's favor. Not only did a reunified Germany outperform France economically; the prospect of EU enlargement to Central and Eastern European countries emphasized Germany's key geo-strategic role between the center and the new periphery of the EU while France was sidelined on the Western march of the EU. Also, the working methods had imperceptibly changed with a consequent erosion of consensus: Mitterrand frequently had to exert pressures to rally an often reluctant German partner. As a result, the German chancellor was often accused at home of giving in to German interests in order to preserve relations with France.

Despite all tensions resulting from German unification and divergent interests, both countries worked together to advance the projects of monetary and political union. They did so by addressing a joint letter to their partners on April 18, 1990, in which they advocated in favor of two IGC: one on monetary union and a parallel one on a "European Union." This European Union was rather vaguely defined since Mitterrand did not want a political union unless it was intergovernmental, while Kohl was in no hurry to achieve economic union. Yet, in the second half of 1990, French and German experts drafted proposals, which were summarized in a joint letter in December 1990. These proposals were adopted soon after the Council meeting in Rome, and on December 15, 1990 the two IGC began their work. Franco–German consultations and input were decisive for the successful outcome of the negotiations and the signing of the Maastricht treaty, creating the EU.[28]

14.4 Conclusion

These duos stand out for their close personal relations, the rhetoric they employed about the Franco–German relationship, which fostered and perpetuated the myth of the Franco–German couple, their deliberate use of the institutional structures of cooperation, which underpinned "their capability to exercise political leadership and . . . to steer the course of the European ship."[29] What set them apart from other Franco–German

couples were their respective abilities to reach bilateral compromises through constructive dialogue (which, however, did not exclude occasional or persistent disagreements),
more realist approaches to the possibilities of their respective countries and their complementarities, but also more pragmatic understandings of what entente could achieve.
Giscard and Schmidt gave the Franco–German entente a new dimension that would be
further developed by their successors: from then on, the Paris–Bonn duo was to play a
true engine role in and for Europe.

Yet, if most of the history-making initiatives and integrationist progress achieved in
the period from the mid-1970s to the mid-1990s were of Franco–German origin,[30] this
was not solely the result of the political will of the leaders on both sides of Rhine.
Domestic and global events also promoted closer Franco–German cooperation. The
end of the Bretton Woods system in 1971 promoted closer monetary cooperation; "stagflation" and the increasing interdependence of leading European economies encouraged
the deepening of economic integration and gave the impetus for the SEA; finally, the
new surge of Cold War tensions in the late 1970s and early 1980s stimulated the development of common policies in the areas of defense and security, with France and Germany
as the main initiators. German unification underscored the need for a deepening of
European integration and significantly reshaped the bilateral relationship. The Franco–
German tandem also found a congenial partner in the European Commission, most
notably under Delors, to support their efforts to advance European integration.

If the most important legacy of these two duos was to have made an operational
Franco–German tandem a key factor of European progress, they also benefitted from an
environment conducive to the assertion of a joint leadership. In the early Community,
Paris and Bonn were able to set the agenda and propose solutions. Franco–German deals,
oftentimes agreed on difficult issues for both of the partners, were usually accepted by the
other member states provided a few amendments. Moreover, France and Germany still
represented the main geographical and political center in the European community of
Nine and the European Community of Twelve and this gave them a decisive advantage to
use their institutionalized "bilateralism"—which until today remains unequalled—to
influence their partners. True, Great Britain's adhesion to the Community in 1973 questioned the early Franco–German take-over of the Community leadership but did not
fundamentally alter the political preponderance of the two countries due to the difficult
relations of Thatcher to the European Community. The accession of the Mediterranean
countries diluted the North-Western dimension of the European Community and introduced new cooperation in areas where France and Germany had little common interests
and thus few incentives to cooperate and deepen European integration. Accordingly, the
expansion of policy areas dealt with by the Community that accompanied enlargement
reduced the leeway of the Franco–German tandem in Europe. Finally, the 2004 enlargement round undermined the Franco–German leadership by altering the traditional coalitions patterns within the Community and moving the European center of gravity farther
to the East. Consequently, present-day Franco–German relations have become more elusive. Yet, a dynamic Franco–German duo remains a necessary, though no longer a sufficient prerequisite for integration progresses in the EU.

NOTES

1. See Douglas Webber, ed., *The Franco–German Relationship in the European Union* (London: Routledge, 1999); Haig Simonian, *The Privileged Partnership: Franco–German Relations in the EC, 1969–1984* (Oxford: Clarendon, 1985); Julius Friend, *The Linchpin. Franco–German Relations 1950–1990* (New York: Praeger, 1990); Valérie Guérin-Sendelbach, *Ein Tandem für Europa? Die deutsch-französische Zusammenarbeit der achtziger Jahre* (Bonn: Europa Union Verlag, 1993); David P. Calleo and Eric R. Staal, eds, *Europe's Franco–German Engine* (Washington, DC: Brookings Institute Press, 1998); Gisela Hendriks and Annette Morgan, eds, *The Franco–German Axis in European Integration* (Cheltenham/Northampton: Edward Elgar Publishing, 2001).

2. On de Gaulle and Adenauer, see Ronald R. Granieri, "More Than a Geriatric Romance. Adenauer, De Gaulle, and the Atlantic Alliance," in Carine Germond and Henning Türk, eds, *A History of Franco–German Relations in Europe: From "Hereditary Enemies" to Partners* (New York: Palgrave Macmillan, 2008), 189–98.

3. Valéry Giscard D'Estaing, *Le pouvoir et la vie* (Paris: Cie 12, 1988), 124–61.

4. Among the numerous biographies and studies devoted to Mitterrand and Kohl, see Ronald Tiersky, *Mitterrand: A Very French President* (Lanham: Rowman & Littlefeld, 2000); Alistair Cole, *François Mitterrand, A Study in Political Leadership* (Abingdon: Routledge, 2000); Hugo Pruys, *Kohl, Genius of the Present. A Biography* (Berlin: Edition Q, 1996); Clay Clemens and William E. Paterson, eds, *The Kohl Chancellorship* (London: F. Cass, 1998).

5. Hubert Védrine, *Les mondes de François Mitterrand. A l'Elysée 1981–1985* (Paris: Fayard, 1996), 120–30.

6. See François Mitterrand, *De l'Allemagne, de la France* (Paris: Odile Jacob, 1996).

7. See Carine Germond, *Partenaires de raison? Le couple France-Allemagne et l'unification de l'Europe (1963–1969)* (Munich: Oldenburg, 2013).

8. On the Elysée Treaty see Corine Defrance and Ulrich Pfeil, eds, *Der Elysée-Vertrag und die deutsch-franzposischen Beziehungen 1945–1963–2003* (Munich: Oldenburg, 2005).

9. William E. Paterson, "Did France and Germany Lead Europe? A Retrospect," in Jack E. Hayward, ed., *Leaderless Europe* (New York: Oxford University Press, 2008), 99.

10. Michèle Weinachter, "Franco–German Relations in the Giscard-Schmidt Era, 1974–1981," in Germond and Türk, *A History of Franco–German Relations in Europe*, 225.

11. Weinachter, "Franco–German Relations in the Giscard-Schmidt Era," 238.

12. Georges Saunier, "Le tandem François Mitterrand-Helmut Kohl," in Wilfried Loth, ed., *La gouvernance supranationale dans la construction européenne* (Bruxelles: Bruylant, 2005), 241.

13. For an in-depth account of Franco–German relations under Giscard and Schmidt, see Michèle Weinachter, *Valéry Giscard d'Estaing et l'Allemagne. Le double rêve inachevé* (Paris: L'Harmattan, 2004); Helène Miard-Delacroix, *Partenaires de choix? Le chancelier Helmut Schmidt et la France (1974–1982)* (Berne: Peter Lang, 1993).

14. See Chapter 13, this volume, for an in-depth discussion of Monnet's role in the early days of European integration.

15. Henri Ménudier, "Valéry Giscard d'Estaing et les relations franco-allemandes (1974–1981)," in Samy Cohen and Marie-Claude Smouts, eds, *La politique extérieure de Valéry Giscard d'Estaing* (Paris: Presses de la fondation nationale des sciences politiques, 1985), 69.

16. Michèle Weinachter, "Le tandem Valéry Giscard d'Estaing–Helmut Schmidt et la gouvernance européenne," in Loth, ed., *La gouvernance supranationale*, 214–15.

17. Weinachter, "Franco–German Relations in the Giscard-Schmidt Era," 227.

18. Giscard, *Le pouvoir et la vie*, 136.

19. Weinachter, "Franco–German Relations in the Giscard-Schmidt Era," 229.

20. A more detailed account of Franco–German military cooperation is provided in Stephen A. Kocs, *Autonomy or Power? The Franco–German Relationship and Europe's Strategic Choices*, 1955–1995 (Westport: Praeger, 1995), 187–244.

21. Hubert Védrine, *Les Mondes de François Mitterrand*.

22. On the Franco–German security dialogue, see Robin Laird, ed., *Strangers and Friends. The Franco-German Security Relationship* (New York: Pinter, 1989); Philip H. Gordon, *France, Germany and the Western Alliance* (Boulder: Westview, 1995).

23. See Thomas Pedersen, *France, Germany and the Integration of Europe. A Realist Interpretation* (London: Pinter, 1998), 88 ff.

24. See Chapter 16, this volume, for an in-depth analysis of Delors' contribution as president of the European Commission.

25. See Hubert Védrine, *Les Mondes de François Mitterrand*, 423–4.

26. Renata Fritsch-Bournazel, "German Unification: A Durability Test for the Franco–German Tandem," *German Studies Review* 14, no. 3 (1991), 575–85.

27. Most critics emphasize Mitterrand's reluctance for a speedy German reunification. See Samy Cohen, ed., *Mitterrand et la sortie de la guerre froide* (Paris: Presses Universitaires de France, 1998); Frédéric Bozo, *Mitterrand, the End of the Cold War, and German Reunification* (New York: Berghahn Books, 2005); Thilo Schabert, *How World Politics is Made. France and the Reunification of Germany* (Missouri: University of Missouri Press, 2002).

28. See Colette Mazzucelli, *France and Germany at Maastricht. Politics and Negotiations to Create the European Union* (New York: Garland, 1997).

29. Alistair Cole, "Franco–German Relations: From Active to Reactive Cooperation," in Hayward, *Leaderless Europe*, 149.

30. See in particular Alistair Cole, *Franco–German Relations* (London: Longman, 2001); Andrew Moravcsik, *The Choice for Europe, Social Purpose and State Power from Messina to Maastricht* (Ithaca: Cornell University Press, 1998).

CHAPTER 15

PROBLEMATIC PARTNERS: DE GAULLE, THATCHER, AND THEIR IMPACT

N. PIERS LUDLOW

EUROPEAN integration has from the outset been a controversial and contested process. Inevitably this has meant that in the course of its half century of existence the European Community/EU has encountered national leaders who have expressed hostility towards it and who have challenged important aspects of its institutions and/or policies. Of such leaders none have been more famous—or notorious in the eyes of pro-European policy-makers—than Charles de Gaulle, the French leader between 1958 and 1969, and Margaret Thatcher, British prime minister between 1979 and 1990. Both had strong views on the integration process which differed significantly from those of their fellow European leaders. Both came from large member states, and might, as such, have been expected to have had significant influence over the course of the European Community's development. Neither was shy about voicing their opinions. And both were in power during periods when the European Community was undergoing particularly rapid transformation, and was hence at the center of political attention. An investigation of how much impact each of them had, and of the manner in which the European Community responded, is thus likely to throw interesting light on the manner in which the European Community/EU is equipped to cope with vociferous internal dissent.

15.1 THE GAULLIST CHALLENGE

General de Gaulle returned to power in France in 1958 with a reputation as a strong opponent of supranational integration within Europe. Much of this resulted from his critique of the planned EDC. In November 1953 for example, de Gaulle had expressed horror at "that artificial monster, that robot, that Frankenstein which...is called the Community."[1] Such forceful words had been followed up by actions, with hostile Gaullist votes contributing significantly to the eventual rejection of the EDC Treaty by the French Parliament in August 1954. And while at least some of the General's ire towards the EDC was directed at its military ineffectiveness, de Gaulle had also made clear that he regarded the whole notion of supranational European cooperation as unsound. Little wonder then that many pro-Europeans looked on with trepidation when the general emerged as the new leader of France just months after the fledgling EEC had begun operating.

In the event, de Gaulle rather confounded expectations by deciding to honor the European commitments into which his IV Republic predecessors had entered. He is reported to have said that had he been in power when the treaties had been negotiated, then Europe would have been organized "in a rather different fashion."[2] But no direct assault was launched. On the contrary, the new government reformed the French economy in such a fashion that Gaullist France did not need to employ the various safeguards against over-rapid liberalization which IV Republic negotiators had secured. And within two years of his return, the French were successfully pushing for the tariff dismantlement timetable to be accelerated and for the customs union to be rapidly flanked by an effective CAP.[3] De Gaulle's initial European actions thus seemed out of line with his earlier rhetorical attacks on supranationality.

Serious doubts remained about the general's commitment to the EEC, however. De Gaulle's principal European interest during his first years back in power was the establishment of some form of political union—a largely intergovernmental structure designed to coordinate the foreign policies of the EEC member states. Viewed charitably this could be seen as a worthwhile ambition, an innovation designed to address Europe's marginalization by the superpowers. If implemented, the 1961 Fouchet Plan might indeed have anticipated the CFSP mechanisms of the Maastricht Treaty by three full decades. But many of de Gaulle's prospective partners were deeply mistrustful of French intentions, suspecting that the general was seeking to construct an intergovernmental alternative to the EEC which would, over time, swallow up the supranational community. The political union proposals were, in other words, interpreted as the attack on the EEC that many had expected from de Gaulle as soon as he had returned to power. Partly for this reason, the general's plans were frustrated by the determined resistance of the Belgians and Dutch.[4] Ambitions to create a coordinated European foreign policy would remain in limbo for the rest of the decade.

De Gaulle reacted to this disappointment by counter-attacking. On May 15, 1962 he told the press that Europe could be built on no reality except that of the member states, denounced those who looked for an external "federator," and ridiculed supranationality.[5] Several pro-European ministers resigned from his government in protest. Over the summer and autumn of 1962 he sought to form a Franco–German partnership capable of replacing his dream of a political Europe. He thus worked hard to cement his relationship with the German Chancellor Konrad Adenauer and to build a durable link with Bonn. These efforts would culminate in January 1963 with the signature of the bilateral Elysée Treaty.[6] This too was seen by his opponents as a move designed to subvert the existing Community structures and to lure Germany away from its previously reliable pro-European stance. And that same month he made his most audacious European move to date, using another of his press conferences on January 14, 1963 to bring to an end the eighteen months of negotiation underway in Brussels on British EEC membership. A maritime country like the UK, linked to the Commonwealth and to the United States could not be included in a continental grouping like the EEC, he declared.[7]

De Gaulle's veto triggered the Community's first major crisis. EEC enlargement to include Britain had been widely supported, but it was the brutally unilateral manner in which it had been dismissed that really appalled France's partners. After a year and a half of painstaking multilateral talks in Brussels, the French president had ruled out British membership on grounds that amounted to little more than the fact that the UK was an island with historical links to its former empire and had done so moreover by means of a public announcement about which not even his most loyal ministers had been forewarned. Even those who had shared some of de Gaulle's misgivings about British membership were shocked by the style of the veto. Taken in conjunction with the signature of the Elysée Treaty just a few days later, the January 14 press conference seemed dramatically to intensify de Gaulle's offensive against the existing Communities. The mood amongst France's partners was volatile and emotional, with widespread talk of retaliation against the French.[8]

It would take several months of careful diplomacy from French representatives in Brussels, and some clever mediation by the Germans, to coax the Community back into effective operation.[9] De Gaulle furthermore was ready to exploit the sense of panic and dismay he had created. In late 1963 and again the following year, he maximized the pressure on Germany to make concessions during negotiations over the CAP by threatening to leave the Community were the talks on farm policy not to advance. The use of such forceful tactics, however, meant that the French were compelled to become yet more radical once their partners began to counter-attack. In May–June 1965, Germany, Italy, The Netherlands, and the European Commission all sought to extract a high price for the final component in the CAP, the financial regulation. De Gaulle was obliged to respond, and did so by withdrawing his permanent representative from Brussels and beginning a six month French boycott of the Community institutions known as the "empty chair crisis." He also took advantage of the stand-off to make public his dislike of certain institutional features of the EEC, notably the growing political ambitions of the European Commission and the planned move to more extensive use of majority voting in the Council of Ministers.[10]

The crisis lasted six months. During this time, the five other member states met anxiously in Brussels, using the Council structures to coordinate their positions and decide on the best response to French brinkmanship. Somewhat to their own surprise, and certainly to that of the French, their resolve did not crack and they stood firm to the line that the Treaty of Rome could not be modified to suit de Gaulle. In January 1966 the two sides finally met once more, at a specially convened Council meeting in Luxembourg, and on January 28 a deal was at last struck which allowed the French to resume their participation in Brussels and the Community to return to normal operation. In terms of substance, the Six did reach consensus on a limited number of suggestions as to how the Commission might alter its behavior, but on the vexed issue of majority voting, the document finally agreed upon merely noted the ongoing difference of views between the French and their partners, without settling the issue one way or the other.[11] Contrary to later legend, no veto right was born as a result of the Luxembourg Compromise.

In the wake of the crisis, both the French and their partners sought to moderate their positions so as to allow the EEC to resume normal operation. Their efforts to do so, however, were derailed by the re-emergence of the British question once the UK reapplied to join the Community in 1967. This time France successfully avoided the opening of membership negotiations. The announcement of the British membership bid was followed almost at once by a press conference from de Gaulle in which he restated his opposition to British entry. No negotiations began, despite several months of careful maneuvering as Britain and its allies amongst the Five sought to force the French to drop their opposition. And in November 1967 a second de Gaulle press conference reaffirmed French opposition to enlargement thereby ending Britain's prospects of entering the EEC in the immediate future. But this turned out to be a Pyrrhic victory for de Gaulle. For whereas in both 1963 and 1965 the French had managed to anger their partners enormously and yet still manage to persuade the Five to resume cooperation once the dust had settled, in 1968–1969 the impasse over British membership would paralyze the Community system for a year and a half. Routine business continued, but no substantive advance was possible while de Gaulle remained in the Elysée. It would thus fall to the general's successor, Georges Pompidou, to begin the slow process of undoing the deadlock that de Gaulle had created.[12]

Throughout his eleven years in power, de Gaulle managed to cast a substantial shadow over the European Community. Speculation about his exact views was rife, whether in the media or in the political world. And the dramatic press conferences at which he announced so many of his policy initiatives were as assiduously listened to in Brussels and other capitals, as they were feared. This capacity to grab the limelight has continued posthumously moreover, with innumerable books and articles devoted to the task of trying to analyze and assess the general's European policy. These advance a bewilderingly wide variety of explanations for de Gaulle's actions, ranging from Cold War calculations about Europe's and France's place in the world, to the desire to use Europe to avert unrest amongst the French peasantry.[13] What is perhaps more relevant for this chapter, however, is the way that the latest wave of historical research has begun to cast doubt on de Gaulle's actual impact on the EEC.

For many years the standard account of the Community's evolution suggested that de Gaulle had seriously damaged the integration process. The Luxembourg Compromise, it was claimed, together with other after-effects of the Community's tussle with de Gaulle, choked off the Community's spectacularly successful early development and ushered in a period of stagnation which endured until the mid-1980s.[14] De Gaulle was thus not just a leader who disliked some aspects of the EEC; he was also someone who significantly affected its subsequent trajectory. Recent archive-based findings cast doubt on this narrative however. For a start, detailed research on the EEC in the 1960s suggests that Gaullist France was far from consistent in its opposition to supranationality. As far as both the CAP and the Kennedy Round of GATT negotiations were concerned, the French tended to favor strong Commission powers rather than opposing them.[15] Second, it is clear that de Gaulle's forceful tactics towards the EEC produced substantial misgivings amongst the French civil service and at the level of French public opinion.[16] This did not always prevent the general from acting as he intended, although it may temporarily have stayed his hand in some instances. But more importantly it contributed to the realization throughout the French elite of how many interests France had at stake in the European Community, and how counterproductive, both in terms of French interests and French public opinion, an anti-European standpoint might be. Both of these lessons long outlived de Gaulle. Third, de Gaulle's successor was obliged to row back from many of the general's more controversial stances, thus doing much to mend relations with both the Five and outside countries like Britain or the United States.[17] The years between 1969 and 1972 thus saw a resumption of constructive advance. Any link between the Gaullist years and the problems that may or may not have afflicted the EEC in the post-1973 period is thus indirect at best and quite possibly entirely spurious. Fourth and most important, a closer look at the Community's institutional development during its first decade of operation suggests that the empty chair crisis and the Luxembourg compromise had much less of an impact on the manner in which the Community functioned than has often been asserted. Instead to the extent that the EEC evolved in a direction that differed from the federalist aspirations of some of its founders, it did so not as a result of a Gaullist coup in 1965–1966, but rather as the consequence of a much more gradual trend, spread out over the whole of the Community's formative decade, and involving multiple member states. The rise of Council power in particular reflected a general realization on the part of the member states that too many of their interests were wrapped up in the Community for the overall direction of EEC development to be left to an independent European Commission that they could not fully control.[18] Any explanation of the Community's development during the 1960s that attributes its institutional evolution primarily to de Gaulle is thus just wrong.

15.2 MRS THATCHER'S CRUSADE

In marked contrast to de Gaulle, Margaret Thatcher did not cause immediate alarm when she triumphed in the 1979 general election. Rather the reverse was true, since both of the preceding Labour prime ministers, Harold Wilson and James Callaghan, had proved to be ambivalent about European integration. Callaghan indeed had recently decided to opt out of the key features of the main new European venture of the period, the EMS launched in 1979.[19] There was hence some relief amongst Britain's European partners at the return to power of a Conservative Party which under Harold Macmillan and Edward Heath had been primarily responsible for leading the UK into the EEC. The party's 1979 manifesto, moreover, seemed to justify the Tories' reputation as "the party of Europe."[20]

The vigor with which Britain's new prime minister launched herself into her quest to reduce the UK's contribution to the EEC budget is hence likely to have been a surprise to Thatcher's European counterparts—as well as to many of the British officials responsible for handling EEC-related matters. The issue itself was not a new one. The question of how to avoid Britain paying a disproportionate amount into the EEC's coffers had first been broached in the course of the abortive 1961–1963 membership negotiations, had briefly resurfaced in 1967, had been hotly contested in the course of the 1970–1972 membership talks, and had been the single biggest issue at stake in the Labour-led renegotiation of Britain's terms of entry in 1974.[21] But the forceful, not to say confrontational style, with which Thatcher embraced the issue immediately soured her relations with the principal European leaders of the day. Helmut Schmidt, the German chancellor, is reputed to have feigned sleep in the middle of one of Thatcher's tirades; Valéry Giscard d'Estaing, the French president, instructed his motorcade to pull up ostentatiously outside the room in which the British prime minister was explaining her position at some length.[22] Thatcher's ten year's in power thus began with a period of turbulence at European level.

The row over what became known as the BBQ—the British Budgetary Question or the Bloody British Question depending on taste[23]—need not necessarily have set Thatcher's European policy on a trajectory of permanent confrontation. For a start neither of the two leaders with whom her relations were most adversely affected—Giscard d'Estaing and Schmidt—remained in power for long, the former losing the 1981 election to François Mitterrand, the latter being replaced by Helmut Kohl in 1982. The new French president indeed would gain a certain amount of credit in Thatcher's eyes for the role he played in finally resolving the BBQ at the Fontainebleau summit in June 1984. More importantly, the agreement of a budgetary rebate mechanism for Britain and the ending of the row about the UK contribution set the scene for the most constructive period of British engagement with the Community during the Thatcher years. It was thus at Fontainebleau that the British presented their partners with a Foreign Office document entitled *Europe: The Future* which set out a series of suggestions about how the integration process could be reinvigorated. This included a section arguing that one of the priorities for a strengthened Community should be the removal of the remaining barriers to intra-Community trade and the development of a "fully integrated common market."[24]

Mrs Thatcher's exact role in the genesis of the single market program, the main catalyst for the EEC's revival in the mid-1980s, is the subject of some disagreement between analysts. Thus, while John Gillingham identifies the British leader as *the* key originator of the Community's drive to eliminate all non-tariff barriers and construct a functioning internal market by the end of 1992, others have pointed out that calls for a further round of European liberalization had been circulating widely ever since the start of the decade amongst European industrialists, politicians of the center and center-right, and European Parliamentarians and Eurocrats.[25] What is beyond dispute, however, is that the single market program was a European scheme that Thatcher was able to support enthusiastically and in pursuit of which she deployed much of her customary energy and determination. For virtually the first time since 1950, Britain thus found itself fleetingly in the vanguard of European advance.

The emergence of a European consensus on the need for a single market masked an important ongoing divide between Britain and its partners, however. For Thatcher, the 1992 program was an essentially economic tool to solve a primarily economic problem, namely Europe's flagging economy and the dwindling competitiveness of European industry. A bigger domestic market would help European companies achieve the same economies of scale and levels of investment that characterized their US and Japanese rivals, thereby reversing the continent's relative economic decline. The initiative was not, by contrast, designed to transform the European political system. For many of Thatcher's European counterparts, however, the economic outcomes, while important in and of themselves, were only part of the attraction. To Mitterrand, to Kohl, or to Jacques Delors, the president of the European Commission, it was as important that the single market program revitalize the European project itself as it was that it regenerate European industrial competitiveness. They therefore always envisaged a Europe open for trade also being a Europe that was advancing much further toward reaching economic and political unity. The 1992 program was a launch pad for further integration more than an end in itself. This underlying philosophical divide would help ensure that Thatcher's period of comfortable involvement with European integration would rapidly come to an end.

The first sign of trouble ahead occurred at the Milan Council in June 1985. At this meeting Thatcher found herself confronted by a majority of European leaders who argued that the single market project would only be possible were the European institutions themselves reformed. In order for this to happen, an IGC would need to be convened and a new European treaty drafted. The British denied that any institutional change was needed. Thatcher thus spoke out against an IGC, but was outmaneuvered by the Italian Prime Minister Bettino Craxi who was chairing the meeting and who took the unprecedented step of calling for a vote on the issue. Those wanting treaty reform carried the motion 7 votes to 3.[26] But in 1985, Thatcher was still too committed to the goal of European trade liberalization to allow this temporary disagreement to undermine her support for the general objective. British negotiators therefore participated constructively in the IGC and Thatcher herself both signed the resultant SEA and threw her personal prestige and that of her government behind the treaty's safe passage through parliament.

In the years that followed, however, the gap between Thatcher and her partners only widened. The very success of the single market project that the Iron Lady had supported stimulated the appearance of multiple other European ambitions to which she was opposed. By 1988, discussions were underway in Brussels and elsewhere about EMU, significant increases in the budgetary transfers from richer European countries to the poorer member states, and decisive steps towards a political union that would enable the newly revitalized European Community to become a significant player in global politics. Also apparent was a sense that the process of institutional reform started with the SEA would need to continue if these new European policy objectives were to be attained. Thatcher hence found herself engaged in a desperate effort to hold back a European tide that appeared in full flood. In the process, her relations with most of her fellow leaders deteriorated disastrously. Successive European Council meetings became pitched battles between an ever-more isolated British leader and the majority of fellow leaders who believed, understandably perhaps, that time and history were on their side. Even more damagingly for Thatcher in the long term, doubts began to grow amongst her own ministers about the efficacy and wisdom of her increasingly ill-tempered rear-guard action. That short-lived period in the middle of the decade when the British had been amongst the European vanguard seemed ever further away. If confirmation of this was needed, it would come in September 1988 when Thatcher made a speech in Bruges that confirmed the gap between her vision of Europe's future evolution and that of her partners.[27]

The European issue that was ultimately to play the most important role in Thatcher's downfall was monetary integration. The British manifestation of this debate was highly distinctive, however, since in London discussion over the more grandiose final objective of EMU and a single currency was to prove much less divisive in the short term than the question of whether Britain should belatedly undo its 1979 decision not to take part in the ERM of the EMS.[28] As early as 1985 the then Chancellor of the Exchequer, Nigel Lawson, had convinced a majority of the British cabinet that membership of the ERM would help control inflation. Thatcher had overruled Lawson, however, and the pound had stayed out of the system. Lawson would return to the attack in 1989, combining forces with the Foreign Secretary Geoffrey Howe, and obliging their leader to admit in principle at the June 1989 Madrid Council that sterling would enter the ERM at some undefined date in the future.[29] Thatcher's revenge was swift: within months Howe had been demoted to leader of the House of Commons and Lawson had resigned as chancellor. Their departure, however, meant that in the autumn of 1990 when their successors, John Major as chancellor and Douglas Hurd as foreign secretary raised the issue again and insisted that a date for sterling's entry be set, the prime minister was ill-placed to resist.[30] On October 5, 1990 the pound entered the ERM—although at a rate against the German mark that was decided unilaterally by the British and would subsequently prove disastrous for the reputation of Britain's pro-Europeans.

In the meantime, Thatcher's relations with the other main European leaders had become even more tense following the fall of the Berlin Wall in November 1989 and the reappearance of the issue of German unification. Many European leaders had misgivings about the speed and the suddenness of Germany's rush to unity. Even Mitterrand conspicuously failed to support Kohl's drive to unity in the manner that might have been expected. But the German chancellor's main tactic for reassuring his fellow leaders that the new Germany would be as reliable a partner as the old divided country was to emphasize Germany's European commitment. This worked well with the majority—and especially well with the French.[31] It only aggravated matters with Thatcher, however, since she liked neither the prospect of a larger and more powerful Germany, nor that of a larger and more powerful European framework to contain it. Her vocal but futile attempts to denounce the consequences of precipitate German unity used up much of her already dwindling stock of credibility amongst her international partners and within her own government.[32]

In November 1990, Thatcher's fall from power was tightly bound up with the European issue. At the Rome Council that month, the British leader was powerless to resist a collective decision on the starting date for stage II of progress towards EMU. The strident terms in which she denounced this decision once back in the House of Commons, however, provoked the resignation of Howe and the crippling valedictory speech that accompanied it.[33] "The tragedy is...that the Prime Minister's perceived attitude towards Europe is running increasingly serious risks for the future of our nation," the former foreign secretary told the Commons.[34] Another discontented pro-European former minister, Michael Heseltine, then announced his decision to stand against the prime minister in a party leadership contest. And it was Thatcher's failure to win an outright majority of votes in the first round of this contest that brought about her resignation. The European issue had been both the trigger and one of the underlying causes of the prime minister's fall.

What impact did Mrs Thatcher have on the integration process during her ten years in power? The answer to this question is likely, perhaps surprisingly, to dwell most on that short period of constructive engagement in the mid-1980s which undoubtedly contributed to the launch of the single market project and the revival of the integration process. The resolution of the budgetary wrangle should probably also be mentioned, whatever its short-term cost, since one of preconditions for the EEC relaunch of the mid-1980s was almost certainly the ending of this ill-tempered dispute. The rebate negotiated has after all endured, however anachronistic it looks today. But those aspects of Thatcher's approach that cast the Iron Lady as an ill-starred but doughty defender of the European status quo against the relentless drive of those intent upon transforming the Community, were much less successful. The British leader's dogged defiance certainly generated much noise and passion. Her presence also turned a number of European Council meetings that might well have been rapid and consensual, into lengthy pitched battles. And the Thatcher decade would firmly consolidate the reputation that Britain had already begun to acquire during the 1970s as an "awkward partner" in the integration process. But very few of those causes against which Thatcher set herself were actually stopped in their tracks. On the contrary, the dominant view around Brussels by the late 1980s was that the British leader would huff and would puff, but would ultimately give way. The wide-ranging expansion of European activities that she had so deplored ultimately took place, symbolized by the signature of a Maastricht Treaty in 1991 that Thatcher herself was no longer around to oppose. The legacy of her Euro-skepticism at a European level was thus arguably surprisingly small, although a case can certainly be made that she has had a more enduring effect on Britain's own debate about European integration and in particular upon opinion within her own party. This longer term effect was very apparent during John Major's premiership, helped quash the putative pro-Europeanism of the early years of Tony Blair's decade in power, and has resurfaced in David Cameron's government in the second decade of the twenty-first century. But while this lasting impact upon Britain and its role in Europe is not without importance, it is certainly very different from the direct influence over the direction of the European integration process to which Thatcher aspired.

15.3 THE PLACE OF "PROBLEM PARTNERS" IN THE INTEGRATION PROCESS

So what can be concluded from this brief review of the Europe's two best-known problem leaders? The first point to make is that both General de Gaulle and Mrs Thatcher generated an immense amount of controversy, perplexity, and genuine anxiety at a European level. This is true of media commentary, subsequent academic analysis, and the reactions of de Gaulle and Thatcher's political colleagues and counterparts. And it highlights the way in which much of the integration process has been based upon the assumption that there existed an underlying consensus about the legitimacy and value of the attempt to build a more united Europe—a consensus that both de Gaulle and Thatcher threatened. Such consensus has not precluded argument about the finer details of how this process should advance. On the contrary, the history of European integration is the history of constant discussions, squabbles, and disputes about how individual policies should work, how the costs and benefits of integration should be distributed, and what the priorities should be at each new stage of development—not to mention the constant jostling between advocates of different institutional visions. But most of these disputes have occurred between constantly shifting coalitions of member states, thereby ensuring that few countries have ever found themselves always on the winning or on the losing side of every Brussels engagement. This has helped sustain the belief that the integration process is in the interests of, and of benefit to, all of those involved—and facilitated the acceptance of the outcome by the losers of each particular argument or confrontation. A situation in which one leader or one participating country could become so out of sympathy with the whole endeavor that they and their representatives would form a constant malcontent minority is therefore something which is viewed, justifiably, with some anxiety. Both de Gaulle and Thatcher generated such fears—although in both cases the reality of their European policy-making included rather more positive and constructive engagement than was often implied by either their own rhetoric or the alarmist analyses of some of their opponents.

The alarm that both leaders generated was not however matched by a lasting impact upon the integration process itself. Both de Gaulle and Thatcher had strong visions of how they wanted Europe to evolve. Neither shied away from expressing their beliefs. And yet neither succeeded in shaping the Community to their liking. At the very most, de Gaulle was able to delay or postpone developments about which he was unhappy: British membership would be the best example since this did not happen while the general remained in power, although revealingly it did happen soon after his resignation. Likewise, Thatcher could do little to halt the broadening of the European agenda in the latter half of the 1980s, although instances could almost certainly be found where British opposition was able to slow movement in a particular direction and there were a few examples of policy areas where the UK was able to secure an opt-out clause. This too underlines a basic reality of the Community/Union decision-making process. In a system where most key decisions are made by consensus, and where even majority votes need to be passed by significantly more than 51 percent of those taking part, it is all but impossible for a single skeptical leader to determine the direction of travel. Instead, any leader wishing really to steer the debate needs to build a coalition of like-minded fellow leaders—something that neither de Gaulle nor Thatcher were consistently able to do. This then leaves the isolated skeptic able to do little more than block advance whenever consensus is required—or occasionally opt out of policies that the other member states decide to adopt.

Even a negative policy of this sort becomes difficult, however, if the leader or country doing the blocking has reasons for wanting other aspects of the integration process to continue. And this highlights the third general conclusion that can be drawn from an investigation of our two problem partners, namely that both de Gaulle and Thatcher were severely limited in the extent to which they could disrupt the European Community during their periods in power by their awareness that 1960s France and 1980s Britain could not afford to leave the European Community. This was something that was repeatedly stressed to de Gaulle by his ministers and officials, most strikingly perhaps during the empty chair crisis of 1965–1966.[35] But it was also the consensus view across Whitehall and most of Westminster during Thatcher's years in power.[36] As a result, both leaders had to limit their European negativism out of the realization that to provoke retaliation from their European partners could be harmful to the many interests that their countries had in play in Brussels and that to precipitate a situation in which either the Community itself was destroyed or that France or Britain were compelled to withdraw would be nothing short of disastrous. Unless actual exit from the European Community/ EU is possible to contemplate, sustained disruptive behavior within the Community or Union is not an easy or a safe course to follow.

A careful look at the European policies of both de Gaulle and Thatcher therefore suggests that isolated Euro-skeptic leaders can only have a comparatively limited impact on the integration process. They certainly cause consternation and controversy. They can to an extent temporarily block moves to which they object. And they may have a lasting impact on the nature of the debate about European integration within their own political system. But such is the nature of European Community/EU decision-making that their capacity actually to seize control of the integration process is almost non-existent and the costs to their own country's interests of sustained obstructionism in Brussels are unacceptably high. De Gaulle and Thatcher were both in their own distinctive ways formidable opponents who caused genuine alarm amongst their European partners. In neither case, however, is there much historical evidence to suggest that they significantly slowed the overall evolution of the integration process during their decades in power.

NOTES

1. Edmond Jouve, *Le Général de Gaulle et la construction de l'Europe*, vol. 1 (Paris: LGDJ, 1967), 255.

2. Cited in Raymond Poidevin, "De Gaulle et l'Europe en 1958," in Institut Charles de Gaulle, *De Gaulle en son siècle*, vol. 5 (Paris: Plon, 1992), 81.

3. Maurice Vaïsse, *La grandeur. Politique étrangère du general de Gaulle 1958–1969* (Paris: Fayard, 1998), 169–75.

4. Pierre Gerbet, "In Search of Political Union: the Fouchet Plan Negotiations (1960–2)," in Roy Pryce, ed., The Dynamics of European Union (London: Routledge, 1989), 105–29.

5. Vaisse, *La grandeur*, 187.

6. Benedikt Schönbrun, *La mésentente apprivoisée. De Gaulle et les Allemands, 1963–1969* (Paris: Presses Universitaires de France, 2007), 29–56.

7. N. Piers Ludlow, *Dealing With Britain: the Six and the First UK Application to the EEC* (Cambridge: Cambridge University Press, 1997), 206–12.

8. Ludlow, *Dealing With Britain*, 213–30.

9. N. Piers Ludlow, *The European Community and the Crises of the 1960s: Negotiating the Gaullist Challenge* (London: Routledge, 2006), 11–39.

10. Ludlow, *The European Community*, 40–70.

11. Ludlow, *The European Community*, 71–103.

12. Ludlow, *The European Community*, 125–98.

13. The best analysis of de Gaulle's approach to the Cold War is Frédéric Bozo, *Two Strategies for Europe: De Gaulle, the United States and the Atlantic Alliance* (Lanham: Rowman and Littlefield, 2001); for an agriculture-centered explanation, see Andrew Moravcsik, "De Gaulle Between Grain and *Grandeur*: the Political Economy of French EC Policy, 1958–1970," *Journal of Cold War Studies* 2, no. 2 (2000) 3–43 and 2, no. 3 (2000) 4–68.

14. Paul Taylor, *The Limits of European Integration* (Beckenham: Croom Helm, 1983), 20.

15. N. Piers Ludlow, "From Words to Actions: Reinterpreting General de Gaulle's European Policy, 1958–69," in Garret Martin, Anna Locher, and Christian Neunlist, eds, *Globalizing de Gaulle: International Perspectives on French Foreign Policies, 1958–1969* (Lanham: Rowman and Littlefield, 2010), 63–83.

16. Ludlow, *The European Community*, 91–2.

17. Eric Roussel, *Georges Pompidou, 1911–1974* (Paris: Jean-Claude Lattès, 1994), 333–42.

18. Ludlow, *The European Community*, 118–24.

19. Peter Ludlow, *The Making of the European Monetary System: A Case Study of the Politics of the European Community* (London: Butterworth, 1982).

20. <http://www.conservative-party.net/manifestos/1979/1979-conservative-manifesto.shtml> (accessed March 2, 2010).

21. David Gowland and Arthur Turner, *Reluctant Europeans. Britain and European Integration 1945–1998* (London: Longman, 2000), 184–97.

22. Roy Jenkins, *European Diary 1977–1981* (London: Collins, 1989), 530; Hugo Young, *This Blessed Plot. Britain and Europe from Churchill to Blair* (London: Macmillan, 1998), 314.

23. Jenkins, *Brussels Diary*, 545.

24. Ronald Reagan Presidential Library, NSC Country Files, Box 20, United Kingdom 7/1/84–1/4/85 (2 of 2), McFarlane to Price, 30/6/1984.

25. John Gillingham, *European Integration, 1950–2003. Superstate or New Market Economy?* (Cambridge: Cambridge University Press, 2003), 164–79; Wayne Sandholtz and John Zysman, "1992——Recasting the European Bargain," *World Politics* 42, no. 1 (1989), 95–128.

26. Young, *This Blessed Plot*, 330–2.

27. <http://www.margaretthatcher.org/speeches/displaydocument.asp?docid=107332> (accessed March 2, 2010).

28. Phillip Stephens, *Politics and the Pound: the Tories, the Economy and Europe* (London: Papermac, 1997), 45–51.

29. Nigel Lawson, *The View from No. 11: Memoirs of a Tory Radical* (London: Bantam Press, 1992), 927–36; Margaret Thatcher, *The Downing St. Years* (London: Harper Collins, 1993), 709–13.

30. Stephens, *Politics and the Pound*, 140–67.

31. Helga Haftendorn, "German Unification and European Integration are but Two Sides of One Coin: the FRG, Europe and the Diplomacy of German Unification," in Frédéric Bozo, Marie-Pierre Rey, N. Piers Ludlow, and Leopoldo Nuti, eds, *Europe and the End of the Cold War: A Reappraisal* (London: Routledge, 2008), 135–47.

32. Patrick Salmon, "The United Kingdom and German Unification," in Bozo et al., *Europe and the End of the Cold War*, 177–90.

33. Stephens, *Politics and the Pound*, 180–2.

34. <http://www.publications.parliament.uk/pa/cm199091/cmhansrd/1990-11-13/Debate-2.html> (accessed March 2, 2010).

35. Ludlow, *European Community*, 91–2.

36. John Young, *Britain and European Unity 1945–1999* (London: Macmillan, 2000), 130.

CHAPTER 16

THE PRESIDENTS AND THE PRESIDENCY OF THE EUROPEAN COMMISSION

HUSSEIN KASSIM

ALTHOUGH the Commission president holds a key position in the EU political system, the powers of the presidency have only recently come to match the importance of the office. The role is broadly similar to that of a prime minister of a national government, but the Commission president confronts a more complex environment, lacks the resources available to most heads of government, and is subject to stricter constraints.[1] Despite these formidable obstacles, however, three incumbents—Walter Hallstein, Roy Jenkins, and Jacques Delors—have been especially effective in this role.[2] This chapter examines the achievements of each in turn, before considering what lessons, if any, can be drawn concerning the conditions for a successful presidency. It begins with a brief description of the role and powers of the Commission president before the treaty changes of the 1990s and after.

16.1 THE COMMISSION PRESIDENCY UNDER THE FOUNDING TREATIES

The Commission president has been a central figure in the Community system since the EEC's inception. One of the few EU office-holders with high visibility across the Union, he is closely and personally identified with "Brussels."[3] As the head of the EU institution charged with a key role in policy initiation, management, enforcement, and external relations, the Commission president is nominally responsible for action on the Commission's part at all stages of EU decision-making and in every area of EU activity. Yet, despite the importance that the office would assume, its powers and responsibilities were largely undefined by the founding treaties. The EEC Treaty entrusted a series of important functions to the Commission, but was silent on its internal organization beyond stipulating how members of the College including the president and the vice-presidents were to be selected.[4]

Partly due to the logistical necessities arising from organizing the Commission's work and the need for the Commission to be represented in its interaction with other actors, and partly to the institutionalization of the office by its first incumbent, Walter Hallstein, the Commission president came to occupy a role in the College similar to that of a prime minister in a national government, albeit in a system where powers are separated rather than fused. The president convenes and chairs meetings of the College, establishes its agenda and approves its minutes, though members of the College may request the addition or postponement of particular dossiers, and minutes must be countersigned by the Secretariat General. The president also decides on the organization and composition of subcommittees of the College, although decision-making cannot be delegated, for example, to groupings of Commissioners. Importantly, the head of the president's personal staff chairs the weekly meeting of the *special chefs* and prepares the weekly Wednesday meeting of the College. In addition, the Commission president receives the accreditation of ambassadors from non-EU states, is a member of the European Council, and represents the EU, with the High Representative for the CFSP, in its external relations.

At the same time, historically, the formal prerogatives associated with the office have been few and its resources sparse compared to those of many prime ministers.[5] Within the College, the Commission president was no more than a *primus inter pares*, with few powers vis-à-vis other Commissioners. Until the 1990s, he had virtually no say in the College's composition and little in the distribution of portfolios.[6] Formally, Commissioners were appointed by common agreement of member-state governments. In practice, each government decided its own nominations unilaterally, then negotiated the distribution of dossiers with the other states. As an appointee of member governments, the Commission president lacked the legitimacy bestowed by a popular mandate.[7] Since, moreover, he was neither a party leader nor the head of a coalition, the president was not able to use party discipline or coalition agreements to control cabinet colleagues or mobilize a supportive parliamentary majority. Furthermore, his administrative resources were few. Although he intervenes across a broader range of policy areas than a prime minister, the Commission president has only a small personal staff. Moreover, whilst the UK prime minister can rely on the Cabinet Office, the chancellor on the Kanzleramt, and the French prime minister on the Secrétariat général du gouvernement, to coordinate the work of government, as well as to communicate the views of the head of government across the administration, the Commission president had no such apparatus at his disposal. Although the body responsible for coordination in the Commission, the Secretariat General, is accountable to the Commission President, it has historically been more a guardian of collegiality than a service of the Commission president.

A further difficulty is that the challenge of heading the Commission is greater than the task of leading a government. The College is the Commission's central decision-making body and decisions are taken collectively, but the College is a super-coalition, whose members are drawn from across the political spectrum. They are not united by ideology, party, or territory, and often nuture quite different political ambitions. At the official level, the Commission services have been competing "baronies" or "silos," where in the absence of concentrated political and administrative authority interdepartmental coordination has been a perennial difficultly. Furthermore, the Commission has only limited powers over its own organization. The size of the College and its composition are set by treaty, which can be amended only by the unanimous agreement of governments at an IGC,[8] while the rules that govern the Commission's operation, as well as the budget, are legislative acts, decided by the Council and the Parliament.

Finally, the Commission operates in a testing and challenging environment. The policy agenda is broader, longer, and more diverse, and the institutional context more complex than in a national setting. The EU combines elements of a mixed system of government with a separation of powers between its institutions. In addition, its decision-making procedures depend upon close cooperation between EU institutions that represent different constituencies with distinct mandates and that are anxious to defend their competencies. Although it has many important responsibilities, the Commission has few direct powers. Decision-making authority is shared with other bodies, and the Commission is "multiply accountable."[9] In this multi-institutional environment, the Commission president is one leader among many,[10] and not the most senior or the most powerful.

In spite of these constraints, three incumbents stand out as effective presidents. The first Commission president, Walter Hallstein, held the office from 1958 until 1967. Roy Jenkins was in post from 1977 until 1981, while Jacques Delors was Commission president from 1985 until 1995.

16.2 THE HALLSTEIN PRESIDENCY

Although he has become one of the "forgotten men" of European integration, Walter Hallstein was a major figure in the Communities' early history.[11] A brilliant academic lawyer, then an adviser and close colleague of Konrad Adenauer, Hallstein was involved in the negotiation of the Schuman Plan and as a senior official at the German foreign ministry played an important role in the negotiations leading up to the Rome Treaty. Appointed as the first president of the EEC Commission, he brought to the office experience of European negotiations and practical experience of administration, as well as legal expertise. Although often portrayed as a supranationalist who wanted to replace European nations with a federal European state,[12] in reality his ambitions were more modest. Hallstein believed that an executive independent of national governments, providing "a constant reminder of a Community interest transcending the interest of each of the participants," was indispensable to integration.[13]

Hallstein considered that it was essential for the Commission to produce work of the highest quality in order for it to demonstrate its value, "to play the role of honest broker between the governments and [to] bring political weight to bear to ensure that formulas for agreement are found."[14] Accordingly, he sought to shape the Commission into "une grande administration" that would match national bureaucracies in caliber and expertise.[15] Organizational independence was also essential if the Commission was to become "a new factor in international life."[16] Thus, while Hallstein was happy for the EEC Commission to cooperate with the executives of the ECSC and Euratom, he was reluctant to create common services. Similarly, though Hallstein accepted financial assistance from the HA of the ECSC, he did so "without any implications for future relations with Luxembourg."[17] More broadly, he sought to defend the independence of the Commission in personnel matters, strongly preferring the model of a career civil servant to an administration populated by secondees from the member states,[18] and attached considerable importance to formal protocol as part of his strategy to secure the Commission's status—an ambition that drew de Gaulle's withering contempt.[19]

Hallstein was quick to establish his status as *primus inter pares* within the College and to define the leadership role of the Commission president. He took responsibility for Directorate General Personnel and Administration, and the Secretariat General, "reserved to himself decisions on structure and personnel," and was personally involved in senior appointments.[20] He also established the convention whereby the Commission president receives the diplomatic credentials of ambassadors from third states. Opting not to take responsibility for a particular portfolio, he enjoyed free rein over the full range of Community activity. Indeed, he made major contributions to policy development in several areas, including external policy, the customs union and the common commercial policy, the common agricultural policy, and competition policy, although such interventions were not always welcome.[21] He was also an effective operator in the Council. Hans von der Groeben, Hallstein's compatriot and fellow Commissioner, offers a number of examples of Hallstein's success, including convincing the Six to shorten the period of transition to forming a customs union.[22]

Hallstein played a key part in the design of the Commission's procedures and organization, creating many of the structures and working practices that have persisted for more than half a century. He established the cabinet system and introduced the system of Directorates-General, Directorates, and Divisions in order to ensure that at each level Commission officials were aligned in terms of seniority with their counterparts in national administrations. He also introduced the principle and practice of collegiality: decisions of the College would be taken collectively by all Commissioners at a weekly meeting devoted to that purpose. In organizational and administrative matters, Hallstein was ably assisted by Emile Noël, executive secretary of the Commission from 1958. His accomplishment in institutionalizing the Commission, creating a flesh-and-blood organization with a purpose, identity, and authority on the basis of few sparse treaty provisions, and in the face of powerful enemies, was genuinely remarkable.

Hallstein also played a key part in the merger of the executives of the three Communities, and the defense against attempts, such as the UK's free trade initiative, to sabotage the Community before it had scarcely become established. Yet these, with his other achievements, are often overlooked or underplayed in the literature, where Hallstein tends to be depicted as a "supranational Icarus,"[23] brought crashing to earth due to his premature efforts to accelerate integration and, as a result of the reaction that his proposals provoked, is held responsible for condemning the Community to years of stagnation.[24] When Hallstein resigned, preferring to leave Brussels when the Six refused to appoint him to head the unified Commission rather than accepting a one-year extension, he left a record of extraordinary accomplishment.

16.3   THE JENKINS PRESIDENCY

According to his former chief of staff, Jenkins' tenure as Commission president marked "the culmination of his European career, the end of his ambition to be a Labour Prime Minister, the opportunity for a major international success, and a time of frustration and eventual disappointment."[25] Yet Jenkins achieved his successes in difficult circumstances.[26] Chancellor Schmidt and President Giscard d'Estaing had attempted to revitalize European cooperation, but from outside existing Community institutions through the European Council, a body whose creation they had instigated. Despite their high regard for Jenkins as a political heavyweight—a former Chancellor of the Exchequer and deputy leader of the Labour Party—who could help revitalize the Community, they had no intention of granting the Commission a leadership role.[27] This tension was to persist throughout the Jenkins presidency.

Jenkins became acquainted with the constraints of the office as soon as he began to assemble his team of Commissioners. Not only was he forced to retain two German Commissioners whom he rated as mediocre, but France insisted on reappointing Francois Ortoli, Jenkins' predecessor as Commission president, one of France's two members of the College.[28] The task was made even more difficult, since Brussels was largely an unknown world for Jenkins. Although he was a committed European and enjoyed the support of a first-rate cabinet, the Commission's sixth president had had little European experience. Nor was he a confident French speaker—the very reason why, according to Crispin Tickell, Jenkins's *chef de cabinet*, French President Giscard d'Estaing chose to address Jenkins in French.

A dispute with Giscard d'Estaing over the Commission's status typified Jenkins' first six months in office. Schmidt and Giscard d'Estaing had been the prime movers behind the launch of regular, informal international summits between the leaders of advanced Western democracies. They had wanted to restrict the gathering to heads of state and government, but their refusal to invite Ortoli, the then Commission President, to a meeting in Puerto Rico, caused ill-feeling among the smaller member states, as well as inside the Commission. The French President maintained his opposition when a year later Jenkins insisted that the Commission, as representative of the world's largest trading bloc, should be present at a London meeting planned for May 1977. However, when six of the Nine made it clear that they wanted the Commission President to attend at the meeting—and following an intervention by Chancellor Schmidt—Jenkins was invited, but only subject to a number of provisos. This was to be the last occasion on which the participation of the Commission President was to be questioned. Jenkins was invited to attend a summit in Bonn the following year and thereafter the Commission President has been routinely involved.

The Commission's rediscovery of its policy-initiating role was a second achievement of the Jenkins presidency. A first attempt to create economic and monetary union (based on the Werner Report) had foundered in the turbulence of the international economic crisis, but Jenkins believed that the moment was ripe to return to the idea. He outlined his thoughts in a speech in Florence in October 1977. Although the initiative was taken over by Schmidt and Giscard d'Estaing, and diluted when eventually implemented, it was clear that Jenkins had restored to the Commission the role in developing a vision of the Community's future that the organization had foregone since the late 1960s.

A third accomplishment was the role played by Jenkins in crafting the 1980 compromise that brought a temporary resolution to the British Budgetary Question. The problem had arisen because Britain was a relatively poor state within the Community. It imported more goods from outside the Community and therefore paid more in levies to the EEC than other member countries. As Britain had a more efficient agricultural sector than its counterparts, it also attracted fewer subsidies under the CAP. The issue was raised by James Callaghan in 1978, but taken up with a vengeance by Margaret Thatcher, for whom "getting our money back" became a crusade (see Chapter 15, this volume). The issue dominated the Council for several years and only after "long, bitter and bad-tempered negotiations in the European Council," meetings of foreign and finance ministers, and "endless bilateral encounters" was a temporary resolution agreed.[29] The experience soured relations between the UK and its partners, and the question of Britain's budgetary contribution has remained a contentious issue.

Jenkins chose not to be considered for a second term as he wanted to return to British political life. Although his achievements as Commission president may not ultimately match those of Hallstein or Delors, Jenkins brought an end to a period of Commission decline and assured the Commission's presence at the top table in international gatherings. He was responsible for a resurgence of the Commission, which he re-established as a source of major policy initiative. As Tickell observes, "the choice of Gaston Thorn to succeed him itself tells a tale."[30] Jenkins' successes were all the more remarkable in view of the ambivalence, and later the hostility, of his home country's government toward Brussels.

16.4 THE DELORS PRESIDENCY

Jacques Delors, the most successful Commission president since Hallstein, acceded to the office after a successful spell as French finance minister.[31] His nomination signaled a renewed commitment to Europe on the part of France. During a decade in which he presided over three successive Commissions (1985–1988, 1989–1992, and 1993–1995), Delors oversaw and played a leading role in the enactment of institutional and policy change which not only relaunched the Community and created the EU, but transformed the ambitions, status, and scope of "Europe" as a collective endeavor.

Delors' first success was the Integrated Mediterranean Programme. This package offered support to Greece and other Southern European states, and its adoption removed a blockage that had prevented the finalization of Portugal's and Spain's accession. Arguably, however, the three most important achievements of his presidency were the single internal market program, EMU, and political union. The first marked a concerted attempt to remove old and new barriers to the freedom of movement of goods, services, capital, and labor between member countries, and mobilized elite and popular support for the Community. Renewed commitment to the Community's original aim of market integration was accompanied by measures that streamlined (and communitarized) European Community decision-making, removing the institutional barriers that had impeded policy development for decades. The "1992" project to complete the internal European market was accompanied by a series of flanking measures—a cohesion policy to support the weaker economies of Southern Europe and modest social provisions—as well as a new budgetary settlement, "Delors I." The package relaunched and transformed the Community. As well as liberalizing sectors that states had kept behind protective barriers for decades, it established Brussels as an authoritative decision-making arena in key policy domains, and gave the Commission a new role as a regulatory actor.

EMU was similarly championed by Delors. Presaged in the SEA, it was negotiated at Maastricht and put into effect by the TEU. Culminating in the adoption of a single currency, monetary union was an historic milestone, marking a step change in relations between the participating states. Political union was also agreed at Maastricht. With the creation of the CFSP (the so-called "second pillar") and the third pillar, JHA, it brought under common institutions cooperation in areas that the member states had historically kept beyond the reach of Brussels. The changes brought about by the Maastricht Treaty were accompanied by a further budgetary settlement ("Delors II").[32]

The achievements of the Delors Commission were not only limited to deepening. As well as the widening of membership in 1995 through the accession of Austria, Finland, and Sweden, much of the groundwork for the "big bang" enlargement to Central, Eastern, and South-Eastern Europe was undertaken during the Delors era. More broadly, the request by the US government that the Commission should be responsible for managing aid and economic support for the former communist states of Central and Eastern Europe underlined the new international stature of the EU's executive.

The president's personal involvement in major initiatives was a distinguishing feature of the Delors presidency. Delors typically worked on the main documents, and took a lead role in selling the central ideas and proposals to heads of state and government. His input into the 1985 and 1991 IGCs, and his authorship of the 1989 Delors report, are key examples. Yet it would be mistaken to attribute the Commission's achievements at this time to Delors alone. The three Colleges over which he presided included many outstanding individuals, such as Lord Cockfield, Peter Sutherland, Sir Leon Brittan, and Karel Van Miert, who made significant and in some cases historic contributions to the Union's development.

At the same time, although the Delors years are often regarded as a golden age,[33] the presidency had negative aspects that must feature in any balanced account of the period. The authoritarian style of the president's cabinet and the use of personal networks to circumvent formal channels is the first (see also below). Second, although the Commission pursued and acquired new competencies, insufficient attention was paid to developing the organization's capacity to take on these responsibilities, many of which were different in kind from its traditional functions. Third, the Commission's continual drive for ever-closer union, combined with the difficulties in ratifying the Maastricht Treaty, led to greater vigilance on the part of governments concerning the actions of the Commission, a reluctance to transfer further competences to the EU, and a reassertion of member-state influence.

16.5 COMPARING THE THREE PRESIDENTS

Extracting lessons from the experience of the Commission's three most effective presidents about what makes a successful presidency is not straightforward. The circumstances under which they occupied the office were very different. Hallstein had the task of leading a nascent institution in the face of pressures from France within and the UK without, while Jenkins became Commission president during a period of "Eurosclerosis," when Schmidt and Giscard d'Estaing were attempting to lead the Community from above. Delors, meanwhile, came to the office after the long-running British Budgetary Question had been resolved,[34] at a moment when, in view of the threat posed by companies in the US and Asia, European capitals were ready to countenance action by Brussels that would improve the competitiveness of European industry, and economic liberalism had spread across the continent. He was also in office when the end of the Cold War called for a collective response from West European states.

Moreover, each president confronted a quite different institutional opportunity structure. The size and composition of the College has changed significantly over time. Hallstein had nine Commissioners from six member states, all of whom had been involved in some capacity in the development of European institutions after 1945. Jenkins presided over a College of thirteen members, with little to bind them together, while the number of Commissioners had grown to fourteen by 1985 when Delors became Commission president. The institutional balance also varied. The Council was in its infancy when Hallstein was in office. Jenkins confronted a mature Council, and a new and assertive actor in the shape of the European Council, while for Delors the European Council was a key interlocutor. The Parliament was weak during the Hallstein and Jenkins presidencies, but increasingly powerful during the Delors era.

Furthermore, the leadership styles of the three presidents varied sharply. Hallstein believed strongly in collegiality. Noël, for example, recalled Hallstein's search for a consensus among his fellow Commissioners and noted that the College did not vote until Hallstein's final year in office. Hallstein used groups of Commissioners to debate policy—perhaps the only time that this device has worked effectively—and had a close relationship with the Secretary General. Jenkins also had a strong commitment to collegiality. Delors, by contrast, was more presidential and his presidency was distinguished by the authoritarian style of his cabinet. Short-circuiting the hierarchy and operating through informal networks was effective, but it marked a departure from the traditions of the house, caused resentment on the part of other Commissioners and senior officials, and led to friction with the Secretary General.[35]

In addition, all three presidents had held high office in national government or administration and were respected for their intellectual prowess, mastery of policy detail, and expertise—legal in the case of Hallstein, financial and economic in the case of Jenkins and Delors. However, the other assets at their disposal varied considerably. Hallstein and Delors had strong support from their national capitals. Jenkins, by contrast, could never count on the same, either with the 1976–1979 Labour government or the Conservative government that replaced it in 1979.

A final observation is that the Commission presidency and the Commission's institutional setting has changed so dramatically since the 1990s that it is not at clear that, beyond the value of certain personal attributes, presidents in the post-Delors era can learn much from their most illustrious predecessors. The office has been strengthened significantly by a series of treaty reforms aimed at strengthening the president's position in the College and introducing greater executive accountability. The TEU gave the nominee for president a voice in the nomination of other members of the cabinet, even if the requirement for "common accord" among member governments remained (Article 158, as amended by Article G(48) TEU). The Amsterdam Treaty included a provision that enshrined the Commission president's pre-eminence within the College: "The Commission shall work under the political guidance of its President."[36] The Treaty of Nice added further elaboration. It provided that the Commission president: "shall decide on [the Commission's] internal organization in order to ensure that it acts consistently, efficiently and on the basis of collegiality."[37] It also gave the president authority over the allocation of portfolios among the members of the College not only at the time of their appointment, but during the Commission's term—an important new power. The president was permitted to appoint vice-presidents from among the members of the College and, significantly, informed no doubt by the events leading to the resignation of the Santer Commission, to require the resignation of a Commissioner, though in both instances the president required the prior approval of the College (Article 217, paras 2–4). While the Lisbon Treaty retained these provisions (Articles 17, 248), it granted the Commission comparable powers in respect to the appointment of the High Representative (Article 81 para. 1), which became a post held jointly in the Commission and the Council.

Moreover, the TEU took an important step in extending the Commission's accountability to the European Parliament. The Treaty introduced a five-year term for the College, which would begin in the January following parliamentary elections in June. The Parliament interpreted this as bestowing on it the right to approve, and therefore also to veto, the member governments' nominations. However, it was the formalization of the principle of parliamentary approval by the Treaty of Amsterdam that led to extensive parliamentary hearings for nominee members of the Commission. After the Parliament has voted on the member governments' nominee for Commission president, the nominee-president and the Council submit the proposed College to a vote of parliamentary approval. Subsequent treaty changes have only extended the parliamentarization of the EU system. While the Treaty of Nice (Article 214) changed the decision rule among member governments from unanimity to QMV, the Lisbon Treaty stipulated that the European Council must take account of the results of elections to the European Parliament (Article 17 para. 7).[38]

Furthermore, under José Manuel Barroso, the Secretariat General has become a service of the president.[39] Although it remains to be seen whether the close relationship between the presidency and the Secretariat General will persist, the change effected by Barroso has given the office an important organizational resource enjoyed by no former Commission president with the possible exception of Hallstein. The expansion of the College to twenty-seven members has also worked to favor a more presidential style of leadership.[40]

Finally, the Commission operates in a more complex, hostile, and challenging environment than previously. The European Council has expanded its range of action, the Parliament is more powerful, and since Lisbon the question of who leads Europe has been further complicated by the creation of European Council president and a Council of President. More generally, governments and publics in Europe are wary of Brussels. In short, although not a "deity,"[41] it is no longer true that "[t]he President has no bargaining position of his own, no sanctions at his disposal, no power to do or to decide anything."[42] It still remains extremely difficult to make a success of the office.[43]

16.6 CONCLUSION

Despite the weakness of the Commission presidency before the 1990s, three incumbents have managed to transcend the limitations of the office. Hallstein, Jenkins, and Delors all made major contributions to the development of the European Communities. All three had intellectual firepower and an ability to command respect in the Council, but differences between the contexts in which they worked, the resources at their disposal, and the opportunity structures they confronted make it difficult to generalize about what makes a successful presidency.

In addition, it is unclear what lessons later presidents might usefully draw from the experience of Hallstein, Jenkins, and Delors. A series of treaty reforms since the early 1990s have given the office greater formal powers and, since 2005, the office has been transformed. José Manuel Barroso succeeded in establishing the presidential model that he had argued was necessary given the expansion of the College to twenty-seven Commissioners following the 2004–2007 enlargement and the increasing demands on the Commission made by the Council and the Parliament. In support of this vision, he also turned the Secretariat General, which had secured a more interventionist role in coordination, into a service of the president. Although the Barroso presidency marked a very significant departure from previous models, it is too early to judge whether its defining traits will prove to be enduring.[44]

NOTES

1. Indeed, according to one author, "The Presidency of the EEC Commission is an impossible job. Indeed, it can hardly be called a job at all—the President has a number of conflicting responsibilities, but no power" (John Campbell, *Roy Jenkins. A Biography* (London: Weidenfeld and Nicolson, 1983), 181).
2. In his memoirs, former UK Commissioner, Christopher Tugendhat, observes that the Commission president "is entirely dependent in his dealing with [heads of state and government] on his own strength of personality and intellectual fire-power" (*Making Sense of Europe* (Harmondsworth: Penguin 2004), 205. He continues: "Only three presidents have overcome this handicap: Walter Hallstein, Roy Jenkins, and Jacques Delors."
3. "He" is used throughout. There has not yet been a female incumbent.
4. Under Article 161 EEC, Commissioners were to be appointed by common accord of governments for a four-year term. The Commission president and vice-presidents were to be similarly chosen, but their term of office was to be only two years. In practice, the president and vice-presidents were automatically reappointed.
5. For discussions of prime ministerial power and political leadership more broadly, see Ludger Helms, *Presidents, Prime Ministers and Chancellors: Executive Leadership in Western Democracies* (Basingstoke: Palgrave Macmillan, 2005), and Robert Elgie, *Political Leadership in Liberal Democracies* (Basingstoke: Macmillan, 1995).
6. See Jacques Delors, *Mémoires* (Paris: Plon, 2004), 221, and Roy Jenkins, *A Life at the Centre* (London: Macmillan, 1991), 450–3.
7. On whether the Commission president should be elected, see Simon Hix, *What's Wrong with the EU and How to Fix It* (Cambridge: Polity, 2008). For an opposing view, see Giandomenico Majone, "The European Commission: The Limits of Centralization and the Perils of Parliamentarianization," *Governance* 15, no. 3 (July 2002), 375–92.
8. Originally, the larger member states appointed two Commissioners and the smaller states one. As the Community grew from six to nine (1973), to ten (1981), twelve (1986), and fifteen (1995), the College expanded from nine to thirteen, to fourteen, seventeen, and twenty, respectively. The Treaty of Nice allowed only one Commissioner per member state. With the 2004 enlargement, one Commissioner from each of the new member states joined the Commission to work alongside existing members. The Prodi Commission temporarily had thirty members. The first Barroso Commission had twenty-five members, which became twenty-seven on the accession of Bulgaria and Romania. For discussion of the College and its impact, see Leo Tindemans, *European Union. Report by Mr. Leo Tindemans, Prime Minister of Belgium, to the European Council. Bulletin of the European Communities, Supplement 1/76. ('The Tindemans Report')* (Brussels: European Communities, 1975), and Dirk Spierenburg, *Proposals for reform of the Commission of the European Communities and its services. Report made at the request of the Commission by an Independent Review Body under*

the chairmanship of Mr. Dirk Spierenburg ('the Spierenburg Report'), 24 September 1979 (Brussels: European Commission–Working Document, 1979).

9. The phrase is from Thomas Christiansen, "A Maturing Bureaucracy? The Role of the Commission in the Policy Process," in Jeremy J. Richardson, ed., *The EU: Policy and Power* (London: Routledge, 1996), 77–95.

10. For discussions of leadership of the EU, see Jack Hayward, "Strategic Innovation by Insider Influence: Monnet to Delors" and Dionyssis G. Dimitrakopoulos, "Collective Leadership in Leaderless Europe: A Sceptical View," both in Jack Hayward, ed., *Leaderless Europe* (Oxford: Oxford University Press, 2008), pages 15–27 and 288–304, respectively.

11. On the Hallstein presidency, see the chapters by Emile Noël, Karl-Heinz Narjes, Wolfgang Wessels, and Hans von der Groeben in Wilfried Loth, William Wallace, and Wolfgang Wessels, eds, *Walter Hallstein. The Forgotten European?* (Basingstoke: Macmillan, 1998). See also N. Piers Ludlow, "A Supranational Icarus: Hallstein, the Early Commission and the Search for an Independent Role," in A. Varsori, ed., *Inside the European Community: Actors and Policies in the European Integration 1957–1972* (Baden-Baden: Nomos, 2006), 37–53, and Chapter 15, this volume; Walter Hallstein, "The EEC Commission: A New Factor in International Life," *International and Comparative Law Quarterly* 14, no. 3 (July 1965), 727–41; and Emile Noël, "Témoignage: l'administration de la Communauté européenne dans la rétrospection d'un ancien haut fonctionnaire," *Jahrbuch für Europäische Verwaltungsgeschichte*, vol. 4 (Die Anfänge de Verwaltung der Europäischen Gemeinschaft) (Baden-Baden: Nomos, 1998), 145–58.

12. See General de Gaulle, *Memoirs of Hope: Renewal, 1958–62; Endeavour, 1962–* (London: Weidenfeld and Nicolson, 1971), 184; and Emile Noël et al., *Walter Hallstein. The Forgotten European?*.

13. See Hallstein, "The EEC Commission," 730.

14. Hallstein, "The EEC Commission," 732.

15. It worth noting that this model differs sharply from Monnet's preferred conception of the HA.

16. Hallstein, "The EEC Commission," 24.

17. Noël, "Témoignage: l'administration de la Communauté européenne," 133.

18. Although he rejected national quotas, Hallstein conceded that a geographical balance would have to be maintained in senior posts.

19. De Gaulle wrote of Hallstein: "He had made Brussels...into a sort of capital. There he sat, surrounded with all the trappings of sovereignty, directing his colleagues, allocating jobs among them, controlling several thousand officials who were appointed, promoted and remunerated at his discretion, receiving the credentials of foreign ambassadors, laying claim to high honor on the occasion of his official visits, concerned above all to further the amalgamation of the Six, believing that the pressure of events would bring about what he envisaged" (*Memoirs of Hope*, 181). Of this portrayal, von der Groeben ("Walter Hallstein as President of the Commission," in Loth et al., *Walter Hallstein. The Forgotten European?*, 108) retorted: "Rarely have a man and his political objectives been so misjudged as in this book."

20. On Hallstein's institutional leadership, see Noël, "Témoignage: l'administration de la Communauté européenne," 132–3; Emile Noël, "Walter Hallstein: A Personal Testimony", in Loth et al., *Walter Hallstein. The Forgotten European?*, 131–4; von der Groeben, "Walter Hallstein as President of the Commission", in Loth et al., *Walter Hallstein. The Forgotten European?*, 95–108; and Karl-Heinz Narjes, "Walter Hallstein and the Early Phase of the

EEC," in Loth et al., *Walter Hallstein. The Forgotten European?*, 109–13; David Coombes, *Politics and Bureaucracy in the European Community* (London: George Allen and Unwin Ltd, 1970), 151–5.

21. For example, Jean Rey, Commissioner for External Affairs, would rather have retained responsibility for handling the UK's first application for EEC membership.

22. "Walter Hallstein as President of the Commission," 96–107.

23. The phrase, but not the view, is expressed by Ludlow, "A Supranational Icarus."

24. As part of a package to reform the CAP, Hallstein had proposed creating a Community budget based on own resources and a move to majority voting in the Council.

25. For the Jenkins presidency, see Roy Jenkins, *European Diary 1977–1981*, (London: Collins, 1989) and *A Life at the Centre* (London: Macmillan, 1991). See also Crispin Tickell, "President of the European Commission," in A. Adonis and K. Thomas, eds, *Roy Jenkins. A Retrospective* (Oxford: Oxford University Press, 2004), 179–204.

26. Four weak presidencies—Jean Rey (1967–1970), Franco Malfatti (1970–1972), Sicco Mansholt (1972–1973), and Francois Ortoli (1973–1977)—separated Hallstein and Jenkins (see Chapter 17, this volume).

27. This was despite Schmidt's description of the role as "a prime minister of Europe."

28. Jenkins, *A Life at the Centre*, 451–3.

29. The quotations are from Tickell, "President of the European Commission," 197.

30. Tickell, "President of the European Commission," 202. See also Chapter 17, this volume.

31. On the Delors presidency, see Ken Endo, *The Presidency of the European Commission under Jacques Delors. The Politics of Shared Leadership* (Basingstoke: Macmillan, 1999); George Ross, *Jacques Delors and European Integration* (Cambridge: Polity Press, 1995); and Charles Grant, *Delors. Inside the House that Jacques Built* (London: Nicholas Brearley Publishing, 2004).

32. The 1993 White Paper on Growth was a further major initiative.

33. In a survey of Commission officials conducted as part of the ESRC-funded project, "The European Commission in Question," Delors was rated considerably more highly than his three successors Jacques Santer, Romano Prodi, and Jose Manuel Barroso in terms of managing the house and promoting the Commission within the EU system. See Hussein Kassim, John Peterson, Michael Bauer, Sara Connolly, Renaud Dehousse, Liesbet Hooghe, and Andrew Thompson, *The European Commission of the Twenty-First Century* (Oxford: Oxford University Press, forthcoming).

34. Thatcher reopened the debate on the expiry of the interim agreement in 1983. The issue was resolved at the Fontainebleau European Council the following year.

35. Noël, remarkably, was still in post when Delors took office, though he retired in 1987.

36. Article 219 TEC.

37. Article 217, para. 1.

38. The incoming Commission usually took office in January. However, due to the delay in appointing its successor, the Santer Commission remained in office in a caretaker capacity until November 1999, when it was replaced by the Prodi Commission. Barroso similarly began his term in November (2004). The delay in implementing the Lisbon Treaty led to an extension of Barroso's first term, so that his second did not begin until February 2010, but its successor was scheduled to take office in October 2014.

39. See Hussein Kassim, "A Silent Transformation: Leadership and Coordination in the European Commission," paper presented at ARENA—Centre for European Studies,

University of Oslo, May 11, 2010, and Kassim et al. *The European Commission of the Twenty First Century*, (Oxford: Oxford University Press, 2012), ch. 6.

40. See Kassim, "A Silent Transformation"; John Peterson, "Enlargement, Reform and the European Commission: Weathering the Perfect Storm," *Journal of European Public Policy* 15, no. 5 (August 2008), 761–80; Peterson, "José Manuel Barroso: Political Scientist and ECPR Member," *European Political Science* 7, no. 1 (March 2008), 64–77; and Hussein Kassim et al., *The European Commission of the Twenty First Century*, ch. 7.

41. Derk Jan Eppink, *Life of a European Mandarin: Inside the Commission* (Tielt: Lannoo, 2007), 211.

42. Campell, *Roy Jenkins*, 182.

43. Michelle Cini, "Political Leadership in the European Commission: The Santer and Prodi Commissions, 1995–2005," in Hayward, *Leaderless Europe*, 113–30; John Peterson "The College of Commissioners," in John Peterson and Michael Shackleton, eds, *The Institutions of the European Union* (Oxford: Oxford University Press), 81–103; Hussein Kassim and Anand Menon, "EU Member States and the Prodi Commission," in Dionyssis G. Dimitrakopoulos, ed., *The Changing Commission* (Manchester: Manchester University Press, 2004), 89–104; Kassim, "A Silent Transformation."

44. Kassim, "A Silent Transformation"; Hussein Kassim et al., *The European Commission of the Twenty First Century*, ch. 7.

....

CHAPTER 17

FAMOUS NON-PERFORMERS: FRANCO MALFATTI, GASTON THORN, AND JACQUES SANTER

....

DESMOND DINAN

FRANCO Malfatti is perhaps the least-known president of the European Commission (1970–1972). He has the distinction of having curtailed his stint in Brussels and returned early to Italy, where he eventually became foreign minister for a brief period. By contrast, Jacques Santer is one of the best-known presidents (1995–1999), but also for an unfortunate reason: the resignation of his Commission in March 1999 to pre-empt what would have been a successful vote of censure by the European Parliament. The Commission's resignation was a major event in the history of the EU, signaling a reversal of political influence in Commission–European Parliament relations. Whether justified or not, Santer will forever be remembered as the president who led the Commission into a disastrous confrontation with the European Parliament, despite having a reasonable record with respect to EMU, enlargement, and internal Commission reform.

Gaston Thorn was a nondescript Commission president (1981–1985), overshadowed at the time by Vice-President Etienne Davignon, known as the best president the Commission never had, and soon thereafter by Jacques Delors, the best president the Commission ever had (see Chapter 16, this volume). Thorn did nothing wrong as Commission president; he was simply unengaged. His presidency was an interregnum between that of Roy Jenkins, who took the first steps toward restoring the Commission's standing in the aftermath of the empty chair crisis (1965–1966), and Delors, under whose leadership the Commission reached its highest point of prestige and power.

Malfatti, Santer, and Thorn are linked by their disappointing presidential performances. Each lacked the drive and ambition associated with holders of high political office. By the standards of other top-level politicians they were relatively laid-back; more Type B than Type A personalities. As Commission presidents, they lacked an intangible though essential attribute of political success: luck. To some extent, a combination of poor judgment, timidity, and misfortune accounts for their poor record in Brussels.

Beyond that, each lead the Commission at markedly different stages in EU history and each faced a set of circumstances that was generally unpropitious. Undoubtedly, individuals with more personal dynamism and political drive, not to mention fortuity, would have fared better in the presidency. Even the most accomplished and astute president, however, would have had difficulty providing powerful leadership in the prevailing circumstances of the early 1970s and late-1990s. The early 1980s, by contrast, was a relatively opportune time for enterprising Commission leadership, which Davignon provided as vice-president and Thorn failed to provide as president (see Chapter 16, this volume).

17.1 Malfatti: A Case Apart

The European Community in which Franco Malfatti arrived as Commission president in July 1970 still had only the six original member states. The memory of the empty chair crisis, when France withdrew its representation from the Council of Ministers to forestall the greater use of QMV and block a budget agreement that would have strengthened the power of the Commission and the European Parliament, was vivid (see Chapter 15, this volume). The fallout from the crisis, still apparent in the early 1970s, greatly damaged the Commission's standing. Internally, the Commission was coping with the administrative implications of the 1967 Merger Treaty, which fused the executive bodies of the three European communities. Externally, the Commission had difficulty asserting itself politically.[1]

France and Germany dominated European Community affairs. Yet the early 1970s was not a period of close Franco–German accord. French President George Pompidou and German Chancellor Willy Brandt did not see eye-to-eye. Nevertheless, in the radically different economic and political circumstances of the post-de Gaulle period—French weakness after the upheaval of 1968; growing German assertiveness; and international financial turmoil—Pompidou and Brandt launched a number of important initiatives intended to reanimate European integration under Franco–German direction.

The post-de Gaulle turn toward a renewal of European integration was consecrated at a summit meeting of European Community leaders in The Hague in December 1969. It was there that Pompidou and Brandt struck an implicit bargain: in return for admitting Britain into the European Community (a preference of Germany and the other member states) governments would agree to switch the basis of Community funding from national contributions to "own resources"—monies that would accrue directly to the European Community budget (a French preference). In addition, governments would explore opportunities for deepening European integration, for instance in the areas of monetary policy and foreign policy cooperation. Pompidou called this new approach "completion, deepening, enlargement"; the media called it "the spirit of The Hague."

July 1970, six months after the successful Hague summit, would seem to have been a fortuitous time for Malfatti to become Commission president. Yet neither Pompidou nor Brandt was interested in the Commission. Pompidou was an intergovernmentalist; Brandt supported supranationalism, but not to the extent of championing either a directly elected Parliament or a strong Commission. Moreover, only one of the initiatives that epitomized the spirit of The Hague—the switch to own resources—would likely enhance the Commission's position, whereas the initiatives associated with "deepening" and "enlargement"—negotiating the accession treaties and reaching agreement on foreign policy cooperation—were largely intergovernmental.

"Deepening" also included a call for EMU, which could have included a central role for the Commission. In October 1970, Pierre Werner, prime minister of Luxembourg, presented an ambitious plan to achieve EMU within ten years.[2] Differences between the governments in Paris and Bonn soon emerged over the scope and possible implementation of the plan, with Pompidou resisting any further sharing of national sovereignty. The circumstances did not favor an enhanced Commission role. By the time that the Six hatched the "snake," a regime to minimize fluctuations among member states' currencies, Malfatti had left Brussels. In the event, fundamental differences between France and Germany over EMU, together with the economic crisis of the mid-1970s, blew EMU off course for the next fifteen years.

A key reason for Malfatti's inability to make an impact on developments in the European Community was that he never wanted to be in Brussels to begin with. By common accord it was Italy's turn to nominate a successor to Jean Rey (1967–1970), who hoped to stay in the presidency. Italy had already passed up the opportunity to nominate Walter Hallstein's successor. This time, Italy felt that it had no choice but to come up with someone to succeed Rey.

It seems remarkable today, when the Commission presidency is one of the most sought-after jobs in the EU, that Italy was uninterested in nominating the president. The explanation lies partly in the fact that the European Community in 1970 was limited in policy scope and political salience. Accordingly, Italy had relatively little interest in what went on in Brussels. For Italy at the time, being a founding member of the European Community was more significant than participating actively in policy-making. Italy's priorities included the twin objectives of regional development (for the poor South) and unrestricted movement for Italian workers among member states, neither of which was on the European Community's agenda in the 1970s.

Italy's disregard for institutional representation in the European Community extended beyond the Commission to the European Parliament, which at the time was indirectly elected. Italy's delegation in the European Parliament was consistently less than full in the 1960s and early 1970s, the main political parties being uninterested in nominating MEPs. When nominated, Italian MEPs had a notoriously high absentee rate.[3]

Similarly, once the Italian government agreed to name Rey's successor, it had difficulty finding a prominent politician from the ruling Christian Democratic party to leave Rome for the political wasteland of Brussels. At the last moment, Malfatti, a Christian

Democratic stalwart, agreed to accept the Commission presidency. He did so not out of conviction, but because of *noblesse oblige* (a fitting reason for the aristocratic Malfatti).

It is hardly surprising, therefore, that Malfatti failed to set Brussels ablaze. He probably could not have done so anyway, given Brandt's and Pompidou's attitude toward the Commission. The two most powerful national leaders treated Malfatti with respect but indifference. Malfatti met Brandt, Pompidou, and other national leaders bilaterally: the European Council did not yet exist and summits were infrequent (the next one, in October 1972, took place after Malfatti had returned to Rome).

Sir Con O'Neill, the chief British negotiator in the accession negotiations, noted how national governments "made it very clear that the Commission must operate as the servant of the Six [member states]."[4] Indeed, national leaders did not allow Malfatti to sign the accession treaties in January 1972. Malfatti may have been unwilling to rock the boat, but he was not entirely subservient. "There are times," he told the European Parliament the following month, "when prejudice replaces judgment, when an academic, legalistic approach replaces considerations of what is politically desirable."[5]

In one respect, at least, Malfatti was a good president: he looked the part and spoke well. Reflecting his roots in Italian politics, he was a good orator; reflecting his roots in Christian Democracy, he espoused European federalism. His short tenure in Brussels is notable mainly for stirring oratory, lamenting the state of European integration, and lauding the cause of European unity.

Malfatti was known in Italy as a capable manager, yet he failed to strengthen administrative procedures in the Commission. The college of commissioners, which had increased in size during an interim period following implementation of the Merger Treaty, reverted to its original composition (two commissioners per large member state; one per small member state) in 1970, when Malfatti became president. The new Commission included a few powerful holdovers from the outgoing administration, notably Raymond Barre (France), Wilhelm Haferkamp (Germany), and Sicco Mansholt (The Netherlands), with whom Malfatti struggled to assert his authority. Mansholt, who succeeded Malfatti on an interim basis and who felt that he (Mansholt) should have been Commission president all along, was especially headstrong.

Malfatti's announcement in March 1972 that he intended to resign and contest the Italian general election reflected the Commission's poor standing at the time. Malfatti's decision embarrassed the Commission but not the Italian government, which was satisfied that it had fulfilled its informal obligation to provide a Commission president. Malfatti's compatriot in the Commission was none other than Altiero Spinelli, the veteran Euro-federalist who subsequently headed the institutional affairs committee of the first directly elected European Parliament and wrote the Draft Treaty on European Union. He and Malfatti were poles apart personally and politically. Spinelli viewed Malfatti's departure with a mixture of relief—Malfatti's successor could hardly be less effective—and disappointment—Malfatti's performance and sudden departure reflected poorly on the Commission, the European Community, and Italy.

17.2 THORN: OUT OF HIS LEAGUE

In the decade between Malfatti's departure and Thorn's arrival as Commission president, the European Community changed in a number of respects. Most visible was the accession of Britain, Denmark, and Ireland in 1973, which brought not only institutional adjustments—for instance, the Commission increased in size from nine to thirteen—but also serious strains as the Community came to terms with a big new member state (Britain) that was unhappy with its terms of membership, disliked the flagship CAP, and had little empathy with the political ethos of European integration. The international economic situation made matters worse, as member states struggled with stagflation (little or no economic growth, high unemployment, and high inflation).[6]

Governments responded institutionally to the challenges confronting the European Community by launching the European Council: regular meetings of national leaders to provide overall direction. The European Council was the brainchild of French President Valéry Giscard d'Estaing who, together with German Chancellor Helmut Schmidt, dominated successive summits. Despite his later incarnation as the father of the Constitutional Treaty, Giscard d'Estaing was an intergovernmentalist who disliked the Commission, opposed direct elections to the European Parliament, and disregarded the small member states. Schmidt instinctively supported supranationalism but, like Brandt before him, had little interest in promoting European federalism. Nevertheless Schmidt espoused and Giscard d'Estaing acquiesced in direct elections to the European Parliament, the first of which took place in June 1979. The newly-elected European Parliament was not as influential as Giscard d'Estaing feared or advocates of ever-closer union hoped, but elections provided a foundation upon which the European Parliament built formidable political power in the years ahead.

In the face of entrenched intergovernmentalism, the early 1980s was not the best time to become Commission president. Roy Jenkins, the outgoing president, had struggled against Giscard d'Estaing. The European Council was their main battleground, with Giscard first attempting to prevent Jenkins' participation and then trying to limit his role. The arrival on the scene of British Prime Minister Margaret Thatcher did not help Jenkins (Thatcher and Jenkins were on opposite sides of the British political divide) or the Commission (Thatcher was every bit as intergovernmentalist as Giscard d'Estaing). Under the circumstances, who would want to become Commission president?

Malfatti notwithstanding, the Commission presidency was always a desirable job, being prestigious if not powerful, and lucrative as well. By common consent it was the turn of a small member state to provide the president. Etienne Davignon, a member of Jenkins' Commission, was eager for the job and had the support of his government (Belgium). But another Belgian (Rey) had already been president, and a Netherlander (Mansholt) had stepped in after Malfatti's departure. Accordingly, it was Luxembourg's turn. Thorn, formerly prime minister (1974–1979), wanted the job. Werner, once again Luxembourg's prime minister, strongly supported Thorn, if only to remove him temporarily from the domestic political scene. Given his experience, Thorn seemed an ideal candidate. As the *Economist* remarked, Thorn "has many obvious qualifications for the post and few known drawbacks."[7]

Nevertheless Giscard d'Estaing stood in his way. At issue was a row between France and Luxembourg over Radio-Television Luxembourg, under joint Franco–Luxembourg ownership, and Giscard d'Estaing's distrust of Thorn's espousal of deeper European integration. Giscard d'Estaing blocked Thorn's appointment at a meeting of the European Council in June 1980. Reacting to the French President's high-handedness, the small member states rallied around Thorn; Belgium no longer pushed Davignon's candidacy; and Thorn in effect became the Benelux candidate. When Giscard relented, the Council of Ministers endorsed Thorn in July 1980.

Never one to forgive or forget, Giscard d'Estaing was determined to put Thorn in his place. Fortunately for Thorn, Giscard d'Estaing lost the French presidential election in May 1981, only four months after Thorn arrived in Brussels. Unfortunately for Thorn, Giscard d'Estaing's successor, François Mitterrand, was preoccupied with internal French affairs for the first two years of his presidency, pursuing policies that were antithetical to deeper integration. By the time that Mitterrand changed tack and championed further integration, in 1984, Thorn's tenure in Brussels was coming to an end.

Without the support of France, in particular, the Commission president could not prosper. Schmidt had little interest in the Commission. Nor, initially, did his successor, Helmut Kohl, who became chancellor in October 1982. Mitterrand and Kohl would spearhead the revival of European integration in the late 1980s in close collaboration with the Commission president, who by that time was Jacques Delors. Even if Thorn had still been president, it is doubtful that he would have been able to exploit the opportunity presented by the new political circumstances in the way that Delors did.

Whereas the leadership of France and Germany changed during Thorn's tenure, the leadership of Britain remained firmly in Thatcher's hands. Even with Thatcher's full support, Thorn could not have asserted himself in the face of France–German indifference. Needless to say, Thorn did not have Thatcher's support. So dismissive was the prime minister that she did not acknowledge Thorn's help in resolving the British budgetary question—Thatcher's demand for a permanent rebate from the Community budget to the British exchequer, an issue that dominated the European Community from 1979 to 1984.

As prime minister of Luxembourg, Thorn had been a founding member of the European Council and knew the institution well. Thorn had seen how Giscard d'Estaing and Schmidt dominated the European Council and how Jenkins had tried, with limited success, to make a mark among the national leaders. Inclined to accept the status quo, Thorn was passive in the European Council when he became Commission president, just as he had been as prime minister of the European Community's smallest member state.

Apart from Giscard d'Estaing's unremitting opposition, another unfortunate legacy of Thorn's selection was Davignon's enduring resentment. During the four years of Thorn's tenure, Davignon behaved as if he (Davignon) should have been president. The aristocratic Davignon, well-connected in the highest political and business circles, having a long history of involvement in European Community affairs, and coming from a bigger member state, completely overshadowed the hapless Thorn. Commissions are generally known by the names of their presidents. In the early 1980s, it was not uncommon to hear reference to the "Davignon Commission."

Thorn's management style did not help. Under his chairmanship, Commission meetings seemed interminable. Thorn was indecisive, soliciting advice from all quarters and often changing his mind. Internally, the Commission was poorly organized and in need of far-reaching reform, as the Spierenburg Report of 1979 had pointed out.[8] But Thorn paid little attention to internal Commission affairs, thereby accentuating the problems that would fester during the Delors presidency and erupt so spectacularly during the Santer and Prodi presidencies.

If he had assigned Commission portfolios differently, Thorn might have been able to restrain Davignon. However, Thorn had no control over the allocation of portfolios. Nor did he have the temperament to stand up to powerful Commission barons. As it was, Davignon received a super-portfolio: industrial affairs and energy.

Despite the seemingly intractable British budgetary question, the Commission and the member states launched various initiatives in the early 1980s that bore fruit later in the decade in the SEA and the single market program. The launch in 1979 of the EMS, intended to establish a zone of monetary stability in a world of wildly fluctuating exchange rates, stood out at an otherwise unremarkable time. After a shaky start, the exchange rate mechanism of the EMS helped participating countries to fight inflation and recover economic growth. The EMS provided a vital underpinning for the single market program and laid a basis for the eventual achievement of EMU. Yet the EMS was not based on the Rome Treaty and did not emerge from a formal Commission proposal. Nor was the Commission centrally involved in its operation.

The Genscher–Colombo initiative of November 1981, named after the German and Italian foreign ministers, was another noteworthy event. It called for more effective decision-making and greater Community competence in external relations and culminated in the Solemn Declaration on European Union, proclaimed by national leaders in June 1983. While seemingly innocuous, the declaration contributed to the incremental deepening of European integration in the early 1980s. In particular, it prefigured the section on foreign policy coordination in the SEA. Although the Genscher–Colombo initiative took place during Thorn's presidency, the Commission did not contribute to the declaration.

By contrast, the Commission was centrally involved in a separate initiative that contributed directly to the revival of European integration: rallying European industry to the cause of cross-border collaboration and the desirability of a single market. This was Davignon's idea. Drawing on extensive contacts at the highest corporate level and experience in the Jenkins Commission, Davignon was instrumental in launching the Round Table of CEOs of major European manufacturers in the high-technology sector, which became a powerful lobby for the single market program. His efforts also resulted in the European Strategic Program for Research and Development in Information Technology (ESPRIT), a basic research program involving major manufacturers, smaller firms, and universities. ESPRIT became both a building block for the single market program and the foundation for the EU's science and technology policy. Impressive though these achievements were for a Commission struggling in the shadow of powerful national interests, they hardly impinged on Thorn.

Apart from helping to resolve the British budgetary question, Thorn's most significant achievement as Commission president was to move the process of Portuguese and Spanish accession along. The Spanish negotiations were especially difficult, due partly to Spanish obduracy and largely to protectionist pressures in France. Issues such as agriculture, fisheries, and the free movement of labor were especially contentious. Thorn took a keen interest in the negotiations, contributing at key moments to breakthroughs on particular issues that contributed to the successful conclusion of negotiations. By the time that Portugal and Spain joined the European Community in January 1986, however, Thorn was out of office.

In 1984, as his presidency drew to a close, Thorn lacked the political support to secure reappointment, even if he had wanted it. Thorn's experience in Brussels had not been happy. Outshone by Davignon, dismissed as a lightweight by many national leaders, and pilloried by the press, Thorn was content to return to Luxembourg as a private citizen. Davignon, Thorn's rival though not his nemesis, hoped finally to become Commission president. But the politics of high-level appointment in the European Community again worked against him and Delors got the top job instead.

17.3 SANTER: STAR-CROSSED

Jacques Santer, another former prime minister of Luxembourg, succeeded Delors. Santer's period as prime minister (1984–1995) had coincided almost exactly with Delors's presidency. As a participant in the European Council, Santer had witnessed the acceleration of European integration from a front-row seat. In particular, he had seen how Delors had mastered the European Council to advance the Commission's and the EU's interests. Delors's success, Santer knew, depended largely on the support of Mitterrand and Kohl, who treated the Commission president almost as an equal. Santer could see that, in the aftermath of the Maastricht Treaty ratification crisis, Delors had lost his luster and the Commission's ascendancy had peaked. Whoever succeeded Delors, Santer knew, would have a difficult time not only dealing with less indulgent national leaders but also managing the Commission, which was badly in need of internal reform.

According to the unofficial rotation, it was the turn of a Christian Democrat from a small member state to succeed Delors, a French socialist. Ruud Lubbers, the Dutch prime minister, seemed the obvious choice, especially as The Netherlands had not previously held the presidency, apart from Mansholt's temporary tenure more than twenty years earlier. Yet Kohl was lukewarm about Lubbers, and cast about for another candidate. He and Mitterrand settled on Jean-Luc Dehaene, like Lubbers a Christian Democrat and prime minister of a small country (Belgium).

Other national leaders were irritated by Mitterrand's and Kohl's behavior but felt powerless to do anything about it, until British Prime Minister John Major forcefully opposed Dehaene. His reason was not principled opposition to Franco–German domination but domestic political opportunism: faced with a shrinking parliamentary majority and growing Euro-skepticism on his own backbenches, Major attempted to score political points by caricaturing Dehaene as a rabid Euro-federalist and vetoing his nomination.

The incoming German Council presidency convened a special summit to resolve the issue. At the last moment, Santer emerged as a compromise candidate. Not only was he a Christian Democrat but also, because he came from Luxembourg, his nomination could be construed as a consolation to Belgium and The Netherlands, the other Benelux countries. Ironically, Santer was as Euro-federalist as Dehaene, but Major was satisfied for the time being with Dehaene's head. Santer seemed destined to succeed Delors.

For the first time in the history of the EU, the selection of the commission president was subject to the European Parliament's approval (under the terms of the Maastricht Treaty). The nature of his selection—the outcome of a bruising intergovernmental battle—did not help Santer's chances; nor did the fact that the Party of European Socialists (PES) held a majority of seats in the European Parliament. As expected, opinion in the European Parliament differed on Santer's qualifications and suitability for the job, as well as on the appropriateness of endorsing a candidate chosen, according to the PES leader, in such a "squalid, shabby, and ill-judged way."[9]

Many MEPs, including some Christian Democrats, thought that the European Parliament should reject Santer in order to force the European Council to choose another candidate more on the basis of merit than expediency, although there was no guarantee that the European Council would have acted any differently next time around. MEPs especially resented governments' warnings that the European Parliament would be held responsible for the consequences of Santer's rejection, and governments' pressure on national delegations in the European Parliament to vote in Santer's favor. In the event, Santer's narrow endorsement in July 1994—by 260 votes to 238 with 23 abstentions—averted a public relations disaster and an inter-institutional crisis, but further weakened the president-designate's stature.[10]

During the debate on his nomination, Santer told the European Parliament that he wanted "to become a strong president at the head of a strong, coherent, determined Commission."[11] Partisan politics in the European Parliament and the institution's increasing assertiveness would make it difficult for Santer to achieve that goal. Moreover, the European Council did not want a new Commission president in the mold of Delors. To make matters worse, Kohl and Mitterrand were disgruntled because Dehaene had not secured the job, and Major's support for Santer was more of a liability than an asset. Jacques Chirac, who replaced Mitterrand as president of France in May 1995, had little time for Santer, whereas Tony Blair, who replaced Major in May 1997, thought Santer perfectly acceptable as Commission president. Given the rivalry that developed between Chirac and Blair, the British prime minister's position did not help to endear Santer to Chirac.[12]

Aware of the handicaps that he faced and unassuming by nature, Santer kept his head down and approached the presidency in a workmanlike manner. The EU had a crowded agenda but was in a consolidating rather than an innovating phase of its development. Issues included absorbing three new member states (Austria, Finland, and Sweden joined the EU in January 1995); developing a pre-accession strategy for the countries of Central and Eastern Europe; negotiating a financial perspective (budget) for the period 2000–2006; devising a new EU–Mediterranean partnership; consolidating the internal market; undertaking economic reform; preparing for the third stage of EMU (the launch of the ECB and the euro); and conducting an IGC on treaty change. While participating in these endeavors, Santer sought to substitute the Commission's current image of ambition and obtrusiveness, personified by Delors, with that of discretion and pragmatism.

Santer was somewhat successful. He was more amenable than Delors to Central and Eastern European enlargement and worked well on the issue with Kohl, for whom enlargement was also a priority. Under Santer's leadership, the Commission took considerable strides toward the eventual accession of the Central and Eastern European states, including initiating Agenda 2000, a proposal for a new financial perspective as well as a set of opinions on the suitability of the candidate countries for EU accession.

At the same time, the Commission helped lay the foundation for the launch of the third stage of EMU in 1999, providing the technical expertise to complement the political push provided primarily by Kohl. In addition, Santer stressed the need to capitalize on the momentum for EMU in order to boost European competitiveness, but few national leaders were willing to undertake far-reaching structural reforms. Santer's signature initiative was the Confidence Pact on Employment, a proposed accord among employers, trade unions, and governments that aimed to generate jobs in the EU by consolidating the single market, curbing state aid, strengthening education and training, and promoting small businesses.

The proposed employment pact sought not simply to alleviate a persistent EU-wide social and economic problem but also to enhance the Commission's standing. In that sense it was analogous to Delors's promotion of cohesion policy in 1988. At that time, however, the political and economic climate was ripe for a bold Commission initiative; despite national resistance to the expense of the proposed structural funds, Delors succeeded in pushing through his ambitious financial package. In so doing, he boosted his own and the Commission's fortunes. In 1996, by contrast, with the EU slowly emerging from recession and governments struggling to meet the EMU convergence criteria, Santer's proposal received only rhetorical support from national leaders. The failure of the employment initiative—although it bore fruit to some extent in the Lisbon Strategy of 2000—showed the limits of Commission activism in the unpropitious circumstances of the mid-1990s.

The extent of the Commission's weakness was painfully evident during the 1996–1997 IGC. Well aware of the prevailing political mood, the Commission, in its preparatory report, pointed out that it sought extra powers neither for itself nor the EU. As in past IGCs, the Commission had a seat at the table, although unlike national delegations it did not have the authority to veto agreement. Santer approached the IGC cautiously, emphasizing his wish to promote the EU's rather than the Commission's interests, although the two are surely inseparable. Santer was right to say in March 1995 that "public opinion has come into play, which we must welcome," but wrong to claim that "there will be a real public debate this time before the end of the IGC."[13]

Compared to previous IGCs, notably the ones that resulted in the SEA and the Maastricht Treaty, the Commission was not influential in the 1996–1997 negotiations. Indeed, the Commission fought a rearguard action to prevent the inclusion in the Amsterdam Treaty of a number of objectionable provisions, such as ending the Commission's exclusive right of legislative initiative in the EU's first (supranational) pillar. From Santer's point of view, the generally disappointing Amsterdam Treaty was the best that could have been hoped for under the circumstances.

Santer was the first Commission president to have a five-year term in office (a change brought about by the Maastricht Treaty). He also presided over the largest European Commission so far (twenty commissioners, thanks to the 1995 enlargement). Santer was not an effective chairman. He ran long and sometimes inconclusive meetings, and failed to rein in powerful colleagues such as Leon Brittan (trade), Mario Monti (internal market), and Karel Van Miert (competition).

Ironically in view of his undoing over allegations of corruption in the Commission, Santer took steps early in his presidency to strengthen financial management. Under his direction, commissioners Anita Gradin (financial control and fraud prevention) and Erkki Liikanen (budget and personnel) spearheaded the reform effort. Significantly, both commissioners came from the new Nordic member states, countries with a reputation for openness and integrity. Going beyond financial control, Santer tried to modernize the civil service, whose organizational problems were rooted in the national governments' determination to retain as much control as possible over the Commission and were compounded by successive enlargements, the proliferation of portfolios, and the excessive power of the cabinets. Staff policy was underused as an instrument of internal reform, new management techniques were rarely introduced, and a decentralization initiative launched in the early 1990s had only mixed results. Delors had made a belated effort to streamline the Commission, but his management style made matters worse. As a result, Santer put internal reform at the top of his presidential agenda.

The Santer reformation included a program to improve administrative practices and personnel policy by means of decentralization, rationalization, and simplification. Easier said than done, its implementation was uneven and aroused the hostility of Commission officials, resentful of what they saw as yet another top-down management initiative with little serious input from the staff itself. A related initiative, "The Commission of Tomorrow," dealt with more politically sensitive issues such as strengthening the Commission presidency, consolidating and reducing the number of portfolios, curbing the power of the cabinets, and basing promotion into the Commission's senior ranks on merit rather than country of origin.

The Commission's ignominious resignation in March 1999, over allegations of corruption and mismanagement, eclipsed Santer's internal reform efforts. The Commission resigned following a confrontation with the European Parliament, the culmination of a series of skirmishes that began in March 1998 when MEPs, incensed by yet another report from the Court of Auditors highly critical of the Commission's handling of the budget, threatened the Commission with censure. Parliament held its fire, but MEPs grew more annoyed throughout the year as additional allegations emerged against the Commission. The most conspicuous case, although it involved a relatively small amount of money, concerned Edith Cresson, a former prime minister of France who allegedly awarded a contract to a friend who was unqualified to carry out the work.[14]

Santer was never accused of financial impropriety, but he showed extraordinary insensitivity and poor political judgment by adopting a tone of indignation and self-righteousness. In effect, he challenged the European Parliament to put up or shut up; to take a vote of censure or not. He left the main political groups little choice but to table a censure motion for the January 1999 plenary session. Santer was confident that the Commission would survive the vote, which it did (the European Parliament failed to muster the necessary two-thirds majority).

Eager to defuse the inter-institutional confrontation, some national politicians urged their counterparts in the European Parliament to drop the matter. Center-right politicians were especially concerned about the vulnerability of Santer, a Christian Democrat, to attacks from the PES. By early 1999, however, the issue transcended party politics: most MEPs were too incensed to back down and wanted to confront the Commission.

Accordingly, the European Parliament decided, with the Commission's agreement, to establish a committee of independent experts to investigate the allegations. The committee's report, published in March 1999, was damning. One widely reported sentence could not have been more injurious: "It is becoming difficult to find anyone [in the Commission] who has even the slightest sense of responsibility."[15] Once the European Parliament made it clear that a Commission that still included Cresson would not survive another censure motion, the Commission's fate was sealed. Santer lacked the authority to dismiss Cresson, especially as the French government backed her to the end; and Cresson herself was unrepentant. The Commission had little choice but to resign as a body; to jump before being pushed by the European Parliament. Santer remained in Brussels, in a caretaker capacity, until a new Commission, under Romano Prodi, took office in September 1999.

Far from being the result of a calculated parliamentary maneuver, the Commission's collapse was the culmination of a series of mistakes and misjudgments on both sides. But the widespread perception was that the European Parliament had come of age and asserted its authority over an arrogant and corrupt Commission. The Commission's forced resignation has therefore gone down in history as one of a series of events in the rise of parliamentary power, on a par with the first direct elections or the introduction of the co-decision procedure for legislative decision-making.[16]

The Commission–Parliament showdown kept Brussels in a tizzy. There was little public sympathy for either of the protagonists, although the European Parliament held the moral high ground against an apparently feckless and wasteful Commission. Lacking flair and largely unknown outside Brussels and Luxembourg, Santer was an easy target for media and public scorn. Much to his chagrin, the events of March 1999 ensured that Santer's presidency is irrevocably linked to allegations of corruption and maladministration in the Commission.

17.4 CONCLUSION

Given that Thorn and Santer came from Luxembourg, one could easily conclude that such a small country simply lacks sufficient talent to supply a politician capable of operating successfully at the highest level in Europe. There may be some merit to that claim, although Jean Claude Juncker, the long-standing Luxembourg prime minister, has been an extremely effective president of the Eurogroup of finance ministers and could well have been a forceful Commission president. Similarly, the fact that Malfatti and Romano Prodi, another less-than-stellar Commission president, came from the same member state could suggest that Italy, for reasons of domestic politics rather than size, is unable to produce a successful Commission president.

Lessons from the underwhelming presidencies of Malfatti, Thorn, and Santer strengthen the conclusion that a Commission president's prospects depend to some extent on country of origin and the attributes of the office itself, but also on the incumbent's personality, acumen, experience, and judgment; prevailing economic and political circumstances; the amount of support from key national leaders, especially of France and Germany; and relations with powerful commissioners. Nevertheless it is difficult to generalize from these three cases. The EU changed markedly from the early 1970, to the early 1980s, to the mid-1990s, and is even more different today. Future Commission presidents could and should draw lessons from the past, but will face circumstances and challenges unique to their times. One thing, at least, is sure: none will want to be linked historically to Malfatti, Thorn, and Santer.

NOTES

1. On Malfatti's presidency, see Michelle Cini, *The European Commission: Leadership, Organization and Culture in the EU Administration* (Manchester: Manchester University Press, 1996), 53–4; on the EU in the early 1970s, see Desmond Dinan, *Europe Recast: A History of European Union* (Basingstoke: Palgrave Macmillan, 2004), 125–45.
2. Commission, "The Werner Report on Economic and Monetary Union," Bulletin EC S/11–1970.
3. See R. E. M. Irving, "Italy's Christian Democrats and European Integration," *International Affairs* 52, no. 3 (July 1976), 400–16.
4. David Hannay, ed., *Britain's Entry into the European Community: Report on the Negotiations of 1970–1972 by Sir Con O'Neill* (London: Routledge, 2000), 71.
5. Quoted in Commission, *Fifth Report on the General Activities of the European Communities* (Luxembourg: European Communities, 1972), p. x.

6. On Thorn's presidency, see Cini, *European Commission*, 63–7; on the EU in the early 1980s, see Dinan, *Europe Recast*, 168–201.

7. *Economist*, May 31, 1980, 58.

8. Commission, Spierenburg Report, Brussels, September 1979.

9. Debates of the European Parliament, *Official Journal of the European Communities*, 4–449, July 19–22, 1994, 79.

10. See Simon Hix and Christopher Lord, "The Making of a President: The EP and the Confirmation of Jacques Santer as President of the Commission," *Government and Opposition* 31, no. 1 (1996), 62–76.

11. Debates of the European Parliament, *Official Journal of the European Communities*, 4–449, July 19–22, 1994, 75.

12. On the Santer Commission, see Cini, *European Commission*, 199–219; and John Peterson, "Jacques Santer: the EU's Gorbachev," *ECSA Review* 12, no. 4 (Fall 1999), 4–6. On the EU in the late 1990s, see Dinan, *Europe Recast*, 265–318.

13. Quoted in *Agence Europe*, March 17, 1995, 2.

14. See Desmond Dinan, "Governance and Institutions 1999: Resignation, Reform and Renewal," *Journal of Common Market Studies* 38, *Annual Review* 2002/2003 (September 2000), 27–30.

15. Committee of Independent Experts, First Report on Allegations Regarding Fraud, Mismanagement and Nepotism in the European Commission, Brussels, March 1999, point 1.6.2.

16. See Julian Priestley, *Six Battles that Shaped Europe's Parliament* (London: John Harper, 2008).

PART IV

MEMBER STATES (CLEAVAGES)

CHAPTER 18

....

LARGE VERSUS SMALL STATES: ANTI-HEGEMONY AND THE POLITICS OF SHARED LEADERSHIP

....

SIMONE BUNSE AND KALYPSO AUDE NICOLAÏDIS

18.1. INTRODUCTION

....

The EU was born first and foremost as an anti-hegemonic project. Anti-hegemony *within* Europe that is, long before any talk of becoming a global anti-hegemon, balancing the US. Peace would require not only the taming of nationalism in general, but a more concrete set of mechanisms to contain the historical appetite for power of continental big states. Napoleons and Bismarks would not do in the halls of Brussels. Instead, the Union-in-the-making would give disproportional voice to smaller states. And the large would gracefully bow. This was the theory at least.

Indeed, "the large versus small" coalition dynamics observed in the EU would otherwise be a puzzle. Interstate coalitions across issues and institutional settings are usually unrelated to size. Other explanations include cultural affinities, geographic proximity, political situation and economic structure, government ideology, or reciprocal agreements between states, trade-offs across issues, and other bargaining factors. In the EU, we can add state preferences regarding integration and the power of supranational institutions. Unsurprisingly, coalitions in Council negotiations are generally highly issue-specific whether structurally so or by circumstance. Amongst the few more durable coalitions over successive enlargements have been the North–South divide or the budget contributors versus receivers. In contrast, size has for fifty years provided the basis for a single-issue coalition, namely that of institutional power. Here the Council splits neatly

into small versus large states—arguably the most persistent and clear-cut country groupings in EU negotiations over time.

That the EU has designed its institutions to accommodate the unequal size of its
constituents is neither surprising nor original. Seeking a difficult equilibrium between
the equality of states and individual citizens is the lot of all federal constructs. After
each enlargement, EU members worry anew about how to accommodate their unequal size and their differing national interests through the complex web of checks and
balances devised by the founding fathers and fine-tuned over half a century. The result
has been a strange mix. On the one hand, the EU has since its early beginnings rested
on the ideal of shared leadership. We are a collective of states, not a nation state. On
the other hand, however, it has obeyed a stringent reality principle. Institutions and
decision-making procedures must reflect power realities between the big and small
member states to be effective and credible. The taming of big state power has been the
best it could do.

This chapter examines the EU's "big versus small problem," or the conflicting views
over institutional design between two opposing coalitions: the more and less populated
member states. It argues that recent rounds of reform have made fundamental changes
to the EU's traditional institutional bargain between big and small states, leading to a
deepening division between them. While not new—the size cleavage had, after all,
played a critical part in dragging out the post-Maastricht institutional agenda—it had
never been as explicit as during the Convention which set the scene for the subsequent
reform debacle.[1] Indeed, the rift between small and big states may—in part—be to blame
for the ratification crisis of the Constitutional and Lisbon Treaties. After eight years of
institutional row and final settlement, the least that can be said is that small states in
Europe are left wounded.[2]

18.2. COALITION PATTERNS IN THE EU

As others demonstrate in this *Handbook*, coalitions in the EU generally form around
issues independent of size. Governments have diverse interests and policy approaches
and face different domestic pressures. Countries have consistently divided along richer–
poorer lines around a cluster of issues related to the distribution of resources within the
EU and agricultural matters. In single market issues the more pro-liberalization and the
more protectionist governments tend to form opposing camps. Depending on the governments in power they may also be more consumer- or more business-oriented.
Alternatively, depending on their degree of industrialization or the power of individual
interest groups they may place greater emphasis on environmental than economic
interests.

In the foreign policy realm, geographic location, a country's colonial past, or its war
history are the most accurate predictors of regional and global priorities or the ambition

it holds for Europe as a global power. For a long time Belgium and France were at odds with the UK and Portugal (all former colonial powers) over their Central Africa approach. Similarly, while Finland, Sweden, and Denmark have all supported Nordic cooperation, the latter two have preferred intergovernmental to supranational forums to do so, as have France and Greece. To be sure, big states sometimes work together simply because they feel they are the most legitimate and credible representatives of the Union, as with the 3 plus 1 talks (Britain, France, and the Commission) with Iran over its nuclear program. But in such instances, and to be effective, the "big" states must generally hold a mandate from their peers. The issue here is one of leadership and control rather than of coalitions per se.

Size does matter however in two instances of policy-making. First, small states may coalesce on specific matters of concern. Small and poor countries, for example, form coalitions to get financial aid or block legislation which could disadvantage them because of their size and limited resources. Small and least industrialized countries may group together to defend lower environmental standards to preserve low production costs and competitiveness. Small countries with governments facing similar industry pressures may together seek to shape legislation reflecting these pressures. However, such constraints, including resources, degree of industrialization, or particular industry interests, tend to be more decisive than population size in forming alliances. Indeed, small countries with their limited voting weight usually try to build alliances with bigger states to ensure that legislation is adopted, win individual concessions, or enhance their blocking power. The second instance, to which we now turn, is of course institutional reform.

18.3. Managing the "Big versus Small Problem"

The EU's founding bargain sought to guarantee a fair balance between big and small states through three complementary mechanisms: a balance between supranational and intergovernmental institutions and policy processes, weighted votes in the Council of Ministers, and sensitive appointment procedures to the Commission, the European Parliament, and the Council presidency.

18.3.1. The EU's Supranational and Intergovernmental Balance

We tend to present the EU's unique brand of interstate cooperation, combining supranational and intergovernmental institutions, as a way to tame and acknowledge sovereignty at the same time. From its origins, however, this design was also meant to accommodate power differentials and reassure smaller states. The relative power of EU institutions depends of course on the underlying legislative procedure and voting arrangements, which vary across areas. In theory, supranational law and institutions are supposed to serve disproportionately the weaker actors, or at least to ensure that size is not mathematically related to influence.[3] So while the intergovernmental Council of Ministers ultimately adopts laws and decides on non-legal matters, the other institutions all contribute to building the EU as a community of law: the Commission with its monopoly right to initiate legislation, the European Parliament and Council as co-legislators, and the ECJ as the interpreter of the Treaties.

Although the small states initially feared Franco–German dominance of the Commission, the collegiality rule has prevented Commissioners from systematically defending their member state's interest. As the Commission developed a reputation as guarantor of the "general interest" against the weight of large states, the "smalls" have generally come to see it as their strongest ally, while big states tend to assert their power in the Council.[4]

The sensitive mix between supranational and intergovernmental processes also manifests itself across issue areas (pillars until the advent of the Lisbon Treaty). While decision-making in pillar I (European Community, ECSC, and Euratom) is managed by the Commission–Council–European Parliament triangle (or Community method), the modus operandi in pillars II and III (CFSP and JHA) is essentially intergovernmental. Deprived of its right of initiative, the Commission has limited power in these areas, as have the ECJ and the European Parliament, both of whom lack jurisdiction or the right to co-legislate here. To balance the lack of power of small states in pillars II and III— often at the expense of efficiency—the prevailing decision-making rule has been unanimity. The areas under each decision mode have changed slightly with the Lisbon Treaty, which moved more issues under the community method. But the basic equation remains: the more sovereignty-sensitive an area, the more (especially big) member states seek to retain control in decision-making.

18.3.2. Weighted Votes

Similarly, the Council of Minister's weighted voting system stems from the enormous size differences of the founding members. It offered small states a degree of security while giving the largest a greater say. The European Community's initial QMV system is a perfect illustration of this logic of "regressive proportionality"—a midway house between the principles of "one country, one vote" and "one citizen, one vote." Initially the largest states were twenty-five times "less represented" than the smallest one and a decision could be blocked by two large states or one large and at least one small state, but not by a small state alliance or one state alone. The qualified majority (QM) represented about 70 percent of the population.

The 1973 enlargement called for a first revision of this bargain: while the UK received the same votes as the three large founders, Denmark and Ireland were given a smaller weight than Belgium and the Netherlands. The original idea of a "blocking minority" (BM) was preserved. Successive enlargements followed the same logic (see Table 18.1). While the rationale for the distribution of votes became more complex with each enlargement, the relative scale of representation—with a factor of one to five between the smallest and biggest state—remained unchanged.

This was, however, an unstable equilibrium. The growing number of "smalls" was diluting the weight of bigger states, who increasingly fell prey to the "gulliver syndrome," picturing themselves as giants held hostage by a crowd of mini-countries.[5] Thus, the Nice Treaty redesigned three parameters of the EU's traditional voting system to reign in the Lilliputs: the number of votes of the big states increased from five to almost ten times that of the smallest member; the majority threshold was raised from 71 to almost 75 percent of the votes (after the 2007 enlargement); and laws were to require a double majority of population (62 percent) and states (or two-thirds if not acting on a Commission proposal). While the implications of these reforms in terms of veto and coalition power are contested, there is no doubt that they heralded a reassertion of "population power" both symbolically and practically.

Yet further boosting the power of the EU's largest members, the Lisbon Treaty has now replaced the EU's system of weighted votes with a double majority system (phased in in 2014 and fully implemented by 2017). When the Council acts on Commission proposals votes must be cast by 55 percent of the member states rather than a simple majority. In addition, the population threshold has been raised to 65 percent. In highly sensitive matters, when the Council acts on its own initiative, or that of a member state, the ECB, or the High Representative, the required QM is 72 percent of states representing 65 percent of the EU population. At the behest of small countries, further safeguards were introduced: a blocking minority must comprise at least four states and—echoing the forty-five-year-old Luxembourg compromise—countries can appeal to the European Council when they feel that vital interests have been violated.[6] Since population thresholds benefit bigger states, while state thresholds benefit the more numerous smalls,[7] the new system may appear carefully balanced. But the introduction of the population criterion as the primary measure of power represents an unmistakable shift. It is no surprise that the French government used enhanced French voting weight in its pro-treaty campaign in 2005 and that the Irish "No-to-Lisbon" campaigns stressed Ireland's loss of voting power.

In the end however, the decision-making game is only very partially defined by the voting system. As former Irish Prime Minister Bertie Ahern once said: "If I had to depend on Ireland's weighted vote to promote our interests in the Council, I would not bother to turn up."[8]

18.3.3. The Composition of the Commission

Disproportional weight has traditionally also been characteristic of the Commission composition and explains, in part, its support by the smalls. From the foundation, each

Table 18.1 Evolution of the qualified majority (QM) in the Council of Ministers

Bigs	1958	1973	1981	1986	1995	May 2004	November 2004 (1)	2007	2014 (3)		Pop. mil.
D	4 (23.5%)	10 (17.2%)	10 (15.9%)	10 (13.2%)	10 (11.5%)	10 (8.1%)	29 (9%)	29 (8.4%)	16.7%	+ 8.3	82.438
F									12.8%	+ 4.4	62.886
I									11.9%	+ 3.5	58.752
GB									12.3%	+ 3.9	60.422
E				8 (10.5%)	8 (9.2%)	8 (6.5%)	27 (8.4%)	27 (7.8%)	8.9%	+ 1.1	43.758
Pl									7.7%	+ 0.1	38.157
Total	12 (70.6%)	40 (69%)	40 (63.5%)	48 (63.2%)	48 (55.2%)	56 (45.2%)	170 (53%)	170 (49.3%)	~70%	~+ 20	346.413
Smalls											
R								14 (4.1)	4.4%	+0.3	21.61
NL	2 (11.8%)	5 (8.6%)	5 (7.9%)	5 (6.6%)	5 (5.7%)	5 (4%)	13 (4%)	13 (3.8%)	3.3%	-0.5	16.334
B									2.1%	-1.4	10.511
Gr									2.3%	-1.2	11.125
P							12 (3.7%)	12 (3.5%)	2.1%	-1.4	10.57
CR									2.1%	-1.4	10.251
H									2.0%	-1.5	10.077
S									1.8%	-1.1	9.048
A					4 (4.6%)	4 (3.2%)	10 (3.1%)	10 (2.9)	1.7%	-1.2	8.266
Bu									1.6%	-1.3	7.719
DK		3 (5.2%)	3 (4.8%)	3 (3.9%)	3 (3.4%)				1.1%	-0.9	5.428
Ire									0.9%	-1.1	4.209
Fin							7 (2.2%)	7 (2%)	1.1%	-0.9	5.256
SR									1.1%	-0.9	5.389

									Pop. %		Pop. (mil)
Li	–	–	–	–	–	3 (2.4%)	–	–	0.7%	-1.3	3.403
La	–	–	–	–	–	–	–	–	0.5%	-0.7	2.295
Slo	–	–	–	–	–	–	–	–	0.49%	-0.8	2.003
Es	–	–	–	–	–	–	4 (1.2%)	4 (1.2%)	0.3%	-0.9	1.344
Cy	–	–	–	–	–	–	–	–	0.2%	-1.0	0.766
L	1 (5.9%)	2 (3.4%)	2 (3.2%)	2 (2.6%)	2 (2.3%)	2 (1.6%)	–	–	0.1%	-1.1	0.46
M	–	–	–	–	–	–	3 (0.9%)	3 (0.9%)	0.1%	-0.8	0.404
Total	5 (29.4%)	18 (31%)	23 (36.5%)	28 (36.8%)	39 (44.8%)	68 (54.8%)	151 (47%)	175 (50.7%)	~30%	~-20	146.468
QM	12 (70.6%)	41 (70.7%)	45 (71.4%)	54 (71.1%)	62 (71.3%)	88 (71%) (2)	232 (72.3%) (2)	258 (74.8%) (2)	65% of pop./55% of MS (4)		–
BM	6 (35.3%)	18 (31%)	19 (30.2%)	23 (30.3%)	26 (29.9%)	37 (29.8%)	90 (28%)	88 (25.5%)	4 MS		–
Total	17	58	63	76	87	124	321	345	100		492.881

Due to rounding, totals may not add up to 100 percent. (1) Nice Treaty. (2) Cast by a majority of MS on a Commission proposal (in other cases, cast by at least two-thirds of MS) and 62 percent of the EU's total population. (3) Double Majority System as per Lisbon Treaty. Full Implementation by 2017. (4) Where the Council is not acting on a proposal of the Commission or initiative of the Union Minister for Foreign Affairs, the QM is obtained with 72 percent of the MS representing 65 percent of the EU population. Council members representing at least three-quarters of a BM (either at the level of MS or population) can demand that the Council should further discuss the issue. The Council may decide to withdraw the latter measure in 2014. Population estimates, Eurostat, 7/11/2006. Commission Doc 15124/06. QM = Qualified Majority; BM = Blocking Minority; MS = Member State; Pop. = Population; mil. = million; D = Germany; F = France; I = Italy; GB = Great Britain; E = Spain; Pl = Poland; R = Rumania; NL = The Netherlands; B = Belgium; Gr = Greece; P = Portugal; CR = Czech Republic; H = Hungary; S = Sweden; A = Austria; Bu = Bulgaria; DK = Denmark; Ire = Ireland; Fin = Finland; SR = Slovak Republic; Li = Lithuania; La = Latvia; Slo = Slovenia; Es = Estonia; Cy = Cyprus; L = Luxembourg; M = Malta.

small state has been guaranteed one Commissioner, while the large states had two. The adoption at Nice of one Commissioner per state up to twenty-seven opened up a short window of complete equality. Despite this strongly degressive rule of proportionality, the asymmetry did not tip the balance of support. The fact that every country has always had a Commissioner is not merely understood in terms of representation (although this matters too, given that many of the high posts in the Commission administration are held by bigger state nationals), but also as a guarantee that the peculiar situation of the small states is understood in the College. Most smaller states see their Commissioner as their eyes, ears, and voice in Brussels and would be loath to abandon the idea. Big states, on the other hand, have increasingly shown dissatisfaction (as in the other areas discussed above) with what they see as an unwarranted equality, and have sought to use the efficiency argument to reduce Commission numbers.

According to the Nice Treaty, from November 2009 the number of Commissioners was supposed to be less than the number of member states. The Commissioners were then to be chosen according to a rotation system reflecting the demographic and geographical range of all states. Given the ratification of the Lisbon Treaty, this system did not see the light of day (except in the fall of 2009, when creative minds competed in finding solutions compatible with both treaties).

Instead, the Lisbon Treaty foresaw a more radical change. The Commission appointed for the period between the entry into force of the treaty and October 31, 2014 would continue to consist of one national per member state. After that, however, the Lisbon Treaty set the number of Commissioners at two-thirds of the number of member states chosen on the basis of a system of equal rotation reflecting the demographic and geographical range of the member states, unless the European Council, acting unanimously, decided to alter this number.

While this provision implied that the Commission would grow with further enlargements, at any time one-third of states would not have a Commissioner. This development, though formally based on equality, was much resented by the smaller states. Bigger states would be able to compensate for the loss of a Commissioner by giving the smaller states more weight in other EU institutions, but the smaller countries would all the same find themselves at a greater disadvantage. As one official argued: "As a small state, if you do not have a Commissioner you are in a sense out of the game."[9] In short, here too, representation was moving away from an interpretation of equality conducive to reassuring small states.

It is no surprise, then, that the one formal concession that was made to assuage the Irish electorate after their "No" vote in June 2008 was that each member state would retain one Commissioner (see below).

18.3.4. Representation in the European Parliament

Predictably, the European Parliament also follows a degressively proportional logic, half way between equal representation and population proportionality. Most small states are either three or four times less represented in the European Parliament than the big ones (see Table 18.2). Up to 2009, the European Parliament had 785 members. The smallest member state, Malta, had 5 seats and the largest, Germany, 99. Lisbon states that representation of citizens should be degressively proportional and raises the minimum number of seats for the smalls to 6, lowers the highest number of MEPs per country to 96, and fixes a maximum of 750 MEPs. To some extent, therefore, the European Parliament appears to offer greater relative power to small states through the formation of ad hoc coalitions within transnational political groups, a fact that may explain their defense of the Commission–European Parliament alliance.

18.3.5. The Rotating Council Presidency

The EU institution which has symbolized the purest reflection of equality and shared leadership has been the rotating Council presidency. Upon its creation, small countries feared a single figurehead in the sway of the big and powerful. Thankfully, such a fear chimed with that of big countries who wanted to avoid the emergence of an autonomous leader that could undermine their own prestige. There was also widely shared agreement that a permanent presidency would risk generating rivalry with the young Commission. Thus, the original model established a system of equal half-yearly rotation among the member governments to chair the different Council formations regardless of size, economic power, or merit.[10]

The rotation principle allowed the member states equal access to an institution which—rather unexpectedly—evolved from a "fairly passive [manager]"[11] and mere administrative function into a crucial agenda setter, a promoter of political initiatives, and a compromise shaper.[12] Enabling states to make diplomatic contributions independent of their political and economic weight,[13] the office has been particularly important for small states:

> The most positive aspect of the rotating presidency is that it gives us a chance to hold an influential role and that you manage to get totally different people to look at the same issue which you move into the spotlight.[14]

It is precisely around this institution that the greatest conflict emerged between big and small EU states in the period 2001–2009.

18.4. A "President for Europe?": The Re-Emergence of the Big versus Small Divide

As the above suggests, the EU's institutional balance between big and small states has been a contested equilibrium. However, only with the Convention's Draft Constitutional Treaty has it been fundamentally put in question by the big states. The following section

Table 18.2 The evolution of the composition of the European Parliament

Bigs	Number of MEPs											Degree of Under–(–)/Over–(+) Representation				
	1958	1973	1976	1981	1986	1991	1995	2004	2007	2009–14[1]	2009–14[2]	% of EU pop.	2007–09 % of seats	2007–09 (–)	2009–14[2] % of seats	2009–14[2] (–)
D	36	36	81	81	81	99	99	99	99	99	96	16.7%	12.6	−4.1	12.8	−3.9
F	36	36	81	81	81	81	87	78	78	72	74	12.8%	9.9	−2.9	9.9	−2.9
I	36	36	81	81	81	81	87	78	78	72	72[3]	11.9%	9.9	−2.0	9.6	−2.3
GB		36	81	81	81	81	87	78	78	72	73	12.3%	9.9	−2.4	9.7	−2.6
E					60	60	64	54	54	50	54	8.9%	6.9	−2.0	7.2	−1.7
Pl								54	54	50	51	7.7%	6.9	−1.8	6.8	−0.9
Seats (%)	76	73	79	75	74	75	68	60	56	56	56	~70	56		56	
Smalls														(+)		(+)
R									35	33	33	4.4%	4.5	0.1	4.4	0.0
NL	14	14	25	25	25	25	31	27	27	25	26	3.3%	3.4	0.1	3.5	0.2
B	14	14	24	24	24	24	25	24	24	22	22	2.1%	3.1	1.0	2.9	0.8
Gr				24	24	24	25	24	24	22	22	2.3%	3.1	0.8	2.9	0.6
P					24	24	25	24	24	22	22	2.1%	3.1	1.0	2.9	0.8
CR								24	24	22	22	2.1%	3.1	1.0	2.9	0.8
H								24	24	22	22	2.0%	3.1	1.1	2.9	0.9
S							22	19	19	18	20	1.8%	2.4	0.6	2.7	0.9
A							21	18	18	17	19	1.7%	2.3	0.6	2.5	0.8
Bu									18	17	18	1.6%	2.3	0.7	2.4	0.8
DK		10	16	16	16	16	16	14	14	13	13	1.1%	1.8	0.7	1.7	0.6
Fin							16	14	14	13	13	0.9%	1.8	0.9	1.7	0.8
SR								14	14	13	13	1.1%	1.8	0.7	1.7	0.6

Ire	–	10	15	15	15	15	13	13	12	12	1.1%	1.7	0.6	1.6	0.5
Li	–	–	–	–	–	–	9	9	8	9	0.7%	1.7	1.0	1.6	0.9
La	–	–	–	–	–	–	9	9	8	8	0.5%	1.1	0.6	1.2	0.7
Slo	–	–	–	–	–	–	7	7	7	8	0.4%	1.0	0.6	1.1	0.7
L	6	6	6	6	6	6	6	6	6	6	0.3%	0.8	0.5	0.8	0.5
Es	–	6	–	–	6	6	6	6	6	6	0.2%	0.8	0.6	0.8	0.6
Cy	–	–	–	–	–	–	6	6	6	6	0.1%	0.8	0.7	0.8	0.7
M	–	–	–	–	–	–	5	5	5	5	0.1%	0.6	0.5	0.8	0.7
Seats (%)	*24*	*27*	*21*	*25*	*26*	*25*	*32*	*40*	*44*	*44*	*~30%*	*44*	*44*	*44*	*44*
Total	*142*	*198*	*410*	*434*	*518*	*536*	*626*	*732*	*785*	*736*	*750³*	*100*	*100*	*100*	*100*

[1] Nice: Distribution of Seats according to Article 189 TEC as modified by Article 9 of the BG/RO–Act of Accession.
[2] Lisbon Treaty and as proposed by European Parliament report of 12/10/2007. Population estimates from Table 18.1.
[3] To be increased by 1.

Abbreviations: D = Germany; F = France; I = Italy; GB = Great Britain; E = Spain; Pl = Poland; R = Rumania; NL = The Netherlands; B = Belgium; Gr = Greece; P = Portugal; CR = Czech Republic; H = Hungary; S = Sweden; A = Austria; Bu = Bulgaria; DK = Denmark; Ire = Ireland; Fin = Finland; SR = Slovak Republic; Li = Lithuania; La = Latvia; Slo = Slovenia; Es = Estonia; Cy = Cyprus; L = Luxembourg; M = Malta.

therefore examines more closely this key moment in the institutional reform debate. It remains to be seen whether the Lisbon Treaty, which to a large extent reflects the 2003 new institutional bargain, will provide a new and stable long-term equilibrium.

18.4.1. Coalitions, Interests, and Power Politics at the Convention

When the Convention started to discuss institutions in 2002, it neatly divided into big and small country camps. While a classic IGC feature, the tensions which developed between the two had never been as stark. The coalition of big countries championed the so-called ABC proposal of José Maria Aznar, Tony Blair, and Jacques Chirac and sought to re-balance influence on all fronts: the election of a full-time European Council presidency; enhanced voting weight; and a reduced Commission.

The coalition of smalls (the "friends of the Community method") fiercely opposed these changes—especially a permanent presidency—with the possible exception of Sweden and Denmark. The Benelux led the group in its efforts to defend their interests and promoted alternative reform proposals. To enhance the Council's effectiveness they suggested separating its executive and legislative functions instead of providing it with a permanent figure head. Moreover, the smalls advocated the reinforcement of the Community method, the election of the Commission president by the European Parliament, and greater executive powers for the Commission. Only on the Commission composition were the Benelux unable to rally their troops: they felt that the Commission's effectiveness would be increased by reducing its size, while other states preferred to retain their Commissioner.

To solve the conflict, France and Germany agreed to a few rather insignificant concessions: the role of the permanent European Council president was watered down, the Commission president would indeed be elected by the European Parliament, and a reduced Commission College would reflect the EU's geographical and demographic diversity. Given the two countries' reputation as the traditional "motor of European integration" and Germany's credentials as a defender of small states, many Convention members welcomed their leadership to bridge the fierce differences over the EU's future institutional set-up.[15]

Moreover, the big states' material resources far outweighed those of the small states' coalition. The Convention was to define its decisions by consensus, and contrary to the EU's historic compromise, Convention President Giscard d'Estaing had defined consensus in terms of the majority of the EU population. Germany and France together already represented more than 30 percent of the EU population, while the sixteen smalls who opposed the permanent presidency particularly fiercely only represented about 25 percent of the EU population. The bargaining power of the big states was further enhanced by the Praesidium's "single negotiating text" approach, which did not leave options open for any last-minute package; by the fact that not all aspects of the Benelux proposal enjoyed the coalition's support; and by the weakness of the Commission and the European Parliament on institutional issues.[16] Finally and crucially, Giscard d'Estaing, who had fleshed out a powerful role for the Convention Praesidium and himself,[17] sided with the EU's big states and supported the idea of a permanent Council presidency. Unsurprisingly, the smalls were to lose on all sides.

The Convention's final institutional bargain resembled the main aspects of the French–German compromise and ignored key criticisms by the smalls (Table 18.3). It made clear that the bargaining space, and hence the outcomes, acceptable by the Convention were bound by the positions and bottom lines of the most powerful states, who kept the most salient issues firmly under their control.

Such intra-state bargains prevailed in a Convention where parliamentarians were a majority for a simple reason: the Convention took place in the shadow of the IGC, whereby any outcome could face a state veto. Once concrete issues were put on the table, the government representatives (and most MPs) loyally defended national interests. The other Convention members, including MEPs and the Commission, anticipating the IGC, had no choice but to adapt their behavior to this constraint. Hence, on institutional issues the Convention was not radically different from IGCs. Much of its endgame was dominated by the kind of hegemonic compromises that have characterized EU politics since its inception.[18]

The Convention's institutional bargain was largely left in place in the ensuing IGC. However, its precise shape and the tactics used to reach it left a "bad taste" among many delegates and observers alike. After the French and Dutch "No" votes, this version of the Constitutional Treaty was abandoned, but its reincarnation under the guise of the Lisbon Treaty did not manage to heal the rift. Concerns over the EU's new institutional balance and divisions between the EU's more and less populated states lingered on, which became clear when the Irish electorate rejected the treaty in June 2008.

18.4.2. "Don't be Bullied": The Irish Referendums and Lisbon Revisited

"Don't be bullied" was one of the rallying cries of the highly successful "No-to-Lisbon" campaign in Ireland. While the Irish voted "No" for many reasons,[19] one of them was the attachment to the "Irish Commissioner" and the desire to protect small states.

As the fate of the Lisbon Treaty hang in the balance, the big–small states divide once again came into sharp relief. Clearly, Irish Prime Minister Brian Cowen could not go back to his electorate and ask for a second vote on the Treaty without some changes between the first and the second version! To allay the key concerns of the naysayers, he convinced his peers to provide legal guarantees that the Lisbon Treaty would not undermine Irish military neutrality or infringe on their right to set taxes and determine abortion policy. The prime minister also convinced them to revisit one of the most contentious issues of the Convention: the Commission composition. Remarkably, even

Table 18.3 Synopsis of small versus big divide and Convention/IGC outcomes

Institution	Position of majority of bigs	Position of majority of smalls	Convention outcome	Constitutional Treaty	Lisbon Treaty	Favours
Council						
- European Council Presidency	Permanent	Rotating	Permanent	Permanent	Permanent	Bigs
- Presidency of the Council of Ministers	Some form of rotation, except for general and foreign affairs, JHA, Ecofin, and the Eurogroup	Rotating	Except foreign affairs, 1-yearly rotation	Except foreign affairs, rotation in accordance with decision by European Council	Except foreign affairs, rotation in accordance with decision by European Council	Status Quo
- QMV	Double majority (except Spain and Poland)	Weighted Votes as per Nice Treaty or sufficient guarantees for smalls	Double majority: 60% of population and a majority or 2/3 of member states No Blocking minority	Double majority: 65% of EU population and 55% or 72% of member states Blocking minority: 4 member states	Double majority: 65% of EU population and 55% or 72% of member states Blocking minority: 4 member states[1]	Bigs
Commission						
- Composition	Less than one Commissioner per member state	One Commissioner per member state (except Benelux)	President, Union Minister for Foreign Affairs (Vice-President) and 13 Commissioners selected on basis of equal rotation reflecting demographic and geographical range of member states	2/3 of the number of member states (unless Council decides otherwise) selected on the basis of equal rotation reflecting demographic and geographical range of member states	Possibility to keep one Commissioner per member state[2]	Status quo

	Not opposed to non-voting Commissioners	Opposed to non-voting Commissioners	Non-voting Commissioners chosen by President according to same criteria that apply for composition	Commission acts as collegiate body	Commission acts as collegiate body	Status quo
- Voting	Not opposed to non-voting Commissioners	Opposed to non-voting Commissioners	Non-voting Commissioners chosen by President according to same criteria that apply for composition	Commission acts as collegiate body	Commission acts as collegiate body	Status quo
- Presidency	Council proposes, European Parliament elects	European Parliament elects, Council confirms	Council proposes, European Parliament elects	Council proposes, European Parliament elects	Council proposes, European Parliament elects	Status quo
European Parliament						
- Composition	Greater proportionality	At least 1 MEP per European Parliament faction (i.e. 7 MEPs per member state)	Degressive proportionality minimum of 4 MEPs per member state; Max. of MEPs 736, Council to decide precise allocation of MEPs	Degressive proportionality minimum of 6, maximum of 96 MEPs per member state; Max of 750 MEPs, Council to decide precise allocation of MEPs	Degressive proportionality minimum of 6, maximum of 96 MEPs per member state; Max of 751 MEPs, Council to decide precise allocation of MEPs	Status quo

[1] To take effect in 2014. Until then, a member state may request that a Commission proposal be adopted according to a QM consisting of at least 255 votes in favor representing a majority of member states. In other cases the Council may request that decisions shall be adopted if there are at least 255 votes in favor representing at least two-thirds of the members.

[2] Upon entering into force of the Treaty of Lisbon, a decision is to be taken to the effect that the Commission beyond 2014 shall continue to include one national per member state.

France, which had strongly advocated reducing the Commission, now seemed to share many of the small countries' concern of losing influence in the Commission (it had agreed to "equal rotation" after all) and to recognize the broader significance of Lisbon's institutional reforms. Reversing previous French thinking, Sarkozy stated in a press interview: "We stop member states from having the [rotating Council] presidency and on top of that we take from them the possibility [of having] a Commissioner...It is a conception and vision of Europe which is not mine."[20] In December 2008, at the urging of Ireland, and to the delight of the "friends of the Community method" and relief of most states, the one-Commissioner-per-country principle was reinstated.[21] It may seem ironic, then, that after all the fuss created by the EU's institutional reforms and the navel-gazing which it induced, we have moved back more than full circle to absolute equality in the Commission—an outcome which had not even been envisaged by the founding fathers. In this one respect, the resistance of the Lilliputs finally paid off!

18.5. CONCLUSION

This chapter has focused on one of the most persistent and clear-cut divisions in EU negotiations since its beginnings: the debate between small and big member states over institutional issues. While coalition formation in the EU usually depends on factors other than size and is highly issue-specific, tensions between large and small states have become ever-more visible with institutional reforms accompanying successive enlargements.

We have argued that European integration has been based on a sophisticated concept of shared leadership to manage the inherent tensions between large and small countries and the need to balance supranational and intergovernmental modes of decision-making. This was reflected particularly in the role and composition of the EU's supranational institutions, its system of weighted votes, and the rotating Council presidency. These mechanisms tried to preserve the basic principle of equality among member states, while still giving the larger ones a predominant say. But as the number of small countries grew, larger states started to question the system's "fairness." By the time the Convention was convened and the EU was about to enlarge to ten new—mostly small—member states, a new bargain was needed to reconcile the principles of equality among states and proportional democratic representation in the EU.

However, neither the Convention nor the subsequent IGCs which eventually led to the Lisbon Treaty narrowed the divide between large and small. Agreeing on a new bargain proved highly difficult. While most of the large states tried to strengthen the role of national governments and the European Council by providing it with a permanent chair, most of the small states defended the Community method, their "representation in the Commission," and the rotation principle.

The final deal brokered in the Convention did not survive the ratification process. In the end, the big states gained strength in the Council—through the new voting procedure and the permanent president/chair—but not in the Commission. The return of the national Commissioner may go a long way to reconciling smaller states with the changes at hand. So might the fact that the new Council presidency post created by the Lisbon Treaty went to Herman Van Rompuy, a former Belgian prime minister, rather than to a representative of one of the bigger member states. The dynamics of coalitional politics between big and small states in the years to come will also depend on other factors, chief among them Germany's behavior under its new "biggest of the big" status: will it continue to seek to play a pivotal role between big and small, old and new member states? Or will it finally claim a role and influence commensurate with its size and formal power in the complex EU system of shared leadership? Despite Germany's traditional reluctance to lead, the ongoing euro crisis, reliance on Germany to solve the crisis, and recent (Franco–) German proposals for a stability union seem to make domination by the EU's big member states much more open ended. The new iteration of the anti-hegemonic bargain in the EU is already proving to be a temporary equilibrium.

Notes

1. The Amsterdam Treaty was to address the key institutional reforms related to member states' disparate size (voting weights and qualified majority in the Council and the number of MEPs and Commissioners), but it did not. The Treaty of Nice tried again and was largely unsuccessful.
2. Given that the present chapter was largely written before the European sovereign debt crisis developed and intensified in early 2010, the analysis does not consider the dynamics between small and big states in the Euro crisis.
3. S. Bunse, P. Magnette, and K. Nicolaidis, "Is the Commission the Small Member States' Best friend?" (Stockholm: SIEPS, 2005).
4. Bunse et al., "Is the Commission the Small Member States' Best friend?"
5. P. Magnette and K. Nicolaïdis, "The European Convention: Bargaining in the Shadow of Rhetoric," *West European Politics* 27, no. 3 (2004), 381–404.
6. If after twelve months no agreement is forthcoming, the countries supporting the proposal may move ahead by themselves.
7. R. Baldwin and M. Widgrén, "Council Voting in the Constitutional Treaty: Devil in the Details," *CEPS Policy Brief*, no. 53 (July 2004) (Brussels: CEPS).
8. T. Brown, "Achieving Balance: Institutions and Member States," *Federal Trust Online Paper* 1/04 (London: Federal Trust, 2004).
9. Interview, March 2, 2005.
10. H. Wallace, "The Presidency: Tasks and Evolution," in C. O'Nuallain and J.-M. Hoscheidt, eds, *The Presidency of the European Council of Ministers; Impacts and Implications for National Governments* (London: Croom Helm in association with EIPA, 1985), 2; M. Westlake, *The Council of the European Union* (London: Cartermill, 1995), 37.
11. H. Wallace and G. Edwards, "The Evolving Role of the Presidency of the Council," *International Affairs* 52, no. 4 (1976), 576.
12. E. J. Kirchner, *Decision-Making in the European Community—The Council Presidency and European Integration* (Manchester: Manchester University Press, 1992); Westlake, *The Council of the European Union*; F. Hayes-Renshaw and H. Wallace, "Executive Power in

the European Union: The Functions and Limits of the Council Ministers," *JEPP* 2, no. 4 (1995), 559–82; P. Sherrington, *The Council of Ministers* (London: Pinter 2002).

13. *Financial Times*, December 4, 2000, 3.

14. Interview, April 26, 2004, cited in S. Bunse, *Small States and EU Governance* (Basingstoke: Palgrave MacMillan, 2009), 203.

15. P. Norman, *The Accidental Constitution* (Brussels: EuroComment, 2003), 174; D. Allen, "The Convention and the Draft Constitutional Treaty," in F. Cameron, ed., *The Future of Europe* (London: Routledge, 2004), 18–34.

16. On the Commission's tactical errors in the Convention, see H. Kassim and A. Menon, "EU Member States and the Prodi Commission," in D. G. Dimitrakopoulos, ed., *The changing European Commission* (Manchester: Manchester University Press, 2004), 89–104.

17. S. Bunse, P. Magnette, and K. Nicolaidis, "Big versus Small: Shared Leadership in the EU and Power Politics in the Convention," in D. Beach and C. Mazucelli, eds, *Leadership in the Big Bangs of European Integration* (Basingstoke: Palgrave MacMillan, 2007), 134–57.

18. P. Magnette and K. Nicolaïdis, "Big vs. Small States in the EU: Reinventing the Balance," *Notre Europe Research Note* 25 (2003), 13.

19. European Commission, *Post Referendum Survey in Ireland*, 18/VI/2008.

20. Cited in D. Dinan, "Institutions and Governance: Saving the Lisbon Treaty," in *JCMS* 47, Annual Review (2009), 113–32, at 124.

21. To avoid re-ratification of the Lisbon Treaty, this will most likely take the form of a protocol to be ratified together with the Croatian Accession Treaty.

CHAPTER 19

··

OLD VERSUS NEW

··

CHRISTIAN LEQUESNE

19.1 INTRODUCTION

The European Community/EU had six enlargements since 1973. It is during the last enlargements of 2004 and 2007 that a distinction has been introduced in the public discourse between "old" and "new" member tates. In political circles (the media but also research), "New Member States" (NMS) is commonly used to single out the former communist countries that joined the EU after the collapse of the Soviet bloc and Yugoslavia. Cyprus and Malta were less concerned by the category NMS. The use of the adjective "new" for the former communist states should be interpreted in a broader context than the sole EU. These countries consider that the "return to Europe" after the end of the Cold War means a "new" departure for their democracy, market economy, and civil society. They are "new" not only as members of the EU, but more generally as sovereign and democratic states. Mostly located in Central Europe and in the Balkans, they did not share with the other member states of the EU the same historical experience of the West in the period 1950–1989. We must immediately add that not all of the fifteen States which were already members of the EU in 2004 considered themselves, by contrast, as "old." A consequence of the move from fifteen to twenty-seven member states in 2004/2007 has been the renaissance of a shared identity among the states which were at the start of the European Community/EU in 1951: France, Germany, Italy, Belgium, Luxemburg, and the Netherlands. Due to the importance (both concrete and symbolic) played by the Franco–German tandem inside the European Community of six, the category "old member state" (OMS) refers more specifically to this group. But beyond the language and the representations (which matter in politics), it is not clear that the difference between OMS and NMS plays such a big role in the decision-making process of the EU. The objective of this chapter is to analyze how the difference operates or does not operate in practice.

19.2 DIFFERENCES IN PREFERENCES

Explorations into the nature of national preferences and their formation in EU member states have generated a large body of scholarly literature.[1] As Nathaniel Copsey and Tim Haughton write: "the fifth wave of enlargement in 2004 and 2007 has provided political scientists with 12 additional cases to examine national policy preferences and behaviour in the EU, and, consequently, the opportunity to refine and develop the existing frameworks for the study of national preference formation."[2] In their study, Copsey and Haughton assume that a NMS versus OMS framework can be used to identify broad differences in preference formation. To test the differences empirically, they examine five policy areas: the institutional design of the EU; the liberalization of the market; the distributional policies; the foreign and security policies; and the further enlargement of the EU. Following Copsey and Haughton's study, we shall see how these five policy areas might highlight concrete differences of policy formation between OMS and NMS.

The institutional design of the EU. The study of public surveys and party manifestos show in all member states of the EU a concern with the functionalist method of integration which has consisted since the 1990s in the development of new EU policies without questioning in detail the finality of the EU and the articulation of national sovereignty. Political parties in every member state are more concerned with the idea that the EU has probably reached a threshold and that national sovereignty does matter. This attitude comes from the lessons drawn after several negative referendums on the EU reform treaties since 1992. Nevertheless, in some OMS political parties could still invoke the further institutional deepening of the EU. This is the case, for instance, of the Christian Democrats in Belgium (both Walloons and Flemings) and in Germany. These parties bear on a federalist legacy that has no real equivalent in the NMS. Due to their constitution or reconstitution in 1990, political parties in the NMS have rarely integrated into their tradition the idealist finality of an EU political union. Most of them have a more pragmatic view of the EU expressed in terms of policy interests, even when they support the current integration stance like the Social Democratic Party in the Czech Republic or the center-right Civic Platform in Poland.

In terms of policy preferences for the future, drawing a clear line between OMS and NMS is also not relevant. Surveys show that the preferences depend first on the political context of each member state behaving as idiosyncratic polities, and that they have no direct link with the date of membership. One sees no clear cleavage in recent Eurobarometers between the NMS and the OMS regarding citizens' views on EU policy priorities. In 2009, 54 percent of the Hungarians think that the policy priority should be an EU energy policy, but 42 percent of the Germans and 41 percent of the Austrians think so too. The explanation for this resides less with the OMS–NMS divide than with the level of dependency on Russian gas.[3]

But as it has been rightly stressed, the defense of national values sometimes plays a more important role in the opposition to the EU developments in the NMS than in the

OMS. In Poland for instance, a significant number of social conservatives inside President Kaczynski's party Law and Justice (PiS) advocated during the negotiation of the Treaty of Lisbon that Poland had to opt out of the Charter of Fundamental Rights, because they felt that rights like gay marriage or adoption of children by homosexual couples could undermine the Catholic values of the Polish society. "Such sentiments have also been articulated by parties elsewhere with a strong Christian base in the NMS such as the Christian Democratic Movement in Slovakia."[4]

The liberalization of the market. Since 1990, political elites defending modernity have been predominantly free marketers in the NMS. The support for the free market goes together with the break with the communist-planned economy and the national transition processes toward market economy. Liberalism, in the conceptions of the NMS's political elites, does not refer naturally to the German model of social market economy. It is more naturally oriented toward the British free market model. Governments dominated by centre-right parties like the ODS in Czech Republic, the Civic Platform in Poland, or Democratic and Christian Union in Slovakia were among the strongest supporters of economic liberalization inside the EU. Some political parties, like the Czech ODS, have even developed a euro-skeptic stance against the EU, because they consider (as the UK Conservative Party in the 1980s and 1990s) that the EU is not enough market oriented. By contrast, the legacy of the welfare state has a stronger impact on the economic views of the political parties in the OMS. French, German, and Belgian center-right as well as center-left parties are more keen to defend social market economies than their equivalents in the NMS. At the EU level, NMS have more regularly been defenders of pro-liberalization policies (like the UK) than the OMS. Of course, the economic crisis of 2008 changed the path of the debates in the NMS. Nevertheless, in March 2009, the Czech Prime minister Topolanek addressing the European Parliament as EU Chairman considered Obama's global plan for economic recovery as a "road to hell." It was a big contrast with the positive comments made by most OMS's leaders, such as Brown and Sarkozy. The 2005 Commission's proposal on the free movement of services got generally a strong support among the NMS whereas it gathered high criticism and opposition in the OMS. It is this directive that gave raise in France to the debate on the Polish plumbers who could massively invade the job market.[5] The NMS versus OMS cleavage on liberalization does not mean that the populations of the NMS are not sensitive to welfare policies. But in general, political elites in these countries have been more neo-liberal than the societies. They are also closer to business interests and less constrained than in OMS by worker unions which, since 1990, are weak and delegitimized organizations. Surveys also show another difference between NMS and OMS which has an impacted on the support for economic liberalization at the EU level: the societies of the NMS consider globalization less of a threat than their OMS counterparts, because they are less inclined to defend the legacy of democratic welfare states that they did not get for fifty years. In 2009, it is clearly in the member states of the former European Community of six that a majority of the citizens consider globalization as a threat to their jobs.[6]

Distributive policies. This policy area refers to the structural and cohesion funds and to the CAP. As regards the latter, there is no cleavage inside the EU between the OMS and the NMS. The difference depends more on the position of each individual member state. It has to do with the transfers each state gets from the EU budget, but also with the "cultural attachment to the CAP."[7] As regards the defense of the CAP, an OMS like France is closer to an NMS like Poland than to the UK or Germany. Even if French farmers do not get as much from the CAP as they did twenty years ago, they are still supported by the EU budget. France is also defending the CAP as a cultural legacy of the European Community against a more "Anglo-Saxon" tradition of support for market liberalization. Poland, with the largest percentage of farmers among the EU-27, is also considering the future of the CAP as questions of interest and culture. Poland is a country like France which has always considered rural life as an important part of its national values and traditions. It is also the country which has discovered after 2004 the benefits of the EU direct income payments to farmers, even if it started with 25 percent of the former EU-15 level to reach 100 percent only by 2012. It explains, for instance, why the Polish Peasant's Party (PSL), which was reluctant to Polish membership to the EU, has changed its views after 2004 when its members discovered the new benefits that the CAP represented for the Polish famers.

The OMS–NMS cleavage is probably more relevant with regards to the allocation of structural and cohesion funds. A majority of NMS still have regions far from the capitals which suffer from underdevelopment or of "peripherization."[8] Most of them are net recipients from the EU budget and receive a vast majority of the EU structural funds since the EU budget reform of 2007. Poland alone concentrates 20 percent of the indicative financial allocations from the structural funds in the period 2007–2013. At the opposite end, OMS are net contributors to the EU budget and are receiving much smaller transfers for their regions. This explains why the OMS are not in favor of a huge increase in the structural funds in the future EU budget; or, as in the case of UK, in fact in favor of a total dismantlement of the EU cohesion policy. If we consider public opinions, solidarity with the poorest regions was in 2009 a policy priority for 20 percent of EU citizens. This percentage was higher in all the NMS, except in Czech Republic where it was below average with 16 percent. But the only percentages superior to 30 percent were found in two Mediterranean countries: Malta and Greece.[9]

Foreign and security policy. This is clearly the policy that resists the most to "communitarization" since the beginning of the European Community. The current CFSP remains an intergovernmental regime and has never achieved huge results in terms of policy coherence. In the OMS, especially in the larger ones like France and Germany, the interests of national diplomacy have the priority on any common European policy. Concerning defense policy in particular, the outcomes have also been modest because OMS (Germany, the Netherlands, UK) have been reluctant to the development of a EU defense policy as NATO appeared a more credible arena. Before the enlargement to CEECs, France was always isolated when it tried to promote an EU defense policy expressing interests different from the US. Of course, the French advocacy in favor of an EU security policy does not echo with the same voice since President Sarkozy decided in 2009 to rejoin the NATO military structures. As regards the NMS, they have been since 1990 strong defenders of the transatlantic relationship. All of them joined the EU and

NATO in parallel with the belief that only the US had the necessary firepower to defend their territorial integrity should the need arise. A couple of months before joining the EU, most heads of governments from Central Europe and the Western Balkans supported George Bush's intervention in Iraq against the Franco–German position of non-intervention. It was at this time that the US defense secretary Donald Rumsfeld opposed in a famous speech a "new" Europe, prepared to follow US leadership, to an "old" Europe withdrawn into itself. But the strong Atlanticism of the NMS's elites has never been a reflection of a similar commitment on the part of the NMS's citizens. For instance, in Poland and in the Czech Republic, a majority of the public opinion has always been against the hosting of US anti-missile defense shields. Surveys showed also that people in the NMS and in the OMS shared, for instance, quite similar views about the illegitimacy of the military intervention in Iraq in the absence of a UN mandate.

Interestingly, Barack Obama's election has been welcomed with more enthusiasm by the OMS's elites than by the NMS's counterparts. The renouncement by the Obama administration to the installation of anti-missile defense shields in the Czech Republic and in Poland, and the new dialogues with Russia and Iran have created doubts about the US political will to remain fully committed to Europe's security. As a consequence, the NMS have discovered a new interest in a European foreign and security policy, especially with regards to Russia.[10] Poland is an interesting example of this recent evolution. In a country which considers itself with a sense of "historical grandeur" (a difference with all the other NMS), European foreign and security policy has become a more important issue since Obama replaced Bush in Washington. The support for a European foreign and security policy is generally high in all member states of the EU, as long as surveys do not ask citizens if they are prepared to invest more public funds for their militaries. In 2009, 75 percent of the EU citizens declared to be in favor of a EDSP. In all the NMS, the rate exceeded the average although it represented only 57 percent in the UK and 48 percent in Ireland.[11]

Further enlargements. This is an issue where the OMS –NMS divide is particularly stark. The NMS (both governments and societies) are more in favor of enlarging the EU-27 than the OMS. In 2009, 76 percent of the Poles, 67 percent of the Lithuanians, and 62 percent of the Czechs considered further enlargements a positive step for the EU, whereas only 32 percent of the French, 28 percent of the Germans, and 25 percent of the Luxembourgers thought the same.[12] Several reasons explain a bigger enthusiasm for further enlargement in the NMS. First, a large number of the NMS constitute now the periphery (Schengen borders) of the EU and expect to become more central in the future. Second, Russia is still perceived as a threat not only to the energy supplies of the EU, but also to the stability of the neighboring countries. To support less dependence on Russia, Poland is pushing the Ukraine into the EU and Romania is doing the same with Moldova. Third, the common experience of communism has developed a sense of solidarity vis-à-vis the former communist countries (for instance in the Western Balkans) which are not yet members of the EU. Finally, the NMS consider that enlargements of the EU toward the East and the South-East constitute a policy area where they can transfer their knowledge and experience. It is not by chance that the Eastern

Partnership of the EU was adopted, in 2009, under a Czech Presidency of the EU. Beyond this global image, differences resulting from privileged bilateralism exist. For examples, Ukraine is particularly supported by Poland, Moldova and Serbia by Romania, Macedonia by Slovenia.[13] The positive stances of the NMS show that they consider EU membership as a geopolitical rather than a purely institutional project. It is a huge contrast with the OMS, where further enlargements mean more of a threat to the current EU polity: dilution of the EU institutions and procedures, more economic heterogeneity, more migratory flows. As regards Turkey, the support for membership is higher in the NMS than in the EU-27 (31 percent versus 27 percent in 2009), however with a decrease since 2004, except in Romania (61 percent in 2009). The cultural argument that Turkey is not a European country has some echo in the societies of the NMS, which are sensitive to an ethnic conception of identity. But no NMS supports the Franco–German proposal to build a privileged partnership with Turkey rather than a full membership. All capitals of the NMS are in favor of following further negotiations with Ankara. Further enlargements remain one of the rare issues of cleavage between the OMS and the NMS (in particular from the former European Community of six).

19.3 Differences in Institutional Involvement

NMS participate in the decision-making of the EU since 2004. Before they joined, a lot of controversial debates went through the OMS about the risks new comers represented for the institutional capabilities of the EU.[14] The treaties of Amsterdam (1997), Nice (2000), and Lisbon (2009) have been adopted with the rationale to adapt the EU institutions to enlargements and to avoid deadlocks. Recent empirical accounts of the impact of enlargements on the EU institutions show that, contrary to a lot of fear in the OMS, the EU institutions have successfully assimilated the NMS into their decision-making dynamics.[15]

Coalition building in the Council of Ministers. The quasi-doubling of the number of member states in 2004/2007 had some inevitable impact on the working methods of the EU Council of ministers. If enlargement has not at all entailed a slower decision-making process, it has lead to what some authors have called a "bureaucratization" of the Council negotiations "in the sense of a further increase in the proportion of decisions which are reached below the ministerial level, and a decrease in the number of real debates which take place in the Council itself."[16] As regards the defense of national interests, the NMS are still on a learning curve with vis-à-vis procedures and norms. Most of them are seen as still remaining somewhat passive and cautious. The exception is Poland, which displayed a more "assertive attitude" during the negotiations than the other NMS.[17] Considering that larger member states (including Poland) continue to play a leading role in the negotiations since 2004, size rather than seniority is the main decision-making resource in the Council of Ministers. Several empirical studies show that there are rarely coalitions of NMS versus OMS in the Council. The reason is that neither the NMS nor the OMS are a "cohesive block of states with the same policy positions."[18] For instance, France and Germany have frequent disagreements during Council negotiations. The Franco–German tandem has always been seen more as a privileged system of conflict management in the Council than as a system to fuse national interests. The four Visegrad countries (the Czech Republic, Hungary, Poland, and Slovakia) also have frequent disagreements over policy options in the Council. Best and Settembri show that during the sugar reform of 2005–2006, roughly equal proportions of OMS and NMS were initially opposed to the Commission's proposal.[19] The absence of a clear division of interests between OMS and NMS confirms what scholars working on the EU Council have regularly stressed, before and after the 2004/2007 enlargement: coalitions are issue-oriented rather than country-oriented.[20] The 2004/2007 enlargement has not modified this structural trend.

Commission, European Parliament, and ECJ. The NMS had to adapt not only to the negotiations in the Council but also to the other EU institutions. To what extend can we observe NMS versus OMS differences inside the Commission, the European Parliament, or the Court of Justice?

As regards the Commission, the enlargements of 2004/2007 have implied a structural change for the College of commissioners which has moved from fifteen to twenty-five, and then to twenty-seven members. A majority of OMS, as of NMS, have supported the principle of one commissioner per member state, considering that the presence of one national inside the Commission will contribute to the defense of the national interest. With the increase of the number of commissioners, there is a tendency toward an "intergovernmentalization" of the Commission. The situation will remain unchanged, the Treaty of Lisbon stating that the College will be reduced from one commissioner per member state to one for two-thirds of member states only in 2014 unless the European Council decides unanimously to alter this number. During the first referendum campaign on the treaty of Lisbon, this question was a sensitive issue in Ireland. There is in general a stronger public support for the Commission in the NMS than in the OMS. In autumn 2009, all citizens from the NMS, except the Latvians, trusted on average more the Commission as an institution than the EU. On the contrary, the French, German, and British citizens on average supported less the Commission than the EU.[21] As two scholars have stressed, "in a sense enlargement appears to be as pro-Commission as the Commission is pro-enlargement."[22] However, the OMS seem to keep the lead inside the Commission in terms of institutional positions. In the Barosso II Commission, which came into office in February 2010, the main portfolios (foreign affairs, trade, internal market and services, competition) have been attributed to nationals from the OMS. Representatives of the NMS have got only two "sensitive" issues: agriculture and rural development; enlargement and neighborhood policy. The pace of absorption of NMS officials into the Directorates-General of the Commission also remains slow: "only 12 per cent of Commission officials hailed from the NMS by mid-2007."[23] There also remain few NMS officials in high-ranking positions like Directors-General or their deputies.

As regards the European Parliament, the MEPs from the NMS represent a bit more than 25 percent of the total members. The vast majority of them exhibit a higher degree of education than the MEPs from the OMS. The number of postgraduate qualifications and doctorates is striking. "This is no doubt linked to the high proportion of them whose previous professional occupation was in education."[24] Most of the MEPs from the NMS have joined the main existing groups inside the European Parliament. Their arrival in Strasbourg has not led to a fundamental restructuring of the European Parliament's party structure.[25] Most joined the European People's Party and European Democrats (Christian Democrats), the Socialist group and the Group of the Alliance of Liberals and Democrats for Europe. There have been only marginal effects of the 2004/2007 enlargements on the party group dynamics inside the European Parliament. The accession of Bulgaria and Romania in 2007 encouraged the creation of a new right-oriented group which quickly disappeared. In 2009, the Czech euro-skeptics from the Civic Democratic Party (ODS) and the Polish euro-skeptics from the party Law and Justice (PiS) joined the British Conservatives to form the new group of the European Conservatives and Reformists. Although the president of the European Parliament elected in 2009, Jerzy Buzek, comes from a NMS, Poland, the OMS remain dominant in the chairmanships of the parliamentary committees, where most of the legislative work is still done. On twenty-three committees operating inside the European Parliament in 2009, only one–the committee for regional development–is chaired by an MEP from an NMS, a Polish member of the European People's Party who is also a former Polish Commissioner. As a point of reference, five committees are chaired by an Italian MEP, five by a German MEP, and four by a French MEP. The voting patterns inside the European Parliament are very fluid and it does not seem that votes pit MNS against OMS. It could happen, as it was the case with the directive on services in the internal market, in November 2006. But the patterns of voting are, as in the Council of Ministers, very much issue focused. They can vary along party lines (right versus left), or along national lines (which does not mean OMS versus NMS), depending on which policy is at stake.

As regards the ECJ, there is a strict parity between the OMS and the NMS in the composition of the Court of Justice and of the General Court; each member state has one judge. In 2009, among the eight advocates-general working at the Court of Justice, six were nationals of an OMS and two of an NMS. Among this community of highly respected lawyers who possess the qualifications required for appointment to the highest judicial offices in their respective countries, professional quality is more important than national origin. For this reason, the ECJ is probably the institution where the distinction between OMS and NMS plays the most limited role for the appointees. If we consider the decision-making process of the Court, the 2004/2007 enlargements has led the ECJ to adapt its structure, especially to "increase the number of chambers and to reduce the number of documents to be translated."[26] The statistics of the Court suggest that there are still more cases coming from the OMS than from the NMS.[27] If we consider the preliminary rulings that allow national courts to ask a question to the ECJ on the interpretation of EU law, the NMS introduced 20 cases out of a total of 288 in 2008, that is to say 7 percent. In the same year, 2008, Belgium alone introduced 24 cases and

Spain 17. It must be stressed that free movement of services between the NMS and the OMS in the new economic context of the enlargement has brought some specific cases to the Court. In the Laval and Partneri case, a question from a Swedish court concerned the right of Swedish trade unions to take collective action in the form of a blockade at building sites where Latvian posted workers were supposed to work. The reason for such a blockade was to compel a service provider from Latvia to subscribe to a rate of pay for the Latvian workers in a collective agreement, as it is ordinary practice in Sweden. In its judgment of December 18, 2007,[28] the ECJ stated that the right to take collective action for the protection of the workers of the host state against possible social dumping may constitute an overriding reason of public interest. But in this particular case, the Court did not see any reasons of public policy, public security, or public health to motivate such an action. The position of the Swedish unions was then refuted. The Laval case became for the unions of the OMS a symbol of the social pressures that an enlarged EU puts on their welfare states.

The transposition of EU law. A huge body of literature exists on the implementation of EU law in the member states. Most of this literature is based on empirical work done in the OMS. However, some works have appeared since 2004 which attempt to assess the state of transposition and implementation not only in the OMS but also in the NMS.[29] For instance, Steuneberger and Toshkov have studied the transposition of a set of directives related in twenty-seven member states. Their conclusion is that "NMS do not systematically perform worse than old member states...We find proof of the opposite. NMS do better than many of the more experienced OMS."[30] Of course, transposition—which describes the legal process of transforming EU law into national law—does not equal to implementation. Focusing on implementation—the enforcement of the directives by economic and social actors—could lead to different findings. Many NMS still have problems making enforcement efficient, because their administrative resources and capabilities remain weak. Moreover, the inclination of politicians and administrators in the NMS to negotiate informal settlements with economic and social actors is an additional brake to fair implementation.

19.4 CONCLUSION

Differences between OMS and NMS exist in policy preferences as well as in institutional involvement in the EU. However, there is a certain risk of overestimating these differences, because OMS and NMS rarely behave as two distinct blocks in the EU arena. In the EU, the relevant analytical unit remains the single member state.[31] Comparisons should be made between individual member states rather than between groups of member states. As the EU-27 develops, comparisons along East–West lines will become less and less relevant. The literature will have to take this into account. Too many EU empirical studies are still focusing either on the OMS, or on the NMS, as if scholars of the former West European integration should still represent a different group from the scholars working on post-communist Europe. Twenty years after the end of the Cold War, EU scholars and post-communist scholars have to realize that they are now working on the same political subject.

NOTES

1. See Andrew Moravcsik, *The Choice for Europe: Social Purpose and State Power from Messina to Maastricht* (London: UCL, 1999); Christian Lequesne and Simon Bulmer, eds, *The Member States of the European Union* (Oxford: Oxford University Press, 2005); Cleave Archer and Neill Nuggent, eds, *Special issue of Journal of European Integration* 28, no. 1 (2006).
2. Nathaniel Copsey and Tim Haughton, "The Choices for Europe: National Preferences in the New and Old Member States," *Journal of Common Market Studies* 47, no. 2 (2009), 264.
3. *Eurobarometer* 70 (2009), 48.
4. Copsey and Haughton, "The Choices for Europe," 274.
5. Christian Lequesne, *La France dans la nouvelle Europe. Assumer le changement d'échelle* (Paris: Presses de Sciences Po, 2008).
6. *Eurobarometer* 70 (2009), 51.
7. Copsey and Haughton, "The choices for Europe," 270.
8. François Bafoil, *Central and Eastern Europe. Europeanization and social change* (New York: Palgrave Macmillan, 2009).
9. *Eurobarometer* 70 (2009), 48.
10. Christian Lequesne, "La génération de la dissidence, l'idée européenne et la divergence transatlantique," *Esprit* (2009), 77–83.
11. *Eurobarometer* 70 (2009), 40.
12. *Eurobarometer* 70 (2009), 43.
13. European Policy Initiative, *Not your Grandfather's Eastern Bloc. The EU New Member States as Agenda Setters in the Enlarged European Union* (Sofia: Open Society Institute, 2009).
14. For France, see Christian Lequesne, *La France dans la nouvelle Europe.*
15. Edward Best, Thomas Christiansen, and Pierpaolo Settembri, eds, *The institutions of the Enlarged European Union. Continuity and Change* (Cheltenham: Edwar Elgar, 2008).
16. Edward Best and Pierpaolo Settembri, "Surviving Enlargement: How the Council Managed?" in Best et al., *The institutions of the Enlarged European Union*, 47.
17. Best and Settembri, "Surviving Enlargement," 47.
18. Javier Arregui and Robert Thomson, "States' Bargaining Success in the European Union," *Journal of European Public Policy* 16, no. 5 (2009), 673.
19. Best and Settembri, "Surviving Enlargement," 49.
20. Fiona Hayes Renshaw, Wim van Acken, and Helen Wallace, "When and Why the Council of Ministers Vote Explicitly," *Journal of Common Market Studies* 44, no. 1 (2006), 161–94.
21. *Eurobarometer* 72 (2009), 29.
22. John Peterson and Andrea Birdsall, "The European Commission: enlargement as reinvention?" in Best et al., *The institutions of the Enlarged European Union*, 59.
23. Peterson and Birdsall, "The European Commission," 58.

24. Brendan Donnelly and Milena Bigatto, "The European Parliament and Enlargement," in Best et al., *The institutions of the Enlarged European Union*, 84.

25. Simon Hix and Abdul Noury, "After Enlargement: Voting Behaviour in the Sixth European Parliament," paper presented at the Federal Trust Conference on "The European Parliament and the European Political Space," London, March 30, 2006.

26. Caroline Naômé, "EU enlargement and the European Court of Justice," in Best et al., *The institutions of the Enlarged European Union*, 100.

27. Statistics can be found on the ECJ's website at http://curia.europa.eu>.

28. Case C-341/05.

29. Gerda Falkner and Oliver Treib, "Three Worlds of Compliance or Four? The EU 15 Compared to the New Member States," *Journal of Common Market Studies* 46, no. 2 (2008), 293–313.

30. Bernard Steuneberger and Dimiter Toshkov, "Comparing Tranposition in 27 Member States of the EU: The Impact of Discretion and Legal Fit," *Journal of European Public Policy* 16, no. 7 (2009), 966.

31. Bulmer and Lequesne, *The Member States of the European Union*.

CHAPTER 20

RICH VERSUS POOR

WALTRAUD SCHELKLE

MOST political economists expect the cleavage of "rich versus poor" member states to be a defining feature of everyday politics in the EU. As the saying goes: "He who pays the piper calls the tune" and so we should expect the rich net payers to dominate the policy agenda. Another line of argument has been repeatedly invoked by EU policy-makers themselves: a union of democratic member states with mostly generous welfare states cannot have too much discrepancy in regional living standards, or mass migration from the poor to the rich and protectionist measures by the rich against the poor will destroy integration. This was a fear expressed in the Southern enlargement of the EU in the 1980s and in the two waves of Eastern enlargement of 2004 and 2007. In the latter cases, these fears manifested themselves in temporary restrictions on free movement by workers from the new member states in the East. The rising share of EU spending on regional aid and cohesion policy, from 17 percent in 1988 to 38 percent in 2013 of the budget, can be read as evidence that the decision-makers in the Council share this concern and try to achieve a convergence of living standards. In fact, Article 174 TFEU obliges the Community to try and reduce "disparities between the levels of development of the various regions and the backwardness of the least favored regions and islands, including rural areas."

And yet, on second thought, each of these arguments can be questioned and the specific relevance of the rich–poor distinction for the EU becomes less obvious. First of all, while bouts of migration become a politically salient issue whenever the receiving countries, sectors, or regions fare badly, it has not been a consistent threat to European integration. The direction is not necessarily from the poor to the rich. Growth, rather than wealth, in the receiving country acts also as an economic pull attracting migrants, and decline rather than low income per se pushes citizens of poor countries out. So the dynamic of getting richer or poorer seems to be as important a consideration as living standards as such. Moreover, many expert observers of EU regional policy doubt that it is about achieving cohesion and convergence since the sums involved are too small to make much difference, amounting to one third of one percent of EU GDP. They suggest, for instance, that aid to the regions serves to fine-tune net contributions to the EU budget or to bribe Euro-skeptic member states. Finally and more generally, it is not clear how a high per capita income of a member state translates into formal political power. Voting rights in the Council or the number of representatives in the European Parliament depend on population size, not on national income. So small versus large is the more relevant distinction for political representation in EU institutions.[1]

This chapter gives first an overview of the countries and regions that are rich and poor and how this pattern evolved over time. The following section analyzes the extent to which socio-economic disparities are politically relevant in the EU and highlights reasons why the rich–poor distinction is less relevant than standard political economy arguments would lead one to expect. The final section takes up a question that may become of unfortunate relevance for the cohesiveness of the Union, namely whether poor member states like Greece are necessarily more crisis-prone, making the poor–rich distinction more salient in the future.

20.1 Who is Rich, Who is Poor—and How are They Doing Over Time?

Member states' income per capita in 2007 is shown in Figure 20.1, both in rank order and relative to the average of the twenty-seven member states indexed as 100.[2] Before the onset of the crisis, the group of countries with above average Gross Domestic Product (GDP), measured at purchasing power parity standard (PPS)[3], contains only member states which have been part of the EU before 2004. In the middle-income group of countries, between 75 and 90 percent of the EU-27 average, we find Greece (GR) and Portugal (PT). The low-income group contains only recent member states, the three Baltic countries (Estonia, Lithuania, and Latvia), Hungary and Poland, as well as the two latest arrivals, Bulgaria and Romania, the latter with income levels of around 40 percent of the EU-average.[4]

Article 174 of the EU Treaty, quoted above, refers only to regions, not to member states. The EU's regional classification scheme, rejoicing in the acronym of NUTS after the French translation for the "Nomenclature of territorial units for statistics," follows in most countries the national administrative divisions but also tries to create units of similar population size.[5] Figure 20.2 shows the disparities between regions within and across member states. Some of the poorer countries, such as Hungary or Slovakia, have capital regions with average or even above-average income levels. One has to keep in mind, however, that regional GDPs of urban agglomerations tend to be overstated because commuters generate large parts of the income and effectively take it with them to the region or country where they live. Hence, the regional GDP as stated is not the income available to the residents of the urban agglomeration.

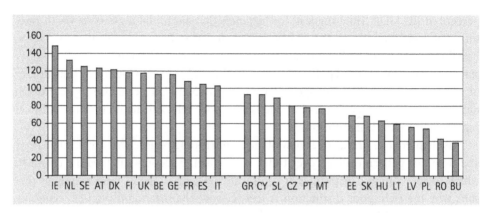

FIGURE 20.1. GDP per head (PPS) in 2007, EU-27 = 100 (Luxembourg Excluded).

Abbreviations: AT = Austria, BE = Belgium, BU = Bulgaria, CY = Cyprus, CZ = Czech Republic,
DK = Denmark, EE = Estonia, ES = Spain, FI = Finland, FR = France, GE = Germany,
GR = Greece, HU = Hungary, IE = Ireland, IT = Italy, LT = Lithuania, LV = Latvia, MT = Malta,
NL = The Netherlands, PL = Poland, PT = Portugal, RO = Romania, SE = Sweden,
SK = Slovakia, SL = Slovenia, UK = United Kingdom

Source: Eurostat

What about changes in this pattern of rich and poor? Are the regional disparities a fairly stable feature or do we see some convergence over time, perhaps even moves up and down the league table? The period of 2000–2005 was a good time for convergence of income levels in the EU. The eight countries with the lowest income, grouped on the right in Figure 20.1, grew on average 5 percent more than the EU-27 in the run-up to enlargement. Over the entire decade, productivity growth in the new member states was 3 percent above that for the EU-27 as Figure 20.3 illustrates.[6] What is particularly encouraging is that not only the small city states in the Baltics but also Poland performed well, the only larger country among the new member states. Disappointing were Spain's and Italy's performance, which meant there was hardly any sustainable rise in living standards. The high growth of nominal income that Spain still experienced in these years was achieved at the cost of competitiveness, i.e. Spanish products became relatively more expensive because productivity did not keep pace with the income growth of those producing them.

A negative correlation between real income growth rates and income per capita levels indicates convergence: high-growth rates for countries with low-income levels and vice versa means that poor countries or regions are catching up. This is shown in Figure 20.4 in a regional breakdown (NUTS2, relevant for the EU's regional policy) and for the most recent period that data is available.[7] We can see that a catch-up dynamic seems to work for low-income regions. But growth rates fall, once regions are in the middle- to high-income range (triangular dots in between 75 and 125 percent of GDP). And quite a number of regions in the high-income range are actually in decline, i.e. they experience negative growth.

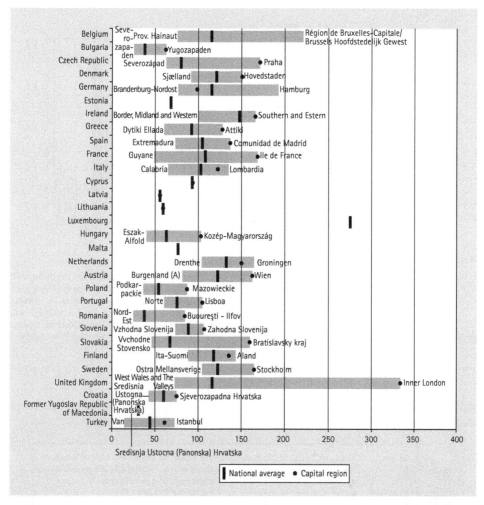

FIGURE 20.2. GDP per head (PPS) in member states and candidate countries with regional extremes, 2007 (EU-27 = 100).

Source: Eurostat, *Regional Yearbook* 2010

The number of citizens living in regions with income below 75 percent of the relevant EU average has not increased in absolute terms between 1995 and 2004 and remained fairly stable in relative terms. This holds even though mostly poor countries and regions joined the EU in the last round of enlargement. In relative terms, about a quarter of the then fictitious EU-27 population lived in poor regions in 1995 and in 2004. This remarkable stability in relative terms came with widening regional disparities in all new member states while the picture for the EU-15 is mixed.[8] This is a well-known feature of rapid growth: agglomeration and scale economies drive growth of particular areas, typically in the capital region, dragging the average growth rate of the country up, until rising real estate prices and congestion keep or drive households and firms out of that region. The

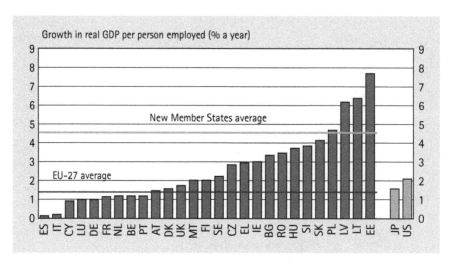

FIGURE 20.3. Productivity growth in member states, 1995–2005.

Abbreviations: AT = Austria, BE = Belgium, BU = Bulgaria, CY = Cyprus, CZ = Czech Republic, DK = Denmark, EE = Estonia, ES = Spain, FI = Finland, FR = France, GE = Germany, GR = Greece, HU = Hungary, IE = Ireland, IT = Italy, JP = Japan, LT = Lithuania, LV = Latvia, MT = Malta, NL = The Netherlands, PL = Poland, PT= Portugal, RO = Romania, SE = Sweden, SK = Slovakia, SL = Slovenia, UK = United Kingdom, US = United States of America

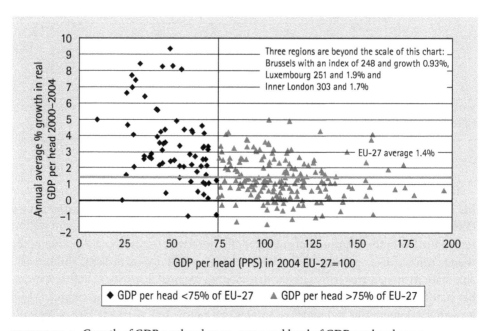

FIGURE 20.4. Growth of GDP per head 2000–2004 and level of GDP per head 2004.

Source: Eurostat

growth trajectory for the country as a whole is then at crossroads: either the surrounding areas benefit from this diversion and also sustain rapid growth by alleviating the bottlenecks; or overall growth declines because the dynamic region has run out of steam and no other area can substitute for it.

In sum, the recent period of European integration, characterized by the onset of monetary union in 1999 and the run-up to the biggest enlargement that the EU ever experienced in 2004, has witnessed both convergence (most noticeably Ireland and the new member states) and stability (share of the population living in areas with less than 75 percent of the EU average). While falling short of the high hopes relentlessly expressed in European Council conclusions, this is good news overall: European integration seems to give a boost to acceding poorer member states while enlargement has not impoverished regions in the pre-2004 member states.

But it is less clear whether this good news is news about the working of EU regional policy. It is notoriously difficult to assess the contribution of EU regional policy to the convergence of regions in the EU.[9] Market opening, that is the EU's single market program, or a rationalization of the policy regime, in the run-up to monetary union, are other contenders for a positive influence of the EU on convergence.[10] The difficulty arises not only because there are mixed motives on the side of EU policy-makers that may divert funds to other causes than helping poor regions to converge. The sums involved, however, are modest and the Commission's institutional self-interest is fairly aligned with that of poor regions that are interested in getting transfers for socio-economic development. It is also difficult to assess the effectiveness of assistance to poor regions because regional policy facilitates the very process, market integration, that can lead to rising disparities, for instance through improving the transport infrastructure. If regional policy achieves this goal, these disparities tend to become a problem within fast-growing poor countries, while the very fact of fast growth reduces disparities between member states. So, far from being an alternative driver, regional aid and market integration tend to be two sides of the same coin in the EU.[11] However, this pattern creates a political problem for the EU: if regional disparities become more and more an intra-national policy problem, it becomes less and less obvious why it should be the EU's business to intervene.

20.2 How Important is "Rich versus Poor" for the Political Economy of European Integration?

The question of why the EU runs a policy for promoting regional and national convergence is typically answered by invoking the value of union solidarity.[12] This is less obvious than it sounds because the EU typically proceeds on the basis of reciprocity. The last round of enlargement to its poorer neighbors was no exception: compliance with the club rules even before membership, such as offering access to national markets and resources, was rewarded with financial and technical assistance to prepare for membership. Consequently, the Commission answers the question for the "value added" of cohesion policy by pointing out two economic advantages (more growth and jobs, faster catching-up) and a third reason that is framed in terms of good governance: "Cohesion policy 'levers in' and safeguards compliance with other EU policies—state aid, environment, transport, support for innovation, the information society. It also improves and modernizes public administrations, enhances transparency and fosters good governance."[13] This can be read as a concession of reciprocity, i.e. regional aid compensates for constraints that the sharing of sovereignty entails, in particular with respect to industrial policy and trade protection.

Given the prominence of distributive issues in political economy, it is remarkable how low the visibility and saliency of the potential cleavage between the rich and the poor in the EU is. Three pieces of evidence can support this proposition. First, and as already indicated, richness does not buy you votes in the EU. In contrast to the UN system, voting shares in the Council or number of representatives in the European Parliament are not determined by GDP but by population size, which is then weighted in favor of smaller countries (see Chapter 19, this volume). Hence, a city state of 400,000 inhabitants like Malta gets 3 votes in the Council and 5 representatives in the Parliament, while a country of 80 million like Germany gets 29 votes in the Council and 99 representatives in Parliament; if equal representation were applied, Germany would have to get 200 votes/representatives for each that Malta gets. This is a well-known feature of second chambers in federal systems: in the US Senate, tiny New Hampshire has as many senators as California or Texas. But in the House of Representatives, the rules try to give roughly equal representation to each citizen by redrawing the boundaries of electoral districts periodically.[14] In the EU, both the Council and the European Parliament overrepresent citizens of small states, irrespective of whether they are rich (Luxembourg) or poor (Latvia). This feature has led to considerable anxieties about Turkey's accession: a large, poor member state does indeed wield more voting power than a smaller, rich member state like the Netherlands which, according to some calculations, is the highest net contributor to the EU budget per capita of its citizens. Successive Dutch legislatures thus acknowledge that the single market benefits Rotterdam as a seaport disproportionately and agree to compensate the Union for this, another sign of the fundamentally reciprocal nature of the EU.

Second, the difference between rich and poor does not play a role for financing the EU budget. It has come to be financed more and more by the so-called GNI-based revenue which is calculated by applying a uniform percentage rate (0.73 percent) to the GNI (Gross National Income) of each member state. This source of revenue finances about two-thirds of EU spending. The other two sources are the "traditional own resources," mostly consisting of duties on imports from outside the EU, and a uniform value added tax that each member state collects on behalf of the union; they finance the remaining budget and have an equal share of 15–17 percent each. All these figures measure obviously only the gross contribution and do not tell us how much the rich versus the poor pay effectively or get eventually. But it is noticeable that there is no progressive taxation or contribution system in place that would make the rich members pay nominally—hence visibly—more for EU expenditures.

Finally, the traditional stance of countries on substantive EU policies is not predictably shaped by them belonging to a club of rich or poor member states. To take a policy where this might be expected to be the case, the CAP, notoriously the biggest single expenditure item in the EU's budget, which favors rural areas that tend to be poor: for a long time, the biggest net contributor overall to the EU budget, Germany before unification, was a strong and decisive supporter of a policy for which it paid a large part of the bill. The explanation for this seemingly irrational behavior was sought in domestic politics: the portfolio for agriculture was reserved for the Bavarian sister party of the Christian Democrats, a rich Land with a sizeable rural population, so an expensive and regressive form of subsidy was needed to please pivotal voters for the conservative party. Similarly, the new member states in Central and Eastern Europe are not predictably for huge handouts from the CAP. While a great bonus for the poor Eastern regions in Poland, where small- scale, undercapitalized agriculture provides a safety net for an underemployed workforce, Hungary has a fairly competitive agricultural sector and would benefit more from liberalization.[15] This conclusion would apply to many other common policies, such as competition policy. Enlargement has weakened the explanatory power of rich versus poor even more since the new member states are more liberal as regards market regulation, hence are prone to join what was traditionally seen as a Nordic position, while they resent the protection for corporatist arrangements inherent in the EU's complex regulation of migration,[16] in line with Southern members.

How can we explain the fact that the socio-economic cleavage of rich versus poor plays a relatively minor role? Why is the calculation of voting rights not at all based on income levels, only on population size, unlike the voting shares in the World Bank or the IMF? Or why is there no progressive element in the financing of the EU budget, unlike what most member states practice in their national tax systems? There is not much research on these questions available. A first answer would challenge the assertion that the EU is based on solidarity, with regional policy as its tangible expression. The fact that there is no redistributive financing—even though, effectively, the EU budget is redistributive through the expenditure side—suggests that union solidarity must not be too conspicuously tested or it tends to be overstretched. The fact that the rich countries can get aid for their poor regions is a way of obscuring how much solidarity there really is exercised between rich and poor members of the union. Similarly, the successful British claim of a rebate is further evidence for the delicate balance between solidarity and reciprocity: because the UK benefits less than other comparable (rich and incumbent) member states from the EU's big expenditure programs, i.e. regional policy and the CAP, the Thatcher government was granted a tax credit on its contribution; and the Labour government did not concede it in subsequent budget negotiations. What all this suggests is that the fact of limited solidarity must avoid the socio-economic cleavage of rich versus poor becoming too prominent in the first place—because if there were stand-offs along these lines, say in the Council or the Parliament, it could lead to a boycott of rich members and the break-up of the union.

This seems to support the view that the EU cannot deal with redistributive issues and therefore concentrates on efficiency-enhancing, market-making regulation.[17] It lacks, for better or worse, an immediate endorsement from general European elections, so-called input legitimacy. Its legitimate role therefore is to conduct policies that potentially increase the pie, such as free trade and competition. This hypothesis can explain why it is politically vital for the EU to be seen as beneficial on economic grounds. For the very same reasons, limited solidarity and reliance on output legitimacy, the Union must avoid to be seen as a hard-nosed club that is run by whoever pays most. Economic distinctions must not determine political distinctions, here: high-income levels and the contribution to the budget must not obviously buy a country more political representation in EU institutions. On the contrary, over-representation gave smaller member states tradition-ally a considerable advantage in receiving agricultural and regional aid.[18]

20.3 ARE POOR COUNTRIES MORE CRISIS-PRONE?

In light of the unprecedented crises, first of the financial system and the rest of the econ-omy in 2008–2009, then of sovereign debt markets since late 2009, one may reasonably ask whether they mark a watershed for the political economy of European integration. Even if it was not predictably marked by a rich–poor cleavage, has the Greek crisis not exposed the stark economic reality that poor countries have current account deficits and high public debt—because they are poor—and that this makes them vulnerable to finan-cial market attacks? If so, the stable members would be repeatedly forced to bail out those in crisis now that financial markets have started to differentiate between the issu-ers of sovereign debt, and the rich–poor distinction may thus become more salient, not as easy to hide or suppress.

The argument that poorer countries must have higher public debt can be easily dis-carded. It is common knowledge that apart from Greece, rather well-off member states, namely Belgium and Italy, have the highest public debt levels. Apart from city state Luxembourg, Ireland had the highest GDP per capita before the crisis. A financial economist would actually expect poorer countries to have lower public debt, simply because they tend to be less creditworthy. That this expectation is often not borne out by the facts, political economists explain with the implicit bailout guarantees that the mere existence of the IMF or EU institutions entail, arguably creating moral hazard on the part of private creditors and finance ministries of poor countries. But even if the IMF or the EU did not project such an assurance that leads to moral hazard, credit markets might still finance budgets of poor or highly indebted countries. This can be explained by the myopia and partisanship of investors: as long as a country grows (Greece before

2007) or pleases with conspicuously technocratic finance ministers (Italy), markets keep on giving credit even when alarm bells should ring.

The link between income level and current account imbalances is less straightforward. One policy conclusion from the Greek crisis that the Commission and the Council have drawn is that external imbalances must be included among the many indicators used in fiscal surveillance (see Chapter 32, this volume); both deficit and surplus countries have now an obligation to avoid permanent imbalances. But is it correct to assume that poorer countries must have higher current account deficits? This was the mainstream view in the early post-war years that justified the creation of the Bretton Woods institutions: poor countries lack capacity and resources to generate enough income, hence they must import more than they can export. This is now widely regarded as defunct reasoning, drawing a false analogy between the individual and the economy, which has led to permanent dependency. Figure 20.5 shows the correlation between countries' GDP per capita (in PPS, see Figure 20.1) and current account balances, taken as the annual average between 2000 and 2007.

At first sight, the rising trend line seems to indicate that there is indeed a strong relationship between income level and current account such that richer countries have surpluses and poorer countries have deficits. Yet the scatter plot also cautions us

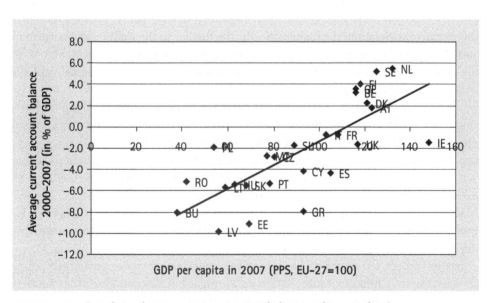

FIGURE 20.5. Correlation between current account balance and income level.

Abbreviations: AT = Austria, BE = Belgium, BU = Bulgaria, CY = Cyprus, CZ = Czech Republic, DK = Denmark, EE = Estonia, ES = Spain, FI = Finland, FR = France, GE = Germany, GR = Greece, HU = Hungary, IE = Ireland, IT = Italy, LT = Lithuania, LV = Latvia, MT = Malta, NL = The Netherlands, PL = Poland, PT = Portugal, RO = Romania, SE = Sweden, SK = Slovakia, SL = Slovenia, UK = United Kingdom

Source: Eurostat

against reading too much into this: just below the horizontal balanced account line we see that countries over the whole range of income levels, from the then richest Ireland, the UK, France, Italy, to the poorer Slovenia, the Czech Republic, Malta, and Poland, all manage with fairly balanced current accounts. There is no reason why there should be a systematic difference between rich and poor countries in this respect. The poor country will simply operate at a lower level of activity than if it were fuelled by higher imports.

There are good economic reasons to believe, however, that rapid growth, i.e. becoming rich, is associated with current account deficits. High growth tends to build up inflationary pressures because bottlenecks emerge, leading to price and wage increases; growth also creates high demand for investment and consumer goods that can easily outstrip exports; and over-optimistic expectations of lasting income growth may fuel asset market bubbles which in turn feed into general price increases. All of which makes these economies extremely vulnerable to any disturbance that may originate somewhere else. This is, in a nutshell, the Greek story as far as macroeconomic imbalances are concerned; and it is the Irish story as far as the vulnerability is concerned. Ireland had become a rich country but had not made the transition from the growth model of an emerging market to that of a mature economy. When the crisis broke, world trade collapsed and the expectations of ever-rising incomes had to be corrected, its FDI-borne economy got into trouble and the housing bubble burst.

So exceptionally rapid growth, for which there is a higher potential in poor countries, can be a source of imbalances, rather than a low level of GDP per se. Figure 20.6 shows this negative correlation: the higher growth (the further to the right on the horizontal axis), the lower the current account balance (the further down on the vertical axis). With the exception of Ireland, no country managed to sustain more than 4.0 percent growth without running into large current account deficits.

Yet, it is also obvious that this is far from a deterministic relationship. Along the horizontal balanced account line, member states with very different growth records are lined up, from the star performer Ireland to the underperformer Italy with only 1.5 percent annual growth over these eight years. If we look beyond Europe, China would show that very high growth rates and current account surpluses can actually go together over an extended period (the country's dot would lie in the North-East of the graph). Macroeconomic restraint, once the economy is booming, and financial market regulation, to rein in excessive optimism and pro-cyclical behavior of investors, can make a big difference.

In this respect, EU members have, however, considerably more constrained policy choices than the Chinese authorities: Greece, Portugal, but also non-eurozone members like Hungary or Latvia have effectively only fiscal policy to deal with macroeconomic imbalances because they cannot run an independent interest rate policy. And none of them can simply suppress financial transactions that fuel current account deficits or asset market bubbles since the freedom of movement of capital and services in the single market rules out this policy option. The reforms of the policy coordination framework in the second half of 2010 have not really tackled this problem of constrained policy

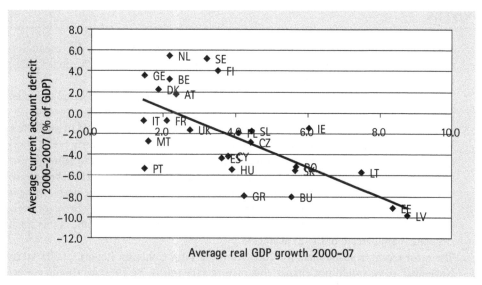

FIGURE 20.6. Correlation between current account balances and real income growth 2000–2007.

Abbreviations: AT = Austria, BE = Belgium, BU = Bulgaria, CY = Cyprus, CZ = Czech Republic, DK = Denmark, EE = Estonia, ES = Spain, FI = Finland, FR = France, GE = Germany, GR = Greece, HU = Hungary, IE = Ireland, IT = Italy, LT = Lithuania, LV = Latvia, MT = Malta, NL = The Netherlands, PL = Poland, PT= Portugal, RO = Romania, SE = Sweden, SK = Slovakia, SL = Slovenia, UK = United Kingdom

Source: Eurostat

choices for stabilization but reinforced the sole reliance on fiscal policy, if somewhat better coordinated fiscal policy. It is this lack of available and admissible policy instruments that makes poorer member states arguably more crisis-prone, rather than their low-income levels as such.

20.4 CONCLUSION

The minor significance of the rich versus poor distinction for the political economy of European integration must come as a surprise to most outside observers of the EU. This chapter argued that the distinction, though manifestly present and justifying a large part of the EU's expenditures, is institutionally played down or even suppressed, for instance in determining a country's weight in the decision-making process or in the financing of the budget. The financial crisis since 2008 is unlikely to change that. Those who pay the piper do not call the tune, in analogy to how market exchange would settle issues. This lends some credence to the claim that the EU is a political union of sorts after all.

NOTES

1. See Chapter 19, this volume, and Jonathan Rodden, "Strength in Numbers? Representation and Redistribution in the European Union," *European Union Politics* 3, no.2 (2002), 151–75.
2. "Growing Regions, growing Europe," *Fourth Report on Economic and Social Cohesion* (Brussels: European Communities, 2007), 4.
3. This means that the currency prices of a particular basket of goods are used to calculate a PPS exchange rate which is then used to translate the GDP of each country into a common standard, instead of the market exchange rate. This typically raises the value of poor countries' income because it takes into account the fact that in such countries labor-intensive services are relatively cheap (undervalued relative to world market prices), while it lowers the value of rich countries' GDP where such services tend to be expensive (or overvalued). Luxembourg as a small financial centre has been left out (the income of this small city state is 275 percent of EU-27 average).
4. The most recent available data for 2008 from the Fifth Cohesion Report, published in November 2010, would not change this picture very much. By 2012, we should expect Ireland to have moved to the bottom of the high-income countries and Greece and Portugal further down in the middle-income range.
5. This regional classification has three hierarchical levels that try to capture units of comparable population size: the Regulation for major socio-economic regions, NUTS1, stipulates a minimum size of 3 million and a maximum of 7 million people; for basic regions, NUTS2, a minimum of 800,000 and a maximum of 3 million; and for specific priority regions, NUTS3, a minimum of 150,000. NUTS2 is the relevant unit for regional aid that intends to promote convergence (Objective 1 of Convergence regions).
6. *Fourth Report on Economic and Social Cohesion* (European Commission 2007), 4, 15.
7. *Fourth Report on Economic and Social Cohesion*, 10.
8. *Fourth Report on Economic and Social Cohesion*, 11.
9. See Robert Leonardi, *Cohesion Policy in the European Union: The Building of Europe* (Basingstoke: Palgrave, 2005), ch. 4, and the *Fourth Report on Economic and Social Cohesion*, ch. 2, for an optimistic view, while more skeptical accounts can be found in Andres Rodríguez-Pose and Ugo Fratesi, "Between Development and Social Policies: The Impact of Structural Funds in Objective 1 Regions," *Regional Studies* 38, no. 1 (2004), 97–119, and David Allen, "The Structural Funds and Cohesion Policy," in Helen Wallace, Mark A. Pollack, and Alistair R. Young, eds, *Policy-Making in the European Union*, sixth edition (Oxford: Oxford University Press, 2010), 250.
10. Raja Shankar and Anwar Shah, *Lessons from European Union Policies for Regional Development*, WPS4977 (Washington DC: The World Bank, 2009), 15–33.
11. This is contrary to the conclusions that the World Bank survey of Shankar and Shah, *Lessons*, 34–5, draw.
12. Leonardi, *Cohesion Policy*, 9–13.
13. "Working for the regions. EU regional policy 2007–2013," *Report of the Commission* (Brussels: Commission of the European Communities, 2008), 5; emphasis in the original.
14. Subject to the constraints that the overall size of the House is fixed at 435 since 1913 and each state must have at least one representative in the House.

15. M. Gorton, S. Davidova, M. Banse, and A. Bailey, "The International Competitiveness of Hungarian Agriculture: Past Performance and Future Projections," *Post-Communist Economies* 18, no.1 (2006), 69–84.

16. An example is the Posted Workers Directive that obliges employers of the home or sending country to apply the minimum standards of labor law in the host or receiving country to the workers they employ.

17. Giandomenico Majone, "A European Regulatory State: The State in Modern Political Economy," in Jeremy Richardson, ed., *European Union: Power and Policy-Making* (London: Routledge, 1996), 263–77, and Fritz W. Scharpf, *Governing in Europe. Effective and Democratic?* (Oxford: Oxford University Press, 1999).

18. Rodden, "Strength in Numbers?" 167.

CHAPTER 21

···

COORDINATED VERSUS LIBERAL MARKET ECONOMIES

···

ORFEO FIORETOS

21.1 INTRODUCTION

···

The 1957 preamble to the treaty establishing the EEC, the precursor to the EU, established that the key means by which that organization was to achieve its chief goals of "an accelerated raising of the standard of living and closer relations between [Member] States," was through "the elimination...of restrictions on the import and export of goods" and "the abolition, as between Member States, of obstacles to freedom of movement for persons, services, and capital." In creating and sustaining such an arrangement, which was eventually termed the internal market, governments have confronted an enduring governance dilemma, namely how to minimize barriers to international economic exchange without undermining national designs that are highly valued domestically. Alternative views on how to resolve this governance dilemma have been at the center of every major intergovernmental bargain and have also defined everyday politics in the EU since 1957. Whether in the context of debates over macroeconomic priorities and a joint currency, or in microeconomic debates concerning the rules governing competition, corporate governance, social insurance, and financial markets, the governance dilemma has presented governments with trade-offs between securing a share of the growing collective benefits of an integrated market and a reduction in national discretion with respect to how markets are regulated nationally and how losers from integration are compensated. This chapter explains how the manner in which governments jointly managed these trade-offs evolved over time as domestic economic priorities changed, more states became members of the EU, and new global economic challenges emerged.

For the purposes of explaining how governments have resolved governance dilemmas and why the integration process followed a particular trajectory, scholars point to many lines of division within the EU. Other chapters in this *Handbook* speak to cleavages between large and small countries, long-standing and recent members, and between rich and less wealthy states in shaping the process and outcome of European integration. This chapter underscores the value of basing the study of how the EU's economic constitution has evolved in historically informed analysis of cleavages between governments promoting alternative models of capitalism. Diversity in national capitalist models has been a persistent feature in post-war Europe, and historical legacies of these models have often cast a long shadow over the type of European designs that governments have championed. Governments favoring a statist market economy model often promoted multilateral designs that permitted great government discretion and strong supranational mandates in the support of specific firms and industries; governments pursuing a liberal market economy model typically sought minimalist solutions to international market regulation; and governments championing a coordinated model of capitalism have tended to seek multilateral designs that preserve significant social protections and constraints on the market for corporate ownership. As governments have reassessed the value of employing alternative economic models, and new members have joined the EU, coalitions within the EU have evolved with significant consequences for the EU's economic architecture.

The following three sections cover distinct phases in the evolution of the EU and document how capitalist diversity, or what at times is termed the EU's internal clash of capitalisms, shaped the content of major intergovernmental bargains and the specific mechanisms that governments have introduced to resolve the governance dilemma. A conclusion speaks to the lessons that a focus on capitalist diversity holds for the future study of the EU.

21.2 FOUNDATIONS

Though Europe's industry suffered major damage during World War II, large parts were intact, and there was a significant backlog of technological innovation that could be exploited for commercial purposes.[1] The major question after the war was thus not whether, but how, industrial capacity could be harnessed to rebuild national economies. While a consensus gradually evolved that greater international economic cooperation was critical to rebuilding national economies, what particular form multilateral designs should take was a subject of great controversy.[2] Much of that controversy can be traced to differences in the domestic programs of reconstruction promoted by European governments and their efforts to secure forms of international cooperation that were compatible with national agendas.

A large literature in comparative political economy documents the historical reasons that European governments adopted diverse national systems of economic governance after the war.[3] Among early members of the EEC, the principal division was between countries that favored a statist model in which economic governance was highly centralized and those championing a coordinated model of capitalism, sometimes described as corporatism, in which societal groups were highly organized and governance functions more decentralized. France and Italy embraced statist models, while Germany and the Benelux favored coordinated models. Conceived of as encompassing and coherent institutional blueprints that would aid countries in rebuilding their economies after the war, the national models of capitalism that governments championed informed their institutional choices in all major areas of the modern market economy, including the nature of macroeconomic policy and the structure of national financial, corporate governance, industrial relations, and social insurance systems.[4]

The economic incentives that governments and domestic interest groups had in supporting European integration are well documented.[5] The prospect of access to foreign markets on non-discriminatory terms was particularly attractive to governments for it promised a foundation on which national economic growth in the industrial sector could be secured and thus also a means by which the expansion of the post-war welfare state could be achieved. But broad agreement on market integration did not generate uniform views among governments on the structure of multilateral designs, in particular on how markets should be regulated. Because international rules would impact national economies in diverse ways depending upon the type of economic programs governments promoted domestically, the latter supported different forms of international market regulation as a means of minimizing domestic adjustment costs.[6]

The 1957 Treaty of Rome that established the EEC committed member states to an open economic regime that would progressively reduce barriers to exchange. Capitalist diversity played a key role in shaping negotiations and their outcome. The primary cleavage was one between two statist market economies, France and Italy, on the one hand, and the coordinated market economies of Germany and the Benelux, on the other. This division was particularly apparent in deliberations over rules governing competition policy which would determine the type of market mechanism that would operate within the EEC and also the discretion that governments would have in supporting domestic producers and in encouraging economic concentration at home.[7] Statist economies favored European rules that permitted greater national discretion in awarding state aid and the use of merger and monopoly rules that encouraged the creation of large enterprises at the national level. By contrast, coordinated market economies, especially Germany, objected to such discretion and sought multilateral rules that limited discriminatory forms of industrial policy and that enforced stricter monopoly and merger rules. While the final agreement was a compromise that fell closer on paper to Germany's preference, the European Commission did little to enforce competition rules in the early period after the Treaty of Rome and thus made it possible for alternative models of capitalism to function side-by-side.

Another area of early disagreement among member states was the nature of European social policy, in particular whether social protections and compensation should be harmonized. With less productive firms and poorly organized societal groups as well as greater involvement by government authorities in wage setting, French governments promoted greater authority for supranational bodies and extensive harmonization in areas affecting wages and non-wage labor costs. Such designs were rejected by Germany, which sought to preserve a legally protected national mandate of autonomy for employers and employees in matters governing wages and some forms of social insurance. To German officials, proposals for the harmonization of social policy represented a threat to a cornerstone of its post-war economic model and were, therefore, vociferously opposed. With support from the Benelux, Germany secured a final agreement that introduced language that committed the EEC to greater social equality but that preserved national discretion in virtually all areas of social policy.

The so-called golden age of post-war capitalism that reached its zenith in the 1960s, when annual growth rates in EEC states averaged about 5 percent, productivity was soaring, and unemployment was in the low single digits, would not have been feasible in the absence of the international institutions that were established in 1957. The EEC served to expand trade within Europe by lengthening the horizons of large-scale capital investors and by providing the outlet for industrial goods.[8] As the benefits of EEC's customs union became more apparent, demands grew for the removal of many remaining barriers to greater economic exchange. But support for such initiatives were not uniform across countries as domestic groups were differently affected by deeper levels of integration. Statist economies were particularly keen on protecting their ability to implement national industrial policies that involved direct subsidies and near-monopolies in major industrial markets. Meanwhile, coordinated market economies were keen to preserve distinct practices in their social, industrial relations, and corporate governance systems.

Because EEC governments retained the ability to veto proposals that entailed unattractive trade-offs between greater economic integration and reductions in national discretion, especially in how to regulate national markets and how to compensate losers from integration, the EEC did not record much progress in the 1960s and 1970s beyond enlarging its membership with the admittance of Britain, Ireland, and Denmark. Indeed, a gradual decline in economic performance led governments to look inward and to resist deeper levels of market integration. As the 1970s drew to a close, the European integration project was therefore frequently characterized as sclerotic and as failing to help governments respond to the international economic crises of that decade.

21.3 MAJOR REFORMS

During the 1980s, the EEC undertook a major reform program that was precipitated by disappointing economic performance in the 1970s and by shifts in the global economy, in particular the emergence of competitive East Asian producers in many of Europe's primary industrial markets. The center of EEC reforms was an ambitious program of market liberalization designed to create the world's largest internal market through the elimination of all barriers to international exchange in capital, goods, services, and labor markets. Both the origin and the form of this program were deeply impacted by the type of domestic market economies that governments promoted at home. First, domestic reassessments of the best model of economic governance, especially in France, created the conditions under which an agreement on the internal market program was feasible. Second, national developments transformed the primary cleavage among member states after the mid-1980s from one between statist and coordinated market economies to one between coordinated and liberal market economies, with important consequences for the nature of EU's economic architecture in the latter half of that decade and beyond.

During the 1980s, the statist market economy model fell out of favor as governments questioned the long-term advantages of centralizing economic regulation, controlling capital markets, overtly discriminating among companies domestically, and shielding select sectors from foreign competition. In particular, following efforts to expand the role of the state in the early 1980s, a French Socialist government suddenly reversed course in 1983 and embarked instead on a program that included a new commitment to macroeconomic stability, economic liberalization, and efforts to emulate features of the coordinated market economy.[9] The French decision to abandon the statist model more closely aligned that country with Europe's other large economies that favored greater levels of international market liberalization.

Parallel to France's radical shift in domestic economic governance, Great Britain implemented a fundamental departure from its post-war approach to economic governance. From having experimented with both statist and coordinated market economy designs for nearly three decades, a British government led by Margaret Thatcher sought to restore a liberal market economy after 1979.[10] Defined by extensive market liberalization and deregulation, the Thatcher agenda signaled the beginnings of a neo-liberal agenda that would eventually also inform reforms in many other countries. The cornerstones of the British reform program were the deregulation of capital and labor markets, a radical reduction in the direct support for national firms, as well as the promotion of an open market for corporate control.

Meanwhile, in Europe's coordinated market economies, the economic challenges of the 1970s and early 1980s generated greater support for post-war designs. In particular the German model, including its constitutional mandate to preserve price stability and an industrial model oriented towards high quality industrial goods became widely seen to be the reason that Germany performed comparatively well when other economies faced serious problems.[11] The positive demonstration case of Germany, and to some extent the Scandinavian economies employing a version of the coordinated market economy, led the EEC's small coordinated market economies to favor an incremental adjustment agenda.

To make the internal market sustainable, substantial changes were needed in basic institutions of political deliberation and decision-making in the EEC. In particular, a multilateral program of economic liberalization could not be expected to function unless a system based on unanimous consent that gave governments veto rights was replaced with some form of majority voting among national representatives. Following extensive negotiations, EEC governments agreed in the SEA of 1986 to replace unanimity voting with QMV in most economic areas.[12] At the same time the oversight functions of the European Commission expanded, while the scope and impact of ECJ adjudication increased significantly.[13] Collectively, these innovations made practicable the implementation of the vast majority of the internal market program by the 1992 target deadline set by governments.

However, greater consensus among the largest economies on the benefits of formalizing international cooperation for the purposes of implementing the ambitious market liberalization program did not spell agreement on the particular nature of international rules.[14] Nor did it bring about uniform views on the nature of discretion that governments would have in maintaining or designing nationally distinct economic institutions. Indeed, new agreements created new concerns for member states, albeit different in nature depending on the type of market economy they favored at home.

For liberal market economies, specifically Britain which in the 1980s was largely on its own in promoting such a model, QMV entailed a potential threat to the ability of governments to support an economic model with lower regulatory standards and social protections than elsewhere in Europe. In particular, British governments feared that supranational mandates requiring higher levels of social protection would be imposed and thus undermine the institutional advantages that the liberal market economy offered employers who benefited from flexible employment contracts. The British government also had strong reservations against the creation of new supranational industrial policy instruments and also expressed great concern that models of corporate governance familiar from coordinated models would be imposed by other states and thus undercut the coherence and sustainability of domestic reforms.

Meanwhile, in Europe's coordinated economies, which remained a majority block in the EEC, market liberalization entailed the prospect of regulatory "races to the bottom" that could potentially erode high social protections and also the core of national financial and corporate governance systems. In these countries, fears of races to the bottom were the product of the anticipated effects of higher levels of competition among producers of goods and services and a 1979 ECJ ruling that institutionalized the principle of mutual recognition. That principle mandates that any good or service produced legally in one member state cannot be excluded through non-tariff barriers in other countries, and it became a core principle behind how regulatory differences among member states would be resolved in the internal market. In coordinated market economies, where social protections were higher, employee representation more extensive, and the market for corporate control entailed many constraints to the benefit of large manufacturing firms and banks, mutual recognition was thought to potentially threaten long-standing national designs. As a consequence, Germany and Benelux, now joined by France, promoted a set of safeguards against the erosion of valued national designs, including various programs that placed Europe's "social dimension" on equal footing with its emerging liberal economic dimension.

Though mutual recognition produced a significant amount of regulatory competition, it also entailed an unexpected boon to further integration by providing new means by which governments could resolve the governance dilemma. It meant that there was agreement in principle that regulatory harmonization was no longer the primary means by which to resolve the governance dilemma. The prospect was therefore diminished that QMV would force members with a minority view, such as Britain, to adopt the designs championed by other member states. At the same time, a series of agreements were reached on common minimum standards in domains with consequences for industrial competitiveness, including social and environmental protections. In a mutual recognition regime, such standards allowed countries with higher standards, typically coordinated market economies, to retain national practices as long as these were non-discriminatory in nature while simultaneously ensuring that egregious races to the bottom would not threaten to undermine national priorities.

The creation of the internal market in the 1980s is rightfully described as the most ambitious international program of market regulation to date and a major watershed in European integration.[15] It impacted virtually every aspect of economic governance and created a genuinely integrated European market. It also represented a significant step toward a more liberal economic constitution for the EEC by reinforcing commitments to market liberalization and deregulation. But at least initially, the reform program did not lead to a convergence in national models of capitalism. Rather, it marked the beginning of a long-lasting cleavage between liberal and coordinated market economies that would also have significant consequences during a third phase of European integration.

21.4 CONSOLIDATION

During the 1990s and 2000s, member states sought to implement programs that had proven elusive and eventually to consolidate the market liberalization and deregulation agendas. The first major accomplishment was an agreement on and the implementation of an EMU that had already been identified as a goal in the 1950s and again in the 1970s. Reached in Maastricht in 1991 when the EU was formally established, and gradually implemented in the course of the 1990s, the EMU agreement entailed a commitment to common macroeconomic priorities and a joint currency. The former part stressed price stability and budget discipline and the latter revolved around establishing irrevocably fixed exchange rates and the introduction of the euro. Like other major initiatives, EMU entailed many economic benefits to member states. The transaction costs of currency exchange would be eliminated among EMU members, markets would become more transparent, and the prospect of negative externalities from currency devaluations would be a matter of history. The potential also existed that the euro would serve as a new international reserve currency and boost the collective economic capacity of the EU.

Though a convergence on national macroeconomic priorities during the 1980s made an agreement on EMU feasible, there were areas of significant disagreement among member states that reflected a clash of capitalism. Led by France, a small number of countries sought to move to EMU quickly and use it as the means by which macroeco-nomic convergence would be realized. This group also sought a broad mandate for an ECB and gave the promotion of economic growth equal if not greater priority than price stability. By contrast, Germany led a larger coalition which advocated that economic convergence be achieved prior to the final operational phase of EMU and that ECB's mandate be narrowly targeted toward price stability. Serving as a positive demonstra-tion case of a macroeconomic regime that had successfully ensured price stability, the blueprint preferred by coordinated market economies prevailed and the German model was closely mirrored both in the priorities enshrined in the Treaty on European Union and in the operational make-up of the ECB.[16]

But not all EU members were willing to support EMU. Facing strong opposition domestically, the British and Danish governments insisted on special provisions that would enable them to opt-in to EMU at a later date. British resistance again reflected concerns over the potential consequences of international programs for the sustainabil-ity of the institutional advantages of the liberal market economy at home. Fixed exchange rates and a powerful ECB were seen as potential threats both to the status of London as Europe's pre-eminent financial hub and to the long-term competitiveness of British firms that remained more price sensitive than their counterparts in Germany and France. After acrimonious negotiations that nearly prevented an agreement on EMU, Britain and Denmark were granted their exemptions and thus made possible the inclu-sion of EMU in the Treaty on European Union.[17]

Britain also objected to efforts by coordinated market economies to expand EU's social dimension during negotiations in Maastricht. Again, a special arrangement was needed to secure a final agreement, this time in the form of an opt-out for Britain from the social chapter of the proposed treaty. While the special provisions that were granted to Britain in the case of EMU and social policy were not the first examples of what is known as variable geometry, an ad hoc practice in which some member states are exempted from specific European mandates, the Maastricht agreement represented the first high-profile use of variable geometry for the purposes of resolving the governance dilemma. By giving Britain the option of choosing if and when to join EMU and to ratify the social chapter, the use of variable geometry avoided the prospect that a clash between liberal and coordinated market economies would undermine the creation of the EU.

In the course of the 1990s and 2000s, competing conceptions of the appropriate form of economic governance became a feature of everyday EU politics. Debates now took place against a backdrop of how the EU and its members could best meet the challenges of greater levels of economic globalization. While seen as an opportunity to enlarge the market for European producers of goods and services, economic globalization also exposed Europe to higher levels of competition. Scholars hypothesized that globaliza-tion and market liberalization in Europe could have similar outcomes and bring about a convergence on a liberal model of economic governance among EU members.[18] But such expectations proved exaggerated, and the degree to which the blueprints of the liberal market economy were adopted varied significantly across member states and issue areas.

Albeit far from complete, convergence on the liberal model was pronounced in the financial and corporate governance systems of France and Germany. Reforms in the financial domain were ostensibly an outgrowth of the internal market program introduced in the 1980s, and corporate governance reform was designed to complement those in the former domain. By the end of the decade, French and German financial and corporate governance systems had more in common with those found in Britain than they had with their own post-war systems.[19] But there were limits to how far these countries were willing to embrace an open market for corporate control. France, for example, became a vociferous opponent of the European Commission's proposals for a takeover directive that would constrain the means by which national companies could defend themselves against hostile takeovers. It also opposed a Commission proposal designed to eliminate privileged voting arrangements in corporate boards in favor of a European-wide commitment to a one-share-one-vote model that is commonly associated with liberal market economies. Revisions were eventually made to the takeover directive that preserved some constraints on the market for corporate control and the Commission withdrew its proposal for a one-share-one-vote corporate governance system. In both cases, then, France successfully defended some features of its corporate governance system by securing European designs that would not undermine it.[20]

Germany recorded similar success in its defense of co-determination which was a defining feature of its post-war corporate governance and industrial relations models. The institution of co-determination gives employees representation in corporate boardrooms, but could potentially be undermined if German companies were able to transform their legal identities into ones that did not require them to observe co-determination. In protracted negotiations over the creation of a European statute that would allow publicly owned companies to eschew national incorporation in favor of a European legal identity, German governments secured a set of constraints that limited the ability of companies to avoid co-determination.[21] This and other cases in which Germany protected features of its post-war model are emblematic of the long shadow that alternative models of capitalism cast on the nature of European integration in the 1990s and 2000s even as countries adopted many features of the liberal market economy model. Thus, while there was greater level of similarity in national models of corporate governance in this period than in previous ones, historic differences persisted in no small part because governments secured EU designs that helped them preserve distinct national institutions.

One of the most significant challenges that EU members faced during the 1990s and 2000s were unprecedented levels of unemployment. Though there were frequent speculations that international market integration would bring about a similar degree of convergence in national systems of social insurance as in the financial and corporate governance systems, this was not the case. Coordinated market economies were opposed to European initiatives that would limit national discretion in devising social insurance programs and labor market institutions that preserved standards of living and individuals' incentives to acquire advanced skills. While governments in most coordinated market economies agreed that the EU ought to make greater flexibility in labor markets a major priority, they differed in their views on what were the best means by which more employment could be promoted and displaced workers helped in adjusting to new labor market conditions.[22]

Liberal market economies sought to limit the expansion of supranational mandates in matters relating to the labor market and social insurance, while coordinated market economies were keen to employ multilateral initiatives as a means of strengthening national programs. To resolve the governance dilemma during the creation and implementation of the Lisbon Strategy—EU's comprehensive strategy during the 2000s to radically improve economic competitiveness—member states introduced a new principle by which they could reconcile common action and non-discrimination with high levels of national discretion. Termed the open method coordination, member states committed themselves to a process guided by common goals and peer review in which they retained the autonomy to reform labor markets and institutions of social insurance in ways that fit national circumstances.[23] While the contributions of the open method of coordination to substantive policy goals have been disputed, its role in resolving the governance dilemma was significant. By avoiding the promotion of a common model to combat unemployment, member states were able to sustain national designs held dear while taking part in a process that served to coordinate European responses. Since its introduction in this area, the open method of coordination has become a popular means by which to resolve the governance dilemma in other areas too, including immigration, macroeconomic coordination, and innovation.

Two enlargements of EU's membership played important roles in this period. The addition of three small economies with roots in a coordinated model of capitalism in 1995 (Sweden, Finland, Austria) strengthened the ability of Germany and Benelux to secure European designs that were palatable with their domestic labor market and social insurance reforms. Meanwhile, the 2004 and 2007 enlargements that saw the inclusion of nearly a dozen formerly Socialist economies raised new concerns about the sustainability of the social model in coordinated market economies. With these latter enlargements, EU's labor market was fundamentally transformed. High unemployment in most formerly Socialist economies and individuals willing to move and work for lower social compensation than in richer member states created large fears in countries with high social protections that these would gradually be undermined. Such concerns were central to the defeat of a proposed European constitution in 2005, when the French electorate rejected the treaty following acrimonious debates over the liberal nature of the proposed constitution and the threats it posed to the French social model.

A period of reassessment followed the defeat of the proposed constitution and revisions to the original text included a less strong embrace of market competition and a boost for the social dimension. With the signing of the Lisbon Treaty in 2007 and its ratification two years later, the EU finally concluded two decades of extensive reform that had seen the implementation of long-standing goals like EMU as well as the consolidation of the internal market. The process that brought about this outcome was not linear, nor was the outcome preordained. Rather, as in the past, European integration was characterized by a series of compromises among member states that entailed trade-offs between reducing barriers to economic integration and the preservation of a diverse set of national designs. While this process made national economic systems more alike than they had been in the 1950s or 1980s, governments also continued a tradition of securing international solutions that gave significant discretion with respect to whether they promoted liberal or coordinated models of capitalism at home.

21.5 CONCLUSION

The diverse national and EU blueprints put forward by governments in the wake of the global financial crisis in the late 2000s are ample evidence that historic differences in national economic models continue to cast a shadow over processes of European integration. Indeed, at least initially, the crisis reinforced a cleavage between liberal and coordinated market economies. While accepting an expansion of regulatory cooperation within the EU, governments in liberal market economies remained skeptical of significantly enhancing such authorities for EU bodies. Meanwhile, governments in coordinated market economies signaled greater openness to such a trajectory and sought multilateral designs that ensured the protection of long-standing national designs in a range of areas, including the banking and securities sectors. As scholars begin to examine how the EU reconciles different views of market regulation after the crisis, what lessons does the past hold?

First, the history of European integration underscores that at no point have governments agreed on what constituted the preferable model of economic governance. Indeed, since the 1950s they have sought to reconcile greater international market integration with the preservation of significant national discretion in order to protect diverse models of capitalism. Yet, divisions between member states have not been static. At various junctures, governments in large economies have undertaken far-reaching reforms with significant consequences for the trajectory of European integration. To wit, the Thatcher revolution, the sudden shift away from the statist market economy in France during the 1980s, and Germany's stronger embrace of market liberalization in the late 1990s had profound consequences for European integration. While rare, similar shifts are likely to occur in the future as well and thus push the EU in new directions. For this reason, a nuanced understanding of the future of EU's economic architecture will depend upon how successfully scholars account for developments within member states and their aggregate effects for reforms at the European level.

While the clash of capitalism has largely been one between member states, it also features within EU bodies. Several studies document the role played by the Commission in pushing member states to adopt more liberal economic policies and in championing designs associated with liberal market economies.[24] The Parliament has also become a venue for the clash of capitalism and through co-decision has expanded its ability to initiate and block legislative initiatives with consequences for EU-level rules. And the ECJ has played a key role in shaping the economic direction of the EU, including through major rulings such as *Cassis de Dijon* and *Centros*. But what the long-term consequences of the clash of capitalism in these bodies will be for member states and for the future of European integration remains largely an open question. Thus, for example, while some studies conclude that the ECJ has ushered in a new era of liberalism that will bring about the end of coordinated market economies,[25] others find that the Court was instrumental in protecting models of social protection closely associated with such economies.[26] To establish what consequences supranational bodies will have for the future of Europe's diverse market economies will require that the political economy field more actively identify the conditions under which EU institutions serve to undermine or sustain distinct national traditions.

Second, the history of European integration underscores that the clash of capitalism has been a central and consistent factor behind major institutional innovations in the EU. It pushed member states to devise and institutionalize means by which to reconcile the creation of a common economic space and the preservation of national discretion in areas valued highly by governments. Institutional innovations like mutual recognition, variable geometry, and the open method of coordination grew out of the clash of capitalism and in turn affected the content and direction of economic reform within the EU. In particular, these innovations enabled member states to sustain the momentum of reducing barriers to exchange while preserving national discretion in periods when integration appeared to stall. These innovations have implications for international cooperation beyond Europe and it may be these, not the formal structure of the EU, that hold the most valuable lessons for non-European countries that seek to reconcile greater international market integration with distinct national priorities in the future.

Finally, the clash of capitalism has implications for the EU's engagement with other international organizations and major economies. In cases where its interests are collectively represented and member states are united, the EU has been successful in shaping global rules.[27] But there are also many instances where the cleavage between liberal and coordinated market economies undermines internal agreement and thus undercuts the prospect that the EU can effectively contribute to the establishment of meaningful global rules. In cases where such divisions are particularly intense and enduring, the EU's ability to muster its potential collective power is circumscribed. For this reason, the ability of the EU's member states to harness their potential collective power in negotiations with other large, global economies and to shape agendas within the G20 and the IMF will be deeply impacted by how successfully they resolve their internal clash of capitalism. Future studies of global regulation must, therefore, avoid treating the EU as a unified organization and pay close attention to the conditions under which member states are successful or not in bridging divides between liberal and coordinated market economies.

NOTES

1. Barry Eichengreen, *The European Economy Since 1945: Coordinated Capitalism and Beyond* (Princeton: Princeton University Press, 2007).

2. Alan Milward, *The European Rescue of the Nation-State* (Berkeley: University of California Press, 1992).

3. Andrew Shonfield, *Modern Capitalism: The Changing Balance of Public and Private Power* (Oxford: Oxford University Press, 1965); Peter Katzenstein, ed., *Between Power and Plenty: Foreign Economic Policies of Advanced Industrial States* (Madison: The University of Wisconsin Press, 1978); Peter A. Hall, *Governing the Economy* (Oxford: Oxford University Press, 1986); Vivien Schmidt, *The Futures of European Capitalism* (Oxford: Oxford University Press, 2002).

4. Peter A. Hall and David Soskice, eds, *Varieties of Capitalism: The Institutional Foundation of Competitive Advantage* (Oxford: Oxford University Press, 2001).

5. Andrew Moravcsik, *The Choice for Europe: Social Purpose and State Power From Messina to Maastricht* (Ithaca: Cornell University Press, 1998); Eichengreen, *The European Economy Since 1945*.

6. Orfeo Fioretos, *Creative Reconstructions: Multilateralism and European Varieties of Capitalism After 1950* (Ithaca: Cornell University Press, 2011).

7. David Gerber, *Law and Competition in Twentieth Century Europe* (Oxford: Clarendon Press, 1998), 334–91.

8. Eichengreen, *The European Economy Since 1945*.

9. Andrea Boltho, "Has France Converged on Germany? Policies and Institutions since 1958," in S. Berger and R. Dore, eds, *National Diversity and Global Capitalism* (Ithaca: Cornell University Press, 1996), 89–104; Vivien Schmidt, *From State to Market? The Transformation of French Business and Government* (Cambridge: Cambridge University Press, 1996).

10. Neil Rollings, *British Business in the Formative Years of European Integration, 1945–1973* (Cambridge: Cambridge University Press, 2007); Hall, *Governing the Economy*.

11. Wolfgang Streeck, *Social Institutions and Economic Performance* (London: Sage, 1992); Michel Albert, *Capitalism vs. Capitalism* (New York: Four Wall Eight Windows, 1993).

12. Moravcsik, *The Choice for Europe*.

13. Mark A. Pollack, *The Engines of European Integration* (Oxford: Oxford University Press, 2003).

14. Liesbet Hooghe and Gary Marks, "The Making of a Polity: The Struggle over European Integration," in H. Kitschelt, P. Lange, G. Marks, and J. D. Stephens, eds, *Continuity and Change in Contemporary Capitalism* (New York: Cambridge University Press, 1999), 427–60; Georg Menz, *Varieties of Capitalism and Europeanization: National Response Strategies to the Single European Market* (Oxford: Oxford University Press, 2005).

15. Neil Fligstein and Jason McNichol, "The Institutional Terrain of the European Union," in W. Sandholtz and A. Stone Sweet, eds, *European Integration and Supranational Governance* (Oxford: Oxford University Press, 1998), 29–55; Moravcsik, *The Choice for Europe*.

16. Kathleen McNamara, *The Currency of Ideas: Monetary Politics in the European Union* (Ithaca: Cornell University Press, 1998).

17. Kenneth Dyson and Kevin Featherstone, *The Road to Maastricht: Negotiating Economic and Monetary Union* (Oxford: Oxford University Press, 1999); Orfeo Fioretos, "The Domestic Sources of Multilateral Preferences: Varieties of Capitalism in the European Community," in P. A. Hall and D. Soskice, eds, *Varieties of Capitalism: The Institutional Foundation of Competitive Advantage* (New York: Oxford University Press), 213–44.

18. See discussions in Schmidt, *The Futures of European Capitalism*; Erik Jones, *Economic Adjustment and Political Transformation in Small States* (Oxford: Oxford University Press, 2008); Helen Callaghan, "Convergence? Divergence? Hybridization? Transnational Law-making and the Clash of Capitalisms," Paper presented at the SASE Conference, Copenhagen (June 26–28, 2007).

19. Pepper Culpepper, "Institutional Change in Contemporary Capitalism: Coordinated Financial Systems since 1990," *World Politics* 57, no. 2 (2005), 173–99; Richard Deeg, "Change from Within: German and Italian Finance in the 1990s," in W. Streeck and T. Kathleen, eds, *Beyond Continuity: Institutional Change in Advanced Political Economies* (New York: Oxford University Press, 2005), 169–202.

20. Helen Callaghan and Martin Höpner, "European Integration and the Clash of Capitalisms: Political Cleavages over Takeover Liberalization," *Comparative European Politics* 3 (2005), 307–32; Ben Clift, "The Second Time as Farce? The EU Takeover Directive, the Clash of Capitalism and the Hamstrung Harmonisation of European (and French) Corporate Governance," *Journal of Common Market Studies* 45, no. 1 (2007), 55–79.

21. Orfeo Fioretos, "The Regulation of Transnational Corporate Identity in Europe," *Comparative Political Studies* 42, no. 9 (2009), 1167–92.

22. André Sapir, "Globalization and the Reform of European Social Models," *Journal of Common Market Studies* 44, no. 2 (2006), 369–90.

23. Jonathan Zeitlin and Philip Pochet, eds, *The Open Method of Coordination in Action: The European Employment and Social Inclusion Strategies* (Brussels: Peter Lang, 2005).

24. Nicolas Jabko, *Playing the Market: A Political Strategy for Uniting Europe, 1985–2005* (Ithaca: Cornell University Press, 2006); Rachel Epstein, *In Pursuit of Liberalism: International Institutions in Postcommunist Europe* (Baltimore: Johns Hopkins University Press, 2008).

25. Martin Höpner and Armin Schäfer, "A New Phase of European Integration: Organized Capitalisms in Post-Ricardian Europe," *West European Politics* 33, no. 2 (2010), 344–68.

26. James Caporaso and Sidney Tarrow, "Polanyi in Brussels: Supranational Institutions and The Transnational Embedding of Capitalism," *International Organization* 63 (2009), 593–620.

27. Daniel Drezner, *All Politics is Global: Explaining International Regulatory Regimes* (Princeton: Princeton University Press, 2007); Wade Jacoby and Sophie Meunier, eds, *Europe and the Management of Globalization*, special issue of *Journal of European Public Policy* 17, no. 3 (2010).

....

CHAPTER 22

LEADERS AND FOLLOWERS: LEADERSHIP AMONGST MEMBER STATES IN A DIFFERENTIATED EUROPE

....

VINCENT DELLA SALA

CAN a polity, such as the EU, that deliberately tries to do away with hierarchical forms of government, whose proponents argue that power is no longer the basis of politics, and that provides even the smallest of its constituent parts a veto over key decisions, have leaders and followers amongst member states? More importantly, does thinking about leaders in the EU help our understanding about its nature and how it works? These are not simply queries about whether there is a core group of states that shape the direction of European integration. They may tell us something about the nature of integration and the extent to which traditional power politics have given way to new ways of conceiving interests by member states.

There has always been interest in trying to identify leaders and followers amongst the member states of the EU, from the early discussion of a Franco–German axis to assessing the impact of British entry on the balance of power between existing members. However, it is in the period since the mid-1990s that there has been a heightened concern with whether there is a "core" Europe that drives the integration process and guides change in the EU rather than being led by it. Both the widening of membership and the heightened but differentiated pace of integration in recent decades have raised questions about whether uniformity amongst member states is giving way to a core group that is ready and willing to push the integration process farther and faster.

The purpose of this chapter is twofold. First, it will demonstrate how the emergence of a differentiated Europe raised the specter of a Europe of leaders and followers, centered around the possibility that a core group of states would race ahead, pulling the rest behind so as not to risk being marginalized. The first section of the chapter will explore how the various forms of differentiation—multi-speed, variable geometry, or à la carte Europe—have different consequences for the question of leadership. Second, it wants to explore to what extent it is possible to speak of leaders and followers within the EU. A political and institutional architecture designed consciously and conspicuously to prevent the concentration of power would seem ill-suited to a discussion of differentiation between leaders and followers amongst member states. Drawing from arguments about "heroic" and "humdrum" leadership and those dealing with policy leaders and laggards, the chapter will illustrate that the EU combines different types of leaders and followers for different tasks, with the possible consequence that leadership is amorphous and fluid. The second section of the chapter will examine the notion of a Franco–German directorate at the core of the EU. It will argue that the bilateral relationship provides the possibility of a heroic form of leadership but that this may not serve well for a great deal of the policy-making that takes place in the EU. The third section will look at policy leaders and laggards to show that there may be different types of leaders and followers, drawing on a range of resources, in various policy areas.

22.1 LEADERSHIP AT ANY SPEED?

First, a small tangent to mention what we mean by leaders and followers. It may seem obvious what both imply but, analytically, it is not always so evident what we mean by the terms. We can refer to leaders simply as those who occupy identified offices or institutions; or more generally, we can refer to power wielders. However, leaders and followers are defined by a dynamic relationship that goes beyond formal institutions. Leadership implies that leaders seek to and can effect change and that followers will go along with those changes.[1] This is why leadership is associated with power—institutional, economic, and military—but it also implies more complex ways in which some have the capacity to effect change while others do not.

A number of issues emerge when defining leaders as those who can bring about change. First, there is the question of whether we expect leaders to always have their preferences met or do we assume that leadership matters only under certain conditions such as periods of instability or to effect first-order changes?[2] Even powerful leaders pick and choose their fights. The important point in trying to assess leadership is to identify when actors give a high priority to a desired outcome and have the capacity to achieve it while others follow along. Second, and along these same lines, do leaders have to constitute monolithic blocs, remaining constant in time and internally coherent? Or can we have collective leadership, where the reins are seized by different actors in different circumstances but they somehow constitute a collective enterprise?[3] These definitional and conceptual issues are especially relevant when discussing leadership between states and in governing structures that they may create.

In international relations, despite the formal equality of sovereign states, a number of terms and concepts have been used to describe a leader: superpower, hegemon, even imperial power.[4] Whereas discussion about hierarchy is not unusual in international relations, the EU is more likely to be discussed in terms of being "leaderless."[5] The entire institutional and decision-making architecture of the EU is designed to ensure that no single institution, member state, or group of member states can concentrate power so that they emerge as leaders. Moreover, a series of delicate balances have been struck—between large and small states, between European institutions, between geographic areas—that have served to put brakes on putative leaders. Yet, change happens and the question is whether it is useful to identify leaders as architects of this change.

We can draw on some of the leadership on policy-making within states to arrive at an understanding of the types of leaders and followers we might find in the EU. Jack Hayward distinguished between heroic and humdrum leadership. In the former, leaders set "explicit long term objectives to be pursued by maximum co-ordination of public policies and by an ambitious assertion of political will,"[6] while decisions with humdrum leadership, "are arrived at by a continuous process of mutual adjustment between a plurality of autonomous policy-makers operating in the context of a highly fragmented multiple flow of influence."[7] He argues that the secret of the Monnet method was to combine both in order for the integration process to proceed. Heroic leadership by stealth meant that the muddling through of decision-making in a range of policy areas would serve long-term objectives set by leaders who had a determined political will to "create an ever closer union." This distinction may help us understand the dynamics between member states in the EU. As we will see below, we can have a core group of member states assuming a leadership role within some parts of the integration process exist alongside a more fluid relationship of policy leaders and laggards who change from one area to the next.

It would be an oversimplification to argue that the larger member states within the EU are the repository of heroic leadership, while EU institutions are the bedrock of humdrum leadership. As we will see below, bold initiatives require the consent, if not support, of key member states, such as France and Germany. It is difficult to imagine important transformations, such as the Treaty of Maastricht, without the leadership of powerful states.[8] However, forming the political will to take those bold steps has often involved European institutions and a plurality of actors influencing incremental change. A core group of powerful member states, then, are necessary for leadership within the EU, but this does not mean that they can always dictate the pace, scale, and nature of change. As Simone Bunse and Kalypso Nicolaidis point out in Chapter 18 of this volume, small states can act not only as a counterweight to more powerful members but can also exert leadership themselves at certain points. Leadership, like integration itself, also takes place by stealth, in the tiny steps taken to solve less politically visible issues. The EU's highly complex decision-making architecture has created the paradoxical situation in which the institutional power of member states has often led to leadership that can only move at the speed set by humdrum leadership.

22.1.1 Differentiated Europe, Different Europe

The debate about hierarchy in relations between sovereign states is especially relevant for the EU, which has tried to go beyond the calculations of power politics to establish relations on the basis of problem-solving, consensus, and the rule of law.[9] Yet, even if power politics were no longer present in the EU, thus negating important differences between member states, the latter could differ amongst themselves according to a whole range of other criteria. More importantly, they could position themselves on the pace and depth they wished to pursue integration, thus raising the prospect of a Union that is not uniform in its membership. A more flexible and differentiated form of integration could reflect, and lead to, the existence of a core group of states that may be leading others. This has led to the creation of an entire lexicon of terms that has tried to understand the extent to which there might be differentiation within the EU.

Discussion about a differentiated Europe emerged prominently in the mid-1990s. One of the central issues at the heart of the 1996–1997 IGC, culminating in the Treaty of Amsterdam, was how to arrive at architecture to accommodate and institutionalize differentiation. Helen Wallace identified a series of factors that shifted the debate from one that saw any form of integration that was not symmetrical and uniform as a failure to one that looked to "flexibility" as the key to propel integration forward.[10] First, the plan to create a single currency clearly created different forms of membership as some states had chosen to opt-out while others might not meet the entry criteria. This was formal recognition that there were EU projects that would involve only the ready and willing. We can add to this the Schengen agreement, which began formally outside of the treaties, as further evidence that differentiation was well and truly now part of the integration process. Second, the enlargements completed by the mid-1990s (EU-15) and the prospect of new members from Eastern and Central Europe, introduced members who perhaps were not willing to travel at the same speed as others. Third, enlargement along with the emergence of a growing range of issues, such as immigration and the environment, had raised expectations of a deepening of the integration process: expectations that, again, were not shared by all member states. There was, then, the growing sense that it was becoming increasingly problematic for the EU to develop broader policy-making powers going forward uniformly as a group of fifteen (or twenty-seven) member states. There were increasing claims that if there was a core group of states that wanted to go further and faster with integration, then this need not be seen as an obstacle to integration. Indeed, it could be a way for leaders to go forward and then eventually have the others follow.[11]

The search for flexibility led to a range of terms that have been used to frame relations between states. The formal legal term used in treaty language is "enhanced cooperation." Title VII of the Treaty on European Union allowed a majority of states, through QMV, to seek closer forms of cooperation provided it was consistent with the *acquis communautaire* and worked to further the objectives of the Treaty. Enhanced cooperation could be used only if it was to push integration forward, not as a way for a majority of states to take steps backwards. Flexibility or differentiation was a way to bring within the EU's institutional framework mechanisms by which member states that wanted to lead could do so.[12]

What was formalized in the treaties in the second half of the 1990s was the recognition that a language and concepts were needed to capture what was increasingly a differentiated or flexible form of integration.[13] It represented an important change in thinking about differentiation and, by consequence, leadership in the EU. Generally, until the Maastricht Treaty, any talk of flexible arrangements was seen as opening a Pandora's box of providing for two different but related possible outcomes. It could pave the way for a "hard core" of states to formally assume a leadership role within the Union and thereby upset the series of delicate balances upon which rested European unity. It also could create an opportunity for those states that did not share the same vision of what should be areas of common action to choose not to take part; possibly fraying unity of purpose in those areas where all members had agreed to cooperate. However, a number of forceful arguments emerged in the wake of the Maastricht Treaty which claimed that a rigid approach that saw common action based only on the participation of all member states would threaten unity more than differentiation. The risk was that those states that wanted to deepen the areas of common action would seek to do so outside of the treaties as they would see their ambitions for Europe thwarted by having to move at the speed of the slowest member state. Indeed, in order to maintain momentum for creating an ever closer union, it was proving to be increasingly clear that some form of differentiation was needed as it would be difficult to get all fifteen members to agree on common action. Especially important in presenting these arguments was a document prepared in 1994 by two German Christian Democrats, Karl Lamers and Wolfgang Schäuble, who argued that a group of core states needed to be able to push ahead within the EU framework.[14] Reflecting on the growing number of member states and the changes introduced by the Maastricht treaty, they called for member states that wanted to embark on more intense forms of integration to begin to find more flexible institutional forms to do so.

Alexander Stubb provides a very useful categorization of the various terms that emerged to understand differentiation and which have been used interchangeably, often erroneously.[15] He identifies three broad categories of differentiation—multi-speed, variable geometry, and à la carte—that operate according to a different logic and, for our purposes, have different consequences for leadership amongst member states. Multi-speed Europe sees a core group of states ready and able to go further in developing close forms of cooperation push forward on the assumption that the others will catch up later. The best example here would be economic and monetary union. As Stubb argues, the element that defines multi-speed differentiation is time; that is, some member states are in a position to go forward at a particular point in time and do so with the assumption that they are blazing a path for others to follow later.[16] This form of differentiation does provide for a hard core of states that can be leaders in the sense that they represent the vanguard for others to follow.

Arguably, a Europe of many speeds is a variation on the neo-functionalist theme of spillover. It allows for the interests of those member states who want a closer union in different areas to co-exist alongside those that see a more limited role for the EU. However, there was also the expectation that enhanced cooperation by the vanguard states would eventually pull along at least those that were willing but not ready for closer integration and possibly even those states that had the capacity but were originally unwilling. Creating institutions that account for a Europe of many speeds would facilitate this process. Former Commission President Romano Prodi had compared the process of European integration to riding a bike; one had to keep pedaling to avoid falling. A multi-speed Europe allows for those states that are willing and able to keep pedaling to do so; and to continue the cycling metaphor, the pack will feel compelled to catch up to the group that has broken away. However, the assumption is that the leadership role played by the core states will be short-lived, as once the other states catch up there is no longer any further need for the vanguard states, and less vertical forms of relations between states will emerge.

Variable geometry, on the other hand, is not about time but about space. It recognizes that not all the member states want to reach the same end point in the integration process so that more durable forms of differentiation are created. A gap emerges between a core group of states that forges ahead and those that have chosen, or have had chosen for them, not to push forward. Given that the aim here is to seek out cooperation only where and with whom it is possible, the existing treaties could serve as a constraint. Variable geometry, then, refers to a range of structures that can bring together a limited number of states, not all of which are EU members. Examples of this form of differentiation include commercial or technological projects such as Airbus or the European Space Agency. However, the structures do not need to be permanently separate as the case of the Schengen Protocols illustrates. What began as something outside of the treaties has slowly been "communitarized," although it is still not entirely uniform as some member states remain outside the agreement while some non-EU states are part of the Schengen area. Variable geometry, as Stubbs argues, can have elements of neo-functionalism as well as realism. It can set in motion pressures for deeper forms of integration and may strengthen the need for supranational institutions and forms of governance. On the other hand, variable geometry might also be simply an intense form of intergovernmental cooperation. It is a strategy, then, that could have some appeal to both those wanting more and those wanting less Europe.

The third form of differentiation identified by Stubb is an "à la carte" Europe, where member states can choose which areas they would like to participate in and opt out from others.[17] There is no statement of common objectives here; rather, states choose to opt out, thus highlighting areas where there is no consensus on the way forward. À la carte differentiation tends to favor more realist views of relations between member states. Thus, it tends to focus on the ways in which states choose not to be led by others in the integration process. This was most evident with the decision by the United Kingdom, Denmark, and Sweden not to take part in the single currency. Opt-outs have come to be used increasingly as a way to solve intractable problems in European negotiations, as witnessed by those granted to Ireland in the wake of the first referendum on the Lisbon treaty.

The discussion of differentiation reveals that there are many ways in which member states can choose to pursue their interests within the EU. Flexibility thus affects the ability of some states to be leaders in a consistent way. The fact that states can have the option in some instances to select which policy areas they will participate in means that they can choose not to be led by others. On the other hand, a multi-speed Europe, as well as variable geometry, does provide greater opportunities, perhaps even more so than uniformity, for a core group of states to exert forms of leadership over others. By choosing to deepen integration in specific policy areas, they may change the calculation of national interests for other states so that they too choose to take part.

22.2 A FRANCO–GERMAN DIRECTORATE?

If there was a core group of states that steered, and perhaps commanded, the integration process and the EU it was to be found in a putative Franco–German axis. The relationship between the two was always going to draw a great deal of interest with respect to their role within the EU: because of their size, the centrality of their economies for Europe, and because the often conflictual relationship between the two had led to the war that resulted in the perceived need for some form of integration.[18] Moreover, throughout the history of the EU, French and German leaders have gone to great lengths to highlight the "special" relationship between the two states. They constituted the "core" of Europe, its "engine," "heart," or the "vanguard" of integration. Implicit in references to a Franco–German leadership is that the "core" Europe that runs at a faster speed is to be found in this axis; and it carries along the rest of the Union. Clearly, there is no other bilateral relationship between member states as intensive and extensive as that between France and Germany; and for the most part, it has been the umbrella of European integration that has been the pretext to closer cooperation and in some instances institutional fusion. Whether this has constituted leadership remains to be explored.

The notion of a special Franco–German relationship as the engine of Europe is based on a number of premises. First, the two states have increasingly fused parts of the machinery of government so that the day-to-day business of governing is no longer seen solely in national terms. Joint military commands have drawn the most attention, but perhaps less visible, though no less important, is the intensive level of exchange between different ministries. The regular meetings of the heads of government no longer generate intense scrutiny as they are seen as normal business. The durability of the relationship is seen in its persistence despite government changes and leaders of different stripes over the decades. More importantly, as Douglas Webber found, French senior public officials see the relationship with their German counterparts as "second nature."[19] The erosion of national borders between the different governments has, over time, become institutionalized so that the "second nature" has also become a set of rules that govern the bilateral relationship.

This leads to a second point highlighted by Webber and others who have explored the different dimensions of the Franco–German relationship. The Elysée Treaty of 1963 committed the two sides to consult on all major foreign policy decisions and to agree, as much as possible, on a common position. This has been, it is argued, especially the case with respect to assuming common positions on and in the EU. The basic premise is that the two states see their national interest as inexorably twined around the relationship and that this is the core of a "European" interest. It is this confluence of French and German national interests with the evolution of a bilateral relationship largely under the umbrella of European integration that has led to the claim that this is where the "core" of the EU rests. Proponents of realism and intergovernmentalism tend to look to the role of the two powerful states in driving forward the process of integration as evidence that the EU is no different from any other relationship between states.[20]

While there is no doubt that Germany and France have worked closely within Europe and their relationship has been pivotal at critical moments in the evolution of the EU, trying to argue that this constitutes a "core" that provides leadership within the EU is more difficult. It may be the case that France and Germany combined to provide forms of heroic leadership at particular points in time, inspired by tandems of political elites such as de Gaulle–Adenauer, D'Estaing–Schmidt, and Mitterrand–Kohl. However, the notion of Franco–German directorate has its limits. First, being a driving force behind European integration does not necessarily mean that the "motor" of the EU steers the process.[21] France and Germany, and the Franco–German relationship, may be indispensable for any major development to take place in the EU but that does not mean that they necessarily exert leadership.[22] Second, as mentioned above, governing in the EU has been led mostly by humdrum leadership partly aiming to achieve some long-term political objective. There is a danger in overstating the importance of a motor in a decision-making system that has so many braking mechanisms. Third, the commitment to find a common position does not always mean that the two will agree or act in a coordinated fashion. The list of instances where they differed is long, ranging from the recognition of the sovereignty of Croatia and Slovenia in 1991 to the more recent differences on how to respond to the global economic recession and the debt crisis in Greece. France and Germany differ, for instance, on the question of the reform of the Security Council of the United Nations. In this instance, clearly national interests are at play and perhaps in conflict as the German path to a possible seat as a permanent member may be impeded by the presence of France. France's (and the United Kingdom's) position in the Security Council is also an obstacle to the two countries assuming a leadership role in making a case for an EU seat.

The Franco–German relationship, then, is a necessary but not sufficient condition for the promotion of the national interest of both states. Moreover, this implies that it is an essential element for decisions to be taken in the EU but not necessarily the only one. It is very hard for things to get done if the two do not share some common ground. But this does not necessarily mean that they can exert leadership and that whatever positions they agree upon become those of the other member states. If there is to be heroic leadership provided by member states, it is likely to start from, and possibly end, with the Franco–German relationship.

22.3 POLICY LEADERS AND LAGGARDS

If the close relationship between the two largest and central member states is not enough to generate the political, economic, and institutional resources to exert leadership over other member states, does it make any sense then to talk about leaders and followers? There is another area of EU activity that has drawn attention with respect to the question of leadership amongst members and this has to do less with what drives the integration process than with how decisions are made and policy outputs produced. It may be the case that the factors and conditions that provide for leadership in the integration process are not be the same as those that create leaders and followers when it comes to making policy decisions.

Realist and intergovernmental approaches would suggest that the ability of member states to affect change would be largely determined by the material resources that they can bring to bear in their relations. If this were the case, we would find that the large member states, despite an institutional architecture that prevented their dominance, prevailed in most if not all areas of policy. Yet, this is not the case and we can identify "policy-makers" and "policy-takers" in different areas. This suggests that there are other resources that may affect the capacity of states to influence others that are not necessarily related to size or material resources.

It is worth examining the case of the role of the Nordic member states—in particular, Sweden, Denmark, and Finland—in some areas of policy to illustrate how leaders can come in many shapes and sizes in the EU. They are useful cases for a number of reasons. First, they are not part of the original six members of the EU (although Denmark did enter nearly twenty years before the other two) so that in some way many important features of the Union were already established when they joined. Second, especially in the case of Denmark, they are sometimes considered to be on the margins of the EU, not because of their geographic location but because they make much use of the differentiation procedures, so that they do not participate in many policy areas. We have, then, in the case of the Nordic countries states that would more likely be followers than leaders, or to stick with the terminology used, policy-takers rather than policy-makers.

Yet, it may be argued that even the Nordic countries have been able to exercise leadership. For instance, the 2002 Danish presidency of the Council has been seen as an example of a strong presidency, providing a degree of leadership and producing important policy outputs.[23] Thomas Pedersen argues that small states, such as Denmark, can provide greater leadership through the presidency because they see it as an important opportunity to punch above their weight on the international stage and will dedicate more time and resources. They also tend to put greater emphasis on negotiation than larger states and come with less political baggage that makes this job easier. Similar patterns have been identified with the Swedish presidency and its successful introduction of conflict prevention in the CFSP during its first ever Council presidency.[24]

What the case of the Nordic countries suggests is that material resources, primarily but not exclusively related to size, are not the only factors that states bring to bear when trying to affect policy outputs. Leadership can also result from the framing of policy questions, the setting of agendas, and diplomacy. This humdrum leadership may not be the drama of a clash between powerful states but this sort of incremental change can reveal elements of leadership amongst member states nonetheless. These are resources that are enhanced by institutional capacity to set clear priorities and to implement short- and longer-term strategies, as well as by policy legacies that bring with them expertise and capacity to control information, not to mention a reputation for being a vanguard in a policy area. For instance, returning to the case of the Nordic countries, they have been able to shape an important part of the ESDP so that civilian crisis management is very much part of Europe's role as a security actor. It did so despite the opposition of large member states, often seen as the architects of ESDP, such as France.[25] Granted, the influence of Nordic countries tends to be restricted to the civilian side of the ESDP, with the broader military questions perhaps still dominated by the larger member states. However, the fact that European definitions of security policy, and a more general understanding of "comprehensive security," contain a civilian component is due to the capacity of member states, such as the Nordic ones, to exploit their reputation in the field of civilian power and the commitment to commit resources to implementing the policy.

The examples of the Nordic states are illustrative of the more general point that material resources may not be the only variable that determines whether member states affect their capacity to lead others in directions they may not have previously thought of or even wanted. It also suggests that while material resources as a source of leadership may remain fairly constant and visible, policy leadership may be more fluid. States do not have the same policy expertise, reputation, and legacy in all areas, so that they may, for instance, be able to set the standard for civilian crisis management or the environment but not telecoms or banking. We cannot speak, therefore, of a "core" Europe in that the member states that matter change from one policy area to the next. So, we have leadership but it is more likely to be of the humdrum rather than the heroic sort.

22.4 CONCLUSION

One can draw upon a whole range of clichés to describe leaders and followers in the EU—"too many cooks spoil the broth," "too many generals, not enough soldiers"—to capture the relationship of sovereign states under an institutional umbrella designed to avoid the emergence of a hegemonic centre. As we have seen, it is not easy to identify a core group of states that may direct not only the long-term strategic interests of the Union, but also its more narrow policy areas that make for the muddling through that has come to characterize the EU. Yet, this has not prevented different types of leaders to emerge in the EU. Indeed, as Jack Hayward argues, the EU lacks leadership, not leaders.[26]

The EU's great challenge is that perhaps the time has come for more heroic forms of leadership to prevail over the reflex to revert to more humdrum relations between different groups of states. It also may be the case that an à la carte Europe, one where states simply opt-out rather than be led, may allow the EU to muddle through but it does make it likely that this will create pressures to eventually catch up with those who have gone ahead. A flexible Europe may be indeed necessary in order not to frustrate the demands of those who want an ever closer union. But it may be the case that it needs to be a flexible union that provides for greater space for heroic forms of leadership.

Notes

1. Barbara Kellerman and Scott W. Webster, "The Recent Literature on Public Leadership: Reviewed and Considered," *The Leadership Quarterly* 12, no. 6 (December 2001), 487.
2. Peter Hall, "Policy Paradigms, Social Learning, and the State: The Case of Economic Policymaking in Britain," *Comparative Politics* 25, no. 3 (April 1993), 275–96.
3. Dionyssis Dimitrakopoulos, "Collective Leadership in a Leaderless Europe: A Sceptical View," in Jack Hayward, ed., *Leaderless Europe* (Oxford: Oxford University Press, 2008), 288–304.
4. Oran Young, "Leadership and Regime Formation: On the Development of Institutions in International Society," *International Organization* 45, no. 3 (Summer 1991), 281–308.
5. Hayward, *Leaderless Europe.*
6. Jack Hayward, "Introduction: Inhibited Consensual Leadership within an Interdependent Confederal Europe," in Hayward, *Leaderless Europe*, 7.
7. Jack Hayward, "Change and choice: the agenda of planning," in Jack Hayward and Michael Watson, eds, *Planning, Politics and Public Policy: The British, French and Italian Experience* (Cambridge: Cambridge University Press, 1975), 4.
8. For a discussion of the role of different types of member states at critical points in the evolution of the EU, see Derek Beach, and Colette Mazzucelli, eds, *Leadership in the Big Bangs of European Integration* (Basingstoke: Palgrave Macmillan, 2007).
9. David Lake, "The New Sovereignty in International Relations," *International Studies Review* 5, no. 3 (September 2003), 303–23.
10. Helen Wallace, "Flexibility: A Tool of Integration or a Restraint on Disintegration?" in Karlheinz Neunreither and Antje Wiener, eds, *European Integration After Amsterdam: Institutional Dynamics and Prospects for Democracy* (Oxford: Oxford University Press, 2000), 177–8.
11. General Secretariat of the Council of the European Union, "Reflection Group Report and Other References for Information Purposes, 1996 Intergovernmental Conference," (Brussels, December 1996).
12. Claus Dieter Ehlermann, "Differentiation, Flexibility, Closer Co-Operation: The New Provisions of the Amsterdam Treaty," *European Law Journal* 4, no. 3 (September 1998), 246–70.
13. For example, see Claus Dieter Ehlermann, "Increased Differentiation or Stronger Uniformity," *EUI Working Paper* RSC No. 95/21 (1995), 1–35.

14. Karl Lamers and Wolfgang Schäuble, "Reflections on European Policy," *Europe Documents* N. 1895/96 (September 7, 1994).

15. Alexander C.-G. Stubb, "A Categorization of Differentiated Integration," *Journal of Common Market Studies* 34, no. 2 (June 1996), 283–95.

16. Stubb, "A Categorization of Differentiated Integration," 285.

17. Stubb, "A Categorization of Differentiated Integration."

18. William E. Paterson, "Did Germany and Germany Lead Europe? A Retrospect," in Hayward, *Leaderless Europe*, 89–111.

19. Douglas Webber, "Introduction," in Douglas Webber, ed., *The Franco-German Relationship in the European Union* (London: Routledge, 1999), 2.

20. Andrew Moravcsik, "Negotiating the Single European Act: National Interests and Conventional Statecraft in the European Community," *International Organization* 45, no. 1 (Winter 1991), 19–56.

21. Webber, "Introduction."

22. Paterson, "Did Germany and Germany Lead Europe? A Retrospect."

23. Thomas Pedersen, "Questions of Leadership," *Cooperation and Conflict* 38, no. 3 (September 2003), 299–304.

24. Annika Björkdahl, "Norm Advocacy: A Small State Strategy to Influence the EU," *Journal of European Public Policy* 15, no. 1 (January 2008), 135–54.

25. Peter Viggo Jakobsen, "Small States, Big Influence: The Overlooked Nordic Influence on the Civilian ESDP," *Journal of Common Market Studies* 47, no. 1 (January 2009), 81–102.

26. Jack Hayward, "Strategic Innovation by Insider Influence: Monnet to Delors," in Hayward, *Leaderless Europe* (Oxford: Oxford University Press, 2008), 15.

PART V

INSTITUTIONS

CHAPTER 23

··

COUNCIL OF MINISTERS
AND EUROPEAN COUNCIL

··

JEFFREY LEWIS

THE EU's Council system is designed to represent national interests and make joint decisions. Descriptively, the Council is a composite organization of committee governance made up of multiple parts, from the heads of state and government who constitute European Council summits to national ministers meeting in different policy configurations of the Council of the European Union (also known by its more familiar name, the Council of Ministers) down to the national experts who comprise working groups and discuss the minutiae of legislative proposals. In total, the Council holds more than 4,500 official meetings per year.[1] Institutionally, the Council is a mixed-motive setting since it serves to safeguard national interests (however narrow or rooted in "special circumstances") *but to also* subject them to a collective legitimation process that can determine what counts as an acceptable interest in the EU context.

The Council's modus operandi—a segmented division of labor by policy specialization, a bias towards *in camera* negotiation, and a reliance on informal group norms to guide appropriate behavior and limit opportunism—endows the institution with a hybrid character, part-intergovernmental and part-supranational.[2] Practitioners refer to the "double hatting" requirements of their work, to deliver both at home and collectively by finding solutions that everyone can live with.[3] Interviews with Council actors regularly produce unprompted self-reflections on this unwritten part of their job description. Some even equate their work as requiring a "Janus face."[4] In this regard, standard textbook imagery of the Council as an intergovernmental bargaining table misleads, since the collectivity dimension of the Council's work imparts a sense of responsibility for national agents to make joint decisions, compromise, and move the legislative workload forward.[5] Taken together, across a wide range of negotiation settings and policy-specialized networks of national officials, the Council defies simple categorization and is an enigmatic construct. Like Mona Lisa's smile, the meaning behind much of the observable behavior in the Council's work—such as the penchant for consensus-seeking or shared expectations to explain positions and not make demands by fiat—remains subject to different interpretation. Helen Wallace equates the Council to the "chameleon" of EU institutions with good cause.[6]

For much of the Council's history, the institution remained a challenging "black box" for researchers to study, but since the 1990s the state-of-the-art has significantly improved thanks to more publically available data (such as voting records) and greater academic attention.[7] Considerable debate remains however on key issues of how power transacts in the Council, how negotiations really work, and the relative importance of formal and informal dimensions of the Council's organization.[8] The remainder of this chapter is organized as follows. The next section looks at the hybrid institutional qualities of the Council in greater detail and examines the deliberate efforts to instill a consensus-inducing environment for joint decision-making. This is followed by an analysis of how the Council has evolved internally, in relations with other key EU institutions like the European Parliament, and in the wake of Eastern enlargement. Finally, a brief conclusion reiterates key themes and underscores the value of pluralistic theories and methods in Council research.

23.1 THE COUNCIL'S AFFINITY FOR CONSENSUS

When the Council was originally established (as the Special Council of Ministers) there was a clear intent to develop something outside the typical mold for multilateral negotiation. Ernst Haas was an early observer of this, and he described the Council as a "novel community-type organ."[9] He thus drew a sharp distinction between the nascent EU's Council and other regional bodies such as the Council of Europe and its Committee of Ministers, which he summed up as "an orthodox intergovernmental agency whose zeal for European unity has been conspicuous by its pallor."[10]

In contrast, the EU Council system was endowed with a qualitatively different institutional environment which had the capacity to alter the calculus of individual rationalities, and notions of "the self" (for more on constructivist views of institutional effects, see Chapter 3, this volume). The joint decision-making style of the EU's Council system is premised on a consensus-seeking culture rather than formal voting.[11] The roots of this consensus culture are as old as the Council itself. There is, of course, a highly ordered system of formal voting rules, minimum blocking thresholds, rights for near blocking minorities, and policy-specific vetoes (including member states' idiosyncratic right to draw "red line" no-go areas, such as European-level fiscal policy). But there is in addition a dynamic, process-level dimension of informal norms which aim toward mutual accommodation for domestic difficulties based on group standards for legitimating such accommodation.

The function of this informal dimension is to routinize a global, collective preference for consensus-based decision-making. The affinity for consensus is reflected in the

Council's voting record, which historically averages about 80 percent of all legislative acts.[12] This means the bulk of legislation formally subject to QMV is adopted by consensus with no pubic dissension and, hence, no need for a formal vote at all.[13] And contested votes tend to cluster in a few policy areas (nearly half involve agricultural and fisheries), frequently involve the political gesture of "abstaining" rather than an explicit "No," and often involve a lone dissenter (rather than multiple dissatisfied members or near blocking minorities).[14] Some forums, especially those more sheltered from public audiences, can use group norms to expose "laughable" reservations or unconvincing arguments and place group pressure on member-state delegations to rethink a position. For example, collective delegitimation of arguments can take the form of shaming, which one permanent representative described as "faked outrage" by the group. There is also occasional recourse to collusive "plotting" of compromise solutions to sell back home.[15] Another variation is to spotlight those who become isolated; the select use of the "silent procedure" can prove instrumental in overcoming stubborn national reserves by putting the onus on a delegation with special problems to speak up by a certain date or else live with a collective agreement.[16] These engrained practices help support Simon Hix's claim that the EU is "perhaps more consensus-oriented in its design than any polity in the history of democratic governance."[17]

Thus, both macro-historical voting evidence and fine-grained case study analyses point to an institutional setting for interstate negotiation which fosters a norm-rich, consensus-inducing social environment for joint decision-making. The policy segmentation tends to instill repeated face-to-face encounters where trust, mutual responsiveness, and unconditional ("diffuse") acts of reciprocity can accumulate social capital and in-group patterns of affect which reinforce compromise- and consensus-seeking behavior. There are group norms that proscribe and prescribe behavior.[18] A simple example is the norm that no one can be a *demandeur* too often and expect the others to listen. A more cognitively complex one is the shared understanding that one must explain arguments with reasoning and/or justification (on the grounds of shared standards, such as non-discrimination, fairness, and proportionality) to gain the sympathy of one's colleagues.[19] Some institutional settings are more thickly bound by shared behavioral standards. For example, it is virtually anathema in COREPER to push for a vote; group consensus norms are so strong that efforts are made to acquire the consent of dissenters to be outvoted *before* a formal vote is called. And in the policy area of CFSP, norms for consensus include "opprobrium attached to blocking or stalling."[20] In a few policy areas—agriculture and the budget stand out— there are thinner norms and, hence, a higher recourse to voting, posturing, and bargaining breakdowns.[21]

While we still lack a systematic understanding of where, when, and why norm-guided behavior adheres in Council venues, there is a growing body of research that documents the scope conditions under which norms operate. For example, denser normative rules are found in Council settings with higher levels of insulation from domestic politics. The tendency for insulated committees to work by norm-governed consensus habits eliminates the need for formal voting which would openly expose divisions and allows member states to reach agreements "without necessarily having to identify winners and losers in the process."[22] Forums with higher levels of issue intensity and/or cross-sectoral mandates also tend to follow more group norms and rely on consensus compared with those who hold a more narrow mandate (compare the foreign ministers in the work of "general affairs" with the ministers of the Agriculture and Fisheries Council (AGFISH) or the preparatory habits of COREPER with the Special Committee on Agriculture (SCA)). Council settings where technical knowledge is highly specialized also have a higher tendency to rely on norm-guided deliberative processes of negotiation.[23] Another plausible scope condition for the Council's normative environment is the enabling force of weak political party dynamics. Markus Jachtenfuchs argues that the EU is a negotiating system with low levels of political party competition which averts issues from "the logic of adversarial politics" and creates "a strong tendency to moderate socioeconomic cleavages" by compromise and consensus.[24]

We also see affirming evidence of normative standards in instances where violations occur. An overt example was when Polish Prime Minister Kaczynski linked the issue of Council voting weight negotiations in June 2007 to the argument that Poland would have a larger population, and hence be entitled to more votes, save for the country's war deaths. As noted by *The Economist*, "this nationalistic sally broke all the rules of European behavior."[25] Another interesting pattern of deviance is seen in Rebecca Adler-Nissen's research on British and Danish opt-outs and the "compensatory practices" by their Brussels' delegations who perceive a responsibility to rebuild goodwill and social influence.[26] More intriguing from a norms perspective is how the legal opt-outs can create a sense of embarrassment for British and Danish officials in the context of Council meetings. Adler-Nissen uses interview evidence to trace how the opt-outs act as a "psychological prison" for negotiators who practice a kind of self-censorship in staying silent during discussions and being overly cautious with legal interpretations.[27] Although they are legally unbound by significant areas of JHA due to the opt-out, she documents how Danish negotiators nevertheless remain normatively bound to participation in JHA deliberations.[28]

In summary, the Council is best viewed as an institution designed to pattern mutually reinforcing habits of cooperation and consensus-seeking around a social environment where trust, reciprocity, and adherence to group norms become habitualized within different segmented "clubs" of policy specialists. To really get at the fine-grained behavioral motivations among Council actors requires better analytical precision (such as identifying underlying scope conditions) as well as broader, more inclusive models of rationality. Supplanting the instrumental logic behind norm conformance with non-instrumental, appropriateness accounts can explain more, and more accurately when it comes to everyday Council behavior. More research is needed on how Council norms can obtain durability from mutually reinforcing effects which act to temper narrower, "thin" conceptions of individual rationality. One highly suggestive example is Elinor Ostrom's work on how reputation, trust, and reciprocity are the core microfoundational relationships that affect cooperation in collective action settings and are positively reinforcing over time.[29]

23.2 THE EVOLVING INSTITUTIONS OF THE COUNCIL SYSTEM

In this section, the focus is on innovation and change in how the Council operates. Compared to other major EU institutions, the Council's internal organization has undergone more incremental and informal revision over time, even in the face of big external "shocks" such as the addition of twelve new members since 2004. Overall, the Council now shares substantial legislative authority with the European Parliament but has enhanced executive functions through European Council summitry, the rotating presidency, and an increasingly powerful Council Secretariat (CGS).

23.2.1 Negotiation via Insulation and "Clan-Like" Networks

Early on, the Council developed a fondness for negotiation away from the limelight of domestic audiences, and created a series of de facto decision-making bodies at the preparatory level. In particular, this applies to COREPER I ("deputies") and II ("ambassadors"), but we should also include the early specialization of the SCA (1960) and the Monetary Committee (now the EFC) (1958). This basic trait, a preference for *in camera* negotiation and a reliance on de facto decision-making, has far reaching implications for how power transacts and where authority resides within the various layers of the Council system. As an institution, the Council has obvious elements of hierarchy: the European Council as the undisputed political heavyweight forum, the ministers' juridical decision-making legitimacy within the Council of Ministers, the Treaty-enshrined "senior preparatory role" for COREPER, and so on. But in terms of inter-organizational power, the hierarchy image can mislead. Or at least it risks overlooking ways in which the Council functions as a network organization of authority rather than as a corporate hierarchy.[30] The saw-tooth quality to how legislative dossiers shuttle through the Council between the ministers, preparatory committees, and working groups obviates any neat distinction between where "technical" and "political" issues are resolved or where substantive components of an agreement are reached. The networking relations of authority within the Council do not match the formal institutional structure since the boundaries between the technical and the political are "constantly blurred."[31] One is struck with the extent to which this pattern is both systematic across the Council's policy competencies and ostensibly by design (rather than patchy and contingent). Jachtenfuchs makes a similar observation, where he notes that "the relatively fluid and complex world of EU committees in the broadest sense is not an indicator of chaos or member state dominance but functional for problem-solving."[32]

This general point also holds true for the misleading clarity of Council agendas separated into "A" (agreed) and "B" (needs discussion) points. Aside from the messy mix of permutations (how to code "false A points," "false B points," etc.) it is nearly impossible to quantify in the aggregate where the *substance* of legislative agreements were reached merely by the metric of whether it appeared on the agenda and if any discussion took place. Attempts to do so, such as recent work by Frank Häge, reveal how difficult it is to answer such straightforward questions as "who decides?" In his findings, ministers decide 63 percent versus 37 percent by committees. But note the coding rules: "A proposal was coded as having been decided at the ministerial level when it had been debated by ministers at some stage"; "only dossiers that showed no direct involvement of ministers were coded as having been decided by a committee."[33] In a footnote, he acknowledges that this coding is "likely to yield figures that exaggerate the influence of ministers" and "what exactly a final decision entails in terms of committee influence is often not clear."[34]

Crude quantification is bound to miss the richness of patterns that can occur in this network environment. One pattern that has been around since at least the 1960s is Emile Noël's observation that the ministers prepare discussions for the permanent representatives (permreps) as much as vice versa.[35] Some permreps are told by their ministers that they are the decision-maker on a given issue. Some, only half-jokingly, say they get the best results when they write their own instructions. Likewise, the working-group level sometimes reaches agreement on substantive definitional issues or frames emerging majority views in path-dependent terms. Sometimes the system relies on the European Council for agreement on technical issues (although participants typically attribute this pattern to the inefficiencies of an individual presidency rather than structural, network characteristics per se). The overall point here is twofold. First, there is often more going on than first meet's the eye in Council negotiations, and this creates huge challenges to operationalize "large-N" formal models of Council decision-making behavior. And second, that this is a challenge stems directly from the purposive design of Council deliberations to operate by networked, "clan-like" relations of power and authority (rather than a straightforward corporate hierarchy).

In recent years, the Council has tried to address the cloaked, behind closed doors image of internal deliberations with a series of "transparency-enhancing" efforts. Foremost has been a loosening of rules on the public availability of documents. Since 1995, the formal voting record has been made public. Select meetings of the ministers are broadcast on TV and the internet, although many are quick to point out that when the cameras switch on behavior changes immediately and the ministers read from preset speeches. Transparency reforms aside, the Council continues to operate in mostly closed settings with a relatively high degree of insulation for national negotiators. One could even argue such insulation was an original design trait of the Council's working methods. From a rational choice perspective, David Stasavage has convincingly shown how the Council benefits from a lack of transparency in removing the incentive for negotiators to engage in posturing and pandering with uncompromising positions for domestic consumption purposes.[36] And Daniel Naurin finds there is a noticeable difference between the behavioral logics of the "public frontstage" and the "private backstage" found in more insulated settings.[37] Even in co-decision with the European Parliament, created to make the legislative process more democratically accountable, the development of more *in camera* methods, such as the "trialogue," has proven instrumental in reaching early agreement.

23.2.2 The European Council as the EU's Ultimate Political Authority

Although it too conducts closed-door negotiations, the European Council was created for the altogether more visible function of providing strategic leadership. Despite intense public attention, and *ex post* journalistic accounts which sometimes contain verbatim reportage of deliberations, the European Council is perhaps the EU's most highly restricted negotiation venue designed to encourage a frank exchange of views and resolve issues too politicized or divisive to be handled elsewhere. Two interrelated facets of the European Council stand out. First, the timing of its innovation and regular use is telling of the underlying purpose for its design. Beginning in the early 1970s and regularized in 1974, the European Council became a high-level political shock absorber during the dark days of Eurosclerosis and economic hard times. The earlier ad hoc method (e.g. in the 1969 Hague Summit) was soon supplanted with a dependence on the European Council to regularly break deadlocks and provide the equivalent of political green lights to other layers of the Council. That the most commonly associated fountainhead of intergovernmental control has over time developed a series of supranationalizing decisions (such as committing to a single market and currency, upgrading foreign policy and homeland security functions, and so on) is a testament to the hybridity of the Council system discussed earlier.[38] Second, there are few parts of the entire institutional system that show such stress fatigue in an enlarged, deepened, and democratically contested Union as the European Council. Agendas have become more and more clogged despite at least one informal and one formal end-of-term capstone summit per presidency and a political agreement from 2002 to hold all meetings in Brussels (which helped pave the way for a new Council headquarters, the Résidence Palace, to be operational by 2013). In response, the Lisbon Treaty created a permanent president of the European Council. While optimists hold that such a position will give EU summitry more coherence and enhance the continuity of leadership, others note that it creates job confusion with the rotating presidency which will continue to operate at most other levels.

23.2.3 Rotating Leadership via the Council Presidency

The office of the Council Presidency, which rotates equally among member states every six months, is both an original design feature and one which has undergone substantial change over time. Until the 1970s, the office of presidency was viewed primarily as an "administrative chore,"[39] but became much more in vogue with the advent of regularized meetings of the heads of government (in 1974) and foreign policy discussions under the auspices of the EPC (started in 1970). Jonas Tallberg convincingly shows how the rotating presidency has evolved to meet growing functional demands for agenda management, brokering compromise efficiently, and representing the Union to the outside world. Even more, by rotating equally, the presidency diffuses power and provides each country "a privileged opportunity to influence the outcomes."[40]

The rotating presidency has also become a high-profile badge of honor among member states, who typically begin preparations eighteen months in advance. The presidency, by rotating equally, not only serves as a leveler of "big state–small state" egos, but creates an institutional role for national officials as stakeholders in the collective output of the Council. The rotating presidency carries with it opportunities for social influence and is seen as a way to prove (or improve) one's "European" credentials. As Elgström and Tallberg have documented, for new member states the presidency is seen as an "entrance exam" while for those "with tainted reputations, conformance to heralded Presidency norms offers a means of changing the established picture."[41] The presidency is also an important institutional mechanism in delivering so many consensus-based outcomes. Disproving the myth of a "neutral" EU president, recent research has shown how the office carries expectations of "procedural impartiality" in order to be able to broker compromise agreements which involve showing partiality and even delegitimizing minority viewpoints in favor of an emerging majority.[42] In this way, the rotating presidency is part of the Council culture to tame individual rationalities with group community standards that are based on distinct role expectations (as an honest broker, compromise builder), codes of conduct (not pushing for a vote), and cues for invoking an impartial or collective perspective (maintaining a separate national delegation at Council meetings, holding confessionals).

23.2.4 The Empowerment of the Council Secretariat

Few aspects of the Council have undergone more substantial internal restructuring in the last two decades than the Secretariat. While the formal aspects of the Council's bureaucracy has changed relatively little—they still keep notes and produce minutes of all meetings, translate documents, provide legal expertise—the informal brokerage functions have expanded widely across the legislative spectrum from co-decision to treaty reform negotiations. A key factor has been the expanded leadership role of the Secretariat's top job, the Secretary-General. During the long tenure of Secretary-General Niels Ersbøll (1980–1994), the CGS was transformed into a much more active participant in Council decision-making. The decision in 1999 to upgrade the position to include foreign policy leadership was a logical extension of the role.[43] While not reflected in any formal rules, informally the Secretariat grew in tasks and responsibilities, all the while staying in the background. In the process, the internal make-up of the CGS has changed significantly. The CGS now provides executive leadership for both CFSP/ESDP and JHA matters. It has also grown significantly in permanent staff, totaling more than 3,300 in the EU-27 (although 1,200 work on translation and document production). Tallberg connects the growth of presidency functions with the pragmatic needs of a more adept Council Secretariat in brokering agreement and providing continuity in Council operations.[44]

Frequently, CGS officials note they work best by staying invisible. The CGS has become more powerful over time primarily by acquiring an "honest broker" reputation that was previously reserved for the Commission.[45] The gradual empowerment of the CGS is one of the subtle ways the supranational entrepreneurship of the Commission is seen to be redundant.[46] The Council Secretariat specializes in finding compromise solutions everyone can live with, having the institutional memory and expertise to identify the middle ground, and occasionally coming up with a creative legal solution. Some presidencies even rely on the Secretariat to help run national coordination meetings in the home capital.[47]

23.2.5 Sharing Legislative Authority with the European Parliament

The advent of the European Parliament as a co-equal legislative partner signifies an important change in the Council's formal legislative powers. Since the 1990s, the tentative sharing of legislative authority (under the Maastricht Treaty) steadily expanded to the point where co-decision is now considered the EU's "ordinary legislative procedure."[48] Some now argue that the EU's legislative system is evolving towards a federal-like arrangement based on a bicameral design.[49] In effect, co-decision remixes the Council's portfolio of legislative–executive competences to share a significant portion of legislative rule with the European Parliament.

According to Michael Shackleton a "shared legislative culture" has emerged in Council–European Parliament relations which has greatly improved the efficiency of finding agreement at the first or second reading and avoiding the lengthy process of conciliation.[50] Now upwards of 85 percent of all co-decision files are concluded prior to conciliation. This is a remarkable change from the early days when Council–European Parliament relations were tense and guarded, and close to half of all files required full conciliation to reach compromise. A procedural innovation which proved key in building this legislative culture was the "trialogue" methodology where negotiations take place in a more restricted setting aided by close contacts between senior officials in the CGS and European Parliament Secretariat and geared toward a frank exchange of views and compromise.[51] It is not without irony that this new legislative process relies so heavily on the Council's venerated traditions of insulated, *in camera* methods for achieving results.

23.2.6 The Effects of Enlargement

The admission of twelve new member states since 2004 was initially feared by many as a qualitative shock to the Council's accustomed decision-making methods.[52] From logistical concerns about the unwieldy size of the negotiating table to more intangible effects on voting and consensus-seeking habits, the worry was that the Council's culture would never be same. However, such concerns now seem unfounded. Enlargement has not altered the Council's consensus culture. Between May 2004 and December 2006, contested votes occurred in less than 15 percent of all legislative acts and only 10.5 percent of all Council actions.[53] Forums designed for insulated deliberation continue to use group norms and standards to assess and accommodate national demands, and there is evidence to suggest the newcomers have adapted to this culture.[54] Some cite the "active observer" period as important in smoothing learning curves and socializing new members to the Council's informal group norms.[55]

Of course, working patterns have changed, such as the increased use of the written procedure, more formalized rules of procedure on "working methods,"[56] and the upgrading of the role of certain preparatory mechanisms such as the Antici group which serves in an advisory capacity to the EU ambassadors. There is a higher reliance on reading "formal statements" into the minutes of legislative acts which may signal a new informal method of expressing political dissatisfaction without the need for a contested vote.[57] Some Council participants cite a more impersonal atmosphere to meetings and a need for conducting more work on informal circuits at the margins of meetings and spending time on the telephone. But overall, the Council's culture and engrained habits of consensus have endured.

23.3 CONCLUSION

As the EU's premier interstate negotiation venue, the Council operates in a distinct institutional social environment. The best single indicator is the body of (mostly informal) group norms which proscribe and prescribe behavior and work to instill consensus-seeking habits. Both the hard data of the public voting record and a rich body of findings from qualitative case study and interview-based research consistently confirm the consensus-seeking tendencies which anchor Council negotiations. Insulation and *in camera* methods of repeat, face-to-face interaction help maintain the high levels of generalized trust and reciprocity that are necessary for mutual accommodation and deliberating collective outcomes that everyone can live with. Group norms are used to legitimate members' pursuit of self-interests. The national actors who participate in this norm-rich environment can develop more empathetic understandings of self-interest as well as other non-instrumental interests in the process of joint decision-making. In this institutional environment both the "self" and "interest" are subject to social construction.

Based on the Council's hybrid institutional environment and deeply embedded normative context for collective decision-making, a healthy range of "new institutionalist" theories are likely to continue to shed light on different aspects of the Council system. Rationalist approaches offer much insight, but narrower conceptions of individualism and strict assumptions of self-interest maximization risk missing the group community standards that undergird a wide range of Council behavior, including the well-seasoned habits of consensus-seeking. (For more on utility maximizing assumptions, see Chapter 1, this volume.) Council studies are thus likely to remain in need of more sociological accounts of persuasion and norm conformance to understand national negotiating behavior and the meaning behind it (see Chapter 4, this volume). This point holds equally true for the benefits of pluralism in methods and epistemology. Even as quantitative studies continue to improve in sophistication and cumulate longitudinal evidence, the added value of qualitative case study research, process tracing, and elite interviewing techniques is also likely to persist. The study of an institutional construct as multilayered and complex as the Council warrants nothing less.

NOTES

1. Fact sheet on the budget of the Council of the European Union available at: www.consilium.europa.eu/showPage.aspx?id=1633&lang=en>.
2. On this theme, see Jens Blom-Hansen and Gijs Jan Brandsma, "The EU Comitology System: Intergovernmental Bargaining and Deliberative Supranationalism?" *Journal of Common Market Studies* 47, no. 4 (2009), 719–40; Uwe Puetter, "Intervening From the Outside: The Role of EU Finance Ministers in the Constitutional Politics," *Journal of European Public Policy* 14, no. 8 (2007), 1293–310; Jeffrey Lewis, "Informal Integration and the Supranational Construction of the Council," *Journal of European Public Policy* 10, no. 6 (2003), 996–1019; Morten Egeberg, Gunther F. Schaefer, and Jarle Trondal, "The Many Faces of EU Committee Governance," *West European Politics* 26, no. 3 (July 2003), 19–40; Jarle Trondal, *Administrative Integration Across Levels of Governance: Integration Through Participation in EU Committees*. ARENA Report No. 01/07 (2001), Oslo, Norway; Wolfgang Wessels, "The EC Council: The Community's Decisionmaking Center," in Robert O. Keohane and Stanley Hoffmann, eds, *The New European Community: Decisionmaking and Institutional Change* (Boulder: Westview Press, 1991), 133–54.
3. On the general pattern, see Brigid Laffan, "The European Union and Its Institutions as 'Identity Builders'," in Richard K. Herrmann, Thomas Risse, and Marilynn B. Brewer, eds, *Transnational Identities: Becoming European in the EU* (Lanham, MD: Rowman and Littlefield, 2004), 75–96; Jeffrey Lewis, "The Janus Face of Brussels: Socialization and Everyday Decision Making in the European Union," *International Organization* 59, no. 4 (2005), 937–71.
4. For some examples, see Jeffrey Lewis, "Is the Hard Bargaining Image of the Council Misleading? The Committee of Permanent Representatives and the Local Elections Directive," *Journal of Common Market Studies* 36, no. 4 (1998), 483–4; David Bostock, "Coreper Revisited," *Journal of Common Market Studies* 40, no. 2 (2002), 215–34; Emile Noël, "Crises and Progress: The Bricks and Mortar of Europe," in *A Tribute to Emile Noël: Secretary-General of the European Commission from 1958 to 1987* (Luxembourg: Office for Official Publications of the European Communities, 1990), 55; Emile Noël, "The Committee of Permanent Representatives," *Journal of Common Market Studies* 5, no. 3 (March 1967), 219–51.
5. See Fiona Hayes-Renshaw and Helen Wallace, *The Council of Ministers*, second edition (New York: St. Martin's Press, 2006), 3, 330–2.

6. Helen Wallace, "The Council: An Institutional Chameleon?" *Governance* 15, no. 3 (July 2002), 325–44.

7. Daniel Naurin and Helen Wallace, "Introduction: From Rags To Riches," in Daniel Naurin and Helen Wallace, eds, *Unveiling the Council of the European Union: Games Governments Play in Brussels* (New York: Palgrave Macmillan, 2008), 2.

8. Compare, for example, the recent exchange between Dorothee Heisenberg and Gerald Schneider. Dorothee Heisenberg, "How Should We Best Study the Council of Ministers?" and Gerald Schneider, "Neither Goethe nor Bismarck: On the Link Between Theory and Empirics in Council Decision-Making Studies," both in Naurin and Wallace, *Unveiling the Council of the European Union*, pages 261–76 and 277–89 respectively.

9. Ernst B. Haas, *The Uniting of Europe: Political, Social, and Economic Forces, 1950–1957* (Stanford, CA: Stanford University Press, 1958), 491.

10. Ernst B. Haas, "Consensus Formation in the Council of Europe," University of California Publications in Political Science, Vol. 11 (1960), 12.

11. Dorothee Heisenberg, "The Institution of 'Consensus' in the European Union: Formal Versus Informal Decision-Making in the Council," *European Journal of Political Research* 44, no. 1 (2005), 65–90.

12. Dorothee Heisenberg, "Informal Decision-Making in the Council: The Secret of the EU's Success?" in Sophie Meunier and Kathleen R. McNamara, eds, *The State of the European Union. Making History: European Integration and Institutional Change at Fifty.* Volume 8 (Oxford: Oxford University Press, 2007), 80.

13. Hayes-Renshaw and Wallace, *The Council of Ministers*, 278.

14. Fiona Hayes-Renshaw, Wim van Aken, and Helen Wallace, "When and Why the EU Council of Ministers Votes Explicitly," *Journal of Common Market Studies* 44, no. 1 (2006), 161–94.

15. See for example, Lewis, "The Janus Face of Brussels"; Uwe Puetter, *The Eurogroup: How a Secretive Group of Finance Ministers Shape European Economic Governance* (Manchester: Manchester University Press, 2006); Jonathan P. Aus, "The Mechanisms of Consensus: Coming to Agreement on Community Asylum Policy," in Naurin and Wallace, *Unveiling the Council of the European Union*, 99–118. On the pattern of faked outrage and for an example of collective plotting, see Jeffrey Lewis, "National Interests: Coreper," in John Peterson and Michael Shackleton, eds, *The Institutions of the European Union*, second edition (Oxford: Oxford University Press, 2002), 286.

16. For an analysis of how the silent procedure overcame Greek and Italian reservations in a sensitive JHA asylum case see Aus, "The Mechanisms of Consensus," 113.

17. Simon Hix, "The European Union as a Polity (I)," in Knud Erik Jørgensen, Mark A. Pollack, and Ben Rosamond, eds, *Handbook of European Union Politics* (London: Sage, 2006), 145.

18. More research needs to be conducted on how group norms can fail or become deactivated. For an example in the context of the open discord over the 2003 Iraq war, see Jeffrey Lewis, "EU Policy on Iraq: The Collapse and Reconstruction of Consensus-Based Foreign Policy," *International Politics* 46, no. 4 (2009), 432–50.

19. Heisenberg, "Informal Decision-Making in the Council," 73, refers to this as a "peer review" quality to Council deliberations. See also, Jürgen Neyer, "Explaining the Unexpected: Efficiency and Effectiveness in European Decision-Making," *Journal of European Public Policy* 11, no. 1 (2004), 19–38; Jürgen Neyer, "Discourse and Order in the EU: A Deliberative Approach to Multi-Level Governance," *Journal of Common Market Studies* 41, no. 4 (2003), 687–706.

20. Simon Duke, "The Role of Committees and Working Groups in the CFSP Area," in Thomas Christiansen and Torbjörn Larsson, eds, *The Role of Committees in the Policy-Process of the European Union: Legislation, Implementation and Deliberation* (Cheltenham: Edward Elgar, 2007), 148.

21. For an analysis of how distributional issues affect negotiation patterns, see Heather Elko McKibben, "Issue Characteristics, Issue Linkage, and States' Choice of Bargaining Strategies in the European Union," *Journal of European Public Policy* 17, no. 5 (2010), 694–707.

22. B. Guy Peters, "Forms of Informal Governance: Searching for Efficiency and Democracy," in Christiansen and Larsson, *The Role of Committees in the Policy-Process of the European Union*, 46–7.

23. For an analysis of the financial services sector, see Lucia Quaglia, "How Does Technical Knowledge Influence Negotiations in the EU?," paper prepared for the conference, "Negotiation Theory and the EU: The State of the Art," University College Dublin, November 14–15, 2008; for a similar argument related to the Article 133 Committee's technical expertise in trade policy, see Arnie Niemann, "Deliberation and Bargaining in the Article 133 Committee and the 1996/97 IGC Representatives Group," in Naurin and Wallace, *Unveiling the Council of the European Union*, 121–43.

24. Markus Jachtenfuchs, "The European Union as a Polity (II)," in Jørgensen, Pollack, and Rosamond, *Handbook of European Union Politics*, 169, 164.

25. *The Economist*, "The Polish Farewell," December 1, 2007, 67.

26. Rebecca Adler-Nissen, "The Diplomacy of Opting Out: A Bourdieudian Approach to National Integration Strategies," *Journal of Common Market Studies* 46, no. 3 (2008), 663–84.

27. Adler-Nissen, "The Diplomacy of Opting Out," 678.

28. Rebecca Adler-Nissen, "Behind the Scenes of Differentiated Integration: Circumventing National Opt-Outs in Justice and Home Affairs," *Journal of European Public Policy* 16, no. 1 (2009), 73–6.

29. Elinor Ostrom, "Collective Action Theory," in Carles Boix and Susan C. Stokes, eds, *The Oxford Handbook of Comparative Politics* (Oxford: Oxford University Press, 2007), 186–208.

30. My own thinking on the Council's organizational form is indebted to the suggestive work of Ouchi on "clans," which rely on informal norms (he calls them "traditions") to govern behavior, limit opportunism, and create a self-policing form of enforcing compliance. See William Ouchi, "Markets, Bureaucracies, and Clans," *Administrative Science Quarterly* 25 (March 1980), 129–41.

31. Eves Fouilleux, Jacques de Maillard, and Andy Smith, "Technical or Political? The Working Groups of the EU Council of Ministers," *Journal of European Public Policy* 12, no. 4 (2005), 610–11.

32. Markus Jachtenfuchs, "The European Union as a Polity (II)," 169.

33. Frank Häge, "Committee Decision-Making in the Council of the European Union," *European Union Politics* 8, no. 3 (2007), 305.

34. Häge, "Committee Decision-Making in the Council," 323, fn. 5. Past efforts at the "who decides" question, such Van Schedelen's study of Agricultural Councils, used a qualitative triangulation method but with data not easy to replicate: he had access to the Dutch permrep's notes from the meetings. See M. P. C. M Van Schendelen, "The Council Decides: Does the Council Decide?" *Journal of Common Market Studies* 34, no. 4 (1996), 531–48.

35. Emile Noël, "The Committee of Permanent Representatives," 248.

36. David Stasavage, "Open-Door or Closed Door? Transparency in Domestic and International Bargaining," *International Organization* 58, no. 2 (2004), 667–703.

37. Daniel Naurin, "Lobbyists in Public and Private Settings in Sweden and the European Union," *Comparative Politics* 29, no. 2 (2007), 209–28.

38. Helen Wallace and Philippe de Schoutheete, "The European Council," *Notre Europe*, Research and European Issues, no. 19 (September 2002); Desmond Dinan, *Ever Closer Union: An Introduction to European Integration*, fourth edition (Boulder: Lynne Rienner, 2010), 205.

39. Hayes-Renshaw and Wallace, *The Council of Ministers*, 133.

40. Jonas Tallberg, *Leadership and Negotiation in the European Union* (Cambridge: Cambridge University Press, 2006), 222.

41. Ole Elgström and Jonas Tallberg, "Conclusion: Rationalist and Sociological Perspectives on the Council Presidency," in Ole Elgström, ed., *European Union Council Presidencies: A Comparative Perspective* (London: Routledge, 2003), 194, 196.

42. Ole Elgström, " 'The Honest Broker?' The Council Presidency as a Mediator," in Elgström, *European Union Council Presidencies*, 38–53; David Metcalfe, "Leadership in European Union Negotiations: The Presidency of the Council," *International Negotiation* 3 (1998), 413–34.

43. The Lisbon Treaty further enhances the High Representative role by "double hatting" the position with the Commission (and access to the sizable external relations budget).

44. Jonas Tallberg, *Leadership and Negotiation in the European Union*, 49.

45. Derek Beach, "The Unseen Hand in Treaty Reform Negotiations: The Role and Influence of the Council Secretariat," *Journal of European Public Policy* 11, no. 3 (2004), 408–39; Thomas Christiansen, "The Role of Supranational Actors in EU Treaty Reform," *Journal of European Public Policy* 9, no. 1 (2002), 33–53.

46. Andrew Moravcsik, "A New Statecraft? Supranational Entrepreneurs and International Cooperation," *International Organization* 53, no. 2 (1999), 267–306.

47. David Galloway, "Keynote Article: Agenda 2000—Packaging the Deal," *Journal of Common Market Studies* 37, Annual Review (September 1999), 9–35.

48. Michael Shackleton, "Parliamentary Government or Division of Powers: Is the Destination Still Unknown?" in Nicolas Jabko and Craig Parsons, eds, *The State of the European Union: With US or Against US? European Trends in American Perspective*. Volume 7 (Oxford: Oxford University Press, 2005), 123–41.

49. See for example, George Tsebelis and Jeannette Money, *Bicameralism* (Cambridge: Cambridge University Press, 1997), 27; Shackleton "Parliamentary Government or Division of Powers"; Jeffrey Lewis, "Is the Council Becoming an Upper House?" in Jabko and Parsons, *The State of the European Union*, 143–71.

50. Michael Shackleton, "The Politics of Codecision," *Journal of Common Market Studies* 38, no. 2 (2000), 325–42.

51. Raunio, Chapter 26, this volume; Shackleton, "The Politics of Codecision"; Julie Garman and Louise Hilditch, "Behind the Scenes: An Examination of the Importance of the Informal Processes at Work in Conciliation," *Journal of European Public Policy* 5, no. 2 (1998), 271–84.

52. See for example, John Peterson and Erik Jones, "Decision Making in an Enlarging European Union," in James Sperling, ed., *Two Tiers or Two Speeds? The European Security Order and the Enlargement of the European Union and NATO* (Manchester: Manchester

University Press, 1999), 25–45; Bart Kerremans, "The Political and Institutional Consequences of Widening: Capacity and Control in an Enlarged Council," in Pierre-Henri Laurent and Marc Maresceau, eds, *The State of the Union, Volume 4: Deepening and Widening* (Boulder: Lynne Rienner, 1998), 87–112; Werner Ungerer, "Institutional Consequences of Broadening and Deepening the Community: The Consequences for the Decision-Making Process," *Common Market Law Review* 30, no. 1 (1993), 71–83.

53. Mikko Mattila, "Voting and Coalitions in the Council After Enlargement," in Naurin and Wallace, *Unveiling the Council of the European Union*, 27, Table 2.1.

54. Jakob Lempp, "'COREPER Enlarged' How Enlargement Affected the Functioning of COREPER," paper presented at the ECPR Third Pan-European Conference, September 21–23, 2006, Istanbul; Dirk Leuffen, "The Impact of Eastern Enlargement on the Internal Functioning of the EU: Why So Much Continuity?," paper presented at the Conference "Europe Twenty Years After the Cold War. The New Europe, New Europes?," Graduate Institute Geneva, October 14–15, 2010.

55. Ana E. Juncos and Karolina Pomorska, "The Deadlock That Never Happened: The Impact of Enlargement on the Common Foreign and Security Policy Council Working Groups," *European Political Economy Review*, no. 6 (March 2007), 4–30.

56. See Annex V, Working Methods for an Enlarged Council, Council Decision of September 15, 2006 adopting the Council's Rules of Procedure (2006/683/EC).

57. Sara Hagemann and Julia De Clerck-Sachsse, "Old Rules, New Game: Decision-Making in the Council of Ministers After the 2004 Enlargement," CEPS Special Report (March 2007).

CHAPTER 24

....

EUROPEAN COMMISSION

....

SUSANNE K. SCHMIDT AND
ARNDT WONKA

24.1 INTRODUCTION
....

The European Commission is one of the most prominent and perhaps also one of the most controversial institutions of the EU, regularly being the subject of heated academic and political debate. The public perception of the European Commission, like that of most other bureaucratic organizations, usually oscillates between ignorance, skepticism, and outright rejection. The Commission's public image hit its negative peak when the Santer Commission had to step down in 1999 due to allegations of mismanagement and nepotism. In less exceptional times, it is common practice among governments and domestic political elites to shift the blame for decisions that meet opposition "at home" on the Commission's "Brussels bureaucrats." Most of the time, therefore, when the Commission makes it to the news it perhaps wished it had not.

Among scholars of the EU there is broad consensus that the European Commission disposes of strong formal institutional as well as informal means to influence the dynamics and outcomes of EU integration. This regularly puts the Commission center stage in inter-institutional bargaining and makes it the target of extensive lobbying activities from a diverse set of regional, national, and European interest groups. Controversy starts when it comes to assessments on the motives driving the Commission's actions as well as the means and extent to which it is able to independently shape the course of European integration. The main conflict line runs between neo-functionalists (see Chapter 2, this volume) and (liberal) intergovernmentalists (see Chapter 1, this volume). While the former attributes to the Commission relative behavioral independence from member-state governments and an independent causal impact on the course of EU politics and integration, the latter denies such influence. Institutionalist perspectives agree on the importance of the respective institutional and political environment in explaining the Commission's influence in EU policy-making, while leaning either toward the intergovernmental or toward the neo-functionalist conception of the Commission's motives and capabilities in EU policy-making. In this chapter's first section we will introduce the Commission's organizational make–up. The subsequent section discusses how this institution changed over time, followed by an analysis in the third section of the Commission's position in the EU's institutional system and its contribution to EU political dynamics.

24.2 Organizational Make—Up

The European Commission is a unique institution, fulfilling functions of a supranational executive. It plays an important role in EU politics in the areas of (legislative) policy-making, EU trade politics, the monitoring of member state's compliance with EU law, and, finally, by providing political impulses for European integration. Its importance in EU policy-making results not least from its monopoly power to draft legislative proposals (Art. 294 TFEU), making it the formal agenda setter in a wide range of EU policy areas.[1] In trade politics the European Commission represents the EU in multi- or bilateral trade negotiations (Art. 207 TFEU). In its function as "guardian of the Treaty" it occupies a central role, in tandem with the ECJ, in monitoring the compliance with EU primary and secondary law in the member states (Art. 258 TFEU). Finally, the Commission acts as a policy entrepreneur, using its institutional position and resources to put topics on the EU's political agenda. Here, it acts together but partly also in rivalry with the Council presidency. With the introduction in the Lisbon Treaty of a new permanent Council president, aimed at strengthening coherence and leadership (see Chapter 23, this volume), this rivalry may augment. Delegating these different preparatory and monitoring functions to the Commission helps member states overcome collective action problems by reducing the transaction costs of bargaining and increasing the credibility of their commitment. Yet, such delegation poses the risk that the supranational agent goes beyond its remit and realizes not only the interests of its principals, the member states, but also its own.[2]

The Commission's most important organizational units are the "College of Commissioners" (College) and the Directorates General and Services, the Commission's bureaucratic apparatus. In addition, each Commissioner has a cabinet, six personal advisors, of which no more than three may have the same nationality as the Commissioner. The College is the Commission's political leadership body, in which Commissioners from all member states and the Commission president discuss and take controversial decisions. It is headed by the Commission president, who leads the weekly meetings and represents the Commission externally, thus formally being a *primus inter pares* amongst the Commissioners (cf. Chapters 16 and 17, this volume).[3] Both the Commission president and the European Commissioners usually are adept party politicians, oftentimes with prior experience in holding national executive office and being members of a party which is in government in the respective country at the time of appointment.[4] The vast majority of decisions in the Commission are taken below the level of the College in the meeting of the heads of cabinets, thus not being subject to collective discussion and decision in the Commission's political leadership body.[5] Whenever conflicts do arise, these seem to run along sectoral lines between Commissioners heading different portfolios, as well as along national lines between groups of Commissioners from different countries sharing common interests in a particular issue. Despite the fact that Commissioners from the same party family regularly meet for consultation also with members of the European Parliament and members of governments, partisan conflicts seem to play a minor role in the Commission. Yet, research on intra-institutional dynamics and decision-making inside the College is still in its infancy, not least due to the unavailability of protocols on internal deliberations and decision-taking.[6]

The Directorates General and Services build the Commission's bureaucratic apparatus and host the Commission's administrative staff.[7] Each Directorate General deals with a particular substantive policy in those areas for which the European Community and the EU Treaties establish competences. Services cover horizontal functions cutting across policy areas such as budget, translation, and legal service. In their institutional make-up, Directorates General and Services are horizontally divided into several directorates with different responsibilities and each directorate again disposing of a number of units. While Commissioners hold political responsibility over Directorates General and the respective policy area, Directorates General's administrations are headed by General Secretaries. The personal cabinets of the Commissioners ease the contact between the political College and the permanent administration. They liaise with the Directorates General in the portfolio of the Commissioner as well as monitoring the developments in the other Directorates General and are at the same time important interlocutors for national interests.[8] Both as regards the size of their staff as and their budget, individual Directorates General and Services vary considerably.[9] Moreover, the work in the Directorates General is supported by a large number of comitology committees, staffed by the Council[10] and expert groups.[11]

In 2009 the Commission's Directorates General and Services were employing a total staff of 33,681, including senior managers (333), middle managers (1247), permanent officials (21,223), and seconded national experts (1106).[12] Although not following a strict rule of proportionality—some of the bigger member states are especially under-represented—the Commission's administrative staff is made up of citizens from all member states and broadly reflect their respective sizes.[13] Though the cost of the administration of all EU institutions amounts to only about five percent of the overall EU budget,[14] Commission administrators are a significant manpower for running the Commission's everyday work in preparing and managing EU programs, drafting policy proposals, and monitoring their implementation. Yet, it is misleading to talk about "the" Commission administrators, as if they held uniform preferences and ideas about European integration. Working in the Commission does affect seconded national officials' and (top) Commission officials' attitudes toward European integration. Administrators in the Commission in general are more supportive of European integration than national elites and electorates.[15] Yet, their attitudes toward both further European integration and interventionist or liberal economic policies are considerably heterogeneous and strongly shaped by their professional and political socialization in their country of origin.[16] Our knowledge of how this domestic imprint on Commission administrators' perceptions and preferences plays out in interactions between them when preparing decisions is still limited. Interactions between administrative staff, however, seem to be running along the lines of formal responsibilities, which is not too surprising for a bureaucratic apparatus, and are not primarily driven by national and cultural affinities.[17]

24.3 DEVELOPMENT OF THE EUROPEAN COMMISSION

Organizational change inside the Commission is rare. There have been repeated discussions on internal organizational changes, and the "Spierenburg Report" in 1979 sketched a broad reform agenda.[18] Far-reaching organizational change, however, only started four decades after the Commission's foundation. In 2000 the so called "Kinnock reform," named after the British Commissioner responsible for personnel and administrative affairs in the 1999–2004 Prodi Commission, led to changes in the areas of service provision, mid-term policy planning, staff policy, and financial control and management. The Kinnock reform was a reaction to the resignation of the Santer Commission in 1999. This pushed at once the reform interests of member-state governments and of administrative elites inside the Commission as organizational change was needed to restore the Commission's public and political reputation.[19] The reform attempts also brought to the fore the difficulties of the Commission as a multinational organization to combine organizational efficiency with member states' fair representation. With informal quotas for different member states and practices of "parachuting" of administrators of the "right" nationality to the top, staff morale was harmed by the lack of a meritocracy.[20] In addition, traditions of "nationalized" Directorates General, like the French agriculture or the German competition Directorates General, lost acceptance in view of successive enlargements. While the reform initiated a rotation system for senior officials, it is not yet clear whether it succeeded in finding a better compromise between the need to represent different member states within the Commission and being an efficient working organization.

More incremental but still significant for the Commission's institutional make-up were the changes caused by the increase in competences through successive treaty reforms as well as territorial enlargements from the original six to the currently twenty-seven member states. Different treaty reforms led to a successive increase in the number of Directorates General and Services to cover newly acquired competences. Starting out with only nine in 1958,[21] the number of Commission Directorates General and Services has more than quadrupled to forty-one in 2009, involving a rising number of administrative staff. In 1970 the European Commission had a staff of about 5000. Successive enlargements, in particular the 2004 Eastern enlargement, brought further growth and diversification of the Commission's administration personnel, but were successfully implemented.[22] Coinciding with the Kinnock reform, these "changes have been dramatic and, in some ways, traumatic."[23]

The number of Commissioners also increased from six member states and nine Commissioners in the 1958 Hallstein Commission to twenty-seven Commissioners (one from each member state) in the 2004 Barroso Commission. Until the coming into force of the Nice Treaty in 2003, the "big" member states—France, Germany, Italy, Spain, and the UK—were entitled to two Commissioners each. The reduction was meant to preserve the Commission's capacity to act and facilitate decision-making in the College. Since the negotiations on the Treaty of Amsterdam, there have been discussions to reduce the number of Commissioners in the College through a rotation system in which not every member state is represented by a Commissioner at any one time. Governments, however, are very reluctant to do without their own Commissioner and to agree on a formula which would have to strike a balance between Commissioners from small and large member states and from different geographical regions. The failed "Constitutional Treaty" as well as its "Lisbon" successor provided for a reduction to two-thirds of member states (postponing, however, its implementation). The compromise agreed in the European Council after the failed Irish referendum includes the permanent representation of all member states in the College. Given the depth of integration and the centrality of the Commission, efficiency advantages have to be weighed against the danger that not having every member state represented might affect the acceptance of Commission decisions.

Another change inside the Commission is the formal role of the Commission president, whose powers in the internal organization of the Commission as well as those vis-à-vis individual Commissioners have been strengthened through subsequent treaty revisions. Since the coming into force of the Amsterdam Treaty in 1999 the Commission president is formally involved in the selection of member states' candidates for Commissioners and has the right to exercise political leadership in the Commission. The Treaty of Nice (2003), moreover, provides the Commission president with the competence to allocate responsibility for the different Directorates General and Services among Commissioners as well as to request, after approval through the College, a Commissioner's resignation. The Lisbon Treaty even dropped the prerequisite of approval by the College. These institutional developments, and the increased size of the College, have been interpreted as leading to a "presidentialization" of the Commission under the presidency of Barroso.[24] Yet, whether this will be a permanent feature of the Commission will depend not least on future appointments of Commission presidents (see Chapters 16 and 17, this volume) and Commissioners.

With respect to Commission appointment, following the Amsterdam and Nice Treaties, the Commission president is nominated by the Council by qualified majority, subject to approval of the Parliament. Although the European Parliament is not formally involved in selecting and approving individual Commissioners, it holds informal hearings with individual candidates in the committee responsible for the policy area which the prospective Commissioner is planned to head. At the end of the process, the

European Parliament approves the Commission as a whole by simple majority. Only after this endorsement can the Council appoint the Commission by qualified majority.[25] Despite its role in the appointment process, the Parliament's influence on the composition of Commissioners should not be overestimated. Governments still have the exclusive right to select their Commissioners and the Commission president and thus set the agenda for the Commission appointment process.

The above paragraphs sketched the development of the European Commission, highlighting its institutional growth and diversification through the successive increase in the number of Directorates General and Services as well as through the growth of its personnel, both at the political top and at the administrative level. These changes are the result of successive Treaty changes, which have delegated new competences to the EU in general and the Commission in particular, as well as the result of the territorial expansion of the EU. It should be noted that these were incremental changes, leading from the small, elitist, and technocratic institution which Jean Monnet planned to the large and powerful executive institution that is the current Commission of the EU.

24.4 THE COMMISSION'S POSITION IN THE EU'S POLITICAL SYSTEM AND ITS CONTRIBUTION TO EU POLICY—MAKING

From its origin as a European Community institution in 1957 (see Chapter 7, this volume), the Commission was institutionally well equipped to play an important role in the actual political realization of the common market. Yet, from the very beginning governments refined the competences they delegated to the EEC and its successors in general and the European Commission in particular by introducing institutional rules that prevent the Commission from taking actions that repeatedly run against their own interests.[26] The Commission's powers in monitoring and implementing competition policies as well as in (external trade) politics have always been great, with the latter being performed under the close supervision of member-state governments.[27] The reverse is true for an area such as social policy.[28] This point is important as it highlights the fact that the Commission's means to leave an imprint on the course of European integration not only varies over time, but also significantly across issue areas.

The Commission has from the very beginning of the EEC held considerable power in legislative policy-making, not least due to its monopoly right to draft all European Community legislative proposals. As the Council and European Parliament can ask the Commission to become active, however, this does not amount to a gatekeeping power, effectively preventing items from entering the legislative arena.[29] The Commission's ability to have an impact on the content of EU policy-making is particularly strong in areas decided under the so called "consultation procedure," where it enjoys formal agenda-setting power. Here, it is easier for the Council to adopt a Commission proposal by a qualified majority than to unanimously agree on a changed proposal (Art. 250 TEC).[30] Up until the introduction of the SEA the consultation procedure was the standard policy-making procedure in the EU. The SEA significantly strengthened the Commission's agenda-setting power, by increasing the number of policy areas in which the Council decided by qualified majority. Even after the introduction of the cooperation procedure (SEA, 1986) and the co-decision procedure (Maastricht (1992) and Amsterdam Treaties (1998), respectively), the consultation procedure accounted for around 50 percent of European Community legislation.[31] The Lisbon Treaty establishes the co-decision procedure, now called ordinary procedure, as the EU's standard legislative procedure and extends its application to almost all policy areas, thereby reducing the Commission's formal agenda-setting power. While the Commission in this procedure still holds monopoly power to draft the initial legislative proposal, negotiations in the co-decision procedure's third stage "conciliation committee" take place between the Council and European Parliament, which can agree on a legislative text without Commission's involvement. In co-decision, the Commission's formal agenda-setting power is therefore closely circumscribed.[32] It would be misleading, however, to characterize the Commission under co-decision as powerless, given its role in formulating the original proposal and the possibility it has of using informal means to try to influence legislation.[33]

The Commission, however, does not only have a direct influence on legislation. During the last decades the Commission repeatedly combined its legislative agenda-setting powers with its strong role as administrator of European competition law and guardian of the Treaty to establish new policies. It did so by threatening member states with Court proceedings or competition decisions, which, if credibly backed by the ECJ, allow the Commission to strategically influence the preferences of member states in the Council:[34] In view of the Commission's actions, the Council may perceive agreeing on European Community legislation as a "lesser evil."[35] Arguing that they were a hindrance to the European Community's common market, the Commission used this mechanism together with the ECJ extensively to bring down member states' public monopolies in formerly well-protected areas such as utilities and telecommunications.[36] The threat of market-making (negative integration) measures may thus facilitate member states' agreement on common regulation (positive integration).[37] Thus, the Commission can make up for its reduced formal agenda-setting role.

The Commission's powers as a guardian of the Treaty are important also beyond its strategic use in the legislative process. Its activities in overseeing member-state governments' implementation of the agreed secondary and primary law increase the credibility of governments' cooperative efforts. The reinvigoration of EU policy-making with the SEA and the "1992" initiative resulted in a greater volume of law across different policy areas, whose implementation the Commission had to oversee. Moreover, the 2004 Eastern enlargement significantly increased the territorial reach of the Commission's monitoring activities and, by being the actor responsible for monitoring the accession process, provided it with new tasks and responsibilities. Since the Copenhagen (accession) criteria include politically sensitive issues such as minority rights, the Commission acquired temporary oversight rights in new areas that might be politically more salient and contentious than the mostly economic *aquis communitaire*.[38] The Commission's activities in opening infringements proceedings, which are its main institutional tool to sanction deficient implementation, vary across countries and policy areas. Often the Commission seems to refrain from non-compliance proceedings, although being aware of implementation deficits. This reluctance apparently does not systematically advantage some (especially large and/or resourceful) member states over others, but rather seems to be caused by a lack of administrative resources and differences in priorities and political preferences of those responsible for opening infringement proceedings in the respective Directorate General.[39] Important for the Commission's role in implementation has also been its cooperation with the increasing numbers of agencies, which complement the Commission's advisory and implementation capacities (see Chapter 28, this volume).

Another development to be mentioned is the EU's turn toward non-legislative means of policy coordination among its member states, such as the Open Method of Coordination. These "new modes of governance," generally draw on soft law or bench-marking, and often include a wider range of private and public actors.[40] Their introduction goes back to EU member states' increased efforts to coordinate their economic and social policy-making, not least expressed through the Lisbon Agenda (2000), which aimed at making the EU the world's most competitive economic region. Given the strong political and institutional heterogeneity of member states' welfare systems, the community method was not considered an option.[41] In 2001, the Commission published a white paper on European governance, proposing principles on good governance and better regulation with a view on the openness and legitimacy of European governance more generally. The white paper was at the same time a response to the crisis of the Santer Commission, trying to re-establish its reputation and legitimacy by asking for an increase in the transparency of EU decision-making and a broader involvement of private actors.[42] The effectiveness of these new modes of governance is strongly contested, some arguing that it is no more than cheap talk and others seeing it as a means to trigger changes in member states' perceptions and behavior.[43]

How then did the Commission make use of its powers during the last decades? Since the establishment of the EEC, the Commission's agenda-setting power has been particularly relevant in the area of customs policy. Yet, its power to make use of its institutional resources in EU policy-making was severely restricted by the "empty chair" crisis provoked by French President De Gaulle in 1965 over a bargain on the European Community's annual budget procedure. The empty chair crisis resulted in the "Luxemburg Compromise" of 1966, according to which decisions in which governments can claim a threat to their country's "vital interests" need to be taken unanimously, even if the formal treaty rules provide for QMV. This severely limited the Commission's room of maneuver in European Community policy-making for almost twenty years. In fact, the years between 1965 and 1985 have been described as years of "Eurosclerosis" during which the Commission lost its leading role in matters ranging from European integration to the ECJ.[44]

The Commission took again center stage, however, in the early 1980s, when it was asked by governments to come up with a proposal to rejuvenate the EU and the single market. The Commission's white paper on the completion of the single market, listing around 300 measures, was adopted by governments at their European Council in Milan in 1985. One year later, the Luxemburg compromise came to an end with the signing of the SEA. QMV in the Council created the institutional conditions for the political realization of the single market. What followed might perhaps be considered the Commission's golden years, when, under its President Jacques Delors, it significantly contributed to the completion of the European Community's internal market and masterminded the future development of the European Community (see Chapter 16, this volume).[45]

The Maastricht Treaty saw significant deepening of integration with the plan for a monetary union. The Commission was not only crucial in attaining this far-reaching integration step,[46] it also gained important monitoring functions over the economies of member states. At the same time, the addition of the second and third pillars indicated that member states saw the competence transfer to the Commission also in part as critical (see Part VIII of this volume). Both pillars were planned as intergovernmental ones with restrained or no roles for the Commission and the Court. The Commission's and the Court's restricted competences in both pillars can be interpreted as member states' attempt to prevent the expansion and self-empowerment of the Commission which they experienced in the first pillar. Particularly the development in JHA subsequently showed, however, that member states soon became aware of the disadvantages of not delegating. Already in Amsterdam the Commission's role was strengthened with part of the policy issues being transferred to the first pillar and the Commission acquiring powers of initiative in the third pillar. For the member states, constraining the Commission had also meant losing cooperation benefits. In the second pillar, the CFSP, the Commission has not made similar progress regarding delegation. It remains intergovernmental also under the Lisbon Treaty, which dissolved the pillar structure. Nevertheless, as in all policy areas, the Commission can have an impact as a coordinator, a broker among different member states, and as a policy-entrepreneur proposing policy ideas[47]—all roles for which the newly introduced permanent Council president may be seen as a competitor.

Proponents of different theoretical perspectives, of course, differ in their interpretations of the role the Commission played in the developments sketched above. The success of the internal-market program and the renewed dynamism of the integration process resulting from the five Treaty revisions in the twenty years between 1986 and 2007 (see Chapters 8–12, this volume) led not only to renewed attention to European integration, but also put the Commission at the center of the theoretical debate between EU scholars. In an influential article of 1989, Sandholtz and Zysman argued that the Commission, linking up with business leaders, had managed to push member states into accepting the "1992" program.[48] This reinvigorated Ernst Haas' neo-functionalist research program, attributing to the Commission, in concert with transnationally active economic and political elites, a strong role in shaping form and content of EU policy-making (see Chapter 2, this volume). The reinvigoration of neo-functionalist or supra-nationalist explanations was quickly countered by Andrew Moravcsik's liberal

intergovernmentalist explanation. Focusing on treaty bargains, liberal intergovernmentalism sees member-state governments and their economic constituencies as the decisive forces behind the process of European integration (see Chapter 1, this volume).
From a liberal intergovernmentalist perspective, the Commission allows member states
to overcome collective action and commitment problems and is considered not to have
an independent causal impact on the course of European integration since the 1950s.[49]

Sidestepping the debate between neo-functionalists and intergovernmentalists and
drawing on the economic literature on regulation and bureaucratic organization,
Majone conceptualizes the Commission as a non-majoritarian institution, acting at
arms length from governments. Majone explains the growth of EU regulation during
the last decades with the Commission's interest in extending its competences, for
which, due to its low budget, it has to resort to regulatory policy-making. In this goal it
is said to be supported by large business, which share a preference for harmonized
European rules.[50]

Over time, the performance of the Commission thus sees the steady increase in competences across policy fields, albeit not in a linear, unambiguous way. Depending on the
political and economic environment which the member states and the EU faces at different times, the Commission has seen successful inroads into new fields, establishing
itself as an important new actor, but has also seen serious drawbacks in core competences. For the latter, the 2005 reform of the Stability and Growth Pact is as much an
example as several annulments of competition decisions of the Commission by the
Court of First Instance in the early 2000s.[51] If ever since the failure of the Santer
Commission, the European Commission has been seen as crisis-prone, this is also
because it has become a victim of its own success. While conditions of low integration
in the late 1980s made it easy for the Commission to have an impact on EU policy-making, it has, in the meantime, seen diminishing returns to its entrepreneurship.[52]
Monitoring policy implementation implies significant workload for the Commission,
and while the mobilization of civil society actors is an important source of support, it
also ties up scarce administrative resources to interact with different groups and might
politicize decision-making and thus make compromise finding and decision-making
much more cumbersome.

As the previous sections make clear, the Commission's impact on the course of
European integration is subject to fluctuation depending on its wider institutional,
political, and economic context, as well as on its internal organization and leadership.
The development which perhaps most strongly influenced the development of the EU's
institutional design was the discussion on the democratic deficit of the EU, of which the
Commission was one addressee. One major consequence was the successive parliamentarization of the EU[53] (see Chapter 26, this volume), which had direct consequences for
the European Commission, both as regards its role in EU policy-making and as regards
the appointment of the Commission president and Commissioners.

To sum up, the institutional development has considerably affected the Commission's
role in the political system of the EU, most remarkably with respect to its appointment
and its role in legislative policy-making. To assess the present-day Commission, these

changes need be seen against the background of the internal changes in the Commission resulting from the successive extension of EU competences, the extended application of supranational (qualified majority) decision-making, and the considerable territorial growth of the EU's territorial scope. The Commission has evolved over time into a highly complex and differentiated organization. The challenge of integrating this multinational and multifunctional organization has been felt repeatedly. Apparently, however, the Commission has successfully managed to cope with these changes and challenges. This is perhaps best exemplified by the way in which the Commission managed, in the wake of the 2004 enlargement, to integrate new personnel, both at the political and at the administrative level, into its organization while still playing a vital role in EU politics. At the same time, however, the advance of integration has made it no longer feasible for the Commission to act as the "motor of integration" by presenting member-state govern-ments with bold policy proposals. The administration of the many successes of coopera-tion in Europe now puts a heavy strain on what is, in principle, a relatively small organization. Having neither the resources nor the mandate to be the exclusive European executive, the Commission has to manage integration by being the hub of different European administrative networks.[54] However, with the need of finding common ground among now twenty-seven member states, the Commission will remain an important actor. Whether it continues to be in a unique position to have an impact on the course of the integration of Europe, or whether it faces increasing competition from the Council President, remains to be seen.

NOTES

1. The establishment of the European Parliament as a co-equal legislator and the introduction of the conciliation committee through the co-decision (Maastricht, Amsterdam) and the ordinary procedure (Lisbon) took away, or at least significantly reduced, the Commission's formal agenda-setting powers; see George Tsebelis and Geoffrey Garrett, "Legislative Politics in the European Union," *European Union Politics* 1, no. 1 (2000), 9–36.
2. Mark A. Pollack, "Delegation, Agency, and Agenda Setting in the European Community," *International Organization* 51, no. 1 (1997), 99–134; Fabio Franchino, *The Powers of the Union. Delegation in the EU* (Cambridge: Cambridge University Press, 2007).
3. David Spence, "The President, the College and the Cabinets," in David Spence and Geoffrey Edwards, eds, *The European Commission* (London: John Harper Publishing, 2006), 25–74.
4. Holger Döring, "The Composition of the College of Commissioners: Patterns of Delegation," *European Union Politics* 8, no. 2 (2007), 209–30; Fabio Franchino, "Experience and the Distribution of Portfolio Payoffs in the European Commission," *European Journal of Political Research* 48, no.1 (2009), 1–30; Edward C. Page, *People Who Run Europe* (Oxford: Clarendon Press, 1997); Arndt Wonka, "Technocratic and Independent? The Appointment of European Commissioners and its Policy Implications," *Journal of European Public Policy* 14, no. 2 (2007), 171–91.
5. Arndt Wonka, "Decision-Making Dynamics in the European Commission: Partisan, National or Sectoral?" *Journal of European Public Policy* 15, no. 8 (2008), 1151.

6. Morten Egeberg, "Executive Politics as Usual: Role Behaviour and Conflict Dimensions in the College of European Commissioners," *Journal of European Public Policy* 13, no. 1 (2006), 1–15; George Ross, ed., *Jacques Delors and European Integration* (Europe and the International Order; Oxford: Polity Press, 1995); Robert Thomson, "National Actors in International Organizations. The Case of the European Commission," *Comparative Political Studies* 41, no. 2 (2008), 169–92; Wonka, "Decision-Making Dynamics."

7. David Spence, "The Directorates General and the Services: Structures, Functions and Procedures," in Spence and Edwards, *The European Commission*, 128–55.

8. Hans J. Michelmann, "Multinational Staffing and Organizational Functioning in the Commission of the European Communities," *International Organization* 32, no. 2 (1978), 477–96.

9. Simon Hix, *The Political System of the European Union* (Houndmills: MacMillan, 2005), 48; Liesbet Hooghe, *The European Commission and the Integration of Europe. Images of Governance* (Cambridge: Cambridge University Press, 2001); Neill Nugent, *The European Commission* (Houndmills: Palgrave, 2001).

10. Christian Joerges and Jürgen Neyer, "Transforming Interaction into Deliberative Problem-Solving: European Comitology in the Foodstuff Sector," *Journal of European Public Policy* 4, no. 4 (1997), 609–25; Mark A. Pollack, *The Engines of Integration. Delegation, Agency and Agenda Setting in the EU* (Oxford: Oxford University Press, 2003), 132.

11. Åse Gornitzka and Ulf Sverdrup, "Who Consults? The Configuration of Expert Groups in the European Union," *West European Politics* 31, no.4 (2008), 725–50; Torbjörn Larsson, *Precooking in the European Union—The World of Expert Groups* (Stockholm: ESO, Fritzes Offentliga Publikationer, 2003).

12. "Human Resources Key Figures Card Staff Members," European Commission, 2009.

13. "Human Resources Key Figures," European Commission, 2009.

14. Hix, *Political System*, 279.

15. Liesbet Hooghe, "Several Roads Lead to International Norms, but Few Via International Socialization: A Case Study of the European Commission," *International Organization* 59 (2005), 876; Jarle Trondal, "Is the European Commission a 'Hothouse' for Supranationalism? Exploring Actor-Level Supranationalism," *Journal of Common Market Studies* 45, no. 5 (2007), 1123.

16. Liesbet Hooghe, "Several Roads."

17. Michelmann, "Multinational Staffing and Organizational Functioning"; Semin Suvarierol, "Beyond the Myth of Nationality: Analysing Networks within the European Commission," *West European Politics* 31, no. 4 (2008), 701–24.

18. Michael W. Bauer, "Introduction: Organizational Change, Management Reform and EU Policy-Making," *Journal of European Public Policy* 15, no. 5 (2008), 627–47.

19. Hussein Kassim, "'Mission Impossible', but Mission Accomplished: the Kinnock Reforms and the European Commission," *Journal of European Public Policy* 15, no. 5 (2008), 648–68.

20. Antonis Ellinas and Ezra Suleiman, "Reforming the Commission: Between Modernization and Bureaucratization," *Journal of European Public Policy* 15, no. 5 (2008), 708–25.

21. David Spence, "The Directorates General and the Services: Structures, Functions and Procedures," in Spence and Edwards, *The European Commission*, 130.

22. Michelle Cini, *The European Commission: Leadership, Organisation, and Culture in the EU Administration* (Manchester: Manchester University Press, 1996), 106. Magali Gravier, "The 2004 Enlargement Staff Policy of the European Commission: The Case for Representative Bureaucracy," *Journal of Common Market Studies* 46, no. 5 (2008), 1025–47.

23. John Peterson, "Enlargement, Reform and the European Commission. Weathering a Perfect Storm?" *Journal of European Public Policy* 15, no. 5 (2008), 761.

24. John Peterson, "Enlargement, Reform," 763.

25. Wonka, "Technocratic and Independent?" 171.

26. Pollack, "Delegation, Agency."

27. Chad Damro, "EU Delegation and Agency in International Trade Negotiations," *Journal of Common Market Studies* 45, no. 4 (2007), 883–903; Dirk De Bièvre and Andreas Dür, "Constituency Interests and Delegation in European and American Trade Policy," *Comparative Political Studies* 38, no. 10 (2005), 1271–96.

28. Tanja Börzel, "Mind the Gap! European Integration Between Level and Scope," *Journal of European Public Policy* 12, no. 2 (2005), 217–36; Pollack, *Engines*, 91–101.

29. Christophe Crombez, Tim Groseclose, and Keith Krehbiel, "Gatekeeping," *Journal of Politics* 68, no. 2 (2006), 322–34.

30. Christophe Crombez, "Legislative Procedures in the European Community," *British Journal of Political Science* 26 (1996), 199–228; Tsebelis and Garrett, "Legislative Politics," 13.

31. Hix, *Political System*, 77.

32. Björn Hörl, Andreas Warntjen, and Arndt Wonka, "Built on Quicksand? A Decade of Procedural Spatial Models on EU Legislative Decision-Making," *Journal of European Public Policy* 12, no. 3 (2005), 592–606; Tsebelis and Garrett, "Legislative Politics."

33. Anne Rasmussen, "Challenging the Commission's Right of Initiative? Conditions for Institutional Change and Stability," *West European Politics* 30, no. 2 (2007), 244–64.

34. Susanne K. Schmidt, "Only an Agenda Setter? The European Commission's Power over the Council of Ministers," *European Union Politics* 1, no. 1 (2000), 37–61.

35. Schmidt, "Agenda Setter."

36. Susanne K. Schmidt, "Commission Activism: Subsuming Telecommunications and Electricity under European Competition Law," *Journal of European Public Policy* 5, no. 1 (1998), 169–84.

37. Fritz W. Scharpf, *Governing in Europe—Democratic and Effective?* (Oxford: Oxford University Press, 1999).

38. Heather Grabbe, "How does Europeanization Affect CEE Governance? Conditionality, Diffusion and Diversity," *Journal of European Public Policy* 8, no. 6 (2001), 1013–31; Ulrich Sedelmeier, "After Conditionality: Post-Accession Compliance with EU Law in East Central Europe," *Journal of European Public Policy* 15, no. 6 (2008), 806–25.

39. Gerda Falkner, Oliver Treib, Miriam Hartlapp, and Simone Lieber, *Complying with Europe. EU Harmonisation and Soft Law in the Member States* (Cambridge: Cambridge University Press, 2005), 201–28; Tanja Börzel, "Non-Compliance in the European Union: Pathology or Statistical Artefact?" *Journal of European Public Policy* 8, no. 5 (2001), 803–24.

40. Burkard Eberlein and Dieter Kerwer, "New Governance in the European Union," *Journal of Common Market Studies* 42, no. 1 (2004), 121–42.

41. Fritz W. Scharpf. "The European Social Model: Coping with the Challenges of Diversity," *Journal of Common Market Studies* 40, no. 4 (2002), 645–70.

42. Laura Cram, "Whither the Commission? Reform, Renewal and the Issue-Attention Cycle," *Journal of European Public Policy* 8, no. 5 (2001), 770–86.

43. Sandra Kröger, "The Open Method of Coordination: Underconceptualisation, Over-determination, De-Politicisation and Beyond," European Integration online Papers 13, no. 5 (2009).

44. Joseph H. H. Weiler, "The Community System: The Dual Character of Supranationalism," *Yearbook of European Law* 1 (1981), 267–306.

45. Ross, *Jacques Delors and European Integration*.

46. Nicolas Jabko, "In the Name of the Market: How the European Commission Paved the Way for Monetary Union," *Journal of European Public Policy* 6, no. 3 (1999), 475–95.

47. Nicolas Jabko, *Playing the Market. A Political Strategy for Uniting Europe, 1985–2005* (Ithaca and London: Cornell University Press, 2006).

48. Wayne Sandholtz and John Zysman, "1992: Recasting the European Bargain," *World Politics* 42, no. 1 (1989), 95–128; Maria Green Cowles, "Setting the Agenda for a New Europe: The ERT and EC 1992," *Journal of Common Market Studies* 33, no. 4 (1995), 501–26.

49. Andrew Moravcsik, "Negotiating the Single European Act: National Interests and Conventional Statecraft in the European Community," *International Organization* 45, no. 1 (1991), 19–56.

50. Giandomenico Majone, "The European Commission as Regulator," in Giandomenico Majone, ed., *Regulating Europe* (London: Routledge, 1996), 61–82.

51. Dirk Lehmkuhl, "On Government, Governance and Judicial Review: The Case of European Competition Policy," *Journal of Public Policy* 28, no. 1 (2008), 148.

52. Mitchell P. Smith, "The European Commission: Diminishing Returns to Entrepreneurship," in Maria Green Cowles and Michael Smith, eds, *The State of the European Union* (Oxford: Oxford University Press, 2000), 207–27.

53. Berthold Rittberger, *Building Europe's Parliament. Democratic Representation Beyond the Nation State* (Oxford: Oxford University Press, 2005).

54. Morten Egeberg, "European Government(s): Executive Politics in Transition?" *West European Politics* 31, no. 1 (2008), 235–57.

....

CHAPTER 25

THE EUROPEAN COURT OF JUSTICE AND THE LEGAL DYNAMICS OF INTEGRATION

....

LOÏC AZOULAI AND RENAUD DEHOUSSE

SINCE the launching of the ECSC in 1951, the logic of power which had essentially characterized the relations between European states until World War II has gradually made way to a logic of cooperation. Calling into question the primacy of state sovereignty is the keystone of the European system of regional integration. For the pioneers of the European cause, right after the two global conflicts which had bled Europe dry, with their trail of ruin and barbarity, it was necessary to go beyond the system inherited from the Peace of Westphalia, constructed on the principle of unlimited state sovereignty, and in which interstate relations were above all power struggles. The idea of a new system, in which the states would be subject to a set of regulatory principles and common objectives, appeared as the only alternative to the "state of nature" in which the state apparatuses had co-existed until that point.

This idea required new legal techniques. Formally, the EU is an international organization. Established by treaty, it rests on the commitment of states to confer limited powers to common organs in order to attain preset objectives, as is common to all international organizations. In the international system, the transfer of competences is generally limited, and states retain a central role in the decision process, which limits possibilities for the organization to impose a will of its own to member countries. On the contrary, the EU system is based on an unconditional transfer of power to institutions exercising autonomous powers by adopting binding acts. This is what has been called, suggestively, a "transfer of sovereign rights." The system of the EU is characterized not only by the allocation of certain limits to states' freedom, but also by the establishment of control mechanisms to ensure the effectiveness of the decisions taken together at the supranational level.

In the EU system, control powers have been granted in particular to a supranational judicial body, the ECJ. This institution is a relatively small and isolated circle: less than 2,000 people currently work at the Court, located in Luxembourg.[1] However, it has gained a major role in the daily lives of most European citizens. This is the result of two main factors: first, the action of the Court itself to fashion a new legal order and to give it the status of the "supreme law" of the European land; second, the political context and the institutional configuration of the EU system which create incentives to systematically turn to the Court as a means to solve problems that meet political blockades at the European or national level. Somewhat unexpectedly, these factors have considerably enlarged the opportunities for private citizens to interfere in interstate relations by submitting cases affecting their interests to the Court, which have ended up altering significantly both the scope and the pace of the integration process.

25.1 Structure and Functions of the Court

At first sight, the ECJ has features similar to that of most judicial bodies. The members of the Court are chosen among individuals whose independence is beyond doubt and who possess the ability required for appointment to higher judicial offices (Article 253 TFEU), and must adhere to a code of conduct meant to shield them from external pressure. Collegiality and the secret of their deliberations guarantee their independence, and therefore the Court's authority. As regards it composition, however, some peculiarities emerge. Formally, the members of the Court are appointed by common accord of the governments of the member states for a term of six years, which is renewable (Article 254 TFEU). As a matter of fact, each country is to be "represented" by one judge. Despite recurrent criticisms, it has remained unchanged under the Lisbon Treaty, notwithstanding the fact that it may appear incompatible with the necessary impartiality expected from such an institution.

True, a supranational court is unlike its domestic counterparts. Its conditions of legitimacy are partially different: first, it must be ensured that a supranational jurisdiction understands properly the national context of the cases; second, governments and their electorates must be able to trust that their legitimate concerns are taken into account in the process of creation of common rules; third, the fact that the different national legal cultures are represented within the Court is an asset for the social acceptability of its judgments.[2] However, two problems remain. On the one hand, as a consequence of recent enlargements, the number of members has almost doubled in size and one must not ignore the impact this may have on the coherence of case law. On the other hand, this allows each government to choose "its" judge, keeping an eye on him, and possibly to renew him, which leaves the door open to possibilities of interference in the Court's work.[3] To address this point, the Lisbon Treaty has introduced a new appointment procedure. Any candidate for the post of member of the Court shall be examined by a panel of seven people, chosen from among former members of the Court, members of national supreme courts, and lawyers of recognized competence. Nonetheless, this panel of experts is confined to giving an opinion. Moreover, the European Parliament has no voice in the selection procedure, even though it may nominate one of the individuals who will sit on the selection panel.

Under Article 19 of the Treaty on European Union, the Court "shall ensure that in the interpretation and application of the Treaties the law is observed." It is quite clear that the framers of the Treaty did not intend to establish a constitutional court as it exists in many member states, that is, a court charged with protecting individual rights and preserving the balance of power within the political system. The Court was entrusted with more modest functions: it was to be an administrative jurisdiction with power to decide on misuse of powers on the part of the Community institutions (in particular the High Authority of the ECSC, and later the European Commission); an international jurisdiction with power to decide on disputes arising between member states and to ensure that the obligations arising out of the Treaties are respected by those states.[4] To this end, it was granted three types of power: the power to review member countries' fulfillment of their obligations, with the so-called infringement procedure, which is usually triggered by the Commission (Article 258 TFEU); the power to assess the validity of EU acts when actions for annulment are brought forward (Article 263 TFUE) or where preliminary questions on the validity of acts are referred by national courts (Article 267 al.1.b TFEU); the power to assist national courts in ensuring a correct application of EU law through a system of "preliminary rulings," enabling domestic courts, whenever they are confronted with a problem involving an EU law dimension, to refer to it any questions they deem fit to ask (Article 267 TFEU).

However, the ECJ has gone far beyond these formal powers. The functions of review and assistance are only one aspect of its activity.[5] First, the Court has committed itself to further the progress of integration. In many cases, the Court pushes the political actors to promote the common goals of integration.[6] Second, the Court has conferred upon itself the task of ensuring the uniform application of EU law. Systematically, the Court insists that the same rule should apply in the whole territory of the Union, irrespective of the peculiarities of national law. This has been made possible by a fairly radical transformation of the main features of the European Community (now EU) legal order.

25.2 THE CONSTITUTIONALIZATION OF THE TREATIES

Through its decisions, the ECJ has fashioned a new legal order, i.e. a system of norms distinct from national legal orders and common to all member states. Originally, this creation was oriented toward the building, promotion, and protection of the common market. To translate the idea of the common market into a reality, the technique of the transfer of competences, common to all international organizations, was not considered efficient enough. The idea was to give the law of the common market a special status, different from that of standard international organizations. Therefore, the Court decided to effectively submit all national measures adopted within the scope of EU law to a requirement of conformity with the objectives provided by the treaties. Three main techniques were employed by the Court to "constitutionalize" the EU Treaties:[7] direct effect, supremacy, and teleological interpretation of EU legal provisions.

In its *Van Gend en Loos* ruling of 1963,[8] the Court took the view that "The objective of the EEC Treaty, which is to establish a common market, the functioning of which is of direct concern to interested parties in the Community, implies that this Treaty is more than an agreement which merely creates mutual obligations between the contracting states." Rights and obligations are not merely attributed to the states but also to individuals. The Treaty is supposed to enable individuals to rely directly on EU law to challenge national measures contrary to EU law. Therefore, if the Treaty establishes an obligation for member states, a subjective right should be derived from that obligation. The remedies granted to individuals amount to creating new means of binding the states. This reasoning was partially instrumental: "when an individual appears before the judge to defend the rights he derives from the Treaties, that individual does not only act in his own interest, he immediately becomes an auxiliary agent of the Community."[9] However, the Court is not in the position to enforce those rights on its own; it had to rely on national courts. The EU system not being a federal system, it has no direct authority over national authorities. It cannot challenge the decisions of national authorities, as it can do with EU provisions. The solution was therefore to empower national judges to enforce EU law.

The principle of supremacy of EU law was invented in the 1964 *Costa v. E.N.E.L.* ruling[10] to ensure that provisions of EU law prevail over any contrary provision. To guarantee its effectiveness, national courts were to be given specific powers that could seem exorbitant within the context of the national legal system to which they belonged, such as the possibility to set aside laws passed by the legislature when they contravene EU rules, or the possibility to short-circuit higher courts when this is required to ensure the effectiveness of EU law.[11] Thanks to the "internal primacy" EU law has been so granted, national judges can be regarded as "European judges."[12] Through the mechanism of preliminary references, the Court has encouraged the gradual establishment, within the national legal systems, of "Europeanized" systems of judicial review and of liability of national authorities. It has gone as far as it could along this "imperfect" path, that of a "quasi-federal" construction of EU law.[13]

In order to further establish the authority of EU provisions, the Court adopted teleological methods of interpretation. These methods are much closer to those of constitutional courts than to those of international tribunals. Far from keeping to the real or supposed intention of the contracting parties—a compulsory point of reference in the interpretation of international agreements—the judges frequently drew inspiration from the ultimate objective of integration, outlined in broad terms in the preamble of the Treaty. The teleological method of interpretation is a two-level construction: as the Court has constantly emphasized in its judgments, "in interpreting a provision of Community law it is necessary to consider not only its wording but also the context in which it occurs and the objects of the rules of which it is part",[14] provided that "every provision of Community law must be placed in its context and interpreted in the light of the provisions of Community law as a whole."[15] The idea is to link each provision of EU law to the normative goals of integration, giving to these provisions the coherence of a complete system of law. Basically, all the interpretative work of the Court was to create a "European teleology," which protects EU law against the dangers of dissolution within the various national legal orders. In constitutionalizing EU law, the Court was seeking to protect EU standards from the national legal constraints, the risks of political negotiations, and all the bureaucratic complexities that EU texts are likely to encounter when they enter the national arena. This case law greatly strengthened the authority of EU law, while at the same time giving the EU judge an absolute control of this new legal order. Here is the paradox: this new sovereign legal order has its origins in a purely subjective perspective, that of the ECJ.

The result of this construction is that EU law is behaving like an "occupying authority" in a foreign country, using internal procedures and mobilizing state bodies to enforce the objectives of the Union. This occupation is not imposed by force; it depends entirely on the voluntary cooperation of national actors. But since these actors are still bound by their constitutional order, it inevitably paves the way for conflicts of sovereignty in exceptional cases in which constitutional norms are challenged by EU law. The Treaty establishing a constitution for Europe meant to consolidate this construction by formally recognizing the supremacy of EU law but, after its defeat in the French and Dutch referendums of 2005, this ambition was abandoned, and the Lisbon Treaty is silent on this issue.

25.3 THE JURIDIFICATION OF THE POLITICAL SPHERE

The EU is a "paradise for lawyers."[16] Given the presence within the European Community system of a judicial body charged with arbitrating inter-institutional conflicts, one could think that the possibility of resorting to the judiciary would rapidly come to be seen as one of the basic features of the European political process. Yet this possibility took some time to take shape in practice. Gradually, the main political actors realized that the legal route could enable them to garner important results, which led to the development of several types of legal strategies. The European Commission, in charge of safeguarding EU law according to the treaty, has not failed to utilize this possibility to compel reluctant states to fulfill their obligations. Some national governments have sometimes accused it of seeking by this means to short-circuit negotiations in hand at the EU Council.[17] This did not prevent them from doing the same when their own interests were at stake, be it to react to what they saw as an intrusion by the Commission into their province,[18] or to "correct" the effects of a decision taken despite their contrary vote in Council.[19] The importance of the legal battles is such that any actor hoping to count has to join in. This explains the keenness with which the European Parliament, which at the outset had only limited access to the Court, fought for its prerogatives to be extended. Now that its right to bring actions before the Court has been recognized, the European Parliament utilizes its legal capacity to defend its own prerogatives or to promote the values that constitute the liberal European ethos.[20]

But inter-institutional disputes are only the tip of the iceberg. Even if not parties to a case before the ECJ, governments and institutions can take part in proceedings through observations they bring before the Court. The closer these observations are to the formal language of law the Court has itself adopted, the more likely it is that they will be well received. This explains why these memoranda are often cast in the rigid mould of legal argument.[21] However, an observer aware of the issue at hand will generally not find it too hard to make out very specific political interests in the background. Of all the political actors, the Commission is the keenest for this type of exercise, making it a point of honor to present its observations on all cases brought before the ECJ by national jurisdictions. National governments have a habit of presenting their observations whenever a dispute raises a question of compatibility of their law with Community law.[22] Even where the Court of Justice is not called upon to intervene, legal considerations are far from being absent from the political process. As a Canadian observer has very rightly pointed out, the juridification of the political game is reflected not just by a change of forum but also by a change in form.[23] The prospect, or sometimes even the mere possibility, of a legal dispute compels political actors to incorporate legal parameters into their strategies so as to avoid possible legal censure. Such questions as the competence of EU institutions, the choice of legal basis, and respect for fundamental principles recognized by the Court of Justice (human rights, the principle of proportionality) may thus play an important part in the political process.

How is one to explain the central role of lawyers in the European political process? Some factors are structural in nature; they have to do with the complex nature of the Community institutional system, where, with all the difficulties this implies, two sorts of distribution of power overlap: "vertical" distribution between the EU and its member states, and "horizontal" distribution among the various EU institutions. As in most separation of powers systems, the need for a judicial umpire has made itself felt, and its activity has enhanced the importance of legal questions. Other factors are of a more political nature. In most systems where institutional conflicts can be submitted to adjudication by a constitutional court, this is only one way among others of settling differences. Alternative proceedings may be used: political parties are often more inclined to favor a negotiated solution rather than embark on legal proceedings where the outcome is always uncertain. This sort of alternative is missing at EU level, where the influence of the political parties remains relatively slight.

Public institutions are not the only ones to have become aware of the potential of the legal sphere. Other actors—private companies, interest groups, or even individuals—have noticed that recourse to the courts could enable them to reach results the ordinary political process could not allow them to aspire to, and they have not refrained from making use of it. A priori there was nothing to foreshadow this development. Reacting against what seemed to them an over-liberal interpretation of the relevant provisions of the ECSC Treaty, the drafters of the Rome Treaty had opted for a formula that strictly limited possibilities of individual appeals by private individuals against acts taken by the institutions. By Article 173 of the EC treaty (now Article 263 of the Treaty on the functioning of the European Union[24]), only persons "directly and individually" concerned by Community acts could ask for them to be set aside.

Two factors, however, enabled private interests to become very active on another front, namely the relationship between national law and EU law. From the outset, with the 1963 *Van Gend en Loos* judgment,[25] the Court of Justice gave a very broad interpretation to the bans on discrimination contained in the treaty. As we said, the Court saw many of these provisions as a source of rights that plaintiffs could invoke before the national courts—for this is what is described as direct effect in EU law—even where the treaty wording clearly suggested they were chiefly addressed to member states. This reading of the treaty, transforming it into a catalogue of individual rights, opened doors to individuals to an arsenal of argument they could make use of whenever the national authorities seemed to them to breach the individual rights granted to them by Community law. Access to the Court was further facilitated by a second revolution—this time of a procedural nature. While the treaty had entrusted to the Commission the task of bringing proceedings aimed at punishing breaches of Community law (Article 258 TFEU), the Court of Justice accepted the national courts' using the channel of the preliminary ruling (Article 267 TFEU) to ask it—in terms often devoid of all ambiguity—about the compatibility of national provisions with EU law, thus bringing about a true decentralization of judicial review of the way EU law was implemented.[26]

The combination of these two developments considerably broadened possibilities for private individuals to utilize the legal sphere. Where they feel that Community rules are more favorable to their interests than national rules, they can in fact lodge an appeal before a national court and endeavor to convince it to send a case to Luxembourg. Through this channel, private plaintiffs can launch a legal offensive at European level against regulatory obstacles they come up against at national level. One has thus seen big shops challenging provisions banning Sunday opening as barriers to free movement; pharmaceutical firms doing the same with rules on the marketing of medicines; women drawing on the principle of equal treatment laid down in Article 157 TFEU to gain social advantages denied to them at national level; and so on. The development of this type of dispute is the fruit of a convergence of specific motivations. Plaintiffs have found in EU law an instrument enabling them to promote their own interests, and the ECJ a way of dismantling the many barriers to trade existing at national level, thus making up for the omissions of a Community legislator hampered by the uncertain search for consensus.[27] In the *Marks & Spencer* case,[28] for instance, the Court had to deal with the problem of the

transfer of losses within groups of companies under the rule on the freedom of establishment of legal persons (Article 49 TFEU), a problem that the Commission had
proposed for a long time (but in vain) to settle through harmonization. In these circumstances, it is not surprising that strategic utilization of European legal procedures is
mostly a matter for big companies[29] or interest groups with sufficient resources to
embark on costly legal battles with uncertain outcomes.

25.4 EXPLAINING THE COURT'S ROLE

While the ECJ's influence may have varied over time, it has always been felt. This is all
the more remarkable considering governments' traditional reluctance to let judicial
bodies interfere in interstate relations, for, despite occasional skirmishes, the ECJ has
not met with systematic resistance on the side of its direct interlocutors. Member states'
governments have occasionally mumbled against some of its rulings, but they have never
attempted to curtail the Court's powers. True, on several occasions they have given evidence of their unwillingness to allow a further expansion of judicial activism. The pillars
structure of the Maastricht Treaty owes much to the willingness to contain the ECJ,
whose influence was to be confined to the Community pillar. Specific protocols were
appended to the Treaties to prevent an unwanted evolution of the Court's case law. But
instances of ratification of judicial inventions weren't rare either: the Maastricht Treaty
validated the Court's recognition of human rights and recognized the European
Parliament's right to bring annulment actions "for the purpose of protecting its prerogatives" which had been first introduced in an earlier ECJ ruling[30] and, as was said, governments had initially envisaged to formally recognize the supremacy of EU law in the
constitutional treaty. The creation by the SEA (1986) of a Court of First Instance, to
which law suits directly introduced by private parties were entrusted, was motivated by
the necessity to enable the ECJ to better perform its task, which can hardly be seen as a
sign of mistrust. Similarly, national courts, called upon to play a key role in the European
legal order, could have reacted negatively against the rulings of the ECJ. Had they done
so, the ECJ would have been faced with great difficulties, since it definitely needs their
support: some 47.9 percent of its rulings in 2008 find their origin in a preliminary reference from national courts. Here again, much attention has gone to the vigorous reactions of some higher courts to the activism displayed by their somewhat intrusive
European counterpart. The decision of the German *Bundesverfassungsgericht* of June 30,
2009 on the Lisbon Treaty, for instance, was a clear warning that further erosions of
Germanys' sovereignty would not be tolerated.[31] But this should not obscure the fact
that, on the whole, national courts (and in particular lower courts) have by and large
played their part with enthusiasm in the Euro-law game: they account for some 48.6
percent of the references that reached the Court's docket in 2008. The first research question is therefore what has prompted most of the ECJ's interlocutors to accept the "quiet
revolution" it has operated with the constitutionalization of the European legal system, a

process without any equivalent on the international plane?[32] Secondly, how can one account for the differences that may be discerned in their reactions?

Glancing at the academic literature, one can distinguish different kinds of responses to these questions. As has been noted, "most of the legal literature begins and ends with law, describing a legalist world that is hermetically closed to considerations of power and self-interest"[33] and has for long been characterized by an uncritical acceptance of the European Court's performance.[34] Legal formalism invites judges and scholars to regard judicial rulings as revealing legal ruler's true meaning, downplaying the amount of discretion it may involve. And in its first years of activity, the ECJ has spared no effort to win national courts' confidence, be it by patiently explaining what it expected them to do and cultivating court-to-court dialogue through the preliminary rulings procedure[35] or by conducting what can be best described as a systematically planned public relations policy, aimed at guaranteeing a smooth cooperation between national and European judges.[36] It could also rely on the active support of the community of EU law specialists, who contributed to spreading the Court's narrative of the necessary construction of an EU legal order.[37]

Some political science accounts offered a neo-institutionalist explanation of the emergence of the European legal system. Burley and Mattli suggested that this process gave incentives to support the European court's case law to a wide range of domestic actors: by pursuing their own personal or professional interests, individual litigants, their lawyers, and lower national courts participated in the construction of the Community legal system.[38] Thus, "the Court created a pro-Community constituency of private individuals by giving them a direct stake in promulgation and implementation of Community law."[39] Many courts, for instance, have seen their power increase under the influence of ECJ case law, which demands that they review the conformity of domestic law with EU law, even though they may be denied a power of judicial review over legislation in their domestic legal order. In a similar vein, Alec Stone Sweet and Thomas Brunel have shown that there is a correlation between the reference rates and trade flows, suggesting that an increase in the latter results in more litigation, with more cases ending up before the ECJ.[40] Yet, the limitation of those analyses is that they treat all national courts alike, whereas there is ample evidence that higher courts do not display the same degree of enthusiasm vis-à-vis the EU as lower courts. Constitutional courts in particular are notorious for their refusal to refer cases to Luxembourg, and several of them have issued clear warnings indicating that they could not accept without qualifications the ECJ's claim to supremacy.[41] Obviously, EU law does not offer the same kind of incentives to all courts.

Turning to national governments, it has been suggested that their overall acceptance of the European Court's jurisprudence could be viewed as a clue that judicial behavior was perhaps more concerned with political interests than it might seem at first sight. On this realist reading, because courts are concerned about the prospect of non-compliance or possible hostile reactions, they tend to calculate how far they can go without eliciting too costly a reaction from politicians.[42] True, such strategic concerns can occasionally be discerned in the ECJ's behavior, witness its tendency to "split the difference" between adverse claims or to use with moderation the broad powers it claims.[43] But there is no shortage of evidence that it is at times willing to challenge the dominant view among governments. Its landmark rulings in *Van Gend and Loos* and *Costa v. ENEL* were taken despite the declared opposition of a majority of states, which had intervened before the Court. But the context of the first decades of integration may explain why the latter's innovation did not meet with stronger resistance: the relative paralysis of the Council following the Luxembourg compromise, the pro-integration stance of a majority of national governments, and the existence of a wide (even if shallow) support for integration within public opinion all concurred to facilitate acceptance of the "constitutionalization" of the Community legal order.[44]

25.5 MARKET-BUILDING AND SOCIAL INTEGRATION

The EJC has been and remains the court of an international organization the primary objective of which is the creation of a common market by the elimination of "all obstacles to intra-community trade in order to merge the national markets into a single market bringing about conditions as close as possible to those of a genuine internal market."[45] The law of the common market is the law of cross-border exchanges. Its aims are to put an end to the compartmentalization of national markets and to allow for the free flow of economic factors. The Court used two main bodies of rules to achieve that objective: the free movement rules designed to eliminate public restrictions of trade; the competition rules designed to ensure conditions of relative equality of opportunities within that market. These rules were promoted to the category of "very foundations of the Community."[46] This promotion was important in establishing a framework in which all the actors engaged in integration must continuously justify themselves with regard to these fundamental legal principles. By imposing this "framework of justification," the Court has set up a constant vigilance over the behavior of EU institutions and national governments. Within the EU context, national governments are subject to the continuous need to justify themselves, before EU bodies and before domestic courts.

This does not mean that the case law of the Court is a closed system. It is also characterized by a certain vulnerability to external forces.[47] The Court had to take into account demands from the member states and from the constitutional courts. The problem was to take into consideration the states' demands without surrendering the autonomy of EU law. The solution was to devise new standards for a better protection of fundamental or social rights, taking into account the needs and specific aims that the Court itself gave to the integration process. Thus, if "respect for fundamental rights forms an integral part of the general principles of law protected by the Court of Justice," it remains that "the protection of such rights, whilst inspired by the constitutional traditions common to the member states, must be ensured within the framework of the structure and objectives of the Community."[48] The structure and the objectives of the common market are thus protected.

A Court acting in this way is a market-building court. Now, any establishment of a new order (economic, political, and legal) presupposes a rupture with the previous order.[49] Through its case law the Court allowed for the modification of the balance of power that was in place in Europe. Some argue that this construction has had a "liberalizing effect" on national economies.[50] What is certain is that it gives the Court an important, perhaps excessive responsibility. It has indeed become the ultimate arbiter of the balance between economic and social concerns in the common market.[51]

From the Treaty of Maastricht onward, the context has changed. The political actors wish to bestow on the Union—founded on pragmatic economic growth—a stronger social and value component. Evidence of this is the wording of Article 2 of the Treaty on European Union, as amended by the Lisbon Treaty: "the Union shall offer its citizens an area of freedom, security and justice without internal frontiers," and the introduction into this provision of a reference to the "social market economy." This concept in the new treaty clearly corresponds to the desire to create a social counterbalance to market considerations. It contains the idea that European integration should not be pursued to the detriment of the integrity of the social systems of the member states. The emphasis is placed on civil and social integration rather than on market integration. The Court cannot ignore this evolution. As a matter of fact, a new integration regime is beginning to emerge in the case law of the Court. Rulings based on market rules reinterpreted in the light of citizenship rights and fundamental rights are designed to ensure the access of Union citizens to those collective goods which are vectors of social integration: markets, but also territories, professions, national systems of social protection, justice, or education.[52]

This seems to imply a "reconstitutionalization" of EU law.[53] The classic type of constitutionalization consisted in establishing the supremacy of the European Community treaty. It was hierarchical in nature. Now, the Court uses constitutional methods of adjudication based on the idea of conciliation between opposing principles and values. In this way, one moves from a hierarchical way of resolving conflicts to a form of legal pluralism. This presupposes a twofold change in the nature of legal integration: an enlargement of its scope and an alteration of its substance. First, it means that virtually no area of economic and social life is, in principle, completely immune from the empire of EU law. The penetration of EU law in all the areas of competence of the member states is perhaps the most important phenomenon in case law in the last ten years.[54]

Second, there is a pressure to reconcile the EU rules favoring free trade with the contradictory requirements of equal constitutional value that arise out of the EU legal order, international law, and national constitutional law. A number of recent judgments bear witness to the birth of a new analytical framework.[55] But, just as the constitutionalization of the Treaties has engendered conflicts of sovereignty, this new trend in case law generates conflicts between values and models. Member countries have espoused very divergent economic, cultural, and social models. In the situation following the accession of twelve new member states, there is an increasing risk of competition between these models, which is potentially destructive for the Union. In the absence of any competence to harmonize social standards transferred to the Union, the task to maintain an equilibrium between the divergent requirements of the national models and the uniform requirements of the internal market is delegated to the Court.[56] So far, it does not seem that the technique of reconciliation used by the Court lives up to the ideal announced in the Lisbon Treaty.[57] The legitimacy of the Court and the consequences of its case law have been occasionally challenged.[58]

25.6 CONCLUSION

The ECJ has played a leading role in the integration process. It has decisively shaped the structure of the EU legal system and its relationships with national legal orders. It is now increasingly called upon to address delicate issues involving fundamental choices between economic freedom and social justice. But the context in which it operates has changed: EU competences have been substantially extended as well as the area is which a majority decision-making is possible in the Council, the Parliament has gained new powers, and there are growing fears of an unequal distribution of the costs and benefits of integration in an enlarged and less homogenous Union.[59] Moreover, the description of a Court "tucked away in the fairyland Duchy of Luxemburg and blessed, until recently, with the benign neglect by the powers that be and the mass media" is no longer true.[60] The Court is operating under greater public scrutiny. The "turning point" can be said to have occurred during the 1990s,[61] as a consequence of a threefold development: the growing importance of fundamental rights issues in case law; the extension of EU competences, in particular in the field of justice and internal affairs; and the widespread recognition of the protection of the constitutional identity of the member states. Moreover, the EU system is above all a system of checks and balances in which each institution enjoys considerable autonomy. Were the role of political groupings to expand, it is not certain that all conflicts could be solved through a political decision. In the current context of crises and uncertainty about the objectives to be pursued by the process of European integration, political negotiations lead to the development of deeply contested legislative agreements, which often represent an uncertain compromise between opposed preferences. This de facto leaves it to the Court to adjudicate disputes and to give the practical meaning of rules.[62]

NOTES

1. R. Grass, "Les ressources humaines à la Cour de justice des Communautés européennes," *in Le droit à la mesure de l'homme. Mélanges en l'honneur de Philippe Léger* (Paris, Pedone, 2006), 69.

2. C. Tomuschat."National Representation of Judges and Legitimacy of International Jurisdictions: Lessons from ICJ to ECJ?" in I. Pernice, J. Kokott, and C. Saunders, eds, *The Future of the European Judicial System in a Comparative Perspective* (Baden-Baden: Nomos Verlag, 2006).

3. J.-V. Louis, "The Court in the Constitution: How Federal?" in I. Pernice et al., *The Future of the European Judicial System*.

4. D. Simon, "Les mécanismes juridictionnels dans la Communauté européenne," in *Perspectives convergentes et divergentes sur l'intégration économique*, Colloque commun SFDI/SQDI de Québec (Paris: Pedone, 1993), 61–78.

5. J. Basedow, "The Judge's Role in European Integration—The Court of Justice and its Critics," in H.-W. Micklitz and B. De Witte, eds. *The European Court of Justice and the Autonomy of the Member States* (Cambridge-Antwerp-Portland: Intersentia, 2012).

6. For example, by ruling in favor of the mobility of students; see case C-147/03, *Commission v. Austria*.

7. J. H. H. Weiler, *The Constitution of Europe* (Cambridge: Cambridge University Press, 1999).

8. Case 26/62.

9. R. Lecourt, *L'Europe des juges* (Brussels: Bruylant, 1976), 260.

10. Case 6/64.

11. Case 106/77, *Simmenthal*.

12. B. de Witte, "Retour à 'Costa': La primauté du droit communautaire à la lumière du droit international," *Revue trimestrielle de droit européen* (1984), 425.

13. Joined Cases C-6/90 and C-9/90CJCE, *Francovich, Bonifaci, and others* v *Italy*.

14. Case C-83/94, *Leifer*.

15. Case 283/81, *CILFIT*.

16. A. Vauchez, "'Integration Through Law': Contribution to a Socio-History of EU Political Common Sense," *EUI Working Paper RSCAS*, no. 2008/10, 2008.

17. See e.g. case 205/84, *Commission v. German Federal Republic*.

18. Joined cases 281, 283–5, 287/85, *FRG et al. v. Commission*.

19. Case 68/86, *UK v. Council*; case C-376/98, *German Federal Republic v. Council*.

20. Case C-540/03, *Parliament v. Council*; Joined cases C-317/04 et C-318/04, *Parliament v. Council*.

21. L. Azoulai, "La fabrication de la jurisprudence communautaire," in P. Mbongo and A. Vauchez, eds, *Dans la fabrique du droit européen. Scènes, acteurs et publics de la Cour de justice des Communautés européennes* (Brussels: Bruylant, 2009), 153.

22. M.-P. Granger, "Les stratégies contentieuses des Etats devant la Cour de justice," in Mbongo and Vauchez, *Dans la fabrique du droit européen. Scènes, acteurs et publics de la Cour de justice des Communautés européennes* (Brussels: Bruylant, 2009), 53.

23. M. Mandel, *The Charter of Rights and the Legalization of Politics in Canada*, second edition (Toronto: Thompson, 1994), 81.

24. Article 263 does not change this rule, it only provides an exception for persons acting against a regulatory act which is of direct concern to them and does not entail implementing measures.

25. Case 26/62.

26. R. Dehousse, *La Cour de justice des Communautés européennes*, second edition (Paris: Montchrestien, 1997), 33–6.

27. Dehousse, *La Cour de justice des Communautés européennes*, 72–6.

28. C-446/03.

29. C. Harding, "Who Goes to Court in Europe? An Analysis of Litigation Against the European Community," *European Law Review* 17 (1992), 104–25.
30. Case C-70/88, *European Parliament v. Council.*
31. D. Halberstam and E. Stein, "The United Nations, the European Union, and the King of Sweden: Economic Sanctions and Individual Rights in a Plural World Order," *Common Market Law Review* 46, no. 1 (2009), 13–72.
32. J. H. H. Weiler, "A Quiet Revolution. The European Court of Justice and its Interlocutors," *Comparative Political Studies* 26 (1994), 510–34.
33. A.-M. Burley and W. Mattli, "Europe Before the Court: A Political Theory of Legal Integration," *International Organization* 47, no. 1 (1993), 41–76, at 45.
34. M. Shapiro, "Comparative Law and Comparative Politics," *Southern California Law Review* 53 (1980), 538.
35. F. Mancini, "The Making of a Constitution of Europe," *Common Market Law Review* 26 (1989), 303–16.
36. Lecourt, *L'Europe des juges.*
37. K. Alter, *The European Court's Political Power: Selected Essays* (Oxford, Oxford University Press, 2009); A. Vauchez, "Droit et politique," in C. Belot, P. Magnette, and S. Saurugger, eds, *Science politique de l'Union européenne* (Paris: Economica, 2008).
38. Burley and Mattli, "Europe Before the Court: A Political Theory of Legal Integration."
39. Burley and Mattli, "Europe Before the Court: A Political Theory of Legal Integration," 60.
40. A. Stone Sweet and T. Brunell, "Constructing a Supranational Constitution: Dispute Resolution and Governance in the European Community," *The American Political Science Review* 92, no 1 (1998), 63–81.
41. K. Alter, *Establishing the Supremacy of European Law: The Making of an International Rule of Law in Europe* (Oxford, Oxford University Press, 2001).
42. G. Garrett and B. Weingast, "Ideas, Interests, and Institutions: Constructing the EC's Internal Market," in J. Goldstein and R. Keohane, eds, *Ideas and Foreign Policy: Beliefs, Institutions, and Political Change* (Ithaca: Cornell University Press, 1993), 173–206.
43. Dehousse, *La Cour de justice des Communautés européennes*, 130–5.
44. J. H. H. Weiler, "The Community System: The Dual Character of Supranationalism," *Yearbook of European Law* 1 (1981), 267.
45. Case 15/81, *Schul.*
46. ECJ opinion, 1/91.
47. M. Rosenfeld, "Comparing Constitutional Review by the European Court of Justice and the U.S. Supreme Court," *International Journal of Constitutional Law* 4, no. 4 (October 2006), 618.
48. Case 44/79, *Liselotte Hauer v Land Rheinland-Pfalz.*
49. H. Lindhal, "Acquiring the Community: The *Acquis* and the Institution of European Legal Order," *European Law Journal* 9, no. 4 (2003), 433–50.
50. F. Scharpf, "The Double Asymmetry of European Integration, Or Why the EU Cannot Be a Social Market Economy," *Max Planck Institute for the Study of Societies Working Paper*, no. 09/12, 2009.
51. M. Poiares Maduro, *We the Court: The European Court of Justice and the European Economic Constitution* (Oxford: Hart Publishing, 1998).
52. See e.g. case C-212/97, *Centros*; case C-117/01, *K.B.*; case C-456/02, *Trojani*; joined cases C-76/05 a C-318/05, *Schwarz*; case C-353/06; *Grunkin & Paul*; case C-127/08, *Metock.*

53. L. Azoulai, "Le rôle constitutionnel de la Cour de justice des Communautés européennes tel qu'il se dégage de sa jurisprudence," *Revue trimestrielle de droit européen*, no. 1 (2008), 29.

54. See e.g. case C-73/08 [2010] § 28. This extension is signalled by a recurrent formula in the Court's rulings: even if, in the areas which fall outside the scope of the EU's competence [such as social protection, tax matters, education, civil status of persons] the Member States are still free, in principle, to lay down the conditions governing the domain in question, the fact remains that, when exercising that competence, the Member States must nevertheless comply with EU law.

55. See e.g. case C-280/00, *Altmark*; case C-309/99, *Wouters*; case C-112/00, *Schmidberger*; case C-36/02, *Omega*.

56. Case C-438/05, *Viking Line*; case C-341/05, *Laval*.

57. L. Azoulai, "The Court of Justice and the Social Market Economy: The Emergence of an Ideal and the Conditions for its Realization," *Common Market Law Review* 45 (2008), 1335.

58. See e.g. case C-144/04, *Mangold*; case C-127/08, *Metock*.

59. N. Fligstein, *Euroclash: The EU, European Identity, and the Future of Europe* (Oxford: Oxford University Press, 2008).

60. E. Stein, "Lawyers, Judges and the Making of a Transnational Constitution," *American Journal of International Law* 75, no. 1 (1981), 1–27.

61. J. Baquero Cruz, "The Changing Constitutional Role of the European Court of Justice," *International Journal of Legal information* 34, no. 2 (2006), 223–45.

62. L. Azoulai, and M. Poiares Maduro, "Introduction," in Azoulai and Poiares Maduro, eds, *The Past and Future of EU Law. The Classics of EU Law Revisited on the 50th Anniversary of the Rome Treaty* (Oxford: Hart Publishing, 2010), xiii–xx.

CHAPTER 26

....

THE EUROPEAN PARLIAMENT

....

TAPIO RAUNIO

26.1 INTRODUCTION

When comparing the various EU institutions, the European Parliament is undoubtedly the one that has changed most over the decades.[1] Initially a purely consultative body with members seconded from national parliaments, the European Parliament is now vested with significant legislative, control, and budgetary powers. The Parliament shapes EU laws, particularly through the co-decision procedure, is involved in the appointment of the Commission and can force the latter to resign, and decides on the EU's annual budget with the Council.

The Parliament has also been directly elected since 1979, with 736 MEPs elected in the seventh round of elections held in 2009. However, at least when measured by turnout, the Parliament has failed to connect with Europeans, with Euro-elections almost exclusively heralded as a disappointment by both the media and political scientists. Turnout has steadily fallen since the first elections, with only 43 percent voting in the 2009 elections. Although the initial expectations regarding turnout were probably unrealistic, the main concern for the European Parliament is that turnout has declined despite the empowerment of the Parliament.

These two themes—the increase in Parliament's powers and European Parliament elections—have also largely dominated the literature. In addition, there is an important body of work on party politics and committees in the Parliament. In fact, it is plausible to argue that the European Parliament is one of the most researched parliaments in the world, and certainly the EU institution we know most about.[2] This chapter examines the state of scholarly understanding on the European Parliament, with the next section focusing on direct elections. Then we turn our attention to European Parliament's party groups before exploring committees and the Parliament's inter-institutional relations with the Council and the Commission. The concluding discussion suggests some avenues for further research.

26.2 ELECTIONS

The literature on European Parliament elections has largely been based on the "second-order" elections model, developed initially by Reif and Schmitt in their article on the first set of Euro-elections held in 1979.[3] According to this analytical framework second-order elections are less important than first-order elections, with the latter referring mainly to domestic parliamentary and/or presidential elections. This research can be divided into two themes: studies focusing on citizens' attitudes and preferences toward voting and European Parliament /EU, and research explaining party strategies and performance in the elections. Much of this research has utilized data generated by the European Election Studies (EES) project that has carried out citizen (all elections except in 1984) and candidate (1994 and 2009) surveys in connection with the elections.[4]

The second-order election model draws on the premise that citizens' behavior is determined more by the national "first-order" context than factors related to the European Parliament elections themselves. The model is based on the following three main hypotheses: (1) turnout is lower in European Parliament elections than in national elections; (2) government parties will suffer losses in Euro-elections; and (3) larger parties will do worse and smaller parties will perform better in European Parliament elections. Regarding the first argument, turnout has indeed declined consistently from 63 percent in 1979 to 43 percent in the 2009 elections. Turnout has thus fallen despite the considerable empowerment of the Parliament. In fact, according to the second-order thesis turnout should have increased when there is "more at stake" in European Parliament elections.[5]

The timing of European Parliament elections plays a crucial part in the second-order model. Government parties will perform worst if European Parliament elections take place halfway through the national parliamentary electoral cycle. But when European Parliament elections are scheduled just after or before national first-order elections, then governing parties do better. The poor success of government or large parties is also explained by the "less at stake" argument. Voters experiment with new parties as they know that European Parliament elections shall not result in major societal changes—at least not in their home country. Hence citizens vote for parties that are either closer to their own preferences or alternatively use European Parliament elections to protest against governing or mainstream parties.[6] The second-order effects also mean that the composition of the Parliament is biased in favor of parties that fare worse in national first-order elections, with national governing parties consistently punished in Euro-elections.[7]

As the second-order model argues, voting decisions in Euro-elections are heavily influenced by the domestic party-political environment. The primacy of domestic factors results in part from the strategies of national parties that control candidate selection and carry out the electoral campaigns. Most national parties fight European Parliament elections on domestic issues. National parties are mainly based on the traditional social cleavages recognized in political science literature, and as the anti/pro-integration dimension tends to cross-cut these cleavages, parties often experience internal fragmentation on EU questions.[8] Moreover, survey data shows that parties are on average more representative of their voters on traditional left–right matters than on issues related to European integration, with the elite more supportive of integration than the electorate.[9] Hence established parties have an incentive to contest the elections along the familiar left–right dimension and to downplay contestation over integration.

Elections to the Parliament are therefore held during the same week and the candidates compete for seats in an EU institution, but there is no common electoral system, and campaigning is conducted by national parties on the basis of largely national agendas. But as Chapter 58 in this volume indicates, Europe as an issue has become increasingly politicized and salient. This has also become apparent in Euro-elections, with the EU as an issue becoming more important in explaining citizens' voting behaviour:

> governing parties may lose votes because of the disconnect between major governing parties and their voters on the issue of EU integration, and the fact that EP elections make this issue, and therefore this disconnect, more prominent. On both the contextual and individual levels, it appears that Europe can matter when voters go to the polls. Governing-party voters who are more sceptical about further integration are more likely to defect or abstain in EP elections.[10]

Research thus indicates that national parties which are out of tune with their electorates over European integration are punished in Euro-elections.

26.3 PARTY SYSTEM

Compared with parties in European national legislatures, European Parliament party groups operate in a very different institutional environment. The political and social heterogeneity of the EU is reflected inside the groups, with around 170 parties from twenty-seven member states winning seats in the 2009 elections. However, European Parliament party groups have gradually consolidated their position in the Parliament. Kreppel shows how the increase in the legislative powers of the European Parliament has contributed to the centralization of power in the hands of the two large party groups—the centre-right European People's Party (EPP) which brings together Christian democrats and conservatives and the centre-left Party of European Socialists (PES; Group of the Progressive Alliance of Socialists and Democrats (S&D) after the 2009 elections)—and in more pragmatic cooperation between them in order to influence the EU policy process. Kreppel also shows how the two main party groups introduced changes to the Parliament's rules of procedure that further marginalized the smaller party groups.[11]

Much of the research on European Parliament party groups is based on roll-call data, with vote data often supplemented by MEP surveys.[12] After the "first generation" of studies that employed rather limited numbers of votes,[13] subsequent research by Hix and others has been far more ambitious, methodologically more sophisticated, and based on larger numbers of votes. This research has produced two main findings. First, European Parliament groups do achieve rather high levels of cohesion, with cohesion levels roughly around 85–90 percent and even above 90 percent. Probably the main reason why MEPs and national parties vote with their group most of the time is policy influence. Cohesive action is essential for achieving group's objectives, while cooperative behavior within groups helps individual MEPs in pursuing their own goals. Moreover, given the huge number of amendments and final resolutions voted upon in plenaries, the voting cues provided by groups and particularly group members in the responsible European Parliament committee are an essential source of guidance for MEPs.[14] Second, the main cleavage structuring competition in the Parliament is the familiar left–right dimension, with the anti/pro-integration dimension constituting the second main structure of competition.[15] Studies based on EES survey data and on expert surveys have produced largely similar results concerning both the dimensionality of the political space in the chamber and levels of group cohesion.[16]

While the primary decision rule in the Parliament is simple majority, in certain issues (mainly budget amendments and second reading legislative amendments adopted under the co-decision procedure) the European Parliament needs to have absolute majorities (50 percent + 1 of MEPs). This absolute majority requirement facilitates cooperation between the two main groups, EPP and S&D, which between them have controlled around two-thirds of the seats. Cooperation between EPP and PES is also influenced by inter-institutional considerations, as the Parliament needed to moderate its resolutions in order to get its amendments accepted by the Council and the Commission.[17] Competition on the left–right has benefited the smaller groups. This has applied particularly to the liberals, named the Alliance of Liberals and Democrats for Europe (ALDE) since the 2004 elections. Situated ideologically between EPP and S&D, the liberals have often been in a "pivotal" position in forming winning coalitions.

The 2004 enlargement did not really change cohesion levels or coalition patterns in the chamber. Party cohesion remained stable and the EPP and PES voted together almost exactly the same amount of times in the 2004–2009 Parliament (68 percent of the time) as in the previous electoral period. However, in the 2004–2009 Parliament there was a clearer centre-right majority bloc (EPP–ALDE–Union for Europe of Nations), while the three leftist groups (PES, Greens/European Free Alliance, European United Left/Nordic Green Left) were often in a minority position and were also less united.[18] In fact, the shift to the right began already in the 1999 elections when the EPP emerged as the largest group.[19]

National parties are crucial to understanding how European Parliament party groups work.[20] MEPs can be regarded as agents serving multiple principals: voters, national parties, and European Parliament party groups. Arguably national parties constitute the most powerful principals as they control candidate selection, especially in countries that use more closed lists. While links between national parties and their MEPs have traditionally been rather loose, recent research indicates that the ties are gradually becoming stronger. There is more policy coordination between MEPs and their parties, with particularly case studies on British and German parties confirming this trend,[21] but national parties nonetheless largely refrain from "mandating" their MEPs.[22] It is also interesting to note that overall the preferences of national MPs and MEPs over integration are quite similar, and that contrary to much accepted wisdom, MEPs do not "go native" in Brussels, becoming considerably more pro-European than their party comrades back home.[23]

Voting behavior in the Parliament provides further evidence of the influence of national parties. Research indicates that when MEPs receive conflicting voting instructions from national parties and their European Parliament groups, they are more likely to side with their national party, particularly in parties where the leadership has better opportunities to punish and reward its MEPs (e.g. through more centralized candidate selection or closed lists): "Despite the fact that the parliamentary principals in the EP control important benefits—such as committee assignments and speaking time—it is the principals that control candidate selection (the national parties) who ultimately determine how MEPs behave. When the national parties in the same parliamentary group decide to vote together, the EP parties look highly cohesive. But when these parties take opposing policy positions, the cohesion of the EP parties breaks down."[24] Hence we can expect particularly those MEPs that are seeking re-election to be reluctant to ignore national party guidelines, with such attentiveness to national party positions higher in the run-up to the Euro-elections.[25]

The main party groups in the Parliament are either officially or in practice the parliamentary wings of their Euro-parties. Maastricht Treaty assigned political parties a specific role to play in the political system of the EU. According to the Treaty's Article 138a, "Political parties at the European level are important as a factor for integration within the Union. They contribute to forming a European awareness and to expressing the political will of the citizens of the Union." This "Party Article" has now been included as Article 10(4) in the Lisbon Treaty: "Political parties at European level contribute to forming European political awareness and to expressing the will of citizens of the Union."

The constitutional recognition in the form of the Party Article in the Maastricht Treaty contributed to the consolidation of Euro-parties. With the exception of the EPP, which had been founded in 1976, the federations of national parties were quickly turned into Euro-parties. The Confederation of Socialist Parties of the European Community (CSP), founded in 1974, was transformed into PES in November 1992. The Federation of European Liberal, Democrat, and Reform Parties, founded in 1976, became ELDR in December 1993. The European Federation of Green Parties (EFGP) was established in June 1993, changing its name to the European Green Party (EGP) in 2004. In addition, a number of smaller Euro-parties have been established since the introduction in 2004 of public funding of Euro-parties from the EU's budget.[26]

Research has mainly focused on individual Euro-parties,[27] with select few comparative works.[28] These studies have largely focused on how an exogenous factor (deepening integration) has produced endogenous reforms within the Euro-parties. However, while there are good case studies of Euro-party influence in the European Council and other EU institutions[29] and in specific policy areas or Treaty negotiations,[30] there is a need for a theory that explains whether and under what conditions Euro-parties impact on EU or national politics. Secondly, there is a lack of comparative studies explaining variation among the Euro-parties. So far such systematic comparison has only been applied to examining the ideologies of the Euro-parties. For example, research by Hix and Gabel shows that Euro-parties have become ideologically increasingly similar, especially after social democrats and greens changed their attitudes to European integration. While support for deeper integration was stronger among the centre-right parties (EPP and ELDR) until the 1990s, since the Maastricht Treaty the centre-left (PES and also partially the Greens) have become the leading advocates of further centralization.[31] This comparative focus could logically be extended to the inner workings of the Euro-parties. We know relatively little in comparative terms about how Euro-parties operate and coordinate policy among the national member parties and whether this policy coordination results in changes in the ideologies of national member parties. Perhaps the existing understanding is best summarized by Ladrech, according to whom Euro-parties are better understood as networks of like-minded national parties that facilitate information-sharing and, within certain constraints, also the advancement of policy objectives.[32]

But can European Parliament party groups and the Parliament influence EU politics? This is the main question addressed in the next section, which first examines committees that are key actors in shaping supranational laws and in forming European Parliament's positions before focusing on the legislative and control powers of the Parliament vis-à-vis the Council and the Commission.

26.4 INFLUENCING EU POLITICS?

Unlike many national constitutions, the Treaties leave it up to the Parliament to design its internal rules. The European Parliament has structured and reformed its internal organization so as to make most of its hard-won powers in the EU political system.[33] As the European Parliament has gained new powers, the full chamber has delegated more authority to committees. The thrust of legislative work is done in committees where individual rapporteurs draft reports that form the basis for parliamentary resolutions. Committees are also key forums for holding institutions such as the Commission and the ECB to account and in shaping the EU's budget and monitoring its implementation. The 2009–2014 Parliament has twenty committees.

Committees of the Parliament have only recently attracted scholarly attention. This research has largely been driven by the debate between informational and distributional models of legislative politics derived from literature on the US Congress. The studies on European Parliament committees have found support for both perspectives, both concerning distribution of committee seats and rapporteurships, with the latter distributed among the groups on the basis of an auction-like points system. As the point total of each party group is proportional to its seat share in the chamber, the most expensive reports, such as those on the EU budget or on important pieces of co-decision legislation, are largely controlled by the large groups.[34]

As committees enjoy extensive procedural rights in the Parliament, it is in the interest of both the party groups and national parties to influence committee work. Party groups monitor committee proceedings, with group working parties and coordinators in key roles.[35] The procedures for allocating committee chairs, seats, and reports, all roughly based on proportionality, can also be seen as mechanisms for the party groups to control the committees. Moreover, national parties are key players in allocating committee seats and reports, and there are signs that they are to an increasing extent using committee assignments for achieving their policy goals. Nonetheless, research suggests that party group influence within committees is ultimately based on coordinating mechanisms for overseeing committee work instead of hierarchical structures for controlling MEP behavior in the committees. But more research is needed on committee decision-making. For example, while committees may act rather consensually,[36] future research should address more carefully the balance of power between rapporteurs, committee chairs, and group coordinators.

But can the Parliament influence EU politics? Or more specifically, has the European Parliament managed to convert its constitutional powers into legislative success? Research on European Parliament's policy influence can be divided into two categories: theoretical modeling and empirical analyses. The former strand of research was really initiated by the article by Tsebelis on the cooperation procedure.[37] Subsequent publications have generated useful insights about the impact of the Parliament under the various legislative procedures, with the debate largely focusing on the respective powers of the Commission, the Council, and the European Parliament under the co-decision procedure.[38] Interestingly, practitioners and academics have not always agreed about the extent to which the co-decision procedure has in fact empowered the Parliament.[39] Empirical analyses have likewise attempted to measure and explain the influence of the Parliament under alternative law-making procedures or in specific issue areas like economic policy.[40]

As the co-decision procedure—officially called the "ordinary legislative procedure" in the Lisbon Treaty—has gradually become the standard mode of adopting EU laws, scholars have also paid attention to the political dynamics of this procedure. Co-decision procedure has resulted in a dramatic increase in interaction between the European Parliament and the Council. This repeated interaction together with worries about legislative delays has contributed to a higher share of early agreements in co-decision procedure. Essentially this means that laws are adopted behind closed doors in informal "trilogues." Reducing inter-institutional rivalry contributes to the technocratization or depoliticization of EU decision-making and makes it difficult to observe what decisions are made and how the different actors involved in the game contribute to them.[41] Currently, an overwhelming majority of co-decision processes are concluded at first reading, hence signaling a need to study the political profiles and policy influence of the MEPs (particularly the rapporteurs[42]) bargaining on behalf of the Parliament in trilogues instead of focusing on the composition of conciliation committees,[43] as the latter are rarely convened any more.

The Parliament has also gradually gained new competences that facilitate stronger control of the Commission. This applies particularly to appointment powers, where the link between European Parliament elections and the composition of the Commission has become more direct since the early 1990s.[44] As both the Commission and its president have to be approved by the Parliament before they can take office (and can also be voted out of office by the MEPs), the European Parliament has explicitly demanded that the verdict of the voters should not be ignored in the make-up of the Commission. This means simply that party politics matters more in EU policy-making, not just inside the Parliament. For example, since the 2004 elections there has been a kind of government and opposition divide in the Parliament. With EPP the largest group and the centre-right groups controlling the majority in the Parliament (and as centre-right cabinets also dominate the Council), the partisan composition of the 2004–2009 and 2009–2014 Commission has leaned toward the centre-right, with a clear majority of the Commissioners and the president representing either EPP or ELDR member parties. Not surprisingly, there has thus been a firm "centre-right" grip on EU politics that has certainly left its mark on legislation.

In fact, there has emerged quite a lively debate about whether the European Parliament should become a fully-fledged "federal" parliament, with the composition of the Commission determined by the results of Euro-elections. The defenders of such a parliamentary model, or stronger supranational democracy in general, argue that as the EU already possesses significant authority over a broad range of policy areas, the choice of who exercises such authority should be based on competition between political forces—in this scenario essentially Euro-parties contesting the European Parliament elections.[45] More cautious voices argue that this is not the right way to address the democratic deficit, partly on account of the lack of common European identity and as issues that are most salient to voters are still decided nationally.[46] Others have pointed out that installing party government at the EU level may not be a good solution in an era when political parties are facing serious difficulties in the context of national democracies.[47]

26.5 CONCLUDING DISCUSSION

The European Parliament has undergone tremendous changes since the 1950s, developing from a non-elected consultative "talking shop" to a directly elected legislature vested with significant law-making powers. At the same time scholarly knowledge of the Parliament has taken major strides forward, even to the extent that the European Parliament is arguably one of the most researched legislatures in the world.

Interestingly, this increase in both the powers of the institution and in the state of academic research has coincided with a growing distance between the Parliament and its electorate. Turnout has declined consistently since the first elections held in 1979 and

Europeans seem to know very little about the Parliament. Future research should focus more on the links between citizens and the Parliament. For example, previous research indicates that the design of the electoral system impacts on MEPs' contacts with their electorates, with MEPs from more "open" systems paying more attention to individual voters and constituency interests.[48] But overall the constituency activities of MEPs—and how these might differ from the constituency work of national MPs—have so far been largely neglected by scholars.

The literature on Euro-elections has perhaps been too tied to the second-order model. The dominance of the second-order paradigm, while a relatively powerful tool for understanding the European Parliament elections, has perhaps unintentionally resulted in somewhat one-sided research on the elections. There is clearly scope for comparative studies between European Parliament and national elections,[49] or between European Parliament elections and other second-order elections. More research is also needed on public perceptions of the Parliament. Who are the "supporters" of the European Parliament and how have voters' views about the Parliament changed over the decades? Do people see the Parliament as an important and trustworthy institution?[50] After all, concerns about the democratic deficit have been one of the key factors behind the gradual empowerment of the Parliament,[51] but whether the European Parliament can actually reduce that deficit depends at least partly on the ability of the institution to connect with the people it represents.

While there is already a substantial body of work on the European Parliament party groups, particularly on their cohesion and coalition formation, future research should focus on the internal dynamics of the party groups. The same applies to committees. Future research could also pay more attention to the smaller party groups to see whether their organization or behavior differs from the larger party groups.[52] More research should also be carried out on explaining variation between the activities of individual MEPs—for example, how often and why they act as rapporteurs, make speeches, or ask questions.[53]

Finally, much of the research on inter-institutional relations has either been in the form of theoretical modeling or of empirical analyses of the legislative success of the various EU organs. Hence future research could focus more on the "partyness" of EU politics. While scholars have paid more attention to the role of parties and party preferences in EU decision-making since the late 1990s, this strand of research is still quite undeveloped, both regarding theory and measuring and explaining partisan links between the EU institutions.[54] As a result, political science still cannot give a good answer to a question that is quite central in EU studies: whether EU laws and policies are shaped more by party preferences or by national interests?

NOTES

1. See Richard Corbett, Francis Jacobs, and Michael Shackleton, *The European Parliament*, seventh edition (London: John Harper Publishing, 2007); David Judge and David Earnshaw, *The European Parliament*, second edition (Houndmills: Palgrave Macmillan, 2008).

2. This is in large part explained by the openness of the Parliament, which enables scholars to gather data on various aspects of the European Parliament's work. In contrast, the other EU organs are much less transparent and hence there is also less empirical research on these institutions.

3. Karlheinz Reif and Hermann Schmitt, "Nine Second-Order National Elections: A Conceptualf Framework for the Analysis of European Election Results," *European Journal of Political Research* 8, no. 1 (1980), 3–44.

4. The main publications of the EES project are Cees van der Cees van der Eijk and Mark N. Franklin, eds, *Choosing Europe? The European Electorate and National Politics in the Face of Union* (Ann Arbor: University of Michigan Press, 1996); Richard S. Katz and Wolfgang Wessels, eds, *The European Parliament, the National Parliaments, and European Integration* (Oxford: Oxford University Press, 1999); Hermann Schmitt and Jacques Thomassen, eds, *Political Representation and Legitimacy in the European Union* (Oxford: Oxford University Press, 1999); Wouter van der Brug and Cees van der Eijk, eds, *European Elections and Domestic Politics: Lessons from the Past and Scenarios for the Future* (Notre Dame: University of Notre Dame Press, 2007); Jacques Thomassen, ed., *The Legitimacy of the European Union after Enlargement* (Oxford: Oxford University Press, 2009); and Hermann Schmitt, ed., "European Parliament Elections after Eastern Enlargement," *Journal of European Integration* 31, no. 5 (2009).

5. Mikko Mattila, "Why Bother? Determinants of Turnout in European Elections," *Electoral Studies* 22, no. 3 (2003), 449–68.

6. See for example van der Eijk and Franklin, *Choosing Europe?*; Jason R. Koepke and Nils Ringe, "The Second-Order Election Model in an Enlarged Europe," *European Union Politics* 7, no. 3 (2006), 321–46; Simon Hix and Michael Marsh, "Punishment or Protest? Understanding European Parliament Elections," *Journal of Politics* 69, no. i (2007), 495–510; van der Brug and van der Eijk, *European Elections and Domestic Politics*; and Till Weber, "Campaign Effects and Second-Order Cycles: A Top-Down Approach to European Parliament Elections," *European Union Politics* 8, no. 4 (2007), 509–36; and Sara B. Hobolt, Jae-Jae Spoon, and James Tilley, "A Vote Against Europe: Explaining Defection at the 1999 and 2004 European Parliament Elections," *British Journal of Political Science* 39, no. 1 (2009), 93–115.

7. Philip Manow and Holger Döring, "Electoral and Mechanical Causes of Divided Government in the European Union," *Comparative Political Studies* 41, no. 10 (2008), 1349–70; and Simon Hix and Michael Marsh, "Second-Order Effects plus Pan-European Political Swings: An Analysis of European Parliament Elections Across Time," *Electoral Studies* 30, no. 1 (2011), 4–15.

8. Simon Hix and Christopher Lord, *Political Parties in the European Union* (Basingstoke: Macmillan, 1997); Simon Hix, "Dimensions and Alignments in European Union Politics: Cognitive Constraints and Partisan Responses," *European Journal of Political Research* 35, no. 1 (1999), 69–106; Gary Marks and Carole J. Wilson, "The Past in the Present: A Cleavage Theory of Party Response to European Integration," *British Journal of Political Science* 30, no. 3 (2000), 433–59; and Gary Marks and Marco R. Steenbergen, eds, *European Integration and Political Conflict* (Cambridge: Cambridge University Press, 2004).

9. Mikko Mattila and Tapio Raunio, "Cautious Voters—Supportive Parties: Opinion Congruence Between Voters And Parties On The EU Dimension," *European Union Politics* 7, no. 4 (2006), 427–49.

10. Hobolt et al., "A Vote Against Europe", 111. See also Catherine E. de Vries, Wouter van der Brug, Marcel H. van Egmond, and Cees van der Eijk, "Individual and contextual variation

in EU issue voting: The role of political information," *Electoral Studies* 30, no. 1 (2011), 16–28.

11. Amie Kreppel, *The European Parliament and the Supranational Party System: A Study of Institutional Development* (Cambridge: Cambridge University Press, 2002).

12. In addition to the EES candidate surveys, the European Parliament Research Group (EPRG) has carried out three MEPs surveys, in 2000, 2006, and 2010 (<www.lse.ac.uk/collections/EPRG/>) that have been utilized in several of the publications referred to in this chapter.

13. Fulvio Attinà, "The Voting Behaviour of the European Parliament Members and the Problem of the Europarties," *European Journal of Political Research* 18, no. 4 (1990), 557–79; Tapio Raunio, *The European Perspective: Transnational Party Groups in the 1989–94 European Parliament* (Aldershot: Ashgate, 1997).

14. Nils Ringe, *Who Decides, and How? Preferences, Uncertainty, and Policy Choice in the European Parliament* (Oxford: Oxford University Press, 2010).

15. See e.g. Simon Hix, Abdul Noury, and Gérard Roland, "Power to the Parties: Cohesion and Competition in the European Parliament, 1979–2001," *British Journal of Political Science* 35, no. 2 (2005), 209–34; Simon Hix, Abdul G. Noury, and Gérard Roland, *Democratic Politics in the European Parliament* (Cambridge: Cambridge University Press, 2007). There is also a debate concerning the validity of the roll-call data. As recorded votes represent only a sample of the totality of votes in the Parliament, the representativeness of that sample is a crucial matter—particularly when studying conflict dimensions in the European Parliament. See Clifford J. Carrubba, Matthew Gabel, Lacey Murrah, Ryan Clough, Elizabeth Montgomery, and Rebecca Schambach, "Off the Record: Unrecorded Legislative Votes, Selection Bias and Roll-Call Vote Analysis," *British Journal of Political Science* 36, no. 4 (2006), 691–704.

16. See for example Jacques Thomassen, Abdul Noury, and Erik Voeten, "Political Competition in the European Parliament: Evidence from Roll Call and Survey Analyses," in Marks and Steenbergen, *European Integration and Political Conflict*, 141–64; Gail McElroy and Kenneth Benoit, "Party Groups and Policy Positions in the European Parliament," *Party Politics* 13, no. 1 (2007), 5–28; and Hermann Schmitt and Jacques Thomassen, "The European Party System after Enlargement," in Thomassen, *The Legitimacy of the European Union after Enlargement*, 23–43.

17. Kreppel, *The European Parliament and the Supranational Party System: A Study of Institutional Development.*

18. Simon Hix and Abdul Noury, "After Enlargement: Voting Patterns in the Sixth European Parliament," *Legislative Studies Quarterly* 34, no. 2 (2009), 159–74; see also Erik Voeten, "Enlargement and the 'Normal' European Parliament," in Thomassen, *The Legitimacy of the European Union after Enlargement*, 93–113.

19. Andreas Warntjen, Simon Hix, and Christophe Crombez, "The Party Political Make-Up of EU Legislative Bodies," *Journal of European Public Policy* 15, no. 8 (2008), 1243–53.

20. See Janina Thiem, *Nationale Parteien im Europäischen Parlament: Delegation, Kontrolle und politischer Einfluss* (Wiesbaden: VS Verlag, 2009).

21. Joey-David Ovey, *Between Nation and Europe: Labour, the SPD and the European Parliament 1994–1999* (Opladen: Leske + Budrich, 2002); William B. Messmer, "Taming Labour's MEPs," *Party Politics* 9, no. 2 (2003), 201–18.

22. Tapio Raunio, "Losing Independence or Finally Gaining Recognition? Contacts Between MEPs and National Parties," *Party Politics* 6, no. 2 (2000), 211–23; Magnus Blomgren,

Cross-Pressure and Political Representation in Europe: A Comparative Study of MEPs and the Intra-Party Arena (Umeå: Department of Political Science, Umeå University, 2003); Stefanie Bailer, "The Puzzle of Continuing Party Cohesion in the European Parliament after Eastern Enlargement," in Daniela Giannetti and Kenneth Benoit, eds, *Intra-Party Politics and Coalition Governments* (Abingdon: Routledge, 2009), 189–204.

23. See Roger Scully, *Becoming Europeans? Attitudes, Behaviour and Socialization in the European Parliament* (Oxford: Oxford University Press, 2005).

24. Simon Hix, "Parliamentary Behavior with Two Principals: Preferences, Parties, and Voting in the European Parliament," *American Journal of Political Science* 46, no. 3, 696. See also Thorsten Faas, "To Defect or Not to Defect? National, Institutional and Party Group Pressures on MEPs and their Consequences for Party Group Cohesion in the EP," *European Journal of Political Research* 42, no. 5 (2003), 841–66; Simon Hix, "Electoral Institutions and Legislative Behavior: Explaining Voting-Defection in the European Parliament," *World Politics* 56, no. 1 (2004), 194–223; Hix et al., *Democratic Politics in the European Parliament*; and Emanuel Emil Coman, "Reassessing the Influence of Party Groups on Individual Members of the European Parliament," *West European Politics* 32, no. 6 (2009), 1099–117.

25. René Lindstädt, Jonathan B. Slapin, and Ryan J. Vander Wielen, "Balancing Competing Demands: Position Taking and Election Proximity in the European Parliament," *Legislative Studies Quarterly* 36, no. 1 (2011), 37–70.

26. This change was based on the revised Party Article (191) included in the Treaty of Nice which stipulated that "Council, acting in accordance with the procedure referred to in Article 251 [co-decision procedure], shall lay down the regulations governing political parties at European level and in particular the rules regarding their funding." See Karl Magnus Johansson and Tapio Raunio, "Regulating Europarties: Cross-Party Coalitions Capitalizing on Incomplete Contracts," *Party Politics* 11, no. 5 (2005), 515–34.

27. Karl Magnus Johansson, *Transnational Party Alliances: Analysing the Hard-Won Alliance Between Conservatives and Christian Democrats in the European Parliament* (Lund: Lund University Press, 1997); Elizabeth Bomberg, *Green Parties and Politics in the European Union* (London: Routledge, 1998); Thomas M. Dietz, "Similar but Different? The European Greens Compared to Other Transnational Party Federations in Europe," *Party Politics* 6, no. 2 (2000), 199–210; Robert Ladrech, *Social Democracy and the Challenge of European Union* (Boulder: Lynne Rienner, 2000); and Simon Lightfoot, *Europeanizing Social Democracy? The Rise of the Party of European Socialists* (Abingdon: Routledge, 2005).

28. David S. Bell and Christopher Lord, eds, *Transnational Parties in the European Union* (Aldershot: Ashgate, 1998); Pascal Delwit, Erol Külachi, and Cédric Van de Walle, eds, *Les federations européennes de parties: Organisation et influence* (Brussels: Editions de l'Universite de Bruxelles, 2001); Karl Magnus Johansson and Peter Zervakis, eds, *European Political Parties between Cooperation and Integration* (Baden-Baden: Nomos, 2002); and David Hanley, *Beyond the Nation State: Parties in the Era of European Integration* (Houndmills: Palgrave Macmillan, 2008).

29. Hix and Lord, *Political Parties in the European Union*; Björn Lindberg, Anne Rasmussen, and Andreas Warntjen, eds, "The Role of Political Parties in the European Union," *Journal of European Public Policy* 15, no. 8 (2008).

30. Karl Magnus Johansson, "Tracing the Employment Title in the Amsterdam Treaty: Uncovering Transnational Coalitions," *Journal of European Public Policy* 6, no. 1 (1999), 85–101; Ladrech, *Social Democracy and the Challenge of European Union*; Karl Magnus

Johansson, "Another Road to Maastricht: The Christian Democrat Coalition and the Quest for European Union," *Journal of Common Market Studies* 40, no. 5 (2002), 871–93; Karl Magnus Johansson, "Party Elites in Multilevel Europe: The Christian Democrats and the Single European Act," *Party Politics* 8, no. 4 (2002), 423–39; and Lightfoot, *Europeanizing Social Democracy?*.

31. Hix, "Dimensions and Alignments in European Union Politics"; Matthew J. Gabel and Simon Hix, "Defining the EU Political Space: An Empirical Study of the European Elections Manifestos, 1979–1999," *Comparative Political Studies* 35, no. 8 (2002), 934–64.

32. Ladrech, *Social Democracy and the Challenge of European Union*; see also Luciano Bardi, "Parties and Party Systems in the European Union," in Kurt Richard Luther and Ferdinand Müller-Rommel, eds, *Political Parties in the New Europe: Political and Analytical Challenges* (Oxford: Oxford University Press, 2002), 293–321; and Lightfoot, *Europeanizing Social Democracy?*.

33. Kreppel, *The European Parliament and the Supranational Party System: A Study of Institutional Development*; Amie Kreppel, "Necessary but Not Sufficient: Understanding the Impact of Treaty Reform on the Internal Development of the European Parliament," *Journal of European Public Policy* 10, no. 6 (2003), 884–911.

34. Shaun Bowler and David M. Farrell,"The Organizing of the European Parliament: Committees, Specialisation and Co-ordination," *British Journal of Political Science* 25, no. 2 (1995), 219–43; Virginie Mamadouh and Tapio Raunio, "The Committee System: Powers, Appointments and Report Allocation," *Journal of Common Market Studies* 41, no. 2 (2003), 333–51; Michael Kaeding, "Rapporteurship Allocation in the European Parliament: Information or Distribution?" *European Union Politics* 5, no. 3 (2004), 353–71; Michael Kaeding, "The World of Committee Reports: Rapporteurship Assignment in the European Parliament," *Journal of Legislative Studies* 11, no. 1 (2005), 82–104; Giacomo Benedetto, "Rapporteurs as Legislative Entrepreneurs: The Dynamics of the Codecision Procedure in Europe's Parliament," *Journal of European Public Policy* 12, no. 1 (2005), 67–88; Bjorn Hoyland, "Allocation of Codecision Reports in the Fifth European Parliament," *European Union Politics* 7, no. 1 (2006), 30–50; Gail McElroy, "Committee Representation in the European Parliament," *European Union Politics* 7, no. 1 (2006), 5–29; Pierre Hausemer, "Participation and Political Competition in Committee Report Allocation: Under What Conditions Do MEPs Represent Their Constituents?" *European Union Politics* 7, no. 4 (2006), 505–30; Nikoleta Yordanova, "The Rationale behind Committee Assignment in the European Parliament: Distributive, Informational and Partisan Perspectives," *European Union Politics* 10, no. 2 (2009), 253–80; and Nikoleta Yordanova, "Inter-institutional Rules and Division of Power in the European Parliament: Allocation of Consultation and Co-decision Reports", *West European Politics* 34, no. 1 (2011), 97–121.

35. Bowler and Farrell,"The Organizing of the European Parliament: Committees, Specialisation and Co-ordination"; Mamadouh and Raunio, "The Committee System"; Richard Whitaker, "Party Control in a Committee-Based Legislature? The Case of the European Parliament," *Journal of Legislative Studies* 7, no. 4 (2001), 63–88; Richard Whitaker, "National Parties in the European Parliament: An Influence in the Committee System?," *European Union Politics* 6, no. 1 (2005), 5–28; Hausemer, "Participation and Political Competition in Committee Report Allocation"; Pierpaolo Settembri and Christine Neuhold, "Achieving Consensus Through Committees: Does the European Parliament Manage?" *Journal of Common Market Studies* 47, no. 1 (2009), 127–51; Ringe, *Who Decides, and How? Preferences, Uncertainty, and Policy Choice in the European*

Parliament; and particularly Richard Whitaker, *The European Parliament's Committees: National Party Control and Legislative Empowerment* (Abingdon: Routledge, 2011).

36. Settembri and Neuhold, "Achieving Consensus Through Committees."

37. George Tsebelis, "The Power of the European Parliament as a Conditional Agenda-Setter," *American Political Science Review* 88, no. 1 (1994), 128–42.

38. For a very good summary of the debate, see Gail McElroy, "Legislative Politics," in Knud Erik Jørgensen, Mark A. Pollack, and Ben Rosamond, eds, *Handbook of European Union Politics* (London: SAGE, 2007), 175–94.

39. Christophe Crombez, Bernard Steunenberg, and Richard Corbett, "Understanding the EU Legislative Process: Political Scientists' and Practitioners' Perspectives," *European Union Politics* 1, no. 3 (2000), 363–81.

40. See for example Amie Kreppel, "Moving Beyond Procedure: An Empirical Analysis of European Parliament Legislative Influence," *Comparative Political Studies* 35, no. 7 (2002), 784–813; Christopher Lord, "The European Parliament in the Economic Governance of the EU," *Journal of Common Market Studies* 41, no. 2 (2003), 249–67; Charlotte Burns, "Who Pays? Who Gains? How do Costs and Benefits Shape the Policy Influence of the European Parliament?" *Journal of Common Market Studies* 43, no. 3 (2005), 485–505; and Raya Kardasheva, "The Power to Delay: The European Parliament's Influence in the Consultation Procedure," *Journal of Common Market Studies* 47, no. 2 (2009), 385–409; Sara Hagemann and Bjørn Høyland, "Bicameral Politics in the European Union," *Journal of Common Market Studies* 48, no. 4 (2010), 811–33; and Daniel Naurin and Anne Rasmussen, eds, "Linking Inter- and Intra-institutional Change in the European Union," *West European Politics* 34, no. 1 (2011). The website of the European Legislative Politics Research Group (<www.elprg.eu>) provides various data sets and other information on research on the European Parliament and EU legislation.

41. Michael Shackleton and Tapio Raunio, "Codecision since Amsterdam: A Laboratory for Institutional Innovation and Change," *Journal of European Public Policy* 10, no. 2 (2003), 171–87.

42. Henry Farrell and Adrienne Hèritier, "Interorganizational Negotiation and Intraorganizational Power in Shared Decision Making: Early Agreements Under Codecision and Their Impact on the European Parliament and Council," *Comparative Political Studies* 37, no. 10 (2004), 1184–212; and Rory Costello and Robert Thomson, "The Policy Impact of Leadership in Committees: Rapporteurs' Influence on the European Parliament's Opinions," *European Union Politics* 11, no. 2 (2010), 219–40.

43. Anne Rasmussen, "The EU Conciliation Committee: One or Several Principals?" *European Union Politics* 9, no. 1 (2008), 87–113.

44. Catherine Moury, "Explaining the European Parliament's Right to Appoint and Invest the Commission," *West European Politics* 30, no. 2 (2007), 367–91.

45. Andreas Follesdal and Simon Hix, "Why There is a Democratic Deficit in the EU: A Response to Majone and Moravcsik," *Journal of Common Market Studies* 44, no. 3 (2006), 533–62; Simon Hix, *What's Wrong With the European Union and How to Fix It* (Cambridge: Polity Press, 2008).

46. Andrew Moravcsik, "In Defence of the 'Democratic Deficit': Reassessing Legitimacy in the European Union," *Journal of Common Market Studies* 40, no. 4 (2002), 603–24.

47. Peter Mair and Jacques Thomassen, "Political Representation and Government in the European Union," *Journal of European Public Policy* 17, no. 1 (2010), 20–35.

48. David M. Farrell and Roger Scully, "Electing the European Parliament: How Uniform are 'Uniform' Electoral Systems?" *Journal of Common Market Studies* 43, no. 5 (2005), 969–84; and David M. Farrell and Roger Scully, *Representing Europe's Citizens? Electoral Institutions and the Failure of Parliamentary Representation* (Oxford: Oxford University Press, 2007); David M. Farrell and Roger Scully, "The European Parliament: One Parliament, Several Modes of Political Representation on the Ground?" *Journal of European Public Policy* 17, no. 1 (2010), 36–54.

49. A good example of such research is Daniele Caramani, "Is There a European Electorate and What Does It Look Like? Evidence from Electoral Volatility Measures, 1976–2004," *West European Politics* 29, no. 1 (2006), 1–27.

50. See for example Roger Scully, "Democracy, Legitimacy, and the European Parliament," in Maria Green Cowles and Michael Smith, eds, *The State of the European Union: Risks, Reform, Resistance, and Revival* (Oxford: Oxford University Press, 2000), 228–45; Matthew Gabel, "Public Support for the European Parliament," *Journal of Common Market Studies* 41, no. 2 (2003), 289–308.

51. See Berthold Rittberger, *Building Europe's Parliament: Democratic Representation beyond the Nation-State* (Oxford: Oxford University Press, 2005); Giacomo Benedetto and Simon Hix, "Explaining the European Parliament's Gains in the EU Constitution," *Review of International Organizations* 2, no. 2 (2007), 115–29.

52. See Christian B. Jensen and Jae-Jae Spoon, "Thinking Locally, Acting Supranationally: Niche Party Behaviour in the European Parliament," *European Journal of Political Research* 49, no. 2 (2010), 174–201.

53. Most of this data is available online at the European Parliament's website. See also the MEP database available at <http://folk.uio.no/bjornkho/MEP/default.htm>. See Bjørn Høyland, Indraneel Sircar, and Simon Hix, "An Automated Database of the European Parliament," *European Union Politics* 10, no. 1 (2009), 143–52. On MEPs' parliamentary questions and plenary speeches, see Sven-Oliver Proksch and Jonathan B. Slapin, "Parliamentary Questions and Oversight in the European Union," *European Journal of Political Research* 50, no. 1 (2011), 53–79; and Jonathan B. Slapin and Sven-Oliver Proksch, "Look Who's Talking: Parliamentary Debate in the European Union," *European Union Politics* 11, no. 3 (2010), 333–57.

54. Lindberg et al., "The Role of Political Parties in the European Union."

....

CHAPTER 27

EXTERNAL SCRUTINY INSTITUTIONS*

....

IAN HARDEN

27.1 INTRODUCTION

....

The editors' working title for this chapter ("Auditors, ombudsmen, etc.") presented a theoretical and a practical challenge. The theoretical challenge was to specify relevant similarities between auditors and ombudsmen so as to fill out the "etc." in a meaningful way. To anticipate: the criteria adopted make it necessary to include the Data Protection Supervisor (EDPS) and the Anti-Fraud Office (OLAF), as well as the Court of Auditors (ECA) and the Ombudsman. Hence the practical challenge of covering four institutions[1] in one chapter.

None of the four was part of the original Community architecture. The ECA dates from 1975 and was elevated to the status of an institution in 1993, by the Maastricht Treaty. It consists of one national of each member state, appointed for six years by the Council, in accordance with the proposals made by each member state and after consulting the European Parliament. The Ombudsman was established by the Maastricht Treaty and began work in 1995. There is only one Ombudsman, who is elected by the European Parliament after each parliamentary election. Neither the Council nor the Commission has any role in the election. OLAF[2] was established in 1999. Its director is appointed by the Commission for a five-year term, renewable once, after consultations with the European Parliament and the Council. The EDPS was established by a Regulation adopted in 2001[3] and began work in 2003. The European Parliament and the Council appoint the EDPS and an Assistant Supervisor, by common accord, for a renewable term of five years, on the basis of a list drawn up by the Commission.

All four institutions play a role in scrutinizing the other EU institutions. (The functions of the ECA and OLAF extend further because their role is basically focused on the EU budget.) Judicial and legislative scrutiny of executive power form part of the constitutional traditions common to the member states. As a result, a shared framework of constitutional understanding provides a starting point for analyzing the scrutiny role of the Union Courts and the European Parliament. The same is not true for the ECA or the Ombudsman.

As regards the former, whilst audit of the public sector exists in all member states, there are wide variations in its purpose, method, organization, and constitutional role. These variations can be analyzed in terms of four models,[4] not all of which find it easy to make sense of the idea that something called a "court" might perform the audit.

As regards the Ombudsman, the institution is relatively new in most member states. Twenty-five now have a national ombudsman, but none of the original six had one when the EEC was founded. Furthermore, there are important differences in the institution's powers, functions, and even its name.[5]

The ECA and the Ombudsman thus supply forms of scrutiny which, at the member state level, (a) are distinct from the checks provided by the legislature and judiciary, and (b) display significant divergences in their role and status. A rapid survey of the EU scene reveals other forms of scrutiny that also fit that description. They differ from the four scrutiny bodies considered in this chapter because they are *internal* mechanisms, reporting primarily to management. In contrast, the ECA, the Ombudsman, and the EDPS are *external* and address their reports to a broader public audience. Despite possessing some internal characteristics, OLAF is also best understood as an external scrutiny body.

Discussion of the significance of the internal/external distinction and its relationship to the intuitively more appealing criterion of independence will be postponed until section 27.6 below.

27.2 THE COURT OF AUDITORS

Decisions about total public expenditure and levels of taxation involve important political and economic choices. The same is true of the allocation of the tax burden and the benefits of spending between competing claims and interests. The budgetary process through which these decisions are made is, therefore, of major constitutional and political significance. In most states, it consists of three successive phases; planning, implementation, and *ex post* accounting and audit. All three phases involve issues of economics, law, and accounting, with the result that political and technical questions are often intertwined.

As a percentage of total economic output, the EU budget is small in comparison to the budgets of the member states.[6] Nonetheless, EU spending and revenue are important because money is one of the two main resources of the EU (the other being law). Moreover, the EU budgetary process is significant in terms of the allocation of power and authority, both among the EU institutions and between the EU and the member states.

As its name suggests, the role of an audit institution in the budgetary process typically focuses on the third phase. However, actors in the earlier phases may change their behavior in anticipation of future audit reactions. Furthermore, audit institutions can help to shape the framework of rules, principles, and standards that govern the planning and execution of the budget. These general points are true of the ECA, which examines whether all revenue and all expenditure have been received and incurred in a lawful and regular manner, and whether the financial management has been sound.[7] The ECA also gives opinions on proposals for EU financial legislation, such as the Financial Regulation.[8]

The Treaty of Maastricht gave the Court the additional task of providing a statement of assurance (known as the "DAS," from the French *déclaration d'assurance*) as to the reliability of the accounts and the legality and regularity of the underlying transactions. The European Parliament takes account of the DAS in granting the Commission "discharge" for the execution of the budget. The discharge procedure normally attracts little attention (the one for 1996, which led to the fall of the Santer Commission in 1999, being the exception). In contrast, the DAS is a focus of media interest because the Court has consistently refused to give an unqualified audit opinion on the accounts as a whole. The political salience of the DAS has enhanced the public visibility of the ECA and reinforced its position in the EU institutional framework as the "financial conscience of the Union."[9] The Treaty of Nice provided for the ECA to supplement the DAS by also making specific assessments for each major area of activity. In recent years, the ECA has given an unqualified opinion on certain areas, including administrative expenditure. For most spending areas, however, the error rate revealed by the audit is still too high for the ECA to give an unqualified opinion on the legality and regularity of the underlying transactions.

In considering the significance of errors detected during the audit, it is important to bear three points in mind. First, errors cannot be equated to fraud, which the ECA suspects in only a small number of cases.[10] Second, the unnecessary complexity of the rules governing certain EU spending programs increases the risk of non-compliance, whether accidental or deliberate. For this reason, the ECA has recommended the simplification of rules and regulations, and a streamlining of internal controls.[11] Finally, efforts to avoid errors are subject to diminishing returns: zero risk implies zero activity. The ECA itself regards an error rate of 2 percent as tolerable, whilst its 2007 Annual Report invited the political authorities of the Union to define a reasonable level of risk. From a rational choice perspective, the definition of an acceptable level of error depends on an overall analysis of the extent to which the specific program concerned is managed so as to ensure economy, efficiency, and effectiveness ("value for money").

The ECA's remit includes value for money ("whether the financial management has been sound"), which it addresses through "performance" audits. In practice, a high proportion of its resources is devoted to legality and regularity for DAS purposes.[12] The ECA's performance is also affected by its internal organization. A generally positive peer review in 2008 criticized the "silo type" structure, which results in the absence of a Court-wide perspective on risk and audit priorities and inconsistencies between the audit groups.[13] These comments are in line with those of some earlier commentators.[14]

The ECA has power to obtain documents and information, and to perform on-the-spot audits in the member states. The ability to conduct such audits is essential because over 80 percent of EU expenditure involves shared management with the member states.[15] The Lisbon Treaty makes cooperation between the Commission and the member states the general principle for implementation of the budget and provides for regulations to lay down the control and audit obligations of the member states and the resulting responsibilities.[16]

The European Parliament's Committee on Budgetary Control has been keen not only to strengthen member states' responsibilities for implementing the budget, but also to find ways to rely on national declarations of assurance, in order to help defuse public criticism that is unfairly directed at the EU and its institutions as a result of the qualified DAS opinions. The ECA has been careful to emphasize that it could not rely on national declarations as such, but only on possible opinions on such declarations produced by national audit bodies.[17] To do so, it would have to satisfy itself about the suitability and quality of the work of the national audit bodies. The main forum for cooperation between the ECA and the national audit bodies is the Contact Committee of the Supreme Audit Institutions of the European Union,[18] which has a working group on common audit standards and comparable audit criteria.

27.3 THE EUROPEAN OMBUDSMAN

"Ombudsman" is a Swedish word and the ombudsman is a Swedish invention. The King's Supreme Ombudsman (or representative) was appointed in 1713 to ensure that the law was observed and that public officials carried out their duties during the King's absence while abroad. In 1809, the Swedish Parliament first elected an Ombudsman to supervise the application of the laws by judges and other public officials.[19] In the second half of the twentieth century, the ombudsman institution was adopted in many countries as a response to problems of bureaucracy associated with the growth of the state and as a mechanism to protect human rights. Typically, the modern ombudsman functions as a moral authority, without power to make legally binding decisions. This is the case for the European Ombudsman.

During the Maastricht Treaty negotiations, Spain proposed a "Mediator" in each member state, possibly supplemented by a European Ombudsman, to help citizens defend their rights vis-à-vis the administrative authorities of both the Union and the member states. In contrast, Denmark proposed an ombudsman with a mandate limited to the Community institutions.[20] The Danish proposal was adopted and the TFEU now provides for the European Parliament to elect an Ombudsman to investigate and report on maladministration in the activities of the Union's institutions, bodies, offices, and agencies. Any citizen or resident, as well as any company or association with a registered office in the EU, may complain to the Ombudsman.

The EU institutions do not provide the public services typical of the welfare state, such as health, housing, social assistance, education, and pensions. Nor do they run prisons, police forces, or systems of immigration control. Consequently, the number of complaints investigated by the European Ombudsman is low compared to the workload of most national ombudsmen, even though the office deals with subjects that many national ombudsmen do not handle, such as contractual and employment disputes.

Transparency is a major theme of the Ombudsman's work. The Regulation giving effect to the fundamental right of public access to documents held by the institutions allows for a refusal to be contested either by application to the General Court, or complaint to the Ombudsman.[21] As well as dealing with such complaints, the Ombudsman was also active in the legislative processes for adoption of the Regulation in 2001 and following the Commission's proposal, made in 2008, for its revision (ongoing at the time of writing). Furthermore, the Ombudsman's efforts to promote transparency are based on a vision of citizenship that implies political participation and empowerment vis-à-vis not only the EU institutions, but also the national authorities in relation to EU matters.[22]

The administration of EU law is largely the responsibility of member states, so it is understandable that many complaints to the Ombudsman concern the activities of their public authorities. Although the Ombudsman cannot inquire into such complaints directly, the office promotes the correct application of EU law by the member states in two main ways. First, the Ombudsman can investigate the Commission in its role as "guardian of the Treaties"[23] and the EIB's role in checking compliance with EU law in relation to the projects it funds. Second, the Ombudsman cooperates closely with ombudsmen and similar bodies in the member states through the European Network of Ombudsmen, which the office organizes.[24] The Ombudsman also deals with cases concerning procedural rights in investigations by OLAF[25] and, more recently, with complaints concerning the Commission's role in enforcing EU competition law.[26]

The Ombudsman has made considerable efforts to develop general principles of good administration and has produced a code of good administrative behavior.[27] The basic philosophy is that good administration requires the institutions to be infused by a culture of service to citizens, which involves more than just compliance with the law.[28] However, whilst an act of maladministration is not necessarily unlawful, any unlawful behavior that falls within the Ombudsman's mandate constitutes maladministration. The Ombudsman thus complements the role of the Courts in promoting the rule of law and a complaint to the Ombudsman constitutes an alternative and often more accessible remedy, despite the fact that it does not lead to a legally binding decision. However, in legal matters, the Ombudsman is clearly subordinate to the Courts, whose judicial role falls outside the Ombudsman's mandate.

27.4 THE EUROPEAN DATA PROTECTION SUPERVISOR

The development of information technology has altered the nature of the social environment. It creates possibilities for surveillance, and for the aggregation and transmission of data, which threaten privacy. This was the original impetus for data protection.

In the 1960s and 1970s, states such as Germany, Sweden, and France adopted laws and established new public authorities to address the issue. At an international level, the Council of Europe adopted a Convention in 1981. Subsequent developments in law and practice have made the relationship between privacy and data protection more complex.[29] The two overlap, but are not identical and EU law now recognizes data protection as a separate fundamental right.[30]

In 1995, an EU Directive on data protection[31] was adopted as a single market provision, to avoid obstacles to the free flow of personal data between member states, which could arise from differing national laws. A major innovation of the Directive compared to the 1981 Convention was to require each member state to establish an independent supervisory authority. The 2008 Framework Decision on data protection in relation to police and judicial cooperation in criminal matters also requires independent supervisory authorities in each member state.[32]

As the supervisory authority for data protection in the Union institutions, the EDPS has both compliance and advisory functions. The EDPS monitors the institutions' processing of personal data in order to ensure respect for the fundamental rights and freedoms of natural persons, in particular their right to privacy. Each institution must appoint an independent data protection officer, who cooperates with the EDPS. The EDPS must be consulted by the Commission on relevant legislative proposals and may also take the initiative to offer advice on the processing of personal data. The EDPS has power to intervene in certain kinds of case before the Court and has done so in a number of high-profile cases.

The compliance function includes enforcement powers and the investigation of complaints. The current EDPS does not, however, see complaint-handling as the primary role of a data protection authority.[33]

A memorandum of understanding between the Ombudsman and the EDPS avoids potential conflict and duplication in complaint-handling and allows the Ombudsman to benefit from the expertise of the EDPS when dealing with complaints that have a data protection dimension. The success of cooperation between the EDPS and the Ombudsman is facilitated by the fact that they have similar views of the relationship between data protection and transparency.[34]

Policing, security, and migration control are the areas in which the balancing of privacy and data protection with other interests is most difficult and controversial. The EDPS supervises the central unit of the Eurodac database of fingerprints of asylum seekers and illegal immigrants. Europol and Eurojust, however, are subject to joint supervisory bodies representing the member states' data protection authorities. The national data protection authorities play an additional role at the EU level through their membership of the independent "Article 29" Working Party, established by the Directive. The Working Party advises the Commission, draws up an annual report, and may also, on its own initiative, make recommendations on all matters relating to the protection of persons with regard to the processing of personal data.

The position of the EDPS has been described as pivotal and strategic for the transfer of learning,[35] which is perhaps another way of saying that the EDPS is one of several players in the European data protection arena,[36] alongside the national supervisory authorities and the Commission, which is not only represented on the Article 29 Working Party but also provides its secretariat.

In addition to recognizing data protection as a fundamental right, the Lisbon Treaty provides a general horizontal legal basis for EU legislation on data protection to apply at both the Union and member-state levels.[37] These provisions seem likely to strengthen the role of the EU in data protection and, perhaps indirectly, give the EDPS a higher profile in the EU data protection landscape.

27.5 THE EUROPEAN ANTI-FRAUD OFFICE (OLAF)

OLAF was established as a rapid response to the fall of the Santer Commission and the first report of the Committee of Independent Experts on allegations regarding fraud, mismanagement, and nepotism in the European Commission.[38] It was given the task, which had not previously existed, of carrying out investigations in all the EU institutions, not just the Commission. Although the OLAF Regulation[39] calls such investigations "internal," OLAF's powers and mode of operation mean that, in terms of the distinction drawn in the present chapter, it operates as an external control.

The functions previously exercised by the Commission's anti-fraud Task Force (UCLAF) were also transferred to OLAF. These include exercising the Commission's powers to carry out investigations in the member states and third countries, including on-the-spot checks and inspections. The Commission also made OLAF responsible for providing support to the member states in the fight against fraud, preparing legislative and regulatory initiatives with the objective of fraud prevention, and all other operational activity of the Commission in relation to the fight against fraud.

OLAF has no power to impose sanctions or to prosecute. Following an investigation, it reports its findings to the competent national authority and/or the relevant institution.

OLAF is part of the Commission and is answerable to the Commission as regards many of its functions. However, it is independent in its investigatory work. The resulting ambivalent or hybrid status[40] is important for any assessment of OLAF's significance for (i) the interaction between supranational and intergovernmental elements in the criminal justice field and (ii) the institutional relationship between the European Parliament and the Commission.[41]

The new "internal" powers of investigation conferred on OLAF in 1999 emphasized the importance of the personal responsibility and liability of the staff of the institutions, as did the amendments of the Staff Regulations adopted in 2004. Whilst this development was necessary and valuable, any assessment of its impact on the functioning of the institutions should take account of two factors. The first is the emphasis, noted above in the discussion of the ECA, on legality and regularity of expenditure. The second is that, despite the word "fraud" in its name, OLAF's power to investigate the conduct of EU staff is not limited to cases of suspected fraud or corruption. Under the Staff Regulations, OLAF may launch an investigation if it becomes aware of evidence of *any* failure by an official to comply with his or her obligations under the Staff Regulations.[42]

Rather than seeking to exercise these powers broadly, OLAF has remained focused on its core mission of protecting EU financial interests. It is an open question, however, whether the combination of overly complex financial provisions and the possibility that *any* error in their application could be grounds for investigation by a body called the anti-*fraud* office could have the perverse effect of encouraging EU staff to adopt a "zero-risk" approach to all decisions involving financial risk. Conversely, the fact that OLAF does not, in practice, pursue cases where no financial interest of the Union is involved may have contributed to a degree of disillusion among staff who have sought to use the "whistleblower" provisions of the 2004 Staff Regulations.[43]

OLAF's status and the method of appointment of its director are subjects of ongoing discussions between the European Parliament and the Commission.

27.6 The Significance of Scrutiny Institutions

None of the four institutions discussed in this chapter can impose formal sanctions and only one, the EDPS, can give legally binding orders and take action to enforce them. The ECA and the Ombudsman are sometimes described as "toothless," because their work does not lead to decisions that can be enforced. To the present author's knowledge, OLAF has not been so described, probably because its investigatory work is sometimes followed up by compulsory recovery of funds, prosecution, or disciplinary action. From a formal legal perspective, however, OLAF's role is purely administrative. As this gap between law and social reality in the case of OLAF demonstrates, sanctions do not always need to be formal to be effective. In particular, the EU institutions and their officials perceive public criticism by the scrutiny institutions as a sanction and make considerable efforts to avoid it.

All four institutions are independent and regard independence as essential to their role. As mentioned above, other EU actors also perform scrutiny functions, including internal auditors, data protection officers, and, within the Commission, the Investigation and Disciplinary Office (IDOC), the staff mediator, and the Impact Assessment Board. Their legal bases also give them independence. The difference between them and the four institutions covered in this chapter is that they are *internal* to the institution concerned. The primary rationale of an internal scrutiny mechanism is to help the organization of which it is part to perform its task better. For this reason, it normally reports to management. In contrast, the primary rationale of an *external* scrutiny mechanism is to make the organization and its management accountable, and it normally reports to the public and/or to the legislature.[44]

Organizations and their management will, if they are wise, draw on the work of external scrutiny bodies in order to correct and improve their own performance. Moreover, external scrutiny bodies take account of, and may recommend or promote, appropriate internal scrutiny mechanisms. Neither these observations, nor the existence of hybrid institutions such as OLAF (or, to take another example, the Commission's hearing officers in competition proceedings) call into question the validity of the conceptual distinction between external and internal scrutiny. What remains to be discussed is whether that distinction has any real significance for an understanding of external scrutiny institutions and their place in the EU institutional landscape.

In many European states, indeed globally, so-called "new public management"[45] has led to a rapid increase in the number and types of evaluation of public sector performance. Both advocates and critics of this phenomenon tend to elide the distinction between internal and external scrutiny, both of which are treated as a form of regulation that takes place inside government[46] (in the broad sense). One immediate problem with this approach is that it offers no explanation for the apparently wasteful duplication in having both internal and external bodies to carry out audits or handle complaints, for example. Moreover, much of the literature on regulation focuses on the problem of aligning the interests of agents with those of their principals. If one seeks to apply principal/agent theory to external scrutiny bodies, a difficulty appears. The Swedish King's Supreme Ombudsman was clearly his agent, but it is less obvious that contemporary ombudsmen can be understood as agents of the legislature, especially when, as in the case of the European Ombudsman, they deal with complaints against Parliament itself. The same is true a fortiori of the other three EU institutions dealt with in this chapter.

An alternative approach is to analyze external scrutiny institutions as basically free-standing forums of accountability, where actors have an obligation to explain and justify their conduct.[47] From this perspective, the four external scrutiny institutions examined in this chapter could be understood as "non-majoritarian."[48] It seems doubtful whether such an analysis accurately captures their full role. It is true that they do not mobilize European citizens in the same way as classical mechanisms of political responsibility.[49] Furthermore, only the Ombudsman functions, in part, as a mechanism of political participation.[50] However, all four help to form and inform public opinion and provide material that the European Parliament can use in making EU decision-makers accountable. In order to be successful, they must not only deploy technical expertise, but do so in a way that makes their outputs understandable and convincing both to the European Parliament and to the public. Moreover, although they are independent of the European Parliament and separate from it, any effort to conceptualize them in terms of a separate "integrity branch"[51] would need to take account of the fact that, albeit to varying degrees, Parliament is a privileged interlocutor for all of them and provides them with a valuable institutional audience.

It is also worth noting that, to do their job at the EU level, all four external scrutiny institutions need to cooperate closely with their counterparts in the member states. The resulting networks also fit uneasily into some existing paradigms. That is to say, whilst they are not supranational, it would also be misleading to describe them as intergovernmental, since they are composed of external scrutiny bodies, rather than being responsible to national governments.

The scrutiny institutions undoubtedly make the institutional framework of the EU more transparent and more accountable than it would be if they did not exist. The thinness of the European public sphere, however, means that their impact is more visible to those working within the institutions than to citizens as a whole.

Notes

* This chapter expresses the personal views of the author and not those of the European Ombudsman.

1. For brevity, the term "institution" is used to refer to all the EU Institutions, bodies, offices, and agencies. Only the Court of Auditors is an institution in the sense of Article 13 TEU.

2. The acronym is from the French *Office de Lutte Anti-Fraude.*

3. Regulation (EC) 45/2001 of December 18, 2000 on the protection of individuals with regard to the processing of personal data by the Community institutions and bodies and on the free movement of such data, 2001 OJ L 8/1.

4. Milagros García Crespo, ed., *Public Expenditure Control in Europe: Coordinating Audit Functions in the European Union* (Cheltenham: Edward Elgar, 2005), 15–16.

5. For a survey, see Gabriele Kucsko-Stadlmayer, *European Ombudsman-Institutions: A Comparative Legal Analysis Regarding the Multifaceted Realisation of an Idea* (Wien-New York: Springer, 2008).

6. Under the 2007–2013 financial perspective, expenditure is limited to just over 1 percent of EU gross national income.

7. Article 287 (2) TFEU. The ECA's role in relation to the ECB is limited to an examination of the operational efficiency of the management.

8. On the significance of the Financial Regulation see, Paul Craig, "The Constitutionalization of Community Administration," Jean Monnet Working Paper no. 3/03 (2003), NYU School of Law.

9. Brigid Laffan, "Auditing and Accountability in the European Union," *Journal of European Public Policy* 10, no. 5 (October 2003), 762–77, at 765.

10. On average, the Court reported 3.5 cases of suspected fraud per year to OLAF in the years 2004–2007; see the Court's Information Note on the 2007 Annual Report on the 2007 EU Budget.

11. House of Lords, European Union Committee, "Financial Management and Fraud in the European Union: Perceptions, Facts and Proposals," 50th Report session 2005–2006, HL Paper 270, (London: the Stationary Office Limited, 2006), paragraph 84.

12. "International Peer Review of the European Court of Auditors,"2008, <http://eca.europa.eu/portal/pls/portal/docs/1/1843517.PDF>, paragraphs 29, 30.

13. "International Peer Review of the European Court of Auditors," paragraphs 22, 23.

14. See for example, Ian Harden, Fidelma White, and Katy Donnelly, "The Court of Auditors and Financial Control and Accountability in the European Community," *European Public Law* 1 (1995), 599–632; House of Lords, European Union Committee, "The European

Court of Auditors: the Case for Reform" HL Paper 270, 12th Report session 2000–2001 (London: the Stationary Office Limited, 2001).

15. Vítor Caldeira, "The Coordination of Internal Controls: The Single Audit—Towards a European Union Internal Control Framework," in Milagros García Crespo, ed., *Public Expenditure Control in Europe: Coordinating Audit Functions in the European Union*, 184–210, at 191.

16. Article 287 TFEU.

17. See the Court's Opinions 2/2004, 2004 OJ C 107/1, and 6/2007, 2007 OJ C 216/3.

18. See <http://contactcommittee.eu>.

19. See the website of the Swedish Parliamentary Ombudsmen: <www.jo.se>.

20. P. Nikiforos Diamandouros, ed., *The European Ombudsman: Origins, Establishment, Evolution* (Luxembourg: Office for Official Publications of the European Communities, 2005).

21. Regulation (EC) No 1049/2001 of the European Parliament and of the Council of May 30, 2001 regarding public access to European Parliament, Council and Commission documents, 2001 OJ L 145/43.

22. See, for example, the Ombudsman's speeches of January 20 and June 12, 2009: <www.ombudsman.europa.eu/activities/speeches.faces>.

23. See generally Melanie Smith, *Centralized Enforcement, Legitimacy and Good Governance in the EU* (London: Routledge, 2009).

24. P. N. Diamandouros, "The European Ombudsman and the Application of EU Law by the Member States," *Review of European Administrative Law* 1, no. 2 (2008), 5–37; Carol Harlow and Richard Rawlings "Promoting Accountability in Multi-Level Governance: A Network Approach," *European Law Journal* 13 (2007), 542–62.

25. Oswald Jansen and Philip M. Langbroek, *Defence Rights During Administrative Investigations* (Oxford: Intersentia, 2007).

26. Bernard E. Amory and Yvan N. Desmedt, "The European Ombudsman's First Scrutiny of the EC Commission in Antitrust Matters," *European Competition Law Review* 30, no. 5 (2009), 205–11.

27. Paul Magnette, "Between Parliamentary Control and the Rule of Law: The Political Role of the Ombudsman in the European Union," *Journal of European Public Policy* 10, no. 5 (October 2003), 677–94.

28. P. N. Diamandouros, "The Relationship Between the Principle of Good Administration and Legal Obligations," in Carl Baudenbacher, Claus Gulmann, Koen Lenaerts, Emmanuel Coulon, and Eric Barbier de la Serre, eds, *Liber Amicorum en l'honneur de/in honour of Bo Vesterdorf* (Brussels: Bruylant, 2007), 315–41.

29. Herke Kranenborg, "Access to Documents and Data Protection in the European Union: On the Public Nature of Personal Data," *Common Market Law Review* 45, no. 4 (2008), 1079–114.

30. Article 16 TFEU; Article 8 Charter of Fundamental Rights.

31. Directive 95/46/EC of the European Parliament and of the Council of October 24, 1995 on the protection of individuals with regard to the processing of personal data and on the free movement of such data, 1995 OJ L 281/31.

32. Framework Decision 2008/977/JHA, 2008 OJ L350/60. The supervisory authorities may be the same as the ones under Directive 95/46.

33. Peter Hustinx, "The Role of Data Protection Authorities" December 23, 2008, available online on the EDPS' website: <www.edps.europa.eu>.

34. See, in particular, EDPS, *Public Access to Documents and Data Protection*, background paper No 1. July 2005 (available on the EDPS website: <www.edps.europa.eu>); the position taken by the EDPS in Case T-194/04, *Bavarian Lager v Commission* [2007] ECR II-4523; and the opinion of the EDPS on the revision of the Regulation on access to documents 2009 OJ C 2/7.

35. Gloria González Fuster and Pieter Paepe, "Reflexive Governance and the EU Third Pillar: Analysis of Data Protection and Criminal Law Aspects," in Elspeth Guild and Florian Geyer, eds, *Security versus Justice?* (Aldershot: Ashgate, 2008), 129–50.

36. Hielke Hijmans, "The European Data Protection Supervisor: The Institutions of the EC Controlled by an Independent Authority," *Common Market Law Review* 43, no. 5 (2006) 1313–42.

37. Article 16 TFEU.

38. Available on the European Parliament's website: <www.europarl.europa.eu/experts>.

39. Regulation 1073/1999 of the European Parliament and of the Council of May 25, 1999 concerning investigations conducted by the European Anti-Fraud Office (OLAF) 1999 OJ L 136/1.

40. European Court of Auditors Special Report No 1/2005 concerning the management of the European Anti-Fraud Office (OLAF), together with the Commission's replies 2005 OJ C 202, page 1, point 6 of the Introduction.

41. Véronique Pujas, "The European Anti-Fraud Office (OLAF): A European Policy to Fight Against Economic and Financial Fraud?" *Journal of European Public Policy* 10, no. 5 (October 2003), 778–97.

42. Article 86 of the Staff Regulations.

43. Whistleblowing Rules: Best Practice; Assessment and Revision of Rules Existing in EU Institutions (2006) commissioned by the European Parliament PE 373.735, available online at: <www.europarl.europa.eu/document/activities/cont/200712/20071213ATT15454/2007 1213ATT15454EN.pdf>.

44. Ian Harden, "When Europeans Complain: The Role of the European Ombudsman," *Cambridge Yearbook of European Legal Studies* 3 (2002), 199–237.

45. For a useful overview of the literature, see Christopher Pollitt, "The New Public Management in International Perspective," in Kate McLaughlin, Stephen P. Osborne, and Ewan Ferlie, eds, *New Public Management: Current Trends and Future Prospects* (London: Routledge, 2001) 274–94.

46. Christopher Hood, Colin Scott, Oliver James, George Jones, and Tony Travers, *Regulation Inside Government: Waste-Watchers, Quality Police and Sleaze-Busters* (Oxford: Oxford University Press, 1999).

47. Mark Bovens, "New Forms of Accountability and EU-Governance," *Comparative European Politics* 5, no. 1 (April 2007), 104–20. See also Carol Harlow, *Accountability in the European Union* (Oxford: Oxford University Press, 2002); F. White and K. Hollingsworth, *Audit, Accountability and Government* (Oxford: Clarendon Press, 1999).

48. On the concept of "non-majoritarian institutions" see Giandomenico Majone, "Regulatory Legitimacy," in Giandomenico Majone, ed., *Regulating Europe* (London: Routledge, 1996) 284–301.

49. Olivier Costa, Nicolas Jabko, Christian Lequesne, and Paul Magnette "Introduction: Diffuse Control Mechanisms in the European Union: Towards a New Democracy?" *Journal of European Public Policy*, 10 no. 5 (October 2003), 666–76.

50. Hijmans, "The European Data Protection Supervisor," 1326.

51. Cf.Bruce Ackerman, "The New Separation of Powers," *Harvard Law Review* 113 (2000), 633–729, at 694.

CHAPTER 28

EUROPEAN UNION AGENCIES

R. DANIEL KELEMEN

OVER the past two decades, the establishment of EU agencies outside the structure of the European Commission has become the primary means of increasing the size and capacity of the EU's bureaucracy. Since the establishment of the European Environment Agency (EEA) in 1990, the EU has established over thirty agencies addressing issues as diverse as pharmaceutical regulation, border control, environmental protection, military procurement, fisheries enforcement, fundamental rights, and network and information security. The agencies have been spread to locations across the EU. Twenty years ago the physical presence of the EU bureaucracy was limited largely to a square kilometer centered on Rond Point Schuman in Brussels. Today, as a result of the dispersal of EU agencies across the continent, one can find bricks-and-mortar outposts of the European Union from Helsinki to Heraklion and from Vilnius to Vigo.

This chapter explores two sets of questions concerning EU agencies—questions concerning their origins and their impact. First, why were EU agencies created and how did politics influence their design? And second, what impact have EU agencies had, both on the policy areas they are designed to address and on the broader EU political system? In recent years, a number of useful case studies have explored the origins and impact of particular EU agencies.[1] Other studies have focused on particular issues concerning the functioning of EU agencies, such as their accountability.[2] The aim here is a much broader one, namely to present a cogent overview of the politics behind the creation of EU agencies and of the place agencies have assumed in the EU's institutional architecture.

Many accounts of the creation of EU agencies posit that they were established to meet functional needs for technical expertise and independence in the EU's regulatory process.[3] By contrast, I have argued that the creation of EU agencies had much more to do with politics than with functional demands.[4] As I explain below, the design of EU agencies was the product of a political compromise between the European Commission, Parliament, and member-state governments. With regard to their impact, the few empirical studies available suggest that EU agencies have proven relatively effective in carrying out their policy mandates.[5] But beyond these sector-specific impacts, the emergence of EU agencies collectively has had a more profound impact on the architecture of EU governance. The delegation of routine regulatory and executive tasks to EU agencies has facilitated a shift in the role of the European Commission from that of independent regulator to that of politicized executive.

The chapter is divided into four sections. Section 28.1 clarifies what an EU agency is and identifies existing EU agencies. Section 28.2 explains why EU agencies were created and how battles between the Commission, Parliament, and Council influenced their design. Section 28.3 presents a brief review of the development of EU agencies from 1989 through 2011. Section 28.4 concludes.

28.1 IDENTIFYING EU AGENCIES

What is an EU agency? The answer is less obvious than it might seem. The Commission, Parliament, and Council have been unable to agree on a common template for EU agencies. They have created a variety of EU-level bodies with a variety of institutional structures and powers, giving them labels including agency, authority, center, office—all of which fall into the general category of "EU agencies." Broadly, we can define an EU agency as an organ of the EU created by an act of secondary legislation with a distinct legal personality and a certain degree of organizational and financial autonomy from other EU bodies.[6]

But what does that really mean? This definition specifies not only what an EU agency is, but also what it is not. First, this definition distinguishes EU agencies from other EU bodies established by member-state governments in EU Treaties, such as the EIB or the ECB.[7] Second, this definition distinguishes EU agencies from comitology committees that advise the Commission and EU sponsored regulatory networks, such as the European Competition Network (ECN) or the European Regulators Group (ERG) in telecoms, that lack the distinct legal personality and the clear institutional core that agencies have. Simply put, if you don't have an address and no one can sue you, you are not an EU agency.

EU agencies differ significantly in their structures, functions, and resources. Broadly, they can be divided into two categories, (1) executive agencies that perform managerial tasks on behalf of the Commission, and (2) regulatory agencies that provide information and advice, make regulatory decisions, and coordinate regulatory networks. The vast majority of these agencies focus on economic and social policies, which formerly fell under the EU's 'first pillar'. Additionally three agencies have been established focusing on CSDP and three focusing on police and judicial cooperation in criminal matters.[8] Table 28.1 summarizes existing European agencies and those in final stages of the legislative process as of 2011.

Table 28.1 EU agencies

NAME	LOCATION	YEAR	PRIMARY FUNCTION
European Centre for the Development of Vocational Training (Cedefop)	Thessaloniki	1975	Dialogue/information
European Foundation for the Improvement of Living and Working Conditions (Eurofound)	Dublin	1975	Dialogue/information
European Environment Agency (EEA)	Copenhagen	1990	Information
European Training Foundation (ETF)	Torino	1990	Executive
The European Monitoring Centre for Drugs and Drug Addiction (EMCDDA)	Lisbon	1993	Information
European Medicines Agency (EMA)	London	1993	Regulation
Office for Harmonization in the Internal Market (OHIM)	Alicante	1993	Regulation
European Agency for Safety and Health at Work (EU OSHA)	Bilbao	1994	Dialogue/information
Community Plant Variety Office (CPVO)	Angers	1994	Regulation
Translation Centre for the Bodies of the European Union (CdT)	Luxembourg	1994	Executive
European Police Office (Europol)	The Hague	1995	Information
European Union Agency for Fundamental Rights (FRA) (previously European Monitoring Centre on Racism and Xenophobia)	Vienna	2007 (1997)	Information
European Police College (CEPOL)	Hook	2000	Training
European Union Institute for Security Studies (ISS)	Paris	2001	Information
European Union Satellite Centre (EUSC)	Torrejón de Ardoz	2001	Information
European Food Safety Authority (EFSA)	Parma	2002	Risk assessment/ regulation
The European Union's Judicial Cooperation Unit—(EUROJUST)	The Hague	2002	Coordination
European Maritime Safety Agency (EMSA)	Lisbon	2002	Regulation
European Aviation Safety Agency (EASA)	Cologne	2002	Regulation
European Network and Information Security Agency (ENISA)	Heraklion	2004	Information/risk assessment
European Railway Agency (ERA)	Lille/Valenciennes	2004	Regulation
European Centre for Disease Prevention and Control (ECDC)	Stockholm	2004	Information
European Defence Agency (EDA)	Brussels	2004	Procurement
European GNSS Agency (GSA)	Brussels	2004	Executive
Community Fisheries Control Agency (CFCA)	Vigo	2005	Regulation
European Agency for the Management of Operational Cooperation at the External Borders (FRONTEX)	Warsaw	2004	Border Control
European Chemicals Agency (ECHA)	Helsinki	2007	Regulation
European Institute for Gender Equality (EIGE)	Vilnius	2007	Information
European Securities and Markets Authority (ESMA)	Paris	2010	Regulation
European Banking Authority (EBA)	London	2010	Regulation

NAME	LOCATION	YEAR	PRIMARY FUNCTION
European Insurance and Occupational Pensions Authority (EIOPA)	Frankfurt	2010	Regulation
Body of European Regulators for Electronic Communications (BEREC)	Riga	2011	Regulation
EU Agency for the Cooperation of Energy Regulators (ACER)	Llubljana	2011	Regulation
European Asylum Support Office	Valletta	2011	Regulation

28.2 WHY WERE EU AGENCIES CREATED?

To understand the creation of EU agencies one must first understand the wider institutional context within which they are designed and the interests of the political principals involved in their creation.[9] EU agencies are designed by—and designed to serve the interests of—the EU's three main political principals—the Council, the Parliament, and the Commission. While the Council and Parliament are the EU's primary legislative actors and the Commission its primary executive arm, all three institutions have acted, to varying extents, as political principals with respect to the design of EU agencies. Their precise role and the extent of their influence over the design of any particular EU regulatory body varies depending on the decision-making procedures in the relevant policy field at the time the new agency is designed. Thus the Council has had near exclusive control over the design of the six EU agencies addressing issues in the areas of CFSP and JHA, where the Commission's and Parliament's powers are limited. By contrast, the Commission, Council, and increasingly the Parliament have all played important roles in the design of the twenty-two agencies addressing issues in the EU's "First Pillar."

The ECJ is of course not involved in agency design, but the ECJ lurks in the background both because an ECJ legal doctrine concerning the "institutional balance" in the EU—the *Meroni*[10] doctrine—limits what powers can be delegated to agencies and because all players involved in the design of agencies recognize that the ECJ may play an important role in reviewing an agency's actions after it is created.

When considering delegating some new regulatory authority or administrative task to the EU level, the Council, Parliament, and Commission face a large range of options in terms of the bureaucratic agents to whom they may delegate.[11] They may delegate authority to EU agencies, or they may instead choose to delegate directly to the European Commission or to loose networks of National Regulatory Authorities (NRAs). And within the category of EU agencies, law-makers may vary the powers they delegate to an agency and the management and oversight structures they put in place to control the agency's discretion.

Confronted with this large menu of institutional choices, what guides the choice and design of executive bodies at the EU level? The design of EU agencies is the result of compromise between the EU's political principals, each of them favoring institutional designs they think will promote their interests. We now explore the preferences of member states, the Commission, and the Parliament regarding these design choices.

Member States. When member states in the Council of Ministers delegate to an EU-level bureaucratic agent, their primary concern is to minimize "bureaucratic drift."[12] For most of the EU's history, when the member states in the Council chose to delegate regulatory tasks to the EU level, they did so by delegating to the EU's primary executive body, European Commission. However, the Commission proved to be a famously slippery agent, prone to bureaucratic drift. The Commission used the power and autonomy it was granted to aggrandize its powers and accelerate integration beyond the scope intended by at least some of the member states. Member states worked to mitigate this loss of control beginning in the 1960s by building a system of intergovernmental "comitology" committees that monitor and to some degree control the Commission's exercise of its executive powers.[13] Given the Council's preference for minimizing supranational bureaucratic drift, one would expect the Council to demand the establishment of mechanisms for intergovernmental oversight when creating any new EU agencies outside the Commission hierarchy. Indeed, one would expect that member states would favor the establishment of EU agencies subject to greater intergovernmental oversight and control than the European Commission.

The European Parliament. Given its well-known preference for deeper European integration, we would expect the Parliament to favor the establishment of powerful, well-resourced EU agencies. Though the Parliament will oppose structures that enable member-state governments to control EU agencies, it will not want the agencies to be completely independent of political control. Rather, given the EU's role in ensuring the democratic accountability of the EU system, we would expect it—like some other legislatures—to favor institutional designs that enhance the transparency and accountability of EU agencies. Given that the Parliament's capacity to monitor agencies is limited, we would expect it to favor mechanisms that facilitate fire-alarm oversight[14] by interest groups (such as the diffuse public interest groups) that are strongly allied to the Parliament.

The European Commission. The European Commission has a clear hierarchy of preferences concerning the structure of regulatory bodies. Unsurprisingly, the Commission's first preference generally would be to expand its own regulatory capacity and authority, through increased financing, staffing, and grants of regulatory powers. However, where member states block delegation to the Commission itself, the Commission may support the establishment of autonomous EU-level regulatory bodies. In that case it will favor the establishment of agencies with considerable autonomy from national governments, but which remain closely tied to and dependent on the European Commission.

EU agencies are products of compromise between the Commission, Parliament, and member states in the Council. The heart of the compromise underlying the creation of nearly all the agencies[15] is the same and unfolds roughly as follows: the EU is taking on a new task, or the burden of existing tasks expands significantly. The European Commission and European Parliament want to expand the EU's bureaucratic capacity in order to address these new demands, and they would prefer to do so by expanding the powers, resources, and staff of the European Commission. The member states recognize the need for added regulatory or administrative capacity at the European level. However, they are unwilling to centralize power, resources, and staff in the hands of the Commission, given its famous track record of going beyond its mandate in its pursuit of deeper integration. Faced with this conundrum, a compromise is struck. Member states agree to delegate power and resources to a new EU-level agency that is autonomous from the Commission and is subject to control by a management board dominated by member-state representatives. Where the European Parliament has influence over agency design (which was increasingly the case after the mid-1990s) it demands the establishment of bureaucratic structures and administrative procedures that enhance the transparency and accountability of agencies to facilitate fire-alarm oversight by its interest group allies.

The precise nature of the compromises struck—and the bureaucratic structures put in place as a result—differ in important ways in the case of each agency. The competences delegated to agencies differ, as do the compositions of their management boards, the procedures for selecting the agency head, and the arrangements for budgetary supervision. Moreover, the politics of agency design has shifted over time, in particular due to the European Parliament's assertion of its growing powers. Nevertheless, the broad compromise underlying the creation of all EU agencies is that described above.

28.3 The Development of EU Agencies

The drive to "complete" the single market by 1992 dramatically increased the regulatory burdens (in terms of data gathering and analysis, rule-making and implementation) on the European Commission. The Commission and European Parliament would have preferred to meet the need for enhanced EU-level administrative capacity by expanding the Commission's staff and budget. However, with Euro-skeptics conjuring the specter of a nascent European superstate there was strong political opposition across the member states to expansion of the Commission bureaucracy. In this context, the Commission sought novel avenues through which to expand the EU's regulatory capacity and turned to the idea of "independent" European agencies.

In January 1989, the European Commission proposed the establishment of the EEA, suggesting the agency would improve the Community's monitoring and implementation capacity.[16] The Parliament quickly endorsed the proposal, though its role in the debate was limited, as the legal basis of Commission's proposal called for a legislative procedure (the Consultation Procedure) that limited the Parliament's involvement. The member states debated the proposal for months, confronting serious disagreements over what powers the agency should be granted and how it should be structured. Ultimately, member states agreed to create a relatively weak EEA focused on information gathering (rather than implementation or enforcement) and put in place a management board composed primarily of member-state appointees to oversee the EEA.

After the establishment of the EEA, proposals for a variety of agencies emerged from various Directorates within the Commission bureaucracy in the early 1990s, and the

Commission Secretariat General then stepped in to coordinate the process of agency design.[17] Eventually the Commission and the Council reached a rough political compromise over how the agencies should be structured and governed. The Commission would have preferred more "supranational" governance structures, but member states in the Council demanded that any new agencies be subject to "intergovernmental" control. All agencies established in the early 1990s were subject to the control of management boards composed overwhelmingly of member-state representatives who could monitor and control agency activities on an ongoing basis. Member-state regulatory authorities were also involved in the day-to-day work of EU agencies. Agencies were generally designed around a hub-and-spoke network model[18] in which the EU agency would coordinate and rely on the resources of existing national regulatory authorities, in some cases (such as the Medicines Agency (EMA)) even delegating tasks to national administrations on a rotating basis. As for the scope of their powers, some agencies were restricted to information gathering roles while others were granted limited regulatory powers.

The EU agency model proved attractive for many reasons. Generally, the notion of delegating tasks to depoliticized, "independent regulatory agencies" was increasingly popular in domestic politics across EU member states in the late 1980s.[19] Therefore the notion of establishing "independent" agencies at the EU level seemed to follow best practices at the national level. For many member states, delegating tasks to EU agencies controlled by management boards that they dominated represented an attractive way to facilitate collective action at the EU level without concentrating too much power in the famously entrepreneurial and self-aggrandizing European Commission. For the European Commission, given member-state opposition to expanding the size and resources of the Commission itself, EU agencies presented an attractive second-best means through which to strengthen the EU's administrative capacity. Importantly, the resources and responsibilities granted to European agencies generally were not taken away from the Commission, but from obscure comitology committees that had long advised and overseen the Commission.[20] To the extent that the Commission did surrender some responsibilities to the EU agencies, these were mostly mundane monitoring and information gathering tasks and losing them did not threaten the Commission's core competences.

The politics of agency design changed significantly in the past decade. Conflicts concerning what powers agencies should have and who should oversee and control the agencies persisted. However, the dynamics shifted as the European Parliament became an increasingly significant player in agency design and oversight. With the growing involvement of the Parliament and heightened profile of existing agencies, questions concerning the transparency and accountability of European agencies became central.[21]

The European Parliament has sought to assert itself as a watchdog of the EU agencies, so as to ensure the transparency and accountability of the regulatory process. Beginning in the mid-1990s, the European Parliament exerted its budgetary powers in order to impose accountability requirements on EU agencies.[22] The Parliament has also demanded that the agencies adopt more formal, transparent, and judicially enforceable administrative procedures than the infamously opaque comitology committees that had long underpinned the Commission's regulatory processes.[23] Finally, the Parliament has called for (though not succeeded in obtaining) a far greater role in the appointment of the management boards that oversee EU agencies, at one point suggesting that all candidates for positions on management boards be submitted to the Parliament for scrutiny.[24]

The transparency and accountability requirements in the founding regulations for the recently established European Aviation Safety Agency (EASA) illustrate the impact of the European Parliament's heightened influence. EASA has been given the authority to issue airworthiness codes and to issue (or suspend or revoke) individual airworthiness and environmental certifications for aircraft products. The regulation (Reg. 1592/2002)[25] establishing the EASA requires the agency to establish "transparent procedures" for issuing certification specifications and demands that the agency "consults widely" with interested parties according to a fixed timetable and that it "make a written response to the consultation process" (Art. 43). When EASA takes individual decisions on aircraft parts it must provide the reasons for the decision to interested parties (Art. 44), providing a potential basis for affected parties to challenge these decisions. At the insistence of the Parliament, similar transparency requirements have been programmed into the founding regulations of other recently established EU agencies.

In the past decade, EU agencies emerged as a central element in the EU's model of governance, and yet efforts to craft a common framework for EU agencies have proven elusive. The 2001 White Paper on European Governance[26] acknowledged the development of European agencies and suggested that the establishment of more such agencies could improve EU regulation. The White Paper also called for the establishment of a formal framework for the creation, operation, and supervision of such agencies. In a 2002 Communication,[27] the Commission proposed a set of guidelines for such a framework. A draft inter-institutional agreement on EU agencies[28] was published in 2005, but adoption of the agreement was blocked in the Council. In March 2008, the Commission published a new Communication on EU agencies[29] again calling for agreement on a common framework for agencies, but none has been agreed as yet.

Very few systematic studies of the effectiveness of EU agencies have been conducted to date. The operations of the EMA have been studied most closely and analysts have concluded that when relying on its centralized procedure, it has proven effective and has made significant contributions to the creation of a true single market for pharmaceuticals.[30] By contrast, Schout's[31] study of the EASA finds that it has not proven effective in its early years of operation. To better understand the effectiveness of EU agencies, many more such studies must be conducted on the operations of other EU agencies. In assessing the effectiveness of EU agencies in promoting regulatory harmonization or other tasks, it is important to consider how EU agencies have performed relative to other potential institutional arrangements. In particular, the establishment of EU-wide networks of NRAs has been touted by some as an alternative to establishing EU agencies.[32] In some sectors such as telecoms and energy, many national governments have long resisted calls for the establishment of EU agencies by insisting that networks of NRAs could achieve the needed cooperation and harmonization. These claims are dubious at best. As Kelemen and Tarrant[33] have argued, networks of NRAs have proven to be a largely ineffectual substitute for EU agencies.

28.4 Conclusion

Confusion concerning EU agencies is abundant. Many observers characterize them as "independent" agencies. In reality, they are anything but independent. Certainly they are not independent of the member states, who have favored delegating to EU agencies—rather than to the European Commission—because agencies are governed by management boards dominated by member state appointees. Nor are they independent of the Parliament, which imposes strict budgetary oversight. And though they are separate from the European Commission, they are not fully independent of it, particularly in that substantive regulatory decisions recommended by the agencies must be formally adopted by the Commission pursuant to the *Meroni* doctrine mentioned above. EU agencies are not designed in order to realize some ideal of independent, technocratic expertise; rather, they are products of political compromise.

The long-term impact of the development of EU agencies may be profound. The development of EU agencies is inextricably bound up with the ongoing politicization of the European Commission. Twenty years ago, the European Commission was viewed essentially as an independent agency charged with promoting European integration and policing the single market. Since then, the European Commission has become more politicized as the EU has moved into more sensitive policy areas, as issues of the democratic accountability of EU institutions have become salient, and as the European Parliament has asserted its power to vet and to oversee the Commission. The delegation of more and more routine regulatory tasks to EU agencies has facilitated the process of transforming the European Commission from an independent regulator to an increasingly politicized executive.

Notes

1. See for instance Thomas Gehring and Sebastian Krapohl, "Supranational Regulatory Agencies Between Independence and Control: The EMEA and the Authorization of Pharmaceuticals in the European Single Market," *Journal of European Public Policy* 14, no. 2 (March 2007), 208–26; Jürgen Feick, "Regulatory Europeanization, National Autonomy and Regulatory Effectiveness: Market Authorization for Pharmaceuticals," Discussion Paper 02/06. Max-Planck-Institut für Gesellschaftsforschung, 2006; Martens, Maria, "Voice or Loyalty? The Evolution of the European Environment Agency," *Journal of Common Market Studies* 48, no. 4 (September 2010), 881–901; M. Groenleer, E. Versluis, and M. Kaeding, "Regulatory Governance Through EU Agencies? The Implementation of Transport Directives," paper presented at the ECPR Standing Group on Regulatory Governance, Utrecht, June 5–7, 2008; Adriaan Schout, "Inspecting Aviation Safety in the EU: EASA as an Administrative Innovation," in *European Risk Governance—Its Science, its Inclusiveness, and its Effectiveness*, CONNEX Report Series No. 6 (February 2008); and Jon Pierre and B. Guy Peters, "From a Club to a Bureaucracy: JAA, EASA, and European Aviation Regulation," *Journal of Public Policy* 16, no. 3 (April 2009), 337–55.

2. Deirdre Curtin, "Holding (Quasi-)Autonomous EU Administrative Actors to Public Account," *European Law Journal* 13, no. 4 (July 2007), 523–41; Williams, Garrath, "Monomaniacs or Schizophrenics?: Responsible Governance and the EU's Independent Agencies," *Political Studies* 53, no. 1 (March 2005), 82–99.

3. See Giandomenico Majone, "The New European Agencies: Regulation by Information," *Journal of European Public Policy* 4, no. 2 (June 1997), 262–75; Giandomenico Majone, "The Credibility Crisis of Community Regulation," *Journal of Common Market Studies* 38, no. 2 (June 2000), 273–302; Giandomenico Majone, "Delegation of Regulatory Powers in a Mixed Polity," *European Law Journal* 8, no. 3 (September 2002), 319–39; Michelle Everson, "Independent Agencies: Hierarchy beaters?," *European Law Journal* 1, no. 2 (July 1995), 180–204; and Alexander Kreher, "Agencies in the European Community—A Step Towards Administrative Integration in Europe," *Journal of European Public Policy* 4, no. 2 (June 1997), 225–45.

4. See R. D. Kelemen, "The European 'Independent' Agencies and Regulation in the EU," CEPS Working Document No. 112 (Brussels: Center for European Policy Studies, 1997); R. D. Kelemen, "The Politics of 'Eurocratic' Structure and the New European Agencies," *West European Politics* 25, no. 4 (October 2002), 93–118; R. D. Kelemen, "The Politics of Eurocracy: Building a New European State?" in Nicolas Jabko and Craig Parsons, eds, *The State of the European Union, Volume 7: With US or Against US? European Trends in American Perspective* (New York: Oxford University Press, 2005), 173–91; Martin Shapiro, "The Problems of Independent Agencies in the United States and the European Union," *Journal of European Public Policy* 4, no. 2 (June 1997), 276–7; and Renaud Dehousse, "Delegation of Powers in the European Union: The Need for a Multi-Principals Model," *West European Politics* 31, no. 4, (July 2008), 789–805.

5. See Jürgen Feick, "Regulatory Europeanization"; and M. Groenleer et al., "Regulatory Governance Through EU Agencies?."

6. See "Communication from the Commission: The Operating Framework for the European Regulatory Agencies"; Commission of the European Communities, COM (2002), 718 final, December 11, 2002, p. 3.

7. A more expansive definition of the concept of "agency" might include these bodies as well—and arguably they should be analyzed alongside agencies in any comprehensive study of the development of the EU's institutional architecture. However, the political dynamics surrounding the creation of bodies like the ECB in an EU Treaty differs profoundly from the process of creating agencies through the EU's regular legislative process. Also, the legal framework (discussed below) that constrains what powers EU agencies may take on does not apply in the case of bodies created through EU Treaties, which can be granted whatever authority the member states agree on. Therefore, whatever the parallels between bodies like the ECB and EU agencies, folding them into the same category would obscure more than it would reveal.

8. Confusingly, the EU has also established additional bodies (six currently) called "Executive Agencies." The "Executive Agencies" have a more limited remit than the Community agencies, as they are established only to implement particular programs for a fixed time period. For our purposes, however, these do not meet the definition of EU agencies. Though these bodies have a legal personality, they are essentially organizational units within the Commission. They can be established and closed by the Commission unilaterally (in accordance with Council Regulation 58/2003) and are not "autonomous agencies" like the others we explore in this chapter. See European Parliament and Council of the European

Union, "Regulation laying down the statue for executive agencies to be entrusted with certain tasks in the management of Community programmes," Regulation No. 58/2003, December 19, 2002.

9. See Renaud Dehousse, "Delegation of Powers in the European Union"; and Kelemen, "The Politics of 'Eurocratic' Structure and the New European Agencies."

10. This is because independent European regulatory agencies are viewed under the *Meroni* doctrine as in principle being unconstitutional since they disturb the "institutional balance" of the Treaty by potentially moving European-level executive powers away from the Commission which should otherwise be the European executive body. In Meroni (1957) the Court held that Community law did not allow delegations of discretionary powers to bodies that were not created by the Treaty (*Meroni v. High Authority* Case 9/56 [1957–58] ECR 133. See also the parallel judgment *Meroni v. High Authority* Case 10/56 [1957–58] ECR 157).

11. See David Coen and Mark Thatcher, "Network Governance and Multi-Level Delegation: European Networks of Regulatory Agencies," *Journal of Public Policy* 28, no. 1 (April 2008), 49–71.

12. On the concept of bureaucratic drift, see John Huber and Charles Shipan, "The Costs of Control: Legislators, Agencies and Transaction Costs," *Legislative Studies Quarterly* 25, no. 1 (February 2000), 25–52.

13. See Mark Pollack, "Delegation, Agency and Agenda Setting in the European Community," *International Organization* 51, no. 1 (Winter 1997), 99–134; and Christian Joerges and Ellen Vos, eds, *EU Committees: Social Regulation, Law and Politics* (Oxford-Portland: Hart Publishing, 1999); Rhys Dogan, "Comitology: Little Procedures with Big Implications," *West European Politics* 20 no. 3 (1997), 31–60.

14. See Matthew McCubbins and Thomas Schwartz, "Congressional Oversight Overlooked: Police Patrols versus Fire Alarms," *American Journal of Political Science* 28, no. 1 (February 1984), 165–79; Mark Pollack, "Delegation, Agency and Agenda Setting"; and Kelemen, "The Politics of 'Eurocratic' Structure," 97.

15. The dynamics surrounding the creation of second pillar (Foreign and Security Policy) and third pillar (Justice and Home Affairs) agencies is rather different, given the minimal Commission and Parliament power in these fields. We will concern ourselves primarily with the twenty-two first pillar agencies. But in all cases, and for similar reasons, EU agencies are created as alternatives to delegating power to the Commission, on the one hand, or to loosen intergovernmental networks and committees, on the other.

16. See Kelemen, "The Politics of 'Eurocratic' Structure."

17. See Kelemen, "The Politics of 'Eurocratic' Structure," 102.

18. See Dehousse, "Delegation of Powers in the European Union."

19. See Mark Thatcher and Alec Stone Sweet, "Theory and Practice of Delegations to Non-Majoritarian Institutions," *West European Politics*, 25, no. 1 (January 2002), 1–22; and Mark Thatcher, "The Third Force? Independent Regulatory Authorities and Elected Politicians in Europe," *Governance* 18, no. 3 (July 2005), 347–73.

20. See Dehousse, "Delegation of Powers in the European Union," 258.

21. See Kelemen, "The Politics of Eurocracy."

22. See Dehousse, "Delegation of Powers in the European Union"; Kelemen, "The Politics of 'Eurocratic' Structure"; and Matthew Flinders, "Distributed Public Governance in the EU," *Journal of European Public Policy* 11, no. 3 (June 2004), 520–44, at 536.

23. See Kelemen, "The Politics of Eurocracy."

24. European Parliament, Report on the Communication from the Commission: "The Opera-
    ting Framework for the European Regulatory Agencies" (COM(2002) 718–2003/2089/
    (INI)), (December 4, 2003), A5-0471/2003, p. 10.
25. See European Parliament and Council of the European Union, "Regulation on common
    rules in the field of civil aviation and establishing a European Aviation Safety Agency,"
    Regulation No. 1592/2002, July 15, 2002.
26. European Governance: A White Paper, Commission of the European Communities, COM
    (2001) 428 final, July 25, 2001.
27. "Communication from the Commission: The Operating Framework for European
    Regulatory Agencies."
28. See "Draft Institutional Agreement on the operating framework for the European regula-
    tory agencies"; Commission of the European Communities, COM (2005) 59 final, February
    25, 2005.
29. See "Communication from the Commission to the European Parliament and the Council:
    European agencies—the way forward"; Commission of the European Communities, COM
    (2008) 135 final, March 11, 2008.
30. See Feick, "Regulatory Europeanization"; and Gehring and Krapohl, "Supernational
    Regulatory Agencies Between Independence and Control."
31. See Schout, "Inspecting Aviation Safety in the EU."
32. See B. Eberlein and E. Grande, "Beyond Delegation: Transnational Regulatory Regimes
    and the EU Regulatory State," *Journal of European Public Policy* 21, no. 1 (February 2005),
    89–112.
33. See R. Daniel Kelemen and Andy Tarrant, "The Political Foundations of the Eurocracy,"
    34, no. 5 (2011), 922–47.

PART VI

ECONOMIC COMPETENCES

CHAPTER 29

··

SINGLE MARKET

··

MICHELLE EGAN

WITH the global economic crisis and increased protectionism within Europe, there are concerns that the single market is under tremendous pressure. As the cornerstone of European integration, and the foundation of market liberalization, the single market has become somewhat neglected in recent years as attention has been given to other new areas of cooperation and integration including foreign policy and justice, freedom and security. Yet the single market is not only a political and economic objective of the EU; it is also a fundamental legal concept, encompassing most of the substantive powers of the European polity. The current economic circumstances, with government bailouts, low growth rates, and rising unemployment, has focused attention back onto the single market and its role in managing globalization and boosting growth and competitiveness.[1]

Yet this will not be easy given the political backlash against further liberalization in the current financial crisis. The global context in which the single market now operates has fundamentally changed, as economies of scale and mass production have been replaced by a knowledge and service economy based on product differentiation.[2] As such, the changing nature of competition should no longer be on removing internal barriers to trade, adopting regulatory and legal standards, and focusing on implementation and compliance across a more diverse economic union. Instead, most analysts argue that the single market should focus on prioritizing certain barriers that restrict innovation, take account of the administrative weaknesses of new member states, avoid comprehensive harmonization, and better coordinate single market policies with competition, trade, and consumer policies.[3] Despite advocating a deeper single market, the new Single Market Act calling for substantial legislative and regulatory action to boost European competitiveness and growth received limited attention. Shifting away from the focus of expanding national markets to achieve economies of scale as articulated in the original single market "1992" program, the new efforts seek to balance social Europe with market integration in order to enhance public support for further market integration based on a "highly competitive social market economy."[4]

This chapter examines the single market by discussing in turn, its origins, development, and impact, and in doing so draws upon the different theoretical approaches used to study the dynamics of market integration. As the cornerstone of market integration, the single market has fostered a breadth and variety of research drawing upon a variety of research traditions.[5] From the launching of the customs union in the 1960s to the "1992 project" in the 1980s, and more recently, the Single Market Act, there is plenty for historians, political scientists, sociologists, lawyers, and economists to study about the process of market-building in Europe. The subsequent section will map out a variety of different research directions for the further study of the single market drawing on different disciplines to show both how the debate has developed and where it may be heading.

29.1 FROM CUSTOMS UNION TO COMMON MARKET

Addressing obstacles to trade within Europe has been a central goal since the Economic Cooperation Act in which the United States pledged economic support for post-war reconstruction. This provided the environment in which European governments coordinated liberalization initiatives, reduced government spending, and opened up economies to foreign trade.[6] The process of market integration that began with the establishment of a common tariff among the members of the ECSC then progressed into the creation of a common market. As negotiations began in Europe among the six original European Community members to foster further market integration, the Spaak report in 1956 envisaged the formation of a continent-wide common market along the lines of the United States.[7] Such economic negotiations within the European Community were perceived as part of a broader set of liberalization measures that were underway in a variety of international institutions.[8]

Yet the Rome Treaty focused primarily on the free movement of goods, particularly the progressive elimination of tariffs and quantitative restrictions and the creation of a common external tariff. However, the common market was not defined in the Rome Treaty, and as such was perceived to be primarily a customs union, with limited attention given to non-tariff barriers.[9] It was clear the treaty placed a priority on trade liberalization in goods rather than other factors of production, with less attention given toward capital and services liberalization due to the assumption about the low mobility of such factors of production compared to goods.[10] The inclusion of common policies such as transport and competition policy, and the emphasis on policing the market through the abolition of state aids and anti-competitive practices pointed to a liberal economic approach. However, this was tempered by specific exemptions written into the treaty, in case member states experienced substantial economic difficulties necessitating corrective measures. But policies requiring intervention such as industrial policy and regional policy were noticeable by their lack of explicit provisions, as the treaty did not have an interventionist slant, at least for industry, in the early period. As such, due to the significant differences in the organization of markets in post-war Europe, with variations in the role of government, the type of market intervention and control, and the role of different institutions (in part the result of different policy objectives and historical legacies), the treaty contained many objectives that were interrelated but conceptually distinct, reflecting the socio-economic preferences of different member states.

29.1.1 Early Market Integration: From Growth to Pessimism

Many European economies experienced rapid expansion in productivity and output in the 1950s and 1960s, although improvement in economic performance was not uniform and underscores the legacy of how different states capitalized on the economic opportunities created by wage moderation, reinvestment, and economic modernization. The economic effects of European integration were considerable. The progressive elimination of tariff barriers in the 1950s and 1960s resulted in major cuts in tariff barriers in the aftermath of the creation of the customs union. Intra-European Community trade increased dramatically, demonstrating the effects of trade creation which were substantially higher than any trade diversion.[11] Throughout the region, many European companies were nationally federated firms, constrained by fragmented markets that prevented them from reaping the benefits of market integration, as restraints of trade existed through a plethora of divergent rules and standards that prevented them from rationalization of production, economies of scale, and factor price differentials.[12] However, the advent of the common market was accompanied by increased foreign direct investment (FDI) which resulted in many European and non-European firms establishing branches and operations in other member states as a way of securing market access, as various kinds of non-tariff barriers often provided special protective measures to preserve domestic sales and market shares.[13]

But by the 1970s, the entire framework of the international economy shifted as the general economic crisis of this decade prompted most European countries to increase non-tariff barriers; European firms experienced a decline in market shares abroad, which heightened concerns about competitiveness. As the exceptionally long period of economic growth gave way to a period of declining investment and competitiveness, and spiraling unemployment and inflation (stagflation), the common market stalled as different conceptions about the agenda for European integration emerged. This crisis sparked different policy responses by member states, and the net effect of the downturn widened the gap in terms of economic performance among member states, and increased economic disparities between the more and less advanced economies and regions.[14]

29.1.2 The Relaunch of Economic Integration: The 1992 Program

As trade deficits soared, attention focused on the completion of the single European market and strengthening of European strategies in areas such as research and development, public purchasing, and technical standards. Efforts also went into improving the environment in which companies operated, and guarded against market outcomes that relegated European firms to the margins of industrial production and exchange.[15] Economists assessed the "costs of non-Europe" in detail, although there were disagreements about the relative static and dynamics effects that would accrue from greater market integration.[16] However, few of these assessments focused on the distribution of gains within the European Community, in terms of which sectors would gain and which would be vulnerable, in a more competitive market.[17] But the design of the single market project was a supply side measure aimed at reducing not only costs but also prices through intensified competition. Thus, the removal of non-tariff barriers would complement the prior reduction in internal tariffs. This would be achieved by lifting the restrictions to goods, capital, services, and labor which was outlined in a White Paper published in 1985, entitled "Completing the Internal Market."[18] This initiative, combined with the SEA, tied the concept of the single market to institutional reform, thus making possible a political deadline of 1992 to address fiscal, technical, and regulatory barriers.[19] The SEA extended QMV to areas of the single market, and defined the "internal market" as an "area without frontiers" in which the "free movement of goods, capital, services and labor" is ensured, thus adding to the older common market concept in the Rome Treaty.[20] However, the economic constitution of the EU not only promotes cross-border liberalization, contingent on specific judicial exemptions, but also provides for the possibility of addressing market failures through the establishment of rules in the common interest.[21] Promising the benefits of increased economies of scale, greater contestability of markets, and substantial economic growth, the single market program quickly becomes a popular policy initiative among business leaders and national politicians.[22]

Previous attempts to address the myriad of border controls, industry standards, state subsidies, and restrictions in areas of health and safety, patents, banking, insurance, and so forth had been unsuccessful. While many proposals were holdovers from the past, they included an alternative way to address different rules that reflected a shift from the original reliance on harmonization of rules to integrate markets.[23] Member states had negotiated common rules which were then binding on all of them, thus overcoming problems of divergent national regulations. However, it is a demanding means to integrate markets as harmonization transfers the rules for compliance and enforcement to the European level.[24] The high decision costs associated with such rule-making were responsible for the limited efforts to address non-tariff barriers as it was tied to the specific provisions in the Rome Treaty. However, the ECJ (pushed by complaints from industry affected by obstacles to trade), and in conjunction with the cooperation of national courts, played a key role in invalidating protectionist measures.[25] Although case law was primarily shaped in the field of goods, the Court, in its efforts to deal with national measures affecting market access, substantially increased member states' obligations to mutually recognize their respective standards, regulations, and certifications. Such legal restrictions have reduced the scope of numerous national provisions in company law, social policy, environmental policy, and other areas.[26] On the one hand, the Court does on occasion respect specific national values and rights to regulate domestically, provided that they are justified. On the other hand, such liberalization pressures limit state regulatory power, leading to competition in rules on goods, but in services leads to fear that such mutual recognition puts pressure on regulatory levels leading to a race to the bottom that necessitates harmonization at the European level to avoid social dumping.

Mutual recognition was thus perceived as an alternative means to integrate markets, as it assumes that rules within each member state are functionally equivalent (although if not, the member state has the right to require host country rather than home country rules for admission to the domestic market). Eliminating the remaining barriers to trade would allow companies to operate on a European-wide basis and encourage firms to rationalize production, exploit cost reduction, and pursue mergers and acquisitions.[27] Companies had to spend considerable effort to meet different national standards, deal with restrictive certification procedures, and import restrictions across a range of industries. While companies with large-scale returns would benefit from the single market, more domestically oriented producers would be exposed to competitive pressures as a result of trade liberalization and increased contestability of markets. As a result, certain sectors were exempt from the single market program (textiles and clothing), others were subject to selective liberalization (modes of transport), and some potentially key sectors received limited attention (service markets and network industries). Yet subsequently, the EU has incrementally widened and deepened the internal market by liberalizing network industries, enhancing intellectual property rights, and creating a vast range of regulatory agencies, although it has also encountered resistance to further integration in labor and services due the competitive pressures resulting from the greater heterogeneity of rules post enlargement.

However, the internal market plan initially neglected the external dimension of its single market program, generating fears about the emergence of "fortress Europe." Yet in several industries, American multinational companies had a long standing European presence, and Japanese companies quickly invested and established local production sites, so that trade rules and regulatory policies could not discriminate between EU and non-EU manufacturers in the single market.[28] Pressure from trading partners forced the EU to announce that the single market was also reducing barriers to entry for foreign corporations due to the principles of non-discrimination and mutual recognition, thus extending the benefits of market access to third countries. Hanson suggests that completing the single market undermined the effectiveness of national trade measures and made it difficult to enact new trade barriers, thus producing a liberal bias in European policies.[29] By contrast, Messerlin and others argue that the EU is a continued user of different administrative and regulatory mechanisms for defensive trade reasons, so that protectionism through quotas, subsidies, and dumping remain a continuing feature of the single market.[30] More recently, Gsohl demonstrates that the growing impact of the internal market depends on issue area and institutional ties.[31] Over the past two decades, the external dimension has become increasingly salient as demands from trading partners for reciprocal market access has led to the conclusion of a number of bilateral free trade agreements. And the EU itself has begun to promote its own internal market norms as a means of leverage in third-country markets. Responding to globalization, the EU has blurred the boundaries between its internal and external market, promoting its rules in international organizations through global standard setting, through preferential trade agreements and customs unions, and through its accession partnerships and enlargement negotiations. Yet despite this externalization of internal market rules, there are few theoretical or empirical studies of the impact of Europeanization in third-country markets, the impact of such policy diffusion and its variation across issue areas.

29.2 Explaining the Origins of the Single Market

Over the past two decades, scholars of European integration have focused on the causes, content, and impact of the single market from a variety of disciplines.[32] The question about where did the ideas and impetus for the single market come from has elicited a variety of explanations ranging from political economy to constructivism. Sandholtz and Zysman felt that the revitalization of the single market was the product of a fear of competition from Japan and the US. Driven by political entrepreneurship by transnational business groups and political actors, the single market package evolved into a more ambitious scheme as different interests saw the single market as an institutional venue to revitalize European economies.[33] Such a view was challenged by Moravscik, who argued that states embraced neo-liberal ideas both to discredit interventionist economic policies of the past, and to offer a new economic vision.[34] Governments advanced their own proposals and the resulting intra-European bargaining based on patterns of asymmetric interdependence produced an outcome that reflected the large member states who were willing to delegate and pool sovereignty to foster specific outcomes. State-centric theorists also argued that an effective European legal order and case law decisions also promoted the interests of specific member states in market integration. Constructivists have challenged this view, arguing that market preferences cannot be derived solely from patterns of interdependence but also reflect socially constructed ideas about economic policies. Fligstein, for example, points to the political opportunity structures that the economic crisis created for a series of actors who were able to construct a broad coalition that supported the revival of the single market. And Jabko depicts the resurgence of market integration as the product of successful framing of ideas in politically strategic ways.[35]

Hooghe and Marks view the resurgence of single market integration as the product of failure of national Keynesian economic policies, necessitating a shift to private actors on the one hand, through deregulation and privatization, and a shift to the supranational level to regulate markets, on the other hand.[36] The resulting single market project brought to the fore different models of capitalism in which proponents of neo-liberalism promoted regulatory competition and mobile factors of production, whereas proponents of regulated capitalism promoted social market solidarity. Caporaso and Tarrow have argued that the single market is part of the political economy of embedded liberalism at the supranational level with the legitimacy of democratic capitalism maintained through the explicit compromise between markets and social protection.[37] Neo-Gramscians have critiqued this model of market integration as reflecting the dynamics of transnational capital and class struggle.[38] Thus, the market liberal bias in both the treaty and case law has prioritized commercial interests over social welfare, favoring the removal of trade barriers over coordinated market regulation.[39] By contrast, Majone views the single market initiatives as designed to address market failures rather than redistributive outcomes. His focus shifts towards understanding the EU in terms of regulation in which the formalization and expansion of policy-making capacity can occur within a polity with limited fiscal and budgetary capacity.[40] As such, the lack of budgetary resources highlights an important feature of how the EU has fostered market integration, namely that regulation is the main instrument of public power in the Union.

29.3 THE GOVERNANCE OF THE SINGLE MARKET

As market integration has deepened, attention has shifted to making the single market deliver—and this has focused on capacities of different governance mechanisms to improve the functioning of the single market through an expansion of impact assessment and monitoring mechanisms. Some authors have studied the compliance with single market rules, looking at notifications and infringement proceedings to assess whether enforcement and implementation of rules affects the functioning of the single market in different policy areas.[41] Other studies have focused on whether the single market has in practice actually fostered market access and trade liberalization. The results are mixed, with mutual recognition proving to be much more difficult than anticipated owing to the fact that member states do not always recognize standards as mutually equivalent.[42] Harmonization of standards has been slow and difficult, service liberalization, where it has occurred, has not functioned properly as restrictive business practices remain, and the lack of a European-wide patent, and limited provisions on debt payments have all arguably impeded the operation of the single market.

Efforts to improve the functioning of the single market have yielded some concrete results, and more attention is being given to credible European economic governance. Some of this is being driven by the financial crisis and the need for supervisory financial regulations.[43] Other initiatives have created new rules and institutions, including

European regulatory agencies, single market scoreboards, and networks of trans-border information and conflict resolution mechanisms (e.g. SOLVIT), as well as new procedures for setting innovative internationally recognized standards. The functioning of the single market has increased in saliency but there are also some contradictory pressures. There has been an increase in soft law, opt-outs, and differentiated integration, which fails to produce uniform comprehensive rules to "implement the principles of economic freedom."[44] There is considerable differentiation and exemptions on labor mobility for example, and the continuation of national practices such as restricted access to networks and variable trading emissions, for example in energy markets. But even with such market integration efforts, recent studies have illustrated the degree of *home bias* in which there is a tendency for goods, services, and investment to be produced and consumed in the "home state."[45] This empirical research highlights the imbalances in integration across markets, suggesting that the EU is not exploiting the synergies between financial, labor, and product markets, as investments and consumption are still heavily national despite efforts to remove national obstacles to trade. As Balta and Delgado conclude, "[in spite of] international specialization and outsourcing and the increasing globalization of capital markets, national borders still matter in Europe," although whether this is due to policy constraints or consumer preference in the single market is hard to establish.[46]

29.4 NEW DIRECTIONS FOR FUTURE RESEARCH

While scholarly accounts of the single market have contributed to our understanding of the dynamics of market integration, and in the process have linked research on the single market to other policy areas, there are some new lines of inquiry. Four are identified here. First, surprisingly little empirical work has been done on the impact of historical–institutional legacies on market integration. Although research on domestic political economies have sought to understand the structural adjustment that is often rooted in the different models of economic governance and market organization, as well as the strategies pursued by interest associations in different member states, few studies have focused on domestic responses to the European impetus for market liberalization and integration. How market integration interacts with different national political economies may be far from uniform given the variation in models of capitalism.[47] More recent debates, especially those informed by the "varieties of capitalism" approach, have focused on the resilience of domestic political–economic institutions, without assessing the impact "on the ground" of European single market initiatives on domestic policy choices and institutional frameworks.

Moreover, more work needs to be done on the changes within the European single market, as part of a larger process of structural transformation in the global economy. Given the recent wave of interest in the nineteenth century as an example of early globalization in which there was unprecedented integration of capital, labor, and commodity markets, the historical precedents have a direct bearing on contemporary market integration.[48] The single market can benefit from testing theoretical arguments longitudinally and comparatively with historical and empirical material.[49] Studies of how single markets have been instituted in other historical periods, drawing on examples from nineteenth-century German unification and integration and nineteenth-century American consolidation and expansion, for example, might provide insights into the relationship between democracy, state-building, and market integration.[50]

A second area of research relates to governance concerns in terms of democratic legitimation and state capacity. In the process of market-building, expanding democratic mechanisms may have a contradictory logic as market integration implies a concentration of authority whereas democracy implies devolution and decentralization of the polity. Yet the conditions for the political sustainability of market integration deserve further attention. Many scholars, particularly those who focus on the compatibility of democracy and economic integration, have drawn attention to the fact that the centralizing tendencies with regard to the market are not entirely benign in their consequences.[51] The increasing constraints on national policy choices, especially the pressures on the welfare states and government-owned monopolies, have in fact contributed to the growing opposition among the populace about further European integration.

Given such political contestation, the need for an effective "state capacity" exists not only during the process of market reform but also after the market system has been instituted. For instance, it is important to have effective governmental regulation of privatized enterprises, reliable guarantees of property rights, an efficient judiciary, and so forth. However, the salient issue of effective public management has at its core the issue of balancing discretionary administration and institutionalized checks and balances. As such, broader concerns about governance have emerged from the choice of regulatory format and instruments in EU. Stated differently, the growth of delegation to non-majoritarian institutions is believed to undermine the legitimacy of political arrangements.[52] By whatever means the single market moves toward greater liberalization, the effectiveness of regulation will be critical for its credibility. Yet much of the work in this area does not evaluate whether the use of cost–benefit analysis, private-market alternatives to government command and control, or other regulatory programs and their economic consequences are the most appropriate tools given the greater economic diversity and regulatory capacity across member states, and the differences between different factors of production, where services are much more complex and heterogeneous than goods in terms of regulation.

Consequently, research on the four freedoms has disproportionately focused on goods, with less attention toward the other freedoms. The case law on the different freedoms raises questions about whether market restrictions are dealt with differently, the effect (if any) of the changing scope of fundamental freedoms, and the impact of judicial action on cross-border market practices in light of home bias. Moreover, the growth of case law and legislation in redistributive policy areas such as tax, corporate governance, and services perhaps accounts for the increasing ideological and redistributive conflict in the European polity.[53] So far, much attention has focused on the need to promote market integration to address transaction costs and market externalities, but regulatory encroachment occurring in fields that are traditionally national spheres such as tax, healthcare, or labor rights (which lack explicit treaty provisions), raises important questions about the boundaries of market integration and state autonomy.

Thus, the functioning of the single market in different sectors has gained in currency, and has engaged scholars of public administration and public management rather than international relations. One of the most thriving research agendas focuses on issues of compliance and implementation of single market regulations across different sectors and states.[54] But further research on how the dynamics internal to the firm affect single market compliance are needed. In addition, we need to see if the new modes of governance, such as decentralized and network-based approaches, social impact assessments, and self-regulation, are more effective than prior instruments or policies such as harmonization or mutual recognition. The capacity to implement the single market should also take account of the regulatory heterogeneity and institutional capacity of states, especially in light of the post-socialist transformation and accession of Central and Eastern European states. While the varied configurations of economic organization—or varieties of capitalism—in Western Europe have led to much theorizing about the impact of institutional adaptation to the common impetus of EU-induced economic liberalization, there has been less research on the functioning of the single market in Central and Eastern Europe and the institutional capacity and market management practices that have evolved.[55]

Third, the persistent economic diversity at the meso- and micro-level within Europe deserves more attention. Few studies, however, have examined the impact of the EU regulatory regime from the perspective of firms, given that they may have conflicting objectives based on industry structure, patterns of trade and investment, and the globalization of production chains. Understanding how institutions change the way economic actors behave can draw upon existing research in economic sociology.[56] Thus, we might focus more on the different initial institutional endowments—based on different varieties of capitalism—to understand divergent responses and industrial outcomes among firms across Europe.[57] How the changing terms of trade resulting from market integration affect the internal organization of firms, the allocation of resources, and the role of intra-firm trade is an important factor in understanding the impact of the single market. Despite the implicit assumption that the single market would transform market practices, there is little research on how business firms responded in terms of corporate strategies to new market opportunities, and only fragmentary data on industry- or sector-level responses to market integration.

Although the single market provides an opportunity to study within sectors, across sectors, and across different factors of production, the role of economic geography is critical. As Krugman notes, regional specialization is another likely consequences of economic integration.[58] Although there is a considerable literature on regional economic development, regional business cycles, and locational economies of scale, the focus of the EU literature has been on the redistributive funds, such as structural and cohesion policies, without much attention to the impact of the single market on regional business practices and economic growth and development. As Sbragia notes, the territorial implications of European regulatory policies have been relatively understudied even though changes in the single market, from innovation and investment to tax policies, can differentially affect different regions.[59] Richer and more empirically focused studies on the impact of the single market—similar to the work on local production regimes and industrial districts—might provide a more nuanced way of understanding the territorial impact of the transformation of market governance across Europe.

Fourth and finally, while research on regional integration initially started with a historical and comparative focus, and acknowledged that regional integration processes are affected by different degrees of economic development and state capacity, societal pluralism, and interest mobilization, there has been much less attention in recent years to broad comparisons with processes and developments elsewhere.[60] At the same time, the deepening of regional integration agreements, and their global expansion in the past decade, has led to increased interest in the European experience as a model. Perhaps the most noticeable change is the rise of economic regionalism as a complement to multilateralism. There are some obvious areas for comparative research, including the role of legal harmonization, the mobilization of business and political elites, the role of ideas, and the diffusion of regulatory practices in evaluating the scope, depth, and shape of integration and harmonization outside of Europe. Focusing on the historical trajectories as well as on variation in institutional design and forms of economic cooperation requires us to theorize about *differentiated* market integration both within Europe and beyond.

29.5 CONCLUSION

Although the economic conditions have changed since the foundation of the European Community—with technological and production changes, the increased tradability of goods and services, and the growing importance of the single market beyond its own borders—internal market liberalization is still a central element of European integration. While the "1992" single market program provided the basis for the expansion into new policy areas, such as monetary union and environmental policy, the research agenda for the single market now requires a shift away from earlier understandings of the political economy of market integration. First, the process is a dynamic one in which technological, political, and economic developments have resulted in new barriers to trade, requiring additional legislative and regulatory action to ensure market integration. Second, the single market is more heterogeneous than in the past, with greater concerns about social dislocation, social dumping, and the constitutional asymmetry resulting from the decoupling of market integration and social protection at the European level. Third, the growing constraints on national policy choices, especially the pressures on welfare states and government-owned monopolies, have in fact contributed to the growing opposition among the populace about further European integration, forcing greater attention to its socio-political legitimacy. Fourth, there is increased attention to the effectiveness of single market policies, not simply in terms of the removal of static barriers to trade and market entry, but as a mechanism to enhance innovation, growth, and competitiveness. And finally, single market policies have gone beyond the traditional "freedoms" to link with structural reforms at the national level, and placed the single market in a wider strategy of promoting market-driven growth. The recent SMA and the Monti Report are aimed at generating new political attention for a series of measures to create a competitive social market economy, deliberately coinciding with the twentieth anniversary of the "1992" single market program.[61]

After much neglect, the single market is again a top priority for the EU. Whether scholars point to the increasing case law in sensitive sectors, the pressures of globalization, or the growth potential of further liberalization, there remain political constraints on deepening market integration in Europe. As important as economic imperatives are, market integration is also the product of politics—most notably, but not exclusively, of the tensions and conflicts about sovereignty and governance. With pressures to regulate market relations and promote economic redistribution, the European polity faces new social demands that compete with notions of market competition, to encompass political and social claims of fairness, equity, and inclusion. The functioning of the single market is crucial, and will depend on further market reforms and liberalization in the context of globalization. This is important given the concerns that political turbulence once again may well constrain or undercut the prospects for further economic and political reforms in Europe. This raises a number of research questions: What are the necessary conditions for market integration? What are the limits? Can social discontent undermine market integration? What lessons from the European "single market" (or other historical market experiences) may be helpful for other regional efforts at market integration? Answering these questions will allow us to think about the comparative dynamics of integrating markets, and to engage with scholars in economic history, economic sociology, political geography, and business policy and strategy in ways that help us conceptualize the single market not merely as a singular exercise in market-building in Europe, but reflective of broader developments in regulating and enhancing economic and social rights, creating innovative and flexible governance structures, and fostering rules of exchange that address both equity and efficiency concerns.[62]

Notes

1. W. Jacoby and S. Meunier, "Europe and Globalization," in M. Egan, N. Nugent, and W. Paterson, eds, *Research Agendas in EU Studies* (Basingstoke: Palgrave Macmillan, 2010), 354–74.
2. M. Canoy et al., *The Single Market Yesterday and Tomorrow*, Bureau of European Policy Advisors, European Commission (no date).
3. Canoy et al., *The Single Market Yesterday and Tomorrow*.
4. Communication from the Commission to the European Parliament, the Council, the Economic and Social Committee, and the Committee of the Regions, Towards a Single Market Act Brussels, 27.10.2010 COM(2010) 608 final p. 1.

5. J. Pelkmans, D. Hanf, and M. Chang, eds, *The EU Internal Market in Comparative Perspective: Economic, Political and Legal Analyses* (Brussels: Peter Lang, 2008); A. Moravscik, *The Choice for Europe: Social Purpose and State Power from Messina to Maastricht* (Cornell: Cornel University Press, 1998); S. Bulmer and K. Amstrong *The Governance of the European Single Market* (Manchester: Manchester University Press, 1998).

6. B. Eichengreen, *The European Economy Since 1945* (Princeton: Princeton University Press, 2007); M. Asbeek Brusse, *Tariffs, Trade and European Integration 1947-1957: From Study Group to Common Market* (New York: St. Martin's Press, 1997).

7. Spaak Report (1956), "Rapport des chefs de délégation aux ministres affaires étrangeres," April 21, 1956.

8. Brusse, *Tariffs, Trade and European Integration 1947-1957*.

9. The original common market derived from three sets of treaty provisions: the common commercial policy, the "four freedoms," and the related articles on harmonization.

10. J. Pelkmans, *Market Integration in the EEC* (The Hague: M. Nijhof, 1984).

11. B. Belassa, *European Economic Integration* (Amsterdam: North Holland, 1975).

12. G. Hufbauer, *Europe 1992: An American Perspective* (Washington DC: Brookings Institution, 1990); M. Egan, *Constructing a European Market: Standards, Regulation and Governance* (Oxford: Oxford University Press, 2001).

13. L. G. Franko, *The European Multinationals* (London: Harper and Row, 1976).

14. A. Boltho, ed., *The European Economy: Growth and Crisis* (Oxford: Oxford University Press, 1982).

15. Egan, *Constructing a European Market*.

16. P. Cecchini, *The "Costs of Non-Europe"* (Luxembourg: Official Publications of the European Communities, 1998).

17. D. Smith and J. Wanke, "1992: Who Wins? Who Loses?" in A. Cafruny and G. Rosenthal, eds, *The State of the European Community* (Boulder: Lynne Reinner, 1993), 353–72.

18. *Completing the Internal Market: White Paper from the Commission to the European Council (Milan, June 28-29, 1985) COM(85) 310, June 1985.*

19. J. Pelkmans and P. Robson, "Aspirations of the White Paper," *Journal of Common Market Studies* 25, no. 3 (1987), 181–92.

20. Article 26 TFEU.

21. The judicial exemptions are often referred to as rule of reason or balancing standards where the Court of Justice may establish restrictions or temporary limitations on free trade principles.

22. See Cecchini, *The "Costs of Non-Europe."*

23. Egan, *Constructing a European Market*.

24. S. Schmidt, "Competing in Markets, Not Rules: The Conflict over the Single Services Market," in C. Joerges and P. Kjaer, eds, *Transnational Standards of Social Protection: Contrasting European and International Governance*, ARENA report series (2008), 31–54.

25. See Egan, *Constructing a European Market*; M. Maduro, *We The Court—The European Court of Justice and the European Economic Constitution* (Oxford: Hart Publishing, 1998).

26. For an overview, see C. Barnard and J. Scott, eds, *The Law of the Single European Market: Unpacking the Premises* (Oxford: Hart, 2002).

27. P. Buigues, F. Ilkowitz, and J. F. Lebrun, "The Impact of the Internal Market by Industrial Sector: The Challenge for Member States," *European Economy*, Special Issue (Brussels: European Commission, 1990).

28. P. Eeckhout, *The European Internal Market and International Trade: A Legal Analysis* (Oxford: Clarendon Press, 2008).

29. B. Hanson, "What Happened to Fortress Europe? External Trade Policy Liberalization in the EU," *International Organization* 52, no. 1 (1998), 55–85.

30. P. Messerlin, *Measuring the Cost of Protection in Europe* (Washington DC: IIE, 2001).

31. S. Gstohl, "The Internal Market's External Dimension Political Aspects," in Pelkmans et al., *The EU Internal Market in Comparative Perspective*, 221–48.

32. Pelkmans et al., *The EU Internal Market in Comparative Perspective*; N. Fligstein, *Euroclash: The EU, European Identity, and the Future of Europe* (Oxford: Oxford University Press, 2008).

33. W. Sandholtz and J. Zysman, "1992: Recasting the European Bargain," *World Politics* 42, no. 1 (1989), 95–128.

34. Moravscik, *The Choice for Europe*.

35. N. Jabko, *Playing the Market: A Political Strategy for Uniting Europe, 1985–2005* (Cornell: Cornell University Press, 2006); N. Fligstein, "Markets as Politics: A Political-Cultural Approach to Market Institutions," *American Sociological Review*, 61, no. 4 (1996), 656–73.

36. L. Hooghe and G. Marks, "Making of A Polity. The Struggle over European Integration," in Herbert Kitschelt, Gary Marks, Peter Lange, and John Stephens, eds, *Continuity and Change in Contemporary Capitalism* (Cambridge: Cambridge University Press, 1999), 70–97.

37. J. Caporaso and S. Tarrow, "Polanyi in Brussels: Supranational Institutions and the Transnational Embedding of Markets," *International Organization* 63, no. 4 (2009), 593–620.

38. B. Van Apeldoorn, "Transnational Class Agency and European Governance: The Case of the European Round Table of Industrialists," *New Political Economy* 5, no. 2 (2000), 157–81.

39. F. Scharpf, "The European Social Model," *Journal of Common Market Studies* 40 (2002), 645–70.

40. G. Majone, *Regulating Europe* (London: Routledge, 1996).

41. G. Falkner, O. Trieb, M. Hartlapp, and S. Leiber, *Complying with Europe: EU Harmonization and Soft Law in Member States* (Cambridge: Cambridge University Press, 2005).

42. J. Pelkmans, "Mutual Recognition in Goods: On Promises and Disillusions," *Journal of European Public Policy* 14, no. 5 (2007), 699–716.

43. S. Donnelley, *The Regimes of European Integration: Constructing Governance in the Single Market* (Oxford: Oxford University Press, 2010).

44. D. Hanf, "Legal Concept and Meaning of the Internal Market," in Pelkmans et al., *The EU Internal Market in Comparative Perspective*, 77–92, at 89.

45. J. Delgado, "Single Market Trails Home Bias," Bruegel Policy Brief, Brussels, 2006.

46. N. Balta and J. Delgado, "Home Bias and Market Integration in the EU," *CESifico Economic Studies* 55, no. 1 (2009), 110–44.

47. G. Menz, *Varieties of Capitalism and Europeanization: National Response Strategies to the Single European Market* (Oxford: Oxford University Press, 2005).

48. M. Egan, "The American Experience," in Pelkmans, et al., *The EU Internal Market in Comparative Perspective*, 249–80.

49. F. Schimmelfennig, "Integration Theory," in Egan et al., *Research Agendas in EU Studies*, 37–59.

50. Egan "The American Experience"; M. Hallerberg and K. Weber, "German Unification 1815–1871 and its Relevance for Integration Theory," *Journal of European Integration* 24, no. 1 (2002), 1–21.

51. Scharpf, "The European Social Model."
52. Majone, *Regulating Europe.*
53. K. Nicolaidis and S. Schmidt, "Mutual Recognition on Trial: The Long Road to Services Liberalization," *Journal of European Public Policy* 14, no. 5 (2007), 717–34.
54. Falkner et al., *Complying with Europe.*
55. L. Bruszt, "Market Making as State Making—Constitutions and Economic Development in Postcommunist Eastern Europe," *Constitutional Political Economy* 13 (2002), 53–72.
56. N. Fligstein, *The Transformation of Corporate Control* (Harvard: Harvard University Press, 1990).
57. D. Bohle and B. Greskovits, "Neoliberalism, Embedded Neoliberalism and Neocorporatism: Towards Transnational Capitalism in Central-Eastern Europe," *West European Politics* 30, no. 3 (2007), 443–66.
58. P. Krugman, *Geography and Trade* (Boston: MIT Press, 2001).
59. A. Sbragia, "Territory, Representation, and Policy Outcome: The United States and the European Union Compared," in C. Ansell and G. Di Palma, eds, *On Restructuring Territoriality: Europe and North America* (Cambridge: Cambridge University Press, 2004), 205–24.
60. J. Caporaso, *EUSA Newsletter* 10, no. 3 (Fall) (Pittsburgh: University of Pittsburgh, 1997).
61. M. Monti, *A New Strategy for the Single Market: At the service of Europe's Economy and Society.* Report to the President of the European Commission, May 2010; Communication from the Commission to the European Parliament, the Council, the Economic and Social Committee and the Committee of the Regions, Single Market Act COM/2011/0206 final.
62. Fligstein, *The Transformation of Corporate Control.*

CHAPTER 30

··

TRADE POLICY

··

ALASDAIR R. YOUNG

TRADE policy is one of the most established areas of cooperation in the EU. The EU's trade policy is the direct product of the decision in the Treaty of Rome to create a customs union, which entails the elimination of tariffs among the members and the creation of a common tariff with respect to imports from non-members. Creating a customs union required establishing the means of agreeing the common trade policy, the CCP, the supranational character of which had important implications for the trajectory of European integration.[1] Moreover, trade policy has been the centerpiece of the EU's engagement with the rest of the world, with the terms of access to the EU's substantial market a key instrument of the EU's external relations.[2]

Despite its central importance to the EU, trade policy-making has received rigorous attention from political scientists only relatively recently, with a burgeoning of literature since the mid-1990s. This literature has crystallized around two central questions: (1) What shapes the EU's trade policy objectives? (2) What affects how effective the EU is in pursuing them? There are not, as yet, very satisfactory answers to either question.

This chapter begins by exploring what trade policy is, before charting, in broad terms, how wider ideational, institutional, and economic changes have influenced the development of the EU's trade policy. It then introduces the key actors in EU trade policy before exploring how the existing literature approaches the motivating questions and highlights areas of agreement and disagreement. It suggests a way forward by encouraging the integration of the two dominant approaches to studying EU trade policy—principle–agent analysis and the two-level game metaphor. The chapter concludes by suggesting how the analysis of EU trade policy might be better integrated with and contribute to the international political economy (IPE) literature on trade policy.

30.1 What is Trade Policy?

The substance of trade policy has changed dramatically since the Treaty of Rome.[3] In the late 1950s trade policy was concerned with the conditions on which goods were imported (and to a lesser extent exported) and focused on tariffs and quantitative restrictions. The EU's customs union was formed in 1968 with the finalization of the common customs tariff, but national quantitative restrictions, supported by restrictions on trade amongst the member states, persisted until the creation of the SEM in the early 1990s. As a result of repeated rounds of multilateral trade negotiations tariffs have become less important obstacles to imports, while non-tariff barriers, including anti-dumping duties (from the 1970s) and regulatory differences (from the 1980s) have became more important. The concept of trade has also become broader. From the mid-1980s, in response to waves of domestic liberalization—deregulation and privatization—the cross-border provision of services began to increase, as did flows of foreign direct investment. As a consequence trade policy is increasingly about how rules with primarily domestic policy objectives affect foreign firms' access to the market.[4]

The EU pursues its trade policy through multilateral negotiations within the context of the WTO (and previously the GATT); through bilateral relations with specific countries or groups of countries; and through unilateral actions. The EU has, at least since the mid-1990s, depicted itself as the most committed advocate of the multilateral trading system.[5] Bilateral trade agreements, however, have been the bedrock of the EU's relations with most countries in the world. These bilateral arrangements provide preferential access to the EU's market such that the products of all but a handful of countries—including Japan and the US—face lower tariffs than those the EU has bound with the WTO. The EU also pursues access to specific foreign markets through bilateral negotiations and, if necessary, through complaints under the WTO's Dispute Settlement Understanding.

The EU also makes extensive use of entirely unilateral trade measures. Its Everything But Arms and GSP Plus initiatives provide improved market access for the least developed countries and developing countries that have signed international environmental and social protocols respectively. Conversely, the EU also makes extensive use of anti-dumping measures—imposing duties on products from specific countries that are found to have been "dumped," that is sold below a fair market price—to protect European producers from "unfair" foreign competition.

30.2 The Changing Context of EU Trade Policy

The context in which EU trade policy is made has changed dramatically since the creation of the customs union. Some of those changes have been broader than the EU itself, such as the spread of neo-liberal economic ideas, the changing nature of trade, and the broadening of the international trade agenda. Other changes have been internal to the EU, including the continuing shift of authority for trade policy from the member states to the EU, the EU's increasing membership, and the impact of the SEM on the trade policy preferences of firms. Many of these changes have reinforced each other resulting in a dramatic transformation of EU trade policy—in both scope and substance—since the creation of the customs union, but that transformation is not the product of steady, incremental change, but of sharp changes and setbacks.

30.2.1 The Changing External Context

One of the most subtle, yet profound, changes to the wider context in which EU trade policy is made has been the increased acceptance of neo-liberal economic ideas by member-state governments and the Commission since the 1980s.[6] The acceptance of the economic argument for free trade has not brought an end to protectionism, but it has arguably made it harder for firms to seek protection in order to preserve employment.[7] Moreover, although there is a strong rhetorical commitment to the EU's opening its market,[8] there is also a heavy emphasis on securing (reciprocal) access to foreign markets.[9]

The dramatic changes to the nature of economic exchange since the mid-1980s, often referred to collectively as globalization, have prompted concern about heightened competition from less developed countries and has contributed to a backlash against the liberal orthodoxy in favor of free trade.[10] In addition, the broader trade agenda has blurred the distinction between international and domestic policies and encouraged the engagement of new actors—non-trade ministries as well as civic interest groups—in the trade policy process.[11] These actors tend to be more skeptical about the benefits of liberalization.[12] Although the impact of these newly mobilized actors on the substance of EU trade policy seems to have been muted,[13] the changed nature of the trade agenda has complicated trade policy-making.

The EU's ability to pursue its trade policy objectives has also been affected by the changing balance of power within the multilateral trading system. Although the GATT had its origins as a transatlantic project,[14] for most of the post-war period the US was the dominant partner. The EU's influence had increased by the Tokyo Round[15] and by the mid-1980s an EU–US consensus was necessary and largely sufficient for concluding the Uruguay Round.[16] Almost as soon as this duopoly emerged, however, it began to erode as developing country governments—particularly those of Brazil, India, and, more quietly, China—began to assert themselves more vigorously.[17] Thus while the EU and US remain the most powerful actors in trade politics they are now only two among several key players.

30.2.2 The Changing EU Context

Arguably, within the EU the competitive challenge posed by globalization has been secondary to that posed by internal liberalization spurred by the SEM program.[18]

The increased competition within the EU caused firms to become competitive or fail, which led to reduced opposition to liberalization (except in agriculture).[19] At least in part as a consequence, EU industrial firms have become more internationally oriented and more supportive of international liberalization.[20] The SEM, by eliminating all trade restrictions among member states, also contributed to external liberalization by altering the default position to the policy (for goods and services) of the most liberal member state.[21] A qualified majority of the Council was, therefore, required to adopt protection, and this was generally difficult to achieve, although there were some notable exceptions, such as the banana trade regime. As a consequence, the SEM generally contributed to liberalization of third-country firms' access to the EU's market,[22] although a few common regulations have been very trade restrictive.[23]

The institutional framework within which trade policy is pursued has also evolved, albeit haltingly, since the Treaty of Rome. From the outset the EU's trade policy has embodied a "two-tier delegation"[24]: from the member states to the EU and, at the EU level, from the Council to the Commission. While the allocation of competence for trade policy between the member states and the EU has long been a source of tension,[25] there has been a gradual shift in authority to the EU level both through the accretion of "implied powers," as internal integration has progressed, and as a result of treaty reforms. The Treaty of Lisbon essentially completes the transfer of authority for trade policy from the member states to the EU, contributing to the establishment of a "comprehensive" trade policy.[26]

The EU's membership has also increased dramatically since the Treaty of Rome. Enlargement has two major implications for trade policy. First, it has increased the size of the EU's market, a source of leverage in negotiations. Second, new member states introduce new political and economic relationships with third countries and different domestic economic concerns and priorities. Thus, enlargement affects both the countries with which the EU seeks to develop special trading relations and the tenor of its trade policies.

Not least because of these changing internal and external contexts, the substance of the EU's trade has changed over time, first becoming more and then becoming protectionist. From the end of World War II until the mid-1960s, the formative period of the common commercial policy, trade policy in Western Europe tended toward greater liberalization.[27] From the late 1960s into the early 1980s, however, in response to slow growth, high inflation, and high unemployment, Western European governments' intervention in the economy and trade policy became more restrictive, most notably in the proliferation of non-tariff barriers (the "new protectionism"[28]). From the mid-1980s, however, the EU's trade policy became more liberal—although there are still substantial levels of protection in agriculture; the EU makes extensive use of anti-dumping measures; common regulatory measures can impede trade; and the EU's preferential trade agreements can divert trade[29]—and more multilateral.[30] Particularly, from the late-1990s the EU began to seek actively to shape the multilateral trading system.[31]

30.3 Key Players in EU Trade Policy?

Before turning to the questions of the EU's trade policy preferences and how it manages to pursue them, several subordinate debates need to be explored: Where do decision-makers' trade policy preferences come from? What are the trade policy preferences of the Commission? What are the trade policy preferences of the member states?

30.3.1 The Sources of Decision-Makers' Trade Policy Preferences

One of the central debates in the IPE literature on trade policy is the extent to which decision-makers are responsive to societal pressures or able to pursue their own trade policy preferences, with much of the literature focused on societal actors.[32] Until recently, however, most of the literature on EU trade policy-making has assumed that decision-makers are quite autonomous from societal pressures, not least because of the two-tiered delegation from member states to the EU and from the Council to the Commission.[33] There has, however, more recently been heightened interest in the impact of interest groups on EU trade policy,[34] with some authors finding evidence that decision-makers are highly responsive to producer pressure.[35]

Unfortunately, the debate has tended to be between two polar extremes: government autonomy and interest group pressure. Woll, however, emphasizes the interaction between policy-makers and pressure groups, with each providing resources to the other.[36] Moreover, this debate would mature if it began to focus on the circumstances under which decision-makers are more/less autonomous from societal actors. The existing literature already suggests some likely avenues of inquiry. Policy-makers are more likely to have a free hand when there are no adversely affected EU interests—such as when the costs of adjustment are expected to fall entirely on the other party, or the domestic costs of liberalization are negligible—or when domestic pressures are evenly balanced.[37] Where institutions are specifically intended to enhance the input of business interests into trade policy, notably the Trade Barriers Regulation and the Anti-Dumping Regulation,[38] societal actors are likely to have more influence. Thus greater attention to the variation in the constellation of preferences and institutional arrangements across aspects of trade policy would facilitate clarifying the relative importance of societal pressures and policy-makers' autonomous preferences and specifying the conditions under which societal influence is more likely.

To the extent that policy-makers have preferences independent of societal pressures, there is an unresolved question about the sources of these preferences. Some cite neoliberal ideas,[39] while others identify foreign policy objectives.[40] Some contend that the incentives of bureaucratic politics encourage the Commission to pursue particular policies in order to justify (or make the case for enhancing) its authority.[41] More constructivist accounts suggest that aspects of the EU's trade policy have been affected by its identity as a regional integration project[42] or the identities of some member states as former colonial powers[43] or by shared norms, such as the principles of "good governance," "WTO compatibility," and "integration into the world economy."[44] Resolving the relative impact of such considerations on policy-makers' preferences will, as with the question of autonomy, require greater attention to the specific circumstances of cases and to the variation between them.

30.3.2 The Council's Pivotal Role

The Council plays the pivotal role the two-tier delegation of trade policy-making in the EU. It is the forum in which the member states aggregate their trade policy preferences, and the body that monitors the implementation of trade policy and ratifies all trade agreements. There is not, however, a Council formation specifically for trade, which falls under the General Affairs and External Relations Council (GAERC), although trade ministers participate on discussions of trade policy and may informally approve the results of a negotiation. The Article 133 Committee, made up of national trade officials, is responsible for monitoring closely the Commission's trade activities and is extensively involved in the making of trade policy.[45]

Analysts often group the member states into the liberal "North" and protectionist "South"; the 2004/2007 enlargements do not seem to have dramatically affected the balance of preferences within Council,[46] although the new member states may be less interested in extra-EU markets.[47] Disappointingly, little scholarly attention has been paid to the trade policy preferences of the member states, and most explanations of EU trade policy tend to take member states' positions as given.[48] While there are some indications that the member states do have broadly consistent trade policy preferences,[49] governments frequently diverge from these tendencies with respect to specific trade policies affecting particular industries.[50] As a result, the member states' general inclinations "are rarely a good predictor of how the Council will react on a given issue on a given day."[51] Moreover, given the rough balance between the supposedly "liberal" and "protectionist" camps, the positions of "swing states"—Austria, the Czech Republic, Finland, Germany, and Spain—are often the key to explaining policy outcomes.[52]

The Council operates largely by consensus in trade policy,[53] with the marked exception of anti-dumping policy. Governments tend to not oppose others' trade policy objectives unless they have very strong countervailing interests, because in the future they might be the *demandeur*.[54] This practice of "diffuse reciprocity"[55] is a common feature of intense, institutionalized, and iterated cooperation.

While most accounts of decision-making in the Council are rationalist, Niemann argues that persuasion, not just bargaining, occurs in trade policy.[56] It is particularly likely to occur at the level of officials (within the Article 133 Committee and involving Commission officials) because issues are less politicized and more cognitively complex, there is more time available for discussion, and there are high levels of interaction and socialization. It is also more likely at the pre-negotiation stage when there is a high degree of uncertainty and negligible countervailing pressures.

Crucially, decision rules vary across different aspects of EU trade policy. The ratification of multilateral trade agreements is formally by qualified majority, although a number of issue areas have been subject to national competence and even under Lisbon require unanimous agreement. Lisbon also formalizes the practice of having the European Parliament give its assent to multilateral trade agreements. Most bilateral trade agreements, because they are concluded as association agreements, are subject to unanimity and the assent of the Parliament. The implementation of Lisbon means that anti-dumping has been brought under the commitology examination procedure, which means that from September 2012 the Commission will be able to impose definitive duties unless there is a qualified majority of member states opposed. Decision rules have implications for the substance of EU policy because they affect which member state is the pivotal player. The implications of the variety of decision rules for the substance of trade policy, however, has been under-researched because of the tendency to focus on case studies located within a single type of trade policy.[57]

30.3.3 The Commission: Policy Entrepreneur?

The Commission is central to EU trade policy. It sets the agenda (as in other policy areas) by advancing proposals for action. It also represents the EU in virtually all international trade negotiations, including in pursuing complaints about market access through the WTO. Given its importance, surprisingly little attention has been paid to the Commission's preferences. Kerremans identifies several key components of the Commission's preferences: desire for greater authority (competence maximization); substantive policy preference; and convincing the member states that it can represent the EU credibly.[58] While the first and third of these considerations are more or less accepted, there is more doubt about the Commission's substantive trade policy preferences, which have not been studied in detail. Nonetheless, there is a common view among scholars and practitioners that the Commission has become markedly more liberal since the mid-1980s and now tends to be more liberal than most of the member states.[59] Woll, however, contends that the Commission does not have an a priori tendency to liberalize; it merely seeks to develop pan-European policy solutions and liberalization tends to be such a solution.[60]

Recently authors have begun to emphasize that the Commission is not a unitary actor and that there can be sharp differences over the substance of trade policy within it. Several authors,[61] for instance, have pointed to the different preferences of the Directorates General for Trade and Development in the EU's relations with developing countries. Others[62] have highlighted differences between Directorate-General Trade and Directorate-General Agriculture in multilateral trade negotiations, although these were sharper during the Uruguay Round than the Doha Round. Moreover, the anti-dumping unit within Directorate-General Trade seems to be more protectionist than the rest of Directorate-General Trade.[63] The Commission, therefore, is a crucial but rather poorly understood player in the EU's trade policy process.

30.4 WHAT SHAPES THE EU'S TRADE POLICY OBJECTIVES?

The EU's trade policy objectives are fundamentally shaped by the crucial and complex relationship between the Council and the Commission; the second "tier of delegation." This interaction is analyzed (implicitly or explicitly) primarily through principal–agent models.[64] Principal–agent analysis recognizes that while there are good reasons why a principal (in this case the member states collectively as the Council) might delegate responsibilities to an agent (the Commission), the principal's and the agent's preferences are not necessarily the same, so the principal needs to find ways of controlling the agent. The three most commonly identified mechanisms through which the Council seeks to control the Commission are: specifying the negotiating directive; monitoring the Commission's performance (particularly through the Article 133 Committee); and ratifying agreements.[65] Kerremans[66] also emphasizes that because delegation in trade policy is iterated (directives must be adopted for each new negotiation) the Commission needs to limit how much autonomy it exercises in the current negotiation so as not to prompt sufficient concern among the member states that Council would seek to constrain the Commission's in future.[67] Crucially, as the Council is a composite principle, the Commission does not necessarily need to worry about the preferences of all of the member states, only enough to secure ratification of the current agreement and/or a flexible mandate for the next negotiations. Consequently, where the agreement of all member states is required, the Commission's influence should be more constrained.[68]

While most analysts find member-state dominance, some identify significant Commission autonomy and influence.[69] One obstacle to resolving the question of Commission influence is the problem of "observational equivalence"; the Council may accept a Commission proposal either because it is influenced by the Commission or because the Commission anticipated the Council's preferences.[70] Kempton, for instance, finds that the Commission "rationally anticipates" the preferences of the member states in anti-dumping decisions because it does not want to lose credibility by having its proposals regularly rejected.[71] This problem could be addressed if more attention were paid to the Commission's preferences and how they relate to the proposals it advances.[72] A second obstacle is that most of the literature focuses on trade negotiations, even though trade negotiations are arguably a "hard case" for Commission influence because the extent of delegation is actually quite limited compared to other EU and non-EU instances of delegation.[73] There is thus significant scope for advancing the debate by broadening the range of empirical cases and by seeking to go beyond whether the

Commission or Council has more influence to trying to specify the conditions under which the Commission (or Council/member states) has more influence.[74]

The literature already suggests some factors that may affect Commission influence. It may have greater autonomy at different stages of the negotiating cycle[75] and when dealing with relatively technocratic issues, but less when issues become politicized,[76] such as when they involve important trade partners;[77] are tied to pursuing foreign policy objectives;[78] or there are significant anticipated costs, as with agriculture.[79] Where the EU is seeking to export its rules or secure non-reciprocal market access, the costs of adjustment fall outside the EU, and the Commission may enjoy greater autonomy.[80] One would also expect to find variation in the degree of the Commission's influence across different trade policies, reflecting the variation in the extent of delegation to the Commission and the decision rule in the Council. More explicitly comparative studies and more careful attention to context should enable significant advances in our understanding of how EU trade policy positions are reached.

30.5 WHAT AFFECTS HOW EFFECTIVE THE EU IS IN PURSUING ITS OBJECTIVES?

There is widespread acceptance that the EU is a "power" in the multilateral trading system,[81] not least because of its economic importance; it is the world's largest market and largest exporter of goods and of services, and the largest importer of services and second-largest importer of goods.[82] There is, however, an abiding sense that the EU is underperforming in international trade negotiations, although the yardstick against which its influence should be assessed is rarely explicitly articulated or justified. Thus a central and recurring concern in the literature has been the EU's ability to translate its economic importance into political leadership.[83]

The dominant approach to analyzing how the EU's influences negotiations is a variant of Putnam's metaphor of the two-level game.[84] The two-level game metaphor focuses on how the interaction between domestic and international constraints and opportunities influences the chief of government's (COG) strategies.[85] In particular it highlights the scope that the COG, who conducts negotiations, has to choose outcomes among a range of options acceptable to the other negotiating parties and for which there is sufficient domestic support for ratification (the "win set"). Most applications to EU trade policy, however, do not take full advantage of the analytical insights of the metaphor.

Rather, the EU tends to be simply inserted as a level between the domestic and international negotiations, creating a "three-level game," although most analyses really only capture the two-level game between the EU and the international levels. While the need to agree a common, EU position in negotiations does add a third level of negotiation, it is not appropriate to characterize the EU's engagement in international negotiations as a three-level game. The key links between the two games in Putnam's metaphor—the

COG and the ratification process—are not the same between the international and EU levels and the EU and national levels.[86] It is thus more appropriate to think in terms of two two-level games that are linked at the EU level.[87]

There are several further problems with how the two-level game metaphor is typically applied to the EU's engagement in international negotiations. First, as with the principal–agent approach, the preferences of the COG (Commission) are poorly specified in advance. Second, the EU's "win set" is rarely delineated.[88] Third, the two-level game approach pays attention to only ratification as a constraint on the negotiator, which does not capture the full range of control mechanisms at the member states' disposal.[89]

The tendency in the two-level game literature to focus on individual negotiations[90] impedes the ability to specify the conditions under which the EU is more likely to prevail in an international trade negotiation. The existing literature does, however, suggest some factors that might influence EU effectiveness. Meunier argues that internal difficulties reaching agreement impede the EU's ability to pursue a reformist agenda, but enhance its ability to resist changes.[91] Others emphasize that the EU is more likely to get its way in negotiations with weaker partners.[92] Dür argues that in reciprocal negotiations foreign firms afraid of losing market access mobilize in favor of domestic liberalization; a particular variant of the asymmetrical negotiation.[93] These suggestions could be developed and tested across a more diverse range of negotiations as a way of enhancing our understanding of what influences the effectiveness of the EU in international trade negotiations.

30.6 ANALYZING TRADE POLICY-MAKING: OF AGENTS, COGs, AND PRINCIPALS

Although most of the EU trade policy literature treats the principal–agent framework and two-level game metaphor as separate, even rival, analytical approaches, this is inaccurate and unhelpful. Putnam explicitly draws on principal–agent models to capture the constraints under which the COG operates in negotiations.[94] Pollack characterizes the Commission's role in external trade policy as analogous to Putnam's COG.[95] Meunier uses principal–agent insights to operationalize the "delegation of competence," a key variable that influences the EU's bargaining power in a two-level game.[96] Thus these approaches can usefully complement each other.[97]

Both approaches draw attention to differences in preferences between the Commission and Council and acknowledge that the Commission enjoys some latitude to pursue its own preferences; how much latitude is a key question for both. Where the two approaches differ, they help to compensate for weaknesses in the other. Applications of the principal–agent model tend to pay more attention to the formation of EU trade preferences than do two-level game approaches, although they cannot easily accommodate societal interests,[98] which the two-level game can capture through the "win set." Two-level game approaches also pay more attention to the international negotiation.[99] The two-level game also puts more emphasis on how the international negotiation affects the internal negotiation.[100] Two-level game applications, however, tend to under-specify how the constraints on the COG operate, paying attention only to ratification.[101] Analyzing the impact of control mechanisms, by contrast, is the great strength of principal–agent models, although there has been a tendency to downplay ratification. Combining the two approaches, therefore, helps to keep the full spectrum of control mechanisms to the fore. Crucially, the proper application of the principal–agent model would provide a way of structuring the relationship between the national–EU and EU–international two-level games, thereby addressing a macro-weakness of the two-level game approach to EU trade policy.

The applications of the two approaches to EU trade policy do, however, share a common shortcoming in that they tend to treat the key European institutions—the Council and Commission—as if they were unitary actors when modeling their interaction. This is a common shortcoming in the literature on the EU's inter-institutional politics,[102] but it denies the analytical richness of the two approaches. Both very explicitly recognize that the Council is a composite actor and there is growing awareness in both literatures that the Commission is a composite agent. Embracing the composite nature of both the Commission and the Council draws attention to the prospect of actors within each institution forming coalitions across institutions in order to realize shared policy objectives. The question thus becomes not whether the Commission or Council has more influence in shaping EU trade policy, but which coalitions of actors across the two institutions prevail on particular issues?

30.7 Conclusions

The literature analyzing EU trade policy is much less developed than one might expect given how established and central the policy is. There have, however, been significant recent advances. The dominant approaches—principal–agent models and the two-level game metaphor—are drawn directly from the wider political science literature and thus there is the potential for the analysis of EU trade policy to feed more directly into wider debates about how trade policy is made. Such a move would be particularly valuable as the general understanding of trade policy-making is heavily colored by the US case.[103]

In order for the analysis of EU trade policy-making to engage fully with wider debates in IPE several further developments are required. First, more precision is needed about how principal–agent models and the two-level game metaphor are applied to the EU's distinctive institutional framework. This chapter is intended to be a step in that direction. Second, there needs to be much more rigorous empirical testing of propositions across cases. This will contribute to a shift from either/or propositions to specifying the conditions under which different factors or actors are more likely to matter. Third, more attention needs to be paid to the trade policy preference of key actors, which would require considering much more carefully the trade policy preferences of firms, and whether and how these preferences influence the trade policy preferences of the member-state governments and the Commission. There is thus significant scope for the analysis of EU trade policy to develop further and real potential for it to make a substantial contribution to our understanding of trade policy-making.

It is important to recognize, however, that the vast majority of the IPE literature on trade is focused on traditional trade policy and the dichotomy between liberalization and protectionism.[104] Such traditional trade policies are becoming less important and "domestic" policies are having greater impact on trade. Attempts to address such trade barriers are characterized by a different kind of politics.[105] In this context the analyses of the EU's experience of overcoming non-traditional barriers to trade among its member states, most notably in the context of the single European market program, albeit with due consideration for the EU's unique institutional framework, may provide a fruitful point of departure for analyzing the trade issues of the twenty-first century.

NOTES

1. L. N. Lindberg and S. A. Scheingold, *Europe's Would-Be Polity: Patterns of Change in the European Community* (Englewood Cliffs, NJ: Prentice-Hall, 1970), 14; A. Moravcsik, *The Choice for Europe* (London: UCL Press, 1998), 153–6; C. Parsons, "Showing Ideas as Causes: The Origins of the European Union," *International Organization* 56, no. 1 (2002), 47–84, at 76.

2. C. Bretherton and J. Vogler, *The European Union as a Global Actor*, second edition (London: Routledge, 2006), 88; C. Hill and M. Smith, "International Relations and the European Union: Themes and Issues," in C. Hill and M. Smith, eds, *International Relations and the European Union* (Oxford: Oxford University Press, 2005), 3–17, at 12; J. McCormick, *The European Superpower* (Basingstoke: PalgraveMacMillan, 2007), 84.

3. A. R. Young and J. Peterson, "The EU and the New Trade Politics," *Journal of European Public Policy* 13, no. 6 (2006), 795–814.

4. W. D. Dymond and M. M Hart, "Post-Modern Trade Policy: Reflections on the Challenges to Multilateral Trade Negotiations after Seattle," *Journal of World Trade* 34, no. 3 (2000), 21–38; B. Hocking, "Changing the Terms of Trade Policy Making: From the 'Club' to the 'Multistakeholder' Model," *World Trade Review* 3, no. 1 (2004), 3–26; A. R. Young, "Trade Politics Ain't What It Used to Be: The European Union in the Doha Round," *Journal of Common Market Studies* 45, no. 4 (2007), 789–811.

5. A. Ahnlid, "Setting the Global Trade Agenda: The European Union and the Launch of the Doha Round," in O. Elgström and C. Jönsson, eds, *European Union Negotiations: Processes, Networks and Institutions* (London: Routledge, 2005), 130–47, at 130; M. Baldwin, "EU Trade Politics—Heaven or Hell?" *Journal of European Public Policy* 13, no. 6 (2006), 926–42, at 933; S. J. Evenett, "Trade Policy: Time for a Rethink," in A. Sapir, ed., *Fragmented Power: Europe and the Global Economy* (Brussels: Bruegel, 2007), 61–93, at 75; M. Smith and S. Woolcock, "European Commercial Policy: A Leadership Role in the New Millennium?" *European Foreign Affairs Review* 4 (1999), 439–62, at 442; L. A. Winters, "European Union Trade Policy: Actually or Just Nominally Liberal?" in H. Wallace, ed., *Interlocking Dimensions of European Integration* (UK: Palgrave, 2001), 25–44, at 28.

6. Baldwin, "EU Trade Politics—Heaven or Hell?," 940; O. Elgström, "The Cotonou Agreement: Asymmetric Negotiations and the Impact of Norms," in Elgström and Jonsson, *European Union Negotiations*, 183–99, at 196; B. T. Hanson, "Opening Europe to the Global Economy: The Politics of Trade Policy Liberalization," paper to the Centre for European Studies Graduate Student Workshop, Harvard University, February 26–28, 1999; S. R. Hurt, "Co-operation and Coercion? The Cotonou Agreement between the European Union and the ACP States and the End of the Lomé Convention," *Third World Quarterly* 24, no. 1 (2003), 161–76, at 174; M. Johnson, *European Community Trade Policy and the Article 113 Committee* (London: Royal Institute of International Affairs, 1998); S. Woolcock, "Theoretical Analysis of Economic Diplomacy," in N. Bayne and S. Woolcock, eds, *The New Economic Diplomacy: Decision-Making and Negotiation in International Economic Relations* (Aldershot: Ashgate, 2003), 21–42, at 31.

7. Hanson, "Opening Europe to the Global Economy."

8. e.g. Commission, "Global Europe: Competing in the World: A Contribution to the EU's Growth and Jobs Strategy," SEC (2006) 1230, 4 October, 6 and 7.

9. e.g. Commission "Global Europe: Competing in the World," 6.

10. Woolcock, "Theoretical Analysis of Economic Diplomacy," 31.

11. Bayne and Woolcock, "What is Economic Diplomacy?"; A. Dür and D. De Bièvre "Inclusion without Influence? NGOs in European Trade Policy," *Journal of Public Policy* 27, no. 1 (2007), 79–101; M. Williams, "Civil Society and the World Trading System," in D. Kelly and W. Grant, eds, *The Politics of International Trade in the Twenty-First Century: Actors, Issues and Regional Dynamics* (Basingstoke: Palgrave Macmillan, 2005), 30–46; A. R. Young, "Trade Politics Ain't What It Used to Be," *Journal of Common Market Studies* 45, no. 4 (2007), 789–811, at 797; Young and Peterson, "The EU and the New Trade Politics," 800.

12. Bayne and Woolcock, "What is Economic Diplomacy?," 3; Commission, "Trade Policy in the Prodi Commission 1999–2004: An Assessment," November 19, 2004, p. 27; B. Hocking and M. Smith, *Beyond Foreign Economic Policy: The United States and the Single European Market and the Changing World Economy* (London: Pinter, 1997); Young, "Trade Politics Ain't What It Used to Be," 797.

13. Dür and De Bièvre, "Inclusion without Influence?.

14. See G. J. Ikenberry, "Creating Yesterday's New World Order: Keynesian 'New Thinking' and the Anglo-American Postwar Settlement," in J. Goldstein and R. O. Keohane, eds, *Ideas and Foreign Policy: Beliefs, Institutions and Political Change* (Ithaca, NY: Cornell University Press, 1993), 57–86; J. G. Ruggie, "International Regimes, Transactions, and Change: Embedded Liberalism in the Postwar Economic Order," *International Organization* 36, no. 2 (1982), 379–415.

15. Smith and Woolcock, "European Commercial Policy," 442; M. Wolf, "The European Community's Trade Policy," in R. Jenkins, ed., *Britain and the EEC* (London: Macmillan, 1983), 151–77, at 151.

16. S. J. Evenett, "EU Commercial Policy in a Multipolar Trading System," *Intereconomics* 42, no. 3 (2007), 143–55, at 143; J. Peterson, "The Politics of Transatlantic Trade Relations," in B. Hocking and S. McGuire, eds, *Trade Politics*, second edition (Routledge: London, 2004), 36–50; Smith and Woolcock, "European Commercial Policy," 442.

17. Baldwin, "EU Trade Politics—Heaven or Hell?"; B. M. Hoekman and M. M. Kostecki, *The Political Economy of the World Trading System*, second edition (Oxford: Oxford University Press, 2001); A. Narlikar, "Developing Countries and the WTO," in Hocking and McGuire,

Trade Politics, 133–45; R. Wilkinson, "The World Trade Organization and the Regulation of International Trade," in Kelly and Grant, *The Politics of International Trade in the Twenty-First Century*, 13–29.

18. C. Hay, and B. Rosamond, "Globalisation, European Integration and the Discursive Construction of Economic Imperatives," *Journal of European Public Policy* 9, no. 2 (2002), 147–67.

19. Baldwin, "EU Trade Politics—Heaven or Hell?," 934; Hanson "Opening Europe to the Global Economy." On the general phenomenon, see R. Sherman, "Endogenous Protection and Trade Negotiations," *International Politics* 39 (2002), 491–509, at 499.

20. Ahnlid, " Setting the Global Trade Agenda," 134; A. Dür, "Bringing Economic Interests Back in the Study of EU Trade Policy-Making," *The British Journal of Politics and International Relations* 10, no. 1 (2008), 27–45; A. van den Hoven, "European Union Regulatory Capitalism and Multilateral Trade Negotiations," in S. Lucarelli and I. Manners, eds, *Values and Principles in European Union Foreign Policy* (London: Routledge, 2006), 185–200; S. Woolcock, "Trade Policy: From Uruguay to Doha and Beyond," in H. Wallace, W. Wallace, and M. A. Pollack, eds, *Policy-Making in the European Union*, fifth edition (Oxford: Oxford University Press, 2005), 377–99.

21. B. T. Hanson, "What Happened to Fortress Europe? External Trade Policy Liberalization in the European Union," *International Organization* 52, no. 1 (1998), 55–85; R. C. Hine, *The Political Economy of European Trade: An Introduction to the Trade Policies of the EEC* (Sussex: Wheatsheaf Books, 1985), 260; A. R. Young, *Extending European Cooperation: The European Union and the "New" International Trade Agenda* (Manchester: Manchester University Press, 2002), 59.

22. Commission, *External Access to European Markets*, The Single Market Review, Subseries IV, Volume 4 (Office for Official Publications of the European Communities, 1998); WTO, *Trade Policy Review: European Union 1995* (Geneva: World Trade Organisation, 1995).

23. Commission, *External Access to European Markets*; A. R Young, "The Incidental Fortress: The Single European Market and World Trade," *Journal of Common Market Studies* 42, no. 2 (2004), 393–414.

24. S. Meunier and K. Nicolaïdis, "Who Speaks for Europe? The Delegation of Trade Authority in the EU," *Journal of Common Market Studies* 37, no. 3 (1999), 477–501, at 481.

25. Young, *Extending European Cooperation*, ch. 2.

26. S. Woolcock, "The Potential Impact of the Lisbon Treaty on the European Union External Trade Policy," European Policy Analysis Issue 8–2008 (Swedish Institute for European Policy Studies); Woolcock, "Trade Policy: A Further Shift towards Brussels," in H. Wallace, M. A. Pollock, and A. R. Young, eds., *Policy-Making in the European Union*, 381–99.

27. M. Wolf, "The European Community's Trade Policy," sixth edition (Oxford: Oxford University Press, 2010), 158.

28. R. Gilpin, *The Political Economy of International Relations* (Princeton, NJ: Princeton University Press, 1987), 204–9; Wolf "The European Community's Trade Policy," 159.

29. See A. Bouët, "Commentaire sur l'article 'Niveau et coût du protectionisme européen' de Patrick Messerlin," *Économie internationale* 89–90 (2002), 65–84; M. Brülhart and A. Matthews, "EU External Trade Policy," in A. M. El-Agraa, ed., *The European Union: Economics and Policies* (Cambridge University Press, 2007), 473–93, at 484; P. Messerlin, *Measuring the Costs of Protection in Europe: European Commercial Policy in the 2000s* (Washington, DC: Institute for International Economics, 2001).

30. Ahnlid, "Setting the Global Trade Agenda," 130; Baldwin, "EU Trade Politics—Heaven or Hell?," 933; S. J. Evenett, "Trade Policy: Time for a Rethink," 75; M. Smith and S. Woolcock, "European Commercial Policy," 442; Woolcock, "Trade Policy: From Uruguay to Doha and Beyond," 381.

31. Ahnlid, "Setting the Global Trade Agenda," 130; Baldwin, "EU Trade Politics—Heaven or Hell?," 933; Evenett "Trade Policy: Time for a Rethink," 75; Smith and Woolcock, "European Commercial Policy," 442; Woolcock, "Trade Policy: From Uruguay to Doha and Beyond," 381.

32. For a survey see H. V. Milner, "International Trade," in W. Carlsnaes, T. Risse, and B. A. Simmons, eds, *Handbook of International Relations* (London: Sage, 2002), 448–61.

33. S. Meunier, *Trading Voices: The European Union in International Commercial Negotiations* (Princeton, NJ: Princeton University Press, 2005), 8–9; M. A. Pollack *The Engines of European Integration: Delegation, Agency and Agenda Setting in the EU* (Oxford: Oxford University Press, 2003), 105, 106; Woolcock, "Trade Policy: From Uruguay to Doha and Beyond," 247; H. Zimmermann, "Realist Power Europe? The EU in the Negotiations about China's and Russia's WTO Accession," *Journal of Common Market Studies* 45, no. 4 (2007), 813–32; for a dissenting view, see D. De Bièvre and A. Dür, "Constituency Interests and Delegation in European and American Trade Policy," *Comparative Political Studies* 38, no. 10 (2005), 1271–96, at 1275.

34. A. Dür, "Bringing Economic Interests Back in the Study of EU Trade Policy-Making"; Dür and De Bièvre, "Inclusion without Influence?"; G. C. Shaffer, *Defending Interests: Public-Private Partnerships in WTO Litigation* (Washington, DC: The Brookings Institution Press, 2003); G. C. Shaffer "What's New in EU Trade Dispute Settlement: Judicialisation, Public-Private Networks and the WTO Legal Order," *Journal of European Public Policy*, 13, no. 6 (2006), 832–50; C. Woll, "Trade Policy Lobbying in the EU: Who Captured Whom?," in D. Coen and J. Richardson, eds, *Lobbying the European Union: Institutions, Actors and Policy* (Oxford: Oxford University Press, 2009), 277–97.

35. De Bièvre and Dür, "Constituency Interests and Delegation in European and American Trade Policy," 1274; and Dür "Bringing Economic Interests Back in the Study of EU Trade Policy-Making."

36. Woll, "Trade Policy Lobbying in the EU," 293–4. See also Johnson, *European Community Trade Policy and the Article 113 Committee*, ch. 5.

37. J. P. Hayes, *Making Trade Policy in the European Community* (London: Macmillan, 1993), 140.

38. De Bièvre, "The WTO and Domestic Coalitions: The Effects of Negotiations and Enforcement in the European Union" (PhD thesis, European University Institute, Florence, 2002); J. Kempton, "Decisions to Defend: Delegations, Rules and Discretion in European Community Anti-Aumping Policy," (D. Phil thesis, University of Sussex, 2001); Shaffer, *Defending Interest*; Shaffer, "What's New in EU Trade Dispute Settlement."

39. Hanson, "What Happened to Fortress Europe?"; "Opening Europe to the Global Economy."

40. Baldwin "EU Trade Politics—Heaven or Hell?"; Messerlin, *Measuring the Costs of Protection in Europe*; Zimmermann, "Realist Power Europe?."

41. B. Kerremans, "What Went Wrong in Cancun? A Principal-Agent View on the EU's Rationale Towards the Doha Development Round," *European Foreign Affairs Review* 9 (2004), 363–93, at 367–8; P. Nedergaard, "The End of Special Interests? The Political

Economy of EC Trade Policy Changes in the 1990s," in O. Nørgaard, T. Pedersen, and N. Petersen, eds, *The European Communities in World Politics* (London: Pinter, 1993), 52–73, at 57; Pollack, *The Engines of European Integration*, 19.

42. V. K. Aggarwal and E. A. Foggarty, "Explaining Trends in EU Interregionalism," in Aggarwal and Fogarty, eds, *EU Trade Strategies: Between Regionalism and Multilateralism* (Basingstoke: Palgrave, 2004), 207–40, at 228.

43. O. Elgström, "The Cotonou Agreement: Asymmetric Negotiations and the Impact of Norms," in Elgström and Jonsson, *European Union Negotiations*, 183–99, at 183.

44. Elgström, "The Cotonou Agreement," 197.

45. Johnson, *European Community Trade Policy and the Article 113 Committee*; A. Murphy, "In the Maelstrom of Change: The Article 113 Committee in the Governance of External Economic Policy," in. T. Christiansen and E. Kirchner, eds, *Committee Governance in the European Union* (Manchester: Manchester University Press, 2000), 98–114.

46. Baldwin "EU Trade Politics—Heaven or Hell?," 931; M. Elsig, "European Union Trade Policy after Enlargement: Does the Expanded Trade Power Have New Clothes?" NCRR Trade Regulation Working Paper 2009/02 (Swiss National Centre of Competence in Research, 2009).

47. Elsig, "European Union Trade Policy after Enlargement."

48. A. Dür and H. Zimmermann, "Introduction: The EU in International Trade Negotiations," *Journal of Common Market Studies* 45, no. 4 (2007), 771–87, at 783.

49. P. Evans, "Is Trade Policy Democratic? And Should It Be?," in N. Bayne and S. Woolcock, eds, *The New Economic Diplomacy: Decision-Making and Negotiations in International Economic Relations* (Aldershot: Ashgate, 2003), 147–59, at 153; H. V. Milner and B. Judkins, "Partisanship, Trade Policy and Globalization: Is there a Left-Right Divide on Trade Policy?," *International Studies Quarterly* 48 (2004), 95–119, at 110.

50. Baldwin, "EU Trade Politics—Heaven or Hell?," 931; Johnson, *European Community Trade Policy and the Article 113 Committee*; Woolcock, "Trade Policy: From Uruguay to Doha and Beyond," 390.

51. Baldwin "EU Trade Politics—Heaven or Hell?," 931; J. Kempton, "Decisions to Defend", 307.

52. Baldwin, "EU Trade Politics—Heaven or Hell?," 931.

53. Johnson, *European Community Trade Policy and the Article 113 Committee*; Meunier and Nicolaïdis, "Who Speaks for Europe?," 480; S. Woolcock, "The Regional Dimension: European Economic Diplomacy," in Bayne and Woolcock, *The New Economic Diplomacy*, 197–213, at 208 and 209.

54. Ahnlid, "Setting the Global Trade Agenda," 137; Hayes, *Making Trade Policy in the European Community*, 131, 132; Johnson, *European Community Trade Policy and the Article 113 Committee*; Kempton, "Decisions to Defend," 187; L. A. Winters, "The EC and Protection: The Political Economy," *European Economic Review* 38 (1994), 596–603, at 600; A. R. Young, "Punching Its Weight? The European Union's Use of WTO Dispute Resolution," in O. Elgström and M. Smith, eds, *The European Union's Roles in International Politics: Concepts and Analysis* (London: Routledge, 2006), 189–207.

55. R. O. Keohane, "Reciprocity in International Relations," *International Organization* 40, no. 1 (1986), 1–27, at 21–5.

56. A. Niemann, "Between Communicative Action and Strategic Action: The Article 113 Committee and the Negotiations on the WTO Basic Telecommunications Services Agreement," *Journal of European Public Policy* 11, no. 3 (2004), 379–407, at 401.

57. Meunier, *Trading Voices* is an exception.

58. Kerremans, "What Went Wrong in Cancun?," 367–8.

59. Aggarwal and Fogarty, "Explaining Trends in EU Interregionalism," 226; Ahnlid, "Setting the Global Trade Agenda," 135; Meunier, *Trading Voices*, 58; Nedergaard, "The End of Special Interests?," 57.

60. Woll, "Trade Policy Lobbying in the EU," 285.

61. M. Frenhoff-Larsen, "Trade Negotiations between the EU and South Africa: A Three Level Game," *Journal of Common Market Studies* 45, no. 4 (2007), 857–81; also Aggarwal and Fogarty, "Explaining Trends in EU Interregionalism," 226–7; G. Forwood, "The Road to Cotonou: Negotiating a Successor to Lomé," *Journal of Common Market Studies* 39, no. 3 (2001), 423–42.

62. e.g. A. van den Hoven, "Assuming Leadership in Multilateral Economic Institutions: The EU's 'Development Round' Discourse and Strategy," *West European Politics* 27, no. 2 (2004), 256–83, at 257.

63. De Bièvre and Dür, "Constituency Interests and Delegation in European and American Trade Policy," 1275; Kempton, "Decisions to Defend," 306 and 310.

64. See, for example, the special issue of the *Journal of European Public Policy*, 18, no. 3 (2011), guest edited by A. Dür and M. Elsig, "Bringing Economic Interests Back in the Study of EU Trade Policy-Making"; M. Elsig, "The EU's Choice of Regulatory Venues for Trade Negotiations: A Tale of Agency Power?," *Journal of Common Market Studies* 45, no. 4 (2007), 927–48; Elsig, "European Union Trade Policy after Enlargement"; Kempton, "Decisions to Defend"; Kerremans, "What Went Wrong in Cancun?"; Kerremans, "Proactive Policy Entrepreneur or Risk Minimizer? A Principal-Agent Interpretation of the EU's Role in the WTO," in Elgström and Smith, *The European Union's Roles in International Politics*, 172–88; Kerremans, "The European Commission in the WTO's DDA Negotiations: A Tale of an Agent, a Single Undertaking, and Twenty-Seven Nervous Principals," in S. Blavoukos and D. Bourantonis, eds, *The EU Presence in International Organizations* (Abingdon: Routledge, 2010), 132–49; Meunier, *Trading Voices*, 57–9; Meunier and Nicolaïdis, "Who Speaks for Europe?," 480; K. Nicolaïdis, "Minimizing Agency Costs in Two-Level Games: Lessons from the Trade Authority Controversies in the United States and European Union," in R. Mnookin and L. Susskind, eds, *Negotiating on Behalf of Others* (London: Sage, 1999), 87–126; Pollack, *The Engines of European Integration*, ch. 5; M. S. Reichert and B. M. E. Jungblut, "European Union External Trade Policy: Multilevel Principal–Agent Relationships," *The Policy Studies Journal* 35, no. 3 (2007), 395–418; A. van den Hoven, "Interest Group Influence on Trade Policy in Multilevel Polity: Analysing the EU Position at the Doha WTO Ministerial Conference," EUI Working Paper RSC 2002/67 (European University Institute, 2002); Woolcock, "Trade Policy: From Uruguay to Doha and Beyond," 390; for a review see Dür and Zimmerman, "Introduction: The EU in International Trade Negotiations," 779–80.

65. See, for example, Meunier, *Trading Voices*, 57–8; Nicolaïdis, "Minimizing Agency Costs in Two-Level Games"; Pollack, *The Engines of European Integration*, 279. Kerremans, "What Went Wrong in Cancun?," 370.

66. Kerremans, "What Went Wrong in Cancun?," 370.

67. See also Kempton, "Decisions to Defend," 311; S. Meunier, "What Single Voice? European Institutions and EU-U.S. Trade Negotiations," *International Organization* 54, no. 1 (2000), 103–35, at 111.

68. Meunier, *Trading Voices*, 64–6; Woolcock, "The Regional Dimension: European Economic Diplomacy," 210.

69. For a review see Dür and Zimmerman, "Introduction: The EU in International Trade Negotiations," 779–80.

70. C. Damro, "EU Delegation and Agency in International Trade Negotiations: A Cautionary Comparison," *Journal of Common Market Studies* 45, no. 4 (2007), 883–903, at 887. Kempton, "Decisions to Defend," 126.

71. Kempton, "Decisions to Defend," 126.

72. Kempton, "Decisions to Defend," 305–11 is an example.

73. Damro, "EU Delegation and Agency in International Trade Negotiations"; Pollack, *The Engines of European Integration*, 94, 278–9; Nicolaïdis 1999, "Minimizing Agency Costs in Two-Level Games," 104.

74. See also Dür and Zimmerman, "Introduction: The EU in International Trade Negotiations," 780.

75. Dür and Zimmerman, "Introduction: The EU in International Trade Negotiations," 780; Hayes, *Making Trade Policy in the European Community*, 124; B. Hocking and M. Smith, *Beyond Foreign Economic Policy: The United States and the Single European Market and the Changing World Economy* (London: Pinter, 1997).

76. Bretherton and Vogler, *The European Union as a Global Actor*; S. Woolcock and M. Hodges, "EU Policy in the Uruguay Round," in H. Wallace and W. Wallace, eds, *Policy-Making in the European Union*, third edition (Oxford: Oxford University Press, 1996), 301–24, at 304.

77. Dür and Zimmerman, "Introduction: The EU in International Trade Negotiations," 780.

78. Baldwin, "EU Trade Politics—Heaven or Hell?."

79. Woolcock and Hodges, "EU Policy in the Uruguay Round," 304; Woolcock, "The Regional Dimension: European Economic Diplomacy," 205.

80. Young, *Extending European Cooperation* and "Punching Its Weight?."

81. Bretherton and Vogler, *The European Union as a Global Actor*; C. Hill and M. Smith, "International Relations and the European Union: Themes and Issues," in Hill and Smith, eds, *International Relations and the European Union* (Oxford: Oxford University Press, 2005), 3–17, at 4; S. Meunier and K. Nicolaïdis, "The European Union as a Conflicted Trade Power," *Journal of European Public Policy* 13, no. 6 (2006), 906; M. Smith and S. Woolcock, "European Commercial Policy: A Leadership Role in the New Millennium?," *European Foreign Affairs Review* 4 (1999), 439–62, at 443.

82. WTO, *International Trade Statistics 2008* (Geneva: World Trade Organization), 13 and 15.

83. Ahnlid, "Setting the Global Trade Agenda," 130; S. Marsh and H. Mackenstein, *The International Relations of the European Union* (Harlow: PearsonLongman, 2005), 30, 31; Meunier and Nicolaïdis, "The European Union as a Conflicted Trade Power," 922; M. Smith, "European Union, Foreign Economic Policy and the Changing World Arena," *Journal of European Public Policy* 1, no. 2 (1994), 283–301, at 291–2; A. R. Young, "The Rise and Fall(?) of the EU's Performance in the Multilateral Trading System,) *Journal of European Integration* 33, no. 6 (2011), 715–29, at 724–6.

84. R. D. Putnam, "Diplomacy and Domestic Politics: The Logic of Two-Level Games," *International Organization* 42, no. 3 (1988), 427–60; see Elgström, "The Cotonou Agreement"; Forwood, "The Road to Cotonou"; Frenhoff-Laursen, "Trade Negotiations between the EU and South Africa"; Meunier, *Trading Voices*; Young, *Extending European Cooperation*; A. R. Young, "Transatlantic Intransigence in the Doha Round: Domestic Politics and the Difficulty of Compromise," in A. Narlikar, ed., *Breaking Deadlocks in Multilateral Settings: An Interdisciplinary Perspective* (Cambridge: Cambridge University

Press, 2010), 123–41; Zimmerman, "Realist Power Europe?." For a review, see Dür and Zimmerman, "Introduction: The EU in International Trade Negotiations."

85. A. Moravcsik, "Introduction: Integrating international and Domestic Theories of International Bargaining," in P. B. Evans, H. K. Jacobson and R. D. Puthan, eds, *Double-Edged Diplomacy: International Bargaining and Domestic Politics* (Berkeley, CA: University of California Press, 1993), 3–42, at 16–17.

86. Frennhoff Larsén, "Trade Negotiations between the EU and South Africa," 860; S. Collinson, "'Issue-Systems', 'Multi-Level Games' and the Analysis of the EU's External Commercial and Associated Policies: A Research Agenda," *Journal of European Public Policy* 6, no. 2 (1999), 206–24, at 219.

87. A. R. Young, "Adapting Two-Level Games to Explain European Foreign Economic Policy," *ECPR News*, 12, no. 2 (2001), 15–16.

88. Forwood, "The Road to Cotonou" is an exception.

89. Nicolaïdis, "Minimizing Agency Costs in Two-Level Games," 94, 98; Woolcock, "Trade Policy: From Uruguay to Doha and Beyond," 391.

90. Meunier's "What Single Voice?" and *Trading Voices*, and Elgström's, "The Cotonou Agreement," are partial exceptions.

91. Meunier, "What Single Voice?"; *Trading Voices*.

92. Elgström, "The Cotonou Agreement," 184; O. Elgström and M. Strömvik, "The European Union as an International Negotiator," in Elgströmadn and Jonsson, *European Union Negotiations*, 117–29, at 122; Forwood "The Road to Cotonou"; A. Dür, "Protecting Exporters: Discrimination and Liberalization in Transatlantic Trade Relations, 1932–2003" (PhD Thesis, European University Institute, 2004).

93. A. Dür, *Protecting Exporters: Tower and Discrimination in Transatlantic Trade Relations, 1930–2010* (Ithaca, NY: Cornell University Press, 2010).

94. Putnam, "Diplomacy and Domestic Politics," 456; see also Nicolaïdis, "Minimizing Agency Costs in Two-Level Games."

95. Pollack, *The Engines of European Integration*, 265.

96. Meunier, "What Single Voice?"; *Trading Voices*, 57–8.

97. See also M. Elsig, *The EU's Common Commercial Policy: Institutions, Interests and Ideas* (Aldershot: Ashgate, 2002), 159 ff.

98. For instance, in order to incorporate societal actors Dür and Elsig have to relax the "strict interpretation of contractual relations" that is at the heart of the principal–agent approach. A. Dür and M. Elsig, "Principals, Agents and the European Union's Foreign Economic Policies," *Journal of European Public Policy* 18, no. 3 (2011), 323–38, at 332.

99. Woolcock, "Theoretical Analysis of Economic Diplomacy," 33.

100. Frenhoff-Larsen, "Trade Negotiations between the EU and South Africa"; Pollack, *The Engines of European Integration*, 266. Dür and Elsig conceptualize the extra-EU relationship as one of delegation (from the EU to international organizations). Dür and Elsig, "Principals, Agents and the European Union's Foreign Economic Policies," 332.

101. Nicolaïdis, "Minimizing Agency Costs in Two-Level Games," 94, 98; Woolcock, "Trade Policy: From Uruguay to Doha and Beyond," 391.

102. See A. R. Young, "The European Policy Process in Comparative Perspective," in Wallace et al., *Policy-Making in the European Union*, sixth edition 45–68.

103. Milner, "International Trade," 458.

104. Milner, "International Trade."

105. C. Woll, *Firm Interests: How Governments Shape Business Lobbying on Global Trade* (Ithaca, NY: Cornell University Press, 2008).

CHAPTER 31

....

COMPETITION POLICY*

....

IMELDA MAHER

COMPETITION policy is a highly technical policy field which nonetheless plays a role in wider EU constitutional and governance developments. It is inextricably linked to the internal market, making it a touchstone for popular (and political) opposition to EU integration. How competition law is governed also reflects recent trends in EU governance and arguably the field more successfully incorporates new governance methods, with networks and soft law a hallmark of law enforcement. This chapter first outlines competition law and policy before examining these two themes. It explores the significance of EU competition law and policy for constitutionalization by analyzing how the Treaties have been repeatedly revised to reflect the changing relationship between the state and the market. The governance of competition policy, including the emergence of an important enforcement network and prevalence of soft law, is then discussed before concluding.

31.1 COMPETITION LAW AND POLICY

....

EU competition policy is supranational. The Commission has extensive enforcement powers and the European Courts have produced a large body of case law. By targeting private and state market behavior that distorts competition, it strongly complements the integration imperative of the internal market.[1] The policy is seen as successful, one measure of which is the extent to which national rules are modeled on the EU rules on restrictive agreements and abuse of market dominance (antitrust rules), in member states and in other jurisdictions.[2] Convergence with the EU rules has been voluntary for "old" member states, while new member states were required to adopt EU-type competition laws for trade with the EU prior to membership.[3] Another measure of success is the Commission's standing as one of the most powerful and influential competition agencies in the world.[4] It exercises considerable power over national governments and private market actors. It has competence, first, to introduce directives liberalizing markets without reference to either the Council or the Parliament[5] in sectors traditionally characterized by state monopolies and/or state-owned firms. In practice, it avails of conventional law-making powers while consistently spearheading market liberalization. The liberalization program has had a major impact on key markets, notably communications and energy, although it has worked more effectively in some sectors and in some member states.[6] Second, national and regional governments are subject to stringent controls with regards to when and to what extent aid can be provided to particular industries, requiring the pre-approval of the Commission (state aid).[7] The Commission also exerts considerable power over private firms.[8] Large[9] mergers can only proceed with its consent and it has the power to impose fines of up to 10 percent of worldwide turnover (which have exceeded 1 billion euros[10]) on firms in breach of the antitrust rules.

The development of competition law can be divided into a number of distinct phases.[11] For the first fifteen years, antitrust rules were enforced in a cautious and restrictive manner as the Commission sought to educate itself, member states, and firms as to the scope and impact of the rules. Caution was combined with a legalistic and over-broad interpretation of the rules. The Commission had exclusive power to exempt agreements notified to it. This exclusivity and the grant of immunity for notified agreements meant that the Commission was swamped with exemption applications from 1963 onward. It acquired the power to enact block exemptions through regulations in 1965—a power exercised cautiously and conservatively reducing its effectiveness.[12]

The second phase—roughly from the oil crisis (1973) to the SEA (1986)—constituted a period of consolidation with the ECJ still broadly supportive of the legalistic approach of the Commission. The 1992 single market program marked the third phase, providing an impetus for change. An EU-wide merger regulation was introduced even though there is no reference to mergers in the Treaty and created a one-stop-shop for very large mergers, attractive to firms and to the Commission who acquired the power of *ex ante* review of mergers for competition compliance.[13] More fundamentally, rules governing state intervention in markets where governments had traditionally conferred special or exclusive rights on firms either through subsidy or regulation were introduced. The aim of these liberalization measures was not privatization per se[14] but to introduce competition to those markets on the basis that market principles of consumer welfare generally bring greater benefits.

Most recently, the modernization of competition policy took place largely in parallel to the Lisbon strategy which emphasized competitiveness and aimed to make the EU the world's leading knowledge-based economy before 2010 through tools of governance, most notably the open method of coordination (see Chapter 33, this volume). Lisbon generated a debate about new governance even though governance methods, especially soft law, are long established in the competition sphere, where the first soft law measure dates from 1962.[15] Thus, care has to be taken in seeing competition policy as a policy apart despite its technocratic nature either in relation to wider political concerns about the state and the market or in relation to governance.

31.2 THE STATE AND THE MARKET

Despite a powerful transnational episteme,[16] considerable if not extraordinary Commission powers, the technical nature of competition and its relative insulation from day-to-day politics, the position of competition law and policy in the EU is still contentious. The negotiation of the relationship between the state and the market, which can be cast as regulation versus competition, public versus private, pervades debates such as what varieties of capitalism should the EU adopt.[17] This has a number of dimensions including market liberalization and the extent to which governments can provide aid to particular industries or geographic areas. Liberalization aims to increase competition and improve market access for EU firms, but the extent to which market principles should apply to public services is controversial. This policy (assisted by technological innovations) has been most influential for telecommunications while change is slower and more highly politicized in other sectors, such as postal services and energy. The market liberalization agenda raises questions about regulation—most of these markets cannot operate without regulatory controls in relation to issues such as third-party access and there is a need to ensure provision of universal service even where service is unprofitable. It is in this context that the role of the state in the market is most contested, as can be seen in the way the Treaty has been revised.

Thus "the establishment of competition rules necessary for the functioning of the internal market" is listed as an exclusive competence of the Union under the TFEU.[18] The link between competition and the internal market is a prerequisite for that exclusivity, underpinning the symbiotic nature of the internal market and competition which has informed much of the development of competition law, even if it has taken a back seat in recent years where a more efficiency-based approach has been developed. On the other hand, the Lisbon Treaty was amended at the last minute at the request of the French president to remove the reference to free and undistorted competition in relation to the establishment of the internal market. This was seen as a response to French concerns that led to a "No" vote in the Constitutional Treaty referendum and highlights the sensitivity of the competing visions of the European economy and, in particular, of what the role of the state should be in that economy.[19] The concerns of some other member states as to the potential negative impact of this revision on state aid policy and market liberalization led to the inclusion of a protocol which states that the member states see the internal market as one that includes a system ensuring competition is not distorted and that if it is, the Union shall if necessary take action, including legislative action.[20] The legal fudge reflects the political compromise that lies at the interface of the internal market and competition law and policy and, more specifically, at the role of the state in that sphere.

The challenge of achieving an appropriate balance between competition and the provision of public services is also reflected in Treaty revisions, highlighting a tension between what can be broadly described as an Anglo-Saxon approach to liberalized markets with a strong emphasis on competition and consumer welfare and continental traditions (especially in France) where social solidarity—the obligation of the state to ensure equal treatment of its citizens irrespective of their economic resources—is seen as fundamental.[21] Initially, the European Courts prioritized market values of competition and market integration over public service provision (referred to as services of general interest in EU law), the provision of such services having to be indispensable before an exception from the competition rules would be granted.[22] This emphasis on market values was reflected in the Treaty of Maastricht (1992), with its aim of adoption of an economic policy that would be conducted according to the principle of an open market economy with free competition.[23] Following a Commission communication on services of general interest[24] (and not just general economic interest, as referred to in Article 106(2) TFEU), the Treaty of Amsterdam added a complex and convoluted provision acknowledging the importance of services of general economic interest.[25] The Lisbon Treaty supplements this in two ways: first, the EU is given legislative competence to determine the principles and conditions underpinning the provision of such services. Second, a new Protocol lists the shared values of these services and emphasizes that member states retain their competence in relation to non-economic services of general interest. The Protocol was required by the Dutch to meet concerns from their "No" vote to the Constitutional Treaty but adds little clarity, leaving much to be decided ultimately by the ECJ.[26] These political tinkerings with the Treaties can be contrasted with the absence of any change in the provisions governing private market behavior since 1958.

The second aspect of state involvement in the market is state aid, which operates at the interface of competition and industrial policy, with governments traditionally having the sovereign power to award aid in various forms to national industries. This power is now subject to internal market and competition policy imperatives designed to level the proverbial playing field while taking cognizance of the special circumstances that apply to particular sectors and regions of the EU. Thus under Article 107TFEU, governments (at national or regional levels) are, in general, not allowed to provide aid to industries or regions where to do so would impact negatively on competition in an interstate context. The reality is that the wealthiest states are best placed to offer assistance.[27] There are huge sums involved with 64,816 million euros in total aid awarded by member states in 2007.[28] The Commission, using transparency principles and a notification system, vets and approves aid. The test is whether a private investor would have acted as the state has done in relation to the particular investment, creating a presumption of market-driven investment which can be departed from in certain circumstances.

The Commission scoreboards show that the amount of aid is not being reduced, but, consistent with the 2005–2009 reform of the rules and the Lisbon agenda,[29] funds are being increasingly directed at general (horizontal) issues such as employment, the environment, and training rather than to specific industries. The Commission remains central to the process with proposed aid notified to and evaluated by it under a balancing test to see if (1) it is aimed at a well-defined objective of common interest; (2) it is well-designed to deliver the objective; and (3) the distortions of competition and effect on trade are limited so that the overall effect is positive.[30] The European Court also has an important role to play in interpreting the scope of the rules and is generally supportive of the Commission's approach, sometimes requiring repayment of funds wrongfully paid.[31]

The state aid regime allows for crisis management, as can be seen in the recent banking crisis. There were two responses: first, applications for aid to individual banks were treated as separate and discrete applications to allow aid. Following the collapse of Lehman Brothers, there was recognition that the crisis was systemic and the Commission changed tack invoking the rarely used Article 107(3)(b)TFEU which allows aid where there is serious disturbance in a national economy.[32] What is noteworthy is that the reformed state aid rules were constantly set out as part of the response to the banking crisis by then-Commissioner Kroes, and not as part of the problem; that the Commission has shown itself to be a policy entrepreneur, filling the gap in governance between the individual responses of national governments (where competence primarily lies for economic policy) by using state aid rules as a tool for "positive" coordination of policy and not just as a "negative" instrument of legal compliance. While it is too early to say, it seems that the reformed state aid framework has worked, with its reform having proved timelier than could have been anticipated.

Competition law has transformed how and to what extent the state can intervene in markets, with market liberalization having radically changed important sectors of the economy. At the same time, the thorny issue of when market values cannot or should not be the primary mechanism determining the provision of certain (public) services remains, reflecting a more fundamental issue in the EU which is the constitutional asymmetry[33] between economic and social Europe.[34] Economic integration is to the fore because the EU has the competence to facilitate such integration. One means of addressing the asymmetry which has grown in importance in recent years has been the emergence of governance tools such as those found in the Lisbon agenda where the issuance of guidelines, creation of benchmarks, and feedback loops characterize measures in the social policy sphere under the moniker of the open method of coordination.[35] The use of soft law is however widespread throughout the EU, and it is an increasingly important characteristic of governance in the competition sphere. In the next section, an analysis of how competition is governed sheds light on the prevalence of soft governance tools in the field.

31.3 GOVERNANCE OF COMPETITION

Competition policy is paradoxically characterized by both legal formalism and extensive use of soft law (rules of conduct which in principle have no legally binding force but can have practical effects[36]). The hybridity[37] of competition law with this mix of binding and soft norms is apparent in the recent modernization of the policy that started in the mid-1990s.[38] This program led to a shift from a notification system for agreements to one where firms self-assess their agreements in the light of the antitrust rules. This freed up Commission resources to allow a shift in focus to detecting and fining cartels. The enhancement of consumer welfare was identified as a key objective.[39] This reflects a trend in competition law enforcement internationally and underlines the synergies between law and economics in this field.[40] The move to an efficiency/consumer welfare approach was essentially a move away from Ordo-liberalism with its emphasis on economic freedom in the context of an economic constitution.[41]

The final element in the reform of antitrust enforcement was decentralization of enforcement to national competition agencies (NCAs) and national courts with the antitrust rules fully directly applicable. The European Competition Network (ECN) was created for the NCAs and the Commission to determine case allocation with powers to exchange confidential information granted through regulation 1.[42] Regulation 1 was supported by a series of soft law measures: including a joint statement of support from the Council and Commission for the ECN[43] and notices on cooperation in the ECN[44] and between the Commission and national courts.[45] Notices dealing with substantive matters were also issued, including guidelines on the concept of interstate trade—a key determinant of EU jurisdiction[46]—and on the application of A101 (3) that exempts agreements and is no longer the exclusive preserve of the Commission.[47] Thus soft law has played a critical role in the modernization of enforcement complementing regulation 1, the centerpiece of the reforms. The hybrid nature of the rules can also be seen in substantive reforms. There are four main elements in addition to the reform of state aid discussed above.

First, cartels (governed by Article 101 TFEU) have become the focus of enforcement. With the abolition of notification, there has been a marked shift in the number of cartels prohibited and fined in recent years. A leniency policy—introduced through guidelines—has been central to this strategy.[48]

Second, the Commission revised the highly formalistic rules (block exemption regulations—BERs) that exempted anti-competitive agreements from notification. With the abolition of notification, logically there should be no need for any BERs but the Commission adopted a twin-track approach, retaining but revising the regulations so they are less prescriptive. The BERs provide guidance to firms as to what provisions will not be exempt, facilitating the self-regulatory regime introduced in 2003. Until the late 1990s, the emphasis on market integration led to outcomes seen as undermining competition, notably regarding vertical distribution agreements.[49] Such agreements were deemed to foreclose the market even though they are important—if not essential—to facilitate market entry, and can promote inter-brand competition (competition between similar products) even where competition between suppliers of the same products is reduced due to the presence of exclusivity clauses. The rules were revised so that exclusivity only became an issue when combined with market dominance, thereby placing competition rather than market integration at the centre of the policy.[50] BERs are supplemented by guidelines that provide details and examples of the clauses (dis)allowed. BERs have a sunset clause every ten years, at which point they are revised following extensive consultation with stakeholders.[51]

Third, Article 102 has been subject to review—within the context of its current Treaty wording and case law. A group of economists at the behest of the Commission published a report which in turn was followed by a Directorate General for Competition staff discussion paper culminating (after an extensive consultation period) in guidance on enforcement priorities for Article 102 in relation to exclusionary conduct.[52] One of the main weaknesses with the guidance is its status—as a soft law measure it does not change the law and the case law is conspicuous for being more formalistic and less welfare economics-orientated than the discussion papers and guidance. It has also been criticized for providing general principles but without the sort of detail necessary to provide effective guidance in practice.[53]

Finally, the merger regulation was revised in 2004, widening the scope of the one-stop-shop principle and the substantive test supplementing the requirement of creating or strengthening a dominant position on the market (which posed difficulties in relation to mergers among collectively dominant firms) with a requirement that the merger must significantly impede effective competition in the common market.[54] The one-stop-shop principle and tight review timetable (a preliminary view offered by the Merger Taskforce in Directorate General for Competition within twenty-five working days of full notification and final decision within ninety working days in the 5–10 percent of cases that proceed to this second phase), is generally welcomed. The quality of analysis of the Commission however was subject to criticism, culminating in a series of damning judgments from the Court of First Instance in 2002.[55] This led to institutional reform with the creation of the post of chief economic advisor with an oversight role on the economic analysis offered in merger decisions. One ongoing institutional concern that has not been fully addressed is that the Commission is prosecutor and judge in its fining decisions. It has sought to address these concerns by using a hearing officer for each case and creating panels to dissect draft decisions to ensure they are rigorously argued. But concerns about compliance with the rule of law remain.

Reforms are characterized by primary legislation supported by a growing body of guidelines and notices designed to improve legal certainty but without any binding legal force. At best, they bind the Commission in its actions[56] and are increasingly taken account of in the competition sphere by the European Courts.[57] The reforms are also presaged by extensive consultation of stakeholders, intense debate in the literature and in submissions, indicative of the strength of the episteme in this policy field. A related characteristic is one associated with new governance—networks. While an advisory committee has existed since the early 1960s[58] and, more recently, networks of sectoral specific regulators have emerged,[59] this form of governance has become central to the enforcement of the antitrust rules through the ECN.[60] Consisting of NCAs and the Commission, the Network enjoys formal legal authority but lacks legal personality. The fact that the Commission can remove any case from any Authority and take charge of it itself creates a formal hierarchy that lends it stability.[61] Policy learning also takes place as a secondary function although the interaction of national officials enforcing common rules further cements the ECN as an intense, secretive, and effective (in so far as there have been no challenges to its case allocation role yet and no public disagreements as to case allocation) governance network.

Thus while on the one hand competition law is characterized by formal legal rules and extensive powers delegated to the Commission and NCAs, on the other hand, governance techniques strongly associated with what are seen as more weakly integrated policy fields are of growing significance in this sphere with soft law and networks prevalent. This would suggest that new governance techniques are neither new, given that they have existed in the competition sphere since the early 1960s, nor perhaps as ineffective as it is sometimes suggested given they act as an appropriate complement to hard law norms in the competition sphere. The main concern yet to be addressed in the competition sphere is that an appropriate balance be maintained between legislative norms enacted with democratic oversight and executive soft law norms that instead look to consultation among (interested) stakeholders who do not necessarily reflect the wider public interest. This is in addition to the more widely aired concerns of legitimacy due to the concentration of investigation and decision-making powers in the Commission when fines are potentially so large.[62]

31.4 CONCLUSION

Competition policy, because of its technical discourse and economic and legal epistemes, is often seen as a policy apart, where politics plays a relatively limited role. Yet, the extent to which the state intervenes in markets lies at the heart of the policy, and was one of the key factors that led to the defeat of the Constitutional Treaty and had a role to play in the Irish "No" vote on the Lisbon Treaty. Thus, the extent to which marketization occurs goes to the heart of the constitutionalization of the EU. The way EU competition law is governed is also a reminder that while reform has taken place to some degree in isolation from major trends in recent European governance, competition governance has availed itself of some of the same techniques—notably soft law and networks—paradoxically to strengthen a legal regime that historically was seen as weakened by its strong adherence to legal formalism. Thus, competition law and policy remain a technical domain, but one which resonates and impacts on wider constitutional and governance trends in the EU.

NOTES

* Thanks to Suzanne Kingston and Colin Scott for comments and to the editors.
1. Intergovernmental Committee on European Integration, *The Brussels Report on the General Common Market* (the Spaak Report) June 1956 Title II Chapter I s. I(b) and s. 2.
2. Peter Holmes, Henrike Müller, and Anestis Papadopoulos, "A Taxonomy of International Competition Provisions," in *Competition Policy Foundations for Trade Reform: Regulatory Reform and Sustainable Development*, January 2006, www.cepr.org/meets/wkcn/6/6641/papers/Holmed.pdf (last accessed March 16, 2012).

3. Michaela Drahos, *Convergence of Competition Laws and Policies in the European Community: Germany, Austria and the Netherlands* (The Hague, Kluwer, 2002); Imelda Maher, "Alignment of Competition Laws in the EC," *Yearbook of European Law* 14 (1996), 223–42; Lee McGowan, "Europeanization Unleashed and Rebounding: Assessing the Modernization of EU Cartel Policy," *Journal of European Public Policy*, 12, no. 6 (2005), 986–1004.

4. Damien Geradin, Marc Reysen, and David Henry, "Extraterritoriality, Comity and Cooperation in EC Competition Law," July 2008, available at SSRN's website <http://ssrn.com/abstract=1175003>.

5. Treaty on the Functioning of the EU (TFEU), Title VII, Chapter 1, Article 106(3).

6. David Coen and Adrienne Héritier, eds, *Refining Regulatory Regimes: Utilities in Europe* (Cheltenham: Edward Elgar, 2005).

7. TFEU Title IV, Chapter 1, Section 2.

8. Any entity engaged in an economic activity, irrespective of its legal form and the way in which it is financed, is categorized as an undertaking—the technical term—see case C-41/90 *Höfner and Elser* [1991] ECR I-1979, paragraph 21, and joined cases C-264/01, C-306/01, C-354/01 and C-355/01 *AOK Bundesverband and Others* [2004] ECR I-2493, paragraph 46.

9. The Merger Regulation applies to mergers with a Community dimension based on European and worldwide turnover thresholds; see Article 1(2) EC Merger Regulation 139/2004 [2004] OJ L24/1. For a compendium of all legislation, see EC Commission, Rules Applicable to Merger Control Situation as at 1 April 2010, <http://ec.europa.eu/competition/mergers/legislation/merger_compilation.pdf>.

10. Article 23, Council Regulation 1/2003 [2003] OJ L 1/1; Commission Decision C(2009) 3726 final of May 13, 2009 in Case COMP/C-3/37.990—Intel where a fine of 1.6 billion euros was imposed. On appeal T-286/09 Intel v. Commission [2009] OJ C 220/41.

11. David Gerber, "The Transformation of European Community Competition Law?," *Harvard International Law Journal* 35, no. 1 (1994), 97–147; Andreas Weitbrecht, "From Freiburg to Chicago and Beyond—the First 50 Years of European Competition Law," *European Competition Law Review* 29, no. 2 (2008), 81–8.

12. D. G. Goyder, *EC Competition Law*, fourth edition (Oxford: Oxford University Press, 2003), ch. 5. Imelda Maher, "Competition Law and Intellectual Property Rights: Evolving Formalism," in Gráinne de Búrca and Paul Craig, eds, *The Evolution of EU Law* (Oxford: Oxford University Press, 1999), 597–624.

13. Regulation 4064/89 [1989] OJ 395/1.

14. Article 345 TFEU.

15. [1962] OJ 139, December 24, 1962 Notice on exclusive dealing contracts with Commercial Agents.

16. Frans van Waarden and Michaela Drahos, "Courts and (Epistemic) Communities in the Convergence of Competition Policies," *Journal of European Public Policy* 6, no. 6 (2002), 913–34. An episteme is a community of experts who share sets of normative and principled beliefs as well as causal beliefs and objective notions of validity, and who belong to a common enterprise. See Peter M. Haas, "Epistemic Communities and International Policy Coordination," *International Organization* 46, no. 1 (1992), 1–35, at 3.

17. See generally Peter Hall and David Soskice, eds, *Varieties of Capitalism: The Institutional Foundations of Comparative Advantage* (Oxford: Oxford University Press, 2001).

18. Title I, Article 3(1)(b).

19. Treaty Establishing a Constitution for Europe, Title I, Article I-3(2) and Treaty on the European Union, Title I, Article 3(3). Sarah Seeger, "From Referendum Euphoria to Referendum Phobia—Framing the Ratification Question," *European Journal of Law Reform* 10, no. 4 (2008), 437–56, at 445.

20. Protocol No. 27. House of Lords European Union Committee, *The Treaty of Lisbon: An Impact Assessment* 10th Report of Session 2007–2008 vol. 1, paragraph 9.13–9.18. Michael Dougan, "The Treaty of Lisbon 2007: Winning Minds not Hearts," *Common Market Law Review* 4, no. 3 (2008), 617–703, at 653. Article 51 TEU gives equal status to Treaty Articles and Protocols.

21. Tony Prosser, *The Limits of Competition Law: Markets and Public Services* (Oxford: Oxford University Press, 2005), chs. 6, 7, and 8.

22. For example case C-18/88 RTT [1991] ECR I-5941.

23. Part I, Article 4(1).

24. The first in a series of communications from the Commission on this topic, the most recent of which is COM(2007)725.

25. Now Part One, Title II, Article 14 TFEU. Malcolm Ross, "Article 16 EC and Services of General Interest: From Derogation to Obligation?," *European Law Review* 25, no. 1 (2000), 22–38.

26. Dragana Damjanovic and Bruno de Witte, "Welfare Integration through EU Law: The Overall Picture in the Light of the Lisbon Treaty," EU Working Papers Law 2008/34, pp. 26–9.

27. Erika Szyszczak, *The Regulation of the State in Competitive Markets in the EU* (Oxford, Hart, 2007), 179.

28. EC Commission, State Aid Scoreboard 31.12.2007, <http://ec.europa.eu/competition/state_aid/studies_reports/studies_reports.html> (last accessed March 16, 2012).

29. EC Commission, *State Aid Action Plan: Less and Better Targeted State Aid: A Road Map for State Aid Reform 005–2009* Brussels, 7.6.2005. COM (2005)107, final.

30. EC Commission Staff Paper, *Common Principles for an Economic Assessment of the Compatibility of State Aid under Article 87.3 EC Treaty*, <http://ec.europa.eu/competition/state_aid/reform/economic_assessment_en.pdf>. On the approach to state aid and services of general economic interest see European Commission, Decision of 20.12.2011 on the application of Article 106(2) TFEU to State aid in the form of public service compensation granted to certain undertakings entrusted with the operation of services of general economic interest SEC(2011)1581.

31. See Jonathan Faull and Ali Nikpay, eds, *The EC Law of Competition*, second edition (Oxford, Oxford University Press, 2007), ch. 16 (D).

32. See for this paragraph Damien Geradin, "Managing the Financial Crisis in Europe: Why Competition Law is Part of the Solution, Not of the Problem," *Global Competition Policy*, issue 1 (December 2008), 1–14.

33. Fritz Scharpf, "The European Social Model: Coping with the Challenge of Diversity," *Journal of Common Market Studies* 40, no. 4 (2002), 645–70, at 645.

34. Jo Shaw, Jo Hunt, and Chloë Wallace, *Economic and Social Law of the European Union* (Basingstoke: Palgrave Macmillan, 2007), ch. 14.

35. Jonathan Zeitlin and Philippe Pochet, eds, *The Open Method of Co-Ordination in Action: The European Employment and Social Inclusion Strategies* (Brussels: Peter Lang, 2005).

36. Francis Snyder, "The Effective of European Community Law: Institutions, Processes, Tools and Techniques," in Terence Daintith, ed., *Implementing EC Law in the United Kingdom: Structures for Indirect Rule* (Chichester: Chancery Law Publishing, 1995), 51–87, at 64.

37. Gráinne de Búrca and Joanne Scott, "Introduction: New Governance, Law and Constitutionalism," in G de Búrca and J Scott, eds, *Law and New Governance in the EU and the US* (Oxford: Hart, 2006), 1–12.

38. Imelda Maher, "Regulation and Modes of Governance in EC Competition Law: What's New in Enforcement?,"*Fordham International Law Journal* 31, no. 6 (2008), 1713–40.

39. Case T-168/01 GlaxoSmithKlineServicesUnlimited v. Commission [2006] EC R II-2969 para. 118 (case dismissed on appeal see C-501/06P [2009] ECR I-9291). See also Commission Guidelines on the Application of Article 81(3) of the Treaty [2004] OJ C 101/97 para 13.

40. D. B. Audretsch, W. J. Baumol, and A. E. Burke, "Competition Policy in Dynamic Markets," *International Journal of Industrial Organization* 19, no. 5 (2001), 613–34.

41. David J. Gerber, *Law and Competition in Twentieth-Century Europe: Protecting Prometheus* (Oxford: Clarendon Press, 1998), 233 ff.

42. Regulation 1/2003, Articles 5, 6, 11, 12, 13, 15, and 16.

43. Interinstitutional File 2000/0243(CNS) Brussels, December 10, 2002.

44. [2004] OJ C 101/03.

45. [2004] OJ C 101/4.

46. [2004] OJ C 101/7.

47. [2004] OJ C 101/08.

48. EC Commission, Notice on Immunity from Fines and Reduction of Fines in Cartel Cases [2006] OJ C 298/17, 8.12.2006.

49. Case 56 & 58/64 *Consten & Grundig* [1966] ECR 299, [1966] CMLR 418; Barry Hawk, "System Failure: Vertical Restraints and EC Competition Law," *Common Market Law Review* 32 (1995), 973–89.

50. Council Regulation 1215/99 June 10, 1999 on Application of Article 85(3) of the Treaty to Certain Categories of Agreements and Concerted Practices [1999] OJ L 148/1, June 15, 1999.

51. For example, EC Commission, Antitrust: Commission Launches Public Consultation on Review of Competition Rules for Distribution sector Press Release IP/09/1197, Brussels, July 28, 2009.

52. Communication from the Commission, Guidance on the Commission's Enforcement Priorities in Applying Article 82 of the EC Treaty to Abusive Exclusionary Conduct by Dominant Undertakings C(2009)864, final. Brussels, 9.2.2009; DG Competition, Discussion Paper on the Application of Article 82 of the Treaty to Exclusionary Abuses, Brussels 2005; Report by the EAGCP (Economic Advisory group for Competition Policy), An Economic Approach to Article July 82, 2005, Brussels, <http://ec.europe.ue/comm/competition/publications/studies/eagcp_july_21_05.pdf>.

53. Ariel Ezrachi, "The European Commission Guidance on Article 82 EC——The Way in which Institutional Realities Limit the Potential for Reform," University of Oxford Legal Research paper Series paper no. 27/2009, August 2009, available at http://ssrn.com/abstract = 1463854>.

54. Regulation 139/2004 of January 20, 2004 on the Control of Concentrations between Undertakings [2004] OJ L 24/1.

55. Cases T-342/99 *Airtours plc v. Commission* [2002] ECR II-5761, [2002] 5 CMLR 7; T-301/01 *Schneider Electric v. Commission* [2002] ECR II-4071, [2003] 4 CML 768; T-5/02 *Tetra Laval v. Commission* [2002] ECR II-4381, [2002] 5 CMLR 1182.

56. Case T-23/99 *LR af 1998 A/S v Commission* [2002] ECR II-1705 para 245.

57. Oana A. Stefan, "European Competition Soft Law in European Courts: A Matter of Hard Principles?," *European Law Journal* 14, no. 6 (2008), 753–72.

58. The Advisory Committee on Restrictive Practices and Dominant Positions; see now Article 14 Regulation 1/2003.

59. David Coen and Mark Thatcher, "Network Governance and Multi-Level Delegation: European Networks of Regulatory Agencies," *Journal of Public Policy* 28, no. 1 (2008), 49–71.

60. Article 11, 12, 13 Regulation 1/2003.

61. Stephen Wilks, "Agencies, Networks, Discourses and the Trajectory of European Competition Enforcement," *European Competition Journal* 3, no. 2 (2007), 437–64.

62. For Commission procedures see Commission Notice on Best Practices for the Conduct of Proceedings concerning Articles 101 and 102 TFEU [2011] OJ C 308, 6–32.

CHAPTER 32

....

ECONOMIC AND MONETARY UNION

....

KENNETH DYSON

ECONOMIC and Monetary Union (EMU) exemplifies in a strikingly vivid manner the enormous extension of the policy scope of the EU over the last thirty years, the EU's asymmetric and "fuzzy" institutional arrangements for handling policies, and the stresses associated with EU enlargement and concomitant increased diversity. In other words, it is bound up in the complex interaction between processes of "broadening," "deepening," and "widening." In terms of scope, EMU is "nested" within and alongside a range of policies: from the single market and competition policy, through the Lisbon process and employment and labor-market policies, to cohesion policies (all discussed in other chapters in this volume). As the traditional "economist" theory emphasized, sustainable monetary union depended on prior economic convergence, which in turn required the implementation of policy measures to create a single market in goods, services, capital, and labor.[1] Hence the policy "core" of EMU could not be sustained without the growth and strength of this supportive infrastructure, including not just freedom of capital movement and flexible market-based adjustment but also financial stability.[2] This policy core comprises fiscal policy coordination, represented by the SGP, and the single monetary policy of the ECB. Though this chapter focuses on the core, the importance of the policy periphery should never be forgotten. Fiscal and monetary policies cannot exist in isolation either from each other or from wider market-making and -shaping policies. As we shall see later, the operation of this policy core of EMU raises even more fundamental issues about political solidarity and legitimacy. In particular, the global financial and economic crisis from 2007 catapulted financial stability from periphery to core of EMU, in the wake of actual and potential cross-national banking failures of systemic significance.[3] Similarly, the shift from banking crises to sovereign debt crises, above all focused on Greece, shifted "bailout" mechanisms and management of "orderly insolvency" to the core of the EMU project.[4]

The unfolding post-2007 crisis was character-defining in illuminating the complexities in "deepening" institutional arrangements to cope with EMU. In managing the crisis the intimate connections of monetary union, financial stability, and fiscal policy were made more transparent.[5] Asymmetry had been built into the institutional design of EMU: monetary policy was Europeanized in the ECB, fiscal policy competence especially for macroeconomic stabilization and banking rescues remained firmly fixed at the national level, whilst competence for financial stability left the EU level uncomfortably poised between global and national regulators and supervisors. There was "fuzziness" in the allocation of these competences between national, eurozone, EU, and international institutions. Functions and territory did not match.[6] There was an EU-wide (actually EEA-wide) single market, with several monetary policies (the major one being the ECB's), with fiscal policies for macroeconomic national stabilization, and with fragmentation into various institutional models of domestic financial market supervision. The weakness of EU-level coordination of fiscal stimulus in 2008–2009, and the continuing lack of clarity about how cross-national banking failures and sovereign debt crises would be managed, highlighted once again the problematic and unresolved issue of how EMU relates to political union.[7] The defeat of the European Constitutional Treaty in referendums in France and the Netherlands, followed by the defeat of the Lisbon Treaty in the first Irish referendum, confirmed that eurozone membership was no simple catalyst for closer political solidarity.

On the third dimension of "widening," EU "big bang" enlargement in 2004 reduced the share of eurozone membership from twelve out of fifteen to twelve out of twenty-five. By 2011, following further EU enlargement in 2007, the share had risen to seventeen out of twenty-seven. Hence the eurozone had enlarged. However, it had been joined by smaller states: Estonia, Greece, Slovenia, Cyprus, Malta, and Slovakia. Larger states like Poland and the UK remained outside, not even participating in the ERM II linking their currencies to the euro. Despite the fact that all but two member states had derogations from monetary union, not the Treaty opt-outs of Denmark and the UK, it was unclear whether de facto some states would shift from being temporary outsiders to semi-permanent outsiders.[8] The likelihood of such a shift derived from diverging attitudes to loss of sovereignty, from asymmetries in the distribution of the costs and gains of euro entry, and from the continuing attractions of "free riding" in exchange-rate and monetary policies.[9] Far less likely was euro "exit." The economic and political costs in credibility, not to mention technical costs, would be huge.[10] The result was that members were constrained to the choice between "loyalty" and "voice."[11]

The birth of the eurozone proved a powerful catalyst for strengthening the principle of differentiation in European integration.[12] Smaller states, with high trade dependence on the eurozone, weakly developed domestic financial markets, and high levels of external indebtedness to the eurozone had powerful incentives to seek early euro entry. The post-2007 crisis increased the attractions of the eurozone as a "shelter" from financial market risks for states with many or all of these characteristics, like the Baltic states (which underwent acutely painful deflations to keep them on the path to meet the convergence criteria for euro entry). However, not all EU states shared these characteristics.

The Czech government was more attracted to retaining the value of domestic exchange-rate policy and interest-rate policy as speedier instruments for adjustment to asymmetric shocks than painful "internal devaluation" through wage and cost cutting. Problems of "real" convergence in GDP and living standards, as well as fiscal challenges of public investment and measures to protect citizens from the harsh effects of transition, meant that many "post-communist" member states shifted from strategies of accelerated euro entry to delay.[13] Hungary was a notable example of the shift from "pacesetter" to "laggard" on euro entry. Perhaps even more strikingly, the UK and Sweden seemed to shift to a "semi-permanent" outsider status; whilst Denmark and the UK retained their Treaty-negotiated opt-outs from monetary union. The result was that the EU had a dominant currency (the euro) and monetary policy (the ECB), whilst the euro played an external role as the main international currency in wider Europe. However, there were still several currencies, several monetary policies, and various exchange-rate regimes (from floating to currency boards) within the EU.

32.1 CHALLENGES: ECONOMIC SHOCKS
AND THEIR LEGACIES

The design of EMU was the foster child of the collapse of the Bretton Woods system in 1971–1973 and the Great Inflation that subsequently dominated the 1970s.[14] It was not originally conceived in this way. Following the completion of the first stages of the EEC, the heads of state and government of the original Six had agreed at The Hague Summit in December 1969 to prioritize EMU. The Werner Report of 1970 embodied the Keynesian orthodoxy of its time. There was to be *parallel* progress in economic and in monetary union, around two poles—the ECOFIN and the system of central banks.[15] Little explicit attention was given to the principle of central bank independence. Indeed, the early collapse of agreement on how to proceed had much to do with French Gaullist reluctance to cede sovereignty over fiscal policy.[16]

The shocks of the collapse of Bretton Woods and of the Great Inflation had paradoxical effects, which in the short term undermined ambitions for EMU and in the longer term recast its foundations more firmly in revived neoclassical economic theory with its focus on the requirements of sustainable economic stabilization. In the short term financial market speculation and currency volatility undermined the unity of the EEC; policy divergence prevailed over convergence. Though affirming their political commitment to realize EMU at the Paris Summit of 1972, they were not able to go beyond modest steps, notably the "Snake" exchange-rate system which proved highly vulnerable to defections. However, the EEC was emboldened to act by the loss of the public good of exchange-rate stability that had previously been provided by the United States. This loss meant serious threat that the gains in trade and investment from the newly established customs union would not be sustained. Hence the first major practical step was the establishment of the ERM in 1978–1979 as in effect a "new Bretton Woods for Europe."[17] The EEC began to organize its own public good. The ERM also offered a tool for importing discipline into domestic economic policies. As it evolved into a D-Mark-anchored system, so commitment to a "hard" ERM offered a means to regain lost domestic credibility. The decisive change was the French decision in the March 1983 crisis to remain in the ERM and to embrace domestic "rigor." The ERM provided a response to the Great Inflation. By stabilizing one's currency against the D-Mark it was possible to rely on the German Bundesbank as the benchmark of credibility. At the same time the continuing vulnerability of the ERM to crisis—demonstrated above all in 1983, 1987, and then again in 1992 and 1993—had two consequences. It bound member states together in crisis management and, more fundamentally, convinced them that in the medium- to long-term the only viable responses were either to opt for floating currencies, with attendant risks to European integration from volatility, or to move to monetary union.[18]

In this context of the collapse of Bretton Woods, the birth of the ERM, and the huge expansion in scale, complexity, and speed of international financial markets, macroeconomic theory erected a new rigorous intellectual edifice that came to remold ideas about EMU as they resurfaced in the 1980s. The new focus was on the primacy of price stability in economic policy, the importance of managing market expectations of inflation through credibility of policies, and the core value of central bank independence for credibility and for the lowest-cost achievement of price stability in growth and employment.[19] This intellectual edifice empowered EU (and other) central bankers and disempowered trade unions and the traditional post-war European institutions of social partnership. The collapse of Bretton Woods had created the gap in which EMU could grow; the Great Inflation and the retreat of Keynesian demand-side economics offered the substantive content that underpinned the design of EMU from 1988. Neoclassical economics combined with German Ordo-liberal ideas to stress the primacy of long-term economic stabilization over short-term fiscal (or monetary) activism and fine-tuning.[20]

The Delors Report of 1989 illustrated the triumph of central banking ideas about EMU, above all of the German Bundesbank.[21] The core organizing principle was to be an independent ECB with a tightly delimited mandate to deliver price stability. As the negotiations proceeded in the EC Monetary Committee, the Committee of Central Bank Governors, ECOFIN, and in 1991 in the IGC on EMU, it became clear that the non-monetary aspects were either side payments (like the Cohesion Fund) and mainly symbolic (like the Employment Chapter inserted in the Amsterdam Treaty in 1997) or supporting props for monetary union. These supporting props included the "no bailout" clause in the Maastricht Treaty, the convergence criteria for entering monetary union, and the excessive deficit procedure in fiscal policy. This ECB-centric character was reinforced in the later German-sponsored SGP proposal (1995–1997), with its stress on the 3 percent fiscal deficit threshold, limits on "exceptional circumstances," and provision for fiscal sanctions for non-compliance.[22] The Euro Group of finance ministers of the eurozone was not established as a "Council" with formal competences. It was informal and had dialogue as its central purpose.[23] The French idea of an "economic government" to act as counterweight to the ECB had very little practical impact.[24]

Hence EMU exhibits a striking historical path-dependence from the shocks of the collapse of Bretton Woods, through the Great Inflation, to the multiple destabilizing crises of the ERM. The question was whether the EU represented an appropriate "Optimum Currency Area" (OCA) to support a sustainable monetary union. The answer depended on the choice of variables with which to assess an OCA. According to the more traditional exogenous model, a sustainable monetary union required a combination of the following characteristics to support macroeconomic stabilization: a low vulnerability to asymmetric shocks because of similarities in economic structure; and, in response to asymmetric shocks, the central capacity to organize fiscal transfers and labor-market mobility and flexibility.[25] By these means domestic business cycles would be closely synchronized so that member states could live with a single interest rate. A one-size monetary policy could fit all.

The EU did not appear to be an OCA in these terms. Its economic structures were too varied (compare Germany and Greece); it lacked an EU budget of any substantial size and that was designed as an instrument for macroeconomic stabilization; whilst cross-border labor mobility was low, principally due to language and cultural differences. However, even in terms of the exogenous model a case could be made for a substantial part of the EU as an OCA, namely the so-called "D-Mark Zone": those member states that had a long record of being in a "hard," narrow-band ERM with Germany (Austria, Benelux, Denmark, France, and Germany). That said, some eurozone members like Greece and Portugal had fewer of the attributes of an OCA with Germany that many EU non-members.[26] Hence, before the post-2007 crisis, the eurozone looked very vulnerable to asymmetric shocks.

Endogenous theories of OCAs offered a different analysis and explanation of whether the EU was an Optimum Currency Area, focusing on its nature as a "regime shift." An independent ECB managing a single currency and mandated to deliver price stability would "lock in" currency and monetary stability. Two benefits would follow. Elimination of exchange-rate risk and reduced transaction costs would expand trade and investment, thereby increasing growth and employment.[27] Additionally, access to much larger and more liquid financial markets on the same terms would provide insurance for borrowers and lenders. Hence it would offer extra financial shelter against asymmetric shocks.

Once again, however, endogenous theories—and the empirical record of the first decade—were not wholly supportive of the belief that the eurozone, let alone the EU, was an OCA. Trade gains were concentrated on the member states closest geographically to Germany, supporting the "gravity" theory of trade (that distance matters). The old "D-Mark" Zone exhibited strong intra-industry trade and synchronized business cycles. However, "periphery" states like Greece, Ireland, Portugal, and Spain benefitted less from EMU-related trade gains, and their business cycles were less synchronized.[28] The result was that "inappropriately" low (for them) interest rates helped spark asset-price bubbles, which resulted in severe asymmetric shocks. Even endogenous theories suggested that the gains from EMU might be asymmetrically distributed.

In consequence, the eurozone appeared highly vulnerable to asymmetric shocks. Its vulnerability was exposed most graphically in the post-2007 global financial and economic crisis. This crisis raised questions not just about the underlying tensions and conflicts from in-built proclivity to asymmetric shocks but also about institutional robustness and flexibility. The eurozone was ill-equipped to deal with mounting internal imbalances between "surplus" states led by Germany and "deficit" states like Greece that were persistently losing competitiveness.[29]

32.2 INSTITUTIONAL ARRANGEMENTS: ASYMMETRY AND "FUZZY" BOUNDARIES

In contrast to the principle of "parallelism" in the Werner Report, the Maastricht EMU "constitution," and its later refinements in domestic fiscal policy coordination and in domestic economic policy coordination, were founded on asymmetry. There was a single monetary policy, managed by the independent ECB, a new European institution with supranational characteristics, and pledged to pursue a narrowly defined Treaty mandate of price stability.[30] However, exchange-rate policy regimes, fiscal policies, and structural reform policies, including employment, wages, and labor-market policies, remained strictly domestic, cases of "constrained discretion." These latter policies were essential to EMU in two senses. Firstly, effective monetary policy depended on domestic exchange-rate, fiscal and structural reform policies "flanking" and supporting price stability. The SGP was designed for this purpose in 1996–1997 as a system of fixed rules on fiscal deficits and public debt.[31] Hence the ECB had a high stake in coordination of these policies, but was confined to a role of exhortation (notably opposing unilateral euroization by non-eurozone member states). Secondly, exchange-rate, fiscal, and structural reform policies remained the main instruments for macroeconomic stabilization. Member states sought accordingly to retain "constrained discretion" to act, especially to deal with economic downturns and recession. The reform of the SGP in 2005, following its crisis in November 2003 when the Council rejected its application against France and Germany, exemplified the member states asserting their role as the "masters of the Treaty."[32] The reformulation of the SGP as "constrained discretion" in fiscal policies was evident in its accommodation of weakly coordinated domestic fiscal stimuli in responding to the 2008–2009 crisis.

This underlying asymmetry in allocation of competences—"cocktail of competences" —was evident in the structure of macroeconomic governance. The Euro Group of eurozone finance ministers was a weak counterweight to the ECB. Under the Treaty it had no role in setting an inflation target for which an independent ECB would be politically accountable. The ECB defined the price stability objective ("below but close to 2 percent") without reference to the Euro Group, making it one of the most independent central banks in the world.[33] Compared to ECOFIN, the Euro Group was small enough to remain a forum for effective debate. However, it lacked formal decision-making competences. The Lisbon Treaty gave it formal recognition and the capacity to strengthen fiscal and economic policy coordination amongst its members. However, core competence remained with ECOFIN. The overall weakness of political leadership in the eurozone was demonstrated by the failure of President Nicolas Sarkozy's initiative in 2008 in trying to use the global crisis to institutionalize meetings of the eurozone heads of state and government. The German government rejected initiatives to strengthen the Euro Group and the eurozone heads of state and government. Such initiatives risked creating serious divisions within the EU, cementing the gap between "ins" and "outs." They also risked jeopardizing the integrity of the single market, with Germany benefiting from the trade gains of a "larger" Europe. And the initiatives were less valuable than opening wider markets by encouraging structural reforms. Above all, the German government feared that the independence of the ECB would be undermined in this way and the euro's reputation as a currency "at least as stable as the D-Mark" destroyed. In consequence, Germany's potentially fragile "permissive consensus" about the euro might be fatally damaged.

The result of this asymmetry in design of EMU was "fuzzy" boundaries. Different functional areas within EMU operated on different spatial scales. The vast edifice of the single market conformed to an EU/EEA scale, alongside competition policy. Access to the wholesale euro payment and settlement system (TARGET) and to the prospective securities settlement system (TARGET2S) were defined as single market issues, about a "level playing field," thereby safeguarding the interest of the City of London despite the decision of the UK government to remain a euro "out." At the same time TARGET was essential for the effective operation of ECB monetary policy and hence needed central Eurosystem management. A similar "fuzziness" was apparent in the emerging retail euro payment and settlement system (the Single Euro Payment Area, SEPA), where again all EEA members participated. The basic principle was that, the closer a policy issue was to the effective operation of the single monetary policy, the more actively the ECB would be involved.

The "fuzziness" was most apparent in the field of financial stability which, with the post-2007 crisis, became much more salient. Because of the global scale of the integration of financial markets and of the intimate interconnections amongst its component parts, the international level of IMF, the Bank for International Settlements (BIS), the G7/8, and—increasingly—the Group of 20 (G20) were seen as essential in setting and monitoring standards, for instance on capital adequacy provisions to mitigate risk. Hence there was a strong bias towards downloading international agreements (like Basel II on banking standards) into EU law. Equally, considerable historical and structural differences among EU banking systems, and the need for proximity of regulators to regulated, meant that detailed supervision was left to national regulators. In turn, different domestic regulatory regimes developed within the EU. Perhaps most crucially, the fact that banking failure would impel national governments to act as "lenders of last resort" to the banking system meant that member-state governments were unwilling to allow a situation to develop in which an EU-level or eurozone body would pre-commit them to costly fiscal policy action. As the post-2007 crisis illustrated graphically, the financial stability function—and failure of "systemically significant" institutions—touched on the politically sensitive core of fiscal sovereignty.

At the same time both the single market in financial services and the transition to monetary union produced new incentives to strengthen arrangements for financial market supervision within the EU. The result was the so-called "Lamfalussy process," with its different levels of regulation and supervision.[34] However, this new system was EU-wide and left wide discretion to national regulators and supervisors. As financial market integration and cross-national financial activities gathered pace with the single market and with monetary union, the inadequacies of this system became apparent. They were laid bare with the 2007–2008 financial crisis, notably the Fortis bank rescue.[35] The European Council accepted the proposals of the de Larosière report of 2009 that the three Lamfalussy bodies for banking, insurance, and securities should be transformed into independent authorities and that the ECB should act as secretariat for a new European Systemic Risk Board (ESRB), which would strengthen macro-prudential regulation of the financial system and monitor systemic risk. Systemic risk and macro-prudential supervision became a new focal point in European economic governance. However, progress here depended on prior agreement that member-state governments could not be pre-committed by the new bodies to undertake fiscal rescues of banks.

32.3 PERFORMANCE AND IMPACT OF EMU ON THE EU AND ITS MEMBER STATES

The influence of EMU on the EU as a whole is crucially dependent on its policy performance, which in turn is conditioned by the extent of the eurozone's vulnerability to asymmetric shocks and by the robustness and flexibility of the institutions of EMU. As we have seen, major question marks continue to hang over the eurozone, mirroring its nature as an "incomplete" project "in the making." In 2010 the European Council committed to doing "whatever it takes" to defend and sustain the euro. It established a new body to provide financial assistance, initially the European Financial Stability Facility (EFSF) and, from 2012, the European Stability Mechanism (ESM). European economic governance was further strengthened with the reform of the SGP, a new procedure for macroeconomic imbalances, the new right of the European Commission to make proposals for prompt corrective measures by member states (only to be overridden by QMV), and the Euro Plus Pact (EPP). Reflecting tenacious German resistance, the EFSF/ESM remained relatively small in its financial firepower. However, their range of instruments was expanded to include loans, precautionary credits, bank recapitalization, purchases in primary soverign bond markets, and interventions secondary bond markets. Though the ESM was an intergovernmental body, it had the attributes of a European Monetary Fund in the making. Eurozone member states that complied with the policies approved in the European Semester were not able to borrow on demand from the EFSF/ESM; whilst they had to ratify the Treaty on Stability, Coordination and Governance in the EMU to qualify for EFSF/ESM assistance. Reforms stopped short of a European public debt management agency able to issue euro bonds or to trade in secondary bond markets. Reforms stopped short of a European public debt management agency able to issue euro bonds or to redeen the bond of member states. In short, whilst reforms appeared considerable, the eurozone continued to lag behind the global financial markets in its capacity to mount large-scale, rapid concerted action to instill financial market confidence. In consequence, its member states remained acutely vulnerable to market fear and contagion.

At a very basic level, monetary union has delivered for its member states shelter from economic crisis by eliminating exchange-rate volatility and crises as sources of asymmetric shock inside the EU. In its absence in 2007–2010 the financial markets would have driven exchange rates apart as they sought to avoid risky currencies for safe havens like the D-Mark. On the other hand, in the absence of autonomous exchange-rate and interest-rate policies, much greater reliance has to be placed on domestic adjustment through wages and costs and on the role of fiscal policy in engineering "internal" devaluation. This process of internal adjustment can be both painful and long and a source of alienation for affected citizens.[36] Potentially it might be dangerously delayed so that major strains develop inside the eurozone, as with Greece and Spain in 2009–2010. In addition to peer pressure, "naming and shaming," and the "nuclear deterrent" of fiscal sanctions under the SGP, the main external discipline remains the bond markets which can impose damage on states seen as at risk of debt rescheduling or default at cost to creditors. There is no EU-wide bond issuance, which has been rejected by creditor states, which fear that higher debt servicing costs will be transferred to fiscally virtuous states like Germany, creating "moral hazard." Member-state governments which are judged to be following unsustainable policies can be punished by higher risk premiums, rising debt servicing costs, and eventually face sovereign default. Prospective market discipline can act as a powerful incentive to corrective action and, in the view of creditor states, avoids moral hazard.

Also, fundamental to the performance of the eurozone has been the success of the ECB in delivering price stability. On two measures it has been successful over the first decade: the actual inflation rate has averaged just over 2 percent, reasonably close to the ECB objective (and a better performance than that of the Bank of England and the US Federal Reserve); whilst market expectations of long-term interest rates have stayed closely aligned with the ECB objective.[37] Despite this gain in credibility, three problems emerged and help explain why the euro remained unloved. Firstly, at the very outset it was clear that *perceived* inflation was significantly higher than officially measured consumer price inflation.[38] This difference helps explain why public perceptions of the record of the ECB were mixed. Perceived inflation is influenced by the frequency of purchases (food, drink, petrol, etc). Secondly, there were serious, persisting inflation differentials across the eurozone. Inflation differentials are typical of monetary unions, but become a worry when they persist so that some parts of the union continue to lose competitiveness. This problem was further highlighted in the post-2007 crisis as it became clear that some states had severe asymmetric shocks from unsustainable asset-price bubbles (notably Ireland and Spain). The ECB made monetary policy for the eurozone as a whole. In the context of this "one-size-fits-all" monetary policy, tackling persisting inflation differentials and regional asset-price bubbles was a matter for national governments. However, it also illustrated that the Eurosystem had made too little use of new instruments to vary lending anti-cyclically.[39]

Thirdly, the crisis opened up the question of whether price stability was enough for a central bank. Though the consensus remained that it was fundamental, attention began to shift toward new policy instruments that might help to better insure against asset-price bubbles and build-up of systemic risks. Following the post-2007 crisis the consensus in monetary economics began to shift toward redefining monetary policy strategy so that it better integrated macro-prudential issues, especially identification and anticipation of systemic risk, into decision-making on interest rates. Here the ECB claimed that its "two-pillar" strategy was superior to the inflation targeting strategy that was pursued by the US Fed and the Bank of England.[40] Its "monetary" pillar focused on the analysis of money and credit growth, which was cross-checked against the broad "economic" pillar (it included inflation forecasts, wages, exchange rates, fiscal policy, etc).

The first large-scale test of the ECB was the post-2007 crisis. In the very early stages it was praised for acting decisively in injecting cheap, plentiful liquidity into the banking system through the operational instruments of monetary policy. These instruments were refined and developed as the crisis matured, especially in the wake of the collapse of Lehman Brothers. After this point the ECB was often criticized for being less bold than the US Fed and the Bank of England, especially in not adopting advanced forms of "quantitative easing" by buying government and corporate bonds. Eventually in May 2010 it began to purchase government bonds as part of the eurozone bailout package, but in a limited way and with great reservations on the part of the Bundesbank. In fact, the ECB's "non-conventional" measures were attuned to the specific bank-based nature of the monetary transmission mechanism in the eurozone. It focused on widening the range of collateral that it would accept from the banks, extending the range of eligible counterparties, and, especially from December 2011, providing unlimited three-year liquidity to the banking system. In effect, the ECB carved out a new, temporary role as orchestrator of the money markets. It threw a lifeline to the banks. However, the risk emerged that banks in some states like Greece, Ireland, Spain, and Portugal became highly dependent on the ECB, creating a serious problem for it in exiting in an orderly way from emergency measures without precipitating a contagious bank solvency crisis.

The endogenous effects of monetary union were also apparent in trade effects of the euro from the elimination of exchange-rate risk and reduced transaction costs. However, though these gains were general, they were asymmetrically distributed. The main positive trade effects were concentrated in the traditional "D-Mark Zone." In consequence, both intra-industry trade and business cycle synchronization were strengthened in this core.[41] At the same time new "borders" within the single market were created, above all on the changing borders of the eurozone. Close to these borders the effects on trade of exchange-rate movements were felt most strongly. Thus, for instance, Slovakia gained generally in trade from euro entry, but suffered specific negative effects as the euro appreciated against the Hungarian and Polish currencies.

Perhaps most negatively of all, and despite these trade gains, the establishment of the eurozone was not associated with any underlying change in the trend output growth rate. There were no statistical signs of an increase in labor productivity, reduction in long-term structural unemployment, or acceleration in economic growth. The relative decline vis-à-vis the United States since the 1980s had not been reversed.[42] Critics of the ECB, like President Jacques Chirac, saw its monetary policy fixation on mastering inflation as part of the problem and contrasted it unfavorably with the US Fed. Conversely, the ECB and most monetary economists identified the problem as a lack of structural reforms to boost growth and employment. In this view, the responsibility rested with national governments. The central problem was that most national governments had failed to demonstrate domestic "ownership" of EMU by making appropriate structural reforms to fiscal institutions and policies, to product and services markets, and to labor markets and wage setting. There was too much rigidity, and a considerable amount of complacency fostered by the loss of the exchange-rate constraint with monetary union and historically low interest rates.[43] A contrast was drawn between small states and large states. The large states—like France, Germany, and Italy—were the worst sinners against the SGP (notably in precipitating the 2003 crisis and the 2005 SGP revision) and weaker on product and labor-market reforms.[44] As they represented the core of the eurozone economy, the effect was negative for all. This tension between large and small states became a feature of the eurozone, especially over the crisis of the SGP in November 2003. Small states appeared to be more exposed through their trade dependency to the effects of monetary union and hence had stronger incentives to comply. Also, many of them had traditions of cooperative management of economic change.

In practice, the performance record was mixed. A focus on measuring "top-down" structural reforms by governments misses the component of "bottom-up" structural change led by firms.[45] On this last dimension the German economy rebounded strongly by 2005–2006 after years of patient and painful corporate restructuring, emerging as the pacesetter in reducing relative unit costs and building up huge current account surpluses. Most other economies, notably Italy, Portugal, and Spain, had lost competitiveness to Germany. In addition, the distinction between strong and weak performances in structural reforms cut across the distinction between euro insiders and outsiders. The Nordic model gained increased credibility from the Lisbon process of ranking states on innovation. It contained a euro outsider (Sweden), an insider (Finland), and an ERM II member (Denmark). In fiscal policy too the record was mixed. Overall, over the first decade the EU performed better in meeting the SGP criteria on deficits and debt than in the previous decade. Post-2007 it recorded an aggregate fiscal performance better than the UK and the USA. This improvement owed much to some eurozone insiders, which had benefitted from lower debt servicing costs in a monetary union as well as in some cases structural reforms. However, camouflaged by unsustainable asset-price booms, some states built up dangerously high structural deficits in their fiscal policies. These deficits were revealed in the 2008–2010 crisis and sparked fears of sovereign debt defaults. They left the SGP looking toothless and ineffective in preparing the EU for the political economy of "bad times" that overtook it from 2007.

In conclusion, the eurozone had experienced a process of limited Europeanization at the domestic level of economic policies. There was a new momentum for domestic reforms to fiscal institutions after the 2005 SGP reform as an essential prerequisite for meeting fiscal commitments. This momentum increased as the post-2007 crisis gathered pace, with Germany's tough constitutionally anchored "debt brake" playing a pacesetting role. The Treaty on Stability, Coordination and Governance in the EMU of 2012 inserted the requirement that the balanced budget rule would be incorporated into national law. There had, however, been a past failure to effectively tackle underlying structural reforms to fiscal policies during economic "good times." The result was that, when the post-2007 crisis struck, states like Italy were constrained from engaging in substantial discretionary fiscal stimulus by the need to avert market penalties. In their cases even the operation of their automatic stabilizers raised serious questions about fiscal sustainability. In short, the room for maneuver of many eurozone states to use fiscal policy for macroeconomic stabilization was severely constrained without serious damage to the SGP and/or risking sovereign debt crisis.

32.4 POLITICAL UNION, PUBLIC OPINION, DEMOCRATIC DEFICIT, AND DIFFERENTIATED INTEGRATION

What impact has EMU had on the wider EU? EMU has acted as a catalyst for pressing ahead with wider political union, whilst at the same time being relatively insulated from these debates. The emphasis has been on protecting the "Maastricht monetary constitution." Economic policy coordination has evolved in a pragmatic manner, essentially as a complement to monetary union: from the Broad Economic Policy Guidelines (BEPGs) and the excessive deficit procedure provided for in the Maastricht Treaty; through the SGP, the Luxembourg process on employment policies, the Cardiff process on structural reforms and the Cologne process on macroeconomic dialogue; to the Lisbon process, above all on innovation. The Lamfalussy process in financial market regulation and supervision can be added. Each of these elements has been reformed and reconstituted over time. In 2011 the new "European Semester" was introduced, integrating economic governance around the agreement and monitoring of measures to ensure stronger fiscal discipline, to correct excessive imbalances, and to strengthen competitiveness and convergence. However, this strengthening of economic governance did not involve the conferral of new formal competences on the EU (or the eurozone), other than a permanent financial assistance mechanism for eurozone member states. As the post-2007 crisis clarified, in economic policy coordination the member states remain "masters of the Treaty." Hence EMU remains asymmetric in being "ECB-centric" and "fuzzy" in its institutional boundaries. The Euro Group remains a shadowy body.

This lack of sharp political profile and convoluted organization summarizes EMU's nature as an elite-driven process that relies on a permissive consensus at the level of public opinion. In this sense it mimics the wider integration process. The euro is neither generally "loved" nor identifiable as a catalyst for a strengthened European identity across eurozone member states.[46] It did not make any appreciable positive impact on the Dutch and the French voters in their referendums in 2005 on the European Constitutional Treaty. Equally, though domestic leaders have been tempted to shift blame to the ECB and EU, the euro had not by early 2011 acted as a source of broad populist mobilization against European integration. Public opinion has tended to fear euro entry or blame the euro after entry for price rises in sensitive areas of consumer purchasing ("perceived" as opposed to "official" inflation). However, it has not attributed blame to the euro for asset-price inflation (e.g. in Ireland and Spain), for anemic growth and employment, or for banking failures. If anything, the euro has made more transparent the failures of domestic political leaders, for instance in fiscal policies and in structural reforms. On the other hand, the eurozone faced the political risk that long, protracted austerity and GDP contraction in some member states, and expensive bailouts by other member states, could trigger populist backlashes. By 2011, riots in Greece, youth protests in Spain, and the electoral success of the True Finns party highlighted this risk.

The post-2007 crisis had ambivalent effects. In one sense it increased the political attractions of the eurozone as a "shelter" from the financial markets. Being outside meant the prospect of IMF interventions (as with Hungary and Latvia); being inside (like Greece, Ireland, and Portugal) meant that collective support was available, notably financial assistance (based on strict conditionality) and more generally from the ECB's generous liquidity provision to banks. A notable innovation was the new EFSF, agreed in 2010 as a three-year special purpose vehicle to assist eurozone states facing severe difficulties. Overall, compared to the 1970s, the crisis showed the value of a "zone of economic stability" in securing both trade and access to finance. However, the crisis revealed the serious flaws in the SGP and in the Lisbon process as crisis prevention mechanisms. The SGP had failed to create sufficient "fiscal space" for member states to let the automatic budget stabilizers operate effectively without risk of sovereign debt crisis; the Lisbon process had been marked by a lack of domestic political ownership of the agenda for strengthening competitiveness. No less seriously, the EU and especially the eurozone were exposed as deficient in crisis management mechanisms: no collective large-scale fiscal "lender of last resort," no collective bond issuance, and no clear procedures for orderly cross-national bank failures or for sovereign insolvency. Lack of capacity for decisive action outside the remit of the ECB invited skepticism within the financial markets. It also left the ECB seriously exposed in crisis management, with serious adverse consequences for the quality of its balance sheet and hence potentially for its reputation.

Despite this continuing, if fragile, permissive consensus, evidence suggests that, given opportunity to vote in referendums on euro entry, popular majorities would reject membership. Supportive evidence includes the failed Danish and Swedish referendums, and the fact that cross-party support for a referendum prior to UK entry acted as a major hurdle that no political leader has been prepared to try to jump. More generally, public opinion tends to demonstrate a residual affection for the former national currencies. Moreover, on balance it can be claimed that EMU has contributed to the wider problem of "democratic deficit" at the heart of the EU. The problem is not so much the ECB. It may be extremely independent of the political process, but its mandate in narrow and it is at least on some key measures accountable and transparent. More problematic is the lack of clear authority, accountability, and transparency in the complex processes of economic policy coordination and in fiscal policy. The key problems derive from the absence of fiscal capacity of the EU. It may claim to be a "regulatory state" but it is not a "fiscal state" empowered to manage public debts. The EU does not posses the capacity to use independent tax-raising and varying powers, large-scale redistributive expenditure programs, deficit financing through EU bond issuance, or the capacity to intervene in secondary debt markets in order to engage in significant macroeconomic stabilization. This problem stems from the lack of democratic political legitimacy through a European government accountable to the European Parliament. In its absence a European *demos* cannot develop. If EMU is supposed to help create a *demos*, it remains an incomplete project.

EMU's "fuzziness" is further demonstrated in its effects on the balance between the principles of unitary and differentiated integration.[47] It has acted to strengthen the unitary principle, especially in financial market regulation and financial stability, though here again the post-2007 crisis was a key catalyst. The euro payment and settlement systems remain an EU/EEA-wide project in construction (if managed by the Eurosystem). Above all, money markets have become highly integrated. However, EMU seems to have cemented the principle of differentiated integration through two Treaty opt-outs and through derogations that leave new member states with discretion over dates for euro entry. At the same time differentiation has combined "multi-speed" with "variable geometry." There has been no formal evolution of the eurozone members into the basis for a "core" Europe, in which monetary union is complemented, for instance, by business tax union, financial market union, foreign and security union, and defense union. The reasons are various, including: the political desire to avoid negating the historic EU enlargement by a new division inside the EU; the fear of losing the mutual gains from an enlarged and enlarging European market, not least of losses from incentivizing free riding for instance in tax and regulatory policies; and the fact that a convergent normative code about monetary union does not translate into convergent policy preferences in wider economic policies, like business taxation, let alone in foreign, security, and defense policies. "Euro" Europe is not necessarily "defense" or "social" Europe.

Notes

1. L. Tsoukalis, *The Politics and Economics of European Monetary Integration* (London: George Allen and Unwin, 1977).
2. O. Issing, *The Birth of the Euro* (Cambridge: Cambridge University Press, 2008).

3. K. Dyson, "The Age of the Euro: A Structural Break? Europeanization, Convergence, and Power in Central Banking," in K. Dyson and M. Marcussen, eds, *Central Banks in the Age of the Euro* (Oxford: Oxford University Press, 2009), 1–50.
4. K. Dyson and L. Quaglia, *European Economic Governance and Policies. Volume II: Commentary on Key Policy Documents* (Oxford: Oxford University Press, 2010).
5. Dyson and Quaglia, *European Economic Governance and Policies.*
6. K. Dyson, "The First Decade: Credibility, Identity, and Institutional 'Fuzziness'," in K. Dyson, ed., *The Euro at 10: Europeanization, Power, and Convergence* (Oxford: Oxford University Press, 2008), 1–34.
7. Dyson and Quaglia, *European Economic Governance and Policies.*
8. K. Dyson, "European States and the Euro Area: Clustering and Covariance in Patterns of Change," in Dyson, *The Euro at 10*, 378–413.
9. On which K. Dyson and A. Sepos, eds, *Which Europe? The Politics of Differentiated Integration* (Houndmills: Palgrave Macmillan, 2010).
10. B. Eichengreen, *The Euro: Love It or Leave It?* November 19, 2007, <http://www.voxeu.org/index.php?q = node/729>.
11. A. Hirschman, *Exit, Voice, and Loyalty* (Cambridge, MA: Harvard University Press, 1970).
12. Dyson and Sepos, *Which Europe?*.
13. K. Dyson, ed., *Enlarging the Euro Area: External Empowerment and Domestic Transformation in East Central Europe* (Oxford: Oxford University Press, 2006).
14. K. Dyson, "Fifty Years of Economic and Monetary Union: A Hard and Thorny Journey," in D. Phinnemore and A. Warleigh-Lack, eds, *Reflections on European Integration: 50 Years of the Treaty of Rome* (Houndmills: Palgrave Macmillan, 2009), 143–71.
15. Tsoukalis, *The Politics and Economics of European Monetary Integration.*
16. K. Dyson, *Elusive Union: The Process of Economic and Monetary Union in Europe* (London: Longman, 1994).
17. Dyson, *Elusive Union.*
18. K. Dyson and K. Featherstone, *The Road to Maastricht: Negotiating Economic and Monetary Union* (Oxford: Oxford University Press, 1999).
19. K. Dyson, *The Politics of the Euro-Zone: Stability or Breakdown?* (Oxford: Oxford University Press, 2000); Dyson, *Elusive Union.*
20. K. Dyson and L. Quaglia. *European Economic Governance and Policies. Volume I: Commentary on Key Historical and Institutional Documents* (Oxford: Oxford University Press, 2010).
21. Dyson and Featherstone, *The Road to Maastricht.*
22. M. Heipertz and A. Verdun, *Ruling Europe: The Politics of the Stability and Growth Pact* (Cambridge: Cambridge University Press, 2010).
23. U. Puetter, *The Eurogroup: How a Secretive Circle of Finance Ministers Shapes European Economic Governance* (Manchester: Manchester University Press, 2006).
24. D. Howarth, *The French Road to European Monetary Union* (Basingstoke: Palgrave, 2001).
25. Dyson, *The Politics of the Euro-Zone.*
26. Dyson, *The Euro at 10*, 378–413.
27. A. Rose, "One Money, One Market: Estimating the Effect of Common Currencies on Trade," *Economic Policy* 30 (2000), 9–45.
28. R. Baldwin. "The Euro's Trade Effects," ECB Working Paper No. 594. Frankfurt am Main, 2006.

29. Dyson and Quaglia, *European Economic Governance and Policies.*
30. D. Howarth and P. Loedel, *The ECB: The New European Leviathan* (Basingstoke: Palgrave, 2005).
31. Heipertz and Verdun, *Ruling Europe.*
32. Heipertz and Verdun, *Ruling Europe.*
33. Issing, *The Birth of the Euro.*
34. On which see H. Macartney and M. Moran, "Banking and Financial Market Regulation and Supervision," in Dyson, *The Euro at 10*, 325–40.
35. See Dyson and M. Marcussen, *Central Banks in the Age of the Euro.*
36. Dyson, *The Euro at 10*, 378–413.
37. See Issing, *The Birth of the Euro.*
38. Dyson, *The Euro at 10*, 1–34.
39. C. Goodhart, "The ECB and the Conduct of Monetary Policy: Goodhart's Law and Lessons from the Euro Area," *Journal of Common Market Studies* 44, no. 4 (2006), 757–78.
40. See Issing, *The Birth of the Euro.*
41. Baldwin, "The Euro's Trade Effects."
42. Dyson, *The Euro at 10*, 1–34.
43. Dyson, *The Euro at 10*, 1–34.
44. R. Duval and J. Elmeskov, *The Effects of EMU on Structural Reforms in Labour and Product Markets*, ECB Working Paper No. 596. Frankfurt am Main, 2006. S. Hauptmeier, M. Heipertz, and L. Schuknecht, *Expenditure Reform in Industrialised Countries: A Case Study Approach.* ECB Working Paper No. 634. Frankfurt am Main, 2006.
45. On which see Dyson, *The Euro at 10*, 378–413.
46. Dyson, *The Euro at 10*, 1–34.
47. Dyson and Sepos, *Which Europe?.*

CHAPTER 33

....

LISBON STRATEGY

....

ANNETTE BONGARDT AND FRANCISCO TORRES

33.1 OBJECTIVES AND BACKGROUND

At its March 2000 summit in Lisbon the European Council launched the European strategy for the knowledge-based economy (Lisbon Strategy).[1] It set a new strategic goal for the EU and defined an overall strategy to transform the European economy, within the ensuing decade (2000–2010), into "the most competitive and dynamic knowledge-based economy in the world capable of sustainable economic growth with more and better jobs and greater social cohesion." It aimed at: "Preparing the transition to a knowledge-based economy and society by better policies for the information society and R&D as well as by stepping up the process of structural reform for competitiveness and innovation and by completing the internal market; Modernizing the European social model, investing in people and combating social exclusion; Sustaining the healthy economic outlook and favorable growth prospects by applying an appropriate macro-economic policy mix."

The European Council thereby envisaged a radical transformation of the European economy towards a knowledge-driven economy, based on information and communication technologies, apt to meet the challenges of globalization. It held that an average economic growth rate of 3 percent of GDP and full employment were possible, provided that a broad range of measures were taken that would, directly or indirectly, facilitate the shift toward the information society. The main political orientations of the Lisbon Strategy comprised better policies for the information society; R&D and innovation policies; enterprise policy; economic reforms; macroeconomic polices; a renewed European social model; new priorities for national education policies; active employment policies, modernizing social protection in member states; national plans to combat social exclusion; and an improved social dialogue in managing change.[2]

The reform agenda was greeted as a new, common response to address the fundamental growth challenges facing the EU, given the accelerating pace of technological change, the internationalization of trade and investment (including outsourcing and the increasing tradability of services), and ageing populations. Growth became increasingly dependent on innovation. It was no longer driven by industrial production economies of scale and imitation of US technological advances, and the EU was approaching the technological frontier. The sustainability of the European model thus came to depend on the reform of outdated economic institutions and the adequate management of the paradigm shift to an innovation-based economic model of growth.[3]

The Lisbon Strategy, developed at subsequent meetings of the European Council, outlines an economic and social strategy meant to relaunch the EU within the changed context of worldwide competition and the paradigm shift to a knowledge economy and an innovation-based model of growth. The economic pillar was to create the basis for the transition to a competitive, dynamic knowledge-based economy, with emphasis on the need to adapt constantly to changes in the information society and to increase research and development. The social pillar was to modernize the European social model, investing in human resources and combating social exclusion. The member states were to invest in education and training and to conduct an active employment policy to facilitate the shift to a knowledge economy. The environmental pillar, added at the Gothenburg European Council meeting in June 2001, called attention for the need to decouple economic growth from natural resource utilization for sustainable development.

The Lisbon Strategy came to feature a multitude of partial targets and an even larger number of indicators.[4] The 2001 Nice Council adopted a list of EU key structural indicators with thirty-six key indicators, covering the general economic background, employment, innovation and research, economic reform, social cohesion, and the environment.[5] However, assessment of progress in the original Lisbon Strategy became based on over one hundred indicators. In 2003 a short list of fourteen main indicators was adopted, accompanied by a longer list of structural indicators.[6] In 2010 the set comprised seventy-nine indicators.[7]

Launching the Lisbon Strategy, the European Council provided a European-level approach to the need to increase productivity and competitiveness if the EU was to raise its living standard in the future and sustain its social model in the face of fiercer competition (the impact of globalization on goods and services sectors in Europe[8]) and new challenges (in particular technological change and the information society; demographic ageing). The importance of faster EU growth, and consequently the need to take advantage of globalization, was attributed to a variety of reasons, such as the sustainability of European varieties of the social model in the face of unfavorable demographics/an ageing population, the need to facilitate catching-up of new and future members, and the fact that low growth makes the political task of reform more difficult (or the EU's political influence[9] negligible). The 2010 sovereign debt crisis highlighted yet another factor, namely economic growth conditioning a country's capacity to service its debts. The need to face up to and make the most of the new drivers of competition shifted the focus on the EU's capacity to grow and on its ability to promote flexible adjustment. Knowledge and innovation were key objectives in the paradigm shift to a knowledge economy that the EU set out to effect, involving institutional, technological, and organizational changes.

The overarching aim of the strategy consisted in improving supply-side conditions so as to make the single European market deliver in the new setting. However, its implementation differed from that of the single market in terms of ultimate aims, intermediate objectives, means, and instruments.[10] The single market aimed at integration and growth. It was associated with narrow intermediate objectives (cuts on cost of cross-border transactions for products and services), precisely defined means (elimination of border controls; harmonization and approximation of laws), and effective instruments (EU directives; enforcement by case law of courts). In contrast, the Lisbon Strategy relied on broader objectives, softer means, and weaker instruments. It aimed at growth but also at social cohesion and employment. Its intermediate objectives were manifold, including advances in education and innovation, increase in R&D spending, liberalization of service industries, and increase in labor force participation and employment rates. Its means featured the definition of common targets, performance reporting, and benchmarking and joint monitoring, with instruments that were mostly national (spending, taxation, regulation).

The Lisbon Strategy came to reach beyond the single market, featuring market liberalization measures and structural reforms for economic, social, and environmental renewal. It thereby came to outline something like a European model.[11] That model may be characterized as aiming to make compatible and furthermore build on the efficiency-enhancing features of social and environmental protection (European values) in order to raise economic performance (EU competitiveness, productivity, and growth). The EU's capacity to shape governance at the global level, in line with its values, hinges on the delivery of the European model. The Lisbon Strategy's success, and that of its successor, the Europe 2020 Strategy formally adopted by the European Council in June 2010, ultimately hinges on achieving the necessary coordination to implement policies with a EU rationale as to realize the efficiency properties of the internal market when increased liberalization and market coordination themselves are not sufficient to do so.[12] The EU agreed on a loosely coordinated approach to welfare state and market-structural reform to make the EU economic system deliver. It allowed for accommodating the different national realities and preferences and could be implemented without Treaty change as such.

33.2 THE COMPETITIVENESS RATIONALE AND ENHANCED ECONOMIC COORDINATION

The Lisbon Strategy was motivated by competitiveness concerns in the context of a changed environment facing the EU. European advances in market liberalization were failing to translate into improved international competitiveness and higher growth. This was attributed to European structural problems and the need to face up to the new market and technological realities of the time, especially to the information society. Liberalization had been asymmetric across markets. In the case of services, market liberalization has lagged behind goods markets in the EU. The difficulty of regulation in the face of diverse national regulation contributed to more limited EU services market integration and network industry liberalization.[13]

The EU had been falling behind its major competitors in terms of productivity growth since the mid-1990s despite progress on the single European market. European productivity growth had gradually declined from levels that were higher than those of the US in the 1970s and 1980s, while US productivity growth had accelerated since 1995; US labor productivity growth had increased (from an average of 1.2 percent in the period 1990–1995 to 1.9 percent in 1995–2000), while EU labor productivity had slowed down (from 1.9 percent to 1.2 percent) in those same periods. At the same time, the EU's convergence process toward US levels of GDP per capita, going on during the late 1980s, had slowed down.[14] Insufficient innovation and under-investment and diffusion of information and communication technologies were regarded as key determinants in explaining the productivity gap between the EU and the US. Nevertheless, there were significant differences between member states, as the EU as a whole (at that time consisting of fifteen member states) but not all of its member states lagged behind the US in the paradigm shift regarding productivity in a knowledge economy.

Still, the existence of a GDP per capita gap between the EU and the US could not be ascribed to institutional failure alone but also to different preferences.[15] While lower GDP per capita in the EU might reflect institutional failure, i.e. a lower employment rate due to a disincentive to work in the face of high tax rates, it also reflects different European societal preferences for more leisure (shorter working days, longer holidays) as well as, for instance in the distribution sector, preferences for more urban, smaller-scale supermarkets rather than large, out-of-town supermarkets. Lower incomes could also provide an incentive for work (substitution and income effects might cancel out). Social systems also condition the (dis)incentives for work.[16]

For the EU to be able to take advantage of globalization and the new economy, the Lisbon Strategy had to target those factors that condition labor productivity and GDP per capita growth.[17] The EU had to tackle a structural productivity problem, rooted in systemic inadequacies of its innovation system, calling for an innovation-based economic model and reforms in the EU's innovation system and in its economic and regulatory environment.[18] In 2006 (the year before the US sub-prime crisis began that triggered the global financial and economic crisis in 2008), the EU productivity gap (GDP per hour worked) with respect to the US was mostly attributable to lower total factor productivity, and to a lesser extent to lower average qualification levels, whereas EU capital intensity was higher. The increase in the gap in growth and labor productivity, which had been observed for a decade, had come to a halt in 2006. EU GDP growth was 3 percent, with a GDP per capita growth rate (EU-27) of 2.6 percent (US 2.3 percent), employment growth increased to 1.6 percent, and the EU productivity per worker rose to 1.5 percent (US 1.4 percent). The upturn was regarded as cyclical, but as displaying a structural component linked to structural reforms in the member states, in particular in labor markets. The policy implication was that to close the gap the EU should give priority to policies that raised total factor productivity (such as information and communication technologies, research and development, innovation, competition, and better regulation, as well as measures that improved human capital).[19]

The Lisbon Strategy set out the case for reform in the EU, but with Lisbon objectives involving member-state competences in most policy areas, the reform agenda required close cooperation between the EU and the member states to achieve results. The changes in the external environment brought about by globalization and the new economy translate into competitive pressures facing economic agents, while their incentives and capacity to react or take a pro-active stance are conditioned by (the design of and incentives provided by) social and economic institutions. The Lisbon Strategy can be regarded as an exercise in policy coordination in response to the common need to create a conducive environment for flexible adjustment and growth.[20] It amounts to the acknowledgment that European competitiveness and growth require enhanced policy coordination between the EU and its member states that extends to many areas of national competency. The recognition of the interrelatedness of member states' economies, with the potentially significant consequences of their action or inaction for the EU, implied a step toward enhanced economic policy coordination and put the Lisbon Strategy at the center of European economic coordination. It translates into the recognition that the EU may transform the new realities—globalization, the new economy, subsequently climate change, but also population ageing—from potential threats into economic opportunities, provided the right framework conditions are created (liberalization, market institutions, policies) for the knowledge-based economy.

In the reality of European mixed economies, this obliged member states to redefine the role of the state in the economy (economic order) and jointly exercise authority in many policy areas formerly under their exclusive control. Member states had to harmonize or otherwise coordinate rules by which they interfere in the economy (regulation), so as to harvest the efficiency advantages of the single market.[21] (Market) institutions in member states were faced with the need for structural reform and coordination at the EU level. Those institutions had often been set up and shaped by the very different market and technological environment in the three decades following the end of World War II (relatively stable markets and technological trajectories, possibility of long-term planning); they had also been shaped by different national traditions and trajectories.

Coordination at the European level rests on economic and political arguments, notably promoting policy learning about best practices; enhancing the quality of reforms by providing a template for reform; spillovers; or working as a lever to counter opposition. The economic case for coordination at the European level importantly rests on the existence of positive or negative spillovers (one-directional externalities or bi-directional complementarities).[22] Coordination produces a net demand externality to the extent that productivity gains in a given member state give rise to an externality, through demand, in other member states.[23] Yet, structural reform in one country also puts pressure on others, thereby providing an incentive for them to become more productive.

The economic case for coordination then rests on the first effect being larger than the second.[24] An example for complementarities is provided by product and labor market (microeconomic) reforms and stabilizing fiscal and monetary (macroeconomic) policies. The political argument for EU coordination goes that reforms are painful. The idea underlying the Lisbon Strategy is therefore that structural reform is of common interest and, in addition, that peer pressure can foster implementation at the level of the European Council.

33.3 GOVERNANCE AND IMPLEMENTATION

The 2000 Lisbon Strategy drew on adapted and strengthened existing policy coordination mechanisms, namely the processes of Luxembourg (employment policies), Cardiff (functioning of goods, services, and capital markets), and Cologne (macroeconomic dialogue, links between macro- and microeconomic policies), besides the Broad Economic Policy Guidelines (BEPG) and the SGP. The BEPG are the central link in the coordination of the member states' economic policies and ensure multilateral surveillance of economic trends in member states, taking the form of a Council recommendation and, since 2003, they have been published for periods of three consecutive years. In addition, the Lisbon 2000 European Council adopted a new open method of coordination (OMC) as an instrument to facilitate implementation of the strategic goal, as the means of spreading best practices and achieving greater convergence towards the main EU goals. Economic reform, taking place principally under the Lisbon Strategy, occurred within the constitutional setting defined by the Maastricht treaty, with small changes under Amsterdam and Nice. Growing resistance to the use of traditional forms of European integration motivated the search for alternative ways of achieving common aims that limit the transfer of power to the Community level.[25]

The origins of the OMC go back to the European Employment Strategy (Luxembourg process), which became an integral part of the Lisbon Strategy. In the European Employment strategy, the OMC provided a new framework for cooperation between member states by directing national policies toward common objectives in areas which fall within the competence of the member states, such as employment, social protection, social inclusion, education, youth, and training.

The definition of the OMC had been undertaken in the run-up to the Lisbon European Council in order to develop the European dimension in new policy areas, and to foster policy learning against the background of common goals but different national realities. Following the Lisbon Summit conclusions, the OMC was implemented in different policy areas, namely information society policy, enterprise policy, the Cardiff process on economic reform, education policy, research policy, and social inclusion.[26]

The OMC designates coordination with open outcomes.[27] The OMC appears in the EU policy process due to structural reasons, most notably the long-term attempt of European policy-makers to get to grips with the problem of competitiveness, but it varies markedly across policy areas in terms of policy practices.[28] Depending on the areas concerned, the OMC involved "soft law" measures (binding on member states to varying degrees but never taking the form of directives, regulations, or decisions). In the context of the Lisbon process the OMC requires member states to draw up national action plans (in the original Lisbon Strategy; national reform programs under the post-2005 revised form of the Lisbon Strategy) and forward them to the Commission.

Before the OMC, policy areas were either of EU or national competence. Under the OMC intergovernmental method of "soft coordination," key policy areas remain a national competence but are recognized as being of common interest. Given that the policies to attain the Lisbon targets fell almost exclusively within the competence of the member states, the OMC provides a new framework for coordinated action between the member states in those areas, so as to direct national policies (and mobilize available resources) toward certain common objectives.

The OMC features four main ingredients: fixing common guidelines for national policies; developing indicators of national performance to compare best practice; asking countries to adopt national action plans to implement the guidelines; joint monitoring and review of results.[29]

Coordination was to be achieved by means of guidelines with specific timetables for reaching goals and by establishing, where appropriate, quantitative and qualitative indicators and benchmarks against the best in the world. The guidelines were to be adapted to national and regional policies by setting specific targets and subjecting their implementation to periodic monitoring, evaluation, and peer review. Member states were evaluated by one another, with the Commission's role being that of surveillance. The OMC operates through peer pressure at the level of the European Council (heads of state and government). Policy-makers from across the member states are to enter a process of comparing national approaches to the common policy goals and engage in dialogue and policy learning, drawing on techniques such as peer review, target and trajectory setting, definition of indicators, and benchmarking best practices.[30]

The European Council (coordinating the various Councils of Ministers and through its Spring Councils evaluating social and economic progress), the BEPG (to improve synergies between macroeconomic policies, structural policies, and employment policy), and the OMC were to provide a reinforced political engine at the European level for policy coordination and adaptation to national settings.[31] The Competitiveness Council was created in 2002 to give an opinion on all matters affecting competitiveness and foster coordination of different policies with an impact on competitiveness (such as the internal market, industrial policy, competition policy, and R&D). In July 2007, it redefined the Lisbon objective of a competitive EU economy as a competitive, low-carbon economy.

The original strategy evolved into an overly complex structure with multiple goals and actions and an unclear division of responsibilities and tasks, particularly between the EU and national levels.[32] In July 2003 the Sapir Report, "An Agenda for a Growing Europe," elaborated by a high-level independent study group established on the initiative of the European Commission president, had confirmed the objectives of the Lisbon

Strategy as rightly ambitious, but criticized an excessive number of targets and a weak method.[33] The report, which came to furnish the intellectual basis for the (revised) Lisbon Strategy, recommended a focus on growth and the improvement of coherence between EU policies and instruments and between decision-makers at the EU and national levels. It proposed a six-point agenda for reforms, composed of policies for promoting growth and modes of delivery (governance and budget).

The Lisbon Strategy was subject to a mid-term review in 2005. The Kok report, prepared under the guidance of Wim Kok, the former prime minister of the Netherlands, took stock of (the lack of) progress on the Lisbon Strategy at the end of 2004.[34] It concluded that the Lisbon Strategy had not delivered on objectives and results and identified four causes, namely an overloaded agenda; poor coordination; conflicting priorities; and lack of determined political action. The report advocated improving the governance of the Lisbon Strategy by a three-legged approach, namely national reform programs (NRP) coordinated by EU guidelines, an EU budget with adequate resources and priorities with respect to the Lisbon objectives, and benchmarking as a coercion mechanism for poor performers. The governance system of the reformed Lisbon Strategy fell short of recommendations and came to rely on NRPs, with EU budget reform postponed and benchmarking through comparative performance indicators watered down. Coordination of reforms rested on the Integrated Guidelines for Growth and Jobs, which established numerous objectives (without priorities and without differentiating between countries) and which were to be the basis for the evaluation of NRPs by the Commission.[35] To overcome member states' lack of willingness to adopt reforms, and given the European Commission's limits (lack of clout, possibility to impose sanctions in order to implement certain kinds of reforms), the Kok report had suggested the method of naming, shaming, and faming, proposing an annual ranking with which the European Commission would praise the positive achievements of member states and criticize negative aspects. However, the 2004 European Council did not accept such a recommendation, thereby critically undermining benchmarking.[36] Stakeholder involvement in NRPs was to augment national ownership of reforms. However, communication remained the Achilles heel of the Lisbon process.[37]

The Lisbon Strategy was relaunched subsequent to the mid-term review in 2005 as the EU's Agenda for Growth and Jobs. It resulted in a refocus on results (the achievement of stronger, lasting growth and the creation of more and better jobs), put in place a new governance structure based on a partnership approach between the EU and the member states, and defined four priority areas for the revised Lisbon Strategy: research and innovation; investing in people/modernizing labor markets; unlocking business potential, particularly of small and medium-sized enterprises (SME); and energy/climate change.

The new governance structure was based on a partnership approach to better guide and monitor economic policy reform for growth and employment through the following principal governance instruments: Integrated Guidelines (instrument of coordination, outlining the key macroeconomic, microeconomic, and labor market reform priorities for the EU as a whole); NRPs (substituting the previous national action plans), designating documents prepared by the member states on their reform efforts for a three-year cycle, which indicate the instruments to be used to achieve their economic policy objectives); Country-specific recommendations (considered a major innovation of the revised Lisbon Strategy of 2005 and the chief mechanism for exerting peer pressure on member states); Community Lisbon Program (European Commission program, created in 2005 with the objective to report on the European dimension of the Lisbon Strategy); Commission's Annual Progress Report (an annual evaluation by the European Commission on progress on the implementation of the Lisbon Strategy that includes policy proposals for the European Council); and the OMC.[38]

The coordination process was simplified in terms of programming and monitoring of results. The Integrated Guidelines for growth and employment were from then on to be presented jointly with the guidelines for macroeconomic and microeconomic policies, over a three-year period. They serve as a basis both for the Community Lisbon Program and for the NRPs. One single progress report was to facilitate better monitoring of implementation. On the whole, the progressive integration of economic governance in the Lisbon process, characterized by the emergence of a new accommodation between hard and soft law, may constitute the biggest change in governance of the last decade. It went together with the adoption of the OMC in additional domains.[39] This raises the question to what extent the Lisbon process has lived up to reform expectations and delivered, notably on improving competitiveness of the EU as a whole and of member states.

33.4 DELIVERY OF RESULTS AND THE PACE OF ECONOMIC REFORM

Despite some progress, the EU has not managed to close the delivery gap between commitments and actions. If measured against its stated objectives, notably the impact on growth, employment, or R&D, the EU has failed to reach its main targets for 2010 on employment—e.g. a total employment rate of 70 percent, a 60 percent employment rate for women, a 50 percent employment rate for workers aged fifty-five or older—and on economic growth—i.e. a 3 percent real GDP growth rate, but also R&D spending (a 3 percent gross domestic expenditure on R&D as percent of GDP). The EU also has still to catch up with the US and Japan in terms of employment and R&D, while EU GDP growth in 2008 was larger than US or Japanese growth.[40]

Disappointment with the underperformance of the Lisbon Strategy met with the difficulty to measure the structural component, complicated by the economic cycle and the impact of public policies, but also external events, such as the sudden burst of the internet bubble, the downturn in the international economic climate in the aftermath of September 11, 2001, the impact of the two EU enlargements in 2004 and 2007 (which raised the number of EU member states from fifteen to twenty-seven), and, last but not least, the 2008 global financial and economic crisis and the 2010 sovereign debt crisis.

The 2009 Swedish presidency[41] concluded that it was necessary "to further improve competitiveness and increase the EU's sustainable growth potential, refocusing policies towards long-term reforms in an ambitious and revamped new strategy." Despite the persisting productivity growth gap with leading industrialized economies and the fact that a causal link between Lisbon reforms and results (growth and jobs) could not always be demonstrated, the European Commission[42] insisted that reforms adopted under the Lisbon Strategy delivered tangible benefits for EU citizens and businesses (in the form of increased employment, a more dynamic business environment with less bureaucracy, and more sustainable growth). Other benefits included the promotion of a broader consensus on reform needs (which set the agenda for reform in member states, focusing on the four priority areas and promoting the flexicurity concept), of policy learning, and of common actions by member states to address the central long-term challenges facing the EU, paving the way for a more coordinated response to the global financial crisis and the subsequent European sovereign debt crisis.

The effectiveness of Lisbon instruments in fostering reforms relevant for growth and employment proved mixed at best.[43] On balance, the (twenty-four) integrated guidelines[44] were too broad (insufficiently action-oriented) as to have a significant influence on member state policy-making. Likewise, country NRP (followed by annual updates, the implementation reports), mirroring the integrated guidelines, largely failed to become effective instruments of mutual learning and were instead used by member states as a low-impact reporting mechanism. The country-specific recommendations, resulting in politically (if not legally) binding guidelines to member states, have been adopted, since March 2007, on an annual basis by the Council upon a Commission recommendation.[45] They increasingly brought to the surface structural problems of member states, yet their impact on the pace of reform was less evident. They could have been more effective if they had better pinned down the issues at stake, had been better integrated with other instruments such as the SGP, and had been supported by a transparent and robust evaluation framework. As for the OMC, it fared poorly as a source of peer pressure and as a forum for sharing good practice. Still, new OMCs were launched under the Lisbon Strategy, including research policy and entrepreneurship.[46]

As for the pace of economic reform in the EU, the EU's overall record on economic policy reform points to a slow pace of reform and uneven progress across member states and policies. On the basis of the EU's short list of structural indicators (including economic, social, and environmental categories) most member states somehow moved toward their Lisbon targets, but few came close to actually meeting them.[47] As a result, in 2010 (EU-27) the gap between the best and the worst performers was wider than in 2000 (EU-15). Well-performing member states went ahead with more ambitious reforms, while others built up a (sizeable) delivery gap.[48] The 2010/2011 World Competitiveness Report[49] confirmed the existence of persistent competitiveness differences between EU members. Other things being equal, the member states with less progress on the Lisbon Strategy will have a lower innovation capacity and lower productivity and employment levels. Progress in chief Lisbon policy areas (innovation, liberalization, enterprise, employment and social inclusion, and sustainable development policies) reveals that overall progress is never excellent although significant differences remain between policy areas; the same holds for member states' progress (best and worst performers) on the Lisbon Agenda[50] (to eurozone and non-eurozone members alike).

The fact that progress in some areas (employment, macroeconomic dimensions) was more pronounced than in others (microeconomic dimensions) caused important benefits and synergies between member state policies to be missed. The objective of promoting more policy integration across macroeconomic, employment, and microeconomic (including environment) dimensions was only partially achieved. Possible synergies of the Lisbon Strategy with existing programs and instruments (such as the SGP, the Sustainable Development Strategy, or the Social Agenda) went unrealized since they operated in isolation and other major policy priorities, such as financial market integration, were absent from the strategy.[51]

33.5 ECONOMIC REFORM UNDER THE EUROPE 2020 STRATEGY AND THE CRISES CONTEXT

The financial and economic crisis and the subsequent sovereign debt crisis have reinforced the case for economic coordination in the EU. The former exposed some member states' persisting structural weaknesses (low progress on the Lisbon Strategy), that is, low competitiveness of national economies and low growth potentials, and the need for economic recovery and growth lent urgency to compliance with the objectives of the Lisbon Strategy and its successor, the Europe 2020 Strategy (smart, sustainable. and inclusive economy, re-establishment of a high potential growth trajectory). The sovereign debt crisis made it plain that member states had insufficiently accounted for negative spillovers from the economic part of the union to the monetary side of EMU (eurozone).

The Europe 2020 Strategy, molded on the Lisbon Strategy, was presented as a response to the global financial and economic, and, one may add, climate crisis. However, its adoption in 2010 came to coincide with the transformation of the crisis into the sovereign debt crisis, whose resolution called for enhanced economic coordination reaching beyond the new strategy.

Europe 2020 builds on the governance framework of the revised Lisbon Strategy of 2005 without substantive innovation in terms of instruments.[52] The Commission is to elaborate, in a synchronized way, reports on member states' progress on augmenting their competitiveness and growth potential with specific recommendations. Specific country reports and recommendations should make member states' non-compliance more visible. The member states' stability and growth programs and their national simplified reform programs are to be evaluated together, thereby reinforcing the cohesion of economic policy coordination between the national budgetary policies and growth-relevant policies. However, the Integrated Guidelines, which guide national economic reforms, still only mention interdependencies among policy areas and do not acknowledge reform interdependencies across member states explicitly. As for coordination between policy areas within and across member states, the situation as compared to the Lisbon Strategy is left unaltered, calling for a careful analysis of the nature and incidence of spillovers, if the latter are to be addressed effectively.[53]

Economic governance advances hence resume, on the one hand, to a stronger recognition of interdependencies between national budgetary policies and national simplified reform programs (competitiveness and growth potential) and, on the other hand, to the attempt to increase pressure on bad performers to implement Lisbon reforms in the continued absence of sanctions.[54] The Europe 2020 Strategy provides instruments to address competitiveness problems (rooted in factors like inflexible labor markets, uncompetitive wage developments, inflated public sectors, unsustainable social systems) and the consequent low growth potential of given member states; it also provides instruments to prioritize spending on those areas that are growth-enhancing and put the economy on a sustainable path. A mix of pressure by financial markets (increasing risk premiums) and the eurozone (member states, ECB) prompted some anticipation of budgetary consolidation in potentially insolvent or illiquid member states so as to cut deficits faster and further than initially agreed to in their stability and growth programs. Member states thereby started to address the need to bring back under control the ballooning deficits and debts after the rescue of national financial systems and/or increased spending in the face of the financial and economic crisis. Member states have begun to implement reforms that may address underlying competitiveness problems and the causes of low growth (hence improve their standing in financial markets), but this can often be ascribed to external (market) pressure rather than the result of soft coordination.

The outbreak of the sovereign debt crisis in 2010 prompted urgent attempts at coordinated action and some step-by-step evolution in economic governance in the face of the unfolding crisis and the risk of contagion to other member states in the eurozone, putting at risk even the survival of the euro. In the first half of the 2010, the eurozone responded to the Greek debt crisis, providing IMF and bilateral credits to Greece; in the summer of 2010 the EFSF was set up as a provisional facility until 2013, used by Ireland in the autumn of 2010; and the European Council December 2010 summit in Brussels agreed on a permanent rescue fund (ESM) for all eurozone members from 2013 onwards, which was subsequently anticipated to mid-2012. The sovereign debt crisis came to expose important spillovers between economic policy coordination (under the Lisbon and Europe 2020 strategies and the SGP) and monetary policy (the need for increased labor market flexibility and sustainable public finances) in the eurozone in the face of the unsustainable financial positions of given member states. The crises led to a wider recognition that the causes of the negative externalities needed to be tackled so as to avoid the insolvency or illiquidity of member states and justify the coordination measures adopted, but were at the outset fraught with insufficient economic and fiscal coordination mechanisms. As for economic coordination (and in the absence of sanctions in the Lisbon and the Europe 2020 Strategies' context), conditionality regarding economic reform made its appearance, but only as a by-product of crisis solution mechanisms in the face of unsustainable fiscal positions. This has meant that financial assistance was also made conditional on progress on the Lisbon Strategy and its successor (implementation of structural reforms and market liberalization measures) to augment competitiveness and potential growth.

Notes

1. Council of the European Union, *Conclusions of the Lisbon European Council*, Council of the European Union SN 100/00, March 23–4, 2000.
2. Maria João Rodrigues, "Introduction: For a European Strategy at the Turn of the Century," in Maria João Rodrigues, ed., *The New Knowledge Economy in Europe* (Cheltenham: Edward Elgar, 2002), 14–23.
3. André Sapir, Philippe Aghion, Giuseppe Bertola, Martin Hellwig, Jean Pisani-Ferry, Dariusz Rosati, José Viñals, and Helen Wallace, *An Agenda for a Growing Europe. Making the EU Economic System Deliver* (Oxford: Oxford University Press, 2004), 35–8.
4. Susan Senior Nello, "The Lisbon Strategy and Beyond," in Susan Senior Nello, *The European Union: Economics, Policies and History* (Maidenhead: McGraw-Hill, 2009), 167–81.
5. European Commission, *Structural Indicators*, COM (2001) 619 final, October 30, 2001b.
6. European Commission, *Commission Staff Working Document in support of the report from the Commission to the Spring European Council, March 22–3, 2005, on the Lisbon Strategy of economic and social and environmental renewal*, SEC (2005) 160 of 28.1.2005.
7. Eurostat, 2010, <http://epp.eurostat.ec.europa.eu/portal/page/portal/structural_indicators/indicators>.
8. Jürgen Kröger, "Globalization: Beneficial for Whom?," in Pompeo Della Posta, Milica Uvalic, and Amy Verdun, eds, *Globalization, Development and Integration—A European Perspective* (Basingstoke: Palgrave Macmillan, 2009), 321–5.
9. Alberto Alesina and Francesco Giavazzi, *The Future of Europe: Reform or Decline* (Cambridge, MA: MIT Press, 2006).
10. Sapir et al., *An Agenda for a Growing Europe*, 103–5.
11. Annette Bongardt and Francisco Torres, "Is the EU Model Viable in a Globalized World?," in Della Posta et al., *Globalization, Development and Integration*, 215–31.
12. Annette Bongardt and Francisco Torres, "Institutions, Governance and Economic Growth in the EU: Is There a Role for the Lisbon strategy?," *Intereconomics—Review of European Economic Policy* 42, no. 1 (January/February 2007), 32–42.
13. Sapir et al., *An Agenda for a Growing Europe*, 105–8.
14. European Commission, *European Competitiveness Report 2001*, SEC 1705, Commission Staff Working Paper, October 30, 2001a.
15. Olivier Blanchard, "The Economic Future of Europe," *Journal of Economic Perspectives* 18, no. 4 (Fall 2004), 3–26.
16. For a categorization of European varieties of the social model and a discussion of the (dis)incentives provided by social systems in Europe, notably their efficiency properties (financial sustainability) and equity (probability of avoiding poverty), see André Sapir, "Globalisation and the Reform of European Social Models," Bruegel Policy Brief 1 (November 2005).

17. The growth rate of GDP per capita is determined by changes in population, employment and labor productivity. GDP per capita growth is determined by the variation of labor productivity (GDP growth divided by hours worked) and the variation of labor utilization (the number of hours worked per capita). The variation of labor utilization can be decomposed into the variation of the employment rate and the variation of the number of hours worked per person. Labor productivity can be explained by investment levels/capital intensity (including human capital, technology adoption) and the effects of this investment (total factor productivity, the residual factor). Total factor productivity captures competitiveness gains, the productive creation and utilization of knowledge, or a favorable regulatory environment.

18. For an analysis of the deterioration of the EU's productivity performance relative to that of the US from the mid-1990s, see European Commission, *Commission Staff Working Document in support of the report from the Commission to the Spring European Council, March 22–3, 2005, on the Lisbon Strategy of economic and social and environmental renewal*, SEC (2005) 160 of 28.1.2005.

19. European Commission, *Raising productivity growth: Key messages from the European Competitiveness Report*, COM (2007) 666 final, 2007.

20. Bongardt and Torres, "Institutions, Governance and Economic Growth in the EU."

21. Jacques Pelkmans, "An EU Subsidiarity Test is Indispensable," *Intereconomics* 41, no. 5 (2006), 249–54; Patrick Messerlin, "Liberalising Services Trade in the EU," *Intereconomics* 40, no. 3 (2005), 120–4.

22. Eckehard Rosenbaum, "Lisbon, Europe 2020, and the Case for Soft Coordination in EU Policymaking," *Intereconomics* 45, no. 5 (2010), 287–92.

23. For every 1000-euros growth in a member state about 200-euros benefits accrue to other member states through trade. European Commission, *Europe 2020. A strategy for sustainable growth and jobs*, contribution from the President of the European Commission to the informal meeting of heads of state and government of February 11, 2010.

24. Charles Wyplosz, "The Failure of the Lisbon Strategy," <VoxEU.org> (January 2010).

25. Iain Begg, "Economic and Social Governance in the Making: EU Governance in Flux," *European Integration* 32, no. 1 (January 2010), 1–16.

26. Maria João Rodrigues, *European Policies for a Knowledge Economy* (Cheltenham: Edward Elgar, 2003), 19–23.

27. Dermot Hodson and Imelda Maher, "The Open Method as a New Mode of Governance: The Case of Soft Economic Policy Coordination," *Journal of Common Market Studies* 39, no. 4 (2001), 719–46; Rodrigues, "Introduction: For a European Strategy at the Turn of the Century."

28. Claudio Radaelli, "The Open Method of Coordination: A New Governance Architecture for the European Union?," Swedish Institute for European Policy Studies, Report no. 1 (March 2003).

29. European Council, *Conclusions of the Lisbon European Council*.

30. Sapir et al., *An Agenda for a Growing Europe*, 103–5.

31. Rodrigues, *European Policies for a Knowledge Economy*, 18–19.

32. European Commission, *Lisbon strategy evaluation document*, Commission Staff Working Document, SEC (2010) 114 final, February 2, 2010b.

33. Sapir et al., *An Agenda for a Growing Europe*.

34. Wim Kok, ed., *Facing the Challenge: the Lisbon Strategy for Growth and Employment*, Report for the High-Level Group chaired by Wim Kok (November 2004).

35. Jean Pisani Ferry and André Sapir, "Last Exit to Lisbon," Bruegel Policy Brief 2 (March 2006).

36. Joachim Fritz-Vannahme, Armando García Schmidt, Dominik Hierlemann, and Robert Vehrkamp, "Lisbon—A Second Shot," *Spotlight Europe* (Bertelsmann Stiftung, February 2010), 3; Wyplosz, "The Failure of the Lisbon Strategy."

37. European Commission, *Lisbon strategy evaluation document.*

38. European Commission, *Lisbon strategy evaluation document.*

39. Begg, "Economic and Social Governance in the Making."

40. See Eurostat, <http://epp.eurostat.ec.europa.eu/portal/page/portal/structural_indicators/indicators>.

41. Council of the European Union, Presidency Conclusions on the Brussels European Council, December 10–11, 2009, <www.europa.eu-un.org/articles/en/article-9310-en.htm>.

42. European Commission, *Lisbon strategy evaluation document.*

43. European Commission, *Lisbon strategy evaluation document.*

44. Adopted by the Council in 2005 and updated in 2008, they were to provide multi-annual general guidance and policy orientations, providing the foundations for the NRP and constituting the basis for country-specific recommendations.

45. That country-specific policy advice, from economic to employment policy, is based on articles 99(2) and 128(4) of the Treaty on the Functioning of the European Union. It is submitted by the European Commission to the European Council and the Council and translates the Commission's assessment of member states' progress toward achieving their objectives set out in their NRP.

46. As for research policy, the OMC approach (including the 2002 Barcelona European Council headline Lisbon target of spending 3 percent of EU GDP on R&D) had proved more useful in terms of policy learning than in terms of policy coordination, leading to the relaunch of the European Research Area with stronger policy coordination in response to a 2008 evaluation. The entrepreneurship OMC is based on benchmarking techniques and includes specific projects and the use of scoreboards.

47. Simon Tilford and Philip Whyte, *The Lisbon Scorecard X. The road to 2020* (Brussels: Centre for European Reform, 2010).

48. Tilford and Whyte, *The Lisbon Scorecard X.* Lisbon league table of ranking of overall member state progress on Lisbon indicators in 2009 (2008 in brackets): 1. Sweden (1), 2. Austria (4), 3. Denmark (2), 4. The Netherlands (3), 5. Finland (5), 6. Germany (8), 7. Ireland (6), 8. United Kingdom (7), 9. France (10), 10. Czech Republic (9), 11. Slovenia (14), 12. Luxembourg (12), 13. Belgium (13), 14. Cyprus (15), 15. Estonia (11), 16. Lithuania (17), 17. Latvia (16), 18. Slovakia (18), 19. Spain (19), 20. Portugal (21), 21. Poland (24), 22. Greece (20), 23. Hungary (23), 24. Italy (22), 25. Bulgaria (25), 26. Romania (26), 27. Malta (27).

49. World Economic Forum, "The Global Competitiveness Report 2010–2011" (2010).

50. Tilford and Whyte, *The Lisbon Scorecard X.*

51. European Commission, *Lisbon strategy evaluation document.*

52. European Commission, *Europe 2020. A strategy for smart, sustainable and inclusive growth,* COM (2010) 2020 final, Brussels, March 3, 2010a.

53. Rosenbaum, "Lisbon, Europe 2020, and the Case for Soft Coordination in EU Policymaking."

54. Annette Bongardt and Francisco Torres, "The Competitiveness Rationale, Sustainable Growth and the Need for Enhanced Economic Coordination," *Intereconomics—Review of European Economic Policy* 45, no. 3 (May/June 2010), 136–41.

....

CHAPTER 34

CAP*

....

FRANCIS SNYDER

34.1 INTRODUCTION
....

The CAP was the EEC's first (and for a long time only) common policy. Following the trauma of World War II, it was based partly on the idea that the EEC should if possible be self-sufficient in food. Its purposes were not solely economic, however.[1] It was premised on the notion of "agricultural exceptionalism." Socially and morally, as well as economically, agriculture was considered a special sector. Based on family farms, it required governmental protection. Though building on pre-war national agricultural policies, the CAP was an essential part of post-war European welfare states; it extended the welfare state to farmers.[2] In the early years of European integration, the CAP also had political objectives; in France its welfarist orientation was intended partly to guarantee rural political stability.[3] These features were clearly visible in the concept of "agriculture" that was elaborated in CAP law.[4] Its basic idea was that public policy should support agricultural production and regulate access to agricultural markets.

Many of the CAP's underlying assumptions and basic principles have remained the same since the 1960s. By the mid-1980s, however, the CAP was no longer central to the politics of European integration.[5] Since then, due to both endogenous and exogenous factors, its policy objectives, fundamental rules, and organizational structures have largely been transformed. This chapter traces its evolution, discusses major reforms, and identifies future challenges. It emphasizes the impact of the international context, changes in regulatory goals and instruments within a stable Treaty framework, the interpretative role of the ECJ, and the need for further reform.

34.2 FOUNDATIONS
....

The 1957 Rome Treaty provided that the common market shall extend to agriculture and trade in agricultural products.[6] It also stated that for agriculture, unlike industrial products, there should be a common policy. The objectives of the CAP were to increase agricultural productivity, thus to ensure a fair standard living for the agricultural community, to stabilize markets, to assure the availability of supplies, and to ensure that supplies reached consumers at reasonable prices. The ECJ has consistently recognized a wide discretion on the part of the Commission and the Council in balancing these competing objectives. The basic European Community rules on free movement of goods applied to agricultural products. However, European Community competition rules often gave way to agricultural policy and law.

The Rome Treaty provided several organizational forms for the CAP, but politics determined which prevailed. In principle, the CAP included a price and market policy and a structural policy on the modernization of farms. Until recently, twenty-one different agricultural products were subject to distinct regulatory schemes called common organizations of the market. Though often diverse, they regulated such matters as product coverage, production year, intervention purchases by governmental authorities, roles of producer associations, product quality, and import and export. For major products, the European Community set target prices and intervention (floor) prices to stabilize markets and guarantee producer incomes. Variable import levies protected European Community producers from less expensive imports. Export subsidies enabled European Community producers to export at low prices ("dump") surplus products on the world market. Costs were underwritten by consumers through high food prices, instead of being recouped in a more equitable way through progressive taxation.

Structural policy initially took second place. Directives on the modernization of farms, cessation of farming, and socio-economic guidance and training were adopted in the early 1970s. They were replaced in 1985 by a regulation on improving the efficiency of agricultural structures. Schemes were introduced in 1987 to preserve the countryside by encouraging conversion from surplus to non-surplus products and extensification in the sense of reducing output without increasing other production costs. A set-aside scheme to take land out of production was introduced in 1988. The CAP gradually expanded to include a regional policy. Numerous initiatives encouraged the formation of producer groups, protection of traditional specialties, and designations of origin, rural development, and environmental protection.

These institutions and mechanisms served to implement the basic principles of common prices, common financing, and Community preference; a further principle, producer responsibility, developed later. The ECJ played an active role in supervising the application of CAP law, interpreting the Treaty and secondary legislation, channeling and legitimating the exercise of legislative and executive discretion, and defining and to some extent protecting the rights and entitlements of litigants. From the legal standpoint, the CAP appeared to be a classic uniform EEC policy.

However, the CAP was distinctive in two respects. First, it was essentially a semi-autonomous sub-sector of EEC law and policy. It always occupied a disproportionate share in EEC policy, at least relative to its contribution to employment or gross domestic product. Even as late as the 1980s, it accounted for more than two-thirds of the EEC budget, Commission staff, EEC legislation, and ECJ case law. Today, the CAP amounts to about 40 percent of the EU budget. Almost inevitably, many basic principles of EU constitutional and administrative law, such as respect for human rights or general principles of law, were elaborated by the ECJ in cases involving the CAP. Nevertheless, the CAP itself was conceived explicitly as a form of economic (and to some extent social) regulation, an essentially technical instrument for achieving specific policy goals in a particular economic sector. Consequently, CAP legislation was overwhelmingly in the form of regulations.[7] It continued to be adopted by the consultative procedure, despite periodic treaty reforms introducing new legislative procedures for other policy areas.

Second, though appearing to be a uniform policy, the CAP actually served as a Community umbrella with considerable room for diverse national policies. Following a brief period of European Community-wide agricultural prices, turbulence on international currency markets led the European Community to introduce special intra-European Community border taxes and levies ("monetary compensatory amounts") and special exchange rates ("green currencies") in the agricultural sector in the early 1970s. This ended common prices, and the ensuing control over exchange rates gave member states scope to operate their own agricultural policies. Agri-monetary differences continued after the establishment of the single currency and are likely to endure until all member states belong to the eurozone. Agri-monetary legislation, incomprehensible to all except a few specialists, accentuated the CAP's character as a semi-autonomous area of European Community policy and law.

34.3 REFORMS

For years, reforms were inhibited by the CAP's complexity, its corporatist governance by national governments, farmers' organizations, and European Community institutions, vested agricultural interests in different member states, and the increasing diversity of agricultural structures with the continual European Community enlargement.[8] Beginning in the mid-1980s, however, three factors contributed to CAP reforms.

First, cost: direct costs of the CAP included increasing expenditure on disposal, destruction or storage of surplus production or, depending on the relation between European Community prices and world market prices, on "dumping" surplus production on the world market. Indirect costs included higher food prices for consumers, welfare costs for citizens, and input costs for the secondary processing industry; environment pollution and health risks, such as the "mad cow" disease (bovine spongiform encephalopathy—BSE), due to productivity-oriented intensive farming; and skewed distribution of expenditure, disproportionately paid to larger farmers and first-stage processing companies.

Second, enlargement: most countries which joined the European Community in May 2004 and January 2007 differed considerably from previous member states in farm structure, agricultural employment, agricultural productivity, environmental protection, health and safety standards, and administrative capacity. In enlargement negotiations direct income payments and production limits were particularly contro-versial issues.[9]

Third, globalization of agriculture and of agricultural regulation: While external fac-tors have always been significant in the CAP,[10] neither endogenous nor external factors alone were sufficient conditions for reform. Nonetheless, the WTO Agreement on Agriculture was decisive in crystallizing pressures for reform at a particular time and in determining the range of acceptable policy instruments.[11] This is not to deny the impor-tance of other factors, including the costs of the CAP, enlargement, or the political acu-men of Agriculture Commissioners Ray MacSharry (1989–1993) and Franz Fischler (1995–2004), but simply to emphasize the complex interrelationship between endog-enous and external factors.

CAP reform began modestly in the mid-1980s. To control agricultural expenditure the Community introduced dairy quotas (1984) and budgetary stabilizers (1988). The ECJ interpreted the Treaty to broaden CAP objectives, for example to include public health, control of agricultural surpluses, availability of agricultural products to non-food industries, and consumer protection.[12] Overall, however, the CAP remained much the same from its origins to 1992.

External factors provided a decisive stimulus for reform. The 1986–1994 Uruguay Round multilateral trade negotiations included agriculture. Negotiations between the US and the EU broke down in 1990 as a result of deadlock on agriculture issues. They resumed only after Ray MacSharry initiated reforms of the CAP. The WTO Agreements came into effect on January 1, 1995. The Agreement on Agriculture established limits on domestic agricultural support, provided for the conversion of variable levies into cus-toms duties ("tariffication"), and placed severe restrictions on export subsidies.

The MacSharry reforms reduced dramatically the price of cereals, a key product; shifted price support partially to direct compensatory payments; and required the set-aside of land from cereals production. They introduced the idea of "multi-functionality." With an agri-environmental program and subsidies for afforestation, farmers were to act as stewards of the environment, though this remained ancillary to their role as pro-ducers. The reforms altered the policy and legal instruments through which farmers were supported, as agricultural policy gradually opened up to broader international, environmental, and consumer interests. Overall, however, they preserved the core of the CAP.

Litigation frequently involved challenges to the reforms.[13] The ECJ legitimated the reforms by continuing to recognize the broad discretion of the European Community legislator in cases concerning priorities among CAP objectives, the changing scope of CAP's legal basis, or the relatively limited role of fundamental rights in the field of agri-culture. The Council was able to reduce domestic prices close to world market prices and to make compensatory payments to cereals producers,[14] or to impose maximum guaranteed quantities for production of raw tobacco.[15] After the Council reformed arrangements for importation of bananas, the ECJ rejected numerous challenges to the new market organization, even though the WTO Appellate Body held that it was con-trary to WTO law.[16] The ECJ found that differential treatment of importers was inherent in market integration, that WTO law, as GATT law, was not directly effective and does not confer rights on individuals, and that the concept of acquired rights and the principle of equality should be interpreted narrowly.[17] It held consistently that there is no legal right to a specific production level, market price, or market share.[18]

Following the Uruguay Round, the US and other countries put greater pressure on the EU to reduce domestic agricultural support as part of the 2001 Doha Development Agenda. Franz Fischler, previously Austrian agricultural minister, became Commissioner for Agriculture in 1996. He initiated reforms culminating in the 2003 "mid-term review" (MTR), which, despite its name, involved the most important CAP reforms to date.

In response to international pressures, increasing surpluses and costs, and forthcoming enlargement, the Commission in 1998 issued a major policy paper.[19] This paved the way for further, partial reforms. In 1999, the European Council in Berlin agreed to reduce price support, extend direct payments, continue to finance set-aside, cap farm payments to the largest farms ("modulation"), and transfer some costs to national governments. These reforms have been described as "a watershed: for the first time a major country was outvoted with respect to a major policy reform."[20] Complementing the price and market policy, a new policy for rural development was introduced.[21] Agri-monetary arrangements were established for the euro. Despite the looming challenge of EU enlargement, these reforms did not reduce total CAP costs.[22] Nevertheless, they provoked a debate on the simplification of the CAP, echoing the broader Community policy shift at the Lisbon Summit and in the Better Regulation agenda. In June 2001, the Small Farmers Scheme (SFS) was adopted to simplify administrative procedures by creating for small farmers a voluntary, flat-rate payment decoupled from production.[23] It provided a model for the Simplified Approach later applied in the CEECs.

Not all reforms stemmed, however, from deliberate European Community policy. Food crises had a major impact on the CAP. The "mad cow" crisis led to the reorganization of the Commission Agricultural Directorate-General and related committees. It set in train fundamental reforms of European food safety policy that contributed to the subsequent disaggregation of the CAP as a semi-autonomous policy field. The ECJ upheld European Community measures in the face of legal challenges.[24] The culmination was the general European Community Food Law in 2002.[25] Legislation was also enacted to prevent certain animal by-products from entering the food chain,[26] to control genetically modified food and feed[27] and to ensure its traceability and labeling,[28] and to control additives used in animal nutrition.[29] Food safety, the management of food risks, and the relationship of Community standards to international standards became major political and legal issues.

The most significant reforms of the CAP were the 2003 Fischler reforms. A Single Farm Payment (SFP) scheme cut the link between income support and production.[30] It was open to farmers who maintained their land in good agricultural condition and complied with standards on public health, animal and plant health, the environment and animal welfare ("cross-compliance").[31] This was closely linked to budgetary reforms. The level of payments to large farms was reduced ("modulation"), and gradually increasing funds were to be switched to rural development. Decoupling of payments from production shifted much European Community agricultural support to the WTO Agreement on Agriculture "green box," meaning that it was classified in WTO law as causing limited or no market distortion. Subsequently the ECJ, in refusing to allow the retroactive application of the post-reform system of penalties concerning cross-compliance, emphasized that the reforms established a "new regulatory context."[32]

Though the Fischler reforms constituted a significant change compared to the 1960s CAP, they were still based on the idea that the government should support farmers' incomes. Due to political compromises, 25 percent of direct area payments remained tied to production.[33] Total agricultural spending was not substantially reduced. There was little change in distribution of expenditure across countries. Only about 3 percent of resources were shifted to rural development. Except for rice, the reforms had little effect on border protection. Export subsidies were not reduced.[34] A major Commission report in 2007 showed that the implementation of cross-compliance was often problematic.[35] Nevertheless, the Fischer reforms reoriented the CAP and facilitated international agricultural negotiations.

34.4 THE CAP TODAY

The reforms led by McSharry and especially by Fischler shaped today's CAP.[36] In 2005, the European Community enacted rules on support from the European Agricultural Fund for Rural Development (EAFRD)[37] and simplified budgetary rules.[38] It applied a Single Area Payment Scheme (SAPS), based on a flat-rate per hectare of land for all farmers, in most new EU member states. Consistently with its "Better Regulation Initiative,"[39] the Commission in 2006 issued proposals for further simplification of the CAP by updating and consolidating legislation and harmonizing rules covering markets for different agricultural products in respect of intervention, private storage aids, import tariff quotas, export refunds, safeguard measures, promotion of the product, state aids, and reporting obligations.[40] New legislation was adopted on tariff import quotas.[41]

The basic regulation on the application of competition rules in the agricultural sector was revised.[42] Legislation was adopted to protect agricultural products and foodstuffs as traditional products guaranteed[43] and geographical indications and designations of origin.[44] In 2007, as part of the CAP "Health Check" foreseen by the 2003 reforms, the Commission proposed a complete shift to flat-rate payments per hectare on a national or regional basis, a cap of payments to larger farmers, the end of export refunds by 2013, the abolition of set-aside, an end to dairy quotas by March 31, 2015, an increased rate of modulation, and a review of cross-compliance conditions.[45]

By October 2008, the twenty-one previously separate sectoral CAP market organizations had been unified in a single legal framework,[46] except for fresh fruit and vegetables and wine to be unified later. The CAP's basic principles, as modified most recently by the

Fischler reforms, continued to apply after this simplification of CAP legislation. These principles applied, however, within a CAP that was more market-oriented, concerned not only with farm incomes but also with rural development and the environment, and that was more flexible, leaving more room for member states.[47] Certain agricultural product markets have been completely restructured; an example is sugar, for which the European Community quota system was reformed following a challenge in the WTO.[48] New rules on private storage aids were adopted.[49]

In the interests of transparency, member states are now required to publish information on the beneficiaries of CAP payments.[50] Reports so far show that large farms, agri-business, and multinational processing and exporting companies are the main beneficiaries.[51] They indicate that further reforms of the CAP are required, including the redefinition of CAP objectives. New common rules for direct support schemes were enacted in January 2009 to extend decoupling of direct support, simplify the Single Payment Scheme, increase flexibility of standards, and provide further for environmental protection.[52] Rules on export refunds were recast,[53] pending eventual abolition foreseen for 2013.

The ECJ has usually rejected challenges to these further reforms. Following its established case law on direct and individual concern, it held that restrictions on forestry aid in a programming document approved by the Commission, in accordance with the basic regulation on support for rural development from the European Agricultural Guidance and Guarantee Fund, should be regarded as a measure of general application.[54] Drawing on the WTO Agreement on Trade-Related Measures of Intellectual Property (TRIPS), bilateral agreements, and/or European Community legislation, it has upheld the strict application of Community legislation on geographical indications protecting Greek feta cheese,[55] Hungarian Tokaj wine,[56] and French Provençal honey,[57] even though enforcement throughout the European Community remains the task of the member state where the protected product originates.[58] On the whole, the ECJ has remained faithful to its established practice of limited judicial review of the exercise of legislative discretion concerning the CAP.

The Lisbon Treaty, amending existing Treaties, resulted in a general TEU and a detailed TFEU.[59] It will to some extent disappoint CAP reformers. It states the same CAP objectives and mechanisms[60] as the 1957 Rome Treaty, though judicial interpretation has of course supplemented the Treaty considerably. Now the Union, not the Community, has responsibility for the CAP,[61] but this can be seen as a reminder of a missed opportunity to redefine the CAP.

There are, however, important changes, and signs of more in future. The CAP is no longer a semi-autonomous policy field. The Lisbon Treaty unified the three pillars inherited from the preceding Treaties. The agricultural provisions are in the TFEU,[62] not the TEU. They can be amended by the simplified procedure.[63] The Union and the member states now share competence for agriculture. Consequently, agricultural law-making is governed by the principle of subsidiarity.[64] This aligns the CAP with the majority of EU policies today and recognizes the increasing role played by member states in making basic rules as well as implementing the CAP. Recent case law testifies to this role concerning matters such as animal welfare,[65] the scope and rates of support in the wine sector,[66] defining certain terms for compensatory allowances,[67] or adapting payments to national agricultural practices.[68]

The voting procedure for adopting CAP legislation is now the co-decision procedure.[69] This represents a major change from previous Treaties, where the European Parliament played a marginal role. It recognizes that wider social perspectives need to be taken into account in making CAP policies. Indeed, in one recent case, the ECJ affirmed that "there can be no question but that the requirements of the protection of public health must take precedence over economic considerations."[70] The European Community legislator continues to enjoy wide discretion. However, the ECJ has held that the legislator must be able to demonstrate that it has taken into consideration all relevant factors, such as labor costs or potential effects of reforms.[71] The CAP today thus differs considerably from that of the 1960s.[72]

34.5 CONCLUSION

Controversial from the outset, the CAP for years represented a distinctive type of economic and social regulation within EU law. Fortunately, this special status has virtually disappeared today. The CAP, though still significant, is now merely one among many EU policies. Its development since the early years of European integration also reflects the broader transformation in the purposes, structure, and functions of EEC/ European Community law more generally. These include broader public participation, an opening-up to diverse interests, simplification and better regulation concerns, and a redefinition of relations between the EU and its member states, for example in matters of competence and subsidiarity. The CAP also offers an instructive example of how government support for domestic agriculture throughout much of the world copes with today's challenges of internationalization and globalization. A steady decline in the agricultural population in most EU member states, EU enlargement, changing public concerns, and integration into the WTO legal framework have altered the role of governments in the EU agricultural sector and have contributed to the redefinition of CAP objectives.[73]

Three questions, however, remain open. First, to what extent should agriculture, farming, rural development, or environmental protection be supported by EU public funds within the framework of the CAP, as distinguished from within other EU policy frameworks or even being paid for by national governments?[74] Particular causes of concern are the facts that EU subsidies continue to play such a large role in farm incomes and that they are so unequally distributed, even to non-farmers. Second, to what extent can the reformed CAP achieve its broader aims, such as consumer protection, animal welfare, and protection of the environment, within the current WTO framework? The challenges to the EU's precautionary principle in the *Beef Hormones*[75] and the *GMO*[76] cases exemplify international constraints on such behind-the-border measures. Third, how can EU policies on agriculture, rural development, food safety, and environmental protection contribute to the achievement of social justice in the world, and notably to the eradication of poverty and hunger? So far, the responses of the EU, other developed countries, and the international community as a whole have proved shockingly inadequate.[77] These questions will occupy policy-makers, scholars, and citizens in the future.

Notes

*   This chapter was written mainly at Peking University Law School, Beijing, China. Thanks to Dean Zhu Suli, Professor Song Ying, and Ms Yin Ming for their support and to Luo Linshan (PKU) and K. L. Thiratayakinant (LSE) for research assistance.

1.   See K. Patel, ed., *Fertile Ground for Europe? The History of European Integration and the Common Agricultural Policy since 1945* (Baden-Baden: Nomos, 2009).

2.   See A.-C. L. Knudsen, *Farmers on Welfare: The Making of Europe's Common Agricultural Policy* (Ithaca: Cornell University Press, 2009).

3.   See *Fertile Ground for Europe?*.

4.   See "The Special Legal Status of Agriculture: Assumptions and Contradictions in Economic Law," in Snyder, *New Directions in European Community Law* (London: Weidenfeld & Nicolson, 1990), 100–45.

5.   N. P. Ludlow, "The Green Heart of Europe? The Rise and Fall of the CAP as the Community's Central Policy, 1858–1985," in Patel, *Fertile Ground for Europe?*, 79–96.

6.   See F. Snyder, *Law of the Common Agricultural Policy* (London: Sweet & Maxwell, 1985).

7.   See F. Snyder, "The Use of Legal Acts in EC Agricultural Policy," in G. Winter, ed., *Sources and Categories of European Union Law: A Comparative and Reform Perspective* (Baden-Baden: Nomos, 1996), 348–84.

8.   On CAP politics, see Grant, *The Common Agricultural Policy* (London: Macmillan, 1997).

9.   Kosior, "New Stakeholders in the Common Agricultural Policy," *European Law Journal* 11, no. 5 (September 2005), 566–85.

10. See A. Swinbank and C. Daugbjerg, "The 2003 CAP Reform: Accommodating WTO Pressures," *Comparative European Politics* 4, no. 1 (2006), 47–64; T. Josling, "External Influences on CAP Reforms: An Historical Perspective," in J. F. M. Swinnen, ed., *The Perfect Storm: The Political Economy of the Fischler Reforms of the Common Agricultural Policy* (Brussels: Centre for European Policy Studies, 2008), 57–75.

11. *EEC Measures on Animal Feed Proteins*, Panel Report adopted March 14, 1978, L/4599, BISD 25S/49, was the first of many challenges to the CAP which the European Community lost in GATT and WTO.

12. See F. Snyder, "The Common Agricultural Policy in the Single European Market," in *Academy of European Law, Collected Courses of the Academy of European Law*, Volume II, Book I (Dordrecht: Martinus Nijhoff, 1992), 303–36.

13. R. Barents, "Recent Developments in Community Case Law in the Field of Agriculture," *Common Market Law Review* 34 (1997), 811–43; C. Blumann, "Les implications de la sécurité alimentaire dans l'évolution de la Politique agricole commune," in J. Bourrinet and F. Snyder, eds, *La sécurité alimentaire dans l'Union européenne* (Brussels: Bruylant, 2003), 69–93; C. Blumann, *Politique agricole commune: Droit communautaire agricole et agro-alimentaire* (Paris: Litec, 1996).

14. Case C-353/92 *Greece v Council* [1994] ECR I-3437.

15. Joined Cases C-300/93 and C-362/93 *Crispoltoni and Others v Fattoria Autonoma Tabacchi and Donatab* [1994] ECR I-4863.

16. *EC—Regime for the Importation, Sale and Distribution of Bananas,* WT/DS/27/R, Appellate Body report adopted September 25, 1997.

17. See e.g. Case C-280/96 *Germany v Council* [1994] ECR I-5039 and Case T-19/01 *Chiquita Brands International and Others v Commission,* [2005] ECR II-315.

18. e.g. Case C-295/03P *Alessandrini and Others v Commission* [2005] ECR I-5673.

19. Commission of the European Communities, *Agenda 2000. The Future of European Agriculture. Explanatory Memorandum* (Brussels: Commission of the European Communities, 1998).

20. J. Pokrivcak, C. Crombez, and J. F. W. Swinnen, "Impact of External Changes and the European Commission on CAP Reforms: Insights from Theory," in Swinnen, *The Perfect Storm,* 9–24, at 12.

21. Council Regulation 1257/1999/EC, May 17, 1999.

22. R. W. Ackrill, "CAP Reform 1999: A Crisis in the Making?," *Journal of Common Market Studies* 38, no. 2 (June 2000), 343–53.

23. Council Regulation 1244/2001/EC, June 19, 2001.

24. See e.g. Case C-180/96 *United Kingdom v Commission and Council* [1998] ECR I-2265; Case C-1/00 *Commission v France* [2010] ECR I-9989; Case C-393/01 *France v Commission* è2003] ECR I-5405; Case C-511/03 *Staat der Nederlanden (Ministerie van Landbouw, Natuurbeheer en Visserij) v Ten Kate Holding Musselkanaal BV and Others* [2005] ECR I-8979.

25. Regulation 178/2002/EC of the European Parliament and of the Council, January 28, 2002.

26. Regulation 1774/2002 of the European Parliament and of the Council, October 3, 2002.

27. Regulation 1829/2003/EC of the European Parliament and of the Council, September 22, 2003.

28. Regulation 1830/2003/EC of the European Parliament and of the Council, September 22, 2003.

29. Regulation 1831/2003/EC of the European Parliament and of the Council, September 22, 2003. See also Case T-13/99 *Pfizer* [2002] ECR 3305.

30. Council Regulation 1782/2003/EC, September 29, 2003 and implementing rules.

31. The Amsterdam Treaty was the first to include a Protocol on Animal Welfare.

32. Case C-420/06 *Rüdiger Jager v Amt für Landwirtschaft Bützow* [2008] ECR I-01315.

33. Daugbjerg, "The Sequencing of Public Policy: The Evolution of the CAP over a Decade," *Journal of European Public Policy* 16, no. 2 (April 2009), 395–411, at 406.

34. See A. Olper, "Constraints and Causes of the 2003 EU Agricultural Policy Reforms" and J. F. M. Swinnen, "The Political Economy of the Fischler Reforms of the EU's Common Agricultural Policy: The Perfect Storm?," in Swinnen, *The Perfect Storm,* 83–101 and 135–66, respectively.

35. European Commission, Report, COM (2007) 147 final, March 29, 2007.

36. See also D. Bianchi and M. Fischer Boel, *La Politique Agricole Commune (PAC): Toute la PAC, rien d'autre que la PAC!* (Brussels, Bruylant, 2006); Blumann, "Les implications de la sécurité alimentaire dans l'évolution de la Politique agricole"; Blumann, *Politique agricole commune:* commune"; J.-C. Bureau, *Politique agricole commune* (Paris: Repères, La Découverte, 2007); J.-C. Bureau and L.-P. Mahé, "CAP Reform Beyond 2013: An Idea for

a Longer View," *Studies & Research* 64, *Notre Europe*, Paris, May 2008; L.-P. Mahé and F. Ortalo-Magné, *Politique Agricole: un modèle européen* (Paris: Presses de Sciences-Po, 2001).

37. Council Regulation 1698/2005/EC, September 20, 2005.
38. Council Regulation 1290/2005/EC, June 21, 2005.
39. Commission, Communication, COM (2005)535 final, October 25, 2005.
40. Commission, Communication, COM (2005)509 final, October 19, 2005.
41. Commission Regulation 1301/2006/EC, August 31, 2006.
42. Council Regulation 1184/2006/EC, July 24, 2006, as amended.
43. Council Regulation 509/2006/EC, March 20, 2006.
44. Council Regulation 1791/2006/EC, November 20, 2006. See also *EC—Protection of Trademarks and Geographical Indications for Agricultural Products and Foodstuffs*, WT/DS174/R, WT/DS290/R, Panel report adopted April 20, 2005.
45. Commission, Communication, COM (2007) 722 final, November 20, 2007.
46. Council Regulation 1234/2007/EC, October 22, 2007.
47. See also A. Burrell, "The CAP: Looking Back, Looking Ahead," *European Integration* 31, no. 3 (May 2009), 271–89.
48. *EC—Export Subsidies on Sugar*, WT/DS265,266, 283/AB/R, Appellate Body report adopted May 19, 2005.
49. Commission Regulation 826/2006/EC, August 20, 2008.
50. Council Regulation 1290/2005/EC, as amended.
51. See <http://ec.europa.eu/agriculture/funding/index_en.htm and www.farmsubsidy.org>. See also D. Carvajal and S. Castle, "Europe's 50 Billion Euro Harvest," *International Herald Tribune*, Friday, July 17, 2009, 1; L. Clavreul, "Et les 'gagnants' sont…," *Le Monde*, jeudi, 30 avril 2009, 3.
52. Council Regulation 73/2009, EC, January 19, 2009, with implementing rules on specific support being provided by Commission Regulation 639/2009/EC, July 22, 2009.
53. Commission Regulation 612/2009/EC, July 7, 2009. For non-Annex I products (secondary processing), see Commission Regulation 1043/2005, June 30, 2005.
54. Case T-108/03 *Elisabeth von Pezold v Commission, Rec.* 2005, II-655, [2005] ECR II-00655.
55. For example, Joined Cases C-465/02 and C-466/02 *Federal Republic of Germany and Kingdom of Denmark v Commission, Rec.* 2005 I-9115, [2005] ECR I-09115.
56. For example, Case C-347/03 *Regione autonoma Friuli-Venezia Giulia and Agenzia regionale per lo sviluppo rurale (ERSA) v Ministero delle Politiche Agricole e Forestali* [2005] ECR I-3785.
57. Case T-35/06 *Hönig-Verband eV v Commission*, 8, [2007] ECR II-02865.
58. Case C-132/06 *Commission v Italy* [2008] ECR I-0547.
59. TEU consolidated version, OJ 9.5.2008 C115/13; TFEU consolidated version OJ 9.5.2008 C115/47.
60. Article 39 TFEU.
61. Article 38(1) TFEU.
62. TFEU, Part Three, Title III.
63. Article 48 TEU, which states that Part III TFEU [including agriculture] can be amended by the simplified procedure.
64. Article 2(2)(d) TFEU. On conferral and subsidiarity, see Article 5 TEU. Environmental policy continues as before to be a matter of shared competence: Article 4(2)(e).
65. e.g. Case C-455/06 *Heemskerk BV and Firma Schaap v Productschap Vee en Vlees* [2008] ECR I-08763; Case C-491/06 *Danske Svineproducenter v Justitsministeriet* [2008] ECR I-03339.

66. e.g., Case T-370/05 *French Republic v Commission* [2008] ECR nyr.

67. Case C-78/07 *Inspettorato Provinciale dell'Agricoltura di Enna and Others v Domenico Valvo* [2008] ECR II-1635.

68. Case C-446/06 *A.G. Winkel v Minister van Landbouw, Natuur en Voedselkwaliteit* [2008] ECR I-1167.

69. Article 43(2) TFEU.

70. Case T-257/07 R *French Republic v Commission* [2007] ECR II-4153, para 141.

71. Case C-310/04 *Kingdom of Spain v Council* [2006] ECR TBA.

72. As a result, "today's critiques often seem to ignore the fact that the reformed CAP no longer generates distortions which approach in magnitude those of the production-oriented CAP of the 1960s"(Bureau and Mahé, "CAP Reform Beyond 2013," 42).

73. The proportion of people employed in agriculture as compared to total employment was about 25 percent in EEC-6 in 1957, 7.6 percent in EC-10 in 1981, and 4.5 percent in EU-25 in 2008. For the first two figures, see Snyder, *Law of the Common Agricultural Policy*, at 6 and 3 respectively. For the last figure, see European Commission, Agriculture and Rural Development, <http://ec.europa.eu/agriculture/agvista/2008/table_fr/3513.pdf> (last accessed October 16, 2009).

74. With due regard for partial comparisons, in the early 1980s subsidies made up 40 percent to 60 percent of agricultural incomes in France; even today, throughout the EU, "incomes net of subsidies are negative in many sectors…, even for top recipients of payments." On the first, see V. Bivar, "Land Reform, European Integration, and the Industrialization of Agriculture in Postwar France," in Patel, *Fertile Ground for Europe?*, 119–37, at 119. On the second, see Bureau and Mahé, "CAP Reform Beyond 2013," 44.

75. *EC—Measures Concerning Meat and Meat Products (Hormones)*, WT/DS26,48/AB/R, Appellate Body report adopted February 13, 1998 was the first among numerous cases in this long-standing saga.

76. *EC—Measures Affecting the Approval and Marketing of Biotech Products*, WT/DS291, 292, 293/R, Panel Report adopted November 21, 2006.

77. See A. Mahiou and F. Snyder, eds, *La sécurité alimentaire/Food Security and Food Safety* (Leiden: Martinus Nijhoff for the Hague Academy of International Law, 2006).

CHAPTER 35

....

REGIONAL AND STRUCTURAL FUNDS

....

DERMOT HODSON

ROADSIDE signs acknowledging support under the cohesion or structural funds—as the principal instruments of EU regional policy are known—are a common sight in many parts of Europe. For some, these signs represent the emergence of the EU as a redistributive power and an expression of solidarity between rich and poor regions. For others, such signs might be seen as evidence of European pork barrel politics and the need for national governments to be seen to win from negotiations over the Community budget.

However EU regional aid is viewed, the fact remains that this area of policy has experienced a rapid rise to prominence in recent decades. In the mid-1970s, Community expenditure on regional policy constituted just 5 percent of the total budget. At the beginning of the 2010s, this figure is closer to 36 percent, making cohesion the second most important category of expenditure after the CAP. EU regional aid is also more widely dispersed than CAP expenditure; the regular farm labor force of the EU-27 currently stands at 27 million people, while an estimated 120 million people live in a region that qualifies for regional funding under the convergence heading alone.

Significant though the sums of money involved in EU regional policy are—347 billion euros were set aside for the cohesion and structural funds over the period 2007–13—they are small when compared to regional transfers in other political systems. The United States, for example, will spend an estimated 2.3 trillion euros on federal grants to state and local governments over the same period.[1] EU regional policy nonetheless provides a valuable case study for students of EU politics and policy-making. The cohesion funds are the original, and still the most important, test case of the EU's emergence as a system of multilevel governance in which national, sub-national, and supranational authorities jostle for position. The comparative development of EU regions also provides a critical case study for understanding the spatial effects of economic integration and the conditions under which policy interventions can and cannot tackle regional inequalities.

This chapter introduces readers to these and other debates concerning the political economy of EU regional policy. Section 35.1 discusses the key stages in the development of this area of EU decision-making from the Treaty of Rome to the Treaty of Lisbon. Section 35.2 introduces the concept of multilevel governance. Section 35.3 explores debates over the economic rationale for the cohesion and structural funds. Section 35.4 looks at ongoing debates concerning the future of EU regional policy.

35.1 THE EVOLUTION OF EU REGIONAL POLICY

The preamble to the Treaty of Rome (1957) expressed the desire of the EEC's founding member states "to strengthen the unity of their economies and to ensure their harmonious development by reducing the differences existing between the various regions and by mitigating the backwardness of the less favored." This intention was not matched by a dedicated regional policy instrument, although the Treaty did provide for the ECSC Funds, which sponsored restructuring in coal-mining regions, the ESF, which offered training to workers, and the EAGGF, which invested in rural communities, indirectly encouraging the economic development of disadvantaged regions.

It was not until 1975 that EEC member states set aside a specific pot of money for regional aid. The European Regional Development Fund (ERDF) allocated 1.3 billion units of account (roughly 4 percent of the Community budget) during the planning period 1975–1977 for investment under two main headings: infrastructure and investment.[2] The first of these headings included support for the chemical, food, and automotive sectors, while upgrading roads and port facilities are among the activities that fell under the second. All regions receiving regional aid from national governments were eligible for funding under the ERDF, which was expected to supplement rather than substitute for national expenditure on regional policy in keeping with the principle of "additionality."

A sharp increase in regional imbalances following the first enlargement of the EEC in 1973 was among the driving factors behind the development of a Community regional policy at this juncture. Denmark's Gross Domestic Product (GDP) per capita at this time was around 114 percent of the Community average, making it the richest member state.[3] Ireland's was around 63 percent, making it by far the poorest. The EEC's ill-fated plans to achieve EMU by 1980, which Kenneth Dyson discusses in Chapter 32, this volume, also encouraged the creation of the ERDF, amid concerns that asymmetric shocks (economic disturbances with a disproportionate impact on specific countries or regions) could make it difficult to irrevocably fix exchange rates. The creation of a regional development fund was also politically convenient, as it helped to compensate the UK for its substantial net contributions to the Community budget.

From the very outset, the ERDF was criticized for allocating too little money to too many regions and objectives.[4] The case for a reform of the structural funds was further strengthened by the Southern enlargement of the EEC—Portugal's GDP per capita, for example, was a little over half of the Community average in 1986—and by fears that poorer and less competitive regions could be disadvantaged by plans to complete the single European market. The SEA (1987) included a new title on strengthening economic and social cohesion—the first time the "c" word was used in the Treaty—and invited the Commission to submit a proposal to the Council to clarify the ERDF and other structural funds.

The Commission's reform proposal resulted in the so-called Delors I package, which allocated ECU 69 billion (roughly 31 percent of the Community budget) to regional policy over the period 1989–93.[5] This substantial increase in EU regional aid was accompanied by a new set of policy priorities. Objective 1, which received around two-thirds of the total funds available, focused on development and structural adjustment in regions with below average incomes. Objectives 2 and 3 focused on areas affected by industrial decline and long-term unemployment respectively. Youth employment was the focus of Objective 4, while Objective 5 concentrated on different aspects of rural, agricultural, and aquacultural development.

The Delors 1 package also established a new set of principles for EU regional policy alongside that of additionality. The principle of concentration called for the structural funds to be targeted at a limited number of regions on the basis of a limited number of objectives. The principle of partnership stressed the need to involve national, subnational, and EU institutions in the formulation and implementation of EU regional policy. Multiannual programming emphasized the importance of strategic planning and analysis for effective regional policy.

The revival of plans for EMU in the late 1980s reignited concerns about the effects of deeper economic integration on poorer regions.[6] EEC leaders responded by creating a new financial instrument to help the poorest member states to meet the Maastricht Treaty's convergence criteria. The Cohesion Fund was aimed primarily at improving transport infrastructure in member states with a GDP per capita below 90 percent of the Community average. Four countries, Ireland, Greece, Portugal, and Spain, received a combined total of ECU 15.5 billion in cohesion funding over the period 1993–1999 as part of the Delors II package, which increased overall funding for EU regional policy to ECU 168 billion (around one-third of the Community budget).[7]

Agenda 2000, the successor to Delors II, set aside 213 billion euros for the structural and cohesion funds (around one-third of the Community budget) over the period 2000–2006.[8] The EU's Eastern enlargement was a key reason for this increase in regional aid, with eight out of the ten Central and Eastern European countries that acceded between 2000 and 2004 doing so with a GDP per capita of less than 60 percent of the Community average. Agenda 2000 also introduced a new streamlined set of policy objectives for EU regional policy focusing on development and structural adjustment on regions facing income inequality (Objective 1), the economic and social conversion of areas facing structural difficulties (Objective 2), and the adaptation and modernization of policies and systems of education, training, and employment (Objective 3).

The EU's financial perspectives for the period 2007–2013 allocated 347 billion euros (35.7 percent of the EU budget) to the structural and cohesion funds.[9] Roughly 80 percent of this funding has been allocated to a new "convergence" objective, which covers regions with GDP per capita below 75 percent of the EU average. Regions that do not meet this criteria are entitled to funding under a new "regional competitiveness and employment" objective, which, in name at least, reflects EU policy-makers' concern that the structural funds should support the Lisbon Strategy for Growth and Jobs and its successor, Europe 2020. This change is accompanied by a new "European territorial cooperation" objective that provides funding for cross-border, transnational, and interregional cooperation.

Among the changes of significance for regional policy introduced by the Lisbon Treaty, which entered into force in December 2009, is the inclusion of policies to promote economic, social, and territorial cohesion among the shared competences of the EU and its member states. The precise meaning of territorial cohesion is unclear— the Commission's 2008 Green Paper on this concept asks for, rather than offers, a definition[10]—but it is likely to place greater weight on concerns over development, sustainability, and good governance in future reforms of EU regional policy.[11]

35.2 Multilevel Governance Under the Microscope

EU regional policy constitutes an important test case for multilevel governance. This theory of EU policy-making, of which George Pagoulatos and Loukas Tsoukalis say more in Chapter 5, this volume, challenges state-centric conceptions of the EU, which view member states as the main driving force behind (and the chief beneficiaries from) European integration. Instead, multilevel governance sees the EU as a battleground between national, sub-national, and supranational authorities in which central governments can, and occasionally do, cede control as a consequence of collective decision-making.

The initial stages of EU regional policy-making are, Marks concedes in his pioneering work on multilevel governance, dominated by national governments.[12] Decisions regarding the allocation of EU financial resources to regional policy and the distribution of these funds between member states take place within the context of the EU financial perspectives, an agreement that sets multi-annual expenditure ceilings for different categories of EU expenditure. The final agreement on the financial perspectives is concluded by the Council of Ministers, the European Parliament, and the European Commission. Before it reaches this stage, however, the financial perspectives go to the European Council, where the heads of state and government must unanimously agree on the size of the budget and the sums allocated to regional aid and other areas of Community expenditure.[13]

Intergovernmental bargaining over the sums spent on EU cohesion policy is intense and issue linkage with other areas of EU policy-making is commonplace. For example, the doubling of the structural funds in the financial perspectives in the Delors I package can be understood as a "side payment" designed to secure the support of poorer member states for plans to complete the single market.[14] Likewise, the decision to stabilize spending on EU cohesion policy in the financial perspectives for 2000–2007 helped to assuage the concerns of net contributors to the EU budget concerning the costs of enlargement.

The need to reach agreement among all member states over the formulation of EU regional policy means that pork barrel politics is hard to avoid. The financial perspectives covering the period 2007–2013 are no exception. The decision to grant an additional 75 million euros in regional funding to Bavaria, one of Europe's richest regions, looked like a fairly blatant attempt to reduce Germany's net contribution to the EU budget.[15] Likewise, the offer of additional "phasing-in" funding under the regional competitiveness objective presumably helped to soften the blow to Spain from losing its entitlement to funding under the convergence objective.

Intergovernmental bargaining reduces the redistributive character of EU cohesion policy and challenges the principle of concentration. In negotiations for the programming period 2007–2013, member states had full discretion to decide on which regions qualify for aid under the regional competitiveness and employment objective. As a result, some 63 percent of the EU's total population lives in a region that is entitled to funding under this heading. The Commission has, in contrast, ensured greater concentration in relation to the convergence heading by restricting entitlement to regions with GDP per head of less than 75 percent of GDP.[16] This might explain why just 35 percent of the total EU population lives in a region entitled to funding under the convergence objective during the period 2007–2013.[17]

The structural programming stage of EU cohesion policy, which determines how funds are spent at the national and sub-national level, provides greater scope for Commission involvement, according to proponents of multilevel governance. The 1988 reform of EU cohesion policy, Hooghe and Marks suggest, made an important difference in this respect by requiring member states to negotiate detailed programming documents, known as Community Support Frameworks, with the Commission.[18] The Commission did not always gain the upper hand in such negotiations, the authors contend, because of a lack of resources and authority, but it did exert significant influence in those member states that were most reliant on the EU as a source of finance for regional development.

Multilevel governance also stresses the involvement of sub-national actors in EU cohesion policy. Under the 1988 reforms, member states were invited to involve local and regional authorities in all stages of structural programming. This invitation was more readily extended and accepted in some member states than in others, Marks and Hooghe find.[19] In Belgium, for example, regional authorities played a pivotal role in the preparation of Regional Development Plans, negotiations with the Commission over the Community Support Frameworks, and the design, implementation, and monitoring of Operational Programmes (OPs). In the United Kingdom, in contrast, the central government dominated all stages of structural programming.

The role of sub-national actors in EU politics is neither exogenously determined nor channeled exclusively though central governments, according to multilevel governance. The process of European integration, it is argued, has encouraged local and regional authorities to become autonomous actors in their own right. This transformation, Hooghe and Marks contend, has affected some member states (e.g. Spain and Germany) more than others (Ireland and the UK) but local and regional authorities are now omnipresent in the EU political arena.[20] The channels of influence in this regard, they suggest, include the establishment of local and regional representations in Brussels, the forging of ties with the Commission, Council, Parliament, and other regions, and the consultative role of the European Committee of the Regions.

Critics of multilevel governance point towards a gradual renationalization of EU cohesion policy over the last two decades. Successive reforms to structural programming, Allen argues, have diluted the dialogue between member states and the Commission over the formulation and implementation of regional policy initiatives.[21] At the beginning of the 2007–2013 programming period, each member state was required to prepare a National Strategic Reference Framework (NSRF) explaining how structural and cohesion funds would be spent and identifying a list of OPs. Although Commission approval is required for (certain aspects of) the NSRF, it is a more strategic and therefore less detailed document than the Community Support Frameworks, making it harder for the Commission to exert influence over member states.

Bachtler and Mendez contest this conclusion.[22] Reforms to the EU cohesion policy have, they concede, made it harder for the Commission to promote detailed changes to specific regional policy measures, but the EU executive can and does influence regional policy priorities. The Commission has, moreover, traded a more hands-off role in relation to structural programming for greater leverage over the management and delivery of structural funds. As such, claims that EU cohesion policy has been renationalized are, in the opinion of the authors, exaggerated.

35.3 THE EQUIVOCAL ECONOMICS OF EU REGIONAL POLICY

Questions over the effectiveness of EU regional policy seem to be of second-order importance for scholars of multilevel governance. This is surprising, as it is unclear why national, sub-national, and supranational actors would battle over comparatively small sums of money unless they served a clear purpose. Economists have looked at this issue in greater detail, although they remain ambivalent about the precise rationale for EU regional policy and its impact on regional inequalities.[23]

The Solow growth model, a mainstay of traditional economic theory, predicts that poor regions will grow faster than rich regions as the rate of return on capital in the latter diminishes, thus reducing differences in per-capita income over the long run. This effect will be reinforced by regional integration, according to traditional trade theory, since the removal of barriers to cross-border capital flows will allow investors to move from rich to poorer regions in search of higher rates of return.

Modern economic theories are more circumspect about the ability of market forces to redress regional inequalities and hence more open to the idea of regional policy. Endogenous growth theory, for example, allows for the possibility that richer regions can experience permanently higher rates of economic growth than poorer regions by relaxing assumptions about the existence of diminishing returns to scale and/or allowing for spillover effects from research and development and other forms of human capital formation. This effect is reinforced in the new economic geography, which suggests that regional integration could lead to a concentration of economic activity in "core" regions as firms seek to take advantage of the economies of scale and access to larger and richer consumer markets.

Empirical estimates concerning the evolution of regional inequalities within the EU are sensitive to the underlying statistical techniques.[24] Early cross-sectional studies, which were based on Ordinary Least Squares (OLS) estimators, conclude that real convergence is occurring between European regions at a very slow pace: 2–3 percent per annum in the 1960s and less than 2 percent thereafter. More recent studies, which employ sophisticated but not undisputed dynamic panel data techniques, suggest that the rate of real convergence between EU regions could be considerably higher.

Economists, as Waltraud Schelkle notes in Chapter 20, this volume, are also divided over the extent to which the EU can claim credit for this reduction of regional inequalities. Boldrin and Canova find no evidence that EU structural funds have had a significant impact on income inequality between EU regions.[25] Leonardi provides a more positive assessment, claiming that roughly one-third of the EU's original Objective 1 regions achieved GDP levels of greater than 75 percent of the EU average within fourteen years.[26] By some measures, the rate of convergence among Objective 1 regions, he suggests, was also significantly higher than for non-Objective 2 regions, suggesting that EU regional policies are reducing regional inequalities.

The effectiveness of EU regional polices appears to vary across EU member states and regions. Sapir et al. find that the bulk of real convergence in the EU over the period 1980–2002 was concentrated in Ireland and Eastern Germany. Spain, Greece, and Portugal experienced only modest catch-up growth during this period while the Mezzogiorno region of Italy experienced none at all.[27] Puga concludes that income inequalities between EU member states fell by 25 percent over the period 1982–1995 but rose by 10 percent between sub-national regions within the EU.[28] This suggests that real convergence between countries is taking place at the expense of real divergence within countries.

There is also a growing body of opinion among economists that the effectiveness of EU regional policies depends on the underlying institutional factors. Ederveen, de Groot, and Nahuis, for example, find that the success of EU structural policies over the period 1960–1995 was conditional on economic openness, institutional quality, corruption and synthetic indicators of good governance.[29] For example, European Regional Development Funding appears to have had a more positive effect in very open economies, such as Ireland, than in comparatively closed economies, such as Spain.

35.4 THE FUTURE OF EU REGIONAL POLICY

EU regional policy has been in a continuous state of reform since the 1980s and this situation is unlikely to change any time soon. Perhaps the most ambitious reform proposals put forward in recent times were those presented by the Sapir Group in July 2003. This high-level body, which was convened by the President of the European Commission, Romano Prodi, and led by a Belgian economist, Andre Sapir, called for a radical reform of EU regional policy, emphasizing the importance of simplification, concentration, and the need to apply conditionality.

The Sapir Report proposed that the cohesion and structural funds should be replaced by two new policy instruments.[30] The first, a convergence fund, would focus on reducing income inequalities between member states and prioritize investment in human and physical capital, on the one hand, and institution building, including upgrading administrative capacity, on the other. The second, a restructuring fund, would provide financial support for workers displaced by technological change, on the one hand, and intra-EU competition and globalization, on the other. As regards conditionality, the Sapir Group argued that member states' entitlement to regional aid should be contingent on the implementation of reforms for which previous funding had been sought.

The innovative ideas presented in the Sapir Report gained only limited traction with EU policy-makers. Plans for a restructuring fund were taken up by the European Commission, which convinced EU member states to establish a Globalisation Adjustment Fund in 2006 to provide (limited) support to workers that lose their job as a result of global competition. The idea of a convergence fund, however, did not catch on. This is unsurprising since, as the Sapir Group recognized, plans to redirect funding from regions to member states are unlikely to receive political support so long as decisions over the financial perspectives are "driven by narrow national calculations of self-interest, bolstered by unanimity voting."[31]

In April 2009, Fabrizio Barca, the Director General of the Italian Ministry of Economy and Finance, presented a report on the future of EU cohesion policy at the request of the Commissioner for Regional Policy, Danuta Hübner.[32] This document, though it remained vague on policy recommendations, was notable for challenging many of the fundamental principles of EU regional policy. Barca's headline message was that EU policy-makers should strive for a "place-based development strategy" targeting specific economic and social challenges in actual places rather than focusing on financial flows to regions created for the express purpose of receiving aid. A example of what Barca might have had in mind was the Border, Midland, and Western Region of Ireland, a grouping which, though it faces genuine economic hardship in places, did not exist until Irish authorities sought a means to continue EU regional aid flows in spite of rising prosperity in the east of the country.

Controversially, the Barca Report also asked whether the EU should really seek to achieve a convergence of incomes between member states and regions. Convergence, the report argues, "is neither a necessary nor a sufficient condition for achieving the efficiency and the social inclusion objectives of cohesion policy and should not be used as a policy target." Efficiency considerations, the report suggests, should encourage policy measures designed to redress the root causes of unemployment and other instance of resource utilization in lagging regions rather than simply redistributing resources from rich to poor. Equity considerations, it argued, should encourage a systemic understanding of social exclusion and include broader measures of well-being that will not necessarily be captured by focusing on income inequalities alone.

A strategic report, adopted by the European Commission in March 2010, put forward an altogether more modest set of ideas for strengthening the implementation of EU cohesion policy.[33] Its recommendations included a more rigorous peer review of how EU member states use regional aid and greater coherence between regional policy initiatives and the Europe 2020 Strategy. Whether these suggestions go far enough or even in the right direction is a matter of debate. What is clear is that debates about the future of cohesion policy will intensify as negotiations over the next programming period (2014–2018) gather pace.

Another factor that is likely to weigh heavily on the future of EU regional policy is the global financial crisis. Following the collapse of the US sub-prime mortgage market in mid-2007 all eyes were focused on Central and Eastern Europe's fragile financial system. Although Hungary, Latvia, and Romania eventually turned to the EU and IMF for financial assistance, the rest of the region proved surprisingly resilient in the short term. In the end, it was an earlier vintage of accession states that caused most concern, with Greece, Ireland, Portugal, and Spain finding themselves on the brink of sovereign default in 2010 and 2011 after their budget deficits and debts spiraled.

That the original cohesion countries ended up in this situation was a blow for those who thought that EU regional policy could prepare member states for the rigors of a monetary union in which national authorities could no longer resort to exchange rate devaluation. It also ensured that EU regional policy moved center stage in debates about managing the sovereign debt crisis and preventing future crises from happening. Some saw EU regional policy as a useful stick, with German finance minister Wolfgang Schäuble suggesting in March 2011 that member states with excessive budget deficits should lose their entitlement to EU regional aid. Others saw EU regional policy as a carrot worth keeping. In August 2011, for instance, the Commission called for the co-financing requirement for EU regional projects to be relaxed for Greece, Ireland, Portugal, Hungary, Latvia, and Romania with a view to counteracting the effects of fiscal austerity and low growth. Whether these proposals will be taken up is not yet known, but a concern for economic instability and inequality in the periphery of the EU in general and the eurozone in particular will be difficult to avoid in debates over the next programming period.

35.5 CONCLUSION

The idea of redressing regional inequalities was a mere afterthought in the Treaty of Rome. Today it is a major part of the EU's economic mantra. Starting in the mid-1980s, successive rounds of negotiation over the EU budget have allocated an increasing share of the Community's resources to regional policy, making this one area of EU governance in which the EU's notoriously prudent policy-makers have been unafraid to put their money where their mouth is.

Regional policy provides rich pickings for students of EU policy-making. Proponents of multilevel governance may find it difficult to defend earlier claims about the empowerment of sub-national and supranational actors through EU regional policy in the light of policy developments, but multilevel governance remains one of the workhorse theories of EU studies. It can also claim some credit for encouraging the discipline of EU studies to look beyond sterile debates between proponents of intergovernmentalism and neo-functionalism.

EU regional policy has also inspired a great deal of theorizing and number crunching among economists. Traditional models of growth and trade saw little need for government intervention, since market forces were expected to reduce regional inequalities over time. Modern theories have challenged these assumptions, although economists remain circumspect about the conditions under which regional policies are likely to be effective. This point is particularly pertinent in relation to the global financial crisis, which has seen member states on the geographic periphery of the eurozone face a severely destabilizing fiscal crisis in spite of the vast sums of EU aid spent on preparing these countries for monetary union.

In the face of such uncertainty, it is hardly surprising that EU regional policy has been in a near continuous state of reform since its relaunch in the 1980s. There has been no shortage of reform proposals in recent times, with the most radical of these suggesting that the EU streamline instruments of EU regional policy and concentrate them on the poorest member states only. Such reforms may make economic sense but they have thus far proved politically untenable under voting arrangements that allow all member states to ask for, and receive a piece of, the EU regional policy pie.

NOTES

1. Author's own calculations based on US Government Printing Office, "Budget of the United States Government, Fiscal Year 2009" (Washington DC: US Government Printing Office, 2008).

2. G. P. Manzella, and C. Mendez, "The Turning Points of EU Cohesion Policy," background paper for the Barca Report (Brussels: DG Regio, 2009).

3. Data on GDP per capita here and elsewhere in this chapter are taken from the European Commission's AMECO database. Figures are adjusted for exchange rates but not inflation. The term "community average" is based on mean income of the EU-15 member states.

4. H. W. Armstrong, "Community Regional Policy: A Survey and Critique," *Regional Studies* 12, no. 5 (1978), 511–28.

5. European Commission, "EU Cohesion Policy 1988–2008: Investing in Europe's Future," *Inforegio* No. 26, June 2008 (Brussels: DG Regio).

6. J. Delors, "Regional Implications of Economic and Monetary Integration" (Brussels: Committee for the Study of Economic and Monetary Union, 1989).

7. European Commission, "EU Cohesion Policy 1988–2008."

8. European Commission, "EU Cohesion Policy 1988–2008."

9. European Commission, "EU Cohesion Policy 1988–2008."

10. European Commission, "Green Paper on Territorial Cohesion: Turning Territorial Diversity into Strength," Brussels, 6.10.2008, COM(2008) 616 final.

11. A. K. F. Faludi, "From European Spatial Development to Territorial Cohesion Policy," *Regional Studies* 40, no. 6 (2006), 667–78.

12. G. Marks, "Structural Policy and Multilevel Governance in the EC," in A. Cafruny and G. Rosenthal, eds, *The State of the European Community* (New York: Lynne Rienner, 1993), 391–410.

13. The Lisbon Treaty retains this requirement for unanimity in relation to the financial perspectives, which become a multiannual financial framework covered by the special legislative procedure (Article 313 TFEU). A passerelle clause is included, however, which would allow the European Council to agree by unanimity to move to QMV on the multiannual financial framework.

14. G. Marks, "Structural Policy in the European Community," in A. Sbragia, ed., *Europolitics: Institutions and Policy Making in the "New" European Community* (Washington, DC: The Brookings Institution, 1992), 191–224.

15. I. Begg and F. Heinemann, "New Budget, Old Dilemmas" (London: Centre for European Reform, 2006).

16. J. Bachtler and C. Mendez, "Who Governs EU Cohesion Policy? Deconstructing the Reforms of the Structural Funds," *Journal of Common Market Studies* 45, no. 3 (2007), 535–64.

17. European Commission, "EU Cohesion Policy 1988–2008."

18. L. Hooghe and G. Marks, *Multi-Level Governance and European Integration* (Boulder, Colorado: Rowman & Littlefield, 2001).

19. Hooghe and Marks, *Multi-Level Governance and European Integration*.

20. Hooghe and Marks, *Multi-Level Governance and European Integration*.

21. D. Allen, "Cohesion and Structural Funds," in H. Wallace, W. Wallace, and M. A. Pollack, eds, *Policy-Making in the European Union* (Oxford: Oxford University Press, 2005), 213–42.

22. Bachtler and Mendez, "Who Governs EU Cohesion Policy?."

23. For an introduction to this literature, see R. Baldwin and C. Wyplosz, *The Economics of European Integration*, third edition (Maidenhead, Berkshire: McGraw-Hill Higher Education, 2006), ch. 10.

24. H. Badinger, W. Müller, and G. Tondl, "Regional Convergence in the European Union, 1985–1999: A Spatial Dynamic Panel Analysis," *Regional Studies* 38, no. 3 (2004), 241–53.

25. M. Boldrin and F. Canova, "Inequality and Convergence in Europe's Regions: Reconsidering European Regional Policies," *Economic Policy* 16, no. 32 (2001), 205–53.

26. R. Leonardi, "Cohesion in the European Union," *Regional Studies* 40, no. 2 (2006), 155–66.

27. A. Sapir, P. Aghion, G. Bertola, M. Hellwig, J. Pisani-Ferry, D. Rosati, J. Viñals, and J. Wallace, *An Agenda for a Growing Europe: The Sapir Report* (Oxford: Oxford University Press, 2004).

28. D. Puga, "European Regional Policies in the Light of Recent Location Theories," *Journal of Economic Geography* 2 (2002), 373–406.

29. S. Ederveen, S. De Groot, and S. Nahuis, "Fertile Soil for Structural Funds? A Panel Data Analysis of the Conditional Effectiveness of European Cohesion policy," *Kyklos* 59, no. 1 (2006), 17–42.

30. Sapir et al., *An Agenda for a Growing Europe*.

31. Sapir et al., *An Agenda for a Growing Europe*, 197.

32. F. Barca, "An Agenda for a Reformed Cohesion Policy: A Place-Based Approach to Meeting European Union Challenges and Expectations" (Brussels: DG Regio, 2009).

33. European Commission, "Cohesion policy: Strategic Report 2010 on the implementation of the programmes 2007–2013" COM(2010)110 final.

PART VII

....

SUBSTANTIVE POLICY DEVELOPMENT

....

CHAPTER 36

....

ENVIRONMENTAL POLICY

....

CHARLOTTE BURNS AND NEIL CARTER

36.1 INTRODUCTION

EU environmental policy is typically identified as a success story; actors within the EU took the creation of the single market as an opportunity to introduce an impressive array of environmental regulation and to place the Union at the forefront of international efforts to combat global environmental problems. Thus the EU has extensive pollution regulations, comprehensive waste laws, an institutional commitment to the pursuit of sustainable development and climate change mitigation, a green growth strategy up to 2020, and an ambitious "Roadmap" spelling out economic and environmental priorities up to 2050.[1] The EU and key states within it are often portrayed as environmental leaders who adopt progressive legislation domestically, thereby driving up European and global standards via a process of regulatory competition.[2] Indeed, there are indications that European leaders are using the EU's environmental successes as a new functional myth to legitimate the Union's activities.[3] However, whilst these portraits of the EU and its "pioneer" states as being environmental leaders are seductive, when subjected to empirical analysis a more nuanced and complex picture emerges.[4] Moreover, there are some long-standing and more recent challenges to the EU's self-perception and wider reputation as an environmental leader. Below we briefly review the development of the EU's environmental policy before addressing the principal challenges that the Union faces in the field of environmental policy, including: the persistent implementation deficit; enlargement to Central and Eastern Europe; and the re-emerging tension between the EU's perception that it is a global environmental leader and its failure to deliver at major international meetings, such as the climate change conferences in Copenhagen (2009) and Cancun (2010).

36.2 THE EVOLUTION OF EU ENVIRONMENTAL POLICY: FROM "SILENCE TO SALIENCE"[5]

There was no formal legal base for environmental policy in the EU until 1986. In the early years only a limited range of legislation was introduced to address technical failures within particular areas such as agricultural or chemicals policy. However, from the 1960s a growing awareness of environmental problems pushed the issue firmly onto the international agenda. Within Europe the 1972 UN conference on the environment in Stockholm, and the emergence of acid rain and *Waldsterben* (forest death in Scandinavia and, crucially, West Germany) as a political issue saw the Commission called upon by the European Council to develop an Environmental Action Programme (EAP) in 1973, the first of six to date.[6] The establishment of an Environmental Directorate-General in the Commission reflected similar developments across Europe as countries sought to deal with the impact of pollution by creating separate government departments to regulate industrial emissions. From the 1970s to early 1980s the member states and the Commission sought to develop legislation to regulate emissions into the key media of air, water, and soil. However, this legislation was typically reactive and end-of-pipe, i.e. it neither anticipated nor prevented environmental damage, but merely sought to mitigate the effects of industrial pollution. As the single market program took off in the 1980s, environmental pollution was recognized as a market failure that would require correction through regulation in order to prevent social and environmental dumping. Thus, the environment was formally included in the Treaty under the SEA (Article 189b) and a swathe of legislation was adopted from 1986 onward to ensure a level playing field between member states, so that a country with weaker environmental regulations does not gain a competitive advantage over those with more stringent rules. The EAPs became increasingly detailed and ambitious, none more so than the fifth EAP published in 1992.[7]

The fifth EAP, with its claim to be moving "Towards Sustainability," represented the apotheosis of the EU's environmental ambition—it called for formal policy integration across the key sectors of agriculture, tourism, transport, energy, and industry; the adoption of a wider range of policy instruments; and the inclusion of a more diverse range of actors in policy-making to allow for the development of more bottom-up initiatives where key stakeholders felt a sense of ownership of policy goals, thereby hopefully improving implementation of policy. This clarion call for environmental policy integration was supplemented a few years later in 1998 by the Council's Cardiff Strategy, which likewise called for greater integration of environmental policy considerations across the affected sectors within the Council of Ministers and the member states.[8] These calls for policy integration reflect one of the most challenging aspects of the environment as a policy problem, namely its transnational and cross-sectoral nature. Environmental pollution respects neither national boundaries nor the bureaucratic division of labor that characterizes the modern machinery of government. Unfortunately, an endemic problem within the EU and more widely has been getting those actors in other policy sectors to incorporate environmental concerns into day-to-day policy-making.[9] The fifth EAP was pilloried for its failure to achieve integration or reach many of its goals. From the late 1990s EU environmental policy entered a period of consolidation.[10] Fewer pieces of legislation were produced; those that were, tended to be large ambitious packages such as the wide-ranging auto-oil package that sought to reduce emissions from cars by tackling engine design and fuel quality, the water framework directive that regulated aquatic pollution via river basin management, and the REACH regulations that brought together in one package the registration and evaluation of chemicals.[11] Thus Directorate-General Environment came to exemplify the shift within the Commission from 2000 onward to do less but do it better.[12] At the same time, the EU has sought to enhance its reputation on the international stage by emerging as a leader in the field of climate change, pushing for ambitious targets and pressurizing states such as Russia to ratify the Kyoto Protocol.[13]

Thus, the EU's environmental policy has moved from being a series of ad hoc incremental pieces of legislation to a fully fledged and comprehensive set of policy measures. The EU is now formally committed in the Treaties and its Sustainability Strategy to sustainable development, typically understood in the classic Brundtland sense as "development that meets the needs of the present without compromising the ability of future generations to meet their own needs."[14] It is important though to note that whilst the EU claims to have embraced sustainable development, it is more accurate to describe the dominant environmental policy paradigm within the Union as ecological modernization. Sustainable development is generally interpreted as encompassing wider global development issues that require an integration of social, economic, and environmental concerns into policy-making. In its more radical forms sustainable development implies the need for radically restructuring economic models of growth.[15] Ecological modernization, whilst sharing some core features of sustainable development, is narrower in its ambition. For example, it assumes that ecological sustainability is achievable without a fundamental transformation of the capitalist system, through the dematerialization of production and decoupling of economic growth and resource use. It is underpinned by the belief that policy-makers should adopt an anticipatory and preventative approach to environmental problems influenced by the precautionary principle, environmental considerations should be integrated into all parts of government, and "new" policy instruments, such as eco-taxes and tradable permits, should be used to encourage environmentally benign behavior and to penalize environmentally damaging activities.[16] By promising "green" capitalism, ecological modernization appeals to European policy-makers because it appears consistent with the wider European "project" of encouraging free trade and continued economic growth. It combines potential commercial benefits, ranging from reduced costs (e.g. by cutting energy use) to the development of new markets in green technologies (e.g. wind turbines) with improved environmental quality, whilst downplaying the politically complex equity issues associated with sustainable development.

36.3 How Did We Get Here?

What then have been the main drivers of the transformation of environmental policy at the European level? First, the nature of the environment as a policy problem lends itself well to European action and integration: it is transnational and therefore regarded by both elites and the public as being a legitimate arena for EU policy-making; for example in the 2009 Standard Eurobarometer public opinion survey 70 percent of respondents felt that environmental policy should be decided jointly at the European level, a consistent finding over the years.[17] The cross-sectoral nature of the environment makes it more likely that policy in one area will spill over into another; for example, regulating the level of pesticides in drinking water has a knock-on effect upon agricultural policy. The decision to regulate emissions from cars requires rules that affect both fuel quality and car engine design, hence the explicit linkage of the two in the auto-oil package.[18]

Second, the primary motivation for environmental regulation at the European level has been economic—key elites have accepted the need for environmental regulation as a way to ensure harmonization and prevent unfair competition. It is no accident that the key turning point for the development of the environmental *acquis* was the launch of the SEM program. This economic rationale has shaped the paradigm that underpins policy, lending it an ecologically modern flavor rather than one based on the more radical principles of sustainable development.

Third, the role of policy entrepreneurs has been crucial. Within the Commission, Directorate-General Environment, and within the European Parliament, the Environment Committee, both played key roles in the 1980s and 1990s in pushing for the wider development of environmental policy, even if partly as a way to advance their own institutional standing.[19] Ironically, as the Parliament's power has increased there is evidence to suggest that whilst it is more successful in shaping legislation it is less radical in its demands.[20] More recently, the emergence of the environment both as a potential legitimating cause for the European project and as a source for growth and jobs has seen it championed by key elites within the institutions.[21] The ECJ's judgments have also played a significant role in shaping the development of environmental policy in the Union, as illustrated in the Danish Bottle Case. When Denmark introduced stringent recycling laws restricting the sale of drinks to those that met the new recycling requirements, the Commission brought an action against Denmark on the grounds that its new law acted as a barrier to trade, as containers that did not meet the Danish requirements could not be sold on the Danish market. The Court held that Denmark was justified in restricting trade on environmental grounds, thereby adding an important green limitation to the pursuit of free trade within the Union.[22]

The other central actors pushing policy have been the so-called pioneer or leader states. Germany, Denmark, and the Netherlands are all Northern, industrially advanced, ecologically modern states that have played a central role in promoting progressive environmental policy at the European level. These states have either purposefully, or as a by-product of domestic policy innovations, shaped EU environmental regulation. For example, by adopting higher standards domestically in relation to container recycling Denmark prompted the Danish Bottle case; Germany actively sought to push its own approach to emissions regulation on the European stage in the 1980s; and The Netherlands successfully uploaded its approach to environmental policy which influenced the shape and structure of the fifth environmental action plan.[23] In 1995 the accession of three further environmental leaders, Austria, Sweden, and Finland, bolstered the position of the other environmental leaders within the Council and saw formal recognition in the Treaties of the right of states to maintain more stringent environmental legislation domestically (the so-called environmental guarantee). The Scandinavian states in particular have played a key role in improving the transparency of both environmental policy and wider EU decision-making.[24]

Whilst these policy entrepreneurs have undoubtedly had a positive effect upon the development of EU environmental policy, it is important to note that the structure of decision-making in the Union means that proposals are subject to dilution or to being rejected altogether. Concurrent majorities are required in each institution before a proposal can be adopted. The dominant process for adopting environmental legislation within the EU is co-decision, which requires agreement from a majority in the Council and the European Parliament with both institutions having the option of a veto. Thus there are numerous veto players who can block or dilute legislation, notwithstanding the efforts of green policy entrepreneurs.[25] For example, the efforts of the Dutch to upload a carbon tax were blocked by the UK and French governments in the early 1990s.[26] The packaging waste legislation was watered down as a consequence of opposition from France, Spain, and the UK.[27] Thus legislation is the result of a compromise with the end product reflecting a process of mediation between agenda setters and veto players.

Two further important agents of change who have helped to shape the behavior of the respective institutional actors have been green parties and environmental non-governmental organizations (ENGOs). The success of the Greens in national elections particularly in the second half of the 1990s saw green ministers command (briefly) a blocking minority in the environment council, a German Green foreign affairs minister (Joschka Fischer), and a Green Commissioner (Michaele Schreyer).[28] The rise of the Greens in Germany in the 1980s contributed to the shift toward ecological modernization domestically prompting Germany to push that agenda on the European stage. Green parties have also done well in European elections—they were the fourth largest party group in the European Parliament in 2004 and 2009—giving them the opportunity to assume key positions of responsibility within the European Parliament, such as vice-presidencies, Committee chairs, and as leaders on key reports. ENGOs and civil society organizations lobby proactively on the European stage; for example, they have successfully shaped policy toward biotechnology and the use of genetically modified organisms (GMOs) in Europe.[29] They also help to implement legislation by bringing breaches of EU law to the attention of the European Parliament and Commission. However, it is important to note that the growth in numbers and activity of ENGOs has been matched by an increase in general interest group activity at the European level as affected groups seek to shape legislation, and invariably the business lobby is better resourced and better connected to key decision-makers.[30]

Given all this activity, what if any impact has the EU had upon domestic environmental policy? Is there evidence of Europeanization? Has there been convergence between the member states? Studies of the objective state of the environment show that the EU performs well compared to other regions of the world and to states at similar levels of development.[31] A large-scale comparative survey of environmental policies globally finds that EU states have adopted relatively ambitious legislation and that EU membership provides part of the explanation for that performance.[32] But evidence of the impact upon national policies and polities is more mixed. There has been some convergence between the member states in policy substance, but a wide degree of divergence in national institutional structures and regulatory styles persists. Thus, Europeanization seems to have been limited to policy rather than to the polity. Indeed, even here its effects have been uneven as the so-called pioneer states demonstrate less evidence of the EU shaping policy than in other states: perhaps a function of successful uploading of domestic policy to the European level.[33] Insofar as it is possible to make generalizations in the face of this varied portrait, the EU seems to have brought the content of policy closer but has seen no radical shift in overall approaches to environmental policy-making.[34]

These findings are perhaps unsurprising given that the dominant instrument used for environmental policy is the directive, which states the aims that member states should strive for, yet leaves the means by which those ends are to be achieved to each member state's discretion. But there are also some structural institutional factors at work—the path-dependency of national administrative structures and norms results in "domestic adaptation with national colors."[35] Thus states try to reduce the costs of implementing legislation by integrating them into existing institutions and structures. Another, less benign way in which states seek to defray costs is by failing to implement EU policies altogether.

36.4 POLICY IMPLEMENTATION

The failure to transpose and implement legislation properly has been a major concern in EU environmental policy since the 1980s. Environmental policy infringements account for the largest percentage of infringement cases dealt with by the Commission (19 percent of the total in 2009). The vast majority of the 2009 infringement cases (55 percent) concerned poor application of the legislation in question, 27 percent concerned the failure to conform to the legislation, and 14 percent with failing to communicate the transposition of legislation.[36] These implementation failures have potentially devastating impacts, as during the time lag between the failure of a member state to implement legislation and action being taken by the Commission, irreparable environmental damage can be caused with knock-on effects for the health of ecosystems. For example, the

Commission took action against Spain for building a road through a protected area (the Santoña Marshes), but although the ECJ found against the Spanish government by the time the case was heard the marshes had silted up and were permanently damaged.[37]

Historically, there was a common assumption that there was a North–South divide in the Union with upright Northern environmental pioneers implementing legislation and Southern laggards failing to do so due to corruption and poor organization. The fact that Greece, Italy, Portugal, and Spain accounted for a substantial proportion of infringement proceedings in the 1980s and 1990s appeared to provide empirical justification for this perception of a "southern problem."[38] However, not all states perform consistently across time and different policy areas. For example, Germany shifted from being a leader in the 1980s to having a relatively poor implementation record in the 1990s.[39] A key explanation for changes in implementation performance is the failure of some states to upload domestic models of regulation to the European level. If a state can successfully shape the style of regulation adopted by the EU it can minimize the domestic costs of adaptation. States who lose this regulatory competition can find themselves having to implement legislation based upon a style of regulation that is alien to their domestic setting, thereby imposing high implementation costs.[40]

Thus, when the Mediterranean enlargements took place in the 1980s the new states found themselves having to implement legislation that they had had no hand in designing and that was ill-suited to their domestic context with regard to both overall governance structures and policy priorities. The heavily industrialized North European states were primarily concerned with industrial emissions whereas in the South the key issues were the rapid expansion of the tourism sector, water supply, and nature protection.[41] Hence the North–South divide that appeared to characterize implementation was at least partly explained by a mismatch of regulatory style and policy priorities. States can also face difficulties if they try to upload policy but as legislation makes its way through the decision-making process it gets amended so that the final version of policy is a departure from the original model, or policy at the national level has shifted so the EU and national regulation are mismatched. For example, various policies uploaded by Germany on air pollution were subject to dilution and compromises at the European level.[42] Similarly, the Dutch successfully uploaded a model of nature protection to the European level that shaped the habitats directive, but changes in policy at the domestic level led to a policy mismatch between EU and Dutch legislation.[43] Notwithstanding these implementation challenges, states are more likely to be able to implement legislation successfully if they can upload national models to the European level. What, then, determines the ability to win this regulatory competition?

Two variables play a critical role in determining success in the regulatory competition: policy preferences and action capacity.[44] A member state with a clear preference for a particular type or style of regulation, perhaps reflecting the dominant environmental issues within that state (e.g. industrial emissions for the North European pioneers), with the political and administrative infrastructure to upload to the European level, is more likely to be successful and so more likely to implement policy down the line. The reason Germany uploaded policy in the fields of industrial emissions and air quality successfully was that it had a clear economic incentive for doing so (i.e. the presence of a large indus-trial sector and powerful car industry) and a model that could be used as the basis of legislation. The presence of policy preferences and action capacity are in turn often linked to levels of economic development. Thus, the perception of the implementation deficit as being a southern problem is too simplistic, and where there have been issues with Southern European states, this can be explained without recourse to crude national stereotyping. Moreover this more nuanced analysis helps explain why states might shift from leader to laggard across time and policy. However, if there is a relationship between levels of economic development and implementation, the accession of the ten Central and East European (CEE) states in 2004 and 2007 suggests that further challenges may emerge.

36.5 ENLARGING EUROPE'S ENVIRONMENT

Certainly, it was widely predicted that the addition of twelve new member states, which were significantly poorer and less economically developed than most existing member states, would seriously impair the quality of EU environmental governance.[45] It was anticipated that a proliferation of new veto players would make it harder to win agree-ment for progressive environmental policies, whilst new member states would be unable to implement those environmental measures that were approved.

Pessimists argued that enlargement should have made it "almost impossible to alter the legislative status quo" in any policy area because the Treaty of Nice introduced a tri-ple majority requirement that Council decisions receive not only a qualified majority, but also an absolute majority of member states and, if a country requests it, a 62 percent majority of the total population of EU countries.[46] The enlarged Council, with a greater diversification of preferences, would therefore find it much harder to secure agreement on any significant changes in existing policy, whilst the Council's increased powers now allow it to veto changes to the status quo.

Environmental policy seemed particularly vulnerable post-enlargement. The politi-cal salience of the environment remains very low across all the accession states: govern-ments and citizens alike emphasize the traditional material concerns of economic growth and welfare policy, rather than environmental protection, particularly when it may conflict with these core concerns. The environmental movement is very weak, with small memberships, while green parties have struggled to establish a footing: for exam-ple, no Greens from CEE states were elected in the 2004 or 2009 European Parliament elections.

Moreover, the CEE states have encountered significant problems in the implementa-tion of environmental legislation. Most accession states still lack the administrative capacity to deliver effective environmental policy.[47] Environmental ministries are under-resourced, weak, and marginalized. There is limited environmental policy expertise and experience, particularly at regional and local levels.[48] Civil society organizations, notably ENGOs, are weak and poorly resourced. But a major obstacle has been the sheer cost of adopting and implementing the full tranche of environmental legislation: one estimate put the total figure for the accession states at 120 billion euros, or an annual investment of 10 billion euros.[49] The EU established various forms of financial assistance to facilitate this transition process, including the Instrument for Structural Policies for Pre-Accession, but these have only partially defrayed the costs of the necessary infrastructure and administrative capacity building. This litany of problems is illustrated in a study of the implementation of the Natura 2000 habitat protection legislation in Hungary, Poland, and Romania.[50] Moreover, the substantial mismatch between the entrenched centralized "top-down" administrative traditions inherited from the Soviet era and the more participatory modes of governance that characterize the Natura 2000 legislation simply "overwhelmed" the CEE state actors. Whilst EU resources have helped ENGOs in CEE countries to become more professional, state actors have been reluctant to grant them an extensive role in policy implementation (in contrast to the major role of ENGOs in older member states) and their actual empowerment has been limited. Progress is under way, but it is slow.

Yet, despite the gloomy prognostications of many observers, the EU has continued to pass important environmental legislation since enlargement. The volume and quality of new environmental legislation has not declined to any significant degree.[51] In the European Parliament, rather than voting as a block, MEPs from the accession states have joined existing party groupings and between 2004 and 2009 rarely voted against their party line. If the European Parliament as a whole became a little less "green," it reflected a general rightward shift in the two major centre-right party groups—the European People's Party (EPP) and Alliance of the Liberals and Democrats for Europe (ALDE)—leading them to become less sympathetic to environmental protection.[52] In the Council, enlargement was initially marked by continuity. It seems that the accession states were learning the ropes initially, only intervening in discussions where a vital national interest was at stake. However, the introduction of the European Climate and Energy Package (ECEP) prompted a shift in attitude, an issue to which we turn in the following section. Suffice to say that enlargement whilst increasing the number of veto players within the EU and posing enormous implementation challenges for the accession states has not led to a freeze on new proposals or an overall downward pressure on standards. Rather the EU continues to operate as before with horse-trading amongst the member states and policy outcomes reflecting this process of mediation between agenda setters and veto players.

36.6 THE EU AS AN INTERNATIONAL ACTOR

As noted above, the EU has since the 1990s emerged as a key player in the field of international environmental politics: it is the signatory to more than forty multilateral environmental agreements and has sought to cast itself as a climate change leader.[53] In the

1980s the coordination challenges associated with developing a coherent position among the member states and between the Council and Commission saw the EU criticized for its behavior at international conferences, particularly for using these events to resolve intra-EU disputes, rather than concentrating on international agreement.[54] Moreover, the opposition of key European chemical industries to the reduction of ozone depleting chemicals saw the US emerge as a leader in relation to ozone depletion in the early 1980s.[55] However, the reluctance of the US to support the Kyoto Protocol saw the EU assume the mantle of leadership in the field of climate change as it pushed for stringent targets and developed the innovative EU bubble, which set an overall target of an 8 percent greenhouse gas reduction on 1990 levels for the EU but required some EU states to reduce their emissions significantly (e.g. Germany and Denmark by 21 percent) whilst others were allowed to increase their emissions (e.g. Greece and Portugal).[56] Moreover, the EU has emerged as a global leader in the use of new market-based approaches to climate change with the development of its pioneering Emissions Trading System (ETS). Whilst the ETS has encountered some major teething problems, such as over-allocation of permits, fluctuating carbon prices, and even a temporary suspension of trading due to fraud, it is nevertheless a genuine example of ground-breaking leadership.

However, the problem of coordination across policy areas and amongst the member states continues to undermine the Union's ability to promote progressive environmental policies at the global level. For example, the EU's ability to promote a coherent sustainable development agenda at the World Summit for Sustainable Development in Johannesburg in 2002 was undermined by the competing interests of the Directorates-General for Agriculture, Development, Trade, and Environment.[57] The addition of more actors post-enlargement seems to have exacerbated this tendency to incoherence and seen a weakening of ambition in relation to climate change, as evinced by the events surrounding the adoption of the ECEP.

The ECEP was the legislative embodiment of the EU's 20/20/20 commitment to reduce emissions of greenhouse gases by 20 percent of 1990 levels, increase the share of renewable energy in the energy mix to 20 percent, and to achieve a 20 percent increase in energy efficiency by 2020. The Package comprised four legislative proposals—directives revising and strengthening the ETS; setting binding national targets for renewable energy; creating a framework for the development of carbon capture and storage technology; and setting binding greenhouse gas emission reduction targets for sectors not covered by the ETS, such as transport and housing.[58] These four proposals were linked together with two further proposals—on cutting CO_2 emissions from cars and improving fuel quality—and they were all adopted together in December 2008. The package was presented by the Commission and Council as evidence of the EU's status as global leader on climate change. However, in anticipation of discontent among CEE states concerned about their cost, these proposals included a range of concessions such as less demanding targets for increasing renewable energy and receiving a disproportionately large share of ETS allowances. Nevertheless, the CEE states were not satisfied and on several issues they acted as a bloc within the Council and in negotiation with the French presidency to win further concessions—notably on increased ETS auction revenue and transitional free allowances for their power sectors. However, it is important not to cast the CEE states as the sole villains of the piece as they were not alone in opposing elements of the ECEP. The package was introduced against the backdrop of a major international economic crisis, which had reduced the appetite for radical climate change legislation amongst many member states, both East and West. For example, the German government, responding to pressure from its domestic car manufacturers, lobbied hard for changes whilst the Italian government used brinkmanship to win last minute concessions.[59] Thus the CEE states found allies right across the EU: there was no sharp East versus West divide, or even an East/South versus West conflict; it was not a simple case of the laggards outvoting the leaders. But the willingness of the CEE states to flex their muscles, after three or four years of passivity, suggests that in the future they might prove more of a stumbling block to the passage of progressive environmental legislation that imposes high domestic costs.

In addition to this potential challenge, the emergence of India and China and the re-emergence of the US as key leaders in environmental negotiations raise the prospect of the EU being excluded from important discussions at international conferences, as happened at the climate change meetings in Copenhagen and Cancun. The persistent problem of failing to present a united front and being unable to respond rapidly to new proposals due to the number of affected actors continues to undermine EU leadership at major international gatherings. That said, the commitment at the Durban Conference of the Parties in 2011 to negotiate a successor treaty to Kyoto came about in large part due to the proactive leadership role adopted by the EU, which stepped in when other states were reluctant to act.[60] Moreover, it is important to note that leadership in environmental policy on the global stage is only partly about performance at the big gatherings. By adopting ambitious targets and shaping the development of new technologies the EU can drive up standards via global regulatory competition.[61] Furthermore, whilst an increase in the number of member states exacerbates the challenge of coordinating policy, it also increases the size of the European market and therefore the economic importance of the Union, making it an actor of considerable global standing that cannot be ignored.

36.7 CONCLUSION

The EU has crafted, particularly since the 1980s, an impressive body of environmental policy and, due to the efforts of key actors, it has also developed a reputation as a global environmental leader. The presence of multiple veto players and the processes of mediation inherent within decision-making have inevitably led to the dilution or shelving of some ambitious policy proposals, such as the carbon tax. Nevertheless, the environmental *acquis* continues to grow and this policy area commands widespread popular support from the Union's citizenry. To maintain its reputation for leadership the Union faces some key challenges. Certainly the wider economic climate since 2008 has been unfavorable for the adoption of progressive environmental policies. Under such circumstances it may be time for the EU to turn to two key areas that need work: securing the implementation of the existing environmental *acquis* and reinvigorating the EU's international leadership in the face of rapidly industrializing economies and a resurgent US. The Council and Commission should concentrate on leading by doing rather than seeking to play a leadership role at international conferences: the ongoing confusion over who speaks for Europe in the field of environmental policy (or indeed any other area) does nothing for Europe's wider reputation. But building upon Europe's market position to develop and deliver cutting-edge technologies that can drive up international standard is not only entirely in-keeping with the dominant paradigm of ecological modernization, it is also the EU's best chance of exercising influence on the international environmental stage.

NOTES

1. European Commission, *A Roadmap for Moving to a Competitive Low Carbon Economy in 2050* (2011), <http://ec.europa.eu/clima/policies/roadmap/index_en.htm>.
2. Mikael Skou Andersen and Duncan Liefferink, eds, *European Environmental Policy: The Pioneers* (Manchester: Manchester University Press, 1997); R. Daniel Keleman, "Globalizing European Union Environmental Policy," *Journal of European Public Policy* 17, no. 3 (April, 2010), 335–49; Rudiger Wurzel and James Connelly, eds, *The European Union as a Leader in International Climate Change Politics* (London: Routledge, 2010).
3. Andrea Lenschow and Carina Sprungk, "The Myth of a Green Europe," *Journal of Common Market Studies* 48, no. 1 (January 2010), 133–54.
4. Tanja Börzel, *Environmental Leaders and Laggards in the European Union: Why There is (Not) a Southern Problem* (London: Ashgate, 2003); Andrew Jordan and Duncan Liefferink, eds, *Environmental Policy in Europe: the Europeanization of National Environmental Policy* (London: Routledge, 2004); Duncan Liefferink, Bas Arts, Jelmer Kamstra, and Jeroen Ooijevaar, "Leaders and Laggards in Environmental Policy: A Quantitative Analysis of Domestic Policy Outputs," *Journal of European Public Policy* 16, no. 5 (August, 2009), 677–700.
5. Albert Weale, Geoffrey Pridham, Michelle Cini, Dimitrios Konstadakopulos, Martin Porter, and Brendan Flynn, *Environmental Governance in Europe* (Oxford: Oxford University Press, 2000), 488.
6. For a history of the EAPs, see Susan Baker, *Sustainable Development* (London: Routledge, 2006); Christopher Knill and Duncan Liefferink, *Environmental Politics in the European Union* (Manchester: Manchester University Press, 2007); Weale et al., *Environmental Governance in Europe.*
7. Commission of the European Communities, *Towards Sustainability: A European Community Programme of Policy and Action in Relation to the Environment and Sustainable Development,* COM 92/23 final (Luxembourg: Commission of the European Communities, 1992).
8. See Andrea Lenschow, ed., *Environmental Policy Integration* (London: Earthscan, 2002).
9. Lenschow, *Environmental Policy Integration.*
10. Knill and Liefferink, *Environmental Politics in the European Union.*

11. See Rüdiger Wurzel, *Environmental Policy-Making in Britain, Germany and the European Union*, (Manchester: Manchester University Press, 2002); Axel Friedrich, Matthias Tappe, and Rüdiger Wurzel, "A New Approach to EU Environmental Policy-Making? The Auto-Oil I Programme," *Journal of European Public Policy* 7, no. 4 (October 2000), 593–612; Dieter Pesendorfer, "EU Environmental Policy Under Pressure: Chemicals Policy Change between Antagonistic Goals," *Environmental Politics* 15, no. 1 (February 2006), 95–114.

12. See Timo Idema and Daniel Robert Keleman, "New Modes of Governance, the Open Method of Co-Ordination and Other Fashionable Red Herrings," *Perspectives on European Politics and Society* 7, no. 1 (May 2006), 108–23.

13. Miranda Schreurs and Yves Tiberghien, "European Union Leadership in Climate Change: Mitigation through Multilateral Reinforcement," in Kathryn Harrison and Lisa Sundstrom, eds, *Global Commons, Domestic Decisions* (Cambridge, MA: MIT Press, 2010), 23–66; John Vogler, "The European Union as a Global Environmental Policy Actor: Climate Change," in Wurzel and Connelly, *The European Union as a Leader in International Climate Change Politics*, 21–37.

14. World Commission on the Environment and Development, *Our Common Future* (Oxford: Oxford University Press, 2000), 43.

15. See Baker, *Sustainable Development*, ch. 2; Neil Carter, *The Politics of the Environment* (Cambridge: Cambridge University Press, 2007), 207–26.

16. Carter, *The Politics of the Environment*, 227–9.

17. European Commission (2009) *Eurobarometer 72, Public Opinion in the European Union*, <http://ec.europa.eu/public_opinion/archives/eb/eb72/eb72_vol1_en.pdf>; Lenschow and Sprungk, "The Myth of a Green Europe," 144.

18. Friedrich et al., "A New Approach to EU Environmental Policy-Making?."

19. David Judge, "Predestined to Save the Earth: The Environment Committee of the European Parliament," *Environmental Politics* 1, no. 4 (Winter 1992), 186–212; Knill and Liefferink, *Environmental Politics in the European Union*; Weale et al., *Environmental Governance in Europe*.

20. Charlotte Burns and Neil Carter, "Is Codecision Good for the Environment?," *Political Studies* 58, no. 1 (February 2010), 123–42.

21. Lenschow and Sprungk, "The Myth of a Green Europe."

22. Weale et al., *Environmental Governance in Europe*, 415–16.

23. Weale et al., *Environmental Governance in Europe*, 415; Jordan and Liefferink, *Environmental Policy in Europe*, 104, 138.

24. Duncan Liefferink and Mikael Skou Andersen, "Strategies of the 'Green' Member States in EU Environmental Policy-Making," *Journal of European Public Policy* 5, no. 2 (June 1998), 254–70.

25. Weale et al., *Environmental Governance in Europe*, 489.

26. Tony Zito, "Integrating the Environment into the European Union: the History of the Controversial Carbon Tax," in Carolyn Rhodes and Sonia Mazey, eds, *The State of the European Union* (Boulder: Lynne Rienner, 1995), 431–48.

27. Weale et al., *Environmental Governance in Europe*, 420.

28. Elizabeth Bomberg and Neil Carter, "The Greens in Brussels," *European Journal for Political Research* 45, Supplement (October 2006), S99–S125.

29. Thomas Bernauer and Erika Meins, "Technological Revolution Meets Policy and the Market: Explaining Cross-National Differences in Agricultural Biotechnology Regulation," *European Journal of Political Research* 42, no. 5 (August 2003), 643–83.

30. See, for example, Wurzel, *Environmental Policy-Making in Britain, Germany and the European Union*, on the car lobby.
31. Lenschow and Sprungk, "The Myth of a Green Europe," 147–8.
32. Liefferink et al., "Leaders and Laggards in Environmental Policy."
33. Jordan and Liefferink, *Environmental Policy in Europe*.
34. Andrew Jordan and Duncan Liefferink, "Europeanization and Convergence," in Jordan and Liefferink, *Environmental Policy in Europe*, 224–45.
35. Maria Cowles, James Caporeso, and Thomas Risse, eds, *Transforming Europe: Europeanization and Domestic Change* (Ithaca: Cornell University Press, 2001), 1.
36. See <http://ec.europa.eu/environment/legal/law/statistics.htm>.
37. C-355/90, Commission vs Spain, Santona Marshes.
38. Börzel, *Environmental Leaders and Laggards in the European Union*.
39. Wurzel, *Environmental Policy-Making in Britain, Germany and the European Union*; Börzel, *Environmental Leaders and Laggards in the European Union*.
40. A Héritier, "The Accommodation of Diversity in European Policy-Making and its Outcomes: Regulatory Policy as a Patchwork," *Journal of European Public Policy* 3, no. 2 (June 1996), 149–67.
41. See Jordan and Liefferink, *Environmental Policy in Europe*.
42. Weale et al., *Environmental Governance in Europe*; Wurzel, *Environmental Policy-Making in Britain, Germany and the European Union*.
43. Duncan Liefferink and Mariëlle van der Zouwen, "The Netherlands: the Advantages of Being 'Mr Average'," in Jordan and Liefferink, *Environmental Policy in Europe*, 136–53.
44. Börzel, *Environmental Leaders and Laggards in the European Union*.
45. Katharina Holzinger and Peter Knoepfel, "The Need for Flexibility: European Environmental Policy on the Brink of Enlargement," in Katharina Holzinger and Peter Knoepfel, eds, *Environmental Policy in a European Union of Variable Geometry? The Challenge of the Next Enlargement* (Basel: Helbing & Lichtenhahn, 2000), 3–35.
46. George Tsebelis and Xenophon Yataganas, "Veto Players and Decision-Making in the EU after Nice," *Journal of Common Market Studies* 40, no. 2 (June 2002), 304.
47. Tanja Börzel, *Coping with Accession to the European Union: New Modes of Environmental Governance* (Basingstoke: Palgrave, 2009).
48. Jon Birger Skærseth and Jørgen Wettestad, "Is EU Enlargement Bad for Environmental Policy? Confronting Gloomy Expectations with Evidence," *International Environmental Agreements* 7, no. 3 (September 2007), 263–80.
49. Liliana Andonova, *Transnational Politics of the Environment* (Cambridge, MA: MIT Press, 2004).
50. Tanja Börzel and Aron Buzogány, "Environmental Organizations and the Europeanization of Public Policy in Central and Eastern Europe: the Case of Biodiversity Governance," *Environmental Politics* 19, no. 5 (September 2010), 708–35.
51. Charlotte Burns, Neil Carter, and Nicholas Worsfold, "Enlargement and the Environment: the Changing Behaviour of the European Parliament," *Journal of Common Market Studies*, 50, no. 1 (January 2012), 54–70.
52. Burns et al., "Enlargement and the Environment."
53. On the EU as an international actor, see Charlotte Bretherton and John Vogler, *The European Union as a Global Actor*, second edition (London: Routledge, 2005); Keleman "Globalizing European Union Environmental Policy"; Schreurs and Tiberghien, "European Union Leadership in Climate Change."

54. See Sebastian Oberthür, "The EU as an International Actor: Protection of the Ozone Layer," *Journal of Common Market Studies* 37, no. 4.
(December 1999), 641–59; Markus Jachtenfuchs, "The European Community and the Protection of the Ozone Layer," *Journal of Common Market Studies* 28, no. 3 (March 1990) 261–77.

55. Oberthür, "The EU as an International Actor."

56. See Loren Cass, *The Failures of American and European Climate Policy* (New York: SUNY Press, 2006); Schreurs and Tiberghien, "European Union Leadership in Climate Change"; Vogler, "The European Union as a Global Environmental Policy Actor."

57. Jon Burchell and Simon Lightfoot, "Leading the Way: the European Union at the WSSD," *European Environment* 14, no. 6 (November/December 2004), 331–441.

58. "The EU Climate and Energy Package," European Commission Climate Action, <http://ec.europa.eu/clima/policies/brief/eu/package_en.htm> (accessed January 27, 2011).

59. Charlotte Burns and Neil Carter, "The European Parliament and Climate Change: from Symbolism to Heroism and Back Again," in Wurzel and Connelly, *The European Union as a Leader in International Climate Change Politics*, 58–73.

60. *The Guardian*, <http://www.guardian.co.uk/environment/2011/dec/11/connie-hedegaard-durban-climate-talks?intcmp=239>.

61. See Keleman, "Globalizing European Union Environmental Policy."

CHAPTER 37

EUROPEAN CONSUMER LAW

HANS-W. MICKLITZ

37.1 WHAT DOES CONSUMER LAW REVEAL ABOUT THE NATURE OF THE EU?

Consumer law has been and still is the spearhead of the European integration process. In a nutshell it reflects the different stages of development, the market focus, and the growing social impact.[1] This chapter aims to demonstrate how the European Commission took the lead in using consumer law and policy in building and completing the internal market. As a result consumer law moved a considerable distance away from its social outlook and was converted into a market-focused law. The emphasis of the Lisbon Agenda[2] on international competitiveness enhances and accelerates the transformation process of consumer law, away from market law toward industrial law. The guiding philosophy is economic efficiency: the consumer has to be made fit and requires the necessary capabilities to be able to reap the benefit of the EU's internal market. However, the streamlining of consumer law and policy leads to social exclusion of all those who do not meet these standards. The social dimension which seems to have been suppressed in the instrumentalization of consumer law as a means to secure the completion of the internal market forcefully reappears on the political agenda. The challenge for the years to come is to find a regulatory scheme for the socially excluded, for the vulnerable, the weak, and the uneducated citizen-consumer.

37.2 The Establishment of Consumer Law as a Building Block in the Internal Market Project

The most fascinating phenomenon is that the European Community got so heavily involved in consumer law and policy at all. The original Treaty of Rome granted no legislative competence in the field of consumer protection—one was inserted into the Treaty only as late as 1993, with the entry into force of the Maastricht Treaty. The first two programs of the European Commission from 1976 and 1981 might be understood as in terms of a "me too" approach. In the aftermath of President Kennedy's declaration in 1962, the member states discovered consumer protection as a field of regulatory activity in reaction to the developing consumer society. In this initial stage the role of the European Commission was rather limited. It sought to coordinate national consumer policy projects bearing a strong social welfare outlook. The major preoccupation was to protect the consumer against information deficits, misleading advertising, and new risks to health and safety; she should be equipped with appropriate rights and be given a voice in law-making and law enforcement. Four legislative projects were brought to fruition under the rule of unanimity in Council during this initial period: Directives 84/450 on misleading advertising, 85/374 on product liability, 85/377 on doorstep selling, and 87/102 on consumer credit.

37.2.1 The Impetus Provided by the SEA

The adoption of the SEA in 1986 changed the scenario dramatically. The newly introduced Art. 100(a)[3] mandated the European Commission to take regulatory measures to complete the internal market, inter alia in the field of consumer protection "at a high level." The equally new rule of QMV in Council paved the way for energetic regulatory activity in the 1990s. The guiding spirit of the European Consumer Policy is to be found in the highly influential Sutherland report.[4] The European consumer and European consumer law were instrumentalized in order to complete the internal market. Step-by-step, the European Commission implemented the two consumer programs and gave regulatory shape to the five identified consumer rights: the right to protection of health and safety, the right to protection of economic interests, the right of redress, the right of information and education, and the right to be heard.

Within the space of less than fifteen years the European Community developed a relatively consistent body of European private law affecting the consumer, even if this was at the time largely unnoticed in political and academic circles. The general part consists of rules governing the pre-contractual stage (Directives 84/450 on misleading advertising and 98/6 on price indication), rules on the modalities of contract conclusion (Directive

85/577 on doorstep selling and Directive 97/7 on distant selling), and rules on the control of unfair contract terms (Directive 93/13). The rules governing the specific part cover contract law (consumer credit in Directive 87/102, package tours in Directive 90/314, time sharing in Directive 94/47, consumer sales in Directive 99/44) and tort law (via Directive 85/374 on product liability). Directive 98/27 on injunctions pays tribute to the growing importance of collective enforcement issues.

The right to protection of health and safety was enshrined in Directive 92/59 on general product safety, which was adopted to complement the so-called "new approach" directives, named after the 1985 "New Approach on Technical Standards and Regulations" which was designed to overcome the burdensome and over-complex harmonization of technical rules within the EU legislative process. The "new approach" set aside non-tariff technical barriers to trade via a new regulatory technique, whereby EU directives formulated "general requirements" with regard to groups of products, which were then given concrete shape by the European Standards Bodies—European Committee for Standardization (CEN) and European Committee for Electrotechnical Standardization (CENELEC). Directive 92/59 was intended to work as a safety net to cover those areas where no "new approach" type directives existed or where gaps in those directives had to be filled. It installed an innovative European-wide post-market control mechanism to withdraw unsafe products from national markets and from the wider internal market.

37.2.2 The European Commission as Key Player and the Minimum Harmonization Approach

Gradually the European Community became the key player in consumer law and policy. Member states were ready to leave the prerogative to the European Commission. A coordinated approach via European rules was presented as better suited and more appropriate as the means to introduce new consumer protection regulation. However, this is only a half-truth. The European Commission could legitimately step in and receive support from the majority of the old member states, because consumer law and policy were already on the decline in the old member states. The development of social welfare policy had lost pace, the economic situation in most of the old member states had become more difficult, criticism of regulatory failure gained ground, and a new paradigm for a more liberal and less intrusive economy policy spilled over from the US via the UK to continental Europe. The remaining conceptual differences were balanced out through preference for the *minimum* harmonization principle. The European Commission managed to convince reluctant member states that the EU rules should establish only a kind of common floor. Without discussing what "minimum standards" meant, member states' sovereignty was explicitly preserved in so far as they chose to maintain or introduce *more* protective standards, going beyond the EU minimum, with the sole exception of Directive 85/374 on product liability. In *Gonzales*[5] the Court of

Justice held, much to the surprise of member states, that the Directive aims at full, not minimum, harmonization.

37.2.3 The Impact of the Internal Market Regime on the Concept of Consumer Law

Viewed retrospectively, the delegation of competences from the member states to the European Community generated major changes in the perception, role, and function of consumer law. Long before the enlargements of the EU in 2004 and 2007, the European Commission succeeded in changing the outlook of consumer law. The original intention of consumer law and policy were to protect the weaker party in the market. The introduction of this new protective target in national legal systems produced strong reactions not only from politicians but also from academics, in particular in continental Europe. "Consumer private law" was accused of challenging the unity of civil law systems by introducing status-related rules and thereby undermining the concept of equality. According to this critique, the protection of the weaker party should not be tied to a particular definition of "the consumer."

The European Community, quite on the contrary, was constitutionally constrained to focus its regulatory activities on a particular understanding of the "European Consumer." The SEA introduced competences only with regard to consumer law, not with regard to the much wider issue of harmonizing civil law systems. All relevant directives, with the exception of Directive 98/6 on price indications, were adopted on the basis of what is today Art. 114 TFEU (formerly Art. 95 EC)—they were therefore tied to the internal market project. Consumer law was capable of being realized and was realized only through its tie to the internal market project. This has consequences for the shape of EU consumer law and policy. The internal market should not only be to the benefit of producers and suppliers; it should also enable consumers to have their fair share of the advantages of breaking down barriers to trade in the form of increased choice, better quality, and lower prices. Therefore the internal market project required a different consumer: not the weak consumer who needs to be protected against risks to her health and violation of her economic interests, but rather a consumer who is willing and competent to play an active role in the completion of the internal market.[6] To achieve this new vision European consumer law had to reduce concern for the initial overwhelmingly protective outlook of consumer policy in the 1960s and 1970s. It might go too far to say that the European consumer law which was established in the 1990s lacks the protective dimension. However, the European consumer behind the internal market project and the Sutherland report is a consumer who might deserve protection, but only as far as protection is needed to enable her to complete the tasks assigned to her in the internal market project. The European concept of protection is a very instrumental one which downplays the passive consumer, who is not interested or not competent enough to benefit from the achievements of the internal market.[7] The European consumer is a normative construct—an ideal average market participant who constantly surveys the market and looks for the best price–quality ratio and who makes use of the mandatory information provided to her prior to the conclusion of a contract. The EU legislator's understanding of the European consumer builds on the normative concept that the Court had already developed in its case law on the four market freedoms. The *Leitbild* (model) is tied to a genuine concept of justice, one which I have termed "access justice" and which differs from national social justice in the sense of distributive justice whose elements can be found in the concept of the weak consumer who is in need of protection.[8] But the choice of minimum harmonization releases this tension: neither conceptual differences between the average, well-informed, and circumspect European consumer and more protective normative and factual designs preferred at national level, nor different models of justice matter, since the EU's minimum standard allows for deviating conceptual criteria at national level.

37.3 THE CURRENT STATE OF PLAY: REAPING THE BENEFITS OF THE INTERNAL MARKET AND MAKING THE EU THE MOST COMPETITIVE ECONOMY IN THE WORLD

The current stage of European consumer law may best be characterized by referring to the spirit of the Lisbon Agenda 2000 from which the above sub-heading is almost literally taken. Whilst the internal market project is the driving force, the Lisbon Agenda has changed and is still about to change the regulatory agenda and the substance of European consumer law.

37.3.1 The New Paradigm: Economic Efficiency—Maximum Harmonization and International Orientation

Two new parameters have entered the European scene: the economic efficiency doctrine and the international orientation of European integration. The economic efficiency doctrine lies behind the current policy shift from minimum to maximum harmonization (not only in consumer law); the international orientation enhances the importance of industrial policy as a device to make Europe fit for the challenges of globalization. Both together initiate a paradigm shift, according to which consumer policy is no longer seen solely as an integral part of the internal market policy but as part of a broader reorientation of the EU to meet the challenges of globalization. Thereby the normative *Leitbild* of the consumer and the prevailing patterns of justice are again subjected to change, from the average consumer to the confident, empowered consumer-entrepreneur, and from access justice to rough justice.[9]

The changing philosophy is only partly reflected in the EU's consumer policy pro-grams, the new agendas, the new impetus, or the new action plans which have been adopted since the Lisbon Agenda in a language which resembles in a frightening way the rhetoric of socialist planning. Perhaps the most outspoken statement can be found in the communication from the Commission on a consumer policy strategy 2002–2006, which gave shape to the Lisbon Agenda: "There is also a need to review and reform existing EU consumer protection directives, to bring them up to date and progressively adapt them from minimum harmonization to 'full harmonization' measures."[10] The current EU Consumer Policy strategy 2007–2013[11] confirms the previous strategy and insists on the implementation of the threefold objective of "Empowering consumers, enhancing their welfare, effectively protecting them." The only new mandate the European Commission received via the Council resolution adopting the strategy concerns the plea to investigate the feasibility of introducing collective redress mechanisms.

The economic thinking behind such a consumer policy is a rather simplistic one. It relies on a crude understanding of law and economics, thereby setting aside more sophisticated arguments which are brought forward in the debate about minimum or maximum harmonization even from a law and economics perspective. It equally neglects twenty to thirty years of empirical research on information economics, on bounded rationality, and on behavioral economics.[12]

37.3.2 The Revision of the Consumer *Acquis* in the Context of the Private Law Codification Project

The policy consequences take shape in consumer contract law through the European Private Law codification project which was launched in the communication of the Commission in 2001,[13] after a decade of pressure from the European Parliament. The European Commission merged the well-established and financially independent Study Group, first run by Ole Lando and then by Christian von Bar, with the newly established Acquis Group headed by Hans Schulte-Nölke. The former had already developed the PECL (Principles of European Contract Law) which relied on a comparative analysis of national private law systems. The latter's concern was to analyze and write down the European private law legislative *acquis*. Both groups developed separate principles, which were eventually merged in the Academic Draft Common Frame of Reference (DCFR). The DCFR is conceptualized as a fully fledged code of European Civil Law (not only contract law). It combines default rules in business to business (b2b) transactions with mandatory rules in business to consumer (b2c) relations. Whilst the political future of the DCFR is still uncertain (a draft regulation for a Common European Sales Law was presented in October 2011[14]), it already serves as a benchmark in the scientific discourse on the future of European private law. As early as 2005, the European Commission decided to single out the revision of the consumer *acquis*[15] from the private law codification project. The European Commission listed eight directives—price indication, two on the modalities of contract conclusion, doorstep selling and distant selling, the directive on unfair terms, three directives on specific types of contracts (package tours, time-sharing, consumer sales), and last but not least the directive on injunctions. The overall objective of the European Commission is to implement the 2002–2006 consumer strategy in transforming minimum into maximum standards, by combining a horizontal approach—uniting the four directives on doorstep, distant selling, unfair terms, and consumer sales—with a vertical approach on package tours and time-sharing.

The European Commission had carefully prepared the ground for its policy shift by way of a comprehensive consultation procedure and impact assessments at the several stages of development. The consultation procedure faces criticism that it does not meet democratic standards and the impact assessment has been accused of employing methodology that is scientifically unsound.[16] The European Commission managed nevertheless to adopt an impressive series of consumer law directives which define maximum standards. The first was Directive 2002/65 on distant selling of financial services, the second and the third (after lengthy political debates) were Directive 2005/29 on unfair commercial practices and Directive 2008/48 on consumer credit. From the eight directives which are part of the revision, the European Commission secured the adoption of one vertical directive (2008/122 on time-sharing), whereas the other one, the revision of the package tour directive, is under consideration. The horizontal directive was planned to become the Directive on Consumer Rights which would cover the other four directives and which is currently heavily and widely discussed. During the legislative discussions, the European Commission vigorously defended the full harmonization project through the legislative procedure—against resistance and reluctance from various sides. In the end it achieved the full harmonization of door step sales and distant sales, now merged in the directive 2011/83. The European Commission does not intend to propose changes to Directive 98/6 on price indications even though it lacks rules on services, nor will it seek to change Directive 98/27 (now re-enacted as Directive 2009/22). The process of consumer law-making as inspired by the Consumer Strategy 2002–2006 is possibly coming to a temporary halt.

The current and the emerging body of consumer law is far from being consistent and coherent. There are many overlaps and inconsistencies; between Directive 97/7 on distant selling (now Directive 2011/83), Directive 2002/65 on distant selling of financial services, and Directive 2001/31 on e-commerce, which deals with the internet in b2b and b2c relations;[17] between the prohibition of misleading omissions in Directive 2005/29 on unfair commercial practices and the information duties in the Directive 2011/83 on Consumer Rights;[18] between the information duties in the two vertical directives, the horizontal Directive on consumer rights, and the directives which are not subject of the revision project; and between the shaping of the right to withdrawal in the various directives in the horizontal, the vertical, and in the directives which remain outside the revision of the consumer *acquis*. The lack of consistency might remain a concern for continental lawyers; from the perspective of economic efficiency and legal certainty it is more than a *quantité negligible*.

37.3.3 Two Important Weaknesses in EU Consumer Policy: Services and Safety

Consumer law issues reach far beyond the eight directives listed by the Commission in 2005 for review and three others that are not listed—distant selling of financial services, commercial practices, and consumer credit. More than 70 percent of today's GDP results from services.[19] The reach of the revised body of consumer law is therefore limited. The main subject matter handled by Directorate-General Sanco in the Commission is in fact late twentieth-century consumer law, perhaps with the exception of rules governing internet shopping. What is excluded in the revision of the consumer law *acquis* is the whole field of services where consumer problems are playing an increasing role and where the EU lacks a horizontal approach, in part due to the fact that regulatory competence is spread over various directorates in the Commission. Directive 2006/123, which is designed to cover services outside regulated markets, impacts on consumer policy via information duties,[20] via securing internet sales across the border, and via technical standards on service contracts elaborated through CEN and CENELEC and national standard bodies.[21] Particular rules on consumer protection are enshrined in (1) Directives 2009/72 on electricity and Directive 2009/73 on gas and specified by the Energy Charter on Consumer Rights; (2) Directive 2009/136 on telecommunication and Directive 2008/6 on postal services, which lay down universal service obligations; (3) Regulation 261/2004 on air passenger rights, Regulation 1371/2007 on railroad passengers, Regulation 181/2011 on the rights of passengers in bus and coach travel and Regulation 1177/2011 concerning the rights of passengers when travelling by sea and inland waterways; (4) MIFID Directive 2004/39 on investment services as specified in Directive 2006/73 and Regulation 2006/1287 adopted under the Lamfalussy procedure, which lay down particular rules applicable to the retail client (the consumer); (5) the Directive 2011/24 on patient rights in trans-border health services. The European Commission does not pursue a full harmonization approach according to a "one fits all" approach—at least not yet. The four regulations on passenger rights aim at full harmonization, the energy directives are restricted to minimum harmonization, the telecommunication directive combines maximum harmonization with further options for the member states in particular areas, and the directive on financial services strives for full harmonization although in a rather narrow field. Once a true competitive market is achieved, full harmonization might become an issue.[22]

The strong focus on private law relations has thrown health and safety somewhat into the background. The original general directive on product safety was replaced in 2001 by Directive 2001/95, which extended the scope of application and broadened the regulatory tools available to public authorities. Although the European Commission launched various initiatives to investigate the safety of services, it does not see any need to take regulatory action with regard to Directive 2001/95, which covers only product-related services, or with regard to the liability for services.[23] Directive 85/374 on product liability remained unchanged and there is nothing which points toward revitalizing the withdrawn proposal on the safety of services. A second deficit results from the outdated focus of European product safety regulation on the producer. This overlooks the fact that the vast majority of consumer products are imported into the EU, mainly from China. The key actors in today's market are dealers, wholesalers, and importers. The European Commission has recently rejected any attempt to upgrade the subsidiary liability of dealers under the Product Liability Directive 85/374. Failing completely to appreciate the increasing importance of dealers in international trade, the *Gonzales* doctrine, which the ECJ confirmed in *Skov*,[24] precludes member states from maintaining more stringent liability rules for non-producers. The general product safety Directive 2001/95 includes distributors to a broader extent, but there is no initiative underway to establish a modern market surveillance system that pays tribute to changing market structures. Directive 2001/95 on general product safety and Regulation 765/2008 on market surveillance with the competences of the custom authorities do not create a coordinated approach to internal market surveillance in the EU.

37.3.4 Individual–Collective and Judicial–Administrative Enforcement

Enforcement of EU rules lies in the hands of the member states. The European legislator developed three different strategies to install rudimentary enforcement structures: first through the competence conferred by Art. 114 TFEU (formerly Art. 95 EC) to combine substantive law-making with obligations imposed on member states to adopt effective, adequate, and deterrent remedies; secondly through the explicit competence under Art. 81 TFEU (formerly Art. 65 EC), which is limited to trans-border enforcement; and thirdly through the steady promotion of alternative dispute mechanisms either under the two above-mentioned competence rules or via soft mechanisms outside and beyond the powers enumerated by the Treaty. Over time the European Community has established a dense set of enforcement rules despite the rather shaky competences. They can be broken down into individual versus collective and private/judicial versus public/administrative enforcement. Setting individual enforcement aside (which is guaranteed by directly enforceable rights as shaped by the Court's case law and alternative dispute resolution (ADR) mechanisms),[25] the European Commission put much emphasis from the very early days of consumer law on the development of collective enforcement mechanisms. The action for an injunction belongs to the minimum protection standards which member states have to guarantee—nationally against unfair contract terms and unfair commercial practices, and in trans-border litigation via Directive 98/27.

During the first twenty-five years of EU consumer policy, the European Commission heavily relied on private collective enforcement through consumer organizations, in particular in the case of trans-border issues. The adoption of Regulation 2006/2004 on Co-Operation in Trans-border Consumer Protection marks the turning point in the development of enforcement policy. Since then, the European Commission promotes the establishment of public agencies to which collective enforcement shall be entrusted. This goes hand in hand with empowered national agencies in regulated markets. This should not only ensure a functioning competitive market but also one in which responsible agencies are increasingly obliged to take consumer protection into consideration.

37.3.5 The Role and Function of the Court of Justice in Secondary Consumer Law

For quite some time the European Commission has been the sole European actor engaged in shaping and developing consumer policy. In the 1990s there were only a few opportunities for the Court of Justice to contribute to European consumer law. Since around 2000 the Court forcefully entered the scene as more and more national courts made use of the preliminary reference procedure to seek advice in the interpretation of the relevant European directives and regulations.[26] Including infringement procedures, and taking into account litigation based on the Brussels Convention and Regulation, there is now an impressive body of more than eighty judgments of the Court, of which some fifty concern preliminary references, which impact on European consumer law.

Most of these references were brought forward by national courts in order to ascertain whether national law should be upgraded given that European minimum standards require a higher level of protection. The maximum harmonization approach will turn the prevailing mode of references upside down. *Gonzales* has triggered a whole series of preliminary references in the field of product liability, all of which involve attempts to show that "higher" national standards have to be set aside as incompatible with the EU's maximum standard. The same scenario can be observed in the references brought forward under Directive 2005/29 on unfair commercial practices, where the Court has taken a harsh stand in *VTB-VAT*[27] against any efforts of the member states to escape or circumvent the fully harmonized scope of application of the Directive. These experiences may serve as a blueprint for the type of conflicts between EU and national law which will come up in the aftermath of the full harmonization approach so successfully implemented in the program on the revision of the consumer *acquis*.

Whereas in primary EU law the Court is said to take a robust interpretation of the consumer which is in line with the internal market ideology, in secondary law the Court is said to be more inclined to take the consumer who is in need of protection as a yardstick.[28] Such a reading, however, does not fully reflect the impression that the Court is oscillating between various concepts of protection, sometimes to the benefit of the consumer, sometimes to her detriment. It is hard to recognize a clear-cut model of protection. In this regard the case law concerning consumers resembles that arising in labor law.

The Court has developed and confirmed in a whole series of cases that the "consumer" has to be narrowly construed, thereby striking down attempts to apply the concept of the consumer to natural persons during the process of setting up business in *Benincasa*[29] or to legal persons in *Idealservice*,[30] giving a rather narrow reading of dual use products in *Gruber*,[31] and of atypical business transactions in *di Pinto*.[32] Whilst most of the judgments concerned the Brussels Convention/Regulation, the Court seems ready to use a consistent approach more broadly, although the EU's consumer contract law, which still relies on minimum harmonization, ensures that the Court's rulings on the meaning of EU law leave room for deviation from stricter standards in the member states. *Océano*[33] stands for a strong protective outlook in the control of unfair terms which is counterbalanced by a more lenient attitude in *Freiburger Kommunalbauten*[34] and *Mostanza Claro*.[35] In *Gysbrechts*[36] the Court rejected stricter national protective standards which seemed justifiable under the minimum harmonization principle on the basis that they violated the proportionality principle; in *Buet*,[37] *Doc Morris*,[38] and *Caja de Ahorros*[39] the Court reached exactly the opposite conclusion on the permissibility of stricter national rules. Given such variation in outcome, it is hard to demonstrate that the Court is guided by the rhetoric and philosophy of the Lisbon Agenda, although *VTB-VAT*, *Gonzales*, and *Gysbrechts* point in this direction.

37.3.6 Impact on the Revised Concept of Protection in Consumer Law

The efficiency doctrine—especially if linked to legal certainty—seems to call for a European regulation laying down consistent and coherent maximum standards on consumer law. Whilst the European Commission would obviously support such a reading of its approach, reality is different. Consumer law, even after the heralded announcement of the revision of the consumer law *acquis*, remains a patchwork in the EU, not only in the traditional set of rules forming the *acquis* in the narrow sense but also in the whole area of services, in particular in regulated markets. The European Commission did not even manage to achieve the intended shift from minimum to maximum harmonization in the adoption of Rome I Regulation[40] and Rome II Regulation.[41] These measures explicitly start from deviations from protective standards in the member states and guarantee the consumer principally that she cannot be deprived of stricter national protective standards in cross-border transactions. However, the proposal on a Common European Sales Law would, if adopted, make the Rome Regulations obsolete.

What has long been missing is a deeper discussion of (a) what maximum harmonization legally means, (b) where it is economically feasible and justifiable, and (c) where it is politically desirable. Maximum harmonization linked to "pre-emption" would require member states to disregard all national rules which could overlap with the scope of fully harmonized EU rules. Such a wide reading of maximum harmonization would create unpredictable effects in national private law systems as each and every fully harmonized rule would have to be tested in the particular factual and regulatory contexts of twenty-seven legal orders. A narrow reading would and could limit the reach of full harmonization to developed conceptual schemes actually set out in the various fully harmonized directives or those which fail to be fully harmonized in the future.[42] It would reduce the destructive potential of full harmonization at the expense of undermining the economic purpose of the directives. A solid economic analysis would make the full harmonization approach much more complex, in particular if a regulatory approach were to take the empirical evidence into account. Nobody reads standard contract terms and conditions—what does this mean for legal rules regulating the insertion of standard terms?[43] The European Commission is proud to have realized a single delay for the execution of the right of withdrawal. Does it make sense not to distinguish between internet sales, time-sharing, and consumer credit?[44] Full harmonization might ideally impose the same regime of protection on all consumers all over Europe, independent of differences between North and South and East and West. But sociological research tells us that Europe is governed by a transnational elite[45] which is relatively homogeneous but which is in no way connected to a particular nation state. The consumer residing in Milan might be much more similar to the consumer in London or Paris than to her compatriot in southern Italy. Maximum harmonization might therefore be desirable for a particular social class which cuts across countries, but it could yield counter-productive effects if applied to all consumers independent of their economic, social, and intellectual capacities wherever they reside. On the other hand, it should not be overlooked that full harmonization might be useful in member states which do not have a genuine consumer policy and which seek orientation from Brussels.

The Lisbon Agenda has even tightened the qualifications the consumer has to meet if she wants to reap the benefits of the internal market. She is there to yield consumer welfare to the benefit of the market and the society. She has to behave like the perfect and efficient "shopper" in internet sales and she has to compare prices of services in regulated markets in order to be able to make use of the often legally guaranteed right to switch. The Lisbon Agenda strives for the transformation of consumers into efficient shoppers and efficient switchers. Empowerment—to use the wording of the 2007–2013 consumer program—requires not only enforceable rights in national and trans-border relations (which, from the perspective of the Commission, European consumer law is on the road to establish through the shift to maximum harmonization). It also calls for appropriate educational training programs to ensure consumers are able to acquire the necessary "capabilities".[46] Such a consumer is obviously multilingual. She is at least able to communicate in English, to read and to write in English, to conclude contracts in English, and to enforce her rights in English. Otherwise, how are we to explain the fact that the whole set of European consumer law rules devote practically no attention to language issues?

37.4 The Challenges Ahead

37.4.1 The Risk of Social Exclusion

The pressure the Lisbon Agenda puts on the new ideal of the European consumer will increase the risk of social exclusion, in particular if full harmonization no longer allows the member states to defend a concept of consumer protection which puts more emphasis on the protection of the weaker party. There are millions of consumers in Europe who do not meet the standards of the "efficient shopper" and the "flexible switcher." What shall happen to them? Can they be defined and distinguished from the successful shopper or switcher? The Lisbon Agenda strives for social cohesion and advocates social inclusion, but it neither distinguishes different groups of consumers according to their capabilities nor does it provide for strategies designed to secure their inclusion. European law marshals the category of "vulnerable consumer" in Directive 2005/29 on unfair commercial practices, in the two energy directives, and recital (26) of the Directive 2009/136 on telecommunications. The regulation on passenger rights and the directive on telecommunications provide for particular rules on the protection of disabled people. Neither of these two categories exists in financial services or in the fully harmonized consumer contract law. The "consumer" is equated with the protection of the weaker party. Hence, there is no need for particular rules on the "vulnerable consumer." Prospective and real problems resulting from the narrow concept of the European ideal-type consumer, which yields and fosters social exclusion, are solved— by way of definition.

37.4.2 A New Social Economic Law for the Vulnerable?

The EU cannot deprive member states of all competence to look after the vulnerable consumer-citizen. Two options can be identified. First, the member states can generalize the notion of the vulnerable consumer already existent or about to exist in the near future in various pieces of EU and national law. Second, they can argue that the weak party or the weak person does not count as a "consumer" according to the European ideal and therefore does not fall under the European definition. Both options lead in the end to a new category of social economic or social private law. The advantage of the first option is that the concept of universal services contains potential for generalizations. In a rather protracted way, social exclusion is linked to the consumer-citizen dimension.[47] The European Commission started using this language in its communications on services of general (economic) interests, thereby pointing to the particular character of former public services and to the need to guarantee the protection of the weakest in the society. The disadvantage of the second option is that such reasoning creates new barriers between the different national legal orders. The concept of universal services could lay down ground rules in the form of a legal framework which might gain importance not only in the field of former public services, but in the area of financial and digital services. Or more broadly, in all those areas where access to certain goods and services is crucial for a person's capacity to participate in society, and not just in the market. Emphasis on the citizen dimension would allow policy-makers to get to grips with the still underdeveloped right to be heard (participation rights).

37.4.3 Installing Appropriate Enforcement Structures

Despite possible lacunae, inconsistencies, and overlaps, European consumer law has gained a certain status within the European legal order. The EU will obviously continue producing new consumer rules. However, these new rules will increasingly aim at amending and supplementing the existing body of rules. That is why there is ample need to shift the focus from law-making to law enforcement. The challenge in the years to come will be to further the development of appropriate enforcement structures which guarantee that European law will be more than merely law in the books.

The European Commission is currently discussing the introduction of collective compensation claims in competition[48] and consumer law.[49] It seems as if the European Commission favors collective compensation via public enforcement agencies instead of granting standing to consumer organizations or ad hoc collective entities (although it is far from clear whether and when the European Commission will be ready to take action). What is still missing in the European debate is an attempt to link collective and individual enforcement, before the courts and through ADR mechanisms.[50] Consumers who enforce their individual rights might be given the opportunity to refer in the litigation to binding regulatory decisions taken by enforcement agencies which affect individual consumers. This entails a need to tackle the issue of access to information which is stored and saved by regulatory agencies but which might be crucial for the enforcement of individual rights. Similar issues arise from judgments taken by competent courts in actions for injunctions prohibiting the use or recommendation of unfair contract terms or prohibiting unfair or misleading advertising. There is a need to discuss the *erga omnes* effects of such judgments to the benefit of individual consumers.

Notes

1. Stephen Weatherill, *EU Consumer Law and Policy* (Cheltenham: Elgar, 2005).
2. Presidency Conclusions, Lisbon European Council, March 23 and 24, 2000, <http://www.europarl.europa.eu/summits/lis1_en.htm>. *Now Europe 2020*, Communication of the Commission, COM (2010) 2020, March 3, 2010.
3. Today Art. 114 of the Treaty on the Functioning of the European Union (TFEU).
4. *Sutherland Report: The Internal Market after 1992: Meeting the Challenge, Report to the EEU Commission by the High Level Group on the Operation of the Internal Market*, <http://aei.pitt.edu/1025>.
5. European Union Journal, *Case C-183/00, 2002 I-3879*, April 25, 2002.
6. Stephen Weatherill, "Who is the Average Consumer?," in S. Weatherill and U. Bernitz, eds, *The Regulation of Unfair Commercial Practices under EC Directive 2005/39: New Rules and New Techniques* (Oxford: Hart Publishing, 2007), 115–38.
7. Thomas Wilhelmsson, "The Abuse of the 'Confident Consumer' as a Justification for EC Consumer Law," *Journal of Consumer Policy* 27 (2004), 317–37.
8. Hans-W. Micklitz, "Social Justice in European Private Law," in Piet Eeckhout and Takis Tridimas, eds, *Yearbook of European Law 19* (Oxford: Clarendon Press, 1999/2000), 167–204.
9. Gralf-Peter Calliess, *Grenzüberschreitende Verbraucherverträge, Rechtssicherheit und Gerechtigkeit auf dem elektronischen Weltmarktplatz* (Tübingen: Mohr Siebeck, 2006). Gralf-Peter Calliess and Peer Zumbansen, *Rough Consensus and Running Code* (Oxford: Hart, 2010).

10. Consumer policy strategy 2002–2006, European Commission, COM (2002) 208 final, June 8, 2002.

11. European Commission, COM (2007) 299 final, March 13, 2007.

12. Lucia A. Reisch and Inge Røpke, eds, *The Ecological Economics of Consumption*. Edward Elgar Series Current Issues in Ecological Economics (Cheltenham: Elgar, 2004).

13. European Commission, COM (2001) 398 final, July 11, 2001.

14. COM (2011) 635 final of 11.10.2011.

15. See already Draft, European Commission, COM (2006) 744 final, February 2, 2007.

16. Thorsten Hüller, *Demokratie und Soziale Regulierung in Europa. Die Online-Konsultationen der EU Kommission* (Frankfurt: Campus, 2010).

17. Martin Schirmbacher, *Verbrauchervertriebsrecht—Die Vereinheitlichung der Vorschriften über Haustürgeschäfte, Fernabsatzverträge und Verträge im elektronischen Geschäftsverkehr* (Baden-Baden: Nomos, 2005).

18. European Commission, COM (2008) 614 final, October 8, 2008.

19. European Commission, COM (2007) 724 final, November 20, 2007, 8.

20. Wulf-Henning Roth, "Freier Dienstleistungsverkehr und Verbraucherschutz," *Verbraucher und Recht* 24 (2007), 161–72.

21. Thomas Ackermann, "Das Informationsmodell im Recht der Dienstleistungen," *Zeitschrift für Europäisches Privatrecht* 17 (2009), 230–67.

22. Beate Gsell and Carsten Herresthal, eds, *Vollharmonisierung im Privatrecht* (Tübingen: Mohr Siebeck, 2009).

23. Ulrich Magnus and Hans-W. Micklitz, *Liability for the Safety of Services* (Baden-Baden: Nomos, 2006).

24. EUJ, 10.1.2006 C-402/03, 2006, I-199.

25. Now under revision. DG Sanco/12360/2011, Draft Directive on ADR; and DG Sanco/12361/2011, Draft Regulation on ODR,

26. Weatherill, *EU Consumer Law and Policy*.

27. European Court of Justice, EUJ, 23.4.2009, 261/07, 2009 I-nyr.

28. H. Unberath and A. Johnston, "The Double-Headed Approach of the ECJ Concerning Consumer Protection," *Common Market Law Review* 44 (2007), 1237–84.

29. Official Journal of the European Union (EUJ), 3.7.1997, C-269/95, 1997, I-3767.

30. EUJ, 22.11.2001, C-541/99, 2001, I-9049.

31. EUJ, 20.1.2005, C-461/01, 2005, I-439.

32. EUJ, 14.3.1991, C-361/89, 1991, I-1189.

33. EUJ, 27.6.2000, Case C-240/98, 2000 ECR I-4941

34. EUJ, 1.4.2002, Case C-237/02, 2004 I-3403

35. EUJ, 26.10.2006, Case C-168/05, 2006 I-10421.

36. EUJ, 17.7.2008, Case, C-205/07, 2008 I-9947.

37. EUJ, 16.5.1989, C-382/87, 1989 ECR-I-1235.

38. EUJ, 11.12.2003, Deutscher Apothekerverband, 2003, I-14887.

39. EUJ, 3.6.2010, C-484/08, 2010/C 209/07.

40. European Parliament and the Council, Regulation No. 593/2008 *(Rome I)*, June 17, 2008.

41. European Parliament and the Council, Regulation No. 864/2007 *(Rome II)*, July 11, 2007.

42. S. Whitaker, "Unfair Contract Terms and Consumer Guarantees: the Proposal for a Directive on Consumer Rights and the Significance of Full Harmonisation," *European Review of Contract Law* 5 (2009), 223–47.

43. Omri Ben-Shahar, "The Myth of the Opportunity to Read in Contract Law," *European Review of Contract Law* 5 (2009), 1–28.

44. Pamaria Rekaiti and Roger van den Bergh, "Cooling-off Periods in the Consumer Laws of the Member States. A comparative Law and Economics Analysis," *Journal of Consumer Policy* 23 (2000), 371–408.

45. Richard Münch, *Die Konstruktion der Europäischen Gesellschaft* (Frankfurt: Campus, 2008).

46. Geraint Howells, "The Potential and Limits of Consumer Empowerment by Information," *Journal of Law Society* 32 (2005), 349–70.

47. Jim Davies, "Entrenchment of New Governance in Consumer Policy Formulation: A Platform for European Consumer Citizenship Practice," *Journal of Consumer Policy* 32, no. 3 (2009), 245–67.

48. European Commission, COM (2005) 672 final, December 19, 2005, and European Commission, SEC (2005) 1732, December 19, 2005; European Commission, COM (2008) 165 final, April 2, 2008 and European Commission, SEC (2008) 404–6, April 2, 2008.

49. European Commission, COM (2008) 794 final, November 27, 2008.

50. J. Stuyck et al., *An analysis and evaluation of alternative means of consumer redress, other than redress through ordinary judicial proceedings, Final Report*, January 2007, <http://ec.europa.eu/consumers/redress/reports_studies/comparative_report_en.pdf>.

....

CHAPTER 38

SOCIAL POLICY AND LABOR MARKET REGULATION

....

CATHERINE BARNARD AND SIMON DEAKIN

38.1 INTRODUCTION

....

Social policy occupies a marginal and contested position in the legal order of the EU. This is the legacy of an approach which saw labor market regulation as, largely, an issue for the member states. In the Treaty of Rome the convergence of national-level labor laws was seen as a consequence of the common market, not one of its preconditions. In one of the few areas explicitly addressed by the Treaty, equal pay between men and women, the Court's activism breathed new life into the law from the mid-1970s onwards, and several directives on equal treatment and employment protection were adopted around the same time, reflecting concern over the implications for social cohesion of the extension of the market. The SEA of 1986 and the Maastricht and Amsterdam Treaties added new powers to harmonize standards in the social policy field, although these left significant gaps in comparison to the range of matters covered by national labor law regimes.

By the early 2000s, a role for EU-level intervention had been identified in terms of "steering" the laws of the member states, preserving diversity, and, at the same time, seeking to avoid a race to the bottom. Thus a "reflexive" perspective informed the design of directives which, in some cases, were based on inputs from the social partners, and left scope for flexible implementation at member-state-level. In this way, the approach to employment policy associated with the open method of coordination (OMC) came to influence the wider social policy field. But any sense of stability proved to be short-lived. The Court's judgments in *Viking* and *Laval* in December 2007 brought to the surface tensions between social policy and the "four freedoms" that had previously been suppressed. The Court's approach opens up the possibility of single market law being used to undermine national labor legislation in contexts where protective standards can be viewed as a "distortion" of the market.

In this chapter we review the evolution of EU-level social policy to this point, consider the various justifications offered for this body of law, and then examine the emergence of single market law as a threat to social policy at national level. Finally, we offer an assessment of possible future developments.

38.2 EVOLUTION OF EU-LEVEL SOCIAL POLICY

The four freedoms were the central pillar of the original Treaty of Rome. The founders believed that from the success of the common market everything else would follow. This idea was encapsulated in the original Article 117 EEC, the first Article in the Title on Social Policy, which expressed the belief that an improvement in working conditions would ensue "from the functioning of the Common Market." Nascent in this observation is the root of problems that have subsequently haunted the evolution of EU social policy. First, it recognizes the (overriding?) importance of the four freedoms and a (naïve?) faith in their ability to improve quality of life in the EU. Secondly, it is implicit from the paltry content of the original Title on Social Policy that social policy was largely a matter of national, not EU, law. As a result, the Treaty failed to provide any clear basis for the creation of social policy at EU level.

The absence of substantive content in the Social Policy Title in the EEC Treaty can be explained by the clash between France and Germany over the place of social policy in the construction of the new Europe. The Germans saw social policy as an issue of national sovereignty which should remain vested in the member states; the French wanted greater harmonization at EU level to avoid perceived "social dumping"—other member states (especially Italy) using their lower labor costs to attract capital. The result was the classic EU compromise. Articles 117 and 118 EEC, on the need to improve working conditions and cooperation between states, reflected the German preference for laissez-faire. By contrast, Articles 119 and 120 EEC on, respectively, equal pay (now Article 157 TFEU) and paid holiday schemes (now Article 158 TFEU) reflected French concerns. These four provisions hardly merited the inclusion of a Title on social policy in the EEC Treaty, so far short did they fall of what is traditionally associated with social policy at national level.

But then the original EEC Treaty did not aspire to create an EU superstate with all the attributes of a nation state. It merely wished to create a common market where the conditions of competition were not distorted. From this perspective, the Court's approach in the 1976 decision of *Defrenne (No.2)* was reflective of the original intention of the Treaty drafters:[1]

> the aim of Article [157] is to avoid a situation in which undertakings established in states which have actually implemented the principle of equal pay suffer a competitive disadvantage in intra-[Union] competition as compared with undertakings established in states which have not yet eliminated discrimination against women workers as regards pay.

However, having recognized the economic purpose of Article 157, the Court then blurred the economic focus of the provisions when it ruled that Article 157 also formed part of the social objectives of the Union. For many this observation was a revelation and marked a sea change in approach. In *Defrenne (No. 3)*[2] the Court went further, elevating the principle of equality to the status of a fundamental right. It argued that "respect for fundamental personal human rights is one of the general principles of [Union] law... there can be no doubt that the elimination of discrimination based on sex forms part of those fundamental rights."

The *Defrenne* line of cases highlights three further points about the evolution of social policy at EU level. First, equality has been the mainstay of EU social policy. Article 157 on equal pay was included in the Treaty of Rome; three of the most important directives adopted in the first wave of social policy legislation in the 1970s concerned equality—Directive 75/117 on equal pay,[3] Directive 76/207 on equal treatment[4] (both now repealed and replaced by Directive 2006/54), and Directive 79/7 on equal treatment in social security.[5] The two most influential social policy directives adopted in the early 2000s (Directives 2000/43 on race and ethnic origin[6] and the framework Directive 2000/78[7]) also concerned equal treatment in respect of the other main grounds of discrimination.

Secondly, the *Defrenne* cases are illustrative of the influential role the Court has played in fleshing out the bones of social policy—or to be more precise—labor law at EU level. Until the decisions in *Viking* and *Laval* (considered below), the Court was generally seen as the defender of the worker against the interests of an (overbearing) employer. For example, it interpreted the original equal treatment Directive 76/207 so as to provide protection for pregnant women[8] and transsexuals.[9] It also said the Directive required the national system to provide effective remedies.[10] Subsequently, it interpreted the framework Directive 2000/78 to cover associative discrimination,[11] and used it as a basis for developing new general principles of law which, it ruled, could be invoked in litigation between private parties.[12] Perhaps most controversially, it ruled in *Barber*[13] that Article 157 TFEU required equality in respect of occupational pension age, despite the derogation to Directive 86/378/EEC for equal treatment in respect of occupational pensions. Trade unions, especially British trade unions, had traditionally been suspicious of courts which they tended to see as biased in favor of employers.[14] As a result of such judgments, however, they increasingly came to view strategic preliminary references to the Court of Justice as a potentially constructive way of leveraging change at national level.

Thirdly, the *Defrenne* cases remind us that the EU's approach to social policy has been largely rights-based. This can be seen in the claims for equal treatment (the *right* to equality) and the constitutionalization of these social rights through the adoption of two charters, the Social Charter of 1989, and the Charter of Fundamental Rights (2000). The 2007 version of the Charter of Fundamental Rights has now been given legal effect by Article 6(1) TEU, introduced by the Lisbon Treaty.[15] One of the striking features of the 2000 Charter is that economic and social rights are put on the same footing as civil and social rights, at least to the extent that they appear in the same document, albeit that certain states, particularly the UK, have tried to downgrade them to "principles" and to "opt-out" from the "Solidarity" Title of the Charter, which contains most social rights.[16]

The EU's approach thus stands in sharp contrast to the traditional "labor" approach, at least in the Anglo-Saxon and Nordic countries, which has not been so much about *individual* rights but *collective* institutions seeking to achieve goods for workers as a whole. In this way, EU law, particularly through the doctrines of supremacy and direct effect, has helped to empower the individual, often to the disadvantage of the collective. This helps to explain some of the concerns in trade union circles about the decisions in *Viking* and *Laval*.

Yet the interests of the collective and the individual are not always in contradiction. One of the distinctive innovations introduced by the Maastricht Treaty was a new "collective" form of law-making to supplement the traditional Community (now Union) method. It gave the social partners (management and labor) the power to negotiate collective agreements which could be extended to all workers via a "decision," in practice a directive, which would then have to be implemented by the member states in the usual way.[17] These powers have not been used as extensively as their proponents might have wished, but the handful of inter-sectoral directives which have been adopted have largely concerned equality matters (Directives on Parental Leave,[18] part-time work,[19] and fixed-term work[20]).

With the amendments to the original EEC Treaty, the competences of the EU in the field of social policy have increased. However, the legislation adopted under these provisions has been confined to a relatively narrow range of areas: equality, health and safety (broadly construed to include pregnant workers,[21] working time,[22] and young workers[23]), information and consultation,[24] rights on restructuring (collective redundancies,[25] the transfer of undertakings,[26] and insolvent employers[27]), and posted workers.[28] This brief list reveals how patchy EU-level social legislation is in practice: key areas traditionally associated with national labor law have not received the attention of the EU legislature, including dismissal, anything to do with the content of the contract of employment, pay, freedom of association, and collective action. In respect of the last three areas, Union competence, at least under Article 153(5) TFEU, is expressly excluded. This has meant that much social policy, an area of shared competence,[29] has remained largely with the member states (see Chapter 40, this volume, for a detailed discussion of the issue of competence).

The Treaty of Nice tidied up the competences introduced under the various legislative amendments. It also expressly made provision for the European Parliament and Council to adopt measures "designed to encourage cooperation through initiatives aimed at improving knowledge, developing exchanges of information and best practices." This is an example of the OMC which has been used most extensively in respect of the European Employment Strategy (EES) introduced by the Amsterdam Treaty.[30] Under the EES, member states and the Union are to "work towards developing a coordinated strategy for employment and particularly for promoting a skilled, trained and adaptable workforce and labour markets responsive to economic change." The coordination is based on "employment guidelines" drawn up by the Commission, structured initially around four pillars of employability, entrepreneurship, adaptability, and equal opportunities. While these pillars have since disappeared, the guidelines continue to place emphasis on these themes.

These developments enabled the Nice European Council to conclude:[31]

> The European social model has developed over the last forty years through a substantial Union *acquis*...It now includes essential texts in numerous areas: free movement of workers, gender equality at work, health and safety of workers, working and employment conditions and, more recently, the fight against all forms of discrimination.

This is a first. Up until Nice, the European Social Model had been defined largely in terms of national social models and common values:[32]

> These include democracy and individual rights, free collective bargaining, the market economy, equality of opportunity for all and social welfare and solidarity. These values...are held together by the conviction that economic and social progress must go hand in hand. Competitiveness and solidarity have both been taken into account in building a successful Europe for the future.

What is clear is that all of the EU institutions recognize that there is such a thing as an EU social model which builds on but is, in many respects, separate from those found in the member states. This raises the fundamental question as to why the EU, a transnational body with limited competence, has a European Social Model that it wishes to call its own. This question has bedevilled the Union since its inception.

38.3 JUSTIFICATIONS FOR EU SOCIAL POLICY

If, as the previous section indicated, social policy remains largely a matter for national law, what then is the rationale for the enactment of social policy at EU level? The justifications have varied over time but four main arguments can be detected in the debates accompanying the adoption of the legislation: (1) response to the effects of the common market; (2) industrial/social citizenship; (3) capabilities; (4) market-making. We shall examine these in turn.

One of the earliest rationales for the enactment of EU social policy was softening the blow of restructuring created by the advent of the single market. This can be seen with the adoption of the Collective Redundancies Directive 75/129/EEC.[33] The purpose of the Directive was twofold:[34] first, that greater protection be afforded to workers in the event of collective redundancies,[35] "while taking into account the need for balanced economic and social development within the [Union]";[36] and second, to promote "approximation...while the improvement (in living and working conditions) is being maintained within the meaning of Article [151 TFEU]."[37]

However, the directive did not prevent redundancies; it merely required employees and their representatives to be informed of them. In this way, it can be seen as part of the process of proceduralization of dismissal. Another way of viewing this directive is through the lens of industrial citizenship. In recent years, the Union has focused particular attention on encouraging dialogue between workers/their representatives and their employers. This is because the Union sees a clear link between dialogue and greater productivity:[38]

> Regular, transparent, comprehensive dialogue creates trust . . . The systematic development of social dialogue within companies, nationally and at European level is fundamental to managing change and preventing negative social consequences and deterioration of the social fabric . . . Social dialogue ensures a balance is maintained between corporate flexibility and workers' [security].[39]

The argument runs that workers who participate in decisions which affect them enjoy a greater degree of job satisfaction and should be more productive than those who simply accept orders.[40] Social dialogue, replacing more traditional hierarchical management arrangements, is therefore seen as a cornerstone of corporate governance designed to create the high-skill, high-effort, high-trust European labor market which lies at the core of the EES.

Others see the gradual adoption of EU social policy as a step toward the creation, not of industrial citizenship, but of social citizenship.[41] In the early days of the EU this was about giving the Union a human face in an attempt to persuade its citizens that the social consequences of growth were being effectively tackled and that the EU was more than a device enabling business to exploit the common market.[42] Later, social policy was seen as putting flesh onto the rather insubstantial bones of the citizenship provisions introduced at Maastricht. This link between citizenship and social policy was made expressly in the Commission's Citizens' Agenda of 2006 *Delivering Results for Europe*.[43] This document was part of the Commission's response to the "No" votes to the Constitutional Treaty in France and the Netherlands. It suggested that:

> A new Citizens' Agenda for Europe must deliver peace, prosperity and solidarity in a new context, globalisation. It should deliver an open and fully functioning single market and effectively turn the four freedoms into reality; promote solidarity, opportunity, access and sustainability; and increase security.

This was followed by the Commission's Social Agenda Package built round the themes of *Opportunities, Access, and Solidarity*.[44]

One of the striking features of the Social Agenda Package was the link it made with Amartya Sen's "capability approach."[45] Thus "the central ambition" of the *Renewed Social Agenda* of 2008 "is to achieve a wider distribution of 'life chances' to allow everyone in the EU to have access to the resources, services, conditions and *capabilities* in order to turn the theoretical equality of opportunities and active citizenship into a meaningful reality."[46] The use of the term "capabilities" in this context implies an active role for social policy in extending the conditions for labor market participation, and for economic opportunity more generally.[47]

The emphasis within EU employment law on the principle of equality can be seen in this light, as can the attempt to marry social protection with labor market flexibility, so-called "flexicurity," which informed the Commission's Green Paper on Labour Law of 2006.[48] This document nevertheless illustrates the tensions inherent in such a project.

The Commission used the language of flexicurity to justify the continuing absence of EU-wide labor standards in the area of dismissal law, arguing that "stringent employment protection tends to reduce the dynamism of the labour market"[49] and advocating elements of the Nordic approach to labor market regulation which it characterized in the following terms:

> Adopting a lifecycle approach to work may require shifting from the concern to protect particular jobs to a framework of support for employment security including social support and active measures to assist workers during periods of transition. This is what Denmark achieved by combining "light" employment protection legislation, intensive active labour market measures, and substantial investment in training as well as high unemployment benefits with strong conditionality.[50]

The analysis of this point contained in the Green Paper was, nevertheless, brief to the point of being superficial; it failed to take into account measures taken at national level to adapt employment protection legislation to firm-level and sector-level conditions, and failed to notice the influence of the OMC on the form of social policy directives, which had incorporated the principle of flexible implementation. The final text of the Green Paper reflected conflicting interpretations of the role of labor law which were being advanced at that time by different Directorates and the difficulty experienced by the Commission in arriving at a policy consensus on the role social policy was to play in the deepening of the integration process, a portent of things to come.[51]

A fourth objective ascribed to social policy has been that of establishing the basis for a "level playing field" between member states on issues of labor market regulation. The Court recognized this aspect of the Union's social provisions in *Commission* v. *UK*[52] in which it said that, in adopting the Directives on Collective Redundancies and Acquired Rights,[53] "the [Union] legislature intended both to ensure comparable protection for employees' rights in the different Member States and *to harmonize the costs* which those protective rules entail for [Union] undertakings" (emphasis added). In practice, this objective has rarely been expressed in a convincing way. The Spaak and Ohlin reports which preceded the Treaty of Rome concluded that regulation was not justified on cost harmonization grounds, as differences in regulation across the member states were generally a reflection of varying levels of economic development. The exception made in the Treaties for equal pay was largely ad hoc.[54] At a time when most European countries remained committed, in their domestic policies, to strong welfare states, the absence of harmonizing measures did not matter much, but this began to change in the 1990s, in part thanks to the EU's own policies of economic and monetary union, followed by enlargement in the 2000s. Member states in the eurozone lost the flexibility in domestic economic policy which fluctuating exchange rates had previously given them, thereby highlighting the need for greater flexibility in national level labor markets, while enlargement created new opportunities for firms to relocate to lower-cost regions within the Union.[55] EU-level social policy failed to provide a countervailing force against the deregulatory pressures arising from these developments, in part because of confusion over what directives in the employment field were trying to achieve. The notion of a "level

playing field" made little sense in the absence of general harmonization of labor legislation.[56] The more limited objective of a "floor of rights," signifying the aim of preventing a
race to the bottom while preserving member states' rights to legislate above the floor
where they chose to do so, represented an uneasy compromise, and even this goal was
not well articulated. When political pressure to deal with the threat of "social dumping"
in the construction industry led to the adoption of the Posted Workers' Directive in
1996,[57] lack of clarity in articulating the purposes of the measure was reflected in dense
and apparently self-contradictory drafting. This was to have far-reaching consequences
in the *Laval* judgment twelve years later.

38.4 THREATS TO (NATIONAL) SOCIAL POLICY

As we have seen, the original constitutional settlement was that the EU would concentrate on achieving free movement but that social policy would be left to the individual
member states.[58] That settlement remained undisturbed so long as the Court took the
view that the principle of non-discrimination was the driving force behind the free movement provisions because social policy provisions generally applied equally to domestic
and migrant labor alike. However, this changed when the Court's focus shifted from the
non-discrimination approach to the "market access" or "restrictions" approach. The dramatic implications of this for domestic social policy can be seen in *Viking* and *Laval*.[59]

Viking concerned a Finnish company wanting to reflag its vessel, the Rosella, under the
Estonian flag so that it could man the ship with an Estonian crew to be paid considerably
less than the existing Finnish crew. The International Transport Workers' Federation
(ITF) told its affiliates to boycott the Rosella and to take other solidarity industrial action.
Viking therefore sought an injunction in the English High Court, restraining the ITF and
the Finnish Seaman's Union (FSU), now threatening strike action, from breaching Article
49 TFEU (ex Article 43 EC) on freedom of establishment.

Laval concerned a Latvian company which won a contract to refurbish a school in
Sweden using its own Latvian workers who earned about 40 percent less than comparable Swedish workers. The Swedish construction union wanted Laval to apply the Swedish
collective agreement but Laval refused, in part because the collective agreement was
unclear as to how much Laval would have to pay its workers, and in part because it
imposed various supplementary obligations on Laval, such as paying a "special building
supplement" to an insurance company to finance group life insurance contracts. There
followed a union picket at the school site, a blockade by construction workers, and sympathy industrial action by the electricians' unions. Although this industrial action was
permissible under Swedish law, Laval brought proceedings in the Swedish labor court,
claiming that it was contrary to *Union* law (in particular Article 56 TFEU (ex Article 49
EC) on freedom to provide services and the Posted Workers' Directive 96/71).

Using the market access approach, the Court ruled that the collective action in both
cases constituted a "restriction" on free movement and so breached Articles 49 and 56

respectively, even though it recognized earlier in the judgments that the right to strike was a fundamental right which formed an integral part of the general principles of Union law.[60] On justification, the Court noted in *Viking* that the right to take collective action for the protection of workers was an overriding reason of public interest provided that jobs or conditions of employment were jeopardized or under serious threat. On the facts, the Court suggested this was unlikely because Viking had given an undertaking that no Finnish workers would be made redundant. If the trade unions could justify the collective action, the Court suggested that it would only be proportionate if it was taken as a last resort. In *Laval*, the Court recognized that the right to take collective action for the protection of Swedish workers "against possible social dumping" was a justification but found on the facts that, using collective action to force Laval to sign a collective agreement whose content on central matters such as pay was unclear, could not be justified. The Court also ruled that the Posted Workers Directive provided no help in this context, as the terms of the collective agreements which the Swedish unions were trying to enforce went beyond the core protections which the directive guaranteed to posted workers. Against the background of uncertainty over the meaning and effects of the directive, the Court interpreted it as imposing a "ceiling" on the laws which member states could adopt to protect posted workers employed on their territory.[61] The Court struck a blow against the previously understood interpretation of social policy directives[62] as setting minimum standards upon which member states could improve.[63]

The unions greeted these rulings with dismay.[64] Addressing the European Parliament in February 2008, John Monks, General Secretary of the ETUC (European Trade Union Confederation), said:

> So we are told that the right to strike is a fundamental right but not so fundamental as the EU's free movement provisions. This is a licence for social dumping and for unions being prevented from taking action to improve matters. Any company in a transnational dispute has the opportunity to use this judgment against union actions, alleging disproportionality.

The ETUC has therefore called for the adoption of a social progress clause which would say that "Nothing in the Treaty, and in particular neither fundamental freedoms nor competition rules shall have priority over fundamental social rights and social progress." It adds: "In case of conflict, fundamental social rights shall take precedence."[65]

This line may find some support from the subsequent judgment of the European Court of Human Rights (ECtHR) in *Demir and Baykara*,[66] ruling that both a right to collective bargaining and a right to take collective action can be inferred from Article 11, the freedom of association provision of the European Convention on Human Rights (ECHR). There are indications in the ECtHR's judgment that the margin of appreciation allowed to states under Article 11(2) will be strictly construed in future. In principle this judgment could have far-reaching implications for EU law.[67] The TEU makes provision for the EU to accede to the ECHR, which may strengthen the case for a realignment of the Court of Justice's approach, but such accession has yet to take place, and its legal implications are unclear.[68] It is also open to the Court to take account of the social rights set out in the EU Charter of Fundamental Rights and Freedoms, given fresh legal impetus by the Lisbon Treaty.[69] However, the potential significance of the Charter as a mechanism for strengthening social policy is tempered by the inclusion of numerous economic rights, including a right to enterprise,[70] which could be invoked to limit the impact of the social rights set out in the Charter.

Perhaps a more promising route for a reconsideration of the balance struck in *Viking* and *Laval* is the inclusion in Article 3(3) TEU by the Lisbon Treaty of the objective for the Union to achieve "a highly competitive social market economy."[71] The significance of this has already been noted by Advocate General Cruz Villalon in *Santos Palhota*.[72] Having referred to Article 3(3) TEU, he said:

> The entry into force of the Lisbon Treaty requires that, if working conditions constitute an imperative reason in the public interest justifying a derogation from the free movement of services, it must no longer be interpreted in a restrictive manner.

38.5 Conclusion: The Future of EU Social Policy

The *Viking* and *Laval* judgments are hardly likely to be the last word on the conflict between single market principles and social policy both at national level and within the EU legal order. In retrospect it is perhaps surprising that this conflict took so long to surface. It was inherent in the original design of the Treaty of Rome, which combined an ordo-liberal conception of the role of the law in promoting competition and market integration, with apparent autonomy for the member states in the social policy field. The idea that differences between the social policy frameworks of the member states could be described as distortions of competition, and regulated as such, was not far from the minds of the framers of the Rome Treaty. However, they rejected this interpretation on the grounds that it would entail far-reaching positive harmonization of social standards. This was thought to be unnecessary at a time when political support for the welfare state regimes was more or less unquestioned at national level, and when, optimistically, it was assumed that improvement and convergence of national laws would occur naturally as a result of the implementation of the common market. Over time, general economic trends associated with the decline of the post-war model of full employment, as well as institutional changes initiated by the EU itself, including monetary union and enlargement, have put paid to that assumption. Prior to *Viking* and *Laval*, social policy faced a legislative deadlock, as the Commission was unwilling to act out of concern for competitiveness and the social partners were increasingly unable to find common ground. After *Viking* and *Laval* the progressive erosion of social policy at national level is a real possibility, and the prospects for consensus for its replacement at EU level look even more remote.

This could be seen as a natural, if somewhat problematic, evolution for a nascent federal structure. The experience of US labor law in the early decades of the twentieth century was one of judicial intervention to strike down state-level labor laws on the grounds of their unconstitutional interference with property rights, an argument which finds echoes in the language of interference with economic freedoms used in *Viking* and *Laval*. Judicial acceptance of the legitimacy of labor legislation at federal level in the 1930s was later qualified by rigid interpretations of those same laws which ruled out experimentation at state level, and which have gradually led to the atrophying of the legislation.[73] Finding a role for social policy in a multi-jurisdictional structure, where competition between states for scarce resources and inter-jurisdictional mobility together threaten to undermine social standards, is set to be a major task for constitutional design on both sides of the Atlantic.

NOTES

1. Case 43/75 [1976] ECR 455. This was emphasized in Case C-50/96 *Deutsche Telekom* v. *Schröder* [2000] ECR I-743, paras. 53–5.
2. Case 149/77 *Defrenne (No. 3)* v. *SABENA* [1978] ECR 1365, 1378; Case 14/83 *Von Colson and Kamann* v. *Land Nordrhein-Westfalen* [1984] ECR 1509.
3. OJ 1975 L45/19.
4. OJ 1976 L39/40.
5. OJ 1979 L6/24.
6. OJ 2000 L180/22.
7. OJ 2000 L303/18.
8. Case C-177/88 *Dekker* v. *Stichting Vormungscentrum voor Jong Volwassenen* [1990] ECR I-3941, Case C-32/93 *Webb* v. *EMO Air Cargo* [1994] ECR I-3567.
9. Case C-13/94 *P* v. *S* [1996] ECR I-2143.
10. e.g. Case 222/84 *Johnston* v. *RUC* [1986] ECR 1651; Joined Cases C-6 and 9/90 *Francovich* v. *Italian Republic* [1991] ECR I-5357.
11. Case C-303/06 *Coleman* [2008] ECR I-5603.
12. Case C-555/07 *Kücükdeveci* [2010] ECR I-000.
13. Case C-262/88 *Barber* v. *Guardian Royal Exchange* [1990] ECR I-1889.
14. A. Davies, "Judicial Self-Restraint in Labour Law," *Industrial Law Journal* 38 (2009), 278, 287.
15. For a full discussion of the effect of the Lisbon Treaty on EU Social Policy, see P. Syrpis, "The Lisbon Treaty. Much Ado…But About What?," *ILJ* 37 (2008), 219.
16. Protocol No. 30. For further discussion, see C. Barnard, "The 'Opt-Out' for the UK and Poland from the Charter of Fundamental Rights: Triumph of Rhetoric Over Reality?," in S. Griller and J. Ziller, eds, *The Lisbon Treaty: EU Constitutionalism without a Constitutional Treaty* (New York: Springer Wien, 2008), 257–83. See also Case C-411/10 *NS*, judgment of 21 Dec. 2011.
17. These collective agreements can also be implemented by national or sub-national collective agreements but such collective agreements (e.g. on work related stress; see <http://europa.eu.int/comm/employment_social/news/2004/oct/stress_agreement_en.pdf>) have proved much less influential.

18. OJ 1996 L145/4.
19. Dir. 97/81/EC (OJ 1998 L14/9).
20. Dir. 99/70/EC (OJ 1999 L175/43). The social partners failed to reach agreement on agency work which was left to the legislature to negotiate: Dir. 2008/114/EC (OJ 2008 L327/9). The Social Partners also reached a framework agreement on work-related stress but this has not been extended to all workers via a directive.
21. Dir. 92/85/EEC (OJ 1992 L348/1).
22. Dir. 93/104/EEC (OJ 1993 L307/18) repealed and replaced by Dir. 2003/88 (OJ 2003 L299/9).
23. Dir. 94/33/EEC (OJ 1993 L216/12).
24. e.g. Dir. 94/45/EC (OJ 1994 L254/64) on the European Works Council, repealed and replaced by Dir. 2009/48 (OJ 2009 L122/28 and Dir. 2002/14 on information and consultation (OJ 2000 L80/29).
25. Dir. 75/129/EEC (OJ No. L48/29) now repealed and replaced by Dir. 98/59/EC (OJ 1998 L225/16).
26. Dir. 77/187/EEC (OJ No. L61/27) now repealed and replaced by Dir. 2001/23 (OJ No. L82/16).
27. Dir. 80/987/EEC (OJ No. L283/23) repealed and replaced by Dir. 2008/94/EC (OJ 2008 L283/36).
28. Dir. 96/71/EEC (OJ 1997 L18/1).
29. Art. 4(2)(b) TFEU.
30. Arts. 145–150 TFEU (ex Arts. 125–130 EC).
31. Para. 12.
32. COM(94) 333, para. 3.
33. Council Directive 75/129/EEC of February 17, 1975 on the Approximation of the Laws of the Member States Relating to Collective Redundancies (OJ [1975] L48/29).
34. Case 215/83 *Commission v. Belgium* [1985] ECR 103.
35. Second recital in the preamble, cited in Case C-449/93 *Rockfon A/S v. Specialarbejderforbundet i Danmark, acting for Nielsen* [1995] ECR I-4291, para. 29; Case C-250/97 *Lauge v. Lønmodtagernes Garantifond* [1998] ECR I-8737, para. 19.
36. Second recital in the Preamble.
37. Case 215/83 *Commission v. Belgium* [1985] ECR I-1039, para. 2.
38. See COM(98) 592.
39. Final Report of the High Level Group on economic and social implications of industrial change, November 9, 1998.
40. B. R. Cheffins, *Company Law: Theory, Structure, and Operation* (Oxford: Oxford University Press, 1997).
41. See, e.g. C. A. Ball, "The Making of a Transnational Capitalist Society: The European Court of Justice, Social Policy, and Individual Rights under the European Community's Legal Order," *Harvard International Law Journal* 37 (1996), 307, 314; I. Bleijenbergh, J. de Bruijn, and J. Bussemaker, "European Social Citizenship and Gender: The Part-Time Work Directive," *EJIR* 10 (2004), 309, 311.
42. M. Shanks, *The European Social Policy Today and Tomorrow* (Oxford: Pergamon, 1977), 378.
43. COM(2006) 211.
44. This started with a Consultation Paper, *Opportunities, Access and Solidarity: Towards a New Social Vision for 21st Century Europe* COM(2007) 726, and was followed up Commission's *Renewed Social Agenda: Opportunities, Access and Solidarity* COM(2008)

412. These are considered in detail in C. Barnard, "Solidarity and the Commission's 'Renewed Social Agenda," in M. Ross and Y. Borgmann-Prebil, eds, *Promoting Solidarity in the European Union* (Oxford: Oxford University Press, 2010), 73.

45. As recently restated in A. Sen, *The Idea of Justice* (London: Allen Lane, 2009).

46. See footnote 46 above (emphasis added).

47. See A. Supiot, ed., *Au delà de l'emploi. Transformations du travail et devenir du droit du travail en Europe* (Paris: Flammarion, 1999); S. Deakin and A. Supiot, eds, *Capacitas: Contract Law and the Institutional Foundations of a Market Economy* (Oxford: Hart Publishing, 2009).

48. COM(2006) 708 final.

49. COM(2006) 708 final, para. 3.

50. COM(2006) 708 final, para. 4a.

51. See S. Sciarra, "EU Commission Green Paper, Modernising Labour Law to Meet the Conditions of the 21st Century," *ILJ* 36 (2007), 375.

52. Case C-382/92 *Commission* v. *UK* [1994] ECR I-2435 and Case C-383/92, [1994] ECR I-2479.

53. Dirs 75/129/EEC (OJ 1975 L48/29) and 77/187/EEC (OJ 1977 L61/27) respectively.

54. See generally S. Deakin, "Labour Law as Market Regulation," in P. Davies, A. Lyon-Caen, S. Sciarra, and S. Simitis, eds, *Principles and Perspectives on EC Labour Law: Liber Amicorum for Lord Wedderburn* (Oxford: Oxford University Press, 1997), 63–93.

55. See e.g. R. Pedersini, "Relocation of Production and Industrial Relations," <http://www.eurofound.europa.eu/eiro/2005/11/study/tn0511101s.htm>. For discussion, see C. Barnard, "Fifty Years of Avoiding Social Dumping," in M. Dougan and S. Currie *Fifty Years of the European Treaties: Looking Back and Thinking Forward* (Oxford: Hart Publishing, 2009).

56. See S. Deakin and F. Wilkinson, "Rights v. Efficiency? The Economic Case for Transnational Labour Standards," *ILJ* 23 (1994), 289.

57. Directive 96/71/EC concerning the posting of workers in the framework of the provision of services (OJ 1997 L18/1).

58. F. Scharpf, "The European Social Model," *JCMS* 40 (2002), 645.

59. Case C-438/05 *Viking Line ABP v The International Transport Workers' Federation, the Finnish Seaman's Union* [2007] ECR I-10779; Case C-341/05 *Laval un Partneri Ltd v Svenska Byggnadsarbetareförbundet* [2007] ECR I-11767.

60. *Viking*, para 44; *Laval*, para 91.

61. To similar effect, see the later (and also highly significant) judgments of the Court in Case C-446/06 *Rüffert* v. *Land Niedersachsen* [2008] IRLR 467 and Case C-319/06 *Commission* v. *Luxembourg* [2009] IRLR 160.

62. The Posted Workers' Directive was adopted under the services provisions of the Treaties, not the social provisions. While labor lawyers assumed that it was a minimum standards directive in the traditional social policy vein, contemporary evidence indicates that it was never intended to be used to allow host states to impose higher labor standards.

63. See S. Deakin, "Regulatory Competition after *Laval*," *CYELS* 10 (2008), 581.

64. "Dumping social: les syndicates européens 'déçus' par la Cour de Justice," lemonde.fr (December 8, 2007).

65. ETUC's Resolution adopted on March 4, 2008; see <http://www.etuc.org/IMG/pdf_ETUC_Viking_Laval_-_resolution_070308.pdf>.

66. *Demir and Baykara v Turkey*, Application No 34503/97, November 12, 2008. See also *Enerji Yapi-Yol (Application no. 68959/01)* confirms right to strike part of Art. 11.

67. K. D. Ewing and J. Hendy, "The Dramatic Implications of *Demir and Baykara*," *ILJ* 39 (2010), 2.
68. Art. 6(2) TFEU.
69. Case C-236/09 Association Belge des Consommateurs Test-Achats v. Conseil des ministers [2011] ECR I-000.
70. Art. 16 of the Charter.
71. For a discussion of this term, see C. Joerges and F. Rödl, "'Social Market Economy' as Europe's Social Model?," EUI Working Paper Law No. 2004/8, who argue that "this concept contained an ordo-liberal basis which was complemented by social and societal policies, whose aims and instruments were supposed to reply on market mechanisms" (page 19). According to Working Group XI on Social Europe (CONV 516/1/03 REV 1, para. 17), the objectives should refer to "social market economy" to underline the link between the economic and social development and the efforts made to ensure greater coherence between economic and social policies.
72. Case C-515/08 *Santos Palhota* [2010] ECR I-000, paras. 51–53 (authors' translation).
73. C. L. Estlund, "The Ossification of American Labor law" *Columbia Law Review* 102 (2002), 1527.

CHAPTER 39

....

EUROPEAN ENERGY POLICY

....

DIETER R. HELM

39.1 INTRODUCTION: THE PLACE OF ENERGY IN THE EU

....

The EU has never had an explicit energy policy in the way that it has, for example, had an agricultural, industrial, or competition policy. Energy policy issues have arisen as part of a more general interest. They were tagged onto the early industrial policies through the ECSC and the Euratom Commission; then they were added into the project to complete the internal market, and finally they have been on the receiving end of the climate change packages.

Yet despite its second class status, energy has never been off the agenda. After World War II, coal mattered for the rebuilding of Europe's industrial economy. In the 1970s, the OPEC shocks left Europe reeling not only economically, but also physically through the selective embargoes. Russian oil (and later gas) played a significant role in the control of the Soviet East, and then in the 1980s, energy featured in the areas of concern raised by the loss of competitiveness.

But it has been since 2000 that the tempo has changed, and for a variety of separate reasons which together started to have a bigger impact on both the economics and politics of Europe. By the end of the first decade of the present century, oil prices had moved from around $10 to $147 a barrel at the peak, back to around $30, and then up to $80 again. There were two significant interruptions of gas supplies from Russia; Europe introduced its first carbon price through the European Union Emissions Trading Scheme (EUETS); and the Renewables Directive mandated a policy-driven investment program. In the lattermost case, the context was the replacement cycle and the impact of the gradual closure of much of the capacity built in the 1970s and before, when Europe had been an energy intensive economy.

The politics of energy also moved up a gear in the 2000s. Europe was mired in the debates and referendums failures of first the Constitution, and then the Lisbon Treaty.

The disconnect between the electorate and the European Commission had widened and Europe needed policies with which it could reconnect. Climate change was an obvious candidate. As the major European political parties gradually fell back in shares of the votes, the "green vote" came to wield greater influence. The Red–Green coalition in Germany was perhaps the starkest example, leading to a major emphasis on wind and solar energy and a decision to phase out nuclear.

For the new members from the East, the legacy of the Soviet Union's use of energy to keep an economic stranglehold meant that energy would inevitably be of great political and economic importance to them. Russia had integrated electricity systems so as to exert a stranglehold—literally to be able to turn off the lights, and heating too. Cheaper energy prices had increased dependency, whilst undermining attempts to increase energy efficiency. In the background was Russia and Gazprom, and in the foreground was the growing Russian–German special relationship. Unsurprisingly Poland feared for its security when the Nord Stream pipelines, agreed between Schröder and Putin, deliberately and more expensively went around its borders. The comparison with the Molotov–Ribbentrop Pact was not surprising—after all, that pact had provided Hitler with much needed oil which in turn had helped the blitz-krieg on Poland. At Europe's new borders, Ukraine and Belarus were especially exposed to Russian energy, not least because they had been given cheap supplies and the main pipelines went through them. Further south and east, the tussle over Caspian supplies, the invasions of South Ossetia and Abkhazia, and the desire to put a pipeline through Turkey and Georgia from Azerbaijan added a further element of political concern—especially when France and Germany were united in opposing Turkey's EU membership application.

It is widely recognized that Europe now needs an energy policy. There is even quite a lot of agreement about what needs to go into it. But the obstacles are formidable, and the legacies of the various component parts which have been built up through the history of the EU provide major constraints. Following a brief description of the early measures up to the end of the 1970s, the three main steps described here are: the internal market; the climate change package; and the first steps toward a security of supply framework. Although it is too early to tell how the EU will bring these components together (and if indeed it will manage to at all), the outlines of a possible way forward are set out by way of a conclusion.

39.2 EARLY ENERGY MEASURES

In the immediate aftermath of World War II, energy—especially coal—was a key component of reconstruction. Germany lost the war for many reasons, but one factor was its lack of indigenous energy resources, having at the outset done the deal with Stalin partly to secure oil supplies, having (unsuccessfully) tried to secure Romanian oil fields, and ending up producing synthetic fuel. The industrial heartlands of the Ruhr, based on the coal fields, were bombed to destruction, and the attempts to build a reconciliation between France and Germany in the aftermath of the war required an understanding of how re-industrialization could be made compatible with peace in general, and France's own industrial interests in particular.

Reconstruction meant industrial policy, and for coal and steel this was encapsulated in the ECSC (for more on this, see Chapter 6, this volume). Initially its task was to deal with coal shortages, but by the end of the 1950s, the position was transformed by competition from oil. As was witnessed later in agriculture, dealing with surpluses was a politically fraught process. In the end, the market determined the outcome. Energy also figured with the development of nuclear power, and the creation of the Euratom Commission. As with the ECSC, national interests limited its effectiveness, and it succumbed to the power of national governments, notably France's.

These early measures were not primarily taken with energy or energy policy in mind. Energy was seen as a national not a European competence, and for the very good reason that for much of the sector, the systems were at least national, and indeed in many cases still local. The early post-war period was characterized by the move from local to national electricity and town gas systems. Britain and France created centralized grids through nationalization—an efficiency gain which took many other European countries another fifty years to achieve, and some not even then. Local and regional authorities proved remarkably reluctant to give up their considerable interests in utilities.

Closely aligned with the development of national energy policies was the emergence of national champions. Electricité de France (EDF), the Central Electricity Generating Board (CEGB), and Rhenish-Westphalian Electric power company (RWE) grew with the major post-war power station building program, whilst mining was also concentrated in few hands. The energy sector became highly concentrated, and with a close corporatist relationship to national governments. In many countries for much of the post-war period, monopoly was statutory, and competition was illegal.

It was against this background that the Treaty of Rome unsurprisingly left energy out of its main framework, an exclusion which was to run right through to the 1980s.

The OPEC oil shocks of the 1970s provided an opportunity for Europe to develop a united response and to grow its energy competence. But it did not. In part this was due to the legacy of the bruising fight with the French and the "empty chair" crisis. But it was also a recognition that oil was international in a way that electricity and gas were not. Thus the International Energy Agency (IEA) was created with a global stocking policy and a global remit, with the Organization for Economic Cooperation and Development (OECD) alongside. To the extent that Europe responded to the oil shocks, it was at the macroeconomic level, notably in respect of exchange rates. The lessons of the 1970s shaped the EMS and then the long march to monetary union and the euro. They did not create an energy policy.

39.3 COMPLETING THE INTERNAL MARKET

In the 1980s, there was an intense debate about the competitiveness of the European economy,[1] resulting in a white paper: *Completing the Internal Market*.[2] It was an ingenious construct: around 300 liberalizing measures were identified, and bundled together in a package so that although there would be objections to individual measures, the net effect was to make everyone a winner. The white paper became the 1992 Programme.

Energy markets did not originally feature in the package but, in part spurred on by the development of privatization and competition in the British energy sector, energy was soon added and the Internal Energy Market programme was promoted by the Commission at the end of the 1980s. The evidence of high and variable prices across Europe was convincing.

The early plans were ambitious. Not deterred by the fact that there was little physical connection between the national markets, the Commission put the cart before the horse. Without the physical interconnections, the Commission instead focused on virtual competition, spot markets, and most of all on access to the existing (largely national) networks by third parties. Instead of directing its energies to creating a European grid for electricity and a European gas pipeline system—the necessary conditions for a Europe-wide internal market—the Commission focused on whether access to existing networks should be regulated (regulated Third Party Access—rTPA) or left to the parties to bargain (negotiated TPA). Naturally the incumbents saw rTPA as a major threat to their regional and national monopolies (as indeed it was intended to be), and there followed a war of attrition between the Commission and the companies.

At the time, the *zeitgeist* was very much on the side of liberalization and competition: incumbents were viewed as monopolies defending their profits. Arguments about the impacts of liberalization on security of supply were largely disregarded, and pressure came early to break up long-term take or pay contracts, particularly in the natural gas sector.[3] With widespread excess supply (a legacy of the investments from the 1970s and the period when Europe had been an energy-intensive economy), the need for long-term contracts to underwrite the sunk costs of new investments was minimal (because the investment was now needed), and vertical integration was similarly treated with suspicion. Competition would, it was argued, largely take care of security of supply. Even at the international level, Europe placed its faith in the Energy Charter, and in particular the Transit Protocol, to extend third-party access elsewhere, notably in Russia.

These arguments would resurface two decades later when the excess capacity was finally eroded away, and the need for investment came to dominate. By the mid-2000s, it was painfully obvious that the failure to build interconnectors and coordinate European networks had left many exposed to interruptions in Ukrainian supplies. But at the time, a battle of wills was conducted between the big companies—notably Germany's Ruhrgas with its long-term contracts; and France's EDF with its nuclear program. The close relationship between these companies and their national governments helped to stave off reform, and it was not until 1996 and 1998 that directives were finally adopted respectively for electricity and gas.[4] These were notably much weaker than the Commission had hoped for.

Unsurprisingly the directives failed to make much impact. Reform did come, but it was overwhelmingly driven by national governments opening up their domestic markets. Following Britain's lead, most member countries started the reform process, and eventually even Germany joined in, leaving France as the outlier. The Commission could claim that it was the threat of intervention that forced the pace, but in practice almost all countries moved for fear of being left behind with higher energy prices. Excess supply undermined the monopolies.

The war of attrition nevertheless continued, and the Commission never gave up on its mission to complete the internal energy market. It continued to promote new directives (the second directives),[5] and eventually in 2006 it launched a major inquiry[6] and the third set of energy directives followed in 2009.[7] The report itself was damning, identifying not only anti-competitive practice but also the damaging consequences to European competitiveness.

By this stage—the high-water mark of the Commission's efforts—the argument had moved on to unbundling—the separating out of the networks from generation and supply either internally within vertically integrated companies (internal unbundling) or through divestment (ownership unbundling). The Commission wanted complete ownership unbundling of the networks. It had two strategies to get there—new directives, and legal action under European competition law. On the former it lost: internal unbundling was the best that could be agreed in the third directives. On the latter, it scored direct hits with competition cases brought against the German companies and exerted major legal pressures on the French and the Italians. By 2009, the Commission could claim considerable success in terms of the legal framework. What it could not claim was that the resulting energy market looked much like a normal competitive commodity market. For whilst the Commission pursued its liberalization agenda, the market itself had set about its great consolidation. From the late 1990s, the Competition Directorate was on the receiving end of a merger wave of unprecedented scale. In response, it treated each member state's market as discrete—as indeed they largely were, given the failure to develop physical interconnections. So when EDF moved into Germany, the move was argued to increase competition in Germany. When E.ON launched its takeover bid for Endesa in Spain, the Commission became in effect a cheerleader, attacking the Spanish government's attempt to maintain national company control. What these mergers did was indeed to increase competition *within* each separate market, but at the price of undermining competition in the wider European market. Thus merger policy, in effect, undermined the overall objective of the internal market—becoming a policy for each national market, not a single integrated European energy market.

At the end of the great merger wave, the energy landscape had been transformed. E.ON was created from an industrial holdings company in 2000, and proceeded to become one of the largest utilities in Europe, incorporating Ruhrgas along the way. EDF spread its wings across a number of countries, buying up the British nuclear industry in the process. By 2009, EDF, E.ON and RWE bestrode the European stage, with a second rank of big players including GdF, ENEL, ENI, Iberdrola and Vattenfall. Thus the important necessary condition for competition—lots of players—had been seriously eroded. Liberalization had been achieved, but not significant competition.

39.4 EUROPE'S CLIMATE CHANGE POLICY

Europe has gradually built up an environmental policy. In the energy sector, the early focus was on acid rain and other air pollution with the Large Combustion Plant Directive (LCPD)[8] as the main instrument. The acid rain problem became acute from the 1970s.[9] It was a problem that lent itself to an EU-based solution: acid rain was a regional problem. The polluters and the polluted were largely within the EU's boundaries.

The solution adopted was classic command-and-control regulation. The LCPD set maximum emission levels, on a plant-by-plant basis. For the energy sector, it meant a clamp down on coal power stations, requiring the fitting of flue gas desulphurization (FGD) or closure. As the policy played out, it would go through a number of revisions, and it now points to a closure of much of the coal-powered generation in the middle of the next decade—which in turn requires a major replacement investment program and carries significant security of supply implications.

The EU's approach to climate change has been more vexed. It is a global, not a European, problem. As early as 1992, the Commission proposed a carbon tax.[10] But with tax as a jealously guarded national competence, it was not until much later that the Commission got round to a carbon price, and it was to be via a permits scheme—the EUETS.[11] This in turn was a response to the Kyoto Protocol, finally agreed in 2003 and coming into force after Russia was persuaded to ratify as part of a broader understanding that Europe would back the Russian bid to join the WTO.

Kyoto was very European. Once the US had changed its mind (it had initially been in favor), Europe led the push for international agreement. The reasons were various. Politically, the green vote had become more important as the votes for the major parties declined across Europe and coalition governments became correspondingly more difficult to form. In Germany, this led to a Red–Green coalition, but elsewhere the major parties felt the pull of green issues and attempted to incorporate the green vote into their mainstream positions.

Economically, Kyoto lent itself to Europe's rapid exit from energy-intensive and polluting Eastern industries, and to the de-industrialization process in the Western countries. The key feature of Kyoto's architecture was that it measured carbon production within countries. It did not measure consumption, and therefore as energy-intensive industries shifted to China, India, and other developing countries, domestic emissions production fell whilst goods were imported back into Europe. Aviation and shipping were also left out of the Kyoto targets. So whilst carbon production fell (looking good in Kyoto terms), consumption increased. In the case of the UK, between 1990 and 2005, carbon production fell by over 15 percent, but carbon consumption went up by around 19 percent.[12]

When the dash-for-gas (displacing coal generation) and the economic crisis from 2007 are added to de-industrialization, Europe's carbon performance since 1990 has had little to do with its climate change policies. These have focused on two dimensions—the EUETS, and the renewables directives.[13] The EUETS was an attempt to impose the Kyoto targets by translating the limits into permits to pollute, and then allowing them to be traded. The theory was that this would guarantee that emissions reductions were actually made, and in the process establish a carbon price.

The EUETS was promoted as an alternative to carbon taxes, and for as long as the permits were grandfathered rather than being auctioned, industry much preferred this approach. But implementation became very political: each country lobbied for its preferred National Allocation Plan (NAP), and industry argued for exemption for the large energy-intensive sectors exposed to international competition (the so-called leakage problem). Given the sheer scale of the economic rents attached to the permits, it was hardly surprising that there was intense political lobbying. In effect, the EUETS formed part of a substantial "carbon pork barrel."[14]

The result was predictable: the EUETS produced low and volatile prices, unrelated to the social cost of carbon. In addition, by setting short periods (2005–2008, 2008–2012, and 2012–2020), there were repeated opportunities to fight for the economic rents, witnessed notably in December 2008 as the Commission pushed through its new climate change package. The result has not been impressive: many of the emissions reductions would probably have been made anyway; and significant profits have been made by traders and incumbent generators. These flaws—and the absence of a longer-term price of carbon relevant to incentivizing technologies coming on-stream after 2020—led the Commission eventually in late 2009 to consider a floor price of carbon (in effect a carbon tax).[15]

There were several coincidental reasons why the Commission pushed forward with a new climate change package in 2007, to be eventually agreed by the Council of Ministers in December 2008. As the Lisbon process rumbled on, the Commission needed a new "project" which might re-engage with the wider electorate. The existing measures were making little difference, and procedurally the Commission needed to take forward the EUETS to the next phase and to prepare its position for the Copenhagen Conference of the Parties (COP) at the end of 2009.

For political presentation rather than economic logic, the Commission presented its program under the slogan of "2020-20-20": a 20 percent reduction in emissions production, a 20 percent target for renewables as a share of total energy; and a 20 percent energy efficiency target. The Commission offered to increase this to a 30 percent emissions reduction target if others were willing to make similar commitments at Copenhagen—which, it turned out, they were not.[16] Of these, the 20 percent renewables target is in practice the binding constraint for many countries, as the economic crisis cut emissions significantly. Each country agreed a NAP with the Commission. For some countries which could back up the intermittent wind generation (the dominant option up to 2020) with hydro—such as Scandinavian countries and Austria—the switch to wind made some sense; for others like the UK, the challenge was immense (requiring an increase from around 5 percent to around 30 percent of electricity generation within just over a decade). Overall, the targets lacked credibility: few expect the targets to be met in a number of countries, but few have an incentive to state this publically given that the targets are set beyond the life of most governments and the terms of office of chief executives.

The dash-for-wind has a number of worrying side effects. The costs are high, imposing a competitive disadvantage and raising fuel poverty. The focus on the period up to 2020 distracts from both the development of new technologies and also large-scale nuclear and Carbon Capture and Storage (CCS) deployment, both of which are predominantly post-2020. Amongst the newer technologies, smart meters, smart grids, batteries, and the electrification of transport (especially cars) are important, and in a credit-constrained world, capital is in shorter supply. Consumers and taxpayers also have a limited ability to absorb higher costs. The impact of the wind program on bills will leave little scope to add more levies and charges to pay for these other new technologies.

For these reasons, the climate change package is likely to be repeatedly revisited in the coming decade. The failures at the Copenhagen Summit in late 2009 and the economic crisis have led to considerable uncertainty about the future of global measures. An immediate European priority has been to try to impose a Europe-wide framework on the rapid development of country-specific carbon taxes. Finland, Sweden, and now France are leading the way. The renewables framework is unlikely to survive to 2020, and the absence of serious penalties and the widespread failure to achieve the target will probably mean that it is replaced by the middle of this decade.

There are likely to be a series of new initiatives. The agenda includes: CCS, (where the Commission is already making tentative moves);[17] common nuclear licensing; incentives to electrify transport; and large-scale solar. The development of intelligent grids will have considerable impact on the internal energy market rules, and energy efficiency measures will bring out the conflict between spot-based markets, and the need for customers to commit to the capital costs through longer-term contracts. This will also put pressure on the internal energy market rules.

But if there are conflicts between the climate change agenda and the internal market emphasis on spot markets and short-term competition, these pale into insignificance beside the problems for security of supply. Europe's dependency on coal for electricity generation (for some countries, like Poland, almost complete) in a context in which the electrification of transport and heating will raise the demand for electricity is in direct conflict with the de-carbonization agenda. The replacement of coal with gas—in part also to back up the intermittent wind generation—may (at least in the short term, before shale gas has its impacts) make security of supply matters worse. By 2020, Europe's gas dependency may be as high as 23 percent of the energy mix, with 77 percent imported.[18]

Of the import sources, Russia has a dominant role—economically at the margin, and politically at Europe's borders.

39.5 SECURITY OF SUPPLY

As the traumatic economic shocks of the 1970s faded from political memories, so too did the security of supply problems. Against expectations after the Iranian Revolution, and despite the Iran–Iraq war, oil prices fell in the 1980s, and only again reached their 1979 peak briefly in 2008, before falling back significantly. Whereas in the late 1970s, it was fashionable to believe that oil prices were on an ever upward path—indeed enough to reinforce France's major nuclear program—the 1980s saw North Sea oil and gas flow into a market with excess supply. Europe's gradual retreat from energy-intensive industries flattened demand too, so that economic growth could be decoupled from energy demand. Whereas 3 percent GDP growth meant around 7 percent growth in electricity demand for much of the post-World War II period, from 1979 the relationship broke down. Europe however inherited all the power stations built to meet a much higher demand in the 1980s and 1990s—hence general excess supply.

Excess supply not only reduces concerns about security of supply; it also shifts the emphasis to sweating existing assets away from investment. Liberalization, competition, and privatization are the obvious policies to force down operating costs. Thus the completion of the internal energy market fitted the times. Without a need to invest, long-term contracts were merely obstacles to short-term competition through spot markets, and with many countries having excess capacity, the need to build interconnectors was not generally a European priority.

The Commission paid lip service to security of supply. In 2000, partly in response to lobbying by the large companies (and the French and German governments) the Commission published a Green Paper on security of supply,[19] highlighting the dash-for-gas, but sidestepping the nuclear question. Both nuclear, and gas imports and pipelines, required commitment to the sunk costs over long-time periods—which meant obligations, long-term contracts, or government guarantees. None of these fitted with the competitive markets model (renewables posed similar problems, but here the Commission found little difficulty in effectively exempting these technologies from the force of competitive markets).

Little followed from the 2000 Green Paper. However, the accession of the Eastern European countries had brought a greater emphasis on security of supply, and at the Hampton Court Summit in 2005 a paper was tabled by the British presidency, proposing a significant shift of emphasis toward completing the physical internal market, and a number of security-boosting initiatives, including strategic gas storage.[20] The Commission built on this paper, with another Green Paper in 2006.[21]

What prevented these ideas being translated into practice was the national policies of a number of countries, notably Germany. Under Schröder's government from 2000, Germany had been building up its bilateral relations with Russia in general, with Gazprom as a company in which Ruhrgas had a shareholding, and between Schröder and Putin personally. Gazprom had fought off European attempts to open up its networks to third-party access, and had rebuffed attempts to use the Energy Charter as a framework for EU–Russian energy negotiations. Rather its strategy had been to do bilateral deals and to deny the EU a locus in energy relationships. From its (monopoly) position, it was rational to close off its pipes to third parties (tightening its internal grip over independent companies like Shell in Sakhalin and BP in Kovykta), and to deal with particular countries bilaterally. Thus Putin and Gazprom (they are intimately related) built up two key counterparties—Germany and Italy—both of which have considerable external energy exposure. Austria played a third part, with its geographical position as an energy crossroads.

These relationships matured into pipeline and contract deals for Russian gas. In Germany's case, it was the Nord Stream pipeline, bypassing Poland and the Baltic states. Though more expensive than the route through its fellow EU member state Poland, Putin insisted on going round the outside and directly linking to Germany. In the Italian case, ENI had considerable interests in Russia and the Caspian, and again pipelines played a key part. The Italian government played its part too, becoming notably pro-Russian in its public statements (especially after the invasions of South Ossetia and Abkhazia).

The Commission struggled to cope with this energy nationalism. Having also had strained relations with France over the internal energy market and nuclear, failure to develop a coherent European policy was inevitable. Instead, Europe focused on what it could agree—climate change and a watered down version of the internal market. It continued to argue that internal competition would solve external security and that intermittent renewables—like wind—would create greater energy independence.

What changed the position was a combination of rising prices and the Ukrainian crises. Whereas Schröder in particular had been keen (with Gazprom) to point to the reliability of Russian supplies and to claim in evidence that Russia had been a reliable supplier throughout the Cold War, in 2006 Russia interrupted supplies of gas through Ukraine. And to compound anxieties at the Commission and in much of Eastern Europe, it did so again in 2009.

In both cases, the arguments between Russia and Ukraine were about both money and politics. Like all the former Soviet satellites in Europe, Ukraine had benefitted from cheap subsidized Russian energy supplies, and the move to market prices was bound to be painful. There was also the question of the charges for transmission, and the extremely murky question of the ownership of the Ukrainian pipelines and who benefitted from the economic rents. But there was also the burden of history, the Russian population in Ukraine (and Putin's interest in them), and the Crimea question (with the Sebastopol naval base). The latter had the potential to be another South Ossetia or Abkhazia and after the Ukrainian election in 2010, the new, more pro-Russian Ukrainian government quickly extended the Russian lease of the naval base.

European efforts in respect of the Ukraine and Russia have been various. At one level, crisis management has had to be developed rapidly as the exposure of the EU members in the South and East has been painful, notably because of the lack of sufficient interconnections. At a second level, the Commission tried to create a role for itself in the interface with Russia. The main countries—Germany, Italy, and increasingly France—in effect ensured that it was them (and not the EU) that called the shots. At a more fundamental level, the Commission pressed for a political dialogue with Russia, and strove (with little success) to replace the original Partnership and Cooperation Agreement (PCA)[22] which expired in 2009 with something more durable.

Finally the Commission got serious about pipelines, and in particular the Nabucco project to build a new supply route from the Caspian into Europe, via Turkey and eventually to Austria. The project was bold, expensive, and an overt attempt to gain a European (as opposed to a German and Italian) solution to energy security. It was also in competition with Russia's South Stream project, and Russia has leant hard on its special relationships with German, Italian, and Austrian companies to support South Stream over Nabucco.

The difficulties were, however, all too apparent. In addition to promoting South Stream, Russia has worked hard to ensure that Caspian gas goes north, not west, in part to make up for its own supply problems. Turkey, seeking EU membership, has played its cards politically, and again the big EU member states have been, at best, lukewarm in support. By the end of 2009, the EU was no nearer to having addressed security of supply. The economic crisis brought temporary relief as the demand for gas fell. Further ahead the prospect of shale gas increasing supplies eased price pressures further.

39.6 FUTURE PROSPECTS

The EU has come some way toward creating an energy policy, but it remains fragmented. The three parts—the internal energy market, climate change, and security of supply—remain distinct, and the national priorities of Germany and France continue to constrain the scope for EU-wide policy.

Over the next decade the pressures are likely to create much greater integration between the three elements, and for national interests to give ground to the European interest. Part of these pressures may be external—after Lisbon, the EU's role in shaping European relations with Russia might expand. Nabucco and the Turkish position at the energy crossroads between the Middle East and Europe will force a reappraisal, and if relations with Iran improve and security in Iraq improves too, southern routes for energy imports will become correspondingly more important. Conversely, if Russia's revisionism at the borders of the EU continues, then the EU will increasingly be pressurized to protect its newer Eastern members, and energy will necessarily be a core component of this. The wild card is shale gas: alternative abundant and cheap supplies would weaken Russia's negotiating hand.

Climate change adds a global dimension. It will not go away, and national governments will find it hard to gain traction in global negotiations that are likely to go on for decades. The EU may continue to be the main interface for European countries, though as the Copenhagen and Durban Summits demonstrated, the "global leadership" role has slipped in the face of US and Chinese pressures. Within Europe, the scale of the challenge to de-carbonize the economy, and developments in new smart grids and smart meters, in electrifying transport, and in a host of new technologies will necessarily generate a continuing sequence of new directives.

The internal market project, so heavily circumvented by the merger wave, will continue to run its course too, though the emphasis may finally swing back from the concepts of spot markets and virtual competition to the creation of capacity markets, physical networks, and interconnections. This physical internal market will be encouraged by ownership unbundling of networks, but the process of bringing national grids together into a more unified power system will involve the ceding of more powers and controls to the Commission, and in consequence the process of national foot-dragging which has plagued the Internal Market Project to date will probably continue.

The trends are therefore in one direction—toward greater emphasis on the European over the national. But they are only trends: a coherent European energy policy may be nearer than at any time since the creation of the Community. But it is still some way off.

Notes

1. See in particular P. Cecchini *The European Challenge, 1992: The Benefits of a Single Market* (Aldershot: Gower, 1988).
2. Commission of the European Communities (1985), *Completing the Internal Market*. White Paper from the Commission to the European Council (Milan, 28–29 June). COM (85) 310 final.
3. Long-term contracts were a natural way to link upstream investments in gas fields and coal mines with investments in pipelines and power stations.
4. European Parliament and Council of the European Union (1996), *Directive 96/92/EC concerning common rules for the internal market in electricity* ("First Electricity Directive"); European Parliament and Council of the European Union (1998), *Directive 98/30/EC concerning common rules for the international market in natural gas* ("First Gas Directive").
5. European Parliament and Council of the European Union (2003), *Directive 2003/54/EC concerning common rules for the internal market in electricity* ("Second Electricity Directive"); European Parliament and Council of the European Union (2003), *Directive 2003/55/EC concerning common rules for the internal market in natural gas* ("Second Gas Directive").
6. Commission of the European Communities (2006), *Communication from the Commission: Inquiry pursuant to Article 17 of Regulation (EC) No 1/2003 into the European gas and electricity sectors (Final Report)*, COM(2006) 851 final.

7. European Parliament and Council of the European Union (2009), *Directive 2009/72/EC concerning common rules for the internal market in electricity ("Third Electricity Directive")*; European Parliament and Council of the European Union (2009), *Directive 2009/73/EC concerning common rules for the internal market in natural gas ("Third Gas Directive")*.

8. Council of the European Communities, (1988). *Council Directive 88/609/EEC of 24th November 1988 on the limitation of emissions of certain pollutants into the air from large combustion plants.*

9. In 1979, the United Nations Economic Commission for Europe (UNECE) implemented the Convention on Long-Range Transboundary Pollution. In 1985 most UNECE members adopted the Protocol on the Reduction of Sulphur Emissions, agreeing to reduce sulphur dioxide emissions by 30 percent (from 1980 levels) by 1993.

10. Commission of the European Communities (1992), *Proposal for a Council Directive Introducing a Tax on Carbon Dioxide Emissions and Energy,* COM(92)226 final.

11. European Parliament and Council of the European Union (2003), Directive 2003/87/EC of the European Parliament and of the Council of 13 October 2003 establishing a scheme for greenhouse gas emission allowance trading within the Community and amending Council Directive 96/61/EC.

12. D. R. Helm, R. Smale, and J. Phillips, *Too Good to be True? The UK's Climate Change Record* (2007). Available at: <http://www.dieterhelm.co.uk/sites/default/files/Carbon_record_2007.pdf> (accessed November 12, 2009).

13. (1) European Parliament and Council of the European Union (2001), *Directive 2001/77/EC on the promotion of electricity produced from renewable energy sources in the internal electricity market.* (2) European Parliament and Council of the European Union (2003), *Directive 2003/30/EC of the European Parliament and of the Council of 8 May 2003 on the promotion of the use of biofuels or other renewable fuels for transport.* (3) European Parliament and Council of the European Union (2009), *Directive 2009/28/EC on the promotion of the use of energy from renewable sources and amending and subsequently repealing directives 2001/77/EC and 2003/30/EC.*

14. D. R. Helm, "Rent-Seeking and Picking Winners: The Evolution of UK Climate Change Policy," *Oxford Review of Economic Policy* 26, no. 2 (2010), 182–96.

15. D. R. Helm, *Caps and Floors for the EU ETS: A Practical Carbon Price* (2008). Available at: <http://www.dieterhelm.co.uk/sites/default/files/Caps_Floors_Oct_2008.pdf> (accessed November 12, 2009); D. R. Helm, "The Case for a Carbon Tax," in Simon Less, ed., *Greener, Cheaper*, Policy Exchange, July 27, 2010.

16. See chapter 12 in D. R. Helm and C. Hepburn, eds, *The Economics and Politics of Climate Change* (Oxford: Oxford University Press, 2009).

17. European Parliament and Council of the European Union (2009), *Directive 2009/31/EC on the geological storage of carbon dioxide.*

18. European Commission Market Observatory for Energy (2008), "Europe's Energy Position, Present and Future.

19. Commission of the European Communities (2000), *Towards a European Strategy for the Security of Energy Supply,* COM(2000)769.

20. D. R. Helm, *European Energy Policy: Securing Supplies and Meeting the Challenge of Climate Change,* Paper for the EU Informal Summit, Hampton Court, London, October 2005. Reprinted in D. R Helm, ed., *The New Energy Paradigm* (Oxford: Oxford University Press, 2007).

21. Commission of the European Communities (2006), *A European Strategy for Sustainable, Competitive and Secure Energy*, COM(2006)105 final, (European Green Paper on energy).

22. European Community, European Coal and Steel Community, European Atomic Energy Community, The 12 Member States, Belgium, Denmark, Federal Republic of Germany, Greece, Spain, France, Ireland, Italy, Luxembourg, Netherlands, Portugal, United Kingdom, Russian Federation (1994), *Agreement on partnership and cooperation establishing a partnership between the European Communities and their Member States, of one part, and the Russian Federation, of the other part—Protocol 1 on the establishment of a coal and steel contact group—Protocol 2 on mutual administrative assistance for the correct application of customs legislation—Final Act—Exchanges of letters—Minutes of signing.*

CHAPTER 40

THE CONSTITUTIONAL CONTEXT OF (EVER-WIDER) POLICY-MAKING

STEPHEN WEATHERILL

40.1 INTRODUCTION

There is a temptation to suppose that the creation and maintenance of an integrated trading area in the EU brings with it a need for a general regulatory competence vested in the EU institutions. The Treaties, however, do not so provide. The competences and powers of the EU are no more than those conferred upon it by its Treaties, and are limited to and by that mandate. That it may seem desirable for the EU to act in a particular way may collide with the constitutional point that its Treaties do not permit such action. In this sense all choices and preferences about the nature and scope of policy-making in the EU are underpinned by constitutional constraints which are particular to the EU. The purpose of this chapter is to present an account of those constitutional constraints in law and in practice.

40.2 THE COMPETENCE OF THE EU: THE BASIC PRINCIPLES

The constitutionally fundamental point that the EU does *not* enjoy a general regulatory competence, but rather that it must operate within the limits set by the Treaties, has long been referred to by rather unmemorable phrases such as the principle of attributed competences, but has, since the entry into force of the Lisbon Treaty, become formally designated the *principle of conferral*. That too is an inelegant label for a matter of the highest constitutional significance, but nevertheless it captures the basic concept, if prosaically: the EU operates on the basis of the competences *conferred* upon it by its member states pursuant to the founding Treaties. Outside those boundaries, the EU has no valid basis for action.

Article 5(1) TEU provides that the limits of Union competences "are governed by the principle of conferral." The issue here is whether a Union competence *exists*. Article 5(1) TEU adds that the use of Union competences is governed by the principles of subsidiarity and proportionality. This relates to the logically subsequent issue of the conditions governing the *exercise* of a Union competence, once it is shown to exist. Subsidiarity and proportionality are considered below.

At a more detailed level, the powers of the individual institutions are limited. Those powers too are defined in and by the Treaties. Just because the EU is equipped with a competence to act in a particular area does not mean that the inquiry into the precise manner in which it may act is at an end. One must understand the detailed nature of the powers attributed to each institution, political and judicial.

Compliance with these foundational rules should be ensured *ex ante* in the law-making process by the political institutions of the EU and, should the necessary restraint be found wanting, the Court stands ready to secure fidelity to these principles by reviewing the validity of adopted legislation *ex post* facto.

40.3 The Nature and Scope of the EU's Competences

But what *are* these competences? What subject matter is involved? And what is their nature, in particular their relationship with state competence? Nothing in Article 5 TEU addresses such issues.

Getting to grips with these matters requires a detailed understanding of the dense undergrowth of the TFEU. Article 1(1) TFEU states that "This Treaty organises the functioning of the Union and determines the areas of, delimitation of, and arrangements for exercising its competences." And so it does, but in a way that is profoundly opaque.

Title I of Part One of the TFEU is entitled *Categories and Areas of Union Competence* and it occupies Articles 2–6 TFEU. Article 2 TFEU defines the several types of competence which are conferred on the Union. There are three principal types: *exclusive* competence (Article 2(1) TFEU), *shared* competence (Article 2(2) TFEU), and *supporting or coordinating competence* (Article 2(5) TEU). Then the TFEU allocates particular areas of activity to each of the available categories.

However, even after reading and absorbing Articles 2–6 TFEU one has acquired only a partial view of the reach of EU law. What is at stake in these foundational provisions is the *legislative* competence of the EU. But the reach of the EU and its legal order extends far beyond the package of competences which authorize legislative intervention. The

Treaty contains a set of "negative" rules: rules which forbid particular types of practice which are hostile to the achievement of the objectives mapped out by the Treaty. Most prominent are the core rules of EU trade law—those which prohibit restrictions on the free movement of goods, persons, services, and capital (albeit in all cases admitting the possibility that such restrictions may be justified) and those which control anti-competitive practices. The prohibition against discrimination based on nationality is another example of a powerfully important prohibition embedded in the Treaty. Public bodies and private parties are (in different ways, to differing extents) subject to these basic rules telling them what they may *not* do. And these core rules operate across the whole sphere of activity covered by the Treaty, which is extremely broad—broader than the scope of legislative competence.

So, as Article 2(6) TFEU makes explicit, the detailed arrangements governing the exercise of the EU's legislative competences are found scattered throughout the Treaty. As Article 2 does *not* make clear, there are a host of relevant prohibitions also scattered throughout the Treaty. It takes a hard, long read to grasp exactly what is the scope of the legislative competences and the applicable institutional powers, combined with appreciation of the scope of the governing prohibitions in EU trade law. The place to go is Part Three of the TFEU, entitled *Union Policies and Internal Actions*. It is huge, containing 24 Titles, and stretching from Article 26 to Article 197 TFEU.

The two dozen titles which comprise Part Three TFEU cover:

> The Internal Market; Free Movement of Goods; Agriculture and Fisheries; Free Movement of Persons, Services and Capital; Area of Freedom, Security and Justice [which is the most institutionally and procedurally atypical]; Transport; Common rules on Competition, Taxation and Approximation of Laws; Economic and Monetary Policy; Employment; Social Policy; European Social Fund; Education, Vocational Training and Sport; Culture; Public health; Consumer protection; Trans-European Networks; Industry; Economic, Social and Territorial Cohesion; Research and Technological Development and Space; Environment; Energy; Tourism; Civil Protection; Administrative Cooperation.

Some of these Articles contain rules of a precision that is sufficient to allow their immediate application (by the CJEU and by national judges) without the need for legislative elaboration; others merely provide a framework for shaping policy through the adoption of secondary legislation at EU level, which commonly requires implementation at national level. So Part Three TFEU is home to free movement law, to competition law—provisions which operate to control practices falling within the scope of EU law largely without the need for legislative amplification. But many of the provisions in Part Three TFEU are drafted to require elaboration through secondary legislation. Their shaping therefore depends, first, on the applicable procedures for law-making and the powers that are made available to the EU institutions, and then to the detailed and sometimes politically controversial process of law-making.

One would certainly be left bemused if one tried to rely only on Articles 2–6 TFEU to understand the nature of the competences available in particular areas. Social policy, for example, is listed as a shared competence in Article 4 TFEU. But one has to pore over Articles 151–61 TFEU to grasp precisely what this entails at the boundaries between Union and state competence. Article 153(2) TFEU envisages the adoption of measures designed to improve cooperation between member states in the fields of social policy listed in Article 153(1), while expressly excluding harmonization of national laws; and also the adoption by directive of minimum rules governing *some* but *not all* of the fields of social policy listed in Article 153(1). And, adding to the complexity, Article 153(2) separates out the several relevant fields of social policy by subjecting *some* to the ordinary legislative procedure and *others* to a special procedure requiring unanimous support in Council.

There are many more instances of the need to reckon with detailed provisions buried deep in the TFEU, and there is no call here to plod through them. The point is only that none of this detail can be satisfactorily gleaned from Articles 2–6 TFEU. So the impression of clean lines governing categories of competence which is conveyed in the early part of the Treaty is rather misleading.

It is nevertheless an improvement on the pre-Lisbon pattern. There was nothing comparable to Articles 2–6 TFEU in the pre-Lisbon texts. Matters of competence— scope, nature—had to be deduced from a messy assortment of materials.[1] The notion of exclusive competence, for example, was created by the Court, and its true scope was always unclear. Article 3 TFEU is plainly drafted with reference to the Court's case law, albeit that some of the detailed choices made are unconvincing.[2] Similarly the notion of supporting competences could be found in the pre-Lisbon Treaty but it was never explicitly explained or defined. Lisbon at least attempts to provide a definition (in Article 6 TFEU).

So, the question "may the EU act in this area of law- and policy-making?" is always answered by "well, it depends on whether the Treaties so provide." And then even if the answer, after inspection of the Treaty texts, turns out to be "Yes! The EU may act" one must then pursue a more detailed examination of exactly how the institutions may exercise their powers.

Why is this so significant? The principle of conferral is fundamentally *constitutional* in character. Tying the EU to the mandate conferred upon it by the founding Treaties emphasizes that member states' democratic political processes, in their different ways in different member states, authorized a transfer of powers from state level to EU level. But the transfer of powers is limited. Any slippage in EU activity beyond the terms of the mandate that is found in the Treaties is illegitimate in the sense that it is devoid of the authorization rooted in national ratification of the original Treaties and the subsequent amending texts.

The Lisbon Treaty has made this root more explicit than it used to be. If, as Article 5(2) TEU provides, the Union is authorized to act only within the limits of the competences conferred on it by the member states, the obvious conclusion is that outwith those limits, the member states retain competence to act unhindered by the constraints of EU law. This was nowhere made explicit in the Treaties pre-Lisbon, but now Article 5(2) TEU makes it explicit in its second sentence: "Competences not conferred upon the Union in the Treaties remain with the Member States." Precisely the same point appears in Article 4(1) TEU. So a point left unmade in the pre-Lisbon texts is now made twice. And it is made yet again in Declaration 18 to the Treaty. It changes nothing: this was always obviously the law. But the fact that the Treaty post-Lisbon hammers home this point confirms a thematic anxiety to enhance the rhetoric of protection of "state rights."

40.4 THE BROADENING OF EU COMPETENCE

So it is possible to pin down the *limits* of EU competence which is central to the character of the principle of conferral found in Article 5 TEU. To get to that place, one must wrestle with Part Three TFEU (in particular) and one must also grasp that the principle of conferral is predominantly concerned with *legislative* competence, whereas the impact of EU law on national autonomy is in fact broader than that, because of the sweep of EU trade law, particularly free movement and competition law.

But the competence of the EU, though *limited*, is not *static*. The member states themselves have extended the scope of EU law by amending the Treaty and adding extra competences to the list. New provisions have been gradually added (such as environmental protection in 1987, consumer protection in 1993), existing provisions widened. And such extension in the scope of EU law does not affect only legislative competence, it also carries with it the unavoidable implication that the prohibitions in free movement law and competition law bite in ever wider areas.

However, what lies at the heart of the increasingly anxious debate about competence in recent years is the perception that the dictates of the principle of conferral tend to be obscured by an open-handed reading of the matter in practice. The problem is captured by the catchphrase: *competence creep*.[3]

So, the complaint runs, the *practice* in this matter of competence definition and competence control is a good deal less clear than the straightforward account based on the text of Article 5 TEU suggests. In part this is attributable to the rules themselves, which in many cases are not conducive to, and are not designed to be conducive to, yielding a clear answer to the question mentioned above, "may the EU act in this area of law- and policy-making?" In part it is attributable to the institutional context in which the rules are applied, *ex ante* and *ex post*, politically and judicially.

40.5 THE NATURE OF THE RULES GOVERNING COMPETENCE

The EU operates according to the principle of conferral, but this means in practice that the Treaty proceeds to set out where the EU is competent to act—not where it is not. There are no bright-line rules which allocate specific functions to the member states, nor are there rules that place areas of activity off-limits to the EU. Moreover, important elements of both the EU's legislative competences and its trade law rules are defined with reference to functionally broad objectives, with the consequence that such limits as they possess are wide and hard to fix. This is true in particular of Articles 114 and 352 TFEU among the legislative competences and of the provisions governing free movement and competition among the trade law rules.

40.5.1 Legislative Competence

There are two Treaty provisions authorizing the adoption of Union legislation which have always been the most sensitive factors in the controversies about legislative competence creep: Article 114 TFEU on the harmonization of laws and Article 352 TFEU which permits legislative action in the absence of provision of the necessary powers elsewhere in the Treaty. In their pre-Lisbon guise they were the only two provisions of the Treaties picked out explicitly for consideration in the Laeken Declaration, where their propensity for provoking competence creep was noted, and Lisbon has done nothing to move them out of the spotlight. Many of the EU's legislative competences are sector-specific and they elaborate rules and impose limits which are attuned to the particular characteristics of the sector in question—environmental policy, energy policy, agricultural policy, and so on. Articles 114 and 352 are profoundly different. Their scope is much broader, their limits much vaguer.

In accordance with the principle of conferral, both provisions have limits—in short, a tie to market-making under Article 114 and a tie to the EU's objectives under Article 352. The Court will not accept legislative harmonization consequent on "a mere finding of disparities between national rules."[4] Nor is harmonization permissible where the measure has only the incidental effect of harmonizing market conditions within the Union.[5] As the Court observed in *Tobacco Advertising*, the most high-profile example of annulment of EU legislation for want of competence, there is no "general power to regulate the internal market."[6] Article 352 possesses a "gap-filling" function but it cannot be used to extend the scope of Union powers or objectives, for that would constitute an impermissible amendment of the Treaty by legislative act and a violation of the principle of conferral.[7]

Nevertheless, any type of national practice which has the requisite impact on the project of market-making—by impeding the free movement of goods or by causing a distortion of competition[8]—may be subjected to the discipline of harmonization. It matters not what the content or purpose of the national laws in question may be, save only that Article 114(2) TFEU excludes harmonization of fiscal provisions, those relating to the free movement of persons and those relating to the rights and interests of employed persons from subjection to the ordinary legislative procedure (which means in practice unanimity among the member states is required for legislative action in these fields). Accordingly the program of legislative harmonization has acquired an extraordinarily wide scope. Similarly Article 352, though limited *in principle* by the requirement that legislation adopted pursuant to it shall attain one of the objectives of the Union, *in practice* offers immense legislative flexibility precisely because those objectives are themselves drawn so broadly.[9]

By conferring on the EU legislative competences of this type, the Treaty is structured in such a way as to make it hard for opponents of legislative initiatives to devise specifically *constitutional* objections. The debate therefore is dominated by majoritarian politics.[10] It is hard too to persuade the Court to invalidate legislation, even if in principle that is precisely the Court's job in so far as the constitutionally central principle of conferral has been violated. These provisions are therefore rather well designed if one's aim is to maximize the flexibility entrusted to the EU law- and policy-making process. In general the EU is deficient in *hard* rules and procedures for restraining legislative creep.[11]

40.5.2 Trade Law

The provisions of the Treaty that forbid particular practices that are incompatible with the EU's objectives display similar characteristics to the provisions that confer legislative competence on the EU: they too are functionally broad in their reach, they are not sector-specific, and they accordingly have a deep impact on national practices. EU trade law pushes into areas of activity that are not mentioned in the Treaty—areas that would not be subject (at all or only under strict limits) to the *legislative* competence of the EU. And then it is necessary to devise some sort of "policy" for respecting the particular concerns and features of the sector in question within the broad framework of application of EU trade law, but this needs to be done without help from the Treaty itself. So spreads the impact of EU law.

The Court's ruling in *Watts* deals with cross-border provision of medical care, but it encapsulates the Court's approach in a number of fields where EU trade law sweeps far beyond the limits of EU legislative competence:

> although ... [Union] law does not detract from the power of the Member States to organise their social security systems and decide the level of resources to be allocated to their operation, the achievement of the fundamental freedoms guaranteed by the Treaty nevertheless inevitably requires Member States to make adjustments to those systems. It does not follow that this undermines their sovereign powers in the field.[12]

This has become a standard formula in cases where the achievement of economic integration collides with national practices in realms where the Union is not competent (at all or only under limited conditions) to act as a substitute *legislator*. Social security is a common example;[13] taxation is another;[14] and even the maintenance of public order has been revealed as a matter of national competence that is nevertheless reviewable in so far as measures taken impede cross-border trade.[15] Free movement law stops states (and to some extent private parties) acting in the absence of justification for chosen practices that impede cross-border trade. The Union cannot go further than this. It cannot set the ground rules for the organization of social security systems or taxation or for preserving public order.

Naturally one may argue that the Court is thoroughly disingenuous when it declares that the achievement of the fundamental freedoms requires an adjustment by the member states which does not undermine "their sovereign powers in the field." EU law radically circumscribes the scope of sovereign state choices. The impetus towards cross-border patient mobility consequent on the *Watts* ruling has confronted health care authorities with wretchedly awkward questions of budget management.[16] However, the Court is choosing to follow what it sees as the logic of the Treaty itself. The Treaty does not place particular sectors of economic activity beyond the reach of its basic rules. Accordingly the Court interprets EU trade law in an expansive manner. As with legislative competence, so with EU trade law: when one is engaged in economic activity, it is very difficult to construct an argument apt to secure insulation from the application of EU law. In EU trade law the principal arguments tend to surround the question whether a particular practice is justified or not. There is little scope for arguing that EU law does not apply *at all*.

Sport is a good example. Sport itself was not mentioned at all in the Treaty pre-Lisbon, and even now it is the subject of only brief reference. But it is part of the economy and the Court has consistently refused to accept the submissions of the football authorities that it should lie beyond the reach of EU law. In *Bosman* the Court had to consider the compatibility of the then-applicable transfer system with EU trade law. It is not for the EU to dictate how football should shape its transfer system. It *is* for the EU—specifically its Court—to rule on how football shall *not* shape its transfer system. It shall not violate EU trade law—the one challenged in the case *did*.[17] So the Court was forced to engage with the purpose of a transfer system, even though the Treaty is utterly silent on such matters. This is the incremental outward drift of "policy-making" driven by the dictates of trade integration yet also appropriately sensitive to the particular needs of the sector in question.[18] In many areas it has proved tempting to shape EU "policies" out of an unpromising collection of material—skeletal Treaty provisions, patchwork secondary legislation, decisions of courts, soft law. EU law- and policy-making typically lacks the systematic character of national practice. That is because of the constitutional constraint of the principle of conferral combined with the appreciation that in practice the EU Treaty is structured to bring a very wide range of activities actually or potentially within its scope.

40.6 SUBSIDIARITY AND PROPORTIONALITY

The principle of conferral limits EU action to the competences conferred upon it by the member states in the Treaties. Article 5(1) TEU adds that the use of Union competences is governed by the principles of subsidiarity and proportionality.

Article 5(3) TEU sets out the principle of subsidiarity. This provides that

> in areas which do not fall within its exclusive competence, the Union shall act only if and in so far as the objectives of the proposed action cannot be sufficiently achieved by the Member States, either at central level or at regional and local level, but can rather, by reason of the scale or effects of the proposed action, be better achieved at Union level.

So the EU may possess a competence to act in an area, but this shall not entitle it to act in particular cases where it cannot (in short) add value to action by the member states. Article 5(4) TEU stipulates that under the principle of proportionality "the content and form of Union action shall not exceed what is necessary to achieve the objectives of the Treaty."

Both provisions assume that the mere *existence* of a competence is not an adequate reason to *exercise* it. Subsidiarity and proportionality are threshold conditions, designed to insert a pause between finding a competence to act and the decision to exploit it. But both, as a general observation, are reckoned to have been of limited value in promoting legislative reflection.

There is a gulf between subsidiarity as a rather self-evident if abstract principle of good governance on the one hand and, on the other, its status as a principle of EU law which should be made operationally useful in concrete debates about whether or not to act. It has proved easy to add the label of "compliance with subsidiarity" to a measure's Preamble, but rare is it to see any serious engagement with what is at stake in making that judgment. So for example, as part of the drive against money laundering the Council in 2006 adopted a "third pillar" Framework Decision, 2006/783 on the application of the principle of mutual recognition to confiscation orders.[19] In Recital 9 it is stated that cooperation between member states presupposes confidence that decisions to be recognized and executed "will always be taken in compliance with the principles of legality, subsidiarity and proportionality." But nowhere else in the twenty-page text is subsidiarity even mentioned.

Subsidiarity, it is widely perceived, has done little to curtail perceived legislative over-enthusiasm at EU level.[20] The Commission is sensitive to being cast as the scapegoat for these trends. It is quick to insist that the application of the subsidiarity principle is not its responsibility alone but also that of the other political institutions, in particular the Council and the Parliament.[21] It is the responsibility of the Court too. But the Court has been reluctant to find adopted legislation incompatible with the principle of subsidiarity. Its orthodox approach has been to find that provided the EU has a competence to adopt common rules, then inevitably the EU, rather than its member states acting individually, is best placed to adopt those common rules. In consequence the dictates of the subsidiarity principle are readily met.[22] It is not difficult to gain the impression that the Court has adopted a narrow approach to subsidiarity as a legal concept according to an assumption that it is in the political sphere in which subsidiarity concerns are most apt to be aired. And the application of the proportionality principle betrays a similar, if slightly milder, judicial anxiety to avoid usurpation of the legislative role.[23]

In EU trade law the principle of subsidiarity has been similarly sidelined. The approach taken in *Bosman* is typical. It was pressed on the Court that the subsidiarity principle dictated that intervention by the EU should be confined to what is strictly necessary, but the Court simply retorted that this could not permit the adoption of sporting rules that run contrary to the Treaty.[24]

40.7 THE INSTITUTIONAL CONTEXT IN WHICH THE RULES ARE APPLIED

One may disagree about the scale of the problem of "competence creep." One may debate how many of its manifestations are endemic to the Treaty and how many are attributable to exploitation of the EU level of law-making by the political institutions as a means to circumvent domestic obstacles to reform and how many to slack control exercised by the Court. But, beginning with the Laeken Declaration, a major preoccupation has been to improve competence definition and competence control, according to an assumption that the legitimacy of the EU is imperiled if it trespasses beyond the competences conferred on by its founding Treaties; and that moreover its legitimacy is damaged if it exercises competences attributed to it in a manner that unnecessarily interferes with the competences that remain in the hands of the member states.

It is, however, striking that the outcome of the recent period of introspection in the EU—the Treaty of Lisbon—has chosen solutions which are toward the modest end of the scale. In the Convention on the Future of Europe several radical proposals were aired, including the adoption of "hard lists" involving exhaustive and tightly-defined lists of the areas in which the Union is competent to act or identification of areas off-limits to the Union and therefore remaining within the exclusive competence of the member states, and the deletion of what have now become Articles 114 and 352 TFEU as the principal problem cases in the corrosion of "competence creep." None was accepted.[25] The Treaty establishing a Constitution preferred two relatively modest adjustments—a reorganization of the material on competence in the Treaty, to improve transparency, and a new monitoring role granted to national parliaments. This model, with small changes of detail, was transplanted to the Treaty of Lisbon. So, first, Articles 2–6 TFEU clarify and reorganize the Treaty rules governing competence and, second, it shall be open to national parliaments to object to alleged misuse of the broadest of all the legislative competences conferred by the Treaty, Article 352 TFEU, and to legislative proposals advanced under any Treaty provision where violation of the subsidiarity principle is alleged.

The detail of this procedure is fleshed out in the Protocols on the role of national parliaments and on subsidiarity and proportionality. Where reasoned opinions on the legislative proposal's non-compliance represent at least one-third of all the votes allocated

to national parliaments, the draft must be reviewed. The Commission may then maintain, amend, or withdraw the draft. Where reasoned opinions on non-compliance represent a simple majority of votes cast by national parliaments, then the Commission
must review the proposal and, if it decides to maintain it, it must itself explain why in its
view the proposal is sound. These opinions are then made available to the Union
legislator.

Plenty of detail associated with the operation of this procedure awaits refinement.
How to contain objections to true matters of subsidiarity rather than broader disagreement with the merits of a proposed act? How to identify what is a "true" matter of subsidiarity? In any event the involvement of national parliaments will not revolutionize
the culture of EU law-making.[26] Many national parliaments are anyway dominated by
the executive and so will hardly be likely to adopt a position any different from that taken
by the member state in Council. The Lisbon reforms have therefore been met with some
skepticism.[27] The core idea, however, is to promote more dialogue—both vertically, by
for the first time connecting national parliaments formally with the EU law-making
process, and also horizontally, between national parliaments which are induced by this
procedure to cooperate since a single voice raised has considerably less legal and political weight than the assembly of a coalition. The aim is to nudge the system in the direction of a more critical approach to EU law-making by bringing in a previously excluded
set of actors, the national parliaments, while emphasizing the predominantly *political*
nature of subsidiarity.[28]

40.8 Conclusion

The sin of "competence creep" has generated proposals designed to confine the EU to an
agenda which can be reliably identified in advance; and to ensure the whistle can be
blown quickly and uncontroversially if the boundary is crossed. The problem is that this
will impose significant costs measured in inflexibility. It will diminish the EU's capacity
to act effectively in order to address (the rather wide range of) objectives assigned to it
by its Treaty. This is why the Lisbon Treaty selected relatively modest reforms, which
assume that the principal place for addressing the problems of "competence creep" must
lie in the institutional culture of the EU, nourished by input from national parliaments.
The principle of conferral, and the associated principles of subsidiarity and proportionality, are in practice more slippery than one would expect of such constitutionally fundamental rules. But many provisions of the EU's Treaties are broad, functionally-driven,
and perhaps vague but for good reason. Although alleged "competence creep" opens the
EU to criticisms rooted in want of formal legitimacy, the more cautious it is about "competence sensitivity," the more it risks being seen as unresponsive and irrelevant, to the
detriment of its ability to gather legitimacy through effective problem-solving on behalf
of its member states.

Notes

1. Armin Von Bogdandy and Jürgen Bast, "The European Union's Vertical Order of Competences: The Current Law and Proposals for its Reform," *Common Market Law Review* 39 (2002), 227–68; Dominik Hanf and Tristan Baumé, "Vers une Clarification de la Répartition des Compétences entre l'Union et ses Etats Membres?," *Cahiers de Droit Européen* 38 (2003), 135–57; Stephen Weatherill, "Better Competence Monitoring," *European Law Review* 30 (2005), 23–43.

2. Robert Schütze, "Lisbon and the Federal Order of Competences: A Prospective Analysis," *European Law Review* 33 (2008), 709–22.

3. Joseph Weiler, "The Transformation of Europe," *Yale Law Journal* 100 (1991), 2403–83; Mark Pollack, "Creeping Competence: The Expanding Agenda of the European Community," *Journal of Public Policy* 14 (1994), 95–145.

4. Cases C-154/04 & C-155/04 *Alliance for Natural Health* [2005] ECR I-6451 para 28.

5. e.g. Cases C-70/88 *Parliament v Council* [1991] ECR I-4529; Case C-209/97 *Commission v Council* [1999] ECR I-8067.

6. Case C-376/98 *Germany v Parliament and Council* [2000] ECR I-8419 para 83.

7. Opinion 2/94 *Accession to the ECHR* [1996] ECR I-1759; Cases C-402/05P & C-415/05P *Kadi and Al Barakaat v Council* [2008] ECR I-6351.

8. e.g. Case 376/98 n 3 above para 95.

9. Robert Schütze, "Organized Change towards an Ever Closer Union: Article 308 EC and the Limits to the Community's Legislative Competence," *Yearbook of European Law* 22 (2003), 79–116.

10. Alexander Somek, *Individualism: An Essay on the Authority of the EU* (Oxford: Oxford University Press, 2008).

11. Lori Thorlakson, "Building Firewalls or Floodgates? Constitutional Design for the European Union," *Journal of Common Market Studies* 44 (2006), 139–60.

12. Case C-372/04 [2006] ECR I-4325 para 121.

13. e.g. Case C-512/03 *J E J Blankaert* [2005] ECR I-7685.

14. e.g. Case C-446/03 *Marks and Spencer v Halsey* [2005] ECR I-10837.

15. e.g. Case C-265/95 *Commission v France* [1997] ECR I-6959.

16. Christopher Newdick, "Citizenship, Free Movement and Health Care: Cementing Individual Rights by Corroding Social Solidarity," *Common Market Law Review* 43 (2006), 1645–68.

17. Case C-415/93 [1995] ECR I-4921.

18. Stephen Weatherill, *European Sports Law* (The Hague: TMC Asser Press, 2007); Richard Parrish and Samuli Miettinen, *The Sporting Exception in European Law* (The Hague: TMC Asser Press, 2008).

19. [2006] OJ L328/59.

20. Gareth Davies, "Subsidiarity: The Wrong Idea, In The Wrong Place, At The Wrong Time," *Common Market Law Review* 43 (2006), 63–84; Jacques Pelkmans, "Testing for Subsidiarity," BEEP Briefing 13, February 2006, http://www.coleurop.be/content/studyprogrammes/eco/publications/BEEPs/BEEP13.pdf>.

21. e.g. "Better Lawmaking 2005" (COM (2006) 289), pp. 6–9.

22. e.g. Case C-491/01 *R v Secretary of State* ex parte *BAT and Imperial Tobacco* [2002] ECR I-11543 paras 177–185; Cases C-154/04 & C-155/04 n 1 above paras 99–108.

23. Takis Tridimas, *The General Principles of EU Law* (Oxford: Oxford University Press, 2006), ch. 4.
24. Case C-415/93 n 10 above para 81.
25. Stephen Weatherill, "Competence Creep and Competence Control," *Yearbook of European Law* 23 (2004), 1–56.
26. Katrin Auel, "Democratic Accountability and National Parliaments: Redefining the Impact of Parliamentary Scrutiny in EU Affairs," *European Law Journal* 13 (2007), 487–504; Philipp Kiiver, *The National Parliaments in the European Union—A Critical View on EU Constitution-Building* (The Hague: Kluwer Law International, 2006).
27. Jukka Snell, "European Constitutional Settlement, An Ever-Closer Union and the Treaty of Lisbon: Democracy or Rrelevance?," *European Law Review* 33 (2008), 619–42.
28. Ian Cooper, "The Watchdogs of Sudsidiarity," *Journal of Common Market Studies* 44 (2006), 281–304; Vlad Constantinesco, "Les compétences et le principe de subsidiarité," *Revue Trimistrielle de Droit Européen* 41 (2005), 305–18; Wilfried Swenden, "Is the EU in Need of a Competence Catalogue? Insights from Comparative Federalism," *Journal of Common Market Studies* 42 (2004), 371–92.

PART VIII

COMPETENCES IN FOREIGN POLICY AND HOME AFFAIRS

CHAPTER 41

....

DEFENSE POLICY

....

ANAND MENON

41.1 INTRODUCTION

....

Initial steps toward post-war intra-European cooperation were rooted in considerations of defense and security. The 1947 Treaty of Dunkirk was an Anglo-French mutual assistance pact; the Brussels Treaty of the following year had as its full title, the "Treaty of Economic, Social and Cultural Collaboration and Collective Self-Defence"; security concerns permeated thinking about the need for collaboration over coal and steel production, whilst the ill-fated EDC took such thinking to its logical conclusion. Yet EDC was both a culmination and a point of rupture. Following its rejection by the French National Assembly, defense policy was removed from the agenda of European integration, with security issues being dealt with primarily in NATO, and, to a far lesser extent, the WEU.

What a contrast to the EU of today. The ESDP is one of the most widely discussed areas of EU activity. Since its inception, the EU has used this new instrument to deploy missions to all parts of the world in a flurry of diplomatic, civilian, and military activity. Europe's pretensions to play a role in the management of global security affairs occupies center stage at many seminar discussions of the Union's future development.

This chapter examines ESDP by discussing, in turn, its origins, development, accomplishments, and, finally, the attempts made by scholars to apply theoretical insights to these. Whilst intended more as a survey than a critical analysis, it does argue that the Union has, to date, failed to live up to the hopes inspired by the creation of ESDP. Equally, however, a burgeoning theoretical literature about it holds out the prospect of many interesting theoretical debates to come.

41.2 ORIGINS

It has become commonplace to regard the emergence of the EU's role in defense policy as an "event," synonymous with the Anglo-French summit in the French seaside resort of Saint Malo in December 1998. One seasoned observer remarks that it is a "truism to date the birth of the EU as a security actor from [that] Franco-British summit."[1] ESDP, however, did not represent a qualitative break with what had gone before but, rather, one step on a path that the European Community, and subsequently EU, had embarked upon many years previously.

That path originated in the 1980s. In 1984, European leaders had agreed on the need to reactivate the WEU, the largely moribund European security organization that had emerged from the 1948 Brussels treaty. Two years later, the SEA for the first time codified their willingness to coordinate their positions more closely within the European Community on the "political and economic aspects of security." These developments were driven largely by external factors, notably a series of disputes with the American administration over issues ranging from Intermediate Nuclear Force deployments to the unveiling of the Strategic Defence Initiative,[2] all of which served to persuade member states of the need for Europeans to have a forum within which to discuss security issues without the Americans.

The end of the Cold War provided a further, and more forceful, impetus for enhanced European cooperation. German unification led to a desire on the part of some member states to "bind" a unified Germany more closely to its Western partners,[3] and convinced the Germans themselves that the price for the abandonment of the Mark should be moves toward a "political union," incorporating defense and foreign policy.[4] The outcome was the security provisions of the Maastricht Treaty, under which the EU was endowed with a CFSP. Defense too was given a place for the first time, with the treaty providing for the "eventual framing of a common defence policy, which might in time lead to a common defence".

Thereafter, two parallel developments provided the impetus for what was to become ESDP. First, West European states immediately attempted to profit from the end of the Cold War by cashing in on their "peace dividends."[5] Second, the Gulf War of 1991 and the outbreak of conflict in Yugoslavia signaled that the end of the bipolar conflict had not ushered in a new age of perpetual peace. Experience during the military operations of the 1990s, moreover, revealed a yawning capabilities gap with the US and increasing differences in terms of both security interests and war fighting doctrines between the Europeans and the United States.[6]

Confronted with these problems, member states turned to the EU as a means of addressing their desire to forge a more effective response to international security problems. The Amsterdam Treaty ushered in modest amendments to the Treaty provisions concerning defense policy, including the incorporation into the EU of the so-called "Petersberg tasks"—namely "humanitarian and rescue tasks, peacekeeping tasks and tasks of combat forces in crisis management, including peacemaking".

At Amsterdam, as at Maastricht, it was the United Kingdom that stymied progress in the sphere of defense. The new British Prime Minister, Tony Blair, arrived in the Dutch capital for his first EU summit armed with the arguments of his predecessors against involving the EU in defense issues. Yet within months of the meeting, the British position began to shift, as Blair, unencumbered in the way his predecessor had been with the problems of managing a minority government with a strong Euro-skeptic element, reacted to the changes that had transformed the European security environment.

Insofar as the Saint Malo meeting of the following year marked a turning point, therefore, it was a turning point in British attitudes rather than in the course of European security cooperation, which had grown steadily tighter over the preceding decade. The stipulation in the ensuing declaration that the Union "must have the capacity for autonomous action, backed up by credible military forces," whilst certainly marking the first explicit foray of European integration into military matters, was largely a logical consequence of what had gone before.

Following Saint Malo, member states moved quickly to put flesh on the bones of ESDP. At the Cologne summit the following June, EU leaders created the institutional framework necessary to take political decisions concerning defense matters. At the Helsinki summit of December 1999 they established the so-called Headline Goals setting force targets for the EU's military capabilities. Foremost amongst these was the decision to create, by December 2003, an EU Rapid Reaction force capable of undertaking the full range of Petersberg tasks and be militarily self-sustaining with the necessary command, control, and intelligence capabilities, logistics, and other combat support services. The Nice Treaty removed virtually all references to the WEU, thereby underlining the fact that the EU itself was now empowered to take and implement defense decisions. Moreover, a report by the French presidency submitted to the summit formalized the existence of the interim ESDP institutions (the Political and Security Committee, the Military Committee, and the Military Staff) which, by then, were up and running. These became permanent institutions in January, April, and June of 2001, respectively. A year later, EU leaders proclaimed ESDP operational in the Laeken Declaration.

41.3 SUBSEQUENT EVOLUTION

Since the inception of ESDP, the Union has launched a total of twenty-two operations, thirteen of which of are ongoing. These latter underline the global nature of EU interventions, ranging from Somalia (operation Atalanta, launched in December 2008) to Guinea Bissau, to two missions in the Democratic Republic of Congo (DRC), to Chad, Kosovo, Bosnia-Herzegovina (two missions), Afghanistan, Georgia, and the Palestinian territories (a further two missions); meanwhile EUJUST LEX has involved the training of Iraqi officials in Brussels. As to the nine missions successfully completed, three were in the DRC, with others in Sudan, the Former Yugoslav Republic of Macedonia (FYROM, three missions), Georgia, and the Indonesian province of Aceh.[7] Operations have ranged in size from the modest (the 15 personnel assigned to the Security Sector Reform mission in Guinea-Bissau) to Operation Althea in Bosnia and Herzegovina that, at its peak, involved 7,000 troops (reduced, in February 2007, to 2,500 backed up by an "over-the-horizon" reserve).

Strikingly, given the strong emphasis on military capabilities and armed intervention in the Saint Malo declaration, only six of these operations have been military (Concordia in FYROM, Artemis and EUFOR in the DRC, Althea in Bosnia, EUFOR Tchad/RCA, and Somalia); seven have been police missions (in Bosnia, FYROM, two in the DRC, Palestine, Macedonia, and Afghanistan); in addition, the Union has carried out four border missions, one planning mission, three rule of law missions, three monitoring missions, two assistance missions, and two Security Sector Reform missions.

Indeed, perhaps one of the most interesting aspects of ESDP has been the way in which its evolution since Saint Malo has seemingly moved away from the military vision laid out at Saint Malo and confounded the predictions of those observers who detected a gradual move toward greater acceptance on the part of EU member states of the use of military force.[8]

One area where tensions between member states have played out has been the EU's relationship with NATO. At issue here were questions about the kinds of missions that would be carried out either autonomously by the EU, by European forces using NATO assets and procedures (under the so-called Berlin plus formula), or by NATO alone.[9] From a French perspective, the assumption characterizing the genesis of ESDP was that "at some stage in the future . . . the EU will have developed sufficient advanced military capacity to be able to cope with, say, a Kosovo crisis without having recourse to either NATO or US assets."[10] For the British, given their belief in the complementary nature of ESDP and NATO, the Union simply did not need to develop capacities on that kind of scale. As UK Defence Secretary Geoffrey Hoon remarked in Washington in January 2000: "For meaningful large-scale military operations, NATO remains, and will remain, the only game in town. It will be the sole organisation for collective defence in Europe. It will be the organization that we expect to turn to for significant crisis management operations."[11]

Tensions over the degree of "autonomy" that ESDP should have from NATO have continued to haunt the undertaking. Even now, a simmering dispute between Cyprus and Turkey means that the two organizations cannot formally discuss their respective ongoing missions in Afghanistan, a failing that potentially puts the lives of EU personnel on the ground at risk. However, the experience of ESDP military missions to date strongly suggests that initial fears amongst some "Atlanticist" states that ESDP represented a potential threat to NATO were misplaced. The modest scope of those few autonomous EU missions carried out without close cooperation with NATO suggest that the latter remains the institution of choice for larger, more demanding interventions.

A further reason for supporters of NATO to feel relaxed is that, for all the ambitious initial talk about the potential for ESDP to enhance EU military capabilities, there are increasingly clear limits to the Union's military ambitions. The Helsinki Headline Goal (HHG) had called for the provision of 60,000 troops, 100 ships, and 400 aircraft, deployable within sixty days and sustainable for one year. The assumption was that, one day, the EU might find itself confronted with a Kosovo-type crisis which it would have to deal with without US assistance. Yet the original HHG has been superseded. The Headline Goal (HG) 2010, formally adopted at the European Council meeting on 17 June, focussed on small, rapidly deployable units capable of high-intensity warfare. "Battle groups," of which up to fifteen are projected, are units of 1,500 troops prepared for combat in jungle, desert, or mountain conditions, deployable within 15 days and sustainable in the field for up to 30 days with potential extension to 120 days. They are defined as "the minimum militarily effective, credible, rapidly deployable, coherent force package capable of stand-alone operations or for the initial phase of larger operations." HG-2010 thus marks a shift away from the large scale military ambitions outlined by its predecessor.

Indeed, and as the record of operations to date illustrates, military power is not the centerpiece of the Union's security policies. Parallel to the development of military capabilities, the Union has developed civilian ESDP. The concept of Civilian Crisis Management (CCM) first appeared in a Council Presidency report following the Helsinki Council meeting of December 1999. Through succeeding presidencies, the European Council emphasized four non-military areas: policing; the administration of justice; civilian administration; and civil protection. In June 2002 the EU established the Committee for the Civilian Aspects of Crisis Management, reporting to the Political and Security Committee.[12] In January 2003, the EU embarked on its first civilian ESDP mission: the deployment of a police training force to Bosnia. The military and non-military aspects of ESDP, therefore, were developed in tandem, with missions reflecting a preference for the latter. In late 2007 and early 2008, the EU drafted a new *Civilian Headline Goal 2010* which featured the launch of an operational *Civilian Planning and Conduct Capability* (CPCC) unit within the Council Secretariat. Within less than a decade, ESDP had moved a long way from the military emphasis of Saint Malo.

41.4 Evaluating ESDP

Evaluating a policy area as complex as ESDP is an arduous undertaking. It is rendered all the more so by the relative youth of the policy. Defense policy is characterized by extremely long-lead times, particularly when it comes to the generation of new military capabilities. It is thus too early for anything but a provisional assessment.

Certainly, ESDP provides the Union with a capability that was previously lacking. The Union had been criticized in the past for "a disproportionately heavy focus on economics, human rights and democratization to the neglect of diplomatic conflict prevention measures that seek to significantly alter the political dynamics of an emerging conflict."[13] Failure in the Balkans led to the creation of a European military instrument that was so conspicuous by its absence during the 1990s.

ESDP therefore responded to a clear need. Yet assessments of the Union's emergent international security role have varied widely. For some, ESDP has "substantially improved Europe's contribution to international security"[14]; others, in contrast, are less sanguine, noting that "the impression isn't of a strong EU, but of a supplicant continent that keeps saying it wants a bigger role on the world stage and then can't deliver."[15]

The ambitions of ESDP were, broadly, twofold: enhancing the Union's ability to intervene in international security affairs, and enhancing European capabilities for such interventions. In terms of the former, enthusiasts have tended to point to the quantity of missions carried out under the aegis of ESDP, arguing that the "number and variety of its operations show that ESDP has made a real difference on the ground."[16] Judging ESDP in this way allows one to compare the EU's activism favorably with the single mission launched by NATO in the twenty-first century—and draw from this the conclusion that the former is now more "usable" than the latter.[17] Yet such an approach leaves much to be desired. Not only does it fail to take into account the varying scale and intensity of the operations undertaken, but it also ignores the qualitative impact of those missions.

Certainly, EU interventions seem to have had a positive impact on the ground. Observers have applauded the outcomes of the various deployments in FYROM,[18] while EU and NATO interventions in Macedonia quite possibly helped avert civil conflict. The peace brokered in Aceh has held, while an Oxfam report acknowledged that EUFOR Chad "has made many civilians feel safer through its activities, which include patrolling known dangerous routes, destroying unexploded ordnance, making contact with local leaders, and positioning itself defensively around civilians during rebel and government fighting."[19]

Nor is it easy to deny the claim made by proponents of ESDP that its missions have tended to achieve their goals.[20] Equally, however, there remain grounds for skepticism, particularly regarding the limited nature of these goals. ESDP missions to date have been "small, lacking in ambition and strategically irrelevant."[21] Military missions in particular have been somewhat unambitious in scope. The first EDSP military deployment—Operation Concordia in the Former Yugoslav Republic of Macedonia—involved only 400 personnel. Operation Artemis has been described as "limited, brief, risk-averse and ultimately ineffective."[22] Indeed, it is striking that a significant proportion of the Union's military interventions have either followed, or accompanied, action on the ground by other institutions (NATO troops preceded those of the EU in both Macedonia and Bosnia, whilst the Union operated alongside UN forces in Congo).

One consequence of the limited nature of the missions undertaken has been their inability fully to resolve problems on the ground. Thus the problems confronting operation Atalanta in its attempts to prevent the activities of Somali pirates are immense—not only the sheer geographical size a limited number of vessels have to patrol (equivalent to that of Western Europe), but also the fact that, ultimately, piracy is merely a symptom of the chaos and instability in Somalia itself.[23] Similarly, EU intervention addressed "only the consequence and not the issues underlying the conflict in Chad."[24] Operation Artemis, deployed to the Democratic Republic of Congo in 2003, was the object of much hostile comment from humanitarian groups because of its limited scope in terms of both space and time.[25] Finally, the Congo operation of 2006 failed to solve fundamental problems in the region, and in fact withdrew whilst tensions were still high.[26] Even when it comes to civilian operations—supposedly the Union's strength—observers have criticized the EU's police training mission in Bosnia, pointing out that crime rates increased after its deployment and that EU officials failed to act on information about war criminals, interpreting their mandate as narrowly as possible.[27]

Moreover, it is hard to avoid the impression that some ESDP missions have been designed with an eye mainly on their consequences for the EU rather than their potential impact on the ground. Observers have argued that missions have sometimes been carried out for purely self-centered motives such as competition with NATO or a desire to test capabilities.[28] There was widespread suspicion that Operation Artemis was conceived for purely political or cosmetic reasons.[29] Others have questioned the added value—apart from allowing the Union to be present—provided by EU participation alongside a NATO mission and multinational "Combined Task Force 150" in the struggle against Somali pirates.[30]

More broadly, even in those cases where the EU has acted, its interventions have been on the margins of international politics, studiously avoiding interactions with the major powers. One Commission official, in making the case for intervention in Darfur in 2004, pointed out that "here we have a low technology, low intensity conflict taking place in a region where we would not trespass on the interest spheres of Russia or the US".[31] Others have argued that Africa has been the location of so many EU military missions precisely because of the possibility of deploying without such trespassing.[32]

So much for the missions themselves. In terms of capability developments, however, the picture is bleaker still. ESDP was, from the start, seen by some as a tool for enhancing member states' military capabilities. Consequently, it has spawned a bewildering variety of initiatives. These have ranged from the Helsinki Headline Goal of December 1999, to annual capabilities pledging conferences, to the November 2001 Capabilities Improvement Conference, itself leading to the creation of the European Capabilities Action Plan of December 2001—drawn up to deal with numerous shortfalls vis-à-vis the original Helsinki targets. In December 2003, member states created the so-called Capability Development Mechanism, whilst the following June saw the unveiling of a brand new Capabilities Plan in the form of the Headline Goal 2010. The following month, the member states created the European Defence Agency to assist them in meeting their objective of capabilities improvements, while 2006 witnessed the drafting of a "Long-Term Vision" for capability needs.

A parallel process was, as we have seen, launched on the civilian side. The Helsinki meeting that produced the Headline Goal also gave birth to a Civilian Crisis Management action plan; at Lisbon in March 2000 a Committee for Civilian Crisis Management was set up; the following June, the Feira Council adopted its four priority areas as the basis for Civilian Crisis Management. In May 2002 a Rule of Law Commitment Conference in

Brussels saw member states commit civilian personnel for crisis management operations. In November 2004 a Civilian Capabilities Commitment Conference was held; in December 2004 a Civilian Headline Goal 2008 was drawn up; in November 2005 the first Civilian Capabilities Improvement Conference was held and, in 2008, a new Civilian Headline Goal was unveiled.

Clearly, member states "have proved no slouches when it comes to delivering on paper."[33] And EU requirements have helped drive forward national defense reform processes and the development of new capabilities,[34] while most member states are taking steps to enhance their force-projection capabilities.[35]

Yet significant substantive improvements have been slow to materialize. The figures here are revealing. In comparison to the roughly 6,000 EU troops currently deployed, the African Union currently fields more than 30,000 and the UN 75,000, while the NATO force is Afghanistan numbers around 45,000 and will rise significantly.[36] In a coruscating critique, the former head of the European Defence Agency baldly characterized as a "failure" attempts to enhance European capabilities.[37] A recent report comments that "institutional initiatives have generated flurries of bureaucratic activity, but achieved limited results."[38] And this while targets are shifted at will. As the former European Defence Agency (EDA) chief has put it, from Helsinki to the Headline Goal 2010 "the goalposts were not so much moved as dismantled altogether."[39]

The simple fact is that European states are not spending enough on defense. SIPRI reported that, in 2005, Europe was the only region in the world where military spending decreased—by some 1.7 percent.[40] Defense spending by European NATO members fell by 35 percent between 1985 and 1995.[41] The disparities between member states, moreover, are huge: France and the UK make up 45 percent of total EU defense spending; they, along with Cyprus, Bulgaria, and Greece are the only member states to spend over the 2 percent of GDP that NATO has deemed a minimum requirement.

Not only are funds scarce, but the cash is often badly spent. Despite the Cold War having ended almost two decades ago, European armed forces still own 10,000 main battle tanks and 2,500 combat aircraft.[42] And despite large manpower budgets—the twenty-seven member states had almost 2 million active service personnel on their books in 2006[43]—only 30 percent of these can actually operate outside European territory because of legal restrictions or inadequate training.[44] Finally, inefficiencies result from the fragmentation of the European defense market. Several small national defense industries producing similar hardware for several small national militaries is a recipe for duplication and waste.

The resultant capabilities shortfalls have had practical implications. Two months after the deployment of a mission to Macedonia in 2003, the Union reported a 30 percent personnel shortfall.[45] A shortage of trainers has also plagued the EU Police Mission in Afghanistan. While US Secretary of Defense Robert Gates spoke of a need for some 3,500 trainers, the Union had, by December 2007, provided only a fraction of the 195 it eventually pledged.

Perhaps most strikingly and most significantly, chronic shortages of airlift capacity continue to bedevil operational capacity.[46] The EU deployment to Chad had to be delayed by six months because of a failure to locate 16 helicopters and 10 transport aircraft. As stop-gap solutions, several member states have resorted to hiring transport aircraft—either renting Ukrainian Antonovs, or attempting to persuading the US Military Air Transport Service to provide C-17s.[47] Meanwhile the long-term solution to such shortfalls—the Airbus A400M—has been the victim of repeated and prolonged delays, with the first deliveries now not expected until 2012.

In sum, and in what is perhaps the most damning critique of ESDP imaginable, "the problem of insufficient European military capacity is arguably more acute than at the time when President Jacques Chirac and Prime Minister Tony Blair met [at Saint Malo]."[48]

41.5 EXPLAINING ESDP

How, then, can one best explain these developments? Theoretical debates about integration had, for many years, and understandably, been preoccupied with areas other than defense policy. Insofar as defense figured at all, it was in an attempt to explain the absence of integration in this realm; the neo-functionalist insistence on the autonomy of different functional contexts was clearly targeted, in part, at the security sector.[49] Thus, the very fact that ESDP emerged at all proved problematic in theoretical terms. This being said, a number of scholars have recently advanced theoretical arguments purporting to explain the development, nature, and workings of ESDP.

41.5.1 Constructivism

Scholars writing in a sociological tradition have been the most active in terms of attempting to explain ESDP. Constructivists have explored the role of discourse in shaping perceptions of it.[50] Others have argued that its emergence is due more to a desire to create some kind of "European identity" and to a need to rally public support for European integration than to any specifically security-related rationale.[51]

Others still have focused on what they see as the convergence between member states over issues such as threat perception.[52] Meyer points to three learning mechanisms. The impact of changing threat perceptions, the socializing effects of ESDP structures, and the way crises act as an impetus to societal learning, may all, he argues, lead strategic cultures to converge.

Finally, Mérand draws on the work of Bourdieu in explaining the emergence of an ESDP "social field."[53] He offers a fascinating insight into the way national social representations interact. National political representations and organizational representations interact within the framework of ESDP, resulting in the particular kinds of institutions that emerge from this process of interaction.

41.5.2 Realism

At around the same time, a separate strand of theoretical work, rooted in power-centered realist accounts of international politics, began to pay attention to developments in the EU. In a series of influential publications dealing with the creation and development of the ESDP,[54] proponents of "soft balancing" have argued that, whilst states may not be engaging in traditional "balancing" against the United States, growing concerns about American power and increasing unilateralism have translated into attempts both to constrain the US and to increase the ability of these states to act. One such strategy is "soft balancing,"[55] whereby "consequential" states seek the ability to act autonomously in order to gain bargaining leverage over that hegemon.[56] Consistent with neo-realist claims that international institutions are simply tools of the "most powerful states in the system" which "create and shape" them,[57] the soft balancers argue that "Britain and France have been the drivers of ESDP."[58]

Thus, the EU is supposedly engaged in an attempt to increase both its autonomy from the United States and its ability to act on the international scene by building up its warfighting potential, with the result that "Europe will, within a decade, be reasonably well prepared to go it alone."[59]

41.5.3 Institutionalist Approaches

Finally, a range of contributions to the debate on ESDP have—implicitly or explicitly—drawn on institutionalist insights to explain its emergence and nature. One recent analysis has criticized the arguments of the "soft balancers" on the grounds that they fail to understand the nature, and inherent limitations, of the EU institutional system, as a consequence of which the Union would be unable to act in the strategic manner they ascribe to it even if it wanted to.[60]

Similarly, recent work on regime complexes has served to shed interesting light on the relationship between the European Union and NATO.[61] In particular, it has served to illustrate the problems inherent in the "chessboard politics" and feedback effects that can characterize situations where overlapping regimes share the same policy space. As we have seen in the case of relations between the EU and NATO, such effects can have significant practical consequences.

Other scholars have explained the nature of ESDP as a function of its institutional structure. Thus, the consensus requirement that governs security policy decisions militates against the rapid deployment of coercive power.[62] ESDP is thus *structurally* better suited to smaller scale crisis management rather than larger military interventions. Similarly, the somewhat ad hoc way in which the Union decides on missions reflects the problems inherent in reaching agreement. Disagreements between member states effectively scuppered EU intervention in the Democratic Republic of Congo in 2008. The need for prolonged negotiations taking into account the sensitivities of the German

Bundestag both shaped and delayed by several months the operation carried out in Kinshasa in 2006. The unanimity requirement also helps explain the apparent lack of ambition of ESDP in that the "lower the level of commitment, the higher the likelihood of achieving consensus."[63]

Such has been the proliferation of institutionalist scholarship in recent years that other, as yet unexplored, lines of inquiry into ESDP also suggest themselves. To take but one example, recent work on the pathologies of international institutions,[64] stemming from their bureaucratic nature, could cast interesting light on some of institutional failings of ESDP. Observers have pointed to the "damaging consequences of excessively complex institutional arrangements,"[65] most notably the resultant tensions and turf wars that have occurred between Commission and Council officials with responsibility for security policy. Even within the Council itself there have been problems of coordination between the various organizations responsible for civilian and military matters.[66]

While scholarly accounts have already, in a relatively short space of time, contributed much to our understanding of ESDP, and, in the process, contributed to the development of social science theory, there is the prospect of much more to come.

41.6 Conclusion

European leaders have not been shy about trumpeting the potential of ESDP. Thus the European Council felt able to declare in June 2004 that the "European Union is a global actor, ready to share in the responsibility for global security."[67] What the foregoing analysis has suggested, however, is that such claims are, at best, premature.

What is not quite so clear is whether this should be a cause for concern. For its proponents, the limited nature of ESDP is, if anything, something to be celebrated. As one disarmingly honest assessment puts it, whilst none of the ESDP missions "have saved the world...they have saved lives; and they have made some parts of the world a better place."[68] Moreover, problems in achieving consensus may themselves represent a blessing in disguise, in that if "the EU is slow to decide it may also be slow to make mistakes—which is not always the case with major powers."[69]

An alternative perspective, however, would hold that the rich countries of Europe should not rely on others when it comes to the deployment of meaningful "hard power." Some twenty five years ago, Hedley Bull had few doubts regarding the unacceptability of European dependence on others in security matters, asserting baldly that a "state of dependence on others...ought not to be compatible with the dignity of nations with the wealth, skills and historical position of those of Western Europe."[70] More recently, another respected observer has noted that, with "27 members already, and more lining up in the western Balkans, the EU cannot pose as a small huddle of vulnerable do-gooders sheltering under the wing of NATO and the United States." Even the former head of EU security policy commented that "we cannot continue to publicly espouse values and principles while calling on others to defend them."[71]

It is difficult, as yet, to rule definitively between these contrasting assessments. What can be said, however, is that opinions regarding the effectiveness of ESDP are crucially contingent on context. During the early part of the twenty-first century, as the Bush administration prepared for war in Iraq, it was relatively easy to praise the virtues of a "normative power Europe" that eschewed all but the limited use of force and preferred to lead others by example.[72] Its relative lack of military capabilities and its focus on non-military missions meant that the EU could boast of its credentials as a "soft power." In the current context of a Democratic American administration desperate for allied support in its campaign in Afghanistan, and as commentators increasingly point to the fact that hard rather than soft power is important in world politics,[73] ESDP suddenly looks somewhat less effective. Only time will tell whether member states will consent to bringing about the capabilities improvements, and reach the kinds of consensus that will allow for a more active role in security affairs.

Whatever the outcome of future developments, and whether or not ESDP eventually matches the expectations of its creators, the one area where it has not disappointed is in the theoretical literature it has spawned. Following on from years of—understandable—neglect, the relationship between defense policy and European integration has become the object of heated theoretical debate. As this literature develops (and it is still in its infancy) we are assured of lively exchanges and of a developing theoretical debate that could contribute not merely to our understanding of this particular policy sector, but of the Union and European integration as a whole.

Notes

1. Jolyon Howorth, *Security and Defence Policy in the European Union* (Basingstoke: Macmillan), 4.
2. Simon Duke, *The Elusive Quest for European Security: From EDC to CFSP* (London: Palgrave, 2000).
3. Seth G. Jones, *The Rise of European Security Cooperation* (Cambridge: Cambridge University Press, 2007).
4. Anand Menon "Defence Policy and Integration in Western Europe," *Contemporary Security Policy* 17, no. 2 (1996), 267–8.
5. Frédéric Mérand, *European Defence Policy: Beyond the Nation State* (Oxford: Oxford University Press, 2008).
6. James P. Thomas, *The Military Challenges of Transatlantic Coalitions* (Oxford: Oxford University Press, 2000).
7. An updated list of missions, along with links to information about each one, is available at <http://www.consilium.europa.eu/cms3_fo/showPage.asp?id = 268&lang = EN>.
8. F. Heisbourg, "Europe's Strategic Ambitions: The Limits of Ambiguity," *Survival* 42, no. 2 (2000), 5–15.
9. See Jolyon Howorth, "France, Britain and the Euro-Atlantic Crisis," *Survival* 45, no. 4 (2003–2004), 33–55.
10. Jolyon Howorth, "European Integration and Defence: The Ultimate Challenge?," *Chaillot Paper no. 43* (Paris: European Union Institute for Security Studies, 2000), 55.

11. Howorth, "European Integration and Defence," 60.
12. Agnieszka Nowak, ed., "Civilian Crisis Management: the European Way," *Chaillot Paper no 90* (Paris: EU Institute for Security Studies, 2006).
13. International Crisis Group. "EU Crisis Response Capability: Institutions and Processes for Conflict Prevention and Management," *ICG Issues Report no. 2* (Brussels: International Crisis Group, 26 June 2001), ii.
14. Daniel Keohane, "Shaping Europe's Military Order," *Irish Times*, November 9, 2009, <http://www.irishtimes.com/newspaper/opinion/2009/1109/1224258393219.html>.
15. Ian Martin, "Europe Looks to the US on Defense," *Wall Street Journal*, November 25, 2009, http://online.wsj.com/article/SB10001424052748704779704574555700693835302.html>.
16. Keohane, "Shaping Europe's Military Order."
17. Jolyon Howorth, *Security and Defence Policy in the European Union* (Basingstoke: Palgrave Macmillan, 2007).
18. J. Dobbins, "Europe's Role in Nation Building," *Survival* 50, no. 3 (2008), 83–110.
19. "Mission Incomplete: Why Civilians Remain at Risk in Eastern Chad," in *Oxfam Briefing Paper* (Oxford: Oxfam, 2008), 13.
20. Keohane, "Shaping Europe's Military Order."
21. Daniel Korski and Richard Gowan, *Can the EU Rebuild Failing States? A Review of Europe's Civilian Capacities* (London: European Council on Foreign Relations, 2009), 11.
22. Jean-Yves Haine and Bastian Giegerich, "In Congo, a Cosmetic EU Operation," *International Herald Tribune*, June 12, 2006, <http://www.nytimes.com/2006/06/12/opinion/12iht-edhaine.1954062.html>.
23. Paul Wood, "Can Somali Pirates be Defeated?," November 24, 2009., Available at <http://news.bbc.co.uk/1/hi/world/africa/8371139.stm> (accessed November 25, 2009).
24. Secretary General of the United Nations, 2008, Report of the Secretary General on the United Nations Mission in the Central African Republic and Chad, para. 52.
25. "Congo Crisis: Military Intervention in Ituri," *ICG Africa Report no. 64* (Brussels: International Crisis Group, 13 June 2003).
26. Catherine Gegout, "The EU and Security in the Democratic Republic of Congo: Unfinished Business," *CFSP Forum* 4, no. 6 (2007), 5–9.
27. "Bosnia's Stalled Police Reform: No Progress, No EU," *ICG Europe Report no. 164* (Brussels: International Crisis Group, 6 Sep 2005).
28. Alyson J. K. Bailes, "The EU and a 'Better World': What Role for the European Security and Defence Policy?," *International Affairs* 84, no. 1 (2008), 115–30.
29. Haine and Giegerich, "In Congo, a Cosmetic EU Operation."
30. Korski and Gowan, *Can the EU Rebuild Failing States?*
31. Cited in Asle Toje, "The Consensus Expectations Gap: Explaining Europe's Ineffective Foreign Policy," *Security Dialogue* 39, no. 1 (2008), 136.
32. Asle Toje, "The European Union as a Small Power, or Conceptualising Europe's Strategic Actorness," *European Integration* 30, no. 1 (2008), 208.
33. Korski and Gowan, "Can the EU Rebuild Failing States?," 43.
34. Nick Witney, "Re-energising Europe's Security and Defence Policy," *ECFR Policy Paper* (London: European Council on Foreign Relations, 29 July 2008).
35. "European Military Capabilities: Building Armed Forces for Modern Operations," *IISS Strategic Dossier* (London: International Institute for Strategic Studies, July 2008).
36. Asle Toje "The EU, NATO and European Defence—A Slow Train Coming," *ISS Occasional Paper no. 74* (Paris: Institute for Security Studies, December, 2008), 12.

37. Witney, *Re-Energising Europe's Security and Defence Policy*, 30.
38. International Institute for Strategic Studies, *European Military Capabilities*, 29.
39. Witney, *Re-Energising Europe's Security and Defence Policy*, 30.
40. *SIPRI Yearbook 2006: Armaments, Disarmament and International Security* (Oxford: Oxford University Press, 2006), 233.
41. International Institute for Strategic Studies, *European Military Capabilities*, 94.
42. Witney, *Re-Energising Europe's Security and Defence Policy*, 30.
43. International Institute for Strategic Studies, *European Military Capabilities*, 6.
44. Witney, *Re-Energising Europe's Security and Defence Policy*, 20.
45. Korski and Gowan, *Can the EU Rebuild Failing States?*, 22.
46. Giegerich and Wallace, "Not Such a Soft Power: The External Deployment," *Survival* 46, no. 2 (2004), 174–5; Wade Jacoby and Christopher Jones, "The EU Battle Groups in Sweden and the Czech Republic: What National Defense Reforms Tell Us about European Rapid Reaction Capabilities," *European Security* 17, no. 2 (2008), 331; Gustav Lindstrom, "Enter the EU Battlgroups," in *Chaillot Paper no. 97* (Paris: European Union Institute for Security Studies, 2007), 31–40.
47. Giegerich and Wallace, "Not Such a Soft Power," 175.
48. Toje, "The EU, NATO, and European Defence," 19.
49. Hanna Ojanen, "The EU and Nato: Two Competing Models for a Common Defence Policy," *Journal of Common Market Studies* 44, no. 1 (2006), 58–60.
50. Henrik Larsen, "The EU: A Global Military Actor?," *Cooperation and Conflict* 37, no. 3 (2002), 283–302.
51. Stephanie Anderson and Thomas R. Seitz, "European Security and Defense Policy Demystified," *Armed Forces and Society* 33, no. 1 (2006), 24–42.
52. C. O. Meyer, *The Quest for a European Strategic Culture: Changing Norms on Security and Defence in the European Union* (Basingstoke: Palgrave Macmillan, 2006).
53. Mérand, *European Defence Policy*.
54. Jones, *The Rise of European Security Cooperation*; Barry R. Posen "European Security and Defense Policy: response to Unipolarity?," *Security Studies* 15, no. 2 (2006), 149–86.
55. See, for example, T. V. Paul, "Soft Balancing in the Age of US Primacy," *International Security* 30, no. 1 (2005), 46–71.
56. Barry R. Posen, "ESDP and the Structure of World Power," *The International Spectator* 39, no. 1 (2004), 5–17.
57. John J. Mearsheimer, "The False Promise of International Institutions," *International Security* 19, no. 3 (1994/5), 13.
58. Robert J. Art, "Striking the Balance," *International Security* 30, no. 3 (2005/6), 183; a similar analysis can be found in Jones, *The Rise of European Security Cooperation*.
59. Posen, "European Union Security and Defense Policy," 153.
60. Jolyon Howorth and Anand Menon, "Still not Pushing Back: Why the European Union is not Balancing the United States," *Journal of Conflict Resolution* 53, no. 5 (2009), 727–44.
61. Stephanie Hoffmann, "Overlapping Institutions in the Realm of International Security: The Case of NATO and ESDP," *Perspectives on Politics* 7, no. 1 (2009), 45–52.
62. Toje, "The European Union as a Small Power," 207; Sten Rynning, "The European Union: Towards a Strategic Culture?," *Security Dialogue* 34, no. 4 (2003), 407.
63. Toje, "The Consensus Expectations Gap," 132.
64. Michael N. Barnett and Martha Finnemore, "The Politics, Power, and Pathologies of International Organizations," *International Organization* 53, no. 4 (1999), 699–732.

65. Jean-Marie Guéhenno, "Forward," in D. Korski and R. Gowan, eds, *Can the EU Rebuild Failing States? A Review of Europe's Civilian Capacities* (London: European Council on Foreign Relations, 2009), 7.

66. Korski and Gowan, *Can the EU Rebuild Failing States?*

67. Council of the European Union 2004, "Presidency Report on ESDP: Annexe 1, Headline Goal 2010, endorsed by the European Council, Brussels, 17 and 18 June 2004." Reproduced in *EU Security and Defence: Core Documents 2004* (Paris: European Union Institute for Security Studies, 2004), 359.

68. Robert Cooper, "Views From the Insiders—Robert Cooper," *ESDP Newsletter Special Issue* (Brussels: Council of the European Union 2009), 14.

69. Cooper, "Views From the Insiders—Robert Cooper," 15.

70. Hedley Bull, "Civilian Power Europe: A Contradiction in Terms?," *Journal of Common Market Studies* 12, no. 2 (1982), 156.

71. Bailes, "The EU and a 'Better World'," 119.

72. Ian Manners, "Normative Power Europe: A Contradiction in Terms?," *Journal of Common Market Studies* 40, no. 2 (2002), 235–58.

73. Kurt M. Campbell and Michael E. O'Hanlon, *Hard Power: The New Politics of National Security* (New York: Basic Books, 2006).

CHAPTER 42

....

THE SHADOW OF SCHENGEN

....

JONATHON W. MOSES

To the ears of many, Schengen rhymes with "borderless Europe." Originally the name of a small wine-making village on the banks of the Moselle in southern Luxembourg, Schengen has come to symbolize the very apex of Europe's integration ideal and ambition. In abolishing border controls between signatory states, the Schengen Agreement made it easier to travel across the breadth of Europe, and prodded a discussion about the need to create a common door to the outside world. This, in a nutshell, is the promise of Schengen.

In practice, the sort of free mobility that we associate with Schengen represents a number of challenges to further integration in Europe. This shadow of Schengen extends over three distinct areas of research, each of which is relatively skeptical of Europe's capacity to integrate. First, Schengen prompts us to consider the role of labor migration within Europe's larger ambitions for economic and monetary union. Second, Schengen prompts a discussion about citizenship, identity, and belonging in an integrated Europe. Finally, Schengen highlights the practical difficulties of getting once sovereign states to agree on how to face the world beyond its borders. This short chapter examines the literature on European migration as it relates to these three, cross-cutting challenges.[1]

42.1 THE ROAD TO SCHENGEN

....

The promise of free mobility in Europe is as old as the Community itself. After all, the Preamble to the 1957 Treaty of Rome, "resolved to ensure the economic and social progress of their countries by common action to eliminate the barriers which divide Europe." But this resolution was placed on hold until the mid-1980s, when Europe's borders were coaxed open by two parallel developments.

In 1985, when the pace of European integration proved too slow for a handful of member states, five countries broke out of the formal confines of the European Community and met on a river boat in Schengen to agree among them on the need to remove their (physical) border controls.[2] In practice, this simply meant that passport checks were to be replaced by visual surveillance of private cars as they passed by (at reduced speed). In 1990, the original agreement was supplemented with a Schengen Implementation Agreement, and both of these were integrated into the EU framework with the 1999 Amsterdam Treaty, introducing the *Schengen-Acquis*.[3]

Schengen abolishes border controls among signatory states and creates a common external border—one that shares common rules of entry into the Schengen area. To facilitate this common border control, signatory states need to pool and share information in the Schengen Information System (SIS)[4] and its supporting network of Supplementary Information Request at the National Entry (SIRENE) offices. This framework, in effect, instituted a system for sharing relevant political and legal information among signatory states.

This Schengen track runs parallel to another set of developments that was occurring within the formal framework provided by the European Community. In 1986, the SEA promised to create "an area without internal frontiers in which the free movement of persons, goods, services and capital is ensured" (Article 8A). This sort of economic right was buttressed with a number of explicitly political rights when the Preamble to the Maastricht Treaty promised "every person holding the nationality of a member state shall be a citizen of the Union."[5]

Together, these developments unleashed an impressive increase in European migration and mobility. For example, in 2006 about 3.5 million people moved to a new country within the EU-27. Most of these (52 percent) came from non-EU countries (roughly distributed across world regions), 34 percent came from other EU member states, and the remaining 14 percent were people returning home after living abroad.[6]

Still, in a comparative context, the level of immigration into the EU remains remarkably low. While the income gap between Europe and its neighbors is comparable with the one that separates North and South America, the net annual immigration rate into the EU (at 2.2 immigrants per thousand) was half of that found in the US and Canada (4.4 per thousand) during the 1990s and early 2000s.[7]

Of course, people are leaving Europe as well, so if we look at the net migration level in the EU-27, we find more sobering numbers: slightly less than two million people (net) entered EU member states from a foreign country. This constitutes much less than 1 percent (actually 0.39 percent) of the total number of inhabitants in the EU-27 that year (2007). As is evident in Figure 42.1, this trend jumped around the turn of the millennium, but it now seems to have stabilized.

In 2007, most of these immigrants ended up entering Spain (701,848), Italy (494,315), and the United Kingdom (174,603). But the heaviest-hit states (in terms of the size of the immigrant flow, relative to the population) were Cyprus, Spain, Ireland, and Luxembourg, as seen in Figure 42.2.[8] These countries experienced immigrant inflows that represented about 1.5 percent of their respective populations. In 2006, the largest internal (EU) source countries of immigrants were Poland and Romania; the largest external source was Morocco.[9]

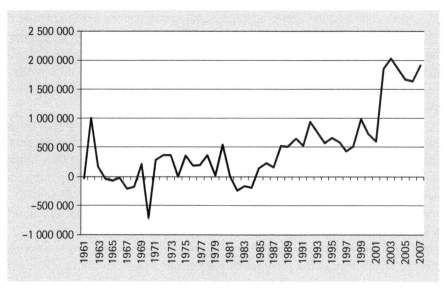

FIGURE 42.1 Net migration, EU-27.

Source: EUROSTAT, *Europe in Figures*, 168.

42.2 LABOR MARKET INTEGRATION

Labor market integration does not happen on its own, and the lifting of formal restrictions could never suffice to bring about a truly integrated European labor market. In practice, the right of free mobility is restricted by a number of other factors. For example, migrants must be able to prove they have sufficient means to support themselves (and their families) and member states retain the prerogative to determine nationality and citizen laws. The constraints are then fortified by cultural and language differences, not to mention dense webs of (national) bureaucratic and legal entanglement. As a result, the European labor market remains very segmented.

From the perspective of several economic approaches, the current scale of mobility in Europe is insufficient to meet at least three daunting tasks and an ideological objective associated with greater European integration. First, economists and demographers have long noted the need to address the threat of shifting demographics in Europe. Low fertility rates, combined with increased life expectancy, will increase Europe's dependency ratio (the ratio of working-age/non-working-age population) substantially. While migration alone is clearly insufficient to correct the problem, it has been discussed as an important facilitating factor, in that targeted immigration can increase the number of working-age contributors and the overall fertility rate (immigrant populations tend to maintain higher fertility rates) as well as supplement the workforce in relevant sectors (e.g. nursing and healthcare) to deal with the aging population.[10]

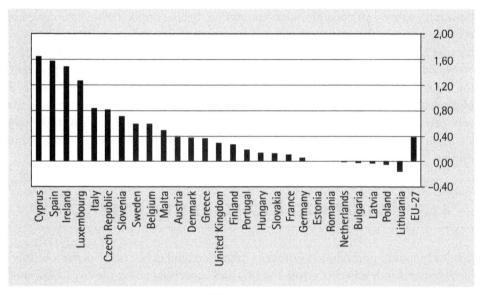

FIGURE 42.2 Net migration, percentage of population, 2007.

Source: EUROSTAT, *Europe in Figures*, figure 3.20.

Second, there are a host of studies that examine how increased migration can affect economic growth, wages, and welfare expenditures in Europe.[11] While the results tend to vary slightly, depending on operationalization choices, the overall consensus is consistent with studies from other countries. Or, in the words of Brücker et al.:

> Our findings by and large confirm the international evidence on this issue: any negative effects in the labour market on wages or employment are hard to detect. In fact, there is evidence that post-enlargement migration contributes to growth prospects of the EU by ensuring a better allocation of human capital, that these migrants are strongly attached to the labour market, and that they are quite unlikely to be among welfare recipients.[12]

Third, Europe suffers from inadequate levels of labor market flexibility in a region that shares a common currency (the euro). Labor mobility and wage flexibility are essential economic attributes, given Europe's ambition to share a common currency area—especially in a context which otherwise lacks significant federal fiscal transfers.[13] But the European labor market is incredibly resilient to the sort of labor market integration that we see in the US (for example). Indeed, EU citizens tend to be about half as mobile as their US counterparts: in the decade preceding the adoption of the euro, 38 percent of EU citizens changed residence, but only about 4 percent of these moved to another member state.[14]

Finally, and at a more ideological level, it is important to note the role played by labor mobility in the broader plan for economic and monetary union in Europe. This is clear, if not explicit, in the way in which the free movement of people, goods, services, and capital are bundled together in Article 8A of the SEA. By unbundling this package, however, we reveal an uncomfortable assumption that lies implicit within the design of economic union: the free movement of goods, services, and capital was embraced because European officials hoped that increased competition among European producers would help consumers and reap the benefits of economies of scale. By implication, the free movement of European labor can be seen as part of an effort to increase the level of competition among European workers, to the benefit of European employers. In the end, perhaps, these gains will benefit European consumers as well (at least those that still have a job)—but these gains will be secured at the expense of organized labor in Europe.[15]

42.3 RESIDENCY, RIGHTS, AND CITIZENSHIP

While economic approaches to European migration tend to be critical of the low levels of migration (both into and across the EU) and concerned about the costs associated with Europe's protected, inflexible, and segmented labor markets, more political approaches tend to focus on Europe's rising xenophobia in the face of this (relatively limited scale of) migration. In this light, Europe suffers from too much mobility and migration.

Europeans appear to be terrified of foreigners and are unable to agree upon a common approach for dealing with them. Whereas American survey respondents wish to limit the rate or *flow* of immigrant entry, most European respondents voice concern about increasing the *stock* of migrants.[16] It would seem that Europe has lost whatever appetite it once had for foreigners.

Nor is this fear of the foreigner limited to the realm of surveys. Foreigners in Europe suffer from an unemployment rate that is more than double that of EU-27 nationals (14.4 percent compared to 6.7 percent for nationals in 2008), although the spread varies significantly from member state to member state.[17] It is also evident in the growing electoral support of radical right, anti-immigrant, parties across Europe.[18] Nearly everywhere it is possible to find a nationalist party that is poised to exploit voter dissatisfaction, alienation, and xenophobia—and Europe's more mainstream parties are being sucked up in the vortex.[19]

Like EU membership in general, immigration challenges national identities and patterns of citizenship. Schengen intensifies these challenges by liberalizing the cross-national flows of people. After all, "If national identity means self-definition and belonging in the national polity, then immigration cuts to the heart of this concept, because it raises political questions about how the nation-state should be defined."[20]

This pressure opens the door on one of the most interesting discussions in contemporary political theory: how immigration challenges the way we conceive of citizenship and rights in the modern polity. While voting rights can be understood as central to the notion of democratic citizenship, civil and social rights are seen to be universal, and are often extended to residents of modern states, even those that are not citizens.

Immigration that results in long-term legal residents without citizenship blurs the lines between citizenship, rights, and obligations.[21] As a result, the European Union offers a fascinating laboratory for balancing the overlapping conceptions of residence, rights, and citizenship.[22]

Actually, the problem is a lack of balance. Despite much rhetoric to the contrary, European citizenship is a rather hollow concept, as member states still control the gates of citizenship; EU citizenship reinforces, rather than detracts from, national citizenship.[23] The hollowness of EU citizenship is most evident when we look at the status of Third-Country Nationals (TCNs).[24] As EU citizenship is reserved for those who already hold citizenship papers in one of the twenty-seven member states, the creation of European citizenship, "effectively froze the 13 million third country nations (TCNs) permanently resident in the European Union out of European citizenship."[25]

Migration into and around Europe continues to challenge existing systems of identity and rights. As migration increases, so does the pressure on nation-based systems of belonging and support—systems which were first developed in Europe, and which enjoy strong traditions and public support. EU efforts to create an alternative (and larger) vessel for organizing identity, rights, and obligations have been entirely insufficient. Into the vacuum has flowed Europe's growing xenophobia.

42.4 A Common Door to the World

There is a general consensus that internal freedom of movement (within the EU) requires the harmonization of EU's external borders with respect to TCNs.[26] Without common external frontiers, a TCN admitted to any Schengen state can freely move to any other Schengen state. Despite this need, and much political smoke, actual harmonization has been very difficult.

This should not come as a surprise. Despite a significant effort to develop a harmonized EU immigration policy with respect to TCNs,[27] there has been much resistance among member states.[28] One reason is that the Treaty of Rome failed to mention external border controls. Another is that member states have long histories, some of which include colonialist pasts, and have several good reasons for maintaining special relationships with some TCNs. Not to be left out is the recognition that states are often leery of seceding political authority, and border control is seen by many as a core instrument of sovereignty.

As a consequence, it has been easier to keep the regulation of TCN immigration located mostly outside of the EU's legal framework. But it is in this area—in the effort to create a common immigration, family-reunion, and asylum policy with respect to TCNs—that the EU is devoting much of its current attention. To catch a glimpse of this effort, we can examine Europe's attempt to build a common border control and monitoring group (which covers each type of TCN movement) and then examine in more detail the development of Europe's nascent common asylum policy.

With respect to the first area, a common border control system, the EU has developed several tools to help forge its common foreign border. In addition to the SIS (already mentioned), Europe has created a common list of countries whose nationals require visas; it has developed common rules for issuing short-stay visas; it has created a Visa Information System; and it has imposed carrier sanctions and passenger data transmission requirements.[29] But the most obvious institutional artifice in securing Europe's common borders is FRONTEX.

FRONTEX was established in 2004 by the Council of the European Union. Based in Warsaw, this European border guard agency was established to coordinate intelligence-driven cooperation at the EU level and to strengthen security along the Union's external borders.[30] The success in establishing FRONTEX might be explained by the heightened security concerns of member states after 2001, although the relationship is complex.[31] Still, the securitization motive was clear in the conclusions of the European Council of Laeken, where "better management of the Union's external border controls will help in the fight against terrorism, illegal immigration networks and the traffic in human beings."[32]

The resulting organization is an interesting blend of intergovernmental and supranational control. The management board of FRONTEX consists of two Commission officials, plus the heads of national border guard services. With a rapidly growing budget and workforce, FRONTEX is responsible for analyzing risks, manning (and training) the border stations, returning the unwanted, along with research and development efforts. It has become the common face of the European Union to TCNs entering into the Schengen space.

Perhaps the most visible manifestation of policy in this area is the Common European Asylum System (CEAS)—an explicit attempt to harmonize the Union's sundry asylum policies and to share responsibility for asylum seekers. Like the effort to create a common border patrol, the pressure to create the CEAS comes from two sources: increasing concerns about security and the unequal distribution of the existing asylum burden across EU member states.[33]

Since the Amsterdam Treaty, one European agreement after the other has signaled an interest in creating a common European asylum policy. The Nice Treaty moved asylum issues from the third to the first pillar of European governance, allowing asylum decision to be carried out by majority voting. This means that member states lost their right to veto policies that they oppose, accelerating the development of a common policy in this area. This development can be traced in four important steps.

First, the (2003) Dublin Regulation aimed to quickly identify the member state responsible for examining an asylum application; to establish reasonable time limits for this; and to prevent multiple applications. Second, the (2003) Reception Conditions Directive introduced minimum standards for reception and detention (e.g. access to information, labor markets, healthcare, etc.). Third, the Qualifications Directive (2004) establishes minimum standards for granting and withdrawing refugee status. Finally, the Asylum Procedures Directive of 2005 obliges states to agree on minimum standards for processing asylum claims.

These four legislative steps have brought the EU much closer to a common asylum policy, and the future will surely bring about even more harmonization and streamlining. Unfortunately, this convergence has brought about a race to the bottom on asylum policy.[34] This was bound to happen, if only because the number of potential asylum hosts has shrunk for those desperately in need of help.

But there is still a very long way to go before Europe's asylum policies and practices are completely harmonized. National governments continue to wield significant power, and national practices are remarkably diverse. This diversity can be seen in the different rates by which member states still reject (or, inversely, recognize) asylum claims. For example, in 2007, the rejection rate ranged from just under 30 percent (in Poland) to 98.6 percent (in Greece)![35] National differences are also evident in the very different ways that member states responded to recent asylum streams from Afghanistan, Iraq, and Chechnya. In short, states interpret common regulations in different ways, and employ derogation clauses that allow them to maintain national policies and interests. The end result is a lack of harmonization, both in terms of recognition and reception conditions.[36]

42.5 CONCLUSION

Contrary to common perceptions, Schengen casts a shadow over Europe's hope for further integration. The Schengen shadow, and this chapter, covers three distinct areas of concern and bodies of literature.

The first two bodies of literature deal with the inadequacies of European immigration policies, but for very different, even conflicting, reasons. On the one hand, European labor markets are seen to be woefully inefficient, fragmented, and closed-off to foreigners and these shortcomings are stifling Europe's economic potential. On the other hand, existing levels of labor market integration—and the influx of foreigners that integration brings along with it—appear to threaten the social and political fabric (not to mention many of the social models) that are uniquely European. In short, Europe seems to be damned if she doesn't open up to increased migration, and yet damned if she does.

At the nexus of these two views lies *A European Dilemma*.[37] After all, there is a huge gap that separates the world views of these two distinct bodies of literature: one sees the promise of immigration in generating economic efficiencies and resolving Europe's demographic crisis; the other finds a xenophobic Europe, full to the gunwales with unwanted foreigners. Like the American dilemma noted by Gunnar Myrdal, Europe faces a "racialization of social relations."[38] But Europe's Dilemma lies in the absence of something akin to the American creed—she still lacks an identity rubric under which the sundry residents of Europe can muster.

The third body of literature examines the difficulty of agreeing on a common policy for dealing with the foreigner at Europe's doorstep: whether he or she is a worker, a relative, or an asylum-seeker. Here too, the difficulties of convincing member states to relinquish control is all too evident, even in the face of what is perceived to be a growing securitization threat.

Each of these bodies of literature is critical of Europe's ability to integrate further. This common pessimism is linked, in part, to the difficulty of expecting workers, as laborers, to behave like other commodities. Herein lays the irony that is Schengen: while viewed as a symbol of European integration, Schengen's shadow casts doubt on this very endeavor.

NOTES

1. For a broader, textbook-level, introduction to this subject matter, see Jonathon W. Moses, "Migration in Europe," in Ronald Tiersky and Erik Jones, eds, *Europe Today*, fourth edition (Lanham: Rowman and Littlefield, 2011), 371–97.
2. For an introduction to the political and historical route to Schengen, see Monica Den Boer and Laura Corrado, "For the Record or Off the Record: Comments About the Incorporation of Schengen into the EU," *European Journal of Migration and Law* 1 (1999), 397–418. On the political difficulties of securing the original agreement and getting other member states to sign, see Andrew Convey and Mark Kupiszewski, "Keeping up with Schengen: Migration and Policy in the European Union," *International Migration Review* 29, no. 4 (1995), 939–40. For a discussion of the closed nature of decision-making in the Schengen executive committee, see Deidre Curtin, "The Principle of Open Government in Schengen and European Union: Democratic Retrogression?," *Common Market Law Review* 32 (1995), 391–442.
3. These provisions where superseded by the Dublin Convention of June 14, 1990, which came into force in September 1997. This was replaced by a Council Regulation which established the criteria for determining the member states responsible for examining asylum regulations: (EC) No. 343/2003. In 2008, the European Commission released a proposal to recast the Dublin Regulation; see European Council on Refugees and Exiles, "Comments From the European Council on Refugees and Exiles on the European Commission Proposal to Recast the Dublin Regulation," April 2009, available at <http://www.ecre.org/files/ECRE_Response_to_Recast_Dublin_Regulation_2009.pdf>.
4. For a description of how the SIS collects and uses this information, see Madeline Colvin, *The Schengen Information System: A Human Rights Audit* (London: JUSTICE, 2000). Work is underway to create a new information system (SIS II), to be launched in 2013.
5. In particular, the Consolidated Version of the European Community Treaty granted the right to vote and to stand as a candidate (Art. 19); the right to protection abroad by diplomatic and consular authorities (Art. 20); and freedom of information rights with respect to Union institutions and the right of petition (Art. 21). Most significantly, in light of recent developments, Article 12 extended the rights of entry, exit, and residence to all nationals of the member states without any discrimination on grounds of nationality. For details of this shift from "market citizenship" to "Union citizenship," see Sergio Carrera, "What Does Free Movement Mean in Theory and Practice in an Enlarged EU?," *European Law Journal* 11, no. 6 (2005), 700–1.
6. EUROSTAT, "Recent Migration Trends: Citizens of EU-27 Member States Become Even More Mobile While EU Remains Attractive to Non-EU Citizens," *Statistics in Focus* 98/2008, 3.

7. Herbert Brücker, Joachim R. Frick, and Gert G. Wagner, "Economic Consequences of Immigration in Europe," in Craig A. Parsons and Timothy M. Smeeding, eds, *Immigration and the Transformation of Europe* (Cambridge: Cambridge University Press, 2006), 111–46.

8. EUROSTAT, *Europe in Figures. EUROSTAT Yearbook 2009* (Luxembourg: European Communities, 2009), Table 3.16, Figure 3.20.

9. EUROSTAT, *Statistics in Focus*, 1.

10. There has been a vibrant debate about whether it is possible to manage Europe's demographic structure in this way. Some authors are critical, e.g. D. A. Coleman, "Does Europe Need Immigrants? Population and Workforce Projects," *International Migration Review* 26 (1992), 413–61; and OECD, *Migration: the Demographic Aspects* (Paris: OECD, 1991). Others are more supportive, suggesting that immigration might buy some needed time to allow the broader economic system to adjust. See T. Straubhaar and K. F. Zimmermann, "Towards a European Migration Policy," *Population Research and Policy Review* 12, no. 93 (1993), 225–41; Axel H. Börsch-Supan, "Migration, Social Security Systems, and Public Finance Source," in Horst Siebert, ed., *Migration: A Challenge for Europe* (Tubingen: Mohr, 1994), 111–14; and Brücker et al., "Economic Consequences of Immigration in Europe," 136.

11. See e.g. Tito Boeri, Gordon Hanson, and Barry McCormick, eds, *Immigration Policy and the Welfare System* (Oxford: Oxford University Press, 2002); Brücker et al. "Economic Consequences of Immigration in Europe"; Ann Morissens, "Immigrants, Unemployment, and Europe's Varying Welfare Regimes," in Parsons and Smeeding, 172–99; and Jonathan Chaloff and Georges Lemaitre, "Managing Highly-Skilled Labour Migration: A Comparative Analysis of Migration Policies and Challenges in OECD Countries," OECD Social, Employment and Migration Working Papers No. 79, March 2009, available at <http://www.oecd.org/officialdocuments/displaydocumentpdf/?cote = DELSA/ELSA/WD/SEM%282009%295&doclanguage = en>.

12. Brücker et al., "Economic Consequences of Immigration in Europe," 37–8. I should point out that Boeri et al. find some evidence that migrants are receiving proportionally more social transfers than the native populations in Europe (see Tito Boeri, "Preface," in Boeri et al., *Immigration Policy and the Welfare System*, p. xx). As some countries will not have lifted restrictions on new-member state immigration before 2011, it is somewhat premature to analyze the effects of immigration from the new member states, but preliminary studies suggest that the economic impact has been positive, if relatively modest. See Martin Kahanec and Klaus F. Zimmermann, "Migration in an Enlarged EU: A Challenging Solution?," *European Economy* 363 (March 2009); and Ray Barrell, John Fitzgerald, and Rebecca Riley, "EU Enlargement and Migration: Assessing the Macroeconomic Impact," *Journal of Common Market Studies* 48, no. 2 (2010), 373–95. More emphasis has been placed on trying to measure the size of the post-enlargement migration flow. Early evidence from the European Commission suggests that these flows have been quite modest in size. See Commission of the European Communities, "Report on the Functioning of Transitional Arrangements set out in the 2003 Accession Treaty (period May 1, 2004–April 30, 2006): Communication from the Commission to the Council, the European Parliament, the European Economic and Social Committee and the Committee of the Regions," February 8, 2006; and Commission of the European Communities, "Enlargement Two Years After: An Economic Evaluation," *European Economy* 24 (2006).

13. The standard references in this area are Barry Eichengreen, Maurice Obstfeld, and Luigi Spaventa, "One Money for Europe? Lessons from the US Currency Union," *Economic*

Policy 5, no. 10 (1990), 160–4; and Paul De Grauwe, *Economics of Monetary Union*, eighth edition (Oxford: Oxford University Press, 2009).

14. Commission of the European Communities, "High Level Task Force on Skills and Mobility: Final Report," Directorate-General for Employment and Social Affairs, Unit EMPL/A.3., December 2001.

15. Fritz W. Scharpf, "The Only Solution is to Refuse to Comply with ECJ Rulings," interview with Cornelia Girndt, *Social Europe Journal* 4, no. 1 (2008), 16–21; Fritz W. Scharpf, "The European Social Model: Coping with the Challenges of Diversity," *Journal of Common Market Studies* 40, no. 4 (2002), 645–70; and Jonathon W. Moses, "Is Constitutional Symmetry Enough? Social Models & Market Integration in the US & Europe," *Journal of Common Market Studies* 49, no. 4 (July 2011), 82343.

16. Boeri, "Preface," vi.

17. EUROSTAT, "Unemployment rates by sex, age groups and nationality (%) [lfsa_urgan]," *Eurostat Dataexplorer*, available at <http://appsso.eurostat.ec.europa.eu/nui/show.do?dataset = lfsa_urgan&lang = en>; and Moses, "Migration in Europe," Figure 5.

18. The voting literature in this area is voluminous, and somewhat beyond the scope of this piece. For reviews, see, e.g. Martin Schain, Aristide R. Zolberg, and Patrick Hossay, eds, *Shadows Over Europe: The Development and Impact of the Extreme Right in Western Europe* (New York: Palgrave Macmillan, 2002) and Antonis A. Ellinas, "Phased Out: Far Right Parties in Western Europe: A Review," *Comparative Politics* 39, no. 3 (2007), 353–71.

19. Joost van Spanje, "Contagious Parties: Anti-Immigration Parties and Their Impact on Other Parties' Immigration Stances in Contemporary Western Europe," *Party Politics* 16, no. 5 (2010), 563–86.

20. Adam Luedtke, "European Integration, Public Opinion and Immigration Policy: Testing the Impact of National Identity," *European Union Politics* 6, no. 1 (2005), 83–112, at 88.

21. Rainer Bauböck, "Expansive Citizenship: Voting beyond Territory and Membership," *PS* 38, no. 4 (2005), 683–7.

22. This discussion is much larger than the EU, in that the *Limits of Citizenship* are global in nature; see Yasemin N. Soysal, *The Limits of Citizenship* (Chicago: University of Chicago Press, 1994). See also Saskia Sassen, "The Repositioning of Citizenship: Emergent Subjects and Space for Politics," *The New Centennial Review* 3, no. 2 (2003), 41–66; Saskia Sassen, "Towards Post-National and Denationalized Citizenship," in E. F. Isin and B. S. Turner, eds, *Handbook of Citizenship Studies* (London: Sage, 2002), 277–91; Saskia Sassen, *Losing Control* (New York: Columbia University Press, 1996); and L. Bosniak, *The Citizens and the Alien: Dilemmas of Contemporary Membership* (Princeton: Princeton University Press, 2006). For a critical view, see Randal Hansen "The Poverty of Postnationalism: Citizenship, Immigration and the New Europe," *Theory and Society* 38 (2009), 1–24. On Europe, see Rainer Bauböck, *Citizenship Policies in the New Europe* (Amsterdam: Amsterdam University Press, 2007); Rainer Bauböck, ed., *Migration and Citizenship: Legal Status, Rights and Political Participation* (Amsterdam: Amsterdam University Press, 2006); Rainer Bauböck, "The Crossing and Blurring of Boundaries in International Migration. Challenges for Social and Political Theory," in Rainer Bauböck and John F. Rundell, eds, *Blurred Boundaries: Migration, Ethnicity, Citizenship* (Aldershot: Ashgate, 1998), 17–52; Rainer Bauböck, Bernhard Perchinig, and Wiebke Sievers, eds, *Citizenship Policies in the New Europe*, expanded and updated edition (Amsterdam: Amsterdam University Press, 2009); Stephen Castles, "Globalization and the Ambiguities of National Citizenship," in Bauböck and Rundell, eds, *Blurred Boundaries: Migration, Ethnicity, Citizenship*, 223–44; Rey

Koslowski, "Intra-EU Migration, Citizenship and Political Union," *Journal of Common Market Studies* 32, no. 3 (1994), 369–402; Hakan G. Sicikkan, "The European Politics of Citizenship and Asylum," Doctoral Dissertation in Comparative Politics (University of Bergen, Norway, 2006); and Jo Shaw, *The Transformation of Citizenship in the European Union* (Cambridge: Cambridge University Press, 2007).

23. Randall Hansen doesn't mince words: "As a derivative status that creates no new rights, EU citizenship in no way challenges national citizenship. This fact is clear from the treaties, yet scholars continue to imbue EU citizenship with an empirical content and theoretical importance that it simply lacks...the European Union has almost nothing to do with immigration and citizenship" (Hansen, "The Poverty of Postnationalism," 6). See also Randal Hansen, "Migration, Citizenship or a Europe of Citizens? Third-Country Nationals in the EU," *Journal of Ethnic and Migration Studies* 24, no. 4 (1998), 751–68; and C. Joppke, *Challenge to the Nation-State* (Oxford: Oxford University Press, 1998).

24. For some history of the relationship between TCNs and European citizenship, see Theodora Kostakopoulou, "Invisible Citizens? Long-Term Resident Third-Country Nationals in the EU and their Struggle for Recognition," in Richard Bellamy and Alex Warleigh, eds, *Citizenship and Governance in the European Union* (London: Continuum, 2001), 180–205; Adam Luedtke, "The European Union Dimension: Supranational Integration, Free Movement of Persons, and Immigration Politics," in Parsons and Smeeding, eds, 419–41; and Willem Maas, "Migrants, States, and EU Citizenship's Unfulfilled Promise," *Citizenship Studies* 12, no. 6 (2008), 583–96.

25. Hansen, "The Poverty of Postnationalism," 17.

26. See, e.g. Demetrios G. Papademetriou, *Coming Together or Pulling Apart? The European Union's Struggle with Immigration and Asylum* (Washington, DC: Carnegie Endowment for International Peace, 1996); Commission of the European Communities, *Communication from the Commission to the Council and the European Parliament: On an open method of coordination for the community immigration policy* (Brussels: CEC, 2001); and Andrew Geddes, *The Politics of Migration and Immigration in Europe* (London: Sage, 2003).

27. Commission of the European Communities, *Communication from the Commission to the Council and the European Parliament: On a community immigration policy* (Brussels: CEC, 2000); and European Parliament, "Movement and residence of EU citizens," *Official Journal of the European Communities,* May C 135, no. 44 (2001), 189–93.

28. e.g. Foreign and Commonwealth Office, *A Partnership Among Nations* (London: FCO, 1996). For details, see Terri Givens and Adam Luedtke, "The Politics of European Union Immigration Policy: Institutions, Salience, and Harmonization," *The Policy Studies Journal* 32, no. 1 (2004), 145–65.

29. E. Guild, "Danger—Borders under Construction: Assessing the First Five Years of Border Policy in an Area of Freedom, Security and Justice," in J. de Zwaan and F. Goudappel, eds, *Freedom, Security and Justice in the European Union: Implementation of the Hague Programme* (The Hague: Asser Press, 2006), 45–72.

30. FRONTEX, "Mission Statement," 2010, available at <http://www.FRONTEX.europa.eu/more_about_FRONTEX/>; see also Andrew W. Neal, "Securitization and Risk at the EU Border: The Origins of FRONTEX," *Journal of Common Market Studies* 47, no. 2 (2009), 333–56.

31. C. Boswell, "Migration Control in Europe after 9/11: Explaining the Absence of Securitization," *Journal of Common Market Studies* 45, no. 3 (2007), 589; and Neal "Securitization and Risk at the EU Border: The Origins of FRONTEX."

32. European Council, "Laeken Presidency Conclusions," SN 300/1/01 Rev 1 (2001),available at http://www.consilium.europa.eu/ueDocs/cms_Data/docs/pressData/en/ec/68827.pdf>.

33. With respect to the former, see Maria Ferreira, "Risk Politicization Strategies in EU Migration and Asylum Policies," *Journal of Global Analysis* 1, no. 2 (2010), 155–83. With respect to the latter, see Ségolène Barbou des Places and Bruno Deffains, "Cooperation in the Shadow of Regulatory Competition: The Case of Asylum Legislation in Europe," *International Review of Law and Economics* 23, no. 4 (2003), 345–64; Eiko R. Thielemann, "Why Asylum Policy Harmonization Undermines Refugee Burden-Sharing," *European Journal of Migration and Law* 6, no. 1 (2004), 47–65; and Eiko R. Thielemann and T. Dewan, "The Myth of Free-Riding: Refugee Protection and Implicit Burden-Sharing," *West European Politics* 29, no. 2 (2006), 351–69. For background, see Mathias Czaika, "Asylum Cooperation Among Asymmetric Countries: The Case of the European Union," *European Union Politics* 10, no. 1 (2009), 89–113.

34. Barbou des Places and Deffains, "Cooperation in the Shadow of Regulatory Competition"; Timothy J. Hatton, "European Asylum Policy," *National Institute Economic Review* 19, no. 4 (2005), 106–19.

35. EUROSTAT, "Decisions on asylum applications by citizenship till 2007 Annual data (rounded) [migr_asydctzy]," *Eurostat Dataexplorer*, available at <http://appsso.eurostat. ec.europa.eu/nui/show.do?dataset = migr_asydctzy&lang = en>.

36. This is not to suggest that these differences matter with respect to influencing the number of asylum applications. Hatton shows that the deterrent effect of asylum policies is remarkably small, given all the political smoke the issue generates. See Timothy J. Hatton, "The Rise and Fall of Asylum: What Happened and Why?," *The Economic Journal* 119 (2009), F183–F213.

37. Carl-Ulrik Schierup, "A European Dilemma: Myrdal, The American Creed and EU Europe," *International Sociology* 10, no. 4 (1995), 347–67; and Carl-Ulrik Schierup, Peo Hansen, and Stephen Castles, *Migration, Citizenship, and the European Welfare State: A European Dilemma* (Oxford: Oxford University Press, 2006).

38. Scheirup et al., *Migration, Citizenship, and the European Welfare State: A European Dilemma*, 4. Gunnar Myrdal, *An American Dilemma: The Negro Problem and Modern Democracy* (New York: Harper & Row, 1944).

CHAPTER 43

....

JUSTICE AND HOME AFFAIRS

....

JÖRG MONAR

43.1 INTRODUCTION

....

The term "justice and home affairs" (JHA) denotes a policy-making domain of the EU covering asylum and immigration policy, external border management, judicial cooperation in both civil and criminal matters, and police cooperation. Although the JHA domain emerged as an EU policy-making domain formally only in 1993 with the Treaty of Maastricht, it has developed into one of the fastest growing fields of EU action with well over a hundred new texts having been adopted every year by the EU "Justice and Home Affairs Council" during the decade 2000–2010.[1]

Since the entry into force of the Treaty of Amsterdam in 1999 JHA have been regrouped under the fundamental treaty objective of creating an EU "area of freedom, security and justice" (AFSJ), an objective which the 2009 Treaty of Lisbon has placed even above the internal market, economic and monetary union, and foreign and security policy in the list of fundamental EU treaty objectives.[2] Two considerations underline the particular significance of the JHA domain for the development of the EU.

The first is that EU action in the JHA domain touches upon fundamental state functions. Since the gradual emergence of the modern nation state in the seventeenth and eighteenth centuries and its conceptualization in the writings of Hobbes, Locke, Montesquieu, and Rousseau, providing security to citizens, controlling access to the national territory, and administering justice have all belonged to the basic justification and legitimacy for the existence of the state. The fact that since the 1990s the EU has developed a steadily increasing role in these fields means that it has entered into one of the last and most sensitive formerly exclusive domains of member-state competence—not by replacing the member states as primary providers of internal security and justice, but by emerging as an increasingly important additional provider of these essential public goods—and can be regarded as a process of major "constitutional" importance for the EU system.

The second is that, although no law enforcement powers have so far been transferred to EU institutions and agencies, measures adopted in the JHA domain can have significant implications for individuals. The mutual recognition of judicial decisions, the harmonization of substantive criminal law, the enhanced cross-border exchange of personal data between law enforcement agencies, the standardization of controls on persons at external borders, and the minimum harmonization of procedural and substantive asylum law all affect the way and the extent to which individuals are subject to the exercise of public power by the competent authorities of the member states. The rather technically sounding term "justice and home affairs" should not make one forget that in this domain the EU is dealing with issues relating to the most invasive forms of state action such as deprivation of liberty, refusal of entry at borders, expulsion, and uncovering of personal data.

This chapter will first explore the origins, obstacles, and driving factors of the EU JHA domain. It will then provide a critical assessment of progress and deficits of the main fields of EU action, i.e. asylum and immigration policy, external border management, internal security, and judicial cooperation in civil matters. The conclusions will attempt an overall assessment and look at key challenges for the further development of this domain.

43.2 FROM TREVI TO THE AFSJ

JHA as an EU policy-making domain can be traced back to three different points of origin, all of which have had a substantial influence on today's AFSJ. The first of these points of origin is the TREVI ("Terrorisme, radicalisme, extrémisme et violence internationale"), which was set up in 1975 by the European Community member states in response to the various terrorist challenges in Europe of the mid-1970s and which lasted until 1993. As a very loose form of intergovernmental cooperation consisting only of information exchange and coordination meetings, TREVI operated outside of the European Community framework as part of European Political Cooperation without any treaty basis or legal instruments. In spite of its structural limitations, TREVI provided the European Community member states with a framework in which they could gradually extend their JHA cooperation into other areas (such as the fight against drug-trafficking and organized crime) and explore more intense mechanisms of information exchange and operational cooperation. As a result TREVI paved the way for the institutionally strengthened JHA cooperation which developed inside the EU after the JHA domain became a formal EU policy-making domain with the Treaty of Maastricht in 1993.[3]

The second—and, because of its ongoing impact, in some respects most important—point of origin is the Schengen system. Set up in 1985 by the Benelux countries, France, and Germany to allow for the abolition of controls on persons at internal borders, the Schengen framework emerged quickly as a laboratory for JHA cooperation. The Schengen countries had to adopt a broad range of so-called "compensatory measures" in the fields of external border management, cross-border police, and judicial cooperation, and even visa, asylum, and migration policy to cope with the actual or potential internal security and migration management risks of the new border control free zone ("Schengenland") they had agreed to establish between themselves. Although the non-participation of other European Community countries—most tenaciously amongst them the UK—meant that Schengen had to develop outside of the European Community/EU until 1999, it was a much stronger framework than TREVI, being founded on the 1985 Schengen Agreement and the 1990 Schengen Implementing Convention, empowered—via its Executive Committee—to adopt binding legal measures and supported by a permanent secretariat. By the time of its incorporation into the EU in 1999 all but two member states (Ireland and the UK) had joined the Schengen system, which had already built up a legally binding *acquis* of over 3,000 pages. Substantial elements of this Schengen *acquis*—such as Schengen rules on external border controls and surveillance, on responsibility for examining an asylum application for asylum, on visas, and on the exchange of liaison police officers and magistrates—became part of the EU *acquis* in 1999, and the Schengen members had also developed a culture of JHA cooperation which helped with policy development after 1999. Still today the Schengen group and its "associated non-EU countries" (Iceland, Norway, and Switzerland)—bound together by the common interests and constraints of their internal border free zone—form a core group which determines much of the agenda of the AFSJ.[4]

The third and final point of origin of the EU JHA domain was the completion of the European Community internal market in 1993. Being essentially a huge liberalization project for cross-border economic activities, the internal market project also generated—as any liberalization project—ample opportunities for abuse of the extended economic freedoms. In order to address enhanced crime risks in the internal market in the process of completion, the member states created between 1986 and 1991 coordination groups and mechanisms to deal with JHA "compensatory measures" relating to the internal market.[5] The rationale for those was similar to the "compensatory measures" of the Schengen group, but with the difference that the intra- European Community JHA cooperation focused on economic and customs aspects only and that it involved all European Community countries and not just the Schengen members. The internal-market-related JHA cooperation was hampered by the absence of specific European Community legislative competences in the JHA field, a fact which contributed to the formal introduction of JHA as a EU policy-making domain by the Treaty of Maastricht.

The Maastricht reforms of 1993 left the Schengen group still in its exile outside of the EU Treaties but absorbed and merged the TREVI cooperation and most of the internal-market-related JHA cooperation in a new Title VI of the TEU, which became known as the EU's "third pillar." Locating the JHA domain in the TEU and not the TEC had been necessary to placate the member states not willing to accept any "communitarization" of the sensitive JHA fields. Negatively affected by the absence of any treaty-defined common objectives, appropriate legal instruments, and majority voting possibilities, the period of the Maastricht "third pillar" (1993–1999) was not very successful in terms of policy output. Yet it secured the full institutionalization of the JHA domain within the EU and a few advances, such as the gradual establishment of the police agency Europol, from 1994 onwards.

It was only with the Treaty of Amsterdam in 1999 that the EU JHA domain—now under the heading of the AFSJ—was placed on a more solid ground. The Amsterdam reforms allowed finally for the incorporation of Schengen, and "communitarized" the fields of asylum, immigration, border controls, and judicial cooperation in civil matters (at the price of opt-outs arrangements for Ireland, the UK, and Denmark) in a new Title IV of the TEC. They also introduced over forty different objectives, more appropriate legal instruments, and the possibility (after a transitional period of five years) to apply QMV and co-decision by the European Parliament to most of the matters of the newly communitarized fields. Only police cooperation and judicial cooperation in criminal matters remained in the thinned-out "intergovernmental" Title VI TEU.[6]

Finally, the Treaty of Lisbon reforms of 2009 have in a sense continued the Amsterdam reforms by communitarizing also police and judicial cooperation in criminal matters, which were merged with previously communitarized Title IV TEC fields in a new Title V of Part III of the TFEU. This has put an end to the separate life of the "third pillar," which had caused a range of legal and decision-making complications for the construction of the AFSJ. The Lisbon Treaty has also extended significantly majority voting and European Parliament co-decision on JHA matters as well as EU action possibilities in a few fields, especially judicial cooperation in criminal matters and border management.[7]

43.3 OBSTACLES AND DRIVING FACTORS

Considering that the European Community founding treaties of the 1950s had not provided for a JHA chapter and that the TREVI and Schengen cooperation of the 1970s and 1980s had still taken place entirely outside of the European Community framework, the JHA domain has made a remarkable "career" in the EU. Today JHA matters are regularly addressed by European Council conclusions; around thirty Council committees and working parties and two EU Commissioners and Commission Directorates-General[8] are focused on the JHA domain; EU budgetary means for the AFSJ have increased more than twenty times from 1999 to 2010;[9] and there is a steadily growing impact of JHA objectives on EU external relations.[10] This is all the more remarkable as EU action had to overcome—and still has to overcome—major obstacles. Since the provision of security and justice belongs to the core functions of the state, member states have been highly reluctant to transfer powers to the EU level and to engage in common policy-making in the JHA domain. Core issues of JHA—such as policing, border controls, and migration management—are intrinsically linked to and protected by national sovereignty and its territorial application—the principle of territoriality. This makes it, for instance, exceedingly difficult to confer law enforcement powers within the national territory on police officers from other member states or Europol. Some JHA fields—such as legal immigration—are politically so sensitive in domestic politics that national governments want to retain a maximum of control. With no single pair of member states having the same organization of law enforcement and judicial authorities, and all of them being embedded in different legal systems and public order cultures, common action in the JHA domain has to struggle with a myriad of both legal and operational difficulties. Last but not least, differences between fundamental political approaches—regarding, for instance, the abolition of controls on persons at internal borders or responses to drug addiction (the Dutch "coffee shops" are a telling and controversial example of EU diversity)—have tended to limit the common ground and slow down or even block common decision-making.

If in spite of these obstacles the JHA domain belongs now—with the AFSJ as overarching objective—to the core of the European project, this can be ascribed to three main driving factors.[11] The first of these has been the emergence of new or increased transnational JHA challenges. The surge of terrorism in the 1970s led to the establishment of TREVI, and the new terrorist threat perception after the September 11, 2001 terrorist attacks—reinforced by the Madrid attacks of 2003 and the London attacks of 2005—gave a major boost to police and criminal justice cooperation as well as to international action of the EU in the JHA domain. New challenges in the fight against organized crime, such as the rapid growth of organized crime originating in Russia and Eastern Europe after the end of the Cold War and new patterns of exploitation of the legal economy by organized crime, led to a gradual strengthening of the role of Europol and the adoption of a range of measures against money laundering and other forms of serious cross-border crime since the mid-1990s. The sharp increase in the number of asylum applications and the mounting illegal immigration pressure at the end of the 1980s were central to the introduction of the "third pillar" by the Maastricht Treaty in 1993, and reinforced illegal immigration pressure played again a key role in the EU's strong emphasis on reinforced "integrated" border management from the June 2002 Seville European Council onward. In all of these cases purely national measures would have been inadequate to address the cross-border nature of these challenges, which made member states accept the need for cooperation and even some degree of common policy-making.

The second driving factor has been a combination of "spillover" effects from other advances of the integration process. As already mentioned, the liberalization of cross-border economic transactions in the context of the internal market programme forced the European Community/EU to consider a range of "compensatory" measures to offset potential internal security risks resulting from the enhanced freedoms of the internal market. The introduction of the euro in 2002—which has also made crime-related cross-border financial transactions easier—has necessitated common measures against counterfeiting and an additional emphasis on anti-money-laundering measures. The "spillover" effects have been even stronger in the case of the Schengen countries, as the abolition of controls on persons at internal border have created de facto a common internal security zone encompassing all of their territories, which has left them with no option but to treat their respective external border as a matter of vital common interest and to develop a whole range of common measures and mechanisms in cross-border law enforcement, judicial and asylum and migration management cooperation. It can also be said that CFSP/ESDP developments have at least encouraged the further development of certain EU JHA fields, as transnational security risks (in particular terrorism and organized crime) have been were firmly put on the EU's global security agenda since the adoption of the EU's "Security Strategy" in December 2003.[12]

Finally, the institutionalization of the JHA domain and its transformation into a fundamental treaty objective—the AFSJ—has also generated a dynamic of its own. Indicators of that are the EU heads of state or government taking a special interest in giving impulses to key JHA areas (starting with the Tampere European Council of October 1999), the Council agreeing on a succession of five-year multi-annual programs defining priorities for the development of the AFSJ (the 1999–2004 Tampere, 2005–2009 Hague, and 2010–2014 Stockholm Programmes) and the European Commission investing heavily in staff resources and starting a stream of initiatives on JHA matters from the 1999–2004 Prodi Commission onward. What can be described as the "own momentum" of JHA policy development has also been reinforced by the range of special JHA structures created to support cross-border cooperation in the JHA domain. Thus, through its pan-EU threat assessments on organized crime and terrorism, Europol has contributed to the perception of a common threat justifying more common action; the external border management agency Frontex is fulfilling a similar role with regard to external border threats and management challenges; the cross-border judicial cooperation unit EUROJUST has helped to identify deficits in cross-border criminal justice cooperation which arguably require further EU action, and through his monitoring of implementation problems of EU measures at both the national and the EU level, the EU's Counter-Terrorism Coordinator has contributed substantially to the further development of the EU strategy and action plan against terrorism. While the aforementioned transnational challenges and spillover effects were the primary factors to make member states accept the need to make JHA a "European" domain of action, its subsequent strong institutionalization has clearly reinforced both its rationale and dynamic evolution.

43.4 ASYLUM AND IMMIGRATION POLICY

Being by any international standard a haven of peace, stability, and prosperity the EU naturally attracts third-country nationals who are fleeing from persecution, oppression, war, and misery in their home countries, or are simply seeking a better economic perspective for them and their relatives. The resulting challenges are reflected both in numbers—over 260,000 asylum applications in 2010[13] and an immigration (legal and illegal) of nearly 1.5 million per year[14]—and in the often heated domestic political debates and occasional outbursts of racism and xenophobia in some of the member states experiencing significant numbers of illegal immigration and/or asylum applications. While there is a strong political consensus amongst the EU governments on the need to reduce illegal immigration, they have found it much more difficult to agree on substantial common asylum standards and a common approach to legal immigration for work purposes. Advances in EU asylum policy have been primarily driven by the Schengen project, as the abolition of controls at internal borders has de facto also created a common zone within which asylum seekers can move freely across borders. The main legal instruments adopted so far include Directive 2001/55/EC on minimum standards for giving temporary protection in the event of a mass influx of displaced persons; the Dublin Regulation 343/2003 establishing the criteria and mechanisms for determining the member state as responsible for examining an asylum application lodged anywhere within the EU; the Reception Conditions Directive 2003/9/EC laying down minimum standards for the reception of asylum seekers; the Qualification Directive 2004/83 on minimum standards for the qualification and status of third-country nationals or stateless persons as refugees or as persons otherwise in need of protection; and the Asylum Procedures Directive 2005/85/EC on minimum standards on procedures in member states for granting and withdrawing refugee status. Of these instruments, the Dublin Regulation can be regarded as the most important one, as it essentially provides for one member state to decide for all on an asylum application, with the result that an asylum applicant has normally no right to apply for a second time in another EU country, a principle whose enforcement is helped by an electronic EU fingerprint database of asylum applicants (EURODAC).

The only justification for having one member state taking an asylum decision for all—under the UN 1951 Geneva Convention member states have an individual obligation to examine asylum applications—is that standards in procedural and substantive asylum law are sufficiently similar across the EU. Yet EU asylum legislation has—especially in the case of the Reception, Procedures, and Qualification Directives—been of a mostly minimalist nature. This means that both the chances of an asylum seeker being accepted and his treatment during the process of application still vary widely from one member state to the other, a situation which has led to repeated accusations of the EU being an "asylum lottery"[15] where everything depends ultimately on the member state in charge of a given application. In other respects, however, the EU's balance sheet is more positive, as it has allowed the definition of common standards previously not adopted by all member states, such as the recognition of the existence of non-state agents of persecution and the codification of temporary protection for refugees. Some of the deficits of the existing instruments are to be addressed in "second-phase" legislation currently under negotiation, which is intended to result in a "common European asylum system" (CEAS) by 2012. In addition to substantive and procedural asylum legislation the EU has also established a European Asylum Support Office (EASO) in Malta, whose tasks include the facilitation of information exchange, the identification and transfer of best pratices and the provision of support to Member States whose asylum and reception system are facing disproportionate pressures. In the latter case the EASO, which started to operate in 2011, can coordinate the deployment of Asylum Support Teams (ASTs) consisting of officials from other Member States and thus make a contribution to solidarity in response to asylum challenges.

In the field of immigration, the EU has adopted a host of measures to curb illegal immigration, ranging from commonly defined sanctions for airlines and other carriers for bringing third-country nationals without the required papers into the EU (Directive 2001/51/EC) through to criminal law measures against facilitators of illegal immigration (Framework Decision 2002/946/JHA) and traffickers in human beings (Directive 2011/36/EU) as well as sanctions for employers of illegally staying third-country nationals (Directive 2009/52/EC) to the tight border control and surveillance standards of the Schengen Borders Code (Regulation (EC) 562/2006) and common procedures and standards for returning illegal immigrants to their country of origin (Directive 2008/115/EC), an instrument which is backed by the conclusion of return agreements with an increasing number of third countries. Much of the operational cooperation at external borders (see below) is also aimed at intercepting illegal immigration across EU external borders. While tackling illegal immigration belongs to the strongest common rationales of the member states within the JHA domain, it has also contributed to the perception of the EU as a "fortress Europe" with ever hardening borders toward asylum seekers and migrants.

With most member states experiencing some shortages of highly skilled workforce in specific sectors of their economies and the rapidly progressing demographic change raising questions about the need for replacement migration, the European Commission has made sustained efforts to get the member states to agree on a common policy on legal immigration. Yet the persistence of essentially national labor markets with different needs and migration absorption capacities as well as strongly diverging demographic change perspectives have so far seriously limited the common political ground. The legislation adopted so far includes directives on the right to family reunification (2003/86/EC), on a long-term resident status for third-country nationals (2003/109/EC), on the admission of students (2004/114/EC), on the facilitation of the admission of researchers into the EU (2005/71/EC), and on the admission of highly skilled migrants on the basis of the so-called "Blue Card" (2009/50/EC).[16] These instruments have in common that they all represent least-common denominator agreements and deal with specific sectors of legal immigration only. The 2009 "Blue Card" Directive is a case in point, as it has not replaced the variety of special national schemes already run by member states to address their respective labor market skill needs and as it applies only to third-country nationals having already been offered a contract in the EU with at least one and a half times the average gross annual salary in the member state concerned. The EU's migration policy has therefore so far developed in a rather asymmetric way, with much more substance on the side of illegal immigration than on legal immigration.

43.5 EXTERNAL BORDER MANAGEMENT

Achieving a high degree of security at external borders—which include land, sea, and air(port) borders—has been at the forefront of the concerns of the Schengen group, as the absence of controls at internal borders means that any lower degree of external border security and immigration control in one country can affect the security and immigration management interests of all others. Although Schengen borders remain legally national borders they have de facto become common borders in the sense that border guards do not only control and patrol them in the interest of their own country only but also in that of all other Schengen members. Hence the need also for a common set of standards and procedures both for external border controls (i.e. control at official border crossing points) and for border surveillance (i.e. at stretches between official border crossing points). The key elements of these standards and procedures were for the first time codified in a single legal instrument in 2006, the aforementioned "Schengen Borders Code" (SBC, Regulation (EC) 562/2006). The provisions of the SBC are the subject of hundreds of pages of implementation rules and guidelines dealing with issues such as the criteria for applying different degrees of density of controls on persons and minimum organizational and technical requirements (including, for instance, even details on the infrared camera equipment of helicopters) for ensuring all-weather, twenty-four hour a day land and sea border surveillance.

A crucial element of the Schengen external border management system is the Schengen Information System (SIS), an electronic network of national databases linked by a central server in Strasbourg (C-SIS) which regroup standardized files on wanted persons, persons to be denied entry into the Schengen zone, and stolen objects. It allows border guard officers at entry or other border points to check on persons wanting to enter the Schengen zone and to take the appropriate action if a "Schengen alert" has been issued regarding them—which can mean, for instance, refusal of entry, arrest, or (in the case of minors reported missing) protection measures. The SIS, which at the end of 2008 was reported to comprise over 27.2 million files,[17] was originally established primarily for border control purposes but has in the meantime become a general law enforcement instrument widely used also by inland police forces (including those of Ireland and the UK). A prior check on the SIS is also an important condition for the issuing of a "Schengen Visa," which opens to its holder the entire "Schengenland" for a maximum of ninety days of stay within six months. A more advanced version of the SIS with capabilities for new cross-file searches and the handling of biometric data—the "SIS II"—should have been in place by 2010 but has been repeatedly delayed by major technical problems.

Since 2002 member states (again including Ireland and the UK, despite their Schengen opt-outs) have increasingly engaged in joint operations primarily aimed at countering illegal immigration and drug-trafficking, involving the deployment of border guard personnel and operational means such as helicopters and patrol boats at external borders. A significant number of those operations have focused on the Mediterranean Sea borders, but there have also been special operations at external eastern borders and airports of several member states. In order to facilitate such joint operations, which also mark a step toward treating external border challenges as a matter of solidarity, the external border management agency Frontex was set up in 2005. Besides planning and coordinating joint operations, Frontex, whose seat is in Warsaw, is also charged with analyzing the threat evolution at external borders and to work on common training standards for member states' border guards and the pooling of technical resources.[18]

43.6 INTERNAL SECURITY: POLICE COOPERATION AND JUDICIAL COOPERATION IN CRIMINAL MATTERS

While external border management forms in a sense the external shield of internal security within the AFSJ, the core of the strong internal security rationale of the JHA domain is formed by police and judicial cooperation in criminal matters. The term "cooperation" used in the treaties well characterizes in fact EU action in these fields, as the main objective is the facilitation of the interaction of national police and judicial systems across borders—and not the creation of an integrated police and/or criminal justice system, which most member states regard as incompatible with national sovereignty and/ or as departing from legal traditions.[19]

In the field of police cooperation EU action has focused on the facilitation of access to and processing of law enforcement relevant data across the entire EU—which has often given rise to concerns about personal data protection—and the facilitation of cross-border police operations. The most important legal instruments include the 2006 Framework Decision on simplifying the exchange of information and intelligence between law enforcement authorities (2006/960/JHA); the 2008 Council Decision on the stepping up of cross-border cooperation, particularly in combating terrorism and cross-border crime (2008/615/JHA—also known as the "Prüm Decision"), which provides for the automated exchange of DNA, fingerprints, and vehicle registration data as well other forms of police cooperation; the 2008 Council Decision on the improvement of cooperation between the special intervention units of the member states of the EU in crisis situations (2008/617/JHA); and the provisions of Article 13 of the EU Convention on Mutual Legal Assistance in Criminal Matters (in force since 2005) on the setting up of Joint Investigation Teams, which can include both police officers and prosecutors from several member states.

EU police cooperation has led to the build-up of the largest special agency established in the JHA domain so far—Europol. Regrouping over 700 police officers and other staff members (2011) at its seat in The Hague, this European police agency focuses on the collection, analysis, and dissemination of data on serious forms of international crime and terrorism. It provides regular threat assessments regarding organized crime and terrorism for the EU as a whole and helps national police forces with intelligence on cross-border crime networks and the build-up of cross-border cooperation and operations to dismantle such networks.[20] While not having any executive powers, Europol has played a central role in facilitating coordinated law enforcement action across EU internal borders and the development of a common EU cross-border organized crime and terrorism threat perception. The role of Europol is complemented by the European Police College (Cepol), which—based on a network of national police academies—provides training to police officers on cross-border policing issues and contributes to best practice identification and transfer.

In the field of judicial cooperation in criminal matters, the primary rationale for EU action is to prevent criminals from exploiting differences between the national judicial systems in order to escape effective prosecution. EU measures have taken two main forms, mutual recognition of judicial decisions and harmonization of national criminal law.[21] Mutual recognition of judicial decisions has often been seen as a less controversial alternative to the harmonization of national criminal law. Yet it raises important questions about adequate protection of judicial rights, and the mutual trust it requires between prosecutors and judges from different countries still cannot be taken for granted. Key mutual recognition instruments include the 2002 Framework Decision on the European Arrest Warrant (2002/584/JHA), which can be issued both for criminal prosecution purposes and for enforcing a custodial sentence, and is valid in all member states; the 2005 Framework Decision on the confiscation of crime-related proceeds, instrumentalities, and property (2005/212/JHA); the 2005 Framework Decision on the application of the principle of mutual recognition to financial penalties (2005/214/JHA); and the 2008 Framework Decisions on the taking into account of convictions handed down in other members states (2008/675/JHA) and on the European evidence warrant for the purpose of obtaining objects, documents, and data for use in proceedings in criminal matters (2008/978/JHA).

Both mutual recognition of judicial decisions and cross-border prosecution can be seriously impaired without at least a minimum of harmonization of substantive and procedural criminal law. The EU has therefore adopted a range of Framework Decisions providing for the common definition of the constituent elements of the most important forms of serious cross-border crime and minimum maximum penalties. Examples are the 2002 Framework Decision on combating terrorism (2002/475/JHA), the 2002 Framework Decision on trafficking in human beings (2002/629/JHA), the 2004 Framework Decision on illicit drug-trafficking (2004/757/JHA), and the 2008 Framework Decision on organized crime (2008/841/JHA). Yet these instruments constitute mainly least-common denominator compromises in which member states have tended to reduce as much as possible the need for substantial changes to their criminal law, with the result that there are wide margins for implementation. A case in point is the Framework Decision on combating terrorism, which provides "only" for a maximum custodial sentence of at least eight years for participating in a terrorist organization and fifteen years for directing one, leaving members states a rather wide implementation margin. Yet it has also to be said that the same legal instrument has at least forced all member states to include specific provisions on terrorist acts in their national criminal law, which several of them had not yet done by the time of the September 11, 2001 attacks.

Cross-border cooperation between national prosecution services is supported by the cross-border prosecution unit EUROJUST which has its seat also in The Hague and a staff of over 300 (2011). EUROJUST can either act through its "national members" (one per member state, normally a senior prosecutor) or as a "college" regrouping all national members. When acting as a "college," EUROJUST can ask the prosecution authorities of member states to undertake a specific investigation or prosecution or to accept that one of them may be in a better position to undertake such an investigation or prosecution to ensure effectiveness and to avoid conflicts of jurisdiction. EUROJUST frequently also assumes an active role in coordinating cross-border prosecution cases.[22]

43.7 JUDICIAL COOPERATION IN CIVIL MATTERS

Civil justice cooperation can be considered a slightly special field in the context of the JHA domain, as it is neither related to internal security nor to migration management which have been given the greatest political attention in the construction of the AFSJ. Yet it is of considerable importance to both citizens and companies, as cooperation in this field is aimed at eliminating the often costly and sometimes prohibitive problems of effective access to justice stemming from the persisting differences between member states' legal and administrative systems. With harmonization of substantive and procedural civil law being at least as complex as it is politically difficult, EU action has focused on the facilitation of mutual recognition and the reduction of conflicts of jurisdiction risks.[23] Key mutual recognition instruments adopted include the 2000 Regulation on mutual recognition in insolvency proceedings ((EC) 1346/2000); the 2001 "Brussels I" Regulation on jurisdiction and the recognition and enforcement of judgments in civil and commercial matters ((EC) 44/2001); the 2003 "Brussels IIa" Regulation concerning jurisdiction and the recognition and enforcement of judgments in matrimonial matters and matters of parental responsibility ((EC) 2201/2003), which was supplemented by the 2009 Regulation on the recognition and enforcement of family law maintenance obligations ((EC) 4/2009); and the 2004 Regulation establishing a "European Enforcement Order" for uncontested claims ((EC) 805/2004).

A considerable effort has also been made to arrive at a harmonization of conflict of laws which has resulted in the adoption of the 2007 "Rome II" Regulation on the law applicable to non-contractual obligations ((EC) 864/2007), the 2008 "Rome I" Regulation on the law applicable to contractual obligations ((EC) 593/2008), and the 2010 "Rome III" Regulation on the law applicable to divorce and legal separation ((EU) 1259/2010). Both instruments enhance legal certainty and the predictability of litigation outcomes, and can help to prevent distortions of competition within the internal market.

The most specific access to justice instrument adopted so far is the 2003 Directive on legal aid (2003/8/EC). It provides for minimum standards of legal aid in cross-border disputes for persons lacking sufficient resources.

43.8 CONCLUSIONS

From rather weak intergovernmental origins in the 1970s, the JHA domain has developed into what today, under the objective of the AFSJ, can be regarded as the largest construction site of the European project in terms of policy areas covered, number of treaty objectives, and action plans in various fields. While significant progress has been achieved on the institutionalization side, the development of a common appreciation of threats and challenges and the development of specific instruments of cooperation (such as the SIS, the special agencies, and the European Arrest Warrant), progress remains uneven and often limited because of considerations of national sovereignty, the tenacious defense of existing national JHA structures and legal provisions, lack of mutual trust, and the differences between member states in terms of national crime, terrorism, and migration challenges.

Three main challenges can be identified for the future development of the ambitious AFSJ project. First, the rapid growth of the JHA domain has led to a proliferation of instruments and objectives with an often inadequate implementation. The potential of Europol, EUROJUST, and Frontex is, for instance, still far from being fully used. A greater focus on implementation and the setting of both fewer and clearer priorities rather than on constantly adding objectives could secure more solid progress in the future.[24]

Second, the strong internal security and migration management rationales for the AFSJ must be kept in a publicly convincing balance with the rights of asylum-seekers, personal data protection, judicial and other rights of individuals. This is not only a question of EU fundamental values but also one of the legitimacy, and hence political sustainability, of the AFSJ project.

Third and finally, with the member states facing rather different burdens in terms of exposure to asylum, migration, border management, and crime challenges, solidarity through the use of EU budgetary means and operational support from other member states by providing personnel and technical means when needed will be increasingly important for the further development potential of the EU JHA domain. An "area of freedom, security and justice" without solidarity in addressing its challenges is likely to remain more of an ambition than a reality.

NOTES

1. Annual lists of adopted texts provided by DG H of the EU Council Secretariat.
2. Article 3(2) TEU.
3. Serge A. Bonnefoi, *Europe et sécurité intérieure: Trevi, Union européenne, Schengen* (Paris: Delmas, 1995).
4. Myriam Massrouri, *Les Accords de Schengen: désaccord à l'unisson?* (Charmey: Éditions de l'Hèbe, 2010); Alexis Pauly, ed., *De Schengen à Maastricht: voie royale et course d'obstacle s* (Maastricht: European Institute of Public Administration, 1996).
5. Wenceslas de Lobkowicz, *L'Europe de la sécurité intérieure: une élaboration par étapes* (Paris: La documentation française, 2002), 34–7.
6. Jörg Monar, "Justice and Home Affairs in the Treaty of Amsterdam: Reform at the Price of Fragmentation," *European Law Review* 23, no. 4 (August), 320–35.
7. Christine Kaddous and Marianne Dony, eds, *D'Amsterdam à Lisbonne: dix ans d'Espace de liberté, de sécurité et de justice* (Basel: Helbing & Lichtenhahn, 2010).
8. The Directorate-General for Home Affairs and the Directorate-General for Justice (and their respective Commissioners).

9. Own calculations based on 1999 and 2010 EU general budgets.

10. Thierry Balzaq, ed., *The External Dimension of EU Justice and Home Affairs* (Basingstoke: Palgrave Macmillan, 2009) and Jörg Monar, "The EU's Externalisation of Internal Security Objectives: Perspectives after Lisbon and Stockholm," *The International Spectator* 45, no. 2 (June), 23–39.

11. For a more detailed coverage and analysis of the dynamics of evolution of the EU JHA domain see Jörg Monar, "The Dynamics of Justice and Home Affairs: Laboratories, Driving Factors and Costs," *Journal of Common Market Studies* 39, no. 4 (November 2001), 747–64 and Thorsten Müller, *Die Innen- und Justizpolitik der Europäischen Union. Eine Analyse der Integrationsentwicklung* (Opladen: Leske + Budrich, 2003) and Elspeth Guild, Alejandro Eggenschwieler, and Sergio Carrera, eds, *The Area of Freedom, Security and Justice Ten Years On: Successes and Future Challenges Under the Stockholm Programme* (Brussels: Centre for European Policy Studies, 2010).

12. "A Secure Europe in a Better World. European Union Security Strategy," Council of the European Union, December 13, 2003.

13. "Asylum in the EU27," Eurostat News Release 47/2011, Eurostat, March 29, 2011.

14. Own calculations based on the "Annual Report on Migration and Integration (2010)", European Commission, COM(2011) 291, May 24, 2011.

15. "Memorandum to the JHA Council: Ending the asylum lottery—Guaranteeing refugee protection in Europe," European Council on Refugees and Exiles, April 2008.

16. For a comprehensive analysis of these instruments, see Anja Wiesbrock, *Legal Migration to the European Union* (Leiden: Martinus Nijhoff, 2010).

17. "Schengen-System funktioniert," *Tagesanzeiger*, Zürich, December 24, 2008.

18. "Frontex, "General Report 2010" (Warsaw: Frontex, 2011).

19. For a critical analysis of key aspects of EU police and criminal justice cooperation, see Cyrille Fijnaut and Jannemieke Ouwerkerk, eds, *The Future of Police and Judicial Cooperation in the European Union* (Leiden: Martinus Nijhoff, 2010).

20. Europol, "Europol Review. General Report on Europol Activities 2010" (The Hague: Europol, 2011).

21. A comprehensive analysis of EU criminal law measures is offered by Valsamis Mitsilegas, *EU Criminal Law* (Oxford: Hart, 2009).

22. Eurojust, "Annual Report 2010" (The Hague: Eurojust, 2011).

23. For the context and content of EU action in the civil law field action, see Eva Storskrubb, *Civil Procedures and EU Law. A Policy Area Uncovered* (Oxford: Oxford University Press, 2008).

24. Jörg Monar and Hans G. Nilsson, "Enhancing the EU's Effectiveness in Response to International Criminality and Terrorism: Current Deficits and Elements of a Realistic Post-2009 Agenda," Olaf Cramme, ed., *Rescuing the European Project: EU legitimacy, Governance and Security* (London: Policy Network, 2009), 109–22.

....

CHAPTER 44

INTELLIGENCE AND THE EUROPEAN UNION*

....

RICHARD J. ALDRICH

In 2004, Christopher Hill argued that the absence of anything even approximating to a common European intelligence service has long been one of the structural weaknesses of the EU CFSP. He added that this was "compounded by the fact that national intelligence services represent powerful bureaucratic interests in favour of intergovernmental-ism and against integration."[1] This chapter begins by examining recent intelligence developments within the EU. Its initial focus is institutional, asking why the intelligence activities of the EU are relatively weak, despite the strong tradition of intelligence coop-eration within Europe. It argues that while intelligence activities that might strictly be described as belonging to the EU remain limited, nevertheless there have been some significant pan-European developments. Since the Madrid bombings of 2004, other multilateral organizations in Europe with an intelligence focus have expanded and have grown stronger links with the EU. Notwithstanding these developments, the gathering of sensitive intelligence from protected sources remains mostly the preserve of states in Europe and its exchange is predominantly bilateral. If the EU has been successful in accelerating intelligence cooperation, then it is with the United States rather than within its own borders. Because many of the new developments are driven by counter-terror-ism, much of this "intelligence" is personal information from mundane sources such as passenger lists and bank statements, rather than the traditional currency of high espio-nage. In turn, these important transatlantic developments raise profound questions about what intelligence has become a decade after the September 11, 2011 attacks.[2]

The United States is the European intelligence partner that dare not speak its name. Washington sees Europe simultaneously as an ally and also a launch pad for future ter-rorist operations against the United States. Accordingly, American intelligence agencies have conducted "action" operations inside Europe, usually with the cooperation of select European partners. The latter part of this chapter considers the controversial efforts of European institutions such as the Council of Europe and the European Parliament to generate oversight and accountability at the European level for multinational intelligence operations that lie beyond the capacity of national systems of inquiry. Some commentators have seen these inquiries as evidence of a restrained and legalistic European approach to intelligence and security, which contrasts with the more muscular American approach. Others have cast doubt on this, arguing that scholars have exaggerated the extent to which Europe and the United States have pursued divergent paths in the realm of intelligence and counter-terrorism. Either way, it is the interface between European and American intelligence that has proved the most controversial.[3]

44.1 INFORMATION OR SECRECY?

Much of the debate about the nature of intelligence within the EU has turned around the distinction between "intelligence" and mere information. Intelligence is best understood as a specialist form of information or research that makes government policy or operations more effective. Nevertheless, in a world of increasingly open sources and ubiquitous computing, intelligence may no longer be so "special." The growing importance of "open-source" intelligence has eroded the barrier between secret and non-secret information. Historically, open-source intelligence has always been present, but the ability to comb this material instantly ensures that it is now more significant than ever. Information technology has also made policy-makers less dependant on the formal intelligence chain and has allowed policy-makers to become their own "DIY analysts" or to outsource alternative views. In turn, the blurring of the boundaries between intelligence, information, and data has meant that international organizations, including the United Nations and the EU, that were once wary of the taint of "spying" have begun to develop their own information services and situation centers.

Some scholars prefer to define intelligence in terms of secrecy rather than information. The sociologist Ken Robertson once described intelligence as "the secret collection of other people's secrets."[4] This captures the traditional notion of intelligence collection as one of the black arts of statecraft. It underlines not only the fact that our opponents have information that they do not want us to know; it also reminds us that the value of discovering those secret things is increased if our opponents believe that their secrets have not been compromised. Partly for this reason, the last half-century has seen the emergence of a range of security processes, including rigid "codeword" compartmentalization, that accompanies the distribution of secret intelligence. This in turn makes the intelligence product difficult to use flexibly and hard to share. Providing timely intelligence to customers from secret sources, or sharing it with allies, without comprising those sources, remains one of the great challenges of intelligence management. In the European context, the excruciating problem of multilateral intelligence sharing has a long and troubled history. Arguably, we are still in the realm of "dark secrets," but we are gradually moving toward an era when intelligence, certainly in the realm of counter-terrorism, will mostly consist of the hoovering up of vast amounts of mundane personal information, some of which is easier to share.

How we conceive of intelligence has profound consequences for the possibility of intelligence cooperation and the construction of pan-European intelligence institutions. Efforts to understand sharing and cooperation in the realm of intelligence have often drawn on economic models. Our outlook on the essential nature of intelligence tends to affect our choice of economic model. If we view intelligence as "mere information," then we might well choose to think of intelligence as public goods whose utility can be multiplied by sharing or "pooling" without increasing its cost. The classic example here is a streetlight that can offer illumination to one or else many people without the need for greater resources. The theoretical underpinning here is a mixture of liberal institutionalism and idealism.[5] By contrast, if we view intelligence as "dark secrets" whose value is lost if they are not protected, then the economic analogy that we choose to illustrate intelligence sharing must be different, emphasizing private goods. We might, instead, think about a producer cartel, like OPEC, where a precious commodity is regulated by the leading exporters, often under the direction of a hegemon. Ultimately, the producer cartel is a realist bargain wherein politics can be rather raw. Arguably, this is not dissimilar to the real world of intelligence alliances and secret sharing.[6]

In Europe, the leading members of the cartel are states like Britain, France, Germany, and Sweden, together with that somewhat peculiar member of the European intelligence club, the United States. Intelligence cartels are normally ruled by the largest producer. Because smaller European states do not generate much intelligence product they find bargaining difficult and are marginalized. For this reason, smaller countries such as Ireland, Austria, and Belgium have, at times, advocated an EU federal intelligence service that would involve "pooling," sometimes described as a European CIA or a European FBI. However these suggestions reveal a fundamental misunderstanding about the real world of intelligence cooperation, which is more about trading than pooling. This also explains why the EU itself has little traction here, since it too is not really an intelligence producer on any scale. Moreover, since 9/11 the larger countries have spent relatively more on intelligence and have become yet more dominant.

Cooperation is now more complicated because the emphasis on counter-terrorism has helped to blur the boundary between domestic intelligence and foreign intelligence. Anxieties about homeland security have contributed to the rise of what might be called the global world of domestic security cooperation. In the 1990s, the painful events in Bosnia and then Kosovo were important in terms of growing a more active European foreign policy. In the minds of EU officials, a federal European intelligence capacity was something they associated with the creation of a CFSP. Their priority was to develop an analytical situation center which would draw intelligence from member states supporting a coherent decision-making process. This has largely been achieved, albeit the EU draws much of its material from national sources. After 9/11 the focus shifted dramatically. The emphasis of the last decade has been upon events inside the EU as much as outside. The new focus on internal security raises awkward issues of jurisdiction. In addition, intelligence and security services are now asked to undertake more disruption and more enforcement. EU officials have recoiled from some of these activities. They have also realized that a pooling of European intelligence information would mean potentially a pooling of responsibility for preventing the next major attack. As a result, even the keenest advocates of a European federal intelligence service have retreated from the ambitions that were articulated only a few years ago.[7]

44.2 EU Intelligence Capabilities

In the decade since 9/11, intelligence and security developments within the EU have largely been shaped by counter-terrorism. Yet there is no clear consensus on the overall texture of Europe's response to terrorism and whether its activities are robust. After 9/11, the European Council developed a "Plan of Action" and secured agreement on significant measures, notably: a European Arrest Warrant; expanding Europol and EUROJUST; a common EU definition of terrorism; the freezing of terrorist finances and the sharing of data with allies. However, some argue that these measures fall far short of what is required, suffer from an implementation deficit and so represent little more than a "paper tiger."[8] Moreover, the EU is often portrayed as a weak intelligence actor.[9] By contrast, others have argued that, away from the media spotlight, lower profile activities such as financial asset freezing and proposals for data retention contain an element of American-style pre-emption and suggest that the EU is actually more proactive than many realize.[10] Indeed, they would argue that the underlying EU intelligence strategy is fundamentally proactive and is driven by alarming practices such as data-mining. There can be no doubt that across both Europe and the United States we are witnessing new technologies that deploy "algorithmic warfare." These work by drawing connections and searching for suspicious patterns across vast aggregations of mundane data.[11] Precisely because much of this new kind of surveillance is conducted through commercialized state—private partnerships, some of it is barely visible, allowing the EU officials to hide the fact that they are perhaps closer to American thinking on some issues than they would care to admit.

Historically, the EU has prioritized analytical intelligence capabilities that are outward-looking with a view to supporting a developing CFSP. From 1992, the EU began to develop an emerging structure with an emphasis upon analysis and elucidation. A great deal of the raw intelligence to support this process comes from the larger member states, often in a slightly sanitized form. The tentative growth in the national intelligence feed is often driven by crisis. Typically, it was the events in the former Yugoslavia during the 1990s that helped to promote the EU Joint Situation Centre or "SitCen." European impotence was increased by the lack of autonomous intelligence, command, and control assets, a situation which contrasted starkly with the United States. This resembled the gradual improvement in the flow of intelligence to similar centers within NATO's political headquarters during the last two decades of the Cold War, which was driven by the need to improve collective crisis decision-making against the background of events such as the invasion of Afghanistan in 1979.[12]

In 1997 the EU adopted what are called the Petersburg tasks which focused on new machinery for an ESDP, effectively a subset of the CFSP. Subsequently, Javier Solana became High Representative for the CFSP and the SitCen was transferred to support the General Secretariat along with the military staff of the EU. The SitCen combines warning and horizon scanning. Working on a twenty-four-hour basis, it concentrates on potential crisis regions, terrorism, and the proliferation of weapons of mass destruction (WMD). Most of its work is strategic analysis designed to support the policy of the EU High Representative and other senior EU officials. The SitCen consists of three parts: a Civilian Intelligence Cell producing political and counter-terrorism assessments; a General Operations Unit providing twenty-four-hour support; and the Communications Unit, handling communications security issues.[13]

Until February 2005, SitCen was primarily focused on CFSP rather than serving JHA. This changed with the creation of a counter-terrorist analytical capacity within the Civilian Intelligence Cell, which constituted a direct response to the bombing of Madrid the previous year. Hitherto, SitCen had received much of its intelligence from the foreign intelligence hubs of member states. Now it also receives internal security intelligence from Europe's internal security services and from counter-terrorism fusion centers such as Germany's Joint Counterterrorism Centre (GTAZ) and the UK's Joint Terrorism Analysis Centre (JTAC).[14] The Dutch intelligence and security service AIVD have been especially energetic in encouraging cross-European comparative studies of radicalization. SitCen's work is used by several Council bodies including the Political and Security Committee, the Terrorism Committee, and the Working Group on Terrorism.[15] The EU Council now requires strategic intelligence-based assessments on counter-terrorism matters, reflecting the priorities of heads of state as set out in the EU Action Plan on Terrorism in 2005. Conceptualized as a cross-pillar work program, it embraces JHA priorities, as well as external issues. Protecting Europe's critical national infrastructure and analyzing trends in terrorist financing have been given priority. In December 2010, SitCen became part of the new European External Action Service.[16]

While SitCen is the most important EU intelligence component, the EU also boasts the Intelligence Division of the European Military Staff or "Intdiv," the European Union Satellite Centre or "EUSC," and Europol. This numbers some thirty officers seconded from member states. Their task is to support crisis planning and to permit the EU political authorities to examine military options. Like SitCen, its focus is strategic. Related to this is the European Union Satellite Centre (EUSC), which answers to the Council of the EU. It is the only major collection asset and is run from Torrejón de Ardoz in Spain, where the core consists of some two-dozen professional imagery analysts. All European countries with an association agreement with the EUSC can draw on its resources. Expanding Europe's military satellite capability is seen as critical if the EU is to avoid over-dependence on the United States for command and control, together with net-centric warfare capability. Currently, there are no less than five satellite observation programs under EU auspices. The most recent, the Pléiades system developed jointly by France, Belgium, Sweden, Spain, and Austria, offers powerful sub-meter imagery of the kind hitherto only deployed by the United States and Russia.[17]

The least convincing aspect of the EU's efforts to develop an intelligence role concerns Europol, a European criminal intelligence agency established in 1999 as the result of the

Maastricht Treaty. In November 2001, Europol announced the creation of a Counter-Terrorism Task Force. The expressed intention was to collect relevant intelligence, conduct analysis, formulate threat assessments, and render assistance to national police forces. However, this proved to be a rather grandiose list of objectives for a small organization. After experiencing difficulties engaging with the secretive intelligence and security services of European states, the Counter-Terrorism Task Force was quietly absorbed into Europol's Serious Crime Department in 2003. However, following the terrorist bombings in Madrid in 2004, Javier Solana insisted it be re-established as a separate entity.[18] Although some thirty staff are now assigned to this group, it remains something of a fifth wheel, since it can only engage on cases when assistance is requested by a national force. In 2005, Gijs de Vries, the EU Counter-terrorism Coordinator, made similar noises about the importance of Europol.[19] Yet it is hard to avoid the conclusion that Europol's counter-terrorism intelligence effort is mostly symbolic.[20] Moreover, as SitCen has gradually developed better relations with the larger national intelligence agencies, it has found it politic to distance itself from less favored elements of the European machine, such as Europol.[21]

Practitioners have argued that trying to develop European "clearing houses" that would pool all European intelligence centrally would be a mistake, since informal networks tend to be more efficient. Instead, rather than trying to centralize data exchange, Europol might be more effective serving as a center for development and training for a new pan-European community of police officers, especially in the East. There is much to be said for a "European criminal intelligence model" which would emphasize coordinating investigations against organized crime within the EU using the methodology of intelligence-led policing.[22] There are signs that the EU is in fact focusing on training and capacity building.[23] The most senior EU figures now seem content to leave the operational realm to others, while focusing on more generalized judicial and administrative issues.[24]

44.3 European Intelligence "Clubs" and EU Expansion

After the bombings in Madrid in 2004 the leading European intelligence and security services resolved to accelerate pre-existing European organizations that provide a framework for regional intelligence cooperation. They also agreed to improve transatlantic linkage. Four substantial multilateral mechanisms are of growing significance. These are the "Club of Berne," the Counter-Terrorist Group, NATO Special Committee, and the Middle European Conference. None of them are formal elements of the EU, but each has gradually synchronized its activities more closely with the EU. The most important is the "Club of Berne," a long-standing group founded in 1965 which consists of the heads of the domestic security services of EU member states, together with

Norway and Switzerland. This meets every six months to discuss intelligence and security matters of all kinds. After 9/11, at the request of the European Council of Ministers of Justice and Home Affairs, the Club of Berne created the Counter Terrorist Group (CTG), a functional body with similar membership (with the Americans also enjoying observer status). Since September 2001, CTG has served mostly as a focus for multilateral exchange. While not an EU body, it has nevertheless provided threat assessments to key EU policy-makers drawing on national resources. CTG also provides a forum for experts to develop practical and technical collaboration on particular projects. This has often taken the form of joint training, allowing European countries with more experience of terrorism to share skills, together with the standardization of some procedures. This has been described by one senior official as "spooks with spooks," adding that the EU has been "kept away" from any operational business.[25] The presence of Switzerland in these groups has been important given its prominent role in multinational operations.[26]

On April 21, 2004, following the attacks in Madrid, the Club of Berne held a meeting in Switzerland to discuss implementation of the objectives of the European Council Declaration on Combating Terrorism. The meeting concluded that the CTG should act as the interface between the EU and the heads of member states' security and intelligence services on terrorist matters. Since 2004, the CTG has worked increasingly closely with the EU and has played a significant part in implementing the relevant sections of the Declaration. Fortuitously, on May 1, 2004, the security services of the ten EU Accession States joined the CTG as full members. Although CTG emphasizes its independence from EU structures, its chairmanship now rotates with that of the EU presidency and CTG has a permanent liaison officer based at SitCen.[27] CTG also held high-level meetings in the wake of the bomb attacks in London in July 2005 and the attempts to attack a transatlantic passenger aircraft at London Heathrow in August 2006. The primary purpose of these meetings was to disseminate information about the "modus operandi" of these novel attacks and the background to the plots.[28]

Formed in December 1952, the Special Committee of NATO is one of the most venerable forums for European intelligence cooperation and consists of the heads of the security services of the member countries. In the 1990s, its role focused on the difficult security problems attendant on sharing sensitive military documents amongst NATO's growing membership in Central and Eastern Europe. However, since NATO's arrival in Afghanistan in 2002, NATO intelligence and security activity has developed a wider remit and the foreign intelligence services of member states have seen more engagement. The NATO Riga summit of November 2006 also saw the creation of a NATO interim information cell consisting of the representatives of the intelligence services of the member states. Close cooperation between NATO, Supreme Headquarters Allied Powers Europe (SHAPE), United States European Command (EUCOM) headquarters, and the French high command has also been important in coordinating an energetic program of special operations in Africa. A fourth body is the Middle European Conference, which has assisted the modernization of Central and East European services since the 1990s and this is discussed below.

The importance of new member states within both the EU and NATO was underlined by Hungary's chairmanship of NATO's Special Committee in 2008. The head of Hungary's security service, who presided over Special Committee in 2008, trained for six years at Soviet intelligence schools in Moscow. For some European countries, residual links between East European services and Russia are a problem because of the recent growth in anxiety about activities by a resurgent Russian foreign intelligence service, the SVR. In 2006, the Czech security service complained that in their country about half of the 153 Russian diplomats and consular staff were undercover intelligence officers engaged in espionage—a return to Cold War levels. This was made worse, they added, by "contacts maintained by officers or persons acting to the benefit of Russian intelligence services with persons from Russian-speaking groups of organized crime in our territory."[29] Counter-intelligence is back on the European agenda, with parallel anxieties about the Chinese and North Korean secret services.

For more than a decade, the issue framing the modernization of the Central and European services has been anxiety about continued Russian influence. With the end of the Cold War in 1989, a vigorous and often public debate developed about whether the old adversaries of the Eastern Bloc could be regarded as partners. In the United States, William Colby, a former Director of CIA, argued for innovative engagement, while Ray Cline, a former Deputy Director, urged caution. Certainly early efforts did not augur well. In May 1993, the United States and Romania jointly hosted the first colloquium of Black Sea intelligence services in Bucharest. The senior CIA officer sent to oversee the event proved to be Aldrich Ames, later revealed to be a Russian double agent. The CIA chief in Bucharest until 1992, Harold James Nicholson, also proved to have been working for the Russians. If nothing else, this prompted some wry remarks about which services actually need to shake themselves loose from Russian influence.[30]

A further initiative was launched the following year in the form of the Dutch-sponsored Middle European Conference, which still meets annually. Also encouraged by the British and Germans, this is a pro-integration group which deliberately excluded those agencies who were felt to be too close to Moscow. It now claims the membership of services from more than a dozen countries including the Baltic states, which joined in 2004. At a recent meeting held on June 12, 2008 in Luxembourg, the Security Information Agency of the Republic of Serbia (BIA) became a new adherent. A NATO working group currently advises the Ukrainian intelligence and security services on the strengthening of democratic control and so the Ukrainian Security Service (SBU) is also scheduled for membership. In short, for European intelligence and security services the "transition to democracy" is very much an ongoing process.[31] Regrettably, some Western intelligence agencies decided that these changes presented tactical opportunities for recruitment and indeed in some cases "transition" meant a garage sale of former assets and agent networks. Moreover, there are now questions as to whether a simple model of policy transfer—the bolting on of Western style accountability committees drawn from parliaments and assemblies—is the right way forward in countries that do not yet have developed traditions of democratic governance or robust general cultures of oversight.[32]

44.4 THE EU AND INTELLIGENCE ACCOUNTABILITY

The efforts of West European states to assist their new Central and East European part-ners in modernizing their intelligence and security services contain a certain irony. With the honorable exception of a few countries such as Holland, which has enjoyed a parlia-mentary oversight committee for intelligence and security since 1952, the majority of states in Western Europe were themselves strangers to meaningful parliamentary accountability until after the Cold War. Change was driven by a number of cases that came before the European Court of Human Rights, notably against the Swedish security service. The European Court criticized the inadequate regulatory frameworks which in turn triggered a headlong rush towards avowal, with most of the European services being placed on a statutory footing in the 1990s. In retrospect, these pan-European develop-ments do not look as impressive as they once did. Parliamentary oversight of intelligence remains quite marginal in a number of European countries, especially France.

The models for the oversight mechanisms that were developed across Western Europe in the 1990s resembled committees pioneered in earlier decades by the United States, Canada, and Australia. Accordingly, these models were borrowed from an era when most of the opponents and threats that concerned intelligence were state-based. Arguably, since 1989, the major change for the intelligence services of Europe has been the shift to deal with transnational threats that are intimately connected with globaliza-tion, including the "new terrorism" and organized crime. As a result we have seen more intelligence cooperation and more joint operations. Even European domestic security services have been required to develop an exotic range of overseas partnerships. Accordingly, the rather old-fashioned national oversight mechanisms that were con-structed in Europe in the 1990s are now ill-equipped to investigate intelligence activities involving cooperation between several countries, since they cannot ask about partners. This mismatch between the cooperative nature of current intelligence activity and weak national oversight mechanisms has been identified by EU institutions.[33]

EU institutions have long been involved in intelligence inquiries. In 1997, the Office of Science and Technology of the European Parliament launched a long-running investi-gation of "Echelon," the popular term for an American-dominated global signals intelli-gence network. More searching inquiries were triggered in November 2005, after path-breaking reports in the *Washington Post* by Dana Priest revealed the existence of CIA "secret prisons" in "several democracies in Eastern Europe" holding high- value detainees.[34] The disturbing idea of "secret prisons" on European territory was the initial point of departure, but EU institutions soon interested themselves in wider issues such as the "ghost flights" that had made their way through European airspace carrying detainees to far-flung destinations. They also looked at extraordinary renditions from European countries such as Sweden, Germany, and Italy to countries outside the EU with dubious human rights records.

The Council of Europe's Committee on Legal Affairs and Human Rights of the Parliamentary Assembly took the lead. The Council of Europe should not be confused with either the European Council or the European Parliament. The Council of Europe is instead a legally orientated body set up in 1949 to oversee the implementation of the European Convention on Human Rights (ECHR). Its time-honored role, its legal basis, and its forty-six nation membership including countries such as Canada and Japan, lent additional weight to its intervention in this sensitive area. The Rapporteur, Swiss Senator Dick Marty, enjoyed only limited resources for his inquiry. However, he was greatly assisted by the Secretary-General of the Council of Europe, who employed his power under Article 52 of the ECHR to request information from member states as to how their laws provided protection against secret detention (including by foreign states) and asked for details of recent instances.

Perhaps the most astute move by Dick Marty was to recognize that the European institutions tend to be politically weak but legally strong. Accordingly, Marty requested a legal opinion on the application of ECHR and other international treaties to these matters from the European Commission for Democracy through Law (the Venice Commission). The intention was to develop an authoritative general statement on the application of ECHR to cooperative intelligence activity. In March 2006, the Venice Commission issued a legal opinion concluding that participation in secret detention is not compatible with ECHR. Remarkably, the Venice Commission asserted that signatories are not only required to avoid such practices themselves, but also obligated to act to police such activity by partner intelligence services within the boundaries of Europe, a requirement that has had profound implications for secret agencies. The European Parliament carried out its own inquiry into renditions, reporting in November 2006, and the European Commission then conducted a third inquiry, reporting in November 2007.[35]

The inquiries identified Poland and Romania as the most likely location of the secret prisons, illuminating the divide between "New Europe," which worked closely with Americans and "Old Europe," which dissented on issues such as the invasion of Iraq. Senior Polish politicians from a number of parties have vehemently denied that CIA "secret prisons" ever existed in Poland. In 2006, the Prime Minister, Kazimierz Marcinkiewicz, denounced this allegation as "groundless slander." In June 2007, the President Lech Kaczyński asserted definitively: "No secret CIA prisons existed in Poland, whether during my term or before that." In August 2008, ex-President Aleksander Kwaœniewski added his weight to the denials, insisting that "the prisons never existed."[36] Yet in June 2008, the New York Times carried a remarkably detailed account of CIA interrogations that reportedly took place at the military intelligence training center in Stare Kiejkuty in north-eastern Poland. Former CIA officers were quoted as describing the fearsome treatment of the key 9/11 suspect Khalid Sheik Mohammed including sleep deprivation, frigid temperatures, and simulated drowning. CIA officers alleged that the Polish prison was "the most important one" for the CIA. These conflicting accounts cannot be reconciled and sooner or later someone will have to amend their narrative.[37]

Revelations by American journalists about the CIA's activities in Eastern Europe have continued to create turmoil. In November 2009, *ABC News* uncovered a secret prison in Lithuania that had existed during 2004 and 2005. The facility was reportedly hidden inside a riding stable north-east of Vilnius and was design to hold up to eight "high-value detainees" at a time. Povilas Malakauskas, chief of Lithuania's State Security department, suddenly resigned following the revelations. In January 2010, German authorities began investigating claims made in an American magazine that a CIA "hit squad" consisting of privateers, tracked an al-Qaeda suspect in Hamburg shortly after 9/11, although the lethal operation was never carried out. The magazine *Vanity Fair* alleges that the team was sent to target Mahmoun Darkazanli, a German-Syrian businessman. Darkazanli has been accused of being close to the 9/11 hijackers. Reportedly, the team was trained by the defense contractor *Blackwater USA*, but neither the German government nor the Hamburg CIA station was aware that the team were operating in the city. Senior German politicians have declared the allegations to be "stunning" and "explosive."[38]

44.5 EUROPE'S ROLE IN TRANSATLANTIC INTELLIGENCE COOPERATION

The ongoing acrimonious public arguments over subjects such as secret prisons, the interrogation of detainees, together with the bitter legacy of the flawed assessments of Iraqi WMD are suggestive of intense transatlantic discord in the realm of intelligence. In late 2005, the EU's Justice Minister, Franco Frattini, warned of "serious consequences," including the suspension of voting rights in the Council, for any EU member state found to have hosted secret CIA detention facilities.[39] At the national level, some political leaders have also been sternly critical of American intelligence activities. The Dutch Foreign Minister, Ben Bot, stated that the Netherlands' contribution of over 1,000 troops to Afghanistan could be in jeopardy if the United States failed to give adequate reassurances on the matter of CIA secret prisons.[40] It is thought that threats by some European countries to reduce or withdraw intelligence cooperation during 2005 and 2006 contributed to Washington's efforts to rethink its approach to counter-terrorism.[41]

Yet improbably, some of those European countries that have expressed strident disagreement with America's "War on Terror" in public are privately the closest intelligence partners of the United States. While the Council of Europe, the European Parliament, and the European Commission have been at loggerheads with American intelligence, simultaneously other elements of the EU have reached agreement on the massive transatlantic sharing of personal electronic data. While French President Jacques Chirac was criticizing the Iraq War sharply, and attacking the intelligence services on the matter of assessments of Iraqi WMD, claiming that the intelligence agencies had a tendency to "intoxicate themselves," France was simultaneously working closely with the United States on field counter-terrorist operations across Europe.

Intelligence services have become more involved in disruption, enforcement, and action since 9/11. Across Europe, we have seen the creation of jointly-run Counter Terrorism Intelligence Centres staffed partly by the CIA. In France, the main center for joint operations is "Alliance Base" located in the seventh arrondissement of Paris. For political and legal reason it is directed by a senior military officer attached to the Directorate-General for External Security and the working language is French, but it is largely funded by the CIA. Participating countries include Germany, the UK, Canada, and Australia. France was chosen for this operational hub because of its tradition of robust action against terrorism and the strong powers of its anti-terrorist magistrates. The dynamic culture of the French intelligence and security services and their unique political frameworks permit a freedom of action that is not possible elsewhere in Europe. Meanwhile, by allocating lead officers from different countries to each operation, problems of access to sensitive intelligence are overcome and legal obstacles surmounted.[42]

The paradox of public criticism and private partnership can be explained partly by viewing intelligence cooperation as a rather specialist kind of "low politics" that is focused on practical arrangements. Whereas collaboration in the area of foreign policy might require a convergence of ideals or at least overall strategy, intelligence cooperation is often built upon mutual trust developed as the result of cooperation at a more tactical level. Like policing, it is often down to individual "cases." Moreover, the predominant pattern of transatlantic intelligence exchange is bilateral, one country to another, resulting in a pattern of transatlantic cooperation that is a dispersed network with few obvious nodes or centers. Each country has several intelligence services, each with their overseas representatives. This allows countries to work together in one area even while they disagree about something else. In short, intelligence is a highly fissiparous activity.[43]

The EU has also worked closely with the United States on intelligence projects that have a greater resonance for the everyday European citizen. Vast amounts of data are now being shared across the Atlantic, despite the very different legal conceptions of privacy deployed by the United States and the EU.[44] Data retention has proved to be the most difficult area for transatlantic intelligence cooperation because the EU believes US data retention procedures to be weak. This initially impeded agreements between the US and Europol. Even more difficult was the battle over Passenger Named Records. Since 2001, Washington has desired detailed information from the European airlines on passengers before they fly from Europe to the United States. The US continually claimed that this foot-dragging revealed that the EU was not a serious partner in counter-terrorism. After difficult negotiations, the European Commission agreed to share some categories of information in May 2004. This was halted by the European Parliament, which took the agreement before the ECJ. After prolonged argument, the Commission moved the agreement under the third pillar, thus evading the European Parliament's objections. A new agreement was drawn up that accommodated the American position and could not be challenged.[45] The United States and the EU are nearing completion of further agreements allowing law enforcement and security agencies to share even more private information, including credit card transactions, travel histories, and Internet browsing habits. The Obama administration has not demonstrated much difference of style on these questions and the US Department of Homeland Security has offered few changes of substance.[46]

The battle over personal data is revealing in two respects. First, it underlines the fact that it is difficult to generalize about a distinct "European style" or culture in the realm of intelligence and security activity. Although the argument that both European governments and the EU favor a law enforcement approach to counter-terrorism and remain allergic to America's "War on Terror" remains broadly true, there are clearly differences within Europe.[47] All European states have become increasingly nervous about US covert action, in other words, instances where secret services go out and actively do things to people, whether it is rendition or other kinds of physical intervention or disruption. However, many European states make a distinction between working with the Americans on "kinetic activity" and working with the Americans on large-scale intelligence sharing and surveillance, which they view as more passive. Indeed, in the area of telecom call data, the EU has actually been used by some member states to introduce intelligence activity which interior ministers could not have hoped to see adopted in their own countries. Within the EU itself, the European Court, European Parliament, and the Council of Europe are foremost in seeking to privilege civil liberties over security interests, while the European Commission remains conspicuously silent on these matters.[48] Other have noted that while EU criminal justice and the European arrest warrant have meant that police and prosecutorial cooperation has improved, the establishment of basic procedural safeguards for suspects has proved near impossible.[49]

Second, in opposing transatlantic exchange on Passenger Named Records, the European Parliament has highlighted a fundamental change in the underlying nature of intelligence. During the Cold War, intelligence communities in both North America and Western Europe were characterized by an emphasis on "foreign intelligence"—that is, the gathering of secret information on nation states' opponents overseas. Even their internal security machinery, which was comparatively small, prioritized the countering of the activities of foreign espionage agents. Since 9/11 this has changed and the lens has gradually turned inward upon our own populations. The intelligence agencies of the West now spend less time trading photos of Russian missiles, and more time trading personal data about each other's citizens. Remarkably, much of this information is not collected by spies, but instead by banks, credit cards companies, airlines, supermarkets, and Internet service providers. This new kind of intelligence—which consists of torrents of rather mundane personal data—is intimately linked to matters such as transport, finance, energy, and communications, which are in turn core areas of EU competency. Moreover, because this material is often conceptualized as "private information" rather than "secret intelligence" it is somewhat easier to share freely.[50] All this promises a stronger future role for the EU in the emerging world of personal data surveillance and data-mining. Accordingly, those who have longed for a larger EU presence in the world of intelligence and security—and who have been singularly disappointed during the last decade—may yet see their ambitions fulfilled.

NOTES

* I am indebted to the Leverhulme Trust for a fellowship that facilitated the writing of this chapter. Confidential interviews were conducted to clarify some of the findings. I would like to thank Matthew Aid, Martin Rudner, Adam Svendsen, and Cees Wiebes for drawing my attention to some of the material below.

1. C. Hill, "Renationalizing or Regrouping? EU Foreign Policy Since September 11, 2001," *Journal of Common Market Studies* 42, no. 1 (2004), 147–9, at 150.

2. W. Rees, *Transatlantic Counter-Terrorism Cooperation: The New Imperative* (New York: Routledge, 2006); D. Omand, *The National Security Strategy: Implications for the UK Intelligence Community* (London: IPPR, 2009).

3. W. Rees and R. J. Aldrich, "Contending Cultures of Counter-Terrorism: Divergence or Convergence?," *International Affairs* 81, no. 5 (2005), 905–24.

4. K. G. Robertson, "Intelligence, Terrorism and Civil Liberties," *Conflict Quarterly* 7, no. 2 (1987), 43 –62, at 47.

5. T. Wetzling, "European Counter-Terrorism Intelligence Liaison," in S. Farson et al. eds, *Global Security and Intelligence: National Approaches,* Vol. 2 (New York: Praeger, 2008), 500–20.

6. M. S. LeClair, *International Commodity Markets and the Role of Cartels* (London: Sharpe, 2000).

7. J. M. Nomikos, "A European Union Intelligence Service for Confronting Terrorism," *International Journal of Intelligence and Counterintelligence* 18, no. 2 (2005), 191–203.

8. R. Bossong, "The Action Plan on Combating Terrorism: A Flawed Instrument of EU Security Governance," *Journal of Common Market Studies* 46, no. 1 (2008), 27–48; O. Bures, "EU Counter-Terrorism Policy: A Paper Tiger?," *Terrorism and Political Violence* 18, no. 1 (2006), 57–78; D. Zimmermann, "The European Union and Post-9/11 Counterterrorism: A Reappraisal," *Studies in Conflict and Terrorism* 29, no. 2 (2006), 123–45.

9. B. Müller-Wille, "The Effect of International Terrorism on EU Intelligence Co-Operation," *Journal of Common Market Studies* 46, no. 1 (2008), 49–73.

10. M. De Goede, "The Politics of Preemption and the War on Terror in Europe," *European Journal of International Relations* 14, no. 1 (2008), 161–85.

11. L. Amoore, "Algorithmic War: Everyday Geographies of the War on Terror," *Antipode: Journal of Radical Geography* 41, no. 1 (2009), 49–69.

12. O. R. Villadsen, "Prospects for a European Common Intelligence Policy," *Studies in Intelligence* 9 (2000), 81–94; R. J. Aldrich, "Intelligence within BAOR and NATO's. Northern Army Group," *Journal of Strategic Studies* 31, no. 1 (2008), 253–7.

13. B. Müller-Wille, "For Our Eyes Only? Shaping an Intelligence Community within the EU," in *EUISS Occasional Paper*, No. 50, (2004), available at: <http://www.iss.europa.eu/uploads/media/occ50.pdf>; S. Duke, "Intelligence, Security and Information Flows in CFSP," *Intelligence & National Security* 21, no. 4 (2006), 604–30.

14. *UK Intelligence and Security Committee Annual Report 2005-6*, Cmnd. 6864 (London: HMSO 2006) p. 29, para. 102.

15. CTIVD no. 22A, Review Committee for the Intelligence and Security Services, *Review Report on the cooperation of GISS (AIVD) with foreign intelligence and/or security services,* August 12, 2009, p. 38. Available at: <http://www.ctivd.nl/?English>.

16. J. I. Walsh, "Intelligence-Sharing in the European Union: Institutions Are Not Enough," *Journal of Common Market Studies* 44, no. 3 (2006), 625–43; HC Deb. June 27, 2005:

Column 1248W Statement on SitCen, available at: <http://www.publications.parliament.uk/pa/cm200506/cmhansrd/vo050627/text/50627w19.htm>.

17. P. C. Nolin, General Rapporteur, "Interoperability: The Need For Transatlantic Harmonisation," 177 Stc o6 E, NATO Parliamentary Assembly Annual Session, 2006; S. Duke, "Intelligence, Security and Information Flows in CFSP."

18. J. Solana, "Intelligent War on Terror," *The Korea Herald,* November 8, 2004, <http://www.consilium.europa.eu/ueDocs/cms_Data/docs/pressdata/EN/articles/82589.pdf>.

19. M. Deflem, "Europol and the Policing of International Terrorism: Counter-Terrorism in a Global Perspective," *Justice Quarterly* 23, no. 3 (2006), 336–59; G. de Vries, "The European Union's Role in the Fight Against Terrorism," *Irish Studies in International Affairs* 16, no. 1 (2005), 3–9.

20. O. Bures, "Europol's Fledgling Counterterrorism Role," *Terrorism and Political Violence* 20, no. 4 (2008), 498–517. Europol has however been praised for its ability to protect privacy in the context of sharing data; see F. Bignami, "Towards a Right to Privacy in Transnational Intelligence Networks," *Michigan Journal of International Law* 28 (2006–2007), 667–72.

21. Duke, "Intelligence, Security and Information Flows," 604–30. Also private information.

22. H. Brady, "Europol and the European Criminal Intelligence Model: A Non-State Response to Organized Crime," *Policing* 2, no. 1 (2008), 103–9.

23. H. of. L., 2008, European Union Committee, Twenty-Ninth Report, October 28, 2008, available at: <http://www.parliament.the-stationery-office.co.uk/pa/ld200708/ldselect/ldeucom/183/18302.htm>.

24. J. Solana, "Intelligent War on Terror."

25. H. of. L, Select Committee on EU Home Affairs (Sub-Committee F) *Inquiry on EU Internal Security Strategy,* Evidence Session No. 2. December 6, 2010.

26. D. Natta and D. Butler, "How Tiny Swiss Cellphone Chips Helped Track Global Terror Web," *New York Times,* March 4, 2004, A1.

27. Swiss Federal Office of Police, "Club de Berne" meeting in Switzerland, Press Release, fedpol, February 28, 2004. Available at: <http://www.ejpd.admin.ch/ejpd/en/home/dokumentation/mi/2004/ref_2004-04-28.html>. See also CTIVD no. 22A, p. 39.

28. Hungarian NBH 2006, Annual Report 2006, "Participation in International Co-operation," available at <http://www.nbh.hu/english/evk2006-eng/06-0035.htm#1>.

29. BIS *Annual Report of the Czech Security Information Service for 2007,* available at: <http://www.bis.cz/n/ar2007en.pdf>.

30. L. L. Watts, "Conflicting Paradigms, Dissimilar Contexts: Intelligence Reform in Europe's Emerging Democracies," *Studies in Intelligence* 48, no. 1 (2004), 11–25.

31. T. Edmunds, "Intelligence Agencies and Democratisation: Continuity and Change in Serbia after Milosevic," *Europe-Asia Studies* 60, no. 1 (2008), 25–48.

32. A. Martin, "The Lessons of Eastern Europe for Modern Intelligence Reform," *Conflict, Security & Development* 7, no. 4 (2007), 551–77. Also private information.

33. I. Leigh and H. Born, eds, *International Intelligence Co-operation and Parliamentary Accountability* (London: Routledge, 2010).

34. Dana Priest, "CIA Holds Terror Suspects in Secret Prisons," *Washington Post,* November 22, 2005, available at <http://www.washingtonpost.com/wp-dyn/content/article/2005/11/01/AR2005110101644.html>.

35. M. Hakimi, "The Council of Europe Addresses CIA Rendition and Detention Program," *American Journal of International Law* 101, no. 2 (2007), 442–52.

36. W. Czuchnowsk, "CIA Prisons in Poland: a Story of Revelation," *gazetta wyborcza*, September 5, 2008, available at: <http://wyborcza.pl2029020,86871,5662023.html> (accessed September 6, 2008).

37. S. Shane, "Inside the Interrogation of a 9/11 Mastermind," *New York Times*, June 22, 2008, A1.

38. AP Report, 2010. "Germany Investigating Report on CIA Hit Team," *New York Times*, January 6, 2010, A1; F. Gathmann and V. Medick, "Did the CIA Plot to Kill German Citizen?," *Der Spiegel*, January 5, 2010.

39. L. Harding, "EU Threat to Countries With Secret CIA Prisons," *The Guardian*, November 29, 2005, 13.

40. G. Kessler, "E.U. Seeks Details On Secret CIA Jails," *Washington Post*, December 1, 2005, A 16.

41. Rees and Aldrich, "Contending Cultures," 920. Also private information.

42. D. Priest, "Help From France Key In Covert Operations," *Washington Post*, July 3, 2005, A1.

43. R. J. Aldrich, "US-European Intelligence Co-Operation on Counter-Terrorism: Low Politics and Constraint," *British Journal of Politics and International Relations* 11, no. 1 (2009), 122–40.

44. F. Bignami, "European Versus American Liberty: A Comparative Privacy Analysis of Anti-Terrorism Data-Mining," *Boston College Law Review* 48, no. 3 (2007), 609–98.

45. D. Heisenberg, *Negotiating Privacy: The European Union, the United States, and Personal Data Protection* (Boulder: Lynne Rienner, 2005); W. Rees, "Securing the Homelands: Transatlantic Co-operation after Bush," *British Journal of Politics and International Relations* 11, no. 1 (2009), 108–21.

46. C. Savage, "US and Europe Near Agreement on Private Data," *New York Times*, June 28, 2008, A1; M. J. Yano, "Come Fly the (Unfriendly?) Skies: Negotiating Passenger Name Record Agreements Between the United States and European Union," *I/S: A Journal of Law & Policy for the Information Society* 5 (2010), 479–505.

47. J. Monar, "The EU's Approach Post-September 11: Global Terrorism as a Multidimensional Law Enforcement Challenge," *Cambridge Review of International Affairs* 20, no. 2 (2007), 267–83; J. Monar, "Common Threat and Common Response? The European Union's Counter-Terrorism Strategy and its Problems," *Government and Opposition* 42, no. 2 (2007), 292–313; D. Keohane, "The Absent Friend: EU Foreign Policy and Counter-Terrorism," *Journal of Common Market Studies* 46, no. 1 (2008), 125–46.

48. I. Cameron, "Beyond the Nation State: The Influence of the European Court of Human Rights on Intelligence Accountability," in Ian Leigh, Hans Born, and Loch K. Johnson, eds, *Who's Watching the Spies? Establishing Intelligence Service Accountability* (Dulles, VA: Potomac Books, 2005), 34–56.

49. J. Hodgson, "Safeguarding Suspects' Rights in EU Criminal Justice: A Comparative Perspective," *New Criminal Law Review* 14, no. 4 (2011), 611–65.

50. See D. Omand, *Securing the State* (London: Hurst/Columbia University Press, 2010), 32–4.

....

CHAPTER 45

THE COMMON FOREIGN AND SECURITY POLICY

....

DAVID ALLEN

SINCE 1954, when the six founding European member states of the ECSC chose not to create an EDC, the member states of the EU (previously the European Community) have been striving to find an effective way of working together on foreign and security policy matters. Had the EDC gone ahead, then it would have been legitimized by a European Political Community (a draft Treaty was drawn up) directed by a European executive (government) which would have been accountable to an elected European Parliament. Such a construction would have been far more state-like than the present EU and there is a sense in which this proposal proved to be "too much integration too soon." The search has been on ever since for an institutional format or political super-structure that could underpin an effective EU foreign and security policy whilst at the same time preserving the "national sovereignty" of the member states.

This chapter describes these efforts, first of all via the EPC process which the European Community member states developed from 1969. This cooperation was formalized as the second pillar of the SEA of 1986—called a "single" act because it bought together in one treaty the supranational European Community and the intergovernmental EPC. In 1991 EPC was transformed by the Maastricht TEU into a commitment to assert the newly established EU's "identity on the international scene, in particular through the implementation of *a common foreign and security policy* including the eventual framing of a common defence policy, which might in time lead to a common defence" (Title 1, Article B). Between the ratification of the TEU in 1993 and the ratification of the Lisbon Treaty in 2009, these provisions have supported the evolution of the CFSP and, after 1999, the establishment and development of a CSDP. Throughout this period however, faced with the need to respond to the perceived likely consequences of further enlarge-ment and to major changes in the global system of international relations, the member states embarked on a long, drawn-out process of further reform. This reform process included a major overhaul of the Union's "external action" provisions, at the center of which lay the CFSP. As the arguments about the "future of Europe" took their tortuous course, the proposals to reform the CFSP remained constant and the ideas about EU external actions that were enshrined in the Constitutional Treaty were, with only minor exceptions, preserved in the Lisbon Reform Treaty. Once the Lisbon Treaty was ratified, the ambition of creating an EU foreign policy moved (theoretically) to a new level. This transformation is evaluated at the end of this survey.

The debate about the CFSP has never been limited to considerations of foreign policy cooperation. The arguments about EPC and the CFSP have been about the practicalities of collaborative foreign policy-making and implementation at the European level that is compatible with the member states' sovereignty concerns. But they have also been about the nature of European integration (supranational or intergovernmental), about the relationship between the member states and the evolving EU institutions, and about the sort of foreign policy that is most appropriate in the contemporary international system.

In the early days, foreign policy at the European level was characterized as "high politics" in comparison to the "low politics" of European Community external relations[1] and this justified the selection of two different sets of policy-making and implementation procedures to cover the "political" and "economic" aspects of the European Community's external actions. The European Community's external relations (low politics) were entrusted to the classical Community method,[2] whereby common European policies replaced national policies using European Community procedures underpinned by supranational law but limited in substance mainly to trade and aid. The development of European Community foreign policy (high politics) was less ambitious in integration terms and was to be achieved by an informal process of consultation between the member states aimed at achieving common positions based on unanimous agreement about a coordination of national foreign policies, the continued existence of which was seen as fundamental to the vital national interests and ongoing sovereignty of the member states. Economic external relations required the involvement of all the European Community institutions (Commission, Council, Parliament, and Court of Justice). Foreign Policy cooperation primarily involved the member states, the Council, and the rotating presidency and, in the early days, was designed to exclude the Commission and the Court of Justice and involve the Parliament only on a consultation basis.

As far as cooperation on military matters was concerned, the failure of the EDC ensured that NATO, under US leadership, remained the international organization of choice for the West Europeans. The European Community's economic and political external actions developed without a military dimension, giving rise to the characterization of the European Community at the end of the Cold War as an "economic giant but a political dwarf" and presumably a military pygmy. A military dimension to European integration remained taboo because it was seen by member states such as the UK and, to a lesser extent West Germany, as symbolic of a French-inspired challenge to the role of the US. This chapter therefore traces the way that European cooperation in the external economic, political, and military fields has gradually progressed from separate development toward the situation that exists today, whereby the EU's CFSP has become the central focus of an attempt to establish an overall "foreign and security policy." Such a policy would ideally be designed to coordinate all the many strands of EU external action including the external implications of various internal policies like the CAP or EMU. Thus the CFSP is seen not just as encompassing a separate and distinct area of external activity but as providing the central organization and purpose for European foreign policy. At the state level, the function of foreign policy is to design, manage, and control the external activities of the state so as to identify, protect, and advance agreed and reconciled "national" interests and objectives.[3] Thus foreign policy can be seen as the pursuit of national interest(s) as defined by the government of the day. It can therefore be argued that if the EU is to have a foreign and security policy but not a government it has to develop ways of providing "governance without government" in this particular policy area. Ways have to be found to carry out the foreign and security functions that are provided by governments at the state level, including identifying the EU interest(s) and then agreeing on the best means of protecting and advancing them. It may well be that with twenty-seven member states with widely differing geopolitical positions and national foreign policy concerns the EU is approaching the limits of governance without government. Certainly the EU's lack of statehood impacts both on the procedural developments traced below as well as on the substance of the foreign policy stances that the EU is able to agree on. Whilst the study of international relations has long ago accepted the importance of non-state actors, there are virtually no examples of such actors having a foreign and security policy. The EU is "more than an international organisation" but it is, and will probably remain, "less than a state" and this has always presented problems for the ambition of an EU foreign policy that the CFSP is designed to facilitate.

This has to be part of the explanation for the EU's early enthusiasm for being seen as a civilian power[4] or a "post-modern power"[5] or as a power seeking to enhance what Arnold Wolfers referred to as "milieu" goals as opposed to "possession" goals.[6] Whilst the EU has achieved a measure of success in dealing with other groups of states, such as the Association of Southeast Asian Nations (ASEAN) or the Asian, Caribbean and Pacific Group (ACP) states of the Cotonou Convention, and in utilizing its undoubted powers of *attraction*[7] to pursue an enlargement policy designed to stabilize its immediate neighborhood, it has been notably less successful in using its powers of *assertion* in taking what some see as its rightful place amongst the great and emerging great powers of the contemporary international system. Despite all its efforts to simulate the appearance of a state whilst preserving the statehood of its twenty-seven member states, the EU as opposed to many of its member states has failed to use EPC/CFSP to establish effective relations with powers such as the US, China, Russia, India, Brazil, and South Africa. The EU is the institutional expression of its member states' desire to manage the realities of interdependence whilst preserving as much as possible of their independence. The CFSP represents an attempt to square this difficult circle.

45.1 EPC IN THE COLD WAR

The decision to initiate the EPC process was taken at The Hague summit of 1969. Its inspiration was more the need to respond collectively to the external political responses that the "economic" Community was generating. It also built on a desire to give the European Community a political dimension. Cooperation in foreign policy was the device chosen to achieve this objective. Ever since, political as opposed to economic integration has been associated with the development of foreign and security policy at the European level.

EPC was not seen as an attack on the supranational "community" method, whose success in completing the common market ahead of time was celebrated at the Hague meeting. EPC was an additional "pillar" that was intergovernmental because of the member states' sensitivities about the relationship between foreign and security policy and their national sovereignty. To use the supranational method of integration in the foreign and security policy domain would have been tantamount to deciding to create a European state and this was not on the cards in 1969 (or since). The decision to create an intergovernmental structure in parallel with the European Community was a practical solution, but it created problems of coherence, coordination, and consistency that the European Community/EU has been grappling with ever since.

EPC[8] established intensive foreign policy consultations between the foreign ministries of the European Community member states plus the four applicant states (UK, Ireland, Denmark, and Norway). These consultations took place at a number of levels; at the top, the occasional meetings of heads of state and government would consider recommendations from the Council of Foreign Ministers who would convene, minus the Commission, on the fringes of European Community Council meetings—at first when an EPC item came onto the agenda the Commission representative would be asked to leave. At the official level, papers would be discussed by a newly established Political Committee consisting of the Political Directors of the member state foreign ministries who were all based in their national capitals. The Political Committee was roughly the same level as COREPER, whose members were permanently based in Brussels. Below the Political Committee, national diplomats met at a variety of levels in specialist working groups under the direction of the representatives from the rotating Council presidency. Decisions were taken by unanimity, giving any member state a veto, and the output consisted mainly of agreed common positions and declarations (usually rather bland and representative of the lowest common denominator). Much of the early discussion around EPC was procedural[9] and gave rise to complex debates about integration "theology" and the role of the European Community's institutions as well as the relationship between national and European foreign policy.[10] One of the challenges was that, to the extent that they existed, the tools of foreign policy at the European level were in the hands of the Commission (trade and aid agreements and finance for instance) and this was one of the reasons why the initial decision to keep EPC and European

Community procedures apart and to avoid in particular the involvement of the Commission was soon amended. Nevertheless there were also substantive policy achievements during the EPC era. The member states managed to orchestrate their participation in the Conference on Security and Cooperation in Europe (CSCE)[11] at a time when the US was not prepared to lead the West in a process that played a significant part in the end of the Cold War. The European Community also used EPC to agree on how the European Community would engage with the newly democratized Mediterranean states of Greece, Spain, and Portugal.[12] Finally in 1980 the Nine produced their "Venice Declaration" on the Middle East Peace Process which served very effectively to move the US position from support for Camp David to the Reagan Plan. Indeed, this is a good example of what Christopher Hill referred to as EPC's achievement of producing on occasions a "second Western voice in international diplomacy."[13]

45.2 CFSP IN THE POST-COLD-WAR ERA 1991–2009

The EU began the post-Cold War with two bold EPC/CFSP statements. In May 1991, as the wars of Yugoslav succession began, Mr. Jacques Poos, the foreign minister of Luxembourg announced, as he departed for Slovenia on a peace negotiation mission as the president in office of EPC, that "this is the hour of Europe, not the hour of the Americans."[14] Shortly after this boast about the European Community's collective diplomatic capabilities the newly agreed TEU recorded that EPC was to be upgraded and that "a common foreign and security policy is hereby established." Although some institutional and procedural progress had been made, the first decade of the CFSP proved to be very difficult.[15]

The break-up of Yugoslavia and the conflicts that followed throughout the 1990s (first in Bosnia and Croatia but later in Kosovo) exposed both the differences between the EU states and their lack of collective resources to implement policies that they could agree on. In the end it took US firepower, utilizing the NATO framework, to bring an end to the bloodshed. The Europeans were mere spectators at the Dayton peace talks that ended the war in Bosnia in 1995. NATO's intervention in Kosovo in 1999 demonstrated how ineffectual the European military capabilities were in comparison to those of the US, although the EU's diplomatic efforts were more effective in persuading Russia to withdraw its unconditional support for Belgrade. It was clear that the 1990s did not herald the "hour of Europe," but the disastrous handling of the Yugoslavian conflicts inspired both academic reflection and a determination within the EU after 1999 to implement and enhance the CFSP provisions of the TEU with a view to improving the EU's foreign policy performance by closing the "capability expectations gap."[16]

During the Cold War, enlargement proved to be one of the most successful European Community external polices. Enlargement decisions were motivated by foreign policy concerns and were orchestrated through EPC, even though their subsequent implementation involved the Commission and community method. This relationship continued in the period between the TEU and the Lisbon Treaty, with the member states reluctant to take the final decisions about enlargement to the East at least until the US sanctioned NATO enlargement. Nevertheless the EU's "power of attraction" continued to be its most effective foreign policy tool, enabling the EU to bring both economic and political stability to its immediate neighborhood by linking the promise of eventual membership to conditions designed to advance democracy, respect for human rights, and the basics of a market economy capable of operating within the EU single market.[17] Thus since the TEU the EU has successfully enlarged to twenty-seven European countries.

Nevertheless, the policy of stabilizing the neighborhood by offering the prospect of membership is proving difficult to sustain. The EU is currently suffering from "enlargement fatigue" and this is partly the result of the previous domination of enlargement policy decisions by foreign policy considerations rather than economic or social considerations. Although the EU is committed to admitting the countries of the Western Balkans, its efforts to stabilize its new post-enlargement neighborhood without the lure of eventual membership have exposed the failure of CFSP to give the EU's external actions strong political guidance. The time is approaching when it will be no longer possible to cite enlargement as the EU's most effective foreign policy.

The pillar structure of the TEU confirmed the fact that the CFSP (the second pillar) would retain intergovernmental procedures but that more efforts would be made to improve the CFSP capabilities of the EU institutions, in particular the Commission and the Council, whilst gradually moving the center of gravity from national capitals to Brussels (for instance by creating a Political and Security Committee based in Brussels to replace the Political Committee in directing the CFSP/ESDP).[18] Such changes did something toward bringing the economic and political aspects of EU external action together, but they did not do much to answer the question, first posed by Henry Kissinger in 1973, of "who speaks for Europe." More important, they did not clarify who decides what the EU's common foreign policy interests are given the ongoing perceptions of "national" interest at the member-state level.

The TEU did not just seek to bring together the twin strands of European foreign policy (CFSP and European Community); it also anticipated the further development of the CFSP to include a defense dimension. Until the very end of the 1990s no significant progress was made with this, other than the relocation of WEU (ambiguously referred to in the TEU as both the "defence arm of the Union" and the "European arm of NATO") to Brussels. Significant change came as CFSP/ESDP's development began to accelerate from 1999 onward. First, rapid progress with ESDP was made following the Anglo–French agreement at St Malo in December 1998. This overshadowed the CFSP in the early 2000s, as the reforms that were perceived as necessary to advance CFSP were held up whilst the member states prevaricated over the "future of Europe." The development of ESDP of course is closely associated with the 1999 appointment of Javier Solana, the former NATO Secretary-General, as the EU's first High Representative (and Secretary-General of the EU Council of Ministers).[19]

Solana was appointed to "assist" the presidency in CFSP matters and he was fortunate, in his first term of office, to work with Chris Patten, the Commissioner responsible for external relations along with the rotating presidency representatives. Solana and Patten worked well together mainly because Patten was strong enough to resist internal Commission pressures to get over-involved in the military aspects of CFSP/ESPD delivery. Patten characterized his role as "occupying the back office of European foreign policy" whilst Solana "occupied the front office."[20] Patten also drew attention to the ongoing problem that the CFSP itself had few resources allocated to it for implementation and was therefore forced to rely on the capabilities that the member states were prepared to share. Meanwhile, considerable financial resources lay in the hands of the Commission to finance its enlargement, neighborhood, and worldwide trade and aid policies. As Patten put it "at least in the back office the levers were connected to machinery; pull them and something happened, if sometimes too slowly."[21]

ESDP dominated the "Solana era," but Solana also played a role in the contributions that the CFSP was able to make toward the Middle East Peace Process, the EU initiative toward Iran, the stabilization of Ukraine, and the diplomatic intervention in the 2008 Georgian crisis.

Despite these achievements, however, the EU failed to make much of an impression on the international stage during the first decade of the twenty-first century. The growing number of ESDP missions suggested activity of sorts and the mix of civilian, police, and military missions indicated that the security element of a foreign and security policy was now more broadly interpreted than in the past—but all this was probably of more interest to internal advocates of European integration than to the EU's international interlocutors. The 2004 and 2007 enlargements underpinned the EU's status as a significant regional actor but globally the EU seemed to be irrelevant. This explains why the reforms finally agreed in the Lisbon Treaty were so eagerly awaited.

2003 is a good illustration. The CFSP plumbed new depths in the first half of the year as the EU member states profoundly disagreed with one another over whether to support the US war in Iraq. Once the major EU states fell out there was little that Solana or the Greek presidency could do about it and their differences were further fuelled by the robust stance taken by the Bush administration.

That said, a characteristic of the CFSP experience is that crisis usually gives way to progress. Just as it had been the case after the Yugoslavian fiasco, so it was again once the Iraq hostilities were over. Although some might have seen the problems over Iraq as indicative of the utter hopelessness of any ambition to construct a meaningful CFSP, others drew solace from the achievements in the second part of 2003, which included agreement for the first time on a European Security Strategy (ESS) laying out the EU's perceived threats and strategic objectives, and making the statement that if the EU was to produce an effective foreign and security policy it needed to be more active, more coherent, and more capable.[22]

The ESS was agreed in 2003 and in 2005 Solana was appointed as the first European foreign minister (elect) in anticipation of the ratification of the Constitutional Treaty. Four years later, when the Lisbon Treaty was at last ratified, it was too late for Solana to take up the revised position of High Representative and Vice President of the European Commission (HR/VP); the EU had spent nearly a decade prevaricating over how best to make the CFSP more active, more coherent, and more capable. However the world had changed significantly since the proposed changes to CFSP were first discussed in the Convention on the Future of Europe, and as the global financial crisis developed from 2008 onward the very basis of the EU came under question. When this happens, the member states usually fall back to the defense of national interests, so the Lisbon Treaty seemed like an irrelevant distraction whose ratification did not inspire much support for the idea that the EU was on the verge of becoming a more significant international actor.

45.3 CFSP AFTER THE LISBON TREATY

The Lisbon Treaty retains most of the proposed changes to the EU's external policy-making system[23] that were originally described in the Constitutional Treaty. Those states like the UK that had problems with the CFSP provisions of the Constitutional Treaty believe that they preserved their sovereignty by insisting that the proposed European foreign minister should continue to be called the High Representative and by the inclusion of two Declarations (30 and 31) which effectively state that nothing in the Treaty impacts on the responsibilities of the member states for the formulation and conduct of their own national foreign policies. Nevertheless the member states remain obliged to seek a common approach to foreign and security matters and to consult one another on any national foreign policy stances or actions that might impact on collective Union policy.

The Lisbon Treaty, unlike the Constitutional Treaty, merely amends the previous EU Treaties (all references here are to the latest consolidated version of the TEU) but a significant proportion of the amendments (twenty-five out of sixty-two) relate to the EU's "external action," which is the new generic term for the totality of the EU's CFSP/CSDP and external relations activities. Title V of the Consolidated Version of the TEU[24] makes it clear that the CFSP is at the center of the EU's external role. Even though a distinction remains between the CFSP and "other areas of the external action of the Union," the role of the HR/VP, with a foot in both the Commission and the Council, is clearly to bring it all together by ensuring consistency. Most of Article V is taken up by Chapter 2, which covers the CFSP (Chapter 1 covers General Provisions on the Union's External Action), and it is significant that the CSDP (covered elsewhere in this *Handbook*) is seen as "an integral part of the CFSP" (Article 42). Although separate pillars of the TEU have gone, the Lisbon Treaty retains the decision-making distinctiveness of the second pillar for CFSP/CSDP activities, which means that there is still no role for the ECJ and most decisions in this policy area will continue to be made unanimously by all the member states except where the Treaty provides for either structured cooperation or, more interestingly, for actions by "coalitions of the able and willing." The possibility for using QMV for some aspects of CFSP implementation remains, but only after a unanimous decision to do so has been taken!

The EU now has legal personality for the first time and an elected president of the European Council charged among other things with representing the Union in foreign and security matters at "his or her level." The first elected president is Hermann Van Rompuy, the former prime minister of Belgium, and he is joined in the European Council by the new HR/VP, Catherine Ashton, the former UK Commissioner, whose powers (Article 27) are more clearly articulated than, and are not to be "prejudiced" by, the president's—a potentially interesting relationship that will be significantly influenced by the personality mix of the two incumbents. The HR/VP was originally charged in 1999 with "assisting the Presidency" on CFSP matters, but under the Lisbon Treaty, the HR/VP effectively replaces the presidency on these matters by chairing the newly established Foreign Affairs Council, by appointing the chair of the Political and Security Committee, by representing the CFSP/CSDP to the European Parliament, and by representing the Union with third parties and in international organizations. Furthermore the HR is now a vice president of the European Commission, effectively taking on the former role of the "Relex" Commissioner, which is why she is known as the HR/VP.

The HR/VP is now supported by the new European External Action Service (EEAS) made up of officials drawn from the Commission, the Council Secretariat, and (eventually) the diplomatic services of the member states.[25] The Commission's external delegations have been renamed as Union delegations with most of their staff employed by the EEAS but some still employed by and answerable to the European Commission, which will probably create some uncertainties about information sharing and lines of reporting responsibility within an EU "embassy." Nevertheless the EEAS does have the potential to provide the services for the Union that one normally associates with the foreign ministry of a state. This can only happen however if the member states are willing. That is a big proviso given the reluctance of the diplomatic services of the larger member states to relinquish their national authority and status and given the financial restrictions that are already impeding the evolution of the EEAS.

Along with the EEAS, the HR/VP is now formally responsible for the appointment and management of the Union's Special and Personal Representatives.[26] Finally, with regard to the CFSP the Lisbon Treaty removes the Common Strategies (that Solana was always so dismissive of) along with Joint Actions and Common Positions. In future, the CFSP/CSDP will be implemented simply by the adoption of "general guidelines" and "decisions defining actions to be taken and positions to be adopted" and by the "strengthening of systematic cooperation between the member states in the conduct of policy" (Article 25). The Treaty also contains a number of changes related to the ongoing development of CSDP (Articles 42–46) which are dealt with in greater detail elsewhere in this *Handbook*.

These Treaty changes to the CFSP have been in force since the end of 2009, but their real impact has yet to be felt. This is partly because the HR/VP, Catherine Ashton, was forced to devote a good part of her first year to the establishment of the EEAS. During this time she was heavily criticized for her lack of action, preparedness, and linguistic fluency, her fondness for appointing UK officials to her staff, and her poor prioritization of relevant issues. Nevertheless her focus on events in the outside world was too often distracted by the turf wars between the Commission and the Council over the EEAS and the demands of the European Parliament, which was apparently determined to take the foreign policy role of the US Congress as its model, as she attempted to negotiate, first the basic structure of the EEAS, then the necessary changes to the EU's staff and financial regulations, and finally a budget for 2011. All of this was necessary to bring the EEAS into being even though it took up most of 2010.[27]

Part of the problem that Ashton faced arose from the fact that, whilst few substantive plans had been made for the introduction of the EEAS or for the implementation of the foreign policy powers granted to the HR/VP and the elected president of the European Council, the EU institutions and the member states had had plenty of time to consider their own positions on these matters and so they were well prepared for the turf wars that then followed. The president of the Commission in particular was anxious to preserve his powers to appoint key officials in the external service. So too was the Spanish presidency of the Council in the first half of 2010, which acted as if the provisions in the Lisbon Treaty designed to hand over the foreign policy responsibilities of the Council presidency to the HR/VP did not exist. In early 2010, President Obama rejected an invitation by the Spanish presidency to attend an EU–US summit in Madrid claiming that there was nothing new to discuss. When he did eventually attend an EU–US meeting in December 2010 it was under the new Lisbon procedures and he met with Presidents Van Rompuy and Barroso with no formal role for the EU Council presidency—which by then had passed to Belgium.

The EEAS formal structures and all senior appointments were in place by early 2011 and the service began its work as a "functionally autonomous body" headed up by the HR/VP. The foreign policy roles of both the HR/VP and the president of the Council have become clearer with Van Rompuy seeking mainly to mediate within the European Council rather than stop the traffic around the world, and with Ashton consolidating her power base within the Council/EEAS structures to the neglect of her position in the Commission (possibly as a result of President Barroso's bid for foreign policy prominence). Viewed from outside the EU, the shared representational roles of Presidents Van Rompuy and Barroso at the expense of the Council presidency, especially at the numerous bilateral summits, has probably given more of an initial impression of change than the activities of the HR/VP, whose inclination, in contrast to her predecessor's, seems to be to shun the international limelight. This was partly because of Ashton's formidable EEAS start-up agenda and partly because it was clear that, whilst she was effectively now acting as the EU's foreign minister, she was ultimately serving the collective interests of the EU member states and their "President" Van Rompuy. The new HR/VP has much more of a potential foreign policy machine under her control than Solana did, but it will be interesting to see how her relationship with both the Foreign Affairs Council and the European Council develops now that she has a fully operational EEAS and a little more time to consider relations between the EU and the outside world rather than relations between the EU's institutions. Nevertheless it is already clear that, regardless of the qualities of the person occupying it, the HR/VP post is an impossible one unless it is supported by some high-profile and competent deputies prepared to work with the HR/VP as a team.

The HR/VP is also handicapped by the unhelpful behavior of the EU's major member states, all of whom face serious internal financial problems which make them inclined to be difficult over the funding for the EEAS and reluctant to cooperate in the necessary agreements to commit their own diplomatic staff to the EEAS, as well as reluctant to take on any further CSDP missions as they seek to cut further their already depleted defense budgets. Most significant of all though is their continued reluctance to honor their commitment, under Article 24 (2), "to support the Union's external and security policy actively and unreservedly in a spirit of loyalty and mutual solidarity" and to "refrain from any action which is contrary to the interests of the Union or likely to impair its effectiveness as a cohesive force in international relations." Ever since EPC was established over forty years ago the member states have resisted any enforceable legal obligation (so important to the success of economic integration in the Union) to subsume their interpretations of their national interests to one of the Union's interests and their national foreign policy positions and actions to collective Union positions and actions. This ongoing barrier to the development of the CFSP suggests that there is a clear role for the president of the European Council to support the HR/VP by reminding his colleagues of their responsibilities under Article 24.

The major problem that the EU faces in using the CFSP to develop an effective and coherent set of European foreign policies is with the EU's "strategic" bilateral relationships with the major powers.[28] The US, China, Russia, Brazil, India, South Africa, Canada, Japan, and Mexico are already "strategic partners" of the EU, with Egypt, Israel, Indonesia, Pakistan, Ukraine, and South Korea likely to join the list in the near future. None of the partnerships can be said to be working well and the Union's poor performance in this aspect of the CFSP has led several commentators[29] to provide negative responses to the question posed by Charles Grant about whether the EU is "doomed to fail as a Power."[30] Although Van Rompuy has spent most of his time on the crisis in the eurozone, his first significant action with regard to foreign policy came when he called a meeting of the European Council in September 2010 specifically to consider strategic partnerships and in particular the management of the bilateral summits that go with them. In the European Council Presidency Conclusions it was noted that there was a need for "improved synergies between the EU and the national levels, for enhanced coordination between institutional actors, the better integration of all relevant instruments and policies and for summit meetings with third countries to be used more effectively."[31]

Mrs. Ashton was sent away by the Council to consider how bilateral relationships might be improved and in December 2010 presented her first progress report on strategic partnerships.[32] Her assessments are slightly tougher and more realistic than previous efforts and all focus on the need for fewer priorities, greater coherence, and more results from bilateral summits. There is also an emphasis on the need for a better linking of foreign and security policies with sectoral policies such as trade, energy, climate, and migration. Finally, there is a need for common messages to be prepared by the EEAS for the use of the EU member states—the "desired outcome" being "not the proverbial 'single voice' but instead one message, twenty-seven voices."[33] There is still much work to be done in this vital area of the CFSP.

45.4 CONCLUSIONS

The most comprehensive and recent account of research on the CFSP has been produced by Karen Smith,[34] who organizes her survey of the literature around six major themes which will also be used to organize the conclusions to this chapter:

(i) The EU member states have agreed to develop the CFSP in order to act collectively in international relations for a variety of reasons. For some it represents the logical development and extension of European integration whilst for others this represents an unfortunate and unintended consequence of seeking to advance national foreign policy objectives collectively because they can no longer be achieved individually. For the larger states the CFSP presents opportunities to retain their former status and to exert leadership, and for the smaller states it represents an opportunity to play a role in a collective policy that they could not hope to play alone. For all the member states the CFSP presents an opportunity to respond collectively to political demands and expectations that are directed at the EU, not at them individually, but which require a response.

(ii) The member states now understand how to make intergovernmental procedures work. They have not really deviated from their determination to maintain unanimity in the CFSP despite attempts to bring in QMV, constructive abstention, and now enhanced cooperation and even "coalitions of the willing." In the Lisbon Treaty they recognized the failings of trying to deal with the outside world via the rotating council presidency but it is too soon to tell whether the new roles for the president of the European Council, the HR/VP, and the EEAS will enable the Union to take coherent and consistent decisions.

(iii) The CFSP institutions have evolved mainly in response to their own failure. The Union has faced a number of crises in the CFSP—the response to the break-up of Yugoslavia and the divisions over the 2003 Iraq war being the most notable—and in every case the reaction has been to reform the institutional arrangements. There are no indications that any member states (with the possible exceptions of Belgium and Luxembourg) are willing to give up what they, and their domestic publics, see as their sovereignty in foreign affairs. The recent changes to the CFSP institutions are radical, but it remains to be seen if they can be made to work in the face of an apparent lack of the political will and political leadership that is vital to their success.

(iv) It is clear that despite the progress that has been made recently there are significant limits to collective action within the CFSP process and it may well be that a process that seeks to deliver "governance without government" to twenty-seven states with very different geopolitical positions and outlooks can progress no further. If anything ideological hostility to further integration both at the governmental and popular level has increased. The major member states continue to undermine collective CFSP stances by their own bilateral activity, especially in relation to the other major powers in the system who do everything they can to encourage this maverick behavior.

It is also the case that the CFSP's development has been significantly affected by influences from outside the EU. The US for example has often been characterized as an external federator both directly and indirectly pushing the EU member states to work more independently and effectively together on foreign policy issues. During the Cold War this was very much in the Kennedy image of the "twin pillars" of the Atlantic Alliance. More recently, the US has put pressure on the CFSP process either by its neglect of international issues which matter to the Europeans or by its selection of policies that concern and divide the Europeans. Although the US supports European integration in principle, it is prepared, as all the other major powers are, to disrupt collective or potential EU stances by exploiting the EU member states' concerns about their individual bilateral relationship with the US.

(v) Participation over the years in both EPC and the CFSP has had a significant impact on the member states themselves.[35] This impact is these days referred to as "Europeanization" which is used to describe and explain the extent to which the EU member states are successful in uploading their national foreign policy concerns to the CFSP level, the extent to which their perceptions of their national foreign policy interests are influenced by the experience of working within CFSP framework (downloading), and the extent to which participation in the CFSP process has given rise to policy transfer or emulation especially from the larger to the smaller member states. It nevertheless remains difficult to isolate the impact of the CFSP and the impact of Europeanization generated by participation in the CFSP process from the wider impact of globalization on national foreign policies and policy-making procedures.[36]

(vi) Finally we should try to evaluate what impact the CFSP has had on outsiders and on international relations in general. Often the subtleties of the distinctions that continue to be made between the EU's many external actions are lost on the EU's interlocutors, who nevertheless play their part in raising expectations about the EU's capacity to act whilst taking advantage of its ongoing inability to do so. The EU has problems behaving like a state. However the EU itself represents an interesting and relatively unique system of international relations on which its most effective foreign policy tool to date is based—its power of attraction. The CFSP has made significant progress since its establishment in 1969, but it remains constrained by the fact that it is still the product of an attempt to reproduce at the EU level foreign policy procedures that are most obviously associated with governments and states.

NOTES

1. Roger Morgan, *High Politics, Low Politics* (The Washington Papers) (London: Sage Publications, 1973).
2. Helen Wallace, "An Institutional Anatomy and Five Policy Modes," in Helen Wallace, Mark Pollack, and Alasdair Young, eds, *Policy-Making in the European Union*, sixth edition (Oxford: Oxford University Press, 2010), 91–4.

3. David Allen, "Who Speaks for Europe? The Search for an Effective and Coherent External Policy," in John Peterson and Helene Sjursen, eds, *A Common Foreign Policy? Competing Visions of CFSP* (London and New York: Routledge, 1998), 43–4.

4. Francois Duchene, "The European Community and the Uncertainties of Interdependence," in Max Kohnstamm and Wolfgang Hager, eds, *A Nation Writ Large? Foreign Policy Problems before the European Community* (London: Macmillan, 1973), 1–21.

5. Robert Cooper, *The Breaking of Nations: Order and Chaos in the Twenty-First Century* (London and New York: Atlantic Books, 2003).

6. Arnold Wolfers, "The Goals of Foreign Policy," in his *Discord and Collaboration: Essays on International Politics* (Baltimore: The Johns Hopkins Press, 1962), 67–80.

7. For a reference to the distinction between the powers of attraction and the powers of assertion, see Michael E. Smith, "A Liberal Grand Strategy in a Realist World? Power, Purpose and the EU's Changing Global Role," *Journal of European Public Policy* 18, no. 2 (March 2011), 161.

8. Philippe de Schoutheete, *La cooperation politique europeene* (Brussels: Editions Labor, 1980); Simon Nuttall, *European Political Cooperation* (Oxford: Clarendon Press, 1992); David Allen, Reinhardt Rummel, and Wolfgang Wessels, eds, *European Political Cooperation: Towards a Foreign Policy for Western Europe* (London: Butterworth Scientific, 1982), 21–32.

9. David Allen and William Wallace, "Political Cooperation: Procedure as Substitute for Policy," in Helen Wallace, William Wallace, and Carole Webb, eds, *Policy-Making in the European Communities* (London and New York: John Wiley, 1977), 227–48.

10. David Allen, "Foreign Policy at the European Level: Beyond the Nation-State," in William Wallace and William Paterson, eds, *Foreign Policy Making in Western Europe* (London: Saxon House, 1978), 135–54.

11. Gotz Von Goll, "The Nine at the Conference on Security and Cooperation in Europe," in David Allen, Reinhardt Rummel, and Wolfgang Wessels, *European Political Cooperation*, 60–9.

12. Nicholas Van Praag, "Political Cooperation and Southern Europe: Case Studies in Crisis Management," in David Allen, Reinhardt Rummel, and Wolfgang Wessels, *European Political Cooperation*, 94–109.

13. Christopher Hill, "The Capability–Expectations Gap or Conceptualising Europe's International Role," *Journal of Common Market Studies* 31, no. 3 (1993), 311.

14. Alan Riding, "Conflict in Yugoslavia; Europeans Send High-Level Team," *The New York Times*, June 29, 1991, available at <http://query.nytimes.com/gst/fullpage.html ?res=9D0C E0DF143CF93AA15755C0A967958260&sec=&spon> (accessed March 6, 2009).

15. For a detailed account of the CFSP provisions of the TEU and of their initial implementation, see Simon Nuttall, *European Foreign Policy* (Oxford: Oxford University Press, 2000).

16. For an astute analysis of the CFSP during the 1990s, see Hill, "The Capability–Expectations Gap," 305–27 and Christopher Hill, "Closing the Capability–Expectations Gap," in John Peterson and Helene Sjursen, eds, *A Common Foreign Policy for Europe*?, 18–38.

17. See Karen Smith, "Enlargement, the Neighbourhood and European Order," in Christopher Hill and Michael Smith, *International Relations and the European* Union, second edition (Oxford: Oxford University Press, 2011), 299–323.

18. For a discussion of "Brusselsization" and of the issues surrounding the arguments about who "speaks for Europe," see Allen, "Who Speaks for Europe," 43–4 and 41–58. For a discussion

of the work of the Political and Security Committee, see Ana Juncos and Christopher Reynolds, "The Political and Security Committee: Governing in the Shadows," *European Foreign Affairs Review* 12, no. 2 (2007), 127–47.

19. For a detailed analysis of Solana's ten-year period in office as EU High Representative, see Gisela Muller Brandeck-Borquet and Carolyn Ruger, eds, *The High Representative for the EU Foreign and Security Policy: Review and Prospects* (Berlin: Nomos, 2011).

20. Chris Patten, *Not Quite a Diplomat: Home Truths about World Affairs* (London: Penguin Books, 2006), 157.

21. Patten, *Not Quite a Diplomat*, 158.

22. For analysis of the European Security Strategy and its subsequent implementation, see Mark Leonard and Richard Gowan, *Implementing the European Security Strategy* (London: Foreign Policy Centre in association with the British Council, 2003); Alfonso De Vasconcelos, *The European Security Strategy 2003–2008: Building on Common Interest* (Brussels: EU Institute for Security Studies, February 2009); Javier Solana, Report on the *Implementation of the European Security Strategy: Providing Security in a Changing World*, Presented to the European Council, Brussels, December 2008, S407/08.

23. For a detailed analyses of the CFSP provisions of the Lisbon Treaty see Richard Whitman, *Foreign, Security and Defence Policy and the Lisbon Treaty: Significant or Cosmetic Reforms?*, Global Europe Papers 2008/1 (Bath: University of Bath, 2008); Federal Trust, *A More Coherent and Effective European Foreign Policy?* (London: Federal Trust Report, 2009); Anthony Gardner and Stuart Eizenstat, "New Treaty, New Influence? Europe's Chance to Punch Its Weight," *Foreign Affairs* 89, no. 2 (2010), 104–19; Joint Report, *The Treaty of Lisbon: A Second Look at the Institutional Innovations* (Brussels: Centre for European Policy Studies/Egmont Institute/European Policy Centre, 2010); Antonio Missiroli, "The New EU 'Foreign Policy' System after Lisbon: A Work in Progress," *European Foreign Affairs Review* 15 (2010), 427–52; Michael Emerson et al., *Upgrading the EU's Role as a Global Actor: Institutions, Law and the Restructuring of European Diplomacy* (Leuven and Brussels: Centre for European Policy Studies/Egmont Institute/European Policy Centre/Leuven Centre for Global Governance Studies, University of Leuven, 2011).

24. *Consolidated Version of the Treaty on European Union*, C115/13 (Luxembourg: Official Journal of the European Union, 2008).

25. On the EEAS, see Simon Duke, "Providing for European-Level Diplomacy After Lisbon: The Case of the European External Action Service," *The Hague Journal of Diplomacy* 4, no. 2 (2009), 211–33; Edith Drieskens and Louise van Schaik, eds, *The European External Action Service: Preparing for Success*, Clingendael Paper 1 (The Hague: Netherlands Institute of International Relations, 2010); Jan Gaspers, "Putting Europe First," *The World Today* (January 2010), 20–2.

26. On the role of EU Special Representatives, see Cornelius Adebahr, "Learning and Change in European Foreign Policy: The Case of the EU Special Representatives" (Berlin: DGAP-Schriften zur Internationalen Politik, 2009); Giovanni Grevi, "Pioneering Foreign Policy: The EU Special Representatives," *Chaillot Paper No. 106* (Paris: European Union Institute for Security Studies, 2007).

27. Joint Report, "The Treaty of Lisbon: A Second Look at the Institutional Innovations" (Brussels: Centre for European Policy Studies/Egmont Institute/European Policy Centre, 2010); Desmond Dinan, "Institutions and Governance," *Journal of Common Market Studies* 49, Annual Review, (September 2011), 103–21.

28. See David Gardner, "Why EU Struggles to Project Itself as a World Power," *Financial Times*, September 20, 2010, 11; Jolyon Howorth, "The EU as a Global Actor: Grand Strategy for a Global Grand Bargain?," *Journal of Common Market Studies* 48, no. 3 (2010), 455–74; Richard Whitman, "The EU: Standing Aside from the Changing Global Balance of Power?," *Politics* 30, Supplement 1 (December 2010), 24–32; Michael Emerson et al., *Upgrading the EU's Role as a Global Actor*; Stephan Keulekaire and Hans Bruyninckx, "The European Union, the BRICs and the Emerging World Order," in Christopher Hill and Michael Smith, *The International Relations of the European Union*, 380–403; and Michael E. Smith, "A Liberal Grand Strategy in a Realist World?."

29. Tony Barber, "Europe is Risking Irrelevance as the World Moves On," *Financial Times*, November 21–22, 2009, 8; Philip Stephens, "Absence of Ambition Leaves Europe in the Slow Lane," *Financial Times*, July 24, 2009, 11.

30. Charles Grant, *Is Europe Doomed to Fail as a Power?* (London: Centre for European Reform, 2009).

31. European Council, "Conclusions," European Council, September 16, 2010, EUCO 21/1/10 REV 1, CO EUR 16, CONCL 3.

32. Catherine Ashton, "Strategic Partners: Progress Report to the European Council," December 16–17, 2010, available at: <http://www.europolitics.info/pdf/gratuit_en/285182-en.pdf>; European Council "Conclusions," European Council, December 16–17, 2010, EUCO 30/1/10 REV 1, CO EUR 21, CONCL 5.

33. Ashton, "Strategic Partners: Progress Report to the European Council."

34. Karen Smith, "The EU in the World: Future Research Agendas," in Michelle Egan, Neill Nugent, and William Paterson, eds, *Studying the European Union: Current and Future Agendas* (London: Palgrave, 2009), 329–53.

35. Christopher Hill has organized collective studies of the impact of EPC/CFSP on the EU member states over an extended period of time. See for instance Christopher Hill, ed., *National Foreign Policies and European Political Cooperation* (London: Allen & Unwin for the Royal Institute of International Affairs, 1983); Christopher Hill, ed., *The Actors in Europe's Foreign Policy* (London: Routledge, 1996); Reuben Wong and Christopher Hill, eds, *National and European Foreign Policy Towards Europeanization* (London: Routledge, 2011). See also Ian Manners and Richard Whitman, eds, *The Foreign Policies of European Union Member States* (Manchester: Manchester University Press, 2000).

36. Compare for instance the very similar conclusions of the following two books on globalization and Europeanization, respectively: Brian Hocking, ed., Foreign Ministries: Change and Adaptation (Basingstoke and New York: Macmillan & St. Martin's Press, 1999) and Brian Hocking and David Spence, eds, *Foreign Ministries in the European Union: Integrating Diplomats* (Basingstoke: Palgrave Macmillan, 2002).

PART IX

POLITICAL
CONCERNS

....

DEMOCRACY AND LEGITIMACY IN THE EUROPEAN UNION

....

VIVIEN A. SCHMIDT

IF the EU can be considered democratic in terms of its institutional set-up, it is so in ways unlike those of nation-state democracies. While democracies in nation states have established governments, the EU has "governance," in which governing occurs without an established government through multiple authorities in highly complex sets of inter-relations with state as well as societal actors.

The EU lacks a directly elected president or parliament-elected prime minister, a fully empowered legislature, vigorous political parties, and a region-wide competitive, parti-san electoral system. Instead, it has strong but indirect representation by nationally elected executives in the Council of Ministers and the European Council, and weak but direct representation by the European Parliament. Although the European Parliament has gained significant co-decision-making powers with the Council over time, making it more independent from the executive than most national parliaments, it remains weaker than any national parliament with regard to executive appointments and legisla-tive initiatives, since it has no say over the appointment of the Council president, has only approval powers over the appointment of the Commission president and members, and has comparatively little input into legislative formulation. European Parliament elections, moreover, which are organized within rather than across member states, con-tinue to be "second-order," given the greater focus on national than European issues.

By comparison, the "non-majoritarian" institutions of the EU have greater powers than in any national democracy. The EU Commission, an unelected bureaucracy whose members are appointed by the Council and approved by the European Parliament, has initiation powers similar to those of federal legislatures and unitary executives while it has oversight and enforcement responsibilities similar to those of national executives generally. A regulatory body like the ECB has more autonomy from political pressures and influence of the member states or EU institutions than any central bank from national governments and institutions. And the Court of Justice of the European Union (CJEU) is even more independent than the most independent of national supreme courts, given EU decision rules that make it very difficult for the member states in the Council to overturn its judgments.

The very make up of the EU, then, means that scholars have had to go beyond the traditional ways of thinking about democracy and legitimacy as tied to national institutional forms and practices. But they have had to consider not just how to legitimate governance at the supranational level but also how this affects national-level democracy and legitimacy. And here, although one can make across-the-board generalizations about member states' loss of national executive autonomy and parliamentary power and gains in judicial independence and sub-national regional autonomy, the impact of EU institutions on its member states' democracies is also more subtly differentiated. This is because the EU has a *highly compound* governance system[1] which is not only multilevel since it includes EU, national, and regional levels (see the relevant chapters in this volume) and "multi-centered" as a result of the geographical dispersion of its governing activities[2] but also "multi-form" along a continuum from "simple" polities where governing activity tends to be channeled through a single authority, as in France or the United Kingdom, to more "compound" polities where governing activity is more dispersed across multiple authorities, as in Germany and Italy.[3]

Scholars remain divided over whether this complicated set of institutional arrangements has engendered a democratic deficit for the EU and/or its member states. They also differ in the analytic framework deployed. Some scholars consider democratic legitimacy in terms of its institutional form and practice as a system of governance, and other scholars focus on its interactive construction in the "European public sphere." But whatever their differences in substantive theory and analytic framework, scholars have tended to summarize their main arguments using concepts borrowed from systems theory, as they analyze the interrelationships between *output* legitimacy, judged in terms of the effectiveness of the EU's policy outcomes *for* the people; *input* legitimacy, judged in terms of the EU's responsiveness to citizen concerns as a result of participation *by* and representation *of* the people; and what we will call "*throughput*" legitimacy, building upon yet another term from systems theory, judged in terms of the accountability, transparency, and efficacy of the EU's decision-making processes along with their openness to pluralist consultation *with* the people.

46.1 EU LEGITIMIZING MECHANISMS: OUTPUT, INPUT, THROUGHPUT

Debates about the democratic legitimacy of the EU have been largely focused on mechanisms that Fritz W. Scharpf has defined as "output" legitimacy—a performance criterion centering on the ability of EU institutions to govern effectively for the people—and "input" legitimacy—involving political participation by the people and citizen representation of the people.[4] These terms have been borrowed from systems theories, originating in particular in the work of David Easton,[5] at the same time that they pick up on Abraham Lincoln's famous dictum about democracy requiring government *by* the people, *of* the people, and *for* the people. Output legitimacy has mostly been tied to the policy-related performance of its "non-majoritarian" institutions such as the ECB, the European Commission's Competition Authority, the CJEU, and other regulatory bodies, while input legitimacy has instead been focused on the EU's "majoritarian" institutions like the European Parliament and the Council and on the practices involving the representation of citizen demands through elections as well as interest-group and grassroot mobilization.

Missing from this theorization, however, is any general theory about the institutional practices that constitute what I will call, borrowing again from systems theory, "throughput" legitimacy. This conceptualization is intended to encompass not only the internal processes and practices of EU governance but also what I have previously termed, adding a preposition to Abraham Lincoln's phrase, interest intermediation *with* the people.[6] "Throughput" legitimacy is a performance criterion centering on what goes on inside the "black box" of EU governance, between the input and the output, which has typically been left blank by political systems theorists. It denotes not just the efficacy of EU governance processes but also, and most importantly, their accountability, meaning that policy actors are responsive and can be held responsible for output decisions; their transparency, meaning that citizens have access to information; and their openness to "civil society," meaning that citizens organized in interest-based organizations have access to and influence in the decision-making process. Curiously enough, there has been little theorization about these processes of "throughput" governance *with* the people taken as a whole,[7] despite the fact that there has been much about the legitimacy of individual aspects of the process within the Commission, the Council, and the European Parliament as well as with civil society.

Output *for* the people, input *by* and *of* the people, and throughput *with* the people are legitimizing mechanisms that are present in all mature national democratic systems. In the EU, they are largely split between the EU and national levels of governance. At the EU level, "output" governing effectiveness *for* the people and "throughput" interest consultation *with* the people are the primary legitimizing mechanisms. At the national level, instead, "input" political participation *by* the people and citizen representation *of* the people are the focus of legitimization. This creates a dynamic in which EU level "output" policies and "throughput" processes alter the equilibria of national legitimizing mechanisms, by putting pressure on national-level "input" politics while diminishing the importance of national throughput processes and the amount of purely national output policies. This can generate legitimacy problems for EU member states generally, and in turn for the EU.

What also emerges from this is that one cannot talk about remedying the problems of EU democracy and legitimacy without recognizing that increasing any one legitimizing mechanism may have negative repercussions on another, as well as on the legitimizing mechanisms of national democracies. For example, more input through greater politicization may complicate throughput efficacy and undermine output performance. Any recommendations for the reform of the EU have to face up to these interactive effects, and the possibility that increasing any one of these legitimizing mechanisms may negatively affect the other two. That said, whereas input and output legitimacy may involve trade-offs, where little input may be offset by good output, or much input may make up for bad output, throughput does not. More accessible and accountable throughput cannot make up for little input or bad output while bad throughput—consisting of oppressive, incompetent, corrupt, or biased governance practices—regularly undermines public perceptions of the legitimacy of EU governance, regardless of how extensive the input or effective the output. The multilevel nature of the EU system, with the split between national level input and EU level output and throughput, further complicates matters. Here, throughput may be used in EU legitimizing arguments as a kind of *"cordon sanitaire"* to suggest that whatever the input, trustworthy throughput processes will ensure that it emerges as uncorrupted output.

46.2 OUTPUT LEGITIMACY

The large majority of scholars of the EU have tended to argue that the EU suffers from a democratic deficit, regardless of the legitimizing mechanism. Only a few scholars defend the EU as democratic enough already, and they generally tend to base their defense on the output legitimacy of the EU's institutional forms and practices. Giandomenico Majone focuses on the "non-majoritarian institutions" that make of the EU a "regulatory state," and argues that the EU's legitimacy is based on the delegated responsibility of its "expertocracy" to produce effective policies and decisions *for* the people.[8] Andrew Moravcsik, who characterizes the EU as more of an intergovernmental organization than a regulatory state, maintains that the EU's institutional checks and balances along with its delegated authorities ensure that the EU is no worse than other democracies in terms of the output legitimacy of its decisions.[9] Anand Menon and Stephen Weatherill argue that the EU's output legitimacy is based on its ability to serve an "efficiency promoting function" by doing things for the member states that they cannot do on their own, such as creating the internal market, speaking for the member states in international trade negotiations, and acting through the ECB to coordinate responses to the economic meltdown.[10] James Caporaso and Sidney Tarrow have additionally contended that output *for* the people comes out of what Polanyi in *The Great Transformation* argued was the constant process of social re-equilibration of economic liberalization through the simultaneous movement/counter-movement of disembedding and re-embedding markets in society, with EU market-correcting alongside EU market-making, as in ECJ rulings in such areas as gender equality, regional equality, environmental protection, and laws promoting family solidarity in the case of labor mobility.[11]

Although these views of the EU's output legitimacy make important points about the ways in which EU institutional forms and practices have ensured a certain kind of non-majoritarian legitimacy, they make three questionable assumptions. Grounding output legitimacy primarily in institutional form or practice, whether through the EU's regulatory functions or its structural checks and balances, seems to assume that output is necessarily good simply because it is produced by independent regulators—an assumption that Majone himself now questions;[12] that its output cannot be bad simply because it has multiple vetoes; and that's its policies intrinsically serve the general interest.

First, the problem with assuming that output is necessarily good because produced by independent regulators fails to deal with the difference between non-majoritarian institutions at the EU and national levels. At the national level, the decisions of non-majoritarian institutions are accepted as legitimate because they operate in the "shadow of politics," as the product of political institutions, with political actors who have the capacity not only to create them but also to alter them and their decisions if they so choose—meaning that they are balanced by institutional input legitimacy. At the EU level, there is no such political balancing, given the EU's decision rules that make it almost impossible to alter such decisions, let alone to alter the non-majoritarian institutions that produce those decisions, in the absence of any kind of political government that could force the issue.

Second, as to the output benefits of the EU's institutional structures, Scharpf has convincingly argued that the "joint decision trap" of the EU's quasi-federal structure is even worse than that of Germany, raising questions about its output effectiveness or its output *tout court*, while the rationalist logic of its multiple veto structure often produces suboptimal substantive policy outcomes.[13] What is more, a structural logic that sees checks and balances as in themselves democratic and legitimate is also problematic because it takes as a fundamental premise the thwarting of majoritarian expressions of the popular will—something that may be accepted in federal systems like Germany or the US but not in unitary states like France and the UK.

Third, with regard to the blanket assumption that the EU's non-majoritarian output policies are legitimate because in the general interest, an increasing number of contested decisions by the EU Commission and the ECJ throw this too into question. These decisions include the Commission's services initiative that privileged home country rules, including pensions and wage rates for service workers in host countries (Directive 2006/123 of the Parliament and the Council on services in the internal market [2006] OJ L376/36), and CJEU decisions focused on freedom of movement that curtailed national unions' rights to strike in the Laval and Viking cases or struck down Austrian medical schools' quotas on German medical students. Although these could be seen positively from a EU-level perspective as promoting a Polanyian, market-correcting governance for all Europeans, it can just as readily be seen negatively from a national-level perspective as a neo-liberal post-Polanyian destruction of national labor relations and welfare systems.[14]

These examples illustrate a fourth drawback to "output" legitimacy, which takes us to the interactive construction of output legitimacy. As Furio Cerutti has argued, the performance-based legitimacy of the "output" variety is insufficient for legitimization, since outcomes also require a kind of "Weberian legitimacy," by which he means the substantive values and principles guiding the performance, that make the performance valued.[15] In other words, even if policy performance is optimal, if the actual content of the policies clashes with national values and principles, as reflected in European citizens' perceptions of EU policies as acceptable and appropriate (or not), then its output legitimacy is in question.

Constructive output legitimacy depends not only on how EU policies resonate with citizen values but also by how well elites' discourse and narratives serve to legitimate those policies and how citizens respond in the context of media-carried "communicative discourses" of deliberation or even contestation. Such discourses may be top-down, as political elites engage in legitimating discourses about the EU and its policies, or bottom-up, as EU-related policies and discourses generate responses and debate from the national media and opinion leaders along with the general public. Such communicative discourses can be centered on internal policies, in efforts to highlight the institutional output performance of, say, the single currency, the internal market, and environmental policies, or to foster positive attitudes toward certain kinds of EU norms and values, such as Commission's campaigns to promote gender equality, oppose racism, or build the concept of "social Europe" to counter perceptions of an EU neo-liberal policy focus. Alternatively, they may be concerned with external policies, say, by promoting human rights in trading partners, casting the EU as a "normative power" in its "neighborhood" as well as in the world more generally.

In the course of generating discussion, deliberation, and even contestation about EU policies, the communicative discourse of national elites may also perform an identity-building function, since the sense of *being* European is generally built not just on *doing*, as in institutional policy outputs, but also on *saying* what the EU is doing, which makes for constructive interactive outputs. The problem here is that national politicians in recent years have tended to engage in comparatively little *saying* about what the EU is doing. Instead, when national politicians do speak on the EU, they have tended to engage mainly in blame-shifting on unpopular policies, claiming that "the EU made me do it," or credit-taking on popular policies, often without even letting on that the policy was generated in Brussels.[16] Studies of media discourse and debate show that, with the exception of the big events like EMU, enlargement, or the Constitutional Treaty, there has been relatively little increase in attention to EU policies over time, and that what attention there has been might be more of an elite than a mass public phenomenon.[17]

Contributing to problems with regard to the building of identity is the fact that the founding, legitimating "grand narrative" that European integration is all about "peace and prosperity" no longer works, given that peace appears assured while prosperity is in question. And there are no persuasive new grand narratives either about what the EU is or does, as Jean Leca has convincingly argued,[18] whether those focused on the EU as "empire," neo-medieval[19] or cosmopolitan,[20] or those evoking new forms of international organization, such as my own notion of the "regional state."[21] Instead, each of the member states could be said to have its very own (often not very grand) narrative about the EU.[22] This said, member-states' visions of what the EU is, should be, and should do, can be grouped into four non-mutually exclusive legitimating discourses:[23] a pragmatic discourse of a borderless, problem-solving entity ensuring free markets and regional security which is generally characteristic of the UK, Scandinavian countries, and some of the

CEECs; a normative discourse of a bordered, values-based community, best identified with France, Germany, Italy, and smaller continental European countries; a principled discourse of a border-free, rights-based post-national union attributed to the Commission and to philosophers like Habermas and Beck and Grande;[24] and a strategic discourse about the EU as global actor "doing international relations differently" through multilateralism, humanitarian aid, and peacekeeping.[25]

This last discourse has increasingly become the preferred one of member-state leaders generally in their efforts to respond to global challenges such as economic crisis, climate change, poverty, and terrorism and to convince the public that the EU can provide another kind of output legitimacy *for* the people based on what it can do in the world. But agreement on what to do can always be undermined by disagreements on what the EU legitimately is—whether a widening free market, deepening values-based community, or democratizing rights-based union. Moreover, no amount of discourse can serve to legitimate the EU if words are not followed by actions, that is, by institutional output. After all, what does "normative power" really mean if the EU cannot deliver, as in the case of the Copenhagen Summit on the environment, or "social Europe," as inequalities rise massively between member states as well as within them in consequence of the economic crisis? This said, the decision in May 2010 to create a financial loan guarantee instrument to protect EU member states from default was a major step forward with regard to economic solidarity. But to make the EU truly live up to the rhetoric, as well as to build greater EU identity and community, it would need much more imagination as well as leadership across domains, say, by creating a European Monetary Fund and a European solidarity tax to alleviate poverty, whether collected through a Tobin-like tax on financial transactions or directly from EU citizens.[26]

46.3 "Input" Legitimacy

Input legitimacy is mostly about the quality of the EU's representative bodies and electoral processes, how these may channel and/or respond to citizen demands, and whether the citizens themselves offer either direct or diffuse support for EU institutions. With regard to all of these issues, scholars focused on institutional form and practices detail the many drawbacks of the EU's "political" system. They find that although the European Parliament does provide for direct citizen representation, it does not make the grade as input legitimacy *by* and *of* the people, in particular with regard to the nature and (low) degree of political participation. Arguably most problematic from the vantage point of traditional (read national) understandings of institutional input legitimacy is the absence of a government that citizens could vote in or out, which makes it impossible for "the people" to express their approval or disapproval of EU policies directly.

Another problem is that the EU has lacked the kind of politics to which citizens can relate, since EU decision-making has not really been much about politics in the traditional sense of party and partisanship (although this has been growing). Instead, it is mostly about the politics of interests, whether the politics of the national interest in the Council, the public interest in the European Parliament, or of organized interests in the Commission. Moreover, at the EU level, party differences and left–right political contestation have long been submerged by the general quest for consensus and compromise—even though politicization has been growing in Council and European Parliament votes while appointments to EU leadership positions now take politics into account. The co-decision procedures with the Council, voted mostly by supermajorities in the European Parliament, also have the effect of submerging partisan divides, as does the Commission's consensus-oriented, technical approach to policy initiation and development, which deliberately seeks to avoid left–right divides as it attempts to balance the representation of all interests. Moreover, European political parties remain weak, underdeveloped, and not very cohesive in the European Parliament, given the diversity of the national-level parties that make up their membership, while European Parliament elections suffer from high rates of abstention (see Chapter 58, this volume).

As a result, policy-making at the EU level can be characterized as "*policy without politics*," which in turn makes for national "*politics without policy*," as increasing numbers of policies are transferred from the national political arena to the EU, leaving national citizens with little direct input on the EU-related policies that affect them, and only national politicians to hold to account for them.[27] This has already had a variety of destabilizing effects on national politics, including citizen demobilization on the one hand and radicalization on the other. At the EU level, moreover, all of these issues have led to a decline in the kind of diffuse support that Easton identified as a key factor in input legitimacy. This is because the "permissive consensus" of the early years, in which citizens largely ignored the EU and its outcomes has been replaced by a "constraining dissensus" along with a rise in Euro-skepticism.[28] What makes matters worse, as Hans-Peter Kriesi and colleagues demonstrate, is that new cleavages have developed between citizens whose ideas for Europe are more open, liberal, and cosmopolitan in orientation and those whose ideas are more closed, xenophobic, and nationalist, or even EU-regionalist oriented.[29] The result has been that national electorates have typically been less mobilized along left–right party lines on EU-related issues than in terms of identity politics, especially on the right.[30] And with the gradual awakening of the "sleeping giant" of cross-cutting cleavages between pro-European "cosmopolitans" and Euro-skeptic "nationalists" in mainstream parties of the right and the left, the EU is likely to see much more hotly contested, politicized European Parliament elections than in the past, even if they remain second-order elections.[31]

For scholars concerned with constructive input legitimacy, all the above problems are compounded by the thinness of the communicative processes that articulate citizen ideas and concerns in the European public sphere. The lack of a common European language, a European media, or a European public opinion ensures that the communicative discourse comes largely by way of national political actors speaking to national publics in national languages reported by national media and considered by national opinion. Although the resulting fragmented communication is attenuated somewhat by the fact that there is a developing European public sphere in which national publics are increasingly aware of European issues and the views of other member-state publics, as noted above, this does not get around the institutional input reality that without a Europe-wide representative politics to focus debate, European political leaders have little opportunity to speak directly to the issues and European publics have little ability to deliberate about them or to state their conclusions directly through the ballot box. And when they have had the opportunity, as in referendums on the Constitutional and Lisbon Treaties, they have tended to prefer to express their concerns about the national impact of EU policies rather than to respond to the question asked (about EU institutions). This said, the fact that citizens were able for once to discuss, deliberate, and contest the issues during such referendums was in itself legitimizing in terms of constructive input, even if the "No" votes were delegitimizing in terms of institutional input.

So, is the answer to bring in more *"policy with politics"* at the EU level, as many scholars advocate, in the effort to diminish the EU's input "democratic deficit"? Some have resisted this suggestion because they see politicization as deleterious to the EU's output governing effectiveness *for* the people. And more politics in such complex institutional structures could also lead to stalemates that would only increase citizens' disaffection from and dissatisfaction with the EU—thus further undermining diffuse input support. Yet others worry that it is too soon for any such politicization given legitimacy problems relating to the lack of citizen identity, collective will, and a fully developed public sphere—which speaks to the interactive construction side of EU input legitimacy.

But the cat is already out of the bag, so the question is how to politicize within the context of the current institutional set-up. Simon Hix's proposal for a greater majoritarian component to the politics of the Council and the European Parliament in order to make it possible to have more clearly demarcated policies of the left or right implemented with greater output efficiency,[32] while a step in the right direction, is premature, since EU political parties lack the kind of cohesion and EU citizens the kind of collective will necessary for any kind of majoritarian politics. The EU might do better with the kind of proportional representation system of a country like Germany in which, once the right–left polarization of elections campaigns is over, compromise and consensus-seeking rule, in particular at times of grand coalitions. Beyond this, greater citizen access to the European Parliament either directly or through the national parliaments is an area crying out for reform. But all of this also demands better working EU institutions to respond to input and to produce output, which is the domain of throughput legitimacy.

46.4 "THROUGHPUT" LEGITIMACY

Throughput legitimacy is focused on the policy-making processes through which decisions go from input to output within the black box of EU governance. This includes not only concern with the workings of the decision-making processes as a whole—that they proceed with efficacy in accountable and transparent manner—but also on the intermediation processes through which citizens *qua* interests as opposed to *qua* voters have an influence. Because throughput has not usually been part of theorizing about EU legitimacy, it has sometimes accompanied discussions of output, where particular institutional or discursive processes are seen as preconditions for better output performance, and occasionally discussions of input, where certain institutional or deliberative processes are assumed better for input participation. Examples include arguments in favor of delegating (throughput) control of monetary policy to the ECB to ensure price stability (output) or of maintaining the elaborate (throughput) system of checks and balances of EU governance to guard against the excesses of majoritarian (input) rule.

For institutional scholars, throughput legitimacy includes not only the workings of the decision-making processes as a whole—that they function efficaciously, in an accountable and transparent manner—but also the intermediation processes through which citizens organized in interest groups have a direct influence on policy-making. Throughput legitimacy via interest-based consultation *with* the people represents a way in which minority interests can gain a voice even without a majority vote. In the EU, such interests include not only well-organized special interests, such as business, but also more diffuse, difficult-to-organize majority interests such as consumer groups and public interest oriented groups such as environmental groups, policy think tanks, or even social movements. This kind of legitimacy has been theorized not only by the pluralist political scientists of the 1950s and 1960s in America but also more recently by theorists of "associative democracy," as another form of democracy in its own right as well as a corrective to representative democracy. For the EU, throughput governance *with* the people through pluralist-type consultation—mainly as part of the joint decision-making process involving a wide range of governmental and non-governmental actors commonly known as the "Community Method"—has deliberately been encouraged as a way of counterbalancing the paucity of governance *by* or *of* the people through political participation and citizen representation. But it is only in recent years that such "functional representation" through interest groups has come to be seen as an additional form of democratic legitimization in the EU.

Within the EU, the Commission and increasingly the European Parliament have sought to promote more pluralist consultation *with* the people, meaning interest groups and members of "civil society," as a way to counterbalance the lack of governance *by* the people and to promote democratic legitimacy.[33] The Commission in particular sought to find ways to make policy-making "more inclusive and accountable" to "civil society"— defined as including special interests like business and labor along with activist citizens—as well as more transparent (as per the *White Paper on European Governance 2001*). Accountability was to be improved through closer controls on expenditures and appointments and transparency by providing greater access to EU documentation for the media and interest groups (see Chapter 47, this volume) as well as through the internet and the development of e-government—which often leads to information overload for any individual trying to sort through the massive amounts of materials available while navigating through EU websites. As for access and openness to civil society, the EU Commission sought to create a more balanced and open playing field among interests groups, including creating "grass roots" interest groups (e.g. of women and consumers) to counterbalance the more powerful, already present business groups.

In addition to such institution-based practices, the EU has sought to increase throughput legitimacy via more and better discursive interaction in the "coordinative" discourses of policy construction among EU actors. Examples of formal processes include the Commission-led, consensus-focused intermediation with experts in comitology and public interest groups, which has been described as a form of "supranational deliberative democracy"[34] or "directly deliberative polyarchy."[35] One might add here the dynamic accountability involved in the deliberative processes of peer reviews, whether in forums, networked agencies, councils of regulators, or the open method of coordination;[36] or the "strong publics" of the European Parliament, with the debates contributing to the greater accountability and transparency of the decision-making process, although one could also see this as contributing to input legitimacy, through the representative nature of MEPs.[37] More ad hoc processes of throughput legitimization include the Constitutional Convention, with arguably the first (and only) creation of an EU deliberative public sphere of communication in which ideas about how to democratize the EU flowed freely, at least at first, in contrast to the IGC that followed, which went back to the same old closed-door bargaining routine.[38] Other informal processes of discursive interaction that contribute to throughput legitimacy "from below" include the role of social movements in advocacy coalitions and grass-roots activism.[39] Moreover, with regard to interest intermediation, rather than competition among interests, the EU Commission sought to foster cooperation in its consensus-based policy formulation process, with rules of the game that entail that in order to play, participants must gain and maintain credibility as trusted actors providing accurate technical information.[40] But regardless of how open to public interest consultation *with* the people the EU may be, the problem for national citizens is that this kind of supranational policy-making is very far from the kind of representative democracy *by* and *of* the people they tend to see as the most legitimate. And it is in any case not open to most of them, given the difficulties of transnational mobilization for most citizens.

Another major problem for efficacious throughput lies in the institutional processes of decision-making themselves. The Lisbon Treaty was touted as the remedy to the institutional decision-making problems of the EU, as all three institutional actors—Commission, Council, and European Parliament—had their powers enhanced. But big legitimacy problems remain, first, with the institutional rules, in particular the fact that once decisions are made, they are nearly impossible to overturn by the member states in the Council; second, with their transparency, given that the Commission-based drive toward greater access to the massive volume of EU-generated information on EU decisions perversely may make it less transparent; and third, with their accountability, given the secrecy of Council meetings. There are also problems with regard to the European Parliament's role, since it has little influence over initiation, no connection to comitology, and so far also little connection to national parliaments—although this could change for the better, given that a procedure for consultation was written into the Lisbon

Treaty. Finally, and arguably most problematic for throughput, are (a) the unanimity rule for treaties, in which the ability of any member state to veto any agreement can lead to treaty delays, dilution, or deadlock; and (b) the uniformity ideal for further integration, in which the fear that differentiated integration will undermine an already diffuse sense of solidarity and community stymies not only deeper integration but also enlargement through graduated membership.[41]

So how would one remedy the problems of throughput legitimacy? With regard to the rules, replacing the unanimity rule with supermajorities with opt-outs on treaties and abandoning the uniformity ideal in favor of more differentiated integration would be steps in the right direction.[42] With regard to pluralist access, why not through more *policy with* pluralist *politics*"? National governments need to find ways of encouraging citizen involvement in supranational decision-making by helping them to organize themselves transnationally so as to gain access and influence in European decision-making—providing funding, information, and strategic advice. Social movements, moreover, could also do more on their own to try to get their message through to Brussels through transnational organization and representation, rather than spending so much of their time and energy organizing "No" votes in treaty referendums. But national governments would need also to improve the national-level inputs, by bringing civil society into national formulation processes focused on EU decision-making. Importantly, however, stakeholder democracy, even if improved, is not necessarily public interest oriented democracy. And however much the EU and national governments seek to promote "*policy with* pluralist *politics*" to enhance "throughput" legitimacy, this cannot be a substitute for input legitimacy, although it can be a supplement to it as well as a way of ensuring better output legitimacy.

46.5 CONCLUSION

As for a final assessment of the quality of democracy and legitimacy of the EU—it is both worse than it seems to some but better than it appears to others. Moreover, the problems of European democratic legitimacy are not confined to the EU level but are arguably as serious if not more so for the EU's member states. And only by reinforcing democracy at the national level as well as by improving national citizens' access to EU decision-making through input and throughput processes can we be sure to shore up the legitimacy of EU output. Finally, in order to explain the problems of the EU, an institutional analysis of EU structures and practices alone is not enough; the ideational and discursive aspects of democracy and legitimacy are as, if not more, important. This is because how citizens think and talk about the EU and its institutions are as important for democratic legitimacy as are the democratic practices that infuse the institutions with legitimacy.

Notes

1. Vivien A. Schmidt, *Democracy in Europe* (Oxford: Oxford University Press, 2006); Sergio Fabbrini, *Compound Democracies* (Oxford: Oxford University Press, 2007).
2. Kalypso Nicolaïdis, "Conclusion," in Kalypso Nicholaïdis and Robert Howse, eds, *The Federal Vision* (Oxford: Oxford University Press, 2001).
3. Schmidt, *Democracy in Europe.*
4. Fritz W. Scharpf, *Governing in Europe* (Oxford: Oxford University Press, 1999).
5. David Easton, *A Systems Analysis of Political Life* (New York: Wiley, 1965).
6. Schmidt, *Democracy in Europe.*
7. The exception is a small cluster of scholars mainly in Germany and bordering countries, although most have limited the definition of throughput to rules-based procedural legitimacy, leaving out interest group participation. See, for example, Michael Zürn, "Democratic Governance Beyond the Nation-State," *European Journal of International Relations* 6, no. 2 (2000), 183–221; Arthur Benz and Yannis Papadopoulos, *Governance and Democracy* (London: Routledge, 2006); R. Holzhacker, "Democratic Legitimacy and the European Union," *Journal of European Integration* 29, no. 3 (2007), 257–69; Thomas Risse and Marieke Kleine, "Assessing the Legitimacy of the EU's Treaty Revision Methods," *Journal of Common Market Studies* 45, no. 1 (2007), 69–80.
8. Giandomenico Majone, "Europe's Democratic Deficit," *European Law Journal* 4, no. 1 (1998), 5–28.
9. Andrew Moravcsik, "Reassessing Legitimacy in the European Union," *Journal of Common Market Studies* 40, no. 4 (2002), 603–24.
10. Anand Menon and Stephen Weatherill, "Transnational Legitimacy in a Globalising World: How the European Union Rescues its States," *West European Politics* 31, no. 3 (2008), 397–416.
11. James Caporaso and Sidney Tarrow Caporaso, "Polanyi in Brussels: European Institutions and the Embedding of Markets in Society." RECON Online Working Paper 2008/01, available at: <www.reconproject.eu/projectweb/portalproject/RECONWorkingPapers.html>.
12. Giandomenico Majone, *Dilemmas of European Integration: The Ambiguities and Pitfalls of Integration by Stealth* (Oxford: Oxford University Press, 2009).
13. Scharpf, *Governing in Europe.*
14. Martin Höpner and Armin Schäfer, "A New Phase of European Integration: Organized Capitalisms in Post-Ricardian Europe." MOIFG Discussion Paper no. 2007/4. Available at SSRN, <http://ssrn.com/abstract = 976162>.
15. Furio Cerutti, "Why Legitimacy and Political Identity are Connected to Each Other, Especially in the Case of the European Union," in Furio Cerutti and Sonia Lucarelli, eds, *The Search for a European Identity* (London: Routledge, 2008), 3–22.
16. Schmidt, *Democracy in Europe.*
17. Ruud Koopmans, "The Transformation of Political Mobilisation and Communication in European Public Spheres," 5th Framework Programme of the European Commission (2004), available at: <http://europub.wz-berlin.de>; Neil Fligstein, *Euroclash* (Oxford: Oxford University Press, 2008); Thomas Risse, *A Community of Europeans? Transnational Identities and Public Spheres* (Ithaca: Cornell University Press, 2010), 128–33.
18. Jean Leca, "'The Empire Strikes Back!' An Uncanny View of the European Union. Part II," *Government and Opposition* 45, no. 2 (2010), 208–90.

19. Jan Zielonka, *Europe as Empire* (Oxford: Oxford University Press, 2006).
20. Ulrich Beck and Edgar Grande, *Cosmopolitan Europe* (Cambridge: Polity Press, 2007).
21. Schmidt, *Democracy in Europe*; Vivien A. Schmidt, "Re-Envisioning the European Union: Identity, Democracy, Economy," *Journal of Common Market Studies* 47 Annual Review (2009), 17–42.
22. Risse, *Community of Europeans*.
23. See Vivien A. Schmidt, "European Elites on the European Union: What Vision for the Future?," in Andrew Gamble and David Lane, eds, *European Union and World Politics: Consensus and Division* (London: Palgrave Macmillan, 2009), 257–73. The definitions of the first three discourses follow E. O. Eriksen and J. E. Fossum, "Europe in Search of Legitimacy," *International Political Science Review* 25, no. 4 (2004), 435–59, and Helen Sjursen, "Enlargement in Perspective: The EU's Quest for Identity" Recon Online Working Paper 2007/15, available at: <www.reconproject.eu/projectweb/portalproject/RECONWorkingPapers.html>. The definition for the fourth discourse follows Jolyon Howorth, *European Security and Defense Policy* (Basingstoke: Palgrave, 2007).
24. Jürgen Habermas, *The Postnational Constellation* (Cambridge, MA: MIT Press 2001); Beck and Grande, *Cosmopolitan Europe*.
25. Howorth, *European Security*.
26. See Schmidt, "Re-Envisioning" for more on this as well as other suggestions.
27. Schmidt, *Democracy in Europe*, ch. 4.
28. Liesbeth Hooghe and Gary Marks, "Postfunctionalist Theory of European Integration: From Permissive Consensus to Constraining Dissensus," *British Journal of Political Science* 39, no. 1 (2009), 1–23.
29. Hans-Peter Kriesi, Edgar Grande, and Romain Lachat, *West European Politics in the Age of Globalization* (Cambridge: Cambridge University Press, 2008).
30. Marks and Hooghe, "Postfunctionalist Theory."
31. Mark Franklin and Cees van der Eijk, "The Sleeping Giant," in Wouter van der Brug and Cees van der Eijk, eds, *European Elections and Domestic Politics* (Notre Dame: University of Notre Dame Press, 2007), 189–208.
32. Simon Hix, *What's Wrong with the European Union and How to Fix It* (Cambridge: Polity Press, 2008).
33. Justin Greenwood, "Organized Civil Society and Democratic Legitimacy in the European Union," *British Journal of Political Science* 37, no. 2 (2007), 333–57.
34. Christian Joerges and and Jürgen Neyer, "Transforming Strategic Interaction Into Deliberative Problem-Solving," *Journal of European Public Policy* 4, no. 4 (1997), 609–25.
35. Oliver Gerstenberg and Charles Sable, "Directly Deliberative Polyarchy: An Institutional Ideal for Europe?" (2000), available at: <http://www.law.columbia.edu/sable/papers/gerst-sable1029.doc>.
36. Charles Sabel and Jonathan Zeitlin, *Experimentalist Governance in the European Union* (Oxford: Oxford University Press, 2010), 12–20.
37. Eriksen and Fossum, "Europe in Search of Legitimacy."
38. E. O. Eriksen, John Erik Fossum, and Augustín José Menendez, *Developing a Constitution for Europe* (London: Routledge, 2004); Risse and Kleine, "EU's Treaty Revision Methods."

39. Klaus Eder and Hans-Jörg Trenz, "Prerequisites of Transnational Democracy and Mechanisms for Sustaining It: The Case of the European Union," B. Kohler-Koch and B. Ritberger, eds, *Debating the Democratic Legitimacy of the European Union* (Lanham, Maryland: Rowman and Littlefield, 2007), 171–2.

40. David Coen, *EU Lobbying* (London: Routledge, 2008).

41. Schmidt, "Re-Envisioning," 28–32.

42. Schmidt, "Re-Envisioning," 28–32.

CHAPTER 47

....

POLICY EFFECTIVENESS AND TRANSPARENCY IN EUROPEAN POLICY-MAKING

....

ADRIENNE HÉRITIER

THIS chapter defines and discusses the concepts of policy evaluation and policy effectiveness, on the one hand, and transparency of public policy-making, on the other.

47.1 DEFINITION OF CONCEPTS

Evaluation describes the scientific activity of measuring the results or effectiveness of a specific policy measure as defined by its originally defined goals. These goals may be defined in more general or in more specific terms. They may relate to concrete measurable actions, or—more difficult to measure—to goals of behavioral change or changes in the physical and natural environment. They may be defined at the top, or be gradually developed from the bottom in the course of implementation. Evaluating the success of a policy measure as defined by the self-defined goals presupposes the existence of a causal link between the measure in question and the measured effect. Evaluating effectiveness poses specific problems and requires special measures depending on when it takes place during the policy cycle: when a policy is defined, when the policy agenda is set, during the formal political decision-making process, or during or after the implementation of a policy measure.

Transparency describes a condition under which a high degree of information concerning a public policy is made accessible and actively spread to the public. It defines which elements of information concerning which public policy aspects are made accessible and spread to whom. Again, transparency implies different activities and problems depending on whether it refers to the definition of a policy problem, the agenda setting process, policy formulation, or policy implementation and policy evaluation.

Transparency itself constitutes a precondition for the successful evaluation of a policy. Without access to information about a policy measure—in all its stages—evaluation would not be possible. However, unlike the creation of transparency, evaluation constitutes a scientific device of assessing the results of a policy decision-making process in all stages of the policy cycle. The critical assessment of transparency, by contrast, refers to practical political and administrative measures designed to create greater openness in public policy-making.

47.2 EVALUATION OF POLICY EFFECTIVENESS AND TRANSPARENCY IN THE CONTEXT OF THE POLICY CYCLE

Both the evaluation of policy effectiveness and the creation of transparent public policy-making involve distinctive activities in different phases of the policy-making cycle. These phases are: problem definition, agenda setting, political decision, policy implementation, evaluation, and feedback loop.[1]

47.2.1 Evaluating Policy Effectiveness in the Context of the Policy Cycle

Evaluation immediately raises the question: "evaluating what?" Without knowledge of what it is that is being evaluated for its effectiveness, evaluating policy effectiveness does not make sense. The objectives of a policy, by which it will be evaluated, are formally defined in the stage of policy formulation, the adoption of legislative or administrative decisions. But prior to that, the policy measure in question has to be defined as a problem of policy-making. Once it has been defined as a policy problem, it still has to compete with many other issues for a place in the political decision-making agenda. Once on the agenda it may be adopted, modified, or discarded in political the decision-making process. The results of the political decision/legislative phase of the policy cycle are *policy outputs*, i.e. legislative and administrative decisions. In the following phase of implementation, these goals are translated into *policy outcomes*, i.e. concrete measures meant to put these formal decisions into place, for example by allocating funds, personnel, and organizational support. If the policy goals are defined at the level of outcomes, evaluating effectiveness is easier than when the goals are defined as *policy impacts*, such as a change of human behavior or an environmental condition. Finally, a policy measure may, after its evaluation, be either continued or abolished.

In the next section we show how each stage focuses on different objects of an evaluation of policy effectiveness: policy outputs, policy outcomes, or policy impacts.

47.2.1.1 *Evaluation: Problem Definition and Agenda Setting*

Describing the definition of a policy problem constitutes a reference point for all subsequent evaluation activities.[2] Once a societal problem has been perceived to be a problem that requires political action, it has obtained the status of a policy problem. This invites the question of why specific problems among hundreds of problems are considered to be *policy* problems, while the rest are not. Three answers may be offered to this question: one from a rationalist power-based perspective, one from a sociological institutionalist perspective, and one which highlights contingency. From a rationalist power-based perspective, the definition of a policy problem is the outcome of an interest-driven, power-based contest among conflicting societal groups and their political organizations, each of them seeking the support of the media. Defining a problem in a particular way has implications as to which political cleavages may emerge and how voters respond to them.[3] From a sociological institutionalist perspective, the definition of a problem depends on whether it corresponds to highly prioritized societal values, beliefs, ideals, or mental frames of specific societal groups.[4] Finally, it may be due to an unforeseen exogenous shock, an international crisis, that a specific problem turns into a policy problem.

Once a problem has obtained the status of a policy problem, it still has to compete with many other policy problems to gain access to the political agenda of a decision-making body. Political agendas, in general, offer very little free space since most of the agenda is taken up by routine problems that need to be processed on a regular basis (e.g. budgetary questions, and so on). Again, the answer to why a specific policy problem gains access to the political agenda can be accounted for by the same three general explanations: the goal-oriented actors and power-based explanation claims that the problems supported by the most powerful actors will achieve this status; the sociological institutionalist approach argues that the strong pressure of specific norms and values leave political actors with no other choice but to insert these issues into their agenda.[5] Finally, an exogenous shock, such an international crisis or a natural crisis, may force policy problems onto the political agenda.

From a methodological viewpoint, answering the question as to why one specific problem became a "policy problem" and then also gained access to the political agenda would require the analysis of the factors and process that led to the narrowing down of a large number of problems discussed at one particular time of a political period. This would in turn require an intensive, detailed analysis of public debates and the subsequent public definition of the policy problem, as well as a qualitative in-depth process analysis of the underlying factors and political processes. Once the most important determinant factors are known, comparative case studies could be conducted along a most-similar systems design or a most-different systems design,[6] varying key factors, such as underlying political cleavage structures and dominant party coalitions.

A different research design based on a large-n quantitative statistical analysis would focus on a large number of polities faced with a comparable problem, such as high unemployment, and analyze in a synchronic and diachronic fashion whether specific unemployment measures become part of the political agenda. Explanatory factors, such as strength of organized labor and dominance of leftist governments, could be systematically varied while controlling for other potentially influential factors.[7]

47.2.1.2 *Evaluating Policy Outputs*

When evaluating effectiveness is conducted at the level of policy outputs, i.e. legislative and administrative decisions, the attention focuses on the similarity or dissimilarity of the problems defined in the public political debate and the formal policy output of the decision-making process. It is asked whether the adopted decision addresses the problem comprehensively and in its full complexity, or whether it limits itself to addressing easily manageable aspects of the problem. If, for instance, unemployment has been defined as the "problem to be solved," evaluation would scrutinize the specific measures proposed to reduce unemployment, such as permanent manpower training, and relate them to their likely effectiveness in contributing to the reduction of unemployment. At the same time, other possible measures not taken to reduce unemployment, such as the creation of public works or childcare facilities for working mothers, would have to be taken into account when evaluating how the chosen measure is likely to contribute to the pursued policy goal.

Methodologically, both large-n quantitative analysis and qualitative case studies' comparisons may be used. A large-n study would compare a large number of polities— with a given identical problem on the agenda—as to their specific policy outputs. In comparative qualitative case studies—again by systematically varying factors favoring or disfavoring the output—the underlying processes leading to the specific output could be analyzed more in detail.

47.2.1.3 *Evaluating Policy Outcomes*

In evaluating the implementation of a legislative act or administrative decree, the investigation focuses on the resources, such as personnel, finances, and organizational means, that have been deployed in order to reach the declared policy goal. Depending on whether the responsibility for implementation lies with central government or with subnational entities, the causes of successful implementation and outcomes are to be identified at the higher or lower level of a polity.[8] To use the above example of permanent manpower training intended to reduce unemployment and, assuming that the implementation responsibility is located at the regional or local level, the necessary teaching personnel and infrastructure has to be provided for at the sub-national level.

Methodologically an effectiveness analysis focusing on the outcomes of implementation would have to scrutinize multiple political and administrative processes at the lower levels as well as target group behavior in order to identify underlying causes and processes of effectiveness or lack of effectiveness. A large-n comparison of expenditures across sub-national units would offer a first overall view of the financial means implementing units have deployed for the implementation of the measure. However, it is only the analysis of the complex interplay of political actors, administrations, and target groups that can reveal whether and why a measure has been implemented or not. This requires an in-depth process analysis of the use of these resources across different political/administrative units.

47.2.1.4 *Evaluating Policy Impact*

The evaluation of the impact of a policy measure is the most challenging task of policy effectiveness analysis. The measurement of impact refers to the mid- and long-term effects of a policy measure, as defined by the "ultimate" goal targeted by a policy measure related to a change in human behavior or in societal condition. Apart from a first difficulty of clearly defining what the original policy goal sought to achieve, there is the problem of identifying a causal link. If the goals have been clearly defined and are easily measurable, this task is straightforward. If the goals are more vaguely defined, the standard by which to evaluate the impact becomes more difficult. Thus, reducing unemployment constitutes a clearly defined goal and is accessible to quantitative measuring. In contrast, improving human health is a goal much more difficult to operationalize. Each definition of what constitutes "human health" would by necessity be very selective and focus on only a few important aspects of human health. The second thorny problem in evaluating the impact of a specific policy measure is the causality problem.[9] It is very difficult to clearly trace an impact to a specific policy measure while controlling for all other possible factors that might have had an influence on the impact. In the case of reduction of unemployment the specific training measure may have had an impact, but at the same time a reduction of unemployment may also have been caused by an upturn of the economy or a change in the demographic structure of a population, to name but two possibilities.

Methodologically, attempts at measuring the impact of a policy measure are made by conducting quasi-experiments or by large-*n* quantitative statistical data analysis. The underlying idea in both cases is to control for all possible influence factors except one, the policy measure in question, in order to observe whether the latter did produce a difference with respect to the goal pursued. In the case of quasi-experiments two units (e.g. school classes) are compared. One class receives a treatment, the other does not. It is observed whether the treatment produced the expected impact. All relevant factors except the treatment variable are controlled for by randomly allocating students to one or the other class. In the case of the large-*n* statistical procedures, a regression analysis is run for a large sample in order to see whether those who have been subject to the policy measure—controlling for all other possible influence factors—reveal an impact in their behavior.[10]

47.2.1.5 *Evaluation and Policy Termination*

A negative evaluation of the effectiveness of a policy measure may be followed by the dismantling of the measure in question. Whether or not a coalition favorable to dismantling the measure will be successful depends on the comparative political costs of terminating the policy. If opposed by a strong political coalition with matching bargaining power, termination is unlikely to materialize.[11] In some instances, under the so-called "sunset legislation," a policy measure from the very beginning has been introduced only for a limited period of time.

47.2.2 Evaluating Policy Effectiveness in the EU

The effectiveness of European policy-making has been subject to a number of evaluation exercises conducted by EU institutions, member states, private consultants, and academic researchers. Fields subject to evaluation include regional/structural funds/cohesion policy; agricultural policy; environmental policy; transport policy; policies on freedom, security, and justice; economic policy; and research policy. According to the point in time or policy-making phase in which an evaluation is conducted, one may distinguish between *ex ante* evaluations, process evaluations/monitoring, and *ex post* evaluations of the effectiveness of a specific policy measure.

Ex ante evaluations or impact assessments seek to calculate the likely costs and benefits of a specific measure before it has been adopted at the political decision-making level. An ambitious *ex ante* evaluation of legislative measures has been the initiative of Better Regulation launched by the renewed Lisbon Strategy focusing on growth and jobs while taking into account social and environmental objectives. The initiative seeks to simplify and improve existing regulation and better design new regulation in order to enforce the effectiveness of regulation. The strategy wants to achieve this by simplification, reduction of administrative burdens, and *ex ante* impact assessments of all regulatory measures,[12] and thereby serve as an aid to political decision-making. The so-called "integrated approach" to the impact assessment of a policy measure was introduced in 2002. It evaluates the likely impact of a measure in economic policy from the perspective of social and environmental affairs. In environmental policy, Sustainability Impact Assessments and Environmental Impact Assessments have been conducted for a number of years. The likely impact of a measure is assessed in scientific terms, but also by wide-ranging consultations with stakeholders. At present all policy initiatives and legislative proposals of the Commission are required to undergo an impact assessment. For this purpose the Commission has developed guidelines on how to conduct them. One of these guidelines includes a standard measurement of the likely administrative costs of a policy measure. In an inter-institutional agreement on better law-making, the European Parliament, the Council, and the Commission agreed on a common approach to impact assessment and defined a set of traffic rules that the institutions will follow in relation to the preparation and use of impact assessment in the legislative process. These rules include a coherent view of the impact, the widening of the possible instrument choices, the consultation of stakeholders, and enhanced transparency (see below). After an external evaluation of the original method of impact assessment, the guidelines were revised, stressing the need to enhance the monitoring of the implementation process of a policy measure.[13]

47.2.2.1 *Process-Evaluation Monitoring*

The implementation process which produces policy outcomes and, ultimately, an impact of European policies is a highly complex process of interaction between and within European institutions (the Commission, the Council of Ministers, the European Parliament, and the ECJ). Moreover, during this process actors of these institutions interact with other levels of government, interest groups, and non-governmental organizations and civil society. This underlines how complex the paths of decision-making and implementation are that lead to specific outcomes and impacts.[14] An example of the constant monitoring of outcomes during the process of implementation is provided by science and research policy, i.e. the Commission-funded research projects. Scientists conducting research during the implementation of the projects are obligated to regularly submit interim results of their research activities—the so-called "deliverables"—allowing the Commission to monitor research results during the process of implementation.[15]

47.2.2.2 *Ex Post Evaluation*

Ex post evaluation of different fields of European policies has been conducted for many years in structural funds policy/cohesion policy; agricultural policy; environmental policy; policies on freedom, security, and justice. In *regional/structural funds policy* various modes of evaluation have been used. All of the criteria and procedures have been critically debated and later revised. The most important criteria have been financial accountability, improved planning, and quality and performance. Methodologically, regional policy evaluation has been haunted by many measurement problems when assessing the effectiveness of structural funds provision on economic growth. While some econometric studies find a positive and statistically significant impact, others find the opposite.[16]

The procedure of evaluation has been subject to criticism as well. It has been decentralized and, therefore, the mode of conducting evaluations have varied greatly across member states. The quality of the evaluation entirely depends on the varying endeavors of individual member states.[17] Another contested issue has been the desirability of a top-down versus a bottom-up approach. The discussion around the organization of the evaluation of rural development programs may serve as an illustration of this debate. The bottom-up approach[18] is based on the assumption that local development factors are very important in determining the outcome and impact of a policy. Therefore, the LEADER program of the Commission is to evaluate local policy-making taking into account the locally diverse contexts of implementation of European policies.[19]

In the area of *Freedom, Security, and Justice*, a particularly diverse area of European policy-making, the Commission set up a system of policy evaluation in 2006, established a unit in JHA to shape and monitor the implementation and monitoring of the adopted measures, and submitted a first report in 2007. Information has been systematically collected on the main instruments used for each policy objective.[20] To achieve a systematic, objective, and balanced evaluation, information input is also sought from stakeholders (Hague Programme). Evaluation in this area explicitly covers all stages of the policy-making progress outlined above and particularly emphasizes the involvement of stakeholders and transparency.

Evaluating policy measures in *transport policy* from the viewpoint of sustainability may serve as an example of a particularly challenging task. Sustainability is a notoriously vague concept, defined as an evolving process of improving management systems with an endpoint not known in advance. For transport policy a number of principles have been developed such as access, equity, individual and community responsibility, health and safety, public participation, integrated planning, and pollution prevention.[21] These vague principles are very hard to evaluate against empirical data unless translated into more objective, but unavoidably more selective, criteria.

Finally, an important example of European *economic policy* evaluation is provided by the SAPIR report on the "Lisbon Agenda for a Growing Europe." The Lisbon agenda meant to make the EU "the most competitive, dynamic and know-how-oriented area with sustainable economic growth, increased social cohesion and rapidly growing standard of life in the new member states" and evaluated the economic efficiency of the European economic system as regards homogeneous markets and related micro- and macroeconomic policies (monetary union and EU budget). The results were measured in terms of economic growth, economic stability, cohesion but also in terms of economic governance.[22]

47.3 TRANSPARENCY IN THE CONTEXT OF THE POLICY CYCLE

Securing transparency as to the substance and the process of political decision-making requires specific conditions and procedures which differ according to the stage of problem definition, agenda setting, political decision-making, policy implementation, evaluation, and termination/continuation. Many of the preconditions are similar to those necessary for the evaluation of policy effectiveness, since an evaluation can only be conducted if enough information is available regarding potential policy problems, the shaping of the agenda, the adoption of policy outputs, and the underlying decision-making processes, as well as the implementation of these policy decisions by administrative and societal actors.

47.3.1 Transparency: Problem Definition and Agenda Setting

Transparency at the stage of problem definition requires accessibility to the debate about which problem (aspect) is to be regarded as a policy problem. This basically means accessibility to the media, and multiple media jointly allow for an unbiased presentation of the debate, informing about the different views of social and political groups as to what aspects of a problem call for political action and reporting about possible political conflicts about which problem aspect is considered to be salient and in need of political action. Why a specific problem definition emerges from a political power struggle eludes transparency. The underlying implicit or explicit bargaining processes between political actors are not out in the open. Whether it appears on the agenda of a government may be seen from the policy goals defined by a governing coalition.

47.3.2 Transparency: Policy Formulation and Policy Outputs

Transparency requirements in the stage of policy formulation relate to the decision-making process as such as well as to its outputs—the substantive policy results. How did the competent political decision-makers arrive at the decision that subsequently is binding for the entire polity? Having access to information about how a policy decision came about, which actors participated in the decision-making process, who took which policy stance, and why a specific decision-making output was produced constitutes the core of transparency requirements. The legislative bodies with their directly elected representatives are the ones to whom the transparency requests are addressed. The political arenas in question are the plenaries of a parliament, but also the parliamentary committees. Executive bodies are less likely to be confronted with transparency requirements as regards internal decision-making processes.

47.3.3 Transparency: Implementation and Policy Outcomes

Transparency in the implementing phase refers to how the resources to realize a policy measure are allocated. While the evaluation question examines the relationship between policy goal and allocated resources, the transparency issue raises the question of where and to what extent these implementing decisions were taken. While the administrative processes of decision-making are unlikely to be governed by transparency rules, the results of the decision-making processes may be questioned by citizens, by asking for the reasons for a decision or by using the institution of the ombudsman.

47.3.4 Transparency: Evaluation and Policy Impact

When evaluating the impact of a policy measure and considering its possible termination, transparency and access to the results of the evaluation are crucial. Transparency rules would describe the type of data accessible to which persons and how the latter could avail themselves of these data.

47.3.5 Transparency Measures in European Policy-Making

European transparency measures—depending on which phase of the policy cycle they refer to—may be of a process- or output/outcomes/impact-related nature. It was the Treaty of Maastricht which first introduced the demand for transparency into EU politics in the form of access to information and the introduction of a European Ombudsman as an instrument of public scrutiny and an instrument against maladministration.[23] Access to documents was the first aspect of transparency to be introduced in European policy-making. The Maastricht Treaty included a Declaration on the right of access to information, recommending that the Commission should draft a report on measures designed to improve public access to information of the institutions. While the Declaration was vaguely formulated, the fact of its adoption was significant. As a result, the Commission and the Council adopted a code of conduct specifying the conditions under which access to information could be requested.[24] The Council altered its rules of procedure. The practices of the Council still remained quite restrictive. The Amsterdam Treaty in the new Art. 255 EC Treaty introduced a right of access to documents, subject to detailed rules set out in secondary European Community legislation in 1997. After long inter-institutional negotiations the Regulation of 2001 adopted rules on access to documents held by the Council, the Commission, and the European Parliament.[25] Even before the Amsterdam Treaty the rules of access to information had spread horizontally to practically all other EU bodies. The Regulation of 2001—applicable to all three pillars of EU activity—still contained a number of very vaguely formulated provisions which were gradually further developed under the influence of ECJ rulings and Ombudsman recommendations.[26] It was subsequently amended to facilitate the access to legislative and non-legislative documents of the European Parliament following an ECJ ruling of 2008. The ruling stated that opinions of the Council's legal service relating to any piece of legislation should be made public. This includes documents originating from member states and received by EU institutions, which should be disclosed after consultation with those member states.[27]

Access to documents, however, constitutes only one aspect of transparency. The latter also requires that the European institutions apply an active policy of spreading information,[28] that it extend transparency to the decision-making process as such (e.g. make the Council of Ministers discuss in public), and that it allow for citizen input (stakeholder consultation).[29] Thus, the Commission's White Paper on Governance (2001) mentions openness as a key to good governance and calls for more cooperation with civil society and the involvement of private parties in the implementation of EU policies. This demand was taken up in the Laeken Declaration and invoked as a central requirement of legitimate governance in Europe. The idea of holding a Convention to draft a Constitution of Europe was closely linked to this more demanding notion and is one of the most salient outcomes of the call for transparency.

47.3.5.1 *Transparency in the Drafting Stage*

When analyzing transparency measures according to policy stages, impact assessments which are conducted before the adoption of legislation may be considered as an important instrument to create transparency about the likely costs and benefits of a planned measure at an early point in time. Impact assessments now have to be conducted for all major policy initiatives. This produced information is subject to transparency requirements. The Better Regulation Strategy mentioned above calls for impact assessment road maps and impact assessment reports, all published on the impact assessment website, accessible to the public.[30]

Similarly, the European Transparency Initiative of 2007 constitutes an important instance of creating transparency at an early stage of decision-making. It requires European institutions to provide information on which interest groups lobbied the institutions in order to influence legislative drafts. For this purpose, a voluntary register for interest representatives was introduced in 2008, linked to a corresponding code of conduct and a monitoring and enforcement mechanism.[31] The stances of interest groups on specific items of legislation should therefore be available to the public on the Commission's website.

47.3.5.2 *Decision-Making Stage*

The rules of procedure of the European Parliament require "utmost transparency" of its activities. This relates to the debates in the plenary and the debates in committees. The committees' agenda, however, is divided into items open and items closed to the public.[32] The Council, in 2005, decided to open to the public the part of their meetings falling under co-decision. The European Ombudsman has concretized the requirements of openness in decision-making processes. For instance, he stated that that the Commission fails to establish a comprehensive register for all the documents it produces and receives. The reason is that the code on access to documents allows for a restriction of the types of documents placed on its public register: only formally transmitted documents by or to an institution are recorded by the Commission.[33]

47.3.5.3 *Implementation Stage*

The access to information regulation allows for some transparency of administrative decision output during implementation. The way in which access to information is handled in member states varies to a great extent. The European Ombudsman can lend support to citizens in actually claiming these rights.

47.4 LINKS BETWEEN EVALUATING EFFECTIVENESS AND TRANSPARENCY

Transparency and the evaluation of policy effectiveness are linked in various ways. Transparency may be a functional prerequisite for the evaluation of policy effectiveness. It may reinforce effective evaluation. However, under specific conditions transparency may also undermine policy effectiveness.

Transparency may be considered a precondition for the evaluation of policy effectiveness since—without information about how a policy has been implemented, or what its outcomes and impact are—an evaluation would not be feasible. Effectiveness may be improved by procedural transparency in the case of the consultation of stakeholders. Since they deal on a daily basis with the issue to be regulated, their views on a legislative draft can contribute to a substantive improvement of the contents of a policy and thereby increase the possibility that the latter will be successful. Finally, however, it is also conceivable that a policy's success may be put at risk if it is subject to transparency requirements and exposure to public attention.[34] A case in point would be the negotiation of a peace agreement in a high-conflict situation.

47.5 CONCLUSION

This chapter analyzed the evaluation of policy effectiveness and transparency in public policy-making from the viewpoint of different policy-making stages. It argued that the evaluation of policy effectiveness depends on a prior problem definition, the output of the political decision-making process, and the implementation of a policy measure. It described core activities of policy evaluation practices as applied in various areas of European policy-making. Providing for transparency of policy-making involves different measures, too, depending on the stage in the policy cycle at which transparency is to be guaranteed. The chapter discussed important steps for the introduction of greater openness in European policy-making and discussed their various forms. Finally, it described possible links between the evaluation of effectiveness of policy-making and transparency, in one case transparency reinforcing while in the other undercutting effectiveness.

NOTES

1. See for instance M. Howlett and M. Ramesh, *Studying Public Policy. Policy Cycles and Policy Subsystems* (Toronto and New York: Oxford University Press, 2003); Guy Peters, "The Policy Process: An Institutionalist Perspective," *Canadian Public Administration Review* 35, no. 2 (1992), 160–80; P. A. Sabatier and D. A. Mazmanian, "The Implementation of Public Policy: A Framework of Analysis," *Policy Studies Journal* 8, no. 4 (1980), 538–60; A. Windhoff-Héritier, *Policy- Analyse. Eine Einführung* (Frankfurt a.M, New York: Campus, 1983); A. Windhoff-Héritier, *Policy-Analyse* (Frankfurt a.M: Campus, 1987).
2. D. Dery, *Problem Definition in Policy Analysis* (Lawrence, KS: University Press of Kansas, 1984); Roger Cobb, Jennie-Keith Ross, and Marc Howard Ross, "Agenda Building as a Comparative Political Process," *The American Political Science Review* 70, no. 1 (1976), 126–38; Windhoff-Héritier, *Policy-Analyse*; J. W. Kingdon, *Agendas, Alternatives, and Public Policies* (New York: Harper Collins, 1984); Adrienne Héritier, *Policy-Analyse: Kritik und Neuorientierung* (PVS-Sonderheft: Opladen, 1993).

3. M. Edelman, *The Symbolic Uses of Politics* (Urbana, IL: University of Illinois Press, 1964); W. Riker, *The Art of Political Manipulation* (New Haven, CT: Yale University Press, 1986).

4. P. A. Hall, "Policy Paradigms, Social Learning and the State: The Case of Economic Policymaking in Britain," *Comparative Politics* 25 (1993), 275–96; A. M. Jacobs, "How Do Ideas Matter? Mental Models and Attention in German Pension Politics," *Comparative Political Studies* 42, no. 2 (2009), 252–79.

5. F. R. Baumgartner and B. D. Jones, eds, *Policy Dynamics* (Chicago; London: University of Chicago Press, 2002); Hall, "Policy Paradigms, Social Learning and the State."

6. A. Przeworski and H. Teune, *The Logic of Comparative Social Inquiry* (New York: John Wiley & Sons, 1970).

7. See among many others, D. Swank and H. G. Betz, "Globalization, the Welfare State and Right-Wing Populism in Western Europe," *Socio-Economic Review* 1, no. 2 (2002), 215–45; E. Huber, C. C. Ragin, and J. D. Stephens, "Social Democracy, Christian Democracy, Constitutional Structure, and the Welfare State," *American Journal of Sociology* 99, no. 3 (1993), 711–49.

8. J. L. Pressman and A. Wildavsky, *Implementation: How Great Expectations in Washington are Dashed in Oakland* (Los Angeles, CA: University of California Press, 1973); E. Bardach, *The Eight-Step Path of Policy Analysis: A Handbook for Practice* (Berkeley, CA: Berkeley Academic Press, 1997); D. A. Mazmanian and P. A. Sabatier, *Implementation and Public Policy* (Glenview, IL: Scott, Foresman, 1983); A. Windhoff-Héritier, *Politikimplementation. Ziel und Wirklichkeit politischer Entscheidungen* (Königstein/Ts: Hain, 1980); R. Mayntz, *Implementation politischer Programme* (Opladen: Westdeutscher Verlag, 1983); R. B. Ripley and G. A. Franklin, *Congress, the Bureaucracy, and Public Policy* (Homewood, IL: The Dorsey Press, 1984).

9. G.-M. Hellstern and H. Wollmann, eds, *Handbuch zur Evaluationsforschung. Bd. 1* (Opladen: Westdeutscher Verlag, 1984); C. Hirschon Weiss, "The Interface between Evaluation and Public Policy," *Evaluation* 5, no. 4 (1999), 468–86.

10. For inferential problems see, for instance, D. A. Freedman, "Statistical Models for Causation: What Inferential Leverage Do They Provide?," *Evaluation Review* 30 (2006), 691–713.

11. J. E. Frantz, "Reviving and Revisiting a Termination Model," *Policy Sciences* 25, no. 1 (1992), 175–86; J. E. Frantz and H. Sato, "Political Resources for Policy Terminators," *Policy Studies Journal* 30, no. 1 (2002), 11–18; P. deLeon, *Democracy and the Policy Sciences* (Albany, NY: State University of New York Press, 1997); M. Bauer and C. Knill, *Politikabbau im europäischen Mehrebenensystem: Nationale Beendigungseffekte europaischer Politik* (manuscript, 2007).

12. C. M. Radaelli, "Whither Better Regulation for the Lisbon Agenda?," *Journal of European Public Policy* 14, no. 2 (2007), 190–207; ec.europa.eu/governance/better_regulation 2009/01/28.

13. ec.europa.eu/governance/better_regulation 2009/01/28.

14. F. McGowan, *The Policy-Making Process in the European Union* (TRANS-TALK Workshop "Policy and Project Evaluation": Brussels, 2000).

15. NewGov Integrated Project funded by the ECE FP6.

16. L. Hooghe and M. Keating, "The Politics of European Union Regional Policy," *Journal of European Public Policy* 1, no. 3 (1994), 367–93; S. Dall'Erba and H. L. F. de Groot, "A Meta-Analysis of EU Regional Policy Evaluation" (manuscript, 2005).

17. S. C. E. Batterbury, "Principles and Purposes of European Union Cohesion Policy Evaluation," *Regional Studies* 40, no. 2 (2006), 179–88; M. Baslé, "Strengths and Weaknesses of European Union Policy Evaluation Methods: Ex-Post Evaluation of Objective 2 1994–99," *Regional Studies* 40, no. 2 (2006), 225–36.

18. R. F. Elmore, "Backward Mapping: Implementation Research and Policy Decisions," *Political Science Quarterly* 94, no. 4 (1979), 601–16.

19. E. Saraceno, "The Evaluation of Local Policy Making in Europe," *Evaluation* 5, no. 4 (1999), 439–57.

20. J. Monar, "The EU's 'Constitutional Crisis' and the Area of Freedom, Security and Justice: Implementation of the Constitution through the Backdoor?," in N. Neuwahl and S. Haack, eds, *Unresolved Issues of the Constitution for Europe. Rethinking the Crisis* (Montreal: Themis, 2007), 309–32.

21. R. Klaus and S. Weinreich, "Criteria for Evaluation Towards Sustainability," in L. Giorgi and A. D. Pearman, eds, *Policy and Project Evaluation in Transport* (Aldershot: Ashgate, 2002), 242–92.

22. A. Sapir, P. Aghion, G. Bertola, M. Hellwig, J. Pisani-Ferry, D. Rosati, J. Viñals, H. Wallace, M. Buti, M. Nava, and P. M. Smith, *An Agenda for a Growing Europe: The Sapir Report* (Oxford: Oxford University Press, 2004).

23. S. C. Van Bijsterveld, *The Empty Throne: Democracy and the Rule of Law in Transition* (Utrecht: Lemma, 2002).

24. Council Decision 93/731/EC Public Access to Council Documents; Commission Decision 94/90/ECSC Access to Information.

25. V. Deckmyn, ed., *Increasing Transparency in the European Union* (Maastricht: European Institute of Public Administration, 2002).

26. S. Peers, "From Maastricht to Laeken: The Political Agenda of Openness and Transparency in the European Union," in V. Deckmyn, ed., *Increasing Transparency in the European Union* (Maastricht: European Institute of Public Administration, 2002), 7–32.

27. Press Release European Parliament March 11, 2009.

28. Deckmyn, *Increasing Transparency in the European Union*.

29. E. Best, "Transparency and European Governance: Clearly Not a Simple Matter," in Deckmyn, *Increasing Transparency in the European Union*, 91–118.

30. ECE Better Regulation, available at: <http://ec.europa.eu/governance/better_regulation>.

31. CEC SEC 2008 1926.

32. Rules of procedure of the European Parliament, July 2009.

33. See <http://Europe.ifj.org.en/articles>.

34. A. Fung, M. Graham, and D. Weil, *Full Disclosure: The Perils and Promise of Transparency* (New York: Cambridge University Press, 2007).

CHAPTER 48

....

IDENTITY AND SOLIDARITY

....

ERIK JONES

THREE major questions in research on European integration consider how Europeans see themselves, how they see one another, and how they interact. The first two questions concern different aspects of identity; the third deals with solidarity. All three are interrelated.

That interrelationship is a problem for researchers. As identity theorists are quick to point out, how we see ourselves in any given context is a loose function of alternative possibilities, also known as the "other." Hence in a room full of Chinese, a Greek and a German may see themselves and each other as Europeans. In a room full of Germans, a Greek might see himself as European but it is likely that the Germans would still regard him as a Greek. These changing perceptions can also influence behavior. Children often complain that their friends treat them one way in the neighborhood and another way at school; adults do the same thing only in bigger arenas. Consider the fate of second- and third-generation immigrants. Even where they have European passports, educations, languages, and accents, they are often treated as though they come from abroad.[1]

Interaction over time only makes matters worse. Identities are not essential characteristics and relationships are not fixed either. Instead, experience shapes both self-identification and perceptions of other groups or individuals; how we relate to others is adaptive as well. Moreover, such changes are endogenous to processes of identification and interaction rather than being driven only by external forces. The brutal reality of German conduct during World War II had a powerful influence on West German attitudes toward the European project that came after. The relative isolation of East Germany both from Western Europe and from its own Nazi past influenced perceptions rather differently.[2]

Finally it is important to distinguish identity from utility, and affection from gain. In essence the question is whether people relate to Europe because of what it is or because of what it offers. Even if both factors are important, it would be interesting to know which has the greater sway.[3] Unfortunately, the boundaries between a sense of belonging and a perception of advantage are difficult to determine; interest is inextricably bound up in self.

With all this complexity, it is no wonder that researchers work hard to isolate discrete components and sharp contrasts. For example, some focus on support for integration while others look at the balance between identification with supranational, national, and sub-national levels. It is also possible to find contributions that focus on support for enlargement or the projection of European values abroad while others choose to examine the rejection of Europe and the embrace of exclusive identities. Some look for evidence of a cosmopolitan Europe; others worry about European xenophobia. The scholars who work in this area not only look for different aspects of identity and solidarity, but they also use a range of different tools and techniques. Subject-directed interviews, focus groups, elite surveys, and public opinion polling lie at one side of the spectrum; historical narrative, process tracing, discourse analysis, and mythology lie at the other. With such diversity of interest and attention, the literature is vast and yet also fragmented.

The temptation when confronted with such diversity of interests and approaches is to push for ever greater specificity in the debate—moving "beyond identity" as a broad concept and embracing different notions of identification or interaction in its place. There is much to be accomplished with such a strategy. Nevertheless, the stakes of achieving a synthesis in this wide-ranging debate are high. Issues of identity and solidarity lie at the heart of our understanding of European integration as a process, they hold the key to its legitimation, and they undergird its stability. They tell us what is Europe, whether and why we should embrace it, and how long it may last. The idea of being European as a category in practice is not in doubt. Self-declared Europeans are easy to find, as are appeals to European identity and solidarity. The challenge is to understand what it means to be European. Categories of practice cannot achieve that objective. Hence, we must also preserve Europe, European identity, and European solidarity as categories for analysis.[4]

The purpose of this chapter is to link the literature on identity and solidarity to those wider considerations of legitimacy, stability, and purpose. My argument is that while the literature is complicated, it is also worth the effort. That argument has five parts. The first introduces the notion that identity may play a causal role in the European process. The second suggests that identity may be less cause than effect. The third looks at the interaction between multiple identities. The fourth makes the link to religion, ethnicity, and immigration. And the fifth concludes with implications for our understanding of European integration.

48.1 IDENTITY AS CAUSALITY

The notion of identity as causality derives from the study of nationalism. In the 1950s, Karl Deutsch wondered whether the same forces behind processes of national integration could give rise to a coherent, stable, and self-preserving Atlantic Community. With the negotiation of the 1958 Rome Treaty, his focus of attention shifted to Europe.

Deutsch's argument is compellingly simple. As different groups interact they begin to build relations of trust and mutual understanding. Eventually, the density of these relationships makes it possible for political leaders to forge appeals that cross not only groups but also the class divisions within them. These appeals identify a project based on common values and mutual responsiveness; they promote a distinctive way of life, they promise to accelerate growth, and they create "an expectation of joint economic reward."[5]

Initially such appeals circulate among elites. Once they find a receptive popular audience, however, the process of integration can "take off." Community building becomes the goal and support for integration consolidates as a political force. Both identity and solidarity are implicit in this argument. They can be found in the common values and mutual responsiveness at its core. The agency lies in the cross-class, inter-group coalition that forms around specific conceptions of identity and solidarity. Therefore if we can recognize those conceptions at the outset and at the same time assess the strength of their appeal, we should be able to anticipate the success with which the subsequent multi-group or multi-ethnic community will form.[6]

There are two qualifications to the argument. The first is that the application of nation-building models to wider processes of integration should not be confused with an assertion that what is happening at the European level is a form of nationalism per se. Deutsch was always careful to distinguish between the specific and the general in that respect. He also conceded that Europe showed little evidence of ethnic or linguistic assimilation. While useful, perhaps, he viewed such assimilation as "non-essential."[7] Europe was no more likely to become a nation state than any multi-ethnic empire was likely to undergo a similar transformation. The distinctiveness of Europe, however, does not rule out the possibility that a coherent European community will emerge via a similar causal mechanism. By analogy, empires can develop along the same lines as nation states while remaining categorically distinct.[8]

The second qualification is that neither identity nor solidarity can be measured directly. It is possible to measure the density of interaction between groups and it is possible to survey their attitudes and opinions—both toward one another and toward their common project both before and after integration starts (or over time along the way). Nevertheless, such measures only approximate the real forces at work within the underlying causal mechanism and so it is useful to incorporate as many different and parallel techniques for data collection as possible. These include but are not limited to the survey (or discourse analysis) of newspaper editorials, face-to-face interviews with elites, public opinion polling, and the like.

Once Deutsch set out to test whether Europe was moving along that causal pathway almost a decade after the negotiation of the Rome Treaty, he came back disappointed: "The spectacular development of formal European treaties and institutions since the mid-1950s has not been matched by any deeper integration of actual behavior."[9] By that he meant that national identities had strengthened and enthusiasm for or interest in European integration as a project had faltered. Specifically in France and Germany, but presumably elsewhere as well, elites and voters were not moving toward common values. And while elites and masses may support integration in principle, they did not agree on what Europe was meant to offer. Moreover, Deutsch did not anticipate that the situation would change within the coming decade, if ever. Hence he concluded his analysis by questioning whether the opportunity to unite Europe would be missed.

Deutsch's pessimistic findings met two different types of criticism—one concerning measurement, the other concerning mechanism. The measurement problem was generational. By surveying public opinion in the present and then projecting attitudes into the future, Deutsch made two assumptions. He assumed that the same people would be around to influence events and he assumed that their personal views might or might not change in the meantime. Yet both of these beliefs may be wrong. Older participants in the survey cohort may no longer hold positions of influence and personal values may be immutable even if the aggregation of those values across society changes over time. Ronald Inglehart made both challenges by disaggregating his survey data into generational cohorts. What he discovered was that younger cohorts showed more support for and identification with the project of European integration than their older counterparts. This led him to suggest that values are received at a given point in time through socialization processes and, once imbedded, that individuals continue to adhere to the same core set of values with only minor degradation for the rest of their lives. There may be some volatility in public opinion polling outcomes due to changes in issue salience, but the broad constellation of values held by individuals should remain relatively stable over time.[10]

Having changed the measurement, however, it was also possible for Inglehart to challenge the mechanism. Rather than having the adoption of a common identity precede the political project of integration, the causality may run the other way around. Young people who have first-hand experience with the benefits of integration may feel more European in response. Their socialization at a young age may make them more supportive of the project later on. Indeed, "awareness" of the integration process may be sufficient to spark the change.[11] The implication here is not that Deutsch was wrong to focus attention on the convergence of attitudes and values as a precursor to integration. Rather it is that the process is more strongly self-reinforcing than Deutsch anticipated in his own analysis of "take off."

Then again it may be possible that integration does not depend upon popular support—or even elite consensus—for its own progress, at least at the early stages if not later on. By measuring the progress of European integration in terms of tangible outputs, it should be possible to check the correlation between what Europe has accomplished with how much support it has garnered along the way. During those early years, the evidence was clear cut. Beneath the high drama in the Council of Ministers, the institutions of Europe continued to expand their output irrespective of popular attitudes.[12] This growth in activity may have yielded dividends in terms of greater popular support and awareness but it did not rely on those factors to get off the ground.

48.2 IDENTITY AS EFFECT

This notion that integration fosters an identification with Europe—including both a convergence on common values and a wider scope of interaction—has roots in the study of nationalism as well. By analogy, it is the macro-cultural version of turning "peasants into Frenchmen."[13] The implications are weaker, of course, but the basic mechanism is the same. The longer groups participate in the integration process and the more extensively they come into contact with one another and with common institutions, the stronger will be the influence of those experiences on their perception of self and group. They will learn patterns of behavior, adopt compatible roles, and become ever more self-consciously interdependent along the way. They will also come together to discuss and narrate their common experience, generating short-hand accounts (or myths) to explain both how they came to participate and why.[14] Ultimately, they will begin to internalize the values that are created and reinforced in this process and so reconstitute their interests in a manner that is more consistent with the community as a whole. The experience of participation will no longer seem foreign and they will identify with the wider community as a result.

There is an appealing logic to this line of argument. Nevertheless, it raises considerable methodological challenges as a focus for research. It assumes that institutionalized communities like the EU are the most important, defining, fora for interaction, when it is clear that other transnational communities exist in Europe (Nordic, Alpine, Mediterranean, Catholic, Protestant, West, East, and so forth) and significant historical cleavage points abound. We may like to imagine that Europe reinvented itself *tabula rasa* soon after the end of World War II, but other historical events—and the unions and divisions they created—loom equally large.[15]

More to the point, it is unclear how we could ever recognize an internalization of new identities until well after the fact. And there is even less reason to believe that the effects of such an internalization would be permanent. Hence what seems like a deterministic mechanism in theory is impossible to distinguish from a highly contingent one in practice.[16] For example, even if Inglehart is right both in terms of the socialization of values at a given age of development and about the influence of environmental factors (such as relative scarcity) on that process, the more intensive interaction offered via European integration is layered onto Inglehart's socialization and does not replace it. Indeed, Inglehart's subsequent research on national cultures has shown that the differences across countries are persistent.[17]

A deeper concern is that Europe is a community in which only a handful of Europeans participate. Where Karl Deutsch's notion of identity as causality rested on the success of cross-class appeals, a European identity as effect may be limited to those with the education, inclination, and resources to interact across national boundaries. This is the prospect raised by Neil Fligstein, who uses a wide range of demographic and public opinion polling data to identify those elements of national societies most likely to be influenced by the spread of European culture, myths, and norms. What he finds is that only 10–15 percent of Europeans have substantial contact with people from other countries, with the remainder divided roughly equally between those who have infrequent contact and those who have essentially none at all. In this sense, European identity reinforces class divisions rather than crossing them. In essence, it is the opposite of what Deutsch intended.[18]

The effect is likely to be even stronger for small countries which have correspondingly small and tightly knit political elites. The recent history of Denmark, for example, shows a consistent pattern of differentiation in support for Europe: the socialization of elites leads them to favor the project while the masses remain more skeptical.[19] The problem may be reinforced by the relative exclusion of small languages. More intense interaction places ever greater efficiency premiums on having a single language for cross-cultural communication. By implication, it also creates greater incentives for those willing and able to master the cross-cultural vernacular. Popular identification with Europe can only suffer as a result.[20]

The political implications of these findings are significant. Fligstein's analysis suggests that the balance of popular support for European integration rests not with the putative Euro-enthusiasts, but with that group in society which has some, and yet only limited contact with people from other European countries. The process of European integration can count on receiving support only so long as this group remains committed. If this group sometimes thinks of itself as European, it also embraces its national identity. This is why the coexistence of unity and diversity in Europe is so important. Should European integration come to be perceived as threatening to national identity, then it is likely to trigger a groundswell of opposition as well.[21] Should elites fail to rally in defense of the European project, such opposition would likely get more intense.[22] Indeed, this appears to be what happened during the 2005 referendum on the European Constitutional Treaty in the Netherlands. Neither economic interests nor the level of interaction across borders played a significant role in determining the referendum outcome. Instead, the Dutch voters rejected the European Constitutional Treaty because they distrusted their national politicians, because they feared immigration, and because they perceived the EU to be a "cultural threat."[23]

48.3 MULTIPLE IDENTITIES

There is no necessary competition between national and European identity. On the contrary, it is possible for people to hold many different identities at once and to use them differentially as well. That was the point about the Greeks and the Germans at the beginning of this chapter. It is also a recurrent theme in the literature. Moreover, it is a theme that resonates strongly with the peculiar institutional structure of Europe. If the EU is a multilevel polity, then it is no surprise that European citizens should have a multilevel identity structure as well. The same could be said about European countries with strong regional or multinational traditions like the United Kingdom, Spain, Italy, or Belgium. This layering of identities is not a sign of illness; if anything, it is a symptom of good health.[24]

The strength of this position about multiple European identities is that it marries the process of socialization among groups with a process of "Europeanization" across institutions at different levels of government. Although it is true that direct socialization at the European level is limited to a small segment of society, as Fligstein argues, it is nevertheless also true that socialization for the rest of society takes places within a national, regional, or local context. Therefore if those other levels of aggregation are being permeated by European norms and values, then the socialization processes they foster must be similarly permeated as well. The result will not be a perfect convergence of identities across Europe. On the contrary, the persistent differences noted by Inglehart (and others) will remain just that, persistent. Nevertheless, the general pattern of identification will shift to become one that is more coherent and more resilient across the EU as a whole. This is the claim made by Thomas Risse in his analysis of the Europeanization of "public spheres."[25]

The implications of Risse's argument are striking for two reasons. The first is that Risse's causal argument builds on foundations of discourse and framing. That is why Risse focuses on public spheres of discourse rather than more narrowly defined political institutions.[26] Identities do not have essential characteristics anymore than individuals have essential identities. Instead, people have to be made aware of their identities and they also need to be mobilized in response to them. Of course it is not always true that European discourse fosters common norms or conventions. On the contrary, efforts to push strong normative positions—like the isolation of Jörg Haider's Austrian Freedom Party—have occasionally proven to be fragile.[27] Nevertheless, Risse marshals considerable evidence that they can be successful in fostering a self-reinforcing pattern of identification and institution-building over the longer term.

Yet if discourse and framing have causal significance, then it should be possible to move the debate in a normative direction as well as a positive one. Even if we cannot find a large group of unambiguously "European" Europeans, we can still recognize the core components of a European identity. By bringing these elements to the center of public debate, we can open a dialogue about their relative merits and shed harsh light on the alternatives. This is the essence of John McCormick's "Europeanism." Ostensibly McCormick offers an ideology rather than an identity—hence the "ism." Nevertheless, it is clear that the emergence of a European identity is a final objective. Drawing on work from Jacques Derrida and Jürgen Habermas, McCormick sketches a cosmopolitan European project that not only promotes welfare and justice at home but projects a model of peaceful reconciliation abroad. In this way, McCormick connects with a growing debate about Europe's external identity—and its corresponding "normative power"—as well as increasing concerns as to whether the EU must reflect the values internally that it hopes to project onto the outside world.[28]

The second implication of Risse's argument is that Europeans may become more "European" without ever necessarily being made aware of that fact. Hence when they claim to hold a national identity, they underestimate the extent to which that national identity has been changed by European integration. This is an intriguing form of cognitive dissonance that poses an important methodological dilemma. Specifically, it suggests that we should find some means to differentiate between the "subjective awareness" of identity, which may or may not change, and a more objective notion of identity "coherence," which should become more European over time. In practical terms, that distinction is hard to make. James Caporaso and Minhyung Kim—who have introduced the distinction in the study of European identity—rely on a contrast between direct expressions of identification and observable behavioral patterns. Their suggestion is that even though Europeans may not express high levels of "we-feeling," they have begun to act more and more alike (at least economically speaking).[29] Yet economic performance is only one possible manifestation of what should be a much broader pattern of social change. Hence, a sociological research agenda might focus on convergence in European "varieties of capitalism," social stratification, class structures, mobility patterns, mass media, or other value-laden structures. Unfortunately for the argument, however, such a wider sociological agenda does not provide unambiguous support. In some ways Europeans are becoming more similar; in others they are becoming more different.[30] Indeed, the same can be said about Europe's neighbors as well.[31]

The formal institutions fare little better as an indicator of value coherence as distinct from subjective awareness. There is a strong argument to be made that the jurisprudence of the EU codifies the common values that constitute a European identity. In this sense, the positive expression of normative power resides in the framework of laws, however Europeans choose to identify themselves publicly. Far more than history or culture, the people of Europe share these things in common. Nevertheless, it would be unwise to overstate the significance of those shared legal commitments. Although European law does embody important points of commonality, there is much to identity that is left out.[32] Hence while the European Constitutional Treaty held out the promise of bringing Europeans together, it also raised the risk that they would react negatively to that prospect. Instead of coming together around the European Constitutional Treaty, the voters began to push apart.[33] Once again we return to the popular referendum in the Netherlands. What is important to note in this context, however, is that the reasons the Dutch voted against the treaty were very different from the motivations in France.

48.4 RELIGION, ETHNICITY, AND IMMIGRATION

The debate over the European Constitutional Treaty also raised a number of issues that have not been explicit in the discussion thus far: religion, ethnicity, and immigration. Nevertheless, these have become the central focus of the debate about European identity—with popular books being written by firebrands touting the "Islamicization" of European culture, appealing to the "wisdom" of Enoch Powell's 1968 "rivers of blood" speech about the perils of immigration, and hinting at the genetic distinctiveness of races. "Why," Thilo Sarrazin asks in his controversial best-seller, "do other immigrants not face the same problems learning German as the Turks?"[34]

The point to note in this debate is that religion, ethnicity, and immigration are not the same—either as categories of practice or as categories of analysis.[35] Both Islam and Christianity are world religions and each contains a strong commitment to universalism. By contrast, ethnicities are exclusive. Some individuals and even groups can be assimilated, but not everyone can be a member. Finally, immigration represents a change of geographical and legal status: first you live in one country, then you live in another. Hence, children born to Italian parents whose own parents emigrated to Argentina become immigrants themselves if they take up residence in Rome. How well they speak the Italian language or enjoy other aspects of Italian culture does not change that simple fact. Hence, while religion, ethnicity, and immigration are intermingled, it is useful to treat them as distinct.[36]

Europe has suffered from religious divisions throughout its history. How else would you explain the Thirty Years War? Moreover, the Westphalian Peace never put matters completely to rest. It created a complex formula for religious cohabitation, but it did not eliminate conflicts over religious difference among Christians.[37] This was true in history and it remains true today. In the past half-century, the troubles in Northern Ireland pitted Catholics and Protestants; the wars in Yugoslavia started between Catholic Croats and Orthodox Serbs. Rocco Buttiglione was rejected as a candidate for the European Commission by a European Parliament that was suspicious of his attitudes toward women and homosexuals—attitudes which he defended as reflecting his devout Catholicism. And two predominantly Catholic countries—France and Belgium— steadfastly refused to make reference in the European Constitutional Treaty to Europe's common Christian heritage (albeit for subtly different reasons).[38]

The introduction of increasingly large numbers of Muslims into Europe did not introduce the notion of religious conflict. But it did broaden the range of religious differences—arguably much more than most Europeans realize. Not only are there differences between Christianity and Islam, but there are also important differences within Islam itself. This is obvious in Germany where Turkish immigrants are divided between Sunni and Alevi, but it is also present in other immigrant populations and in those countries like Albania, Macedonia, Bosnia, and Turkey which have substantial indigenous Islamic populations as well.

The differences in ethnicities tend to fragment and multiply religious divisions—at least for first generation immigrants and possibly for the second generation as well. Then there are new divisions that emerge in the second and third generations as children grow up educated in European languages rather than the languages of their parents. These children are more likely to worship in European languages as well, which creates a division in how Islam is practiced across successive generations.

Finally, these Islamic ethnic minorities remain nested in much larger patterns of migration across European countries as well as into Europe from the global "South." Although labor mobility remains somewhat limited in Europe, it has increased significantly over the past two decades and more particularly since the expansion of the EU in

2004. Hence the real challenge is not to eliminate the ever-increasing diversity in Europe on the altar of some common identity. It may not even be to create a separate identity to which all participants can adhere. Rather, it is to provide a framework within which the tensions created by such diversity can be reconciled. Identity is useful but solidarity is paramount.

At least part of this shift from identity to solidarity can be accomplished by strengthening the notion of citizenship. In a formal sense, citizenship confers a sense of belonging, it defines common interest, it bestows rights and it creates obligations. There may be a deeper form of identification associated with this process.[39] Common citizenship may promote feelings of tolerance as well.[40] The point to note, however, is that these feelings do not have to be shared to be effective. Citizenship is neither religion nor ethnicity; it is membership. It is not normative so much as positive. This is not to say that citizenship is devoid of norms. On the contrary, "citizenship is becoming a normative project" and the goal of that project is to promote peaceful coexistence.[41]

Nevertheless, citizenship represents only a small part of what constitutes relations between groups within Europe. Like identity, European citizenship has many levels. The most important of these levels is not European, however, it is national. European citizenship exists in a formal sense, but it floats on top of national citizenship; the rights it conveys are additional to national rights; and the main agencies for the protection of those rights (and for the enforcement of the obligations that go with them) also reside at the national level. Moreover, there is little sign that Europeans are eager to sever the link between citizenship and the nation state in any major way (if at all). The perceived threat of immigration has led many Europeans to seek a re-nationalization of citizenship. This strong re-assertiveness has become a point of contention between countries and at the European level.[42] Advocates of a true European identity ignore such contestation at their own peril.[43]

48.5 Implications

Perhaps Europe is not the right focus for questions of identity and European solidarity should feed more directly into national, rather than European, political processes. This is the conclusion reached by sociologists like Stefan Auer and Cecile Leconte, who worry about popular backlash against Europe's normative pretensions.[44] Their point is not that Europeans should avoid disagreement on normative matters; rather it is that those disagreements should be made public so that the logic or reasoning behind them can be better understood. This point is somewhat different from McCormick's more ideological form of Europeanism insofar as it does not anticipate that there will be convergence. Europeans do not need a common identity to promote European integration and common identity formation should not be viewed as a measure of European integration's success. Instead, Europeans should accept that they will be different—from one another and from new arrivals as well as from the outside world. What matters is that they live together peacefully and prosperously and not what they call each other or themselves.

Such a conclusion seems almost hopelessly idealistic. Nevertheless, it is grounded in a coherent understanding of European political legitimation. Anand Menon and Stephen Weatherill describe Europe's structure as a form of "multilevel constitutionalism" within which a complex division of labor allows for multiple levels of inputs and outputs, similarities and differences.[45] The success of this system does not lie in its elegance. Neither is it meant to inspire affection all the way down. Like the Westphalian system that preceded it, modern Europe is a complex compromise between aspirations to universality and obvious manifestations of difference. So long as it holds together, it is a success.

Notes

1. Ralph Grillow, "European Identity in a Transnational Era," in Marion Demossier, ed., *The European Puzzle: The Political Structuring of Cultural Identities at a Time of Transition* (New York: Berghahn Books, 2007), 67–9.
2. Eric Langenbacher, "Still the Unmasterable Past? The Impact of History and Memory in the Federal Republic of Germany," *German Politics* 19, no. 1 (March 2010), 24–40; Joyce Marie Mushaben, "Rethinking Citizenship and Identity: 'What it Means to be German' since the Fall of the Wall," *German Politics* 19, no. 1 (March 2010), 72–88.
3. Matthew Gabel, "Public Support for European Integration: An Empirical Test of Five Theories," *Journal of Politics* 60, no. 2 (May 1998), 333–54.
4. Rogers Brubaker and Frederick Cooper, "Beyond 'Identity'," *Theory and Society* 29, no. 1 (February 2000), 4–6.
5. Karl Deutsch, et al., *Political Community and the North Atlantic Area: International Organization in the Light of Historical Experience* (Princeton: Princeton University Press, 1957), 123–54.
6. Deutsch, et al., *Political Community and the North Atlantic Area*, 83–5.
7. Deutsch, et al., *Political Community and the North Atlantic Area*, 154–9.
8. Krishnan Kumar, "Nation-States as Empires, Empires as Nation-State: Two Principles, One Practice?," *Theory and Society* 39, no. 2 (March 2010), 119–43.
9. Karl W. Deutsch, "Integration and Arms Control in the European Political Environment: A Summary Report," *American Political Science Review* 60, no. 2 (June 1966), 355.
10. Ronald F. Inglehart, "An End to European Integration?," *American Political Science Review* 61, no. 1 (March 1967), 92, 96–9. See also, Ronald F. Inglehart, "Changing Values among Western Publics from 1970 to 2006," *West European Politics* 31, nos 1–2 (January–March 2008), 130–46.
11. Inglehart, "Changing Values among Western Publics from 1970 to 2006," 94.
12. William E. Fisher, "An Analysis of the Deutsch Sociocausal Paradigm of Political Integration," *International Organization* 23, no. 2 (Spring 1969), 254–90.
13. Eugen Weber, *Peasants into Frenchmen: Modernization of Rural France, 1870–1914* (Stanford: Stanford University Press, 1976).
14. Vincent Della Sala, "Political Myth, Mythology and the European Union," *Journal of Common Market Studies* 48, no. 1 (January 2010), 3–7.
15. Holly Case, "Being European: East and West," in Jeffrey T. Checkel and Peter J. Katzenstein, eds, *European Identity* (Cambridge: Cambridge University Press, 2009), 112–20.
16. Much of this paragraph draws on Jan Beyers, "Conceptual and Methodological Challenges in the Study of European Socialization," *Journal of European Public Policy* 17, no. 6

(September 2010), 909–20. See also Adrian Favell, "Europe's Identity Problem," *West European Politics* 28, no. 5 (November 2005), 1109–16.

17. Ronald Inglehart, *Modernization and Postmodernization: Cultural, Economic, and Political Change in 43 Societies* (Princeton: Princeton University Press, 1997).

18. Neil Fligstein, *Euroclash: The EU, European Identity, and the Future of Europe* (Oxford: Oxford University Press, 2008), 250. See also Neil Fligstein, "Who are the Europeans and How Does This Matter for Politics?," in Jeffrey T. Checkel and Peter J. Katzenstein, eds, *European Identity* (Cambridge: Cambridge University Press, 2009), 132–66.

19. Trine Flockhart, "Critical Junctures and Social Identity Theory: Explaining the Gap between Danish Mass and Elite Attitudes to Europeanization," *Journal of Common Market Studies* 43, no. 3 (February 2005), 251–71.

20. Peter A. Kraus, *A Union of Diversity: Language, Identity and Polity-Building in Europe* (Cambridge: Cambridge University Press, 2008), 195–8.

21. Lauren M. McLaren, *Identity, Interests and Attitudes to European Integration* (Basingstoke: Palgrave, 2006), 69–92.

22. Liesbet Hooghe and Gary Marks, "Calculation, Community and Cues: Public Opinion on European Integration," *European Union Politics* 6, no. 4 (December 2004), 419–43.

23. Marcel Lubbers, "Regarding the Dutch 'Nee' to the European Constitution: A Test of the Identity, Utilitarian and Political Approaches to Voting 'No'," *European Union Politics* 9, no. 1 (January 2008), 59–86. A similar pattern operates in Central and Eastern Europe. See Raivo Vetik, Gerli Nimmerfelt, and Marti Taru, "Reactive Identity versus EU Integration," *Journal of Common Market Studies* 44, no. 5 (November 2006), 1079–102.

24. Thomas Risse, *A Community of Europeans? Transnational Identities and Public Spheres* (Ithaca: Cornell University Press, 2010), 244. See also John Erik Fossum, "Identity-Politics in the European Union," *Journal of European Integration* 23, no. 4 (October 2001), 373–406.

25. Fossum, "Identity-Politics in the European Union," 127–56. See also Thomas Risse, "Neofunctionalism, European Identity, and the Puzzles of European Integration," *Journal of European Public Policy* 12, no. 2 (April 2005), 291–309.

26. Liesbet Hooghe and Gary Marks, "European Union?," *West European Politics* 31, nos 1–2 (January–March 2008), 119–20.

27. Cécile Leconte, "The Fragility of the EU as a 'Community of Values': Lessons from the Haider Affair," *West European Politics* 28, no. 3 (May 2005), 620–49.

28. John McCormick, *Europeanism* (Oxford: Oxford University Press, 2010). See also Sibylle Scheipers and Daniela Sicurelli, "Normative Power Europe: A Credible Utopia?," *Journal of Common Market Studies* 45, no. 2 (March 2007), 435–57.

29. James A. Caporasa and Min-hyung Kim, "The Dual Nature of European Identity: Subjective Awareness and Coherence," *Journal of European Public Policy* 16, no. 1 (January 2009), 19–42.

30. Adrian Favell and Virginie Guiraudon, "The Sociology of the European Union: An Agenda," *European Union Politics* 10, no. 4 (December 2009), 554, 560–9.

31. John A. Scherpereel, "European Culture and the European Union's 'Turkey Question'," *West European Politics* 33, no. 4 (July 2010), 810–29.

32. Franz C. Mayer and Jan Palmowski, "European Identities and the EU—The Ties that Bind the Peoples of Europe," *Journal of Common Market Studies* 42, no. 3 (October 2004), 573–98.

33. Armin von Bogdandy, "The European Constitution and European Identity: Text and Subtext of the Treaty Establishing a Constitution for Europe," *I-CON* 3, nos 2–3 (May 2005), 313.

34. Thilo Sarrazin, *Deutschland schafft sich ab: Wie wir unser Land aufs Spiel setzen* (München: Deutscher Verlags-Anstalt, 2010), 10. See also Christopher Caldwell, *Reflections on the Revolution in Europe: Immigration, Islam, and the West* (New York: Doubleday, 2009).

35. Bassam Tibi, "The Return of Ethnicity to Europe via Islamic Migration?: The Ethnicization of the Islamic Diaspora," in Roland Hsu, ed., *Ethnic Europe: Mobility, Identity, and Conflict in a Globalized World* (Stanford: Stanford University Press, 2010), 127–8.

36. Saskia van Genugten, "Immigration, Islam, and Political Discourse," in Marco Giuliani and Erik Jones, eds, *Italian Politics: Managing Uncertainty* (New York: Berghahn Books, 2010), 240–57.

37. Peter H. Wilson, *Europe's Tragedy: A History of the Thirty Years War* (London: Allen Lane, 2009).

38. François Foret and Virginie Riva, "Religion between Nation and Europe: The French and Belgian "No" to the Christian Heritage of Europe," *West European Politics* 33, no. 4 (July 2010), 791–809.

39. Percy B. Lehning, "European Citizenship: Towards a European Identity?," *Law and Philosophy* 20, no. 3 (May 2001), 239–82.

40. Ellen Quintelier and Yves Dejaeghere, "Does European Citizenship Increase Tolerance in Young People?," *European Union Politics* 9, no. 3 (July 2008), 339–62.

41. Saskia Sassen, "Membership and Its Politics," in Hsu, *Ethnic Europe*, 26.

42. Randall Hansen, "The Poverty of Postnationalism: Citizenship, Immigration, and the New Europe," *Theory and Society* 38, no. 1 (January 2009), 1–24; Adam Luedtke, "European Integration, Public Opinion and Immigration Policy: Testing the Impact of National Identity," *European Union Politics* 6, no. 1 (January 2005), 83–112.

43. Stefan Auer, "'New Europe': Between Cosmopolitan Dreams and Nationalist Nightmares," *Journal of Common Market Studies* 48, no. 5 (October 2010), 1163–84.

44. Auer, "'New Europe': Between Cosmopolitan Dreams and Nationalist Nightmares"; Cecile Leconte, "Opposing Integration on Matters of Social and Normative Preferences: A New Dimension of Political Contestation in the EU," *Journal of Common Market Studies* 46, no. 5 (October 2008), 1071–91.

45. Anand Menon and Stephen Weatherill, "Transnational Legitimacy in a Globalizing World: How the European Union Rescues Its States," *West European Politics* 31, no. 3 (May 2008), 397–416.

CHAPTER 49

....

POLITICAL TIME
IN THE EU

....

KLAUS H. GOETZ

49.1 POLITICAL TIME: INSTITUTION
AND RESOURCE

....

Political and academic debate about the state and the future of the EU is replete with time-centered arguments. Will the introduction of a president of the European Council, elected for a period of office of two-and-a-half years, increase the efficiency and effectiveness of the European Council and strengthen it vis-à-vis the Council of the EU, whose presidency continues to rotate every six months amongst member states? Are "early agreements" concluded between the European Parliament and the Council of the EU under the co-decision procedure testament to the smooth functioning of the EU legislative process or do they threaten the inter-institutional distribution of powers as envisaged by the Treaties? Is the EU's seven-year budgetary cycle a key source of stability and predictability or should it be shortened and made to coincide with the Parliament's term of office so as "democratize" the budget? As will be discussed below, major debates about the future of the EU—whether they concern differentiated integration, enlargement, or the prospects for further democratization—are intimately connected to arguments about political time. For example, should member states be allowed to move at different speeds in pursuit of common objectives? Does the addition of new member states threaten to slow down decision-making? And how can the requirements of timely and expeditious EU action be reconciled with the inherently time-consuming nature of deliberative bodies, notably the European Parliament?[1]

It is probably not difficult to convince students of the EU of the potential benefits of paying systematic attention to political time. For example, problems of synchronizing EU and national political timetables; the impact of the six-monthly Council presidencies on the temporal ordering of Council business; or the importance of multi-annual planning cycles in shaping the Commission's activities are well known to practitioners and EU scholars alike.[2] But precisely because most aspects of the EU's institutional make-up, its procedures, and its policies are so intimately intertwined with political time and because the latter comes in so many shapes and guises, the key questions to be asked about political time have to be carefully specified.

In order to advance our knowledge of political time in the EU and its consequences, two questions should be prioritized. First, how does the manner in which time is institutionalized along the dimensions of polity, politics, and public policy affect the distribution of power, the efficiency and effectiveness of the EU's actions, and its legitimacy? This question contains some assumptions that deserve spelling out. By referring to the institutionalization of time, attention is drawn to time rules—both formal and informal—that privilege certain courses of action over others. Such time rules refer, in particular, to timing (when something happens); sequence (in what order things happen); speed (how fast they happen); and duration (for how long they happen). Time rules are, thus, understood as part of the institutional setting in which different types of actors operate. It makes sense to examine time rules at the level of *polity*, concerned with the length and configurations of terms, mandates and tenures and the associated time budgets available to, and likely time horizons adopted by, different actors; at the *politics* level, which refers to time-related decision-making rules, as laid down, e.g. in Rules of Procedures, timetables, and schedules; and at the *policy* level, which is concerned with the temporal features of public policy, such as, e.g. the inter-temporal distribution of costs and benefits of environmental or social policies.[3] Finally, the question, as posited, suggests that inquiring into time rules matters because they affect how power is distributed (think, e.g. of the implications of the mid-term reallocation of committee chairmanships in the European Parliament); because they are often critical in enabling or hindering efficient and effective political and administrative action (think, e.g. of the high and regular meeting frequency of COREPER I and II); and because time and legitimacy are closely connected (think, e.g. of rules relating to timing, sequencing and duration of different stages of the legislative process). The totality of such time rules and the temporal regularities with which they are associated constitute the EU timescape.[4]

The second basic question to be asked is: how is time used as a resource in EU political processes? This question concerns the malleability of time. As Schmitter and Santiso have noted, decision-makers "learn how to manipulate time, that is, to turn it from an inexorably limited, linear and perishable constraint into something that could be scheduled, anticipated, delayed, accelerated, dead-lined, circumvented, prolonged, deferred, compressed, parceled out, standardized, diversified, staged, staggered, and even wasted—but never ignored."[5] This perspective revolves around the scarcity of time in democratic politics, since, as Linz and others have noted, democracy is characterized by the fact that it gives power *pro tempore*, i.e. for clearly delimited periods of time.[6] What matters here is the skill with which actors exploit differentials in time budgets and time horizons (e.g. the EU negotiator whose mandate is about to expire may be more likely to agree to a compromise in international negotiations than his counterparts with longer mandates); discretion over the timing, sequence, speed, and duration of actions; and the ability to limit the temporal discretion of others, i.e. to "set the clock." Some of the time games played in the EU are recurrent and well known, such as delaying tactics by the European Parliament to extract substantive concessions from the Council.[7] But whilst it is possible to generalize about the EU timescape, actors' strategic and tactical use of time as a resource is more difficult to describe in general terms, because it is typically tied to particular situations and issues.

To pose the principal questions about time in the EU in this way places the analysis in a specific analytical context, namely that of actor-centered institutionalism, as expounded by Scharpf.[8] Thus, time as an institution is understood as "a system of rules that structure the courses of actions that a set of actors may chose," and these rules may be formal or consist of "social norms that actors will generally respect and whose viola-tion will be sanctioned by loss of reputation, social disapproval, withdrawal of coopera-tion and rewards, or even ostracism."[9] Accusations of "bad timing," "undue haste," or "playing for time" often result from perceived violations of such social norms.[10] Importantly, institutions so understood "define repertoires of more or less acceptable courses of action that will leave considerable scope for the strategic and tactical choices of purposeful actors"[11]—and it is when making those choices that time can also be an important resource.

This way of framing the question of time and the study of the EU also implies a differ-ent agenda from that of historical institutionalism, as most closely associated with the work of Pierson, with its emphasis on explaining developmental trajectories *over time*, i.e. historically, with reference to temporal categories such as timing, sequence, or actors' time horizons.[12] As Bulmer has shown, the study of "politics in time" and the study of the EU timescape and time games are not mutually exclusive or rival enterprises; but what they seek to explain differs.[13]

49.2 TIMESCAPE AND TIME GAMES

What are some first answers that may be given to the two broad questions posed in the preceding section? As regards the contours of the EU timescape, two features stand out: first, the EU is a decidedly heterotemporal political system; second, the timescape, like other elements of the EU's institutional make-up, has been dynamic, with a trend toward the formalization of time rules and increasingly detailed scheduling. Both features require some explication.

The pronounced heterotemporality that characterizes the EU timescape can be observed at polity, politics, and policy levels. Looking first at terms, mandates, and tenures, these differ markedly across the key institutions. The Council of the EU, as a permanent institution, has a presidency that rotates on a six-monthly basis; the ministers who make up the membership of the Council in its various configurations change frequently. The European Council, since the coming into force of the Lisbon Treaty, has a president with a two-and-a-half year tenure, but the composition of the Council changes every time a new head of government assumes office in one of the member states. The High Representative of the Union for CSFP, who doubles as Commissioner for external relations, has a mandate that coincides with the College of Commissioners. The Commission president is appointed and approved before the members of the College of Commissioners. While the European Council nominated José Manuel Barroso for a second five-year term as Commission president in early July 2009 and the European Parliament approved his appointment in September 2009, various delays meant that the Commissioners were only confirmed in February 2010, allowing Barroso plenty of time to develop political guidelines for the future work of the Commission. MEPs are elected for five-year terms, but important posts, including those of the Parliament president and many committee chairmanships, rotate in mid-term. The six members of the ECB serve non-renewable eight-year, staggered terms, so that no more than two members retire in the same year. The judges and Advocates-General of the ECJ are appointed for renewable six-year terms; the Treaties envisage that every three years there shall be a partial replacement of judges and Advocates-General. This list could be continued, but what should emerge is that the configuration of terms, mandates, and tenures across the key EU institutions is scarcely synchronized.

Heterotemporality is further reinforced by the fact that both central political processes and the temporal substance of key policies are more or less decoupled from institutional cycles. Whereas, as the extensive literature on political business cycles shows,[14] in parliamentary democracies the budget process is both procedurally and substantively closely aligned with the terms of the legislature, in the EU, the multi-annual financial framework that establishes upper spending limits and is based on a binding agreement between the Commission, the European Parliament, and the Council, covers seven years; it thus extends across the mandates of both the Commission and the Parliament. The same goes for the framework for the funding of the EU's most costly policy, i.e. agriculture.

These temporal rules have not, of course, remained static. If we seek to characterize the developmental trajectory over time, and especially over the last two decades or so, there is a clear trend towards formalization, as part of a broader process of institutionalization. Time rules—notably as regards decision-making and legislative processes—in the Treaties, the Rules of Procedure of the Commission, the Council, and the Parliament and also in Inter-Institutional Agreements have become more numerous, more detailed, and more binding, in the sense that informal temporal rules become formalized. One example of this dynamic concerns the growing formalization of the Commission's policy processes,[15] with an elaborate strategic planning, programming, and reporting cycle that encompasses, inter alia, five-year strategic objectives adopted by the Commission upon entering office; an annual policy strategy; a Commission work program that builds on the strategy, and includes, in particular, "road maps" for "strategic initiatives" and "priority initiatives"; and still more detailed planning and programming through monthly updated lists of planned and adopted Commission initiatives.

The loss of temporal discretion that results from the growing specificity and formalization of decisional time rules is reinforced by the effects of dense scheduling as regards the meeting frequencies of the main collective decision-makers. Decisions are made in a tight grid of regular meetings in the Parliament, the Commission, the political and administrative levels of the Council of the EU, and the European Council. The de facto deadlines which these meeting schedules impose both mobilize actors at EU- and member-state levels and, by implication, lead to a reordering of short-term and medium-term priorities.[16] Timetables rule.

The interaction between configurations of time rules regarding terms, mandates, and tenures; decisional rules; more or less fixed meeting schedules; and the temporal qualities of policies impose constraints on all actors in the EU system. In accordance with our understanding of time as an institution, they "create and constrain options, and shape perceptions and preferences," but "they cannot influence choices and outcomes in a deterministic sense," since institutionalized "rules, even if they are completely effective, will rarely prescribe one and only one course of action."[17] In other words, they leave scope for strategic and tactical action, which includes, amongst others, time games. The latter may employ a range of tactics and strategies, ranging from the skilful exploitation of discretion within rules, e.g. the well-calculated timing of the announcement of an initiative, to the purposeful violation of time rules in cases where the likely benefits outweigh sanctions for non-observance. The more or less ad hoc creation of new time rules is also part of this repertoire: think, e.g. of the "period of reflection" that was called for following the rejection of the European Constitution in referendums in France and the Netherlands; or of the use of "road maps," i.e. policy schedules—developed by the Commission to steer the enlargement process.[18]

In the EU, such time games matter, in particular, amongst the institutions; within the institutions; and between the EU institutions and those of the member states. A well-documented example that affects inter-institutional relations are the "early agreements" between the European Parliament and the Council under the co-decision procedure, which, as Héritier and Farrell have documented, have been increasingly extended beyond their initially intended domains of application.[19] The inter-institutional effects are far-reaching: the European Parliament

> has gained increasing power in its negotiations with Council representatives because its time horizon on average is longer than that of the Council, which is committed to self-set deadlines and has a Presidency that is eager to use the six-month window of opportunity...if it plays its cards well, it can use early agreements strategically to affect deliberations within the Council itself; negotiations between the Parliament and the Presidency take place before the Council has adopted a formal Common Position.[20]

As regards relations within the EU institutions, it is well understood by analysts of time in organizations that temporal discretion is unequally distributed in organizations:

individuals at the top of the hierarchy tend to possess greater scope for the discretionary uses of time, whilst they also act as the "keeper of the clocks" for others.[21] Time as a resource is, therefore, primarily available to the political and administrative leadership within the EU institutions, and deadlining and its monitoring, in particular, are powerful tools of organizational steering and control. As regards the Commission's above-mentioned temporal instruments of strategic planning, programming, and reporting, for example, it has been suggested that they may have promoted centralization within the Commission:

> The Secretariat General plays a key role in the operation of these instruments and it has contributed to spreading a culture of "upstream coordination," inviting services to plan ahead and revisit the timetable of their initiatives in the light of the overall priorities of the College. It also plays an increasingly pivotal role in steering and screening new policy initiatives, with the possibility to be associated with, or to take over the leadership for, essential files.[22]

Finally, time games, aimed at enhancing and exploiting an actor's own temporal discretion whilst limiting that of others do, of course, take place between the EU institutions and the member states, as, e.g. when individual member states seek to extract concessions from Council presidencies that are approaching the end of their mandate.

49.3 Why European Clocks Matter

Students of comparative politics who have explored empirically the institutionalization of political time and its discretionary uses in politics have tended to concentrate on four themes: the discontinuity inherent in democratic politics and its implications, e.g. the oft-criticized short-termism of decision-makers who will not look beyond the next election date; the cyclical nature of political time in democracies and the fashioning of political business cycles; synchronization problems in political systems with differentiated temporal orders, as they are found, e.g. in federal systems with frequent elections in the constitutive states; and the effects of decisional time rules on power within and amongst political institutions, with a special emphasis on legislative rules.

Such ways of framing problems of political time and the analytical lenses employed to study them also promise insights into the EU timescape, time games played, and their consequences for the distribution of political power in the EU; the efficiency and effectiveness of its actions; and its legitimacy. If we consider, first, the issue of discontinuity and short-termism, it is notable that the EU timescape has some important elements of continuity, which can be expected to act against short-time horizons and short-termism. Thus, both the Council of the EU and the European Council are permanent institutions, although their membership does, of course, change. The administrative level in the Council—notably in the form of COREPER I and II and the General Secretariat—

provides a further element of continuity, not least since Permanent Representatives from the old member states, do, on average, spend about four-and-a half years in post. In the Commission, the Directorates-General with their staff of permanent officials provide both memory and forward-thinking capacity. Moreover, the proliferation of executive agencies, which are not tied directly to the Commission, is likely to promote a partial decoupling between the time horizons of Commissioners with fixed mandates and the European bureaucracy.

Longer-term orientation is arguably reinforced by the lack of an overarching institutional cycle, as already noted above. Elections to the European Parliament do, of course, to some extent set the pace and rhythm of work in the Parliament itself and also in the Commission and the Council. But the electoral cycle is but one amongst several—including, in particular, the cycle of Council presidencies and, since the coming into force of the Lisbon Treaty, the presidency of the European Council—and important policy cycles do not coincide with the electoral cycle. Moreover, as data on the legislative process suggests, the mid-term reallocation of key offices in the European Parliament is important in the temporal sorting of the European Parliament's work.[23] In the absence of empirical studies on political business cycles in the EU, it cannot be excluded that the substance of legislation does, to some extent, take account of impending elections, i.e. that both the timing and the content of legislation are influenced by electoral considerations. But the long-term horizons of both the basic budgetary framework, coupled with the fact that the bulk of EU legislation is regulatory in nature, makes the fashioning of political business cycles unlikely.

The heterotemporality of the EU timescape makes it reminiscent to that found in federal states. In the European context, the parallels to Germany are especially striking. Thus, the Federal Council (*Bundesrat*), like the Council of the EU and the European Council, is a continuous institution, whose membership changes frequently and irregularly. Equally, elections at *Länder* level are not, in principle, synchronized with elections at Federal level (although, in some, it is decided to make election dates coincide), just as there is no synchronization between European and national elections. The oft-heard argument that, as a consequence, German policy-making takes place under conditions of an almost permanent electoral campaign does not directly apply to the EU level. But national election dates, and calculations about their likely outcome, certainly help to define "windows of opportunity" for action at EU level.

A further dominant perspective on political time has focused on time rules and political decision-making, with a strong emphasis on legislative politics. Thus, control over the allocation of parliamentary time and time-related rules favoring the majority during the parliamentary stage of law-making have long been seen as a key resource for government in getting its bills through parliament.[24] Control over timing, sequencing, and duration in parliamentary decision-making are especially important. As already noted, this theme has also been taken up in the literature on the European Parliament and its relations with the Commission and the Council,[25] although the time games played within (the) Parliament have not yet been studied in any great detail.

49.4 Time and EU Scholarship

It should have emerged by now that the manner in which questions of political time are typically approached in comparative politics opens up a broad range of empirical questions about the EU timescape and time games, the answers to which promise valuable insights into the nature of the EU political system. The fundamental question that needs to be addressed is how the specific temporal constitution of the EU affects power relations and institutional performance and how it is linked to the EU's legitimacy. The manifold ways in which this overarching question reaches into discussions about the current state and future of the EU should become even clearer if we consider political time in a multilevel system; political time and societal time; and time, differentiated integration, and enlargement.

Political institutions face at least two basic synchronization problems: inter-institutional synchronization, which, in multilevel system like the EU, is an especially challenging task; and synchronization between political time and the temporality of social, economic, cultural, and technological developments. As regards the former, it has been suggested by various authors that EU time not only reaches into the traditional temporal orders of the member states' political systems, but that the growing fusion of political timetables and time games restricts the temporal discretion of national actors.[26] Thus, the pace of EU policy-making has been explicitly linked to a loss of temporal autonomy of, and a "squeezed present" in, national ministerial bureaucracies, whose calendars are said to be increasingly determined by Brussels.[27] National politicians, too, seem to have little choice but to allocate scarce time to EU-level politics, and their calendars are filled with an ever-increasing number of supranational commitments over whose timing and duration they have little influence. The speed of EU decision-making has also been identified as an obstacle to the effective parliamentarization of EU politics at member-state level, as national legislatures appear to find it difficult to react in time to EU developments.[28] National legislatures' timetables cannot be changed at will to accommodate the needs for speedy parliamentary responses to EU initiatives. Moreover, progressive integration is linked to declining domestic discretion over policy timing, notably the capacity to fashion political business cycles.[29] European economic governance, with monetary policy at its core, has its own distinct timescape that is dissociated from the temporal preferences of domestic political elites.[30] As Majone has repeatedly highlighted, the delegation of authority to the ECB has been effective in addressing time inconsistency in policy—or, to put it more crudely, politicians' temptation to change course in the face of declining popularity and upcoming elections; but this has, in his view, come at the price of a loss of democratic legitimacy.[31]

From such a perspective, it seems that "the slower rhythms of nation states are marginalized by the transnational proliferation of soft law and fast policy."[32] This "temporal disjuncture," it is argued

> sharpens temporal conflicts within the nationally constituted economy and the nationally constituted state. As the upper reaches of the nation state conform to the

temporal urgency of institutionalized supranational decision making, the marginalized national polity is answerable to the slower temporal rhythms of representative
assembly, the election cycle, public policy formation and civil society.[33]

EU analysts and students of Europeanization, in particular, may hesitate to emphasize
the domestic restrictions associated with supranational integration without paying
attention to the "usages of Europe" in member states, since losses of temporal discretion
may well be in the interests of some national actors. At present, references to the problematic effects of integration and EU time on political time in the member states are still
based more on impressions and conjectures than solid systematic data. Moreover, the
power shifts with which they tend to be associated require further empirical probing:
from time-taking member states to EU time-setters; or from decision-makers subject to
electorally bounded time to non-majoritarian institutions. EU scholarship would thus
benefit from paying more systematic attention to the temporality of the multilevel system and its implications.

Synchronization across levels and across institutions is made all the more difficult
when political decisions have to be taken under great time pressure. The theme of acceleration of economic, social, cultural, and technological developments is by no means a
new one. However, recent scholarship that analyzes developmental dynamics in "high-
speed societies"[34] stresses its political implications: an often radical shortening of the
time within which political decisions can be prepared, made, and communicated. This
development is seen to threaten all those political processes and institutions, which,
because of their deliberative character, are time-consuming.[35] Thus, Scheuerman has
suggested that

> acceleration poses fundamental challenges to the temporal fundaments of the sepa-
> ration of powers...High-speed society tends to favor high-speed political institu-
> tions, and traditional liberal democratic assumptions about temporality unwittingly
> aggrandize executive power and weaken broad-based popular legislatures.[36]

In Rosa's view we observe a growing "desynchronization" between politics and its social,
economic, cultural, and technological environments.[37] On the one hand, "the time
needed for democratic political decision-making is not just hard to accelerate, since
processes of deliberation and aggregation in a pluralist democratic society inevitably
take time."[38] On the other, the speed with which societies change accelerates, leading to a
politics that becomes increasingly "situationalist" and the shifting of decisions to other,
faster decision-making arenas.[39]

In case of the EU, the marginalization of deliberative institutions and processes associated with pressures for speediness and its problematic consequences for democratic
legitimacy have, for example, been stressed in Héritier and Farrell's above-mentioned
analysis of "early agreements."[40] Not only do they threaten transparency and accountability in the European Parliament and disadvantage smaller party groups that "now find
themselves increasingly marginalized, as large parties and the Council reach pre-
arranged informal deals, which the large parties then push through by voting down
amendments at Committee."[41] At member-state level, too, parliaments suffer, as

"decisions are typically taken before the Member States have even had a chance to reach a consensus on a Common Position, let alone defend their negotiating strategies to their respective domestic parliaments. Efficiency is enhanced at the expense of accountability."[42] This example underlines the fact that EU scholarship has much to learn from inquiring into time rules and their political consequences.

This also becomes evident if we look at another key debate in EU scholarship—on differentiated integration—which is saturated with time-centered images and metaphors.[43] In Stubb's categorization, time is one of the three main variables of differentiated integration, the others being "space" and "matter,"[44] and more recent contributions have employed similar distinctions.[45] Discussions of temporal differentiation include references to multi-speed Europe, vanguards, and laggards, and major examples of differentiation include transition periods, temporary derogations, phasing in and phasing out arrangements, and differential timing in the full adoption of the euro.[46] Differentiation by means of time is most evident along the policy dimension. One only needs to think of the recent EU enlargements of 2004 and 2007 and the recourse to temporary derogations, provisions regarding the phasing in of policy measures, and transitional arrangements such as the "transition facility," i.e. post-accession financial assistance to the new member states, to recognize its practical importance.

But it is not just the differentiated timescape—i.e. the differentiated time rules—that attest to the intimate connection between political time and enlargement. Successive enlargement rounds have also been characterized by intricate time games, i.e. attempts to use time and time-related governing devices, such as deadlines and timetables, in the pursuit of substantive advantage. As Avery has argued, the 2004 enlargement—with its need for inter-institutional, multilevel and cross-temporal synchronization, mobilization, and commitment over time—confronted policy-makers with huge practical challenges, but it was not clear who would effectively "set the time"—i.e. establish the timeline of enlargement—and how it was best to be ensured that the timeline was adhered to.[47] One important way in which the Commission sought to ensure its own centrality in enlargement governance and drive forward the process was through the use of temporal governing devices, such as the so-called "road maps" produced by the Commission in 2000 to guide the accession negotiations that were to last until 2003.[48] Conversely, enlargement negotiations with Turkey are characterized by the absence of a clear timetable, a case of "playing for time" in the hope that opposition to Turkey's EU accession amongst key member states—most notably France and Germany—will eventually be overcome.

49.5 CONCLUSION

The purpose of this chapter has been to show that EU scholarship has much to gain from exploring more systematically than has hitherto been the case the institutionalization of political time in the EU political system; temporal regularities in its operation; and typical time games that are played within and amongst the main EU institutions. Of course, time rarely matters on its own. Its full implications in terms of the distribution of power, decisional efficiency and effectiveness, and the legitimacy of processes and outcomes can only be grasped if the temporal dimension of institutions and time-centered strategic and tactical behavior of actors are considered in connection with other elements of the institutionalization of the EU political system and other resources that actors have at their disposal. Moreover, as Scharpf's actor-centered institutionalism highlights, institutional analysis must take account of specific actor constellations, interests, and priorities if it wants to understand how institutions help to shape outcomes. But foregrounding political time offers novel perspectives on the nature of EU institutions, decision-making procedures, and EU policy profiles. The time has come to take time seriously in the study of the EU.

Notes

1. William E. Scheuerman, *Liberal Democracy and the Social Acceleration of Time* (Baltimore, MD: The Johns Hopkins University Press, 2004).
2. Klaus H. Goetz, "How Does the EU Tick? Five Propositions on Political Time," *Journal of European Public Policy* 16, no. 2 (2009), 202–20.
3. See Klaus H. Goetz and Jan-Hinrik Meyer-Sahling, "Political Time in the EU: Dimensions, Approaches, Theories," *Journal of European Public Policy* 16, no. 2 (2009), 180–201.
4. See Jan-Hinrik Meyer-Sahling and Klaus H. Goetz, "The EU Timescape: From Notion to Research Agenda," *Journal of European Public Policy* 16, no. 2 (2009), 325–36.
5. Philippe Schmitter and Javier Santiso, "Three Temporal Dimensions to the Consolidation of Democracy," *International Political Science Review* 19, no. 1 (1998), 71.
6. Juan Linz, "Democracy's Time Constraints," *International Political Science Review* 19, no. 1 (1998), 19–37.
7. Berthold Rittberger, "Impatient Legislators and New Issue-Dimensions: A Critique of the Garrett-Tsebelis Standard Version of Legislative Politics," *Journal of European Public Policy* 7, no. 4 (2000), 554–75; Raya Kardasheva, "The Power to Delay: The European Parliament's Influence in the Consultation Procedure," *Journal of Common Market Studies* 47, no. 2 (2009), 385–409.
8. Fritz W. Scharpf, *Games Real Actors Play: Actor-Centred Institutionalism in Policy Research* (Boulder, CO: Westview Press, 1997).
9. Scharpf, *Games Real Actors Play*, 38.
10. Robert E. Goodin, "Keeping Political Time: The Rhythms of Democracy," *International Political Science Review* 19, no. 1 (1998), 39–54.
11. Scharpf, *Games Real Actors Play*, 42.
12. Paul Pierson, *Politics in Time* (Princeton: Princeton University Press, 2004).
13. Simon Bulmer, "Politics in Time Meets the Politics of Time: Historical Institutionalism and the EU Timescape," *Journal of European Public Policy* 16, no. 2 (2009), 307–24.
14. See Allan Drazen, "The Political Business Cycle after 25 Years," *MBER Macroeconomics Annual 2000*, 75–138.
15. Luc Tholoniat, "The Temporal Constitution of the European Commission: A Timely Investigation," *Journal of European Public Policy* 16, no. 2 (2009), 221–38.

16. Magnus Ekengren, *The Time of European Governance* (Manchester: Manchester University Press, 2002).

17. Scharpf, *Games Real Actors Play*, 42.

18. Graham Avery, "The Uses of Time in the EU's Enlargement Process," *Journal of European Public Policy* 16, no. 2 (2009), 256–69; Katja Lass-Lennecke and Annika Werner, "Policies, Institutions and Time: How the European Commission Managed the Temporal Challenge of Eastern Enlargement," *Journal of European Public Policy* 16, no. 2 (2009), 270–85.

19. Adrienne Héritier and Henry Farrell, "The Invisible Transformation of Codecision: Problems in Democratic Legitimacy," in Catherine Moury and Luís de Sousa, eds, *Institutional Challenges in Post-Constitutional Europe* (London: Routledge, 2009), 108–20.

20. Héritier and Farrell, "The Invisible Transformation of Codecision," 112.

21. Ruth Simsa, *Wem gehört die Zeit? Hierarchie und Zeit in Gesellschaft und Organisationen* (Frankfurt a. M.: Campus, 1996).

22. Tholoniat, "The Temporal Constitution of the European Commission," 232.

23. Laszlo Kovats, "Do Elections Set the Pace? A Quantitative Assessment of the Timing of European Legislation," *Journal of European Public Policy* 16, no. 2 (2009), 239–55.

24. Gary Cox, "The Organisation of Democratic Legislatures," in Barry G. Weingast and Donald A. Wittman, eds, *The Oxford Handbook of Political Economy* (Oxford: Oxford University Press, 2005), 141–61; Herbert Döring, "Time as a Scarce Resource: Government Control of the Agenda," in his *Parliaments and Majority Rule in Western Europe* (Frankfurt a. M.: Campus, 1995), 223–46.

25. Rittberger, "Impatient Legislators and New Issue-dimensions"; Kardasheva, "The Power to Delay."

26. Ekengren, *The Time of European Governance*; Magnus Jerneck, "Europeanization, Territoriality and Political Time," *Yearbook of European Studies* 14 (2000), 27–49.

27. Ekengren, *The Time of European Governance*.

28. For further references see Klaus H. Goetz and Jan-Hinrik Meyer-Sahling, "The Europeanisation of Domestic Political Systems," *Living Reviews in European Governance* 3, no. 2, (2008).

29. Kenneth Donahue and Thierry Warin, "The Stability and Growth Pact: A European Answer to the Political Budget Cycle," *Comparative European Politics* 5, no. 4 (2007), 423–40.

30. Kenneth H. Dyson, "The Evolving Timescapes on European Economic Governance: Contesting and Using Time," *Journal of European Public Policy* 16, no. 2 (2009), 286–306.

31. Giandomenico Majone, *Temporal Consistency and Policy Credibility: Why Democracies Need Non-Majoritarian Institutions*, EUI Working Paper RSC No 96/57, 1996; Giandomenico Majone, *Dilemmas of European Integration* (Oxford: Oxford University Press, 2005); Giandomenico Majone, "Transaction Cost Efficiency and the Democratic Deficit," *Journal of European Public Policy* 17, no. 2 (2010), 150–75.

32. Wayne Hope, "Conflicting Temporalities: State, Nation, Economy and Democracy under Global Capitalism," *Time & Society* 18, no. 1 (2009), 79.

33. Hope, "Conflicting Temporalities," 63.

34. Hartmut Rosa and William E. Scheuerman, eds, *High-Speed Society: Social Acceleration, Power, and Modernity* (University Park, PA: Pennsylvania State University Press, 2009).

35. Gisela Riescher, *Zeit und Politik. Zur institutionellen Bedeutung von Zeitstrukturen in parlamentarischen und präsidentiellen Regierungssystemen* (Baden-Baden: Nomos, 1994);

Kari Palonen, *The Politics of Limited Times: The Rhetoric of Temporal Judgement in Parliamentary Democracies* (Baden-Baden: Nomos, 2008).

36. Scheuerman, *Liberal Democracy and the Social Acceleration of Time*, 26.
37. Hartmut Rosa, "Social Acceleration: Ethical and Political Consequences of a Desynchronized High-Speed Society," *Constellations* 10, no. 1 (2003), 3–33; Hartmut Rosa, *Beschleunigung: Die Veränderung von Zeitstrukturen in der Moderne* (Frankfurt a. M.: Suhrkamp, 2005).
38. Rosa, "Social Acceleration," 23.
39. Rosa, "Social Acceleration," 23–4.
40. Héritier and Farrell, "The Invisible Transformation of Codecision."
41. Héritier and Farrell, "The Invisible Transformation of Codecision," 112–13.
42. Héritier and Farrell, "The Invisible Transformation of Codecision," 113.
43. Klaus H. Goetz, "Time and Differentiated Integration," in Kenneth Dyson and Angelos Sepos, eds, *The Politics of Differentiated Integration* (Basingstoke: Palgrave, 2010), 6781.
44. Alexander Stubb, "A Categorization of Differentiated Integration," *Journal of Common Market Studies* 34, no. 2 (1996), 283–95.
45. Svein S. Andersen and Nick Sitter, "Differentiated Integration: What is it and How Much Can the EU Accommodate?," *Journal of European Integration* 28, no. 4 (2006), 313–30.
46. Stubb, "A Categorization of Differentiated Integration"; Dyson, "The Evolving Timescapes on European Economic Governance."
47. Avery, "The Uses of Time in the EU's Enlargement Process."
48. Klaus H. Goetz, "The New Member States and the EU," in Simon Bulmer and Christian Lequesne, eds, *Member States and the European Union* (Oxford: Oxford University Press, 2005), 254–80.

CHAPTER 50

··

PUBLIC OPINION AND INTEGRATION

··

SARA B. HOBOLT

50.1 INTRODUCTION

The times when elites could pursue European integration with no regard to public opinion are long gone. For decades European citizens were viewed as largely irrelevant to the process of integration. Yet, as the EU has evolved from an international organization primarily concerned with trade liberalization to an economic and political union with wide-ranging competences, public opinion has also become more important. With a proliferation of referendums on EU matters, politicization of EU issues in national elections, and increased powers of the European Parliament, future European integration hinges upon public support. There has been a move away from the "permissive consensus"[1] of the early period of integration, where insulated leaders could make decisions without public consultation, toward a "constraining dissensus."[2]

Public opinion has increased its influence on EU policy-making in a number of direct and indirect ways. Notably referendums on treaty revisions have given some national electorates a very direct say on the EU reform process. The number of referendums on EU matters has increased exponentially in recent decades, with only ten EU ballots prior to the signing of the Maastricht Treaty in 1991 and forty-one since then (see Table 50.2). Moreover, since 1979 all European citizens have been able to elect the members of an increasingly powerful European Parliament. Public opinion also shapes policy outcomes in the EU in more indirect ways. Most importantly, political parties increasingly adopt policy positions that mirror public preferences in order to maximize their chances of winning national elections.[3]

Despite these various "routes of representation" available to European citizens, most scholars agree that the electoral connection between elites and citizens in the EU is, if not broken, then at least imperfect. It has been argued that vote choices in referendums and European Parliament elections are about national rather than European matters and thus provide no proper public mandate for EU policy-making,[4] and that national political parties still do not compete on issues relating to European integration.[5] Furthermore, the success of Euro-skeptic parties and the "No" votes in EU referendums have been taken as a sign that elite and public preferences on European integration are out of sync. Even the European Council has expressed concerns that citizens see the EU as "a threat to their identity" and "feel that deals are all too often cut out of their sight."[6]

Understanding the factors that shape public preferences toward the EU and the role of public opinion in the EU is thus of primary importance to the future of European integration. This chapter investigates both *causes* and *effects* of public opinion: what are the origins of public attitudes toward European integration? And, what are the effects of these attitudes on policy-makers and policy-making in the EU? An extensive literature has focused on the origins of attitudes toward European integration. After tracing developments in public support over time, the chapter reviews this body of literature, focusing on utilitarian, cue-taking and identity explanations of EU support. Thereafter, the chapter discusses the constraining role of public opinion in European and national elections and referendums, and considers the implications for democracy in Europe.

50.2 ATTITUDES TOWARD EUROPEAN INTEGRATION

It is noteworthy that the literature on public opinion and integration has shifted its focus from *public support* for European integration to a more recent interest in the determinants of *Euro-skepticism*.[7] After the Danish electorate's rejection of Maastricht Treaty and the decline in support for membership across Europe in the 1990s (see Figure 50.1), the question is no longer "why are people supportive of European integration?," but rather "why are people so opposed to the European Union?" In practice, however, most studies of Euro-skepticism rely on the same operationalization and measurement as earlier studies of EU support. Before turning to the question of what explains attitudes toward European integration it is worthwhile taking a closer look at how public support has been conceptualized and measured in the extant literature.

50.2.1 Definition and Measurement of Public Support

Support for, or opposition to, European integration can entail many different things. Applying David Easton's[8] model of citizen support for politics institutions, we can distinguish between *diffuse* (affective) support for the European project, based on ideological or value-oriented attachments, and *specific* (utilitarian) support for the EU, based on a cost–benefit analysis of the benefits (whether personal or national) derived from membership of the EU.[9] To be sure, these two modes of support are closely interlinked, since utilitarian support may ultimately lead to affective support as protracted positive evaluations of institutions contribute to the emergence of trust and emotional attachment. Importantly, however, Easton argued that diffuse support is fairly constant over time and serves to stabilize a political regime, whereas specific support may fluctuate in the short-term without affecting the stability of the political system as a whole. This poses a challenge to the EU, since most citizens feel less emotionally attached to the EU than to their nation state. When asked how attached they feel to the EU, only 11 percent of Europeans say that they feel "very attached," compared with 52 percent feeling very attached to their country and 49 percent to their city or town.[10] As we will discuss below, this lack of identification with the EU has led many scholars of public opinion to focus on utilitarian, rather than affective, explanations of support for integration.

Conceptually, the distinction between diffuse and specific support is no doubt useful, but empirically it is difficult to distinguish between the two modes of orientation. Most researchers studying public support for European integration have relied on the Eurobarometer, a public opinion survey which has been conducted twice annually since 1973 by the European Commission in all member states. These surveys provide an invaluable source for examining cross-temporal and cross-national patterns in public support for integration. They also contain questions designed to tap into both diffuse and specific support,[11] but the association between the different measures of EU support is very high and they track each other closely over time. Most studies therefore combine various measures to create a generic "EU support" scale, ranging from Euro-skepticism to support for further integration.[12]

Figure 50.1 shows the percentage of citizens stating that their country's EU membership is "generally a good thing" across four groups of countries. The figure clearly illustrates that the founding member states and the Southern European member states have remained the most positive about EU membership across the period, whereas the citizens in Northern Europe (with the exception of Ireland) are generally the most skeptical about EU membership. While commentators and scholars often emphasize a rise in Euro-skepticism across Europe, Figure 50.1 suggests that public support has remained rather stable at around 55 percent stating that membership is "a good thing," which is similar to levels of support in the early 1980s. These aggregate trends of citizen support, however, conceal considerable variation in support not only between member states, but also across individuals within member states. In the next section we turn to the different explanations proposed in the literature for variation in EU support.

50.3 EXPLAINING VARIATION IN SUPPORT

In a series of influential articles on public opinion and integration in the 1970s, Ronald Inglehart forecasted that public support for integration would grow and that public opinion would play an ever more important role in the process of integration: "public preferences are likely to constitute an increasingly effective long-term influence on political decision makers,

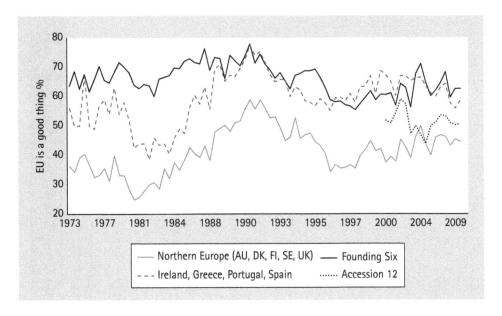

FIGURE 50.1 Public support for EU membership

Source: Eurobarometer surveys, 1973–2009

Note: Percentage of respondents answering "good thing" in response to the following question: "Generally speaking, do you think that [your country's] membership of the European Union is a good thing, a bad thing, or neither good nor bad?"

Founding six: BE, DE, FR, IT, NL, LU;

Accession 12: BG, CY, CZ, EE, HU, LV, LT, MT, PL, RO, SK, SI.

an influence which…is basically favorable to supranational integration."[13] Inglehart based this prediction on two interlinked theoretical arguments. First, his theory of post-material value change posited that people who grow up in times of scarcity and war will value economic and physical security, whereas the individuals socialized in the relatively safe and prosperous post-war era will be more interested in "high-order goals," such as the environment, democracy, and international cooperation. As a consequence, support for European integration will rise through a process of inter-generational replacement.[14] Second, Inglehart argued that those individuals who are more "cognitively mobilized" are less fearful of integration.[15] As levels of education increase, we should therefore expect growing support for European integration. Other scholars have demonstrated that post-materialist values have little explanatory power once we control for political awareness, arguing that cognitive mobilization drives both post-material values and support for integration.[16]

During the period of "Eurosclerosis" from the mid-1960s to the mid-1980s, public opinion was largely ignored in the literature on European integration.[17] Yet after market integration was extended to monetary and political union with the Maastricht Treaty, partisan conflict and public contestation also intensified and a number of studies on the determinants of public support for European integration emerged. The main explanatory approaches, summarized in Table 50.1, are the "utilitarian," the "cue-taking," and the "identity" approaches.

Table 50.1 Explaining support for European integration

	Utilitarian	Cue-Taking	Identity
Individual-level factors	Education, employment, individual economic prospects	Party cues, satisfaction with the government	National identity, fear of other cultures
Country-level factors	EU fiscal transfers, trade benefits, type of capitalism, national economic conditions	Government performance, quality of national political institutions, party polarization on EU issue	National histories and traditions
Key works	Inglehart (1970); Eichenberg & Dalton (1993); Gabel & Palmer (1995); Anderson & Kaltenthaler (1996); Anderson & Reichert (1996); Gabel (1998a, 1998b); Tucker et al. (2002); Brinegar & Jolly (2005)	Franklin et al. (1994); Schneider & Weitsman (1996); Anderson (1998); Sanchez-Cuenca (2000); Rohrschneider (2002); Steenbergen et al. (2007)	Carey (2002); McLaren (2006); Diez-Medrano (2003); Hooghe & Marks (2005)

References: Ronald Inglehart, "Public Opinion and Regional Integration," *International Organization* 24 (1970), 764–95; Richard Eichenberg and Russell Dalton, "Europeans and the European Community: The Dynamics of Public Support for European Integration," *International Organization* 47, no. 4 (1993), 507–34; Matthew J. Gabel and Harvey D. Palmer, "Understanding Variation in Public Support for European Integration," *European Journal of Political Research* 27 (1995), 3–19; Christopher J. Anderson and Karl C. Kaltenthaler, "The Dynamics of Public Opinion toward European Integration, 1973–93," *European Journal of International Relations* 2 (1996), 175–99; Christopher J. Anderson and M. Shawn Reichert, "Economic Benefits and Support for Membership in the EU: A Cross-National Analysis," *Journal of Public Policy* 15 (1996), 231–49; Matthew J. Gabel, *Interest and Integration. Market Liberalization, Public Opinion and European Union* (Ann Arbor: The University of Michigan Press, 1998a); Matthew J. Gabel, "Public Support for European Integration: An Empirical Test of Five Theories," *The Journal of Politics* 60, no. 2 (1998b), 333–54; Joshua A. Tucker, Alexander C. Pacek, and Adam J. Berinsky, "Transitional Winners and Losers: Attitudes Toward EU Membership in Post-Communist Countries," *American Journal of Political Science* 46 (2002), 557–71; Adam Brinegar and Seth Jolly, "Location, Location, Location: National Contextual Factors and Public Support for European Integration," *European Union Politics* 6 (2005), 155–80; Mark Franklin, Michael Marsh, and Lauren McLaren, "The European Question: Opposition to Unification in the Wake of Maastricht," *Journal of Common Market Studies* 35 (1994), 455–72; G. Schneider and P. A. Weitsman, "When in Doubt, Use Proxies: Attitudes Toward Domestic Politics and Support for European Integration," *Comparative Political Studies* 28, no. 4 (1996), 582–607; Christopher Anderson, "When in Doubt, Use Proxies: Attitudes Toward Domestic Politics and Support for European Integration," *Comparative Political Studies* 31, no. 5 (1998), 569–601; Ignacio Sanchez-Cuenca, "The Political Basis of Support for European Integration," *European Union Politics* 1, no. 2 (2000), 147–71; Robert Rohrschneider, "The Democratic Deficit and Support of an EU-Wide Government," *American Journal of Political Science* 46 (2002), 463–75; Marco R. Steenbergen, Erica E. Edwards, and Catherine E. De Vries, "Who's Cueing Whom? Mass-Elite Linkages and the Future of European Integration," *European Union Politics* 8, no. 1 (2007), 13–35; Sean Carey, "Undivided Loyalties: Is National Identity an Obstacle to European Integration?," *European Union Politics* 3, no. 4 (2002), 387–413; Lauren McLaren, *Identity, Interests and Attitudes to European Integration* (Basingstoke: Palgrave Macmillan, 2006); Juan Diez Medrano, *Framing Europe Attitudes to European Integration in Germany, Spain, and the UK* (Princeton, Princeton University Press, 2003); Liesbet Hooghe and Gary Marks, "Community, Calculation and Cues," *European Union Politics* 6, no. 4 (2005), 421–45.

50.3.1 Utilitarian Approach

In the 1990s studies of public support for European integration were dominated by rational-choice explanations. Most scholars rejected the notion that support for integration was based on affective attachments and focused instead on explaining support on the basis of a utilitarian cost–benefit analysis. The basic idea in these studies is that European trade liberalization will favor citizens with higher levels of human capital (education and occupational skills) and income and as a consequence such individuals will be more supportive of European integration.[18] The removal of barriers to trade allows firms to shift production across borders and increases job insecurity for less-skilled workers whereas high-skilled workers and those with capital can take advantage of the opportunities resulting from a liberalized European market. The utilitarian explanation has also been applied to the national level: in countries that profit directly from net fiscal transfers from the EU or indirectly from improved trade and favorable economic conditions, public support for membership will be higher.[19] More recent studies have suggested that national economic institutions moderate attitudes towards integration. For example, Adam Brinegar, Seth Jolly, and Herbert Kitschelt[20] have argued that in social democratic welfare systems, the left will be more opposed to integration than the right, as integration can lead to the dilution of their welfare systems, whereas the opposite is the case in liberal welfare regimes where further integration may increase redistribution.

The utilitarian models provide a compelling framework for understanding differences in support for integration. Yet while studies have consistently shown that socio-economic factors influence public opinion, they only explain a relative small proportion of variance in support, and economic factors do not appear to provide the primary explanation of cross-national differences in support. Moreover, these approaches assume that individuals are able to recognize the implications of European integration and how it affects them. Given the limited knowledge that most citizens have about European integration, scholars have questioned whether public support is driven by sophisticated cost–benefit analyses and have looked for alternative explanations instead.

50.3.2 Cue-Taking Approach

A number of studies have argued that most citizens have too limited interest in and awareness of European integration to base their attitudes on an instrumental evaluation of the implication of the integration process.[21] Instead citizens rely on "proxies" or "cues" to be able to overcome their information shortfalls. Such information shortcuts may take various forms, but since citizens generally pay more attention to the national political arena than European politics it makes sense that they employ domestic cues to form opinions about European integration. The notion of citizens relying on "national proxies" was first developed in the context of research on European elections and referendums,[22] but has also been applied to the study of support for integration. Christopher Anderson[23] has argued that citizens employ proxies from domestic politics, such as satisfaction with democracy, to form opinions about European integration, and other studies have focused on heuristics such as quality of national governance[24] and performance by the nation state.[25] Moreover, it has been shown that the positions of political parties provide information shortcuts that allow voters to infer their own opinions about European integration.[26] Other studies have demonstrated, however, that while integration support is influenced by the national political context, individuals—particularly those who are politically aware—are capable of distinguishing between EU and national institutions when making their evaluations.[27] A recent body of work has emphasized that people's support for European integration is above all shaped by the nature of their attachment to the nation.

50.3.3 Identity Approach

Whereas the utilitarian explanation to EU support takes as starting point rational-choice approaches to opinion formation and the cue-taking explanation originates in political psychology perspectives of how individuals use cognitive short-cues, more recent studies draw on the literature on group conflict and symbolic politics. The major contention is that European integration is not only, or even primarily, about trade liberalization, but also about a pooling of sovereignty that potentially erodes national self-determination and blurs boundaries between distinct national communities.[28] Not surprisingly therefore individuals' attachment to their nation and their perceptions of people from other cultures influence their attitudes toward European integration. Sean Carey[29] has shown that people with strong national identity and pride are less supportive of European integration. There is also evidence in studies by Lauren McLaren[30] and others that Euroskepticism is closely related to a general hostility toward other cultures, such as negative attitudes toward minority groups and immigrants.[31] Liesbet Hooghe and Gary Marks[32] have demonstrated that individuals who conceive of their national identity as exclusive of other territorial identities are likely to be considerably more Euro-skeptic than those who have multiple nested identities.

Since most empirical studies of public support for the EU rely on Eurobarometer survey data, it is possible to compare different theoretical explanations using the same data, and analyses have shown that identity-related concerns are as important, if not more important, than utilitarian factors in explaining support for integration.[33] One concern is that some of the measures used by scholars to measure national and European identity[34] may be endogenous to EU support. That is to say, it is difficult establish whether it is support for the EU that causes people to say that they feel "European" or vice versa. Moreover, while Eurobarometer data allow scholars to compare different explanatory models, the dominance of these data has also meant that researchers often rely on a small set of generic questions to examine public attitudes toward integration, and little work has been done to assess whether attitudes toward European integration is best conceptualized as a single dimension (for or against "Europe") or whether they may be more multifaceted. Another limitation of these studies is that they often examine public support for European integration in isolation from the wider political and electoral processes and thus tell us little about whether public opinion has any discernable effect on European policy-making. That is, the literature has tended to focus on the *origins* of public attitudes towards the EU rather than the *effect* of these attitudes. Recent studies, however, seem to be bridging the gap by investigating the connection between the public and policy-makers in the EU. This connection is explored in greater details in the next section.

50.4 THE ELECTORAL CONNECTION?

In representative democracies, elections are the primary mechanism linking citizens and policy-makers by allowing voters to choose between alternative policy platforms, parties, and ultimately office holders and by making politicians more responsive to public preferences. To assess the impact of public opinion on policy outcomes in the EU, this section thus considers the quality of the electoral connection between citizens and their representatives in European and national elections and referendums.

For many decades, European integration was regarded as an exclusively elite-driven project. Not surprisingly therefore, the dominant theories of integration have largely neglected the role of public opinion.[35] From a neo-functionalist perspective, demands for European integration are articulated by socio-economic interests organized in transnational associations and pressure groups,[36] whereas liberal intergovernmentalists argue that integration is driven by the preferences of powerful member states.[37] This increasing "politicization" of the EU since the 1990s, however, has led scholars to pay more attention to the impact of public opinion on integration. Notably, Liesbet Hooghe and Gary Marks have formulated an ambitious "Postfunctionalist Theory," which incorporates the role of (identity-based) public opinion into a framework for understanding regional integration.[38] They argue that more democratic control over EU decision-making, primarily through European elections and referendums, and increased politicization of the EU issue in domestic party politics have brought the public into EU decision-making. According to other scholars, however, elections and referendums do not (yet) serve to connect public opinion with policy outputs in the EU, and the so-called democratic deficit thus persists.

50.4.1 European Parliament Elections: Still Second-Order?

Elections to the EU's only directly elected institution, the European Parliament, have since 1979 provided European citizens with the most direct way in which to influence EU policy-making. Moreover, successive EU treaty amendments have increased the powers of the European Parliament, which is now a genuine co-legislative body in the EU. Notwithstanding these reforms, scholars have questioned the quality of the electoral connection, arguing that European Parliament elections are not genuinely "European" contests, but rather "second-order national elections" where domestic concerns dominate the agenda.[39] Since less is at stake in European Parliament elections, parties and voters treat them as mid-term national contests rather than opportunities to influence policy-making at the European level. Empirical regularities in all seven European Parliament elections have largely supported the notion that they are second-order elections.[40] First, despite the increasing powers of the Parliament, levels of turnout have been steadily declining from 63 percent in 1979 to 43 percent in 2009. Second, citizens favor smaller parties over larger parties in European Parliament elections; specifically Green and Euro-skeptic parties tend to perform better than in national elections. Third, parties in national governments are punished, especially when European Parliament elections take place during the mid-term of the national election cycle. According to the second-order election model, these empirical regularities owe to the fact that European elections are "determined more by the domestic political cleavages than by alternatives originating in the EC."[41] Recent work, however, has suggested that some voters decide to abstain or defect not because of domestic concerns, but because they disagree with the (pro-) integration positions adopted by mainstream political parties.[42] This debate has important implications for democracy in the Union, since the absence of a "European" element in European elections means that they fail to translate public preferences on issues on the EU policy agenda into policy outcomes. Some scholars have argued that institutional reforms, such as allowing the European Parliament to elect the EU executive, might strengthen the European aspect of these elections,[43] whereas others have suggested that attempts to create a "party government" at the European level would only serve to weaken democracy in Europe.[44] Currently European Parliament elections are rather lackluster affairs in most member states. In contrast, referendums on European matters have often generated more interest among parties and the public and given voters a very direct say on European reforms.

50.4.2 Referendums on European Integration

Direct democracy has become an increasingly common feature of European politics. During the past four decades, European countries have conducted fifty-one referendums on aspects of European integration. Table 50.2 lists all referendums on aspect of European integration to date.

In stark contrast to the otherwise elite-driven nature of the integration project, such national referendums have provided a direct means of involving citizens in the integration process. In the words of Hooghe and Marks, "referendums are elite-initiated events which can have elite-defying consequences."[45] This became very obvious already in 1992 when Danish voters rejected the Maastricht Treaty, and more recently in 2005 when French and Dutch voters sounded the death knell to the Constitutional Treaty, and when the Irish rejected the Lisbon Treaty in their first ballot in 2008. What

Table 50. 2 Referendums on European Integration

Year	Country	Object	Turnout %	Yes %
1972	France	Enlargement of EC (I)	60	68.3
1972	Ireland	EC membership (M)	71	83.1
1972	Norway	EC membership (M)	79	46.5
1972	Denmark	EC membership (M)	90	63.3
1972	Switzerland	EC-EFTA Treaty (T)	52	72.5
1975	United Kingdom	EC membership (M)	64	67.2
1982	Greenland	EC membership (M)	75	45.9
1986	Denmark	Single European Act (T)	75	56.2
1987	Ireland	Single European Act (T)	44	69.6
1989	Italy	Mandate for MEPs (I)	85	88.1
1992	Denmark	Maastricht Treaty (T)	83	49.3
1992	Ireland	Maastricht Treaty (T)	57	68.7
1992	France	Maastricht Treaty (T)	70	51.1
1992	Switzerland	EEA accession (M)	78	49.7
1992	Liechtenstein	EEA accession (M)	87	55.8
1992	Denmark	Maastricht Treaty (T)	87	56.8
1994	Austria	EU membership (M)	82	66.6
1994	Sweden	EU membership (M)	83	52.3
1994	Åland Islands	EU membership (M)	49	73.6
1994	Finland	EU membership (M)	70	56.9
1994	Norway	EU membership (M)	89	47.8
1995	Liechtenstein	EEA accession (M)	82	55.9
1997	Switzerland	EU candidature (M)	35	25.9
1998	Ireland	Amsterdam Treaty (T)	56	61.7
1998	Denmark	Amsterdam Treaty (T)	76	55.1
2000	Switzerland	Bilateral agreements (T)	48	67.2
2000	Denmark	Single currency (I)	88	46.9
2001	Switzerland	EU candidature (M)	55	23.2
2001	Ireland	Nice Treaty (T)	35	46.1
2002	Ireland	Nice Treaty (T)	49	62.9
2003	Malta	EU membership (M)	91	53.6
2003	Slovenia	EU membership (M)	60	89.6
2003	Hungary	EU membership (M)	46	83.7
2003	Lithuania	EU membership (M)	63	89.9
2003	Slovakia	EU membership (M)	52	92.4
2003	Poland	EU membership (M)	59	77.5
2003	Czech Republic	EU membership (M)	55	77.3
2003	Estonia	EU membership (M)	64	66.8
2003	Sweden	Single currency (I)	83	42.0
2003	Latvia	EU membership (M)	73	67.5
2003	Romania	EU membership (M)	56	89.7

Year	Country	Object	Turnout %	Yes %
2005	Spain	Constitutional Treaty (T)	42	76.7
2005	France	Constitutional Treaty (T)	69	**45.3**
2005	The Netherlands	Constitutional Treaty (T)	62	**38.2**
2005	Switzerland	Schengen agreement (I)	56	54.6
2005	Luxembourg	Free movement (I)	88	56.5
2005	Switzerland	Free movement (I)	54	56.0
2006	Switzerland	Cohesion contribution (I)	45	53.4
2008	Ireland	Lisbon Treaty (T)	53	**46.6**
2009	Switzerland	Free movement (I)	51	59.6
2009	Ireland	Lisbon Treaty (T)	59	67.1

Source: Updated from Sara B. Hobolt, *Europe in Question: Referendums on European Integration* (Oxford: Oxford University Press, 2009). "No" votes in bold. I = Single issue referendum; M = Membership referendum; T = Treaty ratification referendum.

is particularly noteworthy about these "No" votes is that the ballot proposals were backed by a broad consensus amongst national elites. Hence, referendums have introduced a popular element into the process of European integration and have forced national and European elites to consider how to garner public support for the integration project. Nevertheless, there is some disagreement over whether the proliferation of EU referendums has indeed strengthened the bond between citizens and politicians in the Union. Several scholars have argued that EU referendums, just like European Parliament elections, are "second-order" ballots determined by domestic political issues and satisfaction with the government,[46] whereas others have suggested that voters do base their vote choices on attitudes toward European integration.[47] If referendum outcomes are plebiscites on the national governments reflecting the will of ill-informed, dissatisfied voters, they are less desirable as a mechanism of decision-making on European integration than if outcomes indicate choices made by knowledgeable voters on the basis of their attitudes toward the issue at stake. Recent work by Sara Hobolt suggests that much depends on the national context, in particular how much information is provided to citizens during the campaign, and that when sufficient information is available voters do consider the issues at stake before they go to the ballot box.[48] Regardless of the "European" nature of vote choices in EU referendums, they are unlikely to provide the panacea for the lack of democratic policy-making in the EU. Not only are referendums only held in a subset of countries, on an isolated number of issues (mainly treaty revisions), but they also represent a rather blunt instrument of policy-making, especially in a multilevel EU where individual national electorates are asked to decide on a treaty that is a political compromise agreed by several nations.

We now turn to the final, and potentially most crucial, link of representation available to citizens, namely the pressure that public opinion can assert on national parties and governments.

50.4.3 The Electoral Connection in Domestic Politics

The Council—which remains the single most powerful decision-making body in the EU—provides national publics with another avenue of representation, namely national elections. National governments will generally seek to adopt policy positions in line with voter preferences in order to ensure re-election. However, the extent to which national political parties adopt EU policy positions in line with public preferences will depend on whether the public cares enough to take notice. During the era of the "permissive consensus," few incentives existed for national governments to take account of public opinion. Hence, most mainstream political parties adopted positions that were largely in favor of further European integration, even if such positions were inconsistent with the preferences of their voters.[49] As decisions taken by the EU have begun to affect citizens in more obvious ways, the potential for politicization of the European issue in the public space has also become greater. In the words of Cees van der Eijk and Mark Franklin, public opinion on European integration is a "sleeping giant" ripe for politicization if and when political entrepreneurs seize the opportunity.[50] There is a debate in the field about the extent to which this sleeping giant has indeed been awoken. Some studies have shown that attitudes towards European integration impact vote choices in at least some national elections.[51] But other scholars have noted that European issues still play a very limited role in domestic political competition.[52] Catherine De Vries[53] has shown that the degree to which European integration issues matter in national elections is conditional upon the salience of the issue for voters and the extent of partisan conflict. In particularly, parties on the far right of the political spectrum can act as effective political entrepreneurs mobilizing voters against further integration.

Any correspondence between public preferences and party positions may of course be due to two different processes: a bottom-up process where elites adapt their positions in line with the voters' preferences (the electoral connection) or a "top-down" process where voters adopt the positions of their preferred political elites (cue-taking). The literature shows considerable evidence for both of these processes.[54] In other words, party elites seem responsive to the views of their supporters, but they also help to shape those views. The strength of these relationships are conditioned by the national context: voters are more responsive to parties when dissent is low, whereas voter preferences have a greater effect on party positions in countries that hold referendums and where parties are polarized on the issue. Existing scholarship thus suggests that there is great potential for an "electoral connection" between national and European politics, but much depends on national political institutions and parties.

50.5 CONCLUSION

In most work on European integration, public opinion has been largely ignored or has been regarded as a by-product of the functional, elite-driven process. Yet, after attempts to reform the EU treaties have been stalled, and even abandoned, due to "No" votes in referendums, scholars have also begun to pay more attention to public opinion. An extensive literature on public support for integration has emerged during the last two decades. While economic cost–benefit models remain the dominant perspective for understanding public support for integration, recent work has returned to a preoccupation with transnational identity (and lack thereof) pioneered in the early neo-functionalist writings.[55] Scholars have acknowledged that while trade liberalization may still be at the heart of the integration process, for many citizens European integration is conceived as a direct threat to their national sovereignty and distinctiveness and thus to their national identity. Moreover, researchers have begun to examine how public opinion is shaped not only by the cues disseminated by party elites, but also by the specific national political and economic context.

The increasing interest in public opinion on European integration also reflects demands for more democratic control of policy-making at the European level. As the scope and level of EU competences have expanded, decision-making by unaccountable elites behind closed doors is no longer regarded as satisfactory. In an attempt to strengthen democracy in the Union, the powers of the European Parliament have been increased. Yet, these reforms have not succeeded in translating public preferences about Europe into policy outputs, due to the second-order nature of European Parliament elections where many voters base their choices on domestic concerns. Referendums have been somewhat more successful in creating a debate about Europe, yet direct democracy has also resulted in institutional deadlock and forced the EU to abandon its attempt to create a Constitution for Europe, designed to make the institutions and decision-making processes more transparent and democratic.

This politicization of the European integration may, however, serve to strengthen the electoral connection at the national level: political entrepreneurs that mobilize opposition to European integration are on the rise in a number of countries. Ironically perhaps, a stronger "electoral connection" between citizens and politicians on European issues also implies a downward pressure on the level and scope of integration, since European publics tend to be more Euro-skeptic than the elites. When given a direct say on the integration process even some of the most pro-European publics have turned down proposals for wider and deeper integration. But this may also suggest that the time is ripe for scholars of public opinion and integration to move beyond the exclusive focus on "more" or "less" integration. As European integration has evolved, it may be that just like the preferences that structure domestic political contestation cannot easily be confined to a single dimension, public opinion on integration is no longer simply concerned with "how much" European integration, but also with "what kind" of European integration. One of the challenges for the next generation of scholarship on public opinion and European integration is therefore to explore the potentially multi-faceted nature of attitudes on European integration, and examine how these attitudes are activated and mobilized by political actors and translated into party positions and policy outcomes.

NOTES

1. Leon Lindberg and Stuart Scheingold, *Europe's Would-Be Polity* (Englewood Cliffs, NJ: Prentice Hall, 1970).
2. Liesbet Hooghe and Gary Marks, "A Postfunctionalist Theory of European Integration: From Permissive Consensus to Constraining Dissensus," *British Journal of Political Science* 39, no. 1 (2009), 1–23.
3. Geoffrey Evans, "Europe: A New Electoral Cleavage?," in Geoffrey Evans and Pippa Norris, *Critical Elections: British Parties and Voters in Long-Term Perspective* (London: Sage Publications, 1999), 207–22; Clifford Carrubba, "The Electorate Connection in European Union Politics," *Journal of Politics* 63 (2001), 141–58; Erik R. Tillman, "The European Union at the Ballot Box? European Integration and Voting Behavior in the New Member States," *Comparative Political Studies* 37, no. 5 (2004), 590–610; Catherine E. De Vries, "Sleeping Giant: Fact or Fairytale? How European Integration Affects National Elections," *European Union Politics* 8, no. 3 (2007), 363–85; Marco R. Steenbergen, Erica E. Edwards, and Catherine E. De Vries, "Who's Cueing Whom? Mass-Elite Linkages and the Future of European Integration," *European Union Politics* 8, no. 1 (2007), 13–35.
4. Mark Franklin, Michael Marsh, and Lauren McLaren, "The European Question: Opposition to Unification in the Wake of Maastricht," *Journal of Common Market Studies* 35 (1994), 455–72; Mark Franklin, Cees Van der Eijk, and Michael Marsh, "Referendum Outcomes and Trust in Government: Public Support for Europe in the Wake of Maastricht," *West European Politics* 18 (1995), 101–7; Cees Van der Eijk and Mark Franklin, *Choosing Europe? The European Electorate and National Politics in the Face of Union* (Ann Arbor: The University of Michigan Press, 1996); Simon Hix and Michael Marsh, "Punishment or Protest? Understanding European Parliament Elections," *The Journal of Politics* 69, no. 2 (2007), 495–510.
5. Andreas Føllesdal and Simon Hix, "Why There is a Democratic Deficit in the EU: A Response to Majone and Moravcsik," *Journal of Common Market Studies* 44, no. 3 (2006), 533–62; Peter Mair, "The Limited Impact of Europe on National Party Systems," *West European Politics* 23, no. 4 (2000), 27–51.
6. European Council, Laeken declaration, December 15, 2001.
7. See e.g. Liesbet Hooghe, "What Drives Euroskepticism?: Party-Public Cueing, Ideology and Strategic Opportunity," *European Union Politics* 8, no. 1 (2007), 5–12.
8. David Easton, *A Systems Analysis of Political Life* (New York: Wiley, 1965); David Easton, "A Re-Assessment of the Concept of Political Support," *British Journal of Political Science* 5 (1975), 435–57.

9. See also Lindberg and Scheingold, *Europe's Would-Be Polity*.

10. Eurobarometer 68 (2007).

11. "In general, are you for or against efforts being made to unify Western Europe?," "Generally speaking, do you think that [your country's] membership of the European Union is a good thing, a bad thing, or neither good nor bad?," and "Would you say that [your country] has on balance benefited from being a member of the EC/EU?."

12. See e.g. Matthew J. Gabel, *Interest and Integration. Market Liberalization, Public Opinion and European Union* (Ann Arbor: The University of Michigan Press, 1998); Lauren McLaren, "Public Support for the European Union: Cost/Benefit Analysis or Perceived Cultural Threat?," *Journal of Politics* 64, no. 12 (2002), 551–66; Liesbet Hooghe and Gary Marks, "Does Identity or Economic Rationality Drive Public Opinion on European Integration?," *PS: Political Science and Politics* 37 (2004), 415–20.

13. Ronald Inglehart, "Public Opinion and Regional Integration," *International Organization* 24 (1970), 795.

14. Ronald Inglehart, *The Silent Revolution. Changing Values and Political Styles among Western Publics* (Princeton, NJ: Princeton University Press, 1977).

15. Inglehart, "Public Opinion and Regional Integration."

16. Joseph I. H. Janssen, "Post-Materialism, Cognitive Mobilization, and Public Support for European Integration," *British Journal of Political Science* 21 (1991), 443–68; Gabel, *Interest and Integration*.

17. A notable exception are the studies on voting behavior in European Parliament elections published in the 1980s: Karlheinz Reif and Hermann Schmitt, "Nine Second-Order National Elections. A Conceptual Framework for the Analysis of European Election Results," *European Journal for Political Research* 8 (1980), 3–44; Karlheinz Reif, "National Election Cycles and European Elections, 1979 and 1984," *Electoral Studies* 3, no. 3 (1984), 244–55.

18. Matthew J. Gabel and Harvey D. Palmer, "Understanding Variation in Public Support for European Integration," *European Journal of Political Research* 27 (1995), 3–19; Christopher J. Anderson and M. Shawn Reichert, "Economic Benefits and Support for Membership in the EU: A Cross-National Analysis," *Journal of Public Policy* 15 (1996), 231–49; Matthew J. Gabel, "Public Support for European Integration: An Empirical Test of Five Theories," *The Journal of Politics* 60, no. 2 (1998), 333–54; Gabel, *Interest and Integration*. See also Joshua A Tucker, Alexander C. Pacek, and Adam J. Berinsky, "Transitional Winners and Losers: Attitudes Toward EU Membership in Post-Communist Countries," *American Journal of Political Science* 46 (2002), 557–71.

19. Richard Eichenberg and Russell Dalton, "Europeans and the European Community: The Dynamics of Public Support for European Integration," *International Organization* 47, no. 4 (1993), 507–34; Christopher J. Anderson and Karl C. Kaltenthaler, "The Dynamics of Public Opinion toward European Integration, 1973–93," *European Journal of International Relations* 2 (1996), 175–99.

20. Adam Brinegar, Seth Jolly, and Herbert Kitschelt, "Varieties of Capitalism and Political Divides over European Integration," in Gary Marks and Marco Steenbergen, eds, *European Integration and Political Conflict* (Cambridge: Cambridge University Press, 2004), 62–89. See also Adam Brinegar and Seth Jolly, "Location, Location, Location: National Contextual Factors and Public Support for European Integration," *European Union Politics* 6 (2005), 155–80; Liesbet Hooghe and Gary Marks, "Community, Calculation and Cues," *European Union Politics* 6, no. 4 (2005), 421–45.

21. Christopher Anderson, "When in Doubt, Use Proxies: Attitudes Toward Domestic Politics and Support for European Integration," *Comparative Political Studies* 31, no. 5 (1998), 569–601; Sylvia Kritzinger, "The Influence of the Nation-State on Individual Support for the European Union," *European Union Politics* 4, no. 2 (2003), 219–41.

22. Reif and Schmitt, "Nine Second-Order National Elections"; Franklin, Marsh and McLaren, "The European Question"; Franklin, Van der Eijk, and Marsh, "Referendum Outcomes and Trust in Government"; G. Schneider and P. A. Weitsman, "The Punishment Trap: Integration Referendums as Popularity Contests," *Comparative Political Studies* 28, no. 4 (1996), 582–607.

23. Anderson, "When in Doubt, Use Proxies."

24. Ignacio Sanchez-Cuenca, "The Political Basis of Support for European Integration," *European Union Politics* 1, no. 2 (2000), 147–71.

25. Robert Rohrschneider, "The Democratic Deficit and Support of an EU-Wide Government," *American Journal of Political Science* 46 (2002), 463–75; Kritzinger, "The Influence of the Nation-State on Individual Support for the European Union."

26. Leonard Ray, "When Parties Matter: The Conditional Influence of Party Positions on Voter Opinion about European Integration," *Journal of Politics* 65, no. 4 (2003), 978–94; Steenbergen, Edwards, and De Vries, "Who's Cueing Whom?."

27. Jeffrey A. Karp, Susan A. Banducci, and Shaun Bowler, "To Know It Is to Love It: Satisfaction with Democracy in the European Union," *Comparative Political Studies* 36, no. 3 (2003), 271–92.

28. Sean Carey, "Undivided Loyalties: Is National Identity an Obstacle to European Integration?," *European Union Politics* 3, no. 4 (2002), 387–413; Hooghe and Marks, "Community, Calculation and Cues"; Lauren McLaren, *Identity, Interests and Attitudes to European Integration* (Basingstoke: Palgrave Macmillan, 2006).

29. Carey, "Undivided Loyalties."

30. McLaren, "Public Support for the European Union"; McLaren, *Identity, Interests and Attitudes to European Integration*.

31. Claes H. De Vreese and Hajo G. Boomgaarden, "Projecting EU Referendums: Fear of Immigration and Support for European Integration," *European Union Politics* 6, no. 1 (2005), 59–82; Sara B. Hobolt, Wouter van der Brug, Claes H. De Vreese, and Hajo G. Boomgaarden, "Religious Intolerance and Euroscepticism," *European Union Politics*, 12, no. 3 (2011), 359–79.

32. Hooghe and Marks, "Community, Calculation and Cues"; Hooghe and Marks, "Does Identity or Economic Rationality Drive Public Opinion on European Integration?."

33. Carey, "Undivided Loyalties"; Hooghe and Marks, "Community, Calculation and Cues"; McLaren, *Identity, Interests and Attitudes to European Integration*.

34. For example: "Do you see yourself as 1) [nationality] only 2) [nationality] and European, 3) European and [nationality] or 4) European only?."

35. In fairness, neo-functionalism scholars are interested in European identity, but primarily as a product, rather than a driver, of the integration process. The two-level game logic at the heart of liberal intergovernmentalism could in principle incorporate the role public opinion at the domestic level, but the focus primary focus has primarily been on national organized interests.

36. Ernst B. Haas, *The Uniting of Europe* (Stanford, CA: Stanford University Press, 1958).

37. Andrew Moravcsik, *The Choice for Europe: Social Purpose and State Power from Messina to Maastricht* (Ithaca: Cornell University Press, 1998).

38. Hooghe and Marks, "A Postfunctionalist Theory of European Integration"; Liesbet Hooghe and Gary Marks, Chapter 58, this volume.

39. Reif and Schmitt, "Nine Second-Order National Elections."

40. Reif, "National Election Cycles and European Elections, 1979 and 1984"; Cees Van der Eijk and Mark Franklin, *Choosing Europe? The European Electorate and National Politics in the Face of Union* (Ann Arbor: The University of Michigan Press, 1996); Michael Marsh, "Testing the Second-Order Election Model After Four European Elections," *British Journal of Political Science* 28, no. 4 (1998), 591–607; Wouter Van der Brug and Cees van der Eijk, eds, *European Elections and Domestic Politics: Lessons from the Past and Scenarios for the Future* (Notre Dame: University of Notre Dame Press, 2007); Hix and Marsh, "Punishment or Protest? Understanding European Parliament Elections."

41. Reif and Schmitt, "Nine Second-Order National Elections," 3.

42. Sara B. Hobolt, Jae-Jae Spoon, and James Tilley, "A Vote against Europe? Explaining Defection at the 1999 and 2004 European Parliament Elections," *British Journal of Political Science* 39, no. 1 (2009), 93–115; Sara B. Hobolt and Jill Wittrock, "The Second-Order Election Model Revisited: An Experimental Test of Vote Choices in European Parliament Elections," *Electoral Studies* 30, no. 1 (2011), 29–40; Catherine E. De Vries, Wouter van der Brug, Cees van der Eijk, and Marcel van Egmond, "Individual and Contextual Variation in EU Issue Voting: The Role of Political Information," *Electoral Studies* 30, no. 1 (2011), 16–28.

43. Føllesdal and Hix, "Why There is a Democratic Deficit in the EU."

44. Peter Mair and Jacques Thomassen, "Political Representation and Government in the European Union," *Journal of European Public Policy* 17, no. 1 (2010), 20–35.

45. Hooghe and Marks, "A Postfunctionalist Theory of European Integration," 20.

46. Franklin, Marsh, and McLaren, "The European Question"; Franklin, Van der Eijk, and Marsh, "Referendum Outcomes and Trust in Government."

47. Karen Siune, Palle Svensson, and Ole Tonsgaard, "The European Union: The Danes Said 'No' in 1992 but 'Yes' in 1993: How and Why?," *Electoral Studies* 13, no. 2 (1994), 107–16; Sara B. Hobolt, *Europe in Question: Referendums on European Integration* (Oxford: Oxford University Press, 2009).

48. Hobolt, *Europe in Question*.

49. Liesbet Hooghe, "Europe Divided? Elites vs. Public Opinion on European Integration," *European Union Politics* 4, no. 3 (2003), 281–305; Hobolt, Spoon, and Tilley, "A Vote against Europe?."

50. Cees Van der Eijk and Mark Franklin, "Potential for Contestation on European Matters at National Elections in Europe," in Gary Marks and Marco Steenbergen, eds, *European Integration and Political Conflict* (Cambridge: Cambridge University Press, 2004), 32–50.

51. Evans, "Europe: A New Electoral Cleavage?"; Tillman, "The European Union at the Ballot Box?"; De Vries, "Sleeping Giant: Fact or Fairytale?."

52. Mair, "The Limited Impact of Europe on National Party Systems"; Nick Sitter, "The Politics of Opposition and European Integration in Scandinavia: Is Euroscepticism a Government-Opposition Dynamic?," *West European Politics* 24, no. 1 (2001), 22–39.

53. De Vries, "Sleeping Giant: Fact or Fairytale?" see also Catherine de Vries, Erica E. Edwards, and Erik R. Tillman, "Clarity of Resporsibility Beyond the Pocketbook: How Political Institutions Condition EU Issue Voting ," *Comparative Political Studies* 44, no. 3 (2011), 339-63.

54. Bernhard Wessels, "Evaluations of the EC: Elite or Mass Driven," in Oskar Neidermayer and Richard Sinott, eds, *Public Opinion and Internationalized Governance* (Oxford: Oxford University Press, 1995), 105–36; Sara B. Hobolt, "How Parties Affect Vote Choice in European Integration Referendums," *Party Politics* 12, no. 5 (2006), 623–47; Carrubba, "The Electorate Connection in European Union Politics"; Steenbergen, Edwards, and De Vries, "Who's Cueing Whom?"; Ray, "When Parties Matter."
55. Haas, *The Uniting of Europe*; Lindberg and Scheingold, *Europe's Would-Be Polity*.

CHAPTER 51

....

RIGHTS (AND OBLIGATIONS) IN EU LAW*

....

JOXERRAMON BENGOETXEA

51.1 INTRODUCTION: APPROACHES TO RIGHTS IN THE EU

....

Studies of rights in the EU can adopt different perspectives. A descriptive approach would identify the rights recognized in EU law, list them, find the Treaty, statutory, and judicial sources upon which they are grounded, survey and compare them. The law of the EU, as regards individuals as citizens and economic actors, is about rights, and the wealth of legislation and case law contributes to a constant fine-tuning of rights, often following from more general Treaties' rights and principles.[1] This approach requires a certain leap of faith: that we have correctly identified the rights according to some rule or practice of recognition or theory of the sources of legal rights, encompassing norms found in written instruments or judgments of the Court, but also in general legal principles; and that we are capable of distinguishing these norms from other types of rights belonging to normative orders to be distinguished from (EU) law.

A second approach would identify types of rights in the EU and their correlative obligations, according to their object: economic, social, political, administrative, and so on. A first category would compare citizenship rights with more general rights of persons, even the rights of aliens, or fundamental rights with the more general human rights. A second category would identify the classical free movement rights together with the non-discrimination principle and free competition rights and perhaps compare them with more recent rights like consumer protection, rights before the administration (governance rights), rights to the environment or sustainable development, rights to universal public services; perhaps even cultural and linguistic rights.[2]

Another approach, namely historical narrative would describe the initial market freedoms and rights and then focus strongly on fundamental rights jurisprudence with its different development stages: from the statement that Community law could not possibly ignore fundamental rights as recognized in the constitutional traditions of the member states, through the incorporation thesis, to the Fundamental Rights review of member states' legislation implementing or applying European Community law.[3] The latest developments concerning the Charter of Fundamental Rights of the EU would receive a prominent position in this analysis, and a discussion would follow concerning its binding versus merely prospective character. This approach would also account for the system developed under the European Convention for the Protection of Human Rights and Fundamental Freedoms. The analysis extends to the accession of the EU to the European Convention and to the legal force of the Charter and the interpretation by the Court of the special opt-outs negotiated for the UK and Poland.

The first approach is apparently more descriptive and less theoretical. The second approach incorporates some type of comparative theory, and the third introduces a historical narrative. Yet another, more philosophical approach would inquire into the common conceptions of the good that eventually permeate rights' discourses and even the models for European integration corresponding to such conceptions of the good. The more ideological versions would identify rights inherited from the liberal tradition or from free market economics, or from social welfare economics, or from the more modern sustainable development and governance ethos. The cultural approaches might see more Western similarities behind these traditionally disputed ideologies sharing concepts of progress and development when compared to other parts of the world and other ways of understanding normative relationships between individuals, groups, authority, nature, and even the cosmic order. In this connection, the extent to which the EU should export its values, standards, and conceptions of the good through the introduction of rights clauses in international treaties has become a contested issue in international relations, especially in the fields of trade and development aid.

Further questions could be asked concerning the holders of the rights or the mechanisms available for rights enforcement.[4] The distinction between classical individual rights and social, cultural rights is easier to draw by looking at the procedural rules concerning standing (locus standi). Sociocultural rights are then reformulated as personal rights with a collective and interpersonal dimension rather than genuine group rights. Even in the more obvious context of industrial relations or civil society, the groups are incorporated in the law as legal persons.[5] Political discourse recognizes group rights and group actors but our legal systems still fail to recognize legal groups or communities other than public law bodies. The mechanisms available for the enforcement of rights are also very complex, especially in the context of a multilevel governance system like that of the EU. Domestic protection of EU law rights in national jurisdictions is the rule, but it does raise the issue whether the existence of a right in EU law also entails a right to effective protection of such right at all levels. Thus, the Court of Justice has insisted time and again on the principle of effective remedies and non-discrimination,[6] but the risk of EU rights being recognized in different degrees throughout the member states haunts case law. The differing normative intensity of the rights and ensuing obligations would jeopardize the project of a harmonized Union based on the principle of equal treatment and non-discrimination.[7] Nowhere is this risk more tenacious than as regards the exhaustion of rights where, because of special procedural rules operative in municipal law, a right-holder might be deprived of the right to bring an action in order to enforce the right.

In this chapter, the general issue of rights (and obligations) in the law of the EU is approached from a theoretical, analytical perspective. This requires, in the first place, a theory of rights: we need to know how to identify rights, and not just fundamental rights, amongst all sorts of jural relations and legal institutes (institutions) (section 51.2 deals with this issue).[8] In a second stage, it will be necessary to consider whether rights in the EU have their very source in instruments of Community law, in the wider law of the EU, or elsewhere (section 51.3). In this latter sense, rights in the EU might be a rather large category comprising all duly recognized and enforceable rights within the EU as a complex set of institutions, and this can include rights derived from, and thereby recognized by EU law, as well as rights derived from other legal systems (member states' legal systems, international law, the European Convention of Human Rights) but recognized also in the EU legal system. Those systems interact when dealing with rights and obligations, especially in the context of directives (or framework decisions), instruments conceived to ensure that rights and obligations created at European Community (or EU) level are recognized in the member states according to their ordinary legislative process.

Fundamental rights are one of the foundations of the EU,[9] and although the discussion whether the ECJ has taken the incorporation thesis to its limits (mostly) with a view to developing a *Grundrechtsgemeinschaft* and the debate concerning the impact of such a move on constitutional pluralism within the EU are theoretically important[10] and not deprived of practical consequences (as the cases in *K.B.*,[11] *Richards*,[12] and *Maruko*[13] show), they go beyond the scope of this chapter.

51.2 THE SYSTEM-RELATIVE CHARACTER OF RIGHTS

Rights are claims to protection of a person's interests under any given normative order: morality, politics, customary law, "folk law," natural law, international law, domestic laws, the regulations and charters of clubs, churches, or other local, national, transnational, or international organizations and undertakings. Since law is institutional normative order,[14] *legal* rights are claims made under a given legal order and protected institutionally within that order, by its legal norms and the officials enforcing them. Obviously, legal rights—and for that matter the rights recognized to members of such associations, organizations, or undertakings—differ from one system to another in a way that moral and human rights do not. Moral and human rights (as modern versions of natural law) lay important claims to universal validity, and although their existence and/or validity do not depend upon their factual recognition within particular systems, their effectiveness and enforceability largely does, even though there is a growing expectation and *opinio iuris* on the part of the world community that states should comply and that intervention on humanitarian (human rights') grounds may be justified.[15] But moral or ethical systems are not institutionally bound to the same extent and intensity as legal systems, and this largely accounts for their universality.

Traditionally state legal systems were the only forum where legal rights could be recognized and awarded legal and judicial protection, and therefore the only forum where legal rights could become effective. The state legal system was the appropriate and probably exclusive forum for imposing and enforcing obligations, thus protecting rights claims. While it is relatively easy to proclaim rights at a supra-state level, it is much more difficult to ensure the imposition of obligations or restrictions correlative to rights and essential for their effectiveness. Even though the nation state remains the chief legal context for rights protection, international human rights movements and instruments such as the European Convention of Human Rights are gaining influence and primacy over domestic regimes. This process is taking place at a global scale, but in Europe it is particularly noteworthy. Complex institutional systems such as the OSCE and (more to the point) the EU have developed, where fundamental rights' protection is bringing about a conceptual redefinition of such rights beyond the sovereign state, thus challenging established municipal views and notions concerning the relationship between citizen, rights, community, and state. "The existence of rights-based protections within the EU raises a plethora of interesting issues concerning the relationship between these rights and those found within the European Convention on Human Rights, national law, and international law."[16]

Rights and obligations are better understood as relations or positions concerning more than one individual arising within concrete institutional normative orders, and appreciated by an interpretation of specific situations read against general rules and principles pertaining to those orders or to the legal cultures in which they develop and to which they contribute. This makes "right" or "obligation" a very markedly relational or system-relative notion, to the extent that they are meaningless when deprived of the social normative networks and relationships in which they occur. Thus, the necessary analysis of the sophisticated techniques and analytical tools developed in (EU) law in order to formalize such relationships should not blind the scholar to the social background of rights and obligations: relations of power, allocations of power in society, imposition of obligations on certain persons, distribution of goods in a society, and theories of fairness in such distribution. Hopefully, all these aspects will enable a further and deeper understanding of social, constitutional, economic, institutional, and political contexts in which reference to rights and obligations takes prominence, all of which are necessary to understand rights' discourses. Understanding the techniques involved in legal reasoning concerning rights and obligations in a legal (contractual or other) relationship between two parties, producer and consumer, large firm and service consumer, or distributor and retailer, or husband and wife, is necessary for an understanding of the rights and (formally voluntary) obligations following from such relationships, but that understanding will need to look at the socio-economic conditions of the actors

involved in the relationships. The intensity of the voluntariness of the parties to a contract can then be put into perspective.

All rights are thus system-relative, but legal rights are relative to those particular legal
orders which recognize them. This relative or dependent nature comes with a greater
effectiveness: the legal system will make it possible to identify the most important features of the right, and the institutional machinery of the law can be mobilized to enforce
the right, following the procedures and within the limits established by law. That legal
rights are effective ultimately means that protection is afforded within the legal order: it
will be possible to identify actors concerned by such rights and officials who can enforce
their correlative obligations.

In the EU, this is a real challenge because it amounts to mobilizing many actors, with
different powers and competences: the right recognized at EU level might require the
imposition of an obligation at state or national level. The most sophisticated instrument
where this dynamics takes place is the directive. The relationship between rights and
obligations is widely accepted in legal and political discourse. However, as Hohfeld
demonstrated a century ago, this binary relation is more complex than the literature
assumes. Rights' discourse is ambiguous or vague; it can refer to claims, liberties, powers, or immunities.

51.2.1 The Attractiveness of Rights and the Spread of Rights Discourses

Rights are an important issue in any society, institution, or community. There is an
inherent attractiveness to rights, a positive emotional charge attaching to rights in any
practical discourse to such an extent that any "serious" normative claim will ultimately
be formulated in terms of rights. This is largely because important human interests are
protected and enhanced when cloaked in rights discourse. On the other hand, reference
to obligations relates to burdens and onus. Claims relating to obligations are normally
directed to other parties, to third persons, and rely on responsibilities or duties. Claims
on obligations are seldom made on oneself. From a contemporary perspective, in which
rights claims are seen as ways of furthering interests, it seems odd and almost counterin-
tuitive to protect one's interest by claiming that some obligation should be imposed on
oneself, beyond those voluntary obligations contractually assumed for which there is
normally a counter-performance of the other party. This might seem awkward but it is
not conceptually wrong. Indeed, sometimes, by claiming new obligations, by assuming
and respecting them, the claim of competence can be strengthened. A person's claim to
custody over a child implies a will to assume obligations concerning that child. An
administration or governance system claiming competence over any specific field, say
competition policy, is implicitly claiming the assumption of obligations to police the
economic behavior of actors, to monitor their compliance with the rules of competition,
and to find and sanction any possible breach of such rules. The party who has control

over the extent of an obligation, duty of care, amounts and conditions of compensation, or the like, has greater control over the legal relationship than the party who claims the recognition of a right.

Some legal and political cultures, such as Western constitutional culture, have historically developed by the claims of rights of the citizen, intended as protection from abuse by public authorities. But to the extent that rights and interests have been extended to other subjects—individual, collective, or even living beings and nature—the accumulation of rights claims has proved to be, if not self-defeating, certainly inflationary and has occasionally weighed and balanced off such claims against each other. (The need to explore other legal techniques and claims of obligations is an avenue worth pursuing.) Invoking rights conveys an implicit claim to legitimacy because rights refer back to serious and important social or political claims to protect valuable human interests. A community where rights are invoked, protected, respected, and fostered is a dynamic, cohesive, and fair one. "Rights" are therefore talked about as something intrinsically valuable. If one adds the qualification "human," "basic," or "fundamental" then even further prestige and weight are added. In this sense, the language of rights is indeed pervasive and encompassing because it relates to fairness.

51.2.2 Fundamental Rights and Fragmentation of Rights

In Euopean Community law, the concepts of fundamental rights and even human rights can be distinguished from the more classical concepts of free movement or common market freedoms. But the former can arguably be distinguished even from the more modern rights of citizenship, which are not *fundamental* or universal, strictly speaking, but only recognized for individuals having the status of "citizen." Fundamental rights are relative latecomers in the rights discourse of European Community law. While there are many possible explanations for this belated inclusion, they are now seen as basic pillars of the EU, ensuring its legitimacy and acceptability. Even the four freedoms of the internal market are reconceptualized as fundamental and ultimately inspired by the leitmotiv of non-discrimination, fairness, and freedom. Talk of free access and free establishment, requiring the abolition of restrictions, opting for a market model which favors intra-community personal and economic transactions, abolishing any measure that might make it less attractive to exercise the right to move within the EU (the internal market), applying the rule of reason or the proportionality tests, or the conditions regarding the justification of restrictions on the four freedoms— all these views of the market-based European Community are now conceived under the fundamental rights rationale and legal reasoning. Thus, the freedom to provide services is further reinforced by the right to marriage and to family life, so that the third-country spouse of a person offering intra-community services cannot be expelled from the member state of residence without infringing on the Treaty.[17] The economic operator enjoying a community right to provide services is, at the same time, a person entitled to the fundamental right to a family.

But rights in European Community law can be further divided into different categories according to their subject matter: economic rights, labor rights, environmental rights, social and welfare rights, sexual and gender rights, political rights, and so on. Does this lead to an inevitable fragmentation of rights discourse, parallel to the implosion of international rights regimes? Or is it only an appearance of diversity and plurality behind the underlying unity and unquestionable attraction of rights, its positive charge, and the elasticity of a concept encapsulating many different elements and legal relationships? The fact that fundamental rights—whether they be negative freedoms, claims to protection *from* state interference, or claims of positive access *to* welfare services—are normally claimed against the state, whereas other rights (especially the jural situations analyzed by Hohfeld) are claimed in binary relations between private individuals, make it difficult to detect a common thread in all rights discourses—fundamental rights, civic rights, citizenship rights, ordinary (Hohfeldian) rights from contract or legislation. Nevertheless, the way the right is protected and enforced does not predetermine its existence or validity.

This dichotomy of unity and fragmentation can also be seen when analyzing the relation between rights and equality, especially in the context of minorities' rights. Equal rights are constitutive of a democratic polity. Ideally, in a fair society, human or fundamental rights are recognized for all persons, no matter what their status or contractual situation might be. Civil and political rights are recognized for all citizens equally, but other legal rights, i.e. rights recognized by legal instruments such as laws, contracts, conventions, agreements, and the like are vested only on the persons concerned by the elements and terms contained in those instruments. They are recognized, not for all citizens and persons universally, but only for classes of people who fulfill certain conditions, and in this sense they are no longer fundamental or human rights (e.g. being a consumer, a tourist, a farmer or economic operator, a worker, or any other condition). Equality and universality go together logically: if the conditions laid out in the definition of the right are fulfilled, the right is recognized to all individuals fulfilling those conditions, without exception or distinction: discrimination is a denial of right. In other words, within each of the categories, rights are recognized irrespective of personal, individual, or subjective features. When such personal features become relevant entitlements to special claims and when other similar cases within the same categories fulfilling the same conditions but different personal features do not qualify for such claims and positions, then we speak of *privileges*, not of rights.

This link between equality and rights is another consideration contributing to the legitimating force of any rights' discourse. However, the idea that rights should be effective and real is also essential to a cohesive society and to any polity that aims to live according to its own values. This means that a discourse stressing the formal equality of rights cannot or should not ignore the fact that certain persons, because of their gender or sex, their age, their origin and color, their language, their (lack of) wealth, their class, and so on, and certain groups, because of their ethnic origin, their language, their religion, or other factors are placed under disadvantaged positions preventing them from enjoying the rights they have as human beings, as citizens, and as classes of people concerned by the laws establishing legal rights or benefits. Minorities' rights and reverse discrimination are then useful conceptual tools to address, or to redress those disadvantages and combat situations of discrimination, which are contrary to a substantial, as opposed to a merely formal, notion of equality.[18] The EU has adopted many instruments in this sense, starting off with sex discrimination and moving into other areas.[19] Correspondingly, at the opposite end of the discrimination spectrum, privileges, special rights or exemptions from duties, or special immunities for specific persons due to a person's power or wealth, name or lineage, personal or family features, are considered contrary to the very concept of equal rights.

51.2.3 The Analysis of Rights

Freedoms and rights are thus resorted to in many different contexts and with possibly different meanings and implications. As a result, there is great confusion on the notion and concept, which potentially generates misunderstandings. The picture can be further complicated by the interference of procedural rules. This situation however has not led to any serious or successful attempt to do away with the term altogether, perhaps because of the special magnetism and definitely positive charge mentioned above (a major feature of the term "rights" which it shares with other terms like "equality," "fairness," or "democracy"). Even those currents of legal theory, such as Scandinavian realism,[20] that take a skeptical attitude toward "rights" as autonomous entities or as conceptual constructs applied in legal reasoning admit their usefulness in the exposition of law for systematizing and pedagogical purposes.

The notion of "rights," when analyzing European Community law, needs closer analytical scrutiny. Hilson and Downes correctly contend that the ECJ has abandoned a simple approach to Community law rights in favor of a more complex and multi-tiered taxonomy of juridical effects; for instance, the effects of the norms contained in directives. The authors[21] examine three contexts where the ECJ elaborates on EU rights: judicial enforceability, the liability of the member states and the Union, and conditions for the effectiveness of directives. This chapter examines all three areas but focuses on the positions affected by directives. Rights, as positions of benefit or advantage recognized by institutional normative orders and developed through legal reasoning, ultimately concern the intersubjective positions of persons. The legal positions of individuals and the legal reasoning involved in the discourse about them need some clarification.

51.2.4 Hohfeld's Analysis

The type of analysis of fundamental legal conceptions, beyond the dichotomy of rights and duties, carried out almost a century ago by Hohfeld can still be considered as illuminating. Wesley Newcomb Hohfeld (1879–1918) published his famous article "Some Fundamental Legal Conceptions as Applied in Judicial Reasoning" in the *Yale Law*

Journal in 1913. He distinguished eight fundamental legal conceptions that enable a more adequate analysis of the legal relations between subjects. According to Hohfeld, the term *right* has in legal language four basic meanings or entitlements:

(1)   as a simple right or a claim(-right)
(2)   as a privilege or a liberty
(3)   as a power or a competence
(4)   as an immunity, shield, or protection

The jural opposites of these entitlements as regards the same interest-holder are referred to as burdens: (1) no-claims (no-rights), (2) duties (no-liberty), (3) disabilities (no-powers), and (4) liabilities (no-immunity). The term "Hohfeldian element" is used to refer to both Hohfeldian entitlements and Hohfeldian burdens. These always operate in specific contexts and not in an abstract general way.

In Hohfeld's system, the concepts form pairs of correlates when they are juxtaposed within the context of a legal relation between two subjects (parties A and B). These correlates are:

$$A: claim \leftrightarrow B: duty$$
$$A: liberty \leftrightarrow B: no\text{-}claim$$
$$A: power \leftrightarrow B: liability$$
$$A: immunity \leftrightarrow B: disability$$

In Hohfeld's system, "power" and "immunity" are second-order concepts in relation to "claims" and "liberties," which concern acts or omissions. On the other hand, powers and immunities concern changes of claims or liberties. Hence, A has a power with respect to B when A can change the elements pertaining to B's position and correlatively B has a liability with respect to A. Similarly A has an immunity against B when B has no power to change A's position, i.e. B has a correlative disability with respect to A. The parties can be individuals, legal persons, authorities, and institutions. Hohfeldian entitlements are not intended to be straightforward descriptions of legal rights in the sense that one could identify individual (subjective) legal rights in isolation; rights like property ownership are complex wholes including all types of elements (entitlements/burdens) as regards different persons.

From this perspective, Hohfeldian elements can be regarded as elementary particles of legal thinking that are combined as atoms and molecules in the various "rights" and "obligations" present at different legal relationships as regulated by different, but coordinated, normative systems. For a judge or a court, the notion of a right always entails the perspective of a binary relation between the parties to the dispute, and possibly tertiary relations involving other interested parties. Thus, the protection of A's liberty consists exactly of B's position as a holder of no-claims, where B can invoke no valid claim against A in the courts or other legal or administrative proceedings. When this absence of claim is extended to all actors within a jurisdiction, A's liberty acquires a universal dimension. We enter the domain of fundamental liberties and B's no-claim becomes a general prohibition on all addressees to interfere with A's liberty. Likewise with immunity or protection, when a person's interests or personal dimensions are protected from inter-ference this becomes a universal protection. The fundamental freedoms of the internal market operate in this manner,[22] as do many of the elements foreseen in directives. The quality or property of a right recognized to an individual by the EU Treaties (or the Charter) or by the EU legislator in a directive projected on third persons in the form of obligations or disabilities is sometimes referred to as horizontal application of funda-mental rights, *Drittwirkung* or *Privatwirkung* in German dogmatics.[23] An example of this property in EU law is personal data protection:[24] all third parties are obliged to respect the privacy of the data they might hold concerning other persons.

51.3 THE SOURCES OF RIGHTS

Legal rights are relative to the legal system or legal order. The question whether a con-sumer, in the EU, has the right unilaterally to annul a contract of sale agreed outwith the premises of the seller[25] is a question that can only be answered according to the law gov-erning such situation in the EU: either European Community law or the laws of the member states. The issue cannot be answered correctly by looking into the laws of another country outside the EU, nor into moral or religious norms.

Theories of natural law have traditionally claimed that the validity and existence of certain rights, like human and fundamental rights, precedes and is not determined by positive laws, that such rights are the same for all individuals regardless of whether they are regulated in the same manner in concrete laws of different polities. In extreme cases, positive law could be invalid and should be left unapplied if it happened to contradict and deny such basic norms and principles when applied to the particular case. The doc-trine of *equity* was developed in some systems to make these correcting operations seem as normal as possible within the law. For those rights at least, their source might be inde-pendent from the concrete system of law of a given polity or it might be a more nuanced and critically inspired interpretation of that system of law, or even of the very concept of law. But even the strongest natural theory would limit the number of such natural rights to the core human rights—life, liberty, due process—and recognize that the develop-ment of fundamental rights and civil and political rights, and especially legal rights as recognized by specific laws (i.e. rights that are inconceivable without a system of law) are relative to and determined by the norms of that legal system.

Legal rights are contained in and defined by legal norms. In other words, the sources of legal rights in any polity are its legal norms, either because those legal norms recog-nize such rights in given circumstances to all those persons who satisfy certain condi-tions, or because those norms make it possible for individuals to enter into legal relations or contracts and thereby voluntarily define or create new individual rights and obliga-tions. So, what are those norms and where are they to be found? There are different views on the concept and nature of legal norms depending on the theoretical standpoint of the observer. For a majority, legal norms are the result of the will of the legislator and integrate the legal system. They are to be found in the sources of the law, the instruments adopted by the legislator, or in judicial decisions known as precedents. In EU law, the legal system would then comprise the norms contained in the Treaties establishing the Union (and its functioning Treaty) (and before the entry into force of the Treaty of Lisbon the Treaties establishing the Communities), and the norms contained in the legislation adopted in pursuance thereof: regulations and directives. The norms contained in the Treaties adopted by the Union with third states or international organizations are also part of the legal system of the EU. General principles of law recognized according to a shared rule of recognition operative throughout the EU are also norms of the EU legal system and can therefore be a source of rights and obligations, although the difficulty will lie in identifying such norms intersubjectively.

In the case of directives, the legal system of the EU will also expand to the legal system of the member states, to include the norms adopted by state and regional legislators in the EU in order to implement them, and generally all the norms contained in instruments dealing with issues where the EU has competence. As a result, the EU legal system might differ and slightly deviate in the different member states because the legal points of contact between member-state law and EU law will differ accordingly. Consequently, we can distinguish between (i) a core legal system of the EU that is uniform and harmonized in all member states, comprising the rights recognized and obligations imposed in the norms following from the Treaties, regulations, or directives, and (ii) a periphery of the EU legal system comprising not only the norms adopted by the different norm-making authorities of the member states (federal, national, central, regional, governmental, parliamentary, social actors) in implementation or development of the uniform norms following from EU directives, but also norms adopted by these same organs in areas of (shared, coordinated, or concerned) competence that are not yet or not fully harmonized throughout the EU.

In this larger periphery (ii), some rights might be recognized in some jurisdictions but not in others. The core (i) will be potentially the same across the EU, and the Court of Justice will ultimately ensure such uniformity. Although it is debatable whether the norms of member-state laws implementing directives or adopted in the areas of EU competence concerned (direct taxation, for instance) are also part of the EU legal system, it remains uncontested that the EU has potential, indirect control over such norms. The Court of Justice can control, for example, whether a given social benefit accorded by a national (central, regional, or local) authority is discriminatory on non-citizens or non-residents, or whether direct taxation norms of the member states (central[26] or regional[27]) are discriminatory or selective and therefore contrary to the rules on establishment or on state aids. This is a negative control of compatibility. These situations can also be described in terms of rights. A right to a certain reduction of the tax rate recognized under certain conditions to the companies established in a given territory, as regulated by the competent legislative authorities of that territory, can be declared discriminatory insofar as it denies the rights of competitors established in other territories of the EU. To this extent, at least, the legal systems of the member states, even in areas of reserved competence, are not immune to the EU legal system and its general principles; e.g. the right not to be discriminated against on the basis of nationality. This general principle of EU law and its application by the ECJ is such that it penetrates, some would say it invades or colonizes,[28] the legal systems of the member states in areas of their reserved or exclusive competence. Hence the theoretical question whether the EU legal system might extend to encompass or overarch the legal systems of the member states as its own federal subsystems.[29]

Rights in EU law will be found in any of the norms of the EU legal system: either in those norms recognizing on person A claims, liberties, capacities (abilities), and immunities, or in those norms imposing on person B duties, no-claims, disabilities, or liabilities. Sometimes those norms will be the result of enactments adopted by combined legislators, each having competence to regulate some specific aspect of the norm. Finally, general principles of law, because of their general nature, make it difficult to operate with Hohfeldian elements: e.g. due diligence, or duty of care. Principles are value-ascriptions rather than concrete allocations of rights and duties. Because of their structure as simple affirmations of value, they are difficult to apply in concrete situations with concrete results. However, through a process of interpretation and legal reasoning, it becomes possible to obtain rights from principles. Sometimes they are resorted to in order to interpret in a particular way rights-creating norms contained in statutes. In such situations, it makes little sense to think of general legal principles as the norms of the legal system: they are rather the source from which the norm will be drawn. But the norm will not exist in the "officially" written and published body of law, before interpretation—at least not in the manner in which a legislative provision can be seen as the norm adopted by the legislator. Principles can be stated by the legislator and incorporated into written provisions, but the principle always needs reconstructing.

51.4 CONCLUSION

The EU legal field is particularly complex as an institutional normative order because it implies complex federal relationships between the EU institutions and the member states, all acting as a coherent legislator. Domestic courts and the ECJ are also seen as a coherent cooperative machinery of interpretation and coherence of the law. The background theory of rights necessary to any institutional normative order we call law needs to address the recognition of rights (where are they recognized and how?) and their operation within the legal system in relation to other legal positions of individuals and authorities. An institutional theory of law relying on a pluralistic rule of recognition of EU (sources and instruments of) law and on the systemic operation of EU law through directives that produce diverse effects on individuals throughout the Union, combined with Hohfeld's analysis of fundamental legal positions, entitlements, and burdens, explain different forms of operation of rights discourse.

There is an aspect of rights, the symbolic one, which was hinted at by Hohfeld and the legal realists: claims of rights within a society are dealt with as serious, legitimate claims that need to be addressed by the legal and political systems. Recognition and enforcement of rights (and other related legal positions) are the means by which the law responds to social needs, formulated also in terms of rights claims, and this gives the law a moral dimension that could be considered inherent to the very concepts of law and right. Ideally these rights should respond to the needs and interests of all people in a given community, and the EU emerges as a complex institutional "lifeworld" encompassing other communities, where rights discourses are generated.[30] Some are strongly linked to the state (federal and pluri-national states or the traditional nation state) and others are public spheres developed independently of state law at the transnational, national, regional, or local levels. In such public spheres and communities, rational communication tends to generate these rights claims which are also claims to (moral, political, and legal) validity, and are often neutralized or weakened by major domains of economic and political life, where other interests are organized—the market, public powers, organizations, complex regulatory regimes—as countervailing forces that tend to drain rights discourses of moral commitment. In this context, engaging with a discourse on rights and obligations engages one in a discourse on justice.

Notes

* This work has been produced within the framework of the Consolidated Research Group (GIC07/86-IT-448-07) with financial assistance from the Education, Universities, and Research Department of the Basque Autonomous Government, and also within the framework of a research project on Fundamental Rights After Lisbon (der 2010–19715, juri) financed by the Spanish Ministry of Science and Innovation.
1. Works in this area are normally restricted to fundamental rights, not to all rights and obligations. An interesting example, Dirk Ehlers, ed., *European Fundamental Rights and Freedoms* (De Gruyter, Berlin 2007), brings together the most refined theories in fundamental rights, namely German dogmatics.
2. One of the classics in this sense, also limited to fundamental rights, is Nannette Neuwahl and Allan Rossas, eds, *The European Union and Human Rights* (Kluwer, The Hague 1995).
3. See e.g. K. Lenaerts, "Respect for Fundamental Rights as a Constitutional Principle of the European Union," in *The Columbia Journal of European Law* 6, no. 1 (2000), 1–25.
4. A study with solid theoretical foundations is Roland Winkler, Die Grundrechte der Europäischen Union (Springer, Wien 2006); it contains a useful summary in English.
5. Judgment of December 11, 2007 in C-438/05, *The International Transport Workers' Federation & The Finnish Seamen's Union* v *Viking* Line ABP & Oü Viking Line Eesti.
6. *Rewe v Lanwirtschaftskammer Saarland* Case 33/76 [1976] ECR 1989.
7. Judgment of November 22, 2005 in C-144/04, *Mangold*, paragraph 77: "it is the responsibility of the national court... to provide, in a case within its jurisdiction, the legal protection which individuals derive from the rules of Community law and to ensure that those rules are fully effective, setting aside any provision of national law which may conflict with that law... even where the period prescribed for transposition of that directive has not yet expired."

8. Following Neil MacCormick's institutional theory of law; see his *Institutions of Law* (Oxford: Oxford University Press, 2007).

9. It follows from Articles 2 and 6 of the Treaty on European Union that the EU is founded on the principles of liberty, democracy, respect for human rights and fundamental freedoms, and the rule of law. These principles are common to all member states. The EU respects fundamental rights, as guaranteed by the European Convention for the Protection of Human Rights and Fundamental Freedoms and as they result from the constitutional traditions common to the member states, as general principles of Community law.

10. A. Von Bogdandy, "The European Union as a Human Rights Organization? Human Rights and the Core of the European Union," *Common Market Law Review* 37 (2000), 1307–38.

11. Judgment of January 7, 2004, case C-117/01.

12. Judgment of April 26, 2006 in case C-423/04.

13. Judgment of April 1, 2008 in case C-267/06.

14. MacCormick, *Institutions of Law*.

15. See generally, Michael Ignatieff, *Human Rights as Politics, Human Rights as Idolatry*, The Tanner Lectures on Human Values (Princeton: Princeton University Press, 2000).

16. Paul Craig, *EU Administrative Law* (Oxford: Oxford University Press, 2006), 483.

17. In Case C-60/00, *Carpenter*, the fact that the family cannot stay together is considered by the Court of Justice as an indirect obstacle to free provision of services and a dissuasion of reliance on free movement (judgment of July 11, 2002).

18. See Patrick Thornberry and María Amor Martín Estébanez, *Minority Rights in Europe*, Council of Europe, 2004.

19. The non-discrimination directives adopted in the year 2000 are noteworthy: 2000/43/EC (combatting non-discrimination generally) and 2000/78/EC (as regards employment and occupation). On age discrimination, which was not explicitly foreseen as a discrimination ground, see case C-144/04, *Mangold*, judgment of November 22, 2005.

20. See Alf Ross, "Tû-tû," *Harvard Law Review* 70 (1957), 812–25.

21. C. Hilson and T. A. Downes, "Making Sense of Rights: Community Rights in E.C. Law," *E.L.Rev.* 24, no. 2 (1999), 121–38.

22. This analysis has been carried out by Joxerramon Bengoetxea and Niilo Jääskinen, "Rights and Diverse Effects in EU Law," in Reza Banakar, ed., *Rights in Context. Law and Justice in Late Modern Society* (Ashgate: Farnham, 2010), 277–300.

23. See Stephan Wernicke, *Die Privatwirkung im Europäischen Gemeinschaftsrecht* (Baden-Baden: Nomos, 2000). See, in English, J. H. Knox, "Horizontal Human Rights Law," *American Journal of International Law* 102, no. 1 (2008), 1–47, and volume 16 of the *European Review of Private Law* (2008).

24. Directive 95/46/EC. See also, Directive 2002/58/EC on privacy and electronic communications. In other jurisdictions this is known as privacy legislation. See case C-101/01, *Lindqvist*, judgment of the ECJ of November 6, 2003.

25. The case refers to C-91/92, *Faccini Dori v. Recreb Srl* [1994] ECR I-3325.

26. See e.g. C-346/04, *Conjin*, judgment of July 6, 2006, at paragraphs 14 and 15.

27. On state aid and regional direct taxation see judgment of September 11, 2008 in Joined Cases C-428/06- C-434/06, *UGT-Rioja e.a. (re. Basque fiscal regime)*.

28. See Marta Cartabia, "La Unión Europea y los derechos fundamentals: 50 años después," *RVAP* (Revista Vasca de Administración Pública) 82, no, 2 (2008), 85–101, at 100.

29. The debate on constitutional pluralism in the EU is illuminating in this regard; see Ingolf Pernice, "Multilevel Constitutionalism in the European Union," *European Law Review*

(2002), 511 and ff. See also generally Miguel Poiares Maduro, *A Constitução Plural* (Estoril: Principia, 2006).

30. On the notion of "lifeworld" and its application to the legal field, see Jürgen Habermas, *Between Facts and Norms. Contributions to a Discourse Theory of Law and Democracy* (Cambridge, MA: MIT Press, 1996), ch. 1.2.

CHAPTER 52

BRINGING THE TERRITORY BACK IN: TOWARD A NEW UNDERSTANDING OF THE REGIONAL DIMENSION OF THE EU

CHARLIE JEFFEREY AND
CAROLYN ROWE

52.1 INTRODUCTION

Analysis of the "regional dimension" of the EU has long since noted how the European integration process reframes the space for political action that regions can access.[1] Clearly, integration has expanded the coalitional possibilities of sub-national and national actors beyond the nation state, allowing both national and sub-national actors to be outflanked.[2]

What remains less clear, however, are the conditions under which European integration, understood here as a new space for political action, is an opportunity for regional governance actors, or a threat. To put it differently, is the EU a "problem" for regions, in need of a resolution?[3] Or is it an opportunity for extending sub-state capacity, particularly by bypassing the national set of controls?[4] It is an issue which separates the complex array of sub-national governmental "forms"—including stateless nations, legislative regions, administrative regions, and municipalities—into those with legislative competencies and those with an executive or administrative role.

Whilst the EU has been regarded variously as an opportunity and a threat by regional actors at different points in its history, contemporary practice shows that the difference in strategy and approach can be directly linked to governmental form at the regional or sub-state level.

A more nuanced analysis of this variation is long overdue.[5] This chapter seeks to unpack what is broadly understood as "the regional dimension" of EU politics, by considering these varying strategies and understandings of Europe as an opportunity space for autonomous political action or as a threat to independent political capacities, as provided for by domestic constitutional and legal arrangements. The picture painted here is one of a much more complex and varied pattern of regional engagement in the EU than the most common metaphors of a "Europe of the Regions" or the EU's "Third Level" would lead us to believe.

52.2 The Opportunities and Constraints of the European Integration Process for the Regions

The extent to which "Europe" is regarded as an opportunity or as a threat by regional actors in the member states varies along the multiple, cross-cutting dimensions of time, space, and sector. As the nature of the European integration process itself has advanced, so too have regional strategies for interacting with political aims and policy goals. Equally, constitutional developments in the member states have redefined the context in which "Europe hits home"[6] at the regional level. Therefore regional strategies for European engagement are not constant, and any categorization is necessarily broad-brush.

We can explore how regional interaction in the EU has been assessed across three principal axes: over time, across policy sectors, and, at an institutional level, within the policy "space."

52.2.1 Time

Several studies have sought to map the history of regional interaction with the European political process. Jeffery has identified three major strategies adopted by regional governments in their attempts to try and influence EU decision-making over the past twenty years.[7] The first strategy centered on an aim to secure sub-state influence in the EU policy process, on a pan-European basis. The resulting outcome failed to secure anything like the goals demanded by the key proponents of this strategy—the German Länder. A "Committee of the Regions" (CoR), the formal and institutionalized embodiment of this strategy, was marginalized in the decision-making process by its limited powers,[8] and was crippled internally by its heterogeneous membership of locally elected politicians, city councillors, and district representatives alongside the political heavyweights such as prime ministers of the German Länder. A second output of this strategy, co-decision rights for regions in the Council of Ministers, was regarded as an achievement by the "strong" regions who could operationalize this new responsibility, but the opportunity was limited by requirements to negotiate with central state authorities on the exact conditions under which this leadership role could be exercised.

In light of this experience, Europe's strong regions had to formulate a "Plan B" to secure greater influence in the EU. To that end, a second strategy, developed in line with Plan A but implemented subsequently, in the late 1990s, focused primarily on the domestic political arena as the core route to influence. This saw the regions in Belgium, Austria, Germany, and Spain, all of which have formal rights of access to relevant information on EU matters from the central state authorities, come to prioritize this internal relationship. The regions began to maximize domestic opportunities for formulating regional opinions on EU issues, and feeding these into the EU decision-making of their respective national governments.[9]

Whilst this remains a core element of regional strategies for maximizing their influence in European decision-making, a further goal has latterly been articulated by the strong, legislative regions, as a way to reinforce this central aim. First put forward in the early 2000s in connection with debates in the Constitutional Convention on the "Future of Europe," regional actors set out demands for more robust constitutional safeguards around regional-level competences in the context of European integration.[10] This goal was again mobilized on a pan-European basis, this time involving only those regions with comparable legislative powers, through a new vehicle for collective action, the "RegLeg" grouping, an advocacy coalition made up of seventy-three EU regions with autonomous legislative powers, from eight EU member states (Austria, Belgium, Finland, Germany, Italy, Portugal, Spain, and the UK). Alongside the group's more obvious benefits of enhanced networking, relationship building, and the exchange of ideas and experience between regional leaderships facing similar governmental concerns, RegLeg's stated aim is to sensitize EU institutions to the specific concerns of this particular *type* of region, and to voice their view on how legislation from the EU impacts on their own legislative capacity. Most recently, their focus has been to articulate a vision of enhanced regional recognition in the debates leading up to the Lisbon Treaty, such as to secure a clearer legal definition of the principle of subsidiarity and an "early warning system" which would allow for "bottom-up" legal challenges to EU legislation on subsidiarty grounds. At a formal level, these principles have indeed formed the lynchpin of the reformulated "regional dimension" of the resulting legal basis of the EU.

There are two problems with this received understanding of "regional engagement in the EU." Firstly, this historical narrative remains limited largely to the analysis of Europe's "strong" or "legislative" regions, that is, those which have elected parliaments and which make laws with direct effect on the public goods and services provided to citizens in that territory.[11] Despite wide-scale decentralization programs in a number of the EU's larger member states, these regions remain in the clear minority. The most recent enlargement rounds in particular have seen regions which are institutionally weak and lack autonomous legislative capacities become the majority of what can be classified as Europe's "Third Level." The analysis of the European strategies pursued by "weak" regions which lack independent legislative powers in the domestic realm is less well defined in the scholarly literature on the EU's "regional dimension," though it is no less valid.

Secondly, the historical narrative focuses principally on the "polity dimension," that is, the formal means through which an institutionalized role for regional levels of authority can be captured within the EU's political process. Beyond periodic opportunities for reconfiguring the institutional architecture of the EU, albeit only on a marginal level, the daily "bread and butter" nature of regional interaction with the EU relates to the outcome of the EU decision-making process, policy, and legislative decisions. It is well documented that two thirds of EU legislation is implemented by local and regional authorities in the member states.[12] Whilst the formal configuration of the EU political space determines the opportunities for regional intermediation, it does not fully delimit the varied nature of regional strategies for engagement with the broader process of European integration, not least action in specific policy sectors.

Thus, whilst this narrative of regional engagement in the EU captures variation over time, it fails to account for variation over alternative dimensions such as sector and space. As a consequence, this account needs further extension in two main directions.

52.2.2 Sector

The majority of analysis on the "regional dimension" of European policies relates to regional policy and the structural funds, notably the suggestion that the "partnership principle," in operation since 1988, has encouraged autonomous lines of communication and control between the supranational and sub-national levels, obviating national channels of control.

The empowering effect of EU structural policy is differential; the new opportunities of structural policy-making ushered in with the 1988 reform of the Structural Funds were distributed among European regions and sub-national authorities according to the "St Matthew" principle: "Those that already had, got more, but those that did not have, remained empty handed."[13]

"Europe" also provides an arena for mutual learning in policy and politics.[14] Networks of policy actors at the regional level are facilitated by the Commission in particular, and are a constant source of ideational change and innovation.[15] Indeed, it is the salience of policy issues which continue to encourage regional engagement with the European integration process, even after the fading of grand visions of constitutional change.[16]

Data from a comprehensive survey of regional representations in the EU[17] found that securing information on European developments remains the most important priority for all types of regional actors in the EU, closely followed by the opportunity to build links with other European regions through EU activity. This then has implications for regions' ability to harness EU funds for broader economic development schemes, such as pan-European regional networks that receive funding assistance from the Commission's "community action" programs. Examples of such opportunities include the European Regions and Innovation Network in Brussels (ERRIN), or the European network of regional and local health authorities (EUREGHA). These networks facilitate the exchange of experience, ideas, and skills, as well as allowing for the development of innovative schemes in particular policy areas.

52.2.3 Space

With regard to the axis of "space," we can consider the varied extent to which regional actors from the member states aim to be active in the emergent European political "space."

The key means through which academic scholarship has sought to assess this particular dimension of regions' strategies for interacting with the EU has been through the lens of regional "mobilization." Mobilization refers to the increased engagement of regional actors with the institutions and process of EU policy-making from the 1980s onward. Though in some cases this mobilization may have reflected an idealistic commitment to integration or attempts to circumvent a domestic conflict by instrumentalizing new opportunities for regional action at the EU level,[18] mostly it had a simple source: as European competence expanded, in particular from the SEA onward, it reached increasingly into fields of policy which within member states fell under the competence of regional actors, with regard both to decisional capacity and to implementation. Even for the weaker regions, the emergent European space was historically seen as an area where long-term tensions in areas relating to language and culture, ethnicity and religion, as well as party politics could be overcome.[19]

But regional mobilization is an empirical phenomenon that takes a variety of different forms and emerges for a variety of different reasons. For those regions who remain marginalized domestically, or those without an explicit political aim from "Europe," the factors encouraging "mobilization" at the EU level are very different from those encouraging the legislative regions to act in Europe. In more recent times, the primary catalyst for regional mobilization is not the ability to present regional policy preferences in the EU policy process independent of nation-state controls. With regard to regions from the new member states in particular, it has become apparent that the socialization effect of precedents set by regions from the EU-15 has led to a degree of what James Mitchell termed "me-tooism" in regional mobilization.[20]

Overall, therefore, the "empowering effect" of the emergent EU political space is differential, and depends largely on intra-state politics, not least the existing provision of the respective region with political, institutional, and socio-economic resources.[21] Strategies for engaging with Europe derive from the domestic politics of Europe within member states and the divergent governmental, constitutional, financial, and ideational resources that different regions have at their disposal, alongside the level of investment they wish to make in a European strategy.[22]

These varied strategic aims and approaches can be seen clearly in empirical analysis of sub-national mobilization which break down patterns of mobilization by clusters of regional actors. Evidently, not all regions are hoping to shape EU legislative outcomes through "mobilization" in the EU. In fact, only "subsets" of regions will use their own Brussels outposts specifically to shape decision-making, and those subsets, in their analysis, are determined on the basis of constitutional entrenchment in their respective national polities.[23]

Fewer regions feel that their activity in Brussels is aimed primarily at either explaining the region's position on policy issues to EU decision-makers, or influencing decision-making in the EU in favor of the region, though regions are more inclined to see this as a core incentive of "mobilization" in Brussels than gaining influence for regions *generally* in the European political process.[24]

This empirical data raises the notion of a paradox of the "Europe of the Regions" idea,[25] a metaphor put forward in the 1980s as the projected endpoint of regional mobilization. Paradoxically, despite the demise of the brave new world of a Europe of the regions—supplanting the role of nation states in the EU—a "Europe of the Regions," still less a Europe *with* the Regions had failed to materialize.[26] Yet despite the lack of a grand project to galvanize pan-regional support, there are still incentives enough to be in the long-term game in Brussels.[27] It is these incentives, motives, and strategies that have tended to dominate analysis of the EU's "regional dimension." On a conceptual level, this remains problematic, however, as mobilization is a variable phenomenon itself, and one which resists systematic categorization. As such, it lacks explanatory power and remains something of a "cause in search of an effect."[28]

52.3 ASSESSING THE DIVERSITY OF THE "REGIONAL DIMENSION": CONCEPTUAL TOOLS

For most of the twenty years of regional mobilization, discourse on the EU's "regional dimension" has been dominated by the concept of multilevel governance (MLG), that is, the empirical analysis of the new multilevel relationships that were established in EU politics, where these can be seen. Early interpretations of this new dynamic suggested that this would have the transformative capacity to unleash a "Europe of the Regions," supplanting a Europe of nation states.[29] The dominance of MLG though has been in line with the overall "governance turn" in EU studies.[30]

The imagery constructed by MLG scholars aims to capture complexity, fluidity, and shifting constellations of resource-dependent actors within the Brussels policy negotiation arena. This powerful narrative brought attention to shifts in the dispersal of power and authority within the European polity.[31] But like the concept of regional mobilization in the EU, ideas on MLG have been unable to deliver systematic insights into the recalibration of politics in the EU that all the various forms of enhanced regional engagement are said to have ushered in, and it has been unable to explain fully the differential patterns of MLG across time, sector, and space, or across politics, policy, and polity.[32]

From an empirical standpoint, it is clear that regions are certainly more present and more active in Brussels; they are more autonomous as political actors within the European governing arena and engage in a dense network of interactions with the European decision-making institutions independently of national governmental controls. But does this activity in any way distinguish itself from mere multilevel "participation" on the one hand,[33] or multilevel "dialogue"[34] on the other? Whilst the increased presence of regional representations in Brussels alongside an expanded portfolio of strategic opportunities for engagement is clearly a shift toward a greater degree of multilevel *participation* in the EU, it is more difficult to assess the actual added value of this greater level of participation, and at what point a shift toward enhanced multilevel *governance* becomes a reality. Theorists of governance (and indeed, MLG) imply a shaping role for those actors engaged in the governing process.[35] Therefore, if we are to classify MLG as an emergent form of social regulation at the EU level,[36] these multilevel interactions in Brussels must be making some form of impact on the outcomes of this process.[37] Under what conditions, then, does regional engagement constitute influence?

Equally, the elasticity of the concept of a system of governance across multiple levels of authority in the EU has led to it being stretched in all directions. Latterly, the original drafters of the MLG idea sought to refine it further, subdividing it into two distinct types: Type 1, constitutionally defined and limited levels of power and governmental authority, such as those found in federal political systems, as opposed to a second variant, Type 2, more ad hoc governing arrangements, such as governmental agencies and partnerships, that are flexible enough to respond to shifting demands. This attempt in and of itself highlights the concept's need for more theoretical underpinning, given the complexity of its empirical object of analysis.

At the other end of the scale, the elasticity of the concept is highlighted by the fact that the term "MLG" has effectively been hijacked for its normative essence. The CoR in particular sees MLG as a means to encourage and facilitate the participation of local and regional perspectives in EU policy process. A recently published "White Paper on Multilevel Governance" uses a politicized definition of MLG as "coordinated action by the EU, the member states, and local and regional authorities, based on partnership and aimed at drawing up and implementing EU policies," arguing in turn that this enhanced role for the local and regional perspective actually helps to meet the Union's fundamental political objectives of a "Europe of citizens," and an enhanced "democratic dimension" of the European Union.[38] The view expressed throughout is that MLG "in practice" equates to greater participation of local and regional authorities in the EU decision-making process and that this in turn equates to respect for the principle of subsidiarity. Such an instrumentalization of the concept has become the chief means by which sub-state authorities, and primarily those that are not "legislative" regions in their domestic systems, try and influence EU decision-making.

52.4 A New Era for Regional Engagement in the EU? The Impact of the Lisbon Treaty

Since its inception as a member-state union, regional tiers of authority have sought progressively to increase their recognition and decision-making capacity within a system originally "blind" to sub-state concerns. The history of treaty revisions throughout the EU's history, and indeed its increasing policy remit, has brought regional and local actors into the governing network in the differentiated ways outlined above.

But with the entry into force of the Lisbon Treaty on December 1, 2009, certain new rules of the game have been established, a number of which will inevitably be of core relevance for sub-state tiers of authority. In particular, the Lisbon Treaty ushers in a new legal context for the understanding and application of the principle of "subsidiarity" which is at the heart of all regional actors claims for greater access to EU decision-making. Potentially, this gives all sub-state authorities an enhanced opportunity to regulate "competence creep" on the part of the EU institutions, particularly in view of the new Articles 2–6 of the "Treaty on the Functioning of the European Union," the remodelled version of the Treaty establishing the European Community which the Treaty of Lisbon has amended, which define precisely the areas of EU competence.

Firstly, the Lisbon Treaty has completely rewritten the Protocol on subsidiarity, and formally obliges the Commission to take into account "the regional and local dimension" in its consultation on proposed legislation. This framework sets a potentially significant new marker in the relations between the EU's key agenda setter and the local and regional level.

Secondly, and again advancing regional input into the EU's decision-making process, the Committee of the Regions has, under Lisbon, finally secured the right to challenge EU legislation viewed as in breach of the subsidiarity principle before the ECJ, achieving an aim that the body had been requesting for fifteen years. This opportunity should offer greater independent scope for action to all types of sub-state actors in the EU, irrespective of their formal legislative powers. For instance, local authorities in Scotland have welcomed this step as allowing them in particular to regulate their own tendering practices in a number of core areas.[39]

Of more significance for constitutional regions in the EU is the fact that the role of national parliaments in the EU's legislative process has also been enhanced under the terms of Lisbon, a factor which will likely have ramifications for regional parliaments and assemblies in those member states where such legislators exist. Under new procedures known respectively as yellow and orange cards, national parliaments have the right to express concerns on subsidiarity directly to the responsible EU institution. Within a time span of eight weeks, that national parliament must then back up its challenge with a fully reasoned opinion. Clearly, in those national parliaments which are in part at least constituted by regional legislators, such as Germany, this system offers a further opportunity for greater sub-state involvement in the legislative process. For less formal multilevel systems of shared authority, the extent to which this will affect sub-state tiers of authority remains to be negotiated in national inter-governmental forums.

The German national position on the Lisbon Treaty has itself further enhanced sub-state control for the German *Länder*, the EU's most powerful regional players, over specific EU integration moves. A ruling by Germany's constitutional court (*Bundesverfassungsgericht*) in June 2009 provided for an enhanced role for the German national parliament in instances where the EU is seeking to apply the simplified treaty revision procedure or the so-called "flexibility clause" which allows for EU action without specific legal basis.[40] This in itself has implications for the future long-term role of sub-national actors in the EU as it fundamentally shifts the balance in favor of a collective, multilevel assessment of the merits of EU proposals, albeit at present in one member state only. Experience has however shown the German domestic arena for inter-governmental accommodation on European matters to have a powerful shaping role beyond its borders.[41]

52.5 CONCLUSIONS

How are we to understand, then, the conditions under which European integration is perceived as an opportunity for regional actors to engage more fully in the European political space, or as a threat to domestic rights and responsibilities? If we are to address this variation, we need to refine the analytical tools which we as scholars have at our disposal.

The engagement of European "regions," in all their various forms, in the European political process is increasing across the board. An increasingly dense network of "mobilized" regional actors and constellations of actors has emerged as new opportunities have been created by the Commission in particular, and through the collective force of political decentralization in the member states, which in turn lead to the growth in an increasingly broad set of regional "strategies" for interaction with Europe. But what is the cumulative effect of these developments? Do they effect real and substantive change to European governance? How can social science address the full complexity of Europe's "regional dimension"? There is a need to break through the circularity of the debate on MLG, and to set out terms for assessing this new dynamic not as a zero-sum game with clear sets of winners and losers.[42]

All of this suggests that the study of the regional dimension of the EU is at something of a juncture. This is where bringing the territory back in to the study of the regional dimension of European integration and politics will advance the development of concepts that travel across time and space and "enable us to grasp the elusive factor of territory and its changing manifestations."[43] The territorial dimension of European politics has been shaped largely by the member states, given their role as chief decision-makers in the institutions with the sole power to transform intergovernmental relations and establish new supranational forums of collective bargaining. But increased regional mobilization, in all its guises, does *suggest* if not *explain* that there has been a collective weakening of the singular dominance of national governments as the controlling territorial actors in the EU political system.[44]

The centre of this territorial politics approach to the study of the EU's regional dimension would be an ontological view of the state as one in constant evolution.[45] This starting point would be the logical place from which to build new conceptual tools which would allow us to better analyze the implications for EU integration of spatial restructuring, and its concomitant impacts in a social, political, and cultural sense. Shifting territorial scales of social and political action pose fundamental challenges to the traditional vantage point of a Europe of multiple tiers of authority. By contrast, a more flexible, sociologically-driven approach, which understands territory not merely a "space" in which things happen, but rather as a socially constructed frame and context for social relationships and action[46] would ultimately deliver insights into the emergent forms of social regulation which are being developed by the complex constellations of variously empowered sub-state actors within the EU's member states. Such an approach would thereby capture the real essence of these new governing networks.

NOTES

1. Charlie Jeffery, "Sub-National Mobilization and European Integration," *Journal of Common Market Studies* 38, no. 1 (2000), 1–23; Liesbet Hooghe and Gary Marks, *Multi-Level Governance and European Integration* (Boulder, CO: Rowman and Littlefield, 2001); Stephen Weatherill and Ulf Bernitz, eds, *The Role of the Regions and Sub-National Actors in Europe* (Oxford: Hart Publishing, 2005).
2. Christopher Ansell, Craig Parsons, and Keith Darden, "Dual Networks in European Regional Development Policy," *Journal of Common Market Studies* 35, no. 3 (1996), 347–75.
3. Charlie Jeffery, "Regions and the European Union: Letting Them In and Leaving Them Alone," in Stephen Weatherill and Ulf Bernitz, *The Role of the Regions and Sub-National Actors in Europe*, 33–46.
4. Ian Bache, *The Politics of European Union Regional Policy: Multi-Level Governance or Flexible Gatekeeping?* (Sheffield: UACES/Sheffield Academic Press, 1998); Ian Bache, *Europeanization and Multilevel Governance. Cohesion Policy in the European Union and Britain* (Plymouth: Rowman and Littlefield, 2008); Ingeborg Tömmel, "Transformation of Governance: The European Commission's Strategy for Creating a Europe of the Regions," *Regional and Federal Studies* 8, no. 2 (1998), 52–80.
5. Michael Bauer and Tanja Börzel, "Regions and the EU," in Hendrik Enderlein, Sonja Wälti, and Michael Zürn, eds, *Handbook on Multilevel Governance* (Cheltenham: Edward Elgar, 2010), 253–66.
6. Tanja Börzel and Thomas Risse. "When Europe Hits Home: Europeanization and Domestic Change," *European Integration Online Papers*, 2009, available at <http://eiop.or.at>; John Loughlin, "Reconfiguring the State: Trends in Territorial Governance in European States," *Regional and Federal Studies* 17, no. 4 (2007), 385–403.
7. Charlie Jeffery, "A Regional Rescue of the Nation-State: Changing Regional Perspectives on Europe," Europa Institute Edinburgh, Working Papers Series 5/2007.
8. Udo Bullmann, "The Politics of the Third Level," in Charlie Jeffery, ed., *The Regional Dimension of the European Union. Towards a Third Level in Europe?* (London: Frank Cass, 1997), 3–19.
9. Jeffery, "A Regional Rescue of the Nation-State.
10. Jeffery, "A Regional Rescue of the Nation-State.
11. Jeffery, "A Regional Rescue of the Nation-State.
12. EUROBAROMETER, The role and impact of local and regional authorities within the European Union, Report, February 2009.
13. Michael Bauer and Tanja Börzel, "Regions and the EU."
14. Michael Keating, "A Quarter Century of the Europe of the Regions," *Regional and Federal Studies* 18, no. 5 (2008), 629–35; Elizabeth Bomberg and N. McEwen, "Intergovernmental

Politics and Climate Change: Scotland, UK, EU." Paper prepared for presentation at UACES conference September 1–3, 2008, Edinburgh, UK.

15. Carolyn Rowe, *Regional Representations in the EU: Between Diplomacy and Interest Mediation* (Basingstoke: Palgrave, 2011).

16. Carolyn Moore, "A Europe of the Regions vs. the Regions in Europe: Reflections on Regional Engagement in Brussels," *Regional and Federal Studies* 18, no. 5 (2008), 517–35.

17. Heather Mbaye, "So What's New? Mapping a Longitudinal Regional Office Footprint in Brussels, paper presented at 11th EUSA biennial conference, Los Angeles, April 23–25, 2009.

18. Jeffery, "A Regional Rescue of the Nation-State."

19. Gary Marks, Francois Nielsen, Leonard Ray, and Jane Salk, "Competencies, Cracks and Conflict: Regional Mobilization in the European Union," *Comparative Political Studies* 29, no. 2 (1996), 164–92.

20. James Mitchell, "Lobbying 'Brussels': The Case of Scotland Europa," *European Urban and Regional Studies* 2, no. 4 (1995), 287–98; Moore, "A Europe of the Regions vs. the Regions in Europe."

21. Bauer and Börzel, "Regions and the EU."

22. Bomberg and McEwen, "Intergovernmental Politics and Climate Change."

23. Gary Marks, Richard Haesly, and Heather Mbaye, "What Do Subnational Offices Think They Are Doing in Brussels," *Regional and Federal Studies* 12, no. 3 (2002), 1–23.

24. Mbaye, "So What's New?."

25. Moore, "A Europe of the Regions vs. the Regions in Europe."

26. Anwen Elias, "Introduction: Whatever Happened to the Europe of the Regions? Revisiting the Regional Dimension of European Politics," *Regional and Federal Studies* 18, no. 5 (December 2008), 483–92.

27. Keating, "A Quarter Century of the Europe of the Regions."

28. Michael Bauer and Diana Pitschel, "Akteurspräferenzen: Schlüssel zur Erklärung subnationaler Mobilisierung," in *Europäisches Zentrum für Föderalismus-Forschung*, ed., *Jahrbuch des Föderalismus* (Baden Baden: Nomos, 2007), 74–85.

29. Liesbet Hooghe, "Subnational Mobilization in the European Union," *West European Politics* 18, no. 3 (1995), 175–98; Hooghe and Marks, *Multi-Level Governance and European Integration*.

30. Beate Kohler-Koch and Berthold Rittberger, "Review Article: The 'Governance Turn' in EU Studies," *Journal of Common Market Studies* 44, Annual Review (2006), 27–49.

31. Michael Keating, "Thirty Years of Territorial Politics," *West European Politics* 31, nos 1–2 (2008), 60–81.

32. Bauer and Börzel, "Regions and the EU"; Simona Piattoni, "Multi-Level Governance: A Historical and Conceptual Analysis," *European Integration* 31, no. 2 (2009), 163–80.

33. Bache, *The Politics of European Union Regional Policy*.

34. David Wilson, "Unravelling Control Freakery: Redefining Central-Local Governmental Relations," *British Journal of Politics and International Relations* 5, no. 3 (2003), 317–46.

35. Hooghe and Marks, *Multi-Level Governance and European Integration*; Kohler-Koch and Rittberger, "Review Article: The 'Governance Turn' in EU Studies."

36. Ian Bache and Matthew Flinders, "Themes and Issues in Multi-Level Governance," in Ian Bache and Matthew Flinders, eds, *Multi-Level Governance* (Oxford: Oxford University Press, 2004), 1–14.

37. Bache, *Europeanization and Multilevel Governance*.

38. Committee of the Regions "White Paper on Multilevel Governance" (CONST-IV-020, 2009), available at <www.cor.europa.eu>.
39. COSLA—The Convention of Scottish Local Authorities, *Response to CoR Consultation on Multi-Level Governance* (2009), available at<www.cor.europa.eu>.
40. Philipp Kiiver, "The Lisbon Judgement of the German Constitutional Court: A Court-Ordered Strengtheninig of the National Legislature in the EU," *European Law Journal* 16, no. 5 (2010), 578–88.
41. S. Bulmer, C. Jeffery, and W. E. Paterson, *Germany's European Diplomacy: Shaping the Regional Milieu* (Manchester: Manchester University Press, 2000).
42. Caitriona Carter and Romain Pasquier, "The Europeanization of Regions as 'Spaces for Politics': A Research Agenda," *Regional and Federal Studies* 21, no. 3 (2010), 295–314.
43. Keating, "Thirty Years of Territorial Politics," 76.
44. Michael Tatham, "Going Solo: Direct Regional Representation in the European Union," *Regional and Federal Studies* 18, no. 5 (2008), 493–515.
45. John Loughlin, "The Regional Question, Subsidiarity and the Future of Europe," in Weatherill and Bernitz, *The Role of the Regions and Sub-National Actors in Europe*, 74–85; Gary Marks, Liesbet Hooghe, and Arjan Schakel, "Measuring Regional Authority," *Regional and Federal Studies* 18, no. 2 (2008), 111–21.
46. Anssi Paasi, "Place and Region: Looking Through the Prism of Scale," *Progress in Human Geography* 28, no. 4 (2004), 536–46.

CHAPTER 53

NEITHER AN INTERNATIONAL ORGANIZATION NOR A NATION STATE: THE EU AS A SUPRANATIONAL FEDERATION

ARMIN VON BOGDANDY*

MY thesis is that the EU is neither an international organization nor a state. Rather, it represents a new kind of polity, here conceived as a supranational federation. This chapter will sketch this understanding not in terms of political theory[1] but from a legal perspective, studying the principles concerning the relationship between the Union and its member states.

53.1 THE FEDERAL CREATION OF UNITY UNDER THE RULE OF LAW PRINCIPLE

53.1.1 Rule of Law and Supranational Law

Among the principles of Article 2 TEU (ex Article 6(1) EU), the rule of law principle has the greatest operative relevance. This principle will be developed in accordance with the guiding thesis of this chapter, namely that the Union can best be explained from the perspective of its relationship with the member states. The corresponding presentation will exhibit continuity *and* innovation vis-à-vis national constitutional thinking and will shed new—constitutional—light on the *acquis communautaire*.

Unity is constitutive for diversity.[2] Consequently, principles advancing unity were the first to develop in the process of integration. In a constitutionalist reconstruction, the rule of law appears to be the most important principle promoting unity. It was the first classical constitutional principle to be claimed for Community, now Union law.[3] Most legal systems subsume the pertinent elements under a term equal or similar to *Rechtsstaatlichkeit* or *l'État de droit*; almost all language versions of the EU Treaty similarly use terminology linked to the state. This terminology is misleading, due to the inclusion of the element of statehood.[4] It seems more accurate to use the term "rule of law" (*prééminence du droit* or *Herrschaft des Rechts*).[5]

The rule of law is fundamental for the trajectory taken by integration. It constitutes a *differentia specifica* in view of international law. The rule of law principle allows for a constitutional interpretation of the Court of Justice of the European Union's (CJEU) jurisprudence, which since the early 1960s has aimed at the juridification of the integration process and at the autonomization of European law.[6] As a principle, it has a "life of its own" and supports far-reaching developments of the law that transformed[7] and constitutionalized[8] Europe. Against this understanding of the rule of law principle the objection may be raised that the CJEU very rarely uses the word *rule of law* in the sense of *Rechtsstaat*. However, the specific terminology of the CJEU, as well as historical motivations, are secondary for a scholarly construction. The decisive factor for doctrinal constructivism lies rather in the cognitive value of a conceptualization of the legal material.

53.1.2 The Effectiveness Principle

The first condition for an actual rule of law is the effectiveness of law with regard to public authorities. In order to achieve this, the CJEU has developed legal concepts in numerous decisions aiming at fostering the obedience of the member states as the most critical addressees of Union law. As a Celex research reveals, the CJEU has thus far employed the argument of the effectiveness of Community/Union law over 10,000 times. The (useful, practical, full) effectiveness (*effet utile*) can be interpreted as a principle created by the judiciary, which more than any other principle structures the relationship between the Union and its member states.[9] It commits the member states to realizing the objectives of a provision of Community law and can generate the requisite legal consequences in cases of conflict.[10] It comprises all judicially developed concepts conveying effectiveness to Community law in the member states' legal orders. The most relevant legal concepts are: the autonomy of Community law,[11] direct effect (of Treaty provisions,[12] decisions,[13] directives,[14] and other legal obligations[15]), primacy,[16] effective and uniform application by member states' authorities,[17] as well as the concept of state liability under Community law.[18] Now with the entry into force of the Lisbon Treaty, these doctrines can be transferred to the entire Union law.

From a national constitutional perspective, this construction might be surprising, as the rule of law principle is generally associated with the *restriction* rather than with the *constitution* of authority. However, the first element of a rule of law principle is the actual rule of law, i.e. the effectiveness of legal norms. A constitutional understanding of the Union's primary law presupposes that the Union actually wields public authority, implying that EU law does not depend upon the addressee's disposition to comply in every single case. At the same time, the principle exercises a legitimating function: effectiveness is indispensable for the so-called output legitimacy of the Union, and the uniform application of the law is indispensable for legal equality.

The effectiveness of Union law is by no means self-evident, given its genesis in international law: in public international law, there exist numerous treaties whose effectiveness vis-à-vis their institutions as well as their state parties is problematic. But herein also lies a major difference between the Union as a bearer of public authority and a state: the missing means of coercion. The effectiveness of national legal norms is usually beyond question due to the common origin of a state's authority. The Union by contrast is (only) a community of law and not also a community of coercion. Considering how many theories conceive of the element of coercion as constitutive for a norm to be law,[19] this is the first challenge for the rule of law principle in Union law. Accordingly, the basic elements of the rule of law were the first aspects of European constitutional thought in the 1960s that coalesced into principles of primary law. The constitutionalization narrative generally starts with exactly those decisions aiming at the strengthening of the effectiveness, normativity, and autonomy of the law.

The federal importance of the effectiveness principle can only be grasped fully if one considers that this principle strengthens the legal subjects of the member states and transforms them into subjects and actors of the supranational legal order, into *market citizens*.[20] In a transnational community of law, the community's systemic interest in the effectiveness of its law and the individual's corresponding interest in the enforcement of a norm that benefits him or her are consonant: the legislator (EU) and the beneficiary (citizen) both need the nation state's domestic courts. The principles establishing the rule of European law indissolubly serve both interests.

Perhaps the Union is even more dependant on the rule of law than an established nation state. The outstanding importance of a common law as a bond that embraces all Union citizens is, in view of the dearth of other integrating factors such as language or history, hardly contestable. Moreover, as already pointed out by de Tocqueville, the bigger and freer a polity is, the more it must rely on the law to achieve integration.[21] So far, then, the notion of a community of law aptly reflects the particular importance of the rule of law in creating a cohesive Union.

The difficulties encountered by a highly centralized institution (located in Brussels and Luxembourg) of securing the effectiveness of its law when this conflicts with national provisions or practices, explain some problematic rigidities of European law, which do not always do justice to other principles. A conflict of the principle of effectiveness with the principles of conferral, subsidiarity, and legal certainty is particularly frequent. The treatment of these conflicts in line with the general doctrines on the collision of principles opens the way for more balanced solutions.[22] Its somewhat erratic jurisprudence regarding the legal effect of acts contrary to Community (now Union) law at least illustrates that the CJEU also does not categorically champion the principle of effectiveness.[23]

The rule of law principle of the Union as concretized by the principle of effectiveness illuminates the *Gestalt* of the Union's legal order by means of its specific relationship with the legal orders of the member states. It is a legal order whose effectiveness equals that of the law of developed federal states, but whose instruments cannot be fully grasped from a traditional federal perspective. This is illustrated clearly by the primacy principle, since it raises the question of hierarchy, the most important instrument for advancing unity. First, merely conceived as an expression of an autonomous legal order, its constitutional and federal dimensions were rapidly understood.[24] The development of the concept of primacy traces the Union's own progression into a supranational federation, rather than a federal state. The decision against supremacy (with the effect of voiding national law) and in favor of primacy of Community (now Union) law (simple non-application of the national law for the conflicting case) comprises a significant pluralist element. Moreover, primacy cannot be fully understood from the perspective of Union law alone, because most member states' high courts do not fully accept such primacy of Union law.[25] The principle of primacy does not succeed in creating complete unity by establishing a strict hierarchy; rather, at the centre of the constitutional interplay one finds an "unregulated" relationship due to the competing jurisdictional claims. This openness is an expression of a constitutional structure adequate for the European legal area, as long as the openness is contained by principles of the legal orders involved, namely by obligations of respect and cooperation.

53.1.3 The Principle of Comprehensive Legal Protection

The principle of effectiveness depends on the possibility of judicial review. This corresponds to the traditional understanding of the rule of law principle. Its development since the nineteenth century has been accompanied by the establishment of judicial control over the exercise of public authority. Whether Sieyès, Bähr, Austin, Orlando, or Dicey, they all argue that law becomes reality only through the settling of conflicts by an unbiased third party.[26] The possibility of judicial review of the exercise of public authority is constitutive for the rule of law.[27]

On closer examination it even becomes apparent that most of the legal concepts depicted in the previous section award judicial competences for the purpose of allowing a court, mostly the CJEU, to control the conformity of the member states' behavior with Union law. For a long time, the respective expansion of the preliminary ruling procedure of Article 267 TFEU (ex Article 234 EC) was at the centre of this development.[28] The cooperation of the CJEU and national courts founded on Article 267 TFEU is constitutive for the juridification and constitutionalization of European integration, since it links the CJEU with the authority of national judgments and thus overcomes a structural weakness of supranational jurisdiction. It is complemented by the duty under Union law to allow for an effective remedy in a competent national court with regard to all acts by the member states violating Union law.[29]

Even though the preliminary ruling procedure of Article 267 TFEU has become the central instrument for judicial control of the Union, it can hardly be grasped in traditional, i.e. hierarchical categories. It does not establish a hierarchical judicial system, but a cooperative procedure.[30] The CJEU is reliant on the willingness of the national courts which can hardly be enforced.[31] This explains many peculiarities of legal protection in the EU.[32] In short: European legal unity is not to be perceived as unitary and hierarchical, but as pluralistic and dialogical. Of course, the principle of legal protection does not solely consist of the control of the member states' action in the procedure established by Article 267 TFEU; it also calls for legal protection against measures by the Union. Nevertheless, the federal relationship is decisively shaped by the preliminary ruling procedure with its specific mixture of cooperative and unitary elements.

53.2 Principles of the Political Process

53.2.1 The Rule of Law and the Legality Principle

The development under the rule of law principle led to the creation of legal unity; it federalized the relationship between Union and member states. However, this development of the law has a clear focus: it facilitates observation and implementation by the member states of the law generated by the Union. As bothersome as this may sometimes be for the member states, it also guarantees them that other authorities will mostly comply with this common law.[33] Law-making in the Union is more than symbolic politics; it exerts actual influence.

This judicial constraint placed on member states entailed an increased significance of the principles of the political process.[34] Accordingly, congenial principles of the political process developed. The rule of law principle does not therefore only refer to the application of the law, but also to European law-making. This has been elaborated by the CJEU in view of competences and procedures, so that the respective principles further shape the federal relationship and the constitutional nature of primary law.

This aspect of the rule of law principle can be labeled the *principle of constitutional legality*.[35] It divides into negative and positive legality. According to the *principle of negative legality* (*Treaty primacy*), every action that can be attributed to the Union has to respect higher-ranking norms. Every secondary law act must be in conformity with all Treaty norms and equal-ranking general principles.[36] This generates a strict internal hierarchy, the layered structure (*Stufenbau*) of the Union's legal order. Article 13(2) (TEU) expresses this yardstick-like character of the Treaties for all actions of the main organs of the Union in all fields, i.e. also CFSP (still to be found in Title V of the TEU) and Police and Judicial Cooperation in Criminal Matters (PJC) (formerly Title VI EU, now to be found in Chapters 1, 4, and 5 of Title IV of Part Three of the TFEU). The principle of negative legality knows no exceptions; the primacy of the Union's constitution is absolute.

Certainly, the primacy of Union law is not under complete judicial control. This holds true in particular for actions under Title V TEU: the European foreign, security, and defense policy is conceived as a governmental *arcanum*, without sufficient control.[37] The European Council's role is also problematic. Similar to the king in the constitutional regimes of the nineteenth century, it is not answerable to any other institution[38] and can "do no wrong."[39]

Nevertheless, the remarkable success of the constitutionalization of the Treaties is illustrated by the fact that the validity of the legality principle with regard to the EC Treaty appears today trivial and its exclusion particularly with regard to Title V EU problematic. As evident as the validity of this principle may seem today, the early Community did not take it for granted.[40] In international law, most international organizations do not conceive their founding treaty as being the yardstick for the law generated by them; this does not therefore amount to an international legal principle.[41] The strict hierarchization is due to the CJEU. From the premise of an autonomous legal order, it deduced the exclusive validity of the treaty amendment procedure (Article 48 TEU) and thus prevented a paralegal development within the EU as well as any paralegal influence of the member states; a similar constitutionalization of international organizations is still in its infancy.[42]

The legality principle protects the member states, since the competence of constitutional development and amendment is reserved to the member states acting jointly. This principle is reflected in Articles 48 and 49 TEU as well as in the principle of attributed (conferred) powers. The legality principle implies that the strict Treaty normativity cannot be temporarily suspended through informal agreements[43] and that even a constant practice of the organs cannot override primary law.[44] Also the law created by unanimous Council decisions has to conform to primary law, protecting the national parliaments from the dynamics of their governments acting jointly at the supranational level. This holds true without restrictions, even when the Council bases its decisions on wide competence clauses such as Article 352 TFEU.[45] If it is not the Council who acts, but a state conference representing the entirety of the member states (the "Representatives of the Governments of the member states meeting within the Council"), the principle of primacy is applied, enforcing negative legality.[46] The consequence is a remarkable dichotomization of the status of the member states. As actors creating and amending the Treaties, the member states operate largely outside the Union's legality, but they can only exert influence through the procedure of Article 48 TEU; in essence this implies a far-reaching autonomization of the Union's constitutional order.

53.2.2 Principles of the Order of Competences

The EU is a bearer of public authority since it has the unilateral power to commit others. This power is constitutionalized at its source by the *principle of positive legality*, also labeled principle of conferral or principle of limited or attributed competences. Every act of secondary Union law must have a legal basis which can be traced back to the founding Treaties. While negative legality is (only) about restricting a preconditioned public authority, the requirement of a competence norm comes in one step earlier at the source of its validity.

Increasingly, the order of competences has been formulated from the perspective of safeguarding the member states' interests. The Treaty of Lisbon continues with this tendency. In accordance with numerous national constitutions,[47] it refers to the competences as being "conferred" by the member states (Article 1(1) TEU, term not used in ex Article 1(1) EU) and stipulates the principles of conferral, subsidiarity, and proportionality (Article 5 TEU). The choice of the wording "confer" marks a distinction from federal constitutions, since a federal state is usually taken to enjoy its own intrinsic constituent power. Nevertheless, "conferral" is not to be understood as technical delegation, since this would commit European public authority to the member states' constitutions and signify the end of the autonomy of Union law.

Doubts have been raised as to whether the Union's institutions always respect these principles, and whether the CJEU enforces them adequately.[48] Whether these doubts are justified does not need to be answered at this point.[49] What is important is that the Union's legal order features principles which allow to legally conceptualize these doubts and—with the exception of Title V TEU—to pursue them before the CJEU. Moreover, the CJEU is not alone in this task, but stands under external control. Institutions of the member states, in particular some national constitutional courts, also credibly enforce the observance of these principles.[50] Herein, the non-hierarchical, pluralist character of the Union's legal order once again becomes apparent.

Since the Union's competences are broad, national autonomy can be considerably limited even when the limitations on the Union's competences are observed. The most important safeguard for the respect of member state autonomy is organizational in nature: the role of the member states in the Union's institutions and processes. This role is safeguarded by the legality principle since measures can only be taken in accordance with the relevant competence norms and with the procedures stipulated therein, including the necessary quorums. The federal tension determines not only the direct relationship between the Union and the member states but also the Union's internal structure, be it the institutions' internal rules or the horizontal inter-institutional relationships. It explains the lack of overarching hierarchical structures, or, to put it another way, the political system's polycentric and horizontal character. This polycentricity is normatively underpinned by the principle of institutional balance: it serves to stabilize the lines of responsibility established by the Treaties[51] as well as compliance with procedural rules[52] without, however, pushing the inter-institutional relationships toward any specific direction.[53] This corresponds to the political science insight that the political process of the Union is an open process of negotiations and is illustrated by the polycentricity of the Council, the most important institution for the pursuit of national interests. The political process is characterized not by hierarchical decree, but rather by contract-like cooperation between different political–administrative systems that are largely independent of each other.

53.2.3 The Principle of the Free Pursuit of Interests

Under the rule of law principle, the political process in the Union has been constitutional-ized: member states and institutions of the Union are effectively bound, and the normativ-ity of law is also promoted with regard to the political organs. This legalization is however largely restricted to the framework of competences and procedures; the positions of the member states remain for the most part undetermined. The Union's constitution provides not much orientation as to the substantive content of the Union's political process.

The member states are free to pursue their "national" interests in the institutions of the Union.[54] The CJEU has not specified the Treaty objectives, in particular concerning the past Articles 2 and 3 EC (which were repealed and have been replaced, in substance, by Article 3 TEU and Articles 3 to 6 TFEU; Article 3(2) EC can now be found in Article 8 TFEU), in a manner that would determine policies. This restraint is by no means imper-ative, the Treaties having been concluded after all in order to realize these objectives and to overcome the national limitations placed on many areas of life and to Europeanize the national societies. Nor does the CJEU infer duties to enact specific rules from the Union's fundamental rights. Furthermore, the CJEU did not develop ex Article 10 EC (now Article 4(3) TEU) into a duty of the member states to cooperate in the institutions of the Union in order to promote the community interest. The principle of loyal cooperation does not require the member states to make compromises in the Council or to use the possibility of majority decisions if a minority opposes a legislative project.[55] This is by no means necessarily so; one can also argue the opposite. After all, the ministers are directly bound by the Union's goals (Article 3 TEU (ex Article 2 EU), Articles 3 to 6, 8 TFEU (ex Articles 2 and 3 EC)) when they participate in the Council. Nevertheless, it has never come to a legal rejection of "national positions." This can be explained by the under-standing of the Union's political system presented above: the European common good is achieved through a synthesis of the various standpoints which are usually brought into the European process by the national governments. The principle therefore only requires participation in the Union's political process.[56]

53.3 PRINCIPLES OF THE COMPOSITE (VERBUND) OF UNION AND MEMBER STATES

53.3.1 The Composite (Verbund) as a New Perspective

An important new line in legal scholarship aims to conceptualize the *whole* of Union and member states.[57] Of particular importance here are the notions "multilevel" and "network," both coined by political science. German legal scholarship, always particu-larly preoccupied with conceptual autonomy, proposes the term *Verbund*, probably best translated using the English nouns "composite" or "compound."

In the European context, the word *Verbund* initially figured in two competing grand interpretations, Paul Kirchhof's (intergovernmental) composite of states (*Staatenverbund*) and Ingolf Pernice's (strongly integrative) composite of constitutions (*Verfassungsverbund*),[58] but it has since been unhinged from this antagonism.

Conceptualizing the whole of Union and member states implies a reorientation of European legal scholarship. Europe's community of law developed as an autonomous legal order.[59] Its autonomy is not merely one principle among others, but rather a normative axiom, defended by the CJEU with utmost resolve.[60] In fact, this concept of an autonomous legal order was fundamental to the supranational legal order's establishment. The actual development both in the political–administrative and in the legal realm led, however, not to separation, but rather to a close-knit interlocking or networking of the Union and the member states.

The dependence of the Union's constitution on the member states' constitutions is greater, in law and in fact, than that of a federal state on its constituent states.[61] In terms of positive law this results from, for instance, Article 6 (1) TEU (ex Article 6(2) EU) and Article 4(2) TEU (ex Article 6(3) EU) or Article 48 TEU (ex Article 48 EU), and conceptually from the principle of dual legitimacy which implies that the Union's legitimacy depends on the legitimacy organized by the national constitutions. The Treaty of Lisbon, for its part, stresses complementarity through such crucial provisions as Articles 1(1), 10(2), and 12 TEU. Yet the member states' constitutions can no longer be adequately grasped without recourse to the Union's constitution, since they no longer constitutionalize all public power in their scope of application.[62] The awareness of this mutual dependence leads to a concept of complementary constitutions. The Union's constitutional law fundamentally determines the member states' constitutions.

53.3.2 Structural Compatibility or Homogeneity?

It was recognized at an early stage in the integration process that a certain structural compatibility among the member states with respect to market economy, democracy, and rule of law is essential for the operation of the Union (on democracy and legitimacy, see Chapter 46, this volume). These conditions were formulated as normative requirements, though they only had a minimal character.[63] In the wake of the realization of a common constitutional area, the question arises whether to tighten such requirements under a legal principle of constitutional homogeneity that furthers constitutional unity.[64] Some derive this from ex Articles 6(1) and 7(1) EU (now Articles 2 and 7 TEU) in particular.[65]

Yet such a principle would face significant objections. To begin with, such a constitutional principle is currently hardly practicable given the diversity among the national constitutions: republics and monarchies, parliamentary and semi-presidential systems, strong and weak parliaments, competitive and consensual democracies, strong and weak political party systems, strong and weak social institutions, unitary and federal systems, strong, weak, or absent constitutional courts, as well as significant divergences in the content and level of the protection of fundamental rights.[66] The Union's eastward and southward expansion has increased this heterogeneity. Neither does the postulation of such a principle derive from ex Articles 6(1) and 7(1) EU (now Articles 2 and 7 TEU). The norms' wording implies a structural consonance only at a rather abstract level; not, however, constitutional homogeneity. Systematically, such a principle of homogeneity could scarcely be justified in light of ex Article 6(3) EU, as national identity finds its expression precisely in the peculiar, individual constitutional arrangements, as confirmed in Article 4(2) TEU. Moreover, the difficulties of making the Charter of Fundamental Rights a binding legal document as well as the modifications in the course of the negotiations of the Treaty of Lisbon also militate against a principle of constitutional homogeneity: many European citizens are concerned that European constitutional law might develop into a force of undesired homogenization, similarly to the basic rights under the German Basic Law or the US constitution.[67]

It seems more promising then to concretize the principles of ex Article 6 EU (now Article 2 TEU) differently for three different settings: the first, with the highest normative density, concerns the Union's own design; the second, with significantly less normative density, concerns the general requirements placed on the member states; and the minimally regulated third setting informs the Union's foreign policy.[68] It results from the cherished diversity in the European constitutional area that the second setting should not be conceived similarly to a principle of homogeneity in a federal state. This should be reflected in the terminology: thus, only a *principle of structural compatibility* should be derived from Articles 2 and 7 TEU (ex Articles 6(1) and 7(1) EU).

This principle of structural compatibility, however, does not exhaust the range of primary law norms comprehensively determining the Union *and* the member states. In particular with regard to the national exercise of public authority within the scope of Union law, jurisprudence, based on Article 4(3) TEU (ex Article 10 EC), aims beyond structural compatibility at a coherence comparable to that of a federal state and which could be conceived as a principle of homogeneity. Thus, the CJEU has of late applied procedural principles developed for the EU's own administrative action to member states' administrative activities.[69] Within the scope of application of Union law, the national administrations are bound by the Union's fundamental rights, the principles of equivalence and effectiveness, and now also through the principles which have been developed for the EU's own administration: a federal constellation through and through. Likewise, a principle of coherent legal protection against any form of public authority applies within the scope of application of Union law.[70] Contrasted with these determinants, it becomes even clearer that the requirements of Articles 2 and 7 TEU (ex Articles 6(1) and 7(1) EU), which set parameters for the member states' legal orders *as a whole*, i.e. outside the scope of application of Union law, are of far lesser density. For reasons of terminological clarity alone they should therefore not be labeled a *principle of homogeneity*.

53.3.3 The Principle of Loyalty and the Federal Balance

Whereas national law brings with it the threat of a sanctioning power, one searches in vain for a European counterpart. Much of European law—namely all legal norms that represent, at their core, a communication between different public authorities—is not even symbolically sanctioned by possible coercion. This aspect shows that loyalty plays a central, indeed fundamental role in European law.

Loyalty as a legal principle plays a seminal role in shaping the manifold relationships between public authorities in the European legal area. Despite the occasional plethora of detailed rules on the cooperation within the composite (*Verbund*), these relationships must be embedded in supplementary duties that secure the law's effectiveness and may solve conflicts. The principle of loyalty (or *principle of cooperation*) generates such duties.[71] The relevant judgments are based mainly on ex Article 10 EC, but the principle has been extended to all Union activities,[72] as now explicitly stated in Article 4(3) TEU. It can both *foster* and *protect diversity*.

The principle of loyalty underlies many important doctrines, often with strongly unifying effects, for instance the requirements regarding judicial cooperation or the domestic implementation of Union law. In light of the protection of diversity, however, it needs to be stressed that the principle protects *only* the integrity of the results of European legislation against *subsequent* disobedience by individual member states. In contrast, duties to formulate "Union-friendly policies" are not derived from it.

The principle of loyalty also imposes duties on the Union's institutions with regard to the member states, as explicitly stated in Article 4(3) TEU.[73] It includes the protection of diversity, although its precise extent still awaits further clarification. It is certain that ex Article 6(3) EU, as an expression of the principle of loyalty, required the Union to take the member states' constitutional principles and fundamental interests into account (now Article 4(2) TEU).[74] However, there cannot be a prohibition on Union action for every infringement of a domestic constitutional position. Otherwise, independent Union politics would be impossible. Rather, the principle is only to be applied in cases of concrete and serious interference with the fundamental requirements of the national constitutional order.

The principle of loyalty thus appears to be another key to understanding the Union. As the European legal order ultimately rests on the voluntary obedience of its member states, and therefore on their loyalty, the principle of loyalty has a key role in generating solutions to open questions and thus containing conflicts that may arise in a polycentric and diverse polity.

53.4 CONCLUDING REMARKS

The Union's founding principles concerning the federal relationship demonstrate its uniqueness, that it should be conceived neither as a state nor as an international organization. The relationship between principles furthering unity and those protecting diversity proves to be philosophically problematic and antinomic.[75] This tension cannot be resolved under the European constitutional law as it stands, because its solution would require European federalism to progress from the supranational to the national.

NOTES

* Nicole Appel and Christian Wohlfahrt provided valuable assistance in the completion of this chapter. This chapter builds on what I have published in "Founding Principles," in Armin von Bogdandy and Jürgen Bast, *Principles of European Constitutional Law* (Oxford: Hart 2009), 11–54.

1. A federal understanding of the EU is becoming ever stronger; see Joseph H. H. Weiler, *The Constitution of Europe* (Cambridge: Cambridge University Press, 1999); Robert Schütze, *From Dual to Cooperative Federalism. The Changing Structure of European Law* (Oxford: Oxford University Press, 2009); Allan Rosas, "The European Union as a Federative Association," *Durham European Law Institute European Law Lecture 2003* (University of Durham, 2004, available at <http://www.dur.ac.uk/resources/deli/annuallecture/2003_DELI_Lecture.pdf) (last accessed January 12, 2012). For my own understanding, see Armin von Bogdandy, "The European Union as a Supranational Federation," *Columbia Journal of European Law* 5 (2000), 27; Armin von Bogdandy, "The Prospect of a European Republic," *CML Rev* 42 (2005), 913–41.

2. Georg Wilhelm Friedrich Hegel, *Wissenschaft der Logik I*, edited by G. Lasson (Leipzig: Verlag von Felix Meiner, 1932 [originally published 1812]), 59.

3. Joseph H. Kaiser, "Bewahrung und Veränderung demokratischer und rechtsstaatlicher Verfassungsstruktur in den internationalen Gemeinschaften," *Veröffentlichungen der Vereinigung der Deutschen Staatsrechtslehrer* 23 (1966), 1–33, at 33.

4. Manfred Zuleeg, in Hans von der Groeben and Jürgen Schwarze, eds, *Kommentar zum EU-/EG-Vertrag* (Baden-Baden: Nomos, 2003), Art 1 EC para. 4.

5. Jörg Gerkrath, *L'émergence d'un droit constitutionnel pour l'Europe* (Bruxelles: Editions de l'Université de Bruxelles, 1997), 347.

6. For a classical example, see Joseph H. H. Weiler, "The Community System," *YEL* 1 (1981), 267–306.

7. See Joseph H. H. Weiler' seminal article, "The Transformation of Europe," *Yale Law Journal* 100 (1991), 2403–83.

8. Eberhard Grabitz, "Der Verfassungsstaat in der Gemeinschaft," *Deutsches Verwaltungsblatt* 92 (1977), 786–94, at 791; Eric Stein, "Lawyers, Judges and the Making of a Transnational Constitution," *AJIL* 75 (1981), 1–27.

9. Sacha Prechal, "Direct Effect, Indirect Effect, Supremacy and the Evolving Constitution of the European Union," in Catherine Barnard, ed., *The Fundamentals of EU Law Revisited* (Oxford: Oxford University Press, 2007), 35. On effectiveness, see further Chapter 47, this volume.

10. Matej Accetto and Stefan Zleptnig, "The Principle of Effectiveness," *European Public Law* 11 (2005), 375–403.

11. Case 6/64, *Costa v E.N.E.L.* [1964] ECR 585 at 593 *et seq.*

12. Case 26/62, *van Gend en Loos* [1963] ECR 1 at 11 *et seq*; Cases C-402/05 P and C-415/05 P, *Kadi* et al. *v Council and Commission* [2008] ECR I-0000, para. 282.

13. Cases 9/70, *Grad* [1970] ECR 825, para. 5.

14. Case 8/81, *Becker* [1982] ECR 53, paras 29 *et seq.*

15. Case 181/73, *Haegeman* [1974] ECR 449, paras 2 *et seq.*

16. Case 92/78, *Simmenthal v Commission* [1979] ECR 777, para. 39; Case C-213/89, *Factortame* [1990] ECR I-2433, para. 18; Case C-285/98, *Kreil* [2000] ECR I-69.

17. Cases 205–215/82, *Deutsche Milchkontor* [1983] ECR 2633, para. 22; Case C-261/95, *Palmisani* [1997] ECR I-4025, para. 27.

18. Cases C-6/90 and C-9/90, *Francovich* [1991] ECR I-5357, paras 33 *et seq.*
19. H. L. A Hart, *The Concept of Law* (Oxford: Oxford University Press, 1994), 20 ff.; Hans Kelsen, *Reine Rechtslehre*, second edition (Wien: Deuticke, 1960), 34.
20. Hans Peter Ipsen, *Europäisches Gemeinschaftsrecht* (Tübingen: Mohr, 1972), 187. On the European citizenship from a federal perspective, see Christoph Schönberger, "European Citizenship as Federal Citizenship," *European Review of Public Law* 19 (2007), 61–81. For a recent case concerning strengthening the citizen's status in view of effective enjoyment of the status, see Case 43/09, *Ruiz Zambrano* [2011] I-0000, para. 45.
21. Alexis de Tocqueville, *Über die Demokratie in Amerika* (1835) (Zürich: Manesse, 1985), 78 ff., 99 ff.; George A Bermann, "The Role of Law in the Functioning of Federal Systems," in Kalypso Nicolaidis and Robert Howse, eds, *The Federal Vision* (Oxford: Oxford University Press, 2001), 191–212. On public opinion and integration, see Chapter 50, this volume.
22. Manfred Zuleeg, *Der rechtliche Zusammenhalt in der Europäischen Union* (Baden-Baden: Nomos, 2004), 104 ff.
23. Concerning final administrative decisions: Case C-224/97, *Ciola* [1999] ECR I-2517, paras 21 *et seq*; concerning decisions which have become definitive: Case C-119/05, *Lucchini* [2007] ECR I-6199, paras 59 *et seq.*
24. On the European Union in the light of the European federal tradition and as a "federation of States," see Robert Schütze, "On 'Federal' Ground: The European Union as an (Inter) national Phenomenon," *Common Market Law Review* 46 (2009), 1069–1105, at 1089 ff. and 1102 ff. For another look "though the federal lens," see Philipp Dann, "Looking through the Federal Lens: The Semi-Parliamentary Democracy of the EU," Jean Monnet Working Paper 5/02, available at <http://centers.law.nyu.edu/jeanmonnet/papers/02/020501.html> (last accessed January 12, 2012).
25. For details, see Franz C. Mayer, *Kompetenzüberschreitung und Letztentscheidung* (München: Beck, 2000), 87 ff.
26. Alexandre Kojève, *Esquisse d'une phénoménologie du droit* (Paris: Gallimard, 1982), § 13.
27. Luc Heuschling, *État de droit, Rechtsstaat, Rule of Law* (Paris: Dalloz, 2002), *passim*, in summary 662.
28. This control might also be achieved through the proceedings of ex Article 230 EC (now Article 263 TFEU), Case C-64/05 P, *Sweden v Commission* [2007] ECR I-11389, paras 93 *et seq.*
29. Case 222/84, *Johnston* [1986] ECR 1651, paras 17 *et seq*, confirmed by Art 47 of the Charter of Fundamental Rights.
30. Andres, Voßkuhle, "Multilevel Cooperation of the European Constitutional Courts," *European constitutional Law Review* 6 (2010), 175–98.
31. For an attempt, see Case C-224/01, *Köbler* [2003] ECR I-10239, paras 30 *et seq.*
32. Renaud Dehousse, *The European Court of Justice* (Basingstoke: Macmillan, 1998), 28 ff.
33. Such a development is much less frequent in international law; see Jan Klabbers, "Compliance Procedures," in Daniel Bodansky et al., eds, *The Oxford Handbook of International Environmental Law* (Oxford: Oxford University Press, 2007), 995–1009.
34. For pioneering work, see Joseph H. H. Weiler, *The European Community in Change: Exit, Voice and Loyalty* (Saarbrücken: Europa-Institut der Universität des Saarlandes, 1987).
35. See Armin von Bogdandy and Jürgen Bast, "The European Union's Vertical Order of Competences," *CML Rev* 29 (2002), 227–68.
36. Opinion 1/91, *EEA I* [1991] ECR I-6079, para. 21.

37. However, the CJEU is developing some means of control, Case C-91/05, *Commission v Council* [2008] ECR I-3651, paras 32 *et seq*. On June 8, 2011 the Court delivered its first judgment annulling a CFSP measure based on its competence in Article 275(2) TFEU in T-86/11, *Nadiany Bamba v Council* [2011] ECR II-00000.
38. Case C-253/94 P, *Roujansky v Council* [1995] ECR I-7, para. 11.
39. Carl von Rotteck, *Lehrbuch des Vernunftrechts und der Staatswissenschaften*, second edition (Stuttgart: Hallberger, 1964 [originally published 1848]), volume II, 249 ff.; Federico Boschi Orlandini, "Principi costitutionali di struttura e Consiglio europeo," in Michele Scudiero, ed., *Il diritto constituzionale comune Europeo* (Napoli: Jovene Editore, 2002), volume I, 165.
40. Karl Carstens, "Die kleine Revision des Vertrags über die Europäische Gemeinschaft für Kohle und Stahl," *Zeitschrift für ausländisches öffentliches Recht und Völkerrecht* 21 (1961), 1–37, at 14, 37.
41. Michael N. Barnett and Martha Finnemore, "The Power of Liberal International Organizations," in Michael N. Barnett and Raymond Duvall, eds, *Power in Global Governance* (Cambridge: Cambridge University Press, 2006), 161–84; Manuel Díez de Velasco Vallejo, *Las Organizaciones Internacionales* (Madrid: Tecnos, 2006), 138.
42. For details, see International Law Association, *Accountability of International Organisations, Final Report* (2004), available at<www.ila-hq.org/en/committees/index.cfm/cid/9 (last accessed January 12, 2012).
43. Case 43/75, *Defrenne* [1976] ECR 455, para. 56.
44. Case 68/86, *UK v Council* [1988] ECR 855, para. 24; Case C-271/94, *Parliament v Council* [1996] ECR I-1689, paras 24, 34.
45. Case 38/69, *Commission v Italy* [1970] ECR 47, paras 12 *et seq*.
46. Case 44/84, *Hurd* [1986] ECR 29, para. 39.
47. Peter M. Huber, "Offene Staatlichkeit: Vergleich," in Armin von Bogdandy et al., ed., *Handbuch Ius Publicum Europaeum* (Heidelberg: C. F. Müller, 2008), volume II, § 26, 403–59.
48. Problematic Opinion 1/91, *EEA I* [1991] ECR I-6079, para. 21.
49. The CJEU made a point especially in Case C-376/98, *Germany v Parliament and Council* [2000] ECR I-8419, para. 83; less explicit Case C-380/03, *Germany v Parliament and Council* [2006] ECR I-11573, paras 36 *et seq*. On this issue, see Chapter 40, this volume.
50. Ground-breaking *Entscheidungen des Bundesverfassungsgerichts* 89, 155 (*Maastricht*). More recently *Entscheidung des Bundesverfassungsgerichts*, BVerfG, 2 BvE 2/08 of June 30, 2009 (*Lisbon*), available at<www.bundesverfassungsgericht.de/entscheidungen/es20090630_2bve000208.htm l> (last accessed January 12, 2012). Concerning control through parliments, the protocols No 1 (on the role of national parliaments in the European Union) and No 2 (on the application of the principles of subsidiarity and proportionality) to the Lisbon Treaty should be noted as well. On the national parliaments and the principle of subsidiarity, see Philipp Kiiver, "The Treaty of Lisbon, the National Parliaments and the Principle of Subsidiarity," *Maastricht Journal of European and Comparative Law* 15 (2008), 77–83. On the Early Warning System, see Philipp Kiiver, "The Early-Warning System for the Principle of Subsidiarity: The National Parliament as a *Conseil d'Etat* for Europe," *European Law Review* 36 (2011), 98–108. On the role of regional parliaments in the Early Warning System, see Gracia Vara Arribas and Delphine Bourdin, "The Role of Regional Parliaments in the Process of Subsidiarity Analysis

within the Early Warning System of the Lisbon Treaty," study for the Committee of the Regions, 2011.

51. Case 9/56, *Meroni v High Authority* [1958] ECR 133 at 152; Case 25/70, *Köster* [1970] ECR 1161, para. 9.

52. Case 139/79, *Roquette Frères v Council* [1980] ECR 3333, para. 33; Jean-Paul Jacqué, "The Principle of Institutional Balance," *CML Rev* 41 (2004), 383–91.

53. An interpretation from the perspective of a federal bicameral system now in Case C-133/06, *Parliament v Council* [2008] ECR I-3189, paras 54 *et seq.*

54. Case 57/72, *Westzucker* [1973] ECR 321, para. 17.

55. cf. the comments in Case 13/83, *Parliament v Council* [1985] ECR 1513 at 1576.

56. An "empty chair policy" (France in 1965) infringes Art 4(3) TEU (ex Art 10 EC); Joseph H. Kaiser, "Das Europarecht in der Krise der Gemeinschaften," *Europarecht* 4 (1966), 4–24.

57. Matthias Ruffert, "Von der Europäisierung des Verwaltungsrechts zum Europäischen Verwaltungsverbund," *Die öffentliche Verwaltung* 60 (2007), 761–70.

58. For details, see Paul Kirchhof, "The European Union of States" and Franz C. Mayer, "Multilevel Constitutional Jurisdiction," both in Armin von Bogdandy and Jürgen Bast, *Principals of European Constitutional Law* (Oxford: Hart, 2009), 735–61 and 399–439 respectively. Ingolf Pernice, "Die Dritte Gewalt im europäischen Verfassungsverbund," *Europarecht* 31 (1996), 27–43.

59. Case 26/62, above n 13, 12; Case 6/64, above n 12, 593; Case C-287/98, *Linster* [2000] ECR I-6719, para. 43.

60. Opinion 1/91, above n 36, paras 30 *et seq*; further Opinion 1/00, *Aviation Agreement* [2002] ECR I-3493, paras 5 *et seq*; Case C-459/03, *Commission v Ireland* [2006] ECR I-4635, paras 123 *et seq.*

61. Peter Häberle, *Europäische Verfassungslehre* (Baden-Baden: Nomos, 2006), 220 ff.

62. For details, see Christoph Grabenwarter, "National Constitutional Law Relating to the European Union" and Mayer, "Multilevel Constitutional Jurisdiction," both in von Bogdandy and Bast, *Principals of European Constitutional Law*, 83–129 and 399–439 respectively.

63. Hans Peter Ipsen, "Über Verfassungs-Homogenität in der Europäischen Gemeinschaft," in Hartmut Maurer, *Das akzeptierte Grundgesetz* (München: Beck, 1990), 159–82.

64. On the concept, Carl Schmitt, *Verfassungslehre*, eighth edition (München: Leipzig, 1993 [originally published 1928]), 65.

65. Stelio Mangiameli, "La clausola di omogeneità," in his *L'ordinamento Europeo: I principi dell'Unione*, (Milano: Giuffré, 2006), 1–42, at 17.

66. Pedro Cruz Villalón, "Grundlagen und Grundzüge staatlichen Verfassungsrechts: Vergleich," in von Bogdandy et al., *Handbuch Ius Publicum Europaeum*, volume I, § 13, 729–77.

67. Allard Knook, "The Court, the Charter, and the Vertical Division of Powers in the European Union," *CML Rev* 42 (2005), 367–98.

68. For details, see Armin von Bogdandy, "The European Union as a Human Rights Organization?," *CML Rev* 37, (2000), 1307–38.

69. Case C-28/05, *Dokter* [2006] ECR I-5431, paras 71 *et seq.*

70. cf. Cases C-46/93 and C-48/93, *Brasserie du pêcheur* [1996] ECR I-1029, para. 42.

71. Case 230/81, *Luxembourg v Parliament* [1983] ECR 255, para. 37; Case 2/88 Imm, *Zwartveld* [1990] ECR I-3365, para. 17; Case C-215/06, *Commission v Ireland* [2008] ECR I-0000, para. 59.

72. Case C-105/03, *Pupino* [2005] ECR I-5285, paras 39 *et seq*; Case C-355/04 P, *Segi* et al. *v Council* [2007] ECR I-1657, para. 52.
73. This provision codifies jurisprudence: Case C-263/98, *Belgium v Commission* [2001] ECR I-6076, paras 94 *et seq*.
74. *Entscheidungen des Bundesverfassungsgerichts* 89, 155 at 174 (*Maastricht*).
75. Immanuel Kant, *Kritik der reinen Vernunft* (Riga: Hartknoch, second edition 1787 = Edition B), 392, 444.

CHAPTER 54

COMPARATIVE REGIONAL INTEGRATION: THEORETICAL DEVELOPMENTS

WALTER MATTLI

54.1 INTRODUCTION

Comparative regional integration has emerged over the last decade as an exciting area of research. Interest was sparked, in part, by a new wave of integration in Asia, Africa, and the Americas that grew in strength in the 1990s. Like earlier waves, this one generated integration schemes that show puzzling differences and variations. Some integration schemes fail to attain most or any of their objectives, whilst others are highly successful. Some integration schemes confer significant authority to supranational agencies, encourage the use of qualified or simple majority in joint decision-making, and make provisions for strong dispute settlement procedures, powerful enforcement tools, as well as extensive common monitoring. Other schemes, however, are strictly intergovernmental in character and shy away from any institutional elements that weaken or undermine national sovereignty. These striking differences in outcomes and in regional governance have prompted scholars to search for comprehensive analytical frameworks of comparative regional integration. This chapter reviews three main such frameworks (and related empirical studies)—neo-functionalism, externality theory, and contracting theory, ponders their strengths and weaknesses, and raises key issues for future research.

54.2 THE NEO-FUNCTIONALIST FRAMEWORK OF COMPARATIVE REGIONAL INTEGRATION

Ernst Haas is the most outstanding and influential early thinker of regional integration processes. He was first and foremost interested in understanding European integration. Nevertheless, Haas insisted that his concern in the end was "not with the... uniqueness of this or that region but with investigating the generality of the integration process" in any region.[1] Remarkably, Haas' analytical framework provides many of the key ideas and elements that later approaches, in particular externality theory and contracting theory, draw on and develop more fully.

What factors account for the varying intensity and fortunes of integration schemes according to Haas? His neo-functionalist framework, which gives pride of place to subnational and supranational actors as key drivers of integration, identifies three sets of internally coherent factors summarized as (1) social and political pluralism, (2) symmetrical regional heterogeneity, and (3) bureaucratized decision-making coupled with supranational agency. The content of each of these factors or explanatory variables can be high or low—a high value favoring integration, a low value rendering success less likely.

High social and political pluralism describes a situation of full mobilization of all segments of society via strong interest groups and political parties, and leadership by elites competing for political survival in democratic contests.[2] Haas hypothesizes that integration proceeds most rapidly when it responds to socio-economic demands emanating from a pluralistic industrial–urban environment. "Because the modern "industrial–political" actor fears that his way of life cannot be safeguarded without structural adaptation, he turns to integration; but by the same token, political actors who are neither industrial, nor urban, nor modern in their outlook usually do not favor this kind of adaptation, for they seek refuge instead in national exclusiveness."[3]

Symmetrical regional heterogeneity is said to be high if two conditions hold: First, each country within a region seeking closer economic ties is fragmented along similar lines of pluralism and, second, each class, political party, or interest group has counterparts in other countries with which it can pursue common cause. Cross-national linkages foster similarity in feelings, expectations, and outlook. Haas suggests that parallel pluralistic socio-political structures in a region are "of far greater importance in explaining... integration['s]... success than is any argument stressing linguistic, cultural or religious unity."[4]

Finally, Haas posits that highly bureaucratized decision-making renders interactions among civil services engaged in policy coordination easier and more productive. And, to the extent that integration treaties allow for supranational agency, national negotiators can rely on experts above the state to "construct patterns of mutual concessions from various policy contexts."[5] Success may persuade political actors to shift more of their "loyalties, expectations, and political activities toward a new and larger center, whose institutions possess or demand jurisdiction over the pre-existing national states."[6]

Integration thus begets integration and generates spillover, i.e. creates a situation where activities associated with sectors integrated initially affect neighboring sectors not yet integrated, thereby becoming the focus of demands for more integration.

The behavioral assumptions underpinning these sets of hypotheses are nicely summarized in a memorable passage of Haas' work on Europe: "The 'good Europeans' are not the main creators of the…community; the process of community formation is dominated by nationally constituted groups with specific interests and aims, willing, and able to adjust their aspirations by turning to supranational means when this course appears profitable."[7] Supranational actors likewise are not immune to utilitarian thinking; they seek to expand the mandate of their own institutions to have a more influential say in integration matters. In other words, the groups driving the process of integration are rational maximizers of their narrow self-interest;[8] they hail from the world of business, politics, and science, and their actions or beliefs need not be infused with pan-regional ideology or commitment.[9] Deeper integration is the intended as well as unintended consequence of their self-serving actions.[10]

How well does Haas' analytical framework explain integration outcomes outside Europe? The first wave of regional integration in Latin America, for example, ended in failure.[11] This came as no surprise to Haas since none of the three factors that he considered essential for success were present in the Latin America of the 1960s.

First, socio-political pluralism was not a given in most of Latin America where dominance of personalistic and familial ties, political authoritarianism, and various forms of socio-economic traditionalism stood in the way of general mobilization of large segments of society through interest groups and political parties. "The kind of pluralism most favorable to rapid integration exists only in spots and its consistency is far from reliable."[12] Second, little symmetrical heterogeneity existed in the region. For example, industrialists across the region tended to have few common commercial interests, and trade unionists in one country would or could not readily establish relationships with their counterparts elsewhere. Finally, decision-making in Latin America was highly politicized. The reason was that "Latin America ha[d] not [yet] reached the end of ideology."[13] Slogans of socialism and capitalism, working class and aristocracy, the military and civilian, and church and state permeated daily political discourse. Dispassionate and pragmatic bureaucrats, the *técnicos*, were few and far between. Most bureaucrats tended to be linked to oligarchic groups, compromising their autonomy as decision-makers.

In short, incrementalism—which depends on institutionalized communication patterns between a wide range of societal groups and national elites, as well as recognized expertise of technicians and secure civil service status—could not develop in Latin America in the 1960s. Haas summed up the difference between Europe and Latin America as follows: "Europe is divided by language and religion, but united by regionally similar social and economic conditions and institutions; Latin America is united merely by language and religion. For automatic integration this is not enough."[14]

Nevertheless, Haas thought it possible that integration in Latin America and other parts of the world could be triggered by common external threats, most notably the "export prowess and possible protectionism of a United Europe."[15] The identification of external threats as trigger or motivator of regional integration is an important insight. However, Haas invokes this new factor in a rather ad hoc fashion, that is, without properly theorizing it. He fails to explain exactly why external threats matter and how and when they succeed in promoting integration—a weakness that externality theory seeks to tackle head-on.[16]

54.3 THE EXTERNALITY THEORY OF COMPARATIVE REGIONAL INTEGRATION

The framework proposed by Walter Mattli in *The Logic of Regional Integration* helped to revive analytical research on comparative regional integration, after a lull of some twenty years.[17] It bears some resemblance with the framework proposed by Haas, most clearly by insisting on the analytical primacy of sub- and supranational actors (see Table 54.2). Like Haas, Mattli seeks to explain within a broadly rationalist framework why some integration schemes succeed while others fail. Central to the Mattli's framework is the concept of cross-border externalities. Different types of such externalities have varying impacts on the incentives of economic and political actors to pursue integration. The concept also permits to integrate the internal and external logics of integration within a single framework. The internal logic elaborates the conditions under which integration succeeds or fails, and the external logic explains why, when, and how successful integration may trigger integrative responses in outsider countries.

54.3.1 The Internal Logic of Regional Integration

The internal logic suggests that two conditions must be satisfied if integration is to succeed, namely demand-side and supply-side conditions. The demand side extrapolates insights derived from economic institutional theories, such as property rights theory and new institutional economics. In short, the argument is that regional governance (i.e. regional rules, regulations, and policies) may be understood as an attempt to internalize externalities that cross borders within a group of countries. Externalities affecting cross-border trade and investment arise from economic and political uncertainty as well as from a wide range of financial risks that market actors face when dealing with firms and governments in the region. The costs of these externalities increase as new technologies raise the potential for gains from cross-border market exchange, thus increasing the pay-offs to regional rules, regulations, and policies capable of alleviating these costs. The demand by economic actors (importers, exporters, transnational investors, etc.) for regional governance depends on the intensity and nature of cross-border transactions. Such transactions are particularly intense and salient in Europe and North America.

However, demand by market actors is not enough for integration to succeed. Supply conditions need to be satisfied too. These are the conditions under which political leaders are willing and able to accommodate demands for integration. Willingness depends on the pay-off of integration to political leaders. The theory assumes that these leaders value political autonomy and power, and that their success in holding on to power depends on their relative success in managing the economy. It follows that leaders may be unwilling to deepen integration if their economies are relatively prosperous. Why sacrifice national sovereignty if the economy is growing relatively quickly and most people are thus content? Put differently, economically successful leaders may not see the need to pursue deeper integration because the expected marginal benefit from further integration in terms of retaining political power is minimal and thus not worth the cost of integration. However, in times of economic difficulties, political leaders will be more concerned with securing their own survival and will thus be more willing to accommodate demands by market players for regional rules, regulations, and policies.

But even willing political leaders may be unable to supply regional rules, regulations, and policies because of collective action problems such as the Prisoners' Dilemma (PD) and, even more importantly, the Coordination Dilemma. The PD problem is one free-riding.[18] It is mitigated if the integration agreement provides for the establishment of "commitment institutions," such as centralized monitoring and third-party enforcement. The provision of such institutions is one supply condition for successful integration, but it is a weak one. In its absence, cooperation may still be possible on the basis of repeat-play, issue-linkage, and reputation. Nevertheless, "commitment institutions" can catalyze the process of regional integration, particularly if they offer direct access to those actors with the greatest vested interest in seeing integration completed—a point forcefully made by Haas' neo-functionalist theory.

The problem in the Coordination Dilemma is not one of freeriding but of agreeing on one of several possible courses of action in a situation in which the states have opposing interests. Coordination problems are particularly salient in integration, because most regional integration schemes, including free-trade areas, customs unions, or economic unions go beyond the removal of border barriers. They may include efforts to adopt common rules of origin, common commercial policies, common investment codes, common health and safety standards, or common macroeconomic policies. Coordination also gives rise to distributional issues, as a chosen course of action benefits some states within the group more than others. Questions of fairness and equitable distribution of the gains from cooperation will need to be addressed to prevent discontent from derailing the integration process. These observations lead to a key supply condition for successful integration, namely the presence of an undisputed leader among the group of countries seeking closer ties. Such a state serves as a focal point in the coordination of rules, regulations, and policies; it may also help to ease distributional tensions by acting as regional "paymaster." In sum, regional groups that satisfy both the demand and supply conditions stand the greatest chance of succeeding, whereas groups that fulfill neither set of conditions are least likely to attain any significant level of integration.

Table 54.1 summarizes the outcomes of several major integration schemes. The major success stories all satisfy these two conditions. They include the EU and the Zollverein; their respective leaders are Germany and Prussia. The North American Free Trade Agreement (NAFTA), led by the United States, is also generally considered to be a success. No integration scheme that satisfies these two conditions has ever failed. Groups in cells with a success rate of 2 have mixed records. The European Free Trade Association (EFTA) lost much of its momentum when the United Kingdom defected to the European Community in 1973. It was further weakened when three of its members, Finland, Sweden, and Austria, switched allegiance to the EU in 1995. Progress within the Asia Pacific Economic Cooperation forum (APEC) has been stalled due to marked differences between the United States and Japan. Their differing economic institutions and policy preferences in development, money, trade, and other domains make coordination difficult. The Central American Common Market (CACM) is a particularly fascinating case. Its place in a cell with a success rate of 2 appears anomalous. However, in CACM, unlike in the Latin American Free Trade Association (LAFTA), the United States came to play the role of the adopted regional leader, easing distributional problems and offering leadership in policy coordination. As a quid pro quo, CACM countries had to accept the rules of integration defined by the United States, heavily favoring American multinational corporations. The outbreak of the "Soccer War" between El Salvador and Honduras in 1969 brought CACM's integration effort to an abrupt end. Finally, the Mercado Común del Sur (MERCOSUR) emerged in the early 1990s from the failed LAFTA. The structure of the economies of its South American members has changed since the early 1960s. Industrialization has broadened the scope for mutually beneficial exchange of goods at the regional level. This has enabled MERCOSUR to raise the percentage of intra-regional trade in total trade. Nevertheless, coordination and redistribution problems are no easier to solve today in Latin America than thirty years ago.

Several recent studies have drawn on the demand- and supply-side conditions of externality theory to shed light on significant developments and variations in regional integration. Roberto Bouzas and Herman Soltz, for example, have assessed the evolving performance of MERCOSUR in terms of changing parameters of demand and supply.[19] And Sebastian Krapohl, Benjamin Faude, and Julia Dinkel have analyzed the influence of the dispute settlement mechanisms of NAFTA and MERCOSUR on integration by drawing on the demand- and supply-side factors, concluding that vigorous economic and social demands within a particular region are at least as important for deep judicial integration as the extent of legalization of a regional integration project.[20] Other scholars have pointed to a limitation of the framework, namely the narrow conception of leadership—leadership provided by the dominant country in the region. Finn Laursen, for example, has correctly pointed out that supranational institutions may sometimes provide critical leadership in forging new rules and regulations or resolving disputes among member states on policy direction.[21] More research is called for to fully flesh out the mechanics and conditions of leadership in comparative regional integration research.

Table 54.1 Integration outcomes

Supply: (Uncontested Regional Leadership)

		YES	No
Demand: (Potential) Market Gains from Integration	RELATIVELY SIGNIFICANT	**3** EUROPEAN UNION NAFTA ZOLLVEREIN EFTA (UNITL 1973)	**2** EFTA (AFTER 1973) ASIA PACIFIC ECONOMIC COOPERATION FORUM (APEC) MERCOSUR
	RELATIVELY INSIGNIFICANT	**2** CENTRAL AMERICAN COMMON MARKET (UNTIL 1969)	**1** BAVARIA-WÜRTTEMBERG CUSTOMS UNION MIDDLE GERMAN COMMERCIAL UNION CENTRAL AMERICAN COMMON MARKET (AFTER 1969) ASEAN ECONOMIC COMMUNITY OF WEST AFRICAN STATES LAFTA ANDEAN PACT CARIBBEAN COMMUNITY ARAB COMMON MARKET

SUCCESS RATES
3 = HIGHEST
1=LOWEST

Source: Walter Mattli, *The Logic of Regional Integration: Europe and Beyond* (Cambridge: Cambridge University Press, 1999).

54.3.2 The External Logic of Regional Integration

A comprehensive explanation of regional integration requires that the discussion of the internal logic of integration be complemented by an account of the external logic, focusing on the effects of regional rules, regulations, and policies on outsider countries. The successful regional process of internalization of externalities can create external effects (i.e. externalities) on countries that do not participate in this process. These effects differ from the externalities that fuel the integration process within a group of countries (as discussed above). What forms do external effects take? Historically, the most important is relative loss of market access. Countries outside an integrated group may face temporary or lasting discriminatory trade policies. Even in the absence of a high common external tariff, discriminating may become lasting because rules of origin associated with free-trade areas can give protected firms a vested interest in maintaining protection. However, discrimination may also be temporary. If trade liberalization within a group has dynamic effects enhancing economic growth, or if scale economies stimulate the demand for imports from outside the region, income effects of liberalization may more than offset trade diversion, thus helping outsiders to raise their welfare.

Another effect is investment diversion. Its importance has grown with the liberalization of capital markets. Rapid economic growth in a union may increase the share of international investment directed to union members at the expense of outsiders. Furthermore, improved competitiveness of the industries in a union could lead to increased production and lower prices, thus putting at a competitive disadvantage producers outside the union that do not experience comparable productivity gains. Finally, to the extent that integration requires a dominant state to assume the role of paymaster dispensing funds to ease distributional frictions within a union, fewer funds may flow to needy outsider states. In other words, integration could have the effect of aid diversion.

How will outsiders react to these externalities? The theory suggests that countries negatively affected by regional integration will pursue one of two strategies. They can either seek to merge with the group generating the external effects—this is the "first integrative response"—or they can respond by creating their own regional group—the "second integrative response." The first integrative response is possible only if the existing group is willing to accept newcomers. If an outsider is not a desirable candidate in the sense of being able to make a net contribution to the union, the union is generally unlikely to accept it. However, a union may have an interest in accepting an "undesirable" candidate when negative externalities originating in an outsider country (perhaps due to exclusion from the regional market) threaten to disrupt the union's prosperity, stability, and security. For example, a dismal economic situation in an outsider country may raise the specter of large-scale migration to the prosperous union, threatening the union's social and political stability. The union may be better off integrating an "undesirable" outsider economy, invigorating export industries in that economy, generating new employment opportunities, and thereby easing migratory pressure.

If an outsider is rejected, or knows it is likely to be rejected if it were to apply, or is unwilling to accept the terms of membership in a given group, it may opt for the "second integrative response." Many examples exist of this logic. The creation of the customs union between Prussia and Hesse-Darmstadt in 1828 triggered the Bavaria-Würtemberg customs union, the Middle German Commercial Union, and the North German Tax Union. The establishment of the European Community triggered numerous integration projects, most notably the European Free Trade Association and LAFTA. Likewise, efforts to deepen integration through the SEA raised fears of a "Fortress Europe," provoking a veritable tidal wave of integration projects throughout the world in the late 1980s. None of the projects of the second integrative response type is guaranteed automatic success. Like any integration scheme, counter-unions must satisfy both demand and supply conditions to be successful.

The discussion of the external logic of integration usefully complements the internal logic of the externality theory. Nevertheless, it overlooks other motivations by regional groups to promote integration externally. Forthcoming work by Tobias Lenz, for example, sheds light on the mechanisms by which the EU model has influenced integration in other regions.[22] More theoretical and empirical research on the external logic of integration is much needed.[23]

54.4 The Contracting Theory of Comparative Regional Integration

The frameworks proposed by Haas and Mattli do not explain why some successful integration schemes have minimalist institutional arrangements whilst others have extensive supranational governance. Similarly, neither framework fully explains why some successful schemes have remained narrow whilst others have gradually grown more expansive. Alexander Cooley and Hendrik Spruyt address these interesting differences head-on in a recent theoretical contribution to comparative regional integration that is bound to generate considerable research.[24]

Cooley and Spruyt argue that two factors determine the dynamics of the integration process: the mode of contracting, and the degree of delegation to supranational institutions. These two factors, in turn, can be explained in terms of two variables, namely the extent of power asymmetry among contracting states and the intensity of demand for integration. Let us consider each of these sets of factors.

Countries seeking integration have to make two fundamental choices: first, do they wish to write an incomplete or a complete regional integration agreement? An incomplete contract is relatively sparse and open-ended and thus likely to be subject to *ex post* negotiations. In contrast, a complete contract requires the parties to draft a fully specified legal text. Second, the parties need to decide whether to allow for the creation of supranational institutions or stick to a strictly intergovernmental arrangement.

Two prominent contrasting cases are the EU and NAFTA. The Treaty of Rome of 1957, the EU's foundational agreement, is an incomplete contract. The text is brief and short on details; its scope, however, is wide. It offers statements of principle and enumerates eleven areas of work, including elimination of customs duties and quantitative restrictions; establishment of a common external tariff and common external policy, freedom of movement of persons, services, and capital; a common agricultural policy, undistorted competition, and coordination of economic policies. The treaty also provides for the creation of supranational institutions, notably the Commission and the ECJ. The modest level of detail in the treaty or *ex ante* legislation indicates a willingness by the signatory states to rely on supranational decision-making and judicial rulings to impart specificity upon statements of principle enshrined in the treaty.

The NAFTA agreement is strikingly different from the Treaty of Rome. It has the hallmarks of a complete contract. It is long (thousands of pages) and highly detailed; yet its aim is limited—NAFTA only seeks to create a free trade area. In addition, NAFTA makes no provisions for supranational agency. It is an intergovernmental integration scheme. Its arbitration panels, for example, are ad hoc and their composition requires the approval of the contracting parties.

The difference between the EU and NAFTA can be summarized in terms of allocation of the residual right of control, i.e. the right or ability to specify or modify contract clauses at time $t + 1$ (that is, after the signing of the original contract). Initially, sovereign states are the holders of residual rights. They then have to decide whether to relinquish these rights in some issue areas (by creating supranational institutions) or retain them. In the EU, states agreed from the onset to grant important residual rights to the Community institutions. In NAFTA, however, these rights remain firmly in the hands of the member-state governments.

54.4.1 Explaining Contractual and Institutional Variations

What explains these differences in contractual choices between the EU and NAFTA? Cooley and Spruyt offer two explanatory factors: relative symmetries in power and in demand for integration among regional states. In NAFTA, the distribution of power is highly asymmetric. The US occupies a hegemonic position; its economy accounts for about 85 percent of the NAFTA region. North American economic integration was demanded first by Canada and later Mexico.[25] Both countries were in serious economic difficulties when they opened trade negotiations with the US, hoping that closer trading ties would improve conditions. In other words, access to the neighboring market was more urgent and important to Canada and Mexico than it was to the US.

As relatively small states, however, Canada and Mexico had to be cautious when dealing with the US. Like any dominant state, the US may be tempted to use its power to its own advantage in future specifications and delineations of an incomplete integration agreement. Canada and Mexico thus had an incentive to seek protection against such risk by demanding a complete contract with the US. Residual rights would remain with the states, giving all signatories a say in future alterations of the agreement.

In theory, small states contracting with a big state can pursue an alternative contractual strategy by agreeing to an incomplete contract but insisting on credible commitments. The creation of supranational institutions or third-party bodies to whom the contractual parties assign residual rights is one such credible commitment mechanism. In practice, however, such institutional protection is rare and weak if one of the parties is hegemonic—like the US in NAFTA. Cooley and Spruyt note:

> Washington signaled strict limits as to how far it would allow its sovereignty to be curtailed...Counterfactually, even if the US had consented to greater delegations to supranational institutions, its commitment to abide by any such legislation or adjudication would be less credible...[T]he very preponderance of the US made it difficult to design institutions that could credibly constrain the hegemon.[26]

Canada and Mexico thus really had little choice but to negotiate a complete contract with the US.

Why did the signatories of the Treaty of Rome agree to an incomplete contract with provisions for supranational institutions? Again, the answer can be found in the distribution of power and the nature of demand for European integration in the late 1950s. France and Germany maintained an uneasy balance of power on the European continent. Germany needed the EU to reintegrate itself economically and regain political respectability; and France viewed the EU as a means to control and perhaps even curtail a rising Germany. Smaller European states also saw benefits; traditionally highly trade-dependent, they stood to gain from easy access to large neighboring markets. In sum, demand for integration was general and strong.

Nevertheless, Belgium, the Netherlands, and Luxembourg had reasons to worry that France and Germany might in the future capitalize on their position as large states and usurp power. They were willing to sign an incomplete integration contract on condition of obtaining a credible commitment from the larger states in the form of supranational institutions. Neither France nor Germany opposed such institutional safeguards. France considered common institutions desirable in order to bind Germany, and German Chancellor Adenauer understood that the acceptance of binding Community institutions was a condition for his country to be regarded as a "normal" state and trustworthy partner. In sum, "the European geopolitical and economic environment ... propelled a disposition among political and social elites to tolerate a significant degree of supranational decision-making with relatively low levels of precision *ex ante* in legislation."[27] Symmetry of power between Germany and France made credible commitments possible, and mutual economic interdependence among all EU founding members made integration desirable.

54.4.2 The Consequences of Contractual and Institutional Variations

Cooley and Spruyt posit that differences in contractual terms and institutional design engender different integration dynamics. Incomplete contracts with residual rights assigned to supranational institutions create incentives for further integration. Intergovernmental complete contracting, by contrast, virtually precludes such developments.

The member states of the EU designed relatively autonomous supranational institutions entrusted with rendering general treaty provision more specific and furthering integration in a wide range of areas. The integration activism displayed by the EU institutions, Cooley and Spruyt argue, is not evidence of a loss of control by the member states over these institutions. Given the logic of incomplete contracting, activism was necessary to give the Treaty of Rome meaning and operationality; in other words, activism was largely intended.

As a result of the incomplete contracting nature of the EEC treaty and because of the need to credibly commit, European Community institutions required the states to give up meaningful authority. This is not simply a question of principal–agent "slippage" but a logical response to how state elites can solve contracting problems.[28]

Nevertheless, Cooley and Spruyt accept that assigning residual rights of control to supranational institutions raises concerns about the possibility of a disjuncture between states' objectives and supranational rule-making. "If residual rights are held by international organizations…, governments will be concerned with the bargaining leverage that flows to such institutions as time progresses."[29] States can prevent such disjuncture by developing means of fire alarm oversight or adopting procedural "reversibility mechanisms," for example, in the form of legislation that counters runaway activism. Rational expectation or anticipation by supranational agents of such measures is likely to keep supranational activism in check.

The dynamic evolution of integration in Europe has not been replicated in North America because of the completeness of the NAFTA agreement. "As a consequence of leaving the residual rights of control with the contracting parties, NAFTA has not progressed much beyond the terms of the initial parties. Unlike European integration, which quickly expanded into various areas of economic and political cooperation…, NAFTA has expanded little."[30] Its scope has remained unchanged since the signing of the agreement.

The propositions of contracting theory travel well beyond Europe and North America. Cooley and Spruyt conclude that "the likelihood that other regional organizations such as ASEAN and Mercosur will come to resemble either the EU or NAFTA will greatly depend on whether their member states choose or adopt incomplete contracting or a complete contract as a governance mechanism."[31] These choices, in turn, will be determined by the distribution of regional power and varying needs of integration.

54.4.3 Outstanding Issues and Summary

Cooley and Spruyt's analytical contribution is significant and timely. However, it also raises several issues for further examination and theoretical refinement. First, Cooley and Spruyt correctly note that supranational institutional safeguards may not be sufficiently strong or credible to constrain a hegemonic state, such as the US in NAFTA. But why should we believe that a complete contract offers greater assurance against future abuses by the powerful? Suppose the hegemonic state wishes after a few years to insert changes into a complete contract—changes that the small states resist. Assuming, as seems plausible, that the small states depend more on access to the market of the hegemon for their prosperity than the hegemon depends on the small markets, the hegemon could credibly threaten to walk away from a complete contract if the small states do not concede. In sum, complete contracts are not necessarily more robust and effective safeguards than institutions. More work is required to define the boundary conditions of effectiveness of alternative safeguarding measures and strategies.

Second, and relatedly, let us assume that a few small states are desperate for an integration agreement but the big neighboring state is only willing to offer an incomplete contract without supranational or third-party institutions. Will the small states necessarily reject such offer? Why, for example, is Mercosur an incomplete contract without provisions for truly supranational institutions? Should Paraguay and Uruguay, and perhaps even Argentina, not be concerned about opportunistic future actions by hegemonic Brazil? Here again, we need greater theoretical specification to provide clear answers.

Third, much more thinking is needed on how to design credible commitment institutions, especially in regions characterized by power asymmetry. Not all supranational institutions are equally vulnerable to usurpation by the powerful. The ECJ's striking effectiveness, for example, derives in large part from its ability to build alliances across Europe with sub-national constituencies that have a vested interest in a truly single European market in goods and services. Such networks have made interference in Court proceedings by governments—and, crucially, even powerful governments—practically impossible for domestic political reasons, boosting the Court's effectiveness as a commitment institution.[32] In sum, certain institutional arrangements may be highly effective, credible commitment devices even in regions characterized by power asymmetry.

Finally, Table 54.2 summarizes some of the key analytical differences among the three frameworks of comparative regional integration. Neo-functionalist and externality theories both privilege sub- and supranational actors as key drivers of integration. Externality theory, however, also models the role played by governments. In contracting theory the main actors are states, though institutions can play a critical supporting role. The first two theories also allow for some level of unintended consequences. Cooley and Spruyt, by contrast, do not deny the existence of spillover but argue that spillover is largely intended; it naturally derives from an incomplete contract and generally is desired by the states. Another difference is that Mattli considers the presence of a dominant state to be necessary to overcome regional coordination dilemmas and resolve distributional problems. Cooley and Spruyt, however, emphasize the risks that contracting with a dominant state entails, and ponder the contracting and governance implications of such risks. Finally, it is noteworthy that all three theories use the term of "(a)symmetry," albeit differently. Haas posits that "symmetrical regional heterogeneity" is a condition for successful integration. In other words, member states need to be fragmented along similar lines of pluralism for the various sub-national groups to be able to pursue common cause with their counterparts in other countries. For Mattli, symmetry of cross-border externalities translates into pan-regional demand by market actors for an integrated governance structure. And for Cooley and Spruyt, power and demand (a)symmetries are the factors that determine contracting type and degree of delegation to supranational institutions.

Table 54.2 Overview of theories of comparative regional integration

	Neo-Functionalist Theory	Externality Theory	Contracting Theory
Main Actors	Sub- and Supranational Actors promote Integration Governments respond	Sub-national actors demand and Supranational Actors facilitate Integration Governments supply	States write integration contracts and Supranational Institutions deepen integration (where they exist)
Demand for Integration	Economic, Political, and Social Sub-national groups	Mainly market players (exporters, importers, and transnational investors)	States (in need of foreign market access)
Regional Leadership/ Hegemony	n/a	Key to overcoming coordination dilemma and solving distributional problems	A Problem/Risk (tackled by complete contracting or credible commitments)
Common Institutions	Co-Drivers of integration	Commitment Devices (help to prevent PD problems)	Commitment Devices (help to prevent usurpation by powerful state at time t+1)
Deeper Integration	Partly intended, partly unintended	Partly intended, partly unintended	Largely intended
External Effects of Integration	Acknowledged (but not theorized)	Central to Theory	n/a

NOTES

1. Ernst Haas and Philippe Schmitter, "Economics and Differential Patterns of Political Integration: Projections about Unity in Latin America," *International Organization* 18, no. 4 (1964), 726.
2. Ernst Haas, *The Uniting of Europe: Political, Social, and Economic Forces 1950–1957*, second edition (Stanford: Stanford University Press, 1968).
3. Ernst Haas, "International Integration: The European and the Universal Process," *International Organization* 15, no. 3 (1961), 375.
4. Ernst Haas, "*The Uniting of Europe* and the Uniting of Latin America," *Journal of Common Market Studies* 5, no. 2 (1967), 319–20.
5. Haas, *The Uniting of Europe*, 152.

6. Haas, *The Uniting of Europe*, 5.

7. Haas, *The Uniting of Europe*, p. xiv.

8. Haas accepts a variant of soft rational-choice ontology—an ontology that is not necessarily materialistic since values shape interests and values include many non-material elements. See Ernst Haas, "Does Constructivism Subsume Neo-Functionalism?," *Journal of European Public Policy* 6, no 4 (2001), 23.

9. Haas, "International Integration," 377.

10. Haas, "*The Uniting of Europe* and the Uniting of Latin America," 325.

11. For a description of regional integration schemes of the 1960s, see Walter Mattli, *The Logic of Regional Integration: Europe and Beyond* (Cambridge: Cambridge University Press, 1999), 140–52.

12. Haas and Schmitter, "Economics and Differential Patterns of Political Integration," 722.

13. Haas and Schmitter, "Economics and Differential Patterns of Political Integration," 334.

14. Haas, "*The Uniting of Europe* and the Uniting of Latin America," 333.

15. Haas, "International Integration," 382.

16. For a more extensive critique of Haas' theorizing of comparative regional integration, see Walter Mattli, "Ernst Haas' Evolving Thinking on Comparative Regional Integration: Of Virtues and Infelicities," *Journal of European Public Policy* 12, no. 2 (2005), 327–48.

17. Mattli, *The Logic of Regional Integration*.

18. "Freeriding" here means defecting from the obligation to contribute to the building of an integrated economy while enjoying the fruits of the joint effort by others.

19. Roberto Bouzas and Herman Soltz, "Institutions and Regional Integration: The Case of Mercosur," in Victor Bulmer-Thomas, ed., *Regional Integration in Latin America and the Caribbean: The Political Economy of Open Regionalism* (London: Institute of Latin American Studies, 2001), 98–118.

20. Sebastian Krapohl, Benjamin Faude, and Julia Dinkel, "Judial Integration in the Americas? A Comparison of Dispute Settlement in NAFTA and MECOSUR," in Finn Laursen, ed., *Comparative Regional Integration: Europe and Beyond* (Farnham Surrey: Ashgate Publishing, 2010), 169–92. For a different perspective, see Francesco Duina, *The Social Construction of Free Trade: The European Union, NAFTA, and Mercosur* (Princeton: Princeton University Press, 2006).

21. Finn Laursen, "Requirements for Regional Integration: A Comparative Perspective of the EU, the Americas and East Asia," in Laursen, *Comparative Regional Integration*, 239–69. See also Jonas Tallberg, *Leadership and Negotiation the European Union* (Cambridge: Cambridge University Press, 2006).

22. Tobias Lenz, "Spurred Emulation: The EU and Regional Integration in Mercosur and SADC," *West European Politics* 35, no 1 (2012), 155–73.

23. For a recent such contribution, see Christina Schneider, *Conflict, Negotiations, and EU Enlargement* (Cambridge: Cambridge University Press, 2009).

24. Alexander Cooley and Hendrik Spruyt, *Contracting States: Sovereign Transfers in International Relations* (Princeton: Princeton University Press, 2009). For a related study, see Kathleen Hancock, *Regional Integration: Choosing Plutocracy* (New York: Palgrave Macmillan, 2009).

25. The Canada–US Free Trade Agreement dates from 1987, and NAFTA from 1994.

26. Cooley and Spruyt, *Contracting States*, 175.

27. Cooley and Spruyt, *Contracting States*, 161.

28. Cooley and Spruyt, *Contracting States*, 182.

29. Cooley and Spruyt, *Contracting States*, 146.
30. Cooley and Spruyt, *Contracting States*, 177.
31. Cooley and Spruyt, *Contracting States*, 185.
32. See Anne-Marie Burley and Walter Mattli, "Europe Before the Court: A Political Theory of Legal Integration," *International Organization* 47, no. 1 (1993), 41–76.

PART X

EU AND THE
MEMBER STATES

CHAPTER 55

....

COORDINATION IN THE EU

....

B. GUY. PETERS

THE EU has become responsible for many aspects of governance within Europe. In its transformation from relatively simple customs union to a complex set of institutions regulating many economic activities and providing a range of services, the need to create coherent and coordinated action has become more crucial. This need for enhanced coordination has been recognized in the Helsinki conclusions and the need appears to be increasing as the scope of activities within the EU continues to expand. The fiscal crisis in the Western world in general, and within the eurozone more specifically, also emphasizes the necessity for coherent and strategic action within the EU.

Creating effective policy coordination is one of the oldest challenges to governing,[1] whether in the EU or national governments. As soon as governments created articulated structures with multiple organizations providing multiple services, the need to have those programs cooperate and function together to produce more effective and efficient services became apparent.[2] In contemporary governments those coordination problems have been exacerbated by the increased number of organizations in the public sector, including many coming from the private and third sectors providing public services. Further, factors such as globalization and regionalization have increased the complexity of governance arrangements, as well as the need for effective policy coordination.

Any number of factors produce problems in policy coordination. The numerous individuals and institutions within a political system all have interests that may be threatened by cooperation with other organizations Those different interests of the individuals and institutions tends to divide them, and to make them focus on pursuing those individual concerns. Indeed, organizations are more likely to be competitive than cooperative and to pursue resources and power at the expense of others. That pursuit of individual interest may be even greater when not constrained by strong political executives or strong central agencies. Also, the New Public Management and other reforms of the public sector have tended to exacerbate the tendencies of organizations to pursue their own interests at the expense of more collective goals.[3]

Even if individuals and organizations within the public sector want to cooperate, they may face numerous barriers to that cooperation. Many organizations within government have relatively little information about the operations of other organizations and therefore may not understand the possibilities for cooperation. This isolation of organizations may be accentuated by professionalization and specialized training of employees in the organizations. Professions tend to provide their members with a particular perception of the world and the ways that are most effective in solving policy problems, and therefore limit cooperation. Finally, the clientele being served by a program may not want that commitment reduced, or appear to be reduced, through cooperation with other programs. In short, although coordination and cooperation may in the end produce better services for citizens and more efficient services, they are not undifferentiated benefits.

The organizational problems encountered in coordination are often increased by the institutional structure of governments and by politics. More complex political systems, e.g. federal systems, may exacerbate the underlying coordination problems.[4] All political systems then have problems of vertical coordination between levels of government, but federalism tends to increase those problems and to politicize them. Likewise, as noted above, the tendency toward disaggregating public administration has made the coordination problem more difficult.[5] Most national governments have been attempting to rectify the problems created by the use of agencies, but there are continuing coordination issues arising from these New Public Management Reforms.[6]

Also, presidential and semi-presidential systems will tend to have greater problems of institutional coordination than parliamentary systems. To the extent that several institutions can rightfully claim a mandate from the public for their policy positions, then putting their views together in coherent packages may be more difficult. Parliamentary regimes are hardly immune to the problems of coordination, especially when as in Germany ministers are empowered to make many decisions on their own,[7] although they do have the advantage of a collective governing organization—the cabinet—that can facilitate the creation of cooperation among ministers and ministries.

Although the structure of parliamentary governments may facilitate coordination, some of that advantage is eliminated by most parliamentary systems being coalition governments. Coalitions governments may be able to negotiate agreements to form a government, but they will still contain parties with different policy priorities, so it is only natural that they encounter some difficulties in developing common, coherent programs for governing.[8] This potential difficulty in coordination is especially true given that parties tend to control the ministries of greatest relevance to their own constituents, and hence have less incentive to make concessions to other parties.

Coordination is therefore a central challenge to any government, including the governing institutions of the EU. Both the underlying policy issues being confronted by governments and the institutions of government pose these problems. Policy ideas and approaches may not be compatible and organizations within the public sector want to maintain their own autonomy and control over policy. Therefore, we need to confront the special case of the EU and determine how those special conditions shape the coordination capacity within that political system.

55.1 The EU as a Special Case of Coordination

Although all political systems have their problems of coordination, the EU constitutes a very special challenge to would-be coordinators. This is especially true if we consider the multiple actors involved in the process and the multiple stages at which coordination must occur in order for there to be effective governance.[9] Likewise, the complexity of the interactions among the levels in this system of multilevel governance makes effective coordination of action more difficult.[10] The resulting process involves both horizontal (cross-policy) and vertical (cross-level) dimensions of coordination. These two processes of coordination occur simultaneously and to some extent difficulties encountered on one dimension can be displaced to the other.[11] Further, given that service delivery in most countries now involves using private sector organizations, the coordination issues become more difficult.

The expanding literature on Europeanization represents the development of coordination through the use of ideas.[12] As Eugene Bardach has discussed with reference to coordination in the United States, coordination can be achieved through reframing policy issues in order to obtain some common understanding of a given issue, and the means of solving it.[13] While producing this agreement on policy requires substantial negotiation and bargaining, if that process is successful then the resulting common understanding is likely to be more enduring than more mechanical coordination devices.

In this context Europeanization implies using both ideational and more hierarchical instruments to produce common policies across Europe. While perhaps more important for the vertical aspects of coordination, the same basic concept of spreading common ideas can be used to think about horizontal coordination. As we will point in detail below, the Open Method of Coordination (OMC) is to some extent based on ideas and creating common understandings about the purposes and mechanisms of policies.

The vertical coordination in the EU also must be understood a being bi-directional. Most of the discussion has been on Brussels coordinating from the center and creating uniformity across the member countries. At the same time, however, there are pressures from the member states below, attempting to create policies that suit their own preferences and brokering deals to have those policies adopted. Further, within the national governments there are pressures for coordinating across policy areas that may be difficult to coordinate even at the national level but for which there is a need for a coordinated position at the European level.

The difficulties of policy-making in the EU may make any coordination that results be more negative than positive.[14] That is, it is relatively easy for programs and their leaders to find ways of avoiding conflicts with one another. The structure of the European Commission, as is true for other public bureaucracies, is highly segmented and that tends to facilitate avoiding direct conflicts.[15] What that segmentation does, however, is to make cooperation and more synergistic interactions among programs less likely. That segmentation also makes moving beyond even positive, cooperative forms of coordination toward more strategic forms of governance even less likely.

55.2 THE NATIONAL LEVEL

One of the most important coordination issues in the EU is that governing within the EU involves a great deal of interaction between the nation states that comprise the Union and the institutions in Brussels itself. If the national governments are to be effective in getting what they want form Brussels, they must coordinate within their own governments, both in the national capitals and in Brussels itself.[16] There has been a good deal of Europeanization of policies across the member states of the EU, but even then the various members have different priorities and preferences, so they need to be effective in coping with the other members and with the Brussels bureaucracy. Different countries have different aspirations concerning the extent to which they present a unified set of positions in Brussels; but all countries can benefit from some internal consistency of their bargaining positions.

55.2.1 Aspirations

One of the most important factors affecting the level of coordination in national governments is the aspiration of the countries to produce that level of policy integration. We might expect all countries to be interested in being as effective as possible in getting what they want from Brussels and in placing a particular stamp on policy; but that is not the case. Some countries such as the United Kingdom invest a great deal of effort in effective coordination relative to the EU, while others such as Denmark have been more casual. Although aspirations do not equate with success in producing coordination, it appears that some political systems do not even have very high aspirations.

As well as general levels of aspirations, countries differ in the range of policies for which they have aspirations for coordination. Some of the member states have a strong emphasis on particular policies, e.g. agriculture or structural funds, and may not be especially concerned about other policy areas. The focus on individual policy areas tends to reduce coordination, albeit maximizing the capacity to reach desired goals for any one government. The economic crisis beginning in 2008 appears to have emphasized the need to coordinate economic policy areas perhaps more than others.

55.2.2 Structures

The capacity to coordinate at the national level is also dependent upon the structures that are involved in making policy decisions. As already noted, federal systems present special challenges for policy coordination, given that the sub-national governments have their own priorities that may make arriving at a common position within the country difficult, especially when those sub-national units are polarized as in Belgium. Further, the multilevel nature of European government means that the coalitions and alliances that are formed across levels of government may produce complex coordination problems that may not be readily addressed through the instrumentalities usually associated with coordination.

The relative powers of ministries with governments may also influence the capacity of national governments to coordinate. For example, although the German government may have a high level of aspiration for good policy coordination, the relative independence of ministers and ministries may make creating that coordination difficult. In contrast, the integration of government decision-making in Sweden means that the individual ministries have relatively little capacity to act autonomously, in general or in relation to the EU. Most governments lie between those two extremes, with varying levels of independence for their ministers when working with Brussels.

The capacity for coordination at the national level is also influenced by the strength of central agencies that are responsible for coordinating domestic policies and can also coordinate national responses to Europe. All countries have powerful ministries of finance, but some are more powerful than others. Further, in some instances the responsibility for coordinating European policy has been assigned to ministries of foreign affairs rather than to finance ministries or to prime minister themselves, and although the foreign ministry may be prestigious, it is generally not so powerful in domestic politics as are the other possible coordinators. Such a choice of institutions may indicate the conception that European-level politics is indeed not like other domestic policy choices but rather is more like international diplomacy.

55.3 Coordination in Brussels

The political process at the national level is difficult and complex, but that in Brussels is perhaps even more complex and requires careful consideration as a mechanism for producing more coherent forms of governing. The need to coordinate is apparent for any governing system, but is perhaps greater in the EU because of the aspirations of creating common forms of governing across Europe. Much of that emphasis on coordination is vertical, attempting to ensure through the community method that the regulations implemented across the Union are as similar as possible—an outcome necessary for ensuring the fairness of the internal market for all the participants.[17]

The coordination problem in the EU is horizontal as well, especially as the policy scope of the Union has become more extensive. There has always been the need to coordinate various aspects of economic policy, again in order to create a coherent economic policy. That need to coordinate naturally increased dramatically when the Union moved from simply regulatory instruments to monetary policy. The increasing need to coordinate aspects of social and labor market policy that impinge on the market has expanded the demands for coordination across a range of domains within the EU, leading at least in part to the development of instruments such as the OMC (see below).

55.3.1 Factors Inhibiting Coordination

Coordination is more difficult in the EU than in most national governments.[18] Some of that difficulty arises from the general complexity of its structures and procedures; there are a number of specific aspects of the EU that make coordination difficult to achieve. Some of these are typical for governments in general, but may be relatively extreme versions of those characteristics. Other features inhibiting coordination are more specific to the EU governing apparatus. The structure of the Union was not designed necessarily to be an effective set of governance institutions and the need to combine an international organization with an economic policy structure makes efficient policy-making, including coordination, difficult.

55.3.2 Bureaucratic Politics

The Commission of the EU is divided into a number of Directorates-General, each responsible for a specific policy area, and these organizations tend to have their own commitments to specific ways of making and implementing policy.[19] Again, this is not dissimilar to government structures at the national level, but there are somewhat fewer instruments to integrate the various policy areas in Brussels than in most national capitals.[20] As already noted, the role of political parties in government is weaker in the EU, so that this common integrative factor is not effective.

There has been some tendency to think of Brussels as some undifferentiated entity while this analysis masks the extreme divisions within the European policy system. The various Directorates-General in the Commission have perhaps more autonomy than would ministries in a national government. The reforms that have tended to strengthen the central executive have tended to reduce some of that autonomy, but there are still strong centrifugal pressures within the European system. Not only are the structures divided by expertise but they are also linked to policy networks that reinforce the differences.

55.3.3 Leadership Instability and Diffusion

Strong executive leadership can enhance the capacity for policy coordination. Part of the effort at enhancing coordination in a number of parliamentary regimes has involved strengthening the center, and empowering prime ministers.[21] The EU does have a relatively strong executive in the president of the European Commission, but the rotating leadership in the European Council[22] does present a problem for steering governance in the EU. If the Treaty of Lisbon is adopted and there is a more permanent president, then some of this executive instability will be alleviated and some greater capacity for coordination will be created.[23]

The executive instability within the EU also may be encountered in the careers of various commissioners themselves. These officials are appointed by their national governments, albeit having to be approved by the other member countries. The members of the European Commission have a set term of office but might not remain in the same commission post for that entire period. Further, relatively few spend more than one or two years in the Commission, so that someone is always coming or going within the structures.[24] Given that a good deal of the work of coordination will be facilitated by political leaders and their cooperation, more frequent changes on those elites are likely to reduce the coordination capacity of this governing system.

A final consideration in the executive structure of the EU is that the Commission as a collectivity has relatively little to unify it as a political actor, or to provide linkages with other political actors.[25] For example, political parties can help to integrate actors across ministries and at least in majoritarian governments can provide a source of coherence.[26] The Commission does not have that sort of integrating political activity, and hence some of the inherent centrifugal forces coming from the different substantive concerns of the Directorates-General and the organizational interests of those organizations are not as readily overcome as they are in other executive structures.

In addition, the Commissioners have been appointed by the member governments and to some extent remain loyal to those governments despite their oaths of loyalty to Europe. It is difficult to ascertain to what extent the Commissioners are indeed agents of their national governments or are they true Europeans, and there is probably no single answer to that question.[27] They therefore may have a range of concerns that is narrowed explicitly by their responsibility for a specific policy area and implicitly by their national political socialization and policy histories. Creating permanent executive officials may help to create more of a strictly European identity within the executive, and that in turn may emphasize the need to coordinate policies across the Directorates-General.

55.3.4 Increasing Administrative Differentiation

The basic structure of the bureaucracy of the EU provides a good deal of autonomy for the various Directorates-General, but it is becoming even more differentiated. Following the fashion of the time, the EU has begun to create a number of quasi-autonomous agencies to address particular issues.[28] As is true in most instances of using these structures, the logic of agencies in the EU is to provide greater capacity of autonomous action and an ability to use better expertise.[29] Agencies have been created in a number of policy areas such as the environment, food safety, and airline regulation that use substantial expertise along with administrative power.

Agencies provide governments with some real administrative advantages but at the same time they present problems for coordination. Several European agencies, e.g. food safety, were themselves established to attempt to bring together a variety of activities that might ordinarily be found in several Directorates-General—but even then, separating food safety from agriculture and biotechnology activities creates yet another set of coordination problems.[30] This agency also represents an important example of the need to bring together horizontal and vertical dimensions of coordination, given the importance of national and sub-national governments for implementing food safety programs.[31]

55.3.5 Facilitating Coordination in the EU

To this point I have been painting a rather bleak picture of the possibilities of policy coordination in the EU. There are indeed a number of barriers to coordination working effectively within this complex set of institutions. That said there are also a number of factors facilitating coordination. These factors may be more effective for creating vertical than horizontal coordination, but there are also some factors that can promote greater horizontality in governing.

55.3.6 The President of the Commission and Staff

As already noted, the president of the European Commission has provided a relatively strong center for the executive of the EU. Two long-serving presidents—Delors and Prodi—were important for setting the policy directions of the EU and integrating the policies of the Union. The Commission does not act as a collectivity as might a cabinet in a parliamentary government, but the policy direction can be supplied by the president, and there has been substantial leadership supplied by the president, including leadership promoting policy integration and coordination.

The leadership of the president of the Commission is important for producing coordinated approaches to policy, but that president also has a substantial staff in the form of his *cabinet* and the general secretariat. The Commission is nominally a collegial organization but the president can be more than *primus inter pares* and can exercise substantial policy coordination functions by shaping the priorities of the Commission as a whole. This is especially important given that the Commission has the power to shape the agenda for policy-making in the EU, both collectively and within individual Directorates-General.

55.3.7 COREPER

Part of the work of the national representations in producing coordination in Brussels is structured by the need to be effective in the COREPER and its working groups.[32] This institution comprises all the permanent representatives of the member countries and does the preparatory work for ministerial meetings of the Council. If the work is done well, then issues that might be problematic for the formal meetings of the ministers can be resolved in advance, and thus reduce conflict within the EU.

COREPER is one of the less researched parts of the EU, but it is central to many aspects of policy-making. By bringing together all the permanent representatives of the member countries, it provides an important means of producing some agreement and coordination on policies across the members.[33] Further, it appears important in creating some common culture among these officials and providing a normative basis for further coordination. That said, however, much of the work of COREPER is done in working groups defined by particular policy areas that may inhibit horizontal coordination.

55.3.8 The Open Method of Coordination

The Lisbon Program adopted in 2000 pledged the EU to develop the most competitive economic area in the world. The various treaties and agreements creating the EU provided ample authority to make economic policy, but there was limited authority for the EU to become involved in other policy areas that affected the competitiveness of Europe. A number of aspects of labor market policy, education and training, and social policy had to be involved in this policy initiative in order to produce the desired economic outcomes. The Lisbon process has helped to demonstrate the complexity of interactions among policy areas and the need for effective coordination.

The OMC was designed to help the EU cope with this mismatch of need and authority.[34] The OMC combines some aspects of vertical policy coordination with some elements of horizontal coordination. The vertical dimension involves producing relatively similar policy responses in all the member states, albeit doing so without the use of direct regulatory authority. This process has then moved the standards for policy harmonization within the EU to a much lower level, allowing the member states to a lower level. The horizontal aspect of coordination is that this method brings together a range of policy areas all of which can contribute to competitiveness.

The method relies on very informal means of producing compliance among the member states, with compliance being produced by negotiation and informal pressures rather than through legal means. There is little to be able to enforce the agreements among the participants at the national level, nor is there any way of ensuring that the various countries will align their own activities with those of their partners. The "logic of appropriateness" about policies that is created through the OMC provides a means of generating coherent policy without the use of formal authority.

55.3.9 Soft Law

The OMC is a specific example of a more general phenomenon in policy-making within the EU, and indeed at the level of national governments. The use of "soft law," meaning instruments such as benchmarks, voluntary agreements, guidelines, and a host of other less authoritative instruments has become a substitute for formal, legal policy-making in most contemporary democracies[35] as a means of facilitating policy-making and especially for enhancing policy implementation. Also described as "New Governance," this approach to policy demands less uniformity than more legalistic mechanisms of governing, although more than might be possible without those mechanisms.[36]

Soft law is a general pattern for policy-making, but it has some special virtues for creating policy coordination within the EU. As with the OMC, the use of all forms of soft law permit gaining some level of compliance and commonality of outcomes without having to enforce direct regulations. Further, the use of softer instruments enables the EU to coordinate policy areas over which it might not ordinarily be able to exercise any substantial controls—even in economic policy, where the Union might be expected to be able to use more formal policy instruments.[37]

55.3.10 Coordination from the Bottom Up

Most discussions of policy coordination begin with an assumption of hierarchical controls and the imposition of authority. Any number of instruments have been developed within national governments in order to use that authority to coordinate public policies. Coordination, however, can be produced through other means, notably through the use of networks of organizations and networks of social actors. In these forms of coordination, the process tends to be more bottom-up than top-down, with the organizations and interests involved working out ways of getting programs to work together.[38]

To some extent these mechanisms for coordination function because they bring together organizations and interests in a range of different settings. For example, the comitology system which is organized to provide advice and permit input from national governments within the EU provides venues in which various national and sectoral interests can help coordinate policies. The working groups that feed their work into the Council through COREPER provide similar loci for discussion and interactions about policy and can thus find potential coordinated responses to policy problems.[39] While not using authority as the basis for coordination, these mechanisms may nonetheless be capable of getting programs to work together more effectively.

55.4 COORDINATING COORDINATION?

We have not discussed a number of different dimensions of coordination within the EU and its member states. Although each can be understood separately, attempting to understand them together and to understand the interactions may be more taxing. There is a vertical dimension of nations attempting to press compatible views of Brussels, and then Brussels attempting to ensure that relatively common policies are being implemented in all member countries. The movement toward softer forms of coordination permits somewhat less stringent forms of vertical coordination and more relaxed standards, but there are still some vertically derived standards.

Each of the nation states is also engaged in a coordination process, attempting to ensure that it presents as coherent a set of bargaining positions as possible in all of the various venues of the EU. This horizontal process is occurring both in the national capital and in the permanent representations in Brussels, and there is substantial interaction between the home offices and Brussels. Once in Brussels, however, that work must to some extent be disaggregated again in order to fit in the rather fragmented policy-making structure of the EU. Although there may have been clear initial positions, the continuing bargaining may require continuing realignment and negotiations within the national delegations.

There are relatively few coordination instruments or venues available to produce that coordination but the leadership from the president of the Commission and staff does provide some capacity for making policy more coherent. Likewise, COREPER tends to bring together national government if not policy areas for effective coordination. Further, the movement toward softer, more negotiated forms of coordination also provides for more coherent, if less directive, formats for coordination.

We can question the extent to which effective policy coordination at one stage or level in this process will tend to limit success at another. For example, to the extent that countries are extremely effective in creating bargaining positions among its various political and administrative organizations, they may inhibit the capacity to produce effective coordination across policy areas. Bargaining to create coherence across policies involves making concessions on national positions, and the firmer those positions are the less likely are agreements. This may, in turn, produce outcomes that are not dissimilar from those Fritz Scharpf describes as resulting from decision situations in which there are veto players.[40]

In addition, increasing use of soft law instruments such as the OMC may enhance the capacity for cross-policy coordination in the EU, but it tends to lessen the level of vertical coordination across the member states. Almost by definition, the utilization of the OMC acknowledges that the uniformity associated with the "community method" may not be as crucial as once thought; and the variations do represent an acceptable decline in policy coherence among the member states. There are strong normative pressures for uniformity across the member states, but with the increasing diversity of countries and a wider range of policies, achieving coherence in policies is difficult.

55.5 Is Coordination Always the Answer?

To this point I have been singing hymns of praise to coordination and its importance in addressing numerous problems in the public sector. While coordination is indeed important, it may not always be the best response, even when policies appear to be discordant and some greater coherence may be beneficial. Thus, this remedy for policy problems, like all others, must be applied carefully and with due consideration to the unintended consequences that may ensue from an overzealous use of that remedy.

The dangers of emphasizing coordination may be seen perhaps most clearly in vertical coordination, and especially in coordinating economic policy among the member state of the EU. The Euro crisis beginning in 2009 has indicated that one common economic and monetary policy, and perhaps one common currency, may not be the best solution to economic management within the EU. The differences in levels of economic development, differences in labor-market policies and differences in the resilience of the banking sectors have all contributed to negative effects for smaller countries such as Greece and Ireland.[41]

Coordination may not be an undivided benefit at a single level of policy-making. The logic of the division of the Commission into so many Directorates-General and for the creation of agencies is to create specialization and to be able to utilize expertise effectively. Attempting to coordinate these expert programs may generate conflicts and may also produce compromise decisions that are in essence a lowest common denominator. Thus, in both political terms and in terms of the actual quality of the decisions being taken, coordination may be sub-optimal. The choice of how far to press for more coordinated solutions therefore involves judgments about how to balance these competing virtues.[42]

55.6 SUMMARY AND CONCLUSIONS

In summary, policy coordination is one goal of making policy in the EU and in the member countries, but it is only one of a number of goals in the policy process. For political leaders or for commission officials pressing through a policy agenda may be more important and emphasizing coordination may diminish the capacity to pursue those policy goals. Top political leaders (and academics) may find effective coordination a crucial aspect of government, but many other participants may consider coordination very much secondary to pursuing specific policies. The problem is that both groups can be correct, especially in the complex policy environment of the EU.

Much of the logic of specialized policy-making and implementation structures is that policy is best made by experts and is best considered in relative isolation from other considerations. The differentiated structure of the Commission, and the addition of many autonomous organizations responsible for public policies, provides for highly expert styles of policy-making. The detailed regulatory style within the EU emphasizes that specialized style of policy formulation. That specialization is not, however, matched by institutions and procedures that are capable of counteracting the centrifugal tendencies within the EU. This should perhaps be expected given the emphasis on the individual policies, and also the reliance on national governments to implement and perhaps to coordinate many of the programs.

Notes

1. Dale Crane and Edward T. Jennings, "Coordination and Welfare Reform: The Search for the Philosopher's Stone," *Public Administration Review* 54 (1994), 341–8; J. E. S. Hayward and Vincent Wright, *Governing from the Centre: Core Executive Coordination in France* (Oxford: Oxford University Press, 2002).
2. Geert Bouckaert, B. Guy Peters, and Koen Verhoest, *Policy Coordinatrion in Seven Industrial Democracies* (Basingstoke: Macmillan, 2010).
3. For example, performance management forces managers to focus their attention on reaching their own targets rather than perhaps cooperating with other organizations.
4. Martin A. Painter, *Collaborative Federalism* (Cambridge: Cambridge University Press, 1998); Thomas O. Hueglin and Alan Fenna, *Comparative Federalism: A Systematic Inquiry* (Toronto: Broadview Press, 2006).
5. Christopher Pollitt and Colin Talbot, *Unbundled Government: A Critical Analysis of the Global Trend to Agencies, Quangos and Contractualisation* (London: Routledge, 2004).
6. Tom Christensen and Per Laegreid, *Transcending New Public Management: The Transformation of Public Sector Reforms* (Aldershot: Ashgate, 2007).
7. Julia Fleischer, "Governing from the German Centre: More Coordination and Less Policy Initiative," in C. Dahlstrom, B. G. Peters, and J. Pierre, eds, *Governing from the Centre* (Toronto: University of Toronto Press, 2010), 54–79.
8. Paul V. Warwick and James N. Druckman, "Portfolio Salience and the Proportionality of Payoffs in Coalition Government," *British Journal of Political Science* 31 (2001), 627–49.
9. John Peterson, "Decision-Making in the European Union: A Framework for Analysis," *Journal of European Public Policy* 2 (1999), 69–93; B. Guy Peters, *Governance in the European Union: The Turn Keeps on Turning* (Stockholm: Utrikespolitska Institutet, 2010).
10. Ian Bache and Matt Flinders, *Multi-Level Governance* (Oxford: Oxford University Press, 2001); Morten Egeberg, *Multi-Level Union Administration: The Transformation of Executive Politics in Europe* (Basingstoke: Macmillan, 2006).
11. Hans-Ulrich Derlien, "Horizontal and Vertical Coordination of German EC Policy," *Hallionen Tutkimus* 15 (1991), 2–16.
12. Johan P. Olsen, "The Many Faces of Europeanization," *Journal of Common Market Studies* 40 (2002), 921–52.
13. Eugene Bardach, *Getting Agencies to Work Together: The Practice and Theory of Managerial Craftsmanship* (Washington, DC: The Brookings Institution, 1998).
14. Fritz W. Scharpf, "Games Real Actors Could Play: Positive and Negative Coordination in Embedded Negotiations," *Journal of Theoretical Politics* 6 (1994), 27–53.
15. Andrew Jordan and A. Schout, *The Coordination of the European Union: Exploring the Capacities of Networked Government* (Oxford: Oxford University Press), 2006.
16. Hussein Kassim, B. Guy Peters, and Vincent Wright, *National Coordination of EU Policy: The Domestic Level* (Oxford: Oxford University Press, 2000).
17. Christopher Preston, "Obstacles to EU Enlargement: The Classical Community Method and the Prospects of a Wider Europe," *Journal of Common Market Studies* 33 (2008), 451–63.
18. The United States government is one possible exception to that generalization given the combination of federalism, a presidential form of government, and a relatively high level of autonomy of administrative agencies. See Sergio Fabrini, *Compound Democracies* (Oxford: Oxford University Press, 2008).

19. B. Guy Peters, "Bureaucratic Politics in Institutions in the European Community," in Alberta, M. Sbragia, ed., *Euro-Politics* (Washington, DC: The Brookings Institution, 1992), 56–89; Mark Rhinard, *Framing Europe: The Policy Shaping Strategies of the European Commission* (Amsterdam: World of Letters, 2009).

20. Vincent Wright, "The National Coordination of European Policymaking: Negotiating the Quagmire," in J. J. Richardson, ed., *European Union: Power and Policymaking* (London: Routledge, 1996), 125–46.

21. Dahlstrom, Peters, and Pierre, *Governing from the Centre.*

22. This leadership has been enhanced after Manuel Barroso gained a second term as the leader of the Commission.

23. Paul Craig, "The Treaty of Lisbon: Process, Architecture and Substance," *European Law Review* (2008), 137–66.

24. A. MacMullen, "European Commissioners: National Routes to a European Elite," in Neill Nugent, ed., *At the Heart of the Union: Studies in the European Commission*, second edition (Basingstoke: Palgrave, 2000), 143–67.

25. Morten Egeberg, "The College of Commissioners: Executive Politics as Usual?," in Morten Egeberg, ed., *Multi-Level Union Administration: The Transformation of Executive Politics in Europe* (Basingstoke: Macmillan, 2006), 76–102.

26. M. Schwartz, "Linkage Processes in Party Networks," in A. Roemmele, D. Farrell, and P. Iganzi, eds, *Political Parties and Political Systems: The Concept of Linkage Revisited* (New York: Praeger, 2005), 146–77.

27. Mark A. Pollack, "The Commission as Agent," in Nugent, *At the Heart of the Union*, 168–91.

28. Matt Flinders, "Distributed Public Governance in the European Union," *Journal of European Public Policy* 11 (2004), 520–44.

29. Jon Pierre and B. Guy Peters, "From a Club to a Bureaucracy: JAA, EASA and Airline Regulation," *Journal of European Public Policy* 16 (2009), 337–55.

30. Rhinard, *Framing Europe.*

31. T. Ugland and F. Veggeland, "The European Commission and the Integration of Food Safety Policy Across Levels," in Egeberg, *Multi-Level Union Administration*, 204–22.

32. J. Lewis, "The Janus Face of Brussels: Socialization and Everyday Decision Making in the European Union," *International Organization* 59 (2005), 937–91; Kassim, Peters, and Wright, *National Coordination of EU Policy: The Domestic Level.*

33. J. Lempp and J. Altenschmidt, "The Prevention of Deadlock Through Informal Processes of 'Supranationalization': The Case of Coreper," *European Integration* 30 (2008), 511–26.

34. Susana Borras and K. Jacobssen, "The Open Method of Coordination and New Governance Patterns in the EU," *Journal of European Public Policy* 11 (2004), 185–208.

35. Ulrika Mörth, *Soft Law in the European Union* (Cheltenham: Edward Elgar, 2004); C. De la Porte, P. Pochet, and G. B. Room, "Social Benchmarking, Policy Making and New Governance in the EU," *Journal of European Social Policy* 11 (2001), 291–307.

36. B. Eberlein and D. Kerwer, "New Governance in the European Union: A Theoretical Perspective," *Journal of Common Market Studies* 42 (2004), 121–42.

37. I. Begg, D. Hodson, and I. Maher, "Economic Policy Coordination in the European Union," *National Institute Economic Review* 183 (2003), 66–77.

38. Chris Ansell, "The Networked Policy: Regional Development in Western Europe," *Governance* 13 (2000), 303–33.

39. E. Fouilleux, J. De Maillard, and A. Smith, "Council Working Groups: Spaces for Sectorized European Policy Deliberation," in Thomas Christensen and Torbjörn Larsson, eds, *The Role of Committees in the Policy-Process of the European Union* (Cheltenham; Edward Elgar, 2007), 168–79.

40. Fritz W. Scharpf, "The Joint Decision Trap: Lessons from German Federalism and European Union," *Public Administration* 66 (1988), 239–78.

41. The difficulties cannot, of course, be attributed entirely to coordination efforts, but those efforts exacerbated underlying difficulties.

42. Just as Harold Simon argued that most of the "proverbs of administration" came in opposing pairs. This is certainly true for coordination and specialization.

CHAPTER 56

....

BURDEN-SHARING

....

EIKO THIELEMANN

56.1 SHARED BURDENS, COMMON RESPONSIBILITIES, AND CROSS-BORDER SOLIDARITY

....

References to "burden-sharing," "responsibility-sharing," or what the Lisbon Treaty now prefers to call "solidarity between the member states" are frequently heard in the context of EU policy-making. Most recently, such references have been prominent in the fields of financial bailouts in the context of EMU, EU climate change policy, and member states' defense collaboration. In the Lisbon Treaty one finds numerous calls for "solidarity" in a number of areas. In its common provisions, it calls for the Union to "promote economic, social and territorial cohesion, and solidarity among Member States" (Article 3).[1] It calls on the Council to act in a spirit of solidarity when it comes to EU energy policy (Articles 122 and 194). In the field of external action, it appeals to solidarity in Common Foreign and Security Matters (Articles 24, 31, and 32) and introduces a new "Solidarity Clause" under Title VII which states that "the Union and its Member States shall act jointly in a spirit of solidarity if a Member State is the object of a terrorist attack or the victim of a natural or man-made disaster" (Article 222). Some of the most explicit calls for burden or responsibility-sharing are found in the "Area of Freedom, Security and Justice" (AFSJ) (Articles 67 and 80). According to Article 80, the policies of the Union and their implementation "shall be governed by the principle of solidarity and fair sharing of responsibility, including its financial implications, between the Member States."

However, the burden-sharing concept is much older than these EU debates. The term "burden-sharing" was first prominently used in the 1950s in the context of NATO debates about sharing defense costs among the members of the North Atlantic alliance (i.e. when the US was trying to get the Europeans to pay more for collective defense efforts). The academic literature on international burden-sharing, i.e. the question how the costs of providing collective goods or common initiatives should be shared between states, has its origins in the 1960s and has since then been prominent among researchers interested in the workings of international organizations.[2] In Europe, these issues initially found their expression in debates about the net contribution of the EU member states to the common European budget.[3] More recently one has been able to observe a widening of the European burden-sharing debate into areas such financial crisis management, security and defense, climate policy, and refugee protection.[4]

This chapter aims to contribute to the nascent debate on European burden-sharing by addressing the following questions: why and under what conditions does burden-sharing among the member states take place? Why are "burdens" so unequally distributed and how can one explain existing patterns of burden distribution among states? Why are effective and equitable burden-sharing arrangements so difficult to achieve? These questions will be addressed by first providing on overview of the theoretical debate on motivations and mechanism of EU burden-sharing and second by illustrating some of the challenges and limitations of equitable burden-sharing in the case of EU refugee management.

56.2 MOTIVATIONS AND MECHANISMS FOR INTERNATIONAL BURDEN-SHARING

How can we explain unequal and inequitable contributions to collective initiatives? What is surprising is not so much that some countries appear to carry disproportionate burdens in providing for collective goods but that these inequitable distributions appear stable over time, with states being unwilling or being unable to change them. The question of why some states put up with bearing larger burdens in the provision of collective goods has sparked strong academic interest. The dominant view in the theoretical literature of alliances is that of Olson and Zeckhauser, who argue that larger countries are exploited by smaller ones in the provision of collective public goods—the latter "freeride" on the commitments of the former.[5] As shown formally by Sandler and Arce, where there is a non-zero-level contribution, the actual contribution made increases in relation to income.[6] Thus, all in all, countries with a larger income bear a larger proportional share of the burden. This is what Olson calls the "exploitation of the big by the small."[7] As a result of such freeriding opportunities, the output for such collective goods will be at sub-optimal levels. Some writers have offered extensions to this model. They argue that pure collective goods are a rare phenomenon. The extent of freeriding is dependent on the degree of publicness of the good in question.[8] Empirically, a number of studies in the area of collective defense have analyzed the correlation of defense spending and Gross National Product (GNP) and have offered support for the "exploitation hypothesis" in the NATO context. These studies have shown that for decades the United States and other large NATO member states have contributed a disproportionately large share of the burden to NATO's collective defense effort and that resource allocation has remained below pareto-optimal levels.[9]

Boyer presents an alternative view based on the idea that countries have a comparative advantage in providing certain types of collective goods over others.[10] This model broadens the scope of analyses of burden-sharing within alliances. In contrast to earlier work, Boyer's analysis opens up the possibility of international burden-sharing across issue areas by hypothesizing that states will specialize in the production of those collective goods (economic, political, and military) for which they possess a comparative advantage. Such specialization allows implicit trades to be made: a country which spends highly upon public goods provision in one area in which it possesses a comparative advantage can effectively trade with another that specializes (and has high expenditures) in another, where it has no such advantage and spends relatively little. Of course it is likely that, if one looks across enough issue dimensions, one will discover some in which contributions correlate negatively. However, the illustrative example used by Boyer is revealing. He shows that countries which spend disproportionate amounts on military defense tend to "underspend" with regard to foreign aid. From this Boyer suggests that countries specialize by contributing to international peace and stability either primarily through military expenditure or through foreign aid payments. Military expenditure and foreign aid can thus be seen as substitutes. If Boyer is correct, focusing on one dimension of alliance contributions misses important aspects of the overall picture. Other forms of non-military security contributions made by members of the alliance should be taken into account when analyzing disparities in international security burdens. The "policy trade model" shows how cross-issue burden-sharing might develop among allies and, more generally, how burdens might be shared among members of any group dealing with multiple public goods. In contrast to the predictions made by freeriding models, size discrepancies in the context of the multiple public goods setting will not necessarily lead to the freerider behavior. Small nations may well make contributions to the collective effort that are commensurate to their size and in accordance with the comparative advantages they possess in the production of certain goods, and according to the Boyer model there is no general incentive for the small to exploit the large.

But what motivates states to address disproportionate distributions of burdens? Or put differently, why do states seek to develop burden-sharing arrangements in the first place? The purpose of any burden-sharing regime is to institutionalize a system of redistribution that allocates burdens differently from how they would otherwise be. While it is unsurprising that the likely winners from such a redistributive mechanism would be in favor of burden-sharing, it is less clear why the potential losers would support it. Unlike processes of market integration in the EU context, which have often been portrayed as being positive-sum (or "win–win") in nature, redistributive burden-sharing agreements will tend to create winners and losers. So, why would the losers agree?

Political sociology identifies two principal logics of social action, a "logic of expected consequences" (informed by a cost–benefit rationale) and a "logic of appropriateness" (informed by a norm-based rationale).[11] The former sees action as being driven by a logic of rational and strategic behavior that anticipates consequences and is based on given preferences. Actors choose among alternatives by evaluating expected consequences of their actions for the achievement of certain objectives, expecting other actors to do the same. In this rational choice informed model, actors assess their goals, interests, and desires independently of institutions. In other words, it is assumed that actors' preference formation is external to the institutional context in which actors find themselves. Institutions affect only the strategic opportunities for achieving certain objectives.[12] The latter "logic of appropriateness" views action as being guided by notions of identity and roles shaped by the institutional context in which actors operate. According to this logic, action is based on rules, practices, and norms that are socially constructed, publicly known, and anticipated. Norm-based approaches emphasize that the motivations, choices, and strategic calculations of political actors are framed by institutional context, which shapes opportunities for action. Behavior often can be associated with what is considered "appropriate" in a particular socio-cultural context. Such a perspective raises the question: to what extent can an actor's broader institutional environment lead to norm-guided behavior that may supplant strategic calculation? These approaches regard institutions as a political environment or cultural context which shape an individual's interests; that is, actors are conditioned (as to their identity, priorities, and interpretations of reality) by institutions over time. Decisions are often taken according to what is considered "appropriate" behavior, with institutional norms being the main shapers of such notions of "appropriateness."[13] This norm-guided account therefore suggests that a calculus of identity and appropriateness is sometimes more important to actors than a calculus of political costs and benefits.[14]

From the above, two possible explanations for cooperation and burden-sharing emerge. On the one hand, one can point out the irrationality of egoism and what the actors would gain by cooperation: it may be rational to sacrifice opportunities for individual action and cooperate to achieve collective goods instead (cost–benefit approach). Side-payments, log-rolling, or insurance systems are often seen as being driven by such cost–benefit calculations. On the other hand, a reflection on the conflict between individual and collective action may denounce egoism as undesirable and seek to attain joint goals by appeals to normative notions such as that of solidarity (norm-based approach). One might ask to what extent the EU, with its stated ambition to represent not only an economic community but also a political one, is fundamentally different from other international organizations. And therefore whether emerging notions of cross-border solidarity beyond the nation state in Europe facilitate burden-sharing agreements beyond the state?

Even if one disagrees about the reasons behind unequal contributions and the motivations for burden-sharing initiatives (which after all are difficult to "test" empirically), it is useful to identify possible ways to address the challenges of unequal responsibilities in this area through multilateral burden-sharing measures. Several different types of burden-sharing mechanisms can be usefully distinguished (see Table 56.1).

Table 56.1 Types of international burden–sharing mechanisms

		Dimensionality	
		One-Dimensional	*Multidimensional*
Distribution Rule	*Hard*	Binding Rules	Explicit Compensation
	Soft	Voluntary Pledging	Implicit Trade

One-dimensional burden-sharing regimes aim to equalize the efforts of states on one particular contribution dimension. This tends to be done in two ways—through binding rules or through voluntary pledging mechanisms. Redistributive quotas are also classic examples of such "binding rules" mechanisms as they try to equalize observed imbalances or inequities in burdens through some agreed distribution key which is usually based on one or several fairness principles such as responsibility, capacity, benefit, or cost. In environmental burden-sharing regimes, the "responsibility" principle is also known as the "polluter pays" principle. The "capacity" principle refers to a state's "ability to pay." The "benefit" principle proposes that states should contribute to a particular regime in relation to the benefit they gain from it and the "cost" principle suggests that states' relative costs in making certain contributions should be taken into account when establishing burden-sharing regimes. Another type of one-dimensional burden-sharing mechanisms is that based on non-binding "pledging" mechanisms. If states cannot agree on a binding distribution key, they can make appeals which ask states with smaller responsibilities to alleviate some of the high burdens that other states are being faced with. In its efforts to enhance solidarity and equalize responsibilities across the member states, existing EU burden-sharing initiatives have largely relied on a one-dimensional burden-sharing logic. Multidimensional burden-sharing regimes are those that do not seek to equalize burdens or responsibilities on one particular contribution dimension alone, but instead operate across several contribution dimensions. On the one hand, some multidimensional regimes are based on an explicit compensation logic. In these cases, a country's disproportionate efforts in one contribution dimension are recognized and that country gets compensated (through benefits or cost reductions) on other dimensions. Financial compensation through a common budget is a common form for such regimes. Finally, a second type of a multidimensional burden-sharing mechanism is based on an implicit trading logic which recognizes that states can contribute to international collective goods in different ways. Here compensation occurs implicitly, without an agreed quota. In the following, the aims and limitations of EU burden-sharing initiatives will be illustrated in the case of EU refugee policy, which is one of the most advanced policy areas from an EU responsibility-sharing perspective.

56.3 Aims and Limitations of EU Burden-Sharing Initiatives: The case of Refugee Protection

EU burden-sharing discussions on asylum and refugee matters go back to the late 1980s but started to receive wider attention in the early 1990s when asylum numbers in Europe increased dramatically. There is a widely held view in some of the larger EU member states that their countries have been most affected by asylum "burdens."[15] This belief, however, is not borne out in the official statistics, which show that while larger states are attracting the largest absolute numbers of asylum applications (Figure 56.1), on a per capita basis, asylum responsibilities in a number of smaller countries are much higher than the responsibilities faced by the larger OECD states (see Figure 56.2). In recent years, Malta and Cyprus, some of the smallest EU members states, have regularly topped the table of relative asylum applications.

Overall asylum trends in Europe over the past twenty-five years have similar features to those in the rest of the developed world. They have been characterized by significant fluctuations in asylum applications, a highly inequitable distribution of asylum responsibilities and restrictive national policy responses. What has been unique in Europe over this period is that these trends have sparked numerous multilateral policy responses at the European level, as member states have increasingly moved toward closer cooperation and more substantive legal harmonization in this field.

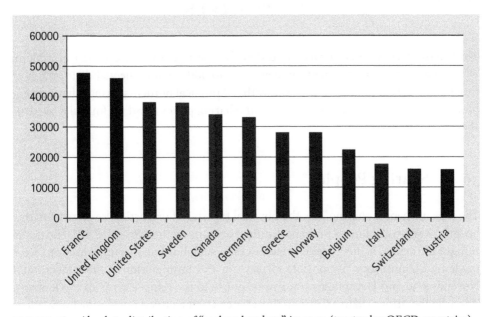

FIGURE 56.1 Absolute distribution of "asylum burdens" in 2009 (top twelve OECD countries)

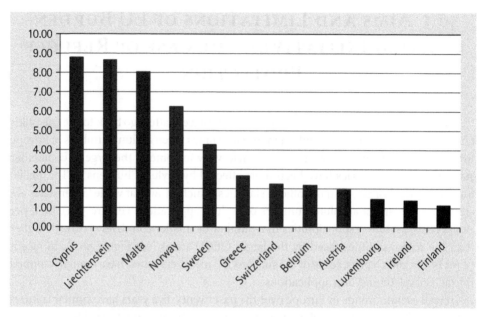

FIGURE 56.2 Relative distribution of "asylum burdens" (per 1000 of population) in 2009 (top twelve OECD countries)

56.4 EU ASYLUM BURDEN-SHARING INITIATIVES

There have been several European burden-sharing initiatives in the area of asylum, which have essentially pursued three avenues to address the unequal distribution of protection-seekers that states are faced with: (1) physical burden-sharing (sharing people); (2) harmonizing of asylum legislation (sharing policy); and (3) financial burden-sharing (sharing money).[16]

56.4.1 Sharing People

The idea of "people sharing," i.e. the physical transfer of protection-seekers from one host territory to another, is perhaps the most obvious method to address disparities in refugee burdens. The first explicit references to such burden-sharing ambitions were made by EU ministers responsible for asylum and immigration at their meeting of November 30 and December 1, 1992 in response to the refugee crisis in the Balkans. These deliberations led to a German Presidency Draft Council Resolution on Burden-Sharing in July 1994.[17] This proposal foresaw the reception of refugees according to a key which was based on three criteria which were given equal weight (population size, size of member state territory, and GDP).[18] The centerpiece of the German draft fore-saw the introduction of a compulsory resettlement mechanism. The text of the pro-posal stated: "Where the numbers admitted by a Member State exceed its indicative figure... other Member States which have not yet reached their indicative figure... will accept persons from the first State." Perhaps unsurprisingly, however, this proposal did not find the necessary support in the Council. In particular, the UK, which had received relatively few asylum-seekers until that point, was strongly opposed to such a scheme.[19]

A more recent EU initiative which is based on a similar mechanism is the 2001 Council Directive on Temporary Protection in the Case of Mass Influx.[20] The directive develops a range of non-binding mechanisms based on the principle of "double volun-tarism": the agreement of both the recipient state and the individual protection-seeker is required before protection-seekers can be moved from one country to another. Under this instrument, member states are expected, in spirit of "European solidarity," to indi-cate their reception capacity and to justify their offers. These pledges are to be made in public, allowing for mechanisms of peer pressure or "naming and shaming." The direc-tive has not yet been used and therefore the effectiveness of this new instrument of "soft" coordination still remains to be tested in practice.

Most recently, we have seen a number of pilot projects for the intra-EU relocation of refugees. For example, EUREMA (EU Relocation Malta) is a project currently running in ten member states (France, Germany, Slovenia, Slovakia, Hungary, Poland, Romania, UK, Luxemburg, and Portugal). Under this program, these states will each relocate a small number of refugees located in Malta. Participating member states set their own criteria: for example, language and job skills; specific nationalities and/or religions; those with family and friends in the country of destination; young people with families; people who are fit and healthy. In addition, there have been a number of small-scale ad hoc bilateral relocation projects between individual member states which have also aimed at sharing refugee burdens among the member states.[21]

56.4.2 Sharing Policy

Another way to achieve a more equitable distribution of asylum burdens is to take a common policy approach through the harmonization of domestic refugee legislation, preventing member states from deflecting asylum-seekers to other member states through particularly restrictive national policy measures. The EU has worked toward the convergence of member states' laws on forced migration since the mid-1980s. What started with initially non-binding intergovernmental instruments has since then been followed by developments in Community law.

The Dublin Convention has sometimes been regarded as the flagship of the EU's asy-lum *acquis*. It provides the rules that determine the responsible member state for deal-ing with a particular asylum claim. In essence, the rule states that asylum-seekers who move to another member state as a secondary movement can be sent back to the "state of first entry." Its principal aim is to "establish which Member State is responsible for the examination of an asylum application lodged on EU territory...and to prevent secondary movements between Member States."[22]

Also noteworthy are several directives that have aimed to level the asylum playing field and to lay the foundations for a Common European Asylum System.[23] The 2003 Reception Conditions Directive guarantees minimum standards for the reception of asylum-seekers, including housing, education, and health. The 2004 Qualification Directive contains a clear set of criteria for qualifying either for refugee or subsidiary protection status and sets out what rights are attached to each status. The 2005 Asylum Procedures Directive seeks to ensure that, throughout the EU, all procedures at first instance are subject to the same minimum standards. The 2008 Directive on common standards and procedures in member states for returning illegally staying third-country nationals ("the Return Directive")[24] provides for a set of rules to be applied throughout the return and removal process (including failed asylum-seekers). The Commission's Green Paper summarizes the underlying logic of EU policy harmonization as a burden-sharing instrument as follows:

> Further approximation of national asylum procedures, legal standards and reception conditions, as envisaged in creating a Common European Asylum System, is bound to reduce those secondary movements of asylum seekers which are mainly due to the diversity of applicable rules, and could thus result in a more fair [*sic*] overall distribution of asylum applications between Member States.[25]

56.4.3 Sharing Money

The EU has also started to introduce multidimensional burden-sharing elements in order to address existing disparities. It has done so through the payment of financial compensation to the most popular destination countries for asylum-seekers. This kind of explicit financial burden-sharing has been taking place since the establishment of the European Refugee Fund (ERF), which was put in place to support and encourage efforts of the member states in receiving and bearing the consequences of receiving refugees and displaced persons.[26] Created on the basis of Article 63(2) (b) of the EC Treaty, the Council Decision of September 28, 2000 established the ERF.[27] The ERF is to allocate resources proportionately to the burden on each member state by reason of their efforts in receiving refugees and displaced persons. This Fund, which is jointly financed by the member states, seeks to support special projects for the reception, integration, and repatriation of refugees and displaced persons. Its rationale is "to demonstrate solidarity between Member States by achieving a balance in the efforts made by those Member States." The decision's text states as its rationale that "it is fair to allocate [EU] resources proportionately to the burden on each Member State by reason of its efforts in receiving refugees and displaced persons."[28] For its first funding period (2000–2004), the ERF had at its disposal a total budget of 216 million euros. In 2007, the Council adopted a

European Commission proposal to extend ERF for the period 2008–2013.[29] At the same time, it was agreed to triple the size of the Fund to 614 million euros.

56.5 Criticism and Proposals for Reform

EU refugee burden-sharing initiatives have attracted criticism, not just in terms of their impact on individual asylum-seekers and refugees, but also with regard to its choice of burden-sharing mechanism and their limited effectiveness.

56.5.1 Physical Relocation

While potentially being the most effective burden-sharing mechanism, the physical relocation of forced migrants also remains the most difficult and controversial. Germany's 1992 proposal for binding refugee quotas for each member states (discussed above), did not receive support in the Council with some member states expressing concern that the proposed "physical" burden-sharing regime, which would have allowed the transfer of refugees without their consent, might violate established human rights. More generally, from an effectiveness perspective, all current EU resettlement or relocation discussion is currently built on a range of non-binding mechanisms based on the principle of double voluntarism, which means that the agreement of both the recipient state and the individuals concerned is required before protection-seekers can be moved from one country to another. However, with its insistence on "double voluntarism," what the EU is left with in terms of physical burden-sharing initiatives is either the unreliability of "voluntary pledging" as enshrined in the "Mass Influx Directive" or merely symbolic relocation like with the EUREMA project.

56.5.2 Common EU Asylum Policies

The EU Asylum Green Paper recognizes that even the establishment of a common asylum procedure and a uniform status will not completely eradicate all reasons why asylum-seekers may find some member states more attractive than others.[30] Policy harmonization can only address imbalances due to differences in domestic legislation in the first place. It is well established that policy differences are only one of several determinants for a protection-seeker's choice of host country, with structural factors such as historic networks, employment opportunities, geography, or a host country's reputation being at least equally, if not more, important. The Commission's belief in the equalizing effect of policy harmonization might therefore be exaggerated. If structural pull factors are indeed crucial for the scale of a country's asylum and refugee burdens, then policy harmonization might actually do more harm than good to the EU's efforts to achieve a more equitable distribution of asylum-seekers across the member states. EU policy harmonization curtails member states' ability to use national asylum policies to counterbalance their country's unique structural pull factors (language, colonial ties, etc.). This is why policy harmonization might in fact undermine rather than facilitate efforts to achieve more equitable responsibility-sharing.[31]

Regarding the specific issues raised by the Dublin Convention, the United Nations High Commissioner for Refugees (UNHCR) laments that the system is based on the flawed assumption that the asylum laws and practices of the participating states have already converged to common standards and produce comparable results. "In reality, asylum legislation and practice still vary widely from country to country, and as a result, asylum-seekers receive different treatment from one Dublin State to another."[32] Moreover, the Commission acknowledges that "the Dublin System may de facto result in additional burdens on member states that have limited reception and absorption capacities and that find themselves under particular migratory pressures because of their geographical location."[33]

56.5.3 Financial Compensation

The Commission emphasizes the need to identify ways to better use money from the ERF "to reduce disparities and to raise standards."[34] It suggests setting up new information-sharing mechanisms to identify more effective projects and programs that could be funded by the ERF. However, this focus seems rather narrow, as it does not address the crucial issue, namely that the ERF has so far failed to provide for effective incentives that would make states with smaller asylum and refugee burdens accept greater responsibilities. While much of the UNHCR's response on this issue engages with the question of how allocated resources from the ERF could be spent better in the future, it does also raise the issue of existing allocation mechanisms that go to the heart of the ERF's functioning as a burden-sharing mechanism. The UNHCR expresses its concern about the fact "that the current allocation based on [the absolute] numbers of asylum claims tends to favour larger Member States with well-established asylum systems."[35]

The European Council for Refugees and Exiles argues that a more effective ERF would need to be large enough to realistically reflect the financial responsibilities faced by states, if it is to provide some states with incentives to accept increased responsibilities in this area.[36] To put the ERF's resources in perspective, it is instructive to compare them with costs incurred at the national level. According to UK Home Office estimates, Britain spends about 30,000 euros per asylum-seeker, if one includes administrative costs, legal bills, accommodation, and subsistence. Compare this with figures from the ERF according to which the UK, as one of the largest recipients of the Fund, received about 100 euros from the ERF per asylum-seeker. Given the limitations of current EU burden-sharing initiatives, there have been repeated calls for broader and more effective EU burden-sharing regimes.

56.6 Toward More Comprehensive EU Burden-Sharing

In the light of the criticism of the existing EU burden-sharing initiatives, it might be time to further explore the fourth burden-sharing mechanism discussed above: trade. The member states have not yet used this mechanism in their burden-sharing efforts. In the refugee area, several objections have been made against a Kyoto-style refugee burden-sharing regime based on the idea of "explicit burden trading," as proposed by Schuck,[37] which raised "unease about treating refugees as commodities in inter-state transactions."[38] An alternative "implicit trade" model suggests that countries can be expected to specialize according to their comparative advantage as to the type and level of contribution they make to international collective goods. Applied to the area of forced migration, Thielemann and Dewan suggest that countries contribute to refugee protection in two principal ways: proactively (e.g. through peacekeeping/making, aid, trade, or investment in regions of origin) and reactively (most commonly through providing protection for displaced persons on a host state's territory).[39] While proactive measures seek to alleviate push factors and aim at preventing a refugee crisis to develop in the first place, reactive measures aim at dealing with the crisis once it has occurred. Empirically, one indeed finds evidence that some countries make disproportionate contributions in "proactive" refugee protection contributions (such as through peacekeeping efforts) while other countries contribute disproportionately with "reactive" measures related to refugee reception. It therefore appears that some implicit trading in refugee protection contributions is already taking place.

From a theoretical perspective, it is not difficult to see why such a division of labor occurs, as countries can be expected to have a comparative advantage in providing certain types of collective goods over others, which means that every country can contribute to some collective goods relatively more cheaply than another country.[40] It seems perfectly reasonable to assume that countries are not equally well placed to contribute to collective goods in the same way. From an economic perspective, the efficiency of countries' specific contributions differs. For example, one might expect a country with well-established asylum/refugee institutions to be relatively more efficient in processing and offering refuge to protection-seekers than a country without such institutions. In contrast, a country with a large army and experience in interventions abroad can be expected to be more efficient in proactive refugee protection efforts than a country with a small army and no such experience. One can extend this argument to the political realm.[41] A country's political comparative advantage is determined by its political environment, with national policy-makers being constrained by the preferences of their constituents. In a country where public attitudes are strongly opposed to its army's intervention abroad but where there is general support for refugee protection in general, granting refuge to displaced persons (i.e. reactive rather than proactive refugee protection measures) might be a government's policy of choice.

The specialization in countries' contributions, suggested by the implicit trade model, has potentially important implications for attempts to develop more effective EU burden-sharing initiatives. First, from a multidimensional burden-sharing perspective, the overall distribution of burdens across several contribution dimensions is perhaps not as inequitable as often assumed. Second, it is possible that burden-sharing initiatives that attempt to force all nations to increase contributions into any particular category of provision are likely to be counterproductive for the efficient provision of collective goods. The provision of collective goods is likely to be more efficient when countries are able to specialize with regard to their contributions. Allowing for specialization in states' contributions can help to increase efficiency. While it might be tempting to conclude from an exclusive focus on one-dimensional burden-sharing (as most current EU burden-sharing initiatives do) that some countries should be brought in line with others, such a conclusion would be simplistic and misleading. It therefore appears reasonable to conclude that attempts to impose exclusively one-dimensional burden-sharing mechanisms can constitute a hindrance for greater specialization and trade which will have adverse overall effects on states' willingness to contribute.

If EU burden-sharing initiatives are to become more effective in addressing collective action problems in fields such as financial management, climate change, defense policy, or refugee protection, member states cannot rely on symbolic expressions of intra-EU solidarity. Moreover for effective collective policy responses to these challenges, the EU needs to be aware of variations in states' preferences on how best to contribute to collective goods like security, a clean environment, or financial stability; it needs to recognize the comparative advantages individual states possess with regard to making certain kinds of contributions to such collective goods. Otherwise, the EU risks undermining the search for more effective burden-sharing in Europe.

NOTES

1. References to Lisbon Treaty articles are based on the Consolidated Version of the Treaty on European Union, Official Journal of the European Communities, 2008/C 115/01.
2. Mancur Olson and Richard Zeckhauser, "An Economic Theory of Alliances," *Review of Economics and Statistics* 48, no. 3 (August 1966), 266–79.
3. Helen Wallace, *Budgetary Politics* (London: Allen and Unwin, 1980); Michael Shackleton, *Financing the European Community* (London: Chatham House/Pinter, 1990); Iain Begg and Nigel Grimwade, *Paying for Europe* (Sheffield, Sheffield Academic Press, 1998).
4. For financial crisis management see: European Commission, *Communication on European Financial Supervision*, Brussels, 27.5.2009, COM (2009) 252 final; for security and defense: Han Dorussen, Emil J. Kirchner, and James Sperling, "Sharing the Burden of Collective Security in the European Union," *International Organization* 63, no. 4 (2009), 789–810; for climate policy: Constanze Haug and Andrew Jordan, "Burden Sharing: Distributing Burdens or Sharing Efforts?," in Andrew Jordan et al., eds, *Climate Change Policy in the European Union: Confronting the Dilemmas of Adaptation and Mitigation?* (Cambridge: Cambridge University Press, 2010), 83–103; and for refugee protection: Eiko Thielemann,

"Between Interests and Norms: Explaining Patterns of Burden-Sharing in Europe," *Journal of Refugee Studies* 16, no. 3 (2003), 253–73.

5. Olson and Zeckhauser, "An Economic Theory of Alliances."

6. Todd Sandler and Daniel Arce, "Pure Public Goods versus the Commons: Benefit-Cost Duality," *Land Economics* 79, no. 3 (2004), 355–68.

7. Mancur Olson, *The Logic of Collective Action: Public Goods and the Theory of Groups* (Cambridge, MA: Harvard University Press, 1965).

8. Sandler and Hartley, "Economics of Alliances."

9. Olson and Zeckhauser, "An Economic Theory of Alliances"; John R. Oneal, "The Theory of Collective Action and Burden Sharing in NATO," *International Organization* 44 (1990), 379–402; Sandler and Hartley, "Economics of Alliances."

10. Mark A. Boyer, "Trading Public Goods in the Western Alliance System," *Journal of Conflict Resolution* 33, no. 4 (December 1989), 700–27.

11. James G. March and Johan P. Olsen, "The Institutional Dynamics of International Political Orders," *ARENA Working Paper* 98/5 (Oslo: ARENA—University of Oslo, 1998), 7–10.

12. Ellen M. Immergut, "The Normative Roots of the New Institutionalism: Historical Institutionalism and Comparative Policy Studies," in Arthur Benz and Wolfgang Seibel, eds, *Theorieentwicklung in der Politikwissenschaft—eine Zwischenbilanz* (Baden Baden: Nomos), 231.

13. Christoph Knill and Andrewa Lenschow, "Coping with Europe: The Impact of British and German Administrations on the Implementation of EU Environmental Policy," *Journal of European Public Policy* 5, no. 4 (1998), 595–614.

14. James March and Johan Olsen, *Rediscovering Institutions: The Organizational Basis of Politics* (New York: Free Press, 1989).

15. The adoption of the "burden-sharing" terminology in the context of forced migration is of course not unproblematic. However, despite its potentially prejudicial connotation in a human rights context in which one might wish the language of costs and benefits to be absent, the term "burden-sharing" is used here to reflect the way the debate about the perceived and real inequalities in the distribution of displaced persons and refugees has been conducted in Europe over recent years. Attempts to replace the term in this area with a call for responsibility-sharing or the "equal balance of efforts" between the member states have had little impact on public policy debates in this area.

16. This categorization is based on Gregor Noll, *Negotiating Asylum* (The Hague: Nijhoff, 2000).

17. Council Document 7773/94 ASIM 124.

18. The form of the suggested redistributive mechanism followed the example of German domestic legislation, which stipulates a population-based key for the distribution of asylum seekers among the German Länder (see section 45 of the German Asylum Procedure Act (Asylverfahrensgesetz)).

19. BMI 1994; *Frankfurter Allgemeine Zeitung*, January 27, 1995, 2; BT-Drs. 13/1070, 55; *Integrationsbericht*, p. 92.

20. Council Directive 2001/55/EC of July 20, 2001, OJ L 212, August 7, 2001.

21. European Commission, *Study on the Feasibility of Establishing a Mechanism for the Relocation of Beneficiaries of International Protection*, JLX/2009/ERFX/PR/1005 (Brussels: European Commission, 2010), 13–18.

22. European Commission 2007, *Green Paper on the Future Common Asylum System*, COM (2007) 301 final.

23. Council Directive 2003/9/EC of January 27, 2003; Council Directive 2004/83/EC of April 29, 2004 and Council Directive 2005/85/EC of December 1, 2005.
24. Directive 2008/115/EC of December 16, 2008. Official Journal L348/98.
25. European Commission, *Study on the Feasibility of Establishing a Mechanism for the Relocation of Beneficiaries of International Protection*, 11.
26. For a more extensive analysis, see Eiko R. Thielemann,"Symbolic Politics or Effective Burden-Sharing? Redistribution, Side-Payments and the European Refugee Fund," *Journal of Common Market Studies* 43, no. 4 (2005), 807–24.
27. OJ L 252/12 of October 6, 2000.
28. OJ L 252/12 of October 6, 2000, para. 11.
29. 2004/904/EC; OJ381/52 of 28/12/2004.
30. OJ381/52 of 28/12/2004, at p. 11.
31. For a more extensive treatment of this argument, see Eiko R. Thielemann "Why European Policy Harmonization Undermines Refugee Burden-Sharing," *European Journal of Migration and Law* 6, no. 3 (2004), 43–61.
32. UNHCR, *Response to the European Commission's Green Paper on the Future Common European Asylum System* (Geneva: UNHCR, September 2007), 38.
33. European Commission, *Green Paper on the Future Common Asylum System*, COM (2007) 301 final (Brussels: European Commission, 2007), 10.
34. European Commission, *Green Paper on the Future Common Asylum System*, 11.
35. UNHCR, *Response to the European Commission's Green Paper on the Future Common European Asylum System*, 42.
36. For all three of these proposals, see also Thielemann, "Symbolic Politics or Effective Burden-Sharing?."
37. Peter Schuck, "Refugee Burden-Sharing: A Modest Proposal," *Yale Journal of International Law* 22 (1997), 243–97.
38. Deborah Anker, Joan Fitzpatrick, and Andrew Shacknove, "Crisis and Cure: A Reply to Hathaway/Neve and Schuck," *Harvard Human Rights Journal* 11 (1998), 295–310.
39. Eiko R. Thielemann and Torun Dewan, "The Myth of Free-Riding: Refugee Protection and Implicit Burden-Sharing," *West European Politics* 29, no. 2 (2006), 351–69.
40. Individual countries need only have a relative (not an absolute) advantage in the production of a particular good to be able to reap benefits from specialization and trade. Even if a country can produce every good more efficiently than other countries, it will still be better off when it specializes in the production of goods in which it holds the greatest relative advantage.
41. Mark Boyer, *International Cooperation and Public Goods* (Baltimore and London: John Hopkins University Press, 1993).

CHAPTER 57

....

EUROPEANIZATION

....

ULRICH SEDELMEIER

SINCE the 1990s, "Europeanization" has developed into one of the main buzzwords in EU studies and is now one of its most dynamic sub-fields. "Europeanization" generally refers to the impact of the EU on nation states. It constitutes a second phase of research on the EU: the first phase was concerned with political integration—the pooling and delegation of powers from nation states to EU institutions. In the second phase, the focus has turned to how this creation of governance structures at the EU level has affected the member states—not their behavior toward each other (which is the traditional focus of international relations) but the behavior of domestic actors, the domestic contexts, and institutional arrangements within states.

In this sense, "Europeanization" is not a theory or a concept, as it is sometimes suggested, but denotes a research area. The absence of a shared definition is not particularly problematic, since definitional differences generally reflect differences in what particular issues research focuses on in its analysis of the EU's impact (which in turn can lead that research to consider different specific types of influences that emanate from the EU). In broad terms, the literature distinguishes three dimensions in which the EU can have a domestic impact: the domestic polity, politics, and policy.

The policy dimension figures most prominently in Europeanization research, both quantitatively and in terms of the development of a common analytical framework. It is in this dimension that Europeanization research originated through studies of the implementation of EU policies[1] before the term became popular. Policy implementation has subsequently developed into its own specialized sub-field on compliance with EU law. The completion of the single market in the early 1990s generated much of the early impetus for studies of the EU's domestic policy impact. More recently, the EU's Eastern enlargement has generated a new wave of research on Europeanization of non-member states. Thus, in addition to different dimensions of Europeanization, we can also distinguish different contexts: member states, candidates for accession, and countries without an explicit membership perspective.

At one level, the key question of Europeanization studies is empirical and descriptive: how much influence does the EU have on domestic politics (which also involves distinguishing its impact from other international influences as well as from unrelated outcomes of domestic politics). The main analytical question is how to explain variation in this impact across different countries, different issue areas, and over time. These questions are highly policy relevant. In the member state context, they are extremely pertinent for the functioning of the internal market and the EU's legal system: are all member states able and willing to play by the jointly agreed rules? This question is also of central importance for the study of international cooperation more generally: how do internal institutions obtain compliance and enforce costly adjustments that are necessary to reap mutual net gains from cooperation? In the context of non-member states, explanations for variation in the EU's domestic impact offer insights into the conditions under which the EU can successfully influence domestic political developments outside its borders. Such insights concern strategies to achieve in candidate countries the necessary adjustments for membership and their sustainability, as well as to shape the EU's neighborhood according to its own economic and political objectives. Moreover, these questions are also normatively highly significant: how does the EU affect democratic processes at the national level?

57.1 ANALYTICAL FRAMEWORK

Europeanization is not a theory, nor is there a theory of Europeanization. Instead, Europeanization research draws on mid-range theories and concepts within the broader discipline of political science to derive its theoretical frameworks. As this section will suggest, rationalist institutionalism and constructivist institutionalism, for example, provide partly competing, partly complementary, explanations for the conditions under which adjustment pressures from the EU lead to domestic policy change. By drawing on such more general theories, rather than attempting to establish a *sui generis* theory of Europeanization, this research area contributes to aligning research on the EU with the study of international and comparative politics. With regard to international relations, Europeanization research draws on explanatory factors derived from studies of the domestic impact of international institutions[2] and national compliance with international institutions. Such studies broadly focus both on the strategies and characteristics of international institutions, the characteristics of their rules, as well as mediating factors in domestic structures. In comparative politics, Europeanization relates to, and can draw on, studies of cross-national variation in response to similar functional pressures, and of the transnational diffusion of ideas. In public administration, it connects well with studies of cross-border policy transfers, and with policy implementation studies.

57.1.1 Categorizing Outcomes of the EU's Influence

Before moving to the theoretical approaches employed in Europeanization research, it is useful to clarify how different studies categorize outcomes on the dependent variable—

the EU's impact on specific aspects of domestic policy, politics, or polity. Where the EU makes specific demands for domestic adjustments (which applies mostly to the policy dimension), one set of studies assesses the outcome narrowly in terms of compliance: the extent to which domestic changes match the EU's demands. This is mainly the case for implementation studies in the context of member states, and in studies of candidate countries that define "Europeanization" as the adoption of EU rules (or compliance with the EU's demand to adopt rules that might not be specifically EU rules). Other studies also consider broader changes in national formal or informal institutions and material or ideational structures that are not as such demanded by the EU, but are by-products of domestic responses to EU demands. These include unintended consequences and may also occur in the absence of (full) compliance.

The notion of unintended consequences of the EU's impact points to a different— often normative—assessments of the outcome. Such studies do not ask primarily whether and how Europeanization happens. Instead, normative impact assessment or policy evaluation analyze the consequences of Europeanization in terms of desired goals and unintended consequences, as well as both for issues where the EU made adjustment demands and where its impact is indirect without explicit demands.

Europeanization research does not usually assess the EU's impact simply in binary terms, whether it happens or not. Instead, different degrees of impact can be distinguished, for example on a continuum from inertia, absorption (incorporation without substantive change to domestic institutions), accommodation (adaption of domestic institutions without change in essential features), to transformation (replacement of fundamental change of domestic institutions).[3] In addition, studies distinguish between different forms of change: formal adoption of rules (formal change of laws and organizations); behavioral rule adoption (rule-conforming practical behavior of the targets of rules); and discursive adoption (incorporation into discourses which may reflect an internalization of rules or merely pay lip service to them).[4] These different forms partly overlaps with the components of implementation that can form different dependent variables in compliance studies: formal (timely and correct) transposition (of EU directives into national law) and their application (in practice), as well as their enforcement (by national public authorities) if application is deficient.

57.1.2 Europeanization in Response to EU Adjustment Pressures: Cost/Benefits and Social Learning

The development of a common analytical framework for Europeanization is most developed with regard to the policy dimension. A key feature that lends itself to such a common framework is that in this dimension, the EU generally makes specific demands for domestic change (irrespective of whether it actually leads to change or whether it is causally relevant for change that occurs). In other words, the EU creates direct adjustment pressures, which is not usually the case for the Europeanization of polity and politics.

The nature of the adjustment pressures differs depending on the context of Europeanization. In the case of member states, adjustment pressures result from the fact that policy rules form part of the *acquis communautaire*, the body of EU rules that member states are obliged to apply domestically. For non-member states, and in particular countries that are candidates for EU membership, adjustment pressures result from the EU's conditionality that sets rewards for the adoption of specific rules. A special case is that of negative externalities of European integration, which create adjustment pressures outside the EU's borders without the EU demanding such adjustment. Adjustment pressures are usually considered a precondition for Europeanization—since otherwise there would be no need for domestic change—but they are not sufficient for the EU to have an impact.[5]

To explain differences in the EU's impact, Europeanization research focuses on variation in the factors that mediate the EU's adjustment pressure and that need to be conducive to domestic change. Most studies explicitly or implicitly derive these factors from the debate between rationalist institutionalism and constructivist institutionalism in international relations and comparative politics. Moreover, this framework is also strongly compatible across different contexts—Europeanization of member states and non-member states.[6]

In a nutshell, rationalist institutionalism conceives of the decision of governments whether to comply with EU rules and conditions as the result of efficiency calculations. Governments consider the benefits of the rewards that the EU offers for compliance (or the costs arising from sanctions for non-compliance) and weigh these against the domestic costs or benefits arising from (non-)compliance. For constructivists, the adoption of EU rules results from processes of social learning that persuade target governments that the EU's rules or demands are legitimate. Rationalist and constructivist institutionalism respectively identify a number of—partly competing, partly complementary—explanatory factors at both the domestic level and the EU level that influence either such costs/benefit calculations or perceived legitimacy.

57.1.3 Domestic Mediating Factors

With regard to the domestic level, from a rationalist institutionalist perspective, EU demands disturb the previously existing domestic equilibrium by offering incentives (positive or negative sanctions) for the adoption of its rules, which usually require costly adjustments. Governments might either directly calculate cost/benefits arising from EU demands, or more indirectly react to pressures from domestic groups affected by domestic adjustments and/or EU rewards. EU adjustment pressures empower those domestic actors that expect benefits from such changes. The key question from a rationalist perspective is then whether the EU's demands lead to a sufficient redistribution of resources in favor of those benefitting from EU rules and demands, which depends on a number of factors.

Since the potential losers of Europeanization oppose an adjustment to EU rules, a key domestic factor that is detrimental for such adjustments are veto players who incur costs from the adoption of EU rules.[7] In a narrower sense, veto players are those actors whose consent is necessary to carry out domestic change, such as parties in a government coalition, an upper house of parliament, or the head of state. In a broader sense, they also include de facto veto players, such as societal groups who cannot formally block decisions, but can raise the political costs for the government, such as threatening their ability to stay in power or win re-election. Societal mobilization and a strong civil society can thus increase the salience of de facto veto players. On the other hand, societal mobilization is also a key condition for the beneficiaries of EU rules to push for the adoption and enforcement of EU rules.[8]

At the same time, while adjustments to EU demands and rules usually generate domestic costs—otherwise they would have been adopted without EU pressures—they can also entail intrinsic benefits for governments. In such cases governments might have been too weak to carry out their preferred domestic changes without the additional legitimacy, pressures, or benefits generated at the international level.[9] Member-state governments try to shape EU policies not only to reduce domestic adjustment pressures, but sometimes also to engineer precisely such domestic adjustment pressures. Likewise, non-member states' governments might pursue EU membership as a strategy to replace domestic rules and lock in such changes. In other cases, EU demands might fit the preferences of new government parties—e.g. the AKP government in Turkey with regard to the role of the military in politics. Governments might also find that a selective application of EU demands can have the—from the EU's perspective—perverse effect of enabling them to tighten their grip on power, as in the case of EU anti-corruption policies in Azerbaijan.[10]

Another mediating factor are domestic political institutions that have a mandate to support those benefitting from EU rules and pushing for their adoption and enforcement.[11] Such institutions are particularly important with regard to enforcing previously adopted EU rules. These institutions include, for example, labor inspectorates (with regard to EU social policy) or environmental agencies, as well as courts more generally and specialized courts in particular. A similar argument, but with regard to the capacity of the public administration more generally, can be derived from "management approaches"[12] in the sub-field of compliance studies. Non-compliance is not necessarily a deliberate act by governments, but can also take the form of involuntary defection if national administrations lack the necessary administrative capacities to transpose, and enforce the correct application of, such policies.[13]

From a constructivist perspective, the EU's impact does not simply depend on the (material) incentive structure that governments face. The perceived legitimacy of EU rules and demands are a key factor that can counterbalance material costs, or form an ideational obstacle—in addition to material costs or in the absence of such costs—to Europeanization. A key domestic mediating factor is therefore whether EU rules have a positive normative resonance with domestic rules and political discourses.[14] The adoption of EU rules is easier if they have a good normative fit with domestic policy paradigms, or at least if domestic rules in a specific issue area are absent, while the lack of cultural match with pre-existing domestic rules is detrimental to Europeanization.

Likewise, EU policies have to be normatively compatible with domestic administrative styles and traditions.[15]

Not only the legitimacy of specific EU rules, but the legitimacy of the EU itself matters, which depends on national identification with the EU and normative attitudes toward European integration. If a target country identifies positively with the EU—i.e. considers the EU to represent an international community of states with which it has a normative affinity—the more likely it is to consider EU rules and demands as legitimate, and the easier it is for the EU to be able to persuade it of their legitimacy.[16]

Additional normative domestic factors include political culture, which creates scope conditions for veto players to matter. A consensual political culture might make it easier to pass major reforms than the formal structure of veto players suggests.[17] Moreover, implementation studies suggest that the domestic impact of EU law depends on national compliance cultures.[18] In this sense, a Nordic culture of "law observance" facilitates the correct domestic implementation of EU policies. Finally, constructivist institutionalism emphasizes that domestic norm entrepreneurs who are persuaded of the normative appropriateness of EU rules can play a key role in facilitating the EU's impact.[19]

57.1.4 EU-Level Mediating Factors

Europeanization research on EU members has focused primarily on domestic mediating factors. By contrast, differences in the EU's enforcement of its demands have not been a prominent concern. This is understandable since the EU's compliance system does not vary across member states.[20] Transposition studies have identified a number of explanatory factors related to the characteristics of EU legislation,[21] but they do not lend themselves easily to the broader study of Europeanization. Studies that explicitly focus on differences in the EU's willingness to pursue compliance problems across issue areas—i.e. the EU's compliance push—are rare.[22] Once studies of Europeanization go beyond the EU's membership, differences in EU strategies and behavior designed to bring about domestic change become much more pronounced. Studies of the Europeanization of candidate countries therefore have also focused much more explicitly and in more detail on such differences.[23]

For rationalist institutionalists, the key point about the Europeanization of non-member states is that the EU can offer incentives, usually positive rewards, for states that comply with its conditions. A number of factors then determine how target governments calculate the benefits of these rewards, which need to outweigh domestic adjustment costs in order for them to comply: the credibility of the EU's conditionality; the clarity of the conditions; and the size of the EU's rewards and their temporal distance.[24]

Starting with the latter, the EU has different types of rewards—positive incentives—at its disposal. The most sizable reward is membership in the EU. Market access and financial assistance are other sizable, but not as powerful rewards. Since membership is such a powerful incentive, the EU has also made progress toward specific steps on the road to membership—such as the start of accession negotiations—a reward for specific conditions. Generally, the greater the asymmetry of interdependence between the EU and a target country, the more powerful these incentives are. The temporal distance of obtaining the reward means that governments are more likely to make costly domestic changes if the reward is imminent, rather than a long-term prospect.

The clarity of the EU's conditionality—and of the rules concerned—is important since a target government needs to know what it is expected to do if it wanted to comply. Moreover, the clearer the rules in question, the easier it is also to monitor (for the EU) and enforce (for the target government) compliance. Moreover, the clarity of rules also relates to the credibility of conditionality since it is less open to interpretation whether compliance has occurred.

Credibility relates to the EU's willingness and ability to pay out the promised reward for compliance with its conditions (and conversely, to withhold the reward unless compliance occurs). Credibility depends on a consistent application of conditionality that rewards all countries equally for compliance—and does not reward a country unless it complies (which becomes more difficult if there is no asymmetrical interdependence in favor of the EU). Likewise, evidence of intra-EU disputes about whether a specific country should obtain the promised reward can damage the credibility of conditionality. A key example here is the case of Turkey, where the expectation to obtain membership in return for meeting the EU's conditions has been diminished by the possibility of a referendum on its accession in France, and by some member-state governments' suggestion that the outcome of accession negotiations should be only a vaguely defined "privileged partnership" rather than full membership. Finally, credibility does not only concern consistency across target countries but also with regard to the application of conditionality with regard to specific issue areas.

A constructivist perspective also identifies a set of factors at the EU level that affect the EU's ability to achieve domestic changes in target countries. A key factor is the perceived legitimacy of the rules that the EU promotes.[25] The legitimacy of rules depends both on the properties of the rules themselves and of the process through which they were set as conditions for EU rewards. The intrinsic legitimacy of rules is higher if they are codified in international treaties[26] as well as widely practiced among the EU's membership. The legitimacy of the process through which EU demands for adjustment are determined increases if the target governments participate in the creation or selection of these rules. Procedural legitimacy is generally problematic in the case of conditionality, since it is usually a top-down process set unilaterally by the EU.[27] Table 57.1 summarizes the key factors that mediate the EU's adjustment pressure and affect whether it leads to domestic change.

57.1.5 Recipient-Driven Europeanization: Emulation and Lesson-Drawing

While much of the Europeanization literature focuses on instances in which the EU attempts to have a domestic impact in target countries, domestic change that meets EU

Table 57.1 Mediating factors of the EU's adjustment pressures inside and outside its membership

	Rationalist institutionalism	Constructivist institutionalism
EU level	- credibility of the EU's (positive or negative) incentives - clarity of rules - size and temporal distance of incentives - power asymmetry between EU institution and target state	- legitimacy of rules - legitimacy of condition-setting process
Domestic level	- governments' positive/negative domestic adjustment costs - veto players - societal mobilization - supportive formal institutions - administrative capacities	- identification with the EU - resonance with domestic rules/ political discourses - consensual political culture - norm entrepreneurs - domestic culture of law observance

requirements is not necessarily the result of active EU initiatives. Countries can also adopt EU rules either independently of EU incentives or persuasion efforts for doing so, or in the absence of such initiatives. The absence of direct EU adjustment pressures is most salient for Europeanization of domestic politics and polities, as well as for countries that are more distant from the EU's immediate neighborhood. It also applies to the policy dimension in the context of member states with regard to issue areas where the EU has no binding rules, but may use softer mechanisms—in particular the Open Method of Coordination—to encourage the diffusion of "good practice."

In such cases, Europeanization results from processes of lesson-drawing and emulation.[28] Such processes are usually triggered by domestic policy failures and/or a delegitimization of domestic rules. Governments look abroad in the search for rules that might improve the efficiency of national policies[29] or imitate foreign rules if they take their appropriateness for granted.[30] It is therefore also possible to distinguish between rationalist institutionalist and constructivist institutionalist variants of emulation, but they are difficult to disentangle in empirical research. For a conceptual framework to study Europeanization, it appears therefore more fruitful to focus on their common characteristic as recipient-driven rule adoption, in which the EU's role is passive, as opposed to instances of Europeanization that are actively induced by the EU.[31]

Conceptually, the research agenda on Europeanization through emulation is much less well developed than Europeanization in response to EU adjustment pressures. Still, we can identify some domestic explanatory factors in recipient countries that make emulation from the EU more likely.[32] Domestic policy failure is a precondition for governments to look for rules to emulate. The likelihood that they would consider EU rules is enhanced through the presence of epistemic communities with expertise in EU rules or involvement of domestic policy-makers in networks involving EU policy-makers.[33] Finally, the rules in question have to be transferable to the national context.

57.2 Empirical Findings

57.2.1 Europeanization of Public Policy

In the policy dimension, Europeanization has been generally strong. At the same time, studies of the member states almost invariably stress that despite the EU's impact, Europeanization has not led to convergence. This frequent claim has to be set against concerns that the internal market might lead to a dramatic erosion of national diversity in the EU. Although the EU has clearly not induced uniformity, it has certainly increased similarities in national public policies. For example, the EU has led to higher environmental and social standards, not only in low-regulation countries, but across the member states. Europeanization is also reflected in the introduction of similar policy instruments, e.g. instruments that are based on economic incentives and societal participation and monitoring in environmental policy. At the same time, since in certain issue areas some member states converge toward similar policies, while others do not, the broader pattern is partial, or "clustered," convergence.[34]

Such patterns of "differential" Europeanization[35] result from variation in domestic mediating factors identified by rationalist and constructivist institutionalism. The literature has not generated a consensus about a dominant explanation, which might be partly related to the difficulties of generalizing across a large number of small-n case studies. Although the narrower field of compliance studies has seen a considerable growth of studies using sophisticated quantitative methods, it has generated a long list of explanatory factors that are significant in some studies, but not an uncontested explanation for cross-country variation either.[36]

On the other hand, research on Europeanization of policies in candidate countries has generated more clear-cut results for its explanatory factors. In the then candidate countries that subsequently joined the EU in 2004 and 2007, the EU generally had a pervasive impact on the public policies that are part of the *acquis communautaire*. The explanatory factors highlighted by rationalist institutionalism account well for this pattern. Governments that were not threatened with prohibitively high costs from compliance with the EU's political conditionality generally adopted the rules of the *acquis* under two conditions. The EU had to offer membership, its most powerful incentive, and this offer had to be credible. For countries with a credible membership perspective, even high costs in specific sectors were outweighed by the overall benefits of accession. High domestic adjustment costs therefore had mainly a delaying effect until membership became more credible and less distant, but did not prevent the adoption of EU policy rules.

By contrast, in the current candidate countries in the western Balkans and Turkey, the EU's impact on public policies has been slower and patchier. In contrast to the East Central European candidates, in many of the countries concerned the EU's political conditions create higher domestic costs as they touch on sensitive questions of national identity and statehood. Moreover, the membership perspective is more distant and, in the case of Turkey, much less credible. The EU's policy impact is even more limited in the countries in its East European neighborhood which the EU has not recognized as potential candidate countries, although they are European.

57.2.2 Europeanization of the Polity

With regard to Europeanization in the polity dimension, we can distinguish three broad sets of issues: impact on national identities, on national executives, and conditionality concerning democracy and human rights in non-members. With regard to the first two issues, the EU does not makes specific demands for adaption, while in the third, it does. The EU's impact on national identities is touched upon in Chapter 48 of this *Handbook* and will not be further elaborated here.

Traditionally, studies of Europeanization in this dimension have focused on the EU's impact on national executives in member states. The EU does not demand the adoption of any particular rules in this area. Instead, its impact results from functional pressures to adjust domestic institutions in such a way that governments can effectively participate in EU policy-making and implement EU policy outputs. Such pressures primarily concern inter-ministerial coordination. National executives have to be able to formulate national positions for EU-level negotiations, and to adapt these positions if necessary. In addition, the executive has to coordinate the timely and correct implementation of EU policies, which also involves national legislatures in the transposition of EU law into national law, and specialized agencies that need to enforce the correct application of legislation.

Although these functional pressures are similar for all member states, research has found some general trends, but the institutional models for inter-ministerial coordination vary significantly across member states.[37] Similar trends across member states include a stronger involvement of prime ministers in EU policy-making and a diminishing role of foreign ministries; the creation and/or subsequent development of inter-ministerial coordination mechanisms that also involve stronger links with the national permanent representations in Brussels; and the creation of administrative units within sectoral ministries with specific expertise on EU affairs.

Despite such trends, arrangements across members differ widely. Studies find a pattern "of limited similarity combined with considerable divergence,"[38] for example with regard to whether the foreign ministry or the prime minister's office plays the dominant role, the extent of centralization of the coordination process, and whether the institutional machinery aims at comprehensive or more selective coordination. The different contributions to this literature do not systematically test comparable explanatory factors that account for this outcome, but some key findings stand out. Among the old member states, the differences appear to relate to the normative fit with broader domestic institutional structures, namely the extent of centralized or decentralized governance in the domestic polity.[39] The new member states do not only display diversity in institutional arrangements, but also rapid and far-reaching changes. These patterns fit neither with a lock-in of initial institutional choices nor with efficiency considerations, but draw attention to institutional choices that maximize partisan actors' benefits in domestic politics following changes in government.[40]

Another key focus of studies of the EU's impact on the national executive concerns its relationship with the legislature. Such studies have tended to see the latter as the losers of European integration. The transfer of legislative powers to the EU level has reduced the direct access of parliaments, leading to a decisive shift in favor of executives in the domestic legislative process.[41] Such tendencies are particular salient in post-communist candidate countries, due to the strong domestic consensus on the overarching goal of accession to the EU.[42] As Sadurski suggests, the inefficiency of post-communist parliaments led governments to use fast-track procedures to enact EU-related laws "with little or no serious parliamentary discussions, and with the executive controlling the process throughout," allowing governments "to by-pass parliament and to justify the centralization of decision-making by the emergency-like circumstances."[43] Yet Goetz and Meyer-Sahling show that some studies come to very different conclusions, namely that parliaments have successfully reasserted their powers.[44] Thus the EU's impact can result in "re-parliamentarization" rather than de-parliamentarization. At one level, these apparently contradictory findings point to the diverse outcomes of Europeanization, but Goetz and Meyer-Sahling argue that they reflect just as much differences in research designs across studies.

The other main area of studies of the EU's impact on the polity has emerged in studies of Europeanization outside the EU. In this context, the EU also makes very direct demands for adjustments with regard to democratic institutions, and human and minority rights. Such rules are key elements of the EU's political conditions for membership but are also increasingly prominent in the EU's relations with neighbors without the prospect of membership and beyond Europe.

In broad terms, studies find only a limited impact of the EU in this area, and the extent of its impact is generally well explained by factors emphasized by rationalist institutionalism, namely governments' domestic adjustment costs.[45] Those countries that adopted democratic institutions and human rights early did so without a causal impact of the EU. For those countries that did not, EU incentives were insufficient to bring about domestic change. Even a credible membership incentive was ineffective, let alone the much weaker rewards that the EU holds out for the countries in the (European) neighborhood for which the EU does not yet consider membership as an option. In these countries, the EU's demands threatened to undermine the ability of authoritarian and/or nationalist parties in government to stay in power. The EU's influence on democratization is therefore mainly observable in fragile democracies, such as Slovakia or Croatia, and to some extent Bulgaria and Romania. In such cases, once a coalition of liberal democratic parties had achieved electoral victories over illiberal parties, they carried out reforms in line with EU demands. Subsequent progress toward EU membership had the effect to lock in such reforms. Even if the former government parties returned to power, they usually had to moderate their platforms to win re-election and did not attempt to roll back reforms, which would have jeopardized the prospect of EU membership and in turn threatened a backlash from voters.

57.2.3 Europeanization of Politics

The politics dimension is generally regarded as least affected by the EU, as captured in Dyson and Goetz's finding of "progressively Europeanized public policies, a semi-Europeanized polity, and a largely non-Europeanized politics."[46] While interest groups have made some adjustments to their organizational structures and strategies, the EU has only had a limited impact on national party systems.[47] However, as Hooghe and Marks (Chapter 58, this volume) note, European integration has increasingly affected political contestation in the member states. This is particularly salient in the new member states, where European integration has become a key dimension that structures competition in the party system.[48]

57.3 Conclusion

The study of Europeanization has grown strongly, especially through a wider focus of the EU's impact outside its membership. Still, it remains a diverse research area due to the broad range of issues on which the EU has an impact across policies, politics, and polity. As a research agenda, it is most cohesive with regard to issue areas where the EU explicitly demands adjustments from member states or non-member states. This is primarily the case in the policy dimension, where studies can draw on a common analytical framework that draws on rationalist institutionalist and constructivist institutionalist approaches from international relations and comparative politics.

Europeanization research in this dimension reflects that the EU has dramatically changed the policy context of its member states and candidate countries. The EU's influence has induced greater policy similarities, but its impact varies across countries and policy areas, leading to clustered convergence rather than uniform policy models. At the same time, continued diversity does not throw into question the EU's ability to elicit compliance with its rules from the member states. Although their compliance with EU law varies, the EU does not seem to have a general compliance problem.[49] Compliance is not only better than in other international organizations, but also than in some federal states.[50] Moreover, the EU has been highly successful in influencing domestic policies outside its borders, in candidate countries, through an effective use of a credible membership incentive.

One key question for further research concerns the sustainability of Europeanization through conditionality after a state has achieved membership. Currently, there are no indications of a backsliding after the incentive structure has changed.[51] Another question is whether the EU can reproduce the successful Europeanization of the countries that joined in 2004 and 2007 in the remaining candidate countries where the conditions are less conducive. In the case of Turkey, the EU is not using its strongest incentive effectively as France and other member states undermine the credibility of the membership perspective. In the Western Balkans, where the political adjustment costs are high and state capacities are weak, the EU faces the dilemma of having to fudge the application of conditionality in order to avoid the prospect of membership remaining too distant for it to serve as an incentive for domestic policy reforms.

NOTES

1. See e.g. H. Siedentopf and J. Ziller, eds, *Making European Policies Work: The Implementation of Community Legislation in the Member States* (London: Sage, 1988).
2. See e.g. A. P. Cortell and J. W. Davis, "How Do International Institutions Matter? The Domestic Impact of International Rules and Norms," *International Studies Quarterly* 40, no. 4 (1996), 451–78.
3. T. A. Börzel and T. Risse, "Conceptualising the Domestic Impact of Europe," in K. Featherstone and C. Radaelli, eds, *The Politics of Europeanization* (Oxford: Oxford University Press, 2003), 55–78, at 69–70.
4. F. Schimmelfennig and U. Sedelmeier, "Introduction: Conceptualizing the Europeanization of Central and Eastern Europe," in F. Schimmelfennig and U. Sedelmeier, eds, *The Europeanization of Central and Eastern Europe* (Ithaca, NY: Cornell University Press, 2005), 1–28, at 8.
5. M. G. Cowles, J. A. Caporaso, and T. Risse, eds, *Transforming Europe: Europeanization and Domestic Change* (Ithaca, NY: Cornell University Press, 2001); Börzel and T. Risse, "Conceptualising the Domestic Impact."
6. P. Kubicek, "International Norms, the European Union, and Democratization: Tentative Theory and Evidence," in P. Kubicek, ed., *The European Union and Democratization* (London: Routledge, 2003), 1–29; Börzel and Risse, "Conceptualising the Domestic Impact"; Schimmelfennig and Sedelmeier, "Introduction."
7. W. Jacoby, "Inspiration, Coalition, and Substitution—External Influences on Postcommunist Transformations," *World Politics* 58, no. 4 (2006), 623–51; Börzel and Risse, "Conceptualising the Domestic Impact"; Schimmelfennig and Sedelmeier, "Introduction."
8. T. A. Börzel, "Participation Through Law Enforcement: The Case of the European Union," *Comparative Political Studies* 39, no. 1 (2006), 128–52; U. Sedelmeier, "After Conditionality: Post-Accession Compliance with EU Law in East Central Europe," *Journal of European Public Policy* 15, no. 6 (2008), 806–25, at 809, 818–19.
9. See R. Putnam, "Diplomacy and Domestic Politics: The Logic of Two-Level Games," *International Organization* 42, no. 3 (1988), 427–60.
10. T. A. Börzel and Y. Pamuk, "Pathologies of Europeanisation: Fighting Corruption in the Southern Caucasus," *West European Politics* 35, no. 1 (2012), 79–97.

11. Börzel and Risse, "Conceptualising the Domestic Impact," 65.

12. J. Tallberg, "Paths to Compliance: Enforcement, Management, and the European Union," *International Organization* 56, no. 3 (2002), 609–43.

13. See T. A. Börzel, T. Hofmann, D. Panke, and C. Sprungk, "Obstinate and Inefficient: Why Member States Do Not Comply With European Law," *Comparative Political Studies* 43, no. 11 (2010), 1363–90.

14. Cortell and Davis, "How Do International Institutions Matter?"; Schimmelfennig and Sedelmeier, "Introduction," 20; Kubicek, "International Norms," 13–14.

15. C. Knill, *The Europeanisation of National Administrations: Patterns of Institutional Change and Persistence* (Cambridge: Cambridge University Press, 2001).

16. R. A. Epstein, *In Pursuit of Liberalism: International Institutions in Postcommunist Europe* (Baltimore, MD: Johns Hopkins University Press, 2008); Schimmelfennig and Sedelmeier, "Introduction," 19; Kubicek, "International norms," 14–15.

17. Börzel and Risse, "Conceptualising the Domestic Impact," 68.

18. G. Falkner, O. Treib, M. Hartlapp, and S. Leiber, *Complying with Europe: EU Harmonisation and Soft Law in the Member States* (Cambridge: Cambridge University Press, 2005).

19. Börzel and Risse, "Conceptualising the Domestic Impact," 67.

20. Tallberg, "Paths to Compliance."

21. See e.g. T. Konig and B. Luetgert, "Troubles with Transposition? Explaining Trends in Member-State Notification and the Delayed Transposition of EU Directives," *British Journal of Political Science* 39, no. 1 (2009), 163–94; B. Steunenberg and D. Toshkov, "Comparing Transposition in the 27 Member States of the EU: the Impact of Discretion and Legal Fit," *Journal of European Public Policy* 16, no. 7 (2009), 951–70.

22. T. A. Börzel, *Environmental Leaders and Laggards in Europe: Why There is (Not) a "Southern Problem"* (Aldershot: Ashgate, 2003).

23. Schimmelfennig and Sedelmeier, "Introduction."

24. Schimmelfennig and Sedelmeier, "Introduction," 12–16.

25. Schimmelfennig and Sedelmeier, "Introduction," 18–19.

26. See T. Freyburg, S. Lavenex, F. Schimmelfennig, T. Skripka, and A. Wetzel, "EU Promotion of Democratic Governance in the Neighbourhood," *Journal of European Public Policy* 16, no. 6 (2009), 916–34.

27. Kubicek, "International Norms," 14–15; W. Jacoby, *The Enlargement of the European Union and NATO. Ordering from the Menu in Central Europe* (Cambridge: Cambridge University Press, 2004), 10; Schimmelfennig and Sedelmeier, "Introduction," 19.

28. See e.g. Schimmelfennig and Sedelmeier, "Introduction," 20–5, Jacoby, "Enlargement"; C. M. Radaelli, "Policy Transfer in the European Union: Institutional Isomorphism as a Source of Legitimacy," *Governance* 13, no. 1 (2000), 25–43.

29. See e.g. D. Dolowitz, and D. Marsh, "Learning from Abroad: The Role of Policy Transfer in Contemporary Policy-Making," *Governance* 13, no. 1 (2000), 5–23.

30. See e.g. J. W. Meyer and B. Rowan, "Institutionalized Organizations: Formal Structure as Myth and Ceremony," in P. DiMaggio and W. Powell, eds, *The New Institutionalism in Organizational Analysis* (Chicago: Chicago University Press, 1991), 41–62.

31. See Schimmelfennig and Sedelmeier, "Introduction."

32. Schimmelfennig and Sedelmeier, "Introduction," 20–5.

33. See S. Lavenex and F. Schimmelfennig, "EU Rules Beyond EU Borders: Theorizing External Governance in European Politics," *Journal of European Public Policy* 16, no. 6 (2009), 791–812, at 797–8.

34. Börzel and Risse, "Conceptualising the Domestic Impact," 73; K. Dyson, "Euro Area Entry in East-Central Europe: Paradoxical Europeanisation and Clustered Convergence," *West European Politics* 30, no. 3 (2007), 417–42.

35. A. Héritier, D. Kerwer, C. Knill, D. Lehmkuhl, M. Teutsch, and A.-C. Douillet, *Differential Europe: the European Union Impact on National Policymaking* (Lanham, MD: Rowman & Littlefield, 2001).

36. O. Treib, "Implementing and Complying with EU Governance," *Living Reviews in European Governance* 3, no. 5 (2008), <http://livingreviews.org/lreg-2008-5>; for the state of the art, see Börzel et al., "Obstinate and Inefficient."

37. H. Kassim, "Meeting the Demands of EU Membership: The Europeanization of National Administrative Systems," in Featherstone and Radaelli, *The Politics of Europeanization*, 83–111; A. Dimitrova and D. Toshkov, "The Dynamics of Domestic Coordination of EU Policy in the New Member States: Impossible to Lock In?," *West European Politics* 30, no. 5 (2007), 961–86; K. H. Goetz, "Making Sense of Post-Communist Central Administration: Modernization, Europeanization or Latinization?," *Journal of European Public Policy* 8, no. 6 (2001), 1032–51.

38. Kassim, "Meeting the Demands," 102.

39. Kassim, "Meeting the Demands," 102.

40. Dimitrova and Toshkov, "The Dynamics of Domestic Coordination."

41. See e.g. A. Maurer and W. Wessels, eds, *National Parliaments on their Ways to Europe: Losers or Latecomers?* (Baden-Baden: Nomos, 2001).

42. H. Grabbe, "How does Europeanization affect CEE Governance? Conditionality, Diffusion and Diversity," *Journal of European Public Policy* 8, no. 6 (2001), 1013–31.

43. W. Sadurski, "Introduction: The Law and Institutions of New Member States in Year One," in W. Sadurski, J. Ziller, and K. Zurek, eds, *Après Enlargement: Legal and Political Responses in Central and Eastern Europe* (Florence: European University Institute, 2006), 3–18, at 7.

44. K. H. Goetz and J.-H. Meyer-Sahling, "The Europeanisation of National Political Systems: Parliaments and Executives," *Living Reviews in European Governance* 3, no. 2 (2008), <http://www.livingreviews.org/lreg-2008-2>.

45. F. Schimmelfennig, "Strategic Calculation and International Socialization: Membership Incentives, Party Constellations, and Sustained Compliance in Central and Eastern Europe," *International Organization* 59 (2005), 827–60; M. A. Vachudova, *Europe Undivided: Democracy, Leverage and Integration after Communism* (Oxford: Oxford University Press, 2005).

46. K. Dyson and K. H. Goetz, *Living with Europe: Germany and the Politics of Constraint* (Oxford: Oxford University Press, 2003), 386.

47. P. Mair, "The Limited Impact of Europe on National Party Systems," *West European Politics* 23, no. 4 (2000), 27–51.

48. L. Hooghe and M. A. Vachudova, "Postcommunist Politics in a Magnetic Field: How Transition and EU Accession Structure Party Competition on European Integration," *Comparative European Politics* 7, no. 2 (2009), 179–212.

49. See e.g. Börzel, "Environmental Leaders and Laggards."

50. M. Zürn and C. Joerges, eds, *Law and Governance in Postnational Europe: Compliance Beyond the Nation-State* (Cambridge: Cambridge University Press, 2005).

51. P. Levitz and G. Pop-Eleches, "Why No Backsliding? The European Union's Impact on Democracy and Governance Before and After Accession," *Comparative Political Studies* 43, no. 4 (2010), 457–85; Sedelmeier, "After Conditionality."

CHAPTER 58

···

POLITICIZATION

···

LIESBET HOOGHE AND
GARY MARKS

POLITICIZATION refers to the increasing contentiousness of decision-making in the process of regional integration. Research has focused on the conditions under which regional integration becomes politicized; how contestation over regional integration connects to domestic conflict; and the consequences of politicization for the speed and direction of regional integration

The early neo-functionalists, who invented the term, believed that politicization would lead to more regional integration. A federal polity, or something like it, would result. According to Schmitter:

> Politicization... refers initially to a process whereby the *controversiality* of joint decision making goes up. This in turn is likely to lead to a *widening of the audience or clientele* interested and active in integration. Somewhere along the line a *manifest redefinition of mutual objectives* will probably occur.... Ultimately,... there will be *a shift in actor expectations and loyalty* toward the new regional center.[1]

Haas argued that "even though supranationality in practice has developed into a hybrid in which neither the federal nor the intergovernmental tendency has clearly triumphed, these relationships have sufficed to create expectations and shape attitudes which will undoubtedly work themselves out in the direction of more integration."[2]

After the debacle of Charles de Gaulle's opposition to supranationalism and the empty chair crisis of 1965–1966, neo-functionalist predictions appeared too rosy. The most influential alternative approach—intergovernmentalism—conceived regional integration as an outcome of bargaining among national states.[3] Neo-functionalists and intergovernmentalists engaged in a decades-long debate about whether the impetus for regional integration came from supra- or transnational actors or from national governments, whether supranational institutions such as the European Commission are autonomous from national governments, and whether regional integration transforms national states.

However, beyond their much-publicized disagreements, neo-functionalists and intergovernmentalists shared an economic conception of regional integration. They conceived its politics as distributional, and hence dominated by functional interest groups. Neo-functionalists hypothesized that such groups would operate at the supranational, as well as at the national level. Intergovernmentalists conceived interest group pressures within discrete national arenas.

This elite conception of European integration survived the creation of a European Parliament and even direct elections from 1979. European elections were merely popularity tests for national governments. European integration remained a non-issue for the general public.[4]

This view rests on three assumptions, none of which now hold. First, the public's attitudes toward European integration are superficial, and therefore incapable of providing a stable structure of electoral incentives for party positioning. Second, European integration is a low salience issue for the general public (in contrast to its high salience for business groups), and therefore has little influence on party competition. And third, the issues raised by European integration are *sui generis*, and therefore unrelated to the basic conflicts that structure political competition.

The experience of the past fifteen years—and the research it generated—has dismantled each of these assumptions. Public opinion on European integration is rather well structured,[5] affects national voting,[6] and is connected to the basic dimensions that structure contestation in European societies.[7]

With the Maastricht Accord of 1991, decision-making on European integration entered the contentious world of party competition, elections, and referendums.[8] Content analysis of media in France, the Netherlands, Germany, Britain, Switzerland, and Austria, reveals that the proportion of statements devoted to European issues in national electoral campaigns increased from 2.5 percent in the 1970s to 7 percent in the 1990s.[9] In the 1990s, between one-tenth and one-eighth of all policy statements in a sample of British and Swiss media contained references to Europe.[10]

Analyzing a dataset of 9,872 protests from 1984 through 1997, Imig concludes that "European integration is highly salient to a growing range of citizens across the continent."[11] On conservative assumptions, the proportion of social movement protest oriented to Europe has risen from the 5 to 10 percent range in the 1980s to between 20 and 30 percent in the second half of the 1990s.

An expert survey conducted by Benoit and Laver finds that European integration was the third most important issue in national party competition in Western Europe in 2003, behind taxes versus spending and deregulation/privatization, but ahead of immigration.[12] European integration topped the list in Britain, France, Cyprus, and Malta. In Eastern Europe, joining the EU was typically the most salient issue.

58.1 LEFT/RIGHT CONFLICT AND
POLITICIZATION

When researchers first tried to make sense of the politicization of European integration after the tumultuous response to the Maastricht Accord, they asked a simple question: how do European issues connect (or fail to connect) to the existing pattern of domestic conflict? An initial hunch was that contestation about the EU would map on left versus right, which structures political conflict in most European countries.[13] The logic of coalition building would then be distributional, pitting parties representing economic factors (mainly labor versus capital) against each other. Coalitions would have to be broad to meet super-majoritarian hurdles within and across EU institutions. One coalition would encompass Christian democrats supporting social market capitalism and social democrats advocating market correcting measures at the European level while seeking to preserve national spaces for redistribution. An opposing coalition would have conservatives and economic liberals as its core, and a Europe-wide (or wider) deregulated market as its goal. Labor and most social movements would undergird the first coalition, business and finance the second.[14]

Evidence has accumulated for this conception of European politics. Left/right contestation structures competition on Europe among national political parties,[15] roll call voting in the European Parliament,[16] social movement contention,[17] interest groups,[18] European Commission officials,[19] the positions adopted by member states in the Council of Ministers,[20] and treaty bargaining.[21]

However, left/right conflict over European issues is not the same as left/right conflict over national policies because the scope for economic redistribution is throttled in Europe. Convergence to a single European model would impose a deadweight cost on diverse national welfare systems.[22]

Moreover, redistribution at the European level is not only from the rich to the poor, but from the rich North and West to the poorer South and East. That is to say, redistribution at the individual level involves redistribution across member states—a large impediment to reform. As if this were not enough, the left is faced with the challenge of cultural diversity which has increased considerably with enlargement to Central and Eastern Europe. Citizens are loath to redistribute income to individuals who are not perceived to belong to the same community.[23] Currently the EU redistributes 0.75 percent of its total economic product through its agricultural and cohesion policies. This is a small proportion when compared to European states, though it is larger than that redistributed by any other international organization. Given the great and growing cultural diversity of the EU, how much higher could this proportion go?

Consequently, left/right conflict at the European level is about social regulation, rather than redistribution. This alienates the radical left which regards the EU as a one-sided capitalist project endangering social protection at the national level. Social democrats also wish to protect national welfare regimes from a European joint-decision trap, but see virtues in coordinating fiscal policy at the European level and in building a "citizens Europe." Social democratic parties, which formed governments or governing coalitions in thirteen of fifteen member states in 1997, pushed through the Amsterdam Treaty which extended EU competence in employment, social regulation, women's rights, human rights, and the environment.[24] The Amsterdam Treaty led to the Lisbon process (2000) with the goal of coordinating policies to combat poverty, raise employment rates, modernize education and training systems, and reform pensions.[25]

In early 2000, the authors of this article were looking at new data on the positioning of national political parties across the EU. They expected to see a strong association between the *left/right* position of a party and its stance on European integration, but to their surprise, this was eclipsed by a *non-economic* left/right dimension, ranging from green/alternative/libertarian (or *gal*) to traditionalism/authority/nationalism (or *tan*). It became clear that their prior analysis of politicization as a conflict between regulated capitalism and market liberalism was seriously incomplete.[26]

The association between *gal/tan* and support for European integration is particularly strong for parties located on the *tan* side of this dimension. *Tan* parties, such as the French *Front National*, the Austrian *Freiheitliche Partei*, or the British Independence Party, reject European integration because they believe it weakens national sovereignty, diffuses self-rule, and introduces foreign ideas. They oppose European integration for the same reasons that they oppose immigration: it undermines national community. These parties attract voters primarily on the basis of their *tan* views, of which their skepticism towards European integration is an integral part, and they downplay their stances on redistribution and the role of government.[27]

Conservative parties are also influenced by their location on the moderate *tan* side of the *gal/tan* dimension. They too defend national culture and national sovereignty against immigrants, against international regimes, and against multiple territorial identities. In conservative parties, however, nationalism competes with neo-liberalism. Nationalists resist dilution of national sovereignty in principle, while neo-liberals are prepared to pool it to achieve economic integration. The clash between nationalism and neo-liberalism has dominated the internal politics of the British Conservative party since the Maastricht Treaty, alienating the party from its traditional constituency— affluent, educated, middle-class voters—whose pragmatic pro-Europeanism fits uncomfortably with the party's Euro-skepticism.[28] Similar disagreements in the Gaullist *Rassemblement pour la République* propelled two anti-Europeanist factions to break away in the early 1990s.[29] In Germany, Angela Merkel, leader of the traditionally pro-European Christian democrats (CDU), has had her hands full with Euro-skeptics in the *Christlich Soziale Union* (CSU). The CDU recently adopted the CSU's opposition to Turkish membership on the grounds that a Muslim country is not European.

The result is that the line-up of supporters and opponents of European integration has changed. In 1984, two years before the single market, the main source of opposition was social-democratic and radical left.[30] By the late 1990s, the largest reservoir of opposition was among radical *tan* parties.[31]

The association between *gal/tan* attitudes and attitudes toward European integration is weaker on the *gal* side. However, the success of *tan* parties in connecting European integration to their core concerns has spurred their opponents. Green parties have come to consider European integration as part of their project for a multicultural European society—notwithstanding their misgivings about the EU's democratic deficit and central bureaucracy. For *left-gal* parties, the EU remains a difficult proposition because it combines *gal* policies with market liberalism. *Les Verts* and *Groenlinks* came out in favor of the Constitutional Treaty in the 2005 French and Dutch referendums, and paid a price in terms of internal dissent and defection of their voters to the "No" camp.[32] In the most recent 2009 European Parliament elections, the European green party championed more EU competence in economic regulation, in sustainable development, and asylum policy, favored giving the European Parliament the power of legislative initiative, and called for transnational party lists to "allow citizens to vote for candidates that represent the whole of the EU, rather than just their national or local constituency."[33]

Party conflict on European integration is simpler and more polarized in Central and Eastern Europe because *gal/tan* and *left/right* positions are mutually reinforcing rather than cross-cutting. The axis of party competition that emerged after the collapse of communism runs from *left-tan* to *right-gal*, pitting market and cultural liberals against social protectionists and nationalists.[34] Hence the two sources of Euro-skepticism in Western Europe—*tan* and *left*—go together in the East. Left parties, including unreformed communist parties, tend to be *tan*, and *tan* parties, including agrarian and populist parties, tend to be left. In Western Europe, the mobilization of national identity and of left concerns about the loss of national protection are expressed in different parties, whereas in Eastern Europe they are fused.[35]

58.2 WHEN DOES AN ISSUE BECOME POLITICIZED?

As European integration has grown in scope and depth, it has proven ripe for politicization. But there is nothing inevitable about this. Whether an issue enters mass politics depends not on its intrinsic importance, but on whether a political party picks it up.

Political parties bundle issues along two dimensions to create distinctive electoral profiles. One is concerned with issues of authority and community, and engages the tension between national autonomy and European integration. A second reflects the basic division between left support for collective allocation of resources and right support for market allocation. This dimension captures the debate between European regulated capitalism and market liberalism. When political parties align themselves on these dimensions in competing for political support, they are making commitments on European decision-making. But what does this mean?

Figure 58.1 conceives a pyramid of connections among dimensions of conflict, EU issues, and EU decisions. There is more structure here than in the preferences of most politically sophisticated individuals, let alone relatively uninformed citizens. When preferences are aggregated over large numbers, idiosyncratic features fall away and we are left with underlying structure. The number of issues in a society is almost infinite, so Figure 58.1 would have to be greatly enlarged if it were to be comprehensive.

Only a few issues at any one time energize the basic dimensions of conflict in a society. Referendums require dichotomous response. Elections allow citizens to express preferences only on issues associated with the dimensions on which political parties compete.

Mass politics trumps interest group politics when both come into play. Interest groups are most effective when they have the field to themselves. When the spotlight of politicization is turned on an issue, when political parties and the public are focused on an issue, interest group lobbying may actually be counterproductive. Public debate in the context of elections and referendums pre-empts the efforts of small, highly motivated, groups to control outcomes.[36]

Issues that are *not* connected with the main dimensions of conflict in a society are decided by government officials and interest groups of diverse kinds, often with little media or public attention. Interest groups are far more effective in influencing this kind of decision-making than they are in elections and party competition. So, when it comes to the price of corn, pharmaceutical product labeling, or the regulation of banking secrecy, the relevant interest groups can be expected to exert significant leverage. On the great issues of the day, e.g. the Constitutional Treaty or monetary union, narrow interests have vastly less influence.

Connections among issues are a human contrivance. Most issues have both communal (*gal/tan*) and distributional (*left/right*) consequences. EU enlargement, for example, increases immigration into Western Europe from societies to the East: it therefore affects the ethnic make-up of local communities, and it affects labor markets. The debate concerning how much authority should be exercised by the European Parliament involves the authority of national institutions, but it also has indirect implications for market regulation.

To understand which issues are politicized and which remain below the horizon of partisan competition, one needs to investigate strategic interaction among political parties.

- The greater a party's potential electoral popularity on an issue, the more it is induced to inject it into competition with other parties. The key term here is "potential," for party leaders strategize under uncertainty. How will opinion shift on an issue when it is debated? Will voters come to perceive the issue as salient, if they do not already? Elections are contests about what issues are important, and a party's decision to raise an issue in party competition rests on its strategic calculation that the issue will count, and will count in a particular direction.

- The ability of party leaders to chase votes by strategic positioning is constrained by reputational considerations and the ideological commitment of party activists. Political parties are not simply machines for aggregating the votes necessary to catapult ambitious individuals into government. Parties are membership organizations with fairly durable programmatic commitments. These commitments constrain strategic positioning. Moreover, a party must strive to convince voters that it will actually do what it says it will do.
- Leaders are reluctant to raise the heat on an issue that threatens to divide their party. Party dissent arises as European integration activates historically rooted tensions.[37] Disunity not only reduces a party's electoral popularity; it is a frequent cause of party death.

Notwithstanding the general reluctance of elites to politicize European integration, some interesting exceptions arose when societies were confronted with basic decisions related to joining, enlarging, or deepening the regime. The sheer existence of constitutional issues that cut against the axis of party competition is both a constant irritation and a standing temptation for party leaders. The flash point is the referendum. Referendums are elite-initiated events which can have elite-defying consequences.[38] They are used for immediate effect, but their institutional impact has a considerable half-life. Referendums are not easily forgotten.

The process of legitimating the Maastricht Accord (1992) was a turning point in the causal underpinnings of European integration. It opened a complex elite bargain to public inspection, and precipitated referendums and a series of national debates that alerted publics to the fact that European integration was diluting national sovereignty. The rejection of the Maastricht Accord in Denmark and its near rejection in France revealed an elite/public gap and sustained the populist notion that important EU decisions could no longer be legitimized by the executive and legislature operating in the normal way—direct popular approval was required.

Most mainstream parties continued to resist politicizing the issue. But a number of populist, non-governing, parties saw opportunity. Their instinctual Euro-skepticism was closer to the pulse of public opinion. On the far left, opposition to European integration expressed antipathy to capitalism; on the populist right, it expressed defense of national community.

The populist demand for national referendums on the so-called grand treaties has shaped popular participation in the EU.[39] Governments in one country after another have come to believe that they need the formal acquiescence of their publics in referendums to go ahead with basic European reform. Parliamentary votes are not deemed sufficient. Public referendums are required even in countries, such as the United Kingdom and the Netherlands, where the legislature is formally supreme. Since the negotiation of the Maastricht Treaty, twenty-nine referendums on Europe have been held in twenty EU countries. The only EU countries never to have held a referendum on Europe are Belgium, Bulgaria, Cyprus, Germany, Greece, Portugal, and Romania. Referendums have blocked the entry of Denmark and Sweden into European monetary union, forced renegotiation of the Maastricht Treaty and the Nice Treaty, derailed the Constitutional Treaty, and have blocked the Lisbon Treaty. Several reforms, such as the entry of the UK into EMU, have been taken off the agenda because governments fear that they would be defeated in a popular referendum.

58.3 IDENTITY AND POLITICIZATION

The jurisdictional shape of Europe has been transformed, but the way in which citizens conceive their identities has not. Since 1992, when the EU's public opinion instrument, *Eurobarometer*, began to ask questions about identity, the proportion of EU citizens who describe themselves as exclusively national, e.g. British, French, or Czech only, rather than national and European, European and national, or European only, has varied between 33 and 46 percent, with no discernable trend. Fligstein argues that the experience of mobility and transnational social interaction spurs European identity, but the pace of such change is much slower than that of jurisdictional reform.[40] Younger people tend to interact across national borders more than older people and, on average, they attest stronger European identity, but there is no evidence of an aggregate shift towards less exclusive national identities since the early 1990s, the period for which we have reasonably good data. Until generational change kicks in, Europe is faced with a tension between rapid jurisdictional change and relatively stable identities.

Two things would have to happen to politically activate such a tension, and both *have* happened. First, the tension must be salient. The scope and depth of European integration have perceptibly increased,[41] and their effects have been magnified because they are part of a broader breakdown of national barriers giving rise to mass immigration and intensified economic competition.

Second, political entrepreneurs must mobilize the tension. Connections between national identity, cultural and economic insecurity, and issues such as EU enlargement, cannot be induced directly from experience, but have to be constructed. Such construction is most influential for individuals who do not have strong prior attitudes and for attitudes toward distant, abstract, or new political objects.[42] Hence, public opinion on Europe is particularly susceptible to construction: i.e. priming (making a consideration salient), framing (connecting a particular consideration to a political object), and cueing (instilling a bias).[43]

It is not unusual for an individual to have a strong national attachment and yet be positively oriented to European integration.[44] What matters is whether a person conceives of her national identity as *exclusive* or *inclusive* of other territorial identities. Individuals with exclusive national identities are predisposed to Euro-skepticism if they are cued to believe that love of their country and its institutions is incompatible with European integration. Recent research by De Vries and Edwards suggests that radical populist parties are decisive in this regard.[45] The stronger the party, the more likely it is that individuals with an exclusive national identity are Euro-skeptic. The association

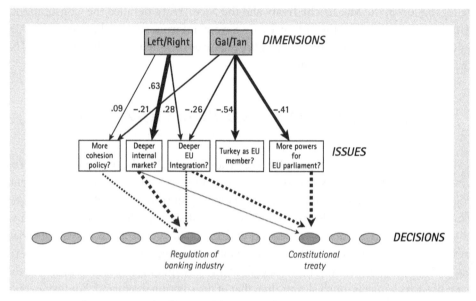

FIGURE 58. 1. The structure of political conflict (2006)

Note: Thickness of arrow indicates strength of association. Dotted arrows are hypothetical relationships. Solid arrows are empirical estimates calculated from the 2006 Chapel Hill party expert data set for EU-27, weighted by party vote. This figure displays only a subset of many possible associations.

indicates the limits as well as the power of framing, for individuals with *inclusive* identities are apparently not affected by either the existence or strength of a populist right party.

This has pushed Europe into national politics and national politics into decision-making on Europe. But this has not led to homogenization. Public responses to Europe are refracted through national institutions and patterns of discourse that reflect distinct historical trajectories. Risse observes that "Europeanness or 'becoming European' is gradually being embedded in understandings of national identities."[46] Public opinion researchers have hypothesized the effects of Catholic versus Protestant beliefs; of civic versus ethnic citizenship models; of coordinated versus market-liberal economic governance; of the communist legacy in Central and Eastern Europe; of distinctive imperial experiences.[47] National peculiarities are more pronounced among publics than elites because publics are more nationally rooted and are more dependent on information filtered by national media.[48]

European politics has become multilevel in a way that few, if any, anticipated. The EU is no longer insulated from domestic politics; domestic politics is no longer insulated from Europe.[49] EU decisions are no longer the exclusive terrain of elites; EU decisions now also engage political parties, social movements, and public opinion. The result is greater divergence of politically relevant perceptions and a correspondingly constricted scope of agreement. A *permissive consensus* has been transformed into a *constraining dissensus.*

Notes

1. Philippe C. Schmitter, "Three Neofunctional Hypotheses About International Integration," *International Organization* 23 (1969), 166.
2. Ernst B. Haas, *The Uniting of Europe* (Stanford: Stanford University Press, 1958), 526–7.
3. Stanley Hoffmann, "Obstinate or Obsolete? The Fate of the Nation-State and the Case of Western Europe," *Daedalus* 95 (1966), 862–914; Alan Milward, *The European Rescue of the Nation-State* (Berkeley: University of California Press, 1992); Andrew Moravcsik, *The Choice for Europe: Social Purpose and State Power from Messina to Maastricht* (Ithaca, NY: Cornell University Press, 1998).
4. Karlheinz Reif and Hermann Schmitt, "Nine National Second-Order Elections: A Systematic Framework for the Analysis of European Election Results," *European Journal of Political Research* 8 (1980), 3–44; Stephan Leibfried and Paul Pierson, eds, *European Social Policy: Between Fragmentation and Integration* (Washington, DC: Brookings Institution, 1995).
5. Cees Van der Eijk and Mark Franklin, eds, *Choosing Europe? The European Electorate and National Politics in the Face of Union* (Ann Arbor: University of Michigan Press, 1996); Mark Franklin and Cees van der Eijk, "Potential for Contestation on European Matters at National Elections in Europe," in Gary Marks and Marco Steenbergen, eds, *European Integration and Political Conflict: Citizens, Parties, Groups* (Cambridge: Cambridge University Press, 2004), 32–50.
6. Catherine De Vries, "Sleeping Giant: Fact or Fairytale? Examining the Impact of European Integration on National Elections in Denmark and the Netherlands," *European Union Politics* 8 (2007), 363–85; Geoffrey Evans, "Europe: A New Electoral Cleavage?," in Geoffrey Evans and Pippa Norris, eds, *Critical Elections: British Parties and Voters in Long-Term Perspective* (London: Sage, 1999), 207–22; Matthew Gabel, "European Integration, Voters and National Politics," *West European Politics* 23 (2000), 52–72.
7. Simon Hix, "Dimensions and Alignments in European Union Politics: Cognitive Constraints and Partisan Responses," *European Journal of Political Research* 35 (1999), 69–106; Gary Marks and Steenbergen, eds, *European Integration and Political Conflict: Citizens, Parties, Groups* (Cambridge: Cambridge University Press, 2004); Paul Pennings, "The Dimensionality of the EU Policy Space," *European Union Politics* 3 (2002), 59–80.
8. Mark Franklin and Cees van der Eijk, "Potential for Contestation on European Matters at National Elections in Europe," in Marks and Steenbergen, *European Integration and Political Conflict*, 32–50.
9. Hanspeter Kriesi, Edgar Grande, Romain Lachat, Martin Dolezal, Simon Bornschier, and Timotheos Frey, "Globalization and the Transformation of the National Political Space: Six European Countries Compared," *European Journal of Political Research* 45 (2006), 921–56; Ruud Koopmans, Hanspeter Kriesi, Juan Diez Medrano, Paul Statham, Virginie Guiraudon, Jos de Beus, and Barbara Pfetsch, *The Transformation of Political Mobilization and Communication in European Public Spheres* (Europub: Integrated Report, 2004), available at <http://europub.wz-berlin.de/project%20reports.en.htm#2> (accessed September 15, 2009).

10. Kriesi et al., "Globalization," 923.
11. Doug Imig, "Contestation in the Streets: European Protest and The Emerging Europolity," in Marks and Steenbergen, *European Integration and Political Conflict*, 232; Sidney Tarrow, *The New Transnational Activism* (Cambridge: Cambridge University Press, 2005).
12. Kenneth Benoit and Michael Laver, *Party Policy in Modern Democracies* (London: Routledge, 2006).
13. Liesbet Hooghe and Gary Marks, "The Making of a Polity: The Struggle over European Integration," in Herbert Kitschelt, Peter Lange, Gary Marks, and John Stephens, eds, *Continuity and Change in Contemporary Capitalism* (Cambridge: Cambridge University Press, 1999), 70–97; Martin Rhodes and Bastiaan van Apeldoorn, "Capitalism versus Capitalism in Western Europe," in Martin Rhodes, Paul Heywood, and Vincent Wright, eds, *Developments in West European Politics* (New York: St. Martin's Press, 1997), 171–89; George Tsebelis and Geoffrey Garrett, "Legislative Politics in the European Union," *European Union Politics* 1 (2000), 9–36.
14. Magnus Johansson, "Party Elites in Multilevel Europe: The Christian Democrats and the Single European Act," *Party Politics* 8 (2002), 423–39; Robert Ladrech, "Social Democratic Parties and EC Integration: Transnational Responses to Europe 1992," *European Journal of Political Research* 24 (1997), 195–210; Gary Marks and Carole Wilson, "The Past in the Present: A Cleavage Theory of Party Positions on European Integration," *British Journal of Political Science* 30 (2000), 433–59; George Ross, *Jacques Delors and European Integration* (Oxford: Oxford University Press 1994).
15. Marks and Steenbergen, *European Integration and Political Conflict*; Paul Taggart and Aleks Szczerbiak, eds, *Opposing Europe? The Comparative Party Politics of Euroscepticism: Volume 1: Case Studies and Country Surveys* (Oxford: Oxford University Press, 2008); Paul Taggart and Aleks Szczerbiak, eds, *Opposing Europe? The Comparative Party Politics of Euroscepticism: Volume 2: Comparative and Theoretical Perspectives* (Oxford: Oxford University Press, 2008).
16. Simon Hix, Abdul Noury, and Roland Gerard, *Democracy in the European Parliament* (Cambridge: Cambridge University Press, 2006); Amie Kreppel, *The European Parliament and the Supranational Party System: A Study of Institutional Development* (Cambridge: Cambridge University Press, 2002); Jacques Thomassen, Abdul Noury, and Erik Voeten, "Political Competition in the European Parliament: Evidence from Roll Call and Survey Analyses," in Marks and Steenbergen, *European Integration and Political Conflict*, 141–64.
17. Imig, "Contestation in the Streets," pp. xx–xx.
18. Bernhard Wessels, "Contestation Potential of Interest Groups in the EU: Emergence, Structure, and Political Alliances," in Marks and Steenbergen, *European Integration and Political Conflict*, 195–215.
19. Liesbet Hooghe, "Euro-Socialists or Euro-Marketeers? Contention about European Capitalism among Senior Commission Officials," *Journal of Politics* 62 (2000), 430–54.
20. Mark Aspinwall, "Preferring Europe: Ideology and National Preferences on European Integration," *European Union Politics* 3 (2002), 81–111; Mikko Mattila, "Contested Decisions: Empirical Analysis of Voting in the EU Council of Ministers," *European Journal of Political Research* 43 (2004), 29–50.
21. Ben Crum, "Politics and Power in the Convention," *Politics* 24 (2004), 1–11; Mark Pollack, "A Blairite Treaty: Neoliberalism and Regulated Capitalism in the Treaty of Amsterdam," in Karl-Heinz Neunreither and Antje Wiener, eds, *European Integration After Amsterdam: Institutional Dynamics and Prospects for Democracy* (Oxford: Oxford University Press, 1999), 266–89.

22. Stephan Leibfried and Paul Pierson, eds, *European Social Policy: Between Fragmentation and Integration* (Washington, DC: Brookings Institution, 1995); Fritz Scharpf, *Governing in Europe: Effective and Democratic?* (Oxford: Oxford University Press, 1999).

23. Claus Offe, "The Democratic Welfare State in an Integrating Europe," in Louis W. Pauly and Michael Th. Greven, eds, *Democracy Beyond the State: The European Dilemma and the Emerging Global Order* (Lanham, MD: Rowman & Littlefield, 2000), 63–90.

24. Pollack, "A Blairite Treaty," 266–89.

25. Mary Daly, "EU Social Policy after Lisbon," *Journal of Common Market Studies* 44 (2006), 461–81.

26. Liesbet Hooghe, Gary Marks, and Carole Wilson, "Does Left/Right Structure Party Positions on European Integration?" *Comparative Political Studies* 35 (2002), 965–89; Gary Marks, Liesbet Hooghe, Moira Nelson, and Erica Edwards, "Party Competition and European Integration in East and West: Different Structure, Same Causality," *Comparative Political Studies* 39 (2006), 155–75.

27. Jan Rovny, "Are Extreme Right Parties Really on the Right? A Dimensional Approach," (unpublished manuscript, 2009).

28. Geoffrey Evans, "Euroscepticism and Conservative Electoral Support: How An Asset Became a Liability," *British Journal of Politics and International Relations* 28 (1998), 573–90.

29. Paul Hainsworth, Carolyn O'Brien, and Paul Mitchell, "The Politics of Euroscepticism on the French Right," in Robert Harmsen and Menno Spiering, eds, *Euroscepticism: Party Politics, National Identity and European Integration* (Amsterdam/New York: Rodopi, 2004), 37–58.

30. Leonard Ray, "Measuring Party Orientation Towards European Integration: Results from an Expert Survey," *European Journal of Political Research* 36 (1999), 283–306.

31. Hooghe, Marks, and Wilson, "Does Left/Right Structure Party Positions on European Integration?" 965–89.

32. It has been argued that the French "No" vote was primarily a vote against a neo-liberal Europe, but detailed analysis of post-election polls suggests a prominent role for *tan* concerns. Among left "No" voters, social concerns were only slightly more important than nationalist threats, while on the political right "the social threat was marginal in its influence; this was not the case for the nationalistic threat" (Sylvain Brouard and Vincent Tiberj, "The French Referendum: The Not So Simple Act of Saying Nay," *PS: Politics and Political Science* 39 (2006), 67).

33. <http://europeangreens.eu/menu/egp-manifesto> (accessed September 18, 2009).

34. Herbert Kitschelt, Zdenka Mansfeldova, Radoslaw Markowski, and Gabor Toka, *Post Communist Party Systems: Competition, Representation, and Inter-Party Cooperation* (Cambridge: Cambridge University Press, 1999); Marks et al., "Party Competition and European Integration in East and West: Different Structure, Same Causality." See also Robert Rohrschneider and Stephen Whitefield, "Understanding Cleavages in Party Systems Issue Position and Issue Salience in 13 Post-Communist Democracies," *Comparative Political Studies* 42 (2009), 280–313.

35. Milada Vachudova and Liesbet Hooghe, "Postcommunist Politics in a Magnetic Field: How Transition and EU Accession Structure Party Competition on European Integration," *Comparative European Politics* 7 (2009), 179–212.

36. Jan Beyers, Rainer Eising, and William Maloney, eds, "The Politics of Organised Interests in Europe: Lessons from EU Studies and Comparative Politics," *West European Politics* 31

(2008), 1103–302; Ken Kollman, *Outside Lobbying* (Princeton: Princeton University Press, 1998); David Lowery, "Why Do Organized Interests Lobby? A Multi-Goal, Multi-Context Theory of Lobbying," *Polity* 39 (2007), 1–54.

37. Erica Edwards, "Products of their Past? Cleavage Theory and Intra-Party Dissent over European Integration," *Papers for the Institut für Höhere Studien (IHS) Political Science Series*, 2009, No. 118.

38. Sarah Binzer Hobolt, "How Parties Affect Vote Choice in European Integration Referendums," *Party Politics* 12 (2006), 623–47; Lawrence Leduc, "Opinion Change and Voting Behaviour in Referendums," *European Journal of Political Research* 41 (2002), 711–32; Claes De Vreese, "Political Parties in Dire Straits? Consequences of National Referendums for Political Parties," *Party Politics* 12 (2006), 581–98.

39. Liesbet Hooghe and Gary Marks, "A Postfunctionalist Theory of European Integration: From Permissive Consensus to Constraining Dissensus," *British Journal of Political Science* 39 (2009), 1–23; Simon Hug, *Voices of Europe: Citizens, Referendums, European Integration* (Lanham, MD: Rowman and Littlefield, 2002); Catherine De Vries, "The Impact of EU Referenda on National Electoral Politics: Evidence from the Dutch Case," *West European Politics* 32 (2009), 142–71.

40. Neil Fligstein, *Euroclash: EU, European Identity, and the Future of Europe* (Oxford: Oxford University Press, 2008).

41. Tanja Börzel, "Mind the Gap! European Integration Between Level and Scope," *Journal of European Public Policy* 12 (2005), 217–36.

42. James N. Druckman, "Political Preference Formation: Competition, Deliberation, and the (Ir)relevance of Framing Effects," *American Political Science Review* 98 (2004), 671–86; Joanne M. Miller and Jon A. Krosnick, "News Media Impact on the Ingredients of Presidential Evaluations: Politically Knowledgeable Citizens are Guided by a Trusted Source," *American Journal of Political Science* 44 (2000), 301–15.

43. Liesbet Hooghe and Gary Marks, "Calculation, Community and Cues: Public Opinion on European Integration," *European Union Politics* 6 (2005), 419–43.

44. Sean Carey, "Undivided Loyalties: Is National Identity an Obstacle to European Integration?," *European Union Politics* 3 (2002), 387–413: Juan Diez Medrano, *Framing Europe: Attitudes to European Integration in Germany, Spain, and the United Kingdom* (Princeton: Princeton University Press, 2003); Lauren McLaren, *Identity, Interests, and Attitudes to European Integration*, (Houndsmill, Basingstoke: Palgrave, 2006): Kees Van Kersbergen, "Political Allegiance and European Integration," *European Journal of Political Research* 37 (2000), 1–17.

45. Catherine De Vries and Erica Edwards, "Taking Europe to Its Extremes: Extremist Parties and Public Euroskepticism," *Party Politics* 15 (2009), 5–28.

46. Thomas Risse, "Neofunctionalism, European Identity and the Puzzles of European Integration," *Journal of European Public Policy* 13 (2005), 291.

47. Michael Bruter, "Winning Hearts and Minds for Europe: The Impact of News and Symbols on Civic and Cultural European Identity," *Comparative Political Studies* 12 (2003), 1148–79; Adam Brinegar and Seth Jolly, "Location, Location, Location: National Contextual Factors and Public Support for European Integration," *European Union Politics* 6 (2005), 155–80; Antonia Ruiz Jimenez, Jaroslaw Jozef Gorniak, Ankica Kosic, Paszkal Kiss, and Maren Kandulla, "European and National Identities in EU's Old and New Member States: Ethnic, Civic, Instrumental and Symbolic Components," *European Integration Online Papers* (2004), No. 8; Brent F. Nelsen, James Guth, and Cleveland R. Fraser, "Does Religion

Matter? Christianity and Public Support for the European Union," *European Union Politics* 6 (2001), 89–112; Hooghe and Marks, "A Postfunctionalist Theory."

48. Fligstein, *Euroclash*; Barbara Pfetsch, Silke Adam, Barbara Berkel, and Juan Diez Medrano, "The Voice of the Media in the European Public Sphere: Comparative Analysis of Newspaper Editorials," *Europub: Integrated Report WP 3* (2004), available at <http://europub.wz-berlin.de/Data/reports/WP3/D3-4%20WP3%20Integrated%20Report.pdf> (accessed September 12, 2009).

49. Hooghe and Marks, "A Postfunctionalist Theory"; Johan P. Olsen, "Unity, Diversity, and Democratic Institutions. What Can We Learn from the European Union as a Large-Scale Experiment in Political Organization and Governing?" *Arena Working Papers*, WP 04/13 (2004).

Index

....

Note: page numbers in *italics* refer to figures and tables. References to endnotes are indicated by the suffix 'n' followed by the note number, e.g. 17n59

1992 Program 107, 410, 417–18, 559
"à la carte" Europe 311, 316
absolute majority requirement, European
       Parliament 368
access to information 685
accountability
  agencies 398–9
  Commission 670–1
  European Parliament 671
  implications of "early agreements" 711–12
acid rain 561
  Convention on Long-Range
     Transboundary Pollution 568n9
Action Committee, 1955–1956 98
Adenauer, K. 86, 181, 183, 185
adjudication 67
adjustment pressures 827–8
  mediating factors 828–31, *832*
Adler-Nissen, R. 324
affective support for integration 717–18
age, relationship to attitude towards
     integration 693
agencies *see* European Union agencies
Agenda 2000 497–8
Agenda for Growth and Jobs, 2005 476
agricultural income, role of subsidies 495n74
agriculture *see* Common Agricultural Policy
    (CAP)
agri-monetary legislation 486, 488
Åland Islands, referendum *725*
algorithmic warfare 630
Allen, D. 501
Alliance Base, Paris 638
Alliance of Liberals and Democrats for
    Europe (ALDE) 368

Alter, K. 89
Amato, G. 155
Ames, A. 634
Amsterdam Treaty 132, 135–6, 151, 843
  actors and processes 137–8
  and Commission 227, 228
    presidency 340
  competition policy 444
  defense policy 586–7
  evaluation 144–5
  flexibility 142–3
  foreign policy 140–1
  institutional reform 141–2
  JHA domain 616
  large versus small states problem 265n1
  negotiation and ratification 136
  provisions for EU citizens 138–40
  Santer's influence 242–3
  on transparency 685
Andean Pact *783*
Anderson, C. 722
anti-dumping measures 423, 425, 428
anti-hegemony 249
antitrust rules 442
appropriateness, logic of 812–13
Arab Common Market *783*
Arbélès, M. 55
Arce, D. 811
Area of Freedom, Security, and Justice
    (AFSJ) 613, 618
  challenges 625
Article K.4 Committee 128
Ashton, C. 170, 651–3
Asia Pacific Economic Cooperation forum
    (APEC) 782, *783*

Assembly, EEC 104
assent ability, European Parliament 116
assertion, powers of 645
Association of Southeast Asian Nations
        (ASEAN) 783
associative democracy 670
asylum burdens 815-16
asylum lottery 619
asylum policy 606-7, 612n36, 618-19
    burden-sharing 815
        common policy approach 817-18,
            819-20
        funding 818-19, 820
        implicit trade model 820
        people sharing 816-17, 823n18
    criticisms and proposals for
        reform 819-20
    sociological perspectives 54
Asylum Procedures Directive, 2005 818
asylum seekers database 385
Asylum Support Teams (ASTs) 619
asymmetric shocks 457-8
asymmetry, EMU 458-9
atomic energy *see* Euratom (European
        Community in Atomic Energy) Treaty
audit, European Court of Auditors
        (ECA) 381-3, 387-9
Auer, S. 699
Austria
    asylum burden 815, 816
    GDP per head, 2007 280
        regional disparities 281
    growth, 1995-2005 282
    net migration 603
    referendum 725
auto-oil package 513, 514

Bache, I. 68
Bachtler, J. 501
Balladur, E. 143, 147n41
Balta, N. 414
banking crisis *see* economic crisis
Barber case 544
Barca, F. 503-4
Bardach, E. 797
Barnier, M. 153

Barroso, J.M. 228-9, 652, 706
Bavaria-Würtemberg Customs Union 783,
        784
Beach, D. 131
Bedault, G. 188
Belgium
    asylum burden 815, 816
    GDP per head, 2007 280
        regional disparities 281
    growth, 1995-2005 282
    net migration 603
    vote allocation, Nice Treaty 157
"benefit" principle 814
Benelux countries
    concerns over High Authority 89
    preference formation, Treaties of
        Paris 84-5
Benoit, K. 841
Benvenuti, L. 97
Best, E. 273
Better Regulation Strategy 686
Beyen, J.-W. 188, 189-90
Beyers, J 41
bilateral trade agreements 412, 423
    ratification 428
binding rules mechanisms, burden-
        sharing 814
Blair, A.
    defense policy 587
    views on Santer 241
block exemption regulations (BERs) 446
blocking minorities 253
"Blue Card" Directive, 2009 620
Body of European Regulators for Electronic
        Communications (BEREC) 395
Boldrin, M. 502
border controls 600-1
    external border management 620-1
    labor market integration 602-4
    Schengen Agreement 600-1
    TCN immigration 605-7
Bosman case 577, 579
Bot, B. 637
"bottom-up" approach 49-50
    role in policy coordination 804
Bourdieu, P. 53-4, 56
Bouzas, R. 782

bovine spongiform encephalopathy (BSE), repercussions 488
Boyer, M. 812
Brandt, W. 235, 236
cooperation with Pompidou 234
Bretherton, R. 97–8
Bretton Woods system 287
cessation 203, 455, 456
Brinegar, A. 721
Britain see United Kingdom
British Budgetary Question (BBQ) 211, 224
Broad Economic Policy Guidelines (BEPG) 474
Brubaker, R. 56
Brücker, H. 603, 609n12
Brunell, T. 25, 358
Brussels Treaty 585
budgetary cycle 703, 706
budgetary process 381
role of ECA 382–3
budgetary stabilizers, CAP 487
Buet directive 536
Bulgaria
GDP per head, 2007 280
regional disparities 281
growth, 1995–2005 282
net migration 603
Bulmer, S. 705
burden-sharing 810–11
inequalities 811–12
mechanisms 813–14
motivations 812–13
refugee protection 815
common policy approach 817–18, 819–20
criticisms and proposals for reform 819–20
funding 818–19, 820
implicit trade model 820
people sharing 816–17, 823n18
bureaucratic drift 396, 402n12
bureaucratized decision-making, impact on integration 778
Burley, A-M. 26, 358
on European Court of Justice 358

Caja de Ahorros directive 536
Callaghan, J. 210

Canada, asylum burden 815
Canova, F. 502
capability approach, social policy 547
"capacity" principle 814
capital, Bourdieusian 53
capitalist diversity 293, 302–3
and consolidation of internal market 298–302
role in EEC foundation 293–5
role in EEC reforms 295–8
Caporaso, J. 413, 664, 697
Carbon Capture and Storage (CCS) 563
carbon performance 561–2
carbon prices 556
carbon taxes 561, 562
Cardiff Strategy 512
Carey, S. 722
Caribbean Community 783
Carrubba, C.J. 26
cartels, competition policy 446
categorization of rights 734
Catholic beliefs 848
causality problems 688n10
policy impact evaluation 680
Cecchini report, 1998 114–15
Cedefop (European Centre for the Development of Vocational Training) 394
CEN (European Committee for Standardization) 528
CENELEC (European Committee for Electrotechnical Standardization) 528
Central American Common Market (CACM) 782, 783
Central and Eastern European Countries (CEECs)
environmental policy implementation 518–19
negotiations for EU membership 40
opposition to ECEP 520–1
Central Intelligence Agency (CIA)
intelligence cooperation 638
secret prisons 635, 636–7
CEPOL (European Police College) 622
Cerutti, F. 665
CGS (Council Secretariat) 328–9
Chad, ESDP intervention 590–1, 592–3

Changing Scales, ERT 1985 113

Charter of Fundamental Rights 544

Chirac, J.

   Amsterdam Treaty negotiations 137

   on Iraq War 637

   Nice Treaty negotiations 152, 153, 154

   views on Santer 241

Christian Democrats, transnational network 85

Christianity, religious divisions 698

Citizens' Agenda 547

citizens' initiative right 168

citizenship 699

citizenship rights 125–6, 601, 604–5, 608n5,

      610n22, 611n23, 739

   impact of Lisbon Treaty 167–8

   provisions of Amsterdam Treaty 138–40, 144

   see also rights

civil justice cooperation 624

civil liberties, conflict with intelligence

      interests 638–9

civil service, Santer's influence 243

Civilian Crisis Management (CCM) 315, 589

   evaluation 591–2

clans, Council 325–6, 333n30

class divisions in support for Europe 692, 695

climate change

   energy policy 561–4, 567

   environmental policy 519–21

Club of Berne 632–3

coal, electricity generation 563

coalition patterns 250–1

coalitions 249–50, 842

   Convention 260–1

   coordination issues 796

   in Council of Ministers, differences

      between old and new member

      states 273

Cockfield White Paper 113, 115

co-decision procedure (ordinary legislative

      procedure) 128–9, 329, 342, 371, 668

   CAP legislation 491

   environmental policy 515

   impact on Commission 346n1

   inter-institutional effects 707

co-determination, Germany 300

coding rules, Council 326

cohabitation, French government 152

cohesion, party groups 368

cohesion funds 126, 496, 498

   Sapir Report, 2003 503

   see also regional aid

cohesion policy *see* regional policy

Cold War, influence on European

      integration 6

collective action, *Viking* and *Laval*

      cases 549–50

collective agreements 545, 552n17, 552n20,

      553n20

collective compensation 539

collective leadership 307

collective public goods, burden-sharing

      811–12, 822, 824n40

Collective Redundancies Directive 546–7, 548

College of Commissioners 220–1, 337–8

   changes over time 226, 229n8

   impact of enlargement 273

condominio 64

comitology committees 396, 398

Commission 336–7

   accountability and transparency 670–1

   approval by European Parliament 340–1, 372

   autonomous operation 65

   balance of power 252

   bureaucratic drift 396

   championing of liberal models 302–3

   changes over time 227–8

   community action programs 752

   competences 345

   competition policy 441–2

   composition 253, 256, 264

   coordination issues 797–8, 800–1, 802, 805

   crisis, 1999 151–2

   EEC 103, 105

   environmental policy 512, 513

   functions 337

      expansion of 297

   impact of conciliation procedure 346n1

   impact on European integration 345, 346

   impact on policy-making 341

      effect of Luxembourg Compromise 343

      governance principles 343

      guardianship of Treaty 342–3

      legislative issues 341–2

      single market program 343–4

theoretical perspectives 344-5
involvement, differences between old and
    new member states 273
neo-functionalist theory 23, 25, 26-7, 28
OLAF (European Anti-Fraud
    Office) 386-7
organizational change 339-40
organizational make-up
    College 337-8
    Directorates General and Services 338
output legitimacy 665
policy evaluation 682-3
policy-initiating role 224
powers 661
resignation, 1999 243-4
role in Amsterdam Treaty negotiations 138
role in cohesion policy 500
role in consumer law 527
    development 528-9, 531-2
    enforcement 534-5
role in creation of agencies 395, 396,
    397-8
role in Nice negotiations 153
role in trade policy-making 428-30
scrutiny institutions 387
size, Nice Summit negotiations 154-5, 156
time rules 706-7
    effects 708
use of legal strategies 354-5
Commission officials, attitudes towards
    integration 338-9
Commission presidency 219, 228-9, 337, 340
    Jacques Delors 224-6
    Walter Hallstein 221-3
    Roy Jenkins 223-4
    comparisons 226-7
    non-performers 233-4, 245
        Franco Malfatti 234-6
        Jacques Santer 240-5
        Gaston Thorn 237-40
    periods of office 706
    powers and responsibilities 220-1, 229n1
    promotion of coordination 802
Commission v. UK 548
Commissioners
    appointment 229n8
    loyalties 801

Committee of Permanent Representatives
    (COREPER) 40, 325
    group consensus norms 323
    promotion of coordination 802-3, 805
Committee of the Regions (CoR) 129, 750
    views on multilevel governance 755
Committee on Budgetary Control 383
committees, European Parliament 370-1
Common Agricultural Policy (CAP) 8, 484,
    491-2
    creation 103, 105
    current policy 489-91
    de Gaulle's negotiation tactics 208
    distinctive features 485-6
    foundations 484-5
    preferences
        differences between old and new
            member states 269-70
        rich versus poor member states 285
    reforms
        contributing factors 486-7
        Fischler Reforms 488-9
        MacSharry Reforms 487
common border system 606
Common European Asylum System
    (CEAS) 606-7, 619
Common Foreign and Security Policy
    (CFSP) 122, 127-8, 132, 270, 630-1,
    643-5
    Amsterdam Treaty 140-1
    conclusions 654-5
    group consensus norms 323
    Lisbon Treaty 166, 650-3
    post-Cold-War era (1991-2009) 647-50
common market 408
common organizations of the market 485
communicative discourses on EU policy 666
    national nature 668
community action programs 752
community building 35-6
Community Fisheries Control Agency
    (CFCA) 394
Community Lisbon Program 477
"Community Method" 121, 670
Community Plant Variety Office (CPVO) 394
Community Support Frameworks 500
comparative development, EU regions 496

comparative regional integration 777
  contractual choices 785–6
    consequences 787–9
    explanatory factors 786–7
  externality theory 780
    external logic of regional
      integration 783–5
    internal logic 780–2
  neo-functionalist framework 778–80
  outcomes of major integration
    schemes 782, 783
  summary of theories 789–90
competence creep 574, 579, 580
competences
  broadening 574
  governing rules 574–5
    institutional context 579–80
    legislative competences 575–6
    trade law 576–7
  impact of Lisbon Treaty 167
  nature and scope 571–4
  principle of conferral 570–1
  principles of the order of
    competences 766–7, 774n50
  provisions of SEA 116–17
  social policy field 545
  subsidiarity and proportionality
    principles 577–9
competition law 359
  administration by Commission 342
  development 442
competition policy 441–2
  governance 445–8
  relationship between state and
    market 443–5
competitiveness
  Europe 2020 Strategy 480
  Lisbon Strategy 471–3
  performance 478
Competitiveness Council 475
complementarities 474
complete contracts 785–6
  consequences 788–9
  explanatory factors 786–7
Completing the Internal Market (Commission,
  1985) 559
compliance 836

  mediating factors 830–1
composite (*Verbund*) perspective 768–9
  loyalty principle 770–1
  structural compatibility 769–70
concentration principle, Delors I
  package 498
conciliation committees 342
confederal consociation 64
Confederation of Socialist Parties of the
  European Community (CSP) 369
Conference on Security and Cooperation in
  Europe (CSCE) 647
conferral, principle of 570–1, 573, 574
Confidence Pact on Employment 242
Congo, Democratic Republic of, ESDP
  intervention 591, 594
consensus-seeking, Council 322–4
conservative parties, stance on
  integration 843
Constitution of Europe 685
constitutional constraints 570
  broadening of competences 574
  nature and scope of competences
    571–4
  principle of conferral 570–1
  rules governing competences 574–5
    institutional context 579–80
    legislative competences 575–6
    trade law 576–7
  subsidiarity and proportionality
    principles 577–9
Constitutional Convention 671
constitutional homogeneity 769–70
constitutional pluralism 747n29
Constitutional Treaty 697
  negotiations 163–4
    coalitions, interests and power
      politics 260–1
    small versus big divide 262–3, 264
  procedures and personalities 172
  ratification failure 164–5
  referendums 692, 844, 851n32
constrained discretion, EMU 458
constraining dissensus 716, 849
constructive abstention 141, 144
constructivism 34–5, 42–3
  ideas and integration preferences 37–9

ideational effects on integration
      outcomes 39–40
interpretation of ESDP 593
on origins of single market 412
and sociological approach 50–1, 54
theory 35–7
constructivist institutionalism, perspective on
      Europeanization 828, 829–30, 831
consultation procedure 341–2
consumer law 526
   challenges
      enforcement 538–9
      risk of social exclusion 537–8
      vulnerable consumers 538
   current stage
      enforcement 534–5
      harmonization 536–7
      paradigm shift 530–1
      Private Law codification project 531–2
      role of European Court of Justice 535–6
      weaknesses: services and safety 533–4
   development 527
      impact of internal market
         regime 529–30
      role of Commission 528–9
      role of SEA 527–8
Contact Committee of the Supreme Audit
      Institutions of the European
      Union 383
contracting theory 785–6, 789, 790
   consequences of contract choices 787–9
   explanatory factors 786–7
Convention 163–4, 264
   coalitions, interests and power
      politics 260–1
   Constitutional Treaty negotiations 163–4,
      172, 175n2
   small versus big divide 262–3
Convention on Long-Range Transboundary
      Pollution 568n9
convergence 280, 283
   Barca Report, 2009 504
   impact of regional policy 502
   regional policy 499
convergence criteria, EMU 124
convergence fund 503
Cooley, A. 785–9

cooperation, party groups 368
cooperation procedure 116, 342
coordinated market models 294
   and market liberalization 297
coordination
   in Brussels 799–800
      facilitating factors 802–4
      inhibiting factors 800–2
   challenges 795–6
   conclusions 806
   EU as a special case 797–8
   Europe 2020 Strategy 479–80
   interacting factors 804–5
   Lisbon Strategy 473–4
   national level
      aspirations 798
      structures 798–9
   negative consequences 805–6
   OMC 474–5
Coordination Dilemma 781
Copsey, N. 268
corporatism 294
cost harmonization, as justification for social
      policy 548–9
"cost" principle 814
Costa v. E.N.E.L. ruling, 1964 353, 359
cost–benefit analyses, relationship to public
      support for integration 721
Council of Europe, intelligence inquiries 636
Council of Ministers (Council of the European
      Union) 104, 321, 321–2, 330–1, 727
   coalition building, differences between old
      and new member states 272–3
   co-decision rights for regions 750–1
   defense of euro 460
   evolving institutions
      Council Presidency 327–8
      effects of enlargement 329–30
      European Council 327
      negotiation methods 325–7
      Secretariat 328–9
      shared legislative culture 329
   interaction with European Parliament 371
   joint decision-making 322–4
   role in creation of agencies 395, 396, 398
   role in trade policy-making 427–8, 429–30
   transparency 686

Council presidency 257, 265, 327–8
    period of office 705–6
Council Secretariat, role in Nice
        negotiations 153
Counter Terrorist Group (CTG) 633
counter-terrorism 631–2, 638
countryside preservation, CAP 485
Court of Auditors (ECA) 380
Court of First Instance (CFI) 107, 357
    origins 116
Court of Justice of the European Union
        (CJEU)
    cooperation with national courts 764–5
    effectiveness principle 762–4
    rule of law principle 762
    see also European Court of Justice (ECJ)
Cowen, B. 261
credibility 831, 833
Cresson, E. 244
Creswell, M. 83
criminal matters
    judicial cooperation 623–4
    police cooperation 622
crisis vulnerability, poor member
        states 286–9
Croatia, GDP per head, 2007, regional
        disparities 281
Crocodile Club 109
cross-border transactors, neo-functionalist
        theory 21–2, 25, 26
cue-taking, as explanation of public
        support 720, 721–2
cultural diversity 842
current account balances
    correlation with GDP 287–8
    negative correlation with rapid
        growth 288, 289
customs union 408, 409, 423
cycles 709
    asynchrony 705–6
    budgetary 703, 706
    policy cycle 677–9
Cyprus
    asylum burden 816
    GDP per head, 2007 280, 281
    growth, 1995–2005 282
    net migration 603

Czech Republic
    attitudes towards further enlargements 271
    GDP per head, 2007 280
        regional disparities 281
    growth, 1995–2005 282
    net migration 603
    referendum 725

dairy quotas 487
Danish Bottle Case 514
DAS (statement of assurance) 382
data, sharing with US 638–9
data protection 743
    EDPS 380, 381, 384–6, 387–9
data surveillance 630, 639
Davignon, E. 233, 237
    ESPRIT 112, 239–40
    resentment of Thorn 238–9
de Gasperi, A. 181, 187, 188, 189
de Gaulle, C. 206
    commitment to EEC 207
    critique of EDC 206–7
    "empty chair crisis," 1965 208
    on Hallstein 230n19
    influence on integration process 209–10,
        215–16
    opposition to British EEC
        membership 208, 209
de Groot, S. 502–3
de Vries, C. 727, 847–8
de Vries, G. 632
decentralization 67, 68
decision-making 67
    time pressures 711
    time rules 704
    transparency 684, 685, 686
decision-making style, impact on regional
        integration 778, 779
defense, provisions of Amsterdam Treaty 141,
        147n30
defense policy 585, 648
    Franco–German cooperation 199–200
    influence of Nordic countries 315
    Lisbon Treaty 170
    Maastricht Treaty 127–8
    Pléven Plan 186

preferences, differences between old and new member states 270–1
sociological perspectives 54–5
see also European Security and Defense Policy
defense spending 592–3
burden-sharing 811–12
defensive realism 5, 7
Defrenne cases 543–4
Dehaene, J.-L. 240–1
Dekker, W., "Europe 1990" plan 113
delegation, principal–agent accounts 12–13
Delgado, J. 414
Delors, J. 107, 113, 114, 115, 802
Commission presidency 52, 224–6, 226–8, 231n33
Delors Committee 122, 131
Delors I package 498
Delors Report, 1989 456
demand-side conditions of integration 780
Demir and Baykara case 550
democracy 661–2, 728
consequences of single market 415–16
elections to European Parliament 723–4
input legitimacy 667–9
legitimizing mechanisms 662–4
output legitimacy 664–7
pro tempore power-giving 704
referendums 724, 725–6, 726
throughput legitimacy 669–72
democratic accountability, risk of multilevel governance 71–2
democratic deficit 173, 191, 664
politicization as solution 669
role of EMU 466
democratization, influence of EU 835–6
demographic shift 602, 609n10
Denmark
Council presidency, leadership 314
GDP per head, 2007 *280*
regional disparities *281*
growth, 1995–2005 *282*
net migration *603*
opt-out of EMU 124
ratification of Maastricht Treaty 129–30
referendums 725
resistance to EMU 299
descriptive approach to rights 734, 735

Deutsch, K. 34, 36, 49, 691–3
developing countries, trade initiatives 423
Dewan, T. 820
di Pinto directive 535
differentiation 309–10, 414, 454–5, 833
categorization 310–11
implications for leadership 312
role of EMU 466
temporal 712
diffuse reciprocity 427
diffuse support for integration *see* affective support for integration
Dinkel, J. 782
Directorates General 338
coordination issues 800, 806
Environment 512, 513
disadvantaged groups 740–1
discharge procedure 382
discontinuity of policy-making 708–9
discrimination, rights issues 741, 744–5, 747n19
discrimination legislation, provisions of Amsterdam Treaty 139
discriminatory trade policies, role in integration 783–4
distributive policy preferences, differences between old and new member states 269–70
"D-Mark Zone" 457
Doc Morris directive 536
Dooge Committee 109
"double hatting," Council members 321
double majority voting system 253
Downes, T.A. 741
Draft Common Frame of Reference (DCFR) 531
Draft Treaty on the European Union (EUT), 1984 109
drug-trafficking, judicial cooperation 623
Dublin Convention 608n3, 817–18, 820
Dublin Regulation, 2003 619
Duchêne, F. 79
Dulles, J.F., influence on Treaties of Rome 101
dumping 412, 423, 425
anti-dumping measures 428
provisions of CAP 485

Dür, A. 431
Dyson, K. 836

"early agreements" 707, 711–12
Eastern Partnership 271–2
Easton, D. 663
Echelon, accountability 635
ECOFIN (Council of Economics and Finance
    Ministers) 125
ecological modernization 513
Economic and Monetary Union (EMU) 453
    asymmetric shock vulnerability 457–8
    central banking 456
    foundations 455–6
    impact of banking crisis 453–4
    impact of enlargement 454–5
    impact on political union 464
    impact on regional policy 497–8
    institutional arrangements
        asymmetry 458–60
        "fuzzy" boundaries 459–60
        Optimum Currency Area (OCA)
            theories 457
        path dependence 457
    performance and impact 464
        ECB 461–2
        economic crisis risk 461
        EFSF/ESM 460–1
        trade effects 462–3
    public opinion 465–6
    role in democratic deficit 466
    role in differentiation 466
    role of labor mobility 603–4
Economic Community of West African
    States 783
Economic Cooperation Act 408
economic coordination
    Europe 2020 Strategy 479–80
    Lisbon Strategy 473–4
        performance 478–9
economic crisis 69, 460, 798
    impact on regional policy 504–5
    implications for EMU 453–4
    performance of ECB 462
    state aid 445
economic crisis risk, impact of EMU 461

economic efficiency doctrine 530–1
economic geography, impact of single
    market 416–17
economic policy, evaluation 683
economic regionalism 417
economic success, relationship to
    integration 781
Ederveen, S., on impact of regional
    policy 502–3
EDF, mergers 560
Edwards, E. 847–8
effectiveness principle, Union law 762–4
efficiency promoting function of EU 664
Eisenhower, D.D., influence on Treaties of
    Rome 100–1
Eising, R. 72
elections to European Parliament 366–7,
    723–4
electoral cycle 709
electricity supply, national policies 558
Elgström, O. 328
Elysée Treaty 195–6, 313
emerging federation 64
emissions targets 562–3
Emissions Trading System (ETS) 520
employment
    agricultural 495n73
    Confidence Pact on Employment 242
    impact of Lisbon Strategy 477
    provisions of Amsterdam Treaty 139
    see also labor market regulation;
        unemployment
"empty chair crisis," 1965 208, 234, 343
emulation, role in Europeanization 832–3
endogenous growth theory 502
energy policy 556–7
    climate change policy 561–4
    early measures 557–8
    future prospects 566–7
    internal market 559–61
    security of supply 564–6
energy services, consumer law 533
enhanced cooperation 151, 309
enlargement
    1973 237
    capitalist diversity 301
    Central and Eastern 242

effects 845
  impact on CAP 486–7
  impact on Commission 339–40, 342–3
  impact on Council 329–30
  impact on European Court of Justice 351
  impact on Franco–German
    cooperation 203
  impact on intelligence "clubs" 634
  impact on party groups 368
  impact on regional policy 497–8
  impact on trade policy 425, 427
  implications for EMU 454–5
  environmental policy implementation 517,
    518–19
  as a foreign policy tool 647–8
  ideational effects on negotiations 40
  new member states 267
  Nice Treaty 149, 152
  preferences, differences between old and
    new member states 271–2
  role in differentiation 309
  role of Delors 225
  Spanish and Portuguese accession 240
  time games 712
  see also old versus new member states
Environmental Action Programs
    (EAPs) 512–13
environmental non-governmental
    organizations (ENGOs) 515–16
  CEE (Central and Eastern European)
    states 519
environmental policy 511
  agents of change 514–16
  burden-sharing 814
  challenges 521–2
  climate change policy 561–4
  evolution 512–13
  impact 516
  impact assessment 681
  impact of enlargement 518–19
  implementation 516–18
  international negotiations 519–21
  provisions of Maastricht Treaty 126–7
  provisions of SEA 117
E.ON, mergers 560
epistemes 449n16
  competition policy 447

equal opportunities, provisions of
    Amsterdam Treaty 139
equal pay, Defrenne cases 543–4
equality, relationship to rights 740–1
equity, doctrine of 743
error detection, audit 382
Estonia
  GDP per head, 2007 280
    regional disparities 281
  growth, 1995–2005 282
  net migration 603
  referendum 725
ethnic assimilation 692
ethnicity, identity issues 697–9
EU Agency for the Cooperation of Energy
    Regulators (ACER) 395
Euratom (European Community in Atomic
    Energy) Treaty 95, 101–2, 558
  influence of United States 100–1
  Messina conference 96–7
  Spaak report 99
    responses 99
  see also Treaties of Rome
EUREMA (EU Relocation Malta) project 817
euro, effect on JHA domain 617
Euro crisis 806
Euro Group 458–9
Euro Payment and Settlement Scheme
    (TARGET) 459
Eurobarometer surveys 718, 719, 722,
    730n11, 847
Euroclash, N. Fligstein 52
EURODAC 619
EUROJUST 618, 623–4
euromissiles crisis 199
Europe 2020 Strategy 471, 479–80
"Europe of the Regions" paradox 754
European Agency for Fundamental Rights
    (FRA) 394
European Agency for Safety and Health at
    Work (EU OSHA) 394
European Agency for the Management of
    Operational Cooperation at the
    External Borders (FRONTEX) 394,
    606, 618, 621
European Agricultural Fund for Rural
    Development (EAFRD) 489

European Agricultural Guarantee and
    Guidance Fund (EAGGF) 497
European Anti-Fraud Office (OLAF) 380,
    381, 386–7
  significance 387–9
European Arrest Warrant 623
European Asylum Support Office
    (EASO) 395, 619
European Aviation Safety Agency
    (EASA) 394
  transparency and accountability 399
European Banking Authority (EBA) 394
European Central Bank (ECB) 124–5, 299,
    456, 458
  autonomy 661–2
  performance 461–2
  periods of office 706
European Centre for the Development of
    Vocational Training (Cedefop) 394
European Centre for Disease Prevention and
    Control (ECDC) 394
European Chemicals Agency (ECHA) 394
European Climate and Energy Package
    (ECEP) 519, 520–1
European Coal and Steel Community
    (ECSC), founding fathers
  Jean Monnet 183–5
  Robert Schuman 185
European Coal and Steel Community (ECSC)
    Treaty 79, 90, 497, 558
  choice of institutions 88–90
  fault lines in literature 80
  link to EEC 190–1
  material versus ideational views 82–5
  negotiation methods 191
  negotiations and ratification 85–8
  state-centric perspectives 81
  transnational perspectives 81–2
European Commission see Commission
European Committee for Electrotechnical
    Standardization (CENELEC) 528
European Committee for Standardization
    (CEN) 528
European Community Food Law 488
European Competition Network (ECN)
    446, 447
European constitutional settlement 173

European consumer concept 529–30,
    535–6, 537
European Convention of Human Rights 737
European Council 321, 327
  formation 237
  Franco–German cooperation 197–8
  impact of Lisbon Treaty 168–9
  origins 116
  timescape 706
European Court of Auditors (ECA) 380,
    381–3
  significance 387–9
European Court of Human Rights (ECHR),
    Demir and Baykara case 550
European Court of Justice (ECJ) 103–4, 121,
    351, 361
  autonomy 65, 662
  clashes of capitalism 303
  constitutionalization of Treaties 352–4
  creation 89
  expansion of scope 297
  explanation of role 357–9
  institutionalization of human rights 40
  involvement, differences between old and
      new member states 274–5
  juridification of political sphere 354–7
  market-building 359–60
  neo-functionalist theory 22–3, 25, 26–7, 28
  output legitimacy 665
  periods of office 706
  provisions of Maastricht Treaty 129
  review of agencies 395
  on rights 741, 744
  role in CAP enforcement 485, 487–8,
      490, 491
  role in consumer law 535–6
  role in development of environmental
      policy 514
  role in enforcement of trade
      liberalization 410–11
  role in social integration 360–1, 364n54
  role in social policy development 543–4
  structure and functions 351–2
  Van Gend en Loos judgment 105
European Currency Unit (ECU) 116, 124
European Data Protection Supervisor
    (EDPS) 380, 381, 384–6

significance 387–9
European Defense Agency (EDA) 170, *394*
European Defense Community (EDC) 643
  de Gaulle's dislike 206–7
  founding fathers 186–9
European Defense Community (EDC)
     Treaty 79–80, 90, 585
  choice of institutions 88–90
  fault lines in literature 80
  material versus ideational views 82–5
  negotiations 85–6, 191
  ratification failure 86, 96
  state-centric perspectives 81
  transnational perspectives 81–2
European Dilemma, A, C.-U Schierup 607
European Economic Community (EEC)
  capitalist diversity 294
  founding fathers 189–90
  growth 295
  link to ECSC 190–1
  social policy 294–5
European Economic Community (EEC)
     reforms, role of capitalist
     diversity 295–8
European Economic Community (EEC)
     Treaty 95, 292
  influence of United States 100–1
  institutional structure 103–4
  legal issues 105
  Messina conference 96–7
  negotiation methods 191
  objectives 102–3
  significance 104–5
  Social Policy Title 543
  Van Gend end Loos judgement 353
  see also Treaties of Rome
European Election Studies (ESS) project 366,
    374n4
European Employment Strategy
    (Luxembourg process) 474, 545
European Environment Agency (EEA) *394*
  establishment 397
European External Action Service
    (EEAS) 170, 651–3, 654
European Federalist Action movement 191
European Federation of Green Parties
    (EFGP) 369

European Financial Stability Facility
    (EFSF) 460–1, 480
European Food Safety Authority (EFSA) *394*
European Foundation for the Improvement of
    Living and Working Conditions
    (Eurofound) *394*
European Free Trade Association
    (EFTA) 104, 782, *783*, 784
European GNSS Agency (GSA) *394*
European Green Party (EGP) 369
European identity 37, 690, 700
  causal role in integration 691–3
  compatibility with national
    identity 695–7
  as effect of integration 694–5
  implications 699–700
  relationship to institutional
    integration 36
  religion, ethnicity, and
    immigration 697–9
  research approaches 691
European Institute for Gender Equality
    (EIGE) *394*
European Insurance and Occupational
    Pensions Authority (EIOPA) *395*
European Maritime Safety Agency
    (EMSA) *394*
European Medicines Agency (EMA) *394*
European Monetary Institute (EMI) 124
European Monetary System (EMS) 239
  Franco–German cooperation 198–9
  inception 196
European Monetary Union (EMU)
  capitalism clashes 298–9
  explanation 131, 132
  Franco–German cooperation 200–1
  influence of Commission 344
  Maastricht Treaty 121, 124–5
    negotiation 122–3
  role of Delors 225
  Santer's influence 242
  Werner's plan, 1970 235
European Monitoring Centre for Drugs
    and Drug Addiction
    (EMCDDA) *394*
European Network and Information Security
    Agency (ENISA) *394*

European Parliament 365
  accountability 671
  approval of Commission 340–1
  clashes of capitalism 303
  Committee on Budgetary Control 383
  committee work 370–1
  composition 256–7
    evolution *258–9*
  elections 366–7
  German Federal Constitutional Court
      judgement 173
  impact of Lisbon Treaty 168
  influence on EU politics 371–2
  involvement, differences between old and
      new member states 274
  new powers under Maastricht
      Treaty 128–9
  party groups 367–70
  power 845
  provisions of Amsterdam Treaty 141–2
  provisions of Nice Treaty 156–8
    distribution of seats *159*
  provisions of SEA 115–16
  role in creation of agencies 395, 396, 397
  role in origins of SEA 109–10
  selection of Commission president 241
  shared legislative culture 329
  sociological perspectives 55
  time games 707
  transparency 374n2, 671, 686
  use of legal strategies 355
  as watchdog of agencies 398–9
  weakness 661
European People's Party (EPP) 367
European Police College (CEPOL)
    394, 622
European Police Office (Europol) *394*, 618,
    622, 631–2
European Political Cooperation (EPC) 82,
    643, 646–7
  provisions of SEA 117
  role in origins of SEA 110
European Railway Agency (ERA) *394*
European Refugee Fund (ERF) 818–19, 820
European Regional Development Fund
    (ERDF) 497
  effectiveness 503

European Roundtable of Industrialists
    (ERT) 112–14
European Securities and Markets Authority
    (ESMA) *394*
European Security and Defense Policy
    (ESDP) 585, 595–6, 648, 649
  effectiveness 595–6
  evaluation 589–90
    Civilian Crisis Management 591–2
    defense spending 592–3
    military capabilities 591
    security missions 590–1
  evolution
    Civilian Crisis Management 589
    military power 589
    relationship with NATO 588
  influence of Nordic countries 315
  interventions 587–8
  origins 586–7
  sociological perspectives 54–5
  theoretical interpretations
    constructivist 593
    institutionalist approaches 594–5
    realism 594
European Security Strategy (ESS) 649
European Social Fund (ESF) 497
European social model 546
European Stability Mechanism (ESM) 460–1,
    480
European Standards Bodies 528
European Strategic on Research in
    Information Technology (ESPRIT)
    112, 239–40
European System of Central Banks
    (ESCB) 124, 125
European Systemic Risk Board (ESRB) 460
European Training Foundation (ETF) *394*
European Transparency Initiative, 2007 686
European Union (EU), establishment in
    Lisbon Treaty 166
European Union agencies 392–3, 400
  coordination issues 801–2, 806
  creation 395–7, 402n15
  definition 393, 401n7
  development 397–8
    common framework 399
    transparency and accountability 398–9

effectiveness 399
Executive Agencies 401n8
executive and regulatory 393
identification 394–5
summary of agencies 394–5
European Union Emissions Trading Scheme
    (EUETS) 561, 562
European Union Institute for Security Studies
    (ISS) 394
European Union of Federalists, Conference,
    1956 191
European Union Satellite Centre
    (EUSC) 394, 631
European Union's Judicial Cooperation Unit
    (EUROJUST) 394
European Venture Capital Association
    (EVCA) 23
"Europeanism" 696
Europeanization 50, 68, 655, 825–6
    categorization of outcomes 826–7
    conclusions 836–7
    mediating factors 832
        domestic 828–30
        EU-level 830–1
    of politics 836
    of the polity 834–6
    of public policy 833–4
    recipient-driven 831–3
    as response to EU adjustment
        pressures 827–8
Europol 394, 618, 622, 631–2
Eurosclerosis 108, 719
Euro-skeptic parties 41
Euro-skepticism 717, 843, 844, 846
    and national identity 847–8
    related factors 722
    see also public support
eurozone summits 169
EUT (Draft Treaty of the European
    Union) 109
evaluation of policy measures
    definition 676
    in EU 681
        ex post evaluation 682–3
        process-evaluation monitoring 682
    links to transparency 686–7
    policy cycle context 677–8

policy impact evaluation 680
policy outcome evaluation 679–80
policy output evaluation 679
policy termination 680–1
problem definition and agenda
    setting 678–9
transparency 677, 684
Everything But Arms initiative 423
ex ante policy evaluations (impact
    assessments) 681
ex post policy evaluations 682–3
exchange rate mechanism (ERM) 456
    Thatcher's views 213
exchange rates, EMU convergence
    criteria 124
exclusionary conduct 447
exclusive competence 573
executive agencies 393, 401n8
    see also European Union agencies
expected consequences, logic of 812–13
explicit compensation mechanisms, burden-
    sharing 814
exploitation hypothesis 811–12
external threats, as stimulus to
    integration 779–80
externality theory 780, 789, 790
    external logic of regional
        integration 783–5
    internal logic of regional
        integration 780–2
extraordinary renditions 635

Faber, A. 172
Farrell, H. 707, 711
Faude, B. 782
Favell, A. 51, 55
federal relationship 761, 772n2, 773n24
federal systems, coordination problems 796,
    798–9
federalist movements 82, 181–2, 191
feedback loops
    ECJ as source 27
    role in integration 20, 21–2
fields, Bourdieusian 53
fields of action 52–3
finance, sources 284–5

financial crisis *see* economic crisis
financial market supervision 460
financial perspectives 499–500
  unanimity 506n13
financial reforms, Santer's influence 243
financial risk 382, 387
financial stability, "fuzzy" boundaries 459
financial vulnerability, poor member
    states 286–9
Finke, D. 172
Finland
  asylum burden *816*
  GDP per head, 2007 *280*
    regional disparities *281*
  growth, 1995–2005 *282*
  net migration *603*
  referendum *725*
firms, impact of single market 416
first integrative response 784
fiscal federalism 68
fiscal policy 125
  constraints 288–9
fiscal surveillance, external imbalances 287
Fischer, J. 173–4
Fischler, F., CAP reforms 488–9
Fleischer, J. 87
"flexibility clause" 756
flexible integration, Amsterdam Treaty 142–3
flexicurity 547–8
Fligstein, N. 25, 51–2, 412, 847
"floor of rights" objective 549
followers, definition 307
Fontainebleau summit, 1984 211
food safety agency 802
food safety legislation 488
football transfer system, *Bosman* case
    577, 579
forced migration, burden-sharing 819, 820,
    823n15
foreign aid, burden-sharing 812
foreign direct investment (FDI) 409, 411
foreign policy 644
  coalition patterns 250–1
  EPC (European Political
      Cooperation) 646–7
  functions 645
  multilevel governance 68

preferences, differences between old and
    new member states 270–1
provisions of Amsterdam Treaty
    140–1, 144
provisions of Lisbon Treaty 170
see also Common Foreign and Security
    Policy
Fortress Europe 620
  as trigger for integration projects 784
Fouchet Plan, 196` 207
founding fathers
  European Coal and Steel Community
    Jean Monnet 183–5
    Robert Schuman 185
  European Defense Community 186–9
  European Economic Community 189–90
  influences 181
  negotiation methods 191
  political experience 182
  political ideology 181–2
  political intentions 190
four freedoms 543
France
  asylum burden *815*
  attitudes towards further enlargements 271
  Constitutional Treaty rejection 165
  convergence towards liberal model 300
  foreign and defense policy 270
  GDP per head, 2007 *280*
    regional disparities *281*
  growth, 1995–2005 *282*
  negotiation position, Treaties of Paris 86, 87
  net migration *603*
  post-war security threats 82–3
  presidency during Nice Treaty
      negotiations 152, 153, 154
  ratification of Maastricht Treaty 130
  referendums *725, 726*, 844, 851n32
  response to Spaak report 99
  views on CAP 270
  vote allocation, Nice Treaty 157
Franco–German brigade 200
Franco–German cooperation 193, 202–3
  De Gaulle and Adenauer 207
  Elysée Treaty 195–6
  European and international
      context 196–202

leadership 312–13
   personal aspects 194–5
   Pompidou and Brandt 234
   selection of Commission president 240–1
Franklin, M. 727
Frattini, F. 637
fraud prevention, OLAF (European Anti-
     Fraud Office) 380, 381, 386–7, 387–9
free market
   preferences, differences between old and
     new member states 269
free pursuit of interests principle 768
free trade agreements 412
Freedom, Security and Justice, policy
     evaluation 682–3
freedom of movement 359, 576–7
   Amsterdam Treaty 139–40
   EEC Treaty 102
   Maastricht Treaty 125
   see also border controls
freeriding 811
   Prisoners' Dilemma 781
Freiberger Kommunalbauten directive 536
French colonies, provisions of EEC
     Treaty 103
FRONTEX 394, 606, 618, 621
functional rational design approach,
     institutional structure 88–9
functions of EU, member-states'
     visions 666–7
fundamental rights 739–40, 746n1, 747n9
"fuzzy" boundaries, EMU 459–60

Gabel, M. 370
Gaillard, F. 97
gal (green/alternative/libertarian)
     stance 843–4, *848*
Garrett, G. 26, 27, 28
gas
   dependency 563–4
   security of supply 564–6
Gazprom 565
General Agreement on Trade and Tariffs
     (GATT) 424
Genscher–Colombo initiative 110, 239
Georgakakis, D. 55

German Länder 750
   impact of Lisbon Treaty 756
Germany
   asylum burden *815*
   attitudes towards further enlargements 271
   co-determination 300
   coordination issues 799
   environmental policy 515
   Federal Constitutional Court, Lisbon
     Treaty judgement 167, 173
   GDP per head, 2007 *280*
     regional disparities *281*
   Green Party 515
   negotiation position, Treaties of Paris
     86, 87
   net migration *603*
   perceived security threat to France 82–3
   political timescape 709
   post-war rehabilitation 182–3
     ECSC 183–5
   rearmament 79, 186
   response to Schuman Plan 83, 84, 86
   response to Spaak report 99
   reunification 122
     impact on Franco–German
       cooperation 201–2, 203, 205n27
     implications 149–50, 151
     role in defense policy 586
     Thatcher's views 213
   stance on CAP 285
   unification, implications 157
   vote allocation, Nice Treaty 157
   see also Franco–German cooperation
Gillingham, J. 86
Giscard d'Estaing, V. 237
   Constitutional Treaty negotiations 163,
     164, 172
   Convention presidency 260–1
   cooperation with Helmut Schmidt
     202–3
     Elysée Treaty 196
     European Council 197–8
     monetary cooperation 198–9
     personal aspects 194, 195
   dispute with Jenkins 223
   response to Margaret Thatcher 211
   and Thorn's Commission presidency 238

global regulation, influence of clashes of
    capitalism 303
globalization 299, 412, 424
    attitudes, differences between old and new
        member states 269
    impact on CAP 487
    implications for European integration 19
    international orientation 529
    and multilevel governance 66
Globalization Adjustment Fund 503
goals, policy impact evaluation 680
Goetz, K.H. 835, 836
Gonzales doctrine 528–9, 534, 535
governance 66, 661
    of competition 445–8
    EMU 124
    influence of Commission 343
    single market 413–14, 415–16
    see also multilevel governance
governance dilemma 292–3
    open method coordination 301
governance system, compound nature 662
government debt, EMU convergence criteria 124
government deficit, EMU convergence
        criteria 124
Gradin, A. 243
Great Inflation, impact on EMU 455–6
Greece
    asylum burden *815, 816*
    debt crisis 480–1
    GDP per head, 2007 *280*
        regional disparities *281*
    net migration *603*
Greek crisis 286, 287
green currencies 486
green parties 561
    role in energy policy development 557
    role in environmental policy development 515
greenhouse gas reduction 520
Greenland, referendum *725*
Grieco, J. 7
gross domestic product (GDP) 290n3, 472,
        482n17
    comparison of member countries 279–*80*
    correlation with current account
        balances 287–8
    regional disparities *281*

gross national income (GNI)-based revenue 284
group norms, Council 323–4, 330
group rights 735
growth 280, 281, 283
    1995–2005 *282*
    GDP per head 472, 482n17
    impact of EMU 463
    impact of regional policy 501–2
    Lisbon Strategy 470, 472, 477–8
    rapid, current account deficits 288, 289
Gruber directive 535
GSP Plus initiative 423
Gstöhl, S. 38, 412
Guiraudon, V. 51, 54, 55
gulliver syndrome 253
Guterres, A., Nice Treaty negotiations 153
Gyllenhammar, P., Marshall Plan for Europe 112
Gysbrechts directive 536

Haas, E. 9, 10, 19, 20, 49, 840
    on Council 322
    on integration 778–80
habitus, Bourdieusian 53
Häge, F. 326, 333n34
Hague me 682–3
Hague summit, 1969 234
Hallstein, W., Commission presidency 108,
        221–3, 226–8
    de Gaulle's views 230n19
Hansen, R. 611n23
Hanson, B. 411
harmonization
    consumer law 530, 531, 536–7
    legislative competences 575–6
    of rights 735, 744, 746n7
Hatton, T.J. 612n36
Haughton, T. 268
Hayward, J. 308, 316
Headline Goal (HG), 2010 589
health and safety, consumer law 528, 533–4
health care, cross-border patient
        mobility 576, 577
Heisenberg, D. 332n19
Helsinki Headline Goal (HHG) 589
Héritier, A. 707, 711
heroic leadership 308, 316

heterotemporality 705–6, 709
High Authority, ECSC 88–9, 184, 185, 189
High Representative for the CFSP 170
    origins of position 140, 144–5
high-speed society 711
Hill, C. 627, 647
Hilson, C. 741
historical approach to rights 734–5
Hitchcock, W. 82–3
Hix, S. 323, 368, 370, 669
Hobolt, S.B. 367, 726
Hoffmann, S 9
Hohfeld, W.N. 741–3
home bias 414
homogeneity, constitutional 769–70
Hooghe, L. 41, 43, 836
    on MLG 64, 65, 67, 70, 72
    on multilevel governance 500–1
    on origins of single market 413
    Postfunctionalist Theory 723
    on referendums 724
Hoon, G. 588
horizontal coordination 805
Howe, G. 213
HR/VP 651–3, 654
human rights 736–7, 739–40
    impact of Lisbon Treaty 167
    parliamentarization and
        institutionalization 40
    see also rights
humanitarian missions, realist perspective 8
humdrum leadership 308
    policy-making 314–15
Hungary
    and CAP 285
    GDP per head, 2007 280
        regional disparities 281
    growth, 1995–2005 282
    net migration 603
    referendum 725
Hyde-Price, A. 8–9
hypocrisy, problem of 8

Idealservice directive 535
ideas and discourses, role in
        constructivism 35, 37

ideational coordination methods 797
ideational factors
    effect on integration outcomes 39–40, 42
    role in European integration 37–9, 42, 85
identity 690, 847–8
    causal role in European integration 691–3
    as effect of European integration 694–5
    implications 699–700
    influence on public support 720, 722–3
    measurement 692, 693
    multilevel structure 695–7
    relationship to European integration 42–3
    religion, ethnicity, and
        immigration 697–9
    research approaches 691
    value coherence 697
    see also national identities
identity building 666
illegal immigrants database 385
illegal immigration 617, 620
Imig, D. 841
immigration 601
    identity issues 697–9
    illegal 617, 620
    as solution to demographic shift 602,
        609n10
    third-country nationals 605–7
    see also migration
immigration policy 620
    sociological perspectives 54
immunities, Hohfeld's concept 742
Impact Assessment Board 387
impact assessments 681
    role in transparency 685–6
implementation of policies
    failures, environmental policy 516–17
    multilevel governance 67
    process-evaluation monitoring 682
    transparency 686
implicit trading mechanisms, burden-
        sharing 814, 820–1
in camera negotiation, Council 325–7, 330
incentives to Europeanization 830–1
incomplete contracts 785
    consequences 787–8
    explanatory factors 787
incrementalism 779

inflation rate
    EMU convergence criteria 124
    performance of ECB 461–2
information society, Lisbon Strategy 469
infrastructure, regional aid 497
infringement procedure 352
Inglehart, R. 693, 694, 694–5
    on public support for integration 718–19
initiation stage, policy-making 67
initiative right, provision of Lisbon
        Treaty 168
input legitimacy 662–3, 667–9
institutional choice, liberal
        intergovernmentalism 11
institutional design
    preferences, differences between old and
        new member states 268–9
institutional involvement, differences
        between old and new member
        states 272
    Commission, European Parliament and
        ECJ 273–5
    Council of Ministers 272–3
    transposition of EU law 275
institutional plateau, Lisbon Treaty 173
institutional rule trajectory 7
institutional structure
    EEC 103–4
    impact of Lisbon Treaty 166–7
    provisions of Amsterdam Treaty
        141–2, 144
    provisions of Maastricht Treaty 128–9
    provisions of SEA 115–16
    as source of coordination problems 796
    Treaties of Paris 88–90
institutionalist approaches, interpretation of
        ESDP 594–5
institutionalization, neo-functionalist
        theory 24
insulation, Council 325–6, 330
integrated approach, impact assessment 681
Integrated Guidelines for Growth and Jobs,
        Lisbon Strategy 476, 477, 478,
        479–80, 483n44
Integrated Mediterranean Program 225
integration, comparative see comparative
        regional integration

integration outcomes, ideational factors
        39–40, 42
integration preferences, ideational
        nature 37–9
integration theories 3–4, 13–14
    constructivism 34–5, 42–3
        ideas and integration preferences 37–9
        ideational effects on integration
            outcomes 39–40
        socialization effects of integration 41–2
        theory 35–7
    intergovernmentalism and liberal
        intergovernmentalism 9–11
    multilevel governance 62–3, 72
        applications 67–9
        comparison with neo-
            functionalism 63
        critiques 69–72
        shift from government to
            governance 66–7
        theoretical project 64–5
    neo-functionalism 27–8
        aims and logic 19–20
        early abandonment 18–19
        empirical hypotheses 24–5
        empirical research 25–7
        updated approach 20–4
    rational-choice institutionalism 11–13
    realism 4–9
    sociological perspectives 48, 57–8
        "bottom-up" approach 49–50
        Bourdieu's work 53–4
        constructivist and interpretative
            approaches 50–1
        distinctiveness 56–7
        Fligstein's work 51–2
        strengths 54–5
integrative responses 784
intelligence 627–8
    distinction from information 628
    EU capabilities 630–2
    European intelligence "clubs" 632–4
    transatlantic cooperation 637–9
intelligence cooperation 629
Intelligence Division of the European
        Military Staff (Intdiv) 631
intelligence management 628

interactive effects, legitimizing
    mechanisms 663–4
interest groups 845
    transparency 686
interest rates
    EMU convergence criteria 124
    performance of ECB 461
intergovernmental bargaining, regional
    policy 499–500
intergovernmental conferences (IGCs)
    negotiation process 137, 145
    role in origins of SEA 111–12
intergovernmental institutions, support of
    small states 251–2
intergovernmentalism 3, 9–11, 17n59, 22, 28,
    34, 840
inter-institutional synchronization 710–11
intermediation processes, throughput
    legitimacy 670, 671
Internal Energy Market Program 559–61, 567
internal logic of regional integration 780–2
internal market
    competition 443
    definition in SEA 410
    impact on consumer law
        development 529–30
    role in origins of JHA domain 615
    see also liberalization of the market
Internal Market Support Committee
    (IMSC) 114
International Energy Agency (IEA) 558
international negotiations, environmental
    policy 519–21
International Political Economy (IPE), and
    trade policy analysis 432–3
interpretivism, and sociological
    approach 50–1
Investigation and Disciplinary Office
    (IDOC) 387
investment diversion, role in integration 784
Iraq war, 2003 7, 649
Ireland
    asylum burden 816
    GDP per head, 2007 280
        regional disparities 281
    growth, 1995–2005 282
    Lisbon Treaty referendums 165–6, 261, 264

net migration 603
Nice Treaty, Seville mandate 159–60
referendums 725, 726
Islam, religious divisions 698
issue linkage, cohesion policy 499–500
Italy
    asylum burden 815
    Commission presidency nomination, 1970
        235
    GDP per head, 2007 280
        regional disparities 281
    growth, 1995–2005 282
    net migration 603
    referendum 725

Jabko, N. 412
Jachtenfuchs, M. 324, 325
Japan
    growth, 1995–2005 282
    multinational companies, investment in
        Europe 411
Jenkins, R., Commission presidency 223–4,
    226–8, 237
Jessop, B. 69
"joint decision trap" 665
Jolly, S. 721
Jordan, A. 69
Jospin, L., Nice Treaty negotiations
    152, 154
judicial cooperation 623–4
    civil matters 624
judicial review 764–5
Juncker, J.C. 245
Justice and Home Affairs (JHA) 122, 132,
    613–14, 624–5
    asylum policy 618–19
    external border management 620–1
    immigration policy 620
    internal security
        judicial cooperation 623–4
        police cooperation 622
    judicial cooperation in civil
        matters 624
    Maastricht Treaty 128
    obstacles and driving factors 616–18
    origins 614–16

Kaczynski, L., deviance from Council
    norms 324
Kagan, R. 8
Kaiser, W. 85
Kauppi, N. 51, 55
Keleman, D.R. 399
Kempton, J. 429
Kerremans, B. 428, 429
Kim, M. 697
Kinnock reform 339
Kinshasa, ESDP intervention 594–5
Kirchhof, P. 769
Kitschelt, H. 721
Klaus, V., Lisbon Treaty ratification 166,
    172–3
Kohl, H. 111, 238
    Amsterdam Treaty negotiations 137, 142
    cooperation with François
        Mitterrand 202–3
        defense policy 199–200
        Elysée Treaty 196
        impact of German reunification 201–2
        monetary cooperation 200–1
        personal aspects 194–5
        political union 200
        selection of Commission
            president 240–1
    on political union 122–3
Kohler-Koch, B. 72
Kok Report, 2005 476
König, T. 172
Krapohl, S. 782
Kreppel, A. 367
Kriesi, H.-P. 668
Krugman, P. 416
Kyoto Protocol 513, 520, 561

labor market flexibility 603
labor market integration 602–4
labor market regulation 542
    evolution 543–6
    future development 551–2
    justifications 546–9
    Viking and Laval cases 549–50
labor utilization and productivity 482n17
Laeken Declaration 587, 685

Lamers, K. 310
Lamfalussy process 460
Large Combustion Plant Directive
    (LCPD) 561
large versus small states problem 249–50,
    264–5
    Convention, coalitions, interests and
        power politics 260–1
    Council presidency, leveling effect 328
    Irish referendums on Lisbon Treaty
        261, 264
    management
        Commission composition 253, 256
        composition of European
            Parliament 256–7, 258–9
        rotating Council presidency 257
        supranational and intergovernmental
            balance 251–2
        weighted votes 252–3
Latin America, regional integration 779
Latin American Free Trade Association
    (LAFTA) 782, 783, 784
Latvia
    GDP per head, 2007 280, 281
    growth, 1995–2005 282
    net migration 603
    referendum 725
Laursen, F. 782
Laval and Partneri case, ECJ 275
Laval case 549–50
Laver, M. 841
law administration, role of Ombudsman 384
Lawson, N. 213
LEADER program 682
leader states, environmental policy 514–15
"leaderless" condition of EU 308
leadership 306, 315–16
    as consequence of differentiation 309–12
    definition 307
    Franco–German cooperation 312–13
    heroic versus humdrum 308
    instability 800–1
    policy leaders 314–15
Leca, J. 666
Leconte, C. 699
left-right conflict 842–4, 848
legal issues

composite (*Verbund*) perspective 768–9
  loyalty principle 770–1
  structural compatibility 769–70
  effectiveness principle 762–4
  principle of comprehensive legal
      protection 764–5
  principle of free pursuit of interests 768
  principles of the order of
      competences 766–7, 774n50
  rule of law principle 761–2
  transposition of EU law, differences
      between old and new member
      states 275
legal norms 743–5
legal order 352–3
legal rights 736
  sources 743–5
  see also rights
legal strategies, use in political process 354–7
legality principle 765–6
legislative competences 571–2
  governing rules 575–6
legislative policy-making, influence of
      Commission 341–2
legislature, Europeanization 835
legitimacy 661–2, 831
legitimizing mechanisms 662–4
  input legitimacy 667–9
  output legitimacy 664–7
  throughput legitimacy 669–72
Legro, J. 6
Lenz, T. 785
Leonardi, R. 502
"level playing field," as justification for social
      policy 548–9
Lewis, J. 40
liberal intergovernmentalism 10–11, 34, 42–3,
      49–50, 723
  interpretation of Treaties of Paris 84–5
  problems 28, 32n52
  views on Commission 336, 344–5
  views on origins of single market 412
liberal model, convergence 299–302
liberalization of the market
  competition policy 443
  consolidation 298–302
  enforcement 410–11

preferences, differences between old and
      new member states 269
  role of capitalist diversity 295–7
  role of European Court of Justice 359–60
  Treaties of Rome 408–9
  see also single market program
liberals, benefits from left–right
      competition 368
Liechtenstein
  asylum burden 816
  referendum 725
"lifeworld" 746, 748n30
Liikanen, E. 243
Lincoln, A. 663
lingual assimilation 692
Linz, J. 704
Lipgens, W. 82
Lisbon Agenda 683
  consumer law 537, 538
Lisbon Strategy 469–71, 843
  competitiveness rationale 471–2
  economic coordination 473–4
  governance and implementation 474–7
  open method coordination 301, 803
  performance 477–9
Lisbon Treaty 132, 301, 327, 334n43, 425
  co-decision procedure 342
  and Commission 227, 228
    composition 256
    presidency 340
  on competition policy 442, 443, 444
  on external action 650, 654
  impact
    on citizens' rights 167–8
    on EU competences 167, 573,
        579–80, 767
    on EU decision-making 168–70
    on EU structure 166–7
    on European and national
        parliaments 168
    on external relations and defense
        policy 170
    provisions for treaty revision 171
    on regional engagement 755–7
  Irish referendums 165–6, 261, 264
  JHA domain 616
  legitimacy problems 671

Lisbon Treaty (*cont.*)
  and nature of EU polity 173–4
  negotiations and ratification 165–6
  Party Article 369
  procedures and personalities 172–3
  provisions for CAP 490
  provisions for data protection 386
  regional policy 499
  on solidarity 810
  voting system reform 253
Lithuania
  alleged CIA secret prisons 637
  attitudes towards further enlargements 271
  GDP per head, 2007 280, 281
  growth, 1995–2005 282
  net migration 603
  referendum 725
living standards disparities 278
London Report, 1981 110
lowest common denominator decisions 64
loyalty principle 770–1
Lubbers, R. 240
Luxembourg
  asylum burden 816
  attitudes towards further enlargements 271
  GDP per head, 2007 281
  growth, 1995–2005 282
  net migration 603
  referendum 726
Luxembourg Compromise 107, 108, 208–9
  impact on Commission 343
Luxembourg process (European Employment
    Strategy) 474
Lynch, F. 84

Maastricht Accord, legitimation process 846
Maastricht Treaty (Treaty on European
    Union) 121–2, 151, 841
  on citizenship 601
  and College term 227
  and Commission 227, 342–3
  competition policy 443, 444
  and differentiation 310
  EMU 124–5
    asymmetry 458
    UK and Danish opt-outs 299

  and European Court of Justice 352, 357
  explanation 130–2
  institutional changes 128–9
  JHA domain 615–16
  liberal intergovernmentalist perspective 11
  main policy changes 125–7
  negotiation 122–3
  new Pillars 127–8
  on political parties 369
  provision for Ombudsman 383
  provisions for further discussion 136, 145n3
  ratification 129–30
  security provisions 586
  significance 132
  social chapter, UK opt-out 299
  social policy, collective agreements 545
  on transparency 685
Macedonia
  ESDP intervention 590
  GDP per head, 2007 281
  support for membership 272
macro-prudential supervision 460
MacSharry, R., CAP reforms 487
"mad cow" disease (BSE), repercussions 488
Majone, G. 345, 413, 664, 665
Major, J., opposition to Dehaene 241
Malfatti, F. 233, 234–6, 245
Malta
  asylum burden 816
    EUREMA project 817
  GDP per head, 2007 280, 281
  growth, 1995–2005 282
  net migration 603
  referendum 725
Manners, I. 8
Mara-Drita, I. 52
market liberalization *see* liberalization of the
    market
Marks, G. 43, 62–3, 65, 836
  on MLG 64, 67, 70, 72
  on multilevel governance 499, 500–1
  on origins of single market 413
  Postfunctionalist Theory 723
  recommendations for treaty reform
    process 174
  on referendums 724
Marks & Spencer case, ECJ 356–7

Martin Report 123
Marty, R. 636
Mattli, W. 26, 358, 780, 789
maximum harmonization 529
    consumer law 530, 531, 536–7
Mayer, R. 190
McCormick, J. 696
McDonagh, R. 137
McLauren, L. 722
Mearsheimer, J. 5, 6
media, communicative discourses on
        EU 666, 668
member state autonomy, safeguards 767
member states, residual rights of control 786
Members of the European Parliament (MEPs)
    constituency activities 373
    elections 366–7, 723–4
    party groups 367–70
    periods of office 706
    see also European Parliament
Mendez, C. 501
Menon, A. 664
Mérand, F. 54, 55, 56–7, 593
Mercado Común del Sur (MERCOSUR) 782, 783
    incomplete contract 789
merger regulation 442, 447, 449n9
mergers, energy companies 560
Merkel, A. 843
    and Lisbon Treaty 165, 172
    proposal of eurozone summits 169
Meroni doctrine 395, 402n10
Messerlin, P. 411–12
Messina conference 96–7
    Spaak report 97–9
Meunier, S. 431
Meyer, C.O. 593
Meyer-Sahling, J.-H. 835
Middle European Conference 633, 634
Middle German Commercial Union 783, 784
migration 278, 601, 602, 603
    citizenship rights 604–5
    labor market integration 602–4
Milan Council, 1985 212
milieu goals 645
military cooperation 644
Milner, H. 81, 86, 87, 88
Milward, A. 86

minimum harmonization principle 528–9
minorities' rights 741
Missing Links, ERT 1984 112
Mitchell, J. 753–4
Mitterrand, F. 111, 122–3, 238
    cooperation with Helmut Kohl 202–3
        defense policy 199–200
        Elysée Treaty 196
        impact of German reunification 201–2,
            205n27
        monetary cooperation 200–1
        personal aspects 194–5
        political union 200
        selection of Commission
            president 240–1
mixed motives, problem of 8
mobilization, regional 753–4
modulation, CAP 488
Moldova, support for membership 271, 272
monetary compensatory amounts 486
monetary policy
    Franco–German cooperation 200–1, 202
    provisions of SEA 116
monetary union see European Monetary
        Union (EMU)
Monnet, J. 79, 183–6
    Action Committee 98
    ECSC negotiations 191
    European army scheme 186
    European Council 197
    role in EEC foundation 189–90
Monnet Plan 84
monolithic myth of realism 6
moral hazard 286–7
moral rights 736–7
    see also rights
Moravcsik, A. 6, 7, 14n1, 26, 27
    on influence of Commission 344–5
    liberal intergovernmentalism 10–11, 13,
        32n52, 33n53, 33n54, 49–50
        problems 28
    on Maastricht Treaty 130–1
    on nature of EU polity 173
    on origins of single market 412
    on output legitimacy 664
    recommendations for treaty reform
        process 174

Mostanza Claro directive 536
multiannual programming principle, Delors I
    package 498
multidimensional burden-sharing 814
multi-functionality, CAP 487
multilateral trading system 423, 424, 425
    ratification of agreements 428
multilevel governance (MLG) 28, 62–3, 72,
        496, 499–501, 754–5, 848
    applications 67–9
    comparison with neo-functionalism 63
    coordination issues 797, 799
    critiques 69–72
    shift from government to
        governance 66–7
    theoretical project 64–5
multiple identities 695–7
multi-speed Europe 310–11
Murrah, L. 26
mutual recognition principle 297–8, 303, 411
    civil justice cooperation 624
    judicial decisions 623

Nabucco project 566
Nahuis, S. 502–3
Napolitano, G., recommendations for treaty
        reform process 174
Narjes, K.-H. 112
national competition agencies (NCAs) 446
national courts
    acceptance of ECJ supremacy 358
    enforcement of principles of the order of
        competences 767, 774n50
national elections, importance of European
        integration issues 841
national executives, Europeanization 834–5
national governments
    acceptance of ECJ 358–9
    coordination 805
        aspirations 798
        structures 798–9
    limited control 65
    reasons to relinquish authority 70
national identities 604, 847
    compatibility with European
        identity 695–7

effects of European integration 697
    influence on public support 720, 722–3
    relationship to European integration 36,
        38–9, 42
    stability 41
    see also identity
national interest school, German post-war
        rehabilitation 182
national interests, free pursuit of interests
        principle 768
national legislature, synchronization
        problems with EU 710–11
national parliaments
    monitoring of rules governing
        competences 579–80
    subsidiarity concerns, provision of Lisbon
        Treaty 756
national parties, links to MEPs 368–9
national politicians, discussion of EU
        666, 668
national politics, positions on integration 727,
        728
national proxies, as explanation of public
        support 721–2
national reform programs (NRPs)
    Lisbon Strategy 476–7, 483n45
    performance 478
national regulatory authority (NRA)
        networks 399
national sovereignty
    impact of globalization 66
    obstacles to JHA domain 616–17
National Strategic Reference Frameworks
        (NSRFs) 501
national values, clashes with EU
        policies 665–6
nationalism 843
nationalism studies
    identity as causality 691–3
    identity as effect 694–5
Natura 2000 legislation, implementation
        problems 519
natural rights 743
Naurin, D, 326
negative legality principle 765–6
"negative" rules, TFEU 572
negotiation methods, Council 323–4

evolution 325–7
neo-classical realism 5–6
    normative power argument 8
neo-functionalism 9, 10, 27–8, 34, 49, 723,
        731n35, 840–1
    aims and logic 19–20
    comparison with multilevel governance 63
    early abandonment 18–19
    empirical hypotheses 24–5
    empirical research
        macro-level processes 25–6
        sectoral outcomes 26–7
    theory of comparative regional
        integration 778–80, 789, 790
    updated approach 20–1
        cross-border transactors 21–2
        institutionalization 24
        supranational organizations 22–3
    views on Commission 336
neo-realism 4–5, 6
neo-realist voice opportunities hypothesis 7
Netherlands
    Constitutional Treaty rejection 165, 692
    environmental policy 515
    GDP per head, 2007 280
        regional disparities 281
    growth, 1995–2005 282
    net migration 603
    referendum 726
    vote allocation, Nice Treaty 157
network environment, Council 325–6
networks, European Competition Network
        (ECN) 446, 447
"new approach" directives 528
New Governance
    role in policy coordination 803–4
    see also soft law
new member states (NMS) 267
    see also old versus new member states
new public management 388
Nice Treaty 149–50, 163
    actors 152–3
    asylum policy 606
    background 151
    on Commission composition 256
    on Commission presidency 227
    and Commission presidency 340

context 151–2
defense policy 587
distribution of European Parliamentary
        seats 159
key issues 154–5
large versus small states problem 265n1
negotiations 155–6
    on composition of the Commission 156
    on QMV 158
    on voting weights and representation
        issues 156–8
presidencies 153–4
Seville mandate 159–60
significance 160
social policy 545–6
voting system reform 253, 254–5
Nicholson, H.J. 634
Niemann, A. 427
Noël, E. 222, 326
Nomenclature of Territorial Units for
        Statistics (NUTS) 279, 290n5
non-governmental organizations,
        environmental (ENGOs) 515–16, 519
non-majoritan institutions, legitimacy 665
Nord Stream pipelines 557, 565
Nordic countries
    leadership 314–15
    see also Denmark; Finland; Norway;
        Sweden
normative effects, role in integration 40,
        42–3
normative power argument 8
North American Free Trade Agreement
        (NAFTA) 782, 783
    complete contract 785–7, 788
North Atlantic Treaty Organization
        (NATO) 644
    burden-sharing 810, 811–12
    intervention in Yugoslavian conflicts 647
    relationship with ESDP 588–9, 594
    Special Committee 633–4
North German Tax Union 784
North–South divide, environmental
        policy 517–18
Norway
    asylum burden 815, 816
    referendums 725

Obama, B. 269, 271, 652
obligations
    attractiveness 738–9
    Hohfeld's analysis 742–3
    system-relative character 737–8
    see also rights
occupational pension age, *Barber* case 544
Océano directive 535
OEEC (Organization for European Economic
    Cooperation), "Plan G" 100
offensive realism 5, 6–7
Office for Harmonization in the Internal
    Market (OHIM) 394
oil prices 556, 564
oil shocks, 1970s, responses 558
OLAF (European Anti-Fraud Office) 380,
    381, 386–7
    significance 387–9
old member states (OMS) 267
old versus new member states 275
    differences in institutional
        involvement 272
        Commission, European Parliament and
            ECJ 273–5
        Council of Ministers 272–3
        transposition of EU law 275
    differences in preferences 268
        distributive policies 269–70
        foreign and security policy 270–1
        further enlargements 271–2
        institutional design 268–9
        liberalization of the market 269
Olson, M. 811
Ombudsman 380, 381, 383–4, 685, 686
    cooperation with EDPS 385
    significance 387–9
one-dimensional burden-sharing 814
O'Neill, C. 236
Open Method of Coordination (OMC) 301,
    303, 343, 474–5, 483n46, 797, 803, 805,
    832
    European Employment Strategy
        (Luxembourg process) 545
    and multi-level governance 68
    performance 478
open-source intelligence 628
Ophuels, C.F. 97

Optimum Currency Area (OCA)
    theories 457
opt-outs 311, 316
    from EMU 124, 455
    implications, Council norms 324
    Lisbon Treaty 166, 167
    Maastricht Treaty 126, 139, 142, 299
    order of competences 766–7, 774n50
ordinary procedure 342
    see also co-decision procedure
Organization for Economic Cooperation and
    Development (OECD) 558
Organization for Security and Cooperation in
    Europe (OSCE) 737
organized crime, impact on JHA domain 617
Ostrom, E. 324
Ouchi, W. 333n30
output legitimacy 662, 663, 664–7
ozone depletion 520

Paris, Treaties of see Treaties of Paris
parliamentary governments
    coordination issues 796
    see also European Parliament; national
        parliaments
Parsons, C. 37–8, 81, 85, 87–8
participation in European community 694–5
participative democracy, provision of Lisbon
    Treaty 168
partnership principle 752
    Delors I package 498
Party Article 369
party groups 372, 373, 668
    electoral profiles 844
    environmental policy 515, 519
    European Parliament 367–70
    funding 375n26
    influence within committees 371
    integration preferences 38
    left-right conflict 842–4
    performance in European Parliament
        elections 724
    strategic interaction 845–6
Party of European Socialists (PES) 367, 369
Passenger Named Records 638, 639
passenger rights, consumer law 533

path-dependence, institutionalization 24
Patijn, M. 139
Patten, C. 649
peacekeeping missions, realist perspective 8
Pedersen, T. 314
people sharing, asylum policy 816–17
permissive consensus 716, 727, 849
Pernice, I. 769
Perraton, J. 68
Peters, B.G. 69, 71
Petersberg tasks 141, 586–7, 630
physical relocation, refugees 819
Pierre, J. 69, 71
Pierson, P. 24, 705
pillar structure, Maastricht Treaty 121, 127–8
Pinto, L. 53, 56
Pitarkis, J-Y. 25–6
"Plan G" 100
pledging mechanisms 814
Pléven Plan 79–80, 83, 186
pluralism, impact on integration 778, 779
Poland
    alleged CIA secret prisons 636
    attitudes towards further enlargements 271
    benefits from CAP 285
    Catholic values 269
    GDP per head, 2007 280
        regional disparities 281
    growth, 1995–2005 282
    net migration 603
    referendum 725
    views on CAP 270
police cooperation 622
policy coordination see coordination
policy cycle
    evaluation of policy measures 677–8
        policy impact evaluation 680
        policy outcome evaluation 679–80
        policy output evaluation 679
        policy termination 680–1
        problem definition and agenda
            setting 678–9
    transparency 683–4
policy effectiveness, evaluation see evaluation
    of policy measures
policy impacts 677–8
    evaluation 680

policy-making
    Europeanization 833–4
    "high" versus "low" politics 644
    impact of Commission 341
        effect of Luxembourg Compromise 343
        governance principles 343
        legislative issues 341–2
        single market program 343–4
        theoretical perspectives 344–5
    influence of Commission, guardianship of
        Treaty 342–3
    leaders and laggards 314–15
    throughput legitimacy 669–72
    see also competition policy; defense policy;
        energy policy; environmental policy;
        Justice and Home Affairs (JHA);
        regional policy; social policy; trade
        policy
policy-making stages 67
policy outcomes 677
    evaluation 679–80
policy outputs 677
    evaluation 679
Policy Planning and Early Warning Unit
    (PPEWU), CFSP 140
policy priorities
    preferences, differences between old and
        new member states 268–9
policy problems 678
    transparency 683–4
policy termination 680–1
policy trade model 812
political business cycles 709
Political Committee 646
political economy
    importance of rich versus poor
        cleavage 284–6
    views on origins of single market 412, 413
political institutions, impact on
    Europeanization 829
political parties see party groups
political pluralism, impact on
    integration 778, 779
political process, use of legal strategies 354–7
political time 703–4
    conclusions 712–13
    priority issues 704–5

political time (*cont.*)
  relevance 708–9
  synchronization problems 710–11
  temporal differentiation 712
  time pressures 711–12
  timescape and time games 705–8
political union
  impact of EMU 464
  Maastricht Treaty, negotiation 122–3
politicization 65, 668, 669, 840–1
  and identity 847–8
  of issues 844–7
  left-right conflict 842–4, *848*
politics, Europeanization 836
polity
  Europeanization 834–6
  time rules 704
Pollack, M. 88–9, 431
"polluter pays" principle 814
pollution, acid rain 561, 568n9
Pompidou, G. 209
  cooperation with Brandt 234
poor member states
  benefits of European integration 283
  comparison of member countries'
    GDP 279–80
  vulnerability to crises 286–9
  see also rich versus poor member states
Poos, J. 647
population versus territory issue 150
Portugal
  GDP per head, 2007 *280*
    regional disparities *281*
  growth, 1995–2005 *282*
  net migration *603*
  presidency during Nice Treaty
    negotiations 153–4
positive legality principle 766–7
Posted Workers' Directive 291n16, 549,
    554n62
Postfunctionalist Theory 723
post-material value theory 719
power asymmetries
  commitment devices 789
  influence on contractual choices 786–7
powers, Hohfeld's concept 742

Praesidium, Constitutional Treaty
    negotiations 164, 172
preliminary rulings procedure, European
    Court of Justice 356, 358
presidencies
  benefits 137–8
  European Council 169
  periods of office 703, 705–6
  see also Commission presidency; Council
    presidency
presidential cycles 709
  coordination issues 800–1
price stability 125
  performance of ECB 461–2
primacy principle 764
principal–agent analysis 12–13
  trade policy 429, 431–2
principles 745
Principles of European Contract Law
    (PECL) 531
Prisoners' Dilemma 781
Private Law codification project 531–2
private plaintiffs, access to European Court of
    Justice 356–7
privileges 740, 741
procedural impartiality, Council
    presidency 328
process-evaluation monitoring 682
Prodi, R. 802
  cycling metaphor 311
product safety, consumer law 533–4
productivity, Lisbon Strategy 472–3
professionalization, as source of coordination
    problems 796
proportionality principle 577–8
protectionism 424, 425
Protestant beliefs 848
Prüm Decision 622
public debt levels 286
public order, rules governing
    competences 576–7
public policy, Europeanization 833–4
public services, competition policy 443–4,
    445
public spheres 696
public support 716–17, 841
  conclusions 728–9

definition and measurement 717–18, *719*
in domestic politics 727
elections to European Parliament 723–4
for EMU 465–6
explanatory factors 718–19, *720*
  cue-taking approach 721–2
  identity approach 722–3
  utilitarian approach 721
referendums 724, *725–6*, 726
Puga, D. 502
purchasing power parity standard
    (PPS) 290n3
Putnam, R.D. 430, 431

Qualification Directive, 2004 818
qualified majority voting (QMV) 108, 121,
    252, 297
  for CFSP implementation 650
  evolution *254–5*
  Nice Summit 155, 158
  provisions of Amsterdam Treaty 140,
    141–2, 147n37
  provisions of Lisbon Treaty 169–70
  provisions of Maastricht Treaty 129
  significance 132
quasi-experiments, policy impact
    evaluation 680

Rapid Reaction force 587
rational-choice institutionalism (RCI) 11–13
rationalist institutionalism, perspective on
    Europeanization 828–9, 830–1
rationality 14n2
realism 4–9, 14n2
  interpretation of ESDP 594
  interpretation of Treaties of Paris 82–3
Reception Conditions Directive, 2003 818
reciprocity principle 283–4, 285
recycling, Danish Bottle Case 514
redistribution of resources 285–6, 415, 842
redistributive quotas 814
referendums 669, 716–17, 724, *725–6*, 726,
    846–7
  on Constitutional Treaty 844, 851n32
Reflection Group, 1995 136

refugee protection
  burden-sharing 815
  common policy approach 817–18,
    819–20
  funding 818–19, 820
  implicit trade model 820
  people sharing 816–17, 823n18
  criticisms and proposals for
    reform 819–20
regional aid 278–9
  see also structural funds
regional classification scheme 279
regional dimension 749–50
  analysis across sectors 752
  analysis over space 753–4
  analysis over time 750–2
  conclusions 757–8
  diversity 754–5
  impact of Lisbon Treaty 755–7
Regional Fund 116
regional mobilization 753–4
regional policy 496, 505
  Barca Report, 2009 503–4
  Commission strategic report, 2010 504
  contribution to convergence 283
  effectiveness 501–3
  evaluation 682
  evolution 497–9
  future 504–5
  motivation 283–4
  multilevel governance 499–501
    unanimity of financial
      perspectives 506n13
  Sapir Report, 2003 503
regional specialization 416
RegLeg grouping 751
regressive proportionality 252
regulatory agencies 393 *see also* European
    Union agencies
Reif, K. 366
religion, identity issues 697–9
renationalization 70–1
  cohesion policy 501
Renewables Directive 556
representation issues 284, 716–17, 728
  Commission composition
    253, 256, 340

representation issues (*cont.*)
  composition of European
      Parliament 256–7
    evolution 258–9
  elections to European Parliament 723–4
  European Court of Justice 351
  legitimacy problems 667
  legitimacy problems 672
  Nice Treaty 149–50, 150, 152, 155, 156–8
    distribution of European Parliamentary
        seats 159
    referendums 724, 725–6, 726
    weighted votes 252–3
research and development
  Lisbon Strategy 469, 477
  provisions of SEA 116–17
resettlement of refugees 819
responsibility-sharing *see* burden-sharing
restructuring fund 503
"Return Directive," 2008 818
rhetorical entrapment, negotiations for EU
    enlargement 40
Rhodes, R.A.W. 66
rich member states, comparison of member
    countries' GDP 279–80
rich versus poor member states 278–9
  importance in political economy 284–6
rights
  analysis 741–3
  attractiveness 738–9
  conclusions 745–6
  definitions 736
  enforcement 735–6
  fragmentation 740–1
  fundamental 739–40, 746n1, 747n9
  harmonization 735, 744, 746n7
  perspectives 734–5
  sources 743–5
  system-relative character 736–8
  see also citizenship rights
rights basis, social policy 544–5
Risse, T. 696
Rittberger, B. 40
Robertson, K. 628
roll-call data, validity 375n15
Romania
  GDP per head, 2007 280

regional disparities *281*
growth, 1995–2005 *282*
net migration *603*
referendum *725*
Rome, Treaties of *see* Treaties of Rome
Romero, F. 101
Rosa, H. 711
Rose, G. 5
Ross, G. 55
rotating presidency, Council 257, 265, 327–8
rule of law principle 761–2
  effectiveness principle 762–4
  and legality principle 765–6
rural development policy 488
Russia
  gas pipelines 557, 565–6
  intelligence services 634

S&D (Group of the Progressive Alliance of
    Socialists and Democrats) 367
Sadurski, W. 835
Saint Malo declaration, defense policy 587
sanctioning powers 770–1
Sandholtz, W. 70, 112, 344, 412
Sandler, T. 811
Santer, J. 233–4
  Commission presidency 240–5
Santiso, J. 704
Santos Palhota case 551
Sapir, A. 502
Sapir Report, 2003 475–6, 503, 683
Sarkozy, N.
  on Lisbon Treaty 264
  proposal of eurozone summits 169
Sarrazin, T. 698
satellite observation programs 631
Saurugger, S. 51
Sbragia, A. 417
Scandinavian countries, reluctance to join
    EU 38
Scharpf, F.W. 662, 665, 705, 805
Schäuble, W. 310, 504
Schäuble–Lamers paper, 1994 143
Schaus, L. 97
Schengen Agreement 139–40, 146n22, 309,
    311, 600–1

influences 607–8
  on citizenship rights 604–5
  on external border control 605–7
  on JHA domain 617–19
  on labor market integration 602–4
Schengen Borders Code 620, 621
Schengen group, external border
    management 620–1
Schengen Information System (SIS) 601, 621
Schengen system, role in origins of JHA
    domain 614–15
Scheuerman, W.E. 711
Schierup, C.-U, *A European Dilemma* 607
Schimmelfennig, F. 11, 13
Schmidt, H. 237
  cooperation with Valérie Giscard
    d'Estaing 202–3
    Elysée Treaty 196
    European Council 197–8
    monetary cooperation 198–9
    personal aspects 194, 195
    response to Margaret Thatcher 211
Schmidt, S.K. 26
Schmitt, H. 366
Schmitter, P.C. 840
Schout, A. 399
Schuck, P. 820
Schuman, R. 79, 181, 185, 186, 188
Schuman Plan 83, 84, 86, 88, 89, 185
Scmitter, P. 704
scrutinizing organizations 380–1
  European Court of Auditors (ECA) 381–3
  European Data Protection Supervisor
    (EDPS) 384–6
  OLAF (European Anti-Fraud
    Office) 386–7
  Ombudsman 383–4
  significance 387–9
Scully, R. 41
second integrative response 784
second-order election model 366, 373
Secreariat General 228
"secret prisons" 635, 636–7
Secretariat, Council 328–9
Secretary-General, Council 328
security dilemma 5
security of energy supply 564–6

Seixas da Costa, F., Nice Treaty
    negotiations 153–4
Sen, A., capability approach 547
Serbia, support for membership 272
Services, Commission 338
services field, consumer law weakness 533
set-aside scheme 485
Settembri, P. 273
Seville mandate, Nice Treaty 159–60
shale gas 566, 567
shared legislative culture 329
short-termism 708–9
Single Area Payment Scheme (SAPS) 489
single currency, Maastricht Treaty 124
Single Euro Payment Area (SEPA) 459
Single European Act (SEA) 63, 107–8, 151, 410
  on border controls 601
  Franco–German cooperation 200
  impact 117–18
    on Commission 342
  key provisions 115–17
  origins 108–9, 114–15
    role of European Parliament 109–10
    role of European Political
      Cooperation 110
    role of intergovernmental
      bargaining 111–12
    role of transnational leadership 112–14
    timeline *113*
  provisions for cohesion 498
  role in consumer law development 527–8,
    529
  role in defense policy 586
Single Farm Payment (SFP) scheme 488
single market program 407, 417–18, 423
  comparison with Lisbon Strategy 471
  directions for future research
    comparative research 417
    compliance and implementation 416
    economic diversity 416–17
    governance concerns 415–16
    historical influences 414–15
  explanation of origins 412–13
  external dimension 411–12
  governance 413–14
  impact of Commission 343–4
  impact on trade policy 424–5

single market program (*cont.*)
  origins 408–9
    1992 program 410
    early integration 409
  role of Delors 225
  role in environmental policy
      development 514
  rule-making and enforcement 410–11
  Thatcher's role 211–12
Single Market Act 407
SitCen (Joint Situation Centre) 630, 631, 632
Slapin, J 17n59
Slovakia
  GDP per head, 2007 *280*
    regional disparities *281*
  growth, 1995–2005 *282*
  net migration *603*
  referendum *725*
Slovenia
  GDP per head, 2007 *280*
    regional disparities *281*
  growth, 1995–2005 *282*
  net migration *603*
  referendum *725*
Small Farmers Scheme (SFS) 488
small states
  coalition patterns 251
  representation 284
  see also large versus small states problem
Smith, A. 55
Smith, K. 654
Smith, M. 68
"snake in the tunnel" 198
Snoy et d'Oppeurs, J.-C. 97
social action logics 812–13
Social Agenda Package 547
Social Charter, 1989 544
social citizenship 547
social constructivism 54
social exclusion, risk from consumer
      law 537–8
"social field," ESDP (European Security and
      Defense Policy) 593
social integration, role of European Court of
      Justice 360–1, 364n54
social learning processes, constructivist
      theories 36

social market economy 551, 555n71
social models 472, 481n16
social pluralism, impact on integration 778, 779
social policy 542
  Amsterdam Treaty 139
  competences 572–3
  EEC Treaty 103, 294–5
  evolution
    Defrenne cases 543–4
    EEC Treaty 543
    Maastricht Treaty 545
    Nice Treaty 545–6
    Treaties of Rome 543
  future development 551–2
  implications for domestic policy 549–51
  justifications
    capabilities 547–8
    industrial/social citizenship 546–7
    market-making 548
    response to single market 546
  left-right conflict 842–3
  Maastricht Treaty 126, 545
  SEA 116
social progress clause 550
social security, rules governing
      competences 576–7
socialization 696
  effects of integration 41–2
  Inglehart's theory 693, 694
societal actors, influence on trade policy 426
sociocultural rights 735
sociological perspectives 57–8
  "bottom-up" approach 49–50
  Bourdieu's work 53–4
  constructivist and interpretative
      approaches 50–1
  distinctiveness 56–7
  Fligstein's work 51–2
  strengths 54–5
"soft balancing" 594
soft law
  competition policy 442, 445, 446, 447–8
  and OMC 475
  role in policy coordination 803–4, 805
Solana, J. 144, 630–1, 632, 648–50
Solemn Declaration on European Union,
      1983 111

solidarity 691, 810
    citizenship 699
    limitations 285–6
    measurement 692
    nationalism 691–2
    see also burden-sharing
Solow growth model 501–2
Soltz, H. 782
Somali pirates, ESDP intervention 590
South Stream project 566
sovereign debt crisis, 2010
    impact on regional policy 504–5
    responses 480–1
sovereignty
    intergovernmentalism 9–11
    rational-choice institutionalism 12
    residual rights of control 786
Soviet Union collapse, impact on EU 6–7,
        122, 135
Spaak, P.-H. 96, 97, 187
    EEC negotiations 191
Spaak report 97–9, 99, 190, 408
Spain
    GDP per head, 2007 280
        regional disparities 281
    net migration 603
    referendum 726
    vote allocation, Nice Treaty 157
Special Committee on Agriculture
        (SCA) 325
specialization, collective goods provision 812,
        822, 824n40
specific support for integration see utilitarian
        support for integration
Spierenburg, D. 89
Spierenburg Report 339
spillover 20, 64, 90, 473, 779
    ECJ as source 27
    effect on JHA domain 617–18
    EMU as 132
    role in integration 21–2
    and sovereign debt crisis 480
Spinelli, A. 104, 109, 187–8, 189, 191
sport, Bosman case 577, 579
Spruyt, H. 785–9
St Matthew principle 752
Stability and Growth Pact, 2005 reform 345

Stability and Growth Pact (SGB)
        proposal 456, 458
Staff Regulations 387
staff mediator 387
stakeholder consultation 685, 687
Stasavage, D. 326
state aid 444–5
state capacity, consequences of single
        market 415–16
state-centric view 14n2
    and multilevel governance 64
    on origins of single market 412
    tension with multilevel governance
        68–9
Treaties of Paris 81
statist models 294
    fall from favor 296
Steuneberger, B. 275
Stone Sweet, A. 25, 52, 70, 358
Strategic Defense Initiative 586
strategic partnerships 653
strong intergovernmentalism 22
structural compatibility 769–70
structural funds 10, 496, 752
    distribution preferences, differences
        between old and new member
        states 270
    effectiveness 502
    evaluation of policy measures 682
    Sapir Report, 2003 503
structural programming 500
structural realism 5
structure/agency debate 181
Stubb, A. 143, 310–11, 712
sub-national actors, role in cohesion
        policy 500–1
subsidiarity principle 125, 577–80, 751
    provisions of Lisbon Treaty 756
"sunset legislation" 681
Supplementary Information Request at the
        National Entry (SIRENE) offices 601
supply-side conditions of integration 781
supporting competences 573
supranational agency, impact on
        integration 778, 779
supranational governance, neo-functionalist
        theory 19–20, 25

supranational institutions, support of small
    states 251–2
supranational organizations, neo-
    functionalist theory 22–3, 25, 26
supranationalism, and Treaties of Paris 81–2
supranationality 840–1
supremacy principle, EU law 353
surveys, Eurobarometer 718, *719*, 722, 730n11
sustainability
    of Europeanization 837
    of transport policy 683
sustainable development 513
    international negotiations 520
Sutherland Report 527
SVR (Foreign Intelligence Service,
    Russia) 634
Sweden
    asylum burden *815*, *816*
    coordination 799
    Council presidency, leadership 314
    GDP per head, 2007 *280*
        regional disparities *281*
    growth, 1995–2005 *282*
    net migration *603*
    Ombudsman 383
    referendums *725*
Switzerland
    asylum burden *815*, *816*
    referendums *725*, *726*
    reluctance to join EU 38
symmetrical regional heterogeneity *778*, *779*
synchronization problems 710–11
systemic risk 460

Tallberg, J. 328, 329
tan (traditionalist/authority/nationalism)
    stance 843–4, 848, *848*
TARGET (Euro Payment and Settlement
    Scheme) 459
Tarrant, A. 399
Tarrow, S. 413, 664
taxation
    rights issues 744
    rules governing competences 576–7
teleological interpretation methods,
    European Court of Justice 353–4

temporal differentiation 712
territorial politics 757–8
territoriality principle 616–17
terrorism 618
    impact on JHA domain 617
    judicial cooperation 623
    responses 630
    TREVI (Terrorisme, radicalisme,
        extrémisme et violence
        internationale) 614, 617
    see also counter-terrorism
TEU (Treaty on European Union) *see*
    Maastricht Treaty
Thatcher, M. 111, 206, 210, 237
    British Budgetary Question (BBQ) 211, 224
    fall from power 214
    influence on European integration 214–16
    market liberalization 296
    and monetary union 213
    relationships with other leaders 211, 212–13
    role in single market program 211–12
    and Thorn's Commission presidency 238
    views on German reunification 213
Thielemann, E.R. 820
third part access, energy networks 559
third-country nationals, asylum
        policy 618–19
Third-Country Nationals (TCNs) 605,
        611n24
Thorn, G. 233–4, 245
three-level game metaphor, trade policy 430
throughput legitimacy 662, 663, 664, 669–72,
        673n7
time
    as an institution 705
    see also political time
time games 704–5, 707–8
    in enlargement negotiations 712
time rules 704, 706–7, 709
timescape 705–7
    elements of continuity 708–9
Tobacco Advertising case 575–6
Toshkov, D. 275
Trachtenberg, M. 83
trade, impact of EMU 462–3
trade law
    governing rules 576–7

"negative" rules 572
trade policy 422–3
  changing context 423–4
    changes in EU 424–5
    external changes 424
  efficacy in pursuit of objectives 430–1
  and IPE literature 432–3
  principal–agent and two-level game
    approaches 429–32
  role of Commission 428–9
  role of Council 427–8
  shaping of objectives 429–30
  sources of policy preferences 426–7
trade-offs
  governance dilemma 292–3
  input and output legitimacy 664
trafficking in human beings, judicial
    cooperation 623
transactionalism 34, 49
transaction-driven theory of integration 22
transfer of sovereign rights 350
transformative effects, constructivist
    theories 36
Translation Centre for the Bodies of the
    European Union (CdT) 394
transnational leadership, role in origins of
    SEA 112–14
transnational society 20
  neo-functionalist theory 21–2, 25, 26
transnationalism, and Treaties of Paris 81–2
transparency
  agencies 398–9
  CAP payments 490
  Commission 670–1
  Council reforms 326
  definition 676–7
  European Parliament 671
  implications of "early agreements" 711
  links to evaluation of policy
    effectiveness 686–7
  policy cycle context 683–4
  in policy-making 685–6
  role of Ombudsman 384
transport policy, evaluation 683
transposition studies 830
treaties
  Elysée Treaty 195–6

negotiation methods 191
unanimity rule 672
see also Amsterdam Treaty; Constitutional
    Treaty; Lisbon Treaty; Nice Treaty;
    Single European Act (SEA)
Treaties of Paris 79, 90
  choice of institutions 88–90
  material versus ideational views 82–5
  negotiations and ratification 85–8
  state-centric perspectives 81
  transnational perspectives 81–2
  see also European Coal and Steel
    Community; European Defense
    Community
Treaties of Rome 18, 95, 294, 408–9
  on border controls 600
  Common Agricultural Policy 484–5
  EEC Treaty
    institutional structure 103–4
    objectives 102–3
    significance 104–5
  Euratom Treaty 101–2
  exclusion of energy 558
  incomplete contract 785, 787–8
  influence of United States 100–1
  liberal intergovernmentalist perspective 11
  Messina conference 96–7
  regional policy 497
  social policy 543, 551
  Spaak report 97–9
    responses 99
Treaty on European Union (TEU) see
    Maastricht Treaty
Treaty on the Functioning of the Union
    (TFEU) 166
  on nature and scope of competences 571–4
treaty reform process
  provisions of Lisbon Treaty 171
  recommendations 174–5
TREVI (Terrorisme, radicalisme, extrémisme
    et violence internationale) 614, 617
Tridimas, G. 25–6
trilogue methodology 329, 371
triple majority, QMV 158
Tsebelis, G. 27, 28
  on Constitutional Treaty negotiations 172
  on cooperation procedure 371

Tuendhat, C. 229n2
Turkey
    accession negotiations 831
    anxieties over accession 284
    GDP per head, 2007, regional
        disparities 281
    support for membership 272
turnout, Euro-elections 366
two-level game metaphor, trade policy 430–2

UCLAF (Anti-Fraud Task Force) 386
Ukraine
    gas pipelines 565–6
    support for membership 271, 272
unbundling, energy policy 560
unemployment
    1990s and 2000s 300–1
    see also employment
uniformity ideal 672
unilateral trade measures 423
United Kingdom
    asylum burden 815
    British Budgetary Question (BBQ) 211,
        224
    de Gaulle's opposition to EEC
        membership 208, 209
    GDP per head, 2007 280
        regional disparities 281
    growth, 1995–2005 282
    impact of EEC Treaty 104
    net migration 603
    opposition to defense policy 587
    opt-out of Maastrict social policy 126
    participation in Spaak Committee 97–8
    "Plan G" 100
    referendum 725
    resistance to EMU 124, 299
    resistance to Maastricht social chapter 299
    stance on QMV 297
United States
    asylum burden 815
    coordination issues 807n18
    economic impact of EEC Treaty 104
    as European intelligence partner 627,
        637–9
    growth, 1995–2005 282

impact of SEA 118
influence on EU foreign policy 655
influence on Treaties of Rome 100–1
invasion of Iraq, 2003 7
multinational companies, investment in
    Europe 411
regional aid 496
relationship with Europe, role in origins of
    SEA 110
utilitarian support for integration 717–18,
    720, 721

value coherence 697
van der Eijk, C. 727
Van Gend en Loos judgement, 1963 105, 353,
    356, 359
Van Rompuy, H., Presidency of European
    Council 169, 651, 652, 653
variable geometry 303, 311
    in Maastricht Treaty 299
Vasquez, J. 6
Venice Commission 636
Venice Declaration 647
Verbund see composite (Verbund) perspective
Verhofstadt, G., Nice Summit
    negotiations 157
Verrijn Stuart, G.M. 97
vertical coordination 804–5
    bi-directional nature 797
    negative consequences 806
veto use
    environmental policy-making 515
    impact on Europeanization 828–9
    impact on policy outcomes 665, 672
Viking case 549–50
Vimont, P., Nice Treaty negotiations 154
visa requirements 606
    Schengen Visas 621
von der Groeben, H. 222
voting behavior
European Parliament 369
    see also qualified majority voting
voting decisions, Euro-elections 366–7
voting weights 252–3
    Nice Summit negotiations 155, 156–8
    provisions of Lisbon Treaty 169–70

VTB-VAT directive 535
vulnerable consumers 538

Waever, O. 38
Wallace, H. 309, 322
Wallace, W. 9–10
Waltz, K. 4–5, 6
Watts case 576, 577
Weatherill, S. 664, 700
Webber, D. 312
Weberian legitimacy 665
weighted votes 252–3, 284
   Nice Summit negotiations 155, 156–8
   provisions of Lisbon Treaty 169–70
welfare systems, relationship to public
     support for integration 721
Wells, P. 68
Werner, P. 235
Wessels, W. 172
Westendorp, C. 136
Western European Union (WEU) 127–8,
   586, 648
   Amsterdam Treaty proposals 141, 144
whistleblowing rules 387, 391n43
wind power 563

withdrawal rights, provisions of Lisbon
   Treaty 171
Wohlforth, W. 6
Wolfers, A. 645
Woll, C. 426, 428
working conditions
   provisions of Amsterdam Treaty 139
   provisions of Maastricht Treaty 126
World Competitiveness Report,
   2010/2011 478
World Trade Organization (WTO)
   423
   Agreement on Agriculture 487, 489

xenophobia 604
   relationship to Euro-skepticism 722

Yugoslavian conflicts 647

Zeckhauser, R. 811
zero-sum decisions 64
Zollverein 782, *783*
Zysman, J. 112, 344, 412